Do your students come to class prepared?
How do you hold your students accountable?

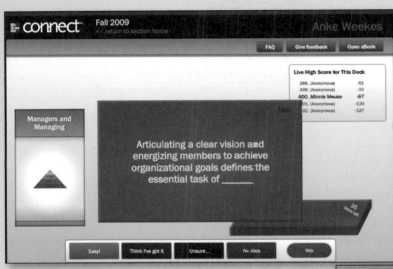

Based on students' self-diagnoses of their proficiency, *LearnSmart* intelligently provides students with a series of adaptive questions. This provides students with a personalized one-on-one tutor experience.

You can incorporate *LearnSmart* into your course in a number of ways to...

- Gauge student knowledge before a lecture
- Reinforce learning after lecture
- Prepare students for assignments and exams

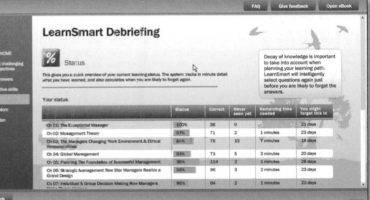

Connect Management powered by *LearnSmart* provides the following Instructor Benefits

- Holds your students accountable and tracks progress
- Assignments are automatically graded
- Students are better prepared for class
- Materials are directly related to textbook and course
- Improves comprehension

Connect Management powered by *LearnSmart* provides the following Student Benefits

- Fun, motivating, and engaging way to learn
- Saves time: efficient and effective way to study
- Improves student grade
- Reinforces concepts

Discover for yourself how *Connect Management* ensures students will **connect** with the content, learn more effectively, and **succeed** in your course.

McGraw Hill **connect**™

|MANAGEMENT

Powered by **LearnSmart**

Management

Leading & Collaborating in a Competitive World

ninth edition

Management

Leading & Collaborating in a Competitive World

Thomas S. Bateman | Scott A. Snell
McIntire School of Commerce | *Darden Graduate*
University of Virginia | *School of Business*
University of
Virginia

MANAGEMENT: LEADING & COLLABORATING IN A COMPETITIVE WORLD
Published by McGraw-Hill/Irwin, a business unit of The McGraw-Hill Companies, Inc., 1221 Avenue of the Americas, New York, NY, 10020. Copyright © 2011, 2009, 2007, 2004, 2002, 1999, 1996, 1993, 1990 by The McGraw-Hill Companies, Inc. All rights reserved. No part of this publication may be reproduced or distributed in any form or by any means, or stored in a database or retrieval system, without the prior written consent of The McGraw-Hill Companies, Inc., including, but not limited to, in any network or other electronic storage or transmission, or broadcast for distance learning.

Some ancillaries, including electronic and print components, may not be available to customers outside the United States.

This book is printed on acid-free paper.

3 4 5 6 7 8 9 0 DOW/DOW 1 0 9 8 7 6 5 4 3 2 1

ISBN 978-0-07-813724-2
MHID 0-07-813724-1

Vice president and editor-in-chief: *Brent Gordon*
Publisher: *Paul Ducham*
Executive editor: *Michael Ablassmeir*
Director of development: *Ann Torbert*
Development editor II: *Laura Griffin*
Editorial assistant: *Andrea Heirendt*
Vice president and director of marketing: *Robin J. Zwettler*
Executive marketing manager: *Anke Braun Weekes*
Marketing coordinator: *Annie Ferro*
Vice president of editing, design and production: *Sesha Bolisetty*
Senior project manager: *Susanne Riedell*
Lead production supervisor: *Michael R. McCormick*
Interior designer: *Pam Verros*
Senior photo research coordinator: *Jeremy Cheshareck*
Photo researcher: *Ira C. Roberts*
Lead media project manager: *Kerry Bowler*
Cover design: *Pam Verros*
Cover image: *© Masterfile*
Typeface: *10/12 Jenson*
Compositor: *Laserwords Private Limited*
Printer: *RR Donnelley*

Library of Congress Cataloging-in-Publication Data

Bateman, Thomas S.
    Management : leading & collaborating in a competitive world / Thomas S. Bateman,
Scott A. Snell.—9th ed.
      p. cm.
    Includes index.
    ISBN-13: 978-0-07-813724-2 (alk. paper)
    ISBN-10: 0-07-813724-1 (alk. paper)
    1. Management. I. Snell, Scott, 1958- II. Title.
HD31.B369485 2011
658—dc22
                                                                2009045059

For my parents, Tom and Jeanine Bateman,
and Mary Jo, Lauren, T.J., and James

and

My parents, John and Clara Snell,
and Marybeth, Sara, Jack, and Emily

About the Authors

Thomas S. Bateman

Thomas S. Bateman is Bank of America Professor and management area coordinator in the McIntire School of Commerce at the University of Virginia. He teaches leadership courses and is director of a new leadership minor open to undergraduate students of all majors. Prior to joining the University of Virginia, he taught organizational behavior at the Kenan-Flager Business School of the University of North Carolina to undergraduates, M.B.A. students, Ph.D. students, and practicing managers. He also taught for two years in Europe as a visiting professor at the Institute for Management Development (IMD), one of the world's leaders in the design and delivery of executive education. Professor Bateman completed his doctoral program in business administration in 1980 at Indiana University. Prior to receiving his doctorate, Dr. Bateman received his B.A. from Miami University. In addition to Virginia, UNC-Chapel Hill, and IMD, Dr. Bateman has taught at Texas A&M, Tulane, and Indiana universities.

Professor Bateman is an active management researcher, writer, and consultant. He has served on the editorial boards of major academic journals and has presented numerous papers at professional meetings on topics including managerial decision making, job stress, negotiation, employee commitment and motivation, group decision making, and job satisfaction. His articles have appeared in professional journals such as the *Academy of Management Journal*, *Academy of Management Review*, *Journal of Applied Psychology*, *Organizational Behavior and Human Decision Processes*, *Journal of Management*, *Business Horizons*, *Journal of Organizational Behavior*, and *Decision Sciences*.

Dr. Bateman's current consulting and research centers on practical wisdom in business executives, leadership in the form of problem solving at all organizational levels, various types of proactive behavior by employees at all levels, and the successful pursuit of long-term work goals. He works with organizations including Nokia, Singapore Airlines, the Brookings Institution, the U.S. Chamber of Commerce, the Nature Conservancy, and LexisNexis.

Scott A. Snell

Scott Snell is the E. Thayer Bigelow Professor of Business Administration at the University of Virginia's Darden Graduate School of Business. He teaches in the Leadership and Organization area and specializes in strategic human resource management. He has worked with a number of Furture 500 companies to address the alignment of investments in talent and strategic capability.

Professor Snell is the author of more than 50 publications in professional journals and edited texts, including the *Academy of Management Journal*, *Academy of Management Review*, *Human Resource Management*, *Human Resource Management Review*, *Industrial Relations*, *Journal of Business Research*, *Journal of Management*, *Journal of Managerial Issues*, *Journal of Management Studies*, *Organizational Dynamics*, *Organization Studies*, *Personnel Psychology*, and *Strategic Management Journal*. He has coauthored four books: *Managing Human Resources. Management: Leading and Collaborating in a Competitive World*, *M: Management*, and *Managing People and Knowledge in Professional Service Firms*, and has coedited the *Sage Handbook of Human Resource Management*. He has served on the boards of the Society for Human Resource Management Foundation, the Academy of Management's Human Resource Division, the *Human Resource Management Journal*, the *Academy of Management Journal*, and the *Academy of Management Review*.

Prior to joining the Darden faculty in 2007, Scott was Professor and Director of Executive Education at Cornell University's Center for Advanced Human Resource Studies and Professor of Management in the Smeal College of Business at Pennsylvania State University. He received a B.A. in psychology from Miami University, as well as M.B.A. and Ph.D. degrees in business administration from Michigan State University. Originally from Lodi, Ohio, Scott now lives in Charlottesville, Virginia, with his wife and three children.

Preface

Welcome to our 9th edition! Thank you to everyone who has used and learned from previous editions, and helped make this book such a success. We are proud to present the newest edition.

As we went to press, stock markets worldwide were rebounding from the previous year's crash. Confidence in the global economy seemed to be returning, until bad news periodically threw new wrenches into the outlook. Sustainability had become a more mainstream and widespread business concern and objective (as reflected in this as well as our previous editions). China had been investing heavily in Africa for years, and Secretary of State Hillary Clinton completed a trip to Africa intended to develop stronger ties with a number of African nations. Iraq's future was highly uncertain, and Afghanistan was getting worse. Under President Obama, health care reform was Topic A but resistance was fierce. Twitter was the new rage, and reality shows were showcasing B-list celebrities and politicians.

But you won't be reading this at the moment we went to press. Those events and trends could still be around, or they may have disappeared or reversed themselves. If they no longer hold, their repercussions still could persist—thus, they may still be relevant (or not). The world continues to change, evolve, and offer new challenges and opportunities.

As things change in the world, they change in business and management. The metaphorical glass sometimes seems half-empty, because unfortunate world events, disconcerting trends, and ineffective and unethical management practices will continue. But good people will continue to "step up" and take on important leadership roles, managing well and making things better, as they always have. In this book, you will read about many managers, some doing things brilliantly, others making mistakes (with some learning from their mistakes, and some not). Some organizations rise from the ashes, or come from seemingly nowhere, to become the next hot investment. Some organizations are high-flyers one day and come crashing down the next. Some achieve greatness, and have occasional downturns, but continue being great.

These performance shifts occur in large part due to the ways in which they are managed, and partly from how circumstances change. Business environments, like pendulums, swing from one extreme to another. These changes will contribute to the fall of some currently successful companies and managers and the rise of others who currently struggle or are now just dreaming of new business ideas.

For you, as a businessperson as in life, uncertainty will be a constant state of affairs. That is, no one knows for certain what will happen, or what to do in pursuit of a successful future. Luck and the right circumstances can help companies (and people) succeed in the short run. But in the long run good management is essential.

Fortunately, you have access to current knowledge about how to manage. We have learned a lot from the companies that have succeeded and failed. The continuing experiment created by the vast array of management practices that exist in the business world, combined with sound research that helps tease out what works from what doesn't, helps us learn from mistakes and identify the most important lessons and useful practices that managers can employ. We hope that you will not only learn as much as you can about this vital activity but also commit to applying it—by reading and learning, and by using it in the best possible ways.

This book and the course you are taking will help you face the managerial challenges of a changing world. In doing so, they will help you identify what's important and what's not, make good decisions, and take effective action on behalf of yourself, your colleagues, and the organizations for which you work.

Our Goals

Our mission with this text hasn't changed from that of our previous editions: to inform, instruct, and inspire. We hope to *inform* by providing descriptions of the important concepts and practices of modern management. We hope to *instruct* by describing how you can take action on the ideas discussed. We hope to *inspire* not only by writing in a positive, interesting, and optimistic way but also by providing a real sense of the opportunities ahead of you. Whether your goal is starting your own company, leading a team to greatness, building a strong organization, delighting your customers, or generally forging a positive future, we want to inspire you to take positive actions.

We hope to inspire you to be both a thinker and a doer. We want you to think about the issues, think about the impact of your actions, think before you act. But being a good thinker is not enough; you also must be a doer. Management is a world of action. It is a world that requires timely and appropriate action. It is a world not for the passive but for those who commit to positive accomplishments.

Keep applying the ideas you learn in this course, read about management in sources outside of this course, and keep learning about management after you leave school and continue your career. Make no mistake about it: learning about management is a personal voyage that will last years, an entire career, your entire lifetime.

Competitive Advantage

Today's world is competitive. Never before has the world of work been so challenging. Never before has it been so imperative to your career that you learn the skills of management. Never before have people had so many opportunities and challenges with so many potential risks and rewards.

You will compete with other people for jobs, resources, and promotions. Your organization will compete with other firms for contracts, clients, and customers. To survive the competition, and to thrive, you must perform in ways that give you an edge over your competitors, that make the other party want to hire you, buy from you, and do repeat business with you. You will want them to choose you, not your competitor.

To survive and thrive, today's managers have to think and act strategically. Today's customers are well educated, aware of their options, and demanding of excellence. For this reason, managers today must think constantly about how to build a capable workforce and manage in a way that delivers the goods and services that provide the best possible value to the customer.

By this standard, managers and organizations must perform. Five essential types of performance, on which the organization beats, equals, or loses to the competition, are *cost*, *quality*, *speed*, *innovation*, and *service*. These five performance dimensions, when managed well, deliver value to the customer and competitive advantage to you and your organization. We will elaborate on all of these topics throughout the book.

The idea is to keep you focused on a type of "bottom line," to make sure you think continually about "delivering the goods" that make both you and your organization a competitive success. This results-oriented approach is unique among management textbooks.

Leading & Collaborating

Yes, business is competitive. But it's not that simple. In fact, to think strictly in terms of competition is overly cynical, and such cynicism can sabotage your performance. The other fundamental elements in the success equation are collaboration and leadership. People working with, rather than against, one another is essential to competitive advantage. Put another way, you can't do it alone—the world is too complex, and business is too challenging.

You need to work with your teammates. Leaders and followers need to work as collaborators more than as adversaries. Work groups throughout your organization need to cooperate with one another. Business and government, often viewed as antagonists, can work productively together. And today more than ever, companies that traditionally were competitors engage in joint ventures and find other ways to collaborate on some things even as they compete in others. Leadership is needed to make these collaborations happen.

How does an organization create competitive advantage through collaboration? It's all about the people, and it derives from good leadership. Three stereotypes of leadership are that it comes from the top of the company, that it comes from one's immediate boss, and that it means being decisive and issuing commands. These stereotypes may contain grains of truth, but the reality is much more complex. First, the person at the top may or may not provide effective leadership—in fact, many observers believe that good leadership is far too rare. Second, organizations need leaders at all levels, in every team and work unit. This includes you, beginning early in your career, and this is why leadership is an important theme in this book. Third, leaders should be capable of decisiveness and of giving commands, but relying too much on this traditional approach isn't enough. Great leadership is far more inspirational than this, and helps people both to think differently and also to work differently—including working collaboratively, with a focus on results.

Leadership—from your boss, as well as from you—generates collaboration, which in turn creates results that are good for the company and good for the people involved.

As Always, Currency and Variety in the 9th Edition

It goes without saying that this textbook, in its 9th edition, remains on the cutting edge of topical coverage, as updated via both current business examples and recent management research. Chapters have been thoroughly updated, and students are exposed to a broad array of important current topics.

We have done our very best to draw from a wide variety of subject matter, sources, and personal experiences. We continue to emphasize throughout the book themes such as real results, ethics, cultural considerations, and leadership and collaboration. Here is just a small sampling of new highlights in the 9th edition, enough to convey the wide variety of people, organizations, issues, and contexts represented throughout the text.

Chapter 1

- Tesla Motors, an electric-car start-up, tries to revolutionize the automotive industry.
- Global reach allows a manufacturer's rep to expand business into China.
- New examples of cost competitiveness include Hewlett-Packard and its strategies to improve efficiencies.

Chapter 2

- Green Mountain Coffee Roasters cultivates fair-trade relationships with suppliers.
- Updated graphics on economic data.
- New examples to demonstrate the concepts of culture (Google and Sprint).

Chapter 3

- Anne Mulcahy's decisions pull Xerox back from the brink.
- An economic crisis forces companies to find innovative alternatives.
- Financial benefits of sustainability.

Chapter 4

- The new unfolding case is about Olli-Pekka Kallasvuo, CEO of Nokia.
- A management coaching firm develops a new strategy to bring in business during an economic downturn.
- Collaborating with key stakeholders.

Chapter 5

- Walmart goes green, responding to critics and helping its bottom line.
- Ethics of blogging and "astroturfing" about companies and products.
- Where the United States stands in the "honesty" rankings.

Chapter 6

- Kraft's unique strategy to improve its global market share.
- Disney opens English schools in China.
- The importance of managers understanding local social norms and cultures.

Chapter 7

- Richard Branson turns to renewable energy in one of his latest endeavors.
- Many new examples of green and socially responsible entrepreneurs.
- Managing risk in the economic downturn.

Chapter 8

- Whirlpool adapts organizational structure to improve growth.
- Company boards rely on more outside directors for guidance.
- Adding middle management layer helps software company grow efficiently.

Chapter 9

- Capitalizing on Corning's strengths to bring the company back to profitability.
- Going "lean" helps Dur-A-Flex maintain its organizational agility.
- Analyzing the American Customer Satisfaction Index.

Chapter 10

- Enterprise Rent-a-Car and its successful HR strategies.
- PriceSpective and its innovative approach to dealing with staffing needs.
- Using simulation games to supplement management training at all levels.

Chapter 11

- Marriott International's commitment to diversity training for all employees.
- The use of social networking Web sites to reach prospective employees.
- The importance of employee support groups within an organization.

Chapter 12

- Amory Lovins may help wean America off of fossil fuels.
- One city administrator's leadership in the aftermath of a devastating Kansas tornado.
- Tips for developing leadership abilities.

Chapter 13

- How Tony Hsieh motivates employees at Zappos .com.
- Examples of how companies motivate employees to take care of their health while lowering health care costs.

- New "psychological contract" example for a frustrated HR manager.

Chapter 14

- Championing teamwork at Cisco Systems.
- Common mistakes team leaders make.
- Challenges that exist in multicultural teams.

Chapter 15

- What customers "Digg" about Kevin Rose's communication style.
- Accenture's employee programs foster communication and strong working relationships.
- Revamping a company Web site to communicate more effectively with customers.

Chapter 16

- How Legal Sea Foods maintains control.
- An accounting firm's formal control process ensures exceptional client service.
- Better business through budgeting.

Chapter 17

- Honda's flexible manufacturing system drives the company's innovation winning streak.
- Too much innovation may be one game designers' downfall.
- A unique lab program allows Intuit employees to focus a percentage of their time on innovation and collaboration.

Chapter 18

- SC Johnson and its environmental sustainability.
- Challenges faced when managing change.
- The right way to shake up a company.

A Team Effort

This book is the product of a fantastic McGraw-Hill/Irwin team. Moreover, we wrote this book believing that we are part of a team with the course instructor and with students. The entire team is responsible for the learning process.

Our goal, and that of your instructor, is to create a positive learning environment in which you can excel. But in the end, the raw material of this course is just words. It is up to you to use them as a basis for further thinking, deep learning, and constructive action.

What you do with the things you learn from this course, and with the opportunities the future holds,

counts. As a manager, you can make a dramatic difference for yourself and for other people. What managers do matters, *tremendously*.

Acknowledgments

This book could not have been written and published without the valuable contributions of many individuals.

Karen Hill and her colleagues at Elm Street Publishing were instrumental in creating a strong 9th edition. Many thanks for their meticulous attention to detail, ideas, and contributions. Karen has become a valued friend throughout the process; we couldn't have done it, or had as much fun, without Karen.

Our reviewers over the last eight editions contributed time, expertise, and terrific ideas that significantly enhanced the quality of the text. The reviewers of the 9th edition are:

J. Dana Clark
Appalachian State University

Laurie Dahlin
Worcester State College

Jordan J. Kaplan
Long Island University–Brooklyn

Eileen Kearney
Montgomery County Community College

John Keeling
Old Dominion University

Richard Kimbrough
University of Nebraska–Lincoln

Gary F. Kohut
The University of North Carolina at Charlotte

Venkatram Krishnamurthy
College of Lake County

William Patrick Leonard
Northwestern College

Flo Lucci
Quinsigamond Community College

Tish Matuszek
Troy University

Carol T. Miller
Community College of Denver

Anthony Narsing
Macon State College

Frank Novakowski
Davenport University

Gregory Schultz
Carroll University

Mansour Sharifzadeh
California State Polytechnic University–Pomona

Marc Siegall
California State–Chico

Brien N. Smith
Ball State University

Edward Von Leffern
California State Polytechnic University–Pomona

Kerry S. Webb
Texas Woman's University

Velvet Weems-Landingham
Kent State University–Geauga

Wendy V. Wysocki
Monroe County Community College

Many individuals contributed directly to our development as textbook authors. Dennis Organ provided one of the authors with an initial opportunity and guidance in textbook writing. Executive Editor John Weimeister has been a friend and adviser from the very beginning. The entire McGraw-Hill/Irwin team, starting with Executive Editor Mike Ablassmeir (who spontaneously and impressively knew *Rolling Stone*'s top three drummers of all time) provided great support and expertise to this new edition. Many thanks to Senior Development Editor Christine Scheid for so much good work on previous editions and for continued friendship. And to our new and superb Development Editor II Laura Griffin, and to Anke Braun Weekes, executive marketing manager and new mom, thank you for your skills, professionalism, collegiality, and for making the new edition *rock!* What a team!

Finally, we thank our families. Our parents, Jeanine and Tom Bateman and Clara and John Snell, provided us with the foundation on which we have built our careers. They continue to be a source of great support. Our wives, Mary Jo and Marybeth, demonstrated great encouragement, insight, and understanding throughout the process. Our children, Lauren, T. J., and James Bateman and Sara, Jack, and Emily Snell, inspire us in every way.

Thomas S. Bateman
Charlottesville, VA

Scott A. Snell
Charlottesville, VA

The Bottom Line

In this ever more competitive environment there are five essential types of performance, on which the organization beats, equals, or loses to the competition: cost, quality, speed, innovation, and service. These five performance dimensions, when done well, deliver value to the customer and competitive advantage to you and your organization.

Throughout the text, Bateman and Snell remind students of these five dimensions and their impact on the "bottom line" with marginal icons. This results-oriented approach is a unique hallmark of this textbook.

From page 61:

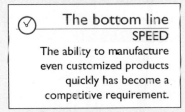

From page 255:

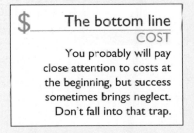

From page 104:

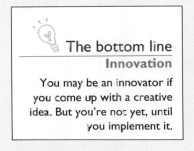

From page 321:

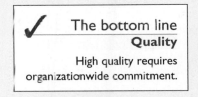

From page 396:

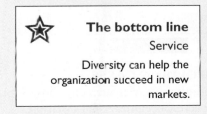

In CASE You Haven't Noticed . . .

Bateman and Snell have once again put together an outstanding selection of case studies of various lengths that highlight companies' ups and downs, stimulate learning and understanding, and challenge students to respond.

Instructors will find a wealth of relevant and updated cases in every chapter, using companies—big and small—that students will enjoy learning about.

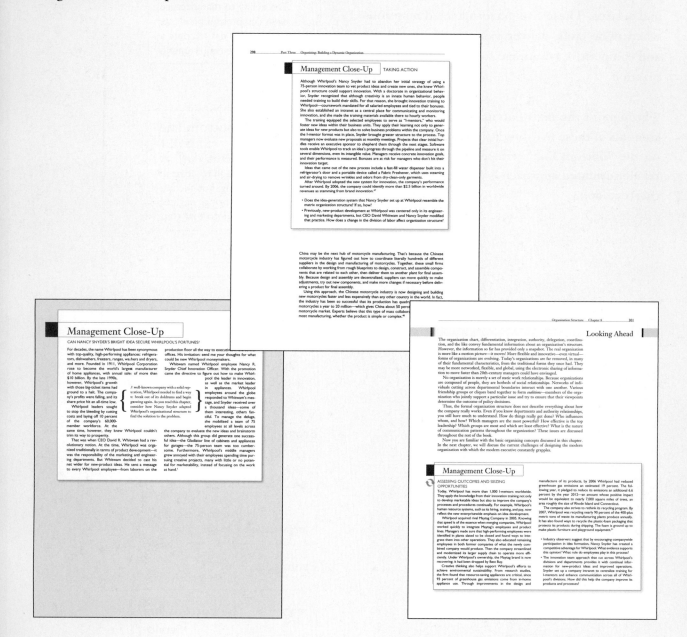

CHAPTER UNFOLDING CASES

Each chapter begins with a Management Close-Up that describes an actual organizational situation, leader, or company. The Management Close-Up is referred to again within the chapter in the Taking Action sections, showing the student how the chapter material relates back to the company, situation, or leader highlighted in the chapter opener. At the end of the chapter, the Assessing Outcomes and Seizing Opportunities sections tie up loose ends and bring the material full circle for the student.

Assurance of Learning

① This 9th edition contains revised learning objectives for each chapter, and ② learning objectives are called out within the chapter where the content begins. ③ The summary for each chapter ties the learning objectives back together as well.

④ Our test bank provides tagging for the learning objective that the question covers, so instructors will be able to test material covering all learning objectives, thus assuring that students have mastered the important topics.

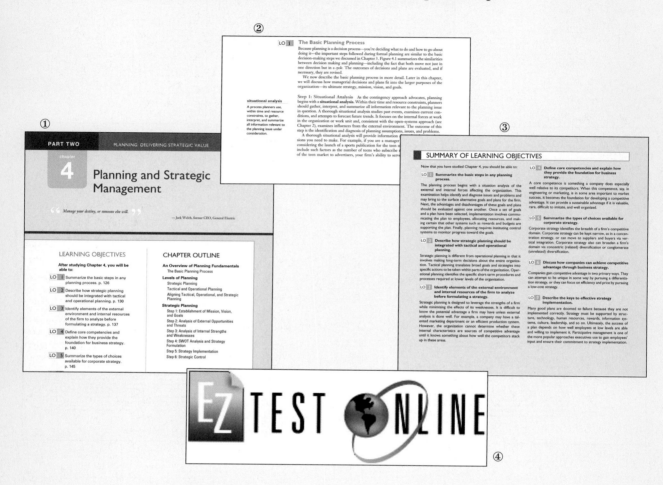

ASSURANCE OF LEARNING READY

Many educational institutions today are focused on the notion of *assurance of learning*, an important element of some accreditation standards. The 9th edition of *Management: Leading & Collaborating in a Competitive World* is designed specifically to support your assurance of learning initiatives with a simple, yet powerful solution.

Each test bank question for *Management: Leading & Collaborating in a Competitive World* maps to a specific chapter learning outcome/objective listed in the text. You can use our test bank software, EZ Test and EZ Test Online, or *Connect Management* to easily query for learning outcomes/objectives that directly relate to the learning objectives for your course. You can then use the reporting features of EZ Test to aggregate student results in similar fashion, making the collection and presentation of assurance of learning data simple and easy.

AACSB STATEMENT

The McGraw-Hill Companies is a proud corporate member of AACSB International. Understanding the importance and value of AACSB accreditation, *Management: Leading & Collaborating in a Competitive World*, 9e recognizes the curricula guidelines detailed in the AACSB standards for business accreditation by connecting selected questions in the text and/or the test bank to the six general knowledge and skill guidelines in the AACSB standards.

The statements contained in *Management: Leading & Collaborating in a Competitive World*, 9e are provided only as a guide for the users of this textbook. The AACSB leaves content coverage and assessment within the purview of individual schools, the mission of the school, and the faculty. While this book and the teaching package make no claim of any specific AACSB qualification or evaluation, we have within *Management: Leading & Collaborating in a Competitive World*, 9e labeled selected questions according to the six general knowledge and skills areas.

Management: Leading & Collaborating in a Competitive World is pedagogically
stimulating and is intended to maximize student learning. With this in mind,
we used a wide array of pedagogical features—some tried and true, others
new and novel:

RANDOM POP-UPS

Throughout the chapter, these marginal boxes
highlight interesting factoids, statistics, and quotes
relating to chapter content.

When managers make decisions, they often draw on other people's insights to help
them evaluate alternatives. In a survey of Canadian executives, more than two-thirds
said the opinion of their assistant was important in deciding which job candidate to
hire—a useful point to remember the next time you are job hunting.[23]

SUSTAINABILITY

Sustainability has become a more maintream and
widespread business concern and objective. Reflected
again in this edition are relevant examples. New
icons with green arrow highlight this content.

A prominent issue today pertains to natural resources: drilling for oil in formerly protected areas in the United States. Firms in the oil industry face considerable public opinion both in favor of preserving the natural environment and against the country's dependence on other countries for fuel. The protection of the natural environment is so important in managerial decisions that we devote Appendix C following Chapter 5 to that subject.

END-OF-CHAPTER ELEMENTS

- **Key terms** are page-referenced to the text and are part of the vocabulary-building emphasis. These terms are defined again in the glossary at the end of the book.

- A **Summary of Learning Objectives** provides clear, concise responses to the learning objectives, giving students a quick reference for reviewing the important concepts in the chapter.

- **Discussion Questions**, which follow the Summary of Learning Objectives, are thought-provoking questions on concepts covered in the chapter and ask for opinions on controversial issues.

- Each chapter ends with a **Concluding Case**, based on disguised but real companies and people, that reinforces key chapter elements and themes.

- Many new **Experiential Exercises** have been added to tried-and-true previous edition favorites. Some exercises allow for personality assessment, some are for use as group activities in the classroom, and some involve outside research.

KEY TERMS

SUMMARY OF LEARNING OBJECTIVES

DISCUSSION QUESTIONS

CONCLUDING CASE

J & G Garden Center: Lawn Care Services Division

EXPERIENTIAL EXERCISES

5.1 Measuring Your Ethical Work Behavior

Comprehensive Supplements

INSTRUCTOR'S MANUAL

Authored by two-time "Excellence in Teaching" award-winner Kimberly Jaussi of SUNY Binghamton, the Instructor's Manual was revised and updated to include thorough coverage of each chapter as well as time-saving features such as an outline on incorporating PowerPoint® slides as well as key student questions, class prepwork assignments, guidance for using the "unfolding" cases, and video supplements.

TEST BANK

Prepared by Carol Johnson, University of Denver, the Test Bank includes more than 100 questions per chapter in a variety of formats. It has been revised for accuracy and expanded to include a greater variety of comprehension and application (scenario-based) questions as well as tagged with Bloom's Taxonomy levels and AACSB requirements. **EZ Test** is a flexible and easy-to-use electronic testing program which allows instructors to create tests from book-specific items. A downloadable desktop version can be found on the IRCD. And **EZ Test Online** (*www.eztestonline.com*) allows you to access the test bank from the OLC virtually anywhere and at anytime. EZ-Test-created exams and quizzes can be administered online, providing instant feedback for students.

POWERPOINT PRESENTATION SLIDES

Prepared by Brad Cox, Midlands Technical College, the PowerPoint presentation collection contains an easy-to-follow outline including figures downloaded from the text. In addition to providing lecture notes, the slides also include questions for class discussion as well as company examples not found in the textbook. This versatility allows you to create a custom presentation suitable for your own classroom experience.

Note: All of the above can be found on the Instructor's Resource CD-ROM. It allows instructors to easily create their own custom presentations using the following resources: Instructor's Manual, Test Bank, EZ Test, and PowerPoint Presentations.

MCGRAW-HILL *CONNECT MANAGEMENT*

LESS MANAGING. MORE TEACHING. GREATER LEARNING

McGraw-Hill *Connect Management* is an online assignment and assessment solution that connects students with the tools and resources they'll need to achieve success.

McGraw-Hill *Connect Management* helps prepare students for their future by enabling faster learning, more efficient studying, and higher retention of knowledge.

MCGRAW-HILL *CONNECT MANAGEMENT* FEATURES

Connect Management offers a number of powerful tools and features to make managing assignments easier, so faculty can spend more time teaching. With *Connect Management*, students can engage with their coursework anytime and anywhere, making the learning process more accessible and efficient. *Connect Management* offers you the features described below.

Diagnostic and Adaptive Learning of Concepts: LearnsSmart Students want to make the best use of their study time. The LearnSmart adaptive self-study technology within *Connect Management* provides students with a seamless combination of practice, assessment, and remediation for every concept in the textbook. LearnSmart's intelligent software adapts to every student response and automatically delivers concepts that advance the student's understanding while reducing time devoted to the concepts already mastered. The result for every student is the fastest path to mastery of the chapter concepts. LearnSmart:

- Applies an intelligent concept engine to identify the relationships between concepts and to serve new concepts to each student only when he or she is ready.
- Adapts automatically to each student, so students spend less time on the topics they understand and practice more those they have yet to master.
- Provides continual reinforcement and remediation, but gives only as much guidance as students need.

- Integrates diagnostics as part of the learning experience.
- Enables you to assess which concepts students have efficiently learned on their own, thus freeing class time for more applications and discussion.

Online Interactives   Online Interactives are engaging tools that teach students to apply key concepts in practice. These Interactives provide immersive, experiential learning opportunities. Students will engage in a variety of interactive scenarios to deepen critical knowledge on key course topics. They receive immediate feedback at intermediate steps throughout each exercise, as well as comprehensive feedback at the end of the assignment. All Interactives are automatically scored and entered into the instructor gradebook.

Student Progress Tracking   *Connect Management* keeps instructors informed about how each student, section, and class is performing, allowing for more productive use of lecture and office hours. The progress-tracking function enables you to:

- View scored work immediately and track individual or group performance with assignment and grade reports.
- Access an instant view of student or class performance relative to learning objectives.
- Collect data and generate reports required by many accreditation organizations, such as AACSB.

Smart Grading   When it comes to studying, time is precious. *Connect Management* helps students learn more efficiently by providing feedback and practice material when they need it, where they need it. When it comes to teaching, your time also is precious. The grading function enables you to:

- Have assignments scored automatically, giving students immediate feedback on their work and side-by-side comparisons with correct answers.
- Access and review each response; manually change grades or leave comments for students to review.
- Reinforce classroom concepts with practice tests and instant quizzes.

Simple Assignment Management   With *Connect Management*, creating assignments is easier than ever, so you can spend more time teaching and less time managing. The assignment management function enables you to:
- Create and deliver assignments easily with selectable end-of-chapter questions and test bank items.

- Streamline lesson planning, student progress reporting, and assignment grading to make classroom management more efficient than ever.
- Go paperless with the eBook and online submission and grading of student assignments.

Instructor Library   The *Connect Management* Instructor Library is your repository for additional resources to improve student engagement in and out of class. You can select and use any asset that enhances your lecture. The *Connect Management* Instructor Library includes:

- Instructor Manual
- PowerPoint files
- TestBank
- Management Asset Gallery
- eBook

Student Study Center   The *Connect Management* Student Study Center is the place for students to access additional resources. The Student Study Center:

- Offers students quick access to lectures, practice materials, eBooks, and more.
- Provides instant practice material and study questions, easily accessible on the go.
- Gives students access to the Personalized Learning Plan described below.

Lecture Capture   Increase the attention paid to lecture discussion by decreasing the attention paid to note taking. For an additional charge Lecture Capture offers new ways for students to focus on the in-class discussion, knowing they can revisit important topics later. Lecture Capture enables you to:

- Record and distribute your lecture with a click of a button.
- Record and index PowerPoint presentations and anything shown on your computer so it is easily searchable, frame by frame.
- Offer access to lectures anytime and anywhere by computer, iPod, or mobile device.
- Increase intent listening and class participation by easing students' concerns about note taking. Lecture Capture will make it more likely you will see students' faces, not the tops of their heads.

Mcgraw-Hill *Connect Plus Management* McGraw-Hill reinvents the textbook learning experience for the modern student with *Connect Plus Management*. A seamless integration of an eBook and *Management, Connect Plus Management* provides all of the *Connect Management* features plus the following:

- An integrated eBook, allowing for anytime, anywhere access to the textbook.
- Dynamic links between the problems or questions you assign to your students and the location in the eBook where that problem or question is covered.
- A powerful search function to pinpoint and connect key concepts in a snap.

In short, *Connect Management* offers you and your students powerful tools and features that optimize your time and energies, enabling you to focus on course content, teaching, and student learning. *Connect Management* also offers a wealth of content resources for both instructors and students. This state-of-the-art, thoroughly tested system supports you in preparing students for the world that awaits.

For more information about Connect, go to **www.mcgrawhillconnect.com**, or contact your local McGraw-Hill sales representative.

TEGRITY CAMPUS: LECTURES 24/7

Tegrity Campus is a service that makes class time available 24/7 by automatically capturing every lecture in a searchable format for students to review when they study and complete assignments. With a simple one-click start-and-stop process, you capture all computer screens and corresponding audio. Students can replay any part of any class with easy-to-use browser-based viewing on a PC or Mac.

Educators know that the more students can see, hear, and experience class resources, the better they learn. In fact, studies prove it. With Tegrity Campus, students quickly recall key moments by using Tegrity Campus's unique search feature. This search helps students efficiently find what they need, when they need it, across an entire semester of class recordings. Help turn all your students' study time into learning moments immediately supported by your lecture.

To learn more about Tegrity watch a two-minute Flash demo at **http://tegritycampus.mhhe.com.**

MCGRAW-HILL CUSTOMER CARE CONTACT INFORMATION

At McGraw-Hill, we understand that getting the most from new technology can be challenging. That's why our services don't stop after you purchase our products. You can e-mail our Product Specialists 24 hours a day to get product-training online. Or you can search our knowledge bank of Frequently Asked Questions on our support Web site. For Customer Support, call 800-331-5094, e-mail **hmsupport@ mcgraw-hill.com**, or visit **www.mhhe.com/ support**. One of our Technical Support Analysts will be able to assist you in a timely fashion.

McGraw-Hill/Irwin Management is excited to now provide a one-stop-shop for our wealth of assets, making it super quick and easy for instructors to locate specific materials to enhance their courses.

The Management Asset Gallery is intuitively organized and designed, allowing instructors ease of use in previewing our wealth of resources. These resources correlate with specific asset categories and more than 40 topics in management.

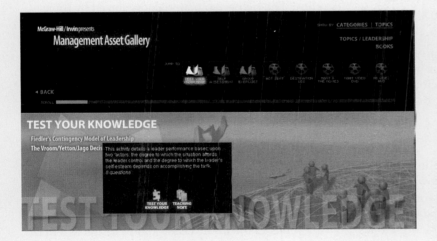

The Asset Gallery includes all of our non-text-specific management resources (Self-Assessments, Test Your Knowledge exercises, Videos and information, additional group and individual exercises) along with supporting PowerPoint® and Instructor Manual materials. Additionally, to help incorporate the assets in the classroom, a guide is provided specific to McGraw-Hill/Irwin texts. Instructors can reach the Asset Gallery through a link from the Instructor area of the Online Learning Center.

MANAGER'S HOT SEAT

NEW Look and Expanded 6 NEW Clips!

This interactive, video-based application puts students in the manager's hot seat, building critical thinking and decision-making skills and allowing students to apply concepts to real managerial challenges. Students watch as 21 real managers apply their years of experience when confronting unscripted issues such as bullying in the workplace, cyber loafing, globalization, intergenerational work conflicts, workplace violence, and leadership vs. management.

SELF-ASSESSMENT GALLERY

Unique among publisher-provided self-assessments, our 23 self-assessments provide students with background information to ensure that students understand the purpose of the assessment. Students test their values, beliefs, skills, and interests in a wide variety of areas allowing them to apply chapter content to their own lives and careers.

Every self-assessment is supported with PowerPoints and an instructor's manual in the Management Asset Gallery, making it easy for the instructor to create an engaging classroom discussion surrounding the assessments.

TEST YOUR KNOWLEDGE

To help reinforce students' understanding of key management concepts, Test Your Knowledge activities provide students a review of the conceptual materials followed by application-based questions to work through. Students can choose practice mode,

which provides them with detailed feedback after each question, or test mode, which provides feedback after the entire test has been completed. Every Test Your Knowledge activity is supported by instructor notes in the Management Asset Gallery to make it easy for the instructor to create engaging classroom discussions surrounding the materials students have completed.

MANAGEMENT HISTORY TIMELINE

This Web application allows instructors to present and students to learn the history of management in an engaging and interactive way. Management history is presented along an intuitive timeline that can be traveled through sequentially or by selected decade. With the click of a mouse students learn the important dates, see the people who influenced the field, and understand the general management theories that have molded and shaped management as we know it today.

VIDEO LIBRARY DVDS

McGraw-Hill/Irwin offers the most comprehensive video support for the Principles of Management classroom through course library video DVDs. This discipline has volume library DVDs tailored to integrate and visually reinforce chapter concepts. The library volume DVDs contain more than 70 clips! The rich video material, organized by topic, comes from sources such as BusinessWeek TV, PBS, NBC, BBC, SHRM, and McGraw-Hill. Video cases and video guides are provided for some clips.

DESTINATION CEO VIDEOS

BusinessWeek-produced video clips feature CEOs discussing a variety of topics. Accompanying each clip are multiple-choice questions and discussion questions to use in the classroom or assign as a quiz.

WWW.MHHE.COM/BATEMAN9E

More and more students are studying online and on the go. As they do, they can refer to the OLC for such benefits as self-grading quizzes, narrated slides, and iPod content.

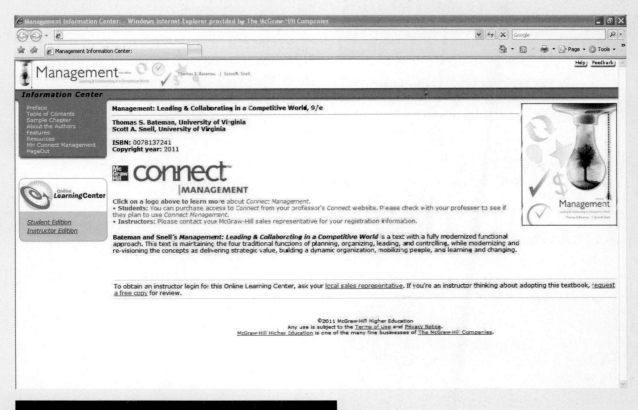

EBOOK OPTIONS

eBooks are an innovative way for students to save money and to "go green." McGraw-Hill's e-books typically cost 55% of bookstore price. Students have the choice between an online and a downloadable CourseSmart eBook.

Through *CourseSmart*, students have the flexibility to access an exact replica of their textbook from any computer that has Internet service without plug-ins or special software via the version, or create a library of books on their hard drive via the downloadable version. Access to the CourseSmart eBooks is one year.

Features: *CourseSmart* eBooks allow students to highlight, take notes, organize notes, and share the notes with other *CourseSmart* users. Students can also search terms across all eBooks in their purchased *CourseSmart* library. *CourseSmart* eBooks can be printed (five pages at a time).

More info and purchase: Please visit **www. coursesmart.com** for more information and to purchase access to our eBooks. *CourseSmart* allows students to try one chapter of the eBook, free charge, before purchase.

CUSTOM TEXTBOOK OPTION

Offer your students a textbook that matches your course exactly in four simple steps! McGraw-Hill's Primis Online digital database offers the flexibility to customize your course including material from the largest online collection of textbooks, readings, and cases. Please visit *www.primisonline.com* for more information, or call (800)962-9342.

CUSTOM E-BOOK OPTION

Primis leads the way in customized e-books with hundreds of titles available at prices that save students over 55% off the regular print purchase price. Additional information is available at (800) 962-9342, or by visiting *www.wbooks.primisonline.com*.

Contents in Brief

Contents

Part One

Foundations of Management

Part Two
Planning: Delivering Strategic Value

Part Three
Organizing: Building a Dynamic Organization

Chapter 11
Managing the Diverse Workforce   380

Part Four
Leading: Mobilizing People

Chapter 12
Leadership   416

Part Five
Controlling: Learning and Changing

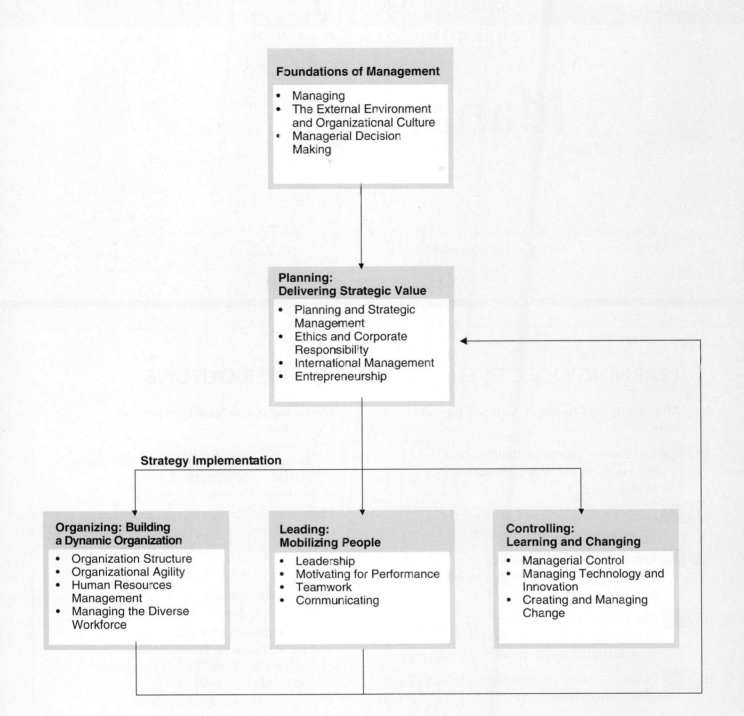

Foundations of Management

- Managing
- The External Environment and Organizational Culture
- Managerial Decision Making

Planning:
Delivering Strategic Value

- Planning and Strategic Management
- Ethics and Corporate Responsibility
- International Management
- Entrepreneurship

Strategy Implementation

Organizing: Building a Dynamic Organization

- Organization Structure
- Organizational Agility
- Human Resources Management
- Managing the Diverse Workforce

Leading:
Mobilizing People

- Leadership
- Motivating for Performance
- Teamwork
- Communicating

Controlling:
Learning and Changing

- Managerial Control
- Managing Technology and Innovation
- Creating and Managing Change

chapter

1

Managing

" Management means, in the last analysis, the substitution of thought for brawn and muscle, of knowledge for folklore and tradition, and of cooperation for force. "

— Peter Drucker

LEARNING OBJECTIVES

After studying Chapter 1, you will be able to:

LO 1 Summarize the major challenges of managing in the new competitive landscape. p. 4

LO 2 Describe the sources of competitive advantage for a company. p. 9

LO 3 Explain how the functions of management are evolving in today's business environment. p. 14

LO 4 Compare how the nature of management varies at different organizational levels. p. 18

LO 5 Define the skills you need to be an effective manager. p. 20

LO 6 Understand the principles that will help you manage your career. p. 22

CHAPTER OUTLINE

Managing in the New Competitive Landscape
Globalization
Technological Change
Knowledge Management
Collaboration across "Boundaries"

Managing for Competitive Advantage
Innovation
Quality
Service
Speed
Cost Competitiveness
Delivering All Five

The Functions of Management
Planning: Delivering Strategic Value
Organizing: Building a Dynamic Organization
Leading: Mobilizing People
Controlling: Learning and Changing
Performing All Four Management Functions

Management Levels and Skills
Top-Level Managers
Middle-Level Managers
Frontline Managers
Working Leaders with Broad Responsibilities
Management Skills

You and Your Career
Be Both a Specialist and a Generalist
Be Self-Reliant
Be Connected
Actively Manage Your Relationship with Your Organization
Survive and Thrive

Management Close-Up

CAN ELON MUSK KEEP TESLA MOTORS RUNNING?

A small player in the struggling global auto market, California-based start-up Tesla Motors is trying to revolutionize its industry. Headed by chief executive Elon Musk, Tesla has an ambitious vision: to mass produce electric cars that end Americans' dependence on fossil fuels and cut greenhouse gas emissions. The South African–born Musk, who holds degrees in both physics and finance, predicts that by 2030, the majority of cars made in the United States will be electric.

A bold prediction? Maybe. But Elon Musk is a skilled manager. By his thirties he had led two successful Internet companies: Zip2 (later sold to Compaq) and X.com (which morphed into what is now known as PayPal). In 2004 Musk became chairman of Tesla Motors, a start-up founded the year before by CEO Martin Eberhard. Self-professed car geeks, Musk and Eberhard saw a bright future for electric cars. But the two often disagreed about how to move the company forward. Costs and conflicts escalated until 2007, when the board of directors ousted Eberhard.

With Tesla at a turning point, Musk helped the company regroup, introducing its first model, the all-electric Roadster, in 2008. The two-seat sports car goes from 0 to 60 miles per hour in four seconds and hits a top speed of 135 mph. Powered solely by a lithium-ion battery, the Roadster operates without engine noise and can travel nearly 250 miles on a single charge. It also doesn't emit any gases to the environment.

Despite its substantial $109,000 price tag, the Tesla Roadster sold out almost immediately. Today, Tesla ships 10 of the cars each week and has a year-long waiting list.[1]

> To be effective, a manager is often compelled to create change. But bringing about change is hard, especially in a difficult business environment. As you read this chapter, think about the challenges Elon Musk faces as his company attempts to fundamentally change the way Americans think about their cars.

Tesla Motors' Elon Musk is arguably one of the most interesting leaders in business today. He combines strong creative skills with a keen ability to see the big picture—and he's been remarkably successful at building organizations. Of course, not every manager or organization succeeds. A recent story of failure that shocked many Americans involved the care provided to wounded soldiers at the Walter Reed Army Medical Center in Washington, D.C. Reporters investigating outpatient facilities of Walter Reed—which ranks among the nation's top military hospitals—discovered that in some facilities, outpatients were coping with mold, roaches, rodents, and damaged walls and doors. Many outpatients, some with serious injuries and mental impairments, complained of paperwork problems that kept them from receiving services. Testifying before Congress, General Richard A. Cody, the Army's vice chief of staff, admitted fundamental management problems:

> Our counselors and case managers are overworked, and they do not receive enough training. We do not adequately communicate necessary information. Our administrative processes are needlessly cumbersome and . . . take too long. Our medical holding units are not manned to the proper level, and we do not assign leaders who can ensure a proper accountability, proper discipline and well-being, . . . and our facilities are not maintained to the standards that we know is [sic] right.[2]

Major General George W. Weightman, who lost his job as Walter Reed's commander as a result of the scandal, acknowledged that the organization had experienced a "failure of leadership."[3]

Companies, like individuals, succeed or fail for a variety of reasons. Some of these reasons are circumstantial. Most are personal and human and include the decisions managers make and the actions they take.

In business, there is no replacement for effective management. Companies may fly high for a while, but they cannot do well for very long without good management. It's the same for individuals: *BusinessWeek*'s Managers of the Year succeed by focusing on fundamentals, knowing what's important, and managing well. The aim of this book is to help you succeed in those pursuits.

Managing in the New Competitive Landscape

LO 1
When the economy is soaring, business seems easy. Starting an Internet company looked easy in the 1990s, and ventures related to the real estate boom looked like a sure thing during much of the past decade. But investors grew wary of dot-com start-ups, and the demand for new homes dropped off the table when the economy crashed in late 2008. At such times, it becomes evident that management is a challenge requiring constant adaptation to new circumstances.

What defines the competitive landscape of today's business? You will be reading about many relevant issues in the coming chapters, but we begin here by highlighting four key elements that make the current business landscape different from the past: globalization, technological change, the importance of knowledge and ideas, and collaboration across organizational "boundaries."

Globalization

Far more than in the past, today's enterprises are global, with offices and production facilities in countries all over the world. Corporations operate worldwide, transcending national borders. Companies that want to grow often need to tap international markets, where incomes are rising and demand is increasing. GE, which became a massive and profitable corporation by selling appliances, light bulbs, and machinery to U.S. customers, recently announced that it expected its foreign sales to equal its sales within the United States. GE's biggest foreign customers are in Europe, but sales volume in China and India is rising fast.[4]

Globalization also means that a company's talent can come from anywhere. As with its sales, half of GE's employees work outside the United States.[5] Cisco, a leader in equipment for computer networking, considers maintaining operations in India to be an essential tactic for staying competitive. Cisco serves the fast-growing Indian Internet market at a crucial time: the growth in demand is attracting low-cost competition from Chinese businesses.[6]

Globalization has changed the face of the workforce. Management in this new competitive landscape will need to attract and effectively manage a talent pool from all over the globe.

Another force that is making globalization both more possible and more inevitable is the Internet. Now that more than a billion users have come online, more and more of the new users are in developing nations such as China, India, Russia, and Brazil.[7] As people in developing nations increasingly turn to the power of the Web, they become a force to develop content in their own languages and suited to their own means of access, such as inexpensive laptops.

The global reach of the Internet pushed Mitch Free to expand his business, MFG.com, into China. MFG.com runs a Web site where manufacturers that need parts post their specifications online, and suppliers bid to provide those parts. Free, who grew up in a small town in Georgia and had barely traveled outside the United States, had never planned to be an international manager, but Chinese suppliers soon began submitting requests to participate. At the same time, manufacturers were pressing MFG.com to include Asian suppliers, which often could offer the best prices.

So Free traveled to Shanghai, China. He learned about the business culture, such as the importance of cultivating business relationships and networks. After a difficult search, he made a key hiring decision: general manager James Jin, who speaks fluent English, studied global management, and has experience in manufacturing both in the United States and China. The effort was well rewarded. Jin has helped Free navigate the fast-growing, ambitious business landscape of his native China. Sales in China accounted for more than 10 percent of MFG.com's total annual sales and are growing faster than overall sales.[8]

Companies can get their message to users on every continent and often are expected to provide service anytime, anywhere. This can affect how and when people work. Laura Asiala, a manager for Dow Corning, based in Midland, Michigan, supervises employees in Tokyo, Seoul, Hong Kong, Shanghai, and Brussels. To keep in touch with them, she may start working at 5:00 a.m. some days and end as late as midnight. She takes a break from 3:30 to 9:30 each day, and technology makes it possible to do some of her communicating from home.[9]

Successful CEOs know that the change from a local to a global marketplace is gaining momentum and is irreversible.[10] For example, PepsiCo's chief executive, Indra Nooyi, brings a much-needed global viewpoint to a company whose international business has been growing three times faster than sales in the United States. Nooyi, who was raised in India and educated there and in the United States, has steered the company toward more "better for you" and "good for you" snacks with acquisitions including a nut packager in Bulgaria and a hummus producer in Israel.[11]

Thus globalization affects small companies as well as large. Many small companies export their goods. Many domestic firms assemble their products in other countries. And companies are under pressure to improve their products in the face of intense competition from foreign manufacturers. Firms today must ask themselves, "How can we be the best in the world?"

For students, it's not too early to think about the personal ramifications. In the words of CEO Jim Goodnight of SAS, the largest privately held software company in the world, "The best thing business schools can do to prepare their students is to encourage them to look beyond their own backyards. Globalization has opened the world for many opportunities, and schools should encourage their students to take advantage of them."[12]

Technological Change

The Internet's impact on globalization is only one of the ways that technology is vitally important in the business world. Technology both complicates things and creates new opportunities. The challenges come from the rapid rate at which communication, transportation, information, and other technologies change.[13] For example, after just a couple of decades of widespread desktop use, customers switched to laptop models, which require different accessories.[14] Any company that serves desktop users has to rethink its customers' wants and needs, not to mention the possibility that these customers are now working at the airport or a local Starbucks outlet, rather than in an office.

Google search sites span the Internet in more than 100 languages.

Later chapters will discuss technology further, but here we highlight the rise of the Internet and its effects. Why is the Internet so important to business?[15] It is a marketplace, a means for manufacturing goods and services, a distribution channel, an information service, and more. It drives down costs and speeds up globalization. It improves efficiency of decision making. It facilitates design of new products, from pharmaceuticals to financial services. Managers can watch and learn what other companies are doing—on the other side of the world. While these advantages create business opportunities, they also create threats as competitors sometimes capitalize on new developments more than you do.

It may be hard to imagine that just a few years ago, going online to order plane tickets, read the news, or share photos was a novelty. Some online success stories, such as Amazon, Monster, and Google, are purely Internet businesses. Other companies, including Barnes & Noble, Best Buy, and Office Depot, have incorporated online channels into an established business strategy.

The Internet's impact is felt not only at the level of businesses as a whole but also by individual employees and managers. Just as globalization has stretched out the workdays of some people, high-tech gadgets have made it possible to stay connected to work anytime, anywhere. This ability is both a convenience and a potential source of stress. The stress comes when employees or their supervisors don't set limits on being connected. Facilities manager Cherri Chiodo loves the convenience of her BlackBerry but finds that it sometimes replaces face-to-face communication with family members. Real estate broker Ted Helgans calls his BlackBerry a "traveling office" and a valuable tool for getting and sharing information. Helgans emphasizes that users can and should decide when to turn the devices off.[17] Jean Chatzkey, an editor for *Money* magazine, found that she constantly interrupted whatever she was doing to check e-mail on her Palm Treo. Realizing that the device had become more of a distraction than a help, Chatzkey began reminding herself that the messages were not emergencies; in fact, many came from subscriptions that Chatzkey

Among people who work long hours in high-stress jobs, 59% said technology lengthens rather than shortens their workday.[16]

decided she could happily live without.[18] Thus, using technology effectively is more than a matter of learning
new skills; it also involves making judgments about when and where to apply
the technology for maximum benefit.

Knowledge Management

Companies and managers face a growing need for good, new ideas. Because
companies in advanced economies have
become so efficient at producing physical goods, most workers have been
freed up to provide services or "abstract
goods" such as software, entertainment,
data, and advertising. Efficient factories
with fewer workers produce the cereals
and cell phones the market demands;

Will Wright, creator of "The
Sims" video games, poses with a
computer image of the game. His
newest creation, "Spore," will
undoubtedly build on the success
of "The Sims."

meanwhile, more and more workers create software and invent new goods and services.
These workers, whose primary contributions are ideas and problem-solving expertise,
are often referred to as *knowledge workers*. Managing these workers poses some particular challenges, which we will examine throughout this book. For example, determining
whether they are doing a good job can be difficult, because the manager cannot simply
count or measure a knowledge worker's output. Also, these workers often are most
motivated to do their best when the work is interesting, not because of a carrot or stick
dangled by the manager.[19]

Because the success of modern businesses so often depends on the knowledge used
for innovation and the delivery of services, organizations need to manage that knowledge. **Knowledge management** is the set of practices aimed at discovering and harnessing an organization's intellectual resources—fully utilizing the intellects of the
organization's people. Knowledge management is about finding, unlocking, sharing,
and altogether capitalizing on the most precious resources of an organization: people's
expertise, skills, wisdom, and relationships. Knowledge managers find these human
assets, help people collaborate and learn, help people generate new ideas, and harness
those ideas into successful innovations.

In hospitals, important knowledge includes patients' histories, doctors' orders,
billing information, dietary requirements, prescriptions administered, and much
more. With lives at stake, many hospitals have embraced knowledge management.
For example, at Virginia Commonwealth University (VCU) Health System, a single
information system lets doctors write prescriptions, look up patient information and
lab results, and consult with one another. Billing also is automated as part of VCU's
knowledge management system, making the process more efficient and connecting with patient data so that it can remind the physician of all the conditions being
treated—and billed for.[20] Hospitals may also give patients access to the knowledge
management system so that they can schedule appointments, request prescription
refills, and send questions to their doctors.

**knowledge
management**

Practices aimed at
discovering and harnessing
an organization's intellectual
resources.

Collaboration across "Boundaries"

One of the most important processes of knowledge management is to ensure that people in different parts of the organization collaborate effectively with one another. This
requires productive communications among different departments, divisions, or other
subunits of the organization. For example, British Petroleum wants "T-shaped" managers who break out of the traditional corporate hierarchy to share knowledge freely

across the organization (the horizontal part of the T) while remaining fiercely committed to the bottom-line performance of their individual business units (the vertical part). This emphasis on dual responsibilities for performance and knowledge sharing also occurs at pharmaceutical giant GlaxoSmithKline, large German industrial company Siemens, and London-based steelmaker Ispat International.[21]

For example, Toyota keeps its product development process efficient by bringing together design engineers and manufacturing employees from the very beginning. Often, manufacturing employees can see ways to simplify a design so that it is easier to make without defects or unnecessary costs. Toyota expects its employees to listen to input from all areas of the organization, so this type of collaboration is a natural part of the organization's culture. Employees use the software to share their knowledge—best practices they have developed for design and manufacturing.[22] Thus, at Toyota, knowledge management supports collaboration, and vice versa.

Collaboration across "boundaries" occurs even beyond the boundaries of the organization itself. Companies today must motivate and capitalize on the ideas of people outside the organization. How can a company best use the services of its consultants, ad agencies, and suppliers? To obtain the product development software that supports collaboration between manufacturing and design, Toyota collaborated with a software developer, PTC. Toyota and PTC together identified how software could support the company's strategy of "lean product development," and they kept meeting regularly to continue improving the software. This collaboration not only helped Toyota obtain a superior product but also helped PTC improve the value of the software it offers to its other customers.[23]

Collaboration with investors helped a pair of entrepreneurs launch their company in the seriously risky business of making games. When Richard Tait and Whit Alexander developed their unusual board game Cranium, they confidently ordered 20,000 units from a Chinese manufacturer before winning any orders from retailers. But retailers generally are reluctant to take a chance on new products. The solution was to collaborate with a different kind of distributor. Howard Schultz, chairman of the Starbucks coffee chain, thought the game was great, so he let Tait and Alexander place samples of Cranium in Starbucks outlets, where customers could try playing it. Customers loved it. Thanks to its track record at Starbucks, Cranium became not only the first game sold at Starbucks but also the first board game sold on Amazon.com, which had earlier turned it down. That success enabled Cranium the company to launch a dozen more games, now sold in 30 countries.[24]

Innovation and collaboration are the key factors in the phenomenal success of Cranium. This board game was the fastest selling game in history when it was released in 1998, with 100,000 units sold within seven months. Creators Richard Tait, left, and Whit Alexander are shown here demonstrating their highly successful board game.

Customers, too, can be collaborators. Companies must realize that the need to serve the customer drives everything else. Best serving the customer can start with involving the customer more in company decisions. For example, companies like Procter & Gamble are getting customers to think creatively and talk with one another online to come up with new product and service ideas.[25] Tapping into the popularity of social networking Web sites like Facebook and MySpace, P&G has set up Web sites aimed at bringing its customers together. One site is a discussion group for women, where they can discuss health and other concerns. Although such sites offer advertising opportunities, P&G uses them primarily as a way to learn more about consumers' attitudes.[26]

Managing for Competitive Advantage

The rise of the Internet turned careers (and lives) upside down. Students dropped out of school to join Internet start-ups or start their own. Managers in big corporations quit their jobs to do the same. Investors salivated, and invested heavily. The risks were often ignored, or downplayed—sometimes tragically, as the boom went bust. Or consider an earlier industry with similar transforming power: automobiles. There have been at least 2,000 car makers, but now only three U.S. car companies are left in the United States. In recent years, even these three have struggled to stay afloat as sales declined. Despite plant closings, layoffs, and other belt-tightening, the financial status of General Motors and Chrysler remained so shaky that, with talk of bankruptcy, President Obama tried to assure the country that the U.S.-based auto industry would not "vanish."[27]

What is the lesson to be learned from the failures in these important transformational industries? A key to understanding the success of a company—whether traditional, Internet-based, or a combination of both—is not how much the industry in which it operates will affect society or how much it will grow. The key is the competitive advantage held by a particular company and how well it can sustain that advantage. Good managers know that they are in a competitive struggle to survive and win.

To survive and win, you have to gain advantage over your competitors and earn a profit. You gain competitive advantage by being better than your competitors at doing valuable things for your customers. But what does this mean, specifically? To succeed, what must managers deliver? The fundamental success drivers are innovation, quality, service, speed, and cost competitiveness.

Innovation

Google's search engine quickly became a hit, and investors bid up the stock price of the company when it went public. But now that the free search service is used around the world, what can the company do next? Competitors are working hard to take away some of Google's share of the market. Google management knows that they need to come up with the next big idea, so they require their engineers to devote one-fifth of their time to special projects of their own.[28]

Innovation is the introduction of new goods and services. Your firm must adapt to changes in consumer demands and to new competitors. Products don't sell forever; in fact, they don't sell for nearly as long as they used to, because so many competitors are introducing so many new products all the time. Your firm must innovate, or it will die. Likewise, you have to be ready with new ways to communicate with customers and deliver the products to them. When the Net allowed merchants to bypass traditional distribution channels and reach buyers directly, traditional marketers had to learn how to innovate to remain competitive.

Sometimes the most important innovation isn't the product itself but the way it is delivered. Borrowing an idea that has proved popular in Europe, Opaque–Dining in the Dark has collaborated with the Braille Institute of America to present dining events at the Hyatt West Hollywood in total darkness. Diners select gourmet meals from a menu in a lighted lounge and then are led into a dark banquet room by blind or visually impaired waiters. The attraction

---

The bottom line
Innovation

Because it's easy for managers to get so caught up in being busy, get distracted, and lose sight of what really drives performance, you will periodically see icons as "bottom-line" reminders of the need for innovation, quality, service, speed, and cost competitiveness.

innovation

The introduction of new goods and services.

People entering the Dans le Noir (In the Black) restaurant in Paris where they will enjoy a dining experience in complete darkness as if they were blind. Blind waiters serve as guides. The concept is an innovative approach to fine dining, and restaurants such as this are spreading around the globe.

is that diners experience the meal in a completely new way because they are forced to concentrate on their senses of taste, smell, and touch.[29]

The need for innovation is driven in part by globalization. One obvious reason is that when facilities in other countries can manufacturer appliances or write software code at a lower cost than facilities in the United States, U.S. facilities are operating at a disadvantage. They have to deliver something that their foreign competitors don't offer—and often that means something new. Philips, which started out making light bulbs in the Netherlands in the 1890s, later expanded into X-ray machines, record albums, and then semiconductors (microchips), which have since become a highly competitive, cost-driven business. Now Philips is moving into higher-end products such as medical equipment and LED-based lighting systems. The company has set up research as well as manufacturing operations of its own in China, because that country is becoming a key source of technical know-how, not just cheap labor.[30] The demand for innovation will only intensify.

Innovation is today's holy grail.[31] Like the other sources of competitive advantage, innovation comes from people, it must be a strategic goal, and it must be managed properly. Later chapters will show you how great companies innovate.

Quality

When Spectrum Health, a hospital chain based in Grand Rapids, Michigan, asked patients how well they were served, patients rated staff low on helpfulness and their attitude toward visitors and said they didn't get good information about procedures or how to take care of themselves after being released to go home. Spectrum set up an advisory council of patients and family members, making visiting hours more flexible, getting patient input into who was allowed to hear medical information and make decisions about treatment, and calling discharged patients at home to make sure they understood the directions they had received. Satisfaction scores of Spectrum patients improved dramatically.[32]

quality

The excellence of your product (goods or services).

Spectrum Health's efforts reflect a commitment to quality. In general, **quality** is the excellence of your product. The importance of quality and the standards for acceptable quality have increased dramatically in recent years. Customers now demand high-quality goods and services, and often they will accept nothing less. In the hospital industry, the government is contributing to that trend. To receive full reimbursement from Medicare, hospitals must participate in a national program of patient satisfaction surveys. Results of these surveys are posted on the Department of Health and Human Service's Medicare information Web site, hospitalcompare.hhs.gov, so that patients can compare the rankings of hospitals in their area when choosing services.[33]

Historically, quality pertained primarily to the physical goods that customers bought, and it referred to attractiveness, lack of defects, reliability, and long-term dependability. The traditional approach to quality was to check work after it was completed and then eliminate defects, using inspection and statistical data to determine whether products were up to standards. But then W. Edwards Deming, J. M. Juran, and other quality gurus convinced managers to take a more complete approach to achieving *total* quality. This includes *preventing* defects before they occur, *achieving zero defects* in manufacturing, and *designing* products for quality. The goal is to solve and eradicate from the beginning all quality-related problems and to live a philosophy of *continuous improvement* in the way the company operates.[34]

Quality is further provided when companies customize goods and services to the wishes of the individual consumer. Choices at Starbucks give consumers thousands of variations on the drinks they can order, whether it's half-caff or all caffeine, skim milk or soy milk, or shots of espresso and any of a variety of flavored syrups. Car buyers can go online to "build their own" Mini Cooper, down to the color of the light for the speedometer. And for a premium price, candy lovers can select M&M's

candies bearing the message of their own creation.[35] Similarly, Jones Soda Company lets visitors to its Web site order a 12-pack of soda with their photo on the bottles. They upload the photo to the myJones Web site (www.myjones.com), choose a soda flavor, and pay by credit card.[36]

Providing world-class quality requires a thorough understanding of what quality really is.[37] Quality can be measured in terms of product performance, customer service, reliability (avoidance of failure or break-downs), conformance to standards, durability, and aesthetics. At the beginning of this section, we mentioned how hospitals are using patient surveys to measure quality and meet Medicare requirements. However, a recent study conducted by the University of Pennsylvania School of Medicine determined that a patient's risk of dying was not significantly less at hospitals that scored well on Medicare's quality measures.[38] But certainly, quality care is more than staying alive! Only when you move beyond broad, generic concepts such as "quality" and identify specific quality requirements can you identify problems, target needs, set performance standards more precisely, and deliver world-class value.

Every time you get a haircut at a salon, you are contributing to the employment of someone in one of the fastest growing job categories, the service sector.

Service

As noted, important quality measures often pertain to the level of service received by customers. This dimension of quality is particularly important because the service sector has come to dominate the U.S. economy. According to the federal government, the value of services produced in the United States is much more than one and a half times the value of tangible goods produced.[39] The Bureau of Labor Statistics projects that the fastest-growing job categories will be almost entirely services and retailing jobs, and the jobs expected to see the greatest declines are almost all in manufacturing.[40] Services include intangible products such as insurance, hotel accommodations, medical care, and haircuts.

In a competitive context, **service** means giving customers what they want or need, when they want it. So service is focused on continually meeting the needs of customers to establish mutually beneficial long-term relationships. Software companies, in addition to providing the actual programs, may help their customers identify requirements, set up computer systems, and perform maintenance. Best Buy adjusted its store environment so that it would be more inviting to female shoppers. The chain's loud music and emphasis on high-tech features had been aimed at young men, but the store found that women today influence 9 out of 10 consumer electronics purchases. So Best Buy lowered the volume and the lighting, and it trained staff to discuss what customers want the technology to do for them, rather than merely pointing out each item's bells and whistles. The chain is also trying to hire more female salespeople.[41]

An important dimension of service quality is making it easy and enjoyable for customers to experience a service or to buy and use products. The Detroit Institute of Arts recently hired Sven Gierlinger, a manager from the Ritz-Carlton hotel chain, noted for its exceptional level of service, to be its vice president of museum operations. As the art museum prepared for a grand reopening following a major renovation, Gierlinger analyzed the types of customer interactions that occur in a museum, identifying ways to make the experience more pleasant. He also worked with his staff to identify ways to customize services, such as offering tours tailored to the interests of particular groups.[42]

service

The speed and dependability with which an organization delivers what customers want.

Speed

Google constantly improves its search product at a rapid rate. In fact, its entire culture is based on rapid innovation. Sheryl Sandberg, a Google vice president, once made a mistake because she was moving too fast to plan carefully. Although the mistake cost the company a few million dollars, Google cofounder Larry Page responded to her explanation and apology by saying he was actually glad she had made the mistake. It showed that she appreciated the company's values. Page told Sandberg, "I want to run a company where we are moving too quickly and doing too much, not being too cautious and doing too little. If we don't have any of these mistakes, we're just not taking enough risks."[43]

While it's unlikely that Google actually favors mistakes over money-making ideas, Page's statement expressed an appreciation that in the modern business environment, **speed**—rapid execution, response, and delivery of results—often separates the winners from the losers. How fast can you develop and get a new product to market? How quickly can you respond to customer requests? You are far better off if you are faster than the competition—and if you can respond quickly to your competitors' actions.

speed

Fast and timely execution, response, and delivery of results.

Speed isn't everything—you can't get sloppy in your quest to be first. But other things being equal, faster companies are more likely to be the winners, slow ones the losers. Even pre-Internet, companies were getting products to market and in the hands of customers faster than ever. Now the speed requirement has increased exponentially. Everything, it seems, is on fast-forward.

Speed is no longer just a goal of some companies; it is a strategic imperative. In the auto industry, getting faster is essential just for keeping up with the competition. A recent study found that the top assembly plant in the United States was Ford's Atlanta facility, where employees needed just 15.4 hours to assemble a vehicle. Compare that with the 1980s, when GM employees needed 40 hours to assemble a vehicle.[44] Another important measure of speed in the auto industry is the time the company takes to go from product concept to availability of the vehicle in the showroom. During the 1980s, that time was about 30 or 40 months. Today Toyota has cut the process to an average of 24 months; it needed just 22 months to launch its Tundra pickup.[45]

Cost Competitiveness

Wal-Mart keeps driving hard to find new ways to cut billions of dollars from its already very low distribution costs. It leads the industry in efficient distribution, but competitors are copying Wal-Mart's methods, so the efficiency no longer gives it as much of an advantage.[46] Wal-Mart has sought to keep costs down by scheduling store employees more efficiently. It recently introduced a computerized system that schedules employees based on each store's sales, transactions, units sold, and customer traffic. The system is intended to schedule just enough workers, with full staffing only at the busiest times of day and days of the week, so it requires more flexibility from Wal-Mart's employees.[47]

cost competitiveness

Keeping costs low to achieve profits and be able to offer prices that are attractive to consumers.

Wal-Mart's efforts are aimed at **cost competitiveness,** which means keeping costs low enough so that the company can realize profits and price its products (goods or services) at levels that are attractive to consumers. Needless to say, if you can offer a desirable product at a lower price, it is more likely to sell.

Start-up firms typically practice cost competitiveness out of necessity. Paul Graham's company, Y Combinator, provides seed funding to start-ups, and he observes how new companies keep their expenses down because they simply don't have much to spend. A start-up's total information technology could be just a few laptops connected to the Internet and running free Web-based software. Graham says lean times can remind managers to think about whether all their expenses are necessary: "You may as well use [a slowdown] as an excuse to clean out all the expensive crap you have lying around."[48]

Managing your costs and keeping them down requires being efficient: accomplishing your goals by using your resources wisely and minimizing waste. Many top executives fly on private jets, which of course is more expensive than buying a ticket on a commercial airline. If the company can arrange to participate in a service such as NetJets, where the company buys only shares in a jet with the rights to use it, this can trim the price and make the arrangement more worthwhile.[49]

One manager with a reputation for meeting this challenge skillfully is Mark Hurd, chief executive of Hewlett-Packard. For Hurd, operating efficiently is the main goal of a necessary and ongoing effort to look hard at all the company's numbers and identify areas where the company can get the job done with less. For example, HP improved the efficiency of its information technology (IT) group by reducing the number of data centers from 85 to 6. Critics question whether HP under Hurd is investing enough in innovation for the future, but at least in the short term, the drive for efficiency has positioned Hewlett-Packard to handle difficult times. In the recent recession, HP forecasted a sales decline but expected its profits would actually rise. That's not so strange when you consider that even as HP reduced staffing in support departments like IT, it was increasing its sales force and helping sales people target HP's most profitable goods and services.[50]

One reason every company must worry about cost is that consumers can easily compare prices on the Internet from thousands of competitors. Consumers looking to buy popular items, such as cameras, printers, and plane fares, can go online to research the best models and the best deals. If you can't cut costs and offer attractive prices, you can't compete.

Delivering All Five

Don't assume that you can settle for delivering just one of the five competitive advantages: low cost alone, or quality alone, for example. The best managers and companies deliver them all.

Virginia Mason Medical Center, like many hospitals, felt challenged in delivering low costs along with high quality and superior services. Virginia Mason has a reputation for high-quality care, but it was losing money treating certain patients. So Virginia Mason collaborated with Aetna, an insurer that pays for 10 percent of the medical center's business, and found ways to treat some of the most expensive conditions so that they became more economical to insure but were paid for at higher rates that would be profitable for Virginia Mason. The medical center has also improved quality through measures that enhance speed—in this case, cutting waiting times for patients, such as a reduction in the 4-hour wait for chemotherapy to 90 minutes.[51]

Trade-offs may occur among the five sources of competitive advantage, but this doesn't need to be a zero-sum game where one has to suffer at the expense of another. Avon focused on cost savings when it contracted with IBM Global Services to handle human resources tasks such as payroll and benefits management. Turning over those responsibilities to a company that specializes in performing them efficiently also frees Avon to concentrate on innovating in areas it knows best: direct selling cosmetics to new customers. Avon's CEO, Andrea Jung, launched an effort to sell cosmetics to Chinese consumers through hundreds of thousands of representatives who are licensed with the government.[52] Avon also has tapped into the trend toward customization by introducing the Hook Up Connector, a packaging product that allows consumers to snap together items of their choice, such as a lipstick and mascara.[53]

These sources of competitive advantage were behind *BusinessWeek*'s choices of best and worst managers. By and large, "best" and "worst" are determined by results, as indicated by the examples in the "From the pages of *BusinessWeek*" feature.

Don't forget:

Don't focus on one aspect of performance and neglect the others. You might be better at or more interested in one than the others, but you should strive for all five.

The Best and Worst Managers of 2008

The best leaders have not only ridden out the crisis so far but also gleaned valuable, often profitable, lessons from it. The worst? Well, some helped set the economic crisis in motion; others became paragons of bad judgment in a time of trouble. Here are the leaders of 2008 with all their successes and failures.

It's not easy to measure excellence in a year like 2008. While some managers can be judged by the bottom line, others merely had the good fortune to be running a food company instead of a financial firm. Then again, with volatile commodity prices, succeeding in the food business wasn't such an easy task.

BusinessWeek has singled out 12 executives who did a remarkable job of navigating stormy waters. Some have posted stellar results. Others are struggling. But there are lessons to be learned from each of them.

David Axelrod, 53
Chief strategist, Obama campaign

The Chicago consultant may have described himself as the "keeper of the message," but he was more an architect. Credited with shaping Obama's mission of hopeful change, he drew campaign themes from the candidate's life story, recruited potent supporters, and made sure any attack on rivals was firm, but seldom angry or demeaning. The tightly run campaign had few leaks and little infighting. And like any good right-hand man, Axelrod stayed focused on the boss. "I see myself simply as helping disseminate the message of Barack Obama," he recently told NBC's *Meet the Press.*

Frank Blake, 59
CEO, Home Depot, Atlanta

He simplified the company and boosted morale. Too bad Blake took over as the housing market went bust.

His valued counselor? "Every year, I do a pilgrimage to go talk to Jack Welch. The first time I sat down with him, he just talked to me about the people [at Home Depot]. Not a number. Not 'How are you going to get your gross margin rates up?' "

Great book: *The War Within,* on the Bush Administration, by Bob Woodward. "That's a good cautionary story. One of the first questions you have to ask as a leader is, to what extent do people feel comfortable saying what's on their minds?"

Jamie Dimon, 52
CEO, JPMorgan, New York

Dimon largely shunned the subprime bets and exotic financial instruments that brought down rivals. As a result, JPMorgan was able to pick up the pieces of Bear Stearns when it imploded in March and later absorb collapsed mortgage lender Washington Mutual.

http://images.businessweek.com/ss/09/01/0108_best_worst/1.htm

SOURCES: Excerpted from "The Best Managers," *BusinessWeek,* January 19, 2009, p. 40; and "The Worst Managers," *BusinessWeek,* January 19, 2009, p. 42.

The Functions of Management

management

The process of working with people and resources to accomplish organizational goals.

 LO 3

Management is the process of working with people and resources to accomplish organizational goals. Good managers do those things both effectively and efficiently. To be *effective* is to achieve organizational goals. To be *efficient* is to achieve goals with minimal waste of resources, that is, to make the best possible use of money, time, materials, and people. Some managers fail on both criteria, or focus on one at the expense of another. The best managers maintain a clear focus on both effectiveness *and* efficiency. These definitions have been around for a long time. But as you know, business is changing radically. The real issue is how to *do* these things.[54]

Although the context of business and the specifics of doing business are changing, there are still plenty of timeless principles that make great managers, and great companies, great. While fresh thinking and new approaches are required now more than ever, much of what has already been learned about successful management practices remains relevant, useful, and adaptable, with fresh thinking, to the 21st-century business environment.

In the business world today, the great executives not only adapt to changing conditions but also apply—fanatically, rigorously, consistently, and with discipline—the fundamental management principles. These fundamentals include the four traditional functions of management: *planning, organizing, leading,* and *controlling.* They remain as relevant as ever, and they still provide the fundamentals that are needed in start-ups as much as in established corporations. But their form has evolved.

Planning: Delivering Strategic Value

Planning is specifying the goals to be achieved and deciding in advance the appropriate actions needed to achieve those goals. Planning activities include analyzing current situations, anticipating the future, determining objectives, deciding in what types of activities the company will engage, choosing corporate and business strategies, and determining the resources needed to achieve the organization's goals. Plans set the stage for action and for major achievements.

The planning function for the new business environment, discussed in Part 2 of this book, is more dynamically described as *delivering strategic value.* **Value** is a complex concept.[55] Fundamentally, it describes the monetary amount associated with how well a job, task, good, or service meets users' needs. Those users might be business owners, customers, employees, society, and even nations. The better you meet those needs (in terms of quality, speed, efficiency, and so on), the more value you deliver. That value is "strategic" when it contributes to meeting the organization's goals. On a personal level, you will do well when you periodically ask yourself and your boss, "How can I add value?" Answering that question will enhance your contributions, your job performance, and your career.

Historically, planning described a top-down approach in which top executives establish business plans and tell others to implement them. Now and in the future, delivering strategic value is a continual process in which people throughout the organization use their brains and the brains of customers, suppliers, and other stakeholders to identify opportunities to create, seize, strengthen, and sustain competitive advantage. This dynamic process swirls around the objective of creating more and more value for the customer. Effectively creating value requires fully considering a new and changing set of stakeholders and issues, including the government, the natural environment, globalization, and the dynamic economy in which ideas are king and entrepreneurs are both formidable competitors and potential collaborators. You will learn about these and related topics in Chapter 4 (planning and strategic management), Chapter 5 (ethics and corporate social responsibility), Chapter 6 (international management), and Chapter 7 (entrepreneurship).

Organizing: Building a Dynamic Organization

Organizing is assembling and coordinating the human, financial, physical, informational, and other resources needed to achieve goals. Organizing activities include attracting people to the organization, specifying job responsibilities, grouping jobs into work units, marshaling and allocating resources, and creating conditions so that people and things work together to achieve maximum success.

Part 3 of the book describes the organizing function as *building a dynamic organization.* Historically, organizing involved creating an organization chart by identifying business functions, establishing reporting relationships, and having a personnel department that administered plans, programs, and paperwork. Now and in the future,

planning

The management function of systematically making decisions about the goals and activities that an individual, a group, a work unit, or the overall organization will pursue.

value

The monetary amount associated with how well a job, task, good, or service meets users' needs.

organizing

The management function of assembling and coordinating human, financial, physical, informational, and other resources needed to achieve goals.

effective managers will be using new forms of organizing and viewing their people as perhaps their most valuable resources. They will build organizations that are flexible and adaptive, particularly in response to competitive threats and customer needs. Progressive human resource practices that attract and retain the very best of a highly diverse population will be essential aspects of the successful company. You will learn about these topics in Chapter 8 (organization structure), Chapter 9 (organizational agility), Chapter 10 (human resources management), and Chapter 11 (managing the diverse workforce).

Shona Brown of Google makes decisions about organizing. She says, "The company's goal is to determine precisely the amount of management it needs—and then use a little bit less."

leading

The management function that involves the manager's efforts to stimulate high performance by employees.

controlling

The management function of monitoring performance and making needed changes.

Leading: Mobilizing People

Leading is stimulating people to be high performers. It includes motivating and communicating with employees, individually and in groups. Leading involves close day-to-day contact with people, helping to guide and inspire them toward achieving team and organizational goals. Leading takes place in teams, departments, and divisions, as well as at the tops of large organizations.

In earlier textbooks, the leading function described how managers motivate workers to come to work and execute top management's plans by doing their jobs. Today and in the future, managers must be good at *mobilizing people* to contribute their ideas—to use their brains in ways never needed or dreamed of in the past.

As described in Part 4, managers must rely on a very different kind of leadership (Chapter 12) that empowers and motivates people (Chapter 13). Far more than in the past, great work must be done via great teamwork (Chapter 14), both within work groups and across group boundaries. Ideally, underlying these processes will be effective interpersonal and organizational communication (Chapter 15).

In a recent nationwide survey, employees had mixed reviews of their manager's leadership skills.[56] As a result, a manager who excels in leadership is especially valuable.

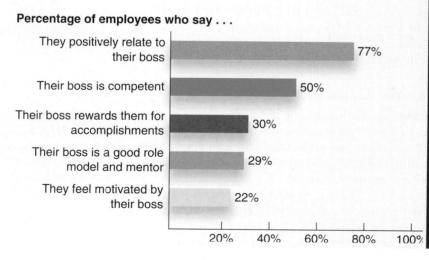

Percentage of employees who say . . .

They positively relate to their boss — 77%

Their boss is competent — 50%

Their boss rewards them for accomplishments — 30%

Their boss is a good role model and mentor — 29%

They feel motivated by their boss — 22%

20%   40%   60%   80%   100%

Controlling: Learning and Changing

Planning, organizing, and leading do not guarantee success. The fourth function, **controlling**, monitors performance and implements necessary changes. By controlling, managers make sure the organization's resources are being used as planned and that the organization is meeting its goals for quality and safety.

Monitoring is an essential aspect of control. If you have any doubts that this function is important, consider some control breakdowns that caused serious problems. After an explosion at BP's Texas oil refinery caused the deaths of 15 people, investigations suggested that widespread failure to implement safety measures was behind the tragedy. In spite of a year of record profits, BP's chief executive announced plans to retire early, and his bonus was cut almost in half.[57] Other lapses in controlling can hurt customers. A recent outbreak of salmonella infections— which can cause fever, diarrhea, dehydration, and even death—was traced to Peter Pan and Great Value peanut butter made by ConAgra Foods in its Sylvester, Georgia, factory. Processing the peanuts generally kills salmonella and other germs, so the likely culprit was contamination of jars or equipment. ConAgra quickly announced a recall, but more than 400 people in 44 states reported being infected, and 71 of them had to be hospitalized. The recall alone was expected to cost ConAgra at least $50 million; lawsuits, cleanup of the facility, and damage to the brands' reputation are adding to those costs.[58] As you can see, control failures can take many forms.

When managers implement their plans, they often find that things are not working out as planned. The controlling function makes sure that goals are met. It asks and answers the question, "Are our actual outcomes consistent with our goals?" It then makes adjustments as needed. To learn how Elon Musk applied this function to make needed adjustments at Tesla Motors, see the "Management Close-Up: Taking Action" feature.

Successful organizations, large and small, pay close attention to the controlling function. But Part 5 of the book makes it clear that today and for the future, the key managerial challenges are far more dynamic than in the past; they involve continually *learning and changing*. Controls must still be in place, as described in Chapter 16. But new technologies and other innovations (Chapter 17) make it possible to achieve controls in more effective ways and to help all the people throughout the company, and across company boundaries (including customers and suppliers), to use their brains, learn, make a variety of new contributions, and help the organization change in ways that forge a successful future (Chapter 18).

The four management functions apply to you personally, as well. You must find ways to create value, organize for your own personal effectiveness, mobilize your own

Management Close-Up   TAKING ACTION

Like many start-ups, Tesla Motors has hit a few potholes along the way. Fundamental differences between Elon Musk and Tesla founder Martin Eberhard led to complications that nearly halted the company's progress. Technical problems during development pushed back the launch of the company's first car, the Roadster, by more than a year. In turn, the production delays caused cash flow problems. Yet, to date Tesla has raised nearly $150 million from investors; $55 million of that has come from Elon Musk.

The company burned through three CEOs before Musk took the reins in 2008. By that time, the world economy had taken a serious downturn, and the United States found itself in a deepening credit crisis. Musk ordered a layoff of nearly 25 percent of the workforce, closed one office in a Detroit suburb, and opened a smaller one nearby. Tesla is also looking to its Roadster, now in full production, to enhance the revenue stream by trimming manufacturing costs.

While Musk is confident Tesla will weather the storm and characterizes the moves as needed belt-tightening, the recession couldn't have come at a worse time for the firm. Tesla was already in development mode on its next model, a four-door luxury sedan called the Model S. Now, Musk has slowed the Model S program, pushing back production until mid-2011, and shelved plans to build an assembly plant.[59]

- What attributes does Elon Musk exhibit that make him an effective manager?
- How can Musk maintain Tesla's momentum in spite of setbacks?

talents and skills as well as those of others, monitor performance, and constantly learn, develop, and change for the future. As you proceed through this book and this course, we encourage you to not merely do your "textbook learning" of an impersonal course subject but to think about these issues from a personal perspective as well, using the ideas for your own personal development.

Performing All Four Management Functions

As a manager, your typical day will not be neatly divided into the four functions. You will be doing many things more or less simultaneously.[60] Your days will be busy and fractionated, spent dealing with interruptions, meetings, and firefighting. There will be plenty to do that you wish you could be doing but can't seem to get to. These activities will include all four management functions.

Some managers are particularly interested in, devoted to, or skilled in one or two of the four functions but not in the others. But you should devote adequate attention and resources to *all four* functions. You can be a skilled planner and controller, but if you organize your people improperly or fail to inspire them to perform at high levels, you will not be realizing your potential as a manager. Likewise, it does no good to be the kind of manager who loves to organize and lead, but who doesn't really understand where to go or how to determine whether you are on the right track. Good managers don't neglect any of the four management functions. Knowing what they are, you can periodically ask yourself if you are devoting adequate attention to *all* of them.

Management Levels and Skills

LO 4

Organizations—particularly large organizations—have many levels. In this section, you will learn about the types of managers found at three different organizational levels: top level, middle level, and frontline.

Top-Level Managers

top-level managers

Senior executives responsible for the overall management and effectiveness of the organization.

Top-level managers are the senior executives of an organization and are responsible for its overall management. Top-level managers, often referred to as *strategic managers*, are supposed to focus on long-term issues and emphasize the survival, growth, and overall effectiveness of the organization.

Top managers are concerned not only with the organization as a whole but also with the interaction between the organization and its external environment. This interaction often requires managers to work extensively with outside individuals and organizations.

The chief executive officer (CEO) is one type of top-level manager found in large corporations. This individual is the primary strategic manager of the firm and has authority over everyone else. Others include the chief operating officer (COO), company presidents, vice presidents, and members of the top management team. As companies are appreciating the potential of modern technology and knowledge management to help them achieve and maintain a competitive advantage, more are creating the position of chief information officer (CIO). At defense contractor Northrop Grumman, CIO Tom Shelman used to focus on managing the company's computer systems. But in the last few years, he has become directly involved with strategy; Shelman's job includes meeting with customers to help identify ways the company can use its technology to serve them better and help the company grow.[61]

Traditionally, the role of top-level managers has been to set overall direction by formulating

In a recent poll of chief information officers, half said their responsibilities extend beyond information technology to include top-level concerns such as developing the company's strategy.[62]

strategy and controlling resources. But now, top managers are more commonly called on to be not only strategic architects but also true organizational leaders. As leaders, they must create and articulate a broader corporate purpose with which people can identify—and one to which people will enthusiastically commit.

Middle-Level Managers

As the name implies, **middle-level managers** are located in the organization's hierarchy below top-level management and above the frontline managers. Sometimes called *tactical managers*, they are responsible for translating the general goals and plans developed by strategic managers into more specific objectives and activities.

Traditionally, the role of the middle manager is to be an administrative controller who bridges the gap between higher and lower levels. Middle-level managers take corporate objectives and break them down into business unit targets; put together separate business unit plans from the units below them for higher-level corporate review; and serve as linchpins of internal communication, interpreting and broadcasting top management's priorities downward and channeling and translating information from the front lines upward.

As a stereotype, the term *middle manager* connotes mediocrity: unimaginative people behaving like bureaucrats and defending the status quo. But middle managers are closer than top managers to day-to-day operations, customers, and frontline managers and employees—so they know the problems. They also have many creative ideas—often better than their bosses'. Good middle managers provide the operating skills and practical problem solving that keep the company working.[63]

middle-level managers

Managers located in the middle layers of the organizational hierarchy, reporting to top-level executives.

Frontline Managers

Frontline managers, or *operational managers*, are lower-level managers who supervise the operations of the organization. These managers often have titles such as *supervisor* or *sales manager*. They are directly involved with nonmanagement employees, implementing the specific plans developed with middle managers. This role is critical in the organization because operational managers are the link between management and nonmanagement personnel. Your first management position probably will fit into this category.

Traditionally, frontline managers have been directed and controlled from above, to make sure that they successfully implement operations in support of company strategy. But in leading companies, the role has expanded. Whereas the operational execution aspect of the role remains vital, in leading companies frontline managers are increasingly called on to be innovative and entrepreneurial, managing for growth and new business development.

Managers on the front line—which usually means newer, younger managers—are crucial to creating and sustaining quality, innovation, and other drivers of financial performance.[64] In outstanding organizations, talented frontline managers are not only *allowed* to initiate new activities but are *expected* to by their top- and middle-level managers. And they are given freedom, incentives, and support to find ways to do so.[65]

Table 1.1 elaborates on the changing aspects of different management levels. You will learn about each of these aspects of management throughout this course.

frontline managers

Lower-level managers who supervise the operational activities of the organization.

Working Leaders with Broad Responsibilities

In small firms—and in those large companies that have adapted to the times—managers have strategic, tactical, *and* operational responsibilities. They are *complete* businesspeople; they have knowledge of all business functions, are accountable for results, and focus on serving customers both inside and outside their firms. All of this requires the ability to think strategically, translate strategies into specific objectives, coordinate resources, and do real work with lower-level people.

TABLE 1.1

Transformation of Management Roles and Activities

	Frontline Managers	Middle-Level Managers	Top-Level Managers
Changing Roles	• From operational implementers to aggressive entrepreneurs	• From administrative controllers to supportive coaches	• From resource allocators to institutional leaders
Key Activities	• Creating and pursuing new growth opportunities for the business	• Developing individuals and supporting their activities	• Establishing high performance standards
	• Attracting and developing resources	• Linking dispersed knowledge and skills across units	• Institutionalizing a set of norms and values to support cooperation and trust
	• Managing continuous improvement within the unit	• Managing the tension between short-term purpose and long-term ambition	• Creating an overarching corporate purpose and ambition

SOURCE: Adapted from C. Bartlett and S. Goshal, "The Myth of the Generic Manager: New Personal Competencies for New Management Roles," *California Management Review* 40, no. 1, Fall 1977, pp. 92–116.

In short, today's best managers can do it all; they are "working leaders."[66] They focus on relationships with other people and on achieving results. They don't just make decisions, give orders, wait for others to produce, and then evaluate results. They get dirty, do hard work themselves, solve problems, and produce value.

What does all of this mean in practice? How do managers spend their time—what do they actually do? A classic study of top executives found that they spend their time engaging in 10 key activities or roles, falling into three categories: interpersonal, informational, and decisional.[67] Table 1.2 summarizes these roles. Even though the study was done decades ago, it remains highly relevant as a description of what executives do. And even though the study focused on top executives, managers at all levels engage in all these activities. As you study the table, you might ask yourself, "Which of these activities do I enjoy most (and least)? Where do I excel (and not excel)? Which would I like to improve?" Whatever your answers, you will be learning more about these activities throughout this course.

Management Skills

Performing management functions and roles, and achieving competitive advantage, are the cornerstones of a manager's job. However, understanding this fact does not ensure success. Managers need a variety of skills to *do* these things *well*. Skills are specific abilities that result from knowledge, information, practice, and aptitude. Although managers need many individual skills, which you will learn about throughout this textbook, there are three essential categories: technical skills, interpersonal and communication skills, and conceptual and decision skills.[68]

LO 5

First-timers can underestimate the challenges of the many technical, human, and conceptual competencies required.[69] But when the key management functions are performed by managers who have these critical management skills, the result is high performance.

Interpersonal Roles	*Leader:* Staffing, training, and motivating people
	Liaison: Maintaining a network of outside contacts who provide information and favors
	Figurehead: Performing symbolic duties (ceremonies and serving other social and legal demands)
Informational Roles	*Monitor:* Seeking and receiving information to develop a thorough understanding of the organization and its environment; serving as the "nerve center" of communication
	Disseminator: Transmitting information from source to source, sometimes interpreting and integrating diverse perspectives
	Spokesperson: Speaking on behalf of the organization about plans, policies, actions, and results
Decisional Roles	*Entrepreneur:* Searching for new business opportunities and initiating new projects to create change
	Disturbance handler: Taking corrective action during crises or other conflicts
	Resource allocator: Providing funding and other resources to units or people; includes making or approving significant organizational decisions
	Negotiator: Engaging in negotiations with parties outside the organization as well as inside (e.g., resource exchanges)

TABLE 1.2

Managerial Roles: What Managers Do

SOURCE: Adapted from H. Mintzberg, *The Nature of Managerial Work* (New York: Harper & Row, 1973), pp. 92–93.

A **technical skill** is the ability to perform a specialized task that involves a certain method or process. Most people develop a set of technical skills to complete the activities that are part of their daily work lives. The technical skills you learn in school will provide you with the opportunity to get an entry-level position; they will also help you as a manager. For example, your accounting and finance courses will develop the technical skills you need to understand and manage the financial resources of an organization.

Conceptual and decision skills involve the ability to identify and resolve problems for the benefit of the organization and everyone concerned. Managers use these skills when they consider the overall objectives and strategy of the firm, the interactions among different parts of the organization, and the role of the business in its external environment. As you acquire greater responsibility, you must exercise your conceptual and decision skills with increasing frequency. You will confront issues that involve all aspects of the organization and must consider a larger and more interrelated set of decision factors. Much of this book is devoted to enhancing your conceptual and decision skills, but experience also plays an important part in their development.

Interpersonal and communication skills influence the manager's ability to work well with people. These skills are often called *people skills.* Managers spend the great majority of their time interacting with people,[70] and they must develop their abilities to lead, motivate, and communicate effectively with those around them. Your people skills often make the difference in how high you go. Management professor Michael Morris explains, "At a certain level in business, you're living and dying on your social abilities. . . . [Knowledge of a particular field] gets you in the door, but social intelligence gets you to the top."[71] Supporting this view, a survey of senior executives and managers found that more than 6 out of 10 say they base hiring and promotion decisions on a candidate's "likability." Almost as many (62 versus 63 percent) said they base these decisions on skills, presumably referring to technical skills.[72]

technical skill

The ability to perform a specialized task involving a particular method or process.

conceptual and decision skills

Skills pertaining to the ability to identify and resolve problems for the benefit of the organization and its members.

interpersonal and communication skills

People skills; the ability to lead, motivate, and communicate effectively with others.

Professor Morris, quoted in the previous paragraph, has helped to teach people skills to MBA candidates at Columbia Business School. He emphasizes that it is vital for future managers to realize the importance of these skills in getting a job, keeping it, and performing well in it, especially in the 21st century, where managers tend to be supervisors of independent-minded knowledge workers. He explains, "You have to get high performance out of people in your organization who you don't have any authority over. You need to read other people, know their motivators, know how you affect them."[73]

The importance of these skills varies by managerial level. Technical skills are most important early in your career. Conceptual and decision skills become more important than technical skills as you rise higher in the company. But interpersonal skills are important throughout your career, at every level of management. Several biomedical companies in California's Orange County collaborated to provide training because they observed that managers originally hired for their technical expertise needed to develop their people skills so that they could handle higher-level assignments successfully.[74]

You and Your Career

LO 6

At the beginning of your career, your contribution to your employer depends on your own performance; that's all you're responsible for. But on becoming a manager, you are responsible for a whole group. To use an orchestra analogy, instead of playing an instrument, you're a conductor, coordinating others' efforts.[75] The challenge is much greater than most first-time managers expect it to be.

Throughout your career you'll need to lead teams effectively, as well as influence people over whom you have no authority; thus, the human skills are especially important. Businesspeople often talk about **emotional intelligence**,[76] or "EQ"—the skills of understanding yourself (including strengths and limitations), managing yourself (dealing with emotions, making good decisions, seeking and using feedback, exercising self-control), and dealing effectively with others (listening, showing empathy, motivating, leading, and so on).

emotional intelligence

The skills of understanding yourself, managing yourself, and dealing effectively with others.

An example of a manager with these skills is Rita Burns, vice president of communications and marketing at Memorial Health System in Colorado Springs. Self-knowledge led Burns to pursue a career that brings together her talent at listening and her love of health care. Burns says she finds it easy to appreciate other points of view: "No matter where I am or what the situation is, I can find something to have a conversation about." Her boss, senior vice president Ron Burnside, describes her as a talented communicator, and a colleague at the American Heart Association says Burns possesses a "collaborative spirit," which helps her see how Memorial Health System can cooperate with the association on joint projects.[77]

A common complaint about leaders, especially newly promoted ones who had been outstanding individual performers, is that they lack what is perhaps the most fundamental of EQ skills: empathy. The issue is not lack of ability to change (you can), but the lack of motivation to change.[78] William George, former chair and CEO of Medtronic, says some people can go a long way in their careers based on sheer determination and aggressiveness, but personal development—including EQ—ultimately becomes essential.[79] Executives who score low on EQ are less likely to be rated as excellent on their performance reviews, and their divisions tend not to perform as well.[80] A vice president at an aerospace company underwent a program to improve her EQ after colleagues kept complaining that she was overly demanding and inclined to put people down. An assessment found that she lacked social awareness. The vice president eventually learned to respond after calming herself, as well as to explore colleagues' ideas rather than demeaning them. Before long, her colleagues began to appreciate the change, and her career took a more successful path.[81]

What should you do to forge a successful, gratifying career? You are well advised to be both a specialist and a generalist, to be self-reliant and connected, to actively manage your relationship with your organization, and to know what is required not only to survive but also to thrive in today's world.

Be Both a Specialist and a Generalist

If you think your career will be as a specialist, think again. Chances are, you will not want to stay forever in strictly technical jobs with no managerial responsibilities. Accountants are promoted to accounting department heads and team leaders, sales representatives become sales managers, writers become editors, and nurses become nursing directors. As your responsibilities increase, you must deal with more people, understand more about other aspects of the organization, and make bigger and more complex decisions. Beginning to learn now about these managerial challenges may yield benefits sooner than you think.

So, it will help if you can become both a specialist and a generalist.[82] Seek to become a *specialist:* you should be an expert in something. This will give you specific skills that help you provide concrete, identifiable value to your firm and to customers. And over time, you should learn to be a *generalist,* knowing enough about a variety of business disciplines so that you can think strategically and work with different perspectives.

Patricia Calkins broadened her focus gradually and ambitiously from specialties in the sciences, expanding first to engineering and then to management. She started her career with AT&T's Western Electric subsidiary as a chemist; when she was considering a master's degree in chemistry, she heeded advice to develop her career opportunities by studying engineering. Once Calkins had her master's in civil and environmental engineering, the company saw her management talent and wanted to promote her, so she returned to school for another master's degree, this time in business administration. She developed her generalist skills by consulting, and from that work moved to her current—and favorite—position as vice president of environment, health, and safety at Xerox.[83]

Patricia Calkins, VP of Environment, Health, and Safety at Xerox, became successful by being both a specialist and a generalist. She developed her specialty skills in the sciences and in business administration, and then acquired her generalist skills as a business consultant. What steps do you need to take to become a specialist and a generalist?

There's another advantage to being both a specialist and a generalist: it can give you the opportunity to indulge in the causes or activities about which you are most passionate. For example, Josh Ruxin, a professor and founder of Access Project, a program that applies American management systems to hospitals in Rwanda, got started on his career path when he traveled to Ethiopia as a teenager. "That changed the rest of my life," Ruxin recalls. "I couldn't believe that people so desperately poor were living on the same planet as we were." So Ruxin earned a doctorate in medical history and joined a management consulting firm, where he honed his management skills. When he got the opportunity to follow a spin-off venture focusing on economic development in underdeveloped regions, he took it.

In Africa, "I realized health care there had to get fixed before these economies had a chance," says Ruxin. So he formed Access Project. Now he uses both his general and his specialized skills to help improve the health care system in Rwanda.[84]

Be Self-Reliant

To be self-reliant means to take full responsibility for yourself, your actions, and your career, as Patricia Calkins did when she furthered her education and tackled consulting assignments that applied her technical knowledge to the business world. You cannot count on your boss or your company to take care of you. A useful metaphor is to think of yourself as a business, with you as president and sole employee. Table 1.3 gives some specific advice about what this means in practice.

Jordan Edelstein took ownership of his career; for him, that meant taking a leap into an industry he loved. General Mills hired him as an assistant marketing manager. He was successful, but during a business trip, as he read about Electronic Arts and its game Sims Online, Edelstein realized that this was an industry he felt passionate about. Edelstein began researching jobs in the industry. When an opening came at Electronic Arts, Edelstein prepared for extensive interviews in which he had to persuade dozens of people that his marketing expertise made up for his lack of experience with high-tech products. Evidently, Edelstein has real marketing talent: he landed what he identified as his dream job.[85]

To be self-reliant, find new ways to make your overall performance better. Take responsibility for change; be an innovator.[86] Don't just do your work and wait for orders; look for opportunities to contribute in new ways, to develop new products and processes, and to generate constructive change that strengthens the company and benefits customers and colleagues. As in Jordan Edelstein's career, success requires more than talent; you also have to be willing to work hard. The elite, world-class performers in many fields reach the top tier only after ten years or more of hard work.[87] The key is to engage in consistent practice, looking at the results and identifying where to improve.

It's easy to see how this works for violinists or basketball players, but what about business managers? The answer is to focus on getting better results each time you try any business task, whether it's writing a report, chairing a meeting, or interpreting a financial statement. To know whether you're getting better, make a point of asking for feedback from customers, colleagues, and bosses.

To develop your full potential, assess yourself, including your interests, aptitudes, and personal character strengths. Think about it, ask others who know you well, conduct a formal exercise in which you learn what others consider to be your "best self,"[88] and use the resources of recent advances in psychology to identify your signature strengths.[89] Consider the professional image and reputation you would like to develop,[90] and continue building your capabilities. Consider the suggestions found throughout this book, and your courses, as you pursue these objectives.

TABLE 1.3
Keys to Career Management

Vicky Farrow of Sun Microsystems gave the following advice to help people assume responsibility for their own careers:
1. Think of yourself as a business.
2. Define your product: What is your area of expertise?
3. Know your target market: To whom are you going to sell this?
4. Be clear on why your customer buys from you. What is your "value proposition"— what are you offering that causes him to use you?
5. As in any business, strive for quality and customer satisfaction, even if your customer is just someone else in your organization—like your boss.
6. Know your profession or field and what's going on there.
7. Invest in your own growth and development, the way a company invests in research and development. What new products will you be able to provide?
8. Be willing to consider changing your career.

Be Connected

Being *connected* means having many good working relationships and interpersonal contacts and being a team player with strong interpersonal skills. For example, those who want to become partners in professional service organizations like accounting, advertising, and consulting firms strive constantly to build a network of contacts. Their "connectedness" goal is to work not only with lots of clients but also with a half dozen or more senior partners, including several from outside their home offices and some from outside their country. A study of new auditors showed that social relationships improved newcomers' knowledge of the organization and their jobs, their social integration into the firm, and their commitment to the organization.[91]

Social capital is the goodwill stemming from your social relationships, and it can be mobilized on your behalf. It aids career success, compensation, employment, team effectiveness, successful entrepreneurship, and relationships with suppliers and other outsiders.[92] Today much of that social capital can be tapped online, at social networking Web sites. Besides the purely social sites like MySpace and Facebook, some of these sites are aimed at helping people tap business networks. For example, LinkedIn has more than 8 million registered users, with membership growing rapidly. Even busy executives are willing to give LinkedIn a try because it allows sharing only among people who agree to be connected; acquaintances can introduce others only with permission.[93]

Look at this another way: All business is a function of human relationships.[94] Building competitive advantage depends not only on you but on other people. Management is personal. Commercial dealings are personal. Purchase decisions, repurchase decisions, and contracts all hinge on relationships. Even the biggest business deals—takeovers—are intensely personal and emotional. Without good work relationships, you are an outsider, not an effective manager and leader.

social capital

Goodwill stemming from your social relationships.

This young professional is "connecting" with her former co-workers through Facebook, a popular social networking tool. Social networking is an important way to stay "connected" and build social relationships within and outside of the workplace. Increasingly, social networking takes place through the use of technology and the Internet.

Actively Manage Your Relationship with Your Organization

Many of the previous comments suggest the importance of taking responsibility for your own actions and your own career. Unless you are self-employed and your own boss, one way to do this is to think about the nature of the relationship between you and your employer. Figure 1.1 shows two possible relationships—and you have some control over which relationship you will be in.

Relationship #1 is one in which you view yourself as an employee and passively expect your employer to tell you what to do and give you pay and benefits. Your employer is in charge, and you are a passive recipient of its actions. Your contributions are likely to be adequate but minimal—you won't make the added contributions that strengthen your organization, and if all organizational members take this perspective, the organization is not likely to be strong for the long run. Personally, you may lose your job, or keep your job in a declining organization, or receive few positive benefits from working there and either quit or become cynical and unhappy in your work.

In contrast, relationship #2 is a two-way relationship in which you and your organization both benefit from one another. The mind-set is different: Instead of doing what you are told, you think about how you can contribute—and you act accordingly. To the extent that your organization values your contributions, you are likely to benefit

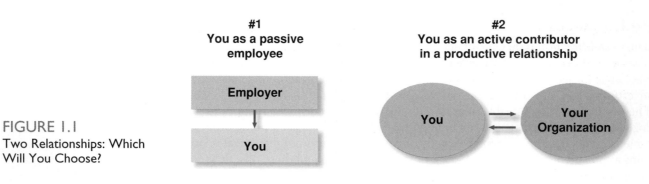

#1
You as a passive employee

#2
You as an active contributor in a productive relationship

Employer

↓

You

You   →
←   Your Organization

FIGURE 1.1
Two Relationships: Which Will You Choose?

in return by receiving full and fair rewards, support for further personal development, and a more gratifying work environment. If you think in broad terms about how you can help your company, and if others think like this as well, there is likely to be continuous improvement in the company's ability to innovate, cut costs, and deliver quality products quickly to an expanding customer base. As the company's bottom line strengthens, benefits accrue to shareholders as well as to you and other employees.

What contributions can you make? You can do your basic work. But you can, and should, go further. You can also figure out new ways to add value—by thinking of and implementing new ideas that improve processes and results. You can do this by using your technical knowledge and skills, as in developing a better information system, accounting technique, or sales technique.

You also can contribute with your conceptual and human skills and your managerial actions (see Figure 1.2). You can execute the essential management functions and deliver competitive advantage. You can deliver strategic value (Part 2 of this book). You can take actions that help build a more dynamic organization (Part 3). You can mobilize people to contribute to their fullest potential (Part 4). And you can learn and change—and help your colleagues and company learn and change—to adapt to changing realities and forge a successful future (Part 5).

Survive and Thrive

Now—far more than ever—you will be accountable for your actions and for results. In the past, people at many companies could show up, do an OK job, get a decent

You

Your Organization

Managerial Actions

1. Delivering Strategic Value
2. Building a Dynamic Organization
3. Mobilizing People
4. Learning and Changing

FIGURE 1.2
Managerial Action Is Your Opportunity to Contribute

evaluation, and get a raise equal to the cost of living and maybe higher. Today, managers must do more, better. Eminent management scholar Peter Drucker, in considering what makes managers effective, notes that some are charismatic while some are not, and some are visionary while others are more numbers-oriented.[95] But successful executives do share some common practices:

- They ask "What needs to be done?" rather than "What do I want to do?"
- They write an action plan. They don't just think, they do, based on a sound, ethical plan.
- They take responsibility for decisions. This requires checking up, revisiting, and changing if necessary.
- They focus on opportunities rather than problems. Problems have to be solved, and problem solving prevents more damage. But exploiting opportunities is what creates great results.

This creative approach can make each employee a standout in some unique way. Career adviser Rachelle Canter advises identifying where you deliver superior results and thinking of that as your "brand." For instance, an executive might develop a track record of consistently improving productivity in various organizations, and an entry-level customer service worker might become the company's go-to employee for handling the toughest customers.[96]

Career success is most likely if you are flexible, creative, and ambitious. You will need to learn how to think strategically, discern and convey your business vision, make decisions, and work in teams. You will need to deliver competitive advantage and thrive on change, just as Elon Musk does at Tesla Motors, as discussed in the "Management Close-Up: Assessing Outcomes and Seizing Opportunities" feature. These and other topics, essential to your successful career, provide the focus for the following chapters.

Management Close-Up

ASSESSING OUTCOMES AND SEIZING OPPORTUNITIES

With Elon Musk's cost-cutting initiatives, Tesla Motors was able to withstand its financial crunch. Musk drew on relationships he formed in the computer industry—with investors ranging from eBay's cofounder to Google's founders to Silicon Valley venture capitalists—to help fund Tesla. Meanwhile, the company focused on filling its backlog of orders for its Roadster sports car to generate needed cash. Musk says, "The reason we started off with a sports car is because initially any new technology's expensive." Sports cars, even with their hefty price tags, do not suffer sales slumps the way an average mom-and-pop car would—buyers still want the latest technology. But their smaller market limits the growth that Tesla can expect. To realize his vision of bringing electric cars to the masses, Musk needs to produce a more mainstream, less expensive model.

So Musk is now working to get his sedan project rolling. In 2009 Tesla previewed its luxury Model S sedan. Designed to travel up to 300 miles on a single charge, the Model S can seat seven passengers. Cars will be assembled in the United States, with full production of up to 20,000 units a year. Though priced at $57,400, the Model S qualifies buyers for a $7,500 federal tax credit through the government's economic stimulus package. That price puts the car in the range of more mainstream buyers.

If it is successful, the Model S could catapult Tesla into industry leadership and allow the company to expand into its planned company-owned dealerships.

Musk has applied for a $350 million loan from the U.S. Department of Energy to help produce the Model S. He also hopes to receive some funding from the government's $25 billion auto-industry bailout package, 10 percent of which is set aside for small business. In addition, Musk has expressed interest in taking Tesla Motors public in the next few years. Of his efforts to bring electric cars to the masses, Musk said, "In all frankness, I don't really need the stress of building a car company. . . . If I didn't think it was extremely important, I wouldn't have done it . . . We need to change the world. There's no choice."[97]

- Consider Elon Musk's background in the computer industry and the difficulty of starting a revolutionary car company. Do you think California is a good place from which to base Tesla Motors? What are some advantages and disadvantages to this strategy?
- Musk has drawn on his background in both physics and finance to get Tesla off the ground. But he has also used his managerial skills to keep the company moving ahead. Which skills has he used? Do you think Musk is more of a specialist or a generalist? Why?

KEY TERMS

Conceptual and decision skills,   p. 21

Controlling,   p. 16

Cost competitiveness,   p. 12

Emotional intelligence,   p. 22

Frontline managers,   p. 19

Innovation,   p. 9

Interpersonal and communication
 skills,   p. 21

Knowledge management,   p. 7

Leading,   p. 16

Management,   p. 14

Middle-level managers,   p. 19

Organizing,   p. 15

Planning,   p. 15

Quality,   p. 10

Service,   p. 11

Social capital,   p. 25

Speed,   p. 12

Technical skill,   p. 21

Top-level managers,   p. 18

Value,   p. 15

SUMMARY OF LEARNING OBJECTIVES

Now that you have studied Chapter 1, you should be able to:

LO 1   Summarize the major challenges of managing in the new competitive landscape.

Managers today must deal with dynamic forces that create greater change than ever before. Among many forces that are creating a need for managers to rethink their approaches, there have recently been four major waves of change: globalization, technological change including the development and applications of the Internet, knowledge management, and collaboration across organizational boundaries.

LO 2   Describe the sources of competitive advantage for a company.

Because business is a competitive arena, you need to deliver value to customers in ways that are superior to what your competitors do. Competitive advantages result from innovation, quality, service, speed, and cost.

LO 3   Explain how the functions of management are evolving in today's business environment.

Despite massive change, management retains certain foundations that will not disappear. The primary functions of management are planning, organizing, leading, and controlling. Planning is analyzing a situation, determining the goals that will be pursued, and deciding in advance the actions needed to pursue these goals. Organizing is assembling the resources needed to complete the job and coordinating employees and tasks for maximum success. Leading is motivating people and stimulating high performance. Controlling is monitoring the progress of the organization or the work unit toward goals and then taking corrective action, as necessary. In today's business environment, these functions more broadly require creating strategic value, building a dynamic organization, mobilizing people, and learning and changing.

LO 4   Compare how the nature of management varies at different organizational levels.

Top-level, strategic managers are the senior executives responsible for the organization's overall management. Middle-level, tactical managers translate general goals and plans into more specific objectives and activities. Frontline, operational managers are lower-level managers who supervise operations. Today, managers at all levels must perform a variety of interpersonal, informational, and decisional roles. Even at the operational level, the best managers think strategically and operate like complete businesspeople.

LO 5   Define the skills you need to be an effective manager.

To execute management functions successfully, managers need technical skills, conceptual and decision skills, and interpersonal and communication skills. A technical skill is the ability to perform a specialized task involving certain methods or processes. Conceptual and decision skills help the manager recognize complex and dynamic issues, analyze the factors that influence those issues or problems, and make appropriate decisions. Interpersonal and communication skills enable the manager to interact and work well with people. As you rise to higher organizational levels, technical skills tend to become less important and conceptual skills become more important, while human skills remain extremely important at every level.

LO 6   Understand the principles that will help you manage your career.

You are more likely to succeed in your career if you become both a specialist and a generalist. You should be self-reliant but also connected. You should actively manage your relationship with your organization and continuously improve your skills so that you can perform in the ways demanded in the changing work environment.

DISCUSSION QUESTIONS

1. Identify and describe a great manager. What makes him or her stand out from the crowd?

2. Have you ever seen or worked for an ineffective manager? Describe the causes and the consequences of the ineffectiveness.

3. Describe in as much detail as possible how the Internet and globalization affect your daily life.

4. Identify some examples of how different organizations collaborate "across boundaries."

5. Name a great organization. How do you think management contributes to making it great?

6. Name an ineffective organization. What can management do to improve it?

7. Give examples you have seen of firms that are outstanding and weak on each of the five pillars of competitive advantage. Why do you choose the firms you do?

8. Describe your use of the four management functions in the management of your daily life.

9. Discuss the importance of technical, conceptual, and interpersonal skills at school and in jobs you have held.

10. What are your strengths and weaknesses as you contemplate your career? How do they correlate with the skills and behaviors identified in the chapter?

11. Devise a plan for developing yourself and making yourself attractive to potential employers. How would you go about improving your managerial skills?

12. Consider the managers and companies discussed in the chapter. Have they been in the news lately, and what is the latest? If their image, performance, or fortunes have gone up or down, what has changed to affect how they have fared?

13. Who are *Business Week*'s most recent "best and worst managers," and why were they selected?

CONCLUDING CASE

Your Job and Your Passion—You Can Pursue Both!

The 21st century offers many challenges to every one of us. As more firms go global, as more economies interconnect, and as the Web blasts away boundaries to communication, we become more informed citizens. This interconnectedness means that the organizations you work for will require you to develop both general and specialized knowledge—such as speaking multiple languages, using various software applications, or understanding details of financial transactions. You will have to develop general management skills to foster your ability to be self-reliant and thrive in a changing marketplace. And here's the exciting part: As you build both types of knowledge, you may be able to integrate your growing expertise with the causes or activities you care most about. Or, your career adventure may lead you to a new passion.

Former presidents George H. W. Bush and Bill Clinton are well known for combining their management skills—running a country—with their passion for helping people around the world. Together they have raised funds to assist disaster victims, those with HIV/AIDS, and others in need. Jake Burton turned his love of snow sports into an entire industry when he founded Burton Snowboards. Annie Withey poured her business and marketing knowledge into her two famous business ventures: Smartfood and Annie's Homegrown. Both products were the result of her passion for healthful foods made from organic ingredients.

As you enter the workforce, you may have no idea where your career path will lead. You may be asking yourself, "How will I fit in?" "Where will I live?" "How much will I earn?" "Where will my business and personal careers evolve as the world continues to change at such a fast pace?" If you are feeling nervous because you don't know the answers to these questions yet, relax. A career is a journey, not a single destination. You may have one type of career or several. It is likely you will work for several organizations, or you may run one or more businesses of your own.

As you ask yourself what you want to do and where you want to be, take a few minutes to review the chapter and its main topics. Think about your personality, what you like and dislike, what you know and what you want to learn, what you fear and what you dream. Then try the following exercise.

QUESTIONS

1. Create a three-column chart in which the first column lists nonmanagement skills you have. Are you good at travel? Do you know how to build furniture? Are you a whiz at sports statistics? Are you an innovative cook? Do you play video games for hours? In the second column, list the causes or activities about which you are passionate. These may dovetail with the first list, but they might not.

2. Once you have your two columns complete, draw lines between entries that seem compatible. If you are good at building furniture, you might have also listed a concern about families who are homeless. Remember that not all entries will find a match—the idea is to begin finding some connections.

3. In the third column, generate a list of firms or organizations you know about that reflect your interests. If you are good at building furniture, you might be interested working for the Habitat for Humanity organization, or you might find yourself gravitating toward a furniture retailer like Ikea or Ethan Allen. You can do further research on organizations via the Internet or business publications.

With this chart, you have begun to create a career plan for yourself. In the next exercise, you will be assessing your management skills. Each of these activities begins to zero in on your own particular combination of general and specialized knowledge—both of which will grow and change throughout your career. Creating a plan is like talking the talk. Making the plan happen requires walking the walk. By the time you finish this course, you will be ready to take those first career steps. You may change direction once or many times, but always your path will lead forward. Good luck!

EXPERIENTIAL EXERCISES

1.1   Personal Assessment of Management Skills (PAMS)

To get an overall profile of your level of skill competence, respond to the following statements using the following rating scale. Please rate your behavior as it is, not as you would like it to be. If you have not engaged in a specific activity, answer according to how you think you would behave based on your experience in similar activities. Be honest; this instrument is designed to help you tailor your learning to your specific needs.

RATING SCALE

1   Strongly disagree

2   Disagree

3   Slightly disagree

4   Slightly agree

5   Agree

6   Strongly agree

In regard to my level of self-knowledge:

_____ 1. I seek information about my strengths and weaknesses from others as a basis for self-improvement.

_____ 2. To improve, I am willing to be self-disclosing to others (i.e., to share my beliefs and feelings).

_____ 3. I am aware of my preferred style in gathering information and making decisions.

_____ 4. I understand how I cope with situations that are ambiguous and uncertain.

_____ 5. I have a well-developed set of personal standards and principles that guide my behavior.

When faced with stressful or time-pressured situations:

_____ 6. I use effective time-management methods such as keeping track of my time, making to-do lists, and prioritizing tasks.

_____ 7. I reaffirm my priorities so that less important things don't drive out more important things.

_____ 8. I maintain a program of regular exercise for fitness.

_____ 9. I maintain an open, trusting relationship with someone with whom I can share my frustrations.

_____ 10. I know and practice several temporary relaxation techniques such as deep breathing and muscle relaxation.

_____ 11. I maintain balance in my life by pursuing a variety of interests outside work.

When I approach a typical, routine problem:

_____ 12. I state clearly and explicitly what the problem is. I avoid trying to solve it until I have defined it.

_____ 13. I generate more than one alternative solution to the problem, instead of identifying only one obvious solution.

_____ 14. I keep steps in the problem-solving process distinct; that is, I define the problem before proposing alternative solutions, and I generate alternatives before selecting a single solution.

When faced with a complex or difficult problem that does not have an easy solution:

_____ 15. I define a problem in multiple ways. I don't limit myself to just one problem definition.

_____ 16. I unfreeze my thinking by asking lots of questions about the nature of the problem before considering ways to solve it.

_____ 17. I think about the problem from both the left (logical) side of my brain and the right (intuitive) side of my brain.

_____ 18. I avoid selecting a solution until I have developed many possible alternatives.

_____ 19. I have specific techniques that I use to help develop creative and innovative solutions to problems.

When trying to foster more creativity and innovation among those with whom I work:

_____ 20. I make sure there are divergent points of view represented or expressed in every complex problem-solving situation.

_____ 21. I try to acquire information from individuals outside the problem-solving group who will be affected by the decision, mainly to determine their preferences and expectations.

_____ 22. I provide recognition not only for those who come up with creative ideas (the idea champions) but also for those who support others' ideas (supporters) and who provide resources to implement them (orchestrators).

_____ 23. I encourage informed rule-breaking in pursuit of creative solutions.

In situations where I have to provide negative feedback or offer corrective advice:

_____ 24. I help others recognize and define their own problems when I counsel them.

_____ 25. I am clear about when I should coach someone and when I should provide counseling instead.

_____ 26. When I give feedback to others, I avoid referring to personal characteristics and focus on problems or solutions instead.

_____ 27. When I try to correct someone's behavior, our relationship is strengthened.

_____ 28. I am descriptive in giving negative feedback to others. That is, I objectively describe events, their consequences, and my feelings about them.

_____ 29. I take responsibility for my statements and point of view, for example, "I have decided" instead of "They have decided."

_____ 30. I identify some area of agreement in a discussion with someone who has a different point of view.

_____ 31. I don't talk down to those who have less power or less information than I.

_____ 32. When discussing someone's problem, I respond with a reply that indicates understanding rather than advice.

In a situation where it is important to obtain more power:

_____ 33. I put forth more effort and take more initiative than expected in my work.

_____ 34. I am continually upgrading my skills and knowledge.

_____ 35. I support organizational ceremonial events and activities.

_____ 36. I form a broad network of relationships with people throughout the organization at all levels.

_____ 37. In my work I strive to generate new ideas, initiate new activities, and minimize routine tasks.

_____ 38. I send personal notes to others when they accomplish something significant or when I pass along important information to them.

_____ 39. I refuse to bargain with individuals who use high-pressure negotiation tactics.

_____ 40. I avoid using threats or demands to impose my will on others.

When another person needs to be motivated:

_____ 41. I determine if the person has the necessary resources and support to succeed in a task.

_____ 42. I use a variety of rewards to reinforce exceptional performances.

_____ 43. I design task assignments to make them interesting and challenging.

_____ 44. I make sure the person gets timely feedback from those affected by task performance.

_____ 45. I help the person establish performance goals that are challenging, specific, and time bound.

_____ 46. Only as a last resort do I attempt to reassign or release a poorly performing individual.

_____ 47. I discipline when effort is below expectations and capabilities.

_____ 48. I make sure that people feel fairly and equitably treated.

_____ 49. I provide immediate compliments and other forms of recognition for meaningful accomplishments.

When I see someone doing something that needs correcting:

_____ 50. I avoid making personal accusations and attributing self-serving motives to the other person.

_____ 51. I encourage two-way interaction by inviting the respondent to express his or her perspective and to ask questions.

_____ 52. I make a specific request, detailing a more acceptable option.

When someone complains about something I've done:

_____ 53. I show genuine concern and interest, even when I disagree.

_____ 54. I seek additional information by asking questions that provide specific and descriptive information.

_____ 55. I ask the other person to suggest more acceptable behaviors.

When two people are in conflict and I am the mediator:

_____ 56. I do not take sides but remain neutral.

_____ 57. I help the parties generate multiple alternatives.

_____ 58. I help the parties find areas on which they agree.

In situations where I have an opportunity to empower others:

_____ 59. I help people feel competent in their work by recognizing and celebrating their small successes.

_____ 60. I provide regular feedback and needed support.

_____ 61. I provide all the information that people need to accomplish their tasks.

_____ 62. I highlight the important impact that a person's work will have.

When delegating work to others:

_____ 63. I specify clearly the results I desire.

_____ 64. I specify clearly the level of initiative I want others to take (e.g., wait for directions, do part of the task and then report, do the whole task and then report, etc.).

_____ 65. I allow participation by those accepting assignments regarding when and how work will be done.

_____ 66. I avoid upward delegation by asking people to recommend solutions, rather than merely asking for advice or answers, when a problem is encountered.

_____ 67. I follow up and maintain accountability for delegated tasks on a regular basis.

When I am in the role of leader in a team:

_____ 68. I know how to establish credibility and influence among team members.

_____ 69. I am clear and consistent about what I want to achieve.

_____ 70. I build a common base of agreement in the team before moving forward with task accomplishment.

_____ 71. I articulate a clear, motivating vision of what the team can achieve along with specific short-term goals.

When I am in the role of team member:

_____ 72. I know a variety of ways to facilitate task accomplishment in the team.

_____ 73. I know a variety of ways to help build strong relationships and cohesion among team members.

When I desire to make my team perform well, regardless of whether I am a leader or member:

_____ 74. I am knowledgeable about the different stages of team development experienced by most teams.

_____ 75. I help the team avoid groupthink by making sure that sufficient diversity of opinions is expressed in the team.

_____ 76. I diagnose and capitalize on my team's core competencies, or unique strengths.

_____ 77. I encourage exceptionally high standards of performance and outcomes that far exceed expectations.

When I am leading change:

_____ 78. I usually emphasize a higher purpose or meaning associated with the work I do.

_____ 79. I keep track of things that go right, not just things that go wrong.

_____ 80. I frequently give other people positive feedback.

_____ 81. I work to close performance gaps—the difference between good performance and great performance.

_____ 82. I express gratitude frequently and conspicuously, even for small acts.

_____ 83. I know how to get people to commit to my vision of positive change.

_____ 84. I know how to unlock the positive energy in other people.

_____ 85. I express compassion toward people who are facing pain or difficulty.

SOURCE: David A. Whetten and Kim S. Cameron, *Developing Management Skills*, 6th ed. (Upper Saddle River, NJ: Pearson/Prentice Hall, 2005), pp. 23–27. Adapted by permission of Pearson Education, Inc., Upper Saddle River, NJ.

1.2 Your Personal Network

1. See the figure on page 33. Working on your own, write down all of your primary contacts—individuals you know personally who can support you in attaining your professional goals. Then begin to explore their secondary connections. Make assumptions about possible secondary connections that can be made for you by contacting your primary connections. For example, through one of your teachers (primary), you might be able to obtain some names of potential employers (secondary). (10–15 min.)

2. Then meet with your partner or small group to exchange information about your primary and secondary networks and to exchange advice and information on how to best use these connections, as well as how you could be helpful to them. (about 5 min. per person; 10–30 min. total, depending on group size)

3. Add names or types of names to your list based on ideas you get by talking with others in your group. (2–5 min.)

4. Discuss with large group or class, using the following discussion questions. (10 min.)

QUESTIONS

1. What were some of the best primary sources identified by your group?

2. What were some of the best sources for secondary contacts identified by your group?

3. What are some suggestions for approaching primary contacts?

4. What are some suggestions for approaching secondary contacts, and how is contacting secondary sources different from contacting primary contacts?

5. What did you learn about yourself and others from this exercise?

SOURCE: Suzanne C. de Janasz, Karen O. Dowd, and Beth Z. Schneider, *Interpersonal Skills in Organizations* (New York: McGraw-Hill, 2002), p. 211. © 2002 The McGraw-Hill Companies.

1.3 Effective Managers

OBJECTIVES

1. To better understand what behaviors contribute to effective management.

2. To conceive a ranking of critical behaviors that you personally believe reflects their importance to your success as a manager.

INSTRUCTIONS

1. Following is a partial list of behaviors in which managers may engage. Rank these items in terms of their importance for effective performance as a manager. Put a 1 next to the item that you think is most important, 2 for the next most important, down to 10 for the least important.

2. Bring your rankings to class. Be prepared to justify your results and rationale. If you can add any behaviors to this list that might lead to success or greater management effectiveness, write them in.

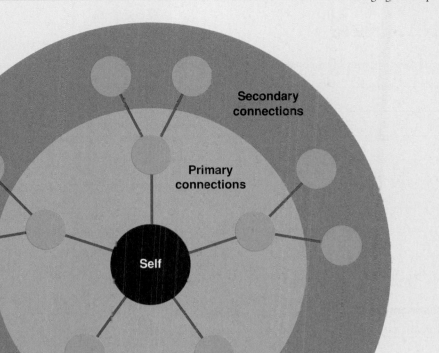

Effective Managers Worksheet

_____ Communicates and interprets policy so that it is understood by the members of the organization.

_____ Makes prompt and clear decisions.

_____ Assigns subordinates to the jobs for which they are best suited.

_____ Encourages associates to submit ideas and plans.

_____ Stimulates subordinates by means of competition among employees.

_____ Seeks means of improving management capabilities and competence.

_____ Fully supports and carries out company policies.

_____ Participates in community activities as opportunities arise.

_____ Is neat in appearance.

_____ Is honest in all matters pertaining to company property or funds.

SOURCE: Excerpted from Lawrence R. Jauch, Arthur G. Bedeian, Sally A. Coltrin, and William F. Glueck, _The Managerial Experience: Cases, Exercises, and Readings_, 5th ed. Copyright © 1989. Reprinted with permission of South-Western, a division of Thomson Learning, www.thomson-rights.com. Fax 800 730-2215.

1.4 Career Planning

OBJECTIVES

1. To explore your career thinking.

2. To visualize your ideal job in terms as concrete as possible.

3. To summarize the state of your career planning, and to become conscious of the main questions you have about it at this point.

INSTRUCTIONS

Read the instructions for each activity, reflect on them, and then write your response. Be as brief or extensive as you like.

Career Planning Worksheet

1. Describe your ideal occupation in terms of responsibilities, skills, and how you would know if you were successful.

_____

_____

_____

_____

_____

_____

_____

_____

2. Identify 10 statements you can make today about your current career planning. Identify 10 questions you need answered for career planning.

10 statements	**10 questions**
1.	1.
2.	2.
3.	3.
4.	4.
5.	5.
6.	6.
7.	7.
8.	8.

9._____

_____

_____

10._____

_____

_____

9._____

_____

_____

10._____

_____

_____

The Evolution of Management

For thousands of years, managers have wrestled with the same issues and problems confronting executives today. Around 1100 B.C., the Chinese practiced the four management functions—planning, organizing, leading, and controlling—discussed in Chapter 1. Between 400 B.C. and 350 B.C., the Greeks recognized management as a separate art and advocated a scientific approach to work. The Romans decentralized the management of their vast empire before the birth of Christ. During medieval times, the Venetians standardized production through the use of an assembly line, building warehouses and using an inventory system to monitor the contents.[1]

But throughout history most managers operated strictly on a trial-and-error basis. The challenges of the industrial revolution changed that. Management emerged as a formal discipline at the turn of the century. The first university programs to offer management and business education, the Wharton School at the University of Pennsylvania and the Amos Tuck School at Dartmouth, were founded in the late 19th century. By 1914, 25 business schools existed.[2]

Thus, the management profession as we know it today is relatively new. This appendix explores the roots of modern management theory. Understanding the origins of management thought will help you grasp the underlying contexts of the ideas and concepts presented in the chapters ahead.

Although this appendix is titled "The Evolution of Management," it might be more appropriately called "The Revolutions of Management," because it documents the wide swings in management approaches over the last 100 years. Out of the great variety of ideas about how to improve management, parts of each approach have survived and been incorporated into modern perspectives on management. Thus, the legacy of past efforts, triumphs, and failures has become our guide to future management practice.

EARLY MANAGEMENT CONCEPTS AND INFLUENCES

Communication and transportation constraints hindered the growth of earlier businesses. Therefore, improvements in management techniques did not substantially improve performance. However, the industrial revolution changed that. As companies grew and became more complex, minor improvements in management tactics produced impressive increases in production quantity and quality.[3]

The emergence of **economies of scale**—reductions in the average cost of a unit of production as the total volume produced increases—drove managers to strive for further growth. The opportunities for mass production created by the industrial revolution spawned intense and systematic thought about management problems and issues—particularly efficiency, production processes, and cost savings.[4]

Figure A.1 provides a timeline depicting the evolution of management thought through the decades. This historical perspective is divided into two major sections: classical approaches and contemporary approaches. Many of these approaches overlapped as they developed, and they often had a significant impact on one another. Some approaches were a direct reaction to the perceived deficiencies of previous approaches. Others developed as the needs and issues confronting managers changed over the years. All the approaches attempted to explain the real issues facing managers and provide them with tools to solve future problems.

Figure A.1 will reinforce your understanding of the key relationships among the approaches and place each perspective in its historical context.

> The oldest company on the *Fortune* 500 list is the Bank of New York, founded in 1784 by Alexander Hamilton. The oldest industrial company is DuPont, begun in 1802 after E. I. du Pont fled persecution during the French Revolution.[5]

CLASSICAL APPROACHES

The classical period extended from the mid-19th century through the early 1950s. The major approaches that emerged during this period were systematic management, scientific management, administrative management, human relations, and bureaucracy.

Systematic Management During the 19th century, growth in U.S. business centered on manufacturing.[6] Early writers such as Adam Smith believed the management of these firms was chaotic, and their ideas helped to systematize it. Most organizational tasks were subdivided and performed by specialized labor. However, poor coordination caused frequent problems and breakdowns of the manufacturing process.

The **systematic management** approach attempted to build specific procedures and processes into operations to ensure coordination of effort. Systematic management emphasized economical

FIGURE A.1
The Evolution of Management Thought

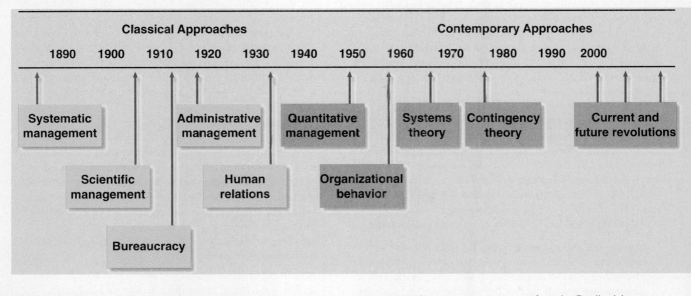

operations, adequate staffing, maintenance of inventories to meet consumer demand, and organizational control. These goals were achieved through:

- Careful definition of duties and responsibilities.
- Standardized techniques for performing these duties.
- Specific means of gathering, handling, transmitting, and analyzing information.
- Cost accounting, wage, and production control systems to facilitate internal coordination and communications.

Systematic management emphasized internal operations because managers were concerned primarily with meeting the explosive growth in demand brought about by the industrial revolution. In addition, managers were free to focus on internal issues of efficiency, in part because the government did

Production costs dropped as mass manufacturing lowered unit costs. Thus economies of scale was born, a concept that persists in the modern manufacturing era.

not constrain business practices significantly. Finally, labor was poorly organized. As a result, many managers were oriented more toward things than toward people.

Systematic management did not address all the issues 19th-century managers faced, but it tried to raise managers' awareness about the most pressing concerns of their job.

An Early Labor Contract

The following rules, taken from the records of Cocheco Company, were typical of labor contract provisions in the 1850s.

1. The hours of work shall be from sunrise to sunset, from the 21st of March to the 20th of September inclusively; and from sunrise until eight o'clock, P.M., during the remainder of the year. One hour shall be allowed for dinner, and half an hour for breakfast during the first mentioned six months; and one hour for dinner during the other half of the year; on Saturdays, the mill shall be stopped one hour before sunset, for the purpose of cleaning the machinery.

2. Every hand coming to work a quarter of an hour after the mill has been started shall be docked a quarter of a day; and every hand absenting him or herself, without absolute necessity, shall be docked in a sum double the amount of the wages such hand shall have earned during the time of such absence. No more than one hand is allowed to leave any one of the rooms at the same time—a quarter of a day shall be deducted for every breach of this rule.

3. No smoking or spiritous liquors shall be allowed in the factory under any pretense whatsoever. It is also forbidden to carry into the factory, nuts, fruits, etc., books, or papers during the hours of work.

SOURCE: W. Sullivan, "The Industrial Revolution and the Factory Operative in Pennsylvania," *The Pennsylvania Magazine of History and Biography* 78 (1954), pp. 478–79.

Scientific Management Systematic management failed to lead to widespread production efficiency. This shortcoming became apparent to a young engineer named Frederick Taylor, who was hired by Midvale Steel Company in 1878. Taylor discovered that production and pay were poor, inefficiency and waste were prevalent, and most companies had tremendous unused potential. He concluded that management decisions were unsystematic and that no research to determine the best means of production existed.

In response, Taylor introduced a second approach to management, known as **scientific management.**[7] This approach advocated the application of scientific methods to analyze work and to determine how to complete production tasks efficiently. For example, U.S. Steel's contract with the United Steel Workers of America specified that sand shovelers should move 12.5 shovelfuls per minute; shovelfuls should average 15 pounds of river sand composed of 5.5 percent moisture.[8]

Taylor identified four principles of scientific management:

1. Management should develop a precise, scientific approach for each element of one's work to replace general guidelines.
2. Management should scientifically select, train, teach, and develop each worker so that the right person has the right job.
3. Management should cooperate with workers to ensure that jobs match plans and principles.
4. Management should ensure an appropriate division of work and responsibility between managers and workers.

To implement this approach, Taylor used techniques such as time-and-motion studies. With this technique, a task was divided into its basic movements, and different motions were timed to determine the most efficient way to complete the task.

After the "one best way" to perform the job was identified, Taylor stressed the importance of hiring and training the proper worker to do that job. Taylor advocated the standardization of tools, the use of instruction cards to help workers, and breaks to eliminate fatigue.

Another key element of Taylor's approach was the use of the differential piecerate system. Taylor assumed workers were motivated by receiving money. Therefore, he implemented a pay system in which workers were paid additional wages when they exceeded a standard level of output for each job. Taylor concluded that both workers and management would benefit from such an approach.

Scientific management principles were widely embraced. Other proponents, including Henry Gantt and Frank and Lillian Gilbreth, introduced many refinements and techniques for applying scientific management on the factory floor. One of the most famous examples of the application of scientific management is the factory Henry Ford built to produce the Model-T.[9]

Scientific Management and the Model-T

At the turn of the century, automobiles were a luxury that only the wealthy could afford. They were assembled by craftspeople who put an entire car together at one spot on the factory floor. These workers were not specialized, and Henry Ford believed they wasted time and energy bringing the needed parts to the car. Ford took a revolutionary approach to automobile manufacturing by using scientific management principles.
After much study, machines and workers in Ford's new factory were placed in sequence so that an automobile could be assembled without interruption along a moving production line. Mechanical energy and a conveyor belt were used to take the work to the workers.
The manufacture of parts likewise was revolutionized. For example, formerly it had taken one worker 20 minutes to assemble a flywheel magneto. By splitting the job into 29 different operations, putting the product on a mechanical conveyor, and changing the height of the conveyor, Ford cut production time to 5 minutes.
By 1914 chassis assembly time had been trimmed from almost 13 hours to 1½ hours. The new methods of production required complete standardization, new machines, and an adaptable labor force. Costs dropped significantly, the Model-T became the first car accessible to the majority of Americans, and Ford dominated the industry for many years.

SOURCE: H. Kroos and C. Gilbert, *The Principles of Scientific Management* (New York: Harper & Row, 1911).

Frederick Taylor (left) and Dr. Lillian Gilbreth (right) were early experts in management efficiency.

The legacy of Taylor's scientific management approach is broad and pervasive. Most important, productivity and efficiency in manufacturing improved dramatically. The concepts of scientific methods and research were introduced to manufacturing. The piecerate system gained wide acceptance because it more closely aligned effort and reward. Taylor also emphasized the need for cooperation between management and workers. And the concept of a management specialist gained prominence.

> The first female executive to head a company on the *Fortune* 500 list was Katharine Graham of *The Washington Post* (first listed in 1972).[10]

Despite these gains, not everyone was convinced that scientific management was the best solution to all business problems. First, critics claimed that Taylor ignored many job-related social and psychological factors by emphasizing only money as a worker incentive. Second, production tasks were reduced to a set of routine, machinelike procedures that led to boredom, apathy, and quality control problems. Third, unions strongly opposed scientific management techniques because they believed management might abuse their power to set the standards and the piecerates, thus exploiting workers and diminishing their importance. Finally, although scientific management resulted in intense scrutiny of the internal efficiency of organizations, it did not help managers deal with broader external issues such as competitors and government regulations, especially at the senior management level.

Administrative Management The **administrative management** approach emphasized the perspective of senior managers within the organization, and argued that management was a profession and could be taught.

An explicit and broad framework for administrative management emerged in 1916, when Henri Fayol, a French mining engineer and executive, published a book summarizing his management experiences. Fayol identified five functions and 14 principles of management. The five functions, which are very similar to the four functions discussed in Chapter 1, are planning, organizing, commanding, coordinating, and controlling. Table A.1 lists and defines the 14 principles. Although some critics claim Fayol treated the principles as universal truths for management, he actually wanted them applied flexibly.[11]

A host of other executives contributed to the administrative management literature. These writers discussed a broad spectrum of management topics, including the social responsibilities of management, the philosophy of management, clarification of business terms and concepts, and organizational principles. Chester Barnard's and Mary Parker Follet's contributions have become classic works in this area.[2]

Barnard, former president of New Jersey Bell Telephone Company, published his landmark book *The Functions of the Executive* in 1938. He outlined the role of the senior executive: formulating the purpose of the organization, hiring key individuals, and maintaining organizational communications.[13] Mary Parker Follet's 1942 book *Dynamic Organization* extended Barnard's work by emphasizing the continually changing situations that managers face.[14] Two of her key contributions—the notion that

TABLE A.1
Fayol's 14 Principles of Management

1. *Division of work*—divide work into specialized tasks and assign responsibilities to specific individuals.
2. *Authority*—delegate authority along with responsibility.
3. *Discipline*—make expectations clear and punish violations.
4. *Unity of command*—each employee should be assigned to only one supervisor.
5. *Unity of direction*—employees' efforts should be focused on achieving organizational objectives.
6. *Subordination of individual interest to the general interest*—the general interest must predominate.
7. *Remuneration*—systematically reward efforts that support the organization's direction.
8. *Centralization*—determine the relative importance of superior and subordinate roles.
9. *Scalar chain*—keep communications within the chain of command.
10. *Order*—order jobs and material so they support the organization's direction.
11. *Equity*—fair discipline and order enhance employee commitment.
12. *Stability and tenure of personnel*—promote employee loyalty and longevity.
13. *Initiative*—encourage employees to act on their own in support of the organization's direction.
14. *Esprit de corps*—promote a unity of interests between employees and management.

managers desire flexibility and the differences between motivating groups and individuals—laid the groundwork for the modern contingency approach discussed later in the chapter.

All the writings in the administrative management area emphasize management as a profession along with fields such as law and medicine. In addition, these authors offered many recommendations based on their personal experiences, which often included managing large corporations. Although these perspectives and recommendations were considered sound, critics noted that they might not work in all settings. Different types of personnel, industry conditions, and technologies may affect the appropriateness of these principles.

> **1955** Ray Kroc's first McDonald's opens. Bill Gates and Steve Jobs are born.[15]

Human Relations A fourth approach to management, **human relations,** developed during the 1930s. This approach aimed at understanding how psychological and social processes interact with the work situation to influence performance. Human relations was the first major approach to emphasize informal work relationships and worker satisfaction.

This approach owes much to other major schools of thought. For example, many of the ideas of the Gilbreths (scientific management) and Barnard and Follet (administrative management) influenced the development of human relations from 1930 to 1955. In fact, human relations emerged from a research project that began as a scientific management study.

Western Electric Company, a manufacturer of communications equipment, hired a team of Harvard researchers led by Elton Mayo and Fritz Roethlisberger. They were to investigate the influence of physical working conditions on workers' productivity and efficiency in one of the company's factories outside Chicago. This research project, known as the *Hawthorne Studies,* provided some of the most interesting and controversial results in the history of management.[16]

The Hawthorne Studies were a series of experiments conducted from 1924 to 1932. During the first stage of the project (the Illumination Experiments), various working conditions, particularly the lighting in the factory, were altered to determine the effects of those changes on productivity. The researchers found no systematic relationship between the factory lighting and production levels. In some cases, productivity continued to increase even when the illumination was reduced to the level of moonlight. The researchers concluded that the workers performed and reacted differently because the researchers were observing them. This reaction is known as the **Hawthorne Effect.**

This conclusion led the researchers to believe productivity may be affected more by psychological and social factors than by physical or objective influences. With this thought in mind, they initiated the other four stages of the project. During these stages, the researchers performed various work group experiments and had extensive interviews with employees. Mayo and his team eventually concluded that productivity and employee behavior were influenced by the informal work group.

Human relations proponents argued that managers should stress primarily employee welfare, motivation, and communication. They believed social needs had precedence over economic needs. Therefore, management must gain the cooperation of the group and promote job satisfaction and group norms consistent with the goals of the organization.

Another noted contributor to the field of human relations was Abraham Maslow.[17] In 1943, Maslow suggested that humans have five levels of needs. The most basic needs are the physical needs for food, water, and shelter; the most advanced need is for self-actualization, or personal fulfillment. Maslow argued that people try to satisfy their lower-level needs and then progress upward to the higher-level needs. Managers can facilitate this process and achieve organizational goals by removing obstacles and encouraging behaviors that satisfy people's needs and organizational goals simultaneously.

Although the human relations approach generated research into leadership, job attitudes, and group dynamics, it drew heavy criticism.[18] Critics believed that one result of human relations—a belief that a happy worker was a productive worker—was too simplistic. While scientific management overemphasized the economic and formal aspects of the workplace, human relations ignored the more rational side of the worker and the important characteristics of the formal organization. However, human

A Human Relations Pioneer

In 1837, William Procter, a ruined English retailer, and James Gamble, son of a Methodist minister, formed a partnership in Cincinnati to make soap and candles. Both were known for their integrity, and soon their business was thriving.

By 1883, the business had grown substantially. When William Cooper Procter, grandson of the founder, left Princeton University to work for the firm, he wanted to learn the business from the ground up. He started working on the factory floor. "He did every menial job from shoveling rosin and soap to pouring fatty mixtures into crutchers. He brought his lunch in a paper bag . . . and sat on the floor [with the other workers] and ate with them, learning their feelings about work."

By 1884, Cooper Procter believed, from his own experience, that increasing workers' psychological commitment to the company would lead to higher productivity. His passion to increase employee commitment to the firm led him to propose a scandalous plan: share profits with workers to increase their sense of responsibility and job satisfaction. The surprise was audible on the first "Dividend Day," when workers held checks equivalent to seven weeks' pay.

Still, the plan was not complete. Workers saw the profit sharing as extra pay rather than as an incentive to improve. In addition, Cooper Procter recognized that a fundamental issue for the workers, some of whom continued to be his good friends, was the insecurity of old age. Public incorporation in 1890 gave Procter a new idea. After trying several versions, by 1903 he had discovered a way to meet all his goals for labor: a stock purchase plan. For every dollar a worker invested in P&G stock, the company would contribute four dollars' worth of stock.

Finally, Cooper Procter had resolved some key issues for labor that paid off in worker loyalty, improved productivity, and an increasing corporate reputation for caring and integrity. He went on to become CEO of the firm, and P&G today remains one of the most admired corporations in the United States.

SOURCES: O. Schisgall, *Eyes on Tomorrow* (Chicago: J. G. Ferguson, 1981): T. Welsh, "Best and Worst Corporate Reputations," *Fortune, February 7, 1994,* pp. 58–66.

relations was a significant step in the development of management thought, because it prompted managers and researchers to consider the psychological and social factors that influence performance.

Bureaucracy Max Weber, a German sociologist, lawyer, and social historian, showed how management itself could be more efficient and consistent in his book *The Theory of Social and Economic Organizations.*[19] The ideal model for management, according to Weber, is the **bureaucracy** approach.

Weber believed bureaucratic structures can eliminate the variability that results when managers in the same organization have different skills, experiences, and goals. Weber advocated that the jobs themselves be standardized so that personnel changes would not disrupt the organization. He emphasized a structured, formal network of relationships among specialized positions in an organization. Rules and regulations standardize behavior, and authority resides in positions rather than in individuals. As a result, the organization need not rely on a particular individual, but will realize efficiency and success by following the rules in a routine and unbiased manner.

1962 The first Wal-Mart store opens n Rogers, Arkansas.
1964 Blue Ribbon Sports ships its first shoes. It's now called Nike.
1969 Don and Doris Fisher open the first Gap store in San Francisco.

According to Weber, bureaucracies are especially important because they allow large organizations to perform the many routine activities necessary for their survival. Also, bureaucratic positions foster specialized skills, eliminating many subjective judgments by managers. In addition, if the rules and controls are established properly, bureaucracies should be unbiased in their treatment of people, both customers and employees.

Many organizations today are bureaucratic. Bureaucracy can be efficient and productive. However, bureaucracy is not the appropriate model for every organization. Organizations or departments that need rapid decision making and flexibility may suffer under a bureaucratic approach. Some people may not perform their best with excessive bureaucratic rules and procedures.

Other shortcomings stem from a faulty execution of bureaucratic principles rather than from the approach itself. Too much authority may be vested in too few people; the procedures may become the ends rather than the means; or managers may ignore appropriate rules and regulations. Finally, one advantage of a bureaucracy—its permanence—can also be a problem. Once a bureaucracy is established, dismantling it is very difficult.

CONTEMPORARY APPROACHES

The contemporary approaches to management include quantitative management, organizational behavior, systems theory, and the contingency perspective. The contemporary approaches have developed at various times since World War II, and they continue to represent the cornerstones of modern management thought.

Quantitative Management Although Taylor introduced the use of science as a management tool early in the 20th century, most organizations did not adopt the use of quantitative techniques for management problems until the 1940s and 1950s.[20] During World War II, military planners began to apply mathematical techniques to defense and logistic problems. After the war, private corporations began assembling teams of quantitative experts to tackle many of the complex issues confronting large organizations. This approach, referred to as **quantitative management,** emphasizes the application of quantitative analysis to management decisions and problems.

Quantitative management helps a manager make a decision by developing formal mathematical models of the problem.

Computers facilitated the development of specific quantitative methods. These include such techniques as statistical decision theory, linear programming, queuing theory, simulation, forecasting, inventory modeling, network modeling, and break-even analysis. Organizations apply these techniques in many areas, including production, quality control, marketing, human resources, finance, distribution, planning, and research and development.

Despite the promise quantitative management holds, managers do not rely on these methods as the primary approach to decision making. Typically they use these techniques as a supplement or tool in the decision process. Many managers will use results that are consistent with their experience, intuition, and judgment, but they often reject results that contradict their beliefs. Also, managers may use the process to compare alternatives and eliminate weaker options.

Several explanations account for the limited use of quantitative management. Many managers have not been trained in using these techniques. Also, many aspects of a management decision cannot be expressed through mathematical symbols and formulas. Finally, many of the decisions managers face are nonroutine and unpredictable.

1971 Intel introduces the first microprocessor and IBM introduces the floppy disk.
1976 Steve Jobs and Steve Wozniak start Apple Computer in their garage.

Organizational Behavior During the 1950s, a transition took place in the human relations approach. Scholars began to recognize that worker productivity and organizational success are based on more than the satisfaction of economic or social needs. The revised perspective, known as **organizational behavior,** studies and identifies management activities that promote employee effectiveness through an understanding of the complex nature of individual, group, and organizational processes. Organizational behavior draws from a variety of disciplines, including psychology and sociology, to explain the behavior of people on the job.

During the 1960s, organizational behaviorists heavily influenced the field of management. Douglas McGregor's Theory X and Theory Y marked the transition from human relations.[21] According to McGregor, Theory X managers assume workers are lazy and irresponsible and require constant supervision and external motivation to achieve organizational goals. Theory Y managers assume employees *want* to work and can direct and control themselves. McGregor advocated a Theory Y perspective, suggesting that managers who encourage participation and allow opportunities for individual challenge and initiative would achieve superior performance.

Other major organizational behaviorists include Chris Argyris, who recommended greater autonomy and better jobs for workers,[22] and Rensis Likert, who stressed the value of participative management.[23] Through the years, organizational behavior has consistently emphasized development of the organization's human resources to achieve individual and organizational goals. Like other approaches, it has been criticized for its limited perspective, although more recent contributions have a broader and more situational viewpoint. In the past few years, many of the primary issues addressed by organizational behavior have experienced a rebirth with a greater interest in leadership, employee involvement, and self-management.

> **1980** Microsoft licenses its operating system to IBM.
> **1981** MTV launches on cable.
> **1995** Netscape goes public and kicks off the dot-com boom.

Systems Theory The classical approaches as a whole were criticized because they (1) ignored the relationship between the organization and its external environment, and (2) usually stressed one aspect of the organization or its employees at the expense of other considerations. In response to these criticisms, management scholars during the 1950s stepped back from the details of the organization to attempt to understand it as a whole system. These efforts were based on a general scientific approach called **systems theory.**[24] Organizations are open systems, dependent on inputs from the outside world, such as raw materials, human resources, and capital. They transform these inputs into outputs that (ideally) meet the market's needs for goods and services. The environment reacts to the outputs through a feedback loop; this feedback provides input for the next cycle of the system. The process repeats itself for the life of the system, and is illustrated in Figure A.2.

Systems theory also emphasizes that an organization is one system in a series of subsystems. For instance, Southwest Airlines is a subsystem of the airline industry and the flight crews are a subsystem of Southwest. Systems theory points out that each subsystem is a component of the whole and is interdependent with other subsystems.

Contingency Perspective Building on systems theory ideas, the **contingency perspective** refutes universal principles of management by stating that a variety of factors, both internal and external to the firm, may affect the organization's performance.[25] Therefore, there is no "one best way" to manage and organize, because circumstances vary.

Situational characteristics are called **contingencies.** Understanding contingencies helps a manager know which sets of circumstances dictate which management actions. You will learn recommendations for the major contingencies throughout this text. The contingencies include

1. Circumstances in the organization's external environment.
2. The internal strengths and weaknesses of the organization.
3. The values, goals, skills, and attitudes of managers and workers in the organization.
4. The types of tasks, resources, and technologies the organization uses.

With an eye to these contingencies, a manager may categorize the situation and then choose the proper competitive strategy, organization structure, or management process for the circumstances.

Researchers continue to identify key contingency variables and their effects on management issues. As you read the topics covered in each chapter, you will notice similarities and differences among management situations and the appropriate responses. This perspective should represent a cornerstone of your own approach to management. Many of the things you will learn about throughout this course apply a contingency perspective.

> **2000** AOL becomes the first pure Internet company to make the *Fortune* 500 list and merges with Time Warner the same year.
> **2001** Enron files for bankruptcy.
> **2002** United Airlines files for bankruptcy.
> **2003** AOL Time Warner posts a record $98.7 billion loss.[26]

AN EYE ON THE FUTURE

All of these historical perspectives have left legacies that affect contemporary management thought and practice. Their undercurrents continue to flow, even as the context and the specifics change.

Times do pass, and things do change. This may sound obvious, but it isn't to those managers who sit by idly while their firms fail to adapt to changing times. Business becomes global. New technologies change how we work, produce goods, and deliver services. Change continually creates both new opportunities and new demands for lowering costs and for achieving greater innovation, quality, and speed. Management knowledge and practices evolve accordingly.

FIGURE A.2
Open-System Perspective of an Organization

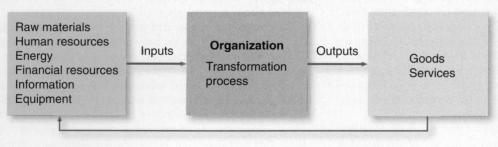

The essential facts about change are these: First, change is happening more rapidly and dramatically than at any other time in history. Second, if you don't anticipate change and adapt to it, you and your firm will not thrive in a competitive business world. The theme of change—what is happening now, what lies ahead, how it affects management, and how you can deal with it—permeates this entire book.

What are the implications of these changes for you and your career? How can you best be ready to meet the challenges? You must ask questions about the future, anticipate changes, know your responsibilities, and be prepared to meet them head-on. We hope you study the remaining chapters with these goals in mind.

KEY TERMS

administrative management   A classical management approach that attempted to identify major principles and functions that managers could use to achieve superior organizational performance, p. 39.

bureaucracy   A classical management approach emphasizing a structured, formal network of relationships among specialized positions in the organization, p. 40.

contingencies   Factors that determine the appropriateness of managerial actions, p. 42.

contingency perspective   An approach to the study of management proposing that the managerial strategies, structures, and processes that result in high performance depend on the characteristics, or important contingencies, or the situation in which they are applied, p. 42.

economies of scale   Reductions in the average cost of a unit of production as the total volume produces increases, p. 36.

Hawthorne Effect   People's reactions to being observed or studied resulting in superficial rather than meaningful changes in behavior, p. 40.

human relations   A classical management approach that attempted to understand and explain how human psychological and social processes interact with the formal aspects of the work situation to influence performance, p. 39.

organizational behavior   A contemporary management approach that studies and identifies management activities that promote employee effectiveness by examining the complex and dynamic nature of individual, group, and organizational processes, p. 41.

quantitative management   A contemporary management approach that emphasizes the application of quantitative analysis to managerial decisions and problems, p. 41.

scientific management   A classical management approach that applied scientific methods to analyze and determine the "one best way" to complete production tasks, p. 38.

systematic management   A classical management approach that attempted to build into operations the specific procedures and processes that would ensure coordination of effort to achieve established goals and plans, p. 36.

systems theory   A theory stating that an organization is a managed system that changes inputs into outputs, p. 42.

DISCUSSION QUESTIONS

1. How does today's business world compare with the one of 40 years ago? What is different about today, and what is not so different?

2. What is scientific management? How might today's organizations use it?

3. Table A.1 lists Fayol's 14 principles of management, first published in 1916. Are they as useful today as they were then? Why or why not? When are they most, and least, useful?

4. What are the advantages and disadvantages of a bureaucratic organization?

5. In what situations are quantitative management concepts and tools applicable?

6. Choose any organization and describe its system of inputs and outputs.

7. Why did the contingency perspective become such an important approach to management? Generate a list of contingencies that might affect the decisions you make in your life or as a manager.

8. For each of the management approaches discussed in the chapter, give examples you have seen. How effective or ineffective were they?

9. The appendix highlighted a few landmark events in recent business history. What additional landmarks during those decades would you include?

10. The final landmark was from 2003—what are the most important landmarks since then, and why?

Experiential Exercises

A.1 Approaches to Management

OBJECTIVES

1. To help you conceive a wide variety of management approaches.
2. To clarify the appropriateness of different management approaches in different situations.

INSTRUCTIONS

Your instructor will divide your class randomly into groups of four to six people each. Acting as a team, with everyone offering ideas and one person serving as official recorder, each group will be responsible for writing a one-page memo to your present class. Subject matter of your group's memo will be "My advice for managing people today is . . ." The fun part of this exercise (and its creative element) involves writing the memo from the viewpoint of the person assigned to your group by your instructor.

Among the memo viewpoints your instructor may assign are:

- An ancient Egyptian slave master (building the great pyramids)
- Henri Fayol
- Frederick Taylor

- Mary Parker Follet
- Douglas McGregor
- A contingency management theorist
- A Japanese auto company executive
- The chief executive officer of IBM in the year 2030
- Commander of the Starship Enterprise II in the year 3001
- Others, as assigned by your instructor

Use your imagination, make sure everyone participates, and try to be true to any historical facts you've encountered. Attempt to be as specific and realistic as possible. Remember, the idea is to provide advice about managing people from another point in time (or from a particular point of view at the present time).

A.2 The University Grading System Analysis

OBJECTIVES

1. To learn to identify the components of a complex system.
2. To better understand organizations as systems.
3. To visualize how a change in policy affects the functioning of an organization system.

INSTRUCTIONS

1. Assume that your university has decided to institute a pass–fail system of grading instead of the letter-grade system it presently has. Apply the systems perspective learned from this chapter to understanding this decision.

Make sure you manage your 20-minute time limit carefully. A recommended approach is to spend 2 to 3 minutes putting the exercise into proper perspective. Next, take about 10 to 12 minutes brainstorming ideas for your memo, with your recorder jotting down key ideas and phrases. Have your recorder use the remaining time to write your group's one-page memo, with constructive comments and help from the others. Pick a spokesperson to read your group's memo to the class.

SOURCE: R. Krietner and A. Kinicki, *Organization Behavior*, 3rd ed. (New York: Richard D. Irwin, 1994), pp. 30–31.

2. Answer the questions on the Grading System Analysis Worksheet individually, or in small groups, as directed by your instructor.

DISCUSSION QUESTIONS

Share your own or your group's responses with the entire class. Then answer the following questions.

1. Did you diagram the system in the same way?
2. Did you identify the same system components?
3. Which subsystems will be affected by the change?
4. How do you explain differences in your responses?

Grading System Analysis Worksheet

DESCRIPTION

1. What subsystems compose the system (the university)? Diagram the system.

_____

_____

_____

2. Identify in this system: inputs, outputs, transformations.

_____

_____

_____

DIAGNOSIS

3. Which of the subsystems will be affected by the change; that is, what changes are likely to occur throughout the system as a result of the policy change?

_____

_____

_____

SOURCE: J. Gordon, *A Diagnostic Approach to Organizational Behavior* (Englewood Cliffs, NJ: Prentice Hall, 1983), p. 38. Reprinted with permission of Prentice Hall, Inc., Englewood Cliffs, NJ.

chapter

2

The External Environment and Organizational Culture

" *The essence of a business is outside itself.* "

— Peter Drucker

LEARNING OBJECTIVES

After studying Chapter 2, you will be able to:

LO 1 Describe how environmental forces influence organizations and how organizations can influence their environments. p. 48

LO 2 Distinguish between the macroenvironment and the competitive environment. p. 48

LO 3 Explain why managers and organizations should attend to economic and social developments. p. 50

LO 4 Identify elements of the competitive environment. p. 55

LO 5 Summarize how organizations respond to environmental uncertainty. p. 63

LO 6 Define elements of an organization's culture. p. 72

LO 7 Discuss how an organization's culture affects its response to its external environment. p. 72

CHAPTER OUTLINE

A Look Ahead

The Macroenvironment
Laws and Regulations
The Economy
Technology
Demographics
Social Issues and the Natural Environment

The Competitive Environment
Competitors
New Entrants
Substitutes and Complements
Suppliers
Customers

Environmental Analysis
Environmental Scanning
Scenario Development
Forecasting
Benchmarking

Responding to the Environment
Adapting to the Environment: Changing Yourself
Influencing Your Environment
Changing the Environment You Are In
Choosing a Response Approach

Culture and the Internal Environment of Organizations
Diagnosing Culture
Managing Culture

Management Close-Up

HOW CAN LARRY BLANFORD KEEP GREEN MOUNTAIN COFFEE ROASTERS PERKING?

In 1981, Bob Stiller began serving his coffee to customers in a tiny Vermont café. He was focused simply on giving them the highest-quality freshly roasted coffee at a reasonable price. As his Green Mountain Coffee Roasters (GMCR) formula caught on, however, nearby restaurants asked him to supply them with coffee and roasting equipment so that they, too, could serve the coffee. Before long, Stiller discovered that he was not only a retailer but a wholesale supplier as well.

The coffee's popularity grew. Ski-season visitors fell in love with Green Mountain coffee and asked if they could ship it home. Thus, GMCR's mail-order business was born.

Stiller wanted to keep growing his business, but he was limited by the times. In the 1980s, coffee was a commodity—something you drank when you ate your piece of pie or a donut. Not until the mid-1990s did coffee brewing became an art form, as the Starbucks-led coffee revolution began to sweep across America.

{ Green Mountain Coffee Roasters started small but ultimately became a large enterprise selling its products through multiple channels. As you read this chapter, consider how this company grew by understanding not only its customers' needs but the needs of its external environment. }

With the emergence of brands like Starbucks, Seattle's Best Coffee, Brothers, and Caribou Coffee, the industry became highly competitive and posed sizable barriers to those who wanted to enter it. To build and maintain retail coffee stores requires a significant monetary outlay, and in a field crowded with competitors, each retail outlet would need high-volume sales to be profitable. Entering the market that way wasn't a good option for Green Mountain Coffee Roasters. What could the company do to expand its growing brand and become a household name beyond New England?[1]

Inputs

Outputs

FIGURE 2.1
Organization Inputs
and Outputs

open systems

Organizations that are affected by, and that affect, their environment.

 LO 1

inputs

Goods and services organizations take in and use to create products or services.

outputs

The products and services organizations create.

external environment

All relevant forces outside a firm's boundaries, such as competitors, customers, the government, and the economy.

competitive environment

The immediate environment surrounding a firm; includes suppliers, customers, rivals, and the like.

macroenvironment

The general environment; includes governments, economic conditions, and other fundamental factors that generally affect all organizations.

As a coffee seller, Green Mountain Coffee Roasters does business all over the world. Its management must therefore keep a sharp watch on a broad spectrum of influences and events that can affect its operations. In this chapter, we discuss in detail how pressures from outside the organization help create the context in which managers and their companies must operate.

As we suggested in the first chapter, organizations are **open systems**—that is, they are affected by and in turn affect their external environments. For example, they take in **inputs** such as goods or services from their environment and use them to create products and services that are **outputs** to their environment, as shown in Figure 2.1. But when we use the term **external environment** here, we mean more than an organization's clients or customers; the external environment includes *all* relevant forces outside the organization's boundaries.

Many of these factors are uncontrollable. Companies large and small are buffeted or battered by recession, government interference, competitors' actions, and other factors. But their lack of control does not mean that managers can ignore such forces, use them as excuses for poor performance, and try to just get by. Managers must stay abreast of external developments and react effectively. Moreover, as we will discuss later in this chapter, sometimes managers can influence components of the external environment. We will examine ways in which organizations can do just that.

Figure 2.2 shows the external environment of a business organization. The organization exists in its **competitive environment,** which is composed of the firm and its rivals, suppliers, customers (buyers), new entrants, and substitute or complementary products. At the more general level is the **macroenvironment,** which includes legal, political, economic, technological, demographic, and social and natural factors that generally affect all organizations.

A Look Ahead

This chapter discusses the basic characteristics of an organization's environment and the importance of that environment for strategic management. We also examine the *internal environment,* or *culture,* of the organization and the way that culture may influence the organization's response to its environment. Later chapters elaborate on many of the basic environmental forces introduced here. For example, technology will be discussed again in Chapter 17. The global environment gets a thorough treatment in Chapter 6, which is devoted to international management. Other chapters focus on ethics, social responsibility, and the natural environment. Chapter 18 reiterates the theme that recurs throughout this text: organizations must change continually because environments change continually.

The Macroenvironment

 LO 2

All organizations operate in a macroenvironment, which is defined by the most general elements in the external environment that potentially can influence strategic decisions. Although a top executive team may have unique internal strengths and ideas about its goals, it must consider external factors before taking action.

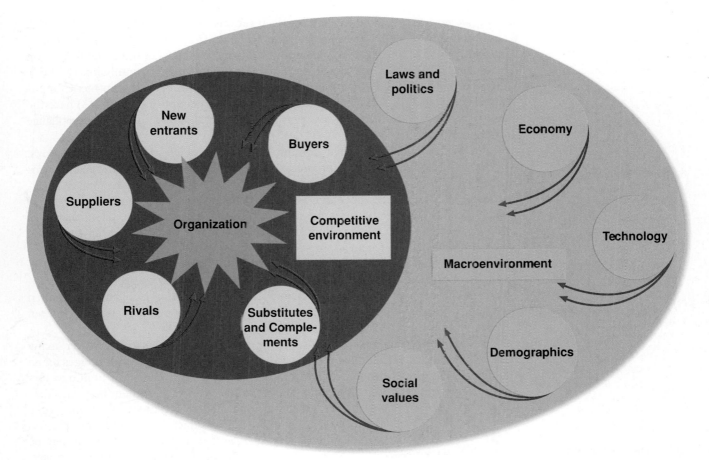

FIGURE 2.2
The External Environment

Laws and Regulations

U.S. government policies impose strategic constraints on organizations but may also provide opportunities. For example, the Library of Congress's Copyright Royalty Board recently alarmed Internet radio companies when it changed its regulations setting the royalty payments these companies owe recording companies and artists. Webcasters had been paying royalties computed as a percentage of their earnings, and because companies like AccuRadio are relatively young and have only begun turning a profit, that arrangement kept costs down. The new regulations would impose a flat fee each time a song is played. AccuRadio complained that this change would raise its annual royalty cost from less than $50,900 to about $600,000 a year—far more than its profits and nearly equal to its entire revenue. Even big Webcasters like RealNetworks and AOL Radio said if the ruling stands, the fees would force them to substantially cut back their offerings. Some companies would benefit from the change, however. Broadcast radio stations pay royalties only to the composers of the songs they play, so they would have an advantage relative to fast-growing but smaller online radio stations. And recording companies would receive more revenue from the new arrangement.[2]

The government can affect business opportunities through tax laws, economic policies, and international trade rulings. An example of restraint on business action is the U.S. government's standards regarding bribery. In some countries, bribes and kickbacks are common and expected ways of doing business, but for U.S. firms they are illegal practices. Some U.S. businesses have, in fact, been fined for using bribery when competing internationally. But laws can also assist organizations. Because U.S. federal and state governments protect property rights, including copyrights, trademarks, and patents, it is economically more attractive to start businesses in the United States than in countries where laws and law enforcement offer less protection.

Regulators are specific government organizations in a firm's more immediate task environment. Regulatory agencies such as the Occupational Safety and Health Administration (OSHA), the Interstate Commerce Commission (ICC), the Federal Aviation Administration (FAA), the Equal Employment Opportunity Commission (EEOC), the National Labor Relations Board (NLRB), the Office of Federal Contract Compliance Programs (OFCCP), and the Environmental Protection Agency (EPA) have the power to investigate company practices and take legal action to ensure compliance with laws.

The Securities and Exchange Commission (SEC) regulates U.S. financial markets. Its regulations are intended to protect investors. For instance, the SEC recently proposed regulations requiring companies to disclose more details about the total compensation paid to executives, including deferred compensation (pensions, severance pay) and perks (such as free housing and personal use of a corporate jet). The objective of the regulations would be to help investors in a company evaluate whether executives are being compensated at an appropriate level.[3]

Another example of a regulatory body is the Food and Drug Administration (FDA), which can prevent a company from selling an unsafe or ineffective product to the public. Following recent highly publicized incidents of illness from people who ate tainted peanuts, lettuce, spinach, and green onions, the FDA came under pressure to tighten its regulations for food safety.

Often the corporate community sees government as an adversary. However, many organizations realize that government can be a source of competitive advantages for an individual company or an entire industry. Public policy may prevent or limit new foreign or domestic competitors from entering an industry. Government may subsidize failing companies or provide tax breaks to some. Federal patents protect innovative products or production process technologies. Legislation may be passed to support industry prices, thereby guaranteeing profits or survival. The government may even intervene to ensure the survival of certain key industries or companies, as it has done to help auto companies, airlines, and agricultural businesses.

The U.S. Department of Commerce's Trade Advocacy Center, at www.export.gov/advocacy/, was established to help U.S. businesses overcome hurdles that make it difficult for them to export goods or compete against foreign firms.

 LO 3

The Economy

Although most Americans think in terms of the U.S. economy, the economic environment for organizations is much larger—created by complex interconnections among the economies of different countries. Wall Street investment analysts begin their workday thinking not just about what the New York Stock Exchange did yesterday but also about how the London and Tokyo exchanges did overnight. Growth and recessions occur worldwide as well as domestically.

The economic environment dramatically affects managers' ability to function effectively and influences their strategic choices. Interest and inflation rates affect the availability and cost of capital, growth opportunities, prices, costs, and consumer demand for products. Unemployment rates affect labor availability and the wages the firm must pay, as well as product demand. Steeply rising energy and health care costs have had a great effect on companies' ability to hire and their cost of doing business. Changes in the value of the dollar on world exchanges may make American products cheaper or more expensive than their foreign competitors.

An important economic influence is the stock market. When investors bid up stock prices, they are paying more to own shares in companies, which means the companies have more capital to fuel their strategies. Observers of the stock market watch trends in major indexes such as the Dow Jones Industrial Average, Standard and Poor's 500, and Nasdaq Composite, which combine many companies' performance into a single

$ The bottom line

COST

With increased competition from foreign and domestic companies, managers must pay particular attention to cost.

Economic forces have caused the fortunes of corn-based ethanol producers to swing wildly. For a time, soaring gasoline prices intensified the demand for alternative fuel sources for automobiles. That fact, coupled with a belief that ethanol fuel would reduce emissions of greenhouse gases, inspired the U.S. government to mandate the use of ethanol. Farmers responded by planting more corn, and energy companies built ethanol refineries.

But soon other forces pummeled the ethanol producers. First, flooding in the Midwest led to forecasts of high corn prices, and many ethanol producers tried to protect themselves by signing contracts for a generous $7 and more per bushel. Then fields dried and prospects for a good harvest improved, so corn prices started falling, leaving producers with contracts for overpriced corn.

More recently, the economy swung downward. A "bubble" of inflated real estate prices burst, contributing to problems for mortgage lenders that quickly spread to the entire financial industry. As credit dried up, the overall pace of business slowed dramatically, and oil prices fell, erasing some of ethanol's competitive advantage in the mar-

The recent economic woes in America have spurred the government to enact new laws to help lift the financial burden off of the shoulders of individuals and businesses that are struggling. Shown here is President Barack Obama signing the economic stimulus bill, as Vice President Joe Biden looks on. What affect do you think this bill will have on the economy?

ketplace for fuel. But prices for corn also fell, keeping production costs down. Ethanol producers are hopeful that in the long run, drivers will need to rely more and more on alternative fuels. Meanwhile, ethanol companies need steady and farsighted management to guide them through the ups and downs of commodity prices and demand.[4]

measurement. Figure 2.3 shows how two of these indexes performed over a year's worth of trading. They are measured against their price level at the beginning of the period, set at an index value of 100. Both indexes had risen to great heights at the beginning of the period, and then they dropped rapidly during the autumn months. The falling prices reflected an economy in which demand for homes and cars had shriveled, credit was difficult to obtain, exports tumbled, and unemployment rates soared.[5] Lower stock values coupled with tight credit made it hard for most businesses to find capital for expansion and innovation. Governments launched a variety of stimulus efforts to help companies get financing and to encourage consumers to start spending again. Stock markets have always rebounded eventually, even after a steep decline such as this one, as investors see hope for renewed business growth.

The stock market may also have a profound effect on the behavior of individual managers. In publicly held companies, managers throughout the organization may feel required to meet Wall Street's earnings expectations. It is quite likely that you, too, at some point in your career, will be asked to improve a budget or estimate because your company does not want to disappoint "the Street." Such external pressures usually have a very positive effect—they help make many firms more efficient and profitable. But failure to meet those expectations can cause a company's stock price to drop,

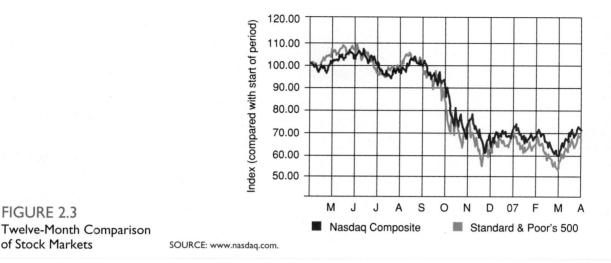

FIGURE 2.3
Twelve-Month Comparison
of Stock Markets

SOURCE: www.nasdaq.com.

making it more difficult for the firm to raise additional capital for investment. The compensation of managers may also be affected, particularly if they have been issued stock options. The net effect of these pressures may sometimes be that managers focus on short-term results at the expense of the long-term success of their organizations. Even worse, a few managers may be tempted to engage in unethical or unlawful behavior that misleads investors.[6] We will discuss managerial ethics in Chapter 5 and stock options in Chapter 10.

Economic conditions change over time and are difficult to predict. Bull and bear markets come and go. Periods of dramatic growth may be followed by a recession. Every trend undoubtedly will end—but when? Even when times seem good, budget deficits or other considerations create concern about the future.

Technology

Today a company cannot succeed without incorporating into its strategy the astonishing technologies that exist and continue to evolve. Technological advances create new products, advanced production techniques, and better ways of managing and communicating. In addition, as technology evolves, new industries, markets, and competitive niches develop. For example, early entrants in biotechnology are trying to establish dominant positions, while later entrants work on technological advances that will give them a competitive niche. Advances in technology also permit companies to enter markets that would otherwise be unavailable to them, such as when cable TV companies adapted their technology to enter the market for Internet services.

The bottom line
SPEED
Managers with ready access to information gain a significant competitive edge.

New technologies also provide new production techniques. In manufacturing, sophisticated robots perform jobs without suffering fatigue, requiring vacations or weekends off, or demanding wage increases. New methods, such as injecting steam into oil fields at high pressure, are enabling Shell, ExxonMobil, and other oil companies to extract that valuable resource from locations that had once been considered depleted. In this case, technological and economic forces overlap: the rising price of oil has made it worthwhile for companies to develop and try the new technology.[7]

In addition, new technologies provide new ways to manage and communicate. Computerized management information systems (MISs) make information available when needed, and networking via the Internet makes it available where it is needed. Computers monitor productivity and note performance deficiencies. Telecommunications allow conferences to take place without requiring people to travel to the same location. Such technological advances create innovations in business. Strategies developed around the cutting edge of technological advances create a competitive advantage; strategies that ignore or lag behind competitors' technology lead to obsolescence and extinction. This issue is so important that we devote an entire chapter (Chapter 17) to the topic.

Demographics

Demographics are measures of various characteristics of the people who make up groups or other social units. Work groups, organizations, countries, markets, and societies can be described statistically by referring to demographic measures such as their members' age, gender, family size, income, education, occupation, and so forth.

Managers must consider workforce demographics in formulating their human resources strategies. Population growth influences the size and composition of the labor force. In the decade from 2004 to 2014, the U.S. civilian labor force is expected to grow at a rate of 10 percent, reaching 162.1 million.[8] This growth is slower than during the previous decade, partly because young workers—those between the ages of 16 and 24—are declining in numbers. The fastest-growing age group will be workers who are 55 and older, who are expected to represent more than one-fifth of the labor force in 2014. What does this mean for employers? They will need to find ways to retain and fully use the talents of their experienced workers while competing for relatively scarce entry-level workers. They may find that many of their older employees are willing to work past the traditional retirement age of 65; one reason is that research suggests that a lack of pensions and adequate savings will make retirement unaffordable for many of today's baby boomers.[9] Eventually, however, declining participation in work by older persons will require managers to find replacements for these highly experienced workers.

The education and skill levels of the workforce are another demographic factor managers must consider. The share of the U.S. labor force with at least some college education has been increasing steadily over the past several decades, from less than one-fourth of the workforce in 1970 to more

Will the next generation of workers change the way we work? Researchers found that teens studying at their computers are also doing something else 65 percent of the time, and 26 percent of teens use several media at once. A study of multitasking and brain activity found that we use different parts of the brain when we multitask while learning. Multitaskers used the part of the brain involved in repetitive skills, while those engaged only in learning used the area associated with memory.[10] Will this influence future managers' ability to think deeply about problems?

than half today.[11] Even so, many companies find that they must invest heavily in training their entry-level workers, who may not have been adequately prepared for some of the more complex tasks the modern workplace requires. (We discuss training in greater detail in Chapter 10.) Also, as college has become a more popular option, employers are finding it difficult to recruit employees for jobs that require knowledge of a skilled trade, such as machinists and toolmakers, especially in areas where the cost of living is so high that most residents are professionals.[12] However, as education levels improve around the globe, more managers find they are able to send even technical tasks to lower-priced but highly trained workers overseas, which we discuss further in Chapter 6.

Another factor that significantly influences the U.S. population and labor force is immigration. Immigrants accounted for approximately 40 percent of the U.S. population growth recently, a trend that has an important impact on the labor force.[13] Immigrants are frequently of working age but have different educational and occupational backgrounds from the rest of the labor force. Immigration is one reason the labor force in the future will be more ethnically diverse than it is today. The biggest percentage employment increases will be by Asian Americans and Hispanic populations, followed by African Americans. The demographic importance of immigration intersects with legal issues governing who is permitted to work in the United States. For example, the federal government has recently cracked down not only on undocumented workers but also on the managers who hired them. Other companies have asked the government to admit more foreign workers with technical expertise that may be hard to find in the United States.

As the number of people in the workforce with a college education increases, managers must consider how this impacts their work.

Since the last quarter of the 20th century, women have joined the U.S. labor force in record numbers. Throughout the 1970s and 1980s, they became much more likely to take paying jobs. In the 1970s, only about one-third of women were in the labor force, but 60 percent had jobs in 1999. Since then, women's labor force participation rate has stayed near that level, declining only slightly. Women's participation contrasts with a participation rate of 73 percent for men, projected to decline to 70 percent by 2020, when a larger share of U.S. adults have retired.[14]

A more diverse workforce has many advantages, but managers have to make certain they provide equality for women and minorities with respect to employment, advancement opportunities, and compensation. They must make strategic plans to recruit, retain, train, motivate, and effectively utilize people of diverse demographic backgrounds who have the skills to achieve the company's mission. We discuss the issue of managing the diverse workforce in detail in Chapter 11.

Social Issues and the Natural Environment

Societal trends regarding how people think and behave have major implications for management of the labor force, corporate social actions, and strategic decisions about products and markets. For example, during the 1980s and 1990s women in the workforce often chose to delay having children as they focused on their careers, but today more women are having children and then returning to the workforce. As a result, companies have introduced more supportive policies, including family leave, flexible working hours, and child care assistance. Many firms also extend these benefits to all employees or allow them to design their own benefits packages, where they can choose from a menu of available benefits that suit their individual situations. Domestic partners, whether they are in a marital relationship or not, also are covered by many employee benefit programs. Firms provide these benefits as a way of increasing a source of competitive advantage: an experienced workforce.

A prominent issue today pertains to natural resources: drilling for oil in formerly protected areas in the United States. Firms in the oil industry face considerable public opinion both in favor of preserving the natural environment and against the country's dependence on other countries for fuel. The protection of the natural environment is so important in managerial decisions that we devote Appendix C following Chapter 5 to that subject.

How companies respond to these and other social issues may also affect their reputation in the marketplace, which in turn may help or hinder their competitiveness. The public health issue of childhood obesity has given videogames a bad name among those who advocate for children to get off the couch and get more exercise. But two games have generated favorable publicity: Konami's Dance Dance Revolution (DDR), where players compete with dance moves, and Nintendo's Wii Sports, where players swing a remote control containing motion sensors to move a virtual tennis racket, bowling ball, baseball bat, or boxing gloves. The games have also been praised as an alternative to the violent themes of many games. Dean Bender, the public relations agent for DDR, said of his client, "With all the bad PR about violence, we became the white knights."[15] And Wii Sports players have reported breaking into a sweat and even straining muscles.[16] However, one side effect of that vigorous play with the Wii system was a safety hazard. The company's first wrist straps for the remote controls occasionally broke. But within weeks, the company began replacing the straps with a stronger version at no charge, a rapid response that cemented customer satisfaction more than the defect harmed Nintendo's reputation.[17]

The Competitive Environment

All managers are affected by the components of the macroenvironment we just discussed. But each organization also functions in a closer, more immediate competitive environment. The competitive environment includes the organizations with which the organization directly interacts. As shown in Figure 2.4, the competitive environment includes rivalry among current competitors and the impact of new entrants, substitute and complementary products, suppliers, and customers. This model was originally developed by Michael Porter, a Harvard professor and a noted authority on strategic management. According to Porter, successful managers do more than simply react to the environment; they act in ways that actually shape or change the organization's environment. In strategic decision making, Porter's model is an excellent method to help managers analyze the competitive environment and adapt to or influence the nature of their competition.

Competitors

Among the various components of the competitive environment, competitors within the industry must first deal with one another. When organizations compete for the same customers and try to win market share at the others' expense, all must react to and anticipate their competitors' actions.

The first question to consider is: Who is the competition? Sometimes the answer is obvious. The major competitors in the market for videogame consoles are Sony (whose brand is the PlayStation), Microsoft (Xbox 360), and Nintendo (maker of the Wii). However, if organizations focus exclusively on traditional rivalries, they miss the emerging ones. Coca-Cola and PepsiCo are obvious competitors, but consumer tastes have shifted away from soda to bottled water and other beverages. The two companies have had to compete in introducing new products, not just in winning consumers over to their brand of cola.

Thus, as a first step in understanding their competitive environment, organizations must identify their competitors. Competitors may include (1) small domestic firms, especially their entry into tiny, premium markets; (2) strong regional competitors; (3) big new domestic companies exploring new markets; (4) overseas firms, especially those that either try to solidify their position in small niches (a traditional Japanese tactic) or are able to draw on an inexpensive labor force on a large scale (as in China); and (5) newer entries, such as firms offering their products on the Web. The growth

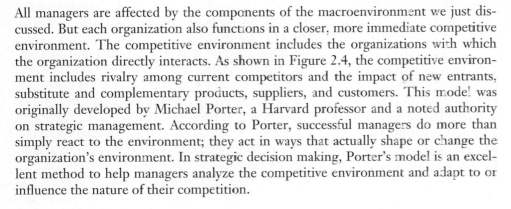

> **The bottom line**
> **Innovation**
>
> Companies often compete through innovation, quality, service, and cost. We will discuss the issue of competitors and strategy in further detail in Chapter 4.

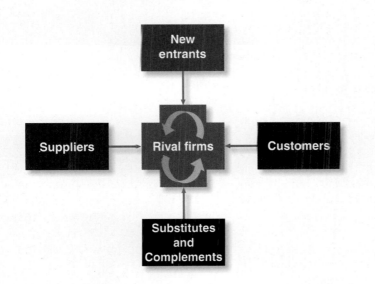

FIGURE 2.4
The Competitive
Environment

in competition from other countries has been especially significant in recent years, with the worldwide reduction in international trade barriers. For example, the North American Free Trade Agreement (NAFTA) sharply reduced tariffs on trade between the United States, Canada, and Mexico. Managers today confront a particular challenge from low-cost producers abroad (see Chapter 6).

Once competitors have been identified, the next step is to analyze how they compete. Competitors use tactics such as price reductions, new-product introductions, and advertising campaigns to gain advantage over their rivals. In the market for videogame consoles, Sony had been a leader and was expected to maintain its dominance when it launched its powerful PS3 model, choosing a technology-based strategy. The PS3 is a technological marvel, which by one account combines "the [processing] speed of a low-end supercomputer with the [component] cooling techniques of a network server" (a high-end computer used to handle the needs of a network of personal computers).[18] Rather than using an existing processor, Sony tapped the expertise of suppliers to develop a new processor and interface. The system generates so much power that engineering teams had to bring in a special team of designers to simulate the air flow with various cooling designs and figure out how to arrange the microchips within the box to keep the whole system from melting down. In addition, Sony's engineers developed a high-definition display, with graphics so detailed that software engineers had to calculate the motions of the game's activities very precisely. If something in a game bounces or breaks, the software must show it moving as the laws of physics would in the real world. These advances generated a lot of excitement—and a high cost. By one estimate, making a top-of-the-line PS3 costs Sony about $840.

It's essential to understand what competitors are doing when you are honing your own strategy. When Sony launched its PS3, it couldn't charge a high enough price to cover its costs. It set the price at $599, which was still far above its competitors. The Xbox 360, which had been on the market for a year, was a less-advanced but comparable product selling for $399. But Nintendo became a surprise winner in the initial competition with PS3 by choosing an entirely different strategy for its Wii. Rather than competing on the basis of advanced graphics and powerful processing, the company chose to offer something new and easy to use—its remote-control motion sensors instead of buttons and knobs. A Wii console costs just $249. While the PS3 and

Nintendo's Wii video game console has been outselling its competitors due to its extremely competitive pricing strategy. Shown here is a young man playing the popular golf simulation game.

Wii both flew off store shelves in the early weeks of the products' launch, PS3 sales over the next few years continually fell below expectations, while Wii became the top-selling game console in the United States. In fact, PS3 fell to *fourth* place in game console units sold, behind the older-generation PS2, which became Sony's lower-priced—and therefore more popular—alternative.[19]

Competition is most intense when there are many direct competitors (including foreign contenders), when industry growth is slow, and when the product or service cannot be differentiated in some way. New, high-growth industries offer enormous opportunities for profits. When an industry matures and growth slows, profits drop. Then, intense competition causes an industry shakeout: Weaker companies are eliminated, and the strong companies survive.[20] We will discuss the issue of competitors and strategy in further detail in Chapter 4.

New Entrants

New entrants into an industry compete with established companies. Wireless telephone advances brought many new competitors into an industry where only a handful of landline companies had operated. Phone companies were further challenged when cable and satellite services began offering consumers attractive packages for broadband Internet services, instead of dial-up or DSL connections. More recently, the introduction of WiMax is poised to shake up cell phone and Internet carriers again. WiMax, which can deliver citywide wireless Internet access and fast download speeds, lets cell phone and computer users go online without hunting for a Wi-Fi hotspot, much less a cord.[21]

If many factors prevent new companies from entering an industry, the threat to established firms is less serious. If there are few such **barriers to entry**, the threat of new entrants is more serious. Some major barriers to entry are government policy, capital requirements, brand identification, cost disadvantages, and distribution channels. The government can limit or prevent entry, as occurs when the FDA forbids a new drug entrant. Some industries, such as liquor retailing, are regulated; more subtle government controls operate in fields such as mining and ski area development. Patents are also entry barriers. When a patent expires, other companies can then enter the market. For example, the patents have recently expired on several drugs made by Pfizer, including antidepressant Zoloft, allergy medicine Zyrtec, and blood pressure medicine Norvasc. At the same time, several research projects to introduce new, patented medicines have failed, so Pfizer was forced to lay off employees and close some facilities to cut costs.[22]

Other barriers are less formal but can have the same effect. Capital requirements may be so high that companies won't risk or try to raise such large amounts of money. Brand identification forces new entrants to spend heavily to overcome customer loyalty. Imagine, for example, the costs involved in trying to launch a new cola against Coke or Pepsi. Or as the *BusinessWeek* box describes, Google's entry into the market for business software surprised many people because Microsoft has dominated that segment for many years. The cost advantages established companies hold—due to large size, favorable locations, existing assets, and so forth—can also be formidable entry barriers.

Finally, existing competitors may have such tight distribution channels that new entrants have difficulty getting their goods or services to customers. For example, established food products already have supermarket shelf space. New entrants must displace existing products with promotions, price breaks, intensive selling, and other tactics.

Substitutes and Complements

Besides products that directly compete, other products can affect a company's performance by being substitutes for or complements of the company's offerings. A *substitute* is a potential threat; customers use it as an alternative, buying less of one kind of product but more of another. A *complement* is a potential opportunity because customers

barriers to entry

Conditions that prevent new companies from entering an industry.

FROM THE PAGES OF

BusinessWeek

Google Steps into Microsoft's Office

Greg Brandeau is itching to dump the decade-old homegrown e-mail system he manages at Pixar Animation Studies Inc. And the senior vice president for technology at the Walt Disney Company unit is sure about one thing: The replacement won't be Microsoft Corporation's Exchange and Outlook duo, whose e-mail, calendar, and other programs dominate corporate computing. Brandeau says it's difficult to manage the software because Pixar uses a variety of computers. His likely choice may surprise you: Google.

After months of dancing around with Web versions of e-mail, group calendars, and the like, Google is finally about to take a big leap onto Microsoft's turf. Since August 2006, the search leader has offered a test version of an online office productivity software suite, called Google Apps for Your Domain, that lets companies offload e-mail systems to Google while keeping their own e-mail addresses. Soon, it's expected to add word-processing and spreadsheet services to the suite, which includes an online calendar, chat service, and Web page builder. In coming weeks, Google Apps will turn into a real business as Google begins charging corporations a subscription fee amounting to a few dollars per person per month. "We're dying to use something like this," says Brandeau. He's "on the cusp" of signing a contract with Google.

For now, Microsoft has little to fear. Many large corporations are wary of having an e-mail system run outside their own walls, where they can't be sure it's secure from hackers and spies. And even Google concedes its services don't have all the bells and whistles of Microsoft's products, such as centralized e-mail backups that help them comply with regulatory rules. "We're not looking to make it us vs. them," swears Dave Girouard, vice president in charge of Google's enterprise group. "We're giving people choices." Still, his 300-person group's very existence—plus Microsoft's stated aim to extend its Office franchise to the Web—suggests that before long these two titans of tech will be battling over many of the same corporate customers.

Google's game is clearly different from Microsoft's. Its new thrust represents a dawning era in corporate computing: software delivered as a service over the Internet, so it's accessible anywhere there is a Web browser handy. This time consumers are leading the way as they flock to Web-based applications such as e-mail, chat, and phone services like eBay's Skype Technologies.

As traditional corporate software has grown complex and expensive to maintain, Web services are getting more capable and reliable every year. "For the first time, consumer-grade applications are good enough that they can be used by enterprises," says Douglas Merrill, a Google vice president for engineering.

It's a testament to Google's popularity that even though Google Apps is still in trial mode, hundreds of thousands of users at thousands of organizations are already using it. That includes a few big ones. Arizona State University reported plans to switch most of its 65,000 students to Gmail, Google Calendar, and a customized "start page."

But corporate users, accustomed to feature-rich applications from the likes of Microsoft and IBM, are more demanding than consumers. Google got a taste last October when it switched over most of its own employees from Outlook and Oracle's calendar program to Gmail and Google Calendar. Some features on the old systems that Googlers considered crucial—such as a way to schedule all those company-paid massages—weren't available on the new system. In all, employees shot back more than 1,000 requests for new features in the first two weeks after the changeover. More traditional companies, with a desire for more control, will be tougher to crack.

Also, competitors aren't standing still—least of all Microsoft. It recently debuted Office Live, which offers Web-based e-mail, calendar, and other services in packages ranging from free to $39.95 a month for a single business. Dozens of start-ups, some of which Google has already bought, also have piled into the nascent market for online office-productivity software.

SOURCE: Excerpted from Robert D. Hof, "Google Steps into Microsoft's Office," *BusinessWeek*, February 12, 2007, http://www.businessweek.com.

buy more of a given product if they also demand more of the complementary product. Table 2.1 lists a dozen products and their potential substitutes and complements.

Technological advances and economic efficiencies are among the ways that firms can develop substitutes for existing products. The introduction of videogame systems created a substitute for television viewing that has drawn a large share of young men away from TV audiences. More recently, the makers of videogames have said that Internet offerings such as YouTube and MySpace have attracted videogame players away from their TV sets to interact with one another online. This example shows that substitute products or services can limit another industry's revenue potential. Companies in those industries are likely to suffer growth and earnings problems unless they improve quality or launch aggressive marketing campaigns. Nintendo's success with the Wii game console partly results from its offering games such as Wii Sports that entice people who want to interact with the game, as well as by allowing them to create avatars to represent themselves in the various games, a feature that computer users enjoy in many online games and worlds. Sony's high-tech strategy for the PS3 aimed in part to make that console a substitute for buying a Blu-ray DVD player. However, prices of Blu-ray players have fallen dramatically, while the price of a PS3 remains high, so for many consumers, the combination of a Blu-ray player plus an Xbox 360 console has become a substitute for a PS3.[23]

$ _____ **The bottom line**
COST
Cost is often a major barrier to entry.

In addition to current substitutes, companies need to think about potential substitutes that may be viable in the near future. For example, as alternatives to fossil fuels, experts suggest that nuclear fusion, solar power, and wind energy may prove useful one day. The advantages promised by each of these technologies are many: inexhaustible fuel supplies, electricity "too cheap to meter," zero emissions, universal public acceptance, and so on. Yet while they may look good on paper—and make us feel good about our choice—they often come up short in economic feasibility or technical viability.

Besides identifying and planning for substitutes, companies must consider complements for their products. When people are buying new homes, they are also buying appliances and landscaping products. When they buy a car, they buy insurance for it.

If the Problem Is . . .	The Solution Might Be . . .
Cotton	Polyester
Coffee	Energy drinks
Fossil fuels	Solar fusion
Music CD	MP3 player
House	Apartment, condo, mobile home
Local telephone	Cell phone
If the Product Is . . .	**The Complement Might Be . . .**
Computer printer	Ink cartridges
Tennis lessons	Tennis racquet
Circular saw	Lumber and nails
Apartment	Furniture
Gaming console	Videogames
New outfit	New shoes
Detergent	Mop
iPod	iTunes

TABLE 2.1

Potential Substitutes for and Complements of Products

And as we have noted, game consoles and videogames are complementary products. For this reason, console makers work closely with developers, giving them the information they need to create products to lure customers to their gaming systems. The complexity of the PS3 created another hurdle for Sony in this area. Because the system is so sophisticated, programming a game for PS3 costs roughly 30 percent more than creating a similar title for Microsoft's Xbox. That has made game developers cautious about launching PS3 titles, which in turn has made game players think twice about buying the new console. In the January following release of the PS3, only 2 of the top 20 games sold ("Resistance: Fall of Man" and "Madden NFL 07") were PS3 games.[24] To collaborate better with the game industry, Sony released programming tools for game developers.[25] The effort was especially important because developers such as Electronic Arts were quick to adjust their own product plans when sales of PS3 titles were lower than expected while sales of Wii titles were better than expected.[26]

As with substitutes, a company needs to watch for new complements that can change the competitive landscape. When the Wii became popular, some programmers saw an opportunity to offer a niche service: tweaking the software to offer customized avatars. Wii players can use Nintendo's software to select from a range of facial characteristics, height, and other features, but some users want a more customized look or perhaps a character modeled after a famous figure. An entrepreneur in Tokyo created Mii Station, which will use a customer-supplied photo to create a Mii look-alike for a $5 fee. A Web developer in Boston started Mii Plaza, a Web site where users can tap a database of more than 8,000 characters to collect and share Miis. Nintendo could have viewed these efforts as copyright infringement, but the company's initial response has been to treat Mii-related businesses as harmless.[27]

Suppliers

Recall from our earlier mention of open systems that organizations must acquire resources (inputs) from their environment and convert those resources into products or services (outputs) to sell. Suppliers provide the resources needed for production, and those resources may come in the form of people (supplied by trade schools and universities), raw materials (from producers, wholesalers, and distributors), information (supplied by researchers and consulting firms), and financial capital (from banks and other sources). But suppliers are important to an organization for reasons that go beyond the resources they provide. Suppliers can raise their prices or provide poor-quality goods and services. Labor unions can go on strike or demand higher wages. Workers may produce defective work. Powerful suppliers, then, can reduce an organization's profits, particularly if the organization cannot pass on price increases to its customers.

One particularly noteworthy set of suppliers to some industries is the international labor unions. Although unionization in the United States has dropped below 10 percent of the private labor force, labor unions are still powerful in industries such as steel, autos, and transportation. Even the Screen Actors Guild, the union representing workers in the entertainment industry, exerts considerable power on behalf of its members. Labor unions represent and protect the interests of their members on matters of hiring, wages, working conditions, job security, and due process appeals. Historically, the relationship between management and labor unions has been adversarial; however, both sides increasingly realize that to improve productivity and competitiveness, management and labor must work together in collaborative relationships. Troubled labor relations can create higher costs and productivity declines and eventually lead to layoffs.[28]

Organizations are at a disadvantage if they become overly dependent on any powerful supplier. A supplier is powerful if the buyer has few other sources of supply or if the supplier has many other buyers. One of the problems plaguing the launch of the PS3 was a shortage of parts, and during the weeks leading up to the console's first Christmas, it was often out of stock in U.S. stores. Sony depended on Panasonic to provide disk drives and on IBM and ATI Technologies to deliver core processors and graphics chips.[29] For such a sophisticated product, the company couldn't go elsewhere for these components.

Switching costs are fixed costs buyers face if they change suppliers. For example, once a buyer learns how to operate a supplier's equipment, such as computer software, the buyer faces both economic and psychological costs in changing to a new supplier.

In recent years, supply chain management has become an increasingly important contributor to a company's competitiveness and profitability. By **supply chain management,** we mean the managing of the entire network of facilities and people that obtain raw materials from outside the organization, transform them into products, and distribute them to customers.[30] In the past, managers did not have to pay as much attention to supply chain management as they do today. Products tended to be standardized, overseas competition was still years in the future, and the pace of change was slower. But increased competition has required managers to pay very close attention to their costs. For example, they can no longer afford to hold large and costly inventories, waiting for orders to come in. Also, once orders do come in, some products still sitting in inventory might well be out of date.

With the emergence of the Internet, customers look for products built to their specific needs and preferences—and they want them delivered quickly, at the lowest available price. This requires the supply chain to be not only efficient but also *flexible*, so that the organization's output can quickly respond to changes in demand.

Today, the goal of effective supply chain management is to have *the right product in the right quantity available at the right place at the right cost.* Boeing, the aircraft and defense systems company, provides a good example of effective supply chain management. Boeing forges partnerships with its suppliers to share knowledge that will help them learn how to operate more efficiently. For example, at Boeing Integrated Defense Systems (IDS), Rick Behrens is senior manager of supplier development, charged with building close supplier relationships and helping them understand Boeing's commitment to "lean" operations, aimed at eliminating waste. Behrens tailors the supplier relationships to each supplier's familiarity with lean processes. He educates some suppliers in the basics of how to run lean operations; for others, he sends a supplier development team to the organization to help them streamline certain activities. He also identifies Boeing specialists who can help suppliers with particularly challenging problems. Along the way, Behrens helps suppliers develop their abilities so that they can move from simply selling parts to providing complete subassemblies. In Behrens's words, "We need suppliers that can grow with us."[31]

In sum, choosing the right supplier is an important strategic decision. Suppliers can affect manufacturing time, product quality, and inventory levels. The relationship between suppliers and the organization is changing in many companies. The close supplier relationship has become a new model for many organizations that are using a just-in-time manufacturing approach (discussed further in Chapters 16 and 17). And in some companies, innovative managers are forming strategic partnerships with their key suppliers in developing new products or new production techniques. We describe this kind of strategic partnership in more detail in Chapter 9. In the "Management Close-Up: Taking Action" feature, consider how Green Mountain Coffee Roasters played an active role with suppliers, collaborating with them by cultivating fair trade relationships and investing in a coffee maker system.

switching costs

Fixed costs buyers face when they change suppliers.

supply chain management

The managing of the network of facilities and people that obtain materials from outside the organization, transform them into products, and distribute them to customers.

The bottom line
SPEED
The ability to manufacture even customized products quickly has become a competitive requirement.

A Keurig single-serving coffee maker is shown at the Green Mountain Coffee Roasters outlet store in Waterbury, Vermont. Green Mountain Coffee Roasters was granted approval by the Federal Trade Commission to buy single-cup brewing systems maker Keurig Incorporated. Green Mountain already owned 35 percent of Keurig and announced that it would acquire the company outright. Do you think this collaboration will benefit the company or the customers?

Management Close-Up | TAKING ACTION

To expand Green Mountain Coffee Roasters, founder Bob Stiller began selling through several channels: in retail stores, in wholesale outlets, through direct-mail catalogs, and on the Web at www.GreenMountainCoffee.com. He also expanded its product line to include more than 100 gourmet coffee varieties under the Green Mountain name. In addition, the more the company learned about the growers who supplied its coffee beans, the more interested it became in the notion of fair trade—ensuring that farmers receive a fair price for their crops. GMCR is now one of the world's leading sellers of fair trade coffee. Recognizing consumers' growing interest in organic foods, GMCR added the Fair Trade Certified organic brand and Newman's Own Organics brand to GMCR's offerings.

During the mid-1990s, managers at Green Mountain discovered Keurig, a manufacturer of a single-serve coffee system. Using the Keurig machine, coffee drinkers could brew a single cup of their favorite blend. The system uses coffee packaged in tiny single-serve "K-cups."

GMCR leadership saw great potential in Keurig. They knew consumers were looking for easy ways to brew a perfect cup of coffee. Only a few competitors operated in the single-cup market. The single-cup brew has the advantage of a premium cup of coffee at a fraction of the price. Once Green Mountain became a Keurig investor, it began working with the company to fine-tune processes and to package and distribute K-cups.[32]

- How did GMCR's awareness of changing consumer preferences help shape the company's business plan?
- GMCR pioneered the concept of fair trade coffee. How did its interest in its suppliers change the face of Green Mountain Coffee Roasters?

Customers

final consumer

Those who purchase products in their finished form.

intermediate consumer

A customer who purchases raw materials or wholesale products before selling them to final customers.

Customers purchase the goods or services an organization offers. Without customers, a company won't survive. You are a **final consumer** when you buy a McDonald's hamburger or a pair of jeans from Aéropostale. **Intermediate consumers** buy raw materials or wholesale products and then sell to final consumers, as when Sony buys components from IBM and ATI Technologies and uses them to make PS3 consoles. Intermediate customers actually make more purchases than individual final consumers do. Types of intermediate customers include retailers, who buy clothes from wholesalers and manufacturers' representatives before selling them to their customers, and industrial buyers, who buy raw materials (such as chemicals) before converting them into final products.

Like suppliers, customers are important to organizations for reasons other than the money they provide for goods and services. Customers can demand lower prices, higher quality, unique product specifications, or better service. They also can play competitors against one another, as occurs when a car buyer (or a purchasing agent) collects different offers and negotiates for the best price. Many companies are finding that today's customers want to be actively involved with their products, as when Wii users create a Mii avatar so that the person playing the game looks like a cartoon version of themselves. Dell Inc. has taken customer input a step further by asking customers what they want the company to develop next. At Dell's IdeaStorm Web site (www.dellideastorm.com), visitors can post ideas for the next generation of computers and vote on the ideas they like best.[33]

The Internet has further empowered customers. It provides an easy source of information—both about product features and about pricing. In addition, today's

Internet users informally create and share messages about a product, which provides flattering free "advertising" at best or embarrassing and even erroneous bad publicity at worst. For example, enthusiastic gamers who favor one device or another have posted their homemade "commercials" pairing scenes from games with musical backgrounds on YouTube, as well as blunt point-by-point product comparisons about competing brands. Fans of the Wii have mocked Sony's claims that its PS3 is popular by visiting stores and filming inventory sitting on shelves. One group of videos on YouTube even portrays an unofficial "brand," Wii60, to drive home the idea that consumers could purchase both a Wii and an Xbox 360 for the price of a PS3.[34] Today's companies may find it difficult to identify, much less respond to, these unofficial messages.

As we discussed in Chapter 1, customer service means giving customers what they want or need, the way they want it, the first time. This usually depends on the speed and dependability with which an organization can deliver its products. Actions and attitudes that provide excellent customer service include the following:

> ★ **The bottom line**
> **Service**
>
> In all businesses—services as well as manufacturing—strategies that emphasize good customer service provide a critical competitive advantage.

Speed of filling and delivering normal orders.
Willingness to meet emergency needs.
Merchandise delivered in good condition.
Readiness to take back defective goods and resupply quickly.
Availability of installation and repair services and parts.
Service charges (that is, whether services are "free" or priced separately).[35]

An organization is at a disadvantage if it depends too heavily on powerful customers. Customers are powerful if they make large purchases or if they can easily find alternative places to buy. If you are the largest customer of a firm and you can buy from others, you have power over that firm, and

> "Your most unhappy customers are your greatest source of learning." Bill Gates

you most likely can negotiate with it successfully. Your firm's biggest customers—especially if they can buy from other sources—will have the greatest negotiating power over you. Customer relationship management is discussed more fully in Chapter 9.

Environmental Analysis

LO 5

If managers do not understand how the environment affects their organizations or cannot identify opportunities and threats that are likely to be important, their ability to make decisions and execute plans will be severely limited. For example, if little is known about customer likes and dislikes, organizations will have a difficult time designing new products, scheduling production, or developing marketing plans. In short, timely and accurate environmental information is critical for running a business.

But information about the environment is not always readily available. For example, even economists have difficulty predicting whether an upturn or a downturn in the economy is likely. Moreover, managers find it difficult to forecast how well their own products will sell, let alone how a competitor might respond. In other words, managers often operate under conditions of uncertainty. **Environmental uncertainty** means that managers do not have enough information about the environment to understand or predict the future. Uncertainty arises from two related factors: (1) complexity and (2) dynamism. Environmental *complexity* refers to the number of issues to which a manager must attend as well as their interconnectedness. For example, industries that have many different firms that compete in vastly different ways tend to be more complex—and uncertain—than industries with only a few key competitors. Similarly, environmental *dynamism* refers to the degree of discontinuous change that occurs within the industry. High-growth industries with products and technologies that change rapidly tend to be more uncertain than stable industries where change is less dramatic and more predictable.[36]

environmental uncertainty

Lack of information needed to understand or predict the future.

As environmental uncertainty increases, managers must develop techniques and methods for collecting, sorting through, and interpreting information about the environment. We discuss some of these approaches in this section of the chapter. (In the next chapter, we will also discuss how managers make decisions under conditions of uncertainty.) By analyzing environmental forces—in both the macroenvironment and the competitive environment—managers can identify opportunities and threats that might affect the organization.

Environmental Scanning

environmental scanning

Searching for and sorting through information about the environment.

Perhaps the first step in coping with uncertainty in the environment is pinning down what might be important. Frequently, organizations and individuals act out of ignorance, only to regret those actions in the future. IBM, for example, had the opportunity to purchase the technology behind xerography but turned it down. Xerox saw the potential, and the rest is history. However, Xerox researchers later developed the technology for the original computer mouse, but not seeing the potential, the company missed an important market opportunity.

To understand and predict changes, opportunities, and threats, organizations such as Monsanto, Weyerhaeuser, and Union Carbide spend a good deal of time and money monitoring events in the environment. **Environmental scanning** means both searching out information that is unavailable to most people and sorting through that information to interpret what is important and what is not. Managers can ask questions such as these:

Who are our current competitors?
Are there few or many entry barriers to our industry?
What substitutes exist for our product or service?
Is the company too dependent on powerful suppliers?
Is the company too dependent on powerful customers?[37]

competitive intelligence

Information that helps managers determine how to compete better.

Answers to these questions help managers develop **competitive intelligence,** the information necessary to decide how best to manage in the competitive environment they have identified. Porter's competitive analysis, discussed earlier, can guide environmental scanning and help managers evaluate the competitive potential of different environments. Table 2.2 describes two extreme environments: an attractive environment, which gives a firm a competitive advantage, and an unattractive environment, which puts a firm at a competitive disadvantage.[38]

scenario

A narrative that describes a particular set of future conditions.

Scenario Development

As managers attempt to determine the effect of environmental forces on their organizations, they frequently develop **scenarios** of the future. Scenarios create alternative

TABLE 2.2
Attractive and Unattractive Environments

Environmental Factor	Unattractive	Attractive
Competitors	Many; low industry growth; equal size; commodity	Few; high industry growth; unequal size differentiated
Threat of entry	High threat; few entry barriers	Low threat; many barriers
Substitutes	Many	Few
Suppliers	Few; high bargaining power	Many; low bargaining power
Customers	Few; high bargaining power	Many; low bargaining power

combinations of different factors into a total picture of the environment and the firm. For example, when Congress and the president must forecast the size of the federal budget deficit, they develop several different scenarios about what the economy is likely to do over the next decade or so. Frequently, organizations develop a *best-case scenario* (the occurrence of events that are favorable to the firm), a *worst-case scenario* (the occurrence of unfavorable events), and some middle-ground alternatives. The value of scenario development is that it helps managers develop contingency plans for what they might do given different outcomes.[39] For example, as a manager, you will quite likely be involved in budgeting for your area. You will almost certainly be asked to list initiatives that you would eliminate in case of an economic downturn and new investments you would make if your firm does better than expected.

Effective managers regard the scenarios they develop as living documents, not merely prepared once and put aside. Instead, they constantly update the scenarios to take into account relevant new factors that emerge, such as significant changes in the economy or actions by competitors.

Forecasting

Whereas environmental scanning is used to identify important factors and scenario development is used to develop alternative pictures of the future, **forecasting** is used to predict exactly how some variable or variables will change in the future. For example, in making capital investments, firms may try to forecast how interest rates will change. In deciding to expand or downsize a business, firms may try to forecast the demand for goods and services or forecast the supply and demand of labor they probably would use. Publications such as *BusinessWeek's Business Outlook* provide forecasts to businesses both large and small.

forecasting

Method for predicting how variables will change the future.

Although forecasts are designed to help executives make predictions about the future, their accuracy varies from application to application. Because they extrapolate from the past to project the future, forecasts tend to be most accurate when the future ends up looking a lot like the past. Of course, we don't need sophisticated forecasts in those instances. Forecasts are most useful when the future will look radically different from the past. Unfortunately, that is when forecasts tend to be less accurate. The more things change, the less confidence we tend to have in our forecasts. The best advice for using forecasts might include the following ideas:

Use multiple forecasts, and perhaps average their predictions.
Remember that accuracy decreases the further into the future you are trying to predict.
Forecasts are no better than the data used to construct them.
Use simple forecasts (rather than complicated ones) where possible.
Keep in mind that important events often are surprises and represent a departure from predictions.[40]

Benchmarking

In addition to trying to predict changes in the environment, firms can undertake intensive study of the best practices of various firms to understand their sources of competitive advantage. **Benchmarking** means identifying the best-in-class performance by a company in a given area, say, product development or customer service, and then comparing your processes to theirs. To accomplish this, a benchmarking team would collect information on its own company's operations and those of the other firm to determine gaps. These gaps serve as a point of entry to learn the underlying causes of performance differences. Ultimately, the team would map out a set of best practices that lead to world-class performance. We will discuss benchmarking further in Chapter 4.

benchmarking

The process of comparing an organization's practices and technologies with those of other companies.

Responding to the Environment

For managers and organizations, responding effectively to their environments is almost always essential. Clothing retailers who pay no attention to changes in the public's style preferences, or manufacturers who don't make sure they have steady sources of supply, are soon out of business. To respond to their environment, managers and companies have a number of options, which can be grouped into three categories: (1) adapting to the environment, (2) influencing the environment, and (3) selecting a new environment.

Adapting to the Environment: Changing Yourself

To cope with environmental uncertainty, organizations frequently make adjustments in their structures and work processes. When uncertainty arises from environmental complexity, organizations tend to adapt by *decentralizing* decision making. For example, if a company faces a growing number of competitors in various markets, if different customers want different things, if the characteristics of different products keep increasing, and if production facilities are being built in different regions of the world, it may be impossible for the chief executive (or a small group of top executives) to keep abreast of all activities and understand all the operational details of a business. In these cases, the top management team is likely to give authority to lower-level managers to make decisions that benefit the firm. The term **empowerment** is used frequently today to talk about this type of decentralized authority. We will address empowerment and decision making in more detail in Chapters 3 and 9.

empowerment

The process of sharing power with employees, thereby enhancing their confidence in their ability to perform their jobs and their belief that they are influential contributors to the organization.

Organizations can compete more effectively in volatile environments if they have knowledgeable and skilled workers. One way to obtain these workers is to sponsor training programs. Alliances among employers, community colleges, universities, and nonprofit training programs are producing workers with much-needed skills in many industries, and those workers now can earn higher wages. One program in New York, Per Scholas, trains computer repair technicians in one of the country's poorest areas—the Bronx. Funded by grants from private foundations and the New York City Council, the program gained momentum through its collaboration with companies such as Time Warner Cable that were looking for skilled employees.

Per Scholas boasts a job placement rate of 80 percent of its graduates, who earn about $12 per hour in the first year and $15 per hour in two years—often double what they would have earned without the training. One such graduate, Cristina Rodriguez, now works at Time Warner Cable as a broadband specialist for a similar wage plus health insurance coverage. Her new skills have empowered her to become a high-performing employee. "What feels great is when I resolve someone's issue," she says. Rodriguez, fluent in both English and Spanish, is able to solve customers' problems in both languages.

Training programs such as Per Scholas have grown more sophisticated in the last few years because of their close association with the companies that hire their graduates. These relationships foster "the deep understanding these programs develop of the workings of industries where they place people," explains MIT Professor Paul Osterman. Connie Ciliberti, vice president of human resources for Time Warner Cable, confirms the importance of this collaboration. "Per Scholas has spent time learning our business, understanding our measures of success," she says.[41]

In response to uncertainty caused by change (dynamism) in the environment, organizations tend to establish more flexible structures. In today's business world, the term *bureaucracy* generally has a bad connotation. Most of us recognize that bureaucratic organizations tend to be formal and very stable; frequently they are unable to adjust to change or exceptional circumstances that "don't fit the rules." And while bureaucratic organizations may be efficient and controlled if the environment is stable, they tend to be slow-moving and plodding when products, technologies, customers, or competitors are changing over time. In these cases, more *organic* structures give organizations the flexibility to adjust to change. We will discuss organic structures in more detail in Chapter 9, but we can simply say here that they are less formal than bureaucratic organizations—making decisions through interaction and mutual adjustment among individuals rather than from a set of predefined rules. Table 2.3 shows four different approaches that organizations can take in adapting to environmental uncertainty.

Adapting at the Boundaries   Because they are open systems, organizations are exposed to uncertainties from both their inputs and outputs. To help them compete, they can create buffers on both the input and output boundaries with the environment. **Buffering** creates supplies of excess resources to meet unpredictable needs. On the input side, organizations establish relationships with employment agencies to hire part-time and temporary help during rush periods when labor demand is difficult to predict. In the U.S. labor force, these workers, known as *contingent workers,* include 2.5 million on-call workers, 1.2 million temporary-help agency workers, and more than 800,000 workers provided by contract firms, suggesting widespread use of this approach to buffering labor input uncertainties.[42] On the output side of the system, most organizations use some type of ending inventories that allow them to keep merchandise on hand in case a rush of customers decide to buy their products. Auto dealers are a common example of this use of buffers, but we can see similar use of buffer inventories in fast-food restaurants, bookstores, clothing stores, and even real estate agencies.[43]

In addition to buffering, organizations may try **smoothing,** or leveling normal fluctuations at the boundaries of the environment. For example, during winter months in the north, when automobile sales drop off, it is not uncommon for dealers to cut the price of their in-stock vehicles to increase demand. At the end of each clothing season, retailers discount their merchandise to clear it out to make room for incoming inventories. These are examples of smoothing environmental cycles to level off fluctuations in demand.

Adapting at the Core   While buffering and smoothing manage uncertainties at the boundaries of the organization, firms also can establish **flexible processes** that allow for adaptation in their technical core. For example, firms increasingly try to customize their goods and services to meet the varied and changing demands of customers. Even in manufacturing, where it is difficult to change basic core processes, firms are adopting techniques of mass customization that help them create flexible factories. Instead of mass-producing large quantities of a "one-size-fits-all" product, organizations can use mass customization to produce individually customized products at an equally low cost. Whereas Henry Ford used to claim that "you could have a Model T in any color you wanted, as long as it was black," auto companies now offer a wide array of colors and trim lines, with different options and accessories. The process of mass customization involves the use of a network of independent operating units in

buffering

Creating supplies of excess resources in case of unpredictable needs.

smoothing

Leveling normal fluctuations at the boundaries of the environment.

flexible processes

Methods for adapting the technical core to changes in the environment.

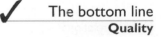 **The bottom line**
Quality

The Internet lets customers quickly find products with the cost and quality features they want.

TABLE 2.3
Four Approaches for Managing Uncertainty

	Stable	Dynamic
Complex	Decentralized	Decentralized
	Bureaucratic (standardized skills)	Organic (mutual adjustment)
Simple	Centralized	Centralized
	Bureaucratic (standardized work processes)	Organic (direct supervision)

which each performs a specific process or task such as making a dashboard assembly on an automobile. When an order comes in, different modules join forces to deliver the product or service as specified by the customer.[44] We will discuss mass customization and flexible factories in more depth in Chapter 9.

Influencing Your Environment

In addition to adapting or reacting to the environment, managers and organizations can develop proactive responses aimed at changing the environment. Two general types of proactive responses are independent action and cooperative action.

independent strategies

Strategies that an organization acting on its own uses to change some aspect of its current environment.

Independent Action   A company uses **independent strategies** when it acts on its own to change some aspect of its current environment.[45] Table 2.4 shows the definitions and uses of these strategies. For example, Southwest Airlines demonstrates competitive aggression by cutting fares when it enters a new market, and Sony used competitive aggression when it aimed to position itself as the gaming industry's technological leader with the launch of the PS3. In contrast, when Kellogg Company promotes the cereal industry as a whole, it demonstrates competitive pacification. Weyerhaeuser Company advertises its reforestation efforts (public relations). The Gap, Motorola, Nike, American Express, Converse, and other companies have signed on to Product Red, a program in which they market special Red-themed products and donate a percentage of the profits to the Global Fund, a project to help end AIDS in Africa (voluntary action). Viacom sued Google for allowing users to post copyrighted video clips on the Google-owned YouTube Web site (legal action). In a recent year, pharmaceutical companies spent $1.1 billion to lobby members of Congress (political action); insurers, the second biggest spenders on lobbying, paid out almost $900 million.[46] Each of these examples shows how organizations—on their own—can have an impact on the environment.

cooperative strategies

Strategies used by two or more organizations working together to manage the external environment.

Cooperative Action   In some situations, two or more organizations work together using **cooperative strategies** to influence the environment.[47] Table 2.5 shows several

TABLE 2.4   Independent Action

Strategy	Definition	Examples
Competitive aggression	Exploiting a distinctive competence or improving internal efficiency for competitive advantage	Aggressive pricing, comparative advertising (e.g., Wal-Mart)
Competitive pacification	Independent action to improve relations with competitors	Helping competitors find raw materials
Public relations	Establishing and maintaining favorable images in the minds of those making up the environment	Sponsoring sporting events
Voluntary action	Voluntary commitment to various interest groups, causes, and social problems	Johnson & Johnson donating supplies to tsunami victims
Legal action	Engaging company in private legal battle	Warner Music lawsuits against illegal music copying
Political action	Efforts to influence elected representatives to create a more favorable business environment or limit competition	Issue advertising; lobbying at state and national levels

SOURCE: Adapted from *Journal of Marketing,* published by the American Marketing Association. C. Zeithaml and V. Zeithaml, "Environmental Management: Revising the Marketing Perspective," Spring 1984.

TABLE 2.5
Cooperative Action

Strategy	Definition	Examples
Contraction	Negotiation of an agreement between the organization and another group to exchange goods, services, information, patents, and so on	Contractual marketing systems
Cooptation	Absorbing new elements into the organization's leadership structure to avert threats to its stability or existence	Consumer and labor representatives and bankers on boards of directors
Coalition	Two or more groups that coalesce and act jointly with respect to some set of issues for some period of time	Industry associations; political initiatives of the Business Roundtable and the U.S. Chamber of Commerce

SOURCE: Reprinted from *Journal of Marketing*, published by the American Marketing Association. C. Zeithaml and V. Zeithaml, "Environmental Management: Revising the Marketing Perspective," Spring 1984.

examples of cooperative strategies. An example of contracting occurs when suppliers and customers, or managers and labor unions, sign formal agreements about the terms and conditions of their future relationships. These contracts are explicit attempts to make their future relationship predictable. An example of cooptation might occur when universities invite wealthy alumni to join their boards of directors.

Finally, an example of coalition formation might be when local businesses band together to curb the rise of employee health care costs and when organizations in the same industry form industry associations and special-interest groups. You may have seen cooperative advertising strategies, such as when dairy producers, beef producers, orange growers, and the like, jointly pay for television commercials. Life Is Good, a New England–based T-shirt company, used the latest economic downturn as an opportunity to strengthen cooperative action with the retailers that stock its products. According to cofounder Bert Jacobs, employees at Life Is Good began calling retailers to ask how they could help them through the slow times. Based on the feedback, Jacobs identified a need to establish online networks that retailers—his company's customers—could use for sharing ideas.[48]

At the organizational level, firms establish strategic alliances, partnerships, joint ventures, and mergers with competitors to deal with environmental uncertainties. Cooperative strategies such as these make most sense when (1) taking joint action will reduce the organizations' costs and risks and (2) cooperation will increase their power, that is, their ability to successfully accomplish the changes they desire.

Changing the Environment You Are In

As we noted previously, organizations can cope with environmental uncertainty by changing themselves (environmental adaptation), changing the environment, or changing the environment they are in. We refer to this last category as **strategic maneuvering**. By making a conscious effort to change the boundaries of its competitive environment, a firm can maneuver around potential threats and capitalize on

Celebrities Bono and Oprah have supported organizations participating in the Product Red Program to help end AIDS in Africa through the Global Fund. What other opportunities do companies have to participate in voluntary actions to change their environment?

Companies or organizations within an industry sometimes form political action committees (PACs) to raise money to help elect lawmakers with favorable points of view. During the most recent presidential-election year, the biggest spenders were labor unions; the most PAC spending by businesses came from companies in finance, insurance, and real estate.[49]

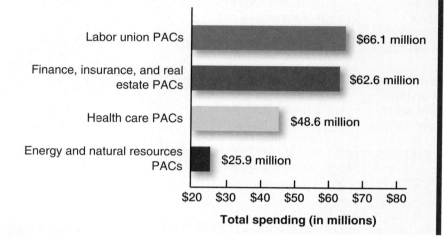

Top four industry/labor sectors for PAC spending

Labor union PACs — $66.1 million
Finance, insurance, and real estate PACs — $62.6 million
Health care PACs — $48.6 million
Energy and natural resources PACs — $25.9 million

Total spending (in millions)

arising opportunities.[50] Managers can use several strategic maneuvers, including domain selection, diversification, merger and acquisition, and divestiture.[51]

Domain selection is the entrance by a company into another suitable market or industry. For example, the market may have limited competition or regulation, ample suppliers and customers, or high growth. An example is Nintendo's decision to create products such as the Wii that appeal to customer segments that have not been enthusiastic to purchase videogames—for instance, people intimidated by complicated game controllers and parents concerned about the violent content and sedentary play involved in videogames. By avoiding head-on competition to be the product with the best graphics or most advanced play, Nintendo was able to enjoy immediate profits from its new console. This approach builds on the company's earlier success with its DS, which lured not only young game players but also women and older-than-average players with its touch screens and games like Brain Age and Nintendogs.[52] Thus, Nintendo has used an existing expertise to broaden the goods and services it offers.

Diversification occurs when a firm invests in different types of businesses or products or when it expands geographically to reduce its dependence on a single market or technology. Apple's launch of the iPod is a good example of effective diversification. While Apple struggled in the highly competitive computer industry, where its Macintosh had only a 3 percent market share, its iPod has gobbled up three-quarters of the market for portable digital music players *and* for online music sales. More recently, its launch of the iPhone has generated considerable buzz. The company's name change from "Apple Computer" to simply "Apple" makes sense in light of these diversification moves.[53]

A **merger** or **acquisition** takes place when two or more firms combine, or one firm buys another, to form a single company. Mergers and acquisitions can offer greater efficiency from combined operations or can give companies relatively quick access to new markets or industries. After Bayer acquired Schering, it announced plans to cut more than 6,000 jobs to "create an internationally successful pharmaceutical company with competitive cost structures," in the words of Werner Wenning, Bayer Schering Pharma's board chairman.[54] Electronic Arts, publisher of videogames, acquired Headgate Studios, a smaller game publisher whose titles include "Tiger Woods PGA Tour" and "Madden NFL." The acquisition helped Electronic Arts add quickly to its list of games for the Wii when sales of the console and its games exceeded expectations.[55]

Divestiture occurs when a company sells one or more businesses. At Ford Motor Company, recent operating losses and the costs of restructuring its workforce have brought about a cash shortage. To raise cash, Ford sold its Aston Martin sports-car brand and its Hertz rental-car unit.[56]

Organizations engage in strategic maneuvering when they move into different environments. Some companies, called **prospectors,** are more likely than others to engage in strategic maneuvering.[57] Aggressive companies continuously change the boundaries of their competitive environments by seeking new products and markets, diversifying, and merging or acquiring new enterprises. In these and other ways, corporations put

strategic maneuvering
An organization's conscious efforts to change the boundaries of its task environment.

domain selection
Entering a new market or industry with an existing expertise.

diversification
A firm's investment in a different product, business, or geographic area.

merger
One or more companies combining with another.

acquisition
One firm buying another.

divestiture
A firm selling one or more businesses.

prospectors
Companies that continually change the boundaries for their task environments by seeking new products and markets, diversifying and merging, or acquiring new enterprises.

their competitors on the defensive and force them to react. **Defenders**, in contrast, stay within a more limited, stable product domain.

Choosing a Response Approach

Three general considerations help guide management's response to the environment. First, organizations should attempt to *change appropriate elements of the environment*. Environmental responses are most useful when aimed at elements of the environment that (1) cause the company problems, (2) provide it with opportunities, and (3) allow the company to change successfully. Thus, Nintendo recognized that its game console would have difficulty competing on superior graphics, so it addressed underserved segments of the market, where customers and favorable publicity made the Wii a successful entrant.

Second, organizations should *choose responses that focus on pertinent elements of the environment*. If a company wants to better manage its competitive environment,

No business likes bad press, but if it occurs, managers must choose a response. They can ignore the negative publicity or address it in such a way that the incident is viewed as neutral, or even positive. When Washington, D.C., restaurateur Mark Sakuta discovered criticisms of his restaurant on the Web site for the *Washington Post,* he was at first puzzled. About 10 negative reviews appeared simultaneously, accusing the restaurant of using cookbook recipes instead of its own original concoctions, claiming that the floor was unstable, and other negative statements. A month later, another harsh review criticized the gratuity policy for large groups.

Sakuta knew that the first group of accusations was simply untrue. He suspected they were written by disgruntled former employees. So he called customer service at the Web site and asked to have them removed. The site manager agreed. But Sakuta did not ask to have the comment about the tipping policy removed because it was accurate. Instead, he decided to adjust the policy. He reasoned that if customers were uncomfortable with it, they might choose to dine elsewhere. Now Sakuta keeps closer tabs on food-related Web sites and blogs, looking for any comments about his business.[58]

competitive aggression and pacification are viable options. Political action influences the legal environment, and contracting helps manage customers and suppliers.

Third, companies should *choose responses that offer the most benefit at the lowest cost*. Return-on-investment calculations should incorporate short-term financial considerations as well as long-term impact. Strategic managers who consider these factors carefully will guide their organizations to competitive advantage more effectively.

In the case of online critics, most responses cost little or nothing. Often, a person just wants to be heard. If it's a customer, "Maybe something they bought isn't working, and customer service says they can't do anything, so now they want to drag that business through the mud," says Joseph Fiore, vice present of CoreX Technology and Solutions. "They're hoping someone will come along and say that happened to me too." Fiore's firm investigates such blogs. Most such situations can be solved with an e-mail or a phone call. But a firm's managers must take action to correct any false information that has been posted so that it doesn't spread and ruin the company's reputation.

Taking a proactive stance can be helpful as well. A company can set up its own site, providing a forum for customers to share feedback. "Some people just need to vent, and if you don't provide a place where you can monitor and do something about those complaints, then they often go elsewhere," warns Alysa Zeltzer, an associate attorney with a law firm in Washington, D.C. Either way, a firm should keep an eye on its Internet reputation—failing to do so can ultimately be costly in both sales and image.[59]

Culture and the Internal Environment of Organizations

organization culture

The set of important assumptions about the organization and its goals and practices that members of the company share.

One of the most important factors that influence an organization's response to its external environment is its culture. **Organization culture** is the set of important assumptions about the organization and its goals and practices that members of the company share. It is a system of shared values about what is important and beliefs about how the world works. In this way, a company's culture provides a framework that organizes and directs people's behavior on the job.[60] The culture of an organization may be difficult for an observer to define easily, yet like an individual's personality, it can often be sensed almost immediately. For example, the way people dress and behave, the way they interact with each other and with customers, and the qualities that are likely to be valued by their managers are usually quite different at a bank than they are at a rock-music company, and different again at a law firm or an advertising agency.

At Nordstrom, the fashion retailer, employees are simply given a five-by-eight-inch card with one rule on it.

Cultures can be strong or weak; strong cultures can have great influence on how people think and behave. A strong culture is one in which everyone understands and believes in the firm's goals, priorities, and practices. A strong culture can be a real advantage to the organization if the behaviors it encourages and facilitates are appropriate ones. For example, the Walt Disney Company's culture encourages extraordinary devotion to customer service; the culture at Apple Inc. encourages innovation. Employees in these companies don't need rule books to dictate how they act, because these behaviors are conveyed as "the way we do things around here"; they are rooted in their companies' cultures.

In contrast, a strong culture that encourages inappropriate behaviors can severely hinder an organization's ability to deal effectively with its external environment—particularly if the environment is undergoing change, as is almost always the case today. A culture that was suitable and even advantageous in a prior era may become counterproductive in a new environment. For instance, a small start-up may have an informal culture that becomes less suitable when the company grows, faces more competition, and requires decision making by a wide range of specialized employees spread out over many locations.

In its relatively short life as a company, Google quickly became a role model for its brainy culture of innovation. Software writers and engineers were attracted to Google not just for its famous perks such as free meals and laundry facilities but also for a climate in which they were encouraged to let their imaginations roam free, dreaming up ideas that could be crazy but just might be the next big thing on the Internet.

During a long-running business boom, that culture served Google well. The best engineers were thrilled to work for a company that let them spend one-fifth of their time on new projects of their own choosing. But when the economy slowed and the stock market nosedived, Google's managers had to cope with a new reality in which money was tight. Google could no longer afford its free-spending culture. Managers had to figure out how to maintain the best of the culture while innovating at a more prudent pace.

Google's modified culture now values setting priorities. New ideas are still welcome if they are focused on core businesses of search, advertising, and Web-based software applications. Managers are reassigning employees away from teams working on unrelated projects and using them to staff teams working on profitable ideas in the core areas. Employees who have an idea that can improve the computer user's experience are asked to consider also what impact that idea might have on Google's bottom line. Similarly, hiring has slowed, because managers must not only justify the talent of a candidate but also target hiring to particular business needs. The challenge will be to keep employees as excited about targeted innovation as they have been about freewheeling innovation.[61]

Similarly, when a merger or acquisition brings together organizations with strong cultures, cultural differences can encourage behaviors that are harmful to the combined organization. After Sprint acquired Nextel, conflicts arose because the two wireless carriers had different cultures. Sprint moved cautiously, whereas Nextel's culture was more entrepreneurial. Such differences in style can be unsettling to employees on both sides and may help to explain why research has found much higher turnover rates among managers at companies that have been acquired.[62]

In contrast to strong cultures, weak cultures have the following characteristics: Different people hold different values, there is confusion about corporate goals, and it is not clear from one day to the next what principles should guide decisions. Some managers may pay lip service to some aspects of the culture ("we would never cheat a customer") but behave very differently ("don't tell him about the flaw"). As you can guess, such a culture fosters confusion, conflict, and poor performance. Most managers would agree that they want to create a strong culture that encourages and supports goals and useful behaviors that will make the company more effective. In other words, they want to create a culture that is appropriately aligned with the organization's competitive environment.[63]

Diagnosing Culture

Let's say you want to understand a company's culture. Perhaps you are thinking about working there and you want a good "fit," or perhaps you are working there right now and want to deepen your understanding of the organization and determine whether its culture matches the challenges it faces. How would you go about making the diagnosis? A variety of things will give you useful clues about culture:

> *Corporate mission statements and official goals* are a starting point, because they will tell you the firm's desired public image. Most companies have a mission statement—even the CIA, as shown in Figure 2.5. Your school has one, and you can probably find it online. But are these statements a true expression of culture? A study of hospital employees and their managers found that managers rated their mission statement more positively than nonmanagers (even though employees had participated in developing it), and 3 out of 10 employees were not

Vision	We will provide knowledge and take action to ensure the national security of the United States and the preservation of American life and ideals.
Mission	We are the eyes and ears of the nation and at times its hidden hand. We accomplish this mission by: • Collecting intelligence that matters. • Providing relevant, timely, and objective all-source analysis. • Conducting covert action at the direction of the president to preempt threats or achieve United States policy objectives.
Values	In pursuit of our country's interests, we put Nation before Agency, Agency before unit, and all before self. What we do matters. • Our success depends on our ability to act with total discretion and an ability to protect sources and methods. • We provide objective, unbiased information and analysis. • Our mission requires complete personal integrity and personal courage, physical and intellectual. • We accomplish things others cannot, often at great risk. When the stakes are highest and the dangers greatest, we are there and there first. • We stand by one another and behind one another. Service, sacrifice, flexibility, teamwork, and quiet patriotism are our hallmarks.

FIGURE 2.5
CIA Vision, Mission, and Values

SOURCE: CIA Web site accessed March 10, 2005, at www.cia.gov/information/mission.html.

even aware that the hospital had a mission statement (even though the hospital had processes for communicating about it).[64] So, even after reading statements of mission and goals, you still need to figure out whether the statements truly reflect how the firm conducts business.

Business practices can be observed. How a company responds to problems, makes strategic decisions, and treats employees and customers tells a lot about what top management really values. The Tribune Company's repeated efforts to cut costs at the *Los Angeles Times* and consolidate its Washington bureau with that of the chain's other newspapers told the acquired company's employees about the parent company's priorities.

Symbols, rites, and ceremonies give further clues about culture. For instance, status symbols can give you a feel for how rigid the hierarchy is and for the nature of relationships between lower and higher levels. Who is hired and fired—and why—and the activities that are rewarded indicate the firm's real values.

The stories people tell carry a lot of information about the company's culture. Every company has its myths, legends, and true stories about important past decisions and actions that convey the company's main values. The stories often feature the company's heroes: people once or still active who possessed the qualities and characteristics that the culture especially values and who act as models for others about how to behave.

A strong culture combines these measures in a consistent way. The Ritz-Carlton hotel chain gives each employee a laminated card listing its 12 service values. Each day it carries out a type of ceremony: a 15-minute meeting during which employees from every department resolve problems and discuss areas of potential improvement. At these meetings, the focus is on the day's "wow story," which details an extraordinary way that a Ritz-Carlton employee lived up to one of the service values. For example, a family arrived at the Bali Ritz-Carlton with special eggs and milk because of their son's allergies, but the food had spoiled. The manager and dining staff couldn't find replacements in town, so the executive chef called his mother-in-law in Singapore and asked her to buy the necessary products and fly with them to Bali.[65]

In general, cultures can be categorized according to whether they emphasize flexibility versus control and whether their focus is internal or external to the organization. By juxtaposing these two dimensions, we can describe four types of organizational cultures, depicted in Figure 2.6:

Group culture. A group culture is internally oriented and flexible. It tends to be based on the values and norms associated with affiliation. An organizational member's compliance with organizational directives flows from trust, tradition, and long-term commitment. It tends to emphasize member development and values participation in decision making. The strategic orientation associated with this cultural type is one of implementation through consensus building. Leaders tend to act as mentors and facilitators.

Hierarchical culture. The hierarchical culture is internally oriented by more focus on control and stability. It has the values and norms associated with a bureaucracy. It values stability and assumes that individuals will comply with organizational mandates when roles are stated formally and enforced through rules and procedures.

Rational culture. The rational culture is externally oriented and focused on control. Its primary objectives are productivity, planning, and efficiency. Organizational members are motivated by the belief that performance that leads to the desired organizational objectives will be rewarded.

FIGURE 2.6
Competing-Values Model of Culture

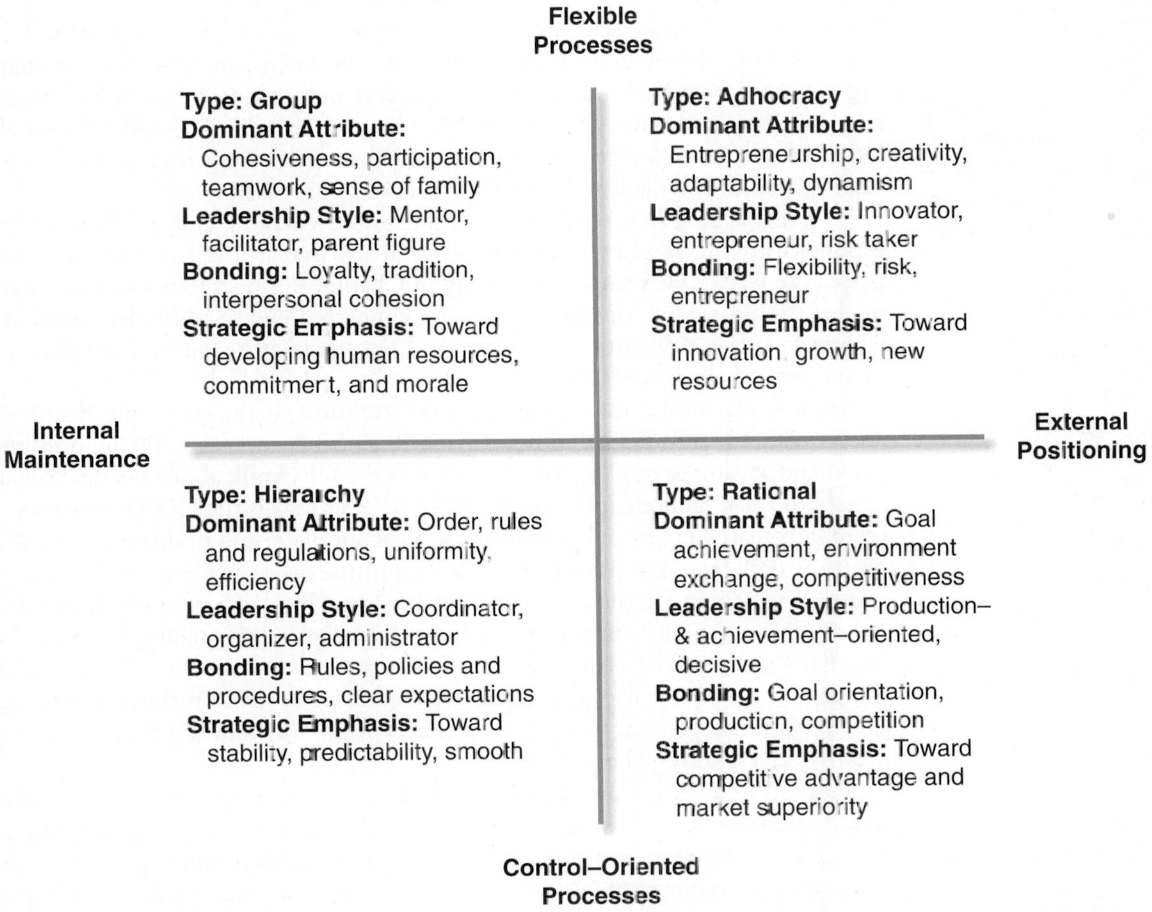

Flexible Processes

Type: Group
Dominant Attribute:
  Cohesiveness, participation, teamwork, sense of family
Leadership Style: Mentor, facilitator, parent figure
Bonding: Loyalty, tradition, interpersonal cohesion
Strategic Emphasis: Toward developing human resources, commitment, and morale

Type: Adhocracy
Dominant Attribute:
  Entrepreneurship, creativity, adaptability, dynamism
Leadership Style: Innovator, entrepreneur, risk taker
Bonding: Flexibility, risk, entrepreneur
Strategic Emphasis: Toward innovation growth, new resources

Internal Maintenance

External Positioning

Type: Hierarchy
Dominant Attribute: Order, rules and regulations, uniformity, efficiency
Leadership Style: Coordinator, organizer, administrator
Bonding: Rules, policies and procedures, clear expectations
Strategic Emphasis: Toward stability, predictability, smooth

Type: Rational
Dominant Attribute: Goal achievement, environment exchange, competitiveness
Leadership Style: Production- & achievement-oriented, decisive
Bonding: Goal orientation, production, competition
Strategic Emphasis: Toward competitive advantage and market superiority

Control–Oriented Processes

SOURCE: Kim S. Cameron and Robert E. Quinn, *Diagnosing and Changing Organizational Culture* (Englewood Cliffs NJ; Addison-Wesley, 1988). Used by permission of the authors.

Adhocracy. The adhocracy is externally oriented and flexible. This culture type emphasizes change in which growth, resource acquisition, and innovation are stressed. Organizational members are motivated by the importance or ideological appeal of the task. Leaders tend to be entrepreneurial and risk takers. Other members tend to have these characteristics as well.[66]

This type of diagnosis is important when two companies are considering combining operations, as in a merger, acquisition, or joint venture, because as we noted, cultural differences can sink these arrangements. In some cases, organizations investigating this type of change can benefit from setting up a "clean team" of third-party experts who investigate the details of each company's culture. For example, they might conduct employee focus groups to learn about leadership styles, the way policies are established, and the kinds of behavior that are rewarded. They can look for systems that indicate employees are empowered to make independent decisions or that directions are handed down from above. They can note how management talks about the company's founder, customers, and employees. In this way, the clean team can identify for the organizations' leaders the types of issues they will have to resolve and the values they must choose among as they try to establish a combined culture.[67]

Managing Culture

We mentioned earlier in this chapter that one important way organizations have of responding to the environment is to *adapt* to it by changing the organization itself. One of the most important tools managers have for implementing such a change lies in their management of their organization's culture. A culture that is inwardly instead of customer focused, for example, when the new competitive environment requires excellence in customer service, can delay or even defeat a manager's efforts to effect change. Simple directives alone are often ineffective; the underlying values of the organization also have to be shifted in the desired direction. Most companies today know that adopting a customer orientation, improving quality, and making other moves necessary to remain competitive are so essential that they require deep-rooted cultural changes. When that kind of change occurs, organization members may then begin to internalize the new values and display the appropriate behaviors on their own.

Top managers can take several approaches to managing culture. First, they should espouse lofty ideals and visions for the company that will inspire organization members. (We will discuss vision more fully in Chapter 4, on strategy, and in Chapter 12, on leadership.) That vision—whether it concerns quality, integrity, innovation, or whatever—should be articulated over and over until it becomes a tangible presence throughout the organization.

Second, executives must give constant attention to the mundane details of daily affairs such as communicating regularly, being visible and active throughout the company, and setting examples. Not only should the CEO talk about the vision, but he or she should also embody it day in and day out. This makes the CEO's pronouncements credible, creates a personal example others can emulate, and builds trust that the organization's progress toward the vision will continue over the long run.

Important here are the moments of truth when hard choices must be made. Imagine top management trumpeting a culture that emphasizes quality and then discovering that a part used in a batch of assembled products is defective. Whether to replace the part at great expense in the interest of quality or to ship the defective part just to save time and money is a decision that will go a long way toward reinforcing or destroying a quality-oriented culture.

To reinforce the organization's culture, the CEO and other executives should routinely celebrate and reward those who exemplify the new values. Another key to managing culture involves hiring, socializing newcomers, and promoting employees on the basis of the new corporate values. In this way, the new culture will begin to permeate

A culture aligned with its environment helps the organization succeed.

the organization. While this may seem a time-consuming approach to building a new culture, effective managers recognize that replacing a long-term culture of traditional values with one that embodies the competitive values needed in the future can take years. But the rewards of that effort will be an organization much more effective and responsive to its environmental challenges and opportunities.

Relationships with customers and suppliers have enabled Green Mountain Coffee Roasters to establish itself as a strong competitor that adapts to and influences its environment. As you read the "Management Close-Up: Assessing Outcomes and Seizing Opportunities" feature, consider what qualities could help the company succeed in its expansion plans.

Management Close-Up

ASSESSING OUTCOMES AND SEIZING OPPORTUNITIES

After initially investing in Keurig's single-cup brewing system, Green Mountain Coffee Roasters' founder Bob Stiller saw a bigger opportunity. Because Keurig brewing systems sell at or near cost, the real money comes from the royalties other brands pay to have their coffee, tea, or cocoa products distributed in K-cups. So GMCR acquired Keurig in 2006. With that acquisition, GMCR's fortunes soared, growing at double-digit rates. The company forecasted a 40 to 45 percent increase in sales for a recent year.

Keurig has captured the single-brew coffee market in offices, hotel rooms, and homes, yet enormous potential remains. The office coffee market has about 2.6 million brewers. About 12 percent have single-cup systems, and half of those are Keurig's. About 80 percent of America's 5 million hotel rooms have traditional coffeemakers. As single-brew popularity spreads, GMCR sees upscale hotels as a prime target. But the fastest-growing market is homes. Keurig is used in just 6 percent so far, but the single-brew system is now available in retail outlets like Costco, Sears, BJ's, and Macy's. On deck is a smaller, portable Keurig brewer with its own travel bag.

Two years after the Keurig acquisition, GMCR founder Stiller stepped down as president and CEO but remains chairman. The experience of his successor, Larry Blanford, helps GMCR continue its unprecedented growth. Blanford has a background in large consumer goods companies such as Maytag and Procter & Gamble.

Under Blanford, GMCR is continuing its expansion by opening roasting and K-cup processing units in Tennessee and buying Seattle-based Tully's Coffee. The Tully's acquisition provides a foothold in office coffee services, food service distributors, and more than 5,000 grocery stores in the West. The link to supermarkets reinforces the sale of Keurig brewers in supermarkets.[68]

- Despite economic and environmental uncertainty, GMCR is growing rapidly while its industry as a whole is struggling. Why do you think this is so?
- What should be Larry Blanford's next move as CEO?

KEY TERMS

SUMMARY OF LEARNING OBJECTIVES

Now that you have studied Chapter 2, you should be able to:

LO 1 **Describe how environmental forces influence organizations and how organizations can influence their environments.**

Organizations are open systems that are affected by, and in turn affect, their external environments. Organizations receive financial, human, material, and information resources from the environment; transform those resources into finished goods and services; and then send those outputs back into the environment.

LO 2 **Distinguish between the macroenvironment and the competitive environment.**

The macroenvironment is composed of international, legal and political, economic, technological, and social forces that influence strategic decisions. The competitive environment is composed of forces closer to the organization, such as current competitors, new entrants, substitute and complementary products, suppliers, and customers. Perhaps the simplest distinction between the macroenvironment and the competitive environment is in the amount of control a firm can exert on external forces. Macroenvironmental forces such as the economy and social trends are much less controllable than are forces in the competitive environment such as suppliers and customers.

LO 3 **Explain why managers and organizations should attend to economic and social developments.**

Developments outside the organization can have a profound effect on the way managers and their companies operate. For example, higher energy costs or increased spending on security may make it harder for managers to keep their prices low. The growing diversity of the labor force gives managers access to a much broader range of talent but also requires them to make sure different types of employees are treated equally. The worldwide increase in free trade can open up overseas markets, but it may also encourage more foreign competition in the domestic market. Effective managers stay aware of trends like these and respond to them effectively.

LO 4 **Identify elements of the competitive environment.**

Elements in the environment can range from favorable to unfavorable. To determine how favorable a competitive environment is, managers should consider the nature of the competitors, potential new entrants, threat of substitutes, opportunities from complements, and relationships with suppliers and customers.

Analyzing how these forces influence the organization provides an indication of potential threats and opportunities. Effective management of the firm's supply chain is one way to achieve a competitive advantage. Attractive environments tend to be those with high industry growth, few competitors, products that can be differentiated, few potential entrants, many barriers to entry, few substitutes, many suppliers (none with much power), and many customers. After identifying and analyzing competitive forces, managers must formulate a strategy that minimizes the power external forces have over the organization.

LO 5 **Summarize how organizations respond to environmental uncertainty.**

Responding effectively to the environment often requires devising proactive strategies to change the environment. Strategic maneuvering involves changing the boundaries of the competitive environment through domain selection, diversification, mergers, and the like. Independent strategies do not require moving into a new environment but rather changing some aspect of the current environment through competitive aggression, public relations, legal action, and so on. Cooperative strategies, such as contracting, cooptation, and coalition building, involve the working together of two or more organizations.

LO 6 **Define elements of an organization's culture.**

An organization's culture is its set of shared values and practices related to what is important and how the world works. The culture provides a framework that organizes and directs people's behavior at work. Elements of the culture may be expressed in corporate mission statements and official goals, assuming these reflect how the organization actually operates. Business practices are a basic measure of culture. Symbols, rites, ceremonies, and the stories people tell express and reinforce their cultural values.

LO 7 **Discuss how an organization's culture affects its response to its external environment.**

A culture may be strong or weak and may be one of four types: group, hierarchical, rational, or adhocracy. These cultures shape whether they are flexible and whether the focus is on the external or internal environment. Managing and changing the culture to align it with the organization's environment will require strong, long-term commitment by the CEO and other managers. Managers should espouse high ideals, pay constant attention to conveying values by communicating and modeling them, making decisions that are consistent with cultural values, and rewarding those who demonstrate the organization's values.

DISCUSSION QUESTIONS

1. This chapter's opening quote by Peter Drucker said, "The essence of a business is outside itself." What do you think this means? Do you agree?

2. What are the most important forces in the macroenvironment facing companies today?

3. Review the example in the three parts of the "Management Close-Up." What other organizations or industries have faced or are facing similar circumstances in their external environments?

4. What are the main differences between the macroenvironment and the competitive environment?

5. What kinds of changes do companies make in response to environmental uncertainty?

6. We outlined several proactive responses that organizations can make to the environment. What examples have you seen recently of an organization's responding effectively to its environment? Did the effectiveness of the response depend on whether the organization was facing a threat or an opportunity?

7. Select two organizations that you are interested in. Research information about the firms or talk with an employee, if possible. What types of cultures do they have? Write a paragraph that describes each culture.

8. When you visited colleges to select one to attend, were there cultural differences in the campuses that made a difference in your choice? Did these differences help you decide which college to attend?

CONCLUDING CASE

Wild Water Gets Soaked

Jason and Marie Salerno, brother and sister, have been running their family business, a water park called Wild Water, since they both graduated from college. The Salernos operate the park, which is located near the New Jersey shore, with help from their parents. Marie's husband and Jason's wife are also involved in the business. Wild Water has now been in business for more than 40 years—it is a landmark to both locals and summer tourists. The water park features such attractions as a wave pool, several water slides, a flume ride, a kiddie pool, and a tube ride. A picnic park, shaded petting zoo, aquarium, snack bar, and restaurant called the Seafood Shack round out the park's offerings.

The park opens on Memorial Day and cuts back to weekends only after Labor Day, typically closing in the fall. With just a few months to accumulate revenue, the family and employees of the park work extremely hard. Marie oversees the financial aspects of the business, while Jason manages the staff. The staff—ride operators, ticket takers, lifeguards, and the like—are very loyal. Some have parents who once worked at the water park, and many have siblings who also work there. By its very nature, the organization culture of Wild Water is hierarchical—but most who work there, including Jason and Marie, would refer to their employees as part of the family. Jason holds weekly staff meetings, where employees are encouraged to voice their ideas about any aspect of the park's operations. Photos of workers and customers line the walls of Jason and Marie's tiny office, and stories about the park and its people abound, including sightings of celebrity visitors and near-disasters such as a close call with a hurricane.

While the organization culture has remained largely unchanged for the past four decades, the environment in which the park operates is changing. A new state safety law requires some expensive updating to meet the code. The Salernos recently learned that some of the smaller beach cottages in the area are going to

be torn down to make way for a development of expensive condominiums. Vacationers who rent the condos are more likely to be looking for entertainment in the form of golf, deep-sea fishing trips, and exclusive restaurants. One of the major amusement park chains has been looking at a piece of real estate nearby. This chain is well known for its high-end rides, shows, and eating establishments. The Salernos point out that an entire family could enter Wild Water for the cost of one ticket at one of the chain's parks.

While the Salernos acknowledge that they have serious challenges ahead, they remain upbeat. Wild Water has been a favorite of families for more than two generations, and they expect it to continue to be a destination for local residents as well as vacationers. But they need to make some changes to keep those visitors—and the new condo owners—coming through the turnstile.

QUESTIONS

1. Imagine that you are a management consultant hired by the Salernos to help them navigate the choppy waters ahead. First, describe the elements of the macroenvironment and competitive environment that affect Wild Water now. Then describe elements that you anticipate will affect the water park in the next few years.

2. Next, describe the organization's culture. Discuss how the current culture affects the way it responds to the organization's external environment.

3. Now, create a plan for Wild Water. In your plan, describe what changes the organization needs to make in its culture to meet upcoming challenges in the external environment. Then describe steps that Wild Water can take to compete successfully against the new amusement park. How can the Salernos keep their loyal customers happy while attracting new ones?

EXPERIENTIAL EXERCISES

2.1 External Environment Analysis

OBJECTIVE

To give you the experience of performing an analysis of a company's external environment

INSTRUCTIONS

Select a company you like in the music industry. Using online and/or library resources, including Web sites on the music industry and your company's Web site and annual report, fill out the following External Environment Worksheet for that company:

External Environment Worksheet

Laws and regulations

What are some key laws and regulations under which this company and the music industry must operate?

_____

_____

The economy

How does the state of the economy influence the sales of this company's products?

_____

_____

Technology

What new technologies strongly affect the company you have selected?

_____

_____

Demographics

What changes in the population might affect the company's customer base?

_____

_____

Social issues

What changes in society affect the market for your company's music products?

_____

_____

Suppliers

How does your company's relationship with suppliers affect its profitability?

_____

_____

Competitors

What companies compete with the firm you have selected? Do they compete on price, on quality, or on other factors?

_____

_____

New entrants

Are new competitors to the company likely? possible?

_____

_____

Substitutes and Complements

Is there a threat of substitutes for the music industry's existing products? Are there complementary products that suggest an opportunity for collaboration?

_____

_____

Customers

What characteristics of the company's customer base influence the company's competitiveness?

_____

_____

DISCUSSION QUESTIONS

1. What has the company done to adapt to its environment?

2. How does the company attempt to influence its environment?

2.2 Corporate Culture Preference Scale

OBJECTIVE

This self-assessment is designed to help you to identify a corporate culture that fits most closely with your personal values and assumptions.

INSTRUCTIONS

Read each pair of the statements in the Corporate Culture Preference Scale and circle the statement that describes the organization you would prefer to work in. This exercise is completed alone so students assess themselves honestly without concerns of social comparison. However, class discussion will focus on the importance of matching job applicants to the organization's dominant values.

Corporate Culture Preference Scale

I would prefer to work in an organization:

1a.	Where employees work well together in teams.	**OR**	1b. That produces highly respected products or services.
2a.	Where top management maintains a sense of order in the workplace.	**OR**	2b. Where the organization listens to customers and responds quickly to their needs.
3a.	Where employees are treated fairly.	**OR**	3b. Where employees continuously search for ways to work more efficiently.
4a.	Where employees adapt quickly to new work requirements.	**OR**	4b. Where corporate leaders work hard to keep employees happy.
5a.	Where senior executives receive special benefits not available to other employees.	**OR**	5b. Where employees are proud when the organization achieves its performance goals.
6a.	Where employees who perform the best get paid the most.	**OR**	6b. Where senior executives are respected.
7a.	Where everyone gets his or her job done like clockwork.	**OR**	7b. That is on top of new innovations in the industry.
8a.	Where employees receive assistance to overcome any personal problems.	**OR**	8b. Where employees abide by company rules.
9a.	That is always experimenting with new ideas in the marketplace.	**OR**	9b. That expects everyone to put in 110 percent for peak performance.
10a.	That quickly benefits from market opportunities.	**OR**	10b. Where employees are always kept informed of what's happening in the organization.
11a.	That can quickly respond to competitive threats.	**OR**	11b. Where most decisions are made by the top executives.
12a.	Where management keeps everything under control.	**OR**	12b. Where employees care for each other.

SOURCE: Steven L. McShane and Mary Ann Von Glinow, *Organizational Behavior*, 3rd ed. (New York: McGraw-Hill/Irwin, 2005), p. 499. © 2005 The McGraw-Hill Companies.

Scoring Key for the Corporate Culture Preference Scale

Scoring Instructions: In each space, write in a "1" if you circled the statement and "0" if you did not. Then add up the scores for each subscale.

Control Culture   _____ + _____ + _____ + _____ + _____ + _____ = _____
                        (2a)   (5a)   (6b)   (8b)   (11b)   (12a)

Performance Culture   _____ + _____ + _____ + _____ + _____ + _____ = _____
                        (1b)   (3b)   (5b)   (6a)   (7a)   (9b)

Relationship Culture   _____ + _____ + _____ + _____ + _____ + _____ = _____
                               (1a)   (3a)   (4b)   (8a)   (10b)   (12b)

Responsive Culture   _____ + _____ + _____ + _____ + _____ + _____ = _____
                               (2b)   (4a)   (7b)   (9a)   (10a)   (11a)

Interpreting Your Score: These corporate cultures may be found in many organizations, but they represent only four of many possible organizational cultures. Also, keep in mind none of these subscales is inherently good or bad. Each is effective in different situations. The four corporate cultures are defined here, along with the range of scores for high, medium, and low levels of each dimension based on a sample of MBA students:

Corporate Culture Dimension and Definition

Control Culture: This culture values the role of senior executives to lead the organization. Its goal is to keep everyone aligned and under control.

Performance Culture: This culture values individual and organizational performance and strives for effectiveness and efficiency.

Relationship Culture: This culture values nurturing and well-being. It considers open communication, fairness, teamwork, and sharing a vital part of organizational life.

Responsive Culture: This culture values its ability to keep in tune with the external environment, including being competitive and realizing new opportunities.

Score Interpretation

High: 3 to 6
Medium: 1 to 2
Low: 0

High: 5 to 6
Medium: 3 to 4
Low: 0 to 2

High: 6
Medium: 4 to 5
Low: 0 to 3

High: 6
Medium: 4 to 5
Low: 0 to 3

Managerial Decision Making

" The business executive is by profession a decision maker. Uncertainty is his opponent. Overcoming it is his mission. "

— John McDonald

LEARNING OBJECTIVES

After studying Chapter 3, you will be able to:

LO 1 Describe the kinds of decisions you will face as a manager. p. 86

LO 2 Summarize the steps in making "rational" decisions. p. 89

LO 3 Recognize the pitfalls you should avoid when making decisions. p. 95

LO 4 Evaluate the pros and cons of using a group to make decisions. p. 98

LO 5 Identify procedures to use in leading a decision-making group. p. 100

LO 6 Explain how to encourage creative decisions. p. 102

LO 7 Discuss the processes by which decisions are made in organizations. p. 104

LO 8 Describe how to make decisions in a crisis. p. 105

CHAPTER OUTLINE

Characteristics of Managerial Decisions
Lack of Structure
Uncertainty and Risk
Conflict

The Stages of Decision Making
Identifying and Diagnosing the Problem
Generating Alternative Solutions
Evaluating Alternatives
Making the Choice
Implementing the Decision
Evaluating the Decision

The Best Decision

Barriers to Effective Decision Making
Psychological Biases
Time Pressures
Social Realities

Decision Making in Groups
Potential Advantages of Using a Group
Potential Problems of Using a Group

Managing Group Decision Making
Leadership Style
Constructive Conflict
Encouraging Creativity
Brainstorming

Organizational Decision Making
Constraints on Decision Makers
Models of Organizational Decision Processes
Decision Making in a Crisis

Management Close-Up

Anne Mulcahy is not your typical English major. After college graduation she joined Xerox Corporation's sales force and rose through the ranks. Twenty-five years later, she became chairman and CEO of the world's leading document management and services enterprise. But her promotion brought a host of problems. King of the hill in the 1970s and 1980s, Xerox had faltered badly with its computer division during the 1990s as competitors undercut it on price. By 2000, once-mighty Xerox Corporation was in the red and sinking fast.

Stepping into the corner office in August 2001, Mulcahy found a company in total disarray. Her predecessor, former IBMer Richard Thoman, had lasted only 13 months in the job. Xerox was nearly $18 billion in debt. It had exhausted a $7 billion line of credit, and its credit ratings were tanking.

{ When Mulcahy took the reins at Xerox, the company was in a mess, seemingly with no way out except bankruptcy. As you read this chapter, consider the decisions managers face—and how Mulcahy approached the decision-making process. }

While Xerox had stayed the course with an outdated business plan, nimbler and more innovative competitors like Ricoh and Canon were snatching away market share. To add to the company's woes, shortly after Mulcahy became CEO, the Securities and Exchange Commission announced that it would investigate Xerox on suspected billing and accounting irregularities.

At that point, Mulcahy could have simply caved to angry shareholders, killed the famed Xerox culture, shut down research and development, filed for bankruptcy, or turned out the lights—all advice she received from many people. But Mulcahy was a Xerox believer. Besides her time in the sales force, she had headed the human resource department and the company's $6 billion desktop printing division. Anne Mulcahy had just begun to fight.[1]

The best managers make decisions constantly. Some are big and difficult, like those Anne Mulcahy faced when she became head of a global empire on the brink of bankruptcy. But managers also make countless smaller decisions that affect day-to-day operations and procedures. Karen Lancaster, chief information officer at Western Marine Insurance, makes many decisions about her firm's computer systems. For example, she had to decide on a plan to back up and store the company's data to protect the company. If Western Marine's computers ever lost power or failed, the company needed to store data off-site. So Lancaster compared offers from three vendors and chose Courtesy Computers, which uses an Internet connection to back up the company's data automatically at the end of each day.

Backing up data is hardly glamorous, but a crisis can bring home the importance of these decisions, as Lancaster well knows. One day the phone company was digging outside Western Marine's building in Stockton, California, and cut a line, causing the company's Internet firewall to go down, which in turn allowed a hacker access to the company's server, clogging it with spam so that it crashed. Another time a power surge caused a loss of data in the computers. In both situations, the online backup solved the problem. Lancaster says, "When you're creating your disaster plan, you need to think about every scenario."[2]

Decisions. If you can't make them, you won't be an effective manager. This chapter discusses what kinds of decisions managers face, how they are made, and how they *should* be made.

Characteristics of Managerial Decisions

LO 1

You'll be making decisions constantly. It may seem obvious, but it's worth stating: If you know how to make good decisions, you'll deliver good results.

Managers face problems and opportunities constantly. Some situations that require a decision are relatively simple; others seem overwhelming. Some demand immediate action, while others take months or even years to unfold.

Actually, managers often ignore problems.[3] M. For several reasons, they avoid taking action.[4] First, managers can't be sure how much time, energy, or trouble lies ahead once they start working on a problem. Second, getting involved is risky; tackling a problem but failing to solve it successfully can hurt a manager's track record. Third, because problems can be so perplexing, it is easier to procrastinate or to get busy with less demanding activities. For these reasons, managers may lack the insight, courage, or will to decide.

It is important to understand why decision making can be so challenging. Figure 3.1 illustrates several characteristics of managerial decisions that contribute to their difficulty and pressure. Most managerial decisions lack structure and entail risk, uncertainty, and conflict.

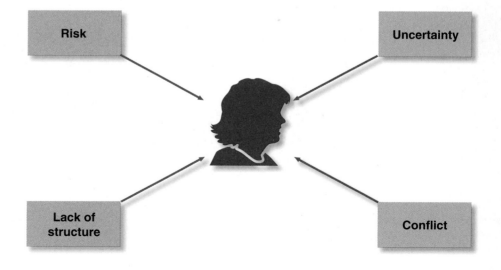

FIGURE 3.1
Characteristics of Managerial Decisions

Lack of Structure

A moderate ego demonstrates wisdom.

Lao-tzu

Lack of structure is the usual state of affairs in managerial decision making.[5] Although some decisions are routine and clear-cut, for most there is no automatic procedure to follow. Problems are novel and unstructured, leaving the decision maker uncertain about how to proceed.

An important distinction illustrating this point is between programmed and nonprogrammed decisions. **Programmed decisions** have been encountered and made before. They have objectively correct answers and can be solved by using simple rules, policies, or numerical computations. If you face a programmed decision, a clear procedure or structure exists for arriving at the right decision. For example, if you are a small-business owner and must decide the amounts for your employees' paychecks, you can use a formula—and if the amounts are wrong, your employees will prove it to you. Table 3.1 gives some other examples.

If most important decisions were programmed, managerial life would be much easier. But managers typically face **nonprogrammed decisions:** new, novel, complex decisions having no certain outcomes. They have a variety of possible solutions, all of which have merits and drawbacks. The decision maker must create or impose a method for making the decision; there is no predetermined structure on which to rely. As Table 3.1 suggests, important, difficult decisions tend to be nonprogrammed, and they demand creative approaches.

programmed decisions

Decisions encountered and made before, having objectively correct answers, and solvable by using simple rules, policies, or numerical computations.

nonprogrammed decisions

New, novel, complex decisions having no proven answers.

Uncertainty and Risk

If you have all the information you need, and can predict precisely the consequences of your actions, you are operating under a condition of **certainty.**[6] Managers are expressing their preference for certainty when they are not satisfied hearing about what *might have* happened or *may* happen, and insist on hearing what *did* or *will* happen.[7] But perfect certainty is rare. For important, nonprogrammed managerial decisions, uncertainty is the rule.

Uncertainty means the manager has insufficient information to know the consequences of different actions. Decision makers may have strong opinions—they may feel sure of themselves—but they are still operating under conditions of uncertainty if

certainty

The state that exists when decision makers have accurate and comprehensive information.

uncertainty

The state that exists when decision makers have insufficient information.

TABLE 3.1

Comparison of Types of Decisions

	Programmed Decisions	Nonprogrammed Decisions
Problem	Frequent, repetitive, routine. Much certainty regarding cause-and-effect relationships.	Novel, unstructured. Much uncertainty regarding cause-and-effect relationships.
Procedure	Dependence on policies, rules, and definite procedures.	Necessity for creativity, intuition, tolerance for ambiguity, creative problem solving.
Examples		
Business firm	Periodic reorders of inventory.	Diversification into new products and markets.
University	Necessary grade-point average for good academic standing.	Construction of new classroom facilities.
Health care	Procedure for admitting patients.	Purchase of experimental equipment.
Government	Merit system for promotion of state employees.	Reorganization of state government agencies.

SOURCE: J. Gibson, J. Ivancevich, and J. Donnelly Jr., *Organizations: Behavior, Structure, Processes,* 10th ed. Copyright © 2000 by The McGraw-Hill Companies. Reprinted with permission of The McGraw-Hill Companies.

they lack pertinent information and cannot estimate accurately the likelihood of different results of their actions.

When you can estimate the likelihood of various consequences but still do not know with certainty what will happen, you are facing **risk.** Risk exists when the probability of an action being successful is less than 100 percent and losses may occur. If the decision is the wrong one, you may lose money, time, reputation, or other important assets.

Risk, like uncertainty, is a fact of life in managerial decision making. But this is not the same as *taking* a risk. Although it sometimes seems as though risk takers are admired and that entrepreneurs and investors thrive on taking risks, the reality is that good decision makers prefer to *manage* risk. They accept the fact that decisions have consequences entailing risk, but they do everything they can to anticipate the risk, minimize it, and control it.

Consider the choices involved in preparing a restaurant menu. The Center for Science in the Public Interest recently criticized restaurant chains for selling entrées, appetizers, and desserts containing 1,400 calories or more (a typical American might eat 2,000 calories in an entire day). Making no changes could give those restaurants a reputation for contributing to obesity, but if a restaurant offers more healthful alternatives, will diners bite? The riskiest approach would be to change the entire menu. Instead, restaurateurs including T.G.I. Friday's are more likely to lower uncertainty by retaining popular choices and adding some new selections. Some entrées are smaller versions of items already being offered, and others are new but similar to popular dishes.[8]

A T-shirt company called Threadless reduces uncertainty and manages risk by basing its whole marketing model on collaboration with customers. Professional and amateur graphic designers submit their ideas for T-shirt designs at the Threadless Web site, where customers vote on the designs they like. From hundreds of submissions, the company selects four to six of the top vote getters each week and pays their designers $1,000. But it makes and sells them only after a minimum number of customers have already ordered the shirt design.[9]

Conflict

Important decisions are even more difficult because of the conflict managers face. **Conflict,** which exists when a manager must consider opposing pressures from different sources, occurs at two levels.

First, individual decision makers experience psychological conflict when several options are attractive, or when none of the options is attractive. For instance, a manager may have to decide whom to lay off, when she doesn't want to lay off anyone. Or she may have three promising job applicants for one position—but choosing one means she has to reject the other two.

Second, conflict arises between people. A chief financial officer argues in favor of increasing long-term debt to finance an acquisition. The chief executive officer, however, prefers to minimize such debt and find the funds elsewhere. A marketing department wants more product lines to sell, and the engineers want higher-quality

---

risk

The state that exists when the probability of success is less than 100 percent and losses may occur.

conflict

Opposing pressures from different sources, occurring on the level of psychological conflict or of conflict between individuals or groups.

T-shirt designers have a chance to get their designs printed through the Threadless Web site, but only after customers have given them high ratings and ordered a shirt.

products. But the production people want to lower costs by having longer production runs of fewer products with no changes. Few decisions are without conflict.

The Stages of Decision Making

LO 2

Faced with these challenges, how can you make good decisions? The ideal decision-making process includes six stages. As Figure 3.2 illustrates, decision makers should (1) identify and diagnose the problem, (2) generate alternative solutions, (3) evaluate alternatives, (4) make the choice, (5) implement the decision, and (6) evaluate the decision.

Identifying and Diagnosing the Problem

The first stage in the decision-making process is to recognize that a problem exists and must be solved. Typically, a manager realizes some discrepancy between the current state (the way things are) and a desired state (the way things ought to be). Such discrepancies—say, in organizational or unit performance—may be detected by comparing current performance against (1) *past* performance, (2) the *current* performance of other organizations or units, or (3) *future* expected performance as determined by plans and forecasts.[10] Larry Cohen, who founded Accurate Perforating with his father, knew his company was having difficulty making a profit, because costs at the metal company were rising while the prices customers were willing to pay remained unchanged. However, when the company's bank demanded immediate payment of its $1.5 million loan, Cohen realized the problem had to be solved, or the company would have to sell off all its assets and close.[11] We will refer to this example throughout this section.

The "problem" may actually be an opportunity that needs to be exploited: a gap between what the organization is doing now and what it can do to create a more positive future. In that case, decisions involve choosing how to seize the opportunity. To recognize important opportunities as a manager, you will need to understand your company's macro- and competitive environments (described in Chapter 2), including the opportunities offered by technological developments. Cisco Systems CEO John Chambers advises managers to stay current by talking to people who challenge you and are willing to teach you. Says Chambers, "When somebody travels with me, they have to teach me a topic. When I review engineers, at the end they have to teach me two topics. I listen."[12]

Recognizing that a problem or opportunity exists is only the beginning of this stage. The decision maker must dig in deeper and attempt to *diagnose* the situation. For example, a sales manager knows that sales have dropped drastically. If he is leaving the company soon or believes the decreased sales volume is due to the economy (which he can't do anything about), he won't take action. But if he does try to solve the problem, he should not automatically reprimand his sales staff, add new people, or increase the advertising budget. He must analyze *why* sales are down and then develop a solution appropriate to his analysis. Asking why, of yourself and others, is essential to understanding the

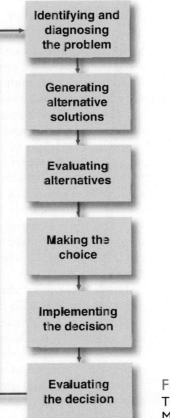

FIGURE 3.2

The Stages of Decision Making

real problem. Unfortunately, in the case of Accurate Perforating, described earlier, Larry Cohen did not ask why profits were declining; he simply assumed that the company's costs were too high.[13]

The following questions are useful to ask and answer in this stage:[14]

Is there a difference between what is actually happening and what should be happening?

How can you describe the deviation, as specifically as possible?

What is/are the cause(s) of the deviation?

What specific goals should be met?

Which of these goals are absolutely critical to the success of the decision?

Bookseller Borders faced a problem: declining sales. The book industry in general had become sluggish, as consumers filled leisure time with other activities. And consumers who did choose to buy books were often doing so online. But Borders didn't recognize that not having its own Web site was a problem, choosing instead to create an alliance with Amazon.com to sell its books online. At the time, CEO Greg Josefowicz defended the decision, saying it would "help us to focus on what we do best," which meant building more stores. But the customers didn't come. As the overall book market declined, online sales soared.

Borders's new CEO, George Jones, admits that the firm's previous strategy was wrong, saying that an online presence will be "a necessary component of our business" going forward. In addition, says Jones, Borders will invest in more superstores, reduce the number of CDs they carry, and strengthen the firm's publishing business—all in an effort to boost those flagging sales.[15]

Generating Alternative Solutions

The second stage of decision making links problem diagnosis to the development of alternative courses of action aimed at solving the problem. Managers generate at least some alternative solutions based on past experiences.[16]

ready-made solutions

Ideas that have been seen or tried before.

custom-made solutions

New, creative solutions designed specifically for the problem.

Solutions range from ready made to custom made.[17] Decision makers who search for **ready-made solutions** use ideas they have tried before or follow the advice of others who have faced similar problems. **Custom-made solutions,** by contrast, must be designed for specific problems. This technique often combines ideas into new, creative solutions. For example, Yamaha Corporation drew on ideas from its customer community, which said that hobby guitarists were interested in an instrument they could play without a lot of practice. Designers at Yamaha created an idea for a guitar that could read electronically entered songs and display lights on the fingerboard showing users where to put their fingers. Customers provided ideas for modifications, and the back and forth eventually generated more than the minimum number of orders for the company to produce the innovative product.[18] Potentially, custom-made solutions can be devised for any challenge. Later in the chapter, we will discuss how to generate creative ideas.

Often, many more alternatives are available than managers may realize. For example, what would you do if one of your competitors reduced prices? Cutting prices in response to a competitor's price cuts is not your only option, although sometimes it is assumed to be. Alternatives include emphasizing consumer risks to low-priced products, building awareness of your products' features and overall quality, and communicating your cost advantage to your competitors so they realize that they can't win a price war. If you do decide to cut your price as a last resort, do it fast—if you do it slowly, your competitors will gain sales in the meantime, which may embolden them to employ the same tactic again in the future.[19]

The case of Accurate Perforating shows the importance of looking for every alternative. The company had become successful by purchasing metal from steel mills, punching many holes in it to make screenlike sheets, and selling this material in bulk to distributors, who sold it to metal workshops, which used it to make custom products. Cohen admits, "We stayed away from sophisticated products, and as a result we wound up in a very competitive situation where the only thing we were selling was price." Management responded by cutting costs wherever possible, avoiding investment in new machinery or processes. The result was an out-of-date factory managed by people who had grown accustomed to resisting change. Only after the bank called in its loan did Cohen begin to see alternatives. The bank offered one painful idea: liquidate the company. It also suggested a management consultant, who advised another alternative: renegotiating payment schedules with the company's suppliers. Cohen also received advice from managers of a company Accurate had purchased a year before. That company, Semrow Perforated & Expanded Metals, sold more sophisticated products directly to manufacturers, and Semrow's managers urged Cohen to invest more in finished metal products such as theirs.[20]

Evaluating Alternatives

The third stage of decision making involves determining the value or adequacy of the alternatives that were generated. In other words, which solution will be the best?

Too often, alternatives are evaluated with insufficient thought or logic. At Accurate Perforating, Cohen made changes to cut costs but dismissed the idea to invest in marketing finished metal products, even though these product lines were more profitable. Accurate's general manager, Aaron Kamins, counseled that money spent on finished metal products would be a distraction from Accurate's core business. That reasoning persuaded Cohen, even though it meant focusing on unprofitable product lines.[21]

Obviously, alternatives should be evaluated more carefully. Fundamental to this process is to predict the consequences that will occur if the various options are put into effect. Managers should consider several types of consequences, including quantitative measures of success, such as lower costs, higher sales, lower employee turnover, and higher profits.

Environmental changes require companies to think through new alternatives and their consequences. When the recent downturn in the U.S. economy required cutbacks, organizations as diverse as the State of California, Gulfstream Aerospace, and Gannett evaluated the alternatives of layoffs (permanent job cuts) versus furloughs (requiring employees to take some unpaid time off until demand picks up again). While layoffs save more money per employee, because the company doesn't have to continue paying for benefits, furloughs attempt to maintain relationships with talented employees, who are more

When managers make decisions, they often draw on other people's insights to help them evaluate alternatives. In a survey of Canadian executives, more than two-thirds said the opinion of their assistant was important in deciding which job candidate to hire—a useful point to remember the next time you are job hunting.[23]

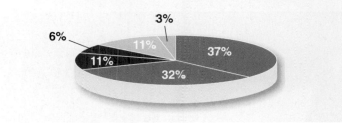

likely than laid-off workers to return when the company needs them again. Furloughs may seem kinder to employees, who can hope to return to work eventually, but workers may not be eligible for unemployment compensation during the furlough period.[22]

To evaluate alternatives, refer to your original goals, defined in the first stage. Which goals does each alternative meet, and fail to meet? Which alternatives are most acceptable to you and to other important stakeholders? If several alternatives may solve the problem, which can be implemented at the lowest cost or greatest profit? If no alternative achieves all your goals, perhaps you can combine two or more of the best ones. Several additional questions help:[24]

> Is our information about alternatives complete and current? If not, can we get more and better information?
> Does the alternative meet our primary objectives?
> What problems could we have if we implement the alternative?

Of course, results cannot be forecast with perfect accuracy. But sometimes decision makers can build in safeguards against an uncertain future by considering the potential consequences of several different scenarios. Then they generate **contingency plans**—alternative courses of action that can be implemented depending on how the future unfolds.

For example, scenario planners making decisions about the future might consider four alternative views of the future state of the U.S. economy:[25] (1) an economic boom with 5 to 6 percent annual growth and the United States much stronger than its global competitors; (2) a moderately strong economy with 2 to 3 percent growth; (3) a pessimistic outlook with no growth, rising unemployment, and recession; or (4) a worse scenario with global depression, massive unemployment, and widespread social unrest.

contingency plans

Alternative courses of action that can be implemented based on how the future unfolds.

> A scenario may use numbers that sound reasonable, but you should look at the data in different ways to check your assumptions. As Dean Kamen's company developed the Segway scooter, Kamen decided that each year Segway could capture 0.1 percent of the world's population. That percentage might sound conservative, but consider that 0.1 percent of 6 billion people is 6 million Segways a year! Kamen decided to build a factory that could produce 40,000 units a month; five years later, sales had reached fewer than 25,000.[26]

Some scenarios will seem more likely than others, and some may seem highly improbable. Ultimately, one of the scenarios will prove to be more accurate than the others. The process of considering multiple scenarios raises important "what if?" questions for decision makers and highlights the need for preparedness and contingency plans. As you read this, what economic scenario is unfolding? What are the important current events and trends? What scenarios could evolve six or eight years from now? How will *you* prepare?

Making the Choice

Once you have considered the possible consequences of your options, it is time to make your decision. Some managers are more comfortable with the analysis stage. Especially with all the advanced technology that is available, quantitatively inclined people can easily tweak the assumptions behind every scenario in countless ways. But the temptation can lead to "paralysis by analysis"—that is, indecisiveness caused by too much analysis rather than the assertive decision making that is essential if an organization is ever to seize new opportunities or thwart challenges. In contrast, as described in the "Management Close-Up: Taking Action" feature, Xerox's Anne Mulcahy behaved decisively.

As you make your decision, important concepts include maximizing, satisficing, and optimizing.[27]

Maximizing is achieving the best possible outcome. The maximizing decision realizes the greatest positive

maximizing

A decision realizing the best possible outcome.

British entrepreneur Richard Branson shows a model of his proposed Spaceship Two, a vehicle he hopes will be developed by his company in the next few years, which would take private passengers on commercial space fights. To what degree do you think Branson's decision to move ahead with this idea was based on the maximizing strategy?

Management Close-Up | TAKING ACTION

As Xerox CEO, Anne Mulcahy stumbled into an environment of uncertainty, but once she learned the full extent of her company's problems, she moved quickly. Mulcahy knew she couldn't fix Xerox by herself; she needed support from the whole team. To gain their cooperation, she would need to inform each person about the new reality for Xerox. So, Mulcahy visited each of Xerox's top 100 executives and, mincing no words about the grim situation, asked whether they were "in." To her credit, all but two stood with her. Today, most of those managers remain at Xerox.

Mulcahy spoke directly and honestly with shareholders, too. While some CEOs avoid giving unpleasant news to shareholders and try to pacify them at all times, that is not Mulcahy's style. What mattered most, she reasoned, were relationships with Xerox's employees and customers. Speaking to the shareholders, she characterized Xerox's old business model as "unsustainable" and warned that unless Xerox cut expenses and increased the profit margin, it would never return to profitability. By the next day, the stock price had tumbled 26 percent.

Yet Mulcahy stuck to her guns. She discontinued paying a dividend to shareholders, then began the difficult task of slashing expenses and eliminating unnecessary jobs. At the same time, she told the sales force she'd go anywhere to meet with Xerox customers and assure them that Xerox was getting back on track.

Where Mulcahy didn't have expertise, she became a quick study. Lacking financial expertise and with Xerox under SEC scrutiny, she asked her finance people for a "crash course" that would enable her to hold her own in meetings with the SEC.[28]

- Unlike many CEOs who put shareholders above everything, Anne Mulcahy decided to put employees and customers first. Why do you think she picked that alternative when it could generate conflict with the shareholders?
- Mulcahy could have declared bankruptcy for Xerox. Instead, she chose a hard program of cutting expenses and reassuring customers that the company would turn around. Why do you think she chose the alternative she did?

---

consequences and the fewest negative consequences. In other words, maximizing results in the greatest benefit at the lowest cost, with the largest expected total return. Maximizing requires searching thoroughly for a complete range of alternatives, carefully assessing each alternative, comparing one to another, and then choosing or creating the very best.

Satisficing is choosing the first option that is minimally acceptable or adequate. When you satisfice, you compare your choice against your goal, not against other options. Satisficing means that a search for alternatives stops at the first one that is okay. Commonly, people do not expend the time or energy to gather more information. Instead, they make the expedient decision based on readily available information.

Let's say you are purchasing new equipment, and your goal is to avoid spending too much money. You would be maximizing if you checked out all your options and their prices, and then bought the cheapest one that met your performance requirements. But you would be satisficing if you bought the first adequate option that was within your budget and failed to look for less expensive options.

Satisficing is sometimes a result of laziness; other times, there is no other known option because time is short, information is unavailable, or other constraints make maximizing impossible. When the consequences are not huge, satisficing can even be the ideal approach. But in other situations, when managers satisfice, they fail to consider important options. Returning to the earlier example of Accurate Perforating, when

satisficing

Choosing an option that is acceptable, although not necessarily the best or perfect.

the company's management initially addressed declining profits, they were satisficing; they assumed they should focus on cutting costs and failed to identify alternatives that would boost profits by investing in new markets where they could charge more.

Optimizing means that you achieve the best possible balance among several goals. Perhaps, in purchasing equipment, you are interested in quality and durability as well as price. So, instead of buying the cheapest piece of equipment that works, you buy the one with the best combination of attributes, even though there may be options that are better on the price criterion and others that are better on the quality and durability criteria. The same idea applies to achieving business goals: one marketing strategy could maximize sales, while a different strategy might maximize profit. An optimizing strategy is the one that achieves the best balance among multiple goals.

optimizing

Achieving the best possible balance among several goals.

Implementing the Decision

The decision-making process does not end once a choice is made. The chosen alternative must be implemented. Sometimes the people involved in making the choice must put it into effect. At other times, they delegate the responsibility for implementation to others, such as when a top management team changes a policy or operating procedure and has operational managers carry out the change.

Unfortunately, sometimes people make decisions but don't take action. Implementing may fail to occur when talking a lot is mistaken for doing a lot; if people just assume that a decision will "happen"; when people forget that merely making a decision changes nothing; when meetings, plans, and reports are seen as "actions," even if they have no effect on what people actually do; and if managers don't check to ensure that what was decided was actually done.[29]

Managers should plan implementation carefully. Adequate planning requires several steps:[30]

1. Determine how things will look when the decision is fully operational.
2. Chronologically order, perhaps with a flow diagram, the steps necessary to achieve a fully operational decision.
3. List the resources and activities required to implement each step.
4. Estimate the time needed for each step.
5. Assign responsibility for each step to specific individuals.

Decision makers should presume that things will *not* go smoothly during implementation. It is very useful to take a little extra time to *identify potential problems* and *identify potential opportunities* associated with implementation. Then you can take actions to prevent problems and also be ready to seize on unexpected opportunities. The following questions are useful:

What problems could this action cause?
What can we do to prevent the problems?
What unintended benefits or opportunities could arise?
How can we make sure they happen?
How can we be ready to act when the opportunities come?

Many of the chapters in this book are concerned with implementation issues: how to implement strategy, allocate resources, organize for results, lead and motivate people, manage change, and so on. View the chapters from that perspective, and learn as much as you can about how to implement properly.

Evaluating the Decision

The final stage in the decision-making process is evaluating the decision. It involves collecting information on how well the decision is working. Quantifiable goals—a 20 percent increase in sales, a 95 percent reduction in accidents, 100 percent on-time

It's easy to become so focused on maximizing on one goal that you lose sight of other important goals. You're optimizing if you make sure that no important result suffers too much, unnecessarily.

deliveries—can be set before the solution to the problem is implemented. Then objective data can be gathered to accurately determine the success or failure of the decision.

Decision evaluation is useful whether the conclusion is positive or negative. Feedback that suggests the decision is working implies that the decision should be continued and perhaps applied elsewhere in the organization. Negative feedback means that either (1) implementation will require more time, resources, effort, or thought or (2) the decision was a bad one.

If the decision appears inappropriate, it's back to the drawing board. Then the process cycles back to the first stage: (re)definition of the problem. The decision-making process begins anew, preferably with more information, new suggestions, and an approach that attempts to eliminate the mistakes made the first time around. This is the stage where Accurate Perforating finally began to see hope. When cost-cutting efforts could not keep the company ahead of the competition or in favor with the company's bank, general manager Aaron Kamins hired a consultant to guide him in identifying more alternatives and making more professional decisions about investment and marketing. This stage of the implementation showed Kamins that the company needed better-educated management, and he began taking executive education courses. Kamins realized that the advice he had received from the managers at the Semrow subsidiary—to invest in producing finished metal products—was wiser than he had realized. He arranged new financing to purchase modern equipment, hired salespeople, developed a Web site, and finally began to see profits from his improved decision making.[31]

The Best Decision

How can managers tell whether they have made the best decision? While nothing can guarantee a "best" decision, managers should at least be confident that they followed proper *procedures* that will yield the best possible decision under the circumstances. This means that the decision makers were appropriately vigilant in making the decision. **Vigilance** occurs when the decision makers carefully and conscientiously execute all six stages of decision making, including making provisions for implementation and evaluation.[32]

vigilance

A process in which a decision maker carefully executes all stages of decision making.

Author and CEO Luda Kopeikina says managers can learn to make better decisions by improving the processes they use. First, she says your decisions will get better if you learn to manage stress, get enough rest, and put distractions aside when you need to make important decisions. Next, you should define the consequences you are trying to achieve and make sure the data you gather match the goals for your decision. Along with this comes the vision of how your decision can play out when you implement it. Finally, you need to develop the strength of character to take responsibility for the consequences of your decision. Encourage debate so that you can see all the alternatives, but if you are the decision maker, you must eventually end the debate, exercise courage, and act on your responsibility as decision maker.[33]

Strong leadership and a vision of the future gave Greg Waldorf confidence to decide on a change in the face of great uncertainty. Waldorf, chief executive of the dating Web site eHarmony, believed the company needed to modify its advertising campaign. The problem, as Waldorf defined it, was that the company's ads, in which several people talked about their experience with the site, were meeting a previous need to explain what the site does. But by now most people had become familiar with what eHarmony does; to persuade new people to sign up, Waldorf believed, the company needed to connect with them on a more emotional level.

Waldorf determined that the best way to generate an emotional response would be with more in-depth examples. But as strongly as he felt, Waldorf also appreciated the risk

Melinda Miller opens her computer to show the eHarmony Web site at Stetson University in Celebration, Florida. Miller vouches for eHarmony where the 32- year-old middle school teacher completed her personality profile. Jack Stevison, an investment officer for a securities firm, submitted his profile the very next day. They met in person and were engaged within four months.

of abandoning an ad campaign that had worked well in favor of new advertisements that had no track record. Waldorf addressed the risk by first testing the new ads, in which one couple per ad talked about their dating relationship, and then airing the campaign first in Canada before moving into the larger U.S. market.

The initial response in Canada was so favorable that Waldorf considered bringing the new ad campaign to the United States ahead of schedule. He ran the idea past his chief operating officer, Greg Steiner, whose business judgment Waldorf values. Steiner agreed with the decision to move ahead, a reaction that helped Waldorf make the call to proceed.[34]

Even if managers reflect on their decision-making activities and conclude that they executed each step conscientiously, they still will not know whether the decision will work; after all, nothing guarantees a good outcome. But they *will* know that they did their best to make the best possible decision.

Barriers to Effective Decision Making

Vigilance and full execution of the six-stage decision-making process are the exception rather than the rule. But when managers use such rational processes, better decisions result.[35] Managers who make sure they engage in these processes are more effective.

Why don't people automatically invoke such rational processes? It is easy to neglect or improperly execute these processes. The problem may be improperly defined, or goals misidentified. Not enough solutions may be generated, or they may be evaluated incompletely. A satisficing rather than maximizing choice may be made. Implementation may be poorly planned or executed, or monitoring may be inadequate or nonexistent. And decisions are influenced by subjective psychological biases, time pressures, and social realities.

Psychological Biases

Decision makers are far from objective in the way they gather, evaluate, and apply information in making their choices. People have biases that interfere with objective rationality. The examples that follow represent only a few of the many documented subjective biases.[36]

The **illusion of control** is a belief that one can influence events even when one has no control over what will happen. Gambling is one example: Some people believe they have the skill to beat the odds, even though most of the time they cannot. In business, such overconfidence can lead to failure because decision makers ignore risks and fail to objectively evaluate the odds of success. In addition, they may believe they can do no wrong, or hold a general optimism about the future that can lead them to believe they are immune to risk and failure.[37] In addition, managers may overrate the value of their experience. They may believe that a previous project met its goals because of their decisions, so they can succeed by doing everything the same way on the next project. Rohit Girdhar admits that he held this type of bias until he tried a computer simulation that he assumed would confirm his skills as an experienced manager of software programmers. In the simulation, the workload increased and he hired more workers, as he had in his prior jobs. But the added workers weren't as productive as his experience told him they would be, and his project fell behind. Girdhar learned to question his assumptions before making decisions.[38]

Framing effects refer to how problems or decision alternatives are phrased or presented and how these subjective influences can override objective facts. In one example, managers indicated a desire to invest more money in a course of action that was reported to have a 70 percent chance of profit than in one said to have a 30 percent chance of loss.[39] The choices were equivalent in their chances of success; it was the way the options were framed that determined the managers' choices.

Managers may be quick to frame a problem as being similar to problems they have already handled, so they don't search for new alternatives. For example, when CEO Richard Fuld tackled financial problems at Lehman Brothers as the mortgage market tumbled, he assumed that the situation was much the same as when he had handled a previous financial crisis in the late 1990s. Unfortunately for Lehman Brothers, the recent crisis was far worse. In late 2008 the firm declared bankruptcy—the largest in U.S. history—helping to send global financial markets into a tailspin. Similarly, when the head of the operations center of the Department of Homeland Security prepared for Hurricane Katrina as it headed for New Orleans, he assumed the storm would be like Florida hurricanes he had prepared for in the past. As information came in, he focused on the data that fit his expectations, but Katrina turned out to be far more devastating.[40]

Often decision makers **discount the future.** That is, in their evaluation of alternatives, they weigh short-term costs and benefits more heavily than longer-term costs and benefits. Consider your own decision about whether to go for a dental checkup. The choice to go poses short-term financial costs, anxiety, and perhaps physical pain. The choice not to go will inflict even greater costs and more severe pain if dental problems worsen. How do you choose? Many people decide to avoid the short-term costs by not going for regular checkups, but end up facing much greater pain in the long run.

The same bias applies to students who don't study, weight watchers who sneak dessert or skip an exercise routine, and people who take the afternoon off to play golf when they really need to work. It can also affect managers who hesitate to invest funds in research and development programs that may not pay off until far into the future. In all these cases, the avoidance of short-term costs or the seeking of short-term rewards results in negative long-term consequences.

In contrast, when U.S. companies sacrifice present value to invest for the future—such as when Weyerhaeuser incurs enormous costs for its reforestation efforts that won't lead to harvest until 60 years in the future—it seems the exception rather than the rule. Discounting the future partly explains governmental budget deficits, environmental destruction, and decaying urban infrastructure.[41]

illusion of control

People's belief that they can influence events, even when they have no control over what will happen.

framing effects

A decision bias influenced by the way in which a problem or decision alternative is phrased or presented.

discounting the future

A bias weighting short-term costs and benefits more heavily than longer-term costs and benefits.

Time Pressures

In today's rapidly changing business environment, the premium is on acting quickly and keeping pace. The most conscientiously made business decisions can become irrelevant and even disastrous if managers take too long to make them.

How can managers make decisions quickly? Some natural tendencies, at least for North Americans, might be to skimp on analysis (not be too vigilant), suppress conflict, and make decisions on one's own without consulting other managers.[42] These strategies may speed up decision making, but they reduce decision *quality*. Carl Camden, CEO of Kelly Services, believed that rapid-fire decisions were the sign of a dynamic executive until he saw how this approach could hurt decision quality. In light of some early mistakes, Camden now believes the habit of fast decisions is related to the "trap of being all-knowing."[43]

In fact, the "speed trap" can be as dangerous as moving too slowly.[44] In an Internet start-up that went bankrupt, fast decisions initially helped the firm achieve its growth objectives. Early on, the founders did everything they could to create a sense of urgency: they planned a meeting to "light a fire under the company," calling it a "state-of-emergency address" with the purpose of creating "the idea of panic with an emerging deadline." Speed became more important than content. They failed to consider multiple alternatives, used little information, didn't fully acknowledge competing views, and didn't consult outside advisers. They never considered slowing down to be an option. This speed trap syndrome is a potential pathology for organizations under pressure to make fast decisions.

Can managers under time pressure make decisions that are timely and of high quality? A recent study of effective decision-making processes in microcomputer firms—a high-tech, fast-paced industry—revealed the tactics that such companies use.[45] First, instead of relying on old data, long-range planning, and futuristic forecasts, they focus on *real-time information:* current information obtained with little or no time delay. For example, they constantly monitor daily operating measures like work in process rather than checking periodically the traditional accounting-based indicators such as profitability.

Second, they *involve people more effectively and efficiently* in the decision-making process. They rely heavily on trusted experts, and this yields both good advice and the confidence to act quickly despite uncertainty. They also take a *realistic view of conflict:* They value differing opinions, but they know that if disagreements are not resolved, the top executive must make the final choice in the end. Slow-moving firms, in contrast, are stymied by conflict. Like the fast-moving firms they seek consensus, but when disagreements persist, they fail to come to a decision.

> ✓ You'll feel pressure to make quick decisions, but then it becomes easier to make mistakes. Fortunately, you can be vigilant while moving quickly, and you can avoid the "speed trap."

Social Realities

Many decisions are made by a group rather than by an individual manager. In slow-moving firms, interpersonal factors decrease decision-making effectiveness. Even the manager acting alone is accountable to the boss and to others and must consider the preferences and reactions of many people. Important managerial decisions are marked by conflict among interested parties. Therefore, many decisions are the result of intensive social interactions, bargaining, and politicking.

The remainder of this chapter focuses on the social context of decisions, including decision making in groups and the realities of decision making in organizations.

Decision Making in Groups

LO 4

Sometimes a manager finds it necessary to convene a group of people for the purpose of making an important decision. Some advise that in today's complex business environment, significant problems should *always* be tackled by groups.[46] As a result, managers must understand how groups operate and how to use them to improve decision making. You will learn much more about how groups work later in the book.

The basic philosophy behind using a group to make decisions is captured by the adage "two heads are better than one." But is this statement really valid? Yes, it is—potentially.

If enough time is available, groups usually make higher-quality decisions than most individuals acting alone. However, groups often are inferior to the *best* individual.[47]

How well the group performs depends on how effectively it capitalizes on the potential advantages and minimizes the potential problems of using a group. Table 3.2 summarizes these issues.

Potential Advantages of Using a Group

If other people have something to contribute, using groups to make a decision offers at least five potential advantages:[48]

1. More *information* is available when several people are making the decision. If one member doesn't have all the facts or the pertinent expertise, another member might.
2. A greater number of *perspectives* on the issues, or different *approaches* to solving the problem, are available. The problem may be new to one group member but familiar to another. Or the group may need to consider other viewpoints— financial, legal, marketing, human resources, and so on—to achieve an optimal solution.
3. Group discussion provides an opportunity for *intellectual stimulation*. It can get people thinking and unleash their creativity to a far greater extent than would be possible with individual decision making.

These three potential advantages of using a group improve the odds that a more fully informed, higher-quality decision will result. Thus, managers should involve people with different backgrounds, perspectives, and access to information. They should not involve only their cronies who think the same way they do.

4. People who participate in a group discussion are more likely to *understand* why the decision was made. They will have heard the relevant arguments both for the chosen alternative and against the rejected alternatives.
5. Group discussion typically leads to a higher level of *commitment* to the decision. Buying into the proposed solution translates into high motivation to ensure that it is executed well.

The last two advantages improve the chances that the decision will be implemented successfully. Therefore, managers should involve the people who will be responsible for implementing the decision as early in the deliberations as possible.

Potential Problems of Using a Group

Things *can* go wrong when groups make decisions. Most of the potential problems concern the process through which group members interact with one another:[49]

1. Sometimes one group member *dominates* the discussion. When this occurs— such as when a strong leader makes his or her preferences clear—the result is

Using a group may seem to slow down decision making. If one person dominates the discussion, it may feel like you're speeding up the decision making. But one dominant person reduces decision quality, and most of you will have wasted your time.

Potential Advantages	Potential Disadvantages
1. Larger pool of information.	1. One person dominates.
2. More perspectives and approaches.	2. Satisficing.
3. Intellectual stimulation.	3. Groupthink.
4. People understand the decision.	4. Goal displacement.
5. People are committed to the decision.	

TABLE 3.2

Pros and Cons of Using a Group to Make Decisions

Keeping focus on the goal is critical for team members, even when there are conflicting viewpoints.

groupthink

A phenomenon that occurs in decision making when group members avoid disagreement as they strive for consensus.

goal displacement

A condition that occurs when a decision-making group loses sight of its original goal and a new, less important goal emerges.

the same as it would be if the dominant individual made the decision alone. Individual dominance has two disadvantages. First, the dominant person does not necessarily have the most valid opinions—and may even have the most unsound ideas. Second, even if that person's preference leads to a good decision, convening as a group will have been a waste of everyone else's time.

2. *Satisficing* is more likely with groups. Most people don't like meetings and will do what they can to end them. This may include criticizing members who want to continue exploring new and better alternatives. The result is a satisficing rather than an optimizing or maximizing decision.

3. *Pressure to avoid disagreement* can lead to a phenomenon called *groupthink*. **Groupthink** occurs when people choose not to disagree or raise objections because they don't want to break up a positive team spirit. Some groups want to think as one, tolerate no dissension, and strive to remain cordial. Such groups are overconfident, complacent, and perhaps too willing to take risks. Pressure to go along with the group's preferred solution stifles creativity and the other behaviors characteristic of vigilant decision making.

4. *Goal displacement* often occurs in groups. The goal of group members should be to come up with the best possible solution to the problem. But when **goal displacement** occurs, new goals emerge to replace the original ones. It is common for two or more group members to have different opinions and present their conflicting cases. Attempts at rational persuasion become heated disagreement. Winning the argument becomes the new goal. Saving face and defeating the other person's idea become more important than solving the problem.

Effective managers pay close attention to the group process; they manage it carefully. You have just read about the pros and cons of using a group to make decisions, and you are about to read *how* to manage the group's decision-making process. Chapter 12, on leadership, helps you decide *when* to use groups to make decisions.

Managing Group Decision Making

LO 5   As Figure 3.3 illustrates, effectively managing group decision making has three requirements: (1) an appropriate leadership style, (2) the constructive use of disagreement and conflict, and (3) the enhancement of creativity.

Leadership Style

The leader of a decision-making body must attempt to minimize process-related problems. The leader should avoid dominating the discussion or allowing another individual to dominate. Less vocal group members should be encouraged to air their opinions and suggestions, and all members should be asked for dissenting viewpoints.

At the same time, the leader should not allow the group to pressure people into conforming. The leader should be alert to the dangers of groupthink and satisficing. Also, she should be attuned to indications that group members are losing sight of the primary objective: to come up with the best possible solution to the problem.

These suggestions have two implications. First, don't lose sight of the problem. Second, make a decision! Slow-moving organizations whose group members can't come to an agreement will be standing still while their competitors move ahead.

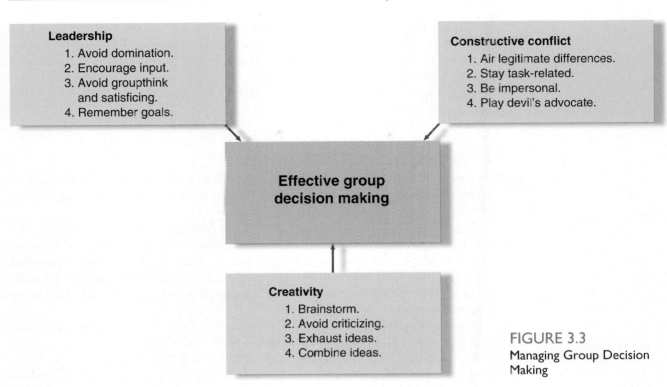

FIGURE 3.3
Managing Group Decision Making

Constructive Conflict

Total and consistent agreement among group members can be destructive. It can lead to groupthink, uncreative solutions, and a waste of the knowledge and diverse viewpoints that individuals bring to the group. Therefore, a certain amount of *constructive* conflict should exist.[50] Some companies, including United Parcel Service, take steps to ensure that conflict and debate are generated within their management teams.[51]

The most constructive type of conflict is **cognitive conflict,** or differences in perspectives or judgments about issues. In contrast, **affective conflict** is emotional and directed at other people. Affective conflict is likely to be destructive to the group because it can lead to anger, bitterness, goal displacement, and lower-quality decisions. Cognitive conflict, in contrast, can air legitimate differences of opinion and develop better ideas and problem solutions. Conflict, then, should be task related rather than personal.[52] But even task-related conflict can hurt performance;[53] disagreement is good only when managed properly.

Conflict can be generated formally through structured processes.[54] Two techniques that purposely program cognitive conflict into the decision-making process are devil's advocacy and the dialectic method.

A **devil's advocate** has the job of criticizing ideas. The group leader can formally assign people to play this role. Requiring people to point out problems can lessen inhibitions about disagreeing and make the conflict less personal and emotional.

An alternative to devil's advocacy is the dialectic. The **dialectic** goes a step beyond devil's advocacy by requiring a structured debate between two conflicting courses of action.[55] The philosophy of the dialectic stems from Plato and Aristotle, who advocated synthesizing the conflicting views of a thesis and an antithesis. Structured debates between plans and counterplans can be useful prior to making a strategic decision. For example, one team might present the case for acquiring a firm while another team advocates not making the acquisition.

Constructive conflict does not need to be generated on such a formal basis and is not solely the leader's responsibility. Any team member can introduce cognitive

cognitive conflict

Issue-based differences in perspectives or judgments.

affective conflict

Emotional disagreement directed toward other people.

devil's advocate

A person who has the job of criticizing ideas to ensure that their downsides are fully explored.

dialectic

A structured debate comparing two conflicting courses of action.

conflict by being honest with opinions, by being unafraid to disagree with others, by pushing the group to action if it is taking too long or making the group slow down if necessary, and by advocating long-term considerations if the group is too focused on short-term results. Introducing constructive conflict is a legitimate and necessary responsibility of all group members interested in improving the group's decision-making effectiveness.

Encouraging Creativity

LO 6

As you've already learned, ready-made solutions to a problem can be inadequate or unavailable. In such cases, custom-made solutions are necessary, so the group must be creative in generating ideas.

Some have said we are in the midst of the next great business revolution: the "creative revolution."[56] Said to transcend the agricultural, industrial, and information revolutions, the most fundamental unit of value in the creativity revolution is ideas. Creativity is more than just an option; it is essential to survival. Allowing people to be creative may be one of the manager's most important and challenging responsibilities.

You might be saying to yourself, "I'm not creative." But even if you are not an artist or a musician, you do have potential to be creative in countless other ways. You are being creative if you (1) bring a new thing into being (*creation*); (2) join two previously unrelated things (*synthesis*); or (3) improve something or give it a new application (*modification*). You don't need to be a genius in school either—Thomas Edison and Albert Einstein were not particularly good students. Nor does something need to change the world to be creative; the "little things" can always be done in new, creative ways that add value to the product and the customer.

How do you "get" creative?[57] Recognize the almost infinite "little" opportunities to be creative. Assume you can be creative if you give it a try. Escape from work once in a while. Read widely, and try new experiences. Take a course or find a good book about creative thought processes; plenty are available. And be aware that creativity is social; your creativity will be affected by your social relationships at work, including your connections with other people outside your immediate close network.[58] Talk to people, often, about the issues and ideas with which you are wrestling.

> "I invented nothing new. I simply assembled into a car the discoveries of other men behind whom were centuries of work."
>
> Henry Ford

How do you "get" creativity out of other people?[59] Give creative efforts the credit they are due, and don't punish creative failures. Avoid extreme time pressure, if possible.[60] Stimulate and challenge people intellectually. Listen to employees' ideas, and allow enough time to explore different ideas. Put together groups of people with different styles of thinking and behaving. Get your people in touch with customers, and let them bounce ideas around. Protect your people from managers who demand immediate payoffs, who don't understand the importance of creative contributions, or who try to take credit for others' successes. And strive to be creative yourself—you'll set a good example.

The bottom line

Innovation

Most creative ideas come, not from the lone genius in the basement laboratory, but from people talking and working together.

People are likely to be more creative if they believe they are capable, if they know that their coworkers expect creativity, and if they believe that their employer values creativity.[61] As a manager, you can do much to help employees develop these beliefs by how you listen, what you allow, and what you reward and punish. At a large consumer products company, management signals that it values creativity by inviting managers to post stories on the company's intranet about ideas their employees have suggested and the results of implementation. The company also awards "innovation bonuses" linked to how these innovations have benefited the organization.[62]

At Miron Construction Company, Theresa Lehman fosters creative thinking about sustainability—the effort to minimize the use of resources, especially those that are polluting and nonrenewable. Besides helping clients plan more sustainable buildings, Lehman, the director of sustainability at the Neenah, Wisconsin, building contractor, helps Miron itself operate more sustainably.

Lehman defines the problem—or opportunity—of running a sustainable construction company as one that extends beyond a building's features. Rather, all efforts to reduce waste contribute to sustainability. Says Lehman, "Everyone needs to focus on doing things more effectively and efficiently by reducing resources and eliminating waste." She seeks ideas from all employees and ensures that every idea receives careful consideration. For example, an employee suggested switching from paper paychecks to direct deposit for all employees. Besides saving paper, that change cuts printing and postage expenses. By taking ideas seriously and then communicating the practical benefits, Lehman reinforces the value of sustainability.

Lehman is ready with plenty of examples about the financial soundness of sustainability. For example, as Miron adds to and renovates its own headquarters, it is installing geothermal heating and cooling, which will pay for itself in five years, and it is replacing interior lights with LED bulbs that are expected to save about $12,000 in energy costs over the life of the bulbs. With benefits like these, it's no wonder that Lehman has been able to make sustainability a widely shared value at Miron.[63]

Brainstorming

A common technique used to elicit creative ideas is brainstorming. In **brainstorming,** group members generate as many ideas about a problem as they can. As the ideas are presented, they are posted so that everyone can read them, and people can use the ideas as building blocks. The group is encouraged to say anything that comes to mind, with one exception: No criticism of other people or their ideas is allowed.

In the proper brainstorming environment—free of criticism—people are less inhibited and more likely to voice their unusual, creative, or even wild ideas. By the time people have exhausted their ideas, a long list of alternatives has been generated. Only then does the group turn to the evaluation stage. At that point, many different ideas can be considered, modified, or combined into a creative, custom-made solution to the problem.

Brainstorming is a technique used to generate as many ideas as possible to solve a problem. You have probably engaged in brainstorming sessions for various class or work projects.

brainstorming

A process in which group members generate as many ideas about a problem as they can; criticism is withheld until all ideas have been proposed.

Brainstorming isn't necessarily as effective as some people think. Sometimes in a brainstorming session people are inhibited and anxious, they conform to others' ideas, they set low standards, and they engage in noncreative behaviors including cocktail party-type conversations—complimenting one another, repeating ideas, telling stories—that are nice but don't promote creativity. Fortunately, there are techniques that help, including brainwriting (taking time to silently write down ideas), using trained facilitators, setting high performance goals, brainstorming electronically so that people aren't competing for air time, and even building a playground with fun elements that can foster creativity.[64]

Organizational Decision Making

LO 7

Individuals and groups make decisions constantly, throughout every organization. To understand decision making in organizations, a manager must consider (1) the constraints decision makers face, (2) organizational decision processes, and (3) decision making during a crisis.

Constraints on Decision Makers

The bottom line

Innovation

You may be an innovator if you come up with a creative idea. But you're not yet, until you implement it.

Organizations—or, more accurately, the people who make important decisions—cannot do whatever they wish. They face various constraints—financial, legal, market, human, and organizational—that inhibit certain actions. Capital or product markets may make an expensive new venture impossible. Legal restrictions may constrain the kinds of international business activities in which a firm can participate. Labor unions may defeat a contract proposed by management, and managers and investors may block a takeover attempt. Even brilliant ideas must take into account the practical matters of implementation.[65]

Suppose you have a great idea that will provide a revolutionary service for your bank's customers. You won't be able to put your idea into action immediately. You will have to sell it to the people who can give you the go-ahead and also to those whose help you will need to carry out the project. You might start by convincing your boss of your idea's merit. Next, the two of you may have to hash it out with a vice president. Then maybe the president has to be sold. At each stage, you must listen to these individuals' opinions and suggestions and often incorporate them into your original concept. Ultimately, you will have to derive a proposal acceptable to others.

In addition, ethical and legal considerations must be thought out carefully. Decision makers must consider ethics and the preferences of many constituent groups—the realities of life in organizations. You will have plenty of opportunity to think about ethical issues in Chapter 5.

bounded rationality

A less-than-perfect form of rationality in which decision makers cannot be perfectly rational because decisions are complex and complete information is unavailable or cannot be fully processed.

Models of Organizational Decision Processes

Just as with individuals and groups, organizational decision making historically was described with rational models like the one depicted earlier in Figure 3.2. But Nobel laureate Herbert Simon challenged the rational model and proposed an important alternative called *bounded rationality*. According to Simon's **bounded rationality,** decision makers cannot be truly rational because (1) they have imperfect, incomplete information about alternatives and consequences; (2) the problems they face are so complex; (3) human beings simply cannot process all the information to which they are exposed; (4) there is not enough time to process all relevant information fully; and (5) people, including managers within the same firm, have conflicting goals.

incremental model

Model of organizational decision making in which major solutions arise through a series of smaller decisions.

When these conditions hold—and they do for most consequential managerial decisions—perfect rationality will give way to more biased, subjective, messier decision processes. For example, the **incremental model** of decision making occurs when decision makers make small decisions, take little steps, move cautiously, and move in piecemeal fashion toward a bigger solution. The classic example is the budget process, which traditionally begins with the budget from the previous period and makes incremental decisions from that starting point.

coalitional model

Model of organizational decision making in which groups with differing preferences use power and negotiation to influence decisions.

The **coalitional model** of decision making arises when people disagree on goals or compete with one another for resources. The decision process becomes political, as groups of individuals band together and try collectively to influence the decision. Two or more coalitions form, each representing a different preference, and each tries to use power and negotiations to sway the decision.

Organizational politics, in which people try to influence organizational decisions so that their own interests will be served, can reduce decision-making effectiveness.[66] One of the best ways to reduce such politics, and to make sure that constructive cognitive conflict does not degenerate into affective conflict, is to *create common goals* for members of the team—that is, make the decision-making process a collaborative, rather than a competitive, exercise by establishing a goal around which the group can rally. In one study, top management teams with stated goals like "build the biggest financial war chest" for an upcoming competitive battle, or "create *the* computer firm of the decade," or "build the best damn machine on the market" were less likely to have dysfunctional conflict and politics between members.[67] On a personal level, if you find yourself in a conflict, you and your adversary may be focused on the wrong goals. Work to find common ground in the form of an important goal that you both want to achieve.

The **garbage can model** of decision making occurs when people aren't sure of their goals, or disagree about the goals, and likewise are unsure of or in disagreement about what to do. This situation occurs because some problems are so complex that they are not well understood and also because decision makers move in and out of the decision process because they have so many other things to attend to as well. This model implies that some decisions are chaotic and almost random. You can see that this is a dramatic departure from rationality in decision making.

garbage can model

Model of organizational decision making depicting a chaotic process and seemingly random decisions.

Decision Making in a Crisis

LO 8

In crises, managers must make decisions under a great deal of pressure.[68] You may know some of the most famous recent crises: the explosion of BP's oil refinery in Texas, the devastation of hurricanes along the Gulf Coast, the sickening of people by tainted peanuts, and the recent economic crisis discussed in the "From the Pages of *BusinessWeek*" feature.

Managing Through a Crisis: The New Rules

FROM THE PAGES OF

BusinessWeek

In times of turmoil, opportunities abound. All managers must do is keep their companies afloat, their eyes peeled for openings, and their bearings—as the old rules wash away. What do Carnegie Steel and Hewlett-Packard (*HPQ*) have in common? Both were born at a time when people thought the world was falling apart. Andrew Carnegie launched his first steel mill during the Panic of 1873, the start of a long depression. He took advantage of low costs to build an industrial giant that made him the world's richest man. Bill Hewlett and Dave Packard showed similar courage when they launched HP from a Palo Alto (Calif.) garage toward the end of the Great Depression.

History has shown that crisis breeds opportunity. Business leaders may have to cut costs to survive 2009, but the smart ones are also out there looking for prospects. They are willing to take the type of bold move that IBM (*IBM*) made during the recessionary days of 1981 when CEO John R. Opel aggressively rolled out the company's landmark personal computer just as PC demand soared. Even in the current downturn, there are companies like AT&T (*T*), which recently announced plans to buy two companies for a total of $1.2 billion. "A recession creates winners and losers just like a boom," observes Mauro F. Guillen, a professor of international management at the University of Pennsylvania's Wharton School.

Managers are now dealing with everything from shattered consumer confidence to tighter credit, not to mention the likelihood of a tougher regulatory environment. Decisions that made sense two years ago may prove disastrous in this climate—from giving outsize rewards to those who take big risks to borrowing heavily just because interest rates are low. Years of excessive borrowing have taken a toll: An unprecedented two-thirds of nonfinancial American companies covered by Standard & Poor's have speculative-grade, or junk-rated, debt. (S&P, like *BusinessWeek*, is a unit of The McGraw-Hill Companies (*MHP*).) On the whole, U.S. businesses face a $238 billion wave of debt maturities that will come due by the end of 2009.

http://www.businessweek.com/magazine/content/09_03/b4116030884620.htm

SOURCE: E. Thornton, "Managing through a Crisis: The New Rules," *BusinessWeek*, January 19, 2009, p. 30.

TABLE 3.3
Two Disasters

Union Carbide	Johnson & Johnson
Failed to identify as a crisis the public perception that the company was a negligent, uncaring killer.	Identified the crisis of public perception that Tylenol was unsafe and J&J was not in control.

No planning before reacting:
 	
  CEO immediately went to India to inspect damage.
 	
  All executives involved.
	Planned before reacting:
	
	  CEO picked one executive to head crisis team.
	
	  Rest of company involved only on a need-to-know basis.

Set no goals.	Set goals to:
	
	  Stop the killings.
	
	  Find reasons for the killings.
	
	  Provide assistance to the victims.
	
	  Restore Tylenol's credibility.

Action: Damage control/stonewalling.
 	
  Distanced itself.
 	
  Misrepresented safety conditions.
 	
  Did not inform spokespeople.
 	
  Adopted bunker mentality.
	Action: Gave complete information.
	
	  Worked with authorities.
	
	  Pulled Tylenol from shelves (first-year cost: $150 million).
	
	  Used strong marketing program.
	
	  Reissued Tylenol with tamper-proof packaging.

Chronic problems continued:
 	
  Public confidence low.
 	
  Costly litigation.
 	
  No formal crisis plan resulted.
	Crisis resolved:
	
	  Public confidence high.
	
	  Sales high again.
	
	  Well-documented crisis management plan.

In two famous cases from the past, Union Carbide's gas leak in Bhopal, India, killed thousands of people, and several people were killed in the cyanide poisonings using Johnson & Johnson's Tylenol. As outlined in Table 3.3, Union Carbide and J&J handled their crises in very different ways. Today, J&J is still known for its effective handling of the crisis, as outlined in the table.

Information technology is a new arena for a crisis. Businesses, homes, government agencies, hospitals, and other organizations send critical information through the Internet and private networks around the clock, and any technical failure—sometimes accidental, sometimes maliciously intentional— could be magnified by the speed and widespread use of information technology. One vulnerable area is the electrical grid, which links utilities and carries power to each user. Information technology systems allow utility employees to control the grid remotely. Recently, information came to light that hackers have gained access to the U.S. electrical grid, leaving behind computer programs that theoretically would permit them to interfere with the grid's operations.[69] Such programs can be purged, but the biggest challenge is preventing or catching each attempt to gain unauthorized access to the system.

The response to IT-related crises must involve senior-level executives in online communication, both to protect the firm's reputation and to communicate with outside experts, news sources, and key external and internal stakeholders. Managers can use IT to monitor and respond immediately to problems including scandals, boycotts, rumors, cyber attacks, and other crises.[70]

Although many companies don't concern themselves with crisis management, it is imperative that it be on management's agenda. An effective plan for crisis management (CM) should include the following elements.[71]

1. *Strategic actions* such as integrating CM into strategic planning and official policies.
2. *Technical and structural actions* such as creating a CM team and dedicating a budget to CM.
3. *Evaluation and diagnostic actions* such as conducting audits of threats and liabilities, and establishing tracking systems for early warning signals.
4. *Communication actions* such as providing training for dealing with the media, local communities, and police and government officials.
5. *Psychological and cultural actions* such as showing a strong top management commitment to CM and providing training and psychological support services regarding the human and emotional impacts of crises.

Ultimately, management should be able to answer the following questions:[72]

What kinds of crises could your company face?
Can your company detect a crisis in its early stages?
How will it manage a crisis if one occurs?
How can it benefit from a crisis after it has passed?

The last question makes an important point: A crisis, managed effectively, can have *benefits*. For example, Hurricanes Katrina and Rita devastated businesses along the Gulf Coast, but some managers were able to respond effectively. Michael de la Houssaye, who with his father runs the C&D Agency, which serves the electricity distribution industry, set up a new office and as soon as possible began communicating with clients via e-mail. As you can imagine, demand for generators and other equipment was enormous in the months following the storm. De la Houssaye took advantage of the demand to shift the focus to selling generators, rather than meeting with clients to discuss new products. More important, perhaps, the agency switched from paper documents to electronic order processing and communications, which yielded greater efficiency. "We're operating here better than I think we were before the hurricane," de la Houssaye concluded.[73]

Thus, with effective crisis management, old as well as new problems can be resolved, new strategies and competitive advantages may appear, and positive change can emerge. And if someone steps in and manages the crisis well, a hero is born. The view that Xerox was floundering, perhaps even near bankruptcy, is one reason that observers are so impressed with Anne Mulcahy's decisions, which turned the company around, as described in the "Management Close-Up: Assessing Outcomes and Seizing Opportunities" feature.

As a leader during a crisis, don't pretend that nothing happened (as did managers at one firm after a visitor died in the hallway despite employees' efforts to save him).[74] Communicate and reinforce the organization's values. Try to find ways for people to support one another, and remember that people will take cues from your behavior. You should be optimistic but brutally honest. Show emotion, but not fear. "You have to be cooler than cool," says Gene Krantz of Apollo 13 ground control fame. But don't ignore the problems or downplay them and reassure too much; don't create false hopes. Give people the bad news straight—you'll gain credibility, and when the good news comes, it will really mean something.

An aerial infrared image of a wildfire area is displayed in the background as California Governor Arnold Schwarzenegger, state fire officials, and NASA employees team up to address the wildfire crisis. This crisis management team met to discuss the important role of NASA's remotely piloted aircraft, named Ikhana. The unmanned aircraft carrying a NASA infrared scanning sensor flew over much of the state gathering information that was delivered to fire commanders in the field, helping them to understand the terrain and behavior of the state's most dangerous fires.

Management Close-Up

ASSESSING OUTCOMES AND SEIZING OPPORTUNITIES

As CEO of a floundering company, Anne Mulcahy had to make hard choices. She closed divisions, eliminated 34,000 jobs, and trimmed billions in expenses. Mulcahy believes companies in crisis need leaders to make speedy decisions, and she claims that "speed trumps perfection." Inaction, when action is needed, she says, is often worse than doing the wrong thing.

With her team, Mulcahy restored Xerox to profitability. The company paid its debts. Revenues are rising, and the company recently hit $1 billion in net profit. In addition, the stock dividend has been restored.

Mulcahy's turnaround strategy emphasized communication and teamwork, and the belief that Xerox would survive only if it made a long-term commitment to innovation. Under Mulcahy, Xerox has stepped up research and development funding, investing nearly $1 billion a year and filling the pipeline with new technologies. Since 2005, the company has introduced 100 new products. Reflecting the spirit of a revived Xerox, the company redesigned its decades-old logo with a lively new one. The logo is a physical symbol of the company's rebirth.

Today, Xerox is moving to an all-color world, where users can print customized work on demand. It is also making strides in digital technologies, helping customers put their records on digital files. Xerox also wants customers to print less. Erasable paper, invented by Xerox, allows users to program what's printed on the sheet to disappear within 24 hours, enabling repeated reuse and eliminating waste.

Anne Mulcahy's brand of tough love seems to have worked. Recently ranked number 10 on *Forbes*'s list of the 100 most powerful women and named CEO of the Year by *CEO Magazine*, she masterminded the plan that pulled Xerox back from the brink.[75]

- Instead of declaring bankruptcy, Mulcahy met with key leaders, employees, and customers to enlist their help in turning the company around. What are the potential advantages and disadvantages to making such group decisions?
- Mulcahy could have focused solely on cost cutting and increasing profits for existing products. How does her decision to invest in research and development demonstrate leadership and creativity in decision making?

KEY TERMS

Affective conflict,   p. 101

Bounded rationality,   p. 104

Brainstorming,   p. 103

Certainty,   p. 87

Coalitional model,   p. 104

Cognitive conflict,   p. 101

Conflict,   p. 88

Contingency plans,   p. 92

Custom-made solutions,   p. 90

Devil's advocate,   p. 101

Dialectic,   p. 101

Discounting the future,   p. 97

Framing effects,   p. 97

Garbage can model,   p. 105

Goal displacement,   p. 100

Groupthink,   p. 100

Illusion of control,   p. 97

Incremental model,   p. 104

Maximizing,   p. 92

Nonprogrammed decisions, p. 87

Optimizing,   p. 94

Programmed decisions,   p. 87

Ready-made solutions,   p. 90

Risk,   p. 88

Satisficing,   p. 93

Uncertainty,   p. 87

Vigilance,   p. 95

SUMMARY OF LEARNING OBJECTIVES

Now that you have studied Chapter 3, you should be able to:

LO 1   Describe the kinds of decisions you will face as a manager.

Most important managerial decisions are ill structured and characterized by uncertainty, risk, and conflict. Yet managers are expected to make rational decisions in the face of these challenges.

LO 2   Summarize the steps in making "rational" decisions.

The ideal decision-making process involves six stages. The first, identifying and diagnosing the problem (or opportunity), requires recognizing a discrepancy between the current state and a desired state and then delving below surface symptoms to uncover the underlying causes of the problem. The second stage, generating alternative solutions, requires adopting ready-made or designing custom-made solutions. The third, evaluating alternatives, means predicting the consequences of different alternatives, sometimes through building scenarios of the future. Fourth, a solution is chosen; the solution might maximize, satisfice, or optimize. Fifth, people implement the decision; this stage requires more careful planning than it often receives. Finally, managers should evaluate how well the decision is working. This means gathering objective, valid information about the impact the decision is having. If the evidence suggests the problem is not getting solved, either a better decision or a better implementation plan must be developed.

LO 3 Recognize the pitfalls you should avoid when making decisions.

Situational and human limitations lead most decision makers to satisfice rather than maximize. Psychological biases, time pressures, and the social realities of organizational life may prevent rational execution of the six decision-making stages. But vigilance and an understanding of how to manage decision-making groups and organizational constraints will improve the process and result in better decisions.

LO 4 Evaluate the pros and cons of using a group to make decisions.

Advantages of using groups include more information, perspectives, and approaches brought to bear on problem solving; intellectual stimulation; greater understanding by all of the final decision; and higher commitment to the decision once it is made. Potential dangers or disadvantages of using groups include individual domination of discussions, satisficing, groupthink, and goal displacement.

LO 5 Identify procedures to use in leading a decision-making group.

Effective leaders in decision-making teams avoid dominating the discussion; encourage people's input; avoid groupthink and satisficing; and stay focused on the group's goals. They encourage constructive conflict via devil's advocacy and the dialectic, posing opposite sides of an issue or solutions to a problem. They also encourage creativity through a variety of techniques.

LO 6 Explain how to encourage creative decisions.

When creative ideas are needed, leaders should set a good example by being creative themselves. They should recognize the almost infinite "little" opportunities for creativity and have confidence in their own creative abilities. They can inspire creativity in others by pushing for creative freedom, rewarding creativity, and not punishing creative failures. They should encourage interaction with customers, stimulate discussion, and protect people from managers who might squelch the creative process. Brainstorming is one of the most popular techniques for generating creative ideas.

LO 7 Discuss the processes by which decisions are made in organizations.

Decision making in organizations is often a highly complex process. Individuals and groups are constrained by a variety of factors and constituencies. In practice, decision makers are boundedly rational rather than purely rational. Some decisions are made on an incremental basis. Coalitions form to represent different preferences. The process is often chaotic, as depicted in the garbage can model. Politics can also enter the process, decisions are negotiated, and crises come and go.

LO 8 Describe how to make decisions in a crisis.

Crisis conditions make sound, effective decision making more difficult. However, it is possible for crises to be managed well. A strategy for crisis management can be developed beforehand, and the mechanisms readied, so that if crises do arise, decision makers are prepared.

DISCUSSION QUESTIONS

1. Discuss Xerox Corporation in terms of risk, uncertainty, and how its managers handled the company's problems. What is the current news on this company?

2. Identify some risky decisions you have made. Why did you take the risks? How did they work out? Looking back, what did you learn?

3. Identify a decision you made that had important unexpected consequences. Were the consequences good, bad, or both? Should you, and could you, have done anything differently in making the decision?

4. What effects does time pressure have on your decision making? In what ways do you handle it well and not so well?

5. Recall a recent decision that you had difficulty making. Describe it in terms of the characteristics of managerial decisions.

6. What do you think are some advantages and disadvantages to using computer technology in decision making?

7. Do you think that when managers make decisions they follow the decision-making steps as presented in this chapter? Which steps are apt to be overlooked or given inadequate attention? What can people do to make sure they do a more thorough job?

8. Discuss the potential advantages and disadvantages of using a group to make decisions. Give examples from your experience.

9. Suppose you are the CEO of a major corporation and one of your company's oil tanks has ruptured, spilling thousands of gallons of oil into a river that empties into the ocean. What do you need to do to handle the crisis?

10. Identify some problems you want to solve. Brainstorm with others a variety of creative solutions.

CONCLUDING CASE

The Wallingford Bowling Center

A group of 12 lifelong friends put together $1,200,000 of their own funds and built a $6,000,000, 48-lane bowling alley, near Norfolk, Virginia. Two of the investors became employees of the corporation. Ned Flanders works full-time as General Manager, and James Ahmad, a licensed CPA, serves as Controller on a part-time basis.

The beautiful, modern-day facility features a multilevel spacious interior with three rows of 16 lanes on two separate levels of the building, a full-service bar, a small restaurant, a game room (pool, videogames, pinball), and two locker rooms. The facility sits on a spacious lot with plenty of parking and room to grow.

The bowling center is located in the small blue-collar town of Wallingford. There is no direct competition within the town. The surrounding communities include a wide-ranging mix of ethnic groups, professionals, middle- to upper-middle-class private homes, and apartment and condominium complexes ranging from singles to young married couples to senior citizen retirement units. Nearly 200,000 people live within 15 miles of Wallingford.

The bowling center is open 24 hours per day and has a staff of 27 part- and full-time employees. After four years of operation, the partners find themselves frustrated with the low profit performance of the business. While sales are covering expenses, the partners are not happy with the end-of-year profit-sharing pool. The most recent income statement follows:

Sales	$1,844,000
CGS	315,000
GM	1,529,000
Operating expenses	1,466,000
Mortgage	460,000
Depreciation	95,000
Utilities	188,000
Maintenance	70,000
Payroll	490,000
Supplies	27,000
Insurance	136,000
Taxable income	63,000
Taxes	19,000
Net income	$ 44,000

The bowling center operates at 100 percent capacity on Sunday through Thursday nights from 6:00 p.m. until midnight. Two sets of men's leagues come and go on each of those nights, occupying each lane with mostly five-person teams. Bowlers from each league consistently spend money at both the bar and restaurant. In fact, the men's leagues combine to generate about 60 percent of total current sales.

The bowling center operates at about 50 percent capacity on Friday and Saturday nights and on Saturday morning. The Friday and Saturday "open bowling" nights include mostly teenagers, young couples, and league members who come to practice in groups of two or three. The Saturday morning group is a kids' league, ages 10 through 14.

There are four ladies leagues that bowl on Monday and Wednesday afternoons.

Business is extremely slow at the bowling center on Monday through Friday and Sunday mornings, and on the afternoons of Tuesday, Thursday, Friday, Saturday, and Sunday. It is not uncommon to have just three or four lanes in operation during those time periods.

The owners have taken a close look at the cost side of their business as a way to improve profitability. They concluded that while the total operating expense of $1,466,000 might appear to be high, there was in fact little room for expense cutting.

At a recent meeting of the partners, James Ahmad reported on the results of his three-month-long investigation into the operating cost side of other bowling alleys and discovered that the Wallingford Bowling Center was very much in keeping with their industry. James went on to report that bowling alleys were considered to be "heavy fixed cost operations" and that the key to success and profitability lies in maximizing capacity and sales dollars.

QUESTIONS

1. Apply the decision-making process described in the chapter to this case. What is the major problem facing Wallingford? List five specific alternative solutions that could be implemented to solve that major problem.

2. As general manager of this company, how could you utilize and manage the group decision-making process and technique to improve company profits? Which employees would you include in the group?

EXPERIENTIAL EXERCISES

3.1 Competitive Escalation: The Dollar Auction

OBJECTIVE

To explore the effects of competition on decision making.

INSTRUCTIONS

Step 1:   5 Minutes. The instructor will play the role of auctioneer. In this auction, the instructor will auction off $1 bills (the instructor will inform you whether this money is real or imaginary). All members of the class may participate in the auction at the same time.

The rules for this auction are slightly different from those of a normal auction. In this version, *both the highest bidder and the next highest bidder will play their last bids* even though the dollar is awarded only to the highest bidder. For example, if Bidder A bids 15 cents for the dollar and Bidder B bids 10 cents, and there is no further bidding, then A pays 15 cents for the dollar and receives the dollar, while B pays 10 cents and receives nothing. The auctioneer will lose 75 cents on the dollar just sold.

Bids must be made in multiples of 5 cents. The dollar will be sold when there is no further bidding. If two individuals bid the same amount at the same time, ties are resolved in favor of the bidder located physically closest to the auctioneer. *During each round, there is to be no talking except for making bids.*

Step 2:   *15 Minutes.* The instructor (auctioneer) will auction off five individual dollars to the class. Any student may bid in an effort to win the dollar. A record sheet of the bidding and winners can be kept in the worksheet that follows.

DISCUSSION QUESTIONS

1. Who made the most money in this exercise—one of the bidders or the auctioneer? Why?

2. As the auction proceeded, did bidders become more competitive or more cooperative? Why?

3. Did two bidders ever pay more for the money being auctioned than the value of the money itself? Explain how and why this happened.

4. Did you become involved in the bidding? Why?

    a. If you became involved, what were your motivations? Did you accomplish your objectives?

    b. If not, why didn't you become involved? What did you think were the goals and objectives of those who did become involved?

5. Did people say things to one another during the bidding to influence their actions? What was said, and how was it influential?

Dollar Auction Worksheet

	Amount paid by winning bidder	Amount paid by second bidder	Total paid for this dollar
First dollar			
Second dollar			
Third dollar			
Fourth dollar			
Fifth dollar			

SOURCE: Excerpted from R. Lewicki, *Experiences in Management and Organizational Behavior*, 3rd ed. Copyright © 1991 John Wiley & Sons, Inc. Reprinted with permission of John Wiley and Sons, Inc.

3.2   Group Problem-Solving Meeting at the Community Agency

OBJECTIVE

To understand the interactions in group decision making through role playing a meeting between a chairman and his subordinates.

INSTRUCTIONS

1. Gather role sheets for each character and instructions for observers.

2. Set up a table in front of the room with five chairs around it arranged in such a way that participants can talk comfortably and have their faces visible to observers.

3. Read the introduction and cast of characters.

4. Five members from the class are selected to role play the five characters. All other members act as observers. The participants study the roles. All should play their roles without referring to the role sheets.

5. The observers read the instructions for observers.

6. When everyone is ready, John Cabot enters his office, joins the others at the table, and the scene begins. Allow 20 minutes to complete the meeting. The meeting is carried to the point of completion unless an argument develops and no progress is evident after 10 or 15 minutes of conflict.

DISCUSSION QUESTIONS

1. Describe the group's behavior. What did each member say? Do?

2. Evaluate the effectiveness of the group's decision making.

3. Did any problems exist in leadership, power, motivation, communication, or perception?

4. How could the group's effectiveness be increased?

INTRODUCTION

The Community Agency is a role-play exercise of a meeting between the chairman of the board of a social service agency and four of his subordinates. Each character's role is designed to recreate the reality of a business meeting. Each character comes to the meeting with a unique perspective on a major problem facing the agency as well as some personal impressions of the other characters developed over several years of business and social associations.

CAST OF CHARACTERS

John Cabot, the Chairman, was the principal force behind the formation of the Community Agency, a multiservice agency. The agency employs 50 people, and during its 19 years of operations has enjoyed better client relations, a better service record, and a better reputation than other local agencies because of a reputation for high-quality service at a moderate cost to funding agencies. Recently, however, competitors have begun to overtake the Community Agency, resulting in declining contracts. John Cabot is expending every possible effort to keep his agency comfortably at the top.

Ron Smith, Director of the agency, reports directly to Cabot. He has held this position since he helped Cabot establish the agency 19 years ago.

Joan Sweet, Head of Client Services, reports to Smith. She has been with the agency 12 years, having worked before that for the government as a contracting officer.

Tom Lynch, Head Community Liaison, reports to Joan Sweet. He came to the Community Agency at Sweet's request, having worked with Sweet previously.

Jane Cox, Head Case Worker, also works for Joan Sweet. Cox was promoted to this position two years ago. Prior to that time, Jane had gone through a year's training program after receiving an MSW from a large urban university.

TODAY'S MEETING

John Cabot has called the meeting with these four managers to solve some problems that have developed in meeting service schedules and contract requirements. Cabot must catch a plane to Washington in half an hour; he has an appointment to negotiate a key contract that means a great deal to the future of the Community Agency. He has only 20 minutes to meet with his managers and still catch the plane. Cabot feels that getting the Washington contract is absolutely crucial to the future of the agency.

SOURCE: Judith R. Gordon, *A Diagnostic Approach to Organizational Behavior.* Copyright © 1983 Pearson Education, Inc. Reprinted by permission of Pearson Education, Inc., Upper Saddle River, NJ.

PART I SUPPORTING CASE

SSS Software In-Basket Exercise

One way to assess your own strengths and weaknesses in management skills is to engage in an actual managerial work experience. The following exercise gives you a realistic glimpse of the tasks faced regularly by practicing managers. Complete the exercise, and then compare your own decisions and actions with those of classmates.

SSS Software designs and develops customized software for businesses. It also integrates this software with the customer's existing systems and provides system maintenance. SSS Software has customers in the following industries: airlines, automotive, finance/banking, health/hospital, consumer products, electronics, and government. The company has also begun to generate important international clients. These include the European Airbus consortium and a consortium of banks and financial firms based in Kenya.

SSS Software has grown rapidly since its inception just over a decade ago. Its revenue, net income, and earnings per share have all been above the industry average for the past several years. However, competition in this technologically sophisticated field has grown very rapidly. Recently, it has become more difficult to compete for major contracts. Moreover, although SSS Software's revenue and net income continue to grow, the rate of growth declined during the last fiscal year.

SSS Software's 250 employees are divided into several operating divisions with employees at four levels: nonmanagement, technical/professional, managerial, and executive. Nonmanagement employees take care of the clerical and facilities support

functions. The technical/professional staff perform the core technical work for the firm. Most managerial employees are group managers who supervise a team of technical/professional employees working on a project for a particular customer. Staff who work in specialized areas such as finance, accounting, human resources, nursing, and law are also considered managerial employees. The executive level includes the 12 highest-ranking employees at SSS Software. There is an organization chart in Figure A that illustrates SSS Software's structure. There is also an Employee Classification Report that lists the number of employees at each level of the organization.

In this exercise, you will play the role of Chris Perillo, Vice President of Operations for Health and Financial Services. You learned last Wednesday, October 13, that your predecessor, Michael Grant, has resigned and gone to Universal Business Solutions, Inc. You were offered his former job, and you accepted it. Previously, you were the Group Manager for a team of 15 software developers assigned to work on the Airbus consortium project in the Airline Services Division. You spent all of Thursday and Friday and most of the weekend finishing up parts of the project, briefing your successor, and preparing for an interim report you will deliver in Paris on October 21.

It is now 7 a.m. Monday, and you are in your new office. You have arrived at work early so you can spend the next two hours reviewing material in your in-basket (including some memos and messages to Michael Grant), as well as your voice mail and e-mail. Your daily planning book indicates that you have no

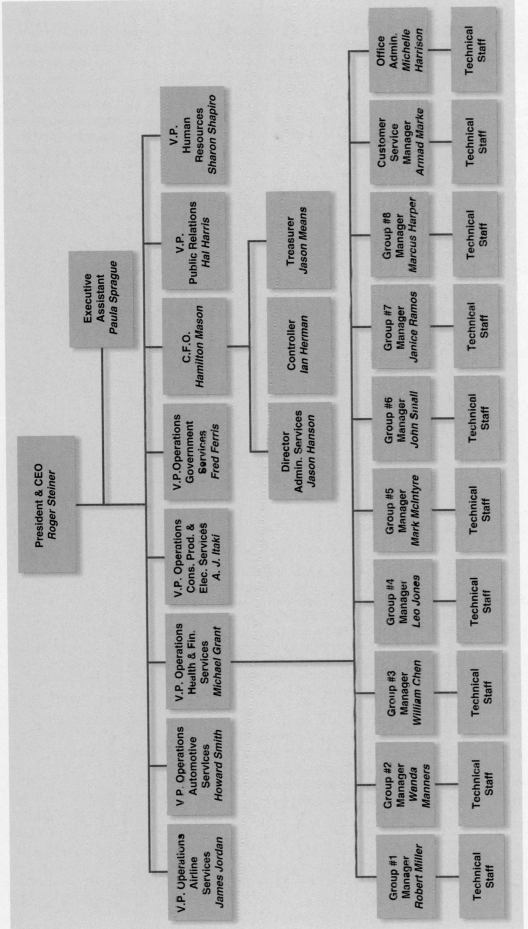

appointments today or tomorrow but will have to catch a plane for Paris early Wednesday morning. You have a full schedule for the remainder of the week and all of next week.

ASSIGNMENT

During the next two hours, review all the material in your in-basket, as well as your voice mail and e-mail. Take only two hours. Using the following response form as a model, indicate how you want to respond to each item (that is, via letter/memo, e-mail, phone/voice mail, or personal meeting). If you decide not to respond to an item, check "no response" on the response form. All of your responses must be written on the response forms. Write your precise, detailed response (do not merely jot down a few notes). For example, you might draft a memo or write out a message that you will deliver via phone/voice mail. You may also decide to meet with an individual (or individuals) during the limited time available on your calendar today or tomorrow. If so, prepare an agenda for a personal meeting and list your goals for the meeting. As you read through the items, you may occasionally observe some information that you think is relevant and want to remember (or attend to in the future) but that you decide not to include in any of your responses to employees. Write down such information on a sheet of paper titled "note to self."

Source: D. Whetten and K. Cameron, *Developing Management Skills,* 3rd ed. (New York: Harper Collins, 1995).

SAMPLE RESPONSE FORM

Relates To:

Memo # _____   E-mail # _____   Voice mail # _____

Response form:

_____ Letter/Memo   _____ Meet with person (when, where)

_____ E-mail   _____ Note to self

_____ Phone call/Voice mail   _____ No response

ITEM I MEMO

TO: All Employees

FROM: Roger Steiner, Chief Executive Officer

DATE: October 15

I am pleased to announce that Chris Perillo has been appointed as Vice President of Operations for Health and Financial Services. Chris will immediately assume responsibility for all operations previously managed by Michael Grant. Chris will have end-to-end responsibility for the design, development, integration, and maintenance of custom software for the health and finance/banking industries. This responsibility includes all technical, financial, and staffing issues. Chris will also manage our program of software support and integration for the recently announced merger of three large health maintenance organizations (HMOs). Chris will be responsible for our recently announced project with a consortium of banks and financial firms operating in Kenya. This project represents an exciting opportunity for us, and Chris's background seems ideally suited to the task.

Chris comes to this position with an undergraduate degree in Computer Science from the California Institute of Technology and an M.B.A. from the University of Virginia. Chris began as a member of our technical/professional staff six years ago and has most recently served for three years as a Group Manager supporting domestic and international projects for our airlines industry group, including our recent work for the European Airbus consortium.

I am sure you all join me in offering congratulations to Chris for this promotion.

ITEM 2 MEMO

TO: All Managers

FROM: Hal Harris, Vice President, Community and Public Relations

DATE: October 15

For your information, the following article appeared on the front page of the business section of Thursday's *Los Angeles Times*.

In a move that may create problems for SSS Software, Michael Grant and Janice Ramos have left SSS Software and moved to Universal Business Solutions Inc. Industry analysts see the move as another victory for Universal Business Solutions Inc. in their battle with SSS Software for share of the growing software development and integration business. Both Grant and Ramos had been with SSS Software for over 7 years. Grant was most recently Vice President of Operations for all SSS Software's work in two industries: health and hospitals, and finance and banking. Ramos brings to Universal Business Solutions Inc. her special expertise in the growing area of international software development and integration.

Hillary Collins, an industry analyst with Merrill Lynch, said "the loss of key staff to a competitor can often create serious problems for a firm such as SSS Software. Grant and Ramos have an insider's understanding of SSS Software's strategic and technical limitations. It will be interesting to see if they can exploit this knowledge to the advantage of Universal Business Solutions Inc."

ITEM 3 MEMO

TO: Chris Perillo

FROM: Paula Sprague, Executive Assistant to Roger Steiner

DATE: October 15

Chris, I know that in your former position as a Group Manager in the Airline Services Division, you probably have met most of the group managers in the Health and Financial Services Division, but I thought you might like some more personal information about them. These people will be your direct reports on the management team.

Group #1: Bob Miller, 55-year-old white male, married (Anne) with two children and three grandchildren. Active in local Republican politics. Well regarded as a "hands-off" manager heading a high-performing team. Plays golf regularly with Mark McIntyre, John Small, and a couple of V.P.s from other divisions.

Group #2: Wanda Manners, 38-year-old white female, single with one school-age child. A fitness "nut," has run in several marathons. Some experience in Germany and Japan. Considered a hard-driving manager with a constant focus on the task at hand. Will be the first person to show up every morning.

Group #3: William Chen, 31-year-old male of Chinese descent, married (Harriet), two young children from his first marriage. Enjoys tennis and is quite good at it. A rising star in the company, he is highly respected by his peers as a "man of action" and a good friend.

Group #4: Leo Jones, 36-year-old white male, married (Janet), with an infant daughter. Recently returned from paternity leave. Has traveled extensively on projects, since he speaks three languages. Has liked hockey ever since the time he spent in Montreal. Considered a strong manager who gets the most out of his people.

Group #5: Mark McIntyre, 45-year-old white male, married (Mary Theresa) to an executive in the banking industry. No children. A lot of experience in Germany and Eastern Europe. Has been writing a mystery novel. Has always been a good "team player," but several members of his technical staff are not well respected and he hasn't addressed the problem.

Group #6: John Small, 38-year-old white male, recently divorced. Three children living with his wife. A gregarious individual who likes sports. He spent a lot of time in Mexico and Central America before he came to SSS Software. Recently has been doing mostly contract work with the federal government. An average manager, has had some trouble keeping his people on schedule.

Group #7: This position vacant since Janice Ramos left. Roger thinks we ought to fill this position quickly. Get in touch with me if you want information on any in-house candidates for any position.

Group #8: Marcus Harper, 42-year-old black male, married (Tamara) with two teenage children. Recently won an award in a local photography contest. Considered a strong manager who gets along with peers and works long hours.

Customer Services: Armand Marke, 38-year-old Armenian male, divorced. A basketball fan. Originally from Armenia. Previously a Group Manager. Worked hard to establish the Technical Services Phone Line, but now has pretty much left it alone.

Office Administrator: Michelle Harrison, 41-year-old white female, single. Grew up on a ranch and still rides horses whenever she can. A strict administrator.

There are a number of good folks here, but they don't function well as a management team. I think Michael played favorites, especially with Janice and Leo. There are a few cliques in this group and I'm not sure how effectively Michael dealt with them. I expect you will find it a challenge to build a cohesive team.

ITEM 4 MEMO

TO: Chris Perillo

FROM: Wanda Manners, Group 2 Manager

DATE: October 15

CONFIDENTIAL AND RESTRICTED

Although I know you are new to your job, I feel it is important that I let you know about some information I just obtained concerning the development work we recently completed for First National Investment. Our project involved the development of asset management software for managing their international funds. This was a very complex project due to the volatile exchange rates and the forecasting tools we needed to develop.

As part of this project, we had to integrate the software and reports with all their existing systems and reporting mechanisms. To do this we were given access to all of their existing software (much of which was developed by Universal Business Solutions Inc.). Of course, we signed an agreement acknowledging that the software to which we were given access was proprietary and that our access was solely for the purpose of our system integration work associated with the project.

Unfortunately, I have learned that some parts of the software we developed actually "borrow" heavily from complex application programs developed for First National Investment by Universal Business Solutions Inc. It seems obvious to me that one or more of the software developers from Group 5 (that is, Mark McIntyre's group) inappropriately "borrowed" algorithms developed by Universal Business Solutions Inc. I am sure that doing so saved us significant development time on some aspects of the project. It seems very unlikely that First National Investment or Universal Business Solutions Inc. will ever become aware of this issue.

Finally, First National Investment is successfully using the software we developed and is thrilled with the work we did. We brought the project in on time and under budget. You probably know that they have invited us to bid on several other substantial projects.

I'm sorry to bring this delicate matter to your attention, but I thought you should know about it.

ITEM 5A MEMO

TO: Chris Perillo

FROM: Paula Sprague, Executive Assistant to Roger Steiner

DATE: October 15

RE: Letter from C.A.R.E. Services (copies attached)

Roger asked me to work on this C.A.R.E. project and obviously wants some fast action. A lot of the staff are already booked solid for the next couple of weeks. I knew that Elise Soto and Chu Hung Woo have the expertise to do this system, and when I checked with them, they were relatively free. I had them pencil in the next two weeks and wanted to let you know. Hopefully, it will take a "hot potato" out of your hands.

ITEM 5B COPY OF FAX

C.A.R.E.
Child and Adolescent Rehabilitative and Educational Services
A United Way Member Agency
200 Main Street
Los Angeles, California 90230

DATE: October 11

Mr. Roger Steiner, CEO
SSS Software
13 Miller Way
Los Angeles, California 90224

Dear Roger,

This letter is a follow-up to our conversation after last night's board meeting. I appreciated your comments during the board meeting about the need for sophisticated computer systems in nonprofit organizations and I especially appreciate your generous offer of assistance to have SSS Software provide assistance to deal with the immediate problem with our accounting system. Since the board voted to fire the computer consultant, I am very worried about getting our reports done in time to meet the state funding cycle.

Thanks again for your offer of help during this crisis.

Sincerely yours,

Janice Polocizwic

Janice Polocizwic
Executive Director

ITEM 5C COPY OF LETTER

SSS SOFTWARE
13 Miller Way
Los Angeles, CA 90224
213-635-2000

DATE: October 12

Janice Polocizwic
Executive Director, C.A.R.E. Services
200 Main Street
Los Angeles, California 90230

Dear Janice,

I received your fax of October 11. I have asked Paula Sprague, my executive assistant, to line up people to work on your accounting system as soon as possible. You can expect to hear from her shortly.

Sincerely,
Roger Steiner
Roger Steiner

cc: Paula Sprague, Executive Assistant

ITEM 6 MEMO

TO: Michael Grant

FROM: Harry Withers, Group 6 Technical Staff

DATE: October 12

PERSONAL AND CONFIDENTIAL

Our team is having difficulty meeting the submission deadline of November 5 for the Halstrom project. Kim, Fred, Peter, Kyoto, Susan, Mala, and I have been working on the project for several weeks, but are experiencing some problems and may need additional time. I hesitate to write this letter, but the main problem is that our group manager, John Small, is involved in a relationship with Mala. Mala gets John's support for her ideas and brings them to the team as required components of the project. Needless to say, this has posed some problems for the group. Mala's background is especially valuable for this project, but Kim and Fred, who have both worked very hard on the project, do not want to work with her. In addition, one member of the team has been unavailable recently because of child-care needs. Commitment to the project and team morale have plummeted. However, we'll do our best to get the project finished as soon as possible. Mala will be on vacation the next two weeks, so I'm expecting that some of us can complete it in her absence.

ITEM 7 VOICE MAIL

Hello, Michael. This is Jim Bishop of United Hospitals. I wanted to talk with you about the quality assurance project that you are working on for us. When José Martinez first started talking with us, I was impressed with his friendliness and expertise. But recently, he doesn't seem to be getting much accomplished and has seemed distant and on-edge in conversations. Today, I asked him about the schedule and he seemed very defensive and not entirely in control of his emotions. I am quite concerned about our project. Please give me a call at 213-951-1234.

ITEM 8 VOICE MAIL

Hi, Michael. This is Armand. I wanted to talk with you about some issues with the Technical Services Phone Line. I've recently received some complaint letters from Phone Line customers whose complaints have included: long delays while waiting for a technician to answer the phone; technicians who are not knowledgeable enough to solve problems; and, on occasion, rude service. Needless to say, I'm quite concerned about these complaints.

I believe that the overall quality of the phone line staff is very good, but we continue to be understaffed, even with the recent hires. The new technicians look strong, but are working on the help line before being fully trained. Antolino, our best tech, often brings her child to work, which is adding to the craziness around here.

I think you should know that we're feeling a lot of stress here. I'll talk to you soon.

ITEM 9 VOICE MAIL

Hi Chris, it's Pat. Congratulations on your promotion. They definitely picked the right person. It's great news—for me, too. You've been a terrific mentor so far, so I'm expecting to learn a lot from you in your new position. How about lunch next week?

ITEM 10 VOICE MAIL

Chris, this is Bob Miller. Just thought you'd like to know that John's joke during our planning meeting has disturbed a few of the women in my group. Frankly, I think the thing's being blown out of proportion, especially since we all know this is a good place for both men and women to work. Give me a call if you want to chat about this.

ITEM 11 VOICE MAIL

Hello. This is Lorraine Adams from Westside Hospital. I read in today's Los Angeles Times that you will be taking over from Michael Grant. We haven't met yet, but your division has recently finished two large million-dollar projects for Westside. Michael Grant and I had some discussion about a small conversion of a piece of existing software to be compatible with the new systems. The original vendor had said that they would do the work but has been stalling, and I need to move quickly. Can you see if Harris Wilson, Chu Hung Woo, and Elise Soto are available to do this work as soon as possible? They were on the original project and work well with our people. You can call me at 213-555-3456.

Um . . . (long pause) I guess I should tell you that I got a call from Michael offering to do this work. But I think I should stick with SSS Software. Give me a call.

ITEM 12 VOICE MAIL

Hi, Chris. This is Roosevelt Moore calling. I'm a member of your technical/professional staff. I used to report to Janice Ramos, but since she left the firm, I thought I'd bring my concerns directly to you. I'd like to arrange some time to talk with you about my experience since returning from six weeks of paternity leave. Some of my major responsibilities have been turned over to others. I seem to be out of the loop and wonder if my career is at risk. Also, I am afraid that I won't be supported or seriously considered for the opening created by Janice's departure. Frankly, I feel I'm being screwed for taking my leave. I'd like to talk with you this week.

ITEM 13 E-MAIL

TO: Michael Grant

FROM: José Martinez, Group 1 Technical Staff

DATE: October 12

I would like to set up a meeting with you as soon as possible. I suspect that you will get a call from Jim Bishop of United Hospitals and want to be sure that you hear my side of the story first. I have been working on a customized system design for quality assurance for them using a variation of the J-3 product we developed several years ago. They had a number of special requirements and some quirks in their accounting systems, so I have had to put in especially long hours. I've worked hard to meet their demands, but they keep changing the ground rules. I keep thinking, this is just another J-3 I'm working on, but they have been interfering with an elegant design I have developed. It seems I'm not getting anywhere on this project. Then Mr. Bishop asked me if the system was running yet. I was worn out from dealing with the Controller, and I made a sarcastic comment to Mr. Bishop. He gave me a funny look and just walked out of the room.

I would like to talk with you about this situation at your earliest convenience.

ITEM 14 E-MAIL

TO: Chris Perillo

FROM: John Small, Group 6 Manager

DATE: October 15

Welcome aboard, Chris. I look forward to meeting with you. I just wanted to put a bug in your ear about finding a replacement for Janice Ramos. One of my technical staff, Mala Abendano, has the ability and drive to make an excellent group manager. I have encouraged her to apply for the position. I'd be happy to talk with you further about this, at your convenience.

ITEM 15 E-MAIL

TO: Chris Perillo

FROM: Paula Sprague, Executive Assistant to Roger Steiner

DATE: October 15

Roger asked me to let you know about the large contract we have gotten in Kenya. It means that a team of four managers will be making a short trip to determine current needs. They will assign their technical staff the task of developing a system and software here over the next six months, and then the managers and possibly some team members will be spending about 10 months on site in Kenya to handle the implementation. Roger would appreciate an email of your thoughts about the issues to be discussed at this meeting, additional considerations about sending people to Kenya, and about how you will put together an effective team to work on this project. The October 15 memo I sent to you will provide you with some information you'll need to start making these decisions.

ITEM 16 E-MAIL

TO: Chris Perillo

FROM: Sharon Shapiro, V. P. of Human Resources

DATE: October 15

RE: Upcoming meeting

I want to update you on the rippling effect of John Small's sexual joke at last week's planning meeting. Quite a few women have been very upset and have met informally to talk about it. They have decided to call a meeting of all the people concerned about this kind of behavior throughout the firm. I plan to attend, so I'll keep you posted.

ITEM 17 E-MAIL

TO: All SSS-Software Managers

FROM: Sharon Shapiro, Vice President, Human Resources

DATE: October 14

RE: Promotions and External Hires

Year-to-date (January through September) promotions and external hires

Level	Race					Sex		Total
	White	Black	Asian	Hispanic	Native American	M	F	
Hires into Executive Level	0 (0%)	0 (0%)	0 (0%)	0 (0%)	0 (0%)	0 (0%)	0 (0%)	0
Promotions to Executive Level	0 (0%)	0 (0%)	0 (0%)	0 (0%)	0 (0%)	0 (0%)	0 (0%)	0
Hires into Management Level	2 (67%)	1 (33%)	0 (0%)	0 (0%)	0 (0%)	2 (67%)	1 (33%)	3
Promotions to Management Level	7 (88%)	0 (0%)	1 (12%)	0 (0%)	0 (0%)	7 (88%)	1 (12%)	8
Hires into Technical/ Professional Level	10 (36%)	6 (21%)	10 (36%)	2 (7%)	0 (0%)	14 (50%)	14 (50%)	28
Promotions to Technical/ Professional Level	0 (0%)	0 (0%)	0 (0%)	0 (0%)	0 (0%)	0 (0%)	0 (0%)	0
Hires into Non-Management Level	4 (20%)	10 (50%)	2 (10%)	4 (20%)	0 (0%)	6 (30%)	14 (70%)	20
Promotions to Non-Management Level	NA	NA	NA	NA	NA	NA	NA	NA

SSS Software employee (EEO) classification report as of June 30

Level	Race					Sex		Total
	White	Black	Asian	Hispanic	Native American	M	F	
Executive Level	11 (92%)	0 (0%)	1 (8%)	0 (0%)	0 (0%)	11 (92%)	1 (8%)	12
Management Level	43 (90%)	2 (4%)	2 (4%)	1 (2%)	0 (0%)	38 (79%)	10 (21%)	48
Technical/ Professional Level	58 (45%)	20 (15%)	37 (28%)	14 (11%)	1 (1%)	80 (62%)	50 (38%)	130
Non-Management Level	29 (48%)	22 (37%)	4 (7%)	4 (7%)	1 (2%)	12 (20%)	48 (80%)	60
Total	141 (56%)	44 (18%)	44 (18%)	19 (8%)	2 (1%)	141 (56%)	109 (44%)	250

CRITICAL INCIDENTS

Employee Raiding

Litson Cotton Yarn Manufacturing Company, located in Murray, New Jersey, decided as a result of increasing labor costs to relocate its plant in Fairlee, a southern community of 4,200. Plant construction was started, and a human resources office was opened in the state employment office, located in Fairlee.

Because of ineffective HR practices in the other three textile mills located within a 50-mile radius of Fairlee, Litson was receiving applications from some of the most highly skilled and trained textile operators in the state. After receiving applications from approximately 500 people, employment was offered to 260 male and female applicants. These employees would be placed immediately on the payroll with instructions to await final installation of machinery, which was expected within the following six weeks.

The managers of the three other textile companies, faced with resignations from their most efficient and best-trained employees, approached the Litson managers with the complaint that their labor force was being "raided." They registered a strong protest to cease such practices and demanded an immediate cancellation of the employment of the 260 people hired by Litson.

Litson managers discussed the ethical and moral considerations involved in offering employment to the 260 people. Litson

clearly faced a tight labor market in Fairlee, and management thought that if the 260 employees were discharged, the company would face cancellation of its plans and large construction losses. Litson management also felt obligated to the 260 employees who had resigned from their previous employment in favor of Litson.

The dilemma was compounded when the manager of one community plant reminded Litson that his plant was part of a nationwide chain supplied with cotton yarn from Litson. He implied that Litson's attempts to continue operations in Fairlee could result in cancellation of orders and the possible loss of approximately 18 percent market share. It was also suggested to Litson managers that actions taken by the nationwide textile chain could result in cancellation of orders from other textile companies. Litson's president held an urgent meeting of his top subordinates to (1) decide what to do about the situation in Fairlee, (2) formulate a written policy statement indicating Litson's position regarding employee raiding, and (3) develop a plan for implementing the policy.

How would you prepare for the meeting, and what would you say at the meeting?

Source: J. Champion and J. James, *Critical Incidents in Management: Decision and Policy Issues*, 6th ed. (Burr Ridge, IL: Richard D. Irwin, 1989). © 1989 The McGraw-Hill Companies.

Effective Management

Dr. Sam Perkins, a graduate of the Harvard University College of Medicine, had a private practice in internal medicine for 12 years. Fourteen months ago, he was persuaded by the Massachusetts governor to give up private practice to be director of the State Division of Human Services.

After one year as director, Perkins recognized he had made little progress in reducing the considerable inefficiency in the division. Employee morale and effectiveness seemed even lower than when he had assumed the position. He realized his past training and experiences were of a clinical nature with little exposure to effective management techniques. Perkins decided to research literature on the subject of management available to him at a local university.

Perkins soon realized that management scholars are divided on the question of what constitutes effective management. Some believe people are born with certain identifiable personality traits that make them effective managers. Others believe a manager can learn to be effective by treating subordinates with a personal and considerate approach and by giving particular attention to their need for favorable working conditions. Still others emphasize the importance of developing a management style characterized by either authoritarian, democratic, or laissez-faire approaches. Perkins was further confused when he learned that a growing number of scholars advocate that effective management is contingent on the situation.

Because a state university was located nearby, Perkins contacted the dean of its college of business administration. The dean referred him to the director of the college's management center, Professor Joel McCann. Discussions between Perkins and McCann resulted in a tentative agreement that the management center would organize a series of management training sessions for the State Division of Human Services. Before agreeing on the price tag for the management conference, Perkins asked McCann to prepare a proposal reflecting his thoughts on the following questions:

1. How will the question of what constitutes effective management be answered during the conference?

2. What will be the specific subject content of the conference?

3. Who will the instructors be?

4. What will be the conference's duration?

5. How can the conference's effectiveness be evaluated?

6. What policies should the State Division of Human Services adopt regarding who the conference participants should be and how they should be selected? How can these policies be best implemented?

Source: J. Champion and J. James, *Critical Incidents in Management: Decision and Policy Issues*, 6th ed. (Burr Ridge, IL: Richard D. Irwin, 1989). © 1989 The McGraw-Hill Companies.

chapter

4

Planning and Strategic Management

" *Manage your destiny, or someone else will.* "

— Jack Welch, former CEO, General Electric

LEARNING OBJECTIVES

After studying Chapter 4, you will be able to:

LO 1 Summarize the basic steps in any planning process. p. 126

LO 2 Describe how strategic planning should be integrated with tactical and operational planning. p. 130

LO 3 Identify elements of the external environment and internal resources of the firm to analyze before formulating a strategy. p. 137

LO 4 Define core competencies and explain how they provide the foundation for business strategy. p. 140

LO 5 Summarize the types of choices available for corporate strategy. p. 145

LO 6 Discuss how companies can achieve competitive advantage through business strategy. p. 148

LO 7 Describe the keys to effective strategy implementation. p. 150

CHAPTER OUTLINE

An Overview of Planning Fundamentals
The Basic Planning Process

Levels of Planning
Strategic Planning
Tactical and Operational Planning
Aligning Tactical, Operational, and Strategic Planning

Strategic Planning
Step 1: Establishment of Mission, Vision, and Goals
Step 2: Analysis of External Opportunities and Threats
Step 3: Analysis of Internal Strengths and Weaknesses
Step 4: SWOT Analysis and Strategy Formulation
Step 5: Strategy Implementation
Step 6: Strategic Control

Management Close-Up

Nokia CEO Olli-Pekka Kallasvuo should have plenty of reasons to be happy these days. More than a billion reasons, you might say. Finland-based Nokia is the world's leading cell phone maker, and more than 1 billion people use its phones. Nokia leads the market in Europe, Asia, the Middle East, and Africa, selling more than its top three competitors combined. In addition, the company regularly wins praise from Greenpeace and *Fortune* magazine for its environmentally responsible practices.

However, Nokia doesn't have bragging rights in North America. Although it posted worldwide sales of $74 billion in a recent year, Nokia has yet to capture the hearts and wallets of U.S. and Canadian consumers. Nokia's high-end models with satellite mapping features do well in Europe and Asia, and in developing countries its low-end phones have been wildly successful. But

> Wireless communication and the Internet have transformed how the world communicates, and new technologies are emerging almost daily. As you read this chapter, consider how Olli-Pekka Kallasvuo needs to bring a different kind of discipline to the planning at Nokia.

when it comes to smart phones in North America, both Apple's iPhone and Research in Motion's BlackBerry models eclipse Nokia. Nokia's strong overall position may more than offset its lesser market share in the United States and Canada, but in the wireless world no manufacturer can afford to be off its game.

Industry observers regarded Nokia's 2006 decision not to produce folding clamshell handsets as a strategic error. Then in 2007 Apple made a splash with the iPhone's alphabetic touch screen—a feature not available in Nokia phones. When Google announced advancements in software that would bring Internet capability to cell phones, Nokia reacted coolly at first. How would the resulting buzz about convergence—the marriage of cell phone mobility and Internet capability—influence the way Nokia plans for the future?[1]

To imagine cell phone giant Nokia—or any organization—dealing with the significant challenges it faces without developing a plan beforehand is almost impossible. Planning is a formal expression of managerial intent. It describes what managers decide to do and how they will do it. It provides the framework, focus, and direction required for a meaningful effort. Without planning, any improvements in an organization's innovation, speed, quality, service, and cost will be accidental, if they occur at all. This chapter examines the most important concepts and processes involved in planning and strategic management. By learning these concepts and reviewing the steps outlined, you will be on your way to understanding the current approaches to the strategic management of today's organizations.

An Overview of Planning Fundamentals

The importance of formal planning in organizations has grown dramatically. Until the mid-1900s, most planning was unstructured and fragmented, and formal planning was restricted to a few large corporations. Although management pioneers such as Alfred Sloan of General Motors instituted formal planning processes, planning became a widespread management function only during the last few decades. Initially, larger organizations adopted formal planning, but today even small firms operated by aggressive, opportunistic entrepreneurs engage in formal planning.[2]

Planning is the conscious, systematic process of making decisions about goals and activities that an individual, group, work unit, or organization will pursue in the future. Planning is not an informal or haphazard response to a crisis; it is a purposeful effort that is directed and controlled by managers and often draws on the knowledge and experience of employees throughout the organization. Planning provides individuals and work units with a clear map to follow in their future activities; at the same time this map may be flexible enough to allow for individual circumstances and changing conditions.

LO 1   The Basic Planning Process

Because planning is a decision process—you're deciding what to do and how to go about doing it—the important steps followed during formal planning are similar to the basic decision-making steps we discussed in Chapter 3. Figure 4.1 summarizes the similarities between decision making and planning—including the fact that both move not just in one direction but in a *cycle*. The outcomes of decisions and plans are evaluated, and if necessary, they are revised.

We now describe the basic planning process in more detail. Later in this chapter, we will discuss how managerial decisions and plans fit into the larger purposes of the organization—its ultimate strategy, mission, vision, and goals.

situational analysis

A process planners use, within time and resource constraints, to gather, interpret, and summarize all information relevant to the planning issue under consideration.

Step 1: Situational Analysis   As the contingency approach advocates, planning begins with a **situational analysis.** Within their time and resource constraints, planners should gather, interpret, and summarize all information relevant to the planning issue in question. A thorough situational analysis studies past events, examines current conditions, and attempts to forecast future trends. It focuses on the internal forces at work in the organization or work unit and, consistent with the open-systems approach (see Chapter 2), examines influences from the external environment. The outcome of this step is the identification and diagnosis of planning assumptions, issues, and problems.

A thorough situational analysis will provide information about the planning decisions you need to make. For example, if you are a manager in a magazine company considering the launch of a sports publication for the teen market, your analysis will include such factors as the number of teens who subscribe to magazines, the appeal of the teen market to advertisers, your firm's ability to serve this market effectively,

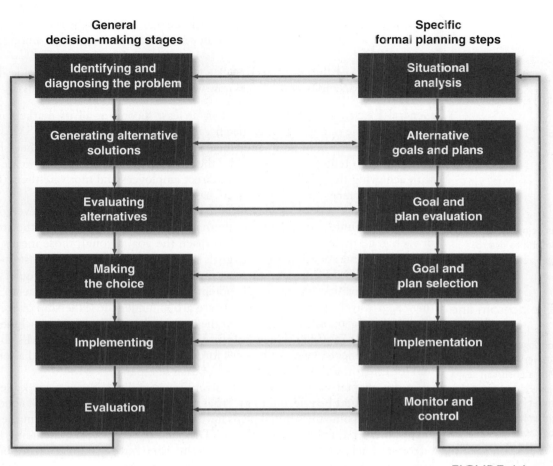

General decision-making stages	Specific formal planning steps
Identifying and diagnosing the problem	Situational analysis
Generating alternative solutions	Alternative goals and plans
Evaluating alternatives	Goal and plan evaluation
Making the choice	Goal and plan selection
Implementing	Implementation
Evaluation	Monitor and control

FIGURE 4.1

Decision-Making Stages (Chapter 3) and Formal Planning Steps (Chapter 4)

current economic conditions, the level of teen interest in sports, and any sports magazines already serving this market and their current sales. Such a detailed analysis will help you decide whether to proceed with the next step in your magazine launch.

Step 2: Alternative Goals and Plans   Based on the situational analysis, the planning process should generate alternative goals that may be pursued in the future and the alternative plans that may be used to achieve those goals. This step in the process should stress creativity and encourage managers and employees to think in broad terms about their jobs. Once a range of alternatives has been developed, the merits of these different plans and goals will be evaluated. Continuing with our magazine publishing example, the alternatives you might want to consider could include whether the magazine should be targeted at young men, young women, or both groups, and whether it should be sold mainly online, through subscriptions, or on newsstands.

Goals are the targets or ends the manager wants to reach. To be effective, goals should have certain qualities, which are easy to remember with the acronym SMART:

goal

A target or end that management desires to reach.

Specific—When goals are precise, describing particular behaviors and outcomes, employees can more easily determine whether they are working toward the goals.

Measurable—As much as possible, the goal should quantify the desired results, so that there is no doubt whether it has been achieved.

Attainable (but challenging)—Employees need to recognize that they can attain the goals they are responsible for, or else they are likely to become discouraged. However, they also should feel challenged to work hard and be creative.

Relevant—Each goal should contribute to the organization's overall mission (discussed later in this chapter), while being consistent with its values, including ethical standards (see Chapter 5). Goals are most likely to be relevant to the organization's overall objectives if they are consistent within and among work groups.

Time-bound—Effective goals specify a target date for completion. Besides knowing what to do, employees should know when they need to deliver results.

General Electric's goal of being first or at least second in all its markets is a well-known example of a goal that is specific, measurable, and challenging. SMART goals such as these not only point individual employees in the direction they should be going but also tend to be accepted by the managers and employees who are charged with achieving them. Thus, they both direct employees and motivate them (for more on the importance of motivation, see Chapter 13).

plans

The actions or means managers intend to use to achieve organizational goals.

Plans are the actions or means the manager intends to use to achieve goals. At a minimum, planning should outline alternative actions that may lead to the attainment of each goal, the resources required to reach the goal through those means, and the obstacles that may develop. IBM has goals to increase its profits, and the fastest-growing area of growth is in software. To meet profit goals, the software unit acquires existing software companies that have high-potential products but lack the means to promote them aggressively enough. IBM's software group, under the leadership of Steve Mills, plans how its giant sales force will sell the new products. Those plans include training the salespeople in what the new software does and how it can help IBM's clients. To improve the effectiveness of the sales force, the software group planned a selling system for categorizing and keeping track of each salesperson's leads.[3]

⭐ **The bottom line**
Service

Contingency plans that keep service levels high during a crisis can seal a company's reputation for caring about customers. But this commitment requires highly dedicated and creative employees, and access to the necessary resources can be expensive. Managers must decide how crucial service is to their strategy—and how willing customers will be to forgive them for service lapses under pressure.

In this chapter we will talk about various types of plans. Some plans, called *contingency plans*, might be referred to as "what if" plans. They include sets of actions to be taken when a company's initial plans have not worked well or if events in the external environment require a sudden change. Disasters of recent years, including the 2001 terrorist attacks and Hurricanes Katrina and Rita, have reminded many businesses how important contingency planning can be.

Most major corporations now have contingency plans in place to respond to a major disaster—to make sure vital data are backed up and can be recovered in an emergency, for instance, or that employees know what to do when a crisis occurs. But contingency plans are important for more-common situations as well. For example, many businesses are affected by snowstorms, increases in gasoline prices, computer breakdowns, or changes in consumer tastes. JetBlue initially achieved success as an airline that would "bring humanity back to air travel" by caring about its customers and employees. But the airline was humiliated by its inability to cope with a February snowstorm during which at least one plane notoriously sat on a runway for 10 hours; the company took days to recover, canceling a thousand flights.[5]

Step 3: Goal and Plan Evaluation Next, managers will evaluate the advantages, disadvantages, and potential effects of each alternative goal and plan. They must prioritize those goals and even eliminate some of them. Also, managers will consider carefully the implications of alternative plans for meeting high-priority goals. In particular, they will pay a great deal of attention to the cost of any initiative and

Are small companies prepared?[4]

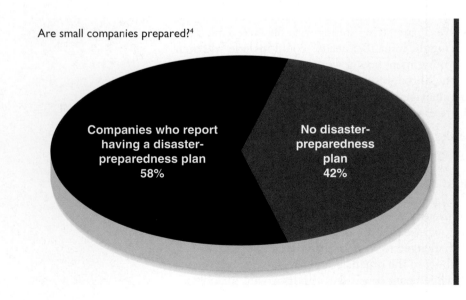

Companies who report having a disaster-preparedness plan
58%

No disaster-preparedness plan
42%

the investment return that is likely to result. In our magazine publishing example, your evaluation might determine that newsstand sales alone wouldn't be profitable enough to justify the launch. Perhaps you could improve profits with an online edition supplemented by Podcasts. To decide, you would estimate the costs and expected returns of such alternatives, trying to following the decision steps advised in Chapter 3.

Step 4: Goal and Plan Selection   Once managers have assessed the various goals and plans, they will select the one that is most appropriate and feasible. The evaluation process will identify the priorities and trade-offs among the goals and plans. For example, if your plan is to launch a number of new publications, and you're trying to choose among them, you might weigh the different up-front investment each requires, the size of each market, which one fits best with your existing product line or company image, and so on. Experienced judgment always

> "Most discussions of decision making assume that only senior executives make decisions or that only senior executives' decisions matter. This is a dangerous mistake."
>
> Peter Drucker

plays an important role in this process. However, as you will discover later in the chapter, relying on judgment alone may not be the best way to proceed.

Typically, a formal planning process leads to a written set of goals and plans that are appropriate and feasible for a particular set of circumstances. In some organizations, the alternative generation, evaluation, and selection steps generate planning **scenarios,** as discussed in Chapter 2. A different contingency plan is attached to each scenario. The manager pursues the goals and implements the plans associated with the most likely scenario. However, the manager will also be prepared to switch to another set of plans if the situation changes and another scenario becomes relevant. This approach helps the firm anticipate and manage crises and allows greater flexibility and responsiveness.

The Hard Rock Café carries its strategy—to be identified with rock 'n' roll—through to its hotel signs.

If a company hasn't already considered relevant scenarios, managers have to be prepared to restart the planning process when an unexpected change brings disappointing results. This flexible approach to planning can help a company survive and even thrive in a turbulent environment. For example, when the economy recently took a downturn, major clients stopped calling on Cor Business, a management coaching firm, for help in developing their managers. Jeffrey Hull and the other partners of Cor Business realized their firm's survival required a new plan for bringing in business.

The partners brainstormed ideas for a new business plan. Looking over the prior year's results, they noticed that most of Cor Business's growth that year had come from small businesses, even though the partners had been directing most of their energy toward large companies like MasterCard and AT&T. As a matter of fact, as the economy had slowed, more and more nervous small-business owners had been looking for help from their firm.

scenario

A narrative that describes a particular set of future conditions.

Hull and the other partners drew up a new plan in which they would focus on serving small clients, helping them do what Cor Business's managers were doing—move beyond their fear of change to find new opportunities in challenging times. Hull counseled the owner of a real estate investment company to set aside his fears about the real estate downturn, reevaluate his data on the prospects for converting a warehouse into a restaurant, and go ahead with plans for what was in fact a well-researched, practical idea.[6]

Step 5: Implementation   Once managers have selected the goals and plans, they must implement the plans designed to achieve the goals. Even the best plans are useless if they are not implemented properly. Managers and employees must understand the plan, have the resources to implement it, and be motivated to do so. Including employees in the previous steps of the planning process paves the way for the implementation phase. As we mentioned earlier, employees usually are better informed, more committed, and more highly motivated when a goal or plan is one that they helped develop.

Finally, successful implementation requires a plan to be linked to other systems in the organization, particularly the budget and reward systems. If the manager does not have a budget with financial resources to execute the plan, the plan is probably doomed. Similarly, goal achievement must be linked to the organization's reward system. Many organizations use incentive programs to encourage employees to achieve goals and to implement plans properly. Commissions, salaries, promotions, bonuses, and other rewards are based on successful performance.

At Wells Fargo, Chairman of the board Dick Kovacevich saw that the bank—one of the nation's largest—could stay competitive by excelling at "cross-selling," the practice of encouraging the bank's existing customers to use more of its financial services. Bank customers typically go to different institutions for different services, but Wells Fargo beat the odds by getting employees at all levels to focus on customer needs, rather than product lines. Tellers and branch managers receive training aimed at this goal, and pay systems reward employees for cross-selling. As a result, Wells Fargo customers use an average of 5.2 of the bank's products, roughly double the average for the industry. Selling to existing customers is much more profitable than winning new ones, so this strategy might seem obvious. Perhaps it is, but Wells Fargo board member Robert Joss says, "It's simple in concept but very hard in execution," adding that this successful implementation reflects Kovacevich's "great capacity to motivate people."[7]

$ **The bottom line**
COST
Tying plans to a firm's financials is a key element of success.

Step 6: Monitor and Control   Although it is sometimes ignored, the sixth step in the formal planning process—monitoring and controlling—is essential. Without it, you would never know whether your plan is succeeding. As we mentioned earlier, planning works in a cycle; it is an ongoing, repetitive process. Managers must continually monitor the actual performance of their work units against the unit's goals and plans. They will also need to develop control systems to measure that performance and allow them to take corrective action when the plans are implemented improperly or when the situation changes. In our magazine publishing example, newsstand and subscription sales reports are essential for letting you know how well your new magazine launch is going. If subscription sales aren't doing as well as expected, you may need to revise your marketing plan. We will discuss the important issue of control systems in greater detail later in this chapter and in Chapter 16.

Levels of Planning

LO 2   In Chapter 1 you learned about the three major types of managers: top-level (*strategic* managers), middle-level (*tactical* managers), and frontline (*operational* managers). Because planning is an important management function, managers at all three levels use it. However, the scope and activities of the planning process at each level of the organization often differ.

Strategic Planning

Strategic planning involves making decisions about the organization's long-term goals and strategies. Strategic plans have a strong external orientation and cover major portions of the organization. Senior executives are responsible for the development and execution of the strategic plan, although they usually do not formulate or implement the entire plan personally.

Strategic goals are major targets or end results that relate to the long-term survival, value, and growth of the organization. Strategic managers—top-level managers—usually establish goals that reflect both effectiveness (providing appropriate outputs) and efficiency (a high ratio of outputs to inputs). Typical strategic goals include growth, increasing market share, improving profitability, boosting return on investment, fostering both quantity and quality of outputs, increasing productivity, improving customer service, and contributing to society.

Organizations usually have a number of mutually reinforcing strategic goals. For example, a computer manufacturer may have as its strategic goals the launch of a specified number of new products in a particular time frame, of higher quality, with a targeted increase in market share. Each of these goals supports and contributes to the others.

A **strategy** is a pattern of actions and resource allocations designed to achieve the goals of the organization. An effective strategy provides a basis for answering five broad questions about how the organization will meet its objectives: (1) Where will we be active? (2) How will we get there (e.g., by increasing sales or acquiring another company)? (3) How will we win in the marketplace (e.g., by keeping prices low or offering the best service)? (4) How fast will we move and in what sequence will we make changes? (5) How will we obtain financial returns (low costs or premium prices)?[8] In setting a strategy, managers try to match the organization's skills and resources to the opportunities found in the external environment. Every organization has certain strengths and weaknesses, so the actions, or strategies, the organization implements should help build on strengths in areas that satisfy the wants and needs of consumers and other key factors in the organization's external environment. Also, some organizations may implement strategies that change or influence the external environment, as discussed in Chapter 2.

Tactical and Operational Planning

Once the organization's strategic goals and plans are identified, they serve as the foundation for planning done by middle-level and frontline managers. As you can see in Figure 4.2, goals and plans become more specific and involve shorter periods of time as they move from the strategic level to the tactical level and then to the operational level. A strategic plan will typically have a time horizon of from three to seven years—but sometimes even decades, as with the successful plan to land a probe on Titan, Saturn's moon. Tactical plans may have a time horizon of a year or two, and operational plans may cover a period of months.

The Chicago Sun-Times and the Chicago Tribune are the only two major daily newspapers that remain in Chicago, a city of 3 million. Both papers are in serious trouble from declining circulation and poor advertising revenues. What kind of new strategy do you think would help to ensure the survival of these two organizations?

strategic planning

A set of procedures for making decisions about the organization's long-term goals and strategies.

strategic goals

Major targets or end results relating to the organization's long-term survival, value, and growth.

strategy

A pattern of actions and resource allocations designed to achieve the organization's goals.

		Managerial Level	Level of Detail	Time Horizon
Strategic		Top	Low	Long (3–7 years)
Tactical		Middle	Medium	Medium (1–2 years)
Operational		Frontline	High	Short (<1 year)

FIGURE 4.2

Hierarchy of Goals and Plans

tactical planning

A set of procedures for translating broad strategic goals and plans into specific goals and plans that are relevant to a distinct portion of the organization, such as a functional area like marketing.

operational planning

The process of identifying the specific procedures and processes required at lower levels of the organization.

Tactical planning translates broad strategic goals and plans into specific goals and plans that are relevant to a definite portion of the organization, often a functional area like marketing or human resources, as discussed in Chapter 10. Tactical plans focus on the major actions a unit must take to fulfill its part of the strategic plan. For example, if the strategy calls for the rollout of a new product line, the tactical plan for the manufacturing unit might involve the design, testing, and installation of the equipment needed to produce the new line.

Operational planning identifies the specific procedures and processes required at lower levels of the organization. Frontline managers usually focus on routine tasks such as production runs, delivery schedules, and human resources requirements, as we discuss in Chapters 16 and 17.

The planning model we have been describing is a hierarchical one, with top-level strategies flowing down through the levels of the organization into more specific goals and plans and an ever-more-limited timetable. But in today's complex organizations, the planning sequence is often not as rigid as this traditional view. As we will see later in this chapter, managers throughout an organization may be involved in developing the strategic plan and contributing critical elements to it. Also, in practice, lower-level managers may be making decisions that shape strategy, whether or not top executives realize it. When Intel senior adviser Andy Grove suggested that the company exit the computer memory business, Intel was directing about one-third of its research dollars to memory-related projects. However, on a practical level, the company had already been exiting the business; only 4 percent of its total sales were for computer memory products. Why was this occurring, if it wasn't yet a defined strategy? Manufacturing managers had been directed by finance executives to set up factories in a way that would generate the biggest margins (revenues minus costs) per square inch of microchips produced. As computer memory became a money-losing commodity, manufacturing made less and less of those products. So, when Intel announced it would get out of the memory business, its strategy was catching up with its operational planning, which had been driven by tactical plans.[9] The lesson for top managers is to make sure they are communicating strategy to all levels of the organization *and* paying attention to what is happening at all levels in the organization.

Aligning Tactical, Operational, and Strategic Planning

Ideally, strategic plans integrate all the bottom-line practices of the firm.

To be fully effective, the organization's strategic, tactical, and operational goals and plans must be *aligned*—that is, they must be consistent, mutually supportive, and focused on achieving the common purpose and direction. Whole Foods Market, for example, links its tactical and operational planning directly to its strategic planning. The firm describes itself on its Web site as a mission-driven company that aims to set the standards for excellence for food retailers. The firm measures its success in

Another company that successfully aligns its levels of goals is Boeing, which has a three-part strategy for achieving "aerospace leadership":

1. Run healthy core businesses.
2. Leverage strengths into new products and services.
3. Open new frontiers.

At one of Boeing's core businesses, Commercial Airplanes, running a healthy core business has required some changes in tactical plans. In the past, a single-minded drive to achieve maximum sales of its 737 and 747 planes at the expense of the division's main competitor, Airbus, resulted in poor operational planning and disastrous relations with customers and suppliers. Salespeople wrote up orders for hundreds of aircraft by pricing many of them too low and promising rapid delivery. Production managers scrambled to hire tens of thousands of workers so that they could double production levels, and suppliers were pressed to ramp-up production. Demand for components became so intense that some were delivered by helicopter and taxicab. Costs rose, but profits suffered.

Today, in contrast, Boeing Commercial Airplanes, led by Scott Carson, is trying to grow at a sustainable pace. Tactical planning is more cautious; the unit now expands its production capabilities only when it determines that the need will continue for at least two years. If a customer is interested in placing a major order, a committee that includes engineers and accountants must sign off on it after ensuring the company has the capacity to meet the contract's time requirements. At the operational level, Boeing also focuses more on collaborating with suppliers, sharing information to ensure that enough parts will be available without the expense of rush orders. Suppliers are relieved not to have to staff production lines for a surge and then lay off workers after a year or two. Production planning covers a time frame of several years, because the backlog can be that long. When some customers are uncertain about their needs, planners adjust the schedule to serve customers who are ready to buy and postpone orders from customers who don't mind waiting, keeping everyone satisfied without the need to hire more workers for peak demand. Thanks to the more even staffing levels, Boeing's operational planning can focus on better training for existing workers, rather than constantly hiring and laying off workers as orders surge and fall.[10]

fulfilling its vision by "customer satisfaction, Team Member excellence and happiness, return on capital investment, improvement in the state of the environment, and local and larger community support."

Whole Foods's strategic goal is "to sell the highest-quality products that also offer high value for our customers." Its operational goals focus on ingredients, freshness, taste, nutritional value, safety, and appearance that meet or exceed its customers' expectations, including guaranteeing product satisfaction. Tactical goals include store environments that are "inviting, fun, unique, informal, comfortable, attractive, nurturing and educational" and safe and inviting work environments for its employees.

One method for aligning the organization's strategic and operational goals is the *strategy map*. The strategy map provides a tool managers can use to communicate their strategic goals and enable members of the organization at every level to understand the parts they will play in helping to achieve them. The map illustrates the four key drivers (or "balanced scorecard") of a firm's long-term success: the skills of its people and their ability to grow and learn; the effectiveness of its internal processes; its ability to deliver value to customers; and, ultimately, its ability to grow its financial assets. The map shows how specific plans and goals in each area link to the others and can generate real improvements in an organization's performance.

> The strategic map shows the relationship between a firm's practices and its long-term success.

Figure 4.3 shows how a strategy map might be built and how the various goals of the organization relate to each other to create long-term value for the firm. As an example, let us assume that a company's primary *financial goal* is "to increase revenues by enhancing the value we offer to existing customers by making our prices the lowest available." (Target and Wal-Mart might be good examples of companies with this kind of strategy.) The company will then have corresponding goals and plans in the other sections of the map to support that strategy. Its *learning and growth goals* might include bringing in the most efficient production technologies or work processes and training the staff to use them. These in turn will lead to the *internal goals* of improved production speed and lower cost, which in turn leads to the *customer goal* of competitive pricing, making the original financial goal feasible. On the other hand, a financial strategy of revenue growth through new products might lead to people and technology goals that speed up product design, to internal processes that lead to innovation, and to a customer goal of perceived product leadership. Whatever the strategy, the strategic map can be used to develop the appropriate measures and standards in each operational area for that strategy and to show how they are all linked.[11]

FIGURE 4.3
The Strategy Map: Creating Value by Aligning Goals

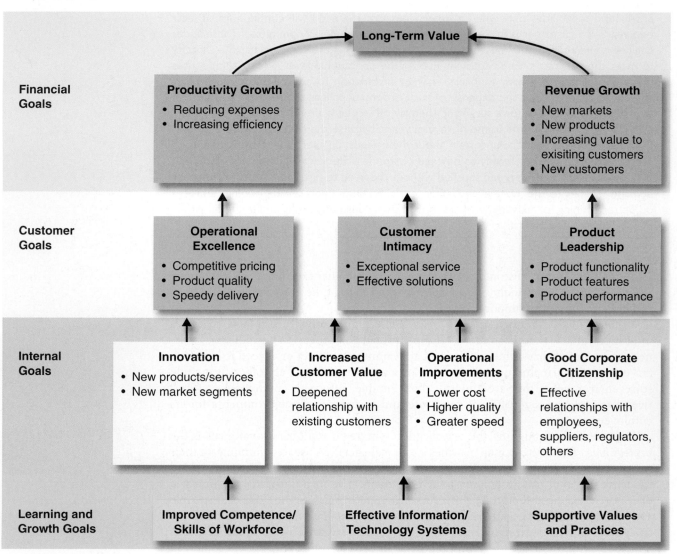

SOURCE: Adapted from Robert Kaplan and David Norton, "Plotting Success with Strategy Maps," *Optimize*, February 2004, online; and Robert Kaplan and David Norton, "Having Trouble with Your Strategy? Then Map It," *Harvard Business Review*, September–October 2000.

Strategic Planning

Strategic decision making is one of the most exciting and controversial topics in management today. In fact, many organizations currently are changing the ways they develop and execute their strategic plans.

Traditionally, strategic planning emphasized a top-down approach—senior executives and specialized planning units developed goals and plans for the entire organization. Tactical and operational managers received those goals and plans, and their own planning activities were limited to specific procedures and budgets for the units.

Over the years, managers and consulting firms innovated with a variety of analytical techniques and planning approaches, many of which have been critical for analyzing complex business situations and competitive issues. In many instances, however, senior executives spent too much time with their planning specialists to the exclusion of line managers in the rest of the organization. As a result, a gap often developed between strategic managers and tactical and operational managers, and managers and employees throughout the organization became alienated and uncommitted to the organization's success.[12]

Today, however, senior executives increasingly are involving managers throughout the organization in the strategy formation process.[13] The problems just described and the rapidly changing environment of the past 25 years have forced executives to look to all levels of the organization for ideas and innovations to make their firms more competitive. Although the CEO and other top managers continue to furnish the strategic direction, or "vision," of the organization, tactical and even operational managers often provide valuable inputs to the organization's strategic plan. In some cases, these managers also have substantial autonomy to formulate or change their own plans. This authority increases flexibility and responsiveness, critical requirements for success in today's organizations.

Because of this trend, a new term for the strategic planning process has emerged: *strategic management*. **Strategic management** involves managers from all parts of the organization in the formulation and implementation of strategic goals and strategies. It integrates strategic planning and management into a single process. Strategic planning becomes an ongoing activity in which all managers are encouraged to think strategically and focus on long-term, externally oriented issues as well as short-term tactical and operational issues.

As shown in Figure 4.4, the strategic management process has six major components:

1. Establishment of mission, vision, and goals.
2. Analysis of external opportunities and threats.

> ## The bottom line
> **Innovation**
>
> New ideas from managers throughout the organization can contribute to a plan's effectiveness.

> **strategic management**
>
> A process that involves managers from all parts of the organization in the formulation and implementation of strategic goals and strategies.

FIGURE 4.4
The Strategic Management Process

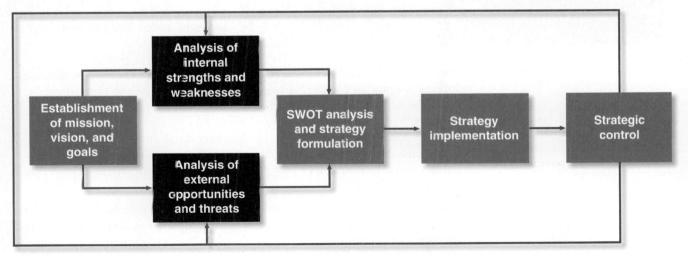

3. Analysis of internal strengths and weaknesses.
4. SWOT (strengths, weaknesses, opportunities, and threats) analysis and strategy formulation.
5. Strategy implementation.
6. Strategic control.

Because this process is a planning and decision process, it is similar to the planning framework discussed earlier. Although organizations may use different terms or emphasize different parts of the process, the components and concepts described in this section are found either explicitly or implicitly in every organization. Even a small entrepreneurial firm can benefit from the kind of planning framework we describe here.

Step 1: Establishment of Mission, Vision, and Goals

The first step in strategic planning is establishing a mission, a vision, and goals for the organization. The **mission** is a clear and concise expression of the basic purpose of the organization. It describes what the organization does, who it does it for, its basic good or service, and its values. Here are some mission statements from firms you will recognize:[14]

> *McDonald's:* "To be our customers' favorite place and way to eat."
> *Microsoft:* "We work to help people and businesses throughout the world to realize their full potential."
> *Allstate:* "To be the best . . . serving our customers by providing peace of mind and enriching their quality of life through our partnership in the management of the risks they face."

mission

An organization's basic purpose and scope of operations.

The mission statemant at McDonald's is "To be our customers' favorite place and way to eat." How do you see that translated into the atmosphere at your local McDonald's?

Smaller organizations, of course, may have missions that aren't as broad as these. For example, the local bar found next to most campuses has this implicit mission: "To sell large quantities of inexpensive beer to college students in a noisily enjoyable environment."

The mission describes the organization as it currently operates. The **strategic vision** points to the future—it provides a perspective on where the organization is headed and what it can become. Ideally, the vision statement clarifies the long-term direction of the company and its *strategic intent.* Here are some actual vision statements:[15]

> *DuPont:* "To be the world's most dynamic science company, creating sustainable solutions essential to a better, safer and healthier life for people everywhere."
> *City of Redmond, Washington:* "Together we create a community of good neighbors."
> *Great Lakes Naval Museum:* "To enhance and become an integral part of the training mission of the Naval Service Training Command, Great Lakes, by instilling in our newest sailors a strong sense of tradition and heritage of Naval service in the United States."

strategic vision

The long-term direction and strategic intent of a company.

The most effective vision statements inspire organization members. They offer a worthwhile target for the entire organization to work together to achieve. Often, these statements are not strictly financial, because financial targets alone may not motivate all organization members. For example, DuPont's vision refers to being a "dynamic science company" that works toward a "better, safer and healthier life" for people. This vision inspires innovation aimed at making the world better—the type of work that is likely to motivate the scientists and other knowledge workers who can give the company an edge, ultimately improving DuPont's competitive position. Likewise, "instilling . . . a strong sense of tradition and heritage" provides an inspirational basis for operating the Great Lakes Naval Museum, in contrast to planning based only on budgets and historical artifacts.

Strategic goals evolve from the mission and vision of the organization. The chief executive officer of the organization, with the input and approval of the board of directors, establishes the mission, vision, and major strategic goals. The concepts and information within the mission statement, vision statement, and strategic goals statement may not be identified as such, but they should be communicated to everyone who has contact with the organization. Large firms generally provide public formal statements of their missions, visions, goals, and even values. For example, in support of its vision that "creating a community of good neighbors" is best done "together" with all sectors of the community, the City of Redmond has established goals such as these:

Enhance citizen engagement in city issues.
Sustain the natural systems and beauty of the community.
Sustain a safe community with a coherent, comprehensive, cohesive approach to
  safety.
Maintain economic vitality.

Different city departments would contribute to various aspects of this vision in the way they carry out their operational plans with an emphasis on collaborating with local businesses and residents.

Lofty words in a vision and mission statement cannot be meaningful without strong leadership support. At McDonald's, the commitment of past and present CEOs has played a large role in the success of the company's strategy implementation. Several years ago, the company was floundering as it lost sight of its commitment to quality, value, speed, and convenience. Under the leadership of James Cantalupo, the company created the mission statement quoted earlier, which placed the emphasis on the customer's experience. In a "Plan to Win," strategic goals such as revamping restaurants for a better drive-through experience and improving the quality of the menu supported the mission. When Jim Skinner took the job of chief executive, he enthusiastically backed the mission statement and its supporting Plan to Win, not hesitating to share credit for the company's continued success.[16]

> "There is no more powerful engine driving an organization toward excellence and long-term success than an attractive, worthwhile, and achievable vision of the future."
> Burt Nanus
>
> SOURCE: *Visionary Leadership* (San Francisco: Jossey-Bass, 1992).

Where leadership is strong, statements of visions and goals clarify the organization's purpose to key constituencies outside the organization. They also help employees focus their talent, energy, and commitment in pursuit of the organization's goals. When the time comes for you to seek employment with a firm, reviewing the firm's statements of mission, vision, and goals is a good first step in determining whether the firm's purposes and values will be compatible with your own.

Step 2: Analysis of External Opportunities and Threats

The mission and vision drive the second component of the strategic management process: analysis of the external environment. Successful strategic management depends on an accurate and thorough evaluation of the competitive environment and macroenvironment. The various components of these environments were introduced in Chapter 2.

TABLE 4.1
Environmental Analysis

Industry and Market Analysis

- *Industry profile:* major product lines and significant market segments in the industry.
- *Industry growth:* growth rates for the entire industry, growth rates for key market segments, projected changes in patterns of growth, and the determinants of growth.
- *Industry forces:* threat of new industry entrants, threat of substitutes, economic power of buyers, economic power of suppliers, and internal industry rivalry (recall Chapter 2).

Competitor Analysis

- *Competitor profile:* major competitors and their market shares.
- *Competitor analysis:* goals, strategies, strengths, and weaknesses of each major competitor.
- *Competitor advantages:* the degree to which industry competitors have differentiated their products or services or achieved cost leadership.

Political and Regulatory Analysis

- *Legislation and regulatory activities* and their effects on the industry.
- *Political activity:* the level of political activity that organizations and associations within the industry undertake (see Chapter 5).

Social Analysis

- *Social issues:* current and potential social issues and their effects on the industry.
- *Social interest groups:* consumer, environmental, and similar activist groups that attempt to influence the industry (see Chapters 5 and 6).

Human Resources Analysis

- *Labor issues:* key labor needs, shortages, opportunities, and problems confronting the industry (see Chapters 10 and 11).

Macroeconomic Analysis

- *Macroeconomic conditions:* economic factors that affect supply, demand, growth, competition, and profitability within the industry.

Technological Analysis

- *Technological factors:* scientific or technical methods that affect the industry, particularly recent and potential innovations (see Chapter 17).

The important activities in an environmental analysis include the ones listed in Table 4.1. The analysis begins with an examination of the industry. Next, organizational stakeholders are examined. **Stakeholders** are groups and individuals who affect and are affected by the achievement of the organization's mission, goals, and strategies. They include buyers, suppliers, competitors, government and regulatory agencies, unions and employee groups, the financial community, owners and shareholders, and trade associations. The environmental analysis provides a map of these stakeholders and the ways they influence the organization.[17]

stakeholders

Groups and individuals who affect and are affected by the achievement of the organization's mission, goals, and strategies.

Collaborating with key stakeholders can help organizations successfully develop and implement their strategic plan. At software company Intuit, CEO Brad Smith launched strategy development by learning what was on the minds of some key stakeholders. He visited with his board of directors and investors and set up meetings with groups of employees who work directly with Intuit's customers.

Smith asked each group of stakeholders some key questions related to strategic analysis: "What is Intuit's biggest untapped opportunity? What is the biggest risk facing Intuit that keeps you up at night? What is the biggest mistake I can make as a CEO in my first year?" From the answers, Smith gained insights that helped him establish priorities for Intuit's strategy.

Smith learned that a sizable number of Intuit's business customers have international activities, so he determined that Intuit would have to become a more global company. Its QuickBooks financial software now handles multiple currencies for international transactions. In response to the competitive threat of a new release of financial software from Microsoft, Smith assembled managers to craft a marketing strategy that would convince customers to wait two more months for the next version of QuickBooks. That campaign caused QuickBooks sales to jump in spite of Microsoft's efforts.[18]

The environmental analysis also should examine other forces in the environment, such as economic conditions and technological factors. One critical task in environmental analysis is forecasting future trends. As noted in Chapter 2, forecasting techniques range from simple judgment to complex mathematical models that examine systematic relationships among many variables. Even simple quantitative techniques outperform the intuitive assessments of experts. Judgment is susceptible to bias, and managers have a limited ability to process information. Managers should use subjective judgments as inputs to quantitative models or when they confront new situations.

Frequently, the difference between an opportunity and a threat depends on how a company positions itself strategically. For example, some states have required that electric utilities get a certain share of their power from renewable sources such as wind and solar energy, rather than from fossil fuels, including coal, oil, and natural gas. This requirement poses an obvious threat to utilities, because the costs of fossil fuel energy are less, and customers demand low prices. However, some companies see strategic opportunities in renewable power. For example, the German conglomerate Schott has developed a solar thermal technology in which sunlight heats oil in metal tubes enclosed in coated glass; the heated oil makes steam, which powers a turbine and generates electricity. Solar thermal energy, although it now costs more than fossil fuels, is more efficient than the solar panels installed on buildings, and it can store extra power to be used on cloudy days.[19] Similarly, overflowing landfills are an expensive challenge for many municipalities, but a growing number are seeing an opportunity in the form of energy generation. As garbage decomposes, it produces methane gas, which is used as a fuel to power generators. In East Brunswick, New Jersey, for example, the Edgeboro landfill generates electricity that powers the county's wastewater treatment plant.[20]

Some changes in the environment can bring one company a combination of threats and opportunities. Recently, the United States and European Union deregulated air travel between their respective countries, allowing any European air carrier to fly to any city in the United States, while U.S. carriers were granted access to all airports in EU countries. Before this agreement, airlines had to negotiate permission with each country whose airport they wanted to use. The deregulation allows American Airlines, for example, to broaden the variety of flights it offers in its oneworld alliance with British Airways—an opportunity. But it also means threats, such as new competition to serve London's Heathrow Airport, where Continental and Delta previously could not land.[21]

> "We wanted Nike to be the world's best sports and fitness company. Once you say that, you have a focus. You don't end up making wing tips or sponsoring the next Rolling Stone world tour."
>
> Philip Knight, Nike Founder

Step 3: Analysis of Internal Strengths and Weaknesses

As managers conduct an external analysis, they will also assess the strengths and weaknesses of major functional areas inside their organization. Table 4.2 lists some of the major components of this internal resource analysis. For example, is your firm strong enough financially to handle the lengthy and costly investment new projects often require? Can your existing staff carry out its part of the plan, or will additional training or hiring be needed? Is your firm's image compatible with the strategy, or will it have to persuade key stakeholders that a change in direction makes sense? This kind of internal analysis provides strategic decision makers with an inventory of the organization's existing functions, skills, and resources as well as its overall performance level. Many of your other business courses will prepare you to conduct an internal analysis.

resources

LO 4

Inputs to a system that can enhance performance.

Amazon's key customer benefits are speed and excellence of service.

Resources and Core Competencies   Without question, strategic planning has been strongly influenced in recent years by a focus on internal resources. **Resources** are inputs to production (recall systems theory) that can be accumulated over time to enhance the performance of a firm. Resources can take many forms, but they tend to fall into two broad categories: (1) *tangible assets* such as real estate, production facilities, raw materials, and so on, and (2) *intangible assets* such as company reputation, culture, technical knowledge, and patents, as well as accumulated learning and experience. The Walt Disney Company, for example, has developed its strategic plan on combinations of tangible assets (e.g., hotels and theme parks) as well as intangible assets (brand recognition, talented craftspeople, culture focused on customer service).[22]

Effective internal analysis provides a clearer understanding of how a company can compete through its resources. Resources are a source of competitive advantage only under certain circumstances. First, if the resource is instrumental for creating customer *value*—that is, if it increases the benefits customers derive from a good or service relative to the costs they incur—the resource can lead to a competitive advantage.[23] For example, Amazon's powerful search technology and its ability to track customer preferences and offer personalized recommendations each time its site is accessed, as

TABLE 4.2
Internal Resource Analysis

Financial Analysis
Examines financial strengths and weaknesses through financial statements such as a balance sheet and an income statement and compares trends to historical and industry figures (see Chapter 18).
Marketing Audit
Examines strengths and weaknesses of major marketing activities and identifies markets, key market segments, and the competitive position (market share) of the organization within key markets.
Operations Analysis
Examines the strengths and weaknesses of the manufacturing, production, or service delivery activities of the organization (see Chapters 9, 16, and 17).
Other Internal Resource Analyses
Examine, as necessary and appropriate, the strengths and weaknesses of other organizational activities, such as research and development (product and process), management information systems, engineering, and purchasing.
Human Resources Assessment
Examines strengths and weaknesses of all levels of management and employees and focuses on key human resources activities, including recruitment, selection, placement, training, labor (union) relationships, compensation, promotion, appraisal, quality of work life, and human resources planning (see Chapters 10 and 11).

well as its quick product-delivery system, are clearly valuable resources that enhance Amazon's competitiveness.

Second, resources are a source of advantage if they are *rare* and not equally available to all competitors. Even for extremely valuable resources, if all competitors have equal access, the resource cannot provide a source of competitive advantage. For companies such as Merck, DuPont, Dow Chemical, and others, patented formulas represent important resources that are both rare and valuable. Amazon, too, sought a patent for its one-click shopping technique.

Third, if resources are *difficult to imitate*, they provide a source of competitive advantage. Earlier in this chapter, we saw that Wells Fargo has managed to compete with larger banks by developing expertise in cross-selling. Unlike, say, free checking accounts, this intangible resource is difficult to imitate because it requires training and motivating employees at all levels to adopt customer-oriented thinking and collaborate across divisions. Under the strong leadership of Dick Kovacevich, Wells Fargo was able to inspire its employees to learn and use the necessary skills. Industry analyst Richard Bove says the strategy succeeded because of a hard-to-imitate resource, "the force of [Kovacevich's] personality, which is so strong and so positive that it infects other people."[24] As in this example, where success relies on leadership and collaboration practices, resources tend to be harder to imitate if they are complex, with many interdependent variables and no obvious links between easily explained behaviors and desired outcomes.[25]

Imagine how skilled Coca-Cola's global network of bottlers are to be able to deliver their product worldwide and more efficiently than any of their competitors. Shown here is a truck delivering Coke in India.

Finally, resources can enhance a firm's competitive advantage when they are well *organized*. For example, Coca-Cola's well-organized and global network of bottlers allows the company to quickly introduce a new soft drink worldwide and to distribute it more efficiently than any competitor. IBM, known primarily for computer hardware until it became more of a commodity than a source of competitive advantage, has organized its staff and systems to efficiently produce a consolidated technology product for its corporate clients—hardware, software, and service in one package. This spares its clients the cost of managing technology on their own.

As shown in Figure 4.5, when resources are valuable, rare, inimitable, and organized, they can be viewed as a company's core competencies. Simply stated, a **core competence** is something a company does especially well relative to its competitors.

core competence

A unique skill and/or knowledge an organization possesses that gives it an edge over competitors.

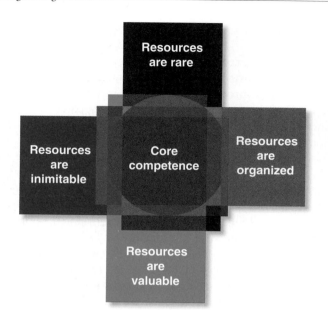

FIGURE 4.5
Resources and Core
Competence

Honda, for example, has a core competence in small engine design and manufacturing; Sony has a core competence in miniaturization; Federal Express has a core competence in logistics and customer service. As in these examples, a core competence typically refers to a set of skills or expertise in some activity, rather than physical or financial assets.

Kodak CEO Antonio Perez is attempting to redefine his firm's core competencies. Once a film-based business, Kodak developed digital camera products that eventually became standard fare. But even though these new products generated huge sales, overall profits for Kodak lagged. So Perez wants Kodak to shift its focus, creating innovative products that will help people organize, classify, and manage their personal photo libraries, much the same way Apple products do for their music libraries. In other words, he wants Kodak to concentrate on digital services instead of tangible products like cameras and film. The new digital services include such offerings as online photo sharing and a rapid-fire scanning system called Scan the World, which takes those old shoe boxes filled with snapshots and transforms them into digital images that are organized and catalogued by date. Perez knows that the change will be difficult. It will be "a very hard transformation," he admits. But he believes this move will ultimately yield greater profits and a longer life for Kodak.[26]

Benchmarking   To assess and improve performance, some companies use benchmarking, the process of assessing how well one company's basic functions and skills compare with those of another company or set of companies. The goal of benchmarking is to thoroughly understand the "best practices" of other firms and to undertake actions to achieve both better performance and lower costs. Benchmarking programs have helped a myriad of companies, such as Ford, Corning, Hewlett-Packard, Xerox, and Anheuser-Busch, make great strides in eliminating inefficiencies and improving competitiveness.

In London, doctors at Great Ormond Street Hospital for Children used benchmarking to improve their procedures for patient handoffs, the times when patients are transferred from one hospital unit or doctor's care to another. A team of doctors benchmarked an organization that excelled in complex procedures: the pit crew for Italy's Formula One Ferrari racing team. They learned, for example, that the pit crew carefully choreographed all their moves, based on information from a human factors engineer and a focus on minor mistakes that wouldn't be obvious. Unlike the surgical teams at Great Ormond, members of the pit crew knew who was in charge, had clearly specific responsibilities, worked in silence, and trained for every imaginable contingency. The doctors developed ways to apply those procedures to their cardiac surgery team, with the result that technical errors declined by 42 percent and failures to share information dropped by half.[27]

Depending on how it is applied, benchmarking may be of limited help in that it only helps a company perform as well as its competitors; strategic management ultimately is about surpassing those companies. Besides benchmarking against leading organizations in other industries, as Great Ormond Street Hospital did, companies may address this problem by engaging in internal benchmarking. That approach involves benchmarking their different internal operations and departments against one another to disseminate the company's best practices throughout the organization and thereby gain a competitive advantage.

Aligning a firm's bottom-line practices with "best practices" can improve its competitiveness.

Step 4: SWOT Analysis and Strategy Formulation

Once managers have analyzed the external environment and the internal resources of the organization, they will have the information they need to assess the organization's strengths, weaknesses, opportunities, and threats. Such an assessment normally is referred to as a **SWOT analysis.** Strengths and weaknesses refer to internal resources. For example, an organization's *strengths* might include skilled management, positive cash flow, and well-known and highly regarded brands. *Weaknesses* might be lack of spare production capacity and the absence of reliable suppliers. Opportunities and threats arise in the macroenvironment and competitive environment. Examples of *opportunities* are a new technology that could make the supply chain more efficient and a market niche that is currently underserved. *Threats* might include the possibility that competitors will enter the underserved niche once it has been shown to be profitable. In the "Management Close-Up: Taking Action" feature, consider what strengths, weaknesses, opportunities, and threats Olli-Pekka Kallasvuo identified at Nokia.

SWOT analysis helps managers summarize the relevant, important facts from their external and internal analyses. Based on this summary, they can identify the primary and secondary strategic issues their organization faces. The managers then formulate a strategy that will build on the SWOT analysis to take advantage of available opportunities by capitalizing on the organization's strengths, neutralizing its weakness, and countering potential threats.

To take an example, consider how SWOT analysis might be carried out at Microsoft. The company's size and earnings from its dominant operating system and Office suite of software are an obvious strength. The company has weaknesses as well. One of the fastest-growing areas of the computer business is Internet applications, especially profits from the sale of online advertising. Microsoft has struggled in this area, with its Internet search engine losing market share year after year, and online ad sales growing but only as a tiny segment of the market. The dominant threat to Microsoft in this area is widely considered to be Google, which not only dominates the search business—and its related advertising—but even has challenged Microsoft with free business applications. This analysis would explain Microsoft's recent efforts to buy DoubleClick, which arranges deals between advertisers and online publishers. DoubleClick is a big player in the online-advertising business and has expertise that Microsoft lacks.[28] By purchasing DoubleClick, Microsoft would use one of its strengths (its capital) to neutralize a weakness (inexperience and small market share in online advertising) and counter a threat (Google). Ironically, before the deal could close, Google emerged as another bidder for DoubleClick.[29] In the real world, as a company is formulating strategy, so are its competitors. As a result, the process must

SWOT analysis

A comparison of strengths, weaknesses, opportunities, and threats that helps executives formulate strategy.

Management Close-Up | TAKING ACTION

When Olli-Pekka Kallasvuo became CEO in 2006, Nokia was viewed as stodgy and slow to react to changes in the cell phone marketplace. What's more, critics characterized its product lineup as "tired." Kallasvuo told the press that despite Nokia's dominant position in most of the world, it could not afford to be overconfident. The company, he said, needed to become flexible and responsive to customer needs and wants.

Kallasvuo also spoke about the importance of humility as a trait in a manager—and a company. He defined a humble company as one that listens to its customers and uses the information in its planning—one whose management teams embrace diversity of opinion. Said Kallasvuo, management teams need to "resist the safe conformity of benchmarking" and embrace change. Kallasvuo also declared that he wanted to move Nokia to a management structure that would better reflect its global presence.

Making these adjustments could be a tall order for a company that, in many respects, already seemed to be doing many things right. Field research has enabled Nokia to learn what consumers in developing economies want and need—for example, a built-in flashlight on the low-cost models Nokia sells in sub-Saharan Africa, where the power grid is often down or spotty. Through high-volume parts purchasing, Nokia has been able to manage unit costs well enough that its competitors can't touch it in the low-end market. Kallasvuo also issued an edict regarding product development: projects must be ready in months, not years.[30]

- Olli-Pekka Kallasvuo says, as a CEO, he can accomplish very little on his own. However, with the Nokia workforce numbering about 100,000, he says there's much that can be accomplished with teams. Do you agree? How does teamwork relate to strategic planning?
- When Google announced it was pioneering software technology to bring Internet capability to cell phones, Nokia's first reaction was that Google did not represent a threat. What do you think of this analysis?

be continually evolving through contingency planning. The more uncertainty that exists in the external environment, the more the strategy needs to focus on building internal capabilities through practices such as knowledge sharing and continuous process improvement.[31] Yet, at a basic level, strategy formulation moves from analysis to devising a coherent course of action, such as Microsoft's plan to purchase (and eventually operate) DoubleClick. In this way, the organization's corporate, business, and functional strategies will begin to take shape.

Before we continue our strategy discussion, we note that many individuals seeking a job or a career change can find a "self-SWOT analysis" helpful. What are you particularly good at? What weaknesses might you need to overcome to improve your employment chances? What firms offer the best opportunity to market your skills to full advantage? Will you have a lot of competition from other job seekers? As with companies, this kind of analysis can be the beginning of a plan of action and can improve the plan's effectiveness.

Corporate Strategy A **corporate strategy** identifies the set of businesses, markets, or industries in which the organization competes and the distribution of resources among those businesses. Figure 4.6 shows four basic alternatives for a corporate strategy, ranging from very specialized to highly diverse. A **concentration** strategy focuses on a single business competing in a single industry. In the food-retailing industry, Kroger, Safeway, and A&P all pursue concentration strategies. Frequently, companies

corporate strategy

The set of businesses, markets, or industries in which an organization competes and the distribution of resources among those entities.

concentration

A strategy employed for an organization that operates a single business and competes in a single industry.

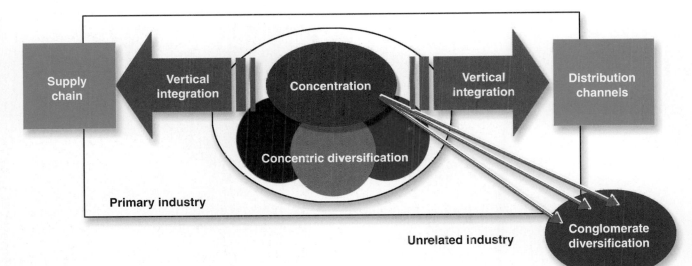

Primary industry

Unrelated industry

Conglomerate diversification

FIGURE 4.6
Summary of Corporate Strategies

LO 5

vertical integration

The acquisition or development of new businesses that produce parts or components of the organization's product.

General Electric's ownership of NBC is an example of conglomerate diversification. Shown from left to right during the giant merger announcement in 1986 are Grant Tinker, outgoing Chairman of NBC; Jack Welch, CEO of GE during the takeover; and Bob Wright, incoming Chairman of NBC.

pursue concentration strategies to gain entry into an industry when industry growth is good, or when the company has a narrow range of competencies. An example is the Chinese company Baidu.com, described in the *BusinessWeek* box. C. F. Martin & Company pursues a concentration strategy by focusing on making the best possible guitars and guitar strings, a strategy that has enabled the family-owned business to operate successfully for more than 150 years.

A **vertical integration** strategy involves expanding the domain of the organization into supply channels or to distributors. At one time, Henry Ford had fully integrated his company from the ore mines needed to make steel all the way to the showrooms where his cars were sold. Vertical integration generally is used to eliminate uncertainties and reduce costs associated with suppliers or distributors.

A strategy of **concentric diversification** involves moving into new businesses that are related to the company's original core business. William Marriott expanded his original restaurant business outside Washington, D.C., by moving into airline catering, hotels, and fast food. Each of these businesses within the hospitality industry is related in terms of the services it provides, the skills necessary for success, and the customers it attracts. Often companies such as Marriott pursue a strategy of concentric diversification to take advantage of their strengths in one business to gain advantage in another. Because the businesses are related, the products, markets, technologies, or capabilities used in one business can be transferred to another. Success in a concentric diversification strategy requires adequate management and other resources for operating more than one business. Guitar maker C. F. Martin once tried expanding through purchases of other instrument companies, but management was stretched too thin to run them all well, so the company eventually divested the acquisitions and returned to its concentration strategy.[32]

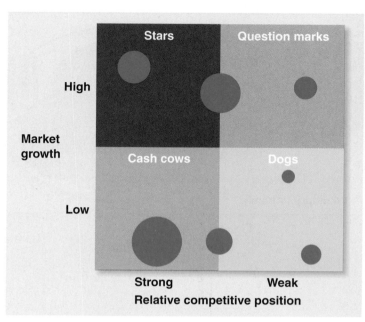

FIGURE 4.7
The BCG Matrix

concentric diversification

A strategy used to add new businesses that produce related products or are involved in related markets and activities.

conglomerate diversification

A strategy used to add new businesses that produce unrelated products or are involved in unrelated markets and activities.

In contrast to concentric diversification, **conglomerate diversification** is a corporate strategy that involves expansion into unrelated businesses. For example, General Electric Corporation has diversified from its original base in electrical and home appliance products to such wide-ranging industries as health, finance, insurance, truck and air transportation, and even media, with its ownership of NBC. Typically, companies pursue a conglomerate diversification strategy to minimize risks due to market fluctuations in one industry.

The diversified businesses of an organization are sometimes called its business *portfolio*. One of the most popular techniques for analyzing a corporation's strategy for managing its portfolio is the BCG matrix, developed by the Boston Consulting Group. The BCG matrix is shown in Figure 4.7. Each business in the corporation is plotted on the matrix on the basis of the growth rate of its market and the relative strength of its competitive position in that market (market share). The business is represented by a circle whose size depends on the business's contribution to corporate revenues.

FROM THE PAGES OF
BusinessWeek

Baidu Thinks It Can Play in Japan

Facing slower growth and increased competition at home, Baidu.com, the dominant search engine in China, is making its first foray overseas. Baidu Chairman and Chief Executive Officer Robin Li said the company will spend $15 million trying to replicate its at-home success in Japan this year.

The company started investing in Japan last year, and management argues that the same magic that made Baidu.com tops in China will give Baidu.jp an edge in Japan. "We are very confident" about Baidu's ability to make an impact in the Japanese market, Li said in a conference call from Beijing.

Baidu certainly has had an impressive run in China. The company reported profits for 2006 of $38.7 million, up 533.9 percent from a year earlier, on sales of $107.4 million, an increase of 162.5 percent from the year before. Baidu has more than half of the total search market in China, and it has formed partnerships with some of the top names in the tech world, from IBM to Intel to Microsoft.

Baidu's accomplishments are all the more impressive given the attempts by both Google and Yahoo to become more competitive in the Chinese search market. Even Baidu, though, can't keep that kind of torrential growth going in China. In the fourth quarter of the previous year, Baidu only added 6,000 new customers on a base of more than 100,000 advertisers. Google and Yahoo aren't the only ones going after Baidu's core business. Local players such as portal Sohu.com and Shenzhen-based instant-messaging provider Tencent are also boosting their Chinese-language search offerings.

That's one reason Baidu is expanding to Japan. Some people who follow the industry believe that Baidu's strengths—especially its ability to cope with tens of thousands of Chinese characters—will help there. Written Japanese uses many of the same characters as written Chinese, and that plays to Baidu's biggest advantage over Western rivals, says Gerhard Fasol, CEO of Tokyo-based consulting firm Eurotechnology Japan. "They may be able to exploit their knowledge of Chinese characters better," he says.

Fasol also believes that Baidu has an opportunity to establish itself in Japan's mobile search market, which is in its infancy. "The momentum on development is moving from fixed-line to mobile," he says, pointing out that search via mobile phones is only about six months old in Japan. "You know, it's very early, so it's not mature at all. The dice have not fallen yet."

Still, some people who follow Chinese companies have their doubts about Baidu's ability to do well in Japan. There are several big-name competitors vying for the same market as Baidu. The field is dominated by Yahoo Japan. Google is stronger in Japan than in China, too. And Japanese cellular operator NTT DoCoMo operates a mobile search service of its own.

Li said Baidu has plenty of experience in coming from behind to take over a market. "Baidu wasn't number one in China from Day One," he said. "We started quite late. So we are familiar with how to play the catch-up game."

SOURCE: Excerpted from Bruce Einhorn, "Baidu Thinks It Can Play in Japan," *BusinessWeek*, February 15, 2007, http://www.businessweek.com.

High-growth, weak-competitive-position businesses are called *question marks*. They require substantial investment to improve their position; otherwise, divestiture is recommended. High-growth, strong-competitive-position businesses are called *stars*. These businesses require heavy investment, but their strong position allows them to generate the needed revenues. Low-growth, strong-competitive-position businesses are called *cash cows*. These businesses generate revenues in excess of their investment needs and therefore fund other businesses. Finally, low-growth, weak-competitive-position businesses are called *dogs*. The remaining revenues from these businesses are realized, and then the businesses are divested.

Concentric diversification can melt national boundaries. Internet search giant Google recently acquired a portion of the rapidly growing Chinese Web site Xunlei.com, which allows users to download music and video clips from the Internet. Google's investment in—and partnership with—Xunlei.com will allow the Chinese site to use Google's search capabilities, while giving Google direct access to China's 130 million Internet users. Google has also formed an alliance with China Mobile, the country's largest mobile phone carrier, to offer mobile Internet search service to Chinese consumers.

Despite its ranking as the world's largest search engine, in China Google is dwarfed by the Chinese search engine Baidu.com, which claims about 63 percent of China's market share. (Google claims only about 19 percent.) In addition, China is filled with tiny start-ups that have, thus far, shut out U.S. Internet firms. So, Google's strategy is to diversify within that country to capture more of the market. Because of government and cultural restraints in China, Google would have a much more difficult time entering the market there alone. By creating alliances with Chinese firms, Google will have a better chance of gaining the attention of Chinese consumers who are in the market for downloads of videos, music, games, software, and cell phone ringtones.[33]

$ **The bottom line**
COST
Companies that integrate vertically often do so to reduce their costs.

The BCG matrix is not intended as a substitute for management judgment, creativity, insight, or leadership. But it is a tool that can, along with other techniques, help managers of the firm as a whole and of its individual businesses evaluate their strategy alternatives.[34] This type of thinking has recently helped Abbott Laboratories succeed. When Miles White took over as Abbott's CEO, he began restructuring the company's portfolio to emphasize growth. He sold off much of the company's diagnostics business, which was earning low returns, and purchased businesses with higher risks but the potential to be stars, including Guidant Corporation's vascular division, which makes drug-coated stents, and Kos Pharmaceuticals, which is working on drugs for raising "good" cholesterol. White says his goal is to have a portfolio of businesses that are innovative, growing, and delivering high returns.[35]

Trends in Corporate Strategy   Corporate America is periodically swept by waves of mergers and acquisitions (M&As). The targets chosen for mergers and acquisitions depend on the organization's corporate strategy of either concentrating in one industry or diversifying its portfolio. Many of the most recent deals, including AT&T's acquisition of BellSouth, have been aimed at helping the companies enjoy the cost advantages of consolidating their marketing, customer service, and other operations. In contrast, during the 1990s, many deals—including the merger of America Online and Time Warner—were made to help traditional businesses enter the hot Internet market.

The value of implementing a diversified corporate strategy depends on individual circumstances. Many critics have argued that unrelated diversification hurts a company more often than it helps it. In recent years, many diversified companies have sold their peripheral businesses so that they could concentrate on a more focused portfolio. In contrast, the diversification efforts of an organization competing in a slow-growth, mature, or threatened industry often are applauded.

Although the merits of diversification are an issue for continued study, most observers agree that organizations usually perform better if they implement a more concentric diversification strategy, in which businesses are related somehow or similar to one another. For example, near the beginning of the chapter, we saw that IBM has a successful strategy of acquiring small software companies. This strategy succeeds because IBM has a competitive advantage in selling software (including a brand with a strong reputation), has expertise in the product category that can help it appreciate the technical applications sold by these sometimes-obscure companies, and uses the acquisitions to grow faster than it could by hiring its programmers to create similar products. The acquired companies benefit because sales of their products increase—by an average of 25 percent in the first year.[37]

The past two decades have seen waves of mergers and acquisitions.[36]

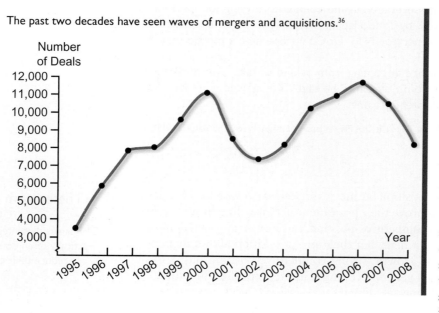

business strategy

The major actions by which a business competes in a particular industry or market.

 Business Strategy   After the top management team and board make the corporate strategic decisions, executives must determine how they will compete in each business area. **Business strategy** defines the major actions by which an organization builds and strengthens its competitive position in the marketplace. A competitive advantage typically results from one of two generic business strategies introduced here and elaborated in Chapter 7.[38]

First, organizations such as Wal-Mart and Southwest Airlines pursue competitive advantage through **low-cost strategies.** Businesses using a low-cost strategy attempt to be efficient and offer a standard, no-frills product. Southwest Airlines' low-cost strategy is simply stated: "to be *the* low-fare airline." That strategy helps with operational planning; when someone suggested offering passengers chicken salad instead of peanuts on some flights, the chief executive simply asked whether chicken salad would help Southwest be "*the* low-fare airline."[39] Companies that succeed with a low-cost strategy often are large and try to take advantage of economies of scale in production or distribution. In many cases, their scale allows them to buy and sell their goods and services at a lower price, which leads to higher market share, volume, and, ultimately, profits. To succeed, an organization using this strategy generally must be the cost leader in its industry or market segment. However, even a cost leader must offer a product that is acceptable to customers compared with competitors' products.

Second, an organization may pursue a **differentiation strategy.** With a differentiation strategy, a company attempts to be unique in its industry or market segment along some dimensions that customers value. This unique or differentiated position within the industry often is based on high product quality, excellent marketing and distribution, or superior service.

Nordstrom's commitment to quality and customer service in the retail apparel industry is an excellent example of a differentiation strategy. For example, Nordstrom's personal shoppers are available online, by phone, or in stores to select items for shoppers' consideration at no charge. Innovation, too, is an important ingredient of a differentiation strategy. In the market for toilet paper, Scott Paper Company once determined that it could not afford to compete for institutional sales based on price. Instead, the company began offering institutions a free dispenser that would hold larger rolls of paper, saving its customers the labor cost of replacing empty rolls more frequently. Scott initially was the only company selling the larger rolls, so it gained market share while competitors scrambled to catch up.[40]

Whatever strategy managers adopt, *the most effective strategy is one that competitors are unwilling or unable to imitate.* If the organization's strategic plan is one that could easily be adopted by industry competitors, it may not be sufficiently distinctive or, in the long run, contribute significantly to the organization's competitiveness. For example, a strategy to gain market share and, ultimately, profits by being the "first mover" to offer an innovative product may or may not succeed, depending in part on competitive responses. In some industries, such as computers, technology advances so fast that the first company to provide a new product is quickly challenged by later entrants offering superior products.[41]

Functional Strategy The final step in strategy formulation is to establish the major functional strategies. **Functional strategies** are implemented by each functional area of the organization to support the business strategy. The typical functional areas include production, human resources, marketing, research and development, finance, and distribution. For example, IBM's plan to grow through acquisitions of software companies requires functional strategies for training its sales force to understand the new products and for training the acquired company's employees to understand IBM's culture and procedures. Part of the functional strategy includes assigning each new employee to an experienced IBM mentor. At Wells Fargo, the strategy to grow through cross-selling requires functional strategies for advertising, training employees to cross-sell, and developing systems for sharing information across department boundaries. And at Boeing, the strategy to grow at a steady pace, rather than ramping-up production until high costs force cutbacks, requires functional strategies related to hiring and training employees, scheduling production, and negotiating sales.[42]

Functional strategies typically are developed by functional area executives with input of and approval from the executives responsible for business strategy. Senior strategic decision makers review the functional strategies to ensure that each major department is operating consistent with the business strategies of the organization. For example, automated production techniques—even if they saved money—would not be appropriate for a piano company like Steinway, whose products are strategically positioned (and priced) as high-quality and hand-crafted. At companies that compete based on product innovation, strategies for research and development are especially critical. But in the recession that occurred at the beginning of this decade, General Electric cut back on research in lighting technology just as other companies were making advances in LED lighting. When the economy recovered, customers were looking for innovative lighting, but GE had fallen behind. Based on that experience, GE committed itself to an R&D strategy of maintaining budgets even when sales slow down. In the latest economic downturn, the company continued to fund a project in which it is developing new aircraft engines with Honda Motor Company.[43]

LO 7 Step 5: Strategy Implementation

As with any plan, simply formulating a good strategy is not enough. Strategic managers also must ensure that the new strategies are implemented effectively and efficiently. Recently, corporations and strategy consultants have been paying more attention to implementation. They realize that clever techniques and a good plan do not guarantee success. This greater appreciation is reflected in two major trends.

First, organizations are adopting a more comprehensive view of implementation. The organization structure, technology, human resources, employee reward systems, information systems, organization culture, and leadership style must all support the strategy. Just as an organization's strategy must be matched to the external environment, so must it also fit the multiple factors through which it is implemented. The remainder of this section discusses these factors and the ways they can be used to implement strategy.

Second, many organizations are extending the more participative strategic management process to implementation. Managers at all levels are involved with formulating strategy and identifying and executing ways to implement it. Senior executives still may oversee the implementation process, but they are placing much greater responsibility and authority in the hands of others. In general, strategy implementation involves four related steps:

Step 1: Define strategic tasks. Articulate in simple language what a particular business must do to create or sustain a competitive advantage. Define strategic tasks to help employees understand how they contribute to the organization, including redefining relationships among the parts of the organization.

Step 2: Assess organization capabilities. Evaluate the organization's ability to implement the strategic tasks. A task force typically interviews employees and managers to identify specific issues that help or hinder effective implementation. Then the results are summarized for top management. In the course of your career, you will likely be asked to participate in a task force. We discuss working effectively in teams in Chapter 14.

Step 3: Develop an implementation agenda. Management decides how it will change its own activities and procedures; how critical interdependencies will be managed; what skills and individuals are needed in key roles; and what structures, measures, information, and rewards might ultimately support the needed behavior. A philosophy statement, communicated in terms of value, is the outcome of this process.

Step 4: Create an implementation plan. The top management team, the employee task force, and others develop the implementation plan. The top management team then monitors progress. The employee task force continues its work by providing feedback about how others in the organization are responding to the changes.

This process, though straightforward, does not always go smoothly. Table 4.3 shows six different barriers to strategy implementation and provides a description of some key principles for overcoming these "silent killers." By paying closer attention to the processes by which strategies are implemented, executives, managers, and employees can make sure that strategic plans are actually carried out.[44]

Step 6: Strategic Control

The final component of the strategic management process is strategic control. A **strategic control system** is designed to support managers in evaluating the organization's progress with its strategy and, when discrepancies exist, taking corrective action. The system must encourage efficient operations that are consistent with the plan while

strategic control system

A system designed to support managers in evaluating the organization's progress regarding its strategy and, when discrepancies exist, taking corrective action.

TABLE 4.3
Attacking the Six Barriers to Strategy Implementation

Change starts with the leader	
The Silent Killers	**Principles for Engaging and Changing the Silent Killers**
Top-down or laissez-faire senior management style	With the top team and lower levels, the CEO/general manager creates a partnership built around the development of a compelling business direction, the creation of an enabling organizational context, and the delegation of authority to clearly accountable individuals and teams.
Unclear strategy and conflicting priorities	The top team, as a group, develops a statement of strategy, and priorities that members are willing to stand behind are developed.
An ineffective senior management team	The top team, as a group, is involved in all steps in the change process so that its effectiveness is tested and developed.
Poor vertical communication	An honest, fact-based dialogue is established with lower levels about the new strategy and the barriers to implementing it.
Poor coordination across functions, businesses, or borders	A set of businesswide initiatives and new organizational roles and responsibilities are defined that require "the right people to work together on the right things in the right way" to implement the strategy.
Inadequate down-the-line leadership skills and development	Lower-level managers develop skills through newly created opportunities to lead change and drive key business initiatives. They are supported with just-in-time coaching, training, and targeted recruitment. Those who still are not able to make the grade must be replaced.

SOURCE: Reprinted from M. Beer and R. A Eisenstat, "The Silent Killers of Strategy Implementation and Learning," *MIT Sloan Management Review* 4, no. 4 (Summer 2000), pp. 29–40, by permission of the publisher. Copyright © 2000 by Massachusetts Institute of Technology. All rights reserved.

allowing flexibility to adapt to changing conditions. As with all control systems, the organization must develop performance indicators, an information system, and specific mechanisms to monitor progress. At Boeing, one obvious measure of its strategy to partner with suppliers is whether suppliers are keeping up with Boeing's need for components that meet its quality standards. In fact, as orders flowed in for the 787 Dreamliner, several suppliers began missing deadlines. Boeing dispatched teams of experts from various functions to visit the suppliers, diagnose the reasons for their difficulties, and help them catch up. It also has modified its strategy by having its own employees do more of the final assembly work in order to avoid falling further behind.[45]

Most strategic control systems include a budget to monitor and control major financial expenditures. In fact, as a first-time manager, you will most likely confront your work unit's budget—a key aspect of your organization's strategic plan. Your executive team may give you budget assumptions and targets for your area, reflecting your part in the overall plan, and you may be asked to revise your budget once all the budgets in your organization have been consolidated and reviewed.

The dual responsibilities of a control system—efficiency and flexibility—often seem contradictory with respect to budgets. The budget usually establishes spending limits, but changing conditions or the need for innovation may require different financial commitments during the period. To solve this dilemma, some companies have created two budgets: strategic and operational. For example, managers at Texas Instruments control two budgets under the OST (objectives-strategies-tactics) system. The strategic budget is used to create and maintain long-term effectiveness, and the operational budget is tightly monitored to achieve short-term efficiency. The topic of control in general—and budgets in particular—is discussed in more detail in Chapter 16. In the "Management Close-Up: Assessing Outcomes and Seizing Opportunities" feature, consider what performance measures indicate the success of Nokia's strategy. What trade-offs, if any, do you see between innovation and efficiency?

Management Close-Up

ASSESSING OUTCOMES AND SEIZING OPPORTUNITIES

After Apple's introduction of the iPhone and its growing multitude of Web applications, how did Nokia respond? Favorably, say industry observers, who have since shifted their outlook on Nokia's prospects. Under Kallasvuo's leadership, they say the company is looking to the future and introducing more interesting phones and services. For example, after Apple introduced its App Store, Nokia upped the ante by launching its Ovi Store on the Internet. The Ovi service, launched in 2007, permits Nokia phone users to access music, games, maps, videos, and more. Ovi applications also provide information targeted to a cell phone user's geographic location.

Nokia's newly launched high-end model, the N97, competes head to head with Apple's iPhone and Research in Motion's BlackBerry. The N97 boasts a slide-out alphabetic keyboard and a 3.5-inch touch screen with 50 percent greater resolution than the iPhone's. What's more, it comes preloaded with Ovi Store.

In another expansion of product capability, Nokia invested $35 million in Obopay, a mobile payment service. Located in India, Obopay enables users to send and receive money using their cell phone. Such services are particularly useful in developing countries, where consumers have little access to banks or credit cards and where holding large amounts of cash can be dangerous.

Nokia is also aggressively building a presence in the United States. Through a joint venture with Siemens AG, it is seeking to buy pieces of bankrupt Canadian carrier Nortel, which had a significant U.S. network and a robust research and development pipeline.

The company also announced it will produce a "green" phone made with recycled steel and environmentally friendly biomaterials. Called the "Remade," the phone has a thin, silver handset whose case is made of renewable materials instead of petroleum-based plastic.[46]

- Olli-Pekka Kallasvuo says that in the mobile-devices industry, one size will not fit all for wireless communications. How does this statement affect strategic planning at Nokia?
- A technology-driven industry like the one in which Nokia operates can be quite fluid. From the discussion in the case, how well do you think Nokia responded to its competition? Do you think its strategic planning has improved overall?

KEY TERMS

SUMMARY OF LEARNING OBJECTIVES

Now that you have studied Chapter 4, you should be able to:

LO 1   Summarize the basic steps in any planning process.

The planning process begins with a situation analysis of the external and internal forces affecting the organization. This examination helps identify and diagnose issues and problems and may bring to the surface alternative goals and plans for the firm. Next, the advantages and disadvantages of these goals and plans should be evaluated against one another. Once a set of goals and a plan have been selected, implementation involves communicating the plan to employees, allocating resources, and making certain that other systems such as rewards and budgets are supporting the plan. Finally, planning requires instituting control systems to monitor progress toward the goals.

LO 2   Describe how strategic planning should be integrated with tactical and operational planning.

Strategic planning is different from operational planning in that it involves making long-term decisions about the entire organization. Tactical planning translates broad goals and strategies into specific actions to be taken within parts of the organization. Operational planning identifies the specific short-term procedures and processes required at lower levels of the organization.

LO 3   Identify elements of the external environment and internal resources of the firm to analyze before formulating a strategy.

Strategic planning is designed to leverage the strengths of a firm while minimizing the effects of its weaknesses. It is difficult to know the potential advantage a firm may have unless external analysis is done well. For example, a company may have a talented marketing department or an efficient production system. However, the organization cannot determine whether these internal characteristics are sources of competitive advantage until it knows something about how well the competitors stack up in these areas.

LO 4   Define core competencies and explain how they provide the foundation for business strategy.

A core competence is something a company does especially well relative to its competitors. When this competence, say, in engineering or marketing, is in some area important to market success, it becomes the foundation for developing a competitive advantage. It can provide a sustainable advantage if it is valuable, rare, difficult to imitate, and well organized.

LO 5   Summarize the types of choices available for corporate strategy.

Corporate strategy identifies the breadth of a firm's competitive domain. Corporate strategy can be kept narrow, as in a concentration strategy, or can move to suppliers and buyers via vertical integration. Corporate strategy also can broaden a firm's domain via concentric (related) diversification or conglomerate (unrelated) diversification.

LO 6   Discuss how companies can achieve competitive advantage through business strategy.

Companies gain competitive advantage in two primary ways. They can attempt to be unique in some way by pursuing a differentiation strategy, or they can focus on efficiency and price by pursuing a low-cost strategy.

LO 7   Describe the keys to effective strategy implementation.

Many good plans are doomed to failure because they are not implemented correctly. Strategy must be supported by structure, technology, human resources, rewards, information systems, culture, leadership, and so on. Ultimately, the success of a plan depends on how well employees at low levels are able and willing to implement it. Participative management is one of the more popular approaches executives use to gain employees' input and ensure their commitment to strategy implementation.

DISCUSSION QUESTIONS

1. This chapter opened with a quote from former CEO of GE Jack Welch: "Manage your destiny, or someone else will." What does this mean for strategic management? What does it mean when Welch adds, "or someone else will"?

2. List the six steps in the formal planning process. Suppose you are a top executive of a home-improvement chain and you want to launch a new company Web site. Provide examples of activities you would carry out during each step to create the site.

3. Your friend is frustrated because he's having trouble selecting a career. He says, "I can't plan because the future is too complicated. Anything can happen, and there are too many choices." What would you say to him to change his mind?

4. How do strategic, operational, and tactical planning differ? How might the three levels complement one another in an organization?

5. How might an organization such as Urban Outfitters use a strategic map? With your classmates and using Figure 4.3 as a guide, develop a possible strategic map for the company.

6. What accounts for the shift from strategic planning to strategic management? In which industries would you be most likely to observe these trends? Why?

7. Review table 4.1, which lists the components of an environmental analysis. Why would this analysis be important to a company's strategic planning process?

8. In your opinion, what are the core competencies of Harley-Davidson Motor Company motorcycles? How do these competencies help Harley-Davidson compete against foreign competitors such as Yamaha and Suzuki?

9. How could SWOT analysis help newspaper companies remain competitive in the new media environment?

10. What are the key challenges in strategy implementation? What barriers might prevent strategy implementation?

CONCLUDING CASE

Custom Coffee & Chocolate

Bonnie Brewer and Stacy Kim were college roommates. While at school, they shared dreams of opening their own business. To prepare themselves, they took business and marketing courses, along with courses in management. When they graduated, they each found jobs in Seattle, near where they'd gone to school.

Several years later, after working at other companies to gain experience, the two women decided to take the plunge together and made a plan to open a small café where they and their customers could indulge their love of good coffee and fine chocolate. They looked at two locations for their café: one near Pike Place Market, which gets a lot of foot traffic from shoppers and businesspeople, and one near the university, where shops and restaurants are patronized by students, faculty, staff, and local residents. They chose the university location because they thought they knew and understood those customers well. The doors to Custom Coffee & Chocolate opened several months later, with both Brewer and Kim working hard to serve unique coffee blends and specialty chocolates, maintain the shop, and handle the finances.

Custom Coffee & Chocolate's business plan included purchasing only fair trade coffee (priced to provide living wages to coffee growers) and chocolates made by a few local suppliers. Their café was small, but it had several comfortable chairs, couches, and coffee tables to encourage customers to stay and chat or read the newspaper between classes. However, the majority of their business was takeout.

At the beginning, business was slow. Brewer and Kim had struggled to find the right price points for their coffee and chocolates, and they worried they might be set too high. But everyone who came in to the café loved what they bought, and came back—and began to bring friends. Business increased over a period of about five months, when Brewer and Kim had to turn their attention toward longer-term planning. They had exhausted their savings and their initial small-business loan, and their six-month lease was up. They needed to decide whether they were in this for the long haul.

The two women met to consider their options. Right away, they decided they wanted to extend their hours and hire two part-time employees. They would investigate a wireless connection that customers could use. Kim would take over more of the finances, while Brewer would handle marketing—which they both agreed they needed for the café to grow. They evaluated whether to expand the menu to include baked chocolate desserts, tea, and other beverages. They considered delivery service to locations on campus, such as dorms and lounges where students were studying. They discussed holding events at the café such as poetry readings or discussion groups. And they talked about establishing a Web site with a menu and phone number, updates on current coffees and chocolate flavors, and a blog written by Brewer with opportunities for customers to respond. They agreed they were not yet ready to accept online orders, but eventually they might.

As Kim and Brewer finalized their planning, they agreed that managing their own business was a challenge, but one they would never regret.

QUESTIONS

1. What do you think Custom Coffee & Chocolate's mission is?

2. Create a SWOT analysis for Custom Coffee & Chocolate.

3. Using the owners' ideas for the future of their café, as well as your own ideas, outline a tactical plan for Custom Coffee & Chocolate.

EXPERIENTIAL EXERCISES

4.1   Strategic Planning

OBJECTIVE

To study the strategic planning of a corporation recently in the news.

INSTRUCTIONS

BusinessWeek magazine frequently has articles on the strategies of various corporations. Find a recent article on a corporation in an industry of interest to you. Read the article and answer the following questions.

Strategic Planning Worksheet

1. Has the firm clearly identified what business it is in and how it is different from its competitors? Explain.

_____
_____
_____
_____
_____
_____

2. What are the key assumptions about the future that have shaped the firm's new strategy?

_____
_____
_____
_____
_____

3. What key strengths and weaknesses of the firm influenced the selection of the new strategy?

_____
_____
_____
_____
_____
_____

4. What specific objectives has the firm set in conjunction with the new strategy?

_____
_____
_____
_____
_____

SOURCE: R. R. McGrath Jr., *Exercises in Management Fundamentals*, p. 15. Copyright © 1984. Reprinted by permission of Pearson Education, Inc., Upper Saddle River, NJ.

4.2 Formulating Business Strategy

OBJECTIVES

1. To illustrate the complex interrelationships central to the formulation of business strategy.

2. To demonstrate the use of SWOT (strengths, weaknesses, opportunities, and threats) analysis in a business situation.

INSTRUCTIONS

1. Your instructor will divide the class into small groups and assign each group a well-known organization for analysis.

2. Each group will

   a. Study the SWOT Introduction and the SWOT Worksheet to understand the work needed to complete the assignment.

   b. Obtain the needed information about the organization under study through library research, interviews, and so on.

   c. Complete the SWOT Worksheet.

   d. Prepare group responses to the discussion questions.

3. After the class reconvenes, group spokespersons will present group findings.

DISCUSSION QUESTIONS

1. Why would most organizations not develop strategies for matches between opportunities and strengths?

2. Why would most organizations not develop strategies for matches between opportunities and weaknesses?

3. Why do most organizations want to deal from strength?

SWOT INTRODUCTION

One of the more commonly used strategy tools is SWOT (strengths, weaknesses, opportunities, and threats) analysis, which is accomplished in four steps:

Step 1: Analyze the organization's internal environment, identifying its strengths and weaknesses.

Step 2: Analyze the organization's external environment, identifying its opportunities and threats.

Step 3: Match (a) strengths with opportunities, (b) weaknesses with threats, (c) strengths with threats, and (d) weaknesses with opportunities.

Step 4: Develop strategies for those matches which appear to be of greatest importance to the organization. Most organizations give top priority to strategies that involve the matching of strengths with opportunities and second priority to strategies that involve the matching of weaknesses with threats. The key is to exploit opportunities in areas where the organization has a strength and to defend against threats in areas where the organization has a weakness.

SWOT Worksheet

Organization being analyzed: _____

Internal Analysis	External Analysis

Strengths

_____

_____

_____

_____

_____

_____

_____

_____

_____

_____

Opportunites

_____

_____

_____

_____

_____

_____

_____

_____

_____

_____

Weaknesses

_____

_____

_____

_____

_____

_____

_____

_____

_____

_____

Threats

_____

_____

_____

_____

_____

_____

_____

_____

_____

_____

Strategies That Match Strengths with Opportunites

_____
_____
_____
_____
_____
_____
_____
_____
_____
_____
_____
_____
_____
_____
_____

Strategies That Match Weaknesses with Threats

_____
_____
_____
_____
_____
_____
_____
_____
_____
_____
_____
_____
_____
_____
_____

Strategies That Match Strengths with Threats

_____
_____
_____
_____
_____
_____
_____
_____
_____
_____
_____
_____

Strategies That Match Weaknesses with Opportunites

_____
_____
_____
_____
_____
_____
_____
_____
_____
_____
_____
_____

chapter

5

Ethics and Corporate Responsibility

" *It is truly enough said that a corporation has no conscience; but a corporation of conscientious men is a corporation with a conscience.* "

— Henry David Thoreau

LEARNING OBJECTIVES

After studying Chapter 5, you will be able to:

LO 1 Describe how different ethical perspectives guide decision making. p. 165

LO 2 Explain how companies influence their ethics environment. p. 167

LO 3 Outline a process for making ethical decisions. p. 173

LO 4 Summarize the important issues surrounding corporate social responsibility. p. 175

LO 5 Discuss reasons for businesses' growing interest in the natural environment. p. 180

LO 6 Identify actions managers can take to manage with the environment in mind. p. 181

CHAPTER OUTLINE

It's a Big Issue
It's a Personal Issue

Ethics
Ethical Systems
Business Ethics
The Ethics Environment
Ethical Decision Making
Courage

Corporate Social Responsibility
Contrasting Views
Reconciliation

The Natural Environment
A Risk Society
Ecocentric Management
Environmental Agendas for the Future

Management Close-Up

At one time, if people used the word "green" to describe Wal-Mart, they were probably referring to the color of money. The world's largest retailer, Wal-Mart posted annual revenues of $400 billion—an amount greater than the gross domestic product of many countries. Operating 7,000 stores worldwide, Wal-Mart has commanded the number-one position on the *Fortune* 500 list nearly every year since 2002, with a workforce of over 2 million people—larger than the population of Philadelphia.

But now, when people use the word "green" to describe Wal-Mart, chances are they're talking about the environmental legacy of H. Lee Scott, who became the company's CEO in 2000 before retiring in 2009 and being succeeded by Michael Duke. Some believe Wal-Mart's environmental transformation began in the aftermath of Hurricane Katrina in late summer of 2005. After providing millions in cash donations and orchestrating a hands-on rescue program for disaster victims, Wal-Mart leaders began to realize how a company of its size had great potential to make a difference.

{ Wal-Mart and its practices have often been debated. The company's focus on the bottom line opened it to criticism on many fronts. Yet, the company has vowed to become a good corporate citizen. As you read this chapter, think about what Wal-Mart will need to do, going forward, to meet its aggressive environmental goals. }

This was a wake-up call, says former CEO Scott. "What struck us was: This world is much more fragile than any of us thought years ago." In an October 2005 speech broadcast to all company employees, Scott announced that Wal-Mart would begin a new sustainability strategy with three ambitious goals:

1. To be supplied 100 percent by renewable energy.
2. To create zero waste.
3. To sell only products that sustain Wal-Mart's resources—and the environment's.

Although Scott set no deadline for achieving those goals, he promised the company would soon begin working toward them. Thereafter, Wal-Mart engaged environmental groups, trade associations, and academics in conversations to educate itself and create a blueprint for long-term change. Scott's bold pronouncement surprised many people—particularly its army of suppliers worldwide. What would an "eco-friendly" Wal-Mart mean for them?[1]

For years, Wal-Mart has been a company its critics have loved to hate. As the retailer grew, so did the size of its stores. Many of its stores average 100,000 to 250,000 square feet, all of which must be heated, cooled, and well lit. The company's global supply and shipping systems operate on a monumental scale—using energy for shipping, trucking fleets, and distribution centers. But Wal-Mart has surprised many of its longtime critics by embracing the value that, as the world's largest retailer, it has not only the capacity but also an obligation to behave responsibly.

This chapter addresses the values and manner of doing business adopted by managers as they carry out their corporate and business strategies. In particular, we will explore ways of applying **ethics,** the system of rules that governs the ordering of values. We do so based on the premise that managers, their organizations, and their communities thrive over the long term when the managers apply ethical standards that direct them to act with integrity. In addition, we consider the idea that organizations may have a responsibility to meet social obligations beyond earning profits within legal and ethical constraints. As you study this chapter, consider what kind of manager you want to be. What reputation do you hope to have? How would you like others to describe your behavior as a manager?

ethics

The system of rules that governs the ordering of values.

It's a Big Issue

Recent scandals have engulfed company executives, independent auditors, politicians and regulators, and shareholders and employees.[2] In some, executives at public companies have made misleading statements to inflate stock prices, undermining the public's trust in the integrity of the financial markets. Often, the scandals are perpetrated by a number of people cooperating with one another, and many of the guilty parties had been otherwise upstanding individuals. Lobbyists have been accused—and some convicted—of buying influence with lavish gifts to politicians. Executives have admitted they received huge bonuses or stock options that were backdated to guarantee they would make money from investing in their company, regardless of whether their performance caused the stock's value to rise or fall. What other news disturbs you about managers' behavior? Tainted products in the food supply . . . actions that harm the environment . . . Internet scams . . . employees pressured to meet sales or production targets by any means? The list goes on, and the public becomes cynical. According to a survey by the public relations firm Edelman, people are often suspicious of their own company's management; only 31 percent said they trust their own CEO.[3] Try to imagine the challenge of leading employees who don't trust you.

Sadly, when corporations behave badly, it's often not the top executives but the rank-and-file employees who suffer most. When companies such as energy trader Enron and insurance brokerage firm Marsh & McLennan saw their stocks tumble following scandals, executives had millions invested from generous pay and bonus packages. In contrast, employees, who had been encouraged to invest their retirement packages heavily in their company's stock, saw their savings disappear along with their company's reputation.

Bernard Madoff was convicted for running a multibillion-dollar ponzi scheme. He was sentenced to 150 years in prison for fraud that totaled an estimated $65 billion. The incident has been referred to as the largest white-collar fraud in history.

Still, simply talking about Enron and other famous cases as examples of lax company ethics doesn't get at the heart of the problem. Clearly, these cases involve "bad guys," and the ethical lapses are obvious. But saying, "I would never do things like that," becomes too easy. The fact is that temptations exist in every organization. Many of the decisions you will face as a manager will pose ethical dilemmas, and the right thing to do is not always evident.

It's a Personal Issue

"Answer true or false: 'I am an ethical manager.' If you answered 'true,' here's an uncomfortable fact: You're probably not."[4] These sentences are the first in a *Harvard Business Review* article called "How (Un)Ethical Are You?" The point is that most of us think we are good decision makers, ethical, and unbiased. But the fact is, most people have unconscious biases that favor themselves and their own group. For example, managers often hire people who are like them, think they are immune to conflicts of interest, take more credit than they deserve, and blame others when they deserve some blame themselves.

To know that you have biases may help you try to overcome them, but usually that's not enough. Consider the basic ethical issue of telling a lie. Many people lie—some more than others, and in part depending on the situation, usually presuming that they will benefit from the lie. At a basic level, we all can make ethical arguments against lying and in favor of honesty. Yet it is useful to think thoroughly about the real consequences of lying.[5] Table 5.1 summarizes the possible outcomes of telling the truth or lying in different situations. People often lie or commit other ethical transgressions somewhat mindlessly, without realizing the full array of negative personal consequences.

TABLE 5.1   Telling the Truth and Lying: Possible Outcomes

Reason and Context of the Lie	Results of Lying	Results of Truth-telling
Conflicting expectations	• Easier to lie than to address the underlying conflict. • Offers quick relief of the issue. • Leaves the underlying problem unresolved. • May have no meaningful consequences, good or bad. • Liar must rationalize the action to preserve positive self-concept.	• Emotionally more difficult than lying. • May correct underlying problem. • May provoke further conflict. • Sometimes difficult to have an impact on an impermeable structure. • Develops one's reputation as an "honest" person.
Negotiation	• Short-term gain. • Economically positive. • Harms long-term relationship. • Must rationalize to oneself.	• Supports high-quality long-term relationship. • Develops reputation of integrity. • Models behavior to others.
Keeping a confidence (that may require at least a lie of omission)	• Protects whatever good reason there is for the confidence. • Maintains a long-term relationship with the party for whom confidence is kept. • May project deceitfulness to the deceived party.	• Violates a trust to the confiding party. • Makes one appear deceitful to all parties in the long run. • Creates the impression of honesty beyond utility.
Reporting your own performance within an organization	• Might advance oneself or one's cause. • Develops dishonest reputation over time. • Must continue the sequence of lies to appear consistent.	• Creates reputation of integrity. • May not always be positive.

SOURCE: From *Academy of Management Executive: The Thinking Manager's Source* by S.L. Gover, "The Truth, the Whole Truth, and Nothing but the Truth: The Causes and Management of Workplace Lying." Copyright © 2005 by Academy of Management via Copyright Clearance Center.

Ethics issues are not easy, and they are not just for newsworthy corporate CEOs. More and more people at work use computers with Internet access. If the employer pays for the computer and the time you spend sitting in front of it, is it ethical for you to use the computer to do tasks unrelated to your work? Maybe you think it's OK to do a little online shopping during your lunch hour or to check scores during the World Series or March Madness. But what if you stream video of the games for your own and your coworkers' enjoyment or take a two-hour lunch to locate the best deal on a flat-panel TV?

Besides lost productivity, employers are most concerned about computer users introducing viruses, leaking confidential information, and creating a hostile work environment by downloading inappropriate Web content.

Sometimes employees write blogs or post comments online about their company and its products. Obviously, companies do not want their employees to say bad things about them, but some companies are concerned about employees who are overly enthusiastic. When employees plug their companies and products on comments pages, this practice is considered spamming at best and deceptive if the employees don't disclose their relationship with their company. Another practice considered deceptive is when companies create fictional blogs as a marketing tactic without disclosing their sponsorship. And in a practice known as Astroturfing—because the "grassroots" interest it builds is fake—businesses pay bloggers to write positive comments about them. A Florida company known as PayPerPost will match advertisers with bloggers but now requires bloggers to disclose the relationship. Companies such as Coca-Cola, UPS, and IBM have established guidelines directing employees to identify themselves accurately in online communications so that they can participate in online conversations about their companies without being accused of deception.[6]

Are these examples too small to worry about? This chapter will help you think through decisions with ethical ramifications.

Here's a small but potentially powerful suggestion.[7] Change your vocabulary: The word "ethics" is too loaded, even trite. Substitute "responsibility" or "decency." And act accordingly.

ethical issue

Situation, problem, or opportunity in which an individual must choose among several actions that must be evaluated as morally right or wrong.

Ethics

The aim of ethics is to identify both the rules that should govern people's behavior and the "goods" that are worth seeking. Ethical decisions are guided by the underlying values of the individual. Values are principles of conduct such as caring, being honest, keeping promises, pursuing excellence, showing loyalty, being fair, acting with integrity, respecting others, and being a responsible citizen.[8]

Most people would agree that all of these values are admirable guidelines for behavior. However, ethics becomes a more complicated issue when a situation dictates that one value overrules others. An **ethical issue** is a situation, problem, or opportunity in which an individual must choose among several actions that must be evaluated as morally right or wrong.[10] Ethical issues arise in every facet of life; we concern ourselves here with business ethics in particular. **Business ethics** comprises the moral principles and standards that guide behavior in the world of business.[11]

Are women more ethical than men? Studies have implied they are, at least by some measures. Surveys of business students found an increase in their interest in studying ethics, with a greater increase among women. Compared with their female counterparts, undergraduate male students in business and psychology showed stronger unethical attitudes and a tendency to behave unethically. When business students took an ethics curriculum, women made greater strides than men in improving their moral awareness and decision-making processes.[9]

business ethics

The moral principles and standards that guide behavior in the world of business.

Ethical Systems

LO 1

Moral philosophy refers to the principles, rules, and values people use in deciding what is right or wrong. This is a simple definition in the abstract but often terribly complex and difficult when facing real choices. How do you decide what is right and wrong? Do you know what criteria you apply and how you apply them?

Ethics scholars point to various major ethical systems as guides.[12] The first ethical system, **universalism,** states that all people should uphold certain values, such as honesty, that society needs to function. Universal values are principles so fundamental to human existence that they are important in all societies—for example, rules against murder, deceit, torture, and oppression.

Some efforts have been made to establish global, universal ethical principles for business. The Caux Roundtable, a group of international executives based in Caux, Switzerland, worked with business leaders from Japan, Europe, and the United States to create the **Caux Principles.** Two basic ethical ideals underpin the Caux Principles: *kyosei* and human dignity. *Kyosei* means living and working together for the common good, allowing cooperation and mutual prosperity to coexist with healthy and fair competition. Human dignity concerns the value of each person as an end, not a means to the fulfillment of others' purposes.

Universal principles can be powerful and useful, but what people say, hope, or think they would do is often different from what they *really* do, faced with conflicting demands in real situations. Before we describe other ethical systems, consider the following example, and think about how you or others would resolve it.

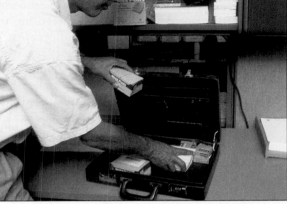

Employees sometimes feel that "borrowing" a few office supplies from their company helps compensate for any perceived inequities in pay or other benefits.

moral philosophy

Principles, rules, and values people use in deciding what is right or wrong.

universalism

The ethical system stating that all people should uphold certain values that society needs to function.

Caux Principles

Ethical principles established by international executives based in Caux, Switzerland, in collaboration with business leaders from Japan, Europe, and the United States.

Suppose that Sam Colt, a sales representative, is preparing a sales presentation on behalf of his firm, Midwest Hardware, which manufactures nuts and bolts. Colt hopes to obtain a large sale from a construction firm that is building a bridge across the Missouri River near St. Louis. The bolts manufactured by Midwest Hardware have a 3 percent defect rate, which, although acceptable in the industry, makes them unsuitable for use in certain types of projects, such as those that might be subject to sudden, severe stress. The new bridge will be located near the New Madrid Fault line, the source of a major earthquake in 1811. The epicenter of that earthquake, which caused extensive damage and altered the flow of the Missouri, is about 190 miles from the new bridge site.

Bridge construction in the area is not regulated by earthquake codes. If Colt wins the sale, he will earn a commission of $25,000 on top of his regular salary. But if he tells the contractors about the defect rate, Midwest may lose the sale to a competitor whose bolts are slightly more reliable. Thus, Colt's ethical issue is whether to point out to the bridge contractor that in the event of an earthquake, some Midwest bolts could fail.

SOURCE: O. C. Ferrell and J. Fraedrich, *Business Ethics: Ethical Decision Making and Cases,* 3rd ed. Copyright © 1997 by Houghton Mifflin Company. Used with permission.

Not everyone would behave the same in this scenario. Different individuals would apply different moral philosophies. Consider each of the following moral philosophies and the actions to which they might lead in the bridge example.[13]

Egoism and Utilitarianism   According to **egoism,** acceptable behavior is that which maximizes benefits for the individual. "Doing the right thing," the focus of

egoism

An ethical system defining acceptable behavior as that which maximizes consequences for the individual.

moral philosophy, is defined by egoism as "do the act that promotes the greatest good for oneself." If everyone follows this system, according to its proponents, the well-being of society as a whole should increase. This notion is similar to Adam Smith's concept of the invisible hand in business. Smith argued that if every organization follows its own economic self-interest, the total wealth of society will be maximized.

utilitarianism

An ethical system stating that the greatest good for the greatest number should be the overriding concern of decision makers.

Unlike egoism, **utilitarianism** directly seeks the greatest good for the greatest number of people. Consider whether utilitarianism would help guide ethical decision making with regard to student loan programs. Recently, New York's attorney general, Andrew Cuomo, investigated 100 colleges and half a dozen lenders for arrangements in which the lenders allegedly offered payments, stock grants, and perks to schools, and the schools listed the companies as "preferred lenders" in information given to students who wanted to borrow tuition money from private sources. Cuomo called the arrangements "kickbacks"; some schools replied that they were not being corrupted but used the money to add to the financial aid they could award to students.[14]

Whereas ethics based on egoism would accept actions that allow the lenders to maximize their earnings and the financial aid officers to pursue whatever arrangements benefit themselves and their schools, utilitarianism requires a broader view. Most obviously, there is the question of what these arrangements cost students who make borrowing decisions on the assumption that "preferred" lenders will give students the best deals. But other students benefited if payments from lenders were used to augment the financial aid given to other students. The utilitarian approach might consider how many students benefited—and by how much—and how many students paid extra for loans and how much more they paid. One company responded to the allegations by agreeing to a code of conduct that forbids gifts in exchange for "preferred" status.[15]

relativism

Philosophy that bases ethical behavior on the opinions and behaviors of relevant other people.

Relativism   Perhaps it seems that an individual makes ethical choices on a personal basis, applying personal perspectives. But this is not necessarily the case. **Relativism** defines ethical behavior based on the opinions and behaviors of relevant other people. In the previous example of student loans, U.S. business, government, and society largely agree that bribes, kickbacks, and conflicts of interest would not be acceptable behaviors for people in the lending industry—perhaps even less so for those charged with serving students. Those standards help to explain the rapid actions taken by the organizations when they found out about the situation.

Relativism acknowledges the existence of different ethical viewpoints. For example, *norms*, or standards of expected and acceptable behavior, vary from one culture to another. A study of Russian versus U.S. managers found that all followed norms of informed consent about chemical hazards in work situations and paying wages on time. But in Russia more than in the United States, businesspeople were likely to consider the interests of a broader set of stakeholders (in this study, keeping factories open for the sake of local employment), to keep double books to hide information from tax inspectors and criminal organizations, and to make personal payments to government officials in charge of awarding contracts.[17] Relativism defines ethical behavior according to how others behave.

In a recent survey ranking 180 nations from most to least honest, the United States came in 18th (tied with Japan and Belgium). The U.S. rating of 7.3 on a 10-point scale placed it among only 22 countries that scored at least a 7.0. The top ratings went to Denmark, Sweden, and New Zealand, each with 9.3. The bottom-ranked nations, including Somalia, Myanmar, and Iraq, tend to be among the poorest. Sadly, the combination of corruption and poverty in these nations can literally amount to a death sentence for many of their citizens.[16]

virtue ethics

Classification of people based on their level of moral judgment.

Virtue ethics   The moral philosophies just described apply different types of rules and reasoning. **Virtue ethics** is a perspective that goes beyond the conventional rules of society by suggesting that what is moral must also come from what a mature person with good "moral character" would deem right. Society's rules provide a moral minimum, and then moral individuals can transcend rules by applying their personal virtues such as faith, honesty, and integrity.

Individuals differ in this regard. **Kohlberg's model of cognitive moral development** classifies people into categories based on their level of moral judgment.[18] People in the *preconventional* stage make decisions based on concrete rewards and punishments and immediate self-interest. People in the *conventional* stage conform to the expectations of ethical behavior held by groups or institutions such as society, family, or peers. People in the *principled* stage see beyond authority, laws, and norms and follow their self-chosen ethical principles.[19] Some people forever reside in the preconventional stage, some move into the conventional stage, and some develop further yet into the principled stage. Over time, and through education and experience, people may change their values and ethical behavior.

Returning to the bolts-in-the-bridge example, *egoism* would result in keeping quiet about the bolts' defect rate. *Utilitarianism* would dictate a more thorough cost-benefit analysis and possibly the conclusion that the probability of a bridge collapse is so low compared to the utility of jobs, economic growth, and company growth that the defect rate is not worth mentioning. The *relativist* perspective might prompt the salesperson to look at company policy and general industry practice, and to seek opinions from colleagues and perhaps trade journals and ethics codes. Whatever is then perceived to be a consensus or normal practice would dictate action. Finally, *virtue ethics*, applied by people in the principled stage of moral development, would likely lead to full disclosure about the product and risks, and perhaps suggestions for alternatives that would reduce the risk.[20]

These major ethical systems underlie personal moral choices and ethical decisions in business.

Business Ethics

Insider trading, illegal campaign contributions, bribery and kickbacks, famous court cases, and other scandals have created a perception that business leaders use illegal means to gain competitive advantage, increase profits, or improve their personal positions. Neither young managers nor consumers believe top executives are doing a good job of establishing high ethical standards.[21] Some even joke that *business ethics* has become a contradiction in terms.

Most business leaders believe they uphold ethical standards in business practices.[22] But many managers and their organizations must deal frequently with ethical dilemmas, and the issues are becoming increasingly complex. For example, many people seek spiritual renewal in the workplace, in part reflecting a broader religious awakening in America, while others argue that this trend violates religious freedom and the separation of church and boardroom.[23] Table 5.2 shows some other important examples of ethical dilemmas in business.

The Ethics Environment

Responding to a series of corporate scandals—particularly the high-profile cases of Enron and WorldCom—Congress passed the **Sarbanes-Oxley Act** in 2002 to improve and maintain investor confidence. The law requires companies to have more independent board directors (not just company insiders), to adhere strictly to accounting rules, and to have senior managers personally sign off on financial results. Violations could result in heavy fines and criminal prosecution. One of the biggest impacts of the law is the requirement for companies and their auditors to provide reports to financial statement users about the effectiveness of internal controls over the financial reporting process.

Companies that make the effort to meet or exceed these requirements can reduce their risks by lowering the likelihood of misdeeds and the consequences if an employee does break the law.[24] But some executives say Sarbanes-Oxley distracts from their real

Kohlberg's model of cognitive moral development

Perspective that what is moral comes from what a mature person with "good" moral character would deem right.

LO 2

Sarbanes-Oxley Act

An act passed into law by Congress in 2002 to establish strict accounting and reporting rules in order to make senior managers more accountable and to improve and maintain investor confidence.

TABLE 5.2
Some Ethical Issues in Business

Artistic control	Rock musicians, independent filmmakers, and other artists are rebelling against control by big media and retail companies.
Brands	In-your-face marketing campaigns have sparked antibrand attitudes among students.
CEO pay	Nearly three-fourths of Americans see executive pay packages as excessive.
Commercialism in schools	Parent groups have mounted battles in hundreds of communities against advertising in the public schools.
Consumerism	Anger and frustration are mounting over high gasoline and drug prices, poor airline service, and HMOs that override doctors' decisions.
Frankenfoods	Europeans' skepticism about genetically modified food is taking hold in the United States, making targets of companies such as Monsanto.
Globalization	Environmentalists, students, and unionists charge that global trade and economic bodies operate in the interests of multinational companies.
Politics	Public revulsion over the corporate bankrolling of politicians has energized campaign-finance reform activists.
Sweatshops	Anti-sweatshop groups have sprung up on college campuses; they routinely picket clothing manufacturers, toymakers, and retailers.
Urban sprawl	Groups in more than 100 cities have blocked big-box superstores by Wal-Mart and other chains.
Wages	Some 56 percent of workers feel they are underpaid, especially as wages since 1992 have topped inflation by 7.6 percent, while productivity is up 17.9 percent.

SOURCE: A. Bernstein, "Too Much Corporate Power?" *BusinessWeek*, September 11, 2000, pp. 146–47. © 2009 Time Inc. All rights reserved.

work and makes them more risk-averse. Some complain about the time and money needed to comply with the internal control reporting—some large companies have reported spending millions of dollars for technology upgrades. Regardless of managers' attitudes toward Sarbanes-Oxley, it creates legal requirements intended to improve ethical behavior.

Ethics are not shaped only by laws and by individual virtue. They also may be influenced by the company's work environment. Unethical corporate behavior may be the responsibility of an unethical individual, but it often also reveals a company culture that is ethically lax.[25] Maintaining a positive ethical climate is always challenging, but it is especially complex for organizations with international activities. Different cultures and countries may have different standards of behavior, and managers have to decide when relativism is appropriate, rather than adherence to firm standards. Table 5.3 gives examples of real situations where ethics-related decisions have arisen in an international context.

The **ethical climate** of an organization refers to the processes by which decisions are evaluated and made on the basis of right and wrong.[26] For example, General Electric's top executives have demonstrated a commitment to promoting high levels of integrity without sacrificing the company's well-known commitment to business results. The measures taken by GE to maintain a positive ethical climate include establishing global standards for behavior to prevent ethical problems such as conflicts of interest and money laundering. As managers monitor the external environment, they are expected to consider legal and ethical developments, along with other concerns, so

ethical climate

In an organization, the processes by which decisions are evaluated and made on the basis of right and wrong.

What would you do in each of these true-life situations, and why?	TABLE 5.3
• You are a sales representative for a construction company in the Middle East. Your company wants very much to land a particular project. The cousin of the minister who will award the contract informs you that the minister wants $20,000 in addition to the standard fees. If you do not make this payment, your competition certainly will—and will get the contract.	Ethical Decision Making in the International Context
• You are international vice president of a multinational chemical corporation. Your company is the sole producer of an insecticide that will effectively combat a recent infestation of West African crops. The minister of agriculture in a small, developing African country has put in a large order for your product. Your insecticide is highly toxic and is banned in the United States. You inform the minister of the risks of using your product, but he insists on using it and claims it will be used "intelligently." The president of your company believes you should fill the order, but the decision ultimately is yours.	
• You are a new marketing manager for a large automobile tire manufacturer. Your company's advertising agency has just presented plans for introducing a new tire into the Southeast Asia market. Your tire is a truly good product, but the proposed advertising is deceptive. For example, the "reduced price" was reduced from a hypothetical amount that was established only so it could be "reduced," and claims that the tire was tested under the "most adverse" conditions ignore the fact that it was not tested in prolonged tropical heat and humidity. Your superiors are not concerned about deceptive advertising, and they are counting on you to see that the tire does extremely well in the new market. Will you approve the ad plan?	

SOURCE: N. Adler, *International Dimensions of Organizational Behavior*, 2nd ed. (Boston: Kent, 1997).

that the company can be prepared for new issues as they arise. Managers at all levels are rewarded for their performance in meeting both integrity and business standards, and when violations occur, even managers who were otherwise successful are disciplined, sending a powerful message that ethical behavior is truly valued at GE.[27]

Danger Signs   Maintaining consistent ethical behavior by all employees is an ongoing challenge. What are some danger signs that an organization may be allowing or even encouraging unethical behavior? Many factors create a climate conducive to unethical behavior, including

1. Excessive emphasis on short-term revenues over longer-term considerations.
2. Failure to establish a written code of ethics.
3. A desire for simple, "quick fix" solutions to ethical problems.
4. An unwillingness to take an ethical stand that may impose financial costs.
5. Consideration of ethics solely as a legal issue or a public relations tool.
6. Lack of clear procedures for handling ethical problems.
7. Responding to the demands of shareholders at the expense of other constituencies.[28]

Do you see danger signs for AutoAdmit? The small company operates a message board Web site targeting college and law school students. Some students have complained that participants on the site's law school message board have posted false and insulting messages about them that have humiliated them and may have interfered with their ability to find summer internships. Many employers use Internet searches as part of their background checks, and sites such as AutoAdmit might surface in search results. AutoAdmit founder Jarret Cohen told the *Washington*

Ethical climate is heating up! Former Enron treasurer Ben Glisan, Jr. pleaded guilty to conspiracy and became the first ex-Enron executive to go to prison. Former Enron executives Jeff Skilling and Ken Lay were later arrested for their participation in the high-profile scandal case that led to the passage of the Sarbanes-Oxley Act in 2002. This case is considered to be one of the biggest business scandals in U.S. history.

Post that he is reluctant to interfere with postings: "I want [the message board] to be a place where people can express themselves freely." He and his partner, Anthony Ciolli, define the matter in terms of free speech, insisting that "one finds overall a much deeper and much more mature level of insight in a community where the ugliest depths of human opinion are confronted, rather than ignored." Ciolli claims that only Cohen has the authority to remove offensive postings, and Cohen refuses to "selectively remove" comments. The site also does not keep information that would identify participants, using only screen names, because "people would not have as much fun" if employers could identify them. Ciolli and Cohen have so far avoided any accusation that their message boards are violating the law; AutoAdmit isn't liable for the content of messages written by visitors to the site.[29] But what do you think about the organization's ethical climate? Should it uphold values other than freedom of expression?

It's been said that your reputation is your most precious asset. Here's a suggestion: Set a goal for yourself to be seen by others as both a "moral person" and also as a "moral manager," someone who influences others to behave ethically. When you are both personally moral and a moral manager, you will truly be an **ethical leader**.[30] You can have strong personal character, but if you pay more attention to other things, and ethics is "managed" by "benign neglect," you won't have a reputation as an ethical leader.

ethical leader

One who is both a moral person and a moral manager influencing others to behave ethically.

Corporate Ethical Standards   To create a culture that encourages ethical behavior, managers must be more than ethical people. They also should lead others to behave ethically.[31] At General Electric, chief executive Jeffrey Immelt demonstrates his concern for ethical leadership by beginning and ending each annual meeting with a statement of the company's integrity principles, emphasizing that "GE's business success is built on our reputation with all stakeholders for lawful and ethical behavior." These words are backed up with a reward system in which managers are evaluated for how well they meet ethics-related standards such as the use of audits, minimal customer complaints and lawsuits, avoidance of compliance actions by government regulators, and high ratings on employee surveys.[32]

Imagine a manager of a used-car dealership working hard to personify ethical business practices, for and with both his customers and his employees.[33] This would create a powerful competitive advantage compared with the industry's reputation (or at least the common stereotype) for shady practices.

IBM uses a guideline for business conduct that asks employees to determine whether under the full glare of examination by associates, friends, and family, they would remain comfortable with their decisions. One suggestion is to imagine how you would feel if you saw your decision and its consequences on the front page of the newspaper.[34] This "light of day" or "sunshine" ethical framework can be powerful.

Such fear of exposure compels people more strongly in some cultures than in others. In Asia, anxiety about losing face often makes executives resign immediately if they are caught in ethical transgressions or if their companies are embarrassed by revelations in the press. By contrast, in the United States, exposed executives might respond with indignation, intransigence, pleading the Fifth Amendment, stonewalling, an everyone-else-does-it self-defense, or by not admitting wrongdoing and giving no sign that resignation ever crossed their minds. Partly because of legal tradition, the attitude often is: Never explain, never apologize, don't admit the mistake, do not resign, even if the entire world knows exactly what happened.[35]

Ethics Codes   The Sarbanes-Oxley Act requires that public companies periodically disclose whether they have adopted a code of ethics for senior financial officers—and if not, why not. Often, the statements are just for show, but when implemented well they can change a company's ethical climate for the better and truly encourage ethical behavior. Executives say they pay most attention to their company's code of ethics when they feel that stakeholders (customers, investors, lenders, and suppliers) try to influence them to do so, and their reasons for paying attention to the code are that doing so will help create a strong ethical culture and promote a positive image.[36]

Ethics codes must be carefully written and tailored to individual companies' philosophies. Aetna Life & Casualty believes that tending to the broader needs of society is essential to fulfilling its economic role. Johnson & Johnson has one of the most famous ethics codes; it is featured in Table 5.4. J&J consistently receives high rankings for community and social responsibility in *Fortune*'s annual survey of corporate reputations.

Most ethics codes address subjects such as employee conduct, community and environment, shareholders, customers, suppliers and contractors, political activity, and technology. Often the codes are drawn up by the organizations' legal departments and begin with research into other companies' codes. The Ethics Resource Center in Washington assists companies interested in establishing a corporate code of ethics.[37]

To make an ethics code effective, do the following: (1) involve those who have to live with it in writing the statement; (2) focus on real-life situations that employees can relate to; (3) keep it short and simple, so it is easy to understand and remember; (4) write about values and shared beliefs that are important and that people can really believe in; and (5) set the tone at the top, having executives talk about and live up to the statement.[38] When reality differs from the statement—as when a motto says people are our most precious asset or a product is the finest in the world, but in fact people are treated poorly or product quality is weak—the statement becomes a joke to employees rather than a guiding light.

The "sunshine" principle encourages employees to consider first if they would like to see their actions displayed on the front page of the newspaper. If yes, then it is likely an appropriate course of action.

Ethics Programs   Corporate ethics programs commonly include formal ethics codes that articulate the company's expectations regarding ethics; ethics committees that develop policies, evaluate actions, and investigate violations; ethics communication systems that give employees a means of reporting problems or getting guidance; ethics officers or ombudspersons who investigate allegations and provide education; ethics training programs; and disciplinary processes for addressing unethical behavior.[39]

Ethics programs can range from compliance-based to integrity-based.[41] **Compliance-based ethics programs** are designed by corporate counsel to prevent, detect, and punish legal violations. Compliance-based programs increase surveillance and controls on people and impose punishments on wrongdoers. Program elements include establishing and communicating legal standards and procedures, assigning high-level managers to oversee compliance,

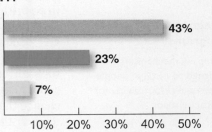

Although many companies have a code of ethics, far fewer have a comprehensive ethics program that includes training, channels for reporting violations, evaluation of ethical conduct, and discipline for violations.[40]

Percentage of organizations that . . .

Measure ethical conduct as part of performance appraisals **43%**
Have a comprehensive ethics and compliance program **23%**
Have no ethics and compliance program **7%**

auditing and monitoring compliance, reporting criminal misconduct, punishing wrongdoers, and taking steps to prevent offenses in the future.

Such programs should reduce illegal behavior and help a company stay out of court. But they do not create a moral commitment to ethical conduct; they merely ensure moral mediocrity. As Richard Breeden, former chairman of the Securities and Exchange Commission, said, "It is not an adequate ethical standard to aspire to get through the day without being indicted."[42]

compliance-based ethics programs

Company mechanisms typically designed by corporate counsel to prevent, detect, and punish legal violations.

TABLE 5.4
Johnson & Johnson's Ethics Code

We believe our first responsibility is to the doctors, nurses, and patients, to mothers and all others who use our products and services. In meeting their needs everything we do must be of high quality. We must constantly strive to reduce our costs in order to maintain reasonable prices. Customers' orders must be serviced promptly and accurately. Our suppliers and distributors must have an opportunity to make a fair profit.

We are responsible to our employees: the men and women who work with us throughout the world. Everyone must be considered as an individual. We must respect their dignity and recognize their merit. They must have a sense of security in their jobs. Compensation must be fair and adequate, and working conditions clean, orderly, and safe. Employees must feel free to make suggestions and complaints. There must be equal opportunity for employment, development, and advancement for those qualified. We must provide competent management, and their actions must be just and ethical.

We are responsible to the communities in which we live and work and to the world community as well.

We must be good citizens—support good works and charities and bear our fair share of taxes. We must encourage civic improvements and better health and education.

We must maintain in good order the property we are privileged to use, protecting the environment and natural resources.

Our final responsibility is to our stockholders. Business must make a sound profit. We must experiment with new ideas. Research must be carried on, innovative programs developed, and mistakes paid for. New equipment must be purchased, new facilities provided, and new products launched. Reserves must be created to provide for adverse times.

When we operate according to these principles, the stockholders should realize a fair return.

SOURCE: Reprinted with permission of Johnson & Johnson.

Yahoo! is struggling with an ethical dilemma as it makes decisions about how to operate in China. The Chinese government arrested Wang Xiaoning for "inciting subversion" in his prodemocracy e-journal and sentenced him to 10 years in prison. According to the case filed against Yahoo! in the United States, the Chinese subsidiary of Yahoo! that Wang used provided the information that enabled officials to track him down. How can an Internet company that values free expression justify support for a repressive government? Yahoo!'s Jim Cullinan points out that the company has to obey the laws of the countries where it operates but adds that the company has been trying to develop operating principles that will help its people make ethical decisions in countries where governments have different values.[43]

integrity-based ethics programs

Company mechanisms designed to instill in people a personal responsibility for ethical behavior.

Integrity-based ethics programs go beyond the mere avoidance of illegality; they are concerned with the law but also with instilling in people a personal responsibility for ethical behavior. With such a program, companies and people govern themselves through a set of guiding principles that they embrace.

For example, the Americans with Disabilities Act (ADA) requires companies to change the physical work environment so it will allow people with disabilities to function on the job. Mere compliance would involve making the changes necessary to avoid legal problems. Integrity-based programs would go further by training people to understand and perhaps change attitudes toward people with disabilities and sending clear signals that people with disabilities also have valued abilities. This effort goes far beyond taking action to stay out of trouble with the law.

When top management has a personal commitment to responsible ethical behavior, programs tend to be better integrated into operations, thinking, and behavior. For example, at a meeting of about 25 middle managers at a major financial services firm, every one of them told the company's general counsel that they had never seen or heard of the company's ethics policy document.[44] The policies existed but were not a part of the everyday thinking of managers. In contrast, a health care products company bases one-third of managers' annual pay raises on how well they carry out the company's ethical ideals. Their ethical behavior is assessed by superiors, peers, and subordinates— making ethics a thoroughly integrated aspect of the way the company and its people do business.

Ethical Decision Making

We've said it's not easy to make ethical decisions. Such decisions are complex. For starters, you may face pressures that are difficult to resist. Furthermore, it's not always clear that a problem has ethical dimensions; they don't hold up signs that say "Hey, I'm an ethical issue, so think about me in moral terms!"[45] Making ethical decisions takes *moral awareness* (realizing the issue has ethical implications), *moral judgment* (knowing what actions are morally defensible), and *moral character* (the strength and persistence to act in accordance with your ethics despite the challenges).[46]

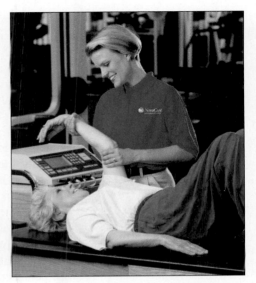

NovaCare is one company with a strong integrity-based ethics program.

Moral awareness begins with considering whether a decision has ramifications that disadvantage employees, the environment, or other stakeholders. Then the challenge is to apply moral judgment.

The philosopher John Rawls created a thought experiment based on the "veil of ignorance."[47] Imagine that you are making a decision about a policy that will benefit or disadvantage some groups more than others. For example, a policy might provide extra vacation time for all employees but eliminate flex time, which allows parents of young children to balance their work and family responsibilities. Or you're a university president considering raising tuition or cutting financial support for study abroad.

Now pretend that you belong to one of the affected groups, but you don't know which one—for instance, those who can afford to study abroad or those who can't, or a young parent or a young single person. You won't find out until after the decision is made. How would you decide? Would you be willing to risk being in the disadvantaged group? Would your decision be different if you were in a group other than your own? Rawls maintained that only a person ignorant of his own identity can make a truly ethical decision. A decision maker can tactically apply the veil of ignorance to help minimize personal bias.

To resolve ethical problems, you can use the process illustrated in Figure 5.1. Understand the various moral standards (universalism, relativism, etc.), as described on pp. 165–167. Go through the problem-solving model from Chapter 3, and recognize the impacts of your alternatives: which people do they benefit and harm, which

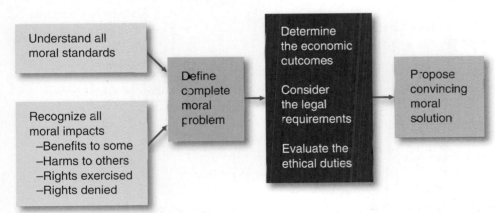

SOURCE: L. T. Hosmer, *The Ethics of Management*, 4th ed. (New York: McGraw-Hill/Irwin, 2003), p. 32. Fig. 5.1A. © 2003 The McGraw-Hill Companies.

FIGURE 5.1

A Process for Ethical Decision Making

are able to exercise their rights, and whose rights are denied? You now know the full scope of the moral problem.

Finding excuses and nationalizations for unethical behavior is easy. Only days after the U.S. government had posted $85 billion to keep insurance giant American International Group from collapsing, AIG sent executives on a luxurious retreat. When questioned about this, executives initially replied with excuses: the $440,000 spent was far, far less than the amount of the government bailout, and the executives who participated in the retreat did not work in the AIG division where the company's financial problems had originated. Eventually they had to concede that these responses did not really address the question of whether the retreat was an ethical use of company money at a time when the company—along with many of the taxpayers whose money was bailing out AIG—was undergoing an economic crisis.[48]

Excuses are often bogus.[49] "I was told to do it" implies a person has no thought and blindly obeys. "Everybody's doing it" often really means that someone is doing it, but it's rarely everybody; regardless, following convention doesn't mean correctness. "Might equals right" is just a rationalization. "It's not my problem" is sometimes a wise perspective, if it's a battle you can't win, but sometimes it's a cop-out. "I didn't mean for that to happen, it just felt right at the time" can be prevented with more forethought and analysis.

You must also consider legal requirements to ensure full compliance, and the economic outcomes of your options, including costs and potential profits. Figure 5.2 shows some of the costs associated with unethical behavior.[50] Some are obvious: fines and penalties. Others, like administrative costs and corrective actions, are less obvious. Ultimately, the effects on customers, employees, and government reactions can be huge. Being fully aware of the potential costs can help prevent people from straying into unethical terrain.

> "Costs" aren't exactly synonymous with "ethics." But by considering all costs to all parties, you can make high-quality ethics decisions that you can more convincingly "sell" to others who might otherwise balk.

Courage

Behaving ethically requires not just moral awareness and moral judgment but also moral character, including the courage to take actions consistent with your ethical decisions. Think about how hard it can be to do the right thing.[51] On the job, how hard would it be to walk away from lots of money in order to "stick to your ethics"?

FIGURE 5.2

The Business Costs of Ethical Failures

SOURCE: From *Academy of Management Executive: The Thinking Manager's Source* by T. Thomas, et al., "Strategic Leadership of Ethical Behavior in Business." Copyright © 2004 by Academy of Management via Copyright Clearance Center.

To tell colleagues or your boss that you believe they've crossed an ethical line? To disobey a boss's order? To go over your boss's head to someone in senior management with your suspicions about accounting practices? To go outside the company to alert others if someone is being hurt and management refuses to correct the problem?

PepsiCo managers faced a difficult choice when an executive secretary from Coca-Cola Company's headquarters contacted them to offer confidential documents and product samples for a price. Rather than seek an unethical (and illegal) advantage, Pepsi's managers notified Coca-Cola. There, management fired the secretary and contacted the FBI. Eventually, the secretary and two acquaintances were convicted of conspiring to steal trade secrets.[52] PepsiCo still doesn't have the secret recipe for Coke, but it did maintain its reputation as a competitor with integrity. Choosing integrity took courage. Courage plays a role in the moral awareness involved in identifying an act as unethical, the moral judgment to fully consider the repercussions, and the moral character to take the ethical action.

Behaving ethically in an ethical climate is complicated enough, but even more courage is necessary when you decide that the only ethical course of action is *whistleblowing*— telling others, inside or outside the organization, of wrongdoing. The road for whistleblowers is rocky. Many, perhaps most, whistleblowers suffer consequences such as being ostracized, treated rudely, or given undesirable assignments. At a Canadian manufacturing company, an employee reported a manager who had an arrangement with suppliers to inflate their invoices; the manager took the extra cash, costing the company more than $100,000. When the other employees found out what had happened, instead of blaming the manager, they began to distrust the whistleblower. Eventually, she quit.[53]

From an organization's point of view, whistleblowing is either an asset or a threat, depending on the situation and management's perspective. In the example of the manager cheating the Canadian manufacturer, it was clearly to the company's advantage to know about the misdeeds so that management could stop the losses. But whistleblowing is a far different

> According to a study by the Association of Certified Fraud Examiners, companies that uncovered fraud most often learned about it from a coworker's tip, rather than from a formal audit.[54]

matter when employees take their complaints to government agencies, report them to the media, or post them on blogs. When problems are resolved in public, the whistleblower is more often seen as acting against the company's interests.

For this reason, and in response to the revised sentencing guidelines under the Sarbanes-Oxley Act, organizations set up channels for employees to report ethics problems so that the organization can respond without the matter becoming a scandal. Ideally, the reporting method should keep the whistleblower's identity secret, management should investigate and respond quickly, and there should be no retaliation against whistleblowers who use proper channels. Besides online reporting systems, such as e-mail and Web-based tools, companies can use drop boxes and telephone hotlines.[55]

Corporate Social Responsibility

LO 4

- Ford Motor Company fights HIV/AIDs in South Africa.
- Levi Strauss fights racism.
- Green Mountain Coffee promotes fair trade coffee around the world.
- Bank Boston fosters economic development in communities of moderate income and in the inner city.
- United Parcel Service works to help people on welfare find employment.
- McDonald's and Bank of America support sustainable development in a variety of strategic ways.[56]

Should business be responsible for social concerns beyond its own economic well-being? Do social concerns affect a corporation's financial performance? The extent of business's responsibility for noneconomic concerns has been hotly debated for years. In the 1960s and 1970s, the political and social environment became more important to U.S. corporations as society turned its attention to issues like equal opportunity, pollution control, energy and natural resource conservation, and consumer and worker protection.[57] Public debate addressed these issues and the ways business should respond to them. This controversy focused on the concept of corporate social responsibility.

Corporate social responsibility is the obligation toward society assumed by business.[58] Corporate social responsibility reflects the social imperatives and the social consequences of business success, and consists broadly of policies and practices that reflect business responsibility for some of the wider societal good. The precise policies and practices underlying this responsibility lie at the discretion of the corporation.[59]

Social responsibilities can be categorized more specifically,[60] as shown in Figure 5.3. The **economic responsibilities** of business are to produce goods and services that society wants at a price that perpetuates the business and satisfies its obligations to investors. For Smithfield Foods, the largest pork producer in the United States, this means selling bacon, ham, and other products to customers at prices that maximize Smithfield's profits and keep the company growing over the long term. Economic responsibility may also extend to offering certain products to needy consumers at a reduced price.

Legal responsibilities are to obey local, state, federal, and relevant international laws. Laws affecting Smithfield cover a wide range of requirements, from filing tax returns to meeting worker safety standards. **Ethical responsibilities** include meeting other societal expectations, not written as law. Smithfield took on this level of responsibility when it responded to requests by major customers, including McDonald's and Wal-Mart, that it discontinue the practice of using gestation crates to house its sows.

corporate social responsibility (CSR)

Obligation toward society assumed by business.

economic responsibilities

To produce goods and services that society wants at a price that perpetuates the business and satisfies its obligations to investors.

legal responsibilities

To obey local, state, federal, and relevant international laws.

ethical responsibilities

Meeting other social expectations, not written as law.

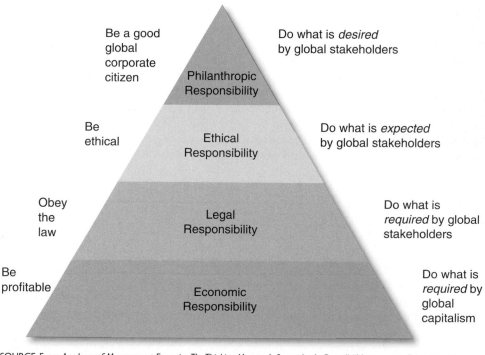

FIGURE 5.3
Pyramid of Global
Corporate Social
Responsibility and
Performance.

SOURCE: From *Academy of Management Executive: The Thinking Manager's Source* by A. Carroll, "Management Ethically with Global Stakeholders: A Present and Future Challenge." Copyright © 2004 by Academy of Management via Copyright Clearance Center.

The customers were reacting to pressure from animal rights advocates who consider it cruel for sows to live in the two-foot by seven-foot crates during their entire gestation period, which means they cannot walk, turn around, or stretch their legs for months at a time. The practice had been to move the sows to a farrowing crate to give birth and then return them to the gestation crate soon after, when they became pregnant again. Smithfield planned to exchange the crates for "group housing," which allows the animals to socialize, even though group housing costs more.[61] Smithfield is not legally required to make the change (except in two states), and the arrangement may not maximize profits, but the company's actions help it maintain good customer relationships and a positive public image.

Finally, **philanthropic responsibilities** are additional behaviors and activities that society finds desirable and that the values of the business support. Examples include supporting community projects and making charitable contributions. Philanthropic activities can be more than mere altruism; managed properly, "strategic philanthropy" can become not an oxymoron but a way to build goodwill in a variety of stakeholders and even add to shareholder wealth.[62]

Robert Giacalone, who teaches business ethics at Temple University, believes that a 21st-century education must help students think beyond self-interest and profitability. A real education, he says, teaches students to leave a legacy that extends beyond the bottom line—a transcendent education.[63] A **transcendent education** has five higher goals that balance self-interest with responsibility to others: *empathy* (feeling your decisions as potential victims might feel them, to gain wisdom); *generativity* (learning how to give as well as take, to others in the present as well as to future generations); *mutuality* (viewing success not merely as personal gain, but a common victory); *civil aspiration* [thinking not just in terms of "don'ts" (lie, cheat, steal, kill), but also in terms of positive contributions]; and *intolerance of ineffective humanity* (speaking out against unethical actions.)

philanthropic responsibilities

Additional behaviors and activities that society finds desirable and that the values of the business support.

transcendent education

An education with five higher goals that balance self-interest with responsibility to others.

Contrasting Views

Two basic and contrasting views describe principles that should guide managerial responsibility. The first holds that managers act as agents for shareholders and, as such, are obligated to maximize the present value of the firm. This tenet of capitalism is widely associated with the early writings of Adam Smith in *The Wealth of Nations*, and more recently with Milton Friedman, the Nobel Prize–winning economist of the University of Chicago. With his now-famous dictum "The social responsibility of business is to increase profits," Friedman contended that organizations may help improve the quality of life as long as such actions are directed at increasing profits.

Some considered Friedman to be "the enemy of business ethics," but his position was ethical: He believed that it was unethical for unelected business leaders to decide what was best for society and unethical for them to spend shareholders' money on projects unconnected to key business interests.[64] Furthermore, the context of Friedman's famous statement includes the qualifier that business should increase its profits while conforming to society's laws and ethical customs.

The second perspective, different from the profit maximization perspective, is that managers should be motivated by principled moral reasoning. Adam Smith wrote about a world different from the one we are in now, driven in the 18th century by the self-interest of small owner-operated farms and craft shops trying to generate a living income for themselves and their families. This self-interest was quite different from that of top executives of modern corporations.[65] It is noteworthy that Adam Smith also wrote *A Theory of Moral Sentiments*, in which he argued that "sympathy," defined as a proper regard for others, is the basis of a civilized society.[66]

Advocates of corporate social responsibility argue that organizations have a wider range of responsibilities that extend beyond the production of goods and services at a profit. As members of society, organizations should actively and responsibly

The Green Movement. David Best, president of Prism Software, unloads a truck full of old computer equipment during an e-cycling event near the Mall of America in Bloomington, Minnesota. Thousands of people lined up for blocks with carloads and truckloads of old consumer appliances needing to be recycled. The event sponsored by the Mall of America and the Materials Processing Corporation (MPC) is designed to help Minnesotans clean house and protect the environment against hazardous waste such as old monitors and televisions.

participate in the community and in the larger environment. From this perspective, many people criticized insurance companies after Hurricanes Katrina and Rita devastated homes and businesses along the Gulf Coast. From a social responsibility perspective, it was wrong for companies to watch out for their bottom line and avoid paying claims where they could make a case that the damage wasn't covered; the insurers should have been more concerned about their devastated customers.

FROM THE PAGES OF
BusinessWeek

Is the Green Movement a Passing Fancy?

With a struggling economy and lower oil prices, we'll get to see how committed to green technology companies really are. Please tell me that "green" isn't a fad.

I don't know about you, but for the past two years I have been on green overload. Everywhere I turned, read, listened, and watched, the race to say "I am greener than you" has been on for individuals and businesses alike.

But that was then. With a struggling economy and oil prices falling fast. I think we will soon see just how real all those green aspirations are. And I for one sure hope the commitment to the environment and green technology is enduring. Unfortunately, I am not so sure that's the case. I just read the results of a recent corporate responsibility survey conducted by Business for Social Responsibility and Cone LLC and found them troubling.

According to the survey, in the face of the current economic conditions, 31% of respondents see their corporate and social responsibility budgets decreasing; another 26% say it's too early to determine the impact of the economic crisis on their corporate responsibility plans.

SMART BUSINESS FOR EVERYONE

So maybe we need to reset the way we think about environmental responsibility. At Xerox (XRX), my job is to meet the needs of our customers and our shareholders. The thing is, what I do at my job and how I do my part for the environment are not mutually exclusive. "Green" is not a corporate function housed in a separate unit devoted to social responsibility; green solutions and sustainable strategies are smart business—for everyone. The greener we get, the more we can reduce costs and boost efficiency. The more we reduce costs, the more productive a business can become and the better we can weather the maladies of the global business market.

http://www.businessweek.com/technology/content/jan2009/tc20090126_136438.htm

SOURCE: U. Burns, "Is the Green Movement a Passing Fancy?" *BusinessWeek*, January 27, 2009.

Reconciliation

Profit maximization and corporate social responsibility used to be regarded as antagonistic, leading to opposing policies. But the two views can converge.[67] The Coca-Cola Company has set up about 70 charitable projects to provide clean water in 40 countries. These projects are helping some of the 1.2 billion people without access to safe drinking water. The company is constructing structures to "harvest" rainwater in India, building extensions of the municipal water supply in Mali, and delivering water purification systems and storage urns to Kenya. These projects are aimed at burnishing the company's image and targeting complaints that the company is using up too much of the world's water supply to manufacture its beverages. From a practical perspective, Coca-Cola's strategic planners have identified water shortages as a strategic risk; from a values perspective, water is, in the words of executive Neville Isdell, "at the very core of our ethos," so "responsible use of that resource is very important to us."[68]

Should pharmaceutical companies be allowed to advertise directly to the consumer if the medicine can be obtained only with a prescription from a doctor? When patients request a particular product, doctors are more likely to prescribe it—even if the patients haven't reported the corresponding symptoms.

Earlier attention to corporate social responsibility focused on alleged wrongdoing and how to control it. More recently, attention has also been centered on the possible competitive advantage of socially responsible actions. DuPont has been incorporating care for the environment into its business in two ways it hopes will put it ahead of the competition. First, the company has been reducing its pollution. It hopes these efforts will give it an advantage in a future where the government more heavily regulates emissions, requiring competitors to play catch-up. In addition, reducing emissions goes hand in hand with reducing waste and unnecessary use of energy, saving the company money and directly benefiting the bottom line. Second, DuPont has been developing products that are sustainable, meaning they don't use up the earth's resources. Examples include corn-based fabrics and new applications of its Tyvek material to make buildings more energy-efficient. DuPont expects these innovations to give the company profitable access to the growing market for environmentally friendly products.[69]

The real relationship between corporate social performance and corporate financial performance is highly complex; socially responsible organizations are not necessarily more or less successful in financial terms.[70] But on net, the accumulated evidence indicates that social responsibility is associated with better financial performance.[71] Some advantages are clear, however. For example, socially responsible actions can have long-term benefits. Companies can avoid unnecessary and costly regulation if they are socially responsible. Honesty and fairness may pay great dividends to the conscience, to the personal reputation, and to the public image of the company as well as in the market response.[72] In addition, society's problems can offer business opportunities, and profits can be made from systematic and vigorous efforts to solve these problems. Firms can perform a cost-benefit analysis to identify actions that will maximize profits while satisfying the demand for corporate social responsibility from multiple stakeholders.[73] In other words, managers can treat corporate social responsibility as they would treat all investment decisions. This has been the case as firms attempt to reconcile their business practices with their effect on the natural environment.

In this way, organizations can identify social issues as part of environmental scanning and SWOT analysis and then choose issues that make the most strategic sense. This approach to social responsibility requires not only careful choice of the initiatives to pursue but also monitoring of results as the company would do for other initiatives. Microsoft has partnered with the American Association of Community Colleges (AACC), whose institutions educate 45 percent of U.S. undergraduates. Microsoft contributes money, equipment, and volunteers to the colleges in the AACC, helping to develop IT curricula and train faculty. In this way, Microsoft is using its own strengths (its volunteers are serving in their areas of expertise) to address an environmental threat (the shortage of IT workers). These accomplishments are all measurable in terms of the number of training programs that meet Microsoft's standards and the number of new IT workers who have completed the programs. Thus, the company is benefiting the community and enhancing its reputation while expanding the market for its products.[75]

> "The essential test that should guide corporate social responsibility is not whether a cause is worthy but whether it presents an opportunity to create shared value—that is, a meaningful benefit for society that is also valuable to the business."
> Michael E. Porter and Mark R. Kramer[74]

The Natural Environment

LO 5

Most large corporations developed in an era of abundant raw materials, cheap energy, and unconstrained waste disposal.[76] But many of the technologies developed during this era are contributing to the destruction of ecosystems. Industrial-age systems follow a linear flow of extract, produce, sell, use, and discard—what some call a "take-make-waste" approach.[77] But perhaps no time in history has offered greater possibilities for a change in business thinking than the 21st century.

Business used to look at environmental issues as a no-win situation: you either help the environment and hurt your business, or help your business at a cost to the environment. But now a paradigm shift is taking place in corporate environmental management: the deliberate incorporation of environmental values into competitive strategies and into the design and manufacturing of products.[78] Why? In addition to philosophical reasons, companies "go green" to satisfy consumer demand, to react to a competitor's actions, to meet requests from customers or suppliers, to comply with guidelines, and to create competitive advantage. Wal-Mart does this by collaborating with its suppliers, as described in the "Management Close-Up: Taking Action" feature.

General Electric CEO Jeff Immelt used to view environmental rules as a burden and a cost. Now he sees environmentally friendly technologies as one of the global economy's most significant business opportunities. Under a business initiative called Ecomagination, GE is looking for business opportunities from solving environmental problems. Ecomagination solutions already include wind turbines, materials for solar energy cells, and energy-efficient home appliances. Over a five-year period, GE's revenues from renewable-energy products rose from $5 million to $7 *billion*.[80]

A Risk Society

We live in a risk society. That is, the creation and distribution of wealth generate by-products that can cause injury, loss, or danger to people and the environment. The fundamental sources of risk in modern society are the excessive production of hazards and ecologically unsustainable consumption of natural resources.[81] Risk has proliferated through population explosion, industrial pollution, and environmental degradation.[82]

Management Close-Up   TAKING ACTION

Months after CEO Lee Scott announced that Wal-Mart would become a better steward of the earth's resources, the retailer introduced a packaging "scorecard" for its more than 60,000 suppliers. By inputting data about its product packaging into the scorecard, a supplier can benchmark its environmentally responsible behavior against that of its peers. Wal-Mart provided the scorecard to help suppliers evaluate their own performance—and to encourage them to improve.

The scorecard is part of Wal-Mart's "Sustainability 360" initiative, which includes aggressive goals for reducing merchandise packaging, cutting solid waste by 25 percent, and making stores 25 percent more energy-efficient. More than 2,000 Wal-Mart suppliers gathered at the company-sponsored Live Better Sustainability Summit in 2007, learning from environmental experts and government groups about manufacturing efficiency, renewable energy, and the movement toward organic food and other green products. At the event, Scott introduced a new Wal-Mart reusable shopping bag labeled "Paper or Plastic? Neither." The bag, made of 85 percent recycled materials, holds more than twice as much as the retailer's disposable plastic bags.[79]

- By introducing a packaging scorecard that lets Wal-Mart suppliers evaluate their own behavior and encourages self-improvement, Lee Scott used persuasion rather than a mandate to urge cooperation. How is this approach consistent with ethical behavior and CSR?
- Wal-Mart's critics claim the firm's sustainability program is merely an attempt to "green-wash" a corporate reputation tainted by its big-box image. How does Scott's behavior illustrate that he's serious about the environment?

Industrial pollution risks include air pollution, smog, global warming, ozone depletion, acid rain, toxic waste sites, nuclear hazards, obsolete weapons arsenals, industrial accidents, and hazardous products. More than 30,000 uncontrolled toxic waste sites have been documented in the United States alone, and the number is increasing by perhaps 2,500 per year. The situation is far worse in other parts of the world. The pattern, for toxic waste and many other risks, is one of accumulating risks and inadequate remedies.

The institutions that create environmental and technological risk (corporations and government agencies) are responsible for controlling and managing the risks.[83] For example, Lockheed Martin Corporation had to contain the spread of a chemical used in industrial degreasers when it leaked from a broken sump pump at an old facility in Florida. Even though Lockheed had sold the facility to another company, it had owned the property when the contamination was first discovered, so it was responsible.[84]

Some of the world's worst environmental problems are in China, because of its rapid industrialization and its huge population and size. Among Asia's capital cities, Beijing has the worst air pollution, with six times the degree of air pollution as in London. About one-third of China's rural population—more than 300 million people—drink unhealthy, unclean water. At least the problem is recognized: local authorities are beginning to experience pressure from the central government to clean up or shut down dirty factories.[85]

ecocentric management

Its goal is the creation of sustainable economic development and improvement of quality of life worldwide for all organizational stakeholders.

Ecocentric Management

Ecocentric management has as its goal the creation of sustainable economic development and improvement of quality of life worldwide for all organizational stakeholders.[86]

sustainable growth

Economic growth and development that meet present needs without harming the needs of future generations.

Sustainable growth is economic growth and development that meet the organization's present needs without harming the ability of future generations to meet their needs.[87] Sustainability is fully compatible with the natural ecosystems that generate and preserve life.[88]

Some believe that the concept of sustainable growth offers (1) a framework for organizations to use in communicating to all stakeholders, (2) a planning and strategy guide, and (3) a tool for evaluating and improving the ability to compete.[89] The principle can begin at the highest organizational levels and be made explicit in performance appraisals and reward systems.

With two-thirds of the world's population expected to experience water scarcity by 2025 and shortages forecast for 36 U.S. states by 2013, businesses are becoming concerned about this essential natural resource. If you haven't experienced a water shortage, water usage might not seem to be an obvious area of concern, but it can be significant. For example, Levi Strauss & Company has determined that making a pair of jeans requires about 500 gallons of water for growing, dying, and processing cotton.

Brewer SABMiller is a leader in making water conservation a part of its strategy. Using an online computer application, the company submitted the GPS coordinates of factory and farm locations and learned where its operations are located in areas of water scarcity. About 30 SABMiller sites were in vulnerable areas. Executives decided to target one of those areas and develop a process they could apply elsewhere. They selected South Africa, whose breweries produce about one-sixth of the company's beer. Not only is South Africa facing water shortages, but its government has yet to provide access to safe drinking water for 5 million of its people.

To get hard information about its water consumption, the company measured water usage at each stage of its processes, from growing crops to rinsing out used bottles before recycling. The most water was used in growing barley, maize (corn), and hops. Together with the water used in factories, 20 gallons of water are needed to produce each pint of beer. Based on the data, SABMiller's initial efforts are focusing on identifying and using more efficient irrigation technology, preventing waste from runoff and evaporation.[90]

life-cycle analysis (LCA)

A process of analyzing all inputs and outputs, though the entire "cradle-to-grave" life of a product, to determine total environmental impact.

Increasingly, firms are paying attention to the total environmental impact throughout the life cycle of their products.[91] **Life-cycle analysis (LCA)** is a process of analyzing all inputs and outputs, through the entire "cradle-to-grave" life of a product, to determine the total environmental impact of the production and use of a product. LCA quantifies the total use of resources and the releases into the air, water, and land.

LCA considers the extraction of raw materials, product packaging, transportation, and disposal. Consider packaging alone. Goods make the journey from manufacturer to wholesaler to retailer to customer; then they are recycled back to the manufacturer. They may be packaged and repackaged several times, from bulk transport, to large crates, to cardboard boxes, to individual consumer sizes. Repackaging not only creates waste but it also costs time. The design of initial packaging in sizes and formats adaptable to the final customer can minimize the need for repackaging, cut waste, and realize financial benefits.

Profitability need not suffer and may be positively affected by ecocentric philosophies and practices. Some, but not all, research has shown a positive relationship between corporate environmental performance and profitability.[92] Of course, whether the relationship is positive, negative, or neutral depends on the strategies chosen and the effectiveness of implementation.

For those interested in reading more about this subject, Appendix B beginning on page 139 discusses in greater detail the reasons for managing with the environment in mind, some history of the environmental movement, economic issues, and a wide array of "green" examples pertaining to strategy, public affairs, legal issues, operations, marketing, accounting, and finance.

Environmental Agendas for the Future

In the past, most companies were oblivious to their negative environmental impact. More recently, many began striving for low impact. Now, some strive for positive impact, eager to sell solutions to the world's problems. IBM has three decades of experience in lowering its environmental impact through efforts such as reducing waste in packaging and measuring carbon emissions. It has begun to use that experience as a strength, a basis for expertise it can sell to other organizations, along with its computing power and other consulting services. Thus, one application might be to help clients measure and forecast the carbon emissions of their entire supply chain. By running calculations on its supercomputers, IBM consultants could help the clients find ways to lower their energy use.[93]

You don't have to be a manufacturer or a utility to jump on the green bandwagon. Web search giant Google is applying a three-pronged strategy aimed at reducing its "carbon footprint," that is, its output of carbon dioxide and other greenhouse gases. At Google, most greenhouse gas emissions are related to electricity consumption by its buildings and computers. So Google is first seeking ways to make buildings and computers more energy-efficient, such as by using high-efficiency lighting and installing power management software in its computers. Second, the company is developing ways to get more of its power from renewable sources, such as the solar power system at its facility in Mountain View, California. Finally, recognizing that its other efforts cannot yet eliminate Google's release of greenhouse gases, the company is purchasing "offsets"—funding projects that reduce greenhouse gas emissions elsewhere.[94]

Webs of companies with a common ecological vision can combine their efforts into high-leverage, impactful action.[95] In Kalundborg, Denmark, such a collaborative alliance exists among an electric power generating plant, an oil refiner, a biotech production plant, a plasterboard factory, cement producers, heating utilities, a sulfuric acid producer, and local agriculture and horticulture. Chemicals, energy (for both heating and cooling), water, and organic materials flow among companies. Resources are conserved, "waste" materials generate revenues, and water, air, and ground pollution all are reduced.

Companies not only have the *ability* to solve environmental problems; they are coming to see and acquire the *motivation* as well, as described in the "Management Close-Up: Assessing Outcomes and Seizing Opportunities" feature. Some companies now believe that solving environmental problems is one of the biggest opportunities in the history of commerce.[96]

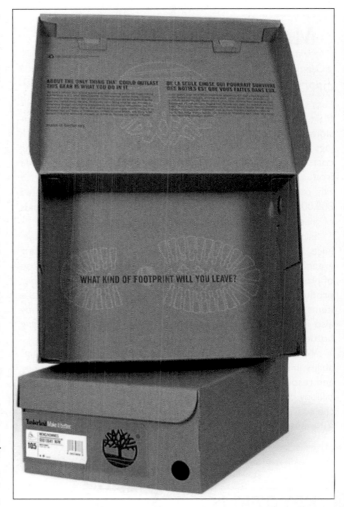

Timberland has paid particular attention to life-cycle analysis, as implied by what is printed on their recycled-material shoe boxes.

Packaging isn't the most glamorous of business topics, but it holds great potential for reducing costs and increasing speed while helping the environment. You can always find opportunities to improve results in unexpected places, where others haven't tried.

Management Close-Up

ASSESSING OUTCOMES AND SEIZING OPPORTUNITIES

Less than a year after introducing its packaging scorecard, Wal-Mart was able to begin using its data to make purchasing decisions. Today, an Ohio dairy supplies Wal-Mart with square milk jugs that pack more efficiently, significantly reducing shipping costs. For its fresh produce, Wal-Mart uses packaging made from a corn-based bioplastic, a renewable resource. Moving to this packaging on only four produce items saved an estimated 800,000 gallons of gas and prevented more than 11 million pounds of greenhouse gases from entering the environment.

Eco-friendly packaging has also been created for yogurt, apple juice, liquid laundry detergent, and other items, greatly reducing greenhouse gas emissions, saving water, and minimizing the use of plastic resin and cardboard. Smaller packaging for many other products has reduced Wal-Mart's logistics costs because the items weigh less. CEO Lee Scott announced that the company also is studying how to reduce the use of plastic in packaging bottled water.

Wal-Mart doesn't disclose financial information on its sustainability initiative, but it says the program is already saving money and resources and predicts the broad array of projects will save billions over time. It also points to the continuing evolution of the scorecard, which has encouraged further learning and innovation from its suppliers.

In 2008 Scott announced that Wal-Mart would require suppliers to comply with strict ethical and environmental standards, including outside audits. Compliance was not an option for companies that sought to do business with Wal-Mart. By 2012, Wal-Mart will require suppliers to source 95 percent of their production from factories that receive the highest audit ratings. For greater openness, the retailer would also begin tracking factories where its products originate.

Scott retired in 2009. During his tenure, Wal-Mart sales nearly tripled. Succeeding Scott is his protégé, Michael T. Duke, who earlier headed Wal-Mart's logistics and international operations. Industry observers expect Duke to advance Scott's policies. With international business comprising nearly a fourth of Wal-Mart's total sales, Duke is also expected to open stores in Russia and China, two high-potential overseas markets.[97]

- When Scott announced Wal-Mart's sustainability initiative, outside research showed that most consumers didn't consider the environment in their buying decisions, and only 16 percent were willing to pay more for a "green" product. By taking the lead on eco-friendly products, how has Wal-Mart's CEO helped change consumer behavior?
- New CEO Michael Duke is known for his "people skills." How will that help him continue the sustainability initiative launched by his predecessor? Would you consider Wal-Mart to have ecocentric management?

KEY TERMS

Business ethics, p. 164

Caux Principles, p. 165

Compliance-based ethics programs, p. 171

Corporate social responsibility (CSR), p. 176

Ecocentric management, p. 181

Economic responsibilities, p. 176

Egoism, p. 165

Ethical climate, p. 168

Ethical issue, p. 164

Ethical leader, p. 170

Ethical responsibilities, p. 176

Ethics, p. 162

Integrity-based ethics programs, p. 172

Kohlberg's model of cognitive moral development, p. 167

Legal responsibilities, p. 176

Life-cycle analysis (LCA), p. 182

Moral philosophy, p. 165

Philanthropic responsibilities, p. 177

Relativism, p. 166

Sarbanes-Oxley Act, p. 167

Sustainable growth, p. 182

Transcendent education, p. 177

Universalism, p. 165

Utilitarianism, p. 166

Virtue ethics, p. 166

SUMMARY OF LEARNING OBJECTIVES

Now that you have studied Chapter 5, you should be able to:

LO 1 Describe how different ethical perspectives guide decision making.

The purpose of ethics is to identify the rules that govern human behavior and the "goods" that are worth seeking. Ethical decisions are guided by the individual's values or principles of conduct such as honesty, fairness, integrity, respect for others, and responsible citizenship. Different ethical systems include universalism, egoism

and utilitarianism, relativism, and virtue ethics. These philosophical systems, as practiced by different individuals according to their level of cognitive moral development and other factors, underlie the ethical stances of individuals and organizations.

LO 2 Explain how companies influence their ethics environment.

Different organizations apply different ethical perspectives and standards. Ethical codes sometimes are helpful, although they must be implemented properly. Ethics programs can range from compliance-based to integrity-based. An increasing number of organizations are adopting ethics codes. Such codes address employee conduct, community and environment, shareholders, customers, suppliers and contractors, political activity, and technology.

LO 3 Outline a process for making ethical decisions.

Making ethical decisions requires moral awareness, moral judgment, and moral character. When faced with ethical dilemmas, the veil of ignorance is a useful metaphor. More precisely, you can know various moral standards (universalism, relativism, and so on), use the problem-solving model described in Chapter 3, identify the positive and negative effects of your alternatives on different parties, consider legal requirements and the costs of unethical actions, and then evaluate your ethical duties using criteria specified in the chapter.

LO 4 Summarize the important issues surrounding corporate social responsibility.

Corporate social responsibility is the extension of the corporate role beyond economic pursuits. It includes not only economic but also legal, ethical, and philanthropic responsibilities. Advocates believe managers should consider societal and human needs in their business decisions because corporations are members of society and carry a wide range of responsibilities. Critics of corporate responsibility believe managers' first responsibility is to increase profits for the shareholders who own the corporation. The two perspectives are potentially reconcilable, especially if managers choose to address areas of social responsibility that contribute to the organization's strategy.

LO 5 Discuss reasons for businesses' growing interest in the natural environment.

In the past, most companies viewed the natural environment as a resource to be used for raw materials and profit. But consumer, regulatory, and other pressures arose. Executives often viewed these pressures as burdens, constraints, and costs to be borne. Now, more companies view the interface between business and the natural environment as a potential win-win opportunity. Some are adopting a "greener" agenda for philosophical reasons and personal commitment to sustainable development. Many also are recognizing the potential financial benefits of managing with the environment in mind, and are integrating environmental issues into corporate and business strategy. Some see entering businesses that help rather than harm the natural environment as one of the great commercial opportunities in history.

LO 6 Identify actions managers can take to manage with the environment in mind.

Organizations have contributed risk to society and have some responsibility for reducing risk to the environment. They also have the capability to help solve environmental problems. Ecocentric management attempts to minimize negative environment impact, create sustainable economic development, and improve the quality of life worldwide. Relevant actions are described in the chapter, including strategic initiatives, life-cycle analysis, and interorganizational alliances. A chapter appendix provides a wide variety of specific examples of strategic, operations, finance, legal and public affairs, marketing, and accounting practices that are environmentally friendly.

DISCUSSION QUESTIONS

1. Has Wal-Mart made headlines recently for any new environmental initiatives? How has the company been progressing toward its goals?

2. Consider the various ethical systems described early in the chapter. Identify concrete examples from your own past decisions or the decisions of others you have seen or read about.

3. Choose one or more topics from Table 5.2 and discuss the ethical issues surrounding them.

4. What would you do in each of the scenarios described in Table 5.3?

5. Identify and discuss illegal, unethical, and socially responsible business actions in the current news.

6. Does your school have a code of ethics? If so, what does it say? Is it effective? Why or why not?

7. You have a job you like at which you work 40 to 45 hours per week. How much off-the-job volunteer work would you do? What kinds of volunteer work? How will you react if your boss makes it clear he or she wants you to cut back on the outside activities and devote more hours to your job?

8. What are the arguments for and against the concept of corporate social responsibility? Where do you stand, and why?

Give your opinions, specifically, with respect to the text examples.

9. What do you think of the concept of a transcendent education, as described in the chapter? What can be done to implement such a vision for education?

10. What is the current status of the Sarbanes-Oxley Act? Have there been any changes? What do executives think of it now? What impact has it had?

11. A company in England slaughtered 70,000 baby ostrich chicks each year for their meat. It told a teen magazine that it would stop if it received enough complaints. Analyze this policy, practice, and public statement using the concepts discussed in the chapter.

12. A Nike ad in the U.S. magazine *Seventeen* showed a picture of a girl, aged perhaps 8 or 9. The ad read,

    If you let me play . . .

    I will like myself more.

    I will have more self-confidence.

    I will suffer less depression.

    I will be 60 percent less likely to get breast cancer.

    I will be more likely to leave a man who beats me.

    I will be less likely to get pregnant before I want to.

I will learn what it means to be strong.
If you let me play sports.

Assess this ad in terms of chapter concepts surrounding ethics and social responsibility. What questions would you ask in doing this analysis?

13. Should companies like GE and Monsanto be held accountable for actions of decades past, then legal but since made

illegal, as their harmful effects became known? Why or why not?

14. Discuss courage as a requirement for ethical behavior. What personal examples can you offer, either as an actor or as an observer? What examples are in the news?

CONCLUDING CASE

J & G Garden Center: Lawn Care Services Division

John and Gloria Weed started a new business in 1986 on the outskirts of Columbus, Ohio. Their original retail store with greenhouse attachment featured fresh-cut flowers, annuals, vegetables, and perennials. The building is on the grounds of Gloria's family farm, enabling the Weeds to grow some of their retail products from scratch. Gloria's parents gave the couple several acres of commercially zoned land as a wedding gift in 1982. The building and greenhouse construction were completed by John with a little help from his brothers. This combination of land acquisition and building construction resulted in very low overhead for the business, which contributed to their start-up success.

An addition to the building completed in 1991 included several new and related product lines such as garden tools, soils and mulch products, gifts, seeds, and related accessories.

Gloria had earned a horticulture degree at the local community college prior to the establishment of the business. In 1997 she was able to fulfill a lifelong dream of starting a landscape design and installation service that became the company's next and newest product line. Gloria set up a small studio and office in the couple's nearby home and was able to acquire some new clients. Her timing was good, as the Columbus area experienced a housing boom during that period. New houses and new developments sprang up in every direction from the city. Their garden center was able to supply the plant materials that each new job required. Soon after, the Weeds expanded their product lines to include a new and wider variety of trees, shrubs, landscape terraces, patios, and walkways as a means to generate new sales and to complement Gloria's new service line.

The original start-up business and each expansion project (building addition, new products, design and installation service) have more than covered their costs, but they have generated only fair to moderate profit margins. The Weeds attribute this mostly to the presence of their competition, which always seems to be growing. As a result, they have been reluctant to raise prices even though some product costs have risen.

One year later, the Weeds completed the final phase of their original long-range business plan with the addition of another new service—Big John, The Lawn & Garden Doctor. This product line was added because of its very high profit projections.

This new division specializes in the treatment and eradication of lawn and garden pests. Many insects and diseases affect plant life, some of which are fatal. In spite of the fact that the Weeds and other local garden centers offer high-quality plants to consumers, nature has a way of wreaking havoc on lawns, gardens, shrubs, and trees over time.

The start-up of this division required a tremendous amount of time, effort, and expense as a result of the environmental and safety-related hazards of some of the products such as insecticides and fungicides. The Weeds were required to train and license two of their employees as certified applications technicians. A custom-built, high-security storage facility was required and built to house all hazardous materials. The building was secured with a locked, barbed-wire fence, an alarm system, and a hazardous material runoff-proof partition. A special liability insurance policy was purchased as well.

As expected, the new division turned out to be very profitable. Demand was strong and the technicians' work was professional and effective. In fact, at the end of its first full year of existence, Big John, The Lawn & Garden Doctor, turned a profit that almost matched that of all other divisions combined. At the company's monthly staff meeting, it therefore came as quite a surprise to everyone when John announced that he was seriously considering dropping the division entirely.

John Weed is a local native of the area. He has very strong family and community values and has always felt responsible for the welfare and happiness of his friends, neighbors, and especially his customers. From the start, he was nervous and apprehensive that something bad would happen as a result of the pesticide or fungicide applications.

And then it happened. A customer's dog became ill, possibly as a result of eating some grass from a recently treated lawn. Big John's technician had taken every precaution. The area was properly treated, marked, and roped off, and the customer was instructed as to the after-care safety precautions, which included a well-written handout and a signed liability waiver form.

Two months later, a lawsuit was filed against the company, claiming that the water runoff from the property of one of their customers had tainted a neighbor's well. The Weeds were forced to hire an attorney. Following a full and costly investigation, they were found not guilty of the charge.

Although the company was clearly not negligent, John was upset. Gloria feels that John is overreacting. She points out that the company is in full compliance with every regulation and that John has gone out of his way to ensure the safety of all. Gloria also noted that no business can control the behavior or be responsible for its customers or the population in general; incidents beyond their control will naturally and always occur. In addition, the high profitability of the division will allow the Weeds to embark on an aggressive advertising campaign aimed at improving the sales and profits of their other divisions.

John is losing sleep over all of this and is not sure what to do. He is worried about the image and reputation of his family and their business. He feels that the lawn and garden doctor business provides a useful service, but his conscience is bothering him.

QUESTIONS

1. Present an argument in favor of retaining the new division that considers and incorporates the ethical conflicts that Mr. Weed is experiencing.

2. Present an argument in favor of eliminating or changing the new division, and make recommendations to improve overall company profits through means that will be acceptable to Mr. Weed.

3. Aside from compliance with the law, how much additional responsibility does a business owner have to his or her customer base, employees, suppliers, and the community at large? How do you feel about the old saying "buyer beware"?

EXPERIENTIAL EXERCISES

5.1 Measuring Your Ethical Work Behavior

OBJECTIVES

1. To explore a range of ethically perplexing situations.
2. To understand your own ethical attitudes.

INSTRUCTIONS

Make decisions in the situations described in the Ethical Behavior Worksheet. You will not have all the background information on each situation, and, instead, you should make whatever assumptions you feel you would make if you were actually confronted with the decision choices described. Select the decision choice that most closely represents the decision you feel you would make personally. You should choose decision options even though you can envision other creative solutions that were not included in the exercise.

Ethical Behavior Worksheet

Situation 1.   You are taking a very difficult chemistry course, which you must pass to maintain your scholarship and to avoid damaging your application for graduate school. Chemistry is not your strong suit, and, because of a just-below-failing average in the course, you will have to receive a grade of 90 or better on the final exam, which is two days away. A janitor, who is aware of your plight, informs you that he found the master for the chemistry final in a trash barrel and has saved it. He will make it available to you for a price, which is high but which you could afford. What would you do?

_____ (a) I would tell the janitor thanks. but no thanks.

_____ (b) I would report the janitor to the proper officials.

_____ (c) I would buy the exam and keep it to myself.

_____ (d) I would not buy the exam myself, but I would let some of my friends, who are also flunking the course, know that it is available.

Situation 2.   You have been working on some financial projections manually for two days now. It seems that each time you think you have them completed your boss shows up with a new assumption or another "what if" question. If you only had a copy of a spreadsheet software program for your personal computer, you could plug in the new assumptions and revise the estimates with ease. Then, a colleague offers to let you make a copy of some software that is copyrighted. What would you do?

_____ (a) I would accept my friend's generous offer and make a copy of the software.

_____ (b) I would decline to copy it and plug away manually on the numbers.

_____ (c) I would decide to go buy a copy of the software myself, for $300, and hope I would be reimbursed by the company in a month or two.

_____ (d) I would request another extension on an already overdue project date.

Situation 3.   Your small manufacturing company is in serious financial difficulty. A large order of your products is ready to be delivered to a key customer when you discover that the product is simply not right. It will not meet all performance specifications, will cause problems for your customer, and will require rework in the field; however, this, you know, will not become evident until after the customer has received and paid for the order. If you do not ship the order and receive the payment as expected, your business may be forced into bankruptcy. And if you delay the shipment or inform the customer of these problems, you may lose the order and also go bankrupt. What would you do?

_____ (a) I would not ship the order and place my firm in voluntary bankruptcy.

_____ (b) I would inform the customer and declare voluntary bankruptcy.

_____ (c) I would ship the order and inform the customer, after I received payment.

_____ (d) I would ship the order and not inform the customer.

Situation 4.   You are the cofounder and president of a new venture, manufacturing products for the recreational market. Five months after launching the business, one of your suppliers informs you it can no longer supply you with a critical raw material because you are not a large-quantity user. Without the raw material, the business cannot continue. What would you do?

_____ (a) I would grossly overstate my requirements to another supplier to make the supplier think I am a much larger potential customer to secure the raw material from that supplier, even though this would mean the supplier will no longer be able to supply another, noncompeting small manufacturer who may thus be forced out of business.

_____ (b) I would steal raw material from another firm (non-competing) where I am aware of a sizable stockpile.

_____ (c) I would pay off the supplier, because I have reason to believe that the supplier could be "persuaded" to meet my needs with a sizable "under the table" pay-off that my company could afford.

_____ (d) I would declare voluntary bankruptcy.

Situation 5.   You are on a marketing trip for your new venture for the purpose of calling on the purchasing agent of a major prospective client. Your company is manufacturing an electronic

system that you hope the purchasing agent will buy. During the course of your conversation, you notice on the cluttered desk of the purchasing agent several copies of a cost proposal for a system from one of your direct competitors. This purchasing agent has previously reported mislaying several of your own company's proposals and has asked for additional copies. The purchasing agent leaves the room momentarily to get you a cup of coffee, leaving you alone with your competitor's proposals less than an arm's length away. What would you do?

_____ (a) I would do nothing but await the man's return.

_____ (b) I would sneak a quick peek at the proposal, looking for bottom-line numbers.

_____ (c) I would put the copy of the proposal in my briefcase.

_____ (d) I would wait until the man returns and ask his per-mission to see the copy.

SOURCE: Jeffry A. Timmons, *New Venture Creation,* 3rd ed. pp. 285–86. Copyright © 1994 by Jeffry A. Timmons. Reproduced with permission of the author. P. 160–161. © 1994 The McGraw-Hill Companies.

5.2 Ethical Stance

Are the following actions ethical or unethical in your opinion? Why or why not? Consider the actions individually, and discuss them in small groups.

• Calling in sick when you really are not.
• Taking office supplies home for personal use.
• Cheating on a test.
• Turning someone in for cheating on a test or paper.
• Overcharging on your company expense report.
• Trying to flirt your way out of a speeding ticket.
• Splicing cable from your neighbor.
• Surfing the net on company time.
• Cheating on income tax.

• Lying (exaggerating) about yourself to influence someone of the opposite sex.
• Looking at pornographic sites on the Web through the company network.
• Lying about your education on a job application.
• Lying about experience in a job interview.
• Making a copy of a rental DVD before returning it to the store.

SOURCE: Suzanne C. de Janasz, Karen O. Dowd, and Beth Z. Schneider, *Interpersonal Skills in Organizations* (New York: McGraw-Hill/Irwin, 2002), p. 391. © 2002 The McGraw-Hill Companies.

Managing in Our Natural Environment

BUSINESS AND THE ENVIRONMENT: CONFLICTING VIEWS

Some people believe everyone wins when business tackles environmental issues.[1] Others disagree.

The Win-Win Mentality Business used to look at environmental issues as a no-win situation: You either help the environment and hurt your business, or help your business only at a cost to the environment. Fortunately, things have changed. "When Americans first demanded a cleanup of the environment during the early 1970s, corporations threw a tantrum. Their response ran the psychological gamut from denial to hostility, defiance, obstinacy, and fear. But today, when it comes to green issues, many U.S. companies have turned from rebellious underachievers to active problem solvers."[2] Table B.1 gives just a few examples of things U.S. corporations are doing to help solve environmental problems.

The Earth Summit in Rio in 1992 helped increase awareness of environmental issues. This led to the Kyoto Protocol, an international effort to control global warming that included an unsuccessful meeting in the Hague in November 2000.[3] "There has been an evolution of most groups—whether industry, governments, or nongovernmental organizations—toward a recognition that everyone plays a part in reaching a solution."[4]

Being "green" is potentially a catalyst for innovation, new market opportunities, and wealth creation. Advocates believe that this is truly a win-win situation; actions can be taken that benefit both business and the environment. For example, Procter & Gamble in a span of five years reduced disposable wastes by over 50 percent while increasing sales by 25 percent.[5] Win-win companies will come out ahead of those companies that have an us-versus-them, we-can't-afford-to-protect-the-environment mentality.

Is the easy part over?[6] Companies have found a lot of easy-to-harvest, "low-hanging fruit"—that is, overly costly practices that were made environmentally friendlier and that saved money at the same time. Many big companies have made these easy changes, and reaped benefits from them. Many small companies still have such low-hanging fruit to harvest,[7] and plenty remains to be done.

The Dissenting View The critics of environmentalism in business are vocal. Some economists maintain that not a single empirical analysis supports the "free lunch view" that spending money on environmental problems provides full payback to the firm.[8] Skepticism should continue, they say; the belief that everyone will come out a winner is naive.

What really upsets many businesspeople is the financial cost of complying with environmental regulations.[9] Consider a few examples:

- GM spent $1.3 billion to comply with California requirements that 10 percent of the cars sold there be emission-free. European automakers spent $7 billion to install pollution-control equipment in all new cars during a five-year period.
- At Bayer, 20 percent of manufacturing costs were for the environment. This is approximately the same amount spent for labor.
- The Clean Air Act alone was expected to cost U.S. petroleum refiners $37 billion, more than the book value of the entire industry.
- California's tough laws are a major reason why manufacturers moved to Arkansas or Nevada.

In industries like chemicals and petroleum, environmental regulations were once considered a threat to their very survival.[10]

Balance A more balanced view is that business must weigh the environmental benefits of an action against value destruction. The advice here is: Don't obstruct progress, but pick your environmental initiatives carefully. Compliance and remediation efforts will protect, but not increase, shareholder value.[11] And it is shareholder value, rather than compliance, emissions, or costs, that should be the focus of objective cost-benefit analyses. Such an approach is environmentally sound but also hard-headed in a business sense, and is the one approach that is truly sustainable over the long term.

Johan Piet maintains, "Only win-win companies will survive, but that does not mean that all win-win ideas will be successful."[12] In other words, rigorous analysis is essential. Thus, some companies maintain continuous improvement in environmental performance, but fund only projects that meet financial objectives.

Most people understand that business has the resources and the competence to bring about constructive change, and that this creates great opportunity—if well managed—for both business and the environment.

TABLE B.1
What Companies Are Doing to Enhance the Environment

Toyota established an "ecotechnologies" division both for regulatory compliance and to shape corporate direction, including the development of hybrid electric-combustion automobiles.

Interface Corporation's new Shanghai carpet factory circulates liquid through a standard pumping loop like those used in most industries. But simply by using fatter pipes and short, straight pipes instead of long and crooked pipes, it cut the power requirements by 92 percent.

Xerox used "zero-waste-to-landfill" engineering to develop a new remanufacturable copier. AT&T cut paper costs by 15 percent by setting defaults on copiers and printers to double-sided mode.

Electrolux uses more environmentally friendly water-based and powder paints instead of solvent-based paints, and introduced the first refrigerators and freezers free of chlorofluorocarbons.

Many chemical and pharmaceutical companies, including Novo Nordisk and Empresas La Moderna, are exploring "green chemistry" and seeking biological substitutes for synthetic materials.

Anheuser-Busch saved 21 million pounds of metal a year by reducing its beer-can rims by 1/8 of an inch (without reducing its contents).

Nissan enlisted a group of ecologists, energy experts, and science writers to brainstorm about how an environmentally responsible car company might behave. Among the ideas: to produce automobiles that snap together into electrically powered trains for long trips and then detach for the dispersion to final destinations.

SOURCES: P. M. Senge and G. Carstedt, "Innovating Our Way to the Next Industrial Revolution," *Sloan Management Review,* Winter 2001, pp. 24–38; M. P. Polonsky and P. J. Rosenberger III, "Reevaluating Green Marketing: A Strategic Approach," *Business Horizons,* September–October, 2001, pp. 21–30; C. Garfield, *Second to None: How Our Smartest Companies Put People First* (Burr Ridge, IL; Business One-Irwin, 1992); H. Bradbury and J. A. Clair, "Promoting Sustainable Organizations with Sweden's Natural Step," *Academy of Management Executive,* November 1999, pp. 63–74; A. Loving, L. Hunter Lovins, and P. Hawken, "A Road Map for Natural Capitalism," *Harvard Business Review,* May–June 1999, pp. 145–58; P. Hawken, A. Lovings, and L. Hunter Lovins, *Natural Capitalism* (Boston: Little Brown, 1999); and S. L. Hart and M. B. Milstein, "Global Sustainability and the Creative Destruction of Industries," *Sloan Management Review,* Fall 1999, pp. 23–32.

WHY MANAGE WITH THE ENVIRONMENT IN MIND?
Business is turning its full attention to environmental issues for many reasons, including legal compliance, cost effectiveness, competitive advantage, public opinion, and long-term thinking.

Legal Compliance Table B.2 shows just some of the most important U.S. environmental laws. Government regulations and liability for damages provide strong economic incentives to comply with environmental guidelines. Most industries already have made environmental protection regulation and liability an

TABLE B.2
Some U.S Environmental Laws

Superfund [Comprehensive Environmental Response, Compensation, and Liability Act (CERCLA)]: Establishes potential liability for any person or organization responsible for creating an environmental health hazard. Individuals may be prosecuted, fined, or taxed to fund cleanup.

Clean Water Act [Federal Water Pollution Control Act]: Regulates all discharges into surface waters, and affects the construction and performance of sewer systems. The Safe Drinking Water Act similarly protects groundwaters.

Clean Air Act: Regulates the emission into the air of any substance that affects air quality, including nitrous oxides, sulfur dioxide, and carbon dioxide.

Community Response and Right-to-Know Act: Mandates that all facilities producing, transporting, storing, using, or releasing hazardous substances provide full information to local and state authorities and maintain emergency-action plans.

Federal Hazardous Substances Act: Regulates hazards to health and safety associated with consumer products. The Consumer Product Safety Commission has the right to recall hazardous products.

Hazardous Materials Transportation Act: Regulates the packaging, marketing, and labeling of shipments of flammable, toxic, and radioactive materials.

Resource Conservation and Recovery Act: Extends to small-quantity generators the laws regulating generation, treatment, and disposal of solid and hazardous wastes.

Surface Mining Control and Reclamation Act: Establishes environmental standards for all surface-mining operations.

Toxic Substances Control Act: Addresses the manufacture, processing, distribution, use, and disposal of dangerous chemical substances and mixtures.

SOURCE: Dennis C. Kinlaw, *Competitive and Green: Sustainable Performance in the Environmental Age* (Amsterdam: Pfeiffer & Co., 1993). Reprinted by permission of the author.

integral part of their business planning.[13] The U.S. Justice Department has handed out tough prison sentences to executives whose companies violate hazardous-waste requirements.

Some businesspeople consider the regulations to be too rigid, inflexible, and unfair. In response to this concern, regulatory reform may become more creative. The Aspen Institute Series on the Environment in the Twenty-First Century is trying to increase the cost-effectiveness of compliance measures through more flexibility in meeting standards and relying on market-based incentives. Such mechanisms, including tradable permits, pollution charges, and deposit refund systems, provide positive financial incentives for good environmental performance.[14]

Cost Effectiveness Environmentally conscious strategies can be cost-effective.[15] In the short run, company after company is realizing cost savings from repackaging, recycling, and other approaches. Union Carbide faced costs of $30 a ton for disposal of solid wastes and $2,000 a ton for disposal of hazardous wastes. By recycling, reclaiming, or selling its waste, it avoided $8.5 million in costs *and* generated $3.5 million in income during a six-month period. Dow Chemical launched a 10-year program to improve its environmental, health, and safety performance worldwide. Dow projected savings of $1.8 billion over the 10-year period.[16]

Environmentally conscious strategies offer long-run cost advantages as well. Companies that are functioning barely within legal limits today may incur big costs—being forced to pay damages or upgrade technologies and practices—when laws change down the road.

A few of the other cost savings include fines, cleanups, and litigation; lower raw materials costs; reduced energy use; less expensive waste handling and disposal; lower insurance rates; and possibly higher interest rates.

Competitive Advantage Corporations gain a competitive advantage by channeling their environmental concerns into entrepreneurial opportunities and by producing higher-quality products that meet consumer demand. Business opportunities abound in pollution protection equipment and processes, waste cleanup, low-water-use plumbing, new lightbulb technology, and marketing of environmentally safe products like biodegradable plastics. With new pools of venture capital, government funding, and specialized investment funds available, environmental technology has become a major sector of the venture-capital industry.[17]

In addition, companies that fail to innovate in this area will be at a competitive *disadvantage*. Environmental protection is not only a universal need; it is also a major export industry. U.S. trade suffered as other countries—notably Germany—took the lead in patenting and exporting anti–air pollution and other environmental technologies. If the United States does not produce innovative, competitive new technologies, it will forsake a growth industry and see most of its domestic spending for environmental protection go to imports.[18]

In short, competitive advantage can be gained by maintaining market share with old customers, and by creating new products for new market opportunities. And if you are an environmental leader, you may set the standards for future regulations—regulations that you are prepared to meet, while your competitors are not.

Public Opinion The majority of the U.S. population believes business must clean up; few people think it is doing its job well. Gallup surveys show that more than 80 percent of U.S. consumers consider environmentalism in making purchases. An international survey of 22 countries found that majorities in 20 countries gave priority to environmental protection even at the risk of slowing economic growth. Consumers seem to have reached the point of routinely expecting companies to come up with environmentally friendly alternatives to current products and practices.[19]

Companies also receive pressure from local communities and from their own employees. Sometimes the pressure is informal and low key, but much pressure is exerted by environmental organizations, aroused citizen groups, societies and associations, international codes of conduct, and environmentally conscious investors.[20]

Another important reason for paying attention to environmental impact is TRI, the Toxic Release Inventory.[21] Starting in 1986, the EPA required all the plants of approximately 10,000 U.S. manufacturers to report annual releases of 317 toxic chemicals into the air, ground, and water. The substances include freon, PCBs, asbestos, and lead compounds. Hundreds of others have been added to the list. The releases are not necessarily illegal, but they provide the public with an annual environmental benchmark. TRI provides a powerful incentive to reduce emissions.

Finally, it is useful to remember that companies recover very slowly in public opinion from the impact of an environmental disaster. Adverse public opinion may affect sales as well as the firm's ability to attract and retain talented people. You can see why companies like P&G consider concern for the environment a consumer need, making it a basic and critical business issue.

Long-Term Thinking Long-term thinking about resources helps business leaders understand the nature of their responsibilities with regard to environmental concerns. For example, you read about sustainable growth in the chapter.[22] Economic arguments and the tragedy of the commons also highlight the need for long-term thinking.

Economic arguments In Chapter 3, we discussed long-term versus short-term decision making. We stated that it is common for managers to succumb to short-term pressure for profits and to avoid spending now when the potential payoff is years down the road. In addition, some economists maintain that it is the responsibility of management to maximize returns for shareholders, implying the preeminence of the short-term profit goal.

But other economists argue that such a strategy caters to immediate profit maximization for stock speculators and neglects serious investors who are with the company for the long haul. Attention to environmental issues enhances the organization's long-term viability because the goal is the long-term creation of wealth for the patient, serious investors in the company[23]—not to mention the future state of our planet and the new generations who will inhabit it.

The tragedy of the commons In a classic article in *Science*, Garrett Hardin described a situation that applies to all business decisions and social concerns regarding scarce resources like clean water, air, and land.[24] Throughout human history, a commons was a tract of land shared by communities of people on which they grazed their animals. A commons has limited **carrying capacity,** or the ability to sustain a population, because it is a finite resource. For individual herders, short-term interest lies in adding as many animals to the commons as they can. But problems develop as more herders add more animals to graze the commons. This leads to tragedy: As each herder acts in his short-term interest, the long-run impact is the destruction of the commons. The solution is to make choices according to long-run rather than short-run consequences.

In many ways, we are witnessing this **tragedy of the commons.** Carrying capacities are shrinking as precious resources, water chief among them, become scarcer. Inevitably, conflict arises—and solutions are urgently needed.

The Environmental Movement The 1990s were labeled the "earth decade" when a "new environmentalism" with new features emerged.[25] For example, proponents of the new environmentalism asked companies to reduce their wastes, use resources prudently, market safe products, and take responsibility for past damages. These requests were formalized in the CERES principles (see Table B.3).

The new environmentalism combined many diverse viewpoints, but initially it did not blend easily with traditional business values. Some of the key aspects of this philosophy are noted in the following discussion of the history of the movement.[26]

Conservation and Environmentalism A strand of environmental philosophy that is not at odds with business management

TABLE B.3
The CERES Principles

Protection of the biosphere: Minimize the release of pollutants that may cause environmental damage.

Sustainable use of natural resources: Conserve nonrenewable resources through efficient use and careful planning.

Reduction and disposal of waste: Minimize the creation of waste, especially hazardous waste, and dispose of such materials in a safe, responsible manner.

Wise use of energy: Make every effort to use environmentally safe and sustainable energy sources to meet operating requirements.

Risk reduction: Diminish environmental, health, and safety risks to employees.

Marketing of safe products and services: Sell products that minimize adverse environmental impact and are safe for consumers.

Damage compensation: Accept responsibility for any harm the company causes the environment; conduct bioremediation; and compensate affected parties.

Disclosure of environmental incidents: Public dissemination of accidents relating to operations that harm the environment or pose health or safety risks.

Environmental directors: Appoint at least one board member who is qualified to represent environmental interests; create a position of vice president for environmental affairs.

Assessment and annual audit: Produce and publicize each year a self-evaluation of progress toward implementing the principles and meeting all applicable laws and regulations worldwide. Environmental audits will also be produced annually and distributed to the public.

SOURCES: *Chemical Week,* September 20, 1989, copyright permission granted by *Chemical Week* magazine. *CERES Coalition Handbook.*

is **conservation.** The conservation movement is anthropocentric (human centered), technologically optimistic, and concerned chiefly with the efficient use of resources. The movement seeks to avoid waste, promote the rational and efficient use of natural resources, and maximize long-term yields, especially of renewable resources.

The **environmental movement,** in contrast, historically has posed dilemmas for business management. Following the lead of early thinkers like George Perkins Marsh (1801–1882), it has shown that the unintended negative effects of human economic activities on the environment often are greater than the benefits. For example, there are links between forest cutting and soil erosion and between the draining of marshes and lakes and the decline of animal life.

Other early environmentalists, such as John Muir (1838–1914) and Aldo Leopold (1886–1948), argued that humans are not above nature but a part of it. Nature is not for humans to subdue but is sacred and should be preserved not simply for economic use but for its own sake—and for what people can learn from it.

Science and the Environment Rachel Carson's 1962 bestselling book, *The Silent Spring,* helped ignite the modern environmental movement by alerting the public to the dangers of unrestricted pesticide use.[27] Carson brought together the findings of toxicology, ecology, and epidemiology in a form accessible to the public. Blending scientific, moral, and political arguments, she connected environmental politics and values with scientific knowledge.

Barry Commoner's *Science and Survival* (1963) continued in this vein. Commoner expanded the scope of ecology to include everything in the physical, chemical, biological, social, political, economic, and philosophical worlds.[28] He argued that all of these elements fit together, and have to be understood as a whole. According to Commoner, the symptoms of environmental problems are in the biological world, but their source lies in economic and political organizations.

Economics and the Environment Economists promote growth for many reasons: to restore the balance of payments, to make nations more competitive, to create jobs, to reduce the deficit, to provide for the elderly and the sick, and to reduce poverty. Environmentalists criticize economics for its notions of efficiency and its emphasis on economic growth.[29] For example, environmentalists argue that economists do not adequately consider the unintended side effects of efficiency. Environmentalists hold that economists need to supplement estimates of the economic costs and benefits of growth with estimates of other factors that historically were not measured in economic terms.[30]

Economists and public policy analysts argue that the benefits of eliminating risk to the environment and to people must be balanced against the costs. Reducing risk involves determining how effective the proposed methods of reduction are likely to be and how much they will cost. There are many ways to consider cost factors. Analysts can perform cost-effectiveness analyses, in which they attempt to figure out how to achieve a given goal with limited resources, or they can conduct more formal risk-benefit and cost-benefit analyses, in which they quantify both the benefits and the costs of risk reduction.[31]

Qualitative Judgments in Cost-Benefit Analysis Formal, quantitative approaches to balancing costs and benefits do not eliminate the need for qualitative judgments. For example, how does one assess the value of a magnificent vista obscured by air pollution? What is the loss to society if a particular genetic strain of grass or animal species becomes extinct? How does one assess the lost opportunity costs of spending vast amounts of money on air pollution that could have been spent on productivity enhancement and global competitiveness?

Fairness cannot be ignored when doing cost-benefit analysis.[32] For example, the costs of air pollution reduction may have to be borne disproportionately by the poor in the form of higher gasoline and automobile prices. Intergenerational fairness also plays a role.[33] Future generations have no representatives in the current market and political processes. To what extent should the current generation hold back on its own consumption for the sake of posterity? This question is particularly poignant because few people in the world today are well off. To ask the poor to reduce their life's chances for the sake of a generation yet to come is asking for a great sacrifice.

International Perspectives Environmental problems present a different face in various countries and regions of the world. The United States and Great Britain lag behind Germany and Japan in mandated emissions standards.[34] In Europe, the Dutch, the Germans, and the Danes are among the most environmentally conscious. Italy, Ireland, Spain, Portugal, and Greece are in the early stages of developing environmental policies. Poland, Hungary, the Czech Republic, and former East Germany are the most polluted of the world's industrialized nations.[35]

U.S. companies need to realize that there is a large growth market in western Europe for environmentally "friendly" products. U.S. managers also need to be fully aware of the environmental movement in western Europe. Environmentalists in Europe have been successful in halting many projects.[36] China has been paying a high ecological price for its rapid economic growth. But the government has begun recognizing the problem and is creating some antipollution laws.[37]

Industries that pollute or make polluting products will have to adjust to the new reality, and companies selling products in certain parts of the world must take into account a growing consumer consciousness about environmental protection. Manufacturers may even be legally required to take products and packaging back from customers after use, to recycle or dispose of. In order to meet these requirements in Germany, and be prepared for similar demands in other countries, Hewlett-Packard redesigned its office-machine packaging worldwide.

WHAT MANAGERS CAN DO

To be truly "green"—that is, a cutting-edge company with respect to environmental concerns—legal compliance is not enough. Progressive companies stay abreast *and* ahead of the laws by going beyond marginal compliance and anticipating future requirements and needs.[38] But companies can go further still by experimenting continually with innovations that protect the environment. McDonald's, for example, conducted tests and pilot projects in composting food scraps and in offering refillable coffee mugs and starch-based (biodegradable) cutlery.[39]

Systems Thinking The first thing managers can do to better understand environmental issues in their companies is to engage in systems thinking. Environmental considerations relate to the organization's inputs, processes, and outputs.[40] *Inputs* include raw materials and energy. Environmental pressures are causing prices of some raw materials, such as metals, to rise. This greatly increases the costs of production. Higher energy costs are causing firms to switch to more fuel-efficient sources.

Firms are considering new *processes* or methods of production that will reduce water pollution, air pollution, noise and vibration, and waste. They are incorporating technologies that sample and monitor (control) these by-products of business processes. Some chemical plants have a computerized system that flashes warnings when a maximum allowable pollution level is soon to be reached. Many companies keep only minimal stocks of hazardous materials, making serious accidents less likely.

Outputs have environmental impact, whether the products themselves or the waste or by-products of processes. To reduce the impact of its outputs, Herman Miller recycles or reuses nearly all waste from the manufacturing process. It sells fabric scraps to the auto industry, leather trim to luggage makers, and vinyl to stereo and auto manufacturers. It buys back its old furniture, refurbishes it, and resells it. Its corporatewide goal is to send zero waste to landfills. Environmental manager Paul Murray says, "There is never an acceptable level of waste at Miller. There are always new things we can learn."[41]

The environmental movement is a worldwide phenomenon. The "Greens," pictured here demonstrating in LePuy, France, are an important growing European political party.

Strategic Integration Systems thinking reveals that environmental issues permeate the firm, and therefore should be addressed in a comprehensive, integrative fashion. Perhaps the first step is to create the proper mindset. Does your firm see environmental concerns merely in terms of a business versus environment trade-off, or does it see in it a potential source of competitive advantage and an important part of a strategy for long-term survival and effectiveness? The latter attitude, of course, is more likely to set the stage for the following strategic actions.

These ideas help to strategically integrate environmental considerations into the firm's ongoing activities:[42]

1. *Develop a mission statement and strong values supporting environmental advocacy.* Table B.4 shows Procter & Gamble's environmental quality policy.
2. *Establish a framework for managing environmental initiatives.* Some industries have created voluntary codes of environmental practice, for example, the chemical industry's Responsible Care Initiative. Not all standard practices are adopted by all companies, however.[43] At J&J, Environmental Regulatory Affairs uses external audit teams to conduct

TABLE B.4
Procter & Gamble's Environmental Quality Policy

Procter & Gamble is committed to providing products of superior quality and value that best fill the needs of the world's consumers. As part of this, Procter & Gamble continually strives to improve the environmental quality of its products, packaging, and operations around the world. To carry out this commitment, it is Procter & Gamble's policy to:

Ensure our products, packaging, and operations are safe for our employees, consumers, and the environment.

Reduce or prevent the environmental impact of our products and packaging in their design, manufacture, distribution, use, and disposal whenever possible.

Meet or exceed the requirements of all environmental laws and regulations.

Continually assess our environmental technology and programs, and monitor programs toward environmental goals.

Provide our consumers, customers, employees, communities, public interest groups, and others with relevant and appropriate factual information about the environmental quality of P&G products, packaging, and operations.

Ensure every employee understands and is responsible and accountable for incorporating environmental quality considerations in daily business activities.

Have operating policies, programs, and resources in place to implement our environmental quality policy.

SOURCE: K. Dechant and B. Altman, "Environmental Leadership: From Compliance to Competitive Advantage," *The Academy of Management Executive,* August 1994, p. 10. Reprinted by permission.

environmental audits.[44] The Community Environmental Responsibility Program includes strategy and planning, and the development of products and processes with neutral environmental impact.

3. *Engage in "green" process and product design.* The German furniture maker Wilkhahn uses an integrated strategic approach that minimizes the use of virgin resources and uses recycled materials in an environmentally designed plant.[45]
4. *Establish environmentally focused stakeholder relationships.* Many firms work closely with the EPA and receive technical assistance to help convert to more energy-efficient facilities. And to defray costs as well as develop new ideas, small companies like WHYCO Chromium Company establish environmental management partnerships with firms like IBM and GM.[46]
5. *Provide internal and external education.* Engage employees in environmental actions. Dow's WRAP program has cut millions of pounds of hazardous and solid waste and emissions, and achieved annual cost savings of over $10 million, all through employee suggestions.[47] At the same time, inform the public of your firm's environmental initiatives. For example, ecolabeling can urge consumers to recycle and communicate the environmental friendliness of your product. And BPAmoco redesigned its logo (BP's logo has always been green) as a sun-based emblem, reflecting its strategic vision of a hydrogen/solar-based energy future.[48]

Implementation How can companies implement "greening" strategies? One tactic you read about in the chapter is life-cycle analysis.[49] That and other approaches begin with a commitment by top management. Specific actions could include commissioning an environmental audit in which an outside company checks for environmental hazards, drafting (or reviewing) the organization's environmental policy, communicating the policy and making it highly visible throughout the organization, having environmental professionals within the company report directly to the president or CEO, allocating sufficient resources to support the environmental effort, and building bridges between the organization and other companies, governments, environmentalists, and local communities.

Ultimately, it is essential to make employees accountable for any of their actions that have environmental impact.[50] Texaco, Du Pont, and other companies evaluate managers on their ideas for minimizing pollution and for new, environment-friendly products. Kodak ties some managers' compensation to the prevention of chemical spills; the company attributes to this policy a dramatic reduction in accidents.[51]

Companies can employ all areas of the organization to meet the challenges posed by pollution and environmental challenges. A variety of companies have responded creatively to these challenges[52] and may serve as models for other organizations. The following sections describe specific actions companies can take to address environmental issues.

Strategy Actions companies can take in the area of strategy include the following:

1. *Cut back on environmentally unsafe businesses.* Du Pont, the leading producer of CFCs, voluntarily pulled out of this $750 million business.[53]

2. *Carry out R&D on environmentally safe activities.* GM is spending millions to develop hydrogen-powered cars that don't emit carbon dioxide. GE is doing research on earth-friendly hydrogen and lower-emission locomotives and jet engines.[54]

3. *Develop and expand environmental cleanup services.* Building on the expertise gained in cleaning up its own plants, Du Pont formed a safety and environmental resources division to help industrial customers clean up their toxic wastes.[55] Global Research Technologies LLC is trying to use solvents to grab carbon dioxide out of the air to isolate it for disposal.[56]

4. *Compensate for environmentally risky projects.* AES has a long-standing policy of planting trees to offset its power plants' carbon emission.[57]

5. *Make your company accountable to others.* Royal Dutch Shell and Bristol-Myers Squibb are trendsetters in green reporting.[58] Danish health care and enzymes company Novo Nordisk purposely asked for feedback from environmentalists, regulators, and other interested bodies from around Europe. Its reputation has been enhanced, its people have learned a lot, and new market opportunities have been identified.[59]

6. *Make every new product environmentally better than the last.* Intel is developing ultra-energy-efficient chips.[60] IBM aims to use recyclable materials, reduce hazardous materials, reduce emissions, and use natural energy and resources in packaging.[61]

7. *Invest in green businesses.* American Electric Power Co. is investing in renewable energy in Chile, as well as retrofitting Bulgarian schools for greater efficiency.[62]

Public affairs In the area of public affairs, companies can take a variety of actions:

1. *Attempt to gain environmental legitimacy and credibility.* The cosponsors of Earth Day included Apple Computer, Hewlett-Packard, and the Chemical Manufacturers Association. McDonald's has tried to become a corporate environmental "educator." Ethel M. Chocolates, in public tours of its Las Vegas factory, showcases effective handling of its industrial wastes.[63]

2. *Try to avoid losses caused by insensitivity to environmental issues.* As a result of Exxon's apparent lack of concern after the *Valdez* oil spill, 41 percent of Americans polled said they would consider boycotting the company.[64] MacMillan Bloedel lost a big chunk of sales almost overnight when it was targeted publicly as a clear-cutter and chlorine user.[65]

3. *Collaborate with environmentalists.* Executives at Pacific Gas & Electric seek discussions and joint projects with any willing environmental group, and ARCO has prominent environmentalists on its board of directors.

The legal area Actions companies can take in the legal area include the following:

1. *Try to avoid confrontation with state or federal pollution control agencies.* W. R. Grace faced expensive and time-consuming lawsuits as a result of its toxic dumps. Browning-Ferris, Waste Management Inc., and Louisiana-Pacific were charged with pollution control violations, damaging their reputations.

2. *Comply early.* Because compliance costs only increase over time, the first companies to act will have lower costs. This will enable them to increase their market share and profits and win competitive advantage. 3M's goal was to meet government requirements to replace or improve underground storage tanks five years ahead of the legally mandated year.

3. *Take advantage of innovative compliance programs.* The EU started a carbon-cutting and trading system in 2005.[66] Instead of source-by-source reduction, the EPA's bubble policy allows factories to reduce pollution at different sources by different amounts, provided the overall result is equivalent. Therefore, 3M installed equipment on only certain production lines at its tape-manufacturing facility in Pennsylvania, thereby lowering its compliance costs.[67] Today, there is greater use of economic instruments like tradable pollution permits, charges, and taxes to encourage improvements.[68] *Joint implementation* involves companies in industrialized nations working with businesses in developing countries to help them reduce greenhouse gas emissions. The company lending a hand then receives credit toward fulfilling its environmental obligations at home. The developing country receives investment, technology, and jobs; the company giving a lending hand receives environmental credits; and the world gets cleaner air.[69]

4. *Don't deal with fly-by-night subcontractors for waste disposal.* They are more likely to cut corners, break laws, and do a poor job. Moreover, the result for you could be bad publicity and legal problems.[70]

Operations The actions companies can take in the area of operations include the following:

1. *Promote new manufacturing technologies.* Louisville Gas and Electric took the lead in installing smokestack scrubbers, Consolidated Natural Gas pioneered the use of clean-burning technologies, and Nucor developed state-of-the-art steel mills.

2. *Practice reverse logistics.* Firms move packaging and other used goods from the consumer back up the distribution channel to the firm. Make them not just costs, but a source of revenue— inputs to production. Fuji Australia believes that remanufacturing has generated returns in the tens of millions of dollars.[71]

3. *Encourage technological advances that reduce pollution from products and manufacturing processes.* Cinergy and AEP are working on technologies that capture carbon as coal is burned and pump it deep into the ground to be stored for thousands of years.[72] 3M's "Pollution Prevention Pays" program is based on the premise that it is too costly for companies to employ add-on technology; instead, they should attempt to eliminate pollution at the source.[73] Pollution prevention, more than pollution control, is related to both better environmental performance and better manufacturing performance, including cost and speed.[74]

4. *Develop new product formulations.* The Chicago Transit Authority and Union Pacific Corporation are replacing traditional wood railroad ties with plastic ties. Other companies are experimenting with making recycled cross-ties of old tires, grocery bags, milk jugs, and Styrofoam

cups.[75] Weyerhaeuser, recognizing the
decreasing supply of timber and growing
demand, is working to produce high-
quality wood on fewer, continuously
regenerated acres.[76] Electrolux has
developed a sun-powered lawn mower
and a chainsaw that runs on vegetable
oil.[77] Many companies are developing
green pesticides.

5. *Eliminate manufacturing wastes.* 3M
replaced volatile solvents with water-
based ones, thereby eliminating the
need for costly air pollution control
equipment. BPAmoco implemented a
similar program.

6. *Find alternative uses for wastes.* When
DuPont halted ocean dumping of acid
iron salts, it discovered that the salts
could be sold to water treatment plants
at a profit. A Queensland sugarcane
facility powers production via sugarcane
waste.[78]

7. *Insist that your suppliers have strong environmental performance.*
Chiquita Banana had a spotty environmental record, but
now its plantations are certified by the Rainforest Alliance,
and Wal-Mart has named Chiquita its most environmentally
conscious supplier.[79] Scott Paper discovered that many of
its environmental problems were "imported" through the
supply chain. Initially focusing on pulp suppliers, the company
sent questionnaires asking for figures on air, water, and land
releases, energy consumption, and energy sources. Scott
was astonished at the variance. For example, carbon dioxide
emissions varied by a factor of 17 among different suppliers.
Scott dropped the worst performers and announced that
the best performers would in the future receive preference
in its purchasing decisions.[80]

8. *Assemble products with the environment in mind.* Make them
easy to snap apart, sort, and recycle, and avoid glues and
screws.

Marketing Companies can also take action in the marketing
area:

1. *Cast products in an environment-friendly light.* Most Americans
believe a company's environmental reputation influences
what they buy.[81] Wal-Mart has made efforts to provide
customers with recycled or recyclable products. A
Chinese entrepreneur is making underwear out of soybean
by-products.[82] Spiegel plans to offer soybean-fiber halter-top
dresses in pink and mocha.[83] Other eco-friendly fibers are
made from hemp and bamboo, which require little pesticide.

2. *Avoid attacks by environmentalists for unsubstantiated or
inappropriate claims.* When Hefty marketed "biodegradable"
garbage bags, that claim was technically true, but it turned
out that landfill conditions didn't allow decomposition to
occur.[84] The extensive public backlash affected not only
Hefty bags but also other Hefty products. Hefty didn't
lie, but it did exaggerate. Its tactics overshadowed well-
intentioned greening actions.

Companies like Toyota use advertising to convey to consumers their
efforts to become more environmentally friendly.

3. *Differentiate your product via environmental services.* ICI takes
back and disposes of customers' waste as a customer service.
Disposal is costly, but the service differentiates the firm's
products. Teach customers how to use and dispose of
products; for instance, farmers inadvertently abuse pesticides.
Make education a part of a firm's after-sales service.

4. *Take advantage of the Net.* The EcoMall (www.ecomall.com/
biz/) promotes a number of environmentally oriented firms
in 68 product categories. Firms using the Net target green
consumers globally, effectively, and efficiently.[85]

Accounting Actions companies can take in the accounting area
include the following:

1. *Collect useful data.* The best current reporters of environmental information include Dow Europe, Danish Steel
Works, BSO/Origin, 3M, and Monsanto. BSO/Origin has
begun to explore a system for corporate environmental
accounting.[86]

2. *Make polluters pay.* CIBA-GEIGY has a "polluter pays
principle" throughout the firm, so managers have the
incentive to combat pollution at the sources they can
influence.[87]

3. *Demonstrate that antipollution programs pay off.* 3M's Pollution
Prevention Pays program is based on the premise that only
if the program pays will there be the motivation to carry
it out. Every company needs to be cost-effective in its
pollution reduction efforts.

4. *Use an advanced waste accounting system.* Do this in addition
to standard management accounting, which can hinder
investment in new technologies. Waste accounting makes
sure all costs are identified and better decisions can be made.

5. *Adopt full-cost accounting.* This approach, called for by Frank
Popoff, Dow's chairman, ensures that the price of a product
reflects its full environmental cost.[88]

6. *Show the overall impact of the pollution reduction program.* Companies have an obligation to account for the costs and benefits of their pollution reduction programs. 3M claims half a *billion* dollars in savings from pollution prevention efforts.[89]

Finance In the area of finance, companies can do the following:

1. *Gain the respect of the socially responsible investment community.* Many investment funds in the United States and Europe take environmental criteria into account. A study by ICF Kaiser concluded that environmental improvements could lead to significant reduction in the perceived risk of a firm, with a possible 5 percent increase in the stock price.[90] Socially responsible rating services and investment funds try to help people invest with a "clean conscience."[91]

2. *Recognize true liability.* Investment houses often employ environmental analysts who search for companies' true environmental liability in evaluating their potential performance. Bankers look at environmental risks and environmental market opportunities when evaluating a company's credit rating.[92] The Securities and Exchange Commission in New York requires some companies to report certain environmental costs. The Swiss Bank Corp. has specialized Environmental Performance Rating Units to include environmental criteria in order to improve the quality of financial analysis.[93]

3. *Fund and then assist green companies.* Ann Winblad of Hummer Winblad Venture Partners was one of the first venture capitalists to coach green entrepreneurs to increase their business skills and chances of success.[94]

4. *Recognize financial opportunities.* Worldwide, one of these great opportunities is water. Water must be purified and delivered reliably to everyone worldwide. Billions of people lack sanitary sewage facilities and have poor access to drinking water. Infrastructures in big cities, including those in the United States, are seriously deteriorating. Supplying clean water to people and companies is a $400 billion-a-year industry—one-third larger than the global pharmaceutical industry. Companies are aggressively pursuing this market. They are betting that water in the 21st century will be like oil in the 20th century. A Bear Stearns analyst called water the best sector for the next century.[95]

KEY TERMS

carrying capacity The ability of a finite resource to sustain a population. p. 191

conservation An environmental philosophy that seeks to avoid waste, promote the rational and efficient use of natural resources, and maximize long-term yields, especially of renewable resources. p. 192

environmental movement An environmental philosophy postulating that the unintended negative effects of human economic activities on the environment are often greater than the benefits, and that nature should be preserved. p. 192

tragedy of the commons The environmental destruction that results as individuals and businesses consume finite resources (the "commons") to serve their short-term interests without regard for the long-term consequences. p. 191

DISCUSSION QUESTIONS

1. To what extent can and should we rely on government to solve environmental problems? What are some of government's limitations? Take a stand on the role and usefulness of government regulations on business activities.

2. To what extent should managers today be responsible for cleaning up mistakes from years past that have hurt the environment?

3. How would you characterize the environmental movement in western Europe? How does it differ from the U.S. movement? What difference will this make to a multinational company that wants to produce and market goods in many countries?

4. What business opportunities can you see in meeting environmental challenges? Be specific.

5. You are appointed environmental manager of XYZ Company. Describe some actions you will take to address environmental challenges. Discuss obstacles you are likely to encounter in the company and how you will manage them.

6. Interview a businessperson about environmental regulations and report your findings to the class. How would you characterize his or her attitude? How constructive is his or her attitude?

7. Interview a businessperson about actions he or she has taken that have helped the environment. Report your findings to the class and discuss.

8. Identify and discuss some examples of the tragedy of the commons. How can the tragedies be avoided?

9. Discuss the status of recycling efforts in your community or school, your perspectives on it as a consumer, and what business opportunities could be available.

10. What companies currently come to mind as having the best and worst reputations with respect to the environment? Why do they have these reputations?

11. Choose one product and discuss its environmental impact through its entire life cycle.

12. What are you, your college or university, and your community doing about the environment? What would you recommend doing?

chapter

6 International Management

It was once said that the sun never set on the British Empire. Today, the sun does set on the British Empire, but not on the scores of global empires, including those of IBM, Unilever, Volkswagen, and Hitachi.

— Lester Brown

LEARNING OBJECTIVES

After studying Chapter 6, you will be able to:

LO 1 Describe how the world economy is becoming more integrated than ever before. p. 200

LO 2 Discuss what integration of the global economy means for individual companies and their managers. p. 207

LO 3 Define the strategies organizations use to compete in the global marketplace. p. 213

LO 4 Compare the various entry modes organizations use to enter overseas markets. p. 218

LO 5 Explain how companies can approach the task of staffing overseas operations. p. 222

LO 6 Summarize the skills and knowledge managers need to manage globally. p. 224

LO 7 Identify ways in which cultural differences across countries influence management. p. 226

CHAPTER OUTLINE

The Global Environment
European Unification
China and the Pacific Rim
The Americas
The Rest of the World

Consequences of a Global Economy
The Role of Outsourcing

Global Strategy
Pressures for Global Integration
Pressures for Local Responsiveness
Choosing a Global Strategy

Entry Mode
Exporting
Licensing
Franchising
Joint Ventures
Wholly Owned Subsidiaries

Managing across Borders
Skills of the Global Manager
Understanding Cultural Issues
Ethical Issues in International Management

Management Close-Up

HOW CAN IRENE ROSENFELD REFORMULATE KRAFT FOODS?

Kraft Foods was struggling in 2006. The world's second-largest food and beverage company—founded in 1903 and the home of venerable brands like Oreo, Chips Ahoy!, Oscar Mayer, and Grey Poupon—was experiencing slumping sales. With American consumers becoming more health conscious about their food choices, suddenly many Kraft brands were losing their appeal. To add to the company's troubles, sales in developing countries were weak. It also didn't help that Kraft was owned by Altria Group, one of the world's largest tobacco companies. Kraft Foods needed a change—and it got one in the form of Irene B. Rosenfeld, named CEO in June of that year.

Rosenfeld is a seasoned veteran of the food and beverage industry. She had spent 20 years at Kraft and General Foods in a variety of senior positions, leading successful turnaround and restructuring efforts in business units in the United States, Canada, and Mexico. Months after taking her place as CEO—and shortly before Altria's long-awaited sale of

As she took the reins at Kraft Foods, Irene Rosenfeld declared, "I genuinely love this company, its brands, its people, and its values." But the once-great company had fallen behind its competitors and was in bad shape. Would Rosenfeld's love—combined with her management skills and experience—be enough to turn it around? As you read this chapter, consider the unique strategy Irene Rosenfeld deployed to capture market share globally.

Kraft—Rosenfeld announced a three-year plan designed to reorganize the company.

Under the turnaround plan, Kraft would focus on its cheese, snacks, and beverage lines. To accomplish this, it would close some factories, cut jobs, and sell off several brands. Her plan included investing as much as $400 million in marketing and research and development. The turnaround, said Rosenfeld, would require aggressive product development beyond existing lines. Aside from its North American markets, clearly one of the greatest opportunities for growth lay overseas.

Could the plan transform Kraft? Rosenfeld remained steadfast, saying it would take about two years for the turnaround plan to begin showing solid results. She emphasized the need for the entire company to focus on innovation and to rethink its approach by considering less what its items contained and more what its consumers wanted—including those in global markets.

The Global Environment

LO 1

The global economy is becoming more integrated than ever before. For example, the World Trade Organization (WTO), formed in 1995, now has 153 member countries involved in more than 95 percent of the world's trade. The newest members are Cambodia, Nepal, Russia, Saudi Arabia, Tonga, Ukraine, and Viet Nam. (The International Monetary Fund, set up by the United Nations in 1945, serves a similar purpose and includes 185 countries.) The WTO provides a forum for nations to negotiate trade agreements and procedures for administering the agreements and resolving disputes. Issues that are currently under negotiation because they have been difficult for the parties to resolve include objections to environmental regulations and subsidies to farmers in developed countries, on the grounds that they conflict with free trade. To follow how these issues are playing out, you can explore the "Trade Topics" section of the WTO Web site, http://www.wto.org.

The global economy is dominated by countries in three regions: North America, western Europe, and Asia. However, other developing countries and regions represent important areas for economic growth as well. Figure 6.1 shows the major international trade areas and countries of the world.

European Unification

Europe is integrating economically to form the biggest market in the world. Under the Maastricht Treaty, which formally established the European Union (EU), the euro was adopted as a common currency among 13 member countries. Currencies with a long history like the franc and the mark are now relics of the past. The EU is also working on a common constitution, and it allows most goods, services, capital, and human resources to flow freely across its national borders. The goal of unification is to strengthen Europe's position as an economic superpower, particularly vis-à-vis the United States. And the EU may have good prospects for eventually doing so, with 27 members and counting, a population of more than 490 million, and a GDP (gross domestic product) at least as big as that of the United States.[2]

The pace of European unification accelerated in 2004, with the addition of former Eastern-bloc countries including Poland and Hungary, and in 2007 Bulgaria and Romania joined. Many of these new members offer a particular challenge to full integration, because as former Communist countries they do not have extensive experience as modern market economies. Other even less wealthy countries—Croatia, Macedonia, and Turkey—have also applied to join the EU.

In addition to the difficulty of integrating widely divergent economies, certain structural issues within Europe need to be corrected for the EU to function effectively. In particular, western Europeans on average work fewer hours, earn more pay, take longer vacations, and enjoy far more social entitlements than do their counterparts in North America and Asia. To be competitive in a global economy, Europeans must increase their level of productivity. In the past, powerful trade unions fiercely defended social benefits, and local governments regulated the labor markets. Some labor markets are slowly being deregulated and more incentives are being offered to create jobs. Deregulation of financial services has already made London a major banking center, attracting an influx of foreign banks, and has permitted the growth of insurance giants such as AXA (based in France), Allianz (Germany), and Generali (Italy).[3] But other problems will present even greater challenges, such as Europe's aging population, low birth rates, and low immigration, all of which are threatening to cause Europe's population to drop, even as America's is increasing.

Still, unification is creating a more competitive Europe, one that U.S. managers will increasingly have to take into account. One reason is that although growth in the developed economies of western Europe has been modest, it is strong in the eastern part of the continent. Companies are investing in Poland, the Czech Republic,

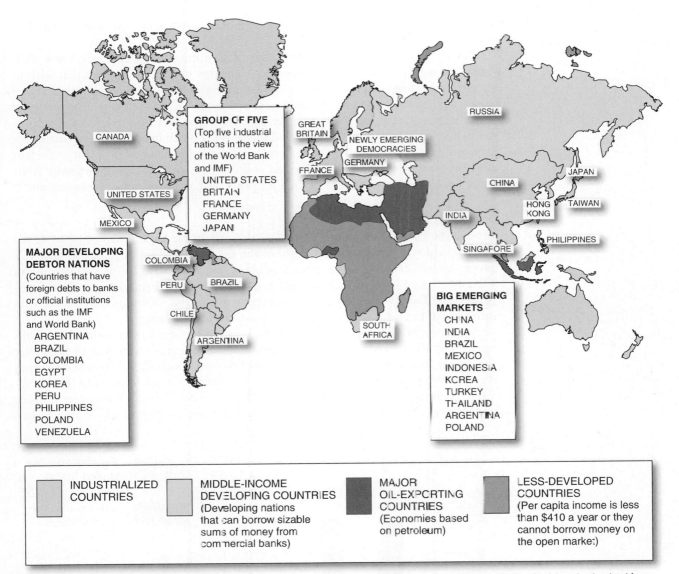

GROUP OF FIVE
(Top five industrial
nations in the view
of the World Bank
and IMF)
    UNITED STATES
    BRITAIN
    FRANCE
    GERMANY
    JAPAN

MAJOR DEVELOPING
DEBTOR NATIONS
(Countries that have
foreign debts to banks
or official institutions
such as the IMF
and World Bank)
    ARGENTINA
    BRAZIL
    COLOMBIA
    EGYPT
    KOREA
    PERU
    PHILIPPINES
    POLAND
    VENEZUELA

BIG EMERGING
MARKETS
    CHINA
    INDIA
    BRAZIL
    MEXICO
    INDONESIA
    KOREA
    TURKEY
    THAILAND
    ARGENTINA
    POLAND

INDUSTRIALIZED
COUNTRIES

MIDDLE-INCOME
DEVELOPING COUNTRIES
(Developing nations
that can borrow sizable
sums of money from
commercial banks)

MAJOR
OIL-EXPORTING
COUNTRIES
(Economies based
on petroleum)

LESS-DEVELOPED
COUNTRIES
(Per capita income is less
than $410 a year or they
cannot borrow money on
the open market)

SOURCE: Michael R. Czinkota and Ilkka A. Ronkainen, *International Marketing*, 7th ed. (Mason, OH: Thomson/South-Western, 2004), p. 91. Adapted and updated from "The Global Economy," *The Washington Post*, January 19, 1986, H1. Reprinted with permission.

FIGURE 6.1
The Global Economy

Globalization
requires
improvements
in all bottom-line
practices.

Romania, and nearby countries because of their relatively low wages, trained workers, and access to markets. Nokia, the Finland-based maker of telecommunications equipment, is building a factory in Romania, where it can provide products not only to European customers but also to Africa and the Middle East. Moving from the other direction, Chinese and Taiwanese companies have seen central Europe as a convenient and affordable location for building facilities to develop their positions in Europe. For example, Sichuan Changhong, a Chinese electronics company, is building a factory in Numburk, Czech Republic and Foxconn, a Taiwanese maker of components for name-brand computers, operates a factory in the Czech city of Pardubice.[4]

The EU also presents a regulatory challenge to the United States and other countries. For example, the EU has supported excluding genetically engineered food products from American firms, over objections from the WTO. It has fined Microsoft for what it says are unreasonable prices Microsoft charges rival software firms to give them the information and documentation they need to develop products compatible with the Windows operating system. The EU required the documentation as a remedy to remove its antitrust charges.[5] In another antitrust case, the EU launched an investigation of the proposed merger between music companies Sony and Bertelsmann; other potential business deals in the industry are on hold as managers watch to see what the EU will require in that case.[6]

The EU's more competitive and regulatory environment clearly presents new challenges to managers and their employees. Managers in U.S. companies that wish to export to that market must become more knowledgeable about the new business environment the EU is creating. Management and labor will have to work cooperatively to achieve high levels of quality to make U.S. goods and services attractive to consumers in Europe and other markets around the world. The United States needs managers who will stay on top of worldwide developments and manage high-quality, efficient organizations as well as a well-educated, well-trained, and continually *retrained* labor force to remain competitive with the Europeans and other formidable competitors.

China and the Pacific Rim

Among the Pacific Rim countries, and particularly in the United States, Japan dominated world attention toward the end of the last century. Today Japan is America's fourth-largest export market, after Canada, China, and Mexico, as you can see in Figure 6.2. And Japan is in fourth place as a source of U.S. imports. Japanese companies like Toyota are both a major source of goods and, as competitors, a growing influence in the ways U.S. managers seek quality and efficiency.

As successful as Japan is, a bigger force is rising in Asia: China. With the world's largest population and increasing industrialization, China is on its way to becoming the largest producer and consumer of many of the world's goods. Its large and growing demand for oil is a cost factor that managers everywhere must consider in their long-range planning. The country has also become the world's largest consumer of basic raw materials like steel and cement, as well as the world's largest cell-phone market.

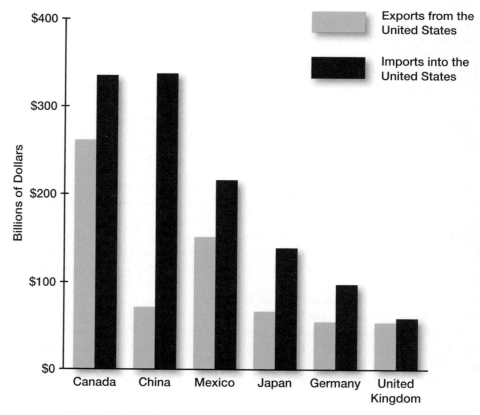

FIGURE 6.2

Top U.S. Trading Partners, Based on Total Imports and Exports

SOURCE: U.S. Census Bureau, *Statistical Abstract of the United States: 2009,* http://www.census.gov.

Not only is China the largest source of imports to the United States (see Figure 6.2), but it is on track to surpass the United States as the world's second-largest exporter overall, after Germany.[7]

As a consuming nation, China's appeal to managers lies in its large population of 1.3 billion people and its extremely rapid economic growth. Even as global economic growth stalled during the recent financial crisis, China's economy continued expanding. During the past decade, it has tripled its imports and quadrupled its exports. The nation was recently ranked as the world's second-largest exporter and third-largest importer, primarily trading manufactured goods but also importing huge quantities of materials used in manufacturing and construction.[8] Several American companies have invested heavily in the Chinese market, with some success. Intel recently announced plans to build a silicon wafer fabrication factory in Dalian, China. Building the facility is an element of Intel's strategy to operate closer to China's information technology market, which the company predicts may become the world's largest. The company already operates laboratories and testing and packaging facilities in China.[9] Microsoft and Chinese computer-maker Lenovo have entered into a partnership in an effort to expand in the Chinese market, as well.

Several U.S. and European companies have sensed opportunity in the estimated 300 million Chinese people learning English—and presumably many millions more who want to learn, given the chance. British publisher Pearson PLC and Sweden-based school operator English First SV have emphasized adult education, but Walt Disney Company sees a profitable niche market in teaching children.

Disney has opened a chain of Disney English schools in Shanghai and drawn up plans to operate in Beijing. Managers insist that the mission of the schools is simply to teach English to Chinese children, but that mission requires books and worksheets, and they just happen to be populated with Buzz Lightyear, Ariel the Mermaid, and other characters from Disney's movies. Young students can earn rewards such as stickers and CDs featuring Disney characters and productions. Rather than being repelled by the marketing angle, Chinese parents see a chance for their children to learn from a company that is familiar and truly international.

For Disney, the schools offer an opportunity to connect with families in an environment that is otherwise politically tricky. While the Chinese government limits movie and television distribution of Disney productions, Disney English can offer students all the Disney-themed worksheets, backpacks, and toys they need to develop a lasting love for Mickey Mouse.[10]

Even with its growing consumption, it is in its role as an exporting nation that China has had an even greater global impact. The enormous size of its labor force, combined with its extremely low labor costs, has given it a huge competitive advantage in manufacturing. Estimates suggest that labor costs in China are less than $1 an hour, compared with $2.92 for manufacturing workers in Mexico and $24.59 for manufacturing workers in the United States.[11] These low wage rates have led many managers to relocate operations to China or to import an increasing number and variety of Chinese products instead of continuing to do business with local manufacturers. This trend is one reason that the value of U.S. imports from China is more than five times the value of U.S exports to China.

This type of trade imbalance may well have contributed to the loss of manufacturing jobs in the United States and Europe. But it has also led to the continuing availability of comparatively low-priced goods, helping consumers everywhere and leading to overall economic and job growth at home. Yet, jobs in certain industries, such as textiles, may have been transferred abroad permanently to lower-cost producers like

China and India. Those affected workers and communities experience real hardships. We will be discussing the effects of *outsourcing* or *offshoring* in more detail later in this chapter.

The world's leading toy maker, Mattel Inc., has announced three recalls of Chinese-made toys, saying it would take back more than 800,000 units globally that contain "impermissible" levels of lead. Now India has specifically banned the import of all Chinese toys for six months, citing public safety and health concerns. Chinese toys dominate a 50 percent market share in the Indian toy industry, with an estimated value of more than $500 million in 2007. How might this affect their ability to continue to offer quality, low-price products?

Threats to China's growing dominance include political instability, as the growing prosperity of its cities and industrial enclaves leave millions of poor rural residents further behind. Also, countries that have experienced job loss may face growing pressure to restrict Chinese imports, particularly in the EU, with its strong labor unions. But for the foreseeable future, China's growing presence in the world economy, as an importer *and* exporter, is one that you as a manager will increasingly have to take into account.

Other rapidly growing countries in the region that have strong trade relationships with the United States include South Korea, Taiwan, and Singapore. These countries are important trading partners not merely because of their wage rates but because many of their companies have developed competitive advantages in areas such as engineering and technological know-how. South Korea's Samsung has the largest share of the world's markets for flat-screen televisions and flash memory cards, and Taiwan's Hon Hai is the leader in contract manufacturing of electronics. The reason you may not have heard of Hon Hai is that it specializes in making components for brand-name products of other companies, including Sony (PlayStations), Apple (iPods), and Dell (computers).[12]

These Asian countries and others have joined with the United States, Australia, and Russia to form the 21-member Asia-Pacific Economic Cooperation (APEC) trade group. Combined, APEC members' economies account for more than half of world output (GDP) and almost half of world trade.[13] In recent years the APEC countries have been working to establish policies that encourage international commerce and reduce trade barriers. APEC members address these objectives through dialogue and nonbinding commitments, rather than treaties.

Another international organization, the Association of Southeast Asian Nations (ASEAN), brings together 10 developing nations, including Indonesia, Malaysia, and the Philippines. Along with economic development, ASEAN is aimed at promoting cultural development and political security.

The Americas

North and South America constitute a mix of industrialized countries, such as Canada and the United States, as well as countries with growing economies, such as Argentina, Brazil, Chile, and Mexico. The winter fruit you eat may come from Chile, the coffee you drink from Jamaica, and the shirt you wear from Honduras. Increasingly, businesses are looking to establish freer trade among countries in the Western Hemisphere—and with other parts of the world.

North American Free Trade Agreement (NAFTA)

An economic pact that combined the economies of the United States, Canada, and Mexico into one of the world's largest trading blocs.

The **North American Free Trade Agreement (NAFTA)** combined the economies of the United States, Canada, and Mexico into one of the world's largest trading blocs with nearly 400 million U.S., Canadian, and Mexican consumers and a total output of $6.5 trillion. By 2008, virtually all U.S. industrial exports into Mexico and Canada were duty-free. Although the United States has had a longer-standing agreement with Canada, Mexico has quickly emerged as the United States's third largest trading partner as a result of NAFTA. U.S. industries that have benefited in the short run include capital-goods suppliers, manufacturers of consumer durables, grain producers and distributors, construction equipment manufacturers, the auto industry, and the financial industry, which now has privileged access into a previously protected market. Besides importing and exporting, companies in the NAFTA countries have invested in facilities across national borders. Mexico-based CEMEX, the world's third-largest cement company, is actually the largest cement supplier in the United States. Twenty-two percent of CEMEX's employees and 27 percent of its sales are in the United States, and it conducts management meetings in English because the majority of its employees do not speak Spanish.[14]

Among the list of the greatest places to work in Mexico are several U.S.-based companies, including McDonald's, which ranked as the 9th best company in 2007.

Economic growth and the easing of import restrictions have also caused trade to rise in South American countries, particularly in agricultural products. Brazil has become the world's largest exporter of orange juice, coffee, and tobacco, and by 2015 it expects to replace the United States as the largest agricultural producer overall. As in Asia, more South American companies are relying on innovation and technology rather than simply cost to compete in the global marketplace. For example, Brazil's Embraer is known as an innovator in the aerospace industry; it operates its own graduate program in aerospace engineering to keep its employees knowledgeable in the latest technology.[15] And one reason that Argentina's Tenaris is the global leader in the market for oil pipes is that management of a predecessor company, Siderca, decided to focus on building a global network of facilities that could research customer needs, develop products, and deliver pipes just as needed by their customers. This focus gave Siderca, now part of Tenaris, a competitive advantage.[16]

Other agreements have been proposed to promote trade with Central and South America. In 2005, President George W. Bush signed into law U.S. participation in a Central America–Dominican Republic–United States Free Trade Agreement (CAFTA-DR). Other nations that have agreed to participate include Costa Rica, the Dominican Republic, El Salvador, Guatemala, Honduras, and Nicaragua. CAFTA-DR creates the second-largest free-trade zone with the United States (NAFTA being the largest). As part of the negotiations for CAFTA-DR, Central American nations promised to protect workers' rights in their countries. Complaints that some countries have not delivered on this promise are making further trade negotiations with Peru, Colombia, and Panama more difficult to sell to the U.S. Congress.[17] Still, those country-by-country talks remain a priority, because talks aimed at going beyond NAFTA to create a Free Trade Area of the Americas (FTAA), extending from Canada to Chile, have recently stalled.[18] At the same time, the countries of South America have formed their own trading bloc, called Mercosur, to promote trade among nations of that continent.

The Rest of the World

We can't begin to fully discuss all the important developments, markets, and competitors shaping the global environment. India, for example, has become an important provider of online support for computer software, software development, and other services. Given that country's fast-growing economy and huge population—the world's second largest—more U.S. businesses are beginning to see India as a source of customers as well as workers. Citigroup, for example, has made plans to open more branches in India and expand service such as microfinance (small loans), as well as to add thousands more staff members there.[19]

These trends leave huge and promising areas of the world—the Middle East, parts of South America, and much of Africa—that have not yet participated as much in globalization. These regions account for a major share of the world's natural resources, and managers are watching the global environment, looking for areas with potential.

The "From the Pages of *BusinessWeek*" feature describes another example of the importance of global business to today's organizations. Ford identified an opportunity in Russia that has enabled the company to ride a wave of growth there even as demand for its vehicles has stagnated at home.

Coffee manufacturers have long conducted business with coffee growers in South America and Africa. And Starbucks has been focused on global growth, expanding its operations to roughly 3,000 stores in 40 countries, and finding new coffees to tempt customers. But expansion hasn't come without challenges. Recently, Starbucks and the Intellectual Property Office of Ethiopia have been mired in a disagreement over the name of one coffee— Shirkana Sun-Dried Sidamo. Starbucks has applied for trademark status for that name, and Ethiopia is seeking protection from that trademark. The reason? Ethiopian officials believe their country deserves trademark status for the coffee that is produced there, despite the fact that Starbucks applied for it first. "There is clearly an intangible value in the specialty coffee of Ethiopia," explains Getachew Mengistie of the Intellectual Property Office. "But it's not being captured here."

Regardless of the outcome of the dispute, Ethiopia is taking a stand—and hoping to claim its place—in the world coffee market.[20]

FROM THE PAGES OF BusinessWeek

They've Driven a Ford Lately

You would think the world's most successful Ford dealer might be in, say, Detroit or Los Angeles. Think again. Last year, New York Motors, on a commercial strip in southwest Moscow, sold more Fords than any other dealership in the world. All told, salesmen in the crowded showroom moved 10,060 vehicles, helping Ford race past rivals Hyundai, Toyota, and Chevrolet to become the top-selling auto nameplate in Russia. "This record has pleased and amazed everyone," says Andrey Pavlovich, general director of New York Motors. "Last year was a boom year."

The brand's success in Russia stands in striking contrast to Ford Motor Company's flagging fortunes elsewhere. The automaker clocked a global loss of $12.7 billion last year, but sales of Ford-branded vehicles in Russia soared 92 percent, to 115,985 cars and trucks, for some $2 billion in revenues. That's partly due to Russia's thriving economy, which has stoked strong demand for foreign models. Last year, foreign brands outsold domestic nameplates for the first time, topping 1 million—a 65 percent increase from 2005 and 20 times the level in 2000, according to the Association of European Businesses in Moscow.

Ford, though, has done more than simply ride the market wave. In 1999, Ford made a big bet on Russia, spending $150 million on a plant near St. Petersburg—the country's first foreign-owned auto factory. The facility opened in 2002, and last year production climbed to 62,400 Focus sedans, hatchbacks, and wagons. "When this decision was taken, in '99, it was of course very daring," says Henrik Nenzen, president of Ford Russia. "But Ford saw that this market would come. . . . And they knew that they needed to enter [it]." Ford's growing network of dealerships is helping boost sales, too. The company now has 150 outlets, some as far away as Vladivostok on the Pacific coast and Murmansk in the far north.

Ford may face a bumpier ride from here on out. Competition is heating up as rivals copy Ford's strategy of local production. Volkswagen, Toyota, General Motors, and Fiat have all announced plans to build plants in Russia. Worse, Ford workers in St. Petersburg, who earn about $650 per month, walked off the job for one day in February 2007 after rejecting an offer of a 14 percent to 20 percent pay raise, interest-free loans, and other benefits. Talks were set to continue.

Still, local production has helped Ford keep prices down. Although about 80 percent of the parts used in the Focus are imported, the company sells the cars for as little as $13,000, or about $3,000 less than similarly equipped imports, which are subject to a 25 percent duty [tax on imports]. While that's not exactly pocket change in Russia, it's low enough for a growing number of middle-class consumers.

Anton Rabotonov, a 28-year-old Moscow economist kicking tires at New York Motors, chose a Focus with air conditioning, antilock brakes, and air bags for $18,950. To pay for his new wheels, Rabotonov is taking advantage of another Ford innovation in Russia: consumer credit. Ford offers two- and three-year car loans at interest rates of just 4.9 percent, a bit more than half the current inflation rate of 9 percent. As far as Rabotonov is concerned, it all adds up to a bargain. "I have driven Russian cars," he says. "Of course, a Ford is much more comfortable."

SOURCE: Excerpted from Jason Bush, "They've Driven a Ford Lately," *BusinessWeek*, February 15, 2007, http://www.businessweek.com.

Consequences of a Global Economy

The increasing integration of the global economy has had many consequences. First, even as the output of the world's economies surged during the middle of the past decade, international trade expanded even faster. When trouble in the financial industry sparked an economic downturn, European and North American imports declined, and other world trade growth slowed. But those trends are expected to be temporary, eventually reversing as economic conditions improve.[21] Years of emphasis on international commerce by major industrial countries; recent liberalized trading brought about by NAFTA, EU, and APEC, as well as market reforms in China have resulted in lowering the barriers to the free flow of goods, services, and capital among nation-states. The impact of these trends is staggering. The dollar value of international trade (merchandise exports and commercial services) is over $16 trillion—up from just a few hundred billion dollars in the 1960s and 1970s. For example, Figure 6.3 shows how the international trade of the United States (particularly for goods) increased relative to the country's output since 1990. The dollar value of trade in goods grew from 12 percent to almost 18 percent of the country's total output of goods, even as total U.S. output also grew. Most experts expect competition to increase as trade is liberalized, and as is often the case, the more efficient players will survive. To succeed in this industrial climate, managers need to study opportunities in existing markets, as well as work to enhance the competitiveness of their firms.

A second consequence of increased global integration is that *foreign direct investment (FDI)* is playing an ever-increasing role in the global economy as companies of all sizes invest overseas. In particular, the foreign direct investment flows to less-developed countries by firms in developed countries has risen substantially.[22] Investment by foreign companies and individuals in U.S. firms is also huge: $1.5 trillion, almost four times the 1990 level, with the majority coming from European investors. In recent years, the United States has received more foreign direct investment than any other country.[23] To give two examples, the Chinese computer maker Lenovo purchased IBM's personal-computer business, and brewing company SABMiller is now under South African ownership.[24] In recent years, China's role as an export

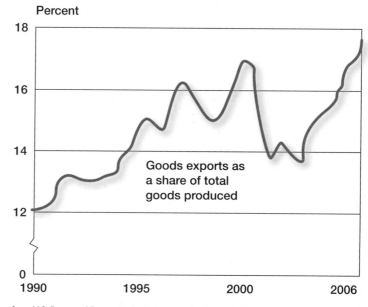

SOURCE: Data from U.S. Bureau of Economic Analysis, as cited in James C. Cooper, "Exports Are Giving the Economy a Surprise Lift," *BusinessWeek*, November 27, 2006, http://www.businessweek.com.

FIGURE 6.3
Growing Proportion of
Goods Being Exported

powerhouse has allowed the Chinese government to amass about $1 trillion in foreign exchange reserves, of which it is expected to invest hundreds of billions of dollars.[25]

A third consequence of an increasingly integrated global economy is that imports are penetrating deeper into the world's largest economies. For example, a high percentage of the clothing and textile products, paper, cut diamonds, and electronics consumed in the United States are imported. If you buy power tools with the Ryobi, Milwaukee, and RIGID brands, they were made by Hong Kong's Techtronic Industries. The top-selling brand of compact refrigerators and number-three maker of freezers is a Chinese company called Haier, which is preparing to move into more-upscale appliances.[26] Figure 6.4 shows how the world trade of manufactured merchandise has grown relative to other product groups. The growth of imports is a natural by-product of the growth of world trade and the trend toward the manufacture of component parts, or even entire products, overseas before shipping them back home for final sale.

Finally, the growth of world trade, FDI, and imports implies that companies around the globe are finding their home markets under attack from foreign competitors. This is true in the United States, where Japanese automakers have captured market share from General Motors, Ford, and Chrysler; and in western Europe, where the once-dominant Dutch company Philips N. V. has lost market share in the consumer electronics industry to Japan's JVC, Matsushita, and Sony.

What does all this mean for today's managers? Compared with only a few years ago, *opportunities are greater* because the movement toward free trade has opened up many formerly protected national markets. The potential for export and for making direct investments overseas is greater today than ever before. *The environment is more complex* because today's manager often has to deal with the challenges of doing business in countries with radically different cultures and coordinating globally dispersed operations. *The environment is more competitive* because in addition to domestic competitors, the manager must deal with cost-efficient overseas competitors.

Companies both large and small now view the world, rather than a single country, as their marketplace. As Table 6.1 shows, the United States has no monopoly on international business. Of the top 25 corporations in the world, 16 are based in countries outside the United States. Also, companies have dispersed their manufacturing, marketing, and research facilities to those locations around the globe where cost and

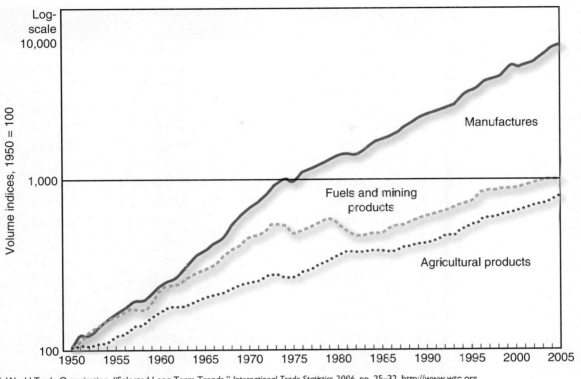

SOURCE: World Trade Organization, "Selected Long-Term Trends," *International Trade Statistics 2006,* pp. 25–32, http://www.wtc.org.

FIGURE 6.4

Relative Growth in World Merchandise Trade by Major Product Group, 1950–2005

skill conditions are most favorable. This trend is now so pervasive in industries such as automobiles, aerospace, and electronics that it is becoming increasingly irrelevant to talk about "American products" or "Japanese products" or "German products."

For example, the headquarters of an automaker no longer says much about where a particular car is made. According to the National Highway Traffic Safety Administration, despite the Jeep Patriot's red-white-and-blue name, only 66 percent of its components are made in the United States. In contrast, although Toyota is a Japanese-headquartered company, 80 percent of the parts in a Toyota Sequoia are produced in the United States. A U.S. headquarters doesn't limit a U.S. car company either. General Motors reports that it employs more people, sells more cars, and sees its best growth prospects outside the United States.[27]

Such internationalization is not limited to the largest corporations. An increasing number of medium-size and small firms also engage in international trade. Some companies have limited their involvement to exporting, while others set up production facilities overseas. Jade Corporation, which started out as a tool-and-die maker, operates three facilities with a few hundred employees. The company found it difficult to compete as U.S. manufacturing operations moved overseas, but creative management continued to find opportunities. As the company moved into making more specialized products, it developed its engineering capabilities and its experience in working with a Singapore manufacturer. Eventually, Jade began working with clients to set up manufacturing facilities in Asia. Jade employees first learn about the customer's product and the way to make it, and then they use their overseas connections to get the customer's foreign plant running.[28] Responding to the dominance of English on the Internet, an Israeli software start-up developed a program called WhiteSmoke, which uses artificial intelligence to analyze written English, not only checking for spelling and grammar errors but also suggesting ways to make the writing clearer and more natural. The company originally found a customer base among Israeli lawyers and tech workers. Since then, the ease of downloading a program online has expanded the market to computer users in the United States. The company next began negotiating with

TABLE 6.1
Top 25 Global Firms

Rank	Firm	Country	Revenues, Millions of U.S. $
1	Royal Dutch Shell	Netherlands	458,361
2	Exxon Mobil	U.S.	442,851
3	Wal-Mart Stores	U.S.	405,607
4	BP	Britain	367,053
5	Chevron	U.S.	263,159
6	Total	France	234,674
7	ConocoPhillips	U.S.	230,764
8	ING Group	Netherlands	226,577
9	Sinopec	China	207,814
10	Toyota Motor	Japan	204,352
11	Japan Post Holdings	Japan	198,700
12	General Electric	U.S.	183,207
13	China National Petroleum	China	181,123
14	Volkswagen	Germany	166,579
15	State Grid	China	164,136
16	Dexia Group	Belgium	161,269
17	ENI	Italy	159,348
18	General Motors	U.S.	148,979
19	Ford Motor	U.S.	146,277
20	Allianz	Germany	142,395
21	HSBC Holdings	Britain	142,049
22	Gazprom	Soviet Union	141,455
23	Daimler	Germany	140,328
24	BNP Paribas	France	136,096
25	Carrefour	France	129,134

SOURCE: From http://money.cnn.com/magazines/fortune/global/500/2009/fullist © 2009 Time Inc. All rights reserved.

distributors to sell WhiteSmoke in China and India. The global nature of the Internet has provided both the need and a major means of distributing WhiteSmoke.[29]

Some of the reasons managers collaborate with their overseas counterparts on trade are obvious. Other countries offer expanded markets for one's own products. In turn, they might have natural resources, products, or cost structures that managers need but that aren't available in the home country. But there are other, perhaps less obvious, benefits to collaborating with other countries on trade. Because trade allows each country to obtain more efficiently what it cannot as easily produce on its own, it lowers prices overall and makes more goods more widely available. This in turn raises living standards—and may broaden the market for a manager's own products, both locally and abroad. Trade also makes new technologies and methods more widely available, again raising the standard of living and improving efficiency. Finally, collaborating with others on trade creates links between people and cultures that, particularly over the long run, can lead to cooperation in other areas.

The Role of Outsourcing

outsourcing

Contracting with an outside provider to produce one or more of an organization's goods or services.

offshoring

Moving work to other countries.

In recent years, the issues of offshoring and outsourcing have become sources of controversy. **Outsourcing** occurs when an organization contracts with an outside provider to produce one or more of its goods or services. **Offshoring** occurs when companies move jobs to another country, typically where wages are lower. This practice does not necessarily require using an outside provider. Companies with large workforces can resource globally. However, most of the concerns expressed about offshoring refer to outsourcing, because people conclude that high-paying U.S. jobs are being lost to low-cost countries overseas. The concern is prompted by widespread reports of major corporations relocating assembly lines, computer programming, help centers, and other parts of their operations to India or China. One study has estimated that by 2015 more than 3 million U.S. jobs will be sent abroad.[30] More recently and dramatically, economist Alan Blinder has raised the possibility that communication technology will lead to the offshoring of at least 30 million jobs over the longer term. For example, the work of bookkeepers, accounting clerks, computer programmers, data entry keyers, and financial analysts can be performed anywhere and submitted to the customer or employer electronically.[31]

The decline in manufacturing employment in the United States is evident. In the first six years of this decade, the United States lost 2 million manufacturing jobs, as well as 1.6 million office and administrative support jobs. But considerable evidence suggests that the cause of this job decline is not offshoring, but innovation. Because of new technology and processes, managers simply need fewer workers to produce the same quantity of goods. Even as manufacturing employment has declined, manufacturing output in the United States has grown. In addition, technology and trade enable the creation of new jobs. Even as manufacturing jobs have been lost, the United States has gained millions of new jobs, including 3.2 million service jobs, 2.5 million professional jobs, and 1.3 million managerial jobs. Thus, the important question may not be how to prevent offshoring from "taking" jobs but how to prepare the workforce for the types of jobs that will be needed in the United States of the future— jobs requiring personal interaction (such as the work of doctors or counselors), hands-on activity (plumbers, janitors), and tailoring to particular situations (identifying a clients' needs, rather than following a routine).[32]

An increasing number of American companies are outsourcing and offshoring divisions and departments of their organizations to save money. Many call centers are now located in India where wages are still much lower than in the U.S. Here is a photo of a typical call center in Hyderabad, India.

The statistics on offshoring often overlook that the job transfers from offshoring represent a small fraction of the 135 million jobs in the United States. Most jobs require workers to be close to their markets—people still shop at their local supermarket and appliance dealer, visit their doctors, and attend a community school. Perhaps most important, as offshoring increases efficiency, it frees funds for expansion and additional employment. The challenge is primarily one in which individual workers are deeply affected when their jobs are lost. Some organizations determine that they have a social responsibility to participate in retraining programs to help these displaced workers identify and prepare for jobs that are less likely to move overseas. The controversy over offshoring also overlooks the extent to which foreign companies hire workers in the United States—for example, when Germany's BMW runs a South Carolina assembly plant for its X5 sport utility vehicle.

One less positive effect of offshoring has been wage stagnation in industries where offshoring is common, as workers in those areas compete with their lower-wage counterparts abroad. On the other hand, wages in some of those other countries have started to rise, reducing the benefits of offshoring.[33] Some firms in India have actually begun to offshore some of *their* work to stay competitive.

"Competitiveness is not a zero-sum game and the success of other economies is not a failure of U.S. competitiveness. As all nations improve their productivity, wages rise and markets expand, creating the potential for rising prosperity for all."
Michael Porter[34]

In recent years automation has reduced the percentage of product costs that can be attributed to labor, making it less necessary to consider moving jobs overseas. Also, managers who offshore to achieve wage savings alone often incur unexpected additional costs in travel, training, quality control, language barriers, and the resistance of some customers who prefer to deal with local personnel. However, offshoring is a continuing trend, because in some cases it delivers advantages other than cost. For some types of work, companies use offshoring as a way to find talent that is in short supply at home. A survey of software firms found that the main reasons for offshoring were to enable the company to grow and to get products to market faster. The companies either have difficulty finding enough programmers in the United States, or they determine that they can keep a project moving ahead around the clock as U.S. and overseas teams hand the project back and forth. Similarly, by outsourcing a project to a specialist firm, a company can quickly have hundreds of people devoted to it, dramatically shortening the turn-around time.[35]

In short, in deciding whether to offshore, managers should not start out with the assumption that it will be cheaper for them to do so. Instead, here are some of the factors they might take into account:

> *What is the competitive advantage of the products they offer?* If, say, rapid delivery, reliability, and customer contact are paramount, then offshoring is a less attractive option. But if the product is widely available and standardized, like a calculator, and the only competitive advantage is price, the lowest possible production cost becomes essential and offshoring becomes something managers will consider.
>
> *Is the business in its early stages?* If so, offshoring may well be inappropriate, as managers need to stay close to the business and its customers to solve problems and make sure everything is going according to plan. When the business is more mature, managers can afford to consider moving some operations overseas.
>
> *Can production savings be achieved locally?* Automation can often achieve significant labor-cost savings and eliminate the advantage of moving production abroad. Where automation savings are not feasible, as with computer call centers, then offshoring becomes a more attractive option.
>
> *Can the entire supply chain be improved?* As we discussed in Chapter 2, enormous productivity savings are possible when managers develop an efficient supply chain, from suppliers to manufacturing to customers. These improvements permit both lower cost and high customer responsiveness. If the supply chain is not a major consideration, or is already highly efficient or routine, and more savings are needed, then offshoring may be one way for managers to achieve additional efficiencies.[36]

These considerations lead to a variety of decisions about where to operate. Hayward Pool Products makes some of its products in China but constantly improves the efficiency of its U.S. factories so that they can do more of the work competitively. And while most clothing sold in the United States today comes from the Asia-Pacific region, Brooks Brothers makes men's ties in New York City, where it can continually adjust production and inventory according to which designs are selling the fastest. For companies selling large volumes or bulky products, a key deciding factor has been transportation costs. When oil prices recently spiked, DESA, which makes heaters, and Emerson, which makes electrical equipment, moved a sizable share of their production from China to North America.[37]

Global Strategy

LO 3

One of the critical tasks an international manager faces is to identify the best strategy for competing in a global marketplace. To approach this issue, managers can plot a company's position on an integration–responsiveness grid, such as that shown in Figure 6.5. The vertical axis measures pressures for *global integration*, and the horizontal axis measures pressures for *local responsiveness*.

Pressures for Global Integration

Managers may have several reasons to want or need a common, global strategy, rather than one tailored to individual markets. These factors include the existence of universal needs, pressures to reduce costs, or the presence of competitors with a global strategy.

Universal needs create strong pressure for a global strategy. Universal needs exist when the tastes and preferences of consumers in different countries with regard to a product are similar. Products that serve universal needs require little adaptation across national markets; thus, global integration is facilitated. This is the case in many industrial markets. For example, electronic products such as semiconductor chips meet universal needs. Certain basic foodstuffs (like colas) and appliances (like can openers) are also increasingly available and regarded in similar ways globally.

Competitive *pressures to reduce costs* may cause managers to seek to integrate manufacturing globally. Cost can be particularly important in industries in which price is the main competitive weapon and competition is intense (e.g., as with hand-held calculators). It is also important if key international competitors are based in countries where labor and other operating costs are low. In these cases, products are more likely to be standardized and perhaps produced in a few locations to capture economies of scale.

The presence of competitors engaged in *global strategic coordination* is another factor that creates pressures for global integration. For example, a competitor that centrally coordinates the purchase of raw materials worldwide may achieve significant price reductions compared with firms that allow subsidiaries to handle purchases locally. Global competition can often create pressures to centralize in corporate headquarters certain decisions being made by different national subsidiaries. And once one multinational company adopts global strategic coordination, its competitors may be forced to do the same.

$ **The bottom line**
COST
The need to lower costs is a key globalization driver.

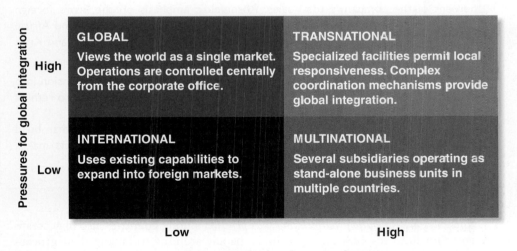

	Low	**High**
High	**GLOBAL** Views the world as a single market. Operations are controlled centrally from the corporate office.	**TRANSNATIONAL** Specialized facilities permit local responsiveness. Complex coordination mechanisms provide global integration.
Low	**INTERNATIONAL** Uses existing capabilities to expand into foreign markets.	**MULTINATIONAL** Several subsidiaries operating as stand-alone business units in multiple countries.

Pressures for global integration

Pressures for local responsiveness

SOURCES: Christopher A. Bartlett and Sumantra Ghoshal, *Managing across Borders: The Transnational Solution* (Boston: Harvard Business School Press, 1991); and Anne-Wil Harzing, "An Empirical Analysis and Extension of the Bartlett and Ghoshal Typology of Multinational Companies," *Journal of International Business Studies* 31, no. 1 (2000), pp. 101–20.

FIGURE 6.5
Organizational Models

Pressures for Local Responsiveness

In some circumstances, managers need to make sure that their companies are able to adapt to different needs in different locations. Strong pressures for local responsiveness emerge when *consumer tastes and preferences differ significantly* among countries. In such cases, products and/or marketing messages have to be customized. In the automobile industry, for example, U.S. consumers' demand for pickup trucks is strong in the South and West, where many families have a pickup truck as a second or third vehicle. In contrast, in Europe pickup trucks are viewed as utility vehicles and are purchased primarily by companies rather than by individuals. As a result, automakers must tailor their marketing messages to these differences in consumer demand. Similarly, as described in the "Management Close-Up: Taking Action" feature, Kraft's global strategy is shaped by differences in consumers' preferences for various foods.

Pressures for local responsiveness also emerge when there are *differences in traditional practices* among countries. For example, in Great Britain people drive on the left side of the road, creating a demand for right-hand-drive cars, whereas in neighboring France people drive on the right side of the road. Obviously, automobiles must be customized to accommodate this difference in traditional practices.

Management Close-Up   TAKING ACTION

When Irene Rosenfeld unveiled her turnaround plan, she knew Kraft would need to win back customers both at home and abroad. To concentrate on the company's core brands, Rosenfeld sold off Minute Rice, Milk-Bone pet snacks, and Cream of Wheat and Post cereals. Also sold were Kraft's Fruit$_2$O water and Veryfine beverage brands, to Sunny Delight Beverages.

Rosenfeld also turned to overseas markets by buying the cookie and cereal division of French firm Groupe Danone, whose LU, Petit Déjeuner, and Tuc cookie brands were big throughout Europe. The $7.2 billion acquisition expanded Kraft's snack food division—already its largest, representing almost one-third of its revenues—and gave Kraft an even larger global presence. Danone's foothold in China doubled Kraft's business in that huge emerging market.

With the acquisition of Groupe Danone, Kraft's international sales increased to over 40 percent of the company's total sales. Rosenfeld's emphasis on the firm's foreign markets yielded strong growth in eastern Europe, Russia, the Middle East, and Africa. Venezuela and Argentina reported double-digit gains, and in Asia, the Oreo and Kraft cheese brands did well.[38]

- What knowledge and skills did Irene Rosenfeld need to include global expansion into her turnaround strategy for Kraft? How did her request for all employees to rethink their products contribute?
- Why do you think Rosenfeld decided to acquire Groupe Danone rather than build new relationships and factories from scratch? What about Kraft's products makes local responsiveness necessary?

Differences in distribution channels and sales practices among countries also may create pressures for local responsiveness. In India, people are used to buying their groceries at small, local shops, creating challenges for Wal-Mart as it develops plans to open supermarkets and larger stores in that

> "When you travel, remember that a foreign country is not designed to make you comfortable. It is designed to make its own people comfortable."
> —Clifton Fadiman

country.[39] And cultural differences in selling have led Apple to adjust its "Mac vs. PC" advertising campaign in some countries. In Japan, people think it's rude to make direct comparisons, so the comedians hired for the Japanese ads deemphasize differences in product features, instead distinguishing them more in terms of the work-oriented PC versus the Mac's appeal for leisure activities. In the United Kingdom, Apple's ad agency hired two British actors to portray the products in terms of the characters the actors play in a sitcom; the more sensible character represents PC, and the more fun-loving character represents Apple. Even with these adjustments, the ads generated some criticism. A poll found that respect for Apple actually declined after the ads started running in Britain, and in Japan the Mac character's casual attire generated some confusion. Instead of seeing the casually dressed character as a hip entrepreneur, some saw him as merely cheap or unsuccessful, wearing low-cost clothing.[40]

Finally, *economic and political demands* that host-country governments impose may necessitate a degree of local responsiveness. Most important, threats of protectionism, economic nationalism, and local content rules (rules requiring that a certain percentage of a product be manufactured locally) dictate that international companies manufacture locally. For example, countries may impose tariffs (taxes on imports) or quotas (restrictions on the number of imports allowed into a country) to protect domestic industries from foreign competition perceived to be unfair or not in the nation's interests. Recently, the United States began imposing tariffs on paper imported from China. The U.S. government justified the tariffs as a response to complaints that the Chinese companies were selling the paper below the cost of the raw materials, presumably because the Chinese government was subsidizing the industry. Others interpret this and other protectionist actions as being motivated primarily by political objectives.[41] Whatever the reasons for them, tariffs and quotas influence managers' decisions about whether it is economically advantageous, or even possible, to operate locally or rely on exporting.

I run Microsoft Office

So do I

See the latest episodes of PC and Mac
apple.com/uk

To re-create the delicate dynamic of its popular U.S. ads, Apple used local TV actors in England, shown here in the U.K. advertisement. They did the same with Japanese actors. Apple faced a difficult issue in bringing its series of ads to different countries since what is funny in one culture can seem ill-mannered in another.

Choosing a Global Strategy

As Figure 6.5 shows, managers can use four approaches to international competition, depending on their company's position on the integration–responsiveness grid: the international model, the multinational model, the global model, and the transnational model. Organizations in each model compete globally, but they differ in the strategy they use and in the structure and systems that drive their operations.

The International Model   In the **international model**, managers use their organization's existing core capabilities to expand into foreign markets. As the grid suggests, it is most appropriate when there are few pressures for economies of scale *or* local responsiveness. Pfizer is an example of a company operating in the international model. It is in an industry that doesn't compete on cost, and its drugs obviously don't need to be tailored for local tastes. The international model uses subsidiaries in each country in which the company does business, with ultimate control exercised by the parent company. In particular, while subsidiaries may have some latitude to adapt products to local conditions, core functions such as research and development tend

international model

An organizational model that is composed of a company's overseas subsidiaries and characterized by greater control by the parent company over the research function and local product and marketing strategies than is the case in the multinational model.

Our vehicles don't just take people to work, they put people to work.

For many Americans, Toyota is more than just a source of transport. It's a source of income. With our eight manufacturing plants, sales and marketing operations, research and design facilities, and through our dealers and suppliers, Toyota's U.S. operations are responsible for more than 190,000 jobs.

Last year, Toyota team members built more than one million vehicles in the U.S.* And with two new manufacturing plants on the way, we're working to create even more jobs and opportunities in the communities where we do business.

*Toyota automobiles and vehicles are made using many U.S.-sourced parts. FS704

toyota.com/usa

TOYOTA

In this ad, Toyota counters the perception that foreign auto companies take jobs from Americans. The production line above is actually its Georgetown, KY, manufacturing plant. According to the organizational model in Figure 6.5, what type of company is Toyota?

✓ The international model helps spread quality and service standards globally.

multinational model

An organizational model that consists of the subsidiaries in each country in which a company does business, with ultimate control exercised by the parent company.

⊘ **The bottom line**
SPEED
The multinational model helps speed up local response.

to be centralized in the parent company. Consequently, the dependence of subsidiaries on the parent company for new products, processes, and ideas requires a great deal of coordination and control by the parent company.

The advantage of this model is that it facilitates the transfer of skills and know-how from the parent company to subsidiaries around the globe. For example, IBM and Xerox profited from the transfer of their core skills in technology and research and development (R&D) overseas. The overseas successes of Kellogg, Coca-Cola, Heinz, and Procter & Gamble are based more on marketing know-how than on technological expertise. Toyota and Honda successfully penetrated U.S. markets from their base in Japan with their core competencies in manufacturing relative to local competitors. Still other companies have based their competitive advantage on general management skills. These factors explain the growth of international hotel chains such as Hilton International, Intercontinental, and Sheraton.

One disadvantage of the international model is that it does not provide maximum latitude for responding to local conditions. In addition, it frequently does not provide the opportunity to achieve a low-cost position via scale economies.

The Multinational Model   Where global efficiency is not required but adapting to local conditions offers advantages, the multinational model is appropriate. The **multinational model,** sometimes referred to as *multidomestic,* uses subsidiaries in each country in which the company does business and provides a great deal of discretion to those subsidiaries to respond to local conditions. Each local subsidiary is a self-contained unit with all the functions required for operating in the host market. Thus, each subsidiary has its own manufacturing, marketing, research, and human resources functions. Because of this autonomy, each multinational subsidiary can customize its products and strategies according to the tastes and preferences of local consumers; the competitive conditions; and political, legal, and social structures.

A good example of a multinational firm is Heineken, a Netherlands-based brewing company. Heineken has three major global brands—Heineken, Amstel, and Murphy's Stout—but it also offers regional and local brands. The company understands that every country is unique, with its own culture and business practices. So it attempts to adapt its products to local attitudes and tastes while maintaining its high quality. As a result, the company produces more than 170 different brands around the world, from its international brands to local and specialty brews. The localized portfolio includes such brands as Primus and Star in Africa, Vitamalt and Piton in the Caribbean, and Tiger in Asia. Individual countries have considerable autonomy in the beer that is brewed locally.[42]

A major disadvantage of the multinational form is higher manufacturing costs and duplication of effort. Although a multinational can transfer core skills among its international operations, it cannot realize scale economies from centralizing manufacturing facilities and offering a standardized product to the global marketplace. Moreover, because a multinational approach tends to decentralize strategy decisions (discussed further in Chapters 8 and 9), launching coordinated global attacks against competitors is difficult. This can be a significant disadvantage when competitors have this ability.

The Global Model   The **global model** is designed to enable a company to market a standardized product in the global marketplace and to manufacture that product in a limited number of locations where the mix of costs and skills is most favorable. The global model has been adopted by companies that view the world as one market and assume that no tangible differences exist among countries with regard to consumer tastes and preferences. Procter & Gamble, for example, has been successful in Europe against Unilever because it has approached the entire continent as a unified whole. Royal Dutch/Shell has been a multinational company for many years but has moved to a global model to reduce costs, increase integration, and improve efficiency.

Companies that adopt the global model tend to construct global-scale manufacturing facilities in a few selected locations so that they can realize scale economies. These scale economies come from spreading the fixed costs of investments in new-product development, plant and equipment, and the like over worldwide sales. By using centralized manufacturing facilities and global marketing strategies, Sony was able to push down its unit costs to the point where it became the low-cost player in the global television market. This advantage enabled Sony to take market share away from Philips, RCA, and Zenith, all of which used traditionally based manufacturing operations in each major national market (a characteristic of the multinational approach). Because operations are centralized, subsidiaries usually are limited to marketing and service functions.

On the downside, because a company pursuing a purely global approach tries to standardize its goods and services, it may be less responsive to consumer tastes and demands in different countries. Attempts to lower costs through global product standardization may result in a product that fails to satisfy anyone. For example, while Procter & Gamble has been quite successful using a global approach, the company experienced problems when it tried to market Cheer laundry detergent in Japan. Unfortunately for P&G, the product did not "suds up" as promoted in Japan because the Japanese use a great deal of fabric softener, which suppresses suds. Moreover, the claim that Cheer worked in all water temperatures was irrelevant in Japan, where most washing is done in cold water. The global model also requires a great deal of coordination, with significant additional management and paperwork costs.

The Transnational Model   In today's global economy, achieving a competitive advantage often requires managers to simultaneously pursue local responsiveness, transfer of know-how, and cost economies.[43] The transnational model is designed to help them do just that. It is an approach that enables managers to "think globally but act locally."

In companies that adopt the **transnational model,** functions are centralized where it makes sense to do so, but a great deal of decision making also takes place at the local level. In addition, the experiences of local subsidiaries are shared worldwide to improve the firm's overall knowledge and capabilities. For example, research, training, and the overall development of the organization's strategy and global brand image tend to be centralized at home. Other functions may be centralized as well, but not necessarily in the home country.

To achieve cost economies, companies may base global-scale production plants for labor-intensive products in low-wage countries such as Mexico, Poland, and China and locate production plants that require a skilled workforce in high-skill countries such as Germany and Japan. Increasingly, companies are able to find locations where the workforce includes the optimal balance of needed skills and relatively low costs. Thus, although wages have begun rising in India, the level of technical skill of its workforce has made that country an attractive place to locate many kinds of knowledge-based operations, such as loan approvals, legal research, and biotech R&D. These types of skilled occupations are growing faster in India than jobs in call centers, the work that once brought India to prominence as an offshoring location.[44]

global model

An organizational model consisting of a company's overseas subsidiaries and characterized by centralized decision making and tight control by the parent company over most aspects of worldwide operations; typically adopted by organizations that base their global competitive strategy on cost considerations.

$ **The bottom line**
                COST
The global model of standardization lowers cost.

transnational model

An organizational model characterized by centralizing certain functions in locations that best achieve cost economies; basing other functions in the company's national subsidiaries to facilitate greater local responsiveness; and fostering communication among subsidiaries to permit transfer of technological expertise and skills.

The transnational model tries to deliver on all bottom-line practices.

Marketing, service, and final-assembly functions tend to be based in the national subsidiaries to facilitate greater local responsiveness. Thus, major components may be manufactured in centralized production plants to realize scale economies and then shipped to local plants, where the final product is assembled and customized to fit local needs.

Caterpillar, which manufactures construction and mining equipment, is a transnational company.[45] The need to compete with low-cost competitors such as Komatsu has forced Caterpillar to look for greater cost economies by centralizing global production at locations where the mix of costs and skills is most favorable. At the same time, variations in construction practices and government regulations across countries mean that Caterpillar must be responsive to local needs. On the integration–responsiveness grid in Figure 6.5, therefore, Caterpillar is situated toward the top right-hand corner.

To deal with these simultaneous demands, Caterpillar has designed its products to use many identical components and has invested in a few large-scale component-manufacturing facilities to fill global demand and realize scale economies. But while the company manufactures components centrally, it has assembly plants in each of its major markets. At these plants Caterpillar adds local product features, tailoring the finished product to local needs. In addition, most of its dealerships, located in more than 200 countries, are locally owned. Thus, Caterpillar is able to realize many of the benefits of global manufacturing while managing pressure for local responsiveness by differentiating its product among national markets.

Perhaps the most important distinguishing characteristic of the transnational organization is the fostering of communications among subsidiaries and the ability to integrate the efforts of subsidiaries when doing so makes sense. For example, when Caterpillar was developing certain medium-size engines, it enlisted the efforts of Caterpillar facilities in the United Kingdom, Mexico, Belgium, and several U.S. locations.

Achieving such communications across subsidiaries requires elaborate formal mechanisms, such as transnational committees staffed by people from the various subsidiaries who are responsible for monitoring coordination among subsidiaries. Equally important is to transfer managers among subsidiaries on a regular basis. This enables international managers to establish a global network of personal contacts in different subsidiaries with whom they can share information as the need arises. Finally, achieving coordination among subsidiaries requires that the head office play a proactive role in coordinating their activities.

Entry Mode

LO 4

When considering global expansion, international managers must decide on the best means of entering an overseas market. The five basic ways to expand overseas are exporting, licensing, franchising, entering into a joint venture with a host-country company, and setting up a wholly owned subsidiary in the host country.[46] Table 6.2 compares the entry modes.

Exporting

$ **The bottom line**
COST

Exporting offers scale economies.

Most manufacturing companies begin global expansion as exporters and later switch to one of the other modes for serving an overseas market. The advantages of exporting are that it (1) provides scale economies by avoiding the costs of manufacturing in other countries and (2) is consistent with a pure global strategy. By manufacturing the product in a centralized location and then exporting it to other national markets, the company may be able to realize substantial scale economies from its global sales volume.

TABLE 6.2   Comparison of Entry Modes

Exporting	Licensing	Franchising	Joint Venture	Wholly Owned Subsidiary
Advantages				
Scale economies	Lower development costs	Lower development costs	Local knowledge	Maintains control over technology
Consistent with pure global strategy	Lower political risk	Lower political risk	Shared costs and risk	Maintains control over operations
			May be the only option	
Disadvantages				
No low-cost sites	Loss of control over technology	Loss of control over quality	Loss of control over technology	High cost
High transportation costs			Conflict between partners	High risk
Tariff barriers				

Television networks have long exported popular U.S. television programs such as *Dallas* and *Friends* to Europe, where they have become hits again. In the old days, Europeans had to wait many months for episodes of their favorite programs. But today, studios such as Buena Vista International (the sales division of Disney's ABC network) and British Sky Broadcasting Group have teamed up to get the hits across the ocean fast. Fans can now view the ABC show *Lost* only four days after its initial airing in the United States. This speed of delivery is an important step as networks scramble to nab their share of the $110 billion overseas television market, which is fast falling prey to online pirating. "Who wants to wait six months to see season three of *Lost* when you can download it?" asks Tom Toumazis, Buena Vista's managing director for Europe, the Middle East, and Africa. So the studios are taking a preemptive step—and exporting their shows as fast as they can.

Still, exporting is not a simple task. Although foreign TV companies have already paid more than $500 million for reruns of NBC's *Law & Order* (with subtitles), the network is beginning to close in on the preference of foreign audiences for shows that reflect their own culture. So, instead of just translating scripts, writers are now adapting certain scenes to reflect France's Napoleonic legal code and changing the set to look like a Paris police station with the Eiffel Tower in the background. The series will even have a new name: *Paris Enquêtes Criminelles*.[47]

However, exporting has a number of drawbacks. First, exporting from the company's home base may be inappropriate if other countries offer lower-cost locations for manufacturing the product. An alternative is to manufacture in a location where the mix of factor costs and skills is most favorable and then export from that location to other markets to achieve scale economies. Several U.S. electronics companies have moved some manufacturing operations to parts of Asia where low-cost, high-skill labor is available, and export from that location to other countries, including the United States.

A second drawback of exporting is that high transportation costs can make it uneconomical, particularly in the case of bulk products. Chemical companies get around this by manufacturing their products on a regional basis, serving several countries in a region from one facility.

Internet communications are making it easier to export services. ValueNotes, based in Pune, India, exports business and legal research services. At the same time, U.S.-based firms such as General Electric, Oracle, and legal-research firm Mindcrest have established offices in India to provide low-cost legal services under their own management umbrellas. In general, U.S. companies are more likely to own a foreign affiliate to sell services than to export the services from the United States to a customer in another country.[48]

International sales of services from U.S. companies

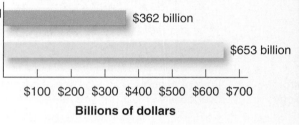

Exports of commercial services — $362 billion
Sales of services through affiliates — $653 billion

$100 $200 $300 $400 $500 $600 $700
Billions of dollars

A third drawback is that host countries can impose (or threaten to impose) tariff barriers. Trade arrangements described earlier, including the World Trade Organization, NAFTA, and APEC, work to minimize this risk. However, tariffs continue to affect trade between particular countries in various industries. Examples include U.S.-imposed tariffs on sugar imported from Mexico and, as mentioned earlier, paper imported from China. Dell has lobbied the Indian government to reduce tariffs on computers exported to that country, where they can increase a computer's price by one-third. In the meantime, the company has decided to manufacture in India, rather than relying on exports.[49]

Licensing

International licensing is an arrangement by which a licensee in another country buys the rights to manufacture a company's product in its own country for a negotiated fee (typically, royalty payments on the number of units sold). The licensee then puts up most of the capital necessary to get the overseas operation going. The advantage of licensing is that the company need not bear the costs and risks of opening up an overseas market.

However, a problem arises when a company licenses its technological expertise to overseas companies. Technological know-how is the basis of the competitive advantage of many multinational companies. But RCA Corporation lost control over its color TV technology by licensing it to a number of Japanese companies. The Japanese companies quickly assimilated RCA's technology and then used it to enter the U.S. market, eventually gaining a bigger share of the U.S. market than RCA held.

Franchising

In many respects, franchising is similar to licensing. However, whereas licensing is a strategy pursued primarily by manufacturing companies, franchising is used primarily by service companies. McDonald's, Hilton International, and many other companies have expanded overseas by franchising. Pretzel maker Auntie Anne's has expanded through franchising in the Asia-Pacific region, where its sales are growing at 30 percent a year, far more quickly than in the United States.[50]

In franchising, the company sells limited rights to use its brand name to franchisees in return for a lump-sum payment and a share of the franchisee's profits. However, unlike most licensing agreements, the franchisee has to agree to abide by strict rules regarding how it does business. Thus, when McDonald's enters into a franchising agreement with an overseas company, it expects the franchisee to run its

Cold Stone Creamery is expanding its franchises overseas, including South Korea, shown here.

restaurants in a manner identical to that used under the McDonald's name elsewhere in the world.

The advantages of franchising as an entry mode are similar to those of licensing. The franchisees put up capital and assume most of the business risk. However, local laws can limit this advantage. Until recently, China required that franchisors had to operate at least two company-owned outlets in that country profitably for at least a year before they would be allowed to offer franchises to Chinese entrepreneurs. Relaxation of that requirement made franchising in China's high-growth market far more attractive to businesses like Ruby Tuesday, all of whose restaurants are operated by franchisees with knowledge of their local markets.[51]

The most significant disadvantage of franchising concerns quality control. The company's brand name guarantees consistency in the company's product. Thus, a business traveler booking into a Hilton International hotel in Hong Kong can reasonably expect the same quality of room, food, and service that he or she would receive in New York. But if overseas franchisees are less concerned about quality than they should be, the impact can go beyond lost sales in the local market to a decline in the company's reputation worldwide. If a business traveler has an unpleasant experience at the Hilton in Hong Kong, she or he may decide never to go to another Hilton hotel—and urge colleagues to do likewise. To make matters worse, the geographic distance between the franchisor and its overseas franchisees makes poor quality difficult to detect.

Franchising is one way to maintain standards globally.

Joint Ventures

Establishing a joint venture (a formal business agreement discussed in more detail in Chapter 11) with a company in another country has long been a popular means of entering a new market. Joint ventures benefit a company through (1) the local partner's knowledge of the host country's competitive conditions, culture, language, political systems, and business systems and (2) the sharing of development costs and/or risks with the local partner. Hershey recently announced a joint venture with India's Godrej Beverages and Foods as a way to achieve growth in an industry that has matured in the United States. Hershey will own a 51 percent share of the joint business, which combines Hershey's brands and recipes with Godrej's manufacturing facilities distribution network. The venture will start by selling Hershey's Syrup in India and later add other products.[52] In addition, many countries' political considerations make joint ventures the only feasible entry mode. Before China opened its borders to trade, many U.S. companies including Eastman Kodak, AT&T, Ford, and GM did business in the country via joint ventures.

But as attractive as they sound, joint ventures have their problems. First, as in the case of licensing, a company runs the risk of losing control over its technology to its venture partner. Second, companies may find themselves at odds with one another. For example, one joint-venture partner may want to move production to a country where demand is growing, while the other would prefer to keep its factories at home running at full capacity. Conflict over who controls what within a joint venture is a primary reason many fail.[53] In fact, many of the early joint ventures American and European companies entered into with companies in China lost money or failed precisely because of conflicts over control. To offset these disadvantages, experienced managers strive to iron out technology, control, and other potential conflicts up front, when they first negotiate the joint-venture agreement.

Wholly Owned Subsidiaries

Establishing a wholly owned subsidiary, that is, an independent company owned by the parent corporation, is the most costly method of serving an overseas market. Companies that use this approach must bear the full costs and risks associated with setting up overseas operations (as opposed to joint ventures, in which the costs and risks are shared, or licensing, in which the licensee bears most of the costs and risks).

Nevertheless, setting up a wholly owned subsidiary offers two clear advantages. First, when a company's competitive advantage is based on technology, a wholly owned subsidiary normally is the preferred entry mode because it reduces the risk of losing control over the technology. This was the case for 3M, which was the first to set up a wholly owned subsidiary in China.[54] Wholly owned subsidiaries are the preferred mode of entry in the semiconductor, electronics, and pharmaceutical industries. And recently, in a twist on the practice of offshoring, U.S. companies have been acquiring outsourcing firms in India, making them subsidiaries. For instance, Texas-based EDS recently announced plans to acquire MphasiS, an Indian provider of computer programming and other services.[55]

Second, a wholly owned subsidiary gives a company tight control over operations in other countries, which is necessary if the company chooses to pursue a global strategy. Establishing a global manufacturing system requires world headquarters to have a high degree of control over the operations of national affiliates. Unlike licensees or joint-venture partners, wholly owned subsidiaries usually accept centrally determined decisions about how to produce, how much to produce, and how to price output for transfer among operations.

Managing across Borders

LO 5

expatriates

Parent-company nationals who are sent to work at a foreign subsidiary.

host-country nationals

Natives of the country where an overseas subsidiary is located.

third-country nationals

Natives of a country other than the home country or the host country of an overseas subsidiary.

Expatriate hiring lowers cost; training raises quality.

When establishing operations overseas, headquarters executives have a choice among sending **expatriates** (individuals from the parent country), using **host-country nationals** (natives of the host country), and deploying **third-country nationals** (natives of a country other than the home country or the host country). While most corporations use some combination of all three types of employees, there are advantages and disadvantages of each. Colgate-Palmolive and Procter & Gamble, for example, use expatriates to get their products to market abroad more quickly. AT&T and Toyota have used expatriates to transfer their corporate cultures and best practices to other countries—in Toyota's case, to its U.S. plants.

Because sending employees abroad can cost three to four times as much as employing host-country nationals, other companies including Texas Instruments have made more limited use of expatriates. Moreover, in many countries—particularly developing countries in which firms are trying to get an economic foothold—the personal security of expatriates is an issue. As a result, more firms may send their expatriates on shorter assignments and engage in telecommuting, teleconferencing, and other electronic means to facilitate communications between their international divisions. In fact, working internationally can be very stressful, even for experienced "globalites." Table 6.3 shows some of the primary stressors for expatriates at different stages of their assignments. It also shows ways for executives to cope with the stress, as well as some of the things that companies can do to help with the adjustment.

Although developing a valuable pool of expatriates is important, local employees are more available, tend to be familiar with the culture and language, and usually cost less because they do not have to be relocated. In addition, local governments often provide incentives to companies that create good jobs for their citizens, or they may place restrictions on the use of expatriates. Only about a thousand of the roughly 7,000 jobs computer-maker Dell added in 2003 were in the United States.

Most of the growth in IBM's workforce is occurring in India, where employees handle software development, services, and customer support. IBM has more employees in India than in any other country outside the United States.[56]

TABLE 6.3   Stressors and Coping Responses in the Developmental Stages of Expatriate Executives

Stage	Primary Stressors	Executive Coping Response	Employer Coping Response
Expatriate selection	Cross-cultural unreadiness.	Engage in self-evaluation.	Encourage expatriate's self- and family evaluation. Perform an assessment of potential and interests.
Assignment acceptance	Unrealistic evaluation of stressors to come. Hurried time frame.	Think of assignment as a growth opportunity rather than an instrument to vertical promotion.	Do not make hard-to-keep promises. Clarify expectations.
Pre- and postarrival	Ignorance of cultural differences.	Do not make unwarranted assumptions of cultural competence and cultural rules.	Provide pre-, during, and postassignment training. Encourage support-seeking behavior.
Arrival	Cultural shock. Stressor reevaluation. Feelings of lack of fit and differential treatment.	Do not construe identification with the host and parent cultures as mutually exclusive. Seek social support.	Provide postarrival training. Facilitate integration in expatriate network.
Novice	Cultural blunders or inadequacy of coping responses. Ambiguity owing to inability to decipher meaning of situations.	Observe and study functional value of coping responses among locals. Do not simply replicate responses that worked at home.	Provide follow-up training. Seek advice from locals and expatriate network.
Transitional	Rejection of host or parent culture.	Form and maintain attachments with both cultures.	Promote culturally sensitive policies in host country. Provide Internet access to family and friends at home. Maintain constant communication and periodic visits to parent organization.
Mastery	Frustration with inability to perform boundary-spanning role. Bothered by living with a cultural paradox.	Internalize and enjoy identification with both cultures and walking between two cultures.	Reinforce rather than punish dual identification by defining common goals.
Repatriation	Disappointment with unfulfilled expectations. Sense of isolation. Loss of autonomy.	Realistically reevaluate assignment as a personal and professional growth opportunity.	Arrange prerepatriation briefings and interviews. Schedule postrepatriation support meetings.

SOURCE: From *Academy of Management Executive: The Thinking Manager's Source* by J. Sanchez, et al. Copyright © 2000 by Academy of Management. Copyright © 2000 by Academy of Management via Copyright Clearance Center.

The company directly employs more than 20,000 people in Asia, Europe, and South America. Similarly, executives at Allen Bradley, a division of Rockwell International, believe that building a strong local workforce is critical to their success overseas, and they transport key host-country nationals to the United States for skills training. The trend away from using expatriates in top management positions is especially apparent in companies that truly want to create a multinational culture. In Honeywell's European division, for example, many of the top executive positions are held by non-Americans.[57]

Companies that engage in 24/7 manufacturing around the world generally benefit from hiring local workers and managers. RollEase, a Connecticut-based manufacturer of manual operating systems for hard and soft window coverings, has an engineer at its facility in China who can work on design changes while the U.S. workers are asleep at night. "We get stuff back from our engineer, and we check it during the day and give it back to him when we leave at night, which is the beginning of his workday," explains Joseph A. Cannaverde, a project manager. "We come in the next morning, and we have a finished drawing. When we walk out the door we are not stopping work."

But this type of management does not always go smoothly. Change orders might be misunderstood or not executed at all, resulting in lost time and productivity. So communication is vital. In the case of RollEase, the Chinese engineer has access to data from the firm's on-demand system so that he knows he has accurate information. He is also an employee of RollEase, not a subcontractor.[58]

<table>
<tr><td>LO 6</td></tr>
</table>

Skills of the Global Manager

failure rate

The number of expatriate managers of an overseas operation who come home early.

It is estimated that nearly 15 percent of all employee transfers are to an international location. However, the **failure rate** among expatriates (defined as those who come home early) ranges from an estimated 20 percent to 70 percent, depending on the country of assignment. The cost of each of these failed assignments ranges from tens of thousands to hundreds of thousands of dollars.[59] Typically, the causes for failure overseas extend beyond technical capability and include personal and social issues. In a recent survey of human resource managers around the globe, two-thirds said the main reason for the failures is family issues, especially dissatisfaction of the employee's spouse or partner.[60] The problem may be compounded in this era of dual-career couples, in which one spouse may have to give up his or her job to accompany the expatriate manager to the new location. To ensure that an overseas posting will succeed, managers can encourage employees to talk to their spouse about what he or she will do in the foreign country. For both the expatriate and the spouse, adjustment requires flexibility, emotional stability, empathy for the culture, communication skills, resourcefulness, initiative, and diplomatic skills.[61] When Kent Millington took the position of vice president of Asia operations for an Internet hosting company, his wife Linda quit her job to move with him to Japan. Especially for Linda Millington, the first three months were difficult, because she didn't speak Japanese, found the transit system confusing, and even struggled to buy food because she couldn't translate the labels. But she persevered and participated in classes and volunteer activities. Eventually, she and her husband learned to enjoy the experience and appreciated the chance to see just how well they could tackle a challenge.[62]

Companies such as Levi Strauss, Bechtel, Monsanto, Whirlpool, and Dow Chemical have worked to identify the characteristics of individuals that will predict their success abroad. Table 6.4 shows skills that can be used to identify candidates who are likely to succeed in a global environment. Interestingly, in addition to such characteristics as cultural sensitivity, technical expertise, and business knowledge, an individual's success abroad may depend greatly on his or her ability to learn from experience.[63]

"If there is any great secret of success in life, it lies in the ability to put yourself in the other person's place and to see things from his point of view as well as your own."
—Henry Ford

Companies such as BPAmocos, Global Hyatt, and others with large international staffs have extensive training programs to prepare employees for international assignments. Table 6.5 suggests ways to improve their likelihood of success. Other organizations, such as Coca-Cola, Motorola, Chevron, and Mattel, have extended this training to include employees who may be located in the United States but who also deal in

TABLE 6.4   Identifying International Executives

End-State Dimensions	Sample Items
1. Sensitivity to cultural differences	When working with people from other cultures, works hard to understand their perspective.
2. Business knowledge	Has a solid understanding of the company's products and services.
3. Courage to take a stand	Is willing to take a stand on issues.
4. Brings out the best in people	Has a special talent for dealing with people.
5. Acts with integrity	Can be depended on to tell the truth regardless of circumstances.
6. Is insightful	Is good at identifying the most important part of a complex problem.
7. Is committed to success	Clearly demonstrates commitment to seeing the organization succeed.
8. Takes risks	Takes personal as well as business risks.
Learning-Oriented Dimensions	**Sample Items**
1. Uses feedback	Has changed as a result of feedback.
2. Is culturally adventurous	Enjoys the challenge of working in countries other than his or her own.
3. Seeks opportunities to learn	Takes advantage of opportunities to do new things.
4. Is open to criticism	Does not appear brittle—as if criticism might cause him or her to break.
5. Seeks feedback	Pursues feedback even when others are reluctant to give it.
6. Is flexible	Doesn't get so invested in things that he or she cannot change when something doesn't work.

SOURCE: Copyright © 1997 by the American Psychological Association. Gretchen M. Sprietzer, Morgan W. McCall, and Joan D. Mahoney, "Early Identification of International Executive Potential," *Journal of Applied Psychology* 82, no. 1 (1997), pp. 6–29. The use of APA information does not imply endorsement by APA.

TABLE 6.5   How to Prevent Failed Global Assignments

- Structure assignments clearly: develop clear reporting relationships and job responsibilities.
- Create clear job objectives.
- Develop performance measurements based on objectives.
- Use effective, validated selection and screening criteria (both personal and technical attributes).
- Prepare expatriates and families for assignments (briefings, training, support).
- Create a vehicle for ongoing communication with expatriates.
- Anticipate repatriation to facilitate reentry when they come back home.
- Consider developing a mentor program that will help monitor and intervene in case of trouble.

international markets. These programs focus on areas such as language, culture, and career development.

Managers who are sent on an overseas assignment usually wonder about the effect such an assignment will have on their careers. Certainly, their selection for a post overseas is usually an indication that they are being groomed to become more effective managers in an era of globalization. In addition, they will often have more responsibility, challenge, and operating leeway than they might have at home. Yet, they may be concerned that they will soon be "out of the loop" on key developments back home. Good companies and managers address that issue with effective communication between subsidiaries and headquarters and by a program of visitations to and from the home office. Communication technology now makes it easy for expatriates to keep in touch with colleagues in their home country on a daily or even more frequent basis, through e-mail and phone calls. Alan Paul, an American journalist working in China, says Internet phone service, a Webcam, and Podcasts of favorite radio programs also enable him to stay in touch with family and friends back home, even to the extent that he has to work hard to have "a fully engaged existence in China."[64]

Understanding Cultural Issues

In many ways, cultural issues represent the most elusive aspect of international business. In an era when modern transportation and communication technologies have created

In this era where people from all over the globe are collaborating on business issues, it is important to continue learning about and respecting different cultures in order to succeed.

a "global village," it is easy to forget how deep and enduring the differences among nations can be. The fact that people everywhere drink Coke, wear blue jeans, and drive Toyotas doesn't mean we are all becoming alike. Each country is unique for reasons rooted in history, culture, language, geography, social conditions, race, and religion. These differences complicate any international activity and represent the fundamental issues that inform and guide how a company should conduct business across borders. For example, while working in Hong Kong, Geoffrey Fowler discovered that his coworkers there choose topics for small talk—people's weight, salary, and the size of their apartment—that would horrify Americans. At the same time, Chinese workers are put off by the American custom of combining lunch with a business meeting, meaning junior employees are chewing away while a superior in the company is talking.[65]

Ironically, while most of us would guess that the trick to working abroad is learning about a foreign culture, in reality our problems often stem from our being oblivious to our own cultural conditioning. Most of us pay no attention to how culture influences our everyday behavior, and because of this, we tend to adapt poorly to situations that are unique or foreign to us. Without realizing it, some managers may even act out of **ethnocentrism**—a tendency to judge foreign people or groups by the standards of one's own culture or group, and to see one's own standards as superior. Such tendencies may be totally unconscious—for example, the assumption that "in England they drive on the *wrong* side of the road," rather than merely on the left. Or they may reflect a lack of awareness of the values underlying a local culture—for example, an assumption that the culture is backward because it does not air American or European television programming, when it is actually focused on maintaining its traditional values and norms.

Assumptions such as these are one reason why people traveling abroad frequently experience **culture shock**—the disorientation and stress associated with being in a foreign environment. Managers are better able to navigate this transition if they are sensitive to their surroundings, including social norms and customs, and readily able to adjust their behavior to such circumstances.[66] Employers can help by identifying some of the cultural norms to expect and by establishing performance measures for behaviors that contribute to success in the host country (for example, the types of communication and direction employees will expect from their manager).

A wealth of cross-cultural research has been conducted on the differences and similarities among various countries. Geert Hofstede, for example, has identified four dimensions along which managers in multinational corporations tend to view cultural differences:

> *Power distance:* the extent to which a society accepts the fact that power in organizations is distributed unequally.

ethnocentrism

The tendency to judge others by the standards of one's group or culture, which are seen as superior.

culture shock

The disorientation and stress associated with being in a foreign environment.

Individualism/collectivism: the extent to which people act on their own or as a part of a group.

Uncertainty avoidance: the extent to which people in a society feel threatened by uncertain and ambiguous situations.

Masculinity/femininity: the extent to which a society values quantity of life (e.g., accomplishment, money) over quality of life (e.g., compassion, beauty).

Figure 6.6 offers a graphic depiction of how 40 different nations differ on the dimensions of individualism/collectivism and power distance. Of course, this depiction

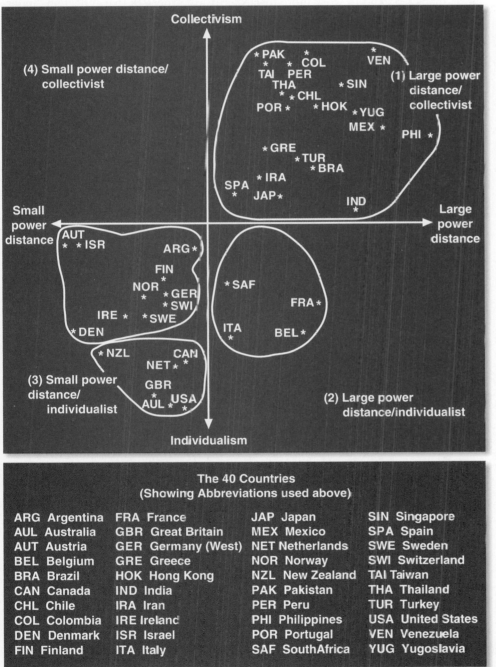

The 40 Countries
(Showing Abbreviations used above)

ARG Argentina	FRA France	JAP Japan	SIN Singapore
AUL Australia	GBR Great Britain	MEX Mexico	SPA Spain
AUT Austria	GER Germany (West)	NET Netherlands	SWE Sweden
BEL Belgium	GRE Greece	NOR Norway	SWI Switzerland
BRA Brazil	HOK Hong Kong	NZL New Zealand	TAI Taiwan
CAN Canada	IND India	PAK Pakistan	THA Thailand
CHL Chile	IRA Iran	PER Peru	TUR Turkey
COL Colombia	IRE Ireland	PHI Philippines	USA United States
DEN Denmark	ISR Israel	POR Portugal	VEN Venezuela
FIN Finland	ITA Italy	SAF SouthAfrica	YUG Yugoslavia

SOURCE: Geert Hofstede, "Motivation, Leadership, and Organization: Do American Theories Apply Abroad?" *Organizational Dynamics* 9, no. 1 (Summer 1980), pp. 42–63. Reprinted by permission.

FIGURE 6.6
Positions of 40 Countries on the Power Distance and Individualism Scales

exaggerates the differences between national traits to some extent. Many Americans prefer to act as part of a group, just as many Taiwanese prefer to act individualistically. And globalization may have already begun to blur some of these distinctions. Still, to suggest no cultural differences exist is equally simplistic. Clearly, cultures such as the United States, which emphasize "rugged individualism," differ significantly from collectivistic cultures such as those of Pakistan, Taiwan, and Colombia. To be effective in cultures that exhibit a greater power distance, managers often must behave more autocratically, perhaps being less participative in decision making. Conversely, in Scandinavian cultures such as Sweden's, for instance, where power distance is low, the very idea that management would make decisions on its own may be questioned. Here, managers tend to work more toward creating processes that reflect an "industrial democracy."

In starting an insurance company in the United Arab Emirates, Texas native Michael Weinberg has learned a lot about that country's business culture. One surprise was the Arabs' far looser sense of time. On an early visit, Weinberg was doubtful when his partners—both Lebanese American and more familiar with the culture—assured him that showing up a few hours late for an appointment would be fine. As it turned out, their hosts were unruffled by their late arrival.

Traditionally, in Arabic culture, people's activities fit around the appointed times for prayer (related to the sun's position) and the climate's cycles of heating and cooling. In addition, participants in a meeting are focused more on the relationships being built than on the next event on their calendar, so appointments often run longer than scheduled. These cultural norms result in a fluid understanding of time.

Still, visitors must be conscientious. They have to take into account the status of their host; a higher-status person expects visitors to be available, even if that means a wait. Weinberg has learned to use waiting time as a chance to catch up on his e-mail. He also calls ahead to confirm meeting times and to notify his host if he'll be late. Also, the office of a company headquartered elsewhere typically follows the customs of its headquarters. Thus, a German company in the UAE will be run with the precision of a German company anywhere else.

Acknowledging the challenges of learning a culture, Weinberg has also experienced the joys, noting the "hospitality, warmth, love, education, and charity" valued by the Arab people he has met.[67]

inpatriate

A foreign national brought in to work at the parent company.

Cross-cultural management extends beyond U.S. employees going abroad. It also includes effective management of **inpatriates**—foreign nationals who are brought in to work at the parent company. These employees provide a valuable service to global companies, because they bring extensive knowledge about how to operate effectively in their home countries. They will also be better prepared to communicate their organization's products and values when they return. But they often have the same types of problems as expatriates and may be even more neglected, because parent-company managers either are more focused on their expatriate program or unconsciously see the home country as normal—requiring no period of adjustment. Yet the language, customs, expense, and lack of local community support in the United States are at least as daunting to inpatriates as the experience of American nationals abroad. Culture shock works both ways.

Effective managers are sensitive to these issues and take them into account in dealing with foreign-national employees. For example, in contrast to American-born employees, coworkers or customers from other countries might tend to communicate less directly, place more emphasis on hierarchy and authority, or make decisions more slowly. For example, an American manager working in Japan sent an e-mail to her American supervisor and Japanese colleagues in which she pointed out flaws in the process they were working on. The supervisor appreciated the alert, but her colleagues were embarrassed by behavior they considered rude; she should have inquired indirectly—say, by wondering what might happen if such a problem did exist. In another situation, a manager from Mexico showed respect for authority by phrasing ideas as questions when he was in a meeting with superiors. Instead of seeing him as appropriately humble, his American colleagues concluded that he was indecisive. In general, managers of international groups can manage these types of misunderstandings by acknowledging cultural differences frankly and finding ways to work around them, by modifying the group (e.g., assigning tasks to subgroups), by setting rules to correct problems that are upsetting group members, or by removing group members who demonstrate they cannot work effectively within a particular situation.[68]

In addition, when working in the United States, foreign nationals will encounter a number of work-related differences Alert managers help their employees adjust. A few basic categories include the following:

Meetings: Americans tend to have specific views about the purpose of meetings and how much time can be spent International workers may have different preconceptions about the nature and length of meetings, and managers should make sure foreign nationals are comfortable with the American approach.

Work(aholic) schedules: Workers from other countries can work long hours but, in countries with strong labor organizations, often get many more weeks of vacation than American workers. And Europeans in particular may balk at working on weekends. Obviously, matters such as these are most helpfully raised and addressed at the beginning of the work assignment.

E-mail: Parts of the world have not yet embraced e-mail and voice mail the way U.S. workers have. Often, others prefer to communicate face to face. Particularly when potential language difficulties exist, at the outset managers will probably want to avoid using e-mail for important matters.

Fast-trackers: Although U.S. companies may take a young MBA graduate and put him or her on the fast track to management, most other cultures still see no substitute for the wisdom gained through experience. (This is something U.S. managers working abroad will also want to keep in mind.) More experienced managers are often a better choice for mentoring inpatriates.

Feedback: Everyone likes praise, but the use of excessive positive feedback tends to be less prevalent in other cultures than in the United States, a useful fact for managers when they give foreign nationals their performance reviews.[69]

Ethical Issues in International Management

If managers are to function effectively in a foreign setting, they must understand how culture influences both how they are perceived and how others behave. One of the most sensitive issues in this regard is how culture plays out in terms of ethical behavior.[70] Issues of right and wrong get blurred as we move from one culture to another, and actions that may be normal and customary in one setting may be unethical—even illegal—in another. The use of bribes, for example, is perceived to be an accepted part of commercial transactions in many Asian, African, Latin American, and Middle Eastern cultures, and even in cultures that view bribery as a form of corruption, some companies offer bribes when they think that it is part of the culture.[71]

In the United States, of course, such behavior is illegal, but what should a U.S. businessperson do when working abroad? Failure to "sweeten" the deal with bribes can result in lost business. Although the Foreign Corrupt Practices Act of 1977 prohibits U.S. employees from bribing foreign officials, one study published in the United States found that less than half of U.S. managers said bribes were unacceptable, and 20 percent actually said they were always acceptable. (Small business gifts or "grease payments" to lower-level officials are permissible under the act, if the dollar amount of the payments would not influence the outcome of the negotiations.) Internationally, countries of the Organization for Economic Cooperation and Development, including the United States, have also prohibited bribes since 1977.[72]

Enforcement of the antibribery law—if only in the United States—did become more vigorous following the high-profile financial scandals at U.S. corporations like Enron and WorldCom. The Sarbanes-Oxley Act, passed in 2002, requires CEOs and CFOs to sign off personally on the veracity of their companies' financial statements. It also requires public companies to establish a confidential system for employees to report wrongdoing and create an ethics code for senior financial officers. Still, even in companies with a solid reputation for ethical conduct, bribery can occur. Johnson & Johnson recently acknowledged that employees in certain subsidiaries were thought to have made bribes related to the sale of medical devices in "two small-market countries." The executive in charge of the subsidiaries accepted responsibility and retired, and the company voluntarily reported the problem to the U.S. Justice Department and the Securities and Exchange Commission, promising to cooperate in any government investigation.[73]

Without an understanding of local customs, ethical standards, and applicable laws, an expatriate may be woefully unprepared to work internationally. To safeguard against the problems and mitigate the punishment if an organization should be found guilty of bribery, the U.S. Sentencing Commission has deemed it essential for firms to establish effective ethics programs and see that they are enforced. Companies such as Caterpillar, General Dynamics, and United Technologies established official codes of conduct for their employees years ago. But since the recent widely publicized scandals at some U.S. corporations, a large number of other companies have hired official ethics officers and increased their ethics efforts.

To put teeth into the corporate ethics initiative, companies with global operations should be at least as engaged in establishing and enforcing standards for ethical behavior as domestic corporations. In Chapter 5, we identified a number of steps organizations should take. They include establishing and communicating the company's values, measuring performance in meeting ethical standards, rewarding employees at all levels for meeting those standards, and taking swift but fair action when violations occur. The primary difference in the international context is that these activities must be carried out with foreign business partners and employees in any subsidiary, franchise, or other company operation.

Interestingly, despite some obvious differences across cultures, research suggests that regardless of nationality or religion, most people embrace a set of five core values: *compassion, fairness, honesty, responsibility,* and *respect for others.* These values lie at the heart of human rights issues and seem to transcend more superficial differences among Americans, Europeans, and Asians. Finding shared values such as these allows companies to build more effective partnerships and alliances, especially across cultures. Perhaps as long as people understand that there is a set of core values, they can permit all kinds of differences in strategy and tactics.[74]

To a large extent, the challenge of managing across borders comes down to the philosophies and systems used to manage people. In moving from domestic to international management, managers need to develop a wide portfolio of behaviors along with the capacity to adjust their behavior for a particular situation. This adjustment, however, should not compromise the values, integrity, and strengths of their home country. When managers can transcend national borders and move among different cultures, they can leverage the strategic capabilities of their organization and take advantage of the opportunities that our global economy has to offer.

Management Close-Up

ASSESSING OUTCOMES AND SEIZING OPPORTUNITIES

Irene Rosenfeld challenged Kraft employees to change their thinking about the company's brands and inspired the firm's local marketers worldwide. Her decision to allow them to tailor products to local tastes freed employees to take a fresh look at their customers' needs.

When studies of Russian consumers revealed a preference for premium instant coffee, Kraft's marketers there repositioned its Carte Noire freeze-dried coffee as an upscale item and offered it at events such as fashion shows, film festivals, and the opera. To capitalize on Europeans' love of dark chocolate, Kraft introduced dark chocolate in Germany under its Milka brand. Knowing that iced tea is popular in the Philippines, Kraft introduced iced-tea-flavored Tang.

But perhaps Kraft's coolest coup was its reinvention of the Oreo in China. Local managers knew the Chinese weren't big cookie eaters. Also, the traditional Oreo, introduced in China in 1996, was too sweet for Chinese tastes and possibly too expensive. A 14-cookie package sold for 72 cents. Kraft tested 20 Oreo prototypes before identifying the right formula. Local managers launched an Oreo ambassador program, using 300 Chinese students riding bikes with wheels resembling Oreo cookies and distributing cookies to passersby. Managers also exploited the growing Chinese interest in milk by extolling the virtues of Oreos with milk. Kraft-sponsored basketball games with an Oreo theme reinforced the concept of "dunking," and TV spots showed children doing the famous "twist, lick, dunk" routine.

Next, Kraft redesigned the Oreo as a chocolate-coated, four-layer wafer stick and repackaged it with fewer cookies at 29 cents. Today, the "new Oreo" is the best-selling cookie in China, even outpacing local brands and doubling its revenues there. Kraft has since introduced the wafer stick in Australia, Canada, and elsewhere in Asia.

Rosenfeld is seeing the benefits of her turnaround plan. But she is not finished: Kraft's global expansion strategy targets 10 markets: Australia, the United Kingdom, Spain, France, Italy, and Germany are countries where the firm hopes to scale up its sales, and China, Russia, Brazil, and Southeast Asia are its highest potential "growth engines." Also, Kraft will focus its overseas efforts on research and development for 10 best-selling brands, which account for about 40 percent of Kraft's international sales and over 60 percent of its profits.[75]

- The Oreo bicycle campaign in China was the idea of local managers, which Irene Rosenfeld characterized as "a stroke of genius that only could have come from local managers." She stated that local managers' opportunities to address local conditions will be "a source of competitive advantage" for Kraft. Do you agree?
- Kraft's strategy for future global growth involves a limited number of markets and products and focuses on going only where management believes the company can win market share. How does this strategy align with Irene Rosenfeld's restructuring plan?

KEY TERMS

Culture shock,   p. 226

Ethnocentrism,   p. 226

Expatriates,   p. 222

Failure rate,   p. 224

Global model,   p. 217

Host-country nationals,   p. 222

Inpatriate,   p. 228

International model,   p. 215

Multinational model,   p. 216

North American Free Trade Agreement (NAFTA),   p. 204

Offshoring,   p. 210

Outsourcing,   p. 210

Third-country nationals,   p. 222

Transnational model,   p. 217

SUMMARY OF LEARNING OBJECTIVES

Now that you have studied Chapter 6, you should be able to:

LO 1 Describe how the world economy is becoming more integrated than ever before.

The gradual lowering of barriers to free trade is making the world economy more integrated. This means that the modern manager operates in an environment that offers more opportunities but is also more complex and competitive than that faced by the manager of a generation ago.

LO 2 Discuss what integration of the global economy means for individual companies and their managers.

In recent years, rapid growth has occurred in world trade, foreign direct investment, and imports. One consequence is that companies around the globe are now finding their home markets under attack from international competitors. The global competitive environment is becoming a much tougher place in which to do business. However, companies now have access to markets that previously were denied to them.

LO 3 **Define the strategies organizations use to compete in the global marketplace.**

The international corporation builds on its existing core capabilities in R&D, marketing, manufacturing, and so on, to penetrate overseas markets. A multinational is a more complex form that usually has fully autonomous units operating in multiple countries. Subsidiaries are given latitude to address local issues such as consumer preferences, political pressures, and economic trends in different regions of the world. The global organization pulls control of overseas operations back into the headquarters and tends to approach the world market as a "unified whole" by combining activities in each country to maximize efficiency on a global scale. A transnational attempts to achieve both local responsiveness and global integration by utilizing a network structure that coordinates specialized facilities positioned around the world.

LO 4 **Compare the various entry modes organizations use to enter overseas markets.**

There are five ways to enter an overseas market: exporting, licensing, franchising, entering into a joint venture, and setting up a wholly owned subsidiary. Each mode has advantages and disadvantages.

LO 5 **Explain how companies can approach the task of staffing overseas operations.**

Most executives use a combination of expatriates, host-country nationals, and third-country nationals. Expatriates sometimes are used to quickly establish new country operations, transfer the company's culture, and bring in a specific technical skill. Host-country nationals have the advantages that they are familiar with local customs and culture, may cost less, and are viewed more favorably by local governments. Third-country nationals often are used as a compromise in politically touchy situations or when home-country expatriates are not available.

LO 6 **Summarize the skills and knowledge managers need to manage globally.**

The causes for failure overseas extend beyond technical capability and include personal and social issues as well. Success depends on a manager's core skills, such as having a multidimensional perspective; having proficiency in line management and decision making; and having resourcefulness, cultural adaptability, sensitivity, team-building skills, and mental maturity. In addition, helpful augmented skills include computer literacy, negotiating skills, strategic vision, and the ability to delegate.

LO 7 **Identify ways in which cultural differences across countries influence management.**

Culture influences our actions and perceptions as well as the actions and perceptions of others. Unfortunately, we are often unaware of how culture influences us, and this can cause problems. Today managers must be able to change their behavior to match the needs and customs of local cultures. For example, in various cultures, employees expect a manager to be either more or less autocratic or participative. By recognizing their cultural differences, people can find it easier to work together collaboratively and benefit from the exchange.

DISCUSSION QUESTIONS

1. Why is the world economy becoming more integrated? What are the implications of this integration for international managers?

2. Imagine you were the CEO of a major company. What approach to global competition would you choose for your firm: international, multinational, global, or transnational? Why?

3. Why have franchises been so popular as a method of international expansion in the fast-food industry? Contrast this with high-tech manufacturing, where joint ventures and partnerships have been more popular. What accounts for the differences across industries?

4. What are the pros and cons of using expatriates, host-country nationals, and third-country nationals to run overseas operations? If you were expanding your business, what approach would you use?

5. If you had entered into a joint venture with a foreign company but knew that women were not treated fairly in that culture, would you consider sending a female expatriate to handle the start-up? Why or why not?

6. What are the biggest cultural obstacles that we must overcome if we are to work effectively in Mexico? Are there different obstacles in France? Japan? China?

CONCLUDING CASE

Travel Wise Spans the Globe

Travel Wise is a small firm with 25 employees based outside Denver, Colorado. "We take travel to new heights," is the firm's slogan, referring to Denver's mile-high elevation above sea level. For more than a decade, Travel Wise has manufactured and sold travel accessories—wallets, passport holders, travel purses, money belts, and the like. Most of the goods are outsourced to overseas manufacturers, where labor and materials are less expensive than they would be in the United States. However, Travel Wise founder Cindy Kirsch works closely with her suppliers in India and China, visiting them frequently to ensure that workers are paid well and treated fairly, earning an income that affords them a comfortable living.

Kirsch wants Travel Wise to expand, and she has discussed her plans with her design, production, marketing, and financial managers. Although each person has an area of expertise, the size of the company dictates that everyone must know the inner workings of the firm. And Kirsch welcomes ideas from all corners. First, Kirsch wants to increase the number of products offered, adding a line of travel clothing. Second, she wants to investigate the possibility of producing the firm's own guidebooks to exotic destinations. Third, she wants to expand the firm's Web site to include blogs, travel information services, and the like. Each of these initiatives requires a strategy that must take into consideration the global business environment. Adding a line of clothing would mean evaluating design and manufacturing alternatives, both in the United States and abroad. Creating a series of travel guides would mean hiring travel writers; establishing relationships with travel bureaus, agencies, and governments; and learning the publishing business. Expanding the Web site would mean determining in which regions of the world most of her customers live and where they want to travel and investigating what types of services consumers might want from the site.

Kirsch and her management staff have several lively discussions before coming up with a plan for the growth of Travel Wise. Then she gathers the entire staff together to discuss the new goals and plans. She solicits ideas from them, and later incorporates those that appear to be viable. Ultimately, Travel Wise has a strategy for its next level of growth. Kirsch is excited but nervous, knowing that her employees are counting on the firm's success. But she knows that they will work around the clock if necessary to make Travel Wise the brand that travelers turn to for more than just accessories—now it will be clothing, guidebooks, and online support. In the next few years, Travel Wise will be taking travel to even greater heights.

QUESTIONS

1. What type of entry mode would you recommend that Travel Wise use for its new line of clothing in U.S. markets? In foreign markets? Should the clothing be outsourced to suppliers overseas, or should Travel Wise consider building its own manufacturing facility here in the United States?

2. What features and services might Travel Wise offer on its expanded Web site that would appeal to travelers from Europe, Asia, and other parts of the world?

3. What types of relationships must Travel Wise forge in other countries to produce accurate, up-to-date, insightful travel guides?

EXPERIENTIAL EXERCISES

6.1 Understanding Multinational Corporations

OBJECTIVE

To gain a more thorough picture of how a multinational corporation operates.

INSTRUCTIONS

Perhaps the best way to gain an understanding of multinational corporations is to study a specific organization and how it operates throughout the world. Select a multinational corporation, find several articles on that company, and answer the questions on the Multinational Worksheet.

Multinational Worksheet

1. What is the primary business of this organization?

_____

_____

_____

_____

2. To what extent does the company engage in multinational operations? For example, does it only market its products and/or services in other countries, or does it also have overseas manufacturing facilities? What portion of the firm's operating income comes from overseas operations?

_____

_____

_____

_____

3. What percentage of the managers in international activities are American (or from the country the corporation considers home)? Are these managers given any special training before their international assignment?

_____

_____

_____

_____

4. What characteristics of the organization have contributed to its success or lack of success in the international marketplace?

_____

_____

_____

_____

SOURCE: R. R. McGrath Jr., *Exercises in Management Fundamentals* (Englewood Cliffs, NJ: Prentice Hall, 1985), p. 177. Reprinted by permission of Prentice Hall, Inc.

6.2 Cross-Cultural Communication Simulation

In this simulation, you will play the part of a manager employed by one of three firms—a commercial bank, a construction firm, and a hotel development company—that are planning a joint venture to build a new hotel and retail shopping complex in Perth, Australia. They come from three different cultures: Blue, Green, and Red. Each has specific cultural values, traits, customs, and practices.

You are a manager in the company to which you have been assigned. You will attend the kickoff get-together for the three-day meeting during which the three companies will negotiate the details of the partnership. Your management team consists of a vice president and a number of other managers. Consider the types of topics that would be discussed by the various corporations at an initial meeting.

INSTRUCTIONS

Your instructor will provide you with information pertaining to your culture. You will be given about 15 minutes to meet with your fellow corporate members, during which you should:

1. Select a leader.
2. Discuss what your objectives and approaches will be at the opening get-together.
3. Using the description of your assigned culture, practice how you will talk and behave until you are reasonably familiar with your cultural orientation. Be sure to practice conversation distance, greeting rituals, and nonverbal behavior.

You will then return to the kick-off meeting where you will meet with the other firms. As the social proceeds, interact with the managers from the other companies. Maintain the role you have been assigned, but do not discuss it explicitly. Notice how other people react to you and how you react to them. We will discuss the experience after it is over.

Upon completing this activity, answer the following questions:

1. In what ways did your perceptions of others and their differences influence how you interacted with them and your ability to achieve your goals?

_____

_____

_____

_____

2. What did you learn about yourself and others through this activity? Discuss your strengths and weaknesses in cross-cultural interaction.

_____

_____

_____

_____

3. What were things you or others did or said that enabled or hindered you from adjusting to other people and their culture: (a) in this activity? (b) in similar real-life situations?

_____

_____

_____

_____

4. What lessons did you learn from this activity? What steps can you take to improve your ability to understand and appreciate differences?

_____

_____

_____

_____

SOURCE: Daphne A. Jameson, "Using a Simulation to Teach Intercultural Communication in Business Communication Courses," *Bulletin of the Association for Business Communication (Business Communication Quarterly)* 55, no. 4 (March 1993), pp. 1–10.

chapter

7 Entrepreneurship

" A man is known by the company he organizes. "

— Ambrose Bierce

LEARNING OBJECTIVES

After studying Chapter 7, you will be able to:

LO 1 Describe why people become entrepreneurs and what it takes, personally. p. 240

LO 2 Summarize how to assess opportunities to start new businesses. p. 243

LO 3 Identify common causes of success and failure. p. 250

LO 4 Discuss common management challenges. p. 252

LO 5 Explain how to increase your chances of success, including good business planning. p. 256

LO 5 Describe how managers of large companies can foster entrepreneurship. p. 260

CHAPTER OUTLINE

Entrepreneurship
Why Become an Entrepreneur?
What Does It Take to Succeed?
What Business Should You Start?
What Does It Take, Personally?
Success and Failure
Increasing Your Chances of Success

Corporate Entrepreneurship
Building Support for Your Idea
Building Intrapreneurship
Management Challenges
Entrepreneurial Orientation

Management Close-Up

Richard Branson seems to have business in his blood. He was only a teen when he started his first company, a magazine called *Student,* in the mid-1960s. In 1970 Branson launched his next enterprise—the one that generated his first fortune, the iconic Virgin Records. Since then, Branson has built 200 other businesses, all under the Virgin umbrella: a global airline, a mobile phone enterprise, and companies in financial services, publishing, and retailing, to name just a few. Today, the Virgin empire has nearly 50,000 employees in 29 countries, and Branson has a mind-boggling net worth of more than $5 billion. In 1999 he was knighted by Queen Elizabeth II.

{ With 200 successful companies to his credit, Richard Branson has a true knack for business. It seems that everything he touches turns to gold. As you read this chapter, consider how Branson's traits and talents have helped him succeed in his different endeavors. }

While Branson's track record is extraordinary, his formula for creating businesses is actually pretty simple. He begins by observing an industry—typically one that has been around a while, is lackluster, and may not treat its customers very well. Then he thinks about what would make the experience more enjoyable. How can he offer customers something better? What would attract them? Then, he builds his better alternative and breaks into the market.

That is how Branson launched Virgin Atlantic Airlines in 1984. The airline industry was controlled by a few carriers offering passengers essentially the same level of service. With passenger complaints on the rise, Branson saw an opportunity to provide a more exciting, more memorable experience. Virgin Atlantic planes have roomy leather seats and video touch screens that enable passengers to choose a movie and order a meal. Many flights have stand-up beverage service so that passengers can stretch their legs and chat to pass the time, and others offer massages. Today, Virgin Atlantic has more than 120 planes, nearly 14,000 employees, and about $5 billion in revenues. The company promotes Virgin Atlantic as "the world's first truly global airline." Virgin Atlantic is looking to become a dominant player in U.S. domestic air travel as well.[1]

entrepreneurship

The pursuit of lucrative opportunities by enterprising individuals.

The bottom line
Innovation

Entrepreneurship is inherently about innovation—creating a new venture where one didn't exist before.

small business

A business having fewer than 100 employees, independently owned and operated, not dominant in its field, and not characterized by many innovative practices.

entrepreneurial venture

A new business having growth and high profitability as primary objectives.

Ryan Clark (bottom) who recently won the 2009 Student Leadership Award from the Black Engineer of the Year Awards, poses with his twin brother, Ashton, at the Coordinated Science Laboratory in Urbana, Illinois. The Clark brothers are both juniors at the University of Illinois and in the past seven years have formed more than a dozen successful Web-based businesses, with products ranging from online music to sports apparel to parking-place reservations.

As Richard Branson and countless others have demonstrated, great opportunity is available to talented entrepreneurs who are willing to work hard to achieve their dreams. **Entrepreneurship** occurs when an enterprising individual pursues a lucrative opportunity.[2] To be an entrepreneur is to initiate and build an organization, rather than being only a passive part of one.[3] It involves creating *new* systems, resources, or processes to produce *new* goods or services and/or serve *new* markets.[4]

Entrepreneurship differs from management generally and from small-business management in particular. An entrepreneur *is* a manager but engages in additional activities that not all managers do.[5] Although managers operate in a more formal management hierarchy, with more clearly defined authority and responsibility, entrepreneurs use networks of contacts more than formal authority. And although managers usually prefer to own assets, entrepreneurs often rent or use assets on a temporary basis. Some say that managers often are slower to act and tend to avoid risk, whereas entrepreneurs are quicker to act and actively manage risk.

How does entrepreneurship differ from managing a small business?[6] A **small business** is often defined as having fewer than 100 employees, being independently owned and operated, not dominant in its field, and not characterized by many innovative practices. Small-business owners tend not to manage particularly aggressively, and they expect normal, moderate sales, profits, and growth. In contrast, an **entrepreneurial venture** has growth and high profitability as primary objectives. Entrepreneurs manage aggressively and develop innovative strategies, practices, and products. They and their financial backers usually seek rapid growth, immediate and high profits, and sometimes a quick sellout with large capital gains.

The Excitement of Entrepreneurship   Consider these words from Jeffry Timmons, a leading entrepreneurship scholar and author: "During the past 30 years, America has unleashed the most revolutionary generation the nation has experienced since its founding in 1776. This new generation of entrepreneurs has altered permanently the economic and social structure of this nation and the world . . . It will determine more than any other single impetus how the nation and the world will live, work, learn, and lead in this century and beyond."[7] Timmons had written previously, "We are in the midst of a silent revolution—a triumph of the creative and entrepreneurial spirit of humankind throughout the world. I believe its impact on the 21st century will equal or exceed that of the Industrial Revolution on the 19th and 20th."[8]

Overhype? Sounds like it could be, but it's not. Entrepreneurship is transforming economies all over the world, and the global economy in general. In the United States since 1980, more than 95 percent of the wealth has been created by entrepreneurs.[9] It's been estimated that since World War II, small entrepreneurial firms have generated 95 percent of all radical innovation in the United States. The Small Business Administration has found that in states with more small-business start-ups, statewide economies tend to grow faster and employment levels tend to be higher than in states with less entrepreneurship.[10] An estimated 20 million Americans are running a young business or actively trying to start one.[11]

The self-employed love the entrepreneurial process, and they report the highest levels of pride, satisfaction, and income. Importantly, entrepreneurship is not about the privileged descendants of the Rockefellers and the Vanderbilts—it provides opportunity and upward mobility for anyone who performs well.[12]

Myths about Entrepreneurship   Simply put, entrepreneurs generate new ideas and turn them into business ventures.[13] But entrepreneurship is not simple, and it is

TABLE 7.1   Some Myths about Entrepreneurs

Myth 1—Anyone can start a business.
Reality—The easiest part is starting up. What is hardest is surviving, sustaining, and building a venture so its founders can realize a harvest.
Myth 2—Entrepreneurs are gamblers.
Reality—Successful entrepreneurs take very careful, calculated risks. They do not deliberately seek to take more risk or to take unnecessary risk, nor do they shy away from unavoidable risk.
Myth 3—Entrepreneurs want the whole show to themselves.
Reality—It is extremely difficult to grow a higher potential venture by working single-handedly. Higher potential entrepreneurs build a team, an organization, and a company.
Myth 4—Entrepreneurs are their own bosses and completely independent.
Reality—Entrepreneurs are far from independent. They have to serve many masters and constituencies, including partners, investors, customers, suppliers, creditors, employees, families, and social and community obligations.
Myth 5—Entrepreneurs work longer and harder than managers in big companies.
Reality—There is no such evidence. Some work more, some less.
Myth 6—Entrepreneurs experience a great deal of stress and pay a high price.
Reality—No doubt about it: Being an entrepreneur is stressful and demanding. But entrepreneurs find their jobs very satisfying. They are healthier, and are much less likely to retire than those who work for others.
Myth 7—Entrepreneurs are motivated solely by the quest for the almighty dollar.
Reality—Entrepreneurs seeking high potential ventures are more driven by building enterprises and realizing long-term capital gains than by instant gratification through high salaries and perks. Feeling in control of their own destinies, and realizing their vision and dreams, are also powerful motivators. Money is viewed as a tool and a way of keeping score.
Myth 8—Entrepreneurs seek power and control over others.
Reality—Successful entrepreneurs are driven by the quest for responsibility, achievement, and results, rather than for power for its own sake. By virtue of their accomplishments, they may be powerful and influential, but these are more the by-products of the entrepreneurial process than a driving force behind it.
Myth 9—If an entrepreneur is talented, success will happen in a year or two.
Reality—An old maxim among venture capitalists says it all: the lemons ripen in two and a half years, but the pearls take seven or eight. Rarely is a new business established solidly in less than three or four years.
Myth 10—Any entrepreneur with a good idea can raise venture capital.
Reality—Of the ventures of entrepreneurs with good ideas who seek out venture capital, only 1 to 3 out of 100 are funded.
Myth 11—If an entrepreneur has enough start-up capital, he or she can't miss.
Reality—Too much money at the outset often leads to lack of discipline and impulsive spending that usually result in serious problems and failure.
Myth 12—Entrepreneurs are lone wolves and cannot work with others.
Reality—The most successful entrepreneurs are leaders who build great teams and effective relationships working with peers, directors, investors, key customers, key suppliers, and the like.
Myth 13—Unless you attained 600 on your SATs or GMATs you'll never be a successful entrepreneur.
Reality—Entrepreneurial IQ is a unique combination of creativity, motivation, integrity, leadership, team building, analytical ability and ability to deal with ambiguity and adversity.

SOURCE: Adapted from J. A. Timmons and S. Spinelli, *New Venture Creation*, 6th ed., pp. 67–68. © 2004 The McGraw-Hill Companies.

frequently misunderstood. Read Table 7.1 to start you thinking about the myths and realities of this important career option.

Here is another myth, not in the table: Being an entrepreneur is great because you can "get rich quick" and enjoy a lot of leisure time while your employees run the company. But the reality is much more difficult. During the start-up period, you

entrepreneur

Individuals who establish a new organization without the benefit of corporate sponsorship.

intrapreneurs

New-venture creators working inside big companies.

are likely to have a lot of bad days. It's exhausting. Even if you don't have employees, you should expect communications breakdowns and other "people problems" with agents, vendors, distributors, family, subcontractors, lenders, whomever. Dan Bricklin, the founder of VisiCalc, advises that the most important thing to remember is this: "You are not your business. On those darkest days when things aren't going so well—and trust me, you will have them—try to remember that your company's failures don't make you an awful person. Likewise, your company's successes don't make you a genius or superhuman."[14]

As you read this chapter, you will learn about two primary sources of new-venture creation: independent entrepreneurship and intrapreneurship. **Entrepreneurs** are individuals who establish a new organization without the benefit of corporate support. **Intrapreneurs** are new-venture creators working inside big companies; they are corporate entrepreneurs, using their company's resources to build a profitable line of business based on a fresh new idea.[15]

Entrepreneurship

LO 1

Table 7.2 lists some extraordinary entrepreneurs. The companies they founded are famously successful—and all of the founders started in their 20s. Two young entrepreneurs who started a highly successful business are Tony Hsieh and Nick Swinmurn. In

Tony Hsieh is listed as an extaordinary entrepreneur. At the age of 24, he had already sold off his first venture and took on Zappos.com, where he continues to work today.

1999, Swinmurn had the then-new idea to sell shoes online, but he needed money to get started. Hsieh, who at age 24 had already just sold his first start-up (LinkExchange, sold to Microsoft for $265 million), agreed to take a chance on the new venture. Swinmurn has moved on, but Hsieh remains at the helm of the company as the CEO of Zappos.com. In a recent year, Zappos.com enjoyed sales of $1 billion.[16]

The real, more complete story of entrepreneurship is not about the famous people in Table 7.2—its mostly about people you've probably never heard of. They have built companies, thrived personally, created jobs, and made positive contributions to their communities through their businesses. Or they're just starting out.

Why Become an Entrepreneur?

Bill Gross has started dozens of companies. When he was a boy, he devised homemade electronic games and sold candy for a profit to friends. In college, he built and sold plans for a solar heating device, started a stereo equipment company, and sold a software product to Lotus. In 1996, he started Idealab, which hatched dozens of start-ups on the Internet. Recently launched Idealab companies include one that is making a three-dimensional (3-D) printer, and another that sells robotics technology to supermarkets and toy companies. Through its Energy Innovations subsidiary, Idealab also has branched out into the now-hot market for alternative-energy technology.[17]

Why do Bill Gross and other entrepreneurs do what they do? Entrepreneurs start their own firms because of the challenge, the profit potential, and the enormous

Entrepreneurial	Company Founder(s)
Microsoft	Bill Gates and Paul Allen
Netscape	Marc Andreessen
Dell Computers	Michael Dell
Gateway 2000	Ted Waitt
McCaw Cellular	Craig McCaw
Apple Computers	Steve Jobs and Steve Wozniak
Digital Equipment Corporation	Ken and Stan Olsen
Federal Express	Fred Smith
Genentech	Robert Swanson
Polaroid	Edward Land
Nike	Phil Knight
Lotus Development Corporation	Mitch Kapor
Facebook	Mark Zuckerberg

TABLE 7.2
Mega-Entrepreneurs Who Started in Their 20s

SOURCES: J. A. Timmons, *New Venture Creation*, 6th ed. (New York: McGraw-Hill/Irwin, 2004), p. 7. © 2004 The McGraw-Hill Companies.

satisfaction they hope lies ahead. People starting their own businesses are seeking a better quality of life than they might have at big companies. They seek independence and a feeling of being part of the action. They feel tremendous satisfaction in building something from nothing, seeing it succeed, and watching the market embrace their ideas and products.

People also start their own companies when they see their progress or ideas blocked at big corporations. When people are laid off, they often try to start businesses of their own. And when employed people believe they will not receive a promotion or are frustrated by bureaucracy or other features of corporate life, they may quit and become entrepreneurs. Years ago, Philip Catron became disillusioned with his job as a manager at ChemLawn because he concluded that the lawn care company's reliance on pesticides contributed to illness in its employees, its customers' pets, and even in the lawns themselves. Catron left the company to start NaturaLawn of America, based on the practice of integrated pest management, which uses natural and nontoxic products as much as possible, reducing pesticide use on lawns by 85 percent. Over two decades, Catron built NaturaLawn into 72 franchises in 25 states—and helped integrated pest management become mainstream, as even his former employer, now part of TruGreen ChemLawn, has changed many of its practices.[18]

Immigrants also may find conventional paths to economic success closed to them and turn to entrepreneurship.[19] For example, the Cuban community in Miami has produced many successful entrepreneurs, as has the Vietnamese community throughout the United States. Sometimes the immigrant's experience gives him or her useful knowledge about foreign suppliers or markets that present an attractive business opportunity. Rakesh Kamdar immigrated to the United States from India to study computer science, but while here, he saw a way he could meet the huge U.S. demand for nursing talent. He set up DB Healthcare to recruit nurses from India to work in the United States. Unlike U.S. competitors that had failed, Kamdar set up meetings at DB's Indian offices, and he invited nurses to attend with their husbands, parents, and in-laws. His staff discussed family and individual questions related to the American jobs. With this strategy, DB Healthcare was earning millions of dollars within a few years.[20]

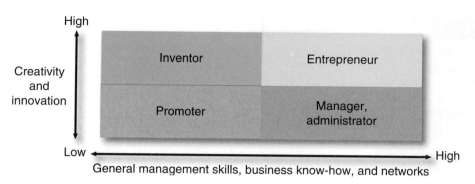

FIGURE 7.1
Who Is the Entrepreneur?

SOURCE: J. A. Timmons, *New Venture Creation,* 6th ed. (New York: McGraw-Hill/Irwin, 2004), p. 67–68 exhibit 20.13. © 2004 The McGraw-Hill Companies.

What Does It Take to Succeed?

What can we learn from the people who start their own companies and succeed? What talents enable entrepreneurs to succeed? We express these characteristics in general terms with Figure 7.1. Successful entrepreneurs are innovators and also have good knowledge and skills in management, business, and networking.[21] In contrast, inventors may be highly creative but often lack the skills to turn their ideas into a successful business. Manager-administrators may be great at ensuring efficient operations but aren't necessarily innovators. Promoters have a different set of marketing and selling skills—useful for entrepreneurs, but those skills can be hired, whereas innovativeness and business management skills remain the essential combination for successful entrepreneurs.

FROM THE PAGES OF
BusinessWeek

Best Entrepreneurs 25 and Under

SmallBiz's top young entrepreneur went from selling shirts out of his car to opening his own stores. Who are the country's most promising young entrepreneurs? With help from our readers, we set out to answer that question in our fourth annual Best Entrepreneurs 25 and Under Special Report. As in previous years, we posted a nomination form on the *SmallBiz* channel of *BusinessWeek*'s Web site and asked readers to recommend business whizzes who were no more than 25 years old and ran their own companies. We received a record number of nominations, ranging from the founder of an online TV network aimed at college students to a maker of flavored plastics.

After the call for nominations ended in July, our staff sifted through the entries, choosing the 25 most impressive. In this we had some high-profile help, from Virgin's Sir Richard Branson, *BusinessWeek* contributor and Duke University executive-in-residence Vivek Wadhwa, and Bo Fishback, vice-president of entrepreneurship at the Kauffman Foundation. As in prior years, some of the finalists were backed by angel investors and venture capitalists, some were already profitable, and most made heavy use of the Internet. The biggest difference? More entrepreneurs voiced a desire not only to make a profit but also to make the world a better place, with a large number focused on education. We posted profiles of the 25 finalists online, asked readers to vote for the most outstanding, and received a record number of votes.

Now (drumroll, please!) the results are in. Music school dropout Johnny Earle, who has since turned 26, led the pack with more than 4,700 votes for Johnny Cupcakes, a line of limited-edition T-shirts.

http://www.businessweek.com/magazine/content/08_70/s0810022684046.htm

SOURCE: Nick Leiber, Stacy Perman, and John Tozzi, "Best Entrepreneurs 25 and Under," *BusinessWeek,* October 17, 2008.

What Business Should You Start?

You need a good idea, and you need to find or create the right opportunity. The following discussion offers some general considerations for choosing a type of business. For guidance in matching your unique strengths and interests to a business type, another helpful resource is *What Business Should I Start? Seven Steps to Discovering the Ideal Business for You*, by Rhonda Abrams.

The Idea   Many entrepreneurs and observers say that in contemplating your business, you must start with a great idea. A great product, a viable market, and good timing are essential ingredients in any recipe for success.

Some of the most exciting ideas today involve products that meet a very basic need at a very low cost. Socially responsible entrepreneurs are combining technological skills with concern for people who live without access to clean water and reliable electricity, creating high-tech projects that can improve lives in poor communities. For example, Nedjip Tozun and Sam Goldman founded D.light Design to develop and sell solar-powered lights, made with low-priced solar panels, efficient LEDs, and sophisticated power management software.

Tozun and Goldman see their market in developing countries, where many people rely on kerosene and diesel lamps, which not only provide a poor quality of lighting but also pollute the air and present a serious danger from fires and serious burns. Although the $25 price tag for a D.light lamp is high for many communities where people earn less than a dollar a day, when family members pool their resources, they find that the lamp allows them to work longer hours, save money spent on fuel, and skip long trips to buy it, so the purchase is a good investment in a cleaner, safer life.

D.light Design is a business, not a charity. Tozun and Goldman see their buyers as "great customers" who see a "clear value proposition" in their product. They also see potential to expand into other solar-powered products, building their business as they meet basic needs.[22]

Many great organizations have been built on a different kind of idea: the founder's desire to build a great organization, rather than to offer a particular product.[23] Examples abound. Bill Hewlett and David Packard decided to start a company and then figured out what to make. J. Willard Marriott knew he wanted to be in business for himself but didn't have a product in mind until he opened an A&W root beer stand. Masaru Ibuka had no specific product idea when he founded Sony in 1945. Sony's first product attempt, a rice cooker, didn't work, and its first product (a tape recorder) didn't sell.

You don't have to be first with a product idea if you can figure out a way to execute an existing idea better than the competition. Federal Express succeeded by borrowing DHL's method of using jets to race ahead of UPS in overnight delivery service in the United States. IBM combined existing components and Microsoft's operating system to launch a personal computer that eventually beat Apple's and Atari's earlier models. And Best Buy raised funds in the stock market to expand a line of stores aimed at competing with Circuit City, which is now out of business.[24]

The company stayed alive by making and selling crude heating pads.

Many now-great companies had early failures. But the founders persisted; they believed in themselves and in their dreams of building great organizations. Be prepared to kill or revise an idea, but never give up on your company—this has been a prescription for success for many great entrepreneurs and business leaders. Think about Sony, Disney, Hewlett-Packard, Procter & Gamble, IBM, and Wal-Mart: their founders' greatest achievements—their greatest ideas—are their organizations.[25]

Harren Jhoti, Chief Executive and founder of a drug discovery and development company called Astex Therapeutics, receives the Chemistry World Entrepreneur of the Year Award at the annual Royal Society of Chemistry Innovations Awards in London. Mr. Jhoti built Astex over eight years, raising over £63 million. The annual award is presented to an individual who has established or contributed to the growth of a small or medium sized chemistry-related company.

The Opportunity Entrepreneurs spot, create, and exploit opportunities in a variety of ways.[26] Entrepreneurial companies can explore domains that big companies avoid and introduce goods or services that capture the market because they are simpler, cheaper, more accessible, or more convenient. While Shayne McQuade was touring Spain, taking a break from his career as a management consultant, he noticed that he had a problem figuring out how to recharge his cell phone. After his trip, McQuade developed a way to make backpacks and messenger bags containing solar panels. His company, Voltaic Systems, contracts to have the bags manufactured in China from material made out of recycled plastic. The products are sold in sporting goods stores, and McQuade is trying to get them stocked by Sam's Club. Eventually he hopes to offer briefcases with the solar power to recharge a laptop.[27]

To spot opportunities, think carefully about events and trends as they unfold. Consider, for example, the following possibilities:[28]

Technological discoveries. Start-ups in biotechnology, microcomputers, and nanotechnology followed technological advances. Howard Berke, who has two Nobel prize winners on his payroll, established Konarka Technologies to offer products based on advances in solar cells. In contrast to the older technology of solar panels, solar cells are based on organic chemicals, so they are more flexible and can be installed in a variety of projects (see the previous example of Voltaic Systems).[29]

Demographic changes. All kinds of health care organizations have sprung up to serve an aging population, from Fit After Fifty exercise studios to assisted-living facilities. One business that targets both the aging American population and the growth in single-parent and dual-career households is Errands Done Right, located in Harrisburg, Pennsylvania. The service, launched by Donna Barber and Dawn Carter, is designed to assist those who are pressed for time or have difficulty getting around.[30]

Lifestyle and taste changes. Start-ups have capitalized on new clothing and music trends, desire for fast food, and growing interest in sports. In recent years, more consumers want to help take care of the environment, and more businesses are concerned about showing consumers that they care, too.

Economic dislocations, such as booms or failures. In recent years, rising oil prices have spurred a variety of developments related to alternative energy or energy efficiency. Howard Berke, the entrepreneur behind Konarka Technologies' solar cells, says, "I don't come at this as an environmentalist. I come at this from good business sense. The cost of renewables . . . is more competitive when compared with fossil fuel."[31]

Calamities such as wars and natural disasters. The terrorist attacks of September 2001 spurred concern about security, and entrepreneurs today are still pursuing ideas to help government agencies prevent future attacks. The more recent hurricanes on the Gulf Coast raised awareness of the importance of preparing for emergencies.

Government initiatives and rule changes. Deregulation spawned new airlines and trucking companies. Whenever the government tightens energy-efficiency requirements, opportunities become available for entrepreneurs developing ideas for cutting energy use.

Franchises One important type of opportunity is the franchise. You may know intuitively what franchising is. Or, at least you can name some prominent franchises: McDonald's, Jiffy Lube, the Body Shop, Dunkin' Donuts, add your favorites here.

Franchising is an entrepreneurial alliance between two organizations, the franchisor and the franchisee.[32] The franchisor is the innovator who has created at least one successful store and seeks partners to operate the same con-

In a recent three-year period, almost 900 new franchise concepts were launched in the United States. The categories with the most new concepts were food retailing, service businesses, and sports and recreation. The categories that added the most new franchise units were service businesses, building and construction, and child-related services.[34]

cept in other local markets. For the franchisee, the opportunity is wealth creation via a proven (but not failureproof) business concept, with the added advantage of the franchisor's expertise. For the franchisor, the opportunity is wealth creation through growth. The partnership is manifest in a trademark or brand, and together the partners' mission is to maintain and build the brand. The Noodles & Company chain of fast-casual restaurants first grew by opening 79 company-owned locations. Management concluded that it could grow at a faster pace through franchising. Establishing standard menus and prices took a year, but franchising has helped the company almost double its revenues in just two years.[33]

People often assume that buying a franchise is less risky than starting a business from scratch, but the evidence is mixed. One study that followed businesses for six years found the opposite of the popular assumption: 65 percent of the franchises studied were operating at the end of the period, while 72 percent of independent businesses were still operating. One reason may be that the franchises involved mostly a few, possibly riskier, industries. A study that compared only restaurants over a three-year period found that 43 percent of the franchises and 39 percent of independent restaurants remained in business.[35]

If you are contemplating a franchise, consider its market presence (local, regional, or national), market share and profit margins, national programs for marketing and purchasing, the nature of the business, including required training and degree of field support, terms of the license agreement (e.g., 20 years with automatic renewal versus less than 10 years or no renewal), capital required, and franchise fees and royalties.[36]

Although some people think success with a franchise is a no-brainer, would-be franchisees have a lot to consider. Luckily, plenty of useful sources exist for learning more, including the International Franchise Association (http://www.franchise.org), the Small Business Administration (http://www.sba.gov), Franchise Chat (http://www.franchise-chat.com), and the Business Franchise Directory (http://www.business-franchisedirectory.com). In addition, the Federal Trade Commission investigates complaints of deceptive claims by franchisors and publishes information about those cases. Dale Cantone, who heads the Franchise and Business Opportunities unit for Maryland's attorney general, advises people to take their time in investigating business opportunities, consulting with an accountant or lawyer who has experience in franchising.[37]

The Next Frontiers The next frontiers for entrepreneurship—where do they lie? Throughout history, aspiring entrepreneurs have asked this question. When a business magazine asked prominent investors in new businesses to name the best ideas for a new start-up, their responses included next-generation batteries with enough juice to power cars after a seconds-long charge, longer-lasting tiny batteries to keep cell phones and

franchising

An entrepreneurial alliance between a franchisor (an innovator who has created at least one successful store and wants to grow) and a franchisee (a partner who manages a new store of the same type in a new location).

A flight into space might become as easy as booking a flight to Florida thanks to Burt Rutan. His idea to launch people into space may have opened the door for an entire space tourism industry.

cameras running for more hours, implantable wireless devices that can monitor heart-beats or blood sugar levels, and online social networking sites that focus on allowing artists and musicians to share and promote their works.[38]

One fascinating opportunity for entrepreneurs is outer space. Historically, the space market was driven by the government and was dominated by big defense contractors such as Boeing and Lockheed Martin. But now, with demand for satellite launches and potential profits skyrocketing, smaller entrepreneurs are entering the field. Some of the most dramatic headlines involve space tourism. Zero Gravity already operates flights in converted Boeing 727 jets that simulate the experience of weightlessness by flying up and down like a roller-coaster 10,000 feet above the earth. Famous passengers who signed up for the $3,500 flights have included business owner Martha Stewart and physicist Stephen Hawking.[39] Other recent ventures in space have included using satellites for automobile navigation, tracking trucking fleets, and monitoring flow rates and leaks in pipelines; testing designer drugs in the near-zero-gravity environment; and using remote sensing to monitor global warming, spot fish concentrations, and detect crop stress for precision farming.

Homeland security is another newly burgeoning industry. A vast number of companies in a wide range of industries are attempting to benefit—for example, baggage screening, smallpox vaccines, capturing arrival and departure information on travelers, explosives detection systems, and sensors for airborne pathogens. Some of the growth is supported by government investment in security-related technology. For example, the state of Illinois recently gave grants to SSS Research, which develops database software that helps terrorism analysts, and RiverGlass, which develops software that connects databases to find patterns describing high-risk people. In Michigan, the state-funded Venture Michigan I Fund supports investment in Michigan-based start-ups in the security and other growth industries.[40]

The Internet　　The Internet is a business frontier that continues to expand. With Internet commerce, as with any start-up, entrepreneurs need sound business models and practices. During the heady days of the Internet rush, many entrepreneurs and investors thought revenues and profits were unimportant and all that mattered was to attract visitors to their Web sites ("capture eyeballs"). But you need to watch costs carefully, and you want to break even and achieve profitability as soon as possible.[41]

At least five successful business models have proven successful in the e-commerce market: transaction fee, advertising support, intermediary, affiliate, and subscription models.[42] In the **transaction fee model,** companies charge a fee for goods or services. Amazon.com and online travel agents are prime examples. In the **advertising support model,** advertisers pay the site operator to gain access to the demographic group that visits the operator's site. More than one-third of online ads are for financial services, and another 22 percent are for Web media. More than half of the ads appear on e-mail pages.[43]

The **intermediary model** has eBay as the premier example, bringing buyers and sellers together and charging a commission for each sale. With the **affiliate model,** sites pay commissions to other sites to drive business to their own sites. Zazzle.com, Spreadshirt.com, and Cafe-Press.com are variations on this model. They sell custom-decorated gift items such as mugs and T-shirts. Designers are the affiliates; they choose basic, undecorated products (such as a plain shirt) and add their own designs, creating the customized products offered to consumers. Visitors to a designer's Web site can link to, say, Zazzle and place an order, or they can go directly to Zazzle to shop. Either

---

transaction fee model

Charging fees for goods and services.

advertising support model

Charging fees to advertise on a site.

intermediary model

Charging fees to bring buyers and sellers together.

affiliate model

Charging fees to direct site visitors to other companies' sites.

Customized products are just a click away. Zazzle.com produces customized T-shirts, posters, and postage stamps. It has built a library of over 500,000 digital images, including more than 3,500 items of copyrighted material licensed from Walt Disney's legendary characters such as Mickey Mouse and Goofy. Shown here is a sample of customized postage stamps provided by Zazzle.

way, Zazzle sets the basic price, and the designer gets about 10 percent. Spreadshirt and CafePress let designers choose how much above the base price they want to charge consumers for the decorated product.[44] Finally, Web sites using the **subscription model** charge a monthly or annual fee for site visits or access to site content. Newspapers and magazines are good examples.

subscription model

Charging fees for site visits.

What about businesses whose primary focus is not e-commerce? Start-ups and established small companies can create attractive Web sites that add to their professionalism, give them access to more customers, and bring them closer to suppliers, investors, and service providers. Traditional companies can move much more quickly than in the past and save money on activities including customer service/support, technical support, data retrieval, public relations, investor relations, selling, requests for product literature, and purchasing. All this is possible even as the costs of computing continue to drop and as more free software tools are being disseminated. As a result, setting up shop online costs less than it ever did.

Munjal Shah's company, Riya, has set up an online shopping service called Like.com, which uses visual recognition software to help shoppers find products that look similar to one another. The search software, Shah says, was based on open-source programs and cost about $50,000; five years ago, it would have been unaffordable. In addition, because current computer chips work more efficiently, the cost to run Riya's Web servers is about one-tenth of what he would have paid a few years ago.[45]

What Does It Take, Personally?

Many people assume that there is an "entrepreneurial personality." No single personality type predicts entrepreneurial success, but you are more likely to succeed as an entrepreneur if you exhibit certain characteristics:[46]

1. *Commitment and determination:* Successful entrepreneurs are decisive, tenacious, disciplined, willing to sacrifice, and able to immerse themselves in their enterprises.
2. *Leadership:* They are self-starters, team builders, superior learners, and teachers. Communicating a vision for the future of the company—an essential component of leadership that you'll learn more about in Chapter 12—has a direct impact on venture growth.[47]
3. *Opportunity obsession:* They have an intimate knowledge of customers' needs, are market driven, and are obsessed with value creation and enhancement.
4. *Tolerance of risk, ambiguity, and uncertainty:* They are calculated risk takers and risk managers, tolerant of stress, and able to resolve problems.
5. *Creativity, self-reliance, and ability to adapt:* They are open-minded, restless with the status quo, able to learn quickly, highly adaptable, creative, skilled at conceptualizing, and attentive to details.
6. *Motivation to excel:* They have a clear results orientation, set high but realistic goals, have a strong drive to achieve, know their own weaknesses and strengths, and focus on what can be done rather than on the reasons things can't be done.

Bill Gross, whom you met in our earlier discussion of "Why Become an Entrepreneur," exemplifies some of these characteristics. He persevered even after his

"Even if you think you know it all, there's a lot of life lessons you're going to learn in school. Develop your network while you're there with peers and professors."
Sam Uisprapassorn, cofounder, Crimson Skateboards[48]

brainchild, Idealab, seemed to have crashed and burned. The company was launched in the mid-1990s to nurture Internet start-ups as they were being formed left and right. Companies that Idealab invested in included eToys, Eve.com, and Pet-Smart.com. If you haven't heard of them, it's probably because they grew fast and then went out of business because sales couldn't keep up with the hype and the hopes. Today Gross explains that he hadn't intended for Idealab to help exclusively dot-com businesses, but that's what entrepreneurs were all starting in the 1990s. When the Internet boom crashed several years ago, Gross laid off employees and shuttered offices, but he didn't abandon his vision of helping entrepreneurs. Instead of giving up, Gross established stricter criteria for funding companies in the future—and determined that he would choose companies whose activities make a difference. Of the company's near failure, Gross says, "We have a lot more wisdom now," admitting that he might have needed to learn wisdom the hard way.[49]

Compare these qualities and examples of successful entrepreneurs with the description of Richard Branson in the "Management Close-Up: Taking Action" feature. How well does Branson fit the mold of a typical entrepreneur?

Management Close-Up | TAKING ACTION

Apparently, winning big in business isn't enough excitement for entrepreneur Richard Branson. He is also a modern-day adventurer. He has set world records for crossing the Atlantic Ocean and the English Channel in boats. In 1987 he became the first person to cross the Atlantic in a hot-air balloon. He has attempted to circle the world nonstop in a balloon and most recently had to abandon an Atlantic crossing in a racing yacht when 40-foot waves shredded his mainsail. But he already has his next challenge in sight—he's attempting to bring outer space to vacationers.

Branson's Virgin Galactic company wants to offer spaceflight for tourists. Galactic's first craft, the mother ship White Knight Two, was unveiled in 2008. It is designed to lift a rocket filled with eight passengers from earth to a launch point at 48,000 feet. Although the spacecraft itself is still under construction, the first passengers have already plunked down $200,000 for their ride; 200 others are on a waiting list.

Although Branson dropped out of school at age 16, he prides himself on being a life-long learner with an interest in creating goods and services that make the world a better place. He has a talent for looking at situations from a completely different perspective than most people.

In addition, despite being a risk taker, Branson says it is important always to have a Plan B. Any business venture can have external risks, so a wise entrepreneur, he declares, takes steps to manage those risks.[50]

- Many Virgin businesses have originated from Richard Branson's own wants and needs. Besides an ability to recognize a want or a need, what other skills did Branson need to become successful?
- Richard Branson seems to thrive on challenge and risk taking. How has this helped him succeed in his various businesses? Could it hurt also? If so, how?

Making Good Choices   Success is a function not only of personal characteristics but also of making good choices about the business you start. Figure 7.2 presents a model for conceptualizing entrepreneurial ventures and making the best possible choices. It depicts ventures along two dimensions: innovation and risk. The new venture may involve high or low levels of *innovation*, or the creation of something new and different. It can also be characterized by low or high *risk*. Risk refers primarily to the probability of major financial loss. But it also is more than that; it is psychological risk as perceived by the entrepreneur, including risk to reputation and ego.[51]

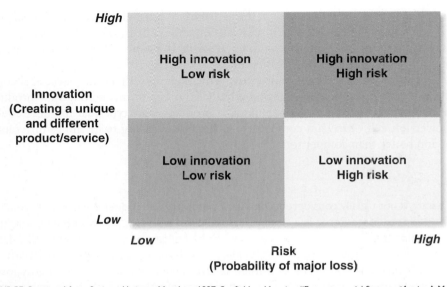

SOURCE: Reprinted from *Business Horizons*, May–June 1997, Sonfield and Lussier, "Entrepreneurial Strategy Matrix. A Model of New and Ongoing Ventures," Copyright © 1997, with permission from Elsevier.

FIGURE 7.2

Entrepreneurial Strategy Matrix

The upper-left quadrant, high innovation/low risk, depicts ventures of truly novel ideas with little risk. As examples, the inventors of Lego building blocks and Velcro fasteners could build their products by hand, at little expense. A pioneering product idea from Procter & Gamble might fit here if there are no current competitors and because, for a company of that size, the financial risks of new product investments can seem relatively small.

In the upper-right quadrant, high innovation/high risk, novel product ideas are accompanied by high risk because the financial investments are high and the competition is great. A new drug or a new automobile would likely fall into this category.

Most small business ventures are in the low innovation/high risk cell (lower right). They are fairly conventional entries in well-established fields. New restaurants, retail shops, and commercial outfits involve high investment for the small business entrepreneur and face direct competition from other similar businesses. Finally, the low innovation/low risk category includes ventures that require minimal investment and/or face minimal competition for strong market demand. Examples are some service businesses having low start-up costs and those involving entry into small towns if there is no competitor and demand is adequate.

Where would you place Second Life in the Entrepreneurial Strategy Matrix (Figure 7.2)? How about the company, Millions of Us, whose CEO is shown here with his virtual avatar? Millions of Us is the source for companies looking to establish a marketing foothold in Second Life.

How is this matrix useful? It helps entrepreneurs think about their ventures and decide whether they suit their particular objectives. It also helps identify effective and ineffective strategies. You might find one cell more appealing than others. The lower-left cell is likely to have relatively low payoffs but to provide more security. The higher risk/return trade-offs are in other cells, especially the upper right. So you might place your new-venture idea in the appropriate cell and determine whether that cell is the one in which you would prefer to operate. If it is, the venture is one that perhaps should be pursued, pending fuller analysis. If it is not, you can reject the idea or take steps to move it toward a different cell.

The matrix also can help entrepreneurs remember a useful point: Successful companies do not always require a cutting-edge technology or an exciting new product. Even companies offering the most mundane products—the type that might reside in the lower-left cell—can gain competitive advantage by doing basic things differently from and better than competitors.

Real estate is not usually considered a pioneering industry, but it does entail risk. Argentina-born developer Jorge Perez is a businessman familiar with risk. Many people credit him with revitalizing much of Miami, beginning with the building and renovation of affordable housing and garden apartment rentals. While most developers spread to the suburbs of Miami, believing that no one really wanted to live downtown, Perez took the opposite course: he focused entirely on the city itself. He began with a pair of condo towers that he built on the Miami River.

Today, Perez's company, The Related Group, is responsible for the three towers of the $1.6 billion Icon Brickell hotel and condominiums, another condo development called 500 Brickell, and the Loft 2—all overlooking Biscayne Bay. In all, The Related Group has constructed or renovated 11 major buildings downtown, giving Miami a fresh look and life. "We're going to finally have a center!" Perez boasts. "This is going to be the epicenter right here!" Not content to rest on past accomplishments, Perez has recently turned his sights toward projects in Atlanta and other cities overseas.[52]

LO 3   Success and Failure

Success or failure lies ahead for entrepreneurs starting their own companies, as well as for those starting new businesses within bigger corporations. Entrepreneurs succeed or fail in private, public, and not-for-profit sectors; in nations of all stages of development; and in all nations, regardless of their politics.[53]

Estimated failure rates for start-ups vary. Most indicate that failure is more the rule than the exception. The failure rate is high for certain businesses like restaurants and lower for successful franchises. Start-ups have at least two major liabilities: newness and smallness.[54] New companies are relatively unknown and need to learn how to be better than established competitors at something that customers value. Regarding smallness, the odds of surviving improve if the venture reaches a critical mass of at least 10 or 20 people, has revenues of $2 million or $3 million, and is pursuing opportunities with growth potential.[55]

You can find a lot of useful hyperlinks at the MIT Enterprise Forum, http://enterpriseforum.mit.edu/.

Acquiring venture capital is not essential to the success of most start-up businesses; in fact, it is rare. Recent numbers from the Census Bureau say that more than three-fourths of start-up companies with employees were financed by entrepreneurs' own assets or assets of their families. Approximately 1 out of 10 businesses were financed with the owners' credit cards.[56] Still, in a recent quarter, venture capital firms invested more than $6 billion in almost 800 deals;[57] that's a sizable amount of money, even if the fraction of total new companies is small. And venture capital firms often provide expert advice that helps entrepreneurs improve the odds for success.

To understand further the factors that influence success and failure, we'll consider risk, the economic environment, various management-related hazards, and initial public stock offerings (IPOs).

Risk You learned about risk in Chapter 3. It's a given: Starting a new business is risky. Entrepreneurs with plenty of business experience are especially aware of this. When Chris McGill was evaluating his idea for Mixx.com, a news Web site that could be personalized based on recommendations by users, he was *USA Today*'s vice president of strategy. To make Mixx succeed, McGill knew he would be leaving a well-paying job for an uncertain future in which he had to line up financing and hire talented people in a

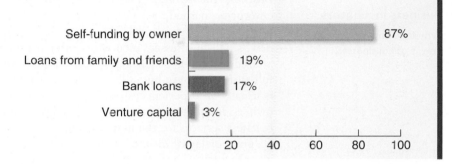

The 5,000 fastest-growing privately held companies in the United States often started modestly. The median amount of money spent to launch these companies was just $25,000. Most of that money came from the entrepreneurs themselves.[58]

Percentage of companies using source of capital

Self-funding by owner	87%
Loans from family and friends	19%
Bank loans	17%
Venture capital	3%

turbulent business environment. But McGill also concluded that his experience at *USA Today* and prior management experience with *Yahoo News* gave him the knowledge and connections for a successful Internet business.[59]

Successful entrepreneurs are realistic about risk. They anticipate difficulties and cushion their business to help it weather setbacks. In downtown Seattle, entrepreneurs Ben and Cindi Raykovich saw a risk when a major construction project began disrupting traffic around their store, Sound Sports. The Raykoviches had built their business around serving running enthusiasts who worked downtown and would stop by on their lunch hour or after work. Concerned that the construction would drive away so much business that the store couldn't survive, they opened a second location in the community of Poulsbo. They intend for the second store to supplement revenue, and if they need to close the first store, they can continue to build their business in Poulsbo. Ben Raykovich is hardly cavalier about the situation: "My life is invested in this business. We need to spread out the risk."[60]

The Role of the Economic Environment Entrepreneurial activity stems from the economic environment as well as the behavior of individuals. For example, money is a critical resource for all new businesses. Increases in the money supply and the supply of bank loans, real economic growth, and improved stock market performance lead to both improved prospects and increased sources of capital. In turn, the prospects and the capital increase the rate of business formation. Under favorable conditions, many aspiring entrepreneurs find early success. But economic cycles soon change favorable conditions into downturns. To succeed, entrepreneurs must have the foresight and talent to survive when the environment becomes more hostile.

Although good economic times may make it easier to start a company and to survive, bad times can offer an opportunity to expand. Ken Hendricks of ABC Supply found a business opportunity in a grim economic situation: a serious downturn in the manufacturing economy of the Midwest contributed to the shutdown of his town's largest employer, the Beloit Corporation. Hendricks purchased the company's buildings and lured a diverse group of new employers to town, in spite of the economic

Richard Foos (left), Bob Emmer (center), and Garson Foos are successful entrepreneurs due to their creativity, innovation, and knowledge of their target customers' desires. They are shown here with a circa 1966–67 Batmobile children's arcade ride in their Shout! Factory headquarters in Los Angeles. As CEO of the Shout! Factory, Richard Foos runs an emporium filled with nostalgia-type collectibles.

challenges. In fact, Hendricks has a track record of turning around the struggling suppliers that ABC acquires.[61] Another silver lining in difficult economic times is that it's easier to recruit talent.

business incubators

Protected environments for new, small businesses.

Business Incubators   The need to provide a nurturing environment for fledgling enterprises has led to the creation of business incubators. **Business incubators,** often located in industrial parks or abandoned factories, are protected environments for new, small businesses. Incubators offer benefits such as low rents and shared costs. Shared staff costs, such as for receptionists and secretaries, avoid the expense of a full-time employee but still provide convenient access to services. The staff manager is usually an experienced businessperson or consultant who advises the new business owners. Incubators often are associated with universities, which provide technical and business services for the new companies.

The heyday of business incubators came in the 1990s, when around 700 of them were financing start-ups, mainly emphasizing technology. Eight out of 10 shut down following the collapse of the Internet bubble, but the idea of nurturing new businesses persists. Naval Ravikant, for example, is developing a company tentatively named Hit Forge, which resembles the dot-com incubators. Hit Forge hired four engineers with experience in launching successful Internet concepts. The engineers have wide latitude to try ideas, but they work under strict deadlines. They must go from concept to product within 90 days, and any enterprises that aren't growing after a year will be terminated. Unlike the older-style incubator, Hit Forge lets engineers work from the location of their choice, and the engineers retain half ownership in the ventures they develop. Also, whereas incubators in the 1990s might have spent $2 million developing an idea, today's launches might cost just $50,000.[62]

LO 4   **Common Management Challenges**   As an entrepreneur, you are likely to face several common challenges that you should understand before you face them, and then manage effectively when the time comes. We next discuss several such challenges.

You Might Not Enjoy It   Some managers and employees can specialize in what they love, whether it's selling or accounting. But entrepreneurs usually have to "do it all," at least in the beginning. If you love product design, you also have to sell what you invent. If you love marketing, get ready to manage the money, too. This last challenge was almost a stumbling block for Elizabeth Busch, Anne Frey-Mott, and Beckie Jankiewicz when they launched The Event Studio to run business conferences for their clients. All three women had experience with some aspect of running conferences, but when they started their company, they didn't fully think out all the accounting decisions they would need for measuring their income and cash flow. With some practical advice, they learned some basic accounting lessons that helped them avoid tax troubles later on.[63] If they hadn't been willing to learn new skills, entrepreneurship might not have been the right career path for them.

Survival Is Difficult   Zappos cofounder Tony Hsieh says, "We thought about going under every day—until we got a $6 million credit line from Wells Fargo."[64] Companies without much of a track record tend to have more trouble lining up lenders, investors, and even customers. When economic conditions cool or competition heats up, a small start-up serving a niche market may have limited options for survival. Gary Gottenbusch worried when orders slowed at his Servatii Pastry Shop and Deli, located in Cincinnati. As a recession hit Ohio hard, customers were deciding that fancy breads and cakes were a luxury they could go without. Servatii might have closed, but Gottenbusch was willing to change. He kept afloat and even added to sales by cultivating new distribution channels (sales in hospitals), new products (distinctive pretzel sticks), and cost-cutting measures (a purchasing association with other bakers in the area).[65]

Failure can be devastating. When Mary Garrison wanted to own a business, she chose the women's fitness industry and decided to buy a franchise from Lady of America Franchise Corporation. But when she held her grand opening, not a single person stopped by. Three months later, she closed. Garrison blames the franchisor for not providing the necessary promotional support, a complaint that Lady of America denies.[66]

While still a student at the University of Missouri, Brian Laoruangroch started Green Mobile to buy, refurbish, and resell used cell phones. Originally, Laoruangroch's business was just a profitable hobby. Looking at phone prices on eBay, he concluded he could earn money by buying and reselling phones. He recruited his brother Brett (another University of Missouri student), and they learned how to repair the phones. Then he launched a Web site to sell the phones. While the "Green" in Green Mobile implies the environmental value of recycling phones, the company's advertising emphasizes its low prices—$30 and up.

As sales grew, keeping up with the business plus school soon got complicated. First Green Mobile began operating a kiosk in a mall. That required employees. Then the company opened a store. That required borrowing. As revenues rose past $500,000, Laoruangroch faced decisions about opening a second store and borrowing from the Small Business Administration. He discovered that managing 30 employees was difficult and not necessarily a profitable scale for his business. He laid off some employees, concluding, "You can get a lot more done with a staff of 14 who care than with 25 or 30 people who don't."

With two stores and all the associated challenges, Laoruangroch finds himself working 60 to 80 hours a week—and wondering how he will ever find the time to finish earning his college degree.[67]

Growth Creates New Challenges   Just one in three *Inc.* 500 companies keeps growing fast enough to make this list of fastest-growing companies two years running. The reason: They are facing bigger challenges, competing with bigger firms, stretching the founders' capacities, and probably burning cash. Consultant Doug Tatum calls this phase of a company's growth "No Man's Land."[68] It's a difficult transition.

The transition is particularly complex for entrepreneurs who quickly face the possibility of expanding internationally. Whether a firm should expand internationally soon after it is created or wait until it is better established is an open question. Entering international markets should help a firm grow, but going global is also likely to create challenges that make survival more difficult, especially when the company is young. For instance, when Lou Hoffman decided to expand his public relations (PR) firm to Japan, to grow alongside existing clients, he was prepared for language and cultural differences but not for the high cost of doing business in that country. He first tried partnering with a translation service, figuring they could share expertise and help each other expand. But the translators really weren't interested in the PR business, so a year later, he was staffing the enterprise from scratch. Then Hoffman decided to open a Chinese office, and in that country, he couldn't find anyone familiar with both Chinese business and the creative business culture that had served his agency well. So he hired a Chinese PR staffer who was willing to spend a year at his California headquarters, just absorbing the business culture. That method worked for the Chinese market but flopped when Hoffman tried it for opening a London office; the British employee didn't want to leave the California lifestyle and return home.[69] Of course, the risks tend to be lower when entrepreneurs (or their company's managers) have experience in serving foreign markets.[70]

In the beginning, the start-up mentality tends to be "we try harder."[71] Entrepreneurs work long hours at low pay, deliver great service, get good word-of-mouth, and their business grows. At first, it's "high performance, cheap labor." But with growth comes the need to pay higher wages to hire more people who are less dedicated than the founders. Then it's time to raise prices, establish efficient systems, or accept lower profits. The founder's talents may not spread to everyone else. You need a unique value proposition that will work as well with 100 employees, because hard work or your instincts alone no longer will get the job done. Complicating matters is the continuing growth in customers' needs and expectations.[72]

Growth seems to be a consuming goal for most entrepreneurs. But some company founders reach the size where they're happy and don't want to grow any further. Reaching a golden mean is possible.[73] Also, sometimes growth needs to be restrained until the company is ready. Only a year after Gregory Wynn, Komichel Johnson, and Robert A. Jones III set up their homebuilding business, JLW Homes and Communities, they had an opportunity to build a 70-unit condominium project called Heritage Pointe. They determined that getting the job done would require a master builder, two assistants, and at least 100 workers. JLW had two master builders, who were already assigned to projects, and too few workers, so the partners reluctantly decided not to take the job. Jones recalls, "It was way too early for us to do this type of deal, . . . and I'm glad we did [turn it down] because if we didn't, we may have lost our shirts."[74] By carefully planning growth at a sustainable pace, JLW has become a successful Atlanta firm.

> Entrepreneurs can stabilize their companies' size, but they still have to keep a high-value business model and provide great customer service.

It's Hard to Delegate   As the business grows, entrepreneurs often hesitate to delegate to other people work that they are used to doing. Leadership deteriorates into micromanagement, in which managers monitor too strictly, to the minutest detail. For example, during the Internet craze many company founders with great technical knowledge but little experience became "instant experts" in every phase of business, including branding and advertising.[75] Turns out, they didn't know as much as they thought, and their companies crashed. In contrast, Darren Herman kept his focus on what he knows. While still in his early 20s, Herman took his passion for videogames and his knowledge of marketing and came up with a business idea: IGA Worldwide, which works with advertisers and game developers to place advertising within videogames. Shortly after he had launched IGA, Herman turned over the job of CEO to a more experienced person and named himself "senior business development director," which means he focuses on spotting new ideas and promoting the company to investors.[76]

Misuse of Funds   Many unsuccessful entrepreneurs blame their failure on inadequate financial resources. Yet failure due to a lack of financial resources doesn't necessarily indicate a real lack of money; it could mean a failure to properly use the available money. A lot of start-up capital may be wasted—on expensive locations, great furniture, and fancy stationery. Entrepreneurs who fail to use their resources wisely usually make one of two mistakes: they apply financial resources to the wrong uses, or they maintain inadequate control over their resources.

> The *Inc.* 500 companies on the 2006 list started with a median of $75,000 in capital. One company reported starting with just $1.[77]

This problem may be more likely when a lucky entrepreneur gets a big infusion of cash from a venture capital firm or an initial offering of stock. For most start-ups, where the money on the line comes from the entrepreneur's own assets, he or she has more incentive to be careful. Tripp Micou, founder of Practical Computer Applications, says, "If all the money you spend is based on what you're bringing in [through sales], you very quickly focus on the right things to spend it on."[78] Micou, an experienced entrepreneur, believes that this financial limitation is actually a management advantage.

Poor Controls   Entrepreneurs, in part because they are very busy, often fail to use formal control systems. One common entrepreneurial malady is an aversion to record keeping. Expenses mount, but records do not keep pace. Pricing decisions are based on intuition without adequate reference to costs. As a result, the company earns inadequate margins to support growth.

Sometimes an economic slowdown provides a necessary alarm, warning business owners to pay attention to controls. When Servatii Pastry Shop and Deli's sales deteriorated even as the prices of ingredients were rising, owner Gary Gottenbusch pushed himself to go "a little out of [his] comfort zone" and consulted with advisers at the Manufacturing Extension Partnership. Besides encouraging him to innovate, the advisers helped him set goals and monitor progress. One problem Gottenbusch tackled was the price of baking commodities, such as shortening and flour. He partnered with other local bakeries to form a purchasing association that buys in bulk and passes along the savings. Keeping costs down helped Servatii stay profitable when customers were trimming their budgets for baked goods.[79]

Even in high-growth companies, great numbers can mask brewing problems. Blinded by the light of growing sales, many entrepreneurs fail to maintain vigilance over other aspects of the business. In the absence of controls, the business veers out of control. So don't get overconfident; keep asking critical questions. Is our success based on just one big customer? Is our product just a fad that can fade away? Can other companies easily enter our domain and hurt our business? Are we losing a technology lead? Do we really understand the numbers, know where they come from, and have any hidden causes for concern?

Mortality   One long-term measure of an entrepreneur's success is the fate of the venture after the founder's death. Founding entrepreneurs often fail to plan for succession. When death occurs, estate tax problems or the lack of a skilled replacement for the founder can lead to business failure.

Management guru Peter Drucker offered the following advice to help family-managed businesses survive and prosper.[80] Family members working in the business must be at least as capable and hard-working as other employees; at least one key position should be filled by a nonfamily member; and someone outside the family and the business should help plan succession. Family members who are mediocre performers are resented by others, outsiders can be more objective and contribute expertise the family might not have. Issues of management succession are often the most difficult of all, causing serious conflict and possible breakup of the firm.

Going Public   Sometimes companies reach a point at which the owners want to "go public." **Initial public stock offerings (IPOs)** offer a way to raise capital through federally registered and underwritten sales of shares in the company.[81] You need lawyers and accountants who know current regulations. The reasons for going public include raising more capital, reducing debt or improving the balance sheet and enhancing net worth, pursuing otherwise unaffordable opportunities, and improving credibility with customers and other stakeholders—"you're in the big leagues now." Disadvantages include the expense, time, and effort involved; the tendency to become more interested in the stock price and capital gains than in running the company properly; and the creation of a long-term relationship with an investment banking firm that won't necessarily always be a good one.[82]

Many entrepreneurs prefer to avoid going public, feeling they'll lose control if they do. States Yvon Chouinard of sports and apparel firm Patagonia: "There's a certain formula in business where you grow the thing and go public. I don't think it has to be that way. Being a closely held company means being able to take risks and try new

---

$ **The bottom line**
                COST
You probably will pay close attention to costs at the beginning, but success sometimes brings neglect. Don't fall into that trap.

---

initial public offering (IPO)

Sale to the public, for the first time, of federally registered and underwritten shares of stock in the company.

things—the creative part of business. If I were owned by a bunch of retired teachers, I wouldn't be able to do what I do; I'd have to be solely concerned with the bottom line. For us to go public would be suicide."[83]

Executing IPOs and other approaches to acquiring capital is complex, legalistic, and beyond the scope of this chapter. Sources for more information include *The Ernst & Young Guide to Raising Capital*, the National Venture Capital Association (www. nvca.org), VentureOne (http://www.ventureone.com), and *VentureWire* (link to this publication from http://www.venturecapital.dowjones.com/).

LO 5   Increasing Your Chances of Success

Aside from financial resources, entrepreneurs need to think through their business idea carefully to help ensure its success. We discuss here the importance of good planning and nonfinancial resources.

Planning   So you think you have identified a business opportunity. And you have the personal potential to make it a success. Now what? Where should you begin?

opportunity analysis

A description of the good or service, an assessment of the opportunity, an assessment of the entrepreneur, specification of activities and resources needed to translate your idea into a viable business, and your source(s) of capital.

business plan

A formal planning step that focuses on the entire venture and describes all the elements involved in starting it.

The Business Plan   Your excitement and intuition may convince you that you are on to something. But they might not convince anyone else. You need more thorough planning and analysis. This effort will help convince other people to get on board and help you avoid costly mistakes.

The first formal planning step is to do an opportunity analysis. An **opportunity analysis** includes a description of the good or service, an assessment of the opportunity, an assessment of the entrepreneur (you), a specification of activities and resources needed to translate your idea into a viable business, and your source(s) of capital.[84] Table 7.3 shows the questions you should answer in an opportunity analysis.

The opportunity analysis, or opportunity assessment plan, focuses on the opportunity, not the entire venture. It provides the basis for making a decision on whether to act. Then, the **business plan** describes all the elements involved in starting the new venture.[85] The business plan describes the venture and its market, strategies, and future directions. It often has functional plans for marketing, finance, manufacturing, and human resources.

Table 7.4 shows an outline for a typical business plan. The business plan (1) helps determine the viability of your enterprise, (2) guides you as you plan and organize, and (3) helps you obtain financing. It is read by potential investors, suppliers, customers, and others. Get help in writing up a sound plan!

TABLE 7.3
Opportunity Analysis

What market need does my idea fill?
What personal observations have I experienced or recorded with regard to that market need?
What social condition underlies this market need?
What market research data can be marshaled to describe this market need?
What patents might be available to fulfill this need?
What competition exists in this market? How would I describe the behavior of this competition?
What does the international market look like?
What does the international competition look like?
Where is the money to be made in this activity?

SOURCE: R. Hisrich and M. Peters, *Entrepreneurship: Starting, Developing, and Managing a New Enterprise, table*, p. 41 Copyright © 1998 by The McGraw-Hill Companies.

TABLE 7.4   Outline of a Business Plan

I. EXECUTIVE SUMMARY
  A. Description of the Business Concept and the Business
  B. The Opportunity and Strategy
  C. The Target Market and Projections
  D. The Competitive Advantages
  E. The Economics, Profitability, and Harvest Potential
  F. The Team
  G. The Offering

II. THE INDUSTRY AND THE COMPANY AND ITS PRODUCT(S) OR SERVICE(S)
  A. The Industry
  B. The Company and the Concept
  C. The Product(s) or Service(s)
  D. Entry and Growth Strategy

III. MARKET RESEARCH AND ANALYSIS
  A. Customers
  B. Market Size and Trends
  C. Competition and Competitive Edges
  D. Estimated Market Share and Sales
  E. Ongoing Market Evaluation

IV. THE ECONOMICS OF THE BUSINESS
  A. Gross and Operating Margins
  B. Profit Potential and Durability
  C. Fixed, Variable, and Semivariable Costs
  D. Months to Break Even
  E. Months to Reach Positive Cash Flow

V. MARKETING PLAN
  A. Overall Marketing Strategy
  B. Pricing
  C. Sales Tactics
  D. Service and Warranty Policies
  E. Advertising and Promotion
  F. Distribution

VI. DESIGN AND DEVELOPMENT PLANS
  A. Development Status and Tasks
  B. Difficulties and Risks

  C. Product Improvement and New Products
  D. Costs
  E. Proprietary Issues

VII. MANUFACTURING AND OPERATIONS PLAN
  A. Operating Cycle
  B. Geographical Location
  C. Facilities and Improvements
  D. Strategy and Plans
  E. Regulatory and Legal Issues

VIII. MANAGEMENT TEAM
  A. Organization
  B. Key Management Personnel
  C. Management Compensation and Ownership
  D. Other Investors
  E. Employment and Other Agreements and Stock Option and Bonus Plans
  F. Board of Directors
  G. Other Shareholders, Rights, and Restrictions
  H. Supporting Professional Advisors and Services

IX. OVERALL SCHEDULE

X. CRITICAL RISKS, PROBLEMS, AND ASSUMPTIONS

XI. THE FINANCIAL PLAN
  A. Actual income Statements and Balance Sheets
  B. Pro Forma Income Statements
  C. Pro Forma Balance Sheets
  D. Pro Forma Cash Flow Analysis
  E. Breakeven Chart and Calculation
  F. Cost Control
  G. Highlights

XII. PROPOSED COMPANY OFFERING
  A. Desired Financing
  B. Offering
  C. Capitalization
  D. Use of Funds
  E. Investor's Return

XIII. APPENDIXES

SOURCE: J. A. Timmons, *New Venture Creation*, 5th ed., p. 374. Copyright © 1999 by Jeffry A. Timmons. Reproduced with permission of the author. © 1999 The McGraw-Hill Companies.

Key Planning Elements   Most business plans devote so much attention to financial projections that they neglect other important information—information that matters greatly to astute investors. In fact, financial projections tend to be overly optimistic. Investors know this and discount the figures. In addition to the numbers, the best plans convey—and make certain that the entrepreneurs have carefully thought through—five key factors: the people, the opportunity, the competition, the context, and risk and reward.[86]

The three founders of AmieStreet.com, an online music retailer, have created competitive advantage by pioneering a new pricing model. It is the first store where the customers collectively determine the price of music. On AmieStreet.com, most songs start free and increase in price up to 98 cents, based on their popularity among members.

The *people* should be energetic and have skills and expertise directly relevant to the venture. For many astute investors, the people are the most important variable, more important even than the idea. Venture capital firms often receive 2,000 business plans per year; many believe that ideas are a dime a dozen and what counts is the ability to execute. Arthur Rock, a legendary venture capitalist who helped start Intel, Teledyne, and Apple, stated, "I invest in people, not ideas. If you can find good people, if they're wrong about the product, they'll make a switch."[87]

The *opportunity* should provide a competitive advantage that can be defended. Customers are the focus here: Who is the customer? How does the customer make decisions? How will the product be priced? How will the venture reach all customer segments? How much does it cost to acquire and support a customer, and to produce and deliver the product? How easy or difficult is it to retain a customer?

It is also essential to fully consider the *competition*. The plan must identify current competitors and their strengths and weaknesses, predict how they will respond to the new venture, indicate how the new venture will respond to the competitors' responses, identify future potential competitors, and consider how to collaborate with or face off against actual or potential competitors. The original plan for Zappos was for its Web site to compete with other online shoe retailers by offering a wider selection than they did. However, most people buy shoes in stores, so Zappos cofounders Nick Swinmurn and Tony Hsieh soon realized that they needed a broader view of the competition. They began focusing more on service and planning a distribution method that would make online shopping as successful as visiting a store.[88]

The environmental *context* should be a favorable one from regulatory and economic perspectives. Such factors as tax policies, rules about raising capital, interest rates, inflation, and exchange rates will affect the viability of the new venture. The context can make it easier or harder to get backing and to succeed. Importantly, the plan should make clear that you know that the context inevitably will change, forecast how the changes will affect the business, and describe how you will deal with the changes.

According to the State New Economy Index, the most hospitable states for starting an innovative, new-economy business are Massachusetts, New Jersey, Maryland, Washington, and California.[89]

The *risk* must be understood and addressed as fully as possible. The future is always uncertain, and the elements described in the plan will change over time. Although you cannot predict the future, you must contemplate head-on the possibilities of key people leaving, interest rates changing, a key customer leaving, or a powerful competitor responding ferociously. Then describe what you will do to prevent, avoid, or cope with such possibilities. You should also speak to the end of the process: how to get money out of the business eventually. Will you go public? Will you sell or liquidate? What are the various possibilities for investors to realize their ultimate gains?[90]

Selling the Plan   Your goal is to get investors to support the plan, so the elements of a great plan, as just described, are essential. It's also important whom you decide to try to convince to back your plan.

Many entrepreneurs want passive investors who will give them money and let them do what they want. Doctors and dentists generally fit this image. Professional venture capitalists do not, as they demand more control and more of the returns. But when a business goes wrong—and chances are, it will—nonprofessional investors are less helpful and less likely to advance more (needed) money. Sophisticated investors have seen sinking ships before and know how to help. They are more likely to solve problems, provide more money, and also navigate financial and legal waters such as going public.[91]

View the plan as a way for you to figure out how to reduce risk and maximize reward, and to convince others that you understand the entire new venture process. Don't put together a plan built on naïveté or overconfidence or one that cleverly hides major flaws. You might not fool others, and you certainly would be fooling yourself.

Nonfinancial Resources   Also crucial to the success of a new business are nonfinancial resources, including legitimacy in the minds of the public and the various ways in which other people can help.

Legitimacy   An important resource for the new venture is **legitimacy**—people's judgment of a company's acceptance, appropriateness, and desirability.[92] When the market confers legitimacy, it helps overcome the "liability of newness" that creates a high percentage of new-venture failure.[93] Legitimacy helps a firm acquire other resources such as top managers, good employees, financial resources, and government support. In a three-year study tracking business start-ups, the likelihood that a company would succeed at selling products, hiring employees, and attracting investors depended most on how skillfully entrepreneurs demonstrated that their business was legitimate.[94]

A business is legitimate if its goals and methods are consistent with societal values. You can generate legitimacy by visibly conforming to rules and expectations created by governments, credentialing associations, and professional organizations; by visibly endorsing widely held values; and by visibly practicing widely held beliefs.[95]

legitimacy

People's judgment of a company's acceptance, appropriateness, and desirability, generally stemming from company goals and methods that are consistent with societal values.

Networks   The entrepreneur is aided greatly by having a strong *network* of people. **Social capital**—being part of a social network, and having a good reputation—helps entrepreneurs gain access to useful information, gain trust and cooperation from others, recruit employees, form successful business alliances, receive funding from venture capitalists, and become more successful.[96] Social capital provides a lasting source of competitive advantage.[97]

To see just some of the ways social capital can help entrepreneurs, consider a pair of examples. Brian Ko, an engineer who founded Integrant Technologies, got useful advice from his investors, including private investors, a bank, and venture-capital firms. One adviser taught Ko that acquiring patents during the start-up phase would help the company stay competitive during the long term, so Integrant spent the money to file applications for 150 patents in six years, positioning the company to protect its ideas as it gains market share and competitors' attention.[98]

Tim Litle has developed several successful innovations and businesses as a result of relationships with business school classmates and customers. Early in his career, a friend in politics wanted to target letters to different groups of citizens, and Litle worked with him to figure out how to do that now-common application with computers. He, the politician, and two other partners eventually built a business to provide the same service to marketers.[99]

social capital

A competitive advantage in the form of relationships with other people and the image other people have of you.

Top-Management Teams   The top-management team is another crucial resource. For example, Sudhin Shahani's start-ups include MyMPO, whose digital media services include Musicane, which lets musicians sell audio and video files and ringtones online at storefronts they create for themselves. The company's head of marketing was singer Will.i.am.[100] Having a musician in that top spot may help Musicane build client relationships with other artists. Also, in companies that have incorporated, a board of directors improves the company's image, develops longer-term plans for expansion, supports day-to-day activities, and develops a network of information sources.

Advisory Boards   Whether or not the company has a formal board of directors, entrepreneurs can assemble a group of people willing to serve as an advisory board. Board members with business experience can help an entrepreneur learn basics such as how to do cash-flow analysis; identify needed strategic changes; and build relationships with bankers, accountants, and attorneys. Musicane has an advisory board whose members include Bob Jamieson, the head of BMG Canada.[101] Jamieson can contribute inside knowledge of the music industry to complement Shahani's business training, as well as giving the organization credibility to investors and to musicians who might be interested in selling online.

Partners   Often, two people go into business together as partners. Partners can help one another access capital, spread the workload, share the risk, and share expertise. One of the strengths of JLW Homes and Communities, the Atlanta construction business described earlier in this chapter, is that the three founding partners bring different areas of expertise to the business. Gregory Wynn was a master homebuilder, Komichel Johnson was a financial expert, and Robert A. Jones III was a successful salesperson. Johnson explains the advantage this way: "We don't all agree on the same issues, and we've had some heated arguments. . . . But we realize that through communication and laying out the facts, that we can overcome any issues that may arise within our organization."[102]

Despite the potential advantages of finding a compatible partner, partnerships are not always marriages made in heaven. "Mark" talked three of his friends into joining him in starting his own telecommunications company because he didn't want to try it alone. He learned quickly that while he wanted to put money into growing the business, his three partners wanted the company to pay for their cars and meetings in the Bahamas. The company collapsed. "I never thought a business relationship could overpower friendship, but this one did. Where money's involved, people change."

To be successful, partners need to acknowledge one another's talents, let each other do what they do best, communicate honestly, and listen to one another. That's what the partners in JLW Homes did when they turned down a chance to build a project they were understaffed for completing. Johnson, the financial expert, believed the company would make a good return, and Jones, the salesperson, was eager to move ahead, but homebuilder Wynn said the company was unprepared for a project of that size. Johnson and Jones bowed to Wynn's experience and were later glad they did.[103] Partners also must learn to trust each other by making and keeping agreements. If they must break an agreement, it is crucial that they give early notice and clean up after their mistakes.

Corporate Entrepreneurship

LO 6   Large corporations are more than passive bystanders in the entrepreneurial explosion. Consider Microsoft. Every spring, the company hosts Techfest, essentially a three-day science fair that spotlights innovations the company may pursue. The first day is open to the public, and the second two are for Microsoft employees. About half of Microsoft's researchers come from around the world to be inspired and energized by the glimpse at their colleagues' creative projects.[104]

Even established companies try to find and pursue new and profitable ideas—and they need in-house entrepreneurs (sometimes called intrapreneurs) to do so. If you work in a company and are considering launching a new business venture, Table 7.5 can help you decide whether the new idea is worth pursuing.

Building Support for Your Idea

A manager who has a new idea to capitalize on a market opportunity will need to get others in the organization to buy in or sign on. In other words, you need to build a network of allies who support and will help implement the idea.

If you need to build support for a project idea, the first step involves *clearing the investment* with your immediate boss or bosses.[105] At this stage, you explain the idea and seek approval to look for wider support.

The bottom line

Innovation

Recall from Chapter 3 that creativity spawns good new ideas, but innovation requires actually implementing those ideas so that they become realities. If you work in an organization and have a good idea, you must convince other people to get on board.

TABLE 7.5
Checklist for Choosing Ideas

Fit with Your Skills and Expertise
Do you believe in the product or service?
Does the need it fits mean something to you personally?
Do you like and understand the potential customers?
Do you have experience in this type of business?
Do the basic success factors of this business fit your skills?
Are the tasks of the enterprise ones you could enjoy doing yourself?
Are the people the enterprise will employ ones you will enjoy working with and supervising?
Has the idea begun to take over your imagination and spare time?

Fit with the Market
Is there a real customer need?
Can you get a price that gives you good margins?
Would customers believe in the product coming from your company?
Does the product or service you propose produce a clearly perceivable customer benefit that is significantly better than that offered by competing ways to satisfy the same basic need?
Is there a cost-effective way to get the message and the product to the customers?

Fit with the Company
Is there a reason to believe your company could be very good at the business?
Does it fit the company culture?
Does it look profitable?
Will it lead to larger markets and growth?

What to Do When Your Idea Is Rejected
As an intrapreneur, you will frequently find that your idea has been rejected. There are a few things you can do.
1. Give up and select a new idea.
2. Listen carefully, understand what is wrong, improve your idea and your presentation, and try again.

3. Find someone else to whom you can present your idea by considering:
  a. Who will benefit most if it works? Can they be a sponsor?
  b. Who are potential customers? Will they demand the product?
  c. How can you get to the people who really care about intrapreneurial ideas?

SOURCE: G. Pinchot III, *Intrapreneuring*, Copyright © 1985 by John Wiley & Sons, Inc. Reprinted by permission of the author, http://www.pinchot.com.

Higher executives often want evidence that the project is backed by your peers before committing to it. This involves *making cheerleaders*—people who will support the manager before formal approval from higher levels. Managers at General Electric refer to this strategy as "loading the gun"—lining up ammunition in support of your idea.

Next, *horse trading* begins. You can offer promises of payoffs from the project in return for support, time, money, and other resources that peers and others contribute.

Finally, you should *get the blessing* of relevant higher-level officials. This usually involves a formal presentation. You will need to guarantee the project's technical and political feasibility. Higher management's endorsement of the project and promises of resources help convert potential supporters into an enthusiastic team. At this point, you can go back to your boss and make specific plans for going ahead with the project.

Along the way, expect resistance and frustration—and use passion and persistence, as well as business logic, to persuade others to get on board.

Building Intrapreneurship

Building an entrepreneurial culture is the heart of the corporate strategy at Acordia, a successful insurance company that recently changed its name to Wells Fargo TPA.[106] Its success in fostering a culture in which intrapreneurs flourish came from making an intentional decision to foster entrepreneurial thinking and behavior, creating new-venture teams, and changing the compensation system so that it encourages, supports, and rewards creative and innovative behaviors. In other words, building intrapreneurship derives from careful and deliberate strategy.

Two common approaches used to stimulate intrapreneurial activity are skunkworks and bootlegging. **Skunkworks** are project teams designated to produce a new product. A team is formed with a specific goal within a specified time frame. A respected person is chosen to be manager of the skunkworks. In this approach to corporate innovation, risk takers are not punished for taking risks and failing—their former jobs are held for them. The risk takers also have the opportunity to earn large rewards.

Bootlegging refers to informal efforts—as opposed to official job assignments—in which employees work to create new products and processes of their own choosing and initiative. Informal can mean secretive, such as when a bootlegger believes the company or the boss will frown on those activities. But companies should tolerate some bootlegging, and some even encourage it. To a limited extent, they allow people freedom to pursue pet projects without asking what they are or monitoring progress, figuring bootlegging will lead to some lost time but also to learning and to some profitable innovations.

Merck, desiring entrepreneurial thinking and behavior in research and development, explicitly rejects budgets for planning and control. New-product teams don't *get* a budget. They must persuade people to join the team and commit *their* resources. This creates a survival-of-the-fittest process, mirroring the competition in the real world.[107] At Merck, as at Wells Fargo TPA, intrapreneurship derives from deliberate strategic thinking and execution.

Management Challenges

Organizations that encourage intrapreneurship face an obvious risk: the effort can fail. One author noted, "There is considerable history of internal venture development by large firms, and it does not encourage optimism."[108] However, this risk can be managed. In fact, failing to foster intrapreneurship may represent a subtler but greater risk than encouraging it. The organization that resists entrepreneurial initiative may lose its ability to adapt when conditions dictate change.

The most dangerous risk in corporate entrepreneurship is the risk of overreliance on a single project. Many companies fail while awaiting the completion of one large, innovative project.[109] The successful entrepreneurial organization avoids overcommitment

skunkworks

A project team designated to produce a new, innovative product.

bootlegging

Informal work on projects, other than those officially assigned, of employees' own choosing and initiative.

to a single project and relies on its entrepreneurial spirit to produce at least one winner from among several projects.

Organizations also court failure when they spread their entrepreneurial efforts over too many projects.[110] If there are many projects, each effort may be too small in scale. Managers will consider the projects unattractive because of their small size. Or those recruited to manage the projects may have difficulty building power and status within the organization.

The hazards in intrapreneurship, then, are related to scale. One large project is a threat, as are too many underfunded projects. But a carefully managed approach to this strategically important process will upgrade an organization's chances for long-term survival and success.

Entrepreneurial Orientation

Earlier in this chapter, we described the characteristics of individual entrepreneurs. To conclude the chapter, we do the same for companies: we describe how companies that are highly entrepreneurial differ from those that are not. CEOs play a crucial role in promoting entrepreneurship within large corporations.[111]

Entrepreneurial orientation is the tendency of an organization to engage in activities designed to identify and capitalize successfully on opportunities to launch new ventures by entering new or established markets with new or existing goods or services.[112] Entrepreneurial orientation is determined by five tendencies: to allow independent action, innovate, take risks, be proactive, and be competitively aggressive. Entrepreneurial orientation should enhance the likelihood of success and may be particularly important for conducting business internationally.[113]

To *allow independent action* is to grant to individuals and teams the freedom to exercise their creativity, champion promising ideas, and carry them through to completion. *Innovativeness* requires the firm to support new ideas, experimentation, and creative processes that can lead to new products or processes; it requires a willingness to depart from existing practices and venture beyond the status quo. *Risk taking* comes from a willingness to commit significant resources, and perhaps borrow heavily, to venture into the unknown. The tendency to take risks can be assessed by considering whether people are bold or cautious, whether they require high levels of certainty before taking or allowing action, and whether they tend to follow tried-and-true paths.

To be *proactive* is to act in anticipation of future problems and opportunities. A proactive firm changes the competitive landscape; other firms merely react. Proactive firms are forward thinking and fast to act, and are leaders rather than followers. Similarly, some individuals are more likely to be proactive, to shape and create their own environments, than others who more passively cope with the situations in which they find themselves.[114] Proactive firms encourage and allow individuals and teams to *be* proactive.

Finally, *competitive aggressiveness* is the tendency of the firm to challenge competitors directly and intensely to achieve entry or improve its position. In other words, it is a competitive tendency to outperform one's rivals in the marketplace. This might take the form of striking fast to beat competitors to the punch, to tackle them head-to-head, and to analyze and target competitors' weaknesses.

What makes a firm "entrepreneurial" is its engagement in an effective combination of independent action, innovativeness, risk taking, proactiveness, and competitive aggressiveness.[115] The relationship between these factors and the performance of the firm is a complicated one that depends on many things. Still, you can imagine how the opposite profile—too many constraints on action, business as usual, extreme caution, passivity, and a lack of competitive fire—will undermine entrepreneurial activities. And without entrepreneurship, how would firms survive and thrive in a constantly changing competitive environment?

Thus, management can create environments that foster more entrepreneurship. If your bosses are not doing this, consider trying some entrepreneurial experiments on

entrepreneurial orientation

The tendency of an organization to identify and capitalize successfully on opportunities to launch new ventures by entering new or established markets with new or existing goods or services.

your own.[116] Seek out others with an entrepreneurial bent. What can you learn from them, and what can you teach others? Sometimes it takes individuals and teams of experimenters to show the possibilities to those at the top. Ask yourself, and ask others: Between the bureaucrats and the entrepreneurs, who is having a more positive impact? And who is having more fun?

Management Close-Up

ASSESSING OUTCOMES AND SEIZING OPPORTUNITIES

With four decades of entrepreneurship behind him, Richard Branson has turned his attention—and his wealth—to preserving the environment. In 2006 he pledged his transportation businesses' profits for ten years—an estimated $3 billion—to fight global warming. Branson is also funding research on renewable energy sources. His Virgin Fuels division has invested nearly $400 million in the effort to date.

Virgin Group has also partnered with NTR, an Ireland-based developer of renewable energy, in a joint venture to build ethanol production plants. The venture, called Virgin Bioverda, has funded two 100-million-gallon plants that convert corn to ethanol in Indiana and Tennessee. Additional biofuel opportunities are under study in North America and Europe.

Virgin is also working with Boeing and GE Aviation, an engine maker, to develop biofuels for aircraft. The company is also working on biofuel production for buses, trains, and cars. Virgin Group also has a train business, Virgin Trains, based in the United Kingdom. That division recently launched a $5.2 million advertising campaign to promote its eco-friendly Pendolino trains. Under the slogan "Go greener, go cheaper," the national campaign includes TV commercials supported by print, radio, outdoor, and online ads as well as brochures.

Branson's financial arm, Virgin Money, has established the Climate Change Fund, a green fund investing only in companies committed to high environmental standards. A majority of the fund will be invested in companies with better-than-average environmental records in their industries.

Branson has announced a high-stakes competition to solve the problem of greenhouse gases. His Virgin Earth Challenge offers a $25 million award to the person or people who come up with a way to remove greenhouse gases from Earth's atmosphere.[117]

- Entrepreneur Richard Branson has said, "Money's a crude measure of success, at best. It is only interesting for what it lets you do." What kinds of challenges have Branson and other entrepreneurs tackled to suggest that this is true? Cite some examples.
- In addition to the environment, Branson says entrepreneurs have a unique role to play in solving global issues like poverty and health crises. Do you agree? Why or why not?

KEY TERMS

SUMMARY OF LEARNING OBJECTIVES

Now that you have studied Chapter 7, you should be able to:

LO 1   Describe why people become entrepreneurs and what it takes, personally.

People become entrepreneurs because of the profit potential, the challenge, the satisfaction they anticipate (and often receive) from participating in the process, and sometimes because they are blocked from more traditional avenues of career advancement. Successful entrepreneurs are innovators, and they have good knowledge and skills in management, business, and networking. While there is no single "entrepreneurial personality," certain characteristics are helpful: commitment and determination; leadership skills; opportunity obsession; tolerance of risk, ambiguity, and uncertainty; creativity, self-reliance, the ability to adapt; and motivation to excel.

LO 2 Summarize how to assess opportunities to start new businesses.

You should always be on the lookout for new ideas, monitoring the current business environment and other indicators of opportunity. Franchising offers an interesting opportunity, and the potential of the Internet is being tapped (after entrepreneurs learned some tough lessons from the dot-bomb era). Trial and error and preparation play important roles. Assessing the business concept on the basis of how innovative and risky it is, combined with your personal interests and tendencies, will also help you make good choices. Ideas should be carefully assessed via opportunity analysis and a thorough business plan.

LO 3 Identify common causes of success and failure.

New ventures are inherently risky. The economic environment plays an important role in the success or failure of the business, and the entrepreneur should anticipate and be prepared to adapt in the face of changing economic conditions. How you handle a variety of common management challenges also can mean the difference between success and failure, as can the effectiveness of your planning and your ability to mobilize nonfinancial resources, including other people who can help.

LO 4 Discuss common management challenges.

When new businesses fail, the causes often can be traced to some common challenges that entrepreneurs face and must manage well. You might not enjoy the entrepreneurial process. Survival—including getting started and fending off competitors—is difficult. Growth creates new challenges, including reluctance to delegate work to others. Funds are put to improper use, and financial controls may be inadequate. Many entrepreneurs fail to plan well for succession. When needing or wanting new funds, initial public offerings provide an option, but they represent an important and difficult decision that must be considered carefully.

LO 5 Explain how to increase your chances of success, including good business planning.

The business plan helps you think through your idea thoroughly and determine its viability. It also convinces (or fails to convince) others to participate. The plan describes the venture and its future, provides financial projections, and includes plans for marketing, manufacturing, and other business functions. The plan should describe the people involved in the venture, a full assessment of the opportunity (including customers and competitors), the environmental context (including regulatory and economic issues), and the risk (including future risks and how you intend to deal with them). Successful entrepreneurs also understand how to develop social capital, which enhances legitimacy and helps develop a network of others including customers, talented people, partners, and boards.

LO 6 Describe how managers of large companies can foster entrepreneurship.

Intrapreneurs work within established companies to develop new goods or services that allow the corporation to reap the benefits of innovation. To facilitate intrapraneurship, organizations use skunkworks—special project teams designated to develop a new product—and allow bootlegging—informal efforts beyond formal job assignments in which employees pursue their own pet projects. Organizations should select projects carefully, have an ongoing portfolio of projects, and fund them appropriately. Ultimately, a true entrepreneurial orientation in a company comes from encouraging independent action, innovativeness, risk taking, proactive behavior, and competitive aggressiveness.

DISCUSSION QUESTIONS

1. On a 1 to 10 scale, what is your level of personal interest in becoming an entrepreneur? Why did you rate yourself as you did?

2. How would you assess your capability of being a successful entrepreneur? What are your strengths and weaknesses? How would you increase your capability?

3. Most entrepreneurs learn the most important skills they need after age 21. How does this affect your outlook and plans?

4. Identify and discuss new ventures that fit each of the four cells in the entrepreneurial strategy matrix.

5. Brainstorm a list of ideas for new business ventures. Where did you get the ideas? Which ones are most and least viable, and why?

6. Identify some businesses that recently opened in your area. What are their chances of survival, and why? How would you advise the owners or managers of those businesses to ensure their success?

7. Assume you are writing a story about what it's really like to be an entrepreneur. To whom would you talk, and what questions would you ask?

8. Conduct interviews with two entrepreneurs, asking whatever questions most interest you. Share your findings with the class. How do the interviews differ from one another, and what do they have in common?

9. Read Table 7.1. Which myths did you believe? Do you still? Why or why not? Interview two entrepreneurs by asking each myth as a true-or-false question. Then ask them to elaborate on their answers. What did they say? What do you conclude?

10. With your classmates, form small teams of skunkworks. Your charge is to identify an innovation that you think would benefit your school, college, or university, and to outline an action plan for bringing your idea to reality.

11. Identify a business that recently folded. What were the causes of the failure? What could have been done differently to prevent the failure?

12. Does franchising appeal to you? What franchises would most and least interest you, and why?

13. The chapter specified some of the changes in the external environment that can provide business opportunity (technological discoveries, lifestyle and taste changes, and so on).

Identify some important recent changes or current trends in the external environment and the business opportunities they might offer.

14. Choose an Internet company with which you are familiar and brainstorm ideas for how its services or approach to business can be improved. How about starting a new Internet company altogether—what would be some possibilities?

CONCLUDING CASE

Shoes With Soul: Two Friends Realize a Dream

Renee Albertelli and Richard Rodriguez shared a dream ever since they met in college: to start their own business. Both took business and marketing courses and began their careers in established businesses so that they could gain experience about what it takes to turn an idea into a business reality. But as they advanced in their careers, the firms they worked for didn't offer the types of challenges they wanted to pursue. They decided they wanted to work for themselves, and they saw an opportunity.

For her job in marketing at a telecommunications firm, Albertelli had traveled to several regions of the world with developing economies, including Africa, Asia, and South America. She became increasingly aware that women in these regions wanted—and needed—to find new ways to earn a living to support and educate their families. Rodriguez, on the other hand, spent his time working in the financial offices of a major U.S. clothing firm that had its own stores nationwide.

During her travels, Albertelli met a group of women who were highly skilled at crafting handmade sandals. They prepared the leather by hand, designed their own shoe patterns, and assembled each pair of sandals with simple tools. Albertelli thought the finished products were beautiful. She was also impressed by the women's desire to operate their own businesses. She thought they would make a great team, if enough sandals could be produced for sale—even in small numbers—in the United States.

Albertelli contacted Rodriguez when she returned from her trip, and the two friends met to create a business plan. Both believed in the product and the cause—they could build a business based on the desire and craftsmanship of small groups of artisans who wanted to band together to form their own businesses and the market for handcrafted goods in the United States. They knew if they could succeed with one group of women and their products, many more would follow. They banked on the fact that U.S. consumers would fall in love with the idea as well—and buy the products.

Albertelli and Rodriguez took a huge risk—they decided to cash in their retirement savings to fund the creation of the first batch of sandals. They devised a plan for acquiring more financial backing so that they could transport and advertise the product. They developed a marketing plan based not only on the beauty of the sandals but also on lives of the women who created them, so that consumers would feel a connection with the makers. They named their company Shoes With Soul. The two entrepreneurs didn't need to worry initially about locating a manufacturing facility because the shoes would continue to be made in the village where they originated.

Albertelli and Rodriguez worked closely with the woman who had started the shoemaking project in her village. When they had enough prototypes, they began to make the rounds to existing stores. They also considered renting kiosks at certain malls and investigated setting up a booth at specific sporting and cultural events. Although they understood the importance of a Web site, they decided not to sell the sandals directly online until they had a more complete line of products to offer consumers.

At first, interest in the shoes was limited to small boutiques—entrepreneurs themselves—until a local TV news show heard about the business and decided to do a story on Albertelli, Rodriguez, and the women. Then things began to change, and Shoes With Soul seemed to take off. Rodriguez and Albertelli were excited by their popularity—but how could they fulfill orders, expand their product line, and grow at a sensible pace?

QUESTIONS

1. Describe the personality characteristics that Renee Albertelli and Richard Rodriguez have that should help them navigate the difficulties of starting a business.

2. Rodriguez and Albertelli decided to focus their marketing efforts on the artisans who made the shoes. Do you think this is a wise decision? Why or why not?

3. What management challenges might cause Shoes With Soul to stumble?

4. Describe several steps that Rodriguez and Albertelli could take to avoid these stumbling blocks and guide their new business to success.

EXPERIENTIAL EXERCISES

7.1   Take an Entrepreneur to Dinner

OBJECTIVES

1. To get to know what an entrepreneur does, how she or he got started, and what it took to succeed.

2. To interview a particular entrepreneur in depth about his or her career and experiences.

3. To acquire a feeling for whether you might find an entrepreneurial career rewarding.

INSTRUCTIONS

1. Identify an entrepreneur in your area you would like to interview.

2. Contact the person you have selected and make an appointment. Be sure to explain why you want the appointment and to give a realistic estimate of how much time you will need.

3. Identify specific questions you would like to have answered and the general areas about which you would like information. (See the following suggested interview questions, although there probably won't be time for all of them.) Using a combination of open-ended questions—such as general questions about how the entrepreneur got started, what happened next, and so forth—and closed-ended questions—such as specific questions about what his or her goals were, if he or she had to find partners, and so forth—will help keep the interview focused yet allow for unexpected comments and insights.

4. Conduct the interview. If *both* you and the person you are interviewing are comfortable, using a small tape recorder during the interview can be of great help to you later. Remember, too, that you most likely will learn more if you are an "interested listener."

5. Evaluate what you have learned. Write down the information you have gathered in some form that will be helpful to you later on. Be as specific as you can. Jotting down direct quotes is more effective than statements such as "highly motivated individual." Also be sure to make a note of what you did not find out.

6. Write a thank-you note. This is more than a courtesy; it will also help the entrepreneur remember you favorably should you want to follow up on the interview.

Suggested Interview

QUESTIONS FOR GATHERING INFORMATION

- *Would you tell me about yourself before you started your first venture?*

  Were your parents, relatives, or close friends entrepreneurial? How so?

  Did you have any other role models?

  What was your education/military experience? In hindsight, was it helpful? In what specific ways?

  What was your previous work experience? Was it helpful? What particular "chunks of experience" were especially valuable or relevant?

  In particular, did you have any sales or marketing experience? How important was this in starting your company?

- *How did you start your venture?*

  How did you spot the opportunity? How did it surface?

  What were your goals? What were your lifestyle or other personal requirements? How did you fit these factors together?

  How did you evaluate the opportunity in terms of the critical elements for success? The competition? The market?

  Did you find or have partners? What kind of planning did you do? What kind of financing did you have?

  Did you have a start-up business plan of any kind? Please tell me about it.

  How much time did it take from conception to the first day of business? How many hours a day did you spend working on it?

  How much capital did it take? How long did it take to reach a positive cash flow and break-even sales volume? If you did not have enough money at the time, what were some ways in which you "bootstrapped" the venture (i.e., bartering, borrowing, and the like)? Tell me about the pressures and crises during that early survival period.

  What outside help did you get? Did you have experienced advisors? Lawyers? Accountants? Tax experts? Patent experts? How did you develop these networks and how long did it take?

  What was your family situation at the time?

  What did you perceive to be your own strengths? Weaknesses?

  What did you perceive to be the strengths of your venture? Weaknesses?

  What was your most triumphant moment? Your worst moment?

  Did you want to have partners or do it solo? Why?

- *Once you got going then:*

  What were the most difficult gaps to fill and problems to solve as you began to grow rapidly?

  When you looked for key people as partners, advisors, or managers, were there any personal attributes or attitudes you were especially seeking because you knew they would fit with you and were important to success? How did you find them?

  Are there any attributes among partners and advisors that you would definitely try to avoid?

  Have things become more predictable? Or less?

  Do you spend more/same/less time with your business now than in the early years?

  Do you feel more managerial and less entrepreneurial now?

  In terms of the future, do you plan to harvest? To maintain? To expand?

  Do you plan ever to retire? Would you explain?

  Have your goals changed? Have you met them?

QUESTIONS FOR CONCLUDING (CHOOSE ONE)

- What do you consider your most valuable asset—the thing that enabled you to "make it"?
- If you had it to do over again, would you do it again, in the same way?

- Looking back, what do you feel are the most critical concepts, skills, attitudes, and know-how you needed to get your company started and grown to where it is today? What will be needed for the next five years? To what extent can any of these be learned?
- Some people say there is a lot of stress being an entrepreneur. What have you experienced? How would you say it compares with other "hot seat" jobs, such as the head of a big company or a partner in a large law, consulting, or accounting firm?

- What are the things that you find personally rewarding and satisfying as an entrepreneur? What have been the rewards, risks, and trade-offs?
- Who should try to be an entrepreneur? Can you give me any ideas there?
- What advice would you give an aspiring entrepreneur? Could you suggest the three most important "lessons" you have learned? How can I learn them while minimizing the tuition?

SOURCE: Jeffry A. Timmons. *New Venture Creation,* 3rd ed. Copyright © 1994 by Jeffry A. Timmons. Reproduced with permission of the author.

7.2   Starting a New Business

OBJECTIVES

1. To introduce you to the complexities of going into business for yourself.
2. To provide hands-on experience in making new business decisions.

INSTRUCTIONS

1. Your instructor will divide the class into teams and assign each team the task of investigating the start-up of one of the following businesses:
   a. Submarine sandwich shop
   b. Day care service
   c. Bookstore
   d. Gasoline service station
   e. Other

2. Each team should research the information necessary to complete the New-Business Start-Up Worksheet. The following agencies or organizations might be of assistance:
   a. Small Business Administration
   b. Local county/city administration agencies
   c. Local chamber of commerce
   d. Local small-business development corporation
   e. U.S. Department of Commerce
   f. Farmer's Home Administration
   g. Local realtors
   h. Local business people in the same or a similar business
   i. Banks and S&Ls

3. Each team presents its findings to the class.

New-Business Start-Up Worksheet

1. *Product*

   What customer need will we satisfy?

   How can our product be unique?

2. *Customer*

   Who are our customers? What are their profiles?

   Where do they live/work/play?

   What are their buying habits?

   What are their needs?

3. *Competition*

   Who/where is the competition?

   What are their strengths and weaknesses?

   How might they respond to us?

4. *Suppliers*

   Who/where are our suppliers?

   What are their business practices?

   What relationships can we expect?

5. *Location*
   Where are our customers/competitors/suppliers?
   What are the location costs?
   What are the legal limitations to location?

6. *Physical Facilities/Equipment*
   Rent/own/build/refurbish facilities?
   Rent/lease/purchase equipment?
   Maintenance?

7. *Human Resources*
   Availability?
   Training?
   Costs?

8. *Legal/Regulatory Environment*
   Licenses/permits/certifications?
   Government agencies?
   Liability?

9. *Cultural/Social Environment*
   Cultural issues?
   Social issues?

10. *International Environment*
    International issues?

11. *Other*

PART 2 SUPPORTING CASE

Global Challenges for ExxonMobil

ExxonMobil is the largest publicly traded oil company in the world. It conducts business in more than 200 countries and territories. *Fortune* magazine ranked ExxonMobil, located in Irving, Texas, Number 2 in its *Fortune* 500 annual listing. In addition, 2004 represented a banner year for the company. It earned more than $25 billion for the year and a record $8.42 billion in the 4th quarter alone. Sales earnings for the year were close to $300 billion, a staggering amount of money for any company by any account.

Despite its stellar financial performance, over the years ExxonMobil has encountered some very serious problems that have in one way or another affected the domestic and international affairs of the company. For example, Exxon, before it merged with Mobil in 1999, never really erased its image problem as a result of the 1989 *Exxon Valdez* debacle—when an oil tanker, the *Exxon Valdez,* spilled more than 10 million gallons of crude oil into Prince William Sound, Alaska, creating an ecological nightmare that almost destroyed this once pristine Alaskan environment. Instead of owning up to the disaster immediately, company management attempted to shift the blame to third parties—the U.S. Coast Guard and the Alaskan governmental agencies; furthermore, the company took what some observers considered an excessive amount of time before management directly addressed cleanup efforts. Incidentally, Exxon paid fines and environmental restoration fees of some $3 billion.

Just last year, ExxonMobil was embroiled in a mega oil bribery scandal. Some top executives were charged by the U.S. Federal Government with attempting to bribe leaders in several African, Asian, and newly independent former USSR satellite countries to secure oil rights. At its annual general meeting in May 2005, slightly more than 28 percent of ExxonMobil shareholders voted on a proposed resolution to force the company to comply with the Kyoto Protocol treaty which calls for the reduction in greenhouse gas emissions. The Kyoto Protocol treaty has been ratified by 140 countries; the United States is one of the countries that has not signed the treaty. Some company critics have openly voiced the opinion that ExxonMobil has failed to meet its corporate responsibility.

In addition to these problems, ExxonMobil needs to resolve other issues. For example, some conflict-ridden oil-rich countries may interrupt the flow of the oil supply and thereby cause the price of oil to fluctuate dramatically. These issues may have an adverse condition on the company's balance sheet, although the recent decline of oil production has not hurt ExxonMobil's profits to date. The company has a very strong cash position and is considered cash rich as a result of fiscal prudence of its long-time chairman and CEO Lee Raymond. According to some estimates, cash accumulations approach the $25 billion mark and there are no plans to spend the money. If ExxonMobil's profits continue, financial projections suggest a nearly $40 billion cash position by the end of 2006. Yet this enviable financial position has created another problem for ExxonMobil. Management has been reluctant to invest in new oil exploration opportunities or to begin the process of building new refineries in the United States.

These current issues present one set of problems for the company. A lesser problem may occur when Chairman and CEO Raymond retires. Rex Tillerson, a 51-year-old civil engineer and 30-year Exxon employee, who began his career as a production engineer, has been designated as Raymond's heir apparent. During his tenure at Exxon, Tillerson has worked in a variety of managerial capacities. He possesses intimate knowledge of both domestic and international markets and has had significant experience in countries such as Russia, Thailand, and Yemen. When he assumes the corporate leadership mantle, Tillerson must grapple with these issues. Can Tillerson translate his various international managerial experiences to deal with some of the key issues confronting ExxonMobil?

QUESTIONS

1. Assume for a moment that you are Rex Tillerson, CEO/chairman heir apparent. Discuss some corporate strategy initiatives you would take with regard to ExxonMobil and the international community.

2. Define corporate responsibility. How well do you think ExxonMobil has met its corporate responsibilities?

3. Are there any other strategies ExxonMobil can implement to help improve its image and performance?

SOURCES: This case was prepared by Joseph C. Santora, professor, business administration at Essex County College, Newark, New Jersey. See also Shelia McNulty, "Key Issues in the Pipeline for Exxon's Heir Apparent," *Financial Times,* June 1, 2005; and "Exxon Hits Kyoto Storm at Annual Meeting," *Financial Times,* May 26, 2005; http://www.forbes.com/business/services/feeds/ap/2005/01/31ap1793587.html; http://www.exxonmobil.com.

Information for Entrepreneurs

If you are interested in starting or managing a small business, you have access to many sources of useful information.

PUBLISHED SOURCES

The first step is a complete search of materials in libraries and on the Internet. You can find a huge amount of published information, databases, and other sources about industries, markets, competitors, and personnel. Some of this information will have been uncovered when you search for ideas. Listed here are additional sources that should help get you started.

Guides and Company Information Valuable information is available in special issues and the Web sites of *BusinessWeek, Forbes, Inc., The Economist, Fast Company,* and *Fortune* and online, in the following:

- Hoovers.com
- ProQuest.com
- Investext.com
- RDS Bizsuite.com

Valuable Sites on the Internet
- Entreworld (http://www.entreworld.org), the Web site of the Kauffman Center for Entrepreneurial Leadership, Ewing Marion Kauffman Foundation
- *Fast Company* (http://www.fastcompany.com)
- Ernst & Young (http://www.ey.com)
- Global Access—SEC documents through a subscription-based Web site (http://www.primark.com)
- Inc. magazine (http://www.inc.com)
- Entrepreneur.com and magazine (http://www.entrepreneur.com)
- EDGAR Database (http://www.sec.gov)—subscription sources, such as ThomsonResearch (http://www.thomsonfinancial.com), provide images of other filings as well.
- Venture Economics (http://www.ventureeconomics.com)

Journal Articles via Computerized Indexes
- Factiva with Dow Jones, *Reuters, The Wall Street Journal*
- EBSCOhost
- FirstSearch
- Ethnic News Watch

- LEXIS/NEXIS
- *The New York Times*
- InfoTrac from Gale Group
- ABI/Inform and other ProQuest databases
- RDS Business Reference Suite
- *The Wall Street Journal*

Statistics
- Stat-USA (http://www.stat-usa.gov)—U.S. government subscription site for economic, trade and business data, and market research
- U.S. Census Bureau (http://www.census.gov)—the source of many statistical data including:
  - Statistical Abstract of the United States
  - American FactFinder—population data
  - Economic Programs (http://www.census.gov/econ/www/index.html)—data by sector
  - County Business Patterns
  - Zip Code Business Patterns
- Knight Ridder . . . CRB Commodity Year Book
- Manufacturing USA, Service Industries USA, and other sector compilations from Gale Group
- Economic Statistics Briefing Room (http://www.whitehouse.gov/fsbr/esbr.html)
- Federal Reserve Bulletin
- Survey of Current Business
- FedStats (http://www.fedstats.gov/)
- Labstat (http://stats.bls.gov/labstat.htm)
- Global Insight, formerly DRI-WEFA
- International Financial Statistics—International Monetary Fund
- World Development Indicators—World Bank
- Bloomberg Database

Consumer Expenditures
- New Strategist Publications

Projections and Forecasts
- ProQuest
- InfoTech Trends
- Guide to Special Issues and Indexes to Periodicals (*Grey House Directory of Special Issues*)
- RDS Business Reference Suite
- Value Line Investment Survey

Market Studies
- LifeStyle Market Analyst
- MarketResearch.com
- Scarborough Research
- Simmons Market Research Bureau

Consumer Expenditures
- New Strategist Publications
- Consumer Expenditure Survey
- Euromonitor

Other Sources
- Wall Street Transcript
- Brokerage House reports from Investext, Multex, etc.
- Company annual reports and Web sites

OTHER INTELLIGENCE

Everything entrepreneurs need to know will not be found in libraries because this information needs to be highly specific and current. This information is most likely available from people—industry experts, suppliers, and the like. Summarized below are some useful sources of intelligence.

Trade Associations Trade associations, especially the editors of their publications and information officers, are good sources of information. Trade shows and conferences are prime places to discover the latest activities of competitors.

Employees Employees who have left a competitor's company often can provide information about the competitor, especially if the employee departed on bad terms. Also, a firm can hire people away from a competitor. While consideration of ethics in this situation is very important, the number of experienced people in any industry is limited, and competitors must prove that a company hired a person intentionally to get specific trade secrets in order to challenge any hiring legally. Students who have worked for competitors are another source of information.

Consulting Firms Consulting firms frequently conduct industry studies and then make this information available. Frequently, in such fields as computers or software, competitors use the same design consultants, and these consultants can be sources of information.

Market Research Firms Firms doing market studies, such as those listed under published sources above, can be sources of intelligence.

Key Customers, Manufacturers, Suppliers, Distributors, and Buyers These groups are often a prime source of information.

Public Filings Federal, state, and local filings, such as filings with the Securities and Exchange Commission (SEC), Patent and Trademark Office, or Freedom of Information Act filings, can reveal a surprising amount of information. There are companies that process inquiries of this type.

Reverse Engineering Reverse engineering can be used to determine costs of production and sometimes even manufacturing methods. An example of this practice is the experience of Advanced Energy Technology, Inc., of Boulder, Colorado, which learned firsthand about such tactics. No sooner had it announced a new product, which was patented, when it received 50 orders, half of which were from competitors asking for only one or two of the items.

Networks The networks mentioned in this chapter can be sources of new venture ideas and strategies.

Other Classified ads, buyers' guides, labor unions, real estate agents, courts, local reporters, and so on can all provide clues.

The U.S. government is engaging in new and more extensive outreach efforts so that small-business owners will use government resources more and understand them more easily. In 2009, the U.S. Small Business Administration launched a community forum, the first government-sponsored online community built specifically for small-business owners, on the Business Gateway site of Business.gov. The forum combines discussion threads, blogs, and resource articles. The goals for the SBA and 21 other federal agencies that cosponsor the site are to engage in dialogue with the public, leverage the expertise that exists in both the public and private sectors, and help government better serve entrepreneurs.

SOURCES: J. A. Timmons and S. Spinelli, *New Venture Creation*, 6th ed. (Burr Ridge, IL: McGraw-Hill/Irwin, 2004), pp. 103–4; Karen Klein, "Government Resources for Entrepreneurs," *Business Week*, March 3, 2009.

chapter

8

Organization Structure

" *Take my assets—but leave me my organization and in five years I'll have it all back.* "

— Alfred P. Sloan Jr.

LEARNING OBJECTIVES

After studying Chapter 8, you will be able to:

LO 1 Explain how differentiation and integration influence an organization's structure. p. 276

LO 2 Summarize how authority operates. p. 278

LO 3 Define the roles of the board of directors and the chief executive officer. p. 279

LO 4 Discuss how span of control affects structure and managerial effectiveness. p. 282

LO 5 Explain how to delegate effectively. p. 284

LO 6 Distinguish between centralized and decentralized organizations. p. 285

LO 7 Summarize ways organizations can be structured. p. 287

LO 8 Identify the unique challenges of the matrix organization. p. 292

LO 9 Describe important integrative mechanisms. p. 296

CHAPTER OUTLINE

Fundamentals of Organizing
Differentiation
Integration

The Vertical Structure
Authority in Organizations
Hierarchical Levels
Span of Control
Delegation
Decentralization

The Horizontal Structure
The Functional Organization
The Divisional Organization
The Matrix Organization
The Network Organization

Organizational Integration
Coordination by Standardization
Coordination by Plan
Coordination by Mutual Adjustment
Coordination and Communication

Looking Ahead

Management Close-Up

CAN NANCY SNYDER'S BRIGHT IDEA SECURE WHIRLPOOL'S FORTUNES?

For decades, the name Whirlpool has been synonymous with top-quality, high-performing appliances: refrigerators, dishwashers, freezers, ranges, washers and dryers, and more. Founded in 1911, Whirlpool Corporation rose to become the world's largest manufacturer of home appliances, with annual sales of more than $10 billion. By the late 1990s, however, Whirlpool's growth with those big-ticket items had ground to a halt. The company's profits were falling, and its share price hit an all-time low.

Whirlpool leaders sought to stop the bleeding by cutting costs and laying off 10 percent of the company's 60,000-member workforce. At the same time, however, they knew Whirlpool couldn't trim its way to prosperity.

That was when CEO David R. Whitwam had a revolutionary notion. At the time, Whirlpool was organized traditionally in terms of product development—it was the responsibility of the marketing and engineering departments. But Whitwam decided to cast his net wider for new-product ideas. He sent a message to every Whirlpool employee—from laborers on the production floor all the way to executives in the corner offices. His invitation: send me your thoughts for what could be new Whirlpool moneymakers.

Whitwam named Whirlpool employee Nancy R. Snyder Chief Innovation Officer. With the promotion came the directive to figure out how to make Whirlpool the leader in innovation, as well as the market leader in appliances. Whirlpool employees around the globe responded to Whitwam's message, and Snyder received over a thousand ideas—some of them interesting, others fanciful. To manage the deluge, she mobilized a team of 75 employees at all levels across the company to evaluate the new ideas and brainstorm others. Although this group did generate one successful idea—the Gladiator line of cabinets and appliances for garages—the 75-person team was too cumbersome. Furthermore, Whirlpool's middle managers grew annoyed with their employees spending time pursuing creative projects, many with little or no potential for marketability, instead of focusing on the work at hand.[1]

> A well-known company with a solid reputation, Whirlpool needed to find a way to break out of its doldrums and begin growing again. As you read this chapter, consider how Nancy Snyder adapted Whirlpool's organizational structure to find the solution to the problem.

Many of us know about Whirlpool and would think of it as enormously successful. Yet, a few years ago, growth at the company had slowed. Profits were falling, and the Whirlpool brands were perceived as "status quo." How could the company respond to this situation? The way in which a company organizes itself to address an issue such as declining profits may well be the most important factor in determining whether its strategy will succeed. Whirlpool, like many other companies, is working hard to make certain that its strategy and structure are aligned.

Whirlpool's profits were falling, growth at the company was slowing down, and their products were perceived as being "status quo." How can the company respond to this situation? Whirlpool Corporation and Chinese electronics company Hisense have recently formed a joint venture. The 50-50 joint venture was formed for the delivery of new world-class and innovative appliances to consumers in the U.S. and China. The companies will share research, technology, and procurement and development resources to produce state-of-the art refrigerators and washing machines to a worldwide market.

This chapter focuses on the vertical and horizontal dimensions of organization structure. We begin by covering basic principles of *differentiation* and *integration*. Next, we discuss the vertical structure, which includes issues of *authority*, hierarchy, delegation, and decentralization. We continue on to describe the horizontal structure, which includes functional, divisional, and matrix forms. Finally, we illustrate the ways in which organizations can integrate their structures: coordination by standardization, coordination by plan, and coordination by mutual adjustment.

In the next chapter, we continue with the topic of organization structure but take a different perspective. In that chapter we focus on the flexibility and responsiveness of an organization, that is, how capable it is of changing its form and adapting to strategy, technology, the environment, and other challenges it confronts.

Fundamentals of Organizing

LO 1

organization chart

The reporting structure and division of labor in an organization.

To get going, let's start simple. We often begin to describe a firm's structure by looking at its organization chart. The **organization chart** depicts the positions in the firm and the way they are arranged. The chart provides a picture of the reporting structure (who reports to whom) and the various activities that are carried out by different individuals. Most companies have official organization charts drawn up to give people this information.

Figure 8.1 shows the traditional organization chart. Note the various types of information that are conveyed in a very simple way:

1. The boxes represent different work.
2. The titles in the boxes show the work performed by each unit.
3. Reporting and authority relationships are indicated by solid lines showing superior–subordinate connections.
4. Levels of management are indicated by the number of horizontal layers in the chart. All persons or units that are at the same rank and report to the same person are on one level.

Although the organization chart presents some important structural features, other design issues related to structure—while not so obvious—are no less significant. Two

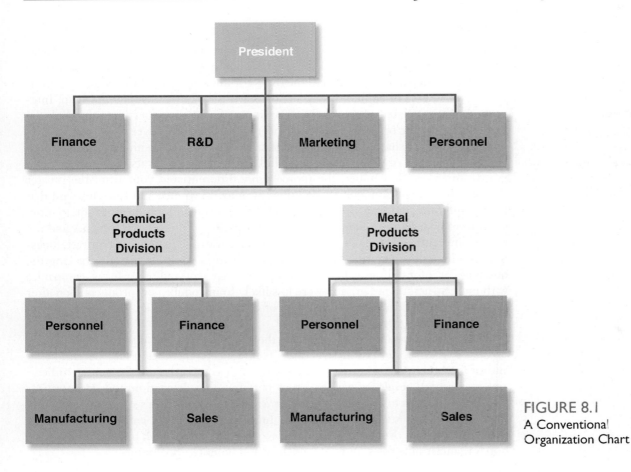

FIGURE 8.1
A Conventional
Organization Chart

fundamental concepts around which organizations are structured are differentiation and integration. **Differentiation** means that the organization is composed of many different units that work on different kinds of tasks, using different skills and work methods. **Integration** means that these differentiated units are put back together so that work is coordinated into an overall product.[2]

Differentiation

Several related concepts underlie the idea of structural differentiation. For example, differentiation is created through division of labor and job specialization. **Division of labor** means the work of the organization is subdivided into smaller tasks. Various individuals and units throughout the organization perform different tasks. **Specialization** refers to the fact that different people or groups often perform specific parts of the larger task. The two concepts are, of course, closely related. Administrative assistants and accountants specialize in, and perform, different jobs; similarly, marketing, finance, and human resources tasks are divided among the respective departments. The many tasks that must be carried out in an organization make specialization and division of labor necessities. Otherwise, the complexity of the overall work of the organization would be too much for any individual.[3]

Differentiation is high when an organization has many subunits and many kinds of specialists who think differently. Harvard professors Lawrence and Lorsch found that organizations in complex, dynamic environments (plastics firms in their study) developed a high degree of differentiation to cope with the complex challenges. Companies in simple, stable environments (container companies) had low levels of differentiation. Companies in intermediate environments (food companies) had intermediate differentiation.[4]

differentiation

An aspect of the organization's internal environment created by job specialization and the division of labor.

integration

The degree to which differentiated work units work together and coordinate their efforts.

division of labor

The assignment of different tasks to different people or groups.

specialization

A process in which different individuals and units perform different tasks.

Integration

As organizations differentiate their structures, managers must simultaneously consider issues of integration. All the specialized tasks in an organization cannot be performed completely independently. Because the different units are part of the larger organization, some degree of communication and cooperation must exist among them. Integration and its related concept, **coordination,** refer to the procedures that link the various parts of the organization to achieve the organization's overall mission.

Integration is achieved through structural mechanisms that enhance collaboration and coordination. Any job activity that links different work units performs an integrative function. Remember, the more highly differentiated your firm, the greater the need for integration among the different units. Lawrence and Lorsch found that highly differentiated firms were successful if they also had high levels of integration. Organizations are more likely to fail if they exist in complex environments and are highly differentiated but fail to integrate their activities adequately.[5] In contrast, focusing on integration may slow innovation, at least for a while. In a study tracking the outcomes at information technology companies that acquired other firms, companies with more structural integration were less likely to introduce new products soon after the acquisition, but integration had less of an impact on product launches involving more experienced target companies.[6]

These concepts permeate the rest of the chapter. First, we discuss *vertical differentiation* within organization structure. This concept includes issues pertaining to authority within an organization, the board of directors, the chief executive officer, and hierarchical levels, as well as issues pertaining to delegation and decentralization. Next, we turn to *horizontal differentiation* in an organization's structure, exploring issues of departmentalization that create functional, divisional, and matrix organizations. Finally, we cover issues pertaining to *structural integration*, including coordination, organizational roles, interdependence, and boundary spanning.

coordination

The procedures that link the various parts of an organization for the purpose of achieving the organization's overall mission.

The Vertical Structure

LO 2

To understand issues such as reporting relationships, authority, responsibility, and the like, we need to begin with the vertical dimension of a firm's structure.

Authority in Organizations

At the most fundamental level, the functioning of every organization depends on the use of **authority,** the legitimate right to make decisions and to tell other people what to do. For example, a boss has the authority to give an order to a subordinate.

Traditionally, authority resides in *positions* rather than in people. Thus, the job of vice president of a particular division has authority over that division, regardless of how many people come and go in that position and who currently holds it.

In private business enterprises, the owners have ultimate authority. In most small, simply structured companies, the owner also acts as manager. Sometimes the owner hires another person to manage the business and its employees. The owner gives this manager some authority to oversee the operations, but the manager is accountable to—that is, reports and defers to—the owner. Thus, the owner still has the ultimate authority.

Formal position authority is generally the primary means of running an organization. An order that a boss gives to a lower-level employee is usually carried out. As this occurs throughout the organization day after day, the organization can move forward and achieve its goals.[7] However, authority in an organization is not always position-dependent. People with particular expertise, experience, or personal qualities may

authority

The legitimate right to make decisions and to tell other people what to do.

"Authority without wisdom is like a heavy axe without an edge, fitter to bruise than polish."

—Anne Bradstreet

have considerable *informal* authority—scientists in research companies, for example, or employees who are computer-savvy. Effective managers are aware of informal authority as a factor that can help or hinder their achievement of the organization's goals; we will say more about informal authority in the next chapter. For now, we discuss the formal authority structure of the organization from the top down, beginning with the board of directors.

Board of Directors   In corporations, the owners are the stockholders. But because there are numerous stockholders and these individuals generally lack timely

LO 3

information, few are directly involved in managing the organization. Stockholders elect a board of directors to oversee the organization. The board, led by the chair, makes major decisions affecting the organization, subject to corporate charter and bylaw provisions. Boards perform at least three major sets of duties: (1) selecting, assessing, rewarding, and perhaps replacing the CEO; (2) determining the firm's strategic direction and reviewing financial performance; and (3) ensuring ethical, socially responsible, and legal conduct.[8] In a move that addresses both the board's responsibility for CEO compensation and public concern that directors have become too cozy with executives, the board of directors at Aflac recently decided they would ask shareholders to vote on the pay packages of the insurance company's executives. The votes serve an advisory purpose. Aflac's directors still decide on the pay packages, but they can see whether they are acting in accordance with shareholders' wishes.[9]

Large corporations have a shareholder-elected board of directors. Small-business leaders can benefit from the expertise of outside executives in the same way by forming peer groups or attending monthly meetings with business owners from noncompeting companies to trade advice.

The board's membership usually includes some top executives—called *inside directors*. Outside members of the board tend to be executives at other companies. The trend in recent years has been toward reducing the number of insiders and increasing the number of outsiders. Today most companies have a majority of outside directors. Boards made up of strong, independent outsiders are more likely to provide different information and perspectives and to prevent big mistakes. Successful boards tend to be those who are active, critical participants in determining company strategies. Even so, in the wake of scandals and lawsuits, many boards have shifted their focus to compliance issues, such as audits, financial reporting, and laws against discrimination. These issues are critically important, but a board staffed mainly with legal and regulatory experts cannot always give management the necessary direction on strategy.[10]

The owner and managers of a small business may need the expertise of a board of directors at least as much as a large company does. To obtain some of these benefits without the expense or loss of day-to-day control, small-business leaders may seek advisers who will hold them accountable for their goals and performance. Some owners set up a board of advisers, such as owners of

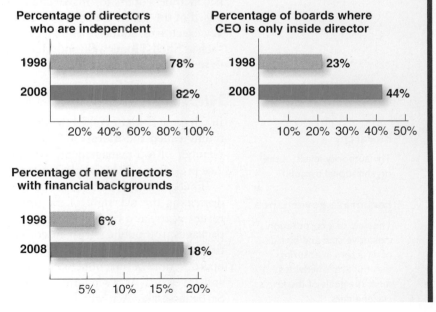

In today's large corporations, most boards of directors have between 9 and 13 directors. Boards are relying more on outside directors, including retired chief executive and chief financial officers.[11]

Percentage of directors who are independent
1998: 78%
2008: 82%

Percentage of boards where CEO is only inside director
1998: 23%
2008: 44%

Percentage of new directors with financial backgrounds
1998: 6%
2008: 18%

Two respected top executives, Bill Gates (left) of Microsoft and Brad Anderson (right) of Best Buy, discuss the Xbox 360 at the grand opening of the store in Bellevue, Washington.

noncompeting companies, retired executives, and perhaps their banker or accountant. Others hire a business consultant or coach, and they have regular meetings at which they discuss progress toward goals. Owners might even take on a partner who has more skills or experience in an area where the owner is relatively weak. Business development coach Jack Tester advocates such efforts based on his own experience, which has taught him that he works harder when he knows someone is watching and will hold him accountable.[12]

Chief Executive Officer The authority officially vested in the board of directors is assigned to a chief executive officer (CEO), who occupies the top of the organizational pyramid. The CEO is personally accountable to the board and to the owners for the organization's performance.

In some corporations, one person holds all three positions of CEO, chair of the board of directors, and president.[13] More commonly, however, one person holds two of those positions, with the CEO serving also as either the chair of the board or the president of the organization. When the CEO is president, the chair may be honorary and may do little more than conduct meetings. In other cases, the chair may be the CEO and the president is second in command.

In recent years the trend has been to separate the position of CEO and chairman of the board. Sometimes this change is related to improved corporate governance; board oversight is easier when the CEO is not quite as dominant a figure. In other cases, the board has acted to reduce an unpopular CEO's power or to help prepare for a successor to the CEO.

Top Management Team Increasingly, CEOs share their authority with other key members of the top management team. Top management teams typically are composed of the CEO, president, chief operating officer, chief financial officer, and other key executives. Rather than make critical decisions on their own, CEOs at companies such as Shell, Honeywell, and Merck regularly meet with their top management teams to make decisions as a unit.[14]

Hierarchical Levels

hierarchy

The authority levels of the organizational pyramid.

corporate governance

The role of a corporation's executive staff and board of directors in ensuring that the firm's activities meet the goals of the firm's stakeholders.

In Chapter 1, we discussed the three broad levels of the organizational pyramid, commonly called the **hierarchy**. The CEO occupies the top position and is the senior member of top management. The top managerial level also includes presidents and vice presidents. They are the strategic managers in charge of the entire organization.

The key responsibilities at this top level include **corporate governance**—a term describing the oversight of the firm by its executive staff and board of directors. In recent years, as a result of corporate scandals and extremely generous executive-pay packages, the public's trust in corporate governance has eroded significantly. Some firms, including Enron and WorldCom, went bankrupt as a result of executive or board action or inaction, with enormous hardship to employees, pension holders, and investors. As we mentioned in Chapter 5, Congress responded by passing the Sarbanes-Oxley Act, which, along with requirements by the Securities and Exchange

Commission, imposed much tighter corporate governance rules. For example, company CEOs and CFOs (chief financial officers) now have to personally certify the accuracy of their firm's financial statements. The "From the Pages of *BusinessWeek*" feature describes how the Sarbanes-Oxley Act has made the role of directors more challenging.

The second broad level of the organization is middle management. At this level, managers are in charge of plants or departments. The lowest level is made up of lower management and workers. It includes office managers, sales managers, supervisors, and other first-line managers, as well as the employees who report directly to them. This level is also called the *operational level* of the organization.

A structure with fewer horizontal layers saves time and money.

Board of Hard Knocks

FROM THE PAGES OF
BusinessWeek

A new era for directors dawned with the passage of the Sarbanes-Oxley Act of 2002. Then board members were hit with the frightening prospect of real financial liability in a smattering of lawsuits that followed the corporate crime wave. Now the heat on directors is growing more intense. Their reputations are increasingly at risk when the companies they watch over are tainted by scandal. Their judgment is being questioned by activist shareholders outraged by sky-high pay packages. And investors and regulators are subjecting their actions to higher scrutiny. Long gone are the days when a director could get away with a quick rubber-stamp of a CEO's plans.

The new dynamic has played out in recent board dramas involving Home Depot, Hewlett-Packard, and Morgan Stanley, among others. If Home Depot's directors had any hope that the spotlight on them would fade in the wake of departure of ex-CEO Robert L. Nardelli on January 3, 2007, they now know better. Unhappy investors are continuing to agitate for new blood in the company's boardroom. "The culpability is not on the CEO for asking [for high pay] but the directors" for approving it, says Richard Ferlauto, director of pensions and benefits policy for the American Federation of State, County & Municipal Employees, one of the more vocal investment funds putting pressure on Home Depot's Board. "Compensation is a symptom. It flags for us a board that is unwilling to challenge a CEO."

And that just won't do. The old rules of civility that discouraged directors from asking managers tough or embarrassing questions are eroding. At the same time, board members are being forced to devote more time and energy to many of their most important duties: setting CEO compensation, overseeing the auditing of financial statements, and, when needed, investigating crises. That's the good news. The bad news is they are so busy delving into the minutiae of compliance that they don't have nearly as much time to advise corporate chieftains on strategy.

The hottest issue for boards is shaping up to be executive compensation. For the first time ever, companies are required to disclose a complete tally of everything they have promised to pay their executives, including such until now hidden or difficult-to-find items as severance, deferred pay, accumulated pension benefits, and perks worth more than $10,000. They will also have to provide an explanation of how and why they've chosen to pay executives as they do. The numbers are likely to be eye-popping. Michael S. Melbinger, a top compensation lawyer in Chicago, thinks that when all the proxies are filed, there could be 50 companies or more with CEO pay packages worth $150 million or more.

And this is, believe it or not, coming as just as big a surprise to many directors as it will be to investors. Up to now, most directors have never seen a tally for the total pay they've promised to executives. "Pay was all compartmentalized: Boards would approve a salary, a certain amount for a bonus, or a certain amount if he got fired, but no one ever added it all up," says Fred Whittlesey, the head of Compensation Venture Group.

Boards are digging deep into compensation consultant reports and questioning the logic of these packages—and even sometimes, in awkward meetings, asking CEOs and other highly paid officers for givebacks. Melbinger tells of a meeting several months ago in which he sat down with a board and the CEO and outlined his perks. The CEO had a provision in his contract that not only required the company to reimburse him for his medical coverage, deductibles, and co-pays, but also had to give him a "tax gross-up" for the payments. One of the stunned board members said, "Now, let me get this straight—not only do you not have to pay the amounts for your medical coverage that every other employee of this company has to pay, we pay your taxes on it, too?" The CEO turned bright red, recognizing how bad that was going to look on the disclosure forms. He quickly agreed to give up the perk.

It's not just compensation committee members who find the world changing. Audit committees used to meet only twice a year: once when it was time to take the audit in and once more to ratify it. Dick Swanson, chair of the audit committees of two companies, says he now holds 8 to 12 meetings a year for each committee.

Some argue that as a result of the heightened pressure, boards are getting better. "One of the reasons bad stuff went on so much in the past," says Warren L. Batts, former chairman and CEO of Tupperware Brands Corporation and now a director of Methode Electronics, "was the board wasn't organized to deal with them."

SOURCE: Excerpted from Nanette Byrnes and Jane Sasseen, "Board of Hard Knocks," *BusinessWeek*, January 22, 2007, downloaded from Business & Company Resource Center, http://galenet.galegroup.com.

An authority structure is the glue that holds these levels together. Generally, but not always, people at higher levels have the authority to make decisions and tell lower-level people what to do. For example, middle managers can give orders to first-line supervisors; first-line supervisors, in turn, direct operative-level workers.

A powerful trend for U.S. businesses over the past few decades has been to reduce the number of hierarchical layers. General Electric used to have 29 levels; today it has only a handful of layers and its hierarchical structure is basically flat. Most executives today believe that fewer layers create a more efficient, fast-acting, and cost-effective organization. This also holds true for the **subunits** of major corporations. A study of 234 branches of a financial services company found that branches with fewer layers tended to have higher operating efficiency than did branches with more layers.[15]

This trend and research might seem to suggest that hierarchy is a bad thing, but entrepreneur Joel Spolsky learned that a completely flat structure is not necessarily ideal. When Spolsky and Michael Pryor started Fog Creek Software, they decided they would empower employees by having everyone report to the two owners. The system worked fine for a few years until Fog Creek grew to 17 full-time employees. At that size, the company was no longer one small happy family; employees had concerns and were finding it difficult to approach the partners and set up three-way meetings with them. So Spolsky and Pryor tapped two of the employees to serve as leaders of programming teams. Employees found it easier to talk to their team leader, and Spolsky concludes that this layer of "middle management" is helping his company run more smoothly.[16]

subunits

Subdivisions of an organization.

LO 4

Span of Control

The number of people under a manager is an important feature of an organization's structure. The number of subordinates who report directly to an executive or supervisor is called the **span of control.** The implications of differences in the span of control for the shape of an organization are straightforward. Holding size constant, narrow spans build a *tall* organization that has many reporting levels. Wide spans create a *flat* organization with fewer reporting levels. The span of control can be too narrow or too wide. The optimal span of control maximizes effectiveness because it is

span of control

The number of subordinates who report directly to an executive or supervisor.

(1) narrow enough to permit managers to maintain control over subordinates but (2) not so narrow that it leads to overcontrol and an excessive number of managers who oversee a small number of subordinates.

What is the optimal number of subordinates? Five, according to Napoleon Bonaparte.[17] Some managers today still consider five a good number. At one Japanese bank, in contrast, several hundred branch managers report to the same boss.

Actually, the optimal span of control depends on a number of factors. The span should be wider when (1) the work is clearly defined and unambiguous, (2) subordinates are highly trained and have access to information, (3) the manager is highly capable and supportive, (4) jobs are similar and performance measures are comparable, and (5) subordinates prefer autonomy to close supervisory control. If the opposite conditions exist, a narrow span of control may be more appropriate.[18]

Delegation

As we look at organizations and recognize that authority is spread out over various levels and spans of control, the issue of delegation becomes paramount. **Delegation** is the assignment of authority and responsibility to a subordinate at a lower level. It often requires that the subordinate report back to his or her boss about how effectively the assignment was carried out. Delegation is perhaps the most fundamental feature of management, because it entails getting work done through others. Thus, delegation is important at all hierarchical levels. The process can occur between any two individuals in any type of structure with regard to any task.

Some managers are comfortable fully delegating an assignment to subordinates; others are not. Consider the differences between these two office managers and the ways they gave out the same assignment in the following example. Are both of these examples of delegation?

> **delegation**
>
> The assignment of new or additional responsibilities to a subordinate.

Manager A: "Call Tom Burton at Nittany Office Equipment. Ask him to give you the price list on an upgrade for our personal computers. I want to move up to a Core 2 Duo processor with 4 gigs of RAM and at least a 500-gigabyte hard drive. Ask them to give you a demonstration of the Vista operating system and Microsoft Office Communication Services (OCS). I want to be able to establish collaboration capability for the entire group. Invite Cochran and Snow to the demonstration, and let them try it out. Have them write up a summary of their needs and the potential applications they see for the new systems. Then prepare me a report with the costs and specifications of the upgrade for the entire department. Oh, yes, be sure to ask for information on service costs."

Manager B: "I'd like to do something about our personal computer system. I've been getting some complaints that the current systems are too slow, can't run current software, and don't allow for networking. Could you evaluate our options and give me a recommendation on what we should do? Our budget is around $2,500 per person, but I'd like to stay under that if we can. Feel free to talk to some of the managers to get their input, but we need to have this done as soon as possible."

Responsibility, Authority, and Accountability   When delegating work, it is helpful to keep in mind the important distinctions among the concepts of authority, responsibility, and accountability. **Responsibility** means that a person is assigned a task that he or she is supposed to carry out. When delegating work responsibilities, the manager also should delegate to the subordinate enough authority to get the job done. *Authority*, recall, means that the person has the power and the right to make decisions, give orders, draw on resources, and do whatever else is necessary to fulfill the responsibility. Ironically, it is quite common for people to have more responsibility than authority; they must perform as well as they can through informal influence

> **responsibility**
>
> The assignment of a task that an employee is supposed to carry out.

tactics instead of relying purely on authority. More will be said about informal power and how to use it in Chapter 12.

As the manager delegates responsibilities, subordinates are held accountable for achieving results. **Accountability** means that the subordinate's manager has the right to expect the subordinate to perform the job, and the right to take corrective action if the subordinate fails to do so. The subordinate must report upward on the status and quality of his or her performance of the task.

However, the ultimate responsibility—accountability to higher-ups—lies with the manager doing the delegating. Managers remain responsible and accountable not only for their own actions but also for the actions of their subordinates. Managers should not resort to delegation to others as a means of escaping their own responsibilities. In many cases, however, managers refuse to accept responsibility for subordinates' actions. Managers often "pass the buck" or take other evasive action to ensure they are not held accountable for mistakes.[19] Ideally, however, empowering employees to make decisions or take action results in an increase in employee responsibility.

Advantages of Delegation   Delegating work offers important advantages, particularly when it is done effectively. Effective delegation leverages the manager's energy and talent and those of his or her subordinates. It allows managers to accomplish much more than they would be able to do on their own. Conversely, lack of delegation, or ineffective delegation, sharply reduces what a manager can achieve. The manager also saves one of his or her most valuable assets—time—by giving some of his or her responsibility to somebody else. He or she is then free to devote energy to important, higher-level activities such as planning, setting objectives, and monitoring performance.

Another very important advantage of delegation is that it helps develop effective subordinates. Look again at the different ways the two office managers gave out the same assignment. The approach that is more likely to empower subordinates and help them develop will be obvious to you. (You may also quickly conclude which of the two managers you would prefer to work for.) Delegation essentially gives the subordinate a more important job. The subordinate acquires an opportunity to develop new skills and to demonstrate potential for additional responsibilities and perhaps promotion. In essence, the subordinate receives a vital form of on-the-job training that could pay off in the future. In addition, there is evidence that, at least for some employees, delegation promotes a sense of being an important, contributing member of the organization, so these employees tend to feel a stronger commitment, perform their tasks better, and engage in more innovation.[20]

Through delegation, the organization also receives payoffs. Allowing managers to devote more time to important managerial functions while lower-level employees carry

However, imagine delegation taken to the extreme—allowing managers to institute takeovers of other companies. That's exactly what Illinois Tool Works has done. ITW has built a reputation on its ability to acquire smaller firms, quickly and efficiently. Now a conglomerate with 750 business units worldwide, ITW was originally a toolmaker. Its products still tend to be small and industrial—screws, auto parts, the plastic rings that hold a six-pack of soda, and the like. But ITW makes much of its money by buying and selling smaller firms. That's where managers like John Stevens, a mechanical engineer, come in.

Stevens, and many others like him, are being trained in the art of acquisition. CEO David Speer believes that employees like this are the perfect choice for the task because they know and understand the business they are in. So ITW executives are now giving two-day acquisition workshops for business-unit managers, then sending them out to buy. "We weren't necessarily banging on doors as we should have," explains Speer. "It was a question of getting people trained and re-energized."[21]

---

accountability

The expectation that employees will perform a job, take corrective action when necessary, and report upward on the status and quality of their performance.

Effective delegation raises the quality of subordinates and the service they provide to customers or coworkers.

out assignments means that jobs are done more efficiently and cost effectively. In addition, as subordinates develop and grow in their own jobs, their ability to contribute to the organization increases as well.

How Should Managers Delegate?   To achieve the advantages we have just discussed, delegation must be done properly. As Figure 8.2 shows, effective delegation proceeds through several steps.[22]

The first step in the delegation process, defining the goal, requires the manager to have a clear understanding of the outcome he or she wants. Then the manager should select a person who is capable of performing the task. Delegation is especially beneficial if you can identify an employee who would benefit from developing skills through the experience of taking on the additional responsibility.

The person who gets the assignment should be given the authority, time, and resources to carry out the task successfully. The required resources usually involve people, money, and equipment, but often they may also involve critical information that will put the assignment in context. ("Review every cost item carefully, because if we're the low bidder, we'll get the account.") Throughout the delegation process, the manager and the subordinate must work together and communicate about the project. The manager should know the subordinate's ideas at the beginning and inquire about progress or problems at periodic meetings and review sessions. Thus, even though the subordinate performs the assignment, the manager is available and aware of its current status. These checkups also provide an important opportunity to offer encouragement and praise.

Some tasks, such as disciplining subordinates and conducting performance reviews, should not be delegated. But when managers err, it usually is because they delegated too little rather than too much. The manager who wants to learn how to delegate more effectively should remember this distinction: If you are not delegating, you are merely *doing* things; but the more you delegate, the more you are truly *building* and *managing* an organization.[23]

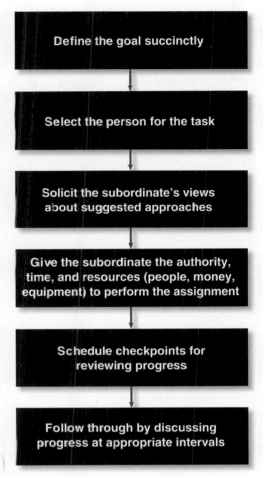

FIGURE 8.2
The Steps in Effective Delegation

Decentralization

The delegation of responsibility and authority *decentralizes* decision making. In a **centralized organization,** important decisions usually are made at the top. In **decentralized organizations,** more decisions are made at lower levels. Ideally, decision making occurs at the level of the people who are most directly affected and have the most intimate knowledge about the problem. This is particularly important when the business environment is fast-changing and decisions must be made quickly and well. Balanced against these criteria, centralization may be valuable when departments have different priorities or conflicting goals, which need to be mediated by top management. For example, when researchers modeled the search for new ideas in organizations, they found that the worst performance occurred in decentralized organizations where the search for new ideas was carried out at lower levels, because ideas were presented for approval only if they benefited the particular department doing the search.[24]

Sometimes organizations change their degree of centralization, depending on the particular challenges they face. Tougher times often cause senior managements to take charge, whereas in times of rapid growth, decisions are pushed farther down the chain of command. For example, in the 1980s Harley-Davidson was in great financial difficulty and faced tough competition from Honda, Suzuki, and Yamaha. It needed strong, centralized leadership that could react quickly and decisively to survive. But once the crisis was past, this approach wasn't as effective in gaining the commitment

 LO 6

centralized organization

An organization in which high-level executives make most decisions and pass them down to lower levels for implementation.

decentralized organization

An organization in which lower-level managers make important decisions.

The traditional hierarchy at Harley-Davidson has been replaced with collaborative leadership, based on the assumption that all employees can make decisions and take responsibility for meeting the organization's goals. Why would this be an effective form of decision making?

☑ **The bottom line**
SPEED

Decentralization often speeds decision making.

and energy of employees, who were the ones building the products and the relationships with customers. Harley-Davidson made the transition to a flatter, more empowered organization that decentralizes decision making. Today, the traditional hierarchy at the company has been replaced with collaborative leadership, based on the assumption that all employees can make decisions and take responsibility for meeting the organization's goals.[25]

Most American executives today understand the advantages of pushing decision-making authority down to the point of the action. The level that deals directly with problems and opportunities has the most relevant information and can best foresee the consequences of decisions. Executives also see how the decentralized approach allows people to take timelier action.[26]

When times get tough, people tend to want to seize greater control over their situation, and if you're a senior executive, a centralized structure often seems to be the safest course. Nevertheless, executives at Johnson & Johnson have been sticking to decentralization, even during the recent severe recession.

Johnson & Johnson, best known for brands like Band-Aid bandages and Splenda artificial sweetener, operates 250 business units in 57 countries. Besides the famous consumer brands, it also makes medical devices and pharmaceuticals—all products linked to health care. With so many product lines in so many geographic areas, executives at the company's New Jersey headquarters couldn't possibly make all the right decisions. So within the three broad divisions of consumer products, medical devices and diagnostics, and pharmaceuticals, line managers are charged with running business units specializing in particular products and regions.

Not only does this arrangement push decisions closer to the customers, but it also helps J&J develop a huge pool of management talent. Managers can improve their skills while serving a small market segment and take on additional responsibilities as they learn. The company's chief executive officer and chief financial officer both built careers at J&J by working in various businesses to develop broad skills. Similarly, Sheri McCoy, who leads the pharmaceuticals division, held various positions in devices and diagnostics. That kind of experience is hard to get in a company that is smaller or more centralized, so J&J is using its organizational structure as a source of competitive advantage.[27]

According to Raj Gupta, president of Environmental Systems Design (ESD), the engineering design firm decentralized as a necessary response to growth. A traditional "command and control" approach to management worked fine when the company was starting out, but now with 240 engineering and design professionals designing for diverse clients working on commercial, transportation, residential, manufacturing, energy, and other projects, it would be impossible for a few people at the top to dictate solutions. In fact, it wouldn't even be desirable, given the diverse expertise of its employees. So instead of grouping staff into functional departments such as sustainable design or electrical work, ESD has a structure in which studios of professionals serve particular clients, making decisions to meet their specialized needs.[28]

The Horizontal Structure

LO 7

Up to this point, we've talked primarily about vertical aspects of organization structure. Issues of authority, span of control, delegation, and decentralization are important because they give us an idea of how managers and employees relate to one another at different levels. Yet, separating discussion of vertical differentiation from horizontal differentiation is a bit artificial because the elements work simultaneously.

As the tasks of organizations become increasingly complex, the organization inevitably must be subdivided—that is, *departmentalized*—into smaller units or departments. One of the first places this can be seen is in the distinction between line and staff departments. **Line departments** are those that have responsibility for the principal activities of the firm. Line units deal directly with the organization's primary goods or services; they make things, sell things, or provide customer service. At General Motors, for example, line departments include product design, fabrication, assembly, distribution, and the like. Line managers typically have much authority and power in the organization. They have the ultimate responsibility for making major operating decisions. They also are accountable for the bottom-line results of their decisions.

Staff departments are those that provide specialized or professional skills that support line departments. They include research, legal, accounting, public relations, and human resources departments. Each of these specialized units often has its own vice president, and some are vested with a great deal of authority, as when accounting or finance groups approve and monitor budgetary activities.

In traditionally structured organizations, conflicts could arise between line and staff departments. One reason was that career paths and success in many staff functions have depended on being an expert in that particular functional area, while success in line functions is based more on knowing the organization's industry. Thus, while line managers might be eager to pursue new products and customers, staff managers might seem to stifle these ideas with a focus on requirements and procedures. Line managers might seem more willing to take risks for the sake of growth, while staff managers seem more focused on protecting the company from risks. But in today's organizations, staff units tend to be less focused on monitoring and controlling performance and more interested in moving toward a new role focused on strategic support and expert advice.[29] For example, human resource managers have broadened their focus from merely creating procedures that meet legal requirements to helping organizations plan for, recruit, develop, and keep the kinds of employees who will give the organization a long-term competitive advantage. This type of strategic thinking not only makes staff managers more valuable to their organizations but also can reduce the conflict between line and staff departments.

As organizations divide work into different units, we can detect patterns in the way departments are clustered and arranged. The three basic approaches to **departmentalization** are functional, divisional, and matrix. We will talk about each and highlight some of their similarities and differences.

The Functional Organization

In a **functional organization,** jobs (and departments) are specialized and grouped according to *business functions* and the skills they require: production, marketing, human resources, research and development, finance, accounting, and so forth. Figure 8.3 illustrates a basic functional organization chart.

Functional departmentalization is common in both large and small organizations. Large companies may organize along several different functional groupings, including groupings unique to their businesses. For example, Carmike Cinema, which operates

line departments

Units that deal directly with the organization's primary goods and services.

staff departments

Units that support line departments.

departmentalization

Subdividing an organization into smaller subunits.

functional organization

Departmentalization around specialized activities such as production, marketing, and human resources.

FIGURE 8.3
The Functional
Organization

more than 2,400 screens in 289 theaters in 37 states, has vice presidents of finance, concessions, film, and entertainment and digital cinema, as well as a general manager of theater operations.

The traditional functional approach to departmentalization has a number of potential advantages for an organization:[30]

$ **The bottom line**

COST

When like functions are grouped, savings often result.

1. *Economies of scale can be realized.* When people with similar skills are grouped, more efficient equipment can be purchased, and discounts for large purchases can be used.
2. *Monitoring of the environment* is more effective. Each functional group is more closely attuned to developments in its own field and therefore can adapt more readily.
3. *Performance standards* are better maintained. People with similar training and interests may develop a shared concern for performance in their jobs.
4. People have greater opportunity for *specialized training* and *in-depth skill development.*
5. Technical specialists are relatively *free of administrative work.*
6. *Decision making* and *lines of communication* are simple and clearly understood.

The functional form does have disadvantages, however. People may care more about their own function than about the company as a whole, and their attention to functional tasks may make them lose focus on overall product quality and customer satisfaction. Managers develop functional expertise but do not acquire knowledge of the other areas of the business; they become specialists, but not generalists. Between functions, conflicts arise, and communication and coordination fall off. In short, while functional differentiation may exist, *functional integration* may not.

As a consequence, the functional structure may be most appropriate in rather simple, stable environments. If the organization becomes fragmented (or *dis*integrated), it may have difficulty developing and bringing new products to market and responding quickly to customer demands and other changes. Particularly when companies are growing and business environments are changing, organizations need to integrate work areas more effectively so that they can be more flexible and responsive. Other forms of departmentalization can be more flexible and responsive than the functional structure.

One organization that has capitalized on the benefits of integrating functions is pharmaceutical firm AstraZeneca. Developing and bringing a new drug to market is a complex procedure, particularly for a company with global reach, so AstraZeneca brought employees from different functions and regions together on product teams. For example, when the company was working on approvals for its anticholesterol drug, Crestor, it set up a global product team, with both technical research and commercial heads to oversee the drug's development and marketing. Communication among the team members not only helped the drug through its clinical trials in various countries but also allowed the marketers who would be responsible for disseminating information to physicians and patients learn about the drug early in its development.[31]

Demands for total quality, customer service, innovation, and speed have made clear the shortcomings of the functional form for some firms. Functional organizations are highly differentiated and create barriers to coordination across functions. Cross-functional coordination is essential for total quality, customer service, innovations, and speed. The functional organization will not disappear, in part because functional specialists will always be needed, but functional managers will make fewer decisions. The more important units will be cross-functional teams that have integrative responsibilities for products, processes, or customers.[32]

The Divisional Organization

The discussion of a functional structure's weaknesses leads us to the **divisional organization.** As organizations grow and become increasingly diversified, they find that functional departments have difficulty managing a wide variety of products, customers, and geographic regions. In this case, organizations may restructure to group all functions into a single division and duplicate each of the functions across all the divisions. In the divisional organization chart in Figure 8.4, Division A has its own operations, marketing, and finance department, Division B has its own operations, marketing, and finance department, and so on. In this structure, separate divisions may act almost as separate businesses or profit centers and work autonomously to accomplish the goals of the entire enterprise. Table 8.1 presents examples of how the same tasks would be organized under functional and divisional structures.

Organizations create a divisional structure in several ways. It can be created around products, customers, or geographic regions. Each of these is described in the following sections.

Product Divisions   In the product organization, all functions that contribute to a given product are organized under one manager. In the product organization, managers in charge of functions for a particular product report to a product manager. Johnson & Johnson is one example of this form. J&J has more than 250 independent company divisions, many of which are responsible for particular product lines. For example, its subsidiary Cordis Corporation has divisions that develop and sell products for treating vascular diseases, while McNeil-PPC's products include Listerine and Plax mouthwashes.

The product approach to departmentalization offers a number of advantages:[33]

1. *Information needs are managed more easily.* Less information is required, because people work closely on one product and need not worry about other products.

divisional organization

Departmentalization that groups units around products, customers, or geographic regions.

Functional Organization	Divisional Organization
A central purchasing department.	Each division has its own purchasing unit.
Separate companywide marketing, production, design, and engineering departments.	Each product group has experts in marketing, design, production, and engineering.
A central-city health department.	The school district and the prison have their own health units.
Plantwide inspection, maintenance, and supply departments.	Production Team Y does its own inspection, maintenance, and supply.
A university statistics department teaches statistics for the entire university.	Each department hires statisticians to teach its own students.

TABLE 8.1

Examples of Functional and Divisional Organization

SOURCE: George Strauss and Leonard R. Sayles, *Strauss and Sayles's Behavioral Strategies for Managers,* © 1980. p. 221. Reprinted by permission of Prentice Hall, Inc., Englewood Cliffs, New Jersey.

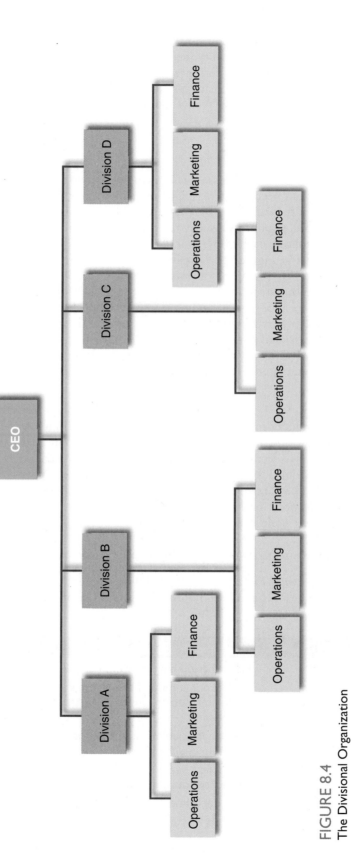

FIGURE 8.4
The Divisional Organization

2. *People have a full-time commitment to a particular product line.* They develop a greater awareness of how their jobs fit into the broader scheme.
3. *Task responsibilities are clear.* When things go wrong in a functional organization, functional managers can pass the buck ("That other department is messing up, making it harder for us to do our jobs"). In a product structure, managers are more independent and accountable because they usually have the resources they need to perform their tasks. Also, the performances of different divisions can be compared by contrasting their profits and other measures.
4. *People receive broader training.* General managers develop a wide variety of skills, and they learn to be judged by results. Many top executives received crucial early experience in product structures.

Because the product structure is more flexible than the functional structure, it is best suited for unstable environments, when an ability to adapt rapidly to change is important. But the product structure also has disadvantages. It is difficult to coordinate across product lines and divisions. And although managers learn to become generalists, they may not acquire the depth of functional expertise that develops in the functional structure.

Furthermore, functions are not centralized at headquarters, where they are done for all product lines or divisions. Such duplication of effort is expensive. Also, decision making is decentralized in this structure, and so top management can lose some control over decisions made in the divisions. Proper management of all the issues surrounding decentralization and delegation, as discussed earlier, is essential for this structure to be effective.[34]

Customer and Geographic Divisions   Some companies build divisions around groups of customers or around different geographic areas. Pfizer recently replaced divisions based on location with three based on customer groups: primary care, specialty care, and emerging markets. The pharmaceutical company hopes that this structure will make the company more responsive to the needs of doctors and their patients in each group.[35] Similarly, a hospital may organize its services around child, adult, psychiatric, and emergency cases. Bank loan departments commonly have separate groups handling consumer and business needs.

In contrast to customers, divisions can be structured around geographic regions. Sears, for example, was a pioneer in creating *geographic divisions*. Geographic distinctions include district, territory, region, and country. Macy's Group, formerly Federated Department Stores, has geographic divisions for its operations serving particular states or regions of the United States: Macy's East, Macy's Florida, Macy's Midwest, Macy's North, Macy's Northwest, Macy's South, and Macy's West, as well as Macys.com for online shoppers. Executives at Ford Motor Company include the CEO of Ford of Europe, the CEO of Ford of Mexico, and the president of Ford Motor (China) Ltd.

Customer and geographic divisions often serve customers faster.

The primary advantage of both the product and customer/regional approaches to departmentalization is the ability to focus on customer needs and provide faster, better service. But again, duplication of activities across many customer groups and geographic areas is expensive.

Establishing customer divisions improved strategic decisions at Det Norske Veritas (DNV), a Norwegian firm that provides services related to risk management. Initially, the company's management assumed that any collaboration across divisions would build sales and profits, but the first effort flopped. Management tried combining the efforts of two business units: its consulting group and a unit that inspects food companies' production chains. The idea was that the combined groups could help food companies reduce risks in their supply chains. However, the group members were slow to share information about customers, thought that time spent on the joint project undermined the work of their own division (which was how their performance was measured), and engaged in conflicts that caused project delays and cost overruns.

Disappointed with these early results, DNV's executives evaluated their decision making and realized they were assembling a collaboration project without first prioritizing the market opportunities, identifying the impact on each division's profits, and rewarding employees for collaborating. To improve future decisions, they restructured the company into business units serving particular markets. With their market knowledge, each unit then investigated where collaboration would make sense to serve its market's needs. Because the whole unit would benefit, it was now easier to tie rewards to collaboration. One success came from the business unit serving the maritime industry. Managers determined that the information technology specialists in this unit could collaborate with the risk management group to help shipping companies manage the risk of their computer systems' malfunctioning. This time, customers *and* employees were enthusiastic.[36]

The Matrix Organization

matrix organization

An organization composed of dual reporting relationships in which some managers report to two superiors—a functional manager and a divisional manager.

A **matrix organization** is a hybrid form of organization in which functional and divisional forms overlap. Managers and staff personnel report to two bosses—a functional manager and a divisional manager. Thus, matrix organizations have a dual rather than a single line of command. In Figure 8.5, for example, each project manager draws employees from each functional area to form a group for the project. The employees working on those projects report to the individual project manager as well as to the manager of their functional area.

A good example of the matrix structure can be found at Time Inc., the top magazine publisher in the United States and United Kingdom. At major Time Inc. titles such as *Time*, *Sports Illustrated*, and *People*, production managers who are responsible for getting the magazines printed report both to the individual publishers and editors of each title *and* to a senior corporate executive in charge of production. At the corporate level, Time Inc. achieves enormous economies of scale by buying paper and printing in bulk and making sure production activities in the company as a whole are

FIGURE 8.5
Matrix Organizational Structure

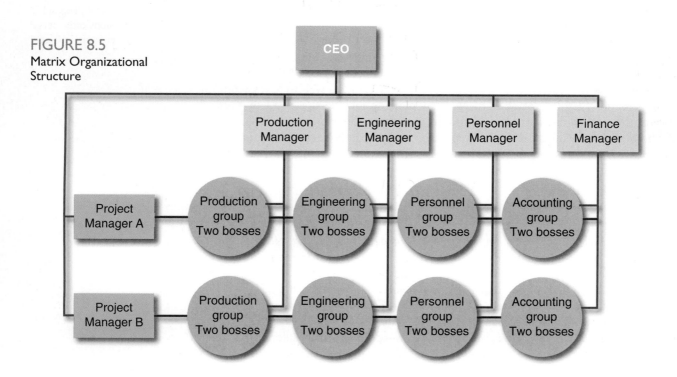

coordinated. At the same time, production managers working at each title make sure the different needs and schedules of their individual magazines are being met. Similar matrix arrangements are in place for other key managers, such as circulation and finance. In this way, the company attempts to gain the benefits of both the divisional and functional organization structure.

The matrix form originated in the aerospace industry, first with TRW in 1959 and then with NASA. Applications now occur in hospitals and health care agencies, entrepreneurial organizations, government laboratories, financial institutions, and multinational corporations.[37] Other companies that have used or currently use the matrix form include IBM, Boeing, Xerox, Shell Oil, Texas Instruments, Bechtel, and Dow Corning.

Organizations with highly specialized staff, such as NASA astronaut Susan J. Helms (left), shown here with Russian cosmonaut Yury V. Usachev in the International Space Station, typically use a matrix structure.

Pros and Cons of the Matrix Form   Like other organization structures, the matrix has both strengths and weaknesses. Table 8.2 summarizes the advantages of using a matrix structure. The major potential advantage is a higher degree of flexibility and adaptability.

Table 8.3 summarizes the potential shortcomings of the matrix form. Many of the disadvantages stem from the matrix's inherent violation of the **unity-of-command principle,** which states that a person should have only one boss. Reporting to two superiors can create confusion and a difficult interpersonal situation, unless steps are taken to prevent these problems from arising.

Matrix Survival Skills   The value of collaboration is particularly pronounced in a matrix organization. For example, in the kind of structure illustrated in Figure 8.5, project group members may not be permanently assigned to the project manager. They will return to their functional area once the project has been completed. For this group to work effectively, the traditional command-and-control management style

unity-of-command principle

A structure in which each worker reports to one boss, who in turn reports to one boss.

- Decision making is decentralized to a level where information is processed properly and relevant knowledge is applied.
- Extensive communications networks help process large amounts of information.
- With decisions delegated to appropriate levels, higher management levels are not overloaded with operational decisions.
- Resource utilization is efficient because key resources are shared across several important programs or products at the same time.
- Employees learn the collaborative skills needed to function in an environment characterized by frequent meetings and more informal interactions.
- Dual career ladders are elaborated as more career options become available on both sides of the organization.

SOURCE: H. Kolodny, "Managing in a Matrix," *Business Horizons*, March–April 1981, pp. 17–24.

TABLE 8.2
Advantages of the Matrix Design

- Confusion can arise because people do not have a single superior to whom they feel primary responsibility.
- The design encourages managers who share subordinates to jockey for power.
- The mistaken belief can arise that matrix management is the same thing as group decision making—in other words, everyone must be consulted for every decision.
- Too much democracy can lead to not enough action.

SOURCE: H. Kolodny, "Managing in a Matrix," *Business Horizons*, March–April 1981, pp. 17–24.

TABLE 8.3
Disadvantages of the Matrix Design

may not be the most appropriate; it might gain *compliance* from group members, but not their full *commitment*, making it harder to achieve the project's goals. Also, as the matrix organization draws on members of functional groups to tap their expertise, it is very important to get their full contribution. A collaborative process, in which the manager and participants develop a shared sense of ownership for the work they are doing, will generate better ideas, participation, and commitment to the project and its outcomes.

To a large degree, problems can be avoided if the key managers in the matrix learn the behavioral skills demanded in the matrix structure.[38] These skills vary depending on the job in the four-person diamond structure shown in Figure 8.6.

The *top executive*, who heads the matrix, must learn to balance power and emphasis between the product and functional orientations. *Product or division managers* and *functional managers* must learn to collaborate and manage their conflicts constructively. Finally, the *two-boss managers* or employees at the bottom of the diamond must learn how to be responsible to two superiors. This means prioritizing multiple demands and sometimes even reconciling conflicting orders. Some people function poorly under this ambiguous, conflictual circumstance; sometimes this signals the end of their careers with the company. Others learn to be proactive, communicate effectively with both superiors, rise above the difficulties, and manage these work relationships constructively.

The Matrix Form Today   The popularity of the matrix form waned during the late 1980s, when many companies had difficulty implementing it. But recently, it has come back strong. Reasons for this resurgence include pressures to consolidate costs and be faster to market, creating a need for better coordination across functions in the business units, and a need for coordination across countries for firms with global business strategies. Many of the challenges created by the matrix are particularly acute in an international context, mainly because of the distances involved and the differences in local markets.[39]

The key to managing today's matrix is not the formal structure itself but the realization that the matrix is a *process*. Managers who have appropriately adopted the matrix structure because of the complexity of the challenges they confront, but have had trouble implementing it, often find that they haven't changed the employee and managerial relationships within their organizations in ways that make the matrix

§ The matrix structure can speed decisions and cut costs.

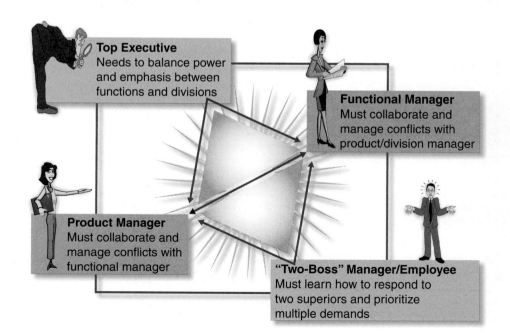

FIGURE 8.6
The Matrix Diamond

effective. It is not enough to create a flexible organization merely by changing its structure. To create an environment that allows information to flow freely throughout the organization, managers must also attend to the norms, values, and attitudes that shape how people within their organizations behave.[40] We will address these issues in the next chapter and in Part Four of the book, which focuses on how to lead and manage people.

The Network Organization

So far, the structures we have been discussing are variations of the traditional, hierarchical organization, within which all the business functions of the firm are performed. In contrast, the **network organization** is a collection of independent, mostly single-function firms that collaborate to produce a good or service. As depicted in Figure 8.7, the network organization describes not one organization but the web of relationships among many firms. Network organizations are flexible arrangements among designers, suppliers, producers, distributors, and customers where each firm is able to pursue its own distinctive competence, yet work effectively with other members of the network. Often members of the network communicate electronically and share information to be able to respond quickly to customer demands. In effect, the normal boundary of the organization becomes blurred or porous, as managers within the organization interact closely with network members outside it. The network as a whole, then, can display the technical specialization of the functional structure, the market responsiveness of the product structure, and the balance and flexibility of the matrix.[41]

A very flexible version of the network organization is the **dynamic network**—also called the *modular* or *virtual* corporation. It is composed of temporary arrangements among members that can be assembled and reassembled to meet a changing competitive environment. The members of the network are held together by contracts that stipulate results expected (market mechanisms) rather than by hierarchy and authority. Poorly performing firms can be removed and replaced.

Such arrangements are common in the electronics, toy, and apparel industries, each of which creates and sells trendy products at a fast pace. Dynamic networks also are suited to organizations in which much of the work can be done independently by experts. For example, the more than 200 graphic designers affiliated with Logoworks provide design services to small-business customers looking for professional work without the overhead expense of an advertising agency. A popular Logoworks product is a $399 set of logo design ideas from three designers; the client picks his or her

network organization

A collection of independent, mostly single-function firms that collaborate on a good or service.

dynamic network

Temporary arrangements among partners that can be assembled and reassembled to adapt to the environment.

Networks can improve cost, quality, service, speed, and innovation.

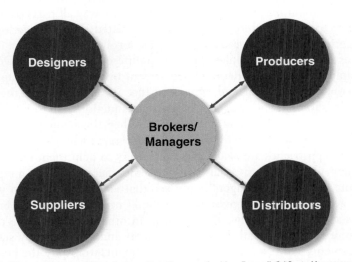

SOURCE: From R. Miles and C. Snow, "Organizations: New Concepts for New Forms," *California Management Review*, Spring 1986, p. 65. Copyright © 1986 by The Regents of the University of California. Reprinted from the *California Management Review*, vol. 28, no. 3.

FIGURE 8.7
A Network Organization

favorite, all the designers are paid a set fee, and the designer whose idea is chosen earns a bonus. Logoworks conducts marketing online, hires some designers, and negotiates freelance contracts with the rest.[42]

Successful networks potentially offer flexibility, innovation, quick responses to threats and opportunities, and reduced costs and risk. But for these arrangements to be successful, several things must occur:

The firm must choose the right specialty. It must be something (good or service) that the market needs and which the firm is better at providing than other firms.

The firm must choose collaborators that also are excellent at what they do and that provide complementary strengths.

The firm must make certain that all parties fully understand the strategic goals of the partnership.

Each party must be able to trust all the others with strategic information and also trust that each collaborator will deliver quality products even if the business grows quickly and makes heavy demands.

The role of managers shifts in a network from that of command and control to more like that of a **broker.** Broker/managers serve several important boundary roles that aid network integration and coordination:

broker

A person who assembles and coordinates participants in a network.

Designer role. The broker serves as a network architect who envisions a set of groups or firms whose collective expertise could be focused on a particular good or service.

Process engineering role. The broker serves as a *network co-operator* who takes the initiative to lay out the flow of resources and relationships and makes certain that everyone shares the same goals, standards, payments, and the like.

Nurturing role. The broker serves as a network developer who nurtures and enhances the network (like team building) to make certain the relationships are healthy and mutually beneficial.[43]

Organizational Integration

At the beginning of this chapter, we said organizations are structured around differentiation and integration. So far, our discussion has focused on *differentiation*—the way the organization is composed of different jobs and tasks, and the way they fit on an organization chart. But as organizations differentiate their structures, they also need to be concerned about *integration* and *coordination*—the way all parts of the organization will work together. Often, the more differentiated the organization, the more difficult integration may be. Because of specialization and the division of labor, different groups of managers and employees develop different orientations. Depending on whether employees are in a functional department or a divisional group, are line or staff, and so on, they will think and act in ways that are geared toward their particular work units. In short, people working in separate functions, divisions, and business units literally tend to forget about one another. When this happens, it is difficult for managers to combine all their activities into an integrated whole.

A variety of approaches are available to managers to help them make certain that interdependent units and individuals will work together to achieve a common purpose. In some situations, managers might see that employees need to work closely together to achieve joint objectives, so they build mutual trust, train employees in a common set of skills, and reward teamwork. In other situations, the organization might rely more on individuals with unique talents and ideas, so they set up flexible work arrangements and reward individual achievements to inspire the best from each individual, while encouraging individual employees to share knowledge and develop respect for one another's contributions.[44] In general, however, coordination methods include standardization, plans, and mutual adjustment.[45]

Coordination by Standardization

When organizations coordinate activities by establishing routines and standard operating procedures that remain in place over time, we say that work has been standardized. **Standardization** constrains actions and integrates various units by regulating what people do. People often know how to act—and how to interact—because standard operating procedures spell out what they should do. For example, managers may establish standards for which types of computer equipment the organization will use. This simplifies the purchasing and computer-training process—everyone will be on a common platform—and makes it easier for the different parts of the organization to communicate with each other.

Banks are among the most standardized of organizations, from operating procedures through dress codes, reinforcing to their customers and employees that the organization and their dealings with it are stable and reliable.

To improve coordination, organizations may also rely on **formalization**—the presence of rules and regulations governing how people in the organization interact. Simple, often written, policies regarding attendance, dress, and decorum, for example, may help eliminate a good deal of uncertainty at work. But an important assumption underlying both standardization and formalization is that the rules and procedures should apply to most (if not all) situations. These approaches, therefore, are most appropriate in situations that are relatively stable and unchanging. In some cases, when the work environment requires flexibility, coordination by standardization may not be very effective. Who hasn't experienced a time when rules and procedures—frequently associated with a slow bureaucracy—prevented timely action to address a problem? In these instances, we often refer to rules and regulations as "red tape."[46] As you read the "Management Close-Up: Taking Action" feature, consider how employees are likely to view the new formal innovation procedures at Whirlpool.

standardization

Establishing common routines and procedures that apply uniformly to everyone.

formalization

The presence of rules and regulations governing how people in the organization interact.

Coordination by Plan

If laying out the exact rules and procedures by which work should be integrated is difficult, organizations may provide more latitude by establishing goals and schedules for interdependent units. **Coordination by plan** does not require the same high degree of stability and routinization required for coordination by standardization. Interdependent units are free to modify and adapt their actions as long as they meet the deadlines and targets required for working with others.

In writing this textbook, for example, we (the authors) sat down with a publication team that included the editors, the marketing staff, the production group, and support staff. Together we ironed out a schedule for developing this book that covered approximately a two-year period. That development plan included dates and "deliverables" that specified what was to be accomplished and forwarded to the others in the organization. The plan allowed for a good deal of flexibility on each subunit's part, and the overall approach allowed us to work together effectively.

coordination by plan

Interdependent units are required to meet deadlines and objectives that contribute to a common goal.

Coordination by Mutual Adjustment

Ironically, the simplest and most flexible approach to coordination may just be to have interdependent parties talk to one another. **Coordination by mutual adjustment** involves feedback and discussions to jointly figure out how to approach problems and devise solutions that are agreeable to everyone. The popularity of teams today is in part due to the fact that they allow for flexible coordination; teams can operate under the principle of mutual adjustment.

But the flexibility of mutual adjustment as a coordination device does not come without some cost. Hashing out every issue takes time and may not be the most

coordination by mutual adjustment

Units interact with one another to make accommodations to achieve flexible coordination.

Management Close-Up   TAKING ACTION

Although Whirlpool's Nancy Snyder had to abandon her initial strategy of using a 75-person innovation team to vet product ideas and create new ones, she knew Whirlpool's structure could support innovation. With a doctorate in organizational behavior, Snyder recognized that although creativity is an innate human behavior, people needed training to build their skills. For that reason, she brought innovation training to Whirlpool—coursework mandated for all salaried employees and tied to their bonuses. She also established an intranet as a central place for communicating and monitoring innovation, and she made the training materials available there to hourly workers.

The training equipped the selected employees to serve as "I-mentors," who would foster new ideas within their business units. They apply their learning not only to generate ideas for new products but also to solve business problems within the company. Once the I-mentor format was in place, Snyder brought greater structure to the process. Top managers now evaluate new proposals at monthly meetings. Projects that clear initial hurdles receive an executive sponsor to shepherd them through the next stages. Software tools enable Whirlpool to track an idea's progress through the pipeline and measure it on several dimensions, even its intangible value. Managers receive concrete innovation goals, and their performance is measured. Bonuses are at risk for managers who don't hit their innovation target.

Ideas that came out of the new process include a fast-fill water dispenser built into a refrigerator's door and a portable device called a Fabric Freshener, which uses steaming and air-drying to remove wrinkles and odors from dry-clean-only garments.

After Whirlpool adopted the new system for innovation, the company's performance turned around. By 2006, the company could identify more than $2.5 billion in worldwide revenues as stemming from brand innovation.[47]

- Does the idea-generation system that Nancy Snyder set up at Whirlpool resemble the matrix organization structure? If so, how?
- Previously, new-product development at Whirlpool was centered only in its engineering and marketing departments, but CEO David Whitwam and Nancy Snyder modified that practice. How does a change in the division of labor affect organization structure?

China may be the next hub of motorcycle manufacturing. That's because the Chinese motorcycle industry has figured out how to coordinate literally hundreds of different suppliers in the design and manufacturing of motorcycles. Together, these small firms collaborate by working from rough blueprints to design, construct, and assemble components that are related to each other, then deliver them to another plant for final assembly. Because design and assembly are decentralized, suppliers can move quickly to make adjustments, try out new components, and make more changes if necessary before delivering a product for final assembly.

Using this approach, the Chinese motorcycle industry is now designing and building new motorcycles faster and less expensively than any other country in the world. In fact, the industry has been so successful that its production has quadrupled from 5 million motorcycles a year to 20 million—which gives China about 50 percent of the worldwide motorcycle market. Experts believe that this type of mass collaboration is the future of most manufacturing, whether the product is simple or complex.[48]

General
Strategies

Specific
Techniques

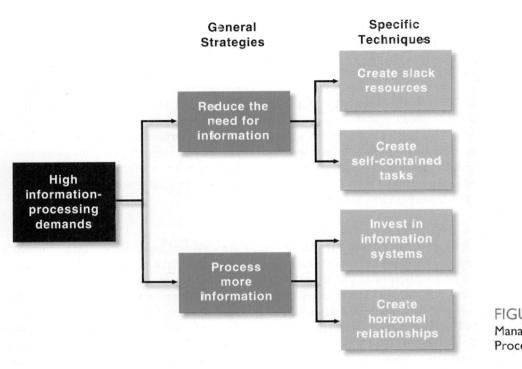

FIGURE 8.8
Managing High Information-
Processing Demands

expedient approach for organizing work. Imagine how long it would take to accomplish even the most basic tasks if subunits had to talk through every situation. At the same time, mutual adjustment can be very effective when problems are novel and cannot be programmed in advance with rules, procedures, or plans. Particularly during crises, in which rules and procedures don't apply, mutual adjustment is likely to be the most effective approach to coordination.

Coordination and Communication

Today's environments tend to be complex, dynamic, and therefore uncertain. Huge amounts of information flow from the external environment to the organization and back to the environment. To cope, organizations must acquire, process, and respond to that information. Doing so has direct implications for how firms organize. To function effectively, organizations need to develop structures for processing information.

Information sharing is vital at the National Counterterrorism Center, shown here. Technology is used to enable the efficient and safe sharing of this information.

To cope with high uncertainty and heavy information demands, managers can use the two general strategies shown in Figure 8.8. First, management can act to reduce the need for information. Second, it can increase its capacity to handle more information.[49]

Option 1: Reducing the Need for Information

Managers can reduce the need for information in two ways: (a) creating slack resources and (b) creating self-contained tasks. *Slack resources* are simply extra resources on which organizations can rely in a pinch so that if they get caught off guard, they can still adjust. Inventory, for example, is a type of slack resource that provides extra stock on hand in case it is needed. With extra inventory, an organization does not have to have as much information about sales demand, lead time, and the like.

Employees also can be a type of slack resource. For example, many companies augment their full-time staffs with part-time and temporary employees. This way, they do not have to perfectly forecast sales peaks but can rely on supplementary workers to handle irregularities.

Like slack resources, *creating self-contained tasks* allows organizations to reduce the need for some information. Creating self-contained tasks refers to changing from a functional organization to a product or project organization and giving each unit the resources it needs to perform its task. Information-processing problems are reduced because each unit has its own full complement of specialties instead of functional specialties that have to share their expertise among a number of different product teams. Communications then flow within each team rather than among a complex array of interdependent groups.

Option 2: Increasing Information-Processing Capability

Instead of reducing the need for information, an organization may take the approach of increasing its information-processing capability. It can *invest in information systems*, which usually means employing or expanding computer systems. But increasing an organization's information-processing capability also means what we referred to in Chapter 1 as *knowledge management*—capitalizing on the intellect and experience of the organization's human assets to increase collaboration and effectiveness. One way to do that is by creating horizontal relationships between units to foster coordination. Such horizontal relationships are effective because they increase integration, which Lawrence and Lorsch suggest is necessary for managing complex environments. As uncertainty increases, the following horizontal processes may be used, ranging from the simplest to the most complex:[50]

> **The bottom line**
> **Innovation**
> Cross-unit coordination can lead to effective problem solutions.

1. *Direct contact (mutual adjustment)* among managers who share a problem. In a university, for example, a residence hall adviser might call a meeting to resolve differences between two feuding students who live in adjacent rooms.
2. *Liaison roles*, or specialized jobs to handle communications between two departments. A fraternity representative is a liaison between the fraternity and the interfraternity council, the university, or the local community.
3. *Task forces*, or groups of representatives from different departments, brought together temporarily to solve a common problem. For example, students, faculty, and administrators may be members of a task force charged with bringing distinguished speakers to campus for a current-events seminar.
4. *Teams*, or permanent interdepartmental decision-making groups. An executive council made up of department heads might meet regularly to make decisions affecting a college of engineering or liberal arts.

> "An organization's ability to learn, and translate that learning into action rapidly, is the ultimate competitive advantage."
>
> —Jack Welch

5. *Product, program, or project managers* who direct interdisciplinary groups with a common task to perform. In a college of business administration, a faculty administrator might head an executive education program of professors from several disciplines.
6. *Matrix organizations*, composed of dual relationships in which some managers report to two superiors. Your instructors, for example, may report to department heads in their respective disciplines and also to a director of undergraduate or graduate programs.

Several of these processes are discussed further in Chapter 14, where we examine managing teams and intergroup relations.

Looking Ahead

The organization chart, differentiation, integration, authority, delegation, coordination, and the like convey fundamental information about an organization's structure. However, the information so far has provided only a snapshot. The real organization is more like a motion picture—it moves! More flexible and innovative—even virtual—forms of organizations are evolving. Today's organizations are far removed, in many of their fundamental characteristics, from the traditional forms they once had. They may be more networked, flexible, and global, using the electronic sharing of information to move faster than 20th-century managers could have envisaged.

No organization is merely a set of static work relationships. Because organizations are composed of people, they are hotbeds of social relationships. Networks of individuals cutting across departmental boundaries interact with one another. Various friendship groups or cliques band together to form *coalitions*—members of the organization who jointly support a particular issue and try to ensure that their viewpoints determine the outcome of policy decisions.

Thus, the formal organization structure does not describe everything about how the company really works. Even if you know departments and authority relationships, you still have much to understand. How do things really get done? Who influences whom, and how? Which managers are the most powerful? How effective is the top leadership? Which groups are most and which are least effective? What is the nature of communication patterns throughout the organization? These issues are discussed throughout the rest of the book.

Now you are familiar with the basic organizing concepts discussed in this chapter. In the next chapter, we will discuss the current challenges of designing the modern organization with which the modern executive constantly grapples.

Management Close-Up

ASSESSING OUTCOMES AND SEIZING OPPORTUNITIES

Today, Whirlpool has more than 1,000 I-mentors worldwide. They apply the knowledge from their innovation training not only to develop marketable ideas but also to improve the company's processes and procedures continually. For example, Whirlpool's human resource systems, such as its hiring, training, and pay, now reflect the new enterprisewide emphasis on idea development.

Whirlpool acquired rival Maytag Company in 2005. Knowing that speed is of the essence when merging companies, Whirlpool worked quickly to integrate Maytag's employees and product lines. Managers made sure that high-performing employees were identified in plants slated to be closed and found ways to integrate them into other operations. They also educated remaining employees in both former companies of what the newly combined company would produce. Then the company streamlined and modernized its larger supply chain to operate more efficiently. Under Whirlpool's ownership, the Maytag brand is now recovering; it had been dropped by Best Buy.

Creative thinking also helps support Whirlpool's efforts to achieve environmental sustainability. From research studies, the firm found that resource-saving appliances are critical, since 93 percent of greenhouse gas emissions come from in-home appliance use. Through improvements in the design and manufacture of its products, by 2006 Whirlpool had reduced greenhouse gas emissions an estimated 19 percent. The following year, it pledged to reduce its emissions an additional 6.6 percent by the year 2012—an amount whose positive impact would be equivalent to nearly 7,000 square miles of trees, an area roughly the size of Rhode Island and Connecticut.

The company also strives to rethink its recycling program. By 2007, Whirlpool was recycling nearly 90 percent of the 400-plus metric tons of waste its manufacturing plants produce annually. It has also found ways to recycle the plastic-foam packaging that protects its products during shipping. The foam is ground up to make plastic furniture and playground equipment.[51]

- Industry observers suggest that by encouraging companywide participation in idea formation, Nancy Snyder has created a competitive advantage for Whirlpool. What evidence supports this opinion? What role do employees play in this process?

- The innovation team approach that cut across Whirlpool's divisions and departments provides it with continual information for new-product ideas and improved operations. Snyder set up a company intranet to centralize training for I-mentors and enhance communication across all of Whirlpool's divisions. How did this help the company improve its products and processes?

KEY TERMS

Accountability, p. 284

Authority, p. 278

Broker, p. 296

Centralized organization, p. 285

Coordination, p. 278

Coordination by mutual
    adjustment, p. 297

Coordination by plan, p. 297

Corporate governance, p. 280

Decentralized organization, p. 285

Delegation, p. 283

Departmentalization, p. 287

Differentiation, p. 277

Division of labor, p. 277

Divisional organization, p. 289

Dynamic network, p. 295

Formalization, p. 297

Functional organization, p. 287

Hierarchy, p. 280

Integration, p. 277

Line departments, p. 287

Matrix organization, p. 292

Network organization, p. 295

Organization chart, p. 276

Responsibility, p. 283

Span of control, p. 282

Specialization, p. 277

Staff departments, p. 287

Standardization, p. 297

Subunits, p. 282

Unity-of-command principle, p. 293

SUMMARY OF LEARNING OBJECTIVES

Now that you have studied Chapter 8, you should be able to:

LO 1 Explain how differentiation and integration influence an organization's structure.

Differentiation means that organizations have many parts. Specialization means that various individuals and units throughout the organization perform different tasks. The assignment of tasks to different people or groups often is referred to as the division of labor. But the specialized tasks in an organization cannot all be performed independently of one another. Coordination links the various tasks in order to achieve the organization's overall mission. An organization with many different specialized tasks and work units is highly differentiated; the more differentiated the organization is, the more integration or coordination is required.

LO 2 Summarize how authority operates.

Authority is the legitimate right to make decisions and tell other people what to do. Authority is exercised throughout the hierarchy, as bosses have the authority to give orders to subordinates. Through the day-to-day operation of authority, the organization proceeds toward achieving its goals. Owners or stockholders have ultimate authority.

LO 3 Define the roles of the board of directors and the chief executive officer.

Boards of directors report to stockholders. The board of directors controls or advises management, considers the firm's legal and other interests, and protects stockholders' rights. The chief executive officer reports to the board and is accountable for the organization's performance.

LO 4 Discuss how span of control affects structure and managerial effectiveness.

Span of control is the number of people who report directly to a manager. Narrow spans create tall organizations, and wide spans create flat ones. No single span of control is always appropriate; the optimal span is determined by characteristics of the work, the subordinates, the manager, and the organization.

LO 5 Explain how to delegate effectively.

Delegation—the assignment of tasks and responsibilities—has many potential advantages for the manager, the subordinate, and the organization. But to be effective, the process must be managed carefully. The manager should define the goal, select the person, solicit opinions, provide resources, schedule checkpoints, and discuss progress periodically.

LO 6 Distinguish between centralized and decentralized organizations.

In centralized organizations, most important decisions are made by top managers. In decentralized organizations, many decisions are delegated to lower levels.

LO 7 Summarize ways organizations can be structured.

Organizations can be structured on the basis of function, division (product, customers, or geographic), matrix, and network. Each form has advantages and disadvantages.

LO 8 Identify the unique challenges of the matrix organization.

The matrix is a complex structure with a dual authority structure. A well-managed matrix enables organizations to adapt to change. But it can also create confusion and interpersonal difficulties. People in all positions in the matrix—top executives, product and function managers, and two-boss managers—must acquire unique survival skills.

LO 9 Describe important integrative mechanisms.

Managers can coordinate interdependent units through standardization, plans, and mutual adjustment. Standardization occurs when routines and standard operating procedures are put in place. They typically are accompanied by formalized rules. Coordination by plan is more flexible and allows more freedom in how tasks are carried out but keeps interdependent units focused on schedules and joint goals. Mutual adjustment involves feedback and discussions among related parties to accommodate each other's needs. It is at once the most flexible and simple to administer, but it is time-consuming.

DISCUSSION QUESTIONS

1. Based on the description of Whirlpool in this chapter, give some examples of differentiation in that organization. In other words, what specialized tasks have to be performed, and how is labor divided at Whirlpool? Also, how does Whirlpool integrate the work of these different units? Based on what you have learned in this chapter, would you say Whirlpool has an effective structure? Why or why not?

2. What are some advantages and disadvantages of being in the CEO position?

3. Would you like to sit on a board of directors? Why or why not? If you did serve on a board, what kind of organization would you prefer? As a board member, in what kinds of activities do you think you would most actively engage?

4. Interview a member of a board of directors, and discuss that member's perspectives on his or her role.

5. Pick a job you have held, and describe it in terms of span of control, delegation, responsibility, authority, and accountability.

6. Why do you think managers have difficulty delegating? What can be done to overcome these difficulties?

7. Consider an organization in which you have worked, draw its organization chart, and describe it by using terms in this chapter. How did you like working there, and why?

8. Would you rather work in a functional or divisional organization? Why?

9. If you learned that a company had a matrix structure, would you be more or less interested in working there? Explain your answer. How would you prepare yourself to work effectively in a matrix?

10. Brainstorm a list of methods for integrating interdependent work units. Discuss the activities that need to be undertaken and the pros and cons of each approach.

CONCLUDING CASE

Down East Spud Busters

Down East Spud Busters is part of a conglomerate that represents the potato growers of eastern Canada and northern Maine and that also oversees the collection, processing, and distribution of potatoes and potato products.

For many years, the industry functioned as a local cooperative. The cooperative was simply a collection center where potatoes were weighed and received, washed and graded, bagged and distributed. Potatoes were the only product. Potatoes were distributed in a variety of bag sizes and weights and were also sold loosely in large bins.

The first phase of Down East Spud Busters' strategic plan resulted in the building of a large manufacturing plant in northern Maine with a focus on value-added products. The major strategy is to process higher-value potato products. Those products include a frozen division line (French fries, home fries, gourmet stuffed potatoes, flavored potato skins, and so on), a dried-food division line (instant mashed potatoes, freeze-dried potatoes, potato pancake mix, and so on), and the traditional potato line (bagged potatoes, loose potatoes, microwave singles, baby potatoes, and so on). The corporate group figures that it can triple sales revenues from the existing yield of potatoes.

The second phase of Down East Spud Busters' strategic plan calls for a nationwide sales and distribution program. A gigantic market in retail food sales has gone untouched by this group of growers and producers. The major strategy is to recruit the appropriate sales force and to set up a system for selling and distributing the products. The major markets are supermarket chains, smaller retail grocers, major hotel chains, and governmental/school institutional kitchens.

Down East Spud Busters is leaning toward the concept of hiring sales associates who will work out of their own homes in strategic locations throughout the United States. Those sales associates will be assigned to specific territories and will be challenged to meet or exceed specific quotas of each of the conglomerate's products. The sales associates will also be responsible for overseeing the distribution and delivery of the products, and for dealing with any and all after-sale problems or issues.

The third and final phase of Down East Spud Busters' strategic plan is to build a second manufacturing plant in Idaho in five years and to possibly facilitate and oversee an increase in crop planting and yield in both territories. The company also plans to expand its market territories into selected locations in Europe and the Pacific Rim.

QUESTIONS

1. Select options from the chapter text, and prepare an organizational chart for the national distribution program that this company is about to embark on. Be sure to incorporate the company's goals into your overall structure.

2. Given the vast geographic expanse and logistical challenges of this new program, what recommendations do you have for the company regarding HR policies and procedures?

3. What other types of industries could use the model from this case as a means to expand sales nationally or internationally?

EXPERIENTIAL EXERCISES

8.1   The Business School Organization Chart

OBJECTIVES

1. To clarify the factors that determine organization structure.

2. To provide insight into the workings of an organization.

3. To examine the working relationships within an organization.

INSTRUCTIONS

1. Draw an organization chart for your school of business. Be sure to identify all the staff and line positions in the school. Specify the chain of command and the levels of administration. Note the different spans of control. Are there any advisory groups, task forces, or committees to consider?

2. Review the chapter material on organization structure to help identify both strong and weak points in your school's organization. Now draw another organization chart for the school, incorporating any changes you believe would improve the quality of the school. Support the second chart with a list of recommended changes and reasons for their inclusion.

DISCUSSION QUESTIONS

1. Is your business school well organized? Why or why not?

2. In what ways is the school's structure designed to suit the needs of students, faculty, staff, the administration, and the business community?

8.2   Designing a Student-Run Organization That Provides Consulting Services

OBJECTIVES

1. To appreciate the importance of the total organization on group and individual behavior.

2. To provide a beginning organization design experience that will be familiar to students.

BACKGROUND

The Industry Advisory Council for your school has decided to sponsor a student-run organization that will provide business consulting services to nonprofit groups in your community. The council has donated $20,000 toward start-up costs and has agreed to provide office space, computer equipment, and other materials as needed. The council hopes that the organization will establish its own source of funding after the first year of operation.

Task 1   The dean of the school wants you to develop alternative designs for the new organization. Your task is to identify the main design dimensions or factors to be dealt with in establishing such an organization and to describe the issues that must be resolved for each factor. For example, you might provide an organization chart to help describe the structural issues

involved. Before jumping ahead with your design, you may also have to think about (1) groups in the community that could use your help and (2) problems they face. Remember, though, your task is to create the organization that will provide services, not to provide an in-depth look at the types of services provided.

You and your team are to brainstorm design dimensions to be dealt with and to develop a one- or two-page outline that can be shared with the entire class. You have one hour to develop the outline. Select two people to present your design. Assume that you will all be involved in the new organization, filling specific positions.

Task 2   After the brainstorming period, the spokespersons will present the group designs or preferred design and answer questions from the audience.

Task 3   The instructor will comment on the designs and discuss additional factors that might be important for the success of this organization.

SOURCE: A. B. (Rami) Shani and James B. Lau, *Behavior in Organizations: An Experimental Approach* (New York: McGraw-Hill/Irwin, 2005), p. 369. © 2005 The McGraw-Hill Companies.

8.3   Decentralization: Pros and Cons

OBJECTIVE

To explore the reasons for, as well as the pros and cons of, decentralizing.

INSTRUCTIONS

The following Decentralization Worksheet contains some observations on decentralization. As you review each of the statements, provide an example that illustrates why this statement is important and related problems and benefits of the situation or condition indicated in the statement.

Decentralization Worksheet

A large number of factors determine the extent to which a manager should decentralize. Clearly, anything that increases a manager's workload creates pressure for decentralization because only a finite level of work can be accomplished by a single person. As with many facets of management, there are advantages and disadvantages to decentralization.

1. The greater the diversity of products, the greater the decentralization.

_____

_____

_____

2. The larger the size of the organization, the more the decentralization.

_____

_____

_____

3. The more rapidly changing the organization's environment, the more decentralization.

_____

_____

_____

4. Developing adequate, timely controls is the essence of decentralizing.

_____

_____

_____

5. Managers should delegate decisions that involve large amounts of time but minimal erosions of their power and control.

_____

_____

_____

6. Decentralizing involves delegating authority, and therefore, the principles of delegation apply to decentralization. (List the principles of delegation before you start your discussion.)

_____

_____

_____

SOURCE: R. R. McGrath Jr., *Exercises in Management Fundamentals* (Englewood Cliffs, NJ: Prentice Hall, 1985), pp. 59–60. Reprinted by permission of Prentice Hall, Inc.

Organizational Agility

It is change, continuing change, inevitable change, that is the dominant fact in society today. No sensible decision can be made any longer without taking into account not only the world as it is, but the world as it will be.

— Isaac Asimov

LEARNING OBJECTIVES

After studying Chapter 9, you will be able to:

LO 1 Discuss why it is critical for organizations to be responsive. p. 308

LO 2 Describe the qualities of an organic organization structure. p. 310

LO 3 Identify strategies and dynamic organizational concepts that can improve an organization's responsiveness. p. 311

LO 4 Explain how a firm can be both big and small. p. 314

LO 5 Summarize how firms organize to meet customer requirements. p. 318

LO 6 Identify ways that firms organize around different types of technology. p. 324

CHAPTER OUTLINE

The Responsive Organization

Strategy and Organizational Agility
Organizing around Core Competencies
Strategic Alliances
The Learning Organization
The High-Involvement Organization

Organizational Size and Agility
The Case for Big
The Case for Small
Being Big and Small

Customers and the Responsive Organization
Customer Relationship Management
Total Quality Management
ISO 9001
Reengineering

Technology and Organizational Agility
Types of Technology Configurations
Organizing for Flexible Manufacturing
Organizing for Speed: Time-Based Competition

Final Thoughts on Organizational Agility

Management Close-Up

HOW CAN WENDELL WEEKS KEEP CORNING'S FUTURE BRIGHT?

Corning chairman and CEO Wendell Weeks could be a poster child for the American success story. Weeks grew up outside Scranton, Pennsylvania, a coal town that had seen better days, and was from a middle-class family. After graduating from Lehigh University, he joined New York–based Corning during the 1980s and rose steadily, leaving only briefly to earn a Harvard MBA.

His company, founded in 1851 by Avery Houghton Sr., specializes in inventing and producing glass and high-tech ceramics. For generations Corning discoveries have helped make our everyday lives better. In 1912, for example, Corning's invention of heat-resistant glass for railroad lanterns enabled it to create Pyrex glass for science labs and kitchen cookware worldwide. The 1972 development of a ceramic that could filter pollutants led to the invention of the catalytic converter for a car's exhaust system. Over the years, Corning's process and product developments have boosted production efficiencies in other industries, including aeronautics, automotives, and consumer electronics.

{ During the telecom boom of the 1990s, Wendell Weeks led Corning Inc. to spectacular success. When the boom went bust, however, Corning had to start over. As you read this chapter, consider how Weeks capitalized on Corning's strengths to work the company back to profitability. }

Leading Corning's fiber-optics division during the telecom boom of the 1990s, Weeks helped generate huge profits for the company. The future of fiber optics seemed limitless. But when the telecom bubble burst in 2001, the fall could have literally wiped out the company. At that time, about 80 percent of Corning's business was built on fiber optics. The company's share price plummeted from a high of $113 to $1.10.

Former Corning CEO—and great-great-grandson of the founder—Jamie Houghton came out of retirement to help struggling Corning find its way. Instead of blaming Weeks for the failure and booting him out, Corning promoted him and assigned him the monumental task of turning the company around. Houghton reportedly told Weeks, "You got us here; now, get us out." Surprised that he still had a job, Weeks began searching for ways to rescue his ailing firm.[1]

Like Corning, today's successful companies can't afford to stand still. They cannot rest on their previous accomplishments. If they do, they can all too easily become vulnerable—to a competitor's new product, shifts in customer preferences, or other changes in their environment. Instead, they use their current successes to continue to build a competitive advantage for the future, constantly seeking new ways to remain flexible, innovative, efficient, and responsive to their customers. One of the most important ways they have of doing that is to make sure that their organization structures and systems remain *adaptable*—prepared to meet the complex and ever-changing challenges that managers and their organizations constantly confront.

In Chapter 8, we described the formal structure of the organization. We discussed hierarchical levels, reporting relationships, division of labor, coordination—all the basic, traditional elements of structure that are fundamental for understanding the way organizations work. But a firm's formal structure is only part of the story. Organizations are not static structures but complex systems in which many people do many different things at the same time. The overall behavior of organizations does not just pop out of a chart; it emerges out of all the processes, systems, and relationships within the organization, and the ways they interact. The task of organizing, then, is a matter of designing not just the appropriate formal structure for the organization but also the appropriate processes, information flows, and technology that make the organization effective. The "structuring" of these elements is critical for the flexibility and agility today's dynamic organizations require. The organization forms that enable that agility are the subject of this chapter.

The Responsive Organization

The bottom line
SPEED
Speed is vital to an organization's survival.

mechanistic organization

A form of organization that seeks to maximize internal efficiency.

organic structure

An organizational form that emphasizes flexibility.

The formal structure is put in place to *control* people, decisions, and actions. But in today's fast-changing business environment, *responsiveness*—quickness, agility, the ability to adapt to changing demands—is more vital than ever to a firm's survival.[2]

Many years after Max Weber wrote about the concept of bureaucracy, two British management scholars (Burns and Stalker) described what they called the **mechanistic organization**.[3] The common mechanistic structure they described was similar to Weber's bureaucracy, but they went on to suggest that in the modern corporation, the mechanistic structure is not the only option. The **organic structure** stands in stark contrast to the mechanistic organization. It is much less rigid and, in fact, emphasizes flexibility. The organic structure can be described as follows:

1. Jobholders have broader responsibilities that change as the need arises.
2. Communication occurs through advice and information rather than through orders and instructions.
3. Decision making and influence are more decentralized and informal.
4. Expertise is highly valued.
5. Jobholders rely more heavily on judgment than on rules.
6. Obedience to authority is less important than commitment to the organization's goals.
7. Employees depend more on one another and relate more informally and personally.

Figure 9.1 contrasts the formal structure of an organization—epitomized by the organization chart—to the informal structure, which is much more organic. Astute managers are keenly aware of the network of interactions among the organization's members, and they structure around this network to increase agility. People in organic organizations work more as teammates than as subordinates who take orders from the boss, thus breaking away from the traditional bureaucratic form.[4]

The ideas underlying the organic structure and networks are the foundation for the newer forms of organization described in this chapter. The more organic a firm

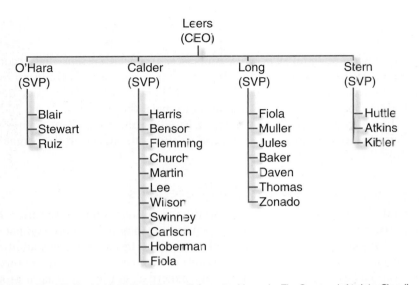

FIGURE 9.1(a)
Organization Chart Shows Who's on Top

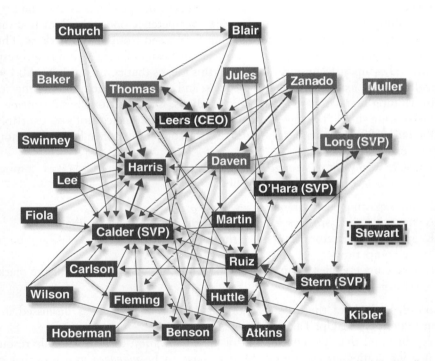

FIGURE 9.1(b)
Advice Network Reveals Knowledge Flow

is, the more responsive it will be to changing competitive demands and market realities. Managers in progressive companies place a premium on being able to act, and act fast. They want to act in accordance with customer needs and other outside pressures. They want to take actions to correct past mistakes and also to prepare for an uncertain future. They want to be able to respond to threats and opportunities. The particular form—and degree—of organic structure the organization adopts to accomplish these goals will depend on its *strategy*, its *size*, its *customers*, and its *technology*. We will consider each of these in turn.

Strategy and Organizational Agility

Certain strategies, and the structures, processes, and relationships that accompany them, seem particularly well suited to improving an organization's ability to respond quickly and effectively to the challenges it faces. They reflect its managers' determination to fully leverage its people and assets to make the firm more agile and competitive. These strategies and structures are based on the firm's core competencies, its strategic alliances, its ability to learn, and its ability to engage all the people in the organization in achieving its objectives.

Organizing around Core Competencies

A recent, different, and important perspective on strategy and organization hinges on the concept of *core competence*.[5] As you learned in Chapter 4, a core competence is the capability—knowledge, expertise, skill—that underlies a company's ability to be a leader in providing a range of specific goods or services. It allows the company to compete on the basis of its core strengths and expertise, not just on what it produces. For example, Barnes & Noble's core competence is book merchandising. A core competence gives value to customers, makes the company's products different from—and better than—those of competitors, and can be used in creating new products. Think of core competencies as the roots of competitiveness and products as the fruits.

Successfully developing a world-class core competence opens the door to a variety of future opportunities; failure means being foreclosed from many markets. Thus, a well-understood, well-developed core competence can enhance a company's responsiveness and competitiveness. Strategically, this means that companies should commit to excellence and leadership in competencies, and strengthen them, before they commit to winning market share for specific products. Organizationally, this means that the corporation should be viewed as a portfolio of competencies, not just a portfolio of specific businesses. Companies should strive for core competence leadership, not just product leadership.

Managers who want to strengthen their firms' competitiveness via core competencies need to focus on several related issues:

> Identify existing core competencies.
> Acquire or build core competencies that will be important for the future.
> Keep investing in competencies so that the firm remains world class and better than competitors.
> Extend competencies to find new applications and opportunities for the markets of tomorrow.[6]

Consider which of these issues Corning's CEO addressed, as discussed in the "Management Close-Up: Taking Action" feature.

Keep in mind that it's not enough for an organization to *have* valuable resources that provide competencies; those resources have to be *managed* in a way that gives the organization an advantage over competitors.[8] That means managers have to do three things. First, they must accumulate the right resources (such as talented people) by determining what resources they need, acquiring and developing those resources, and eliminating resources that don't provide value. Next, they combine the resources in ways that give the organization capabilities, such as researching new products or resolving problems for customers. These combinations may involve knowledge sharing and alliances between departments or with other organizations. Finally, managers need to leverage or exploit their resources. They do this by identifying the opportunities where their competencies deliver value to customers—say, by creating new products or by delivering existing products better than competitors—and then by coordinating and deploying the employees and other resources needed to respond to those opportunities.

Core competence can be a source of quality and innovation.

Management Close-up | TAKING ACTION

To fix Corning, Wendell Weeks first considered what the company represents at its core: its values, its people, and a culture built around innovation. He thought about how Corning added value: by making what Corning calls "keystone components" for the world's major industries. As Weeks put it, "We are never about the products we make, because those will continue to change."

Meeting with his top 200 managers, Weeks described the situation facing Corning, as well as his plans for turning the company around. Vowing that Corning would stay true to its core ideals, he took the message to Corning's plants around the world.

Weeks examined the company's research and development pipeline for the best opportunities. Before his promotion to Corning's fiber-optics unit in 1992, Weeks had worked in its liquid crystal display (LCD) glass business. Although the LCD business had been losing money for years, Corning scientists knew the glass had many applications: televisions and computer monitors, laptop and notebook computers, and many other portable devices. As the technology for big-screen TVs evolved, demand for LCD glass grew. Corning increased its production of LCD glass, and soon the glass drove the bulk of the company's profits. For 2006, the company posted record earnings, based largely on the production of LCD glass.

Aside from its domestic business, Corning opened its first LCD glass manufacturing plant in China. With China's growing manufacturing capabilities and rising middle class, Corning promised more investment in that emerging market. The company projected growing global demand for the glass in 2008.[7]

- Wendell Weeks began the turnaround of Corning by considering what he called "the core of the company": an innovative culture that responded to the changing demands of the marketplace. How did this attribute lead to Corning's turnaround?
- Corning operates in five business units: Display Technologies, Telecommunications, Environmental Technologies, Specialty Materials, and Life Sciences. How did these core competencies influence Weeks's turnaround strategy?

Strategic Alliances

LO 3

As we discussed in Chapter 8, the modern organization has a variety of links with other organizations. These links are more complex than the standard relationships with traditional stakeholders such as suppliers and clients. Today even fierce *competitors* are working together at unprecedented levels to achieve their strategic goals. For example, Federal Express has drop-off boxes at U.S. Postal Service facilities. The New York Times Company and Monster Worldwide formed an alliance in which job advertisements for 19 newspapers will carry the Monster.com brand. The arrangement gives the newspaper company, whose papers include the *New York Times* and *Boston Globe*, a stronger online presence and gives Monster better visibility in local job markets, which have traditionally been dominated by local papers.[9] In these and other examples, strategic alliances allow participants to respond to customer demands or environmental threats far faster and less expensively than each would be able to do on its own.

A **strategic alliance** is a formal relationship created with the purpose of joint pursuit of mutual goals. In a strategic alliance, individual organizations share administrative authority, form social links, and accept joint ownership. Such alliances are blurring firms' boundaries. They occur between companies and their competitors, governments, and universities. Such partnering often crosses national and cultural boundaries. Companies form strategic alliances to develop new technologies, enter

strategic alliance

A formal relationship created among independent organizations with the purpose of joint pursuit of mutual goals.

Airlines, which are fierce competitors as they each try to secure their space in the skies, actually form alliances designed to improve customer service. Member airlines of Star Alliance share ground facilities such as baggage claim, customer lounges, ticketing, and check-in counters. They also share check-in lanes during peak travel times. All of these shared activities help smooth the way for travelers, particularly those with tight connections and who are traveling on multiple airlines. Star Alliance staff (employees of member airlines) notify each other when flights are late, asking them to wait for connecting passengers, if possible. And although the alliance makes every effort to make sure passengers' luggage is not lost, those who do come up empty handed receive a Star Alliance overnight kit. Star Alliance airlines also purchase joint advertising and even make large fuel purchases together, reducing costs. In the future the alliance may begin making joint purchases of such items as coffee and airsick bags.

Although Star Alliance seeks to offer uniformity of ground services, the group encourages individual airlines to maintain their own unique character in the air, such as specialty meals or specific in-flight services.[10]

Music and Coffee—A Harmonious Strategic Alliance! Apple and Starbucks created a partnership that allows Apple customers to sync to the Starbucks wireless internet network instantly from their iPod Touch, Macs, and iPhones to download music. Shown here is a Starbucks customer, Steve Carpenter (right), using his iPhone to capture a song at a Starbucks in Miami Beach, Florida.

Alliances can increase speed and innovation and lower costs.

learning organization

An organization skilled at creating, acquiring, and transferring knowledge, and at modifying its behavior to reflect new knowledge and insights.

new markets, and reduce manufacturing costs. Not only can alliances enable companies to move ahead faster and more efficiently, but they also are sometimes the only practical way to bring together the variety of specialists needed for operating in today's complex and fast-changing environment. Rather than hiring the experts who understand the technology and market segments for each new product, companies can form alliances with partners that already have those experts on board.[11]

Managers typically devote plenty of time to screening potential partners in financial terms. But for the alliance to work, the partners also must consider one another's areas of expertise and the incentives involved in the structure of the alliance. A comparison of research and development alliances found that the most innovation occurred when the partners were experts in moderately different types of research. If the partners were very different, they shared ideas and innovated more when the alliance was set up through equity (stock) ownership; for similar partners, a contract to do the research was associated with more innovation.[12]

Managers also must foster and develop the human relationships in the partnership. Asian companies seem to be the most comfortable with the nonfinancial, "people" side of alliances; European companies the next so; and U.S. companies the least. Thus, U.S. companies may need to pay extra attention to the human side of alliances. Table 9.1 shows some recommendations for how to do this. In fact, most of the ideas apply not only to strategic alliances but to any type of relationship.[13]

The Learning Organization

Being responsive requires continually changing and learning new ways to act. Some experts have stated that the only sustainable advantage is learning faster than the competition. This has led to a new term that is now part of the vocabulary of most managers: the learning organization.[14] A **learning organization** is an organization skilled at creating, acquiring, and transferring knowledge, and at modifying its behavior to reflect new knowledge and insights.[15] Google, Toyota, and IDEO are good examples of learning organizations. Such organizations are skilled at solving problems,

The best alliances are true partnerships that meet these criteria:
1. *Individual excellence:* Both partners add value, and their motives are positive (pursue opportunity) rather than negative (mask weaknesses).
2. *Importance:* Both partners want the relationship to work because it helps them meet long-term strategic objectives.
3. *Interdependence:* The partners need each other; each helps the other reach its goal.
4. *Investment:* The partners devote financial and other resources to the relationship.
5. *Information:* The partners communicate openly about goals, technical data, problems, and changing situations.
6. *Integration:* The partners develop shared ways of operating; they teach each other and learn from each other.
7. *Institutionalization:* The relationship has formal status with clear responsibilities.
8. *Integrity:* Both partners are trustworthy and honorable.

TABLE 9.1
How I's Can Become We's

experimenting with new approaches, learning from their own experiences, learning from other organizations, and spreading knowledge quickly and efficiently.

How do firms become true learning organizations? There are a few important ingredients.[16]

1. Their people engage in disciplined thinking and attention to details, making decisions based on data and evidence rather than guesswork and assumptions.
2. They search constantly for new knowledge and ways to apply it, looking for expanding horizons and opportunities rather than quick fixes to current problems. The organization values and rewards individuals who expand their knowledge and skill in areas that benefit the organization.
3. They carefully review both successes and failures, looking for lessons and deeper understanding.
4. Learning organizations benchmark—they identify and implement the best business practices of other organizations, stealing ideas shamelessly.
5. They share ideas throughout the organization via reports, information systems, informal discussions, site visits, education, and training. Employees work with and are mentored by more-experienced employees.

The High-Involvement Organization

Participative management is becoming increasingly popular as a way to create a competitive advantage. Particularly in high-technology companies facing stiff international competition, the aim is to generate high levels of commitment and involvement as employees and managers work together to achieve organizational goals.

In a **high-involvement organization,** top management ensures that there is a consensus about the direction in which the business is heading. The leader seeks input from his or her top management team and from lower levels of the company. Task forces, study groups, and other techniques are used to foster participation in decisions that affect the entire organization. Also fundamental to the high-involvement organization

high-involvement organization

A type of organization in which top management ensures that there is consensus about the direction in which the business is heading.

When companies need to be highly responsive, a high-involvement organization is key. Especially in high-technology companies where competition is tough, it's important for all employees to be on the front line and be able to react quickly to change.

is continual feedback to participants regarding how they are doing compared with the competition and how effectively they are meeting the strategic agenda.

Structurally, this usually means that even lower-level employees have a direct relationship with a customer or supplier and thus receive feedback and are held accountable for a good or service delivery. The organizational form is a flat, decentralized structure built around a customer, good, or service. Employee involvement is particularly powerful when the environment changes rapidly, work is creative, complex activities require coordination, and firms need major breakthroughs in innovation and speed—in other words, when companies need to be more responsive.[17]

Organizational Size and Agility

LO 4

One of the most important characteristics of an organization—and one of the most important factors influencing its ability to respond effectively to its environment—is its size. Large organizations are typically less organic and more bureaucratic. For example, Unilever, whose many consumer brands include Hellman's, Ben & Jerry's, Lipton, Vaseline, Dove, and Slim-Fast, has more than 200,000 employees worldwide. In many countries, the company has operated as three independent business lines—food, personal care, and ice cream and frozen food—each with its own supply chain and marketing budget.[18]

In large organizations, jobs become more specialized. More distinct groups of specialists get created because large organizations can add a new specialty at lower proportional expense. The complexity created by these numerous specialties makes the organization harder to control. As a result, in the past management added more levels to keep spans of control from becoming too large. To cope with complexity, large companies tend to become more bureaucratic. Rules, procedures, and paperwork are introduced.

Thus, with size comes greater complexity, and complexity brings a need for increased control. In response, organizations adopt bureaucratic strategies of control. The conventional wisdom is that bureaucratization increases efficiency but decreases a company's ability to innovate. So, are larger companies more responsive to competitive demands or not? Let's see.

The Case for Big

Bigger was better after World War II, when foreign competition was limited and growth seemed limitless. To meet high demand for its products, U.S. industry embraced high-volume, low-cost manufacturing methods. IBM, General Motors (GM), and Sears all grew into behemoths during those decades.

Alfred Chandler, a pioneer in strategic management, noted that big companies were the engine of economic growth throughout the 20th century.[19] Size creates *scale economies*, that is, lower costs per unit of production. And size can offer specific advantages such as lower operating costs, greater purchasing power, and easier access to capital. Wal-Mart, among the largest companies in America, has the purchasing power to buy merchandise in larger volumes

$ **The bottom line**
COST

Large size often leads to scale economies.

Walmart's huge size has enabled it to set up a highly efficient distribution system in which suppliers work to keep costs low, an important competitive advantage for its low-price strategy.

and sell it at lower prices than its competitors can. Size also creates **economies of scope;** materials and processes employed in one product can be used to make other, related products. With such advantages, huge companies with lots of money may be the best at taking on large foreign rivals in huge global markets.

The Case for Small

But a huge, complex organization can find it hard to manage relationships with customers and among its own units. Bureaucracy can run rampant. Too much success can breed complacency, and the resulting inertia hinders change. Experts suggest that this is a surefire formula for being "left in the dust" by hungry competitors. As consumers demand a more diverse array of high-quality, customized products supported by excellent service, giant companies have begun to stumble. Some evidence exists, for example, that as firms get larger and their market share grows, customers begin to view their products as having lower quality. Also, once a company has captured a big share of the market, future growth is complicated because winning over more customers requires costlier efforts or a fresh approach. When growth was slowing at Walmart, the company tried branching into affordable but fashionable clothing. But cutting-edge fashion has not been an area of expertise for the company, and the initial efforts flopped.[20]

Larger companies also are more difficult to coordinate and control. While size may enhance efficiency by spreading fixed costs out over more units, it also may create administrative difficulties that inhibit efficient performance. Unilever not only has three organizations selling different product lines in each country it serves, but until recently it was run by two chairmen-CEOs, an artifact of a merger that took place decades ago. This cumbersome structure has held back Unilever's efficiency and agility, making competition more difficult.[21] To describe this type of problem, a new term has entered the business vocabulary: *diseconomies of scale*, or the costs of being too big. "Small is beautiful" has become a favorite phrase of entrepreneurial business managers.[22]

Smaller companies can move fast, provide quality goods and services to targeted market niches, and inspire greater involvement from their people. Nimble, small firms frequently outmaneuver big bureaucracies. They introduce new and better products, and they steal market share. The premium now is on flexibility and responsiveness—the unique potential strengths of the small firm. An extreme example is Kobold Watch, staffed by founder Michael Kobold and three employees. The small company makes and sells premium mechanical wristwatches priced at thousands of dollars each. Kobold advertises online and through word-of-mouth generated by sales to celebrities, including former president Bill Clinton and actors Kiefer Sutherland and James Gandolfini. When sales surge, Kobold calls on two other watchmakers to help out as needed. He intentionally limits production to 2,500 watches a year—not just to keep his company lean but also to maintain the prestige of his brand.[23]

economies of scope

Economies in which materials and processes employed in one product can be used to make other, related products.

The bottom line
SPEED
Small size may improve speed.

To keep its flexibility as it grew, Dur-A-Flex became a learning organization. The company started out primarily installing commercial and industrial flooring, but it gradually expanded into manufacturing the flooring systems and related products. After a decade of rapid growth, the company's structure had become rigid, divided into separate manufacturing systems operating on three shifts. Maintaining quality and speed across departments and shifts was sometimes awkward.

Under CEO Bob Smith, Dur-A-Flex embarked on a change program known as "lean," an approach (described later in this chapter) that involves studying and improving every process. Going lean introduced a climate that fostered learning. Every employee is trained in the methods and philosophy behind the lean approach. The company set up its own program, called Dur-A-Flex University, which holds classes mainly during lunch breaks.

According to Bill Greider, who led the lean initiative, "Once our focus turned to learning, everything changed." As employees began interacting in the classes, divisions among groups slipped away. Employees now are encouraged to learn about all aspects of Dur-A-Flex's business, from financial matters to flooring installation methods. Employees also can teach or sign up for a variety of fun Dur-A-Flex University "electives" such as beer making. CEO Smith says the learning approach not only helps employees cut costs and boost sales but also builds their enthusiasm and empowers them.[24]

Being Big and Small

Small *is* beautiful for unleashing energy and speed. But in buying and selling, size offers market power. The challenge, then, is to be both big and small to capitalize on the advantages of each.

When Intuit grew from a software start-up to an established company selling popular accounting software, the company brought in a CEO recruited from General Electric, Steve Bennett, to mesh big-company skills with Intuit's entrepreneurial energy. Managers had plenty of new ideas but needed to build their skill in choosing and implementing the best ideas. Bennett helped the company reevaluate its strategy to find areas of new growth. Popular Intuit products like QuickBooks have already captured most of the market for accounting software, so the company needs to focus less on competitors for its existing products and more on areas of untapped opportunity, which is why Intuit has begun to develop new areas such as online banking and software for managing health care expenses.[25]

> "When I got [to Intuit], . . . I changed only one word in the operating values: I changed 'Think fast, move fast' to 'Think smart, move fast.' Because doing dumb things faster doesn't get you anywhere."
>
> —Steve Bennett, Intuit CEO[26]

From a different angle, companies such as Starbucks and Amazon are very large companies that work hard to act small and maintain a sense of intimacy with employees and customers. Both are considered among the best-managed companies in the world. To avoid problems of growth and size, they decentralize decision making and organize around small, adaptive, team-based work units.

Verizon Communications is one large company that collaborates with its smaller customers to spread word about the benefits of its services. The company recently made an offer that some of its small-business customers decided to accept. The big firm asked the small ones if they would like to be featured in upcoming advertising. Jill Gizzio, founder of DogToys.com, which sells pet products, agreed to participate. The story of her seven-employee firm—which happens to use Verizon's broadband telecommunications technology—was featured along with two other small firms in a regional ad. Gizzio was pleased with the result, which gave her tiny company more exposure than it had ever had. "It was the easiest thing I've ever done," says Gizzio.

Business experts believe that the joint effort benefits both sides. Small-business customers get a chance to reach a wider audience and Verizon is profiled for its commitment and attention to small-business owners. "The Verizon commercial is helping to brand my company," says Gizzio. But it's important for the relationship to make sense—by partnering with companies that have similar outlooks and objectives. Says one industry observer, "A small-business owner might avoid teaming up with a large firm that is having ethical problems or whose image doesn't mesh with that of the small business." Similarly, a large firm might wait until a small firm has an established track record before offering it the spotlight. But when the relationship between the two works, the result can be very powerful.[27]

Downsizing   As large companies attempt to regain the responsiveness of small companies, they often face the dilemma of downsizing. **Downsizing** is the planned elimination of positions or jobs. Common approaches to downsizing include eliminating functions, hierarchical levels, or even whole units.[28] Another growing trend has been to replace full-time employees with less-expensive part-time or temporary workers.

Recognizing that people will be unemployed, frightened, and perhaps unable to pay their bills, managers usually opt for downsizing only in response to some kind of pressure. Traditionally, companies have downsized when demand falls and seems unlikely to rebound in the short run. Laying off workers is a way to avoid paying people who aren't needed to produce and ship goods, as well as to lower costs so that the company remains profitable—or at least viable—until the next upturn in business. More recently, however, global competition forced companies to cut costs even when sales were strong, and technological advances made it possible to produce the same amount of work with fewer employees. As a result, in recent decades, many companies have used downsizing as a way to become more efficient. This trend changed the types of positions that were eliminated. Downsizing in response to a slowdown in demand has tended to have the most impact on operating-level jobs in manufacturing firms. Downsizing to improve efficiency has focused on eliminating layers of management and bureaucratic structures, so those layoffs target "white-collar" middle managers.

The recent recession has forced widespread downsizing across a variety of industries, not just manufacturing. For example, Microsoft faced a severe downturn in demand, driven in part by a rare decline in the number of personal computers sold. The company announced that, for the first time in its history, it would have to downsize, laying off about 5,000 employees (about 5 percent of its workforce). The company started with 1,400 job cuts, and several months later announced that another 3,000 workers would lose their jobs, bringing the company near the end of its downsizing plan. In a memo to employees, CEO Steve Ballmer acknowledged the risks of such an approach: "Our success at Microsoft has always been the direct result of the talent, hard work, and commitment of our people."[29] In effect, downsizing runs the risk of eliminating the very source of a company's success.

Done appropriately, with inefficient layers eliminated and resources focused more on adding customer value than on wasteful internal processes, downsizing can indeed lead to a more agile, flexible, and responsive firm. In that case, downsizing can be called **rightsizing**—arrival at the size at which the company performs most effectively. But even under the best circumstances, downsizing can be traumatic for an organization and its employees. What can be done to manage downsizing effectively, to help make it more effective?

First, firms should avoid excessive (cyclical) hiring to help reduce the need to engage in major or multiple downsizings. But beyond that, firms must avoid common mistakes such as making slow, small, frequent layoffs; implementing voluntary early retirement programs that entice the best people to leave; and laying off so many people that the company's work can no longer be performed. Instead, firms can engage in a number of positive practices to ease the pain and increase the effectiveness of downsizing:[30]

> Use downsizing only as a last resort, when other methods of improving performance by innovating or changing procedures have been exhausted.
> Choose positions to be eliminated by engaging in careful analysis and strategic thinking.
> Train people to cope with the new situation.
> Identify and protect talented people.
> Give special attention and help to those who have lost their jobs.

downsizing

The planned elimination of positions or jobs.

rightsizing

A successful effort to achieve an appropriate size at which the company performs most effectively.

Communicate constantly with people about the process, and invite ideas for alternative ways to operate more efficiently.

Identify how the organization will operate more effectively in the future, and emphasize this positive future and the remaining employees' new roles in attaining it.

The management practices of high-involvement organizations, described earlier in this chapter, also play a role. In general, the negative consequences of downsizing are greater at high-involvement organizations—but not as bad if the organization continues the high employee involvement after the layoffs.[31]

Interestingly, the people who lose their jobs because of downsizing are not the only ones deeply affected. Those who survive the process—who keep their jobs—tend to exhibit what has become known as **survivor's syndrome**.[32] They struggle with heavier workloads; wonder who will be next to go; try to figure out how to survive; lose commitment to the company and faith in their bosses; and become narrow-minded, self-absorbed, and risk-averse. As a consequence, morale and productivity usually drop.

You will learn more about some of these ideas in later chapters on human resources management, leadership, motivation, communication, and managing change. You might also refer back to our discussion in Chapter 1 about some of the things you can do to successfully manage your own career in an era where downsizing is a normal occurrence.

survivor's syndrome

Loss of productivity and morale in employees who remain after a downsizing.

Customers and the Responsive Organization

 LO 5

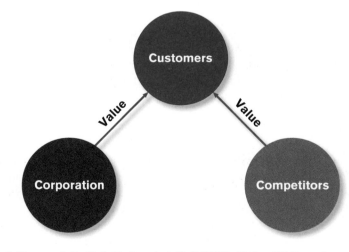

Today's customers demand excellent service and new high-quality, low-cost products—fast.

So far, we have discussed how an organization's agility, adaptability, and structure are influenced by its *strategy* and *size*. But in the end, the point of structuring a responsive, agile organization lies in enabling it to meet and exceed the expectations of its *customers*—the people it must attract to purchase a good or service and whose continued patronage and involvement with the organization constitute the fundamental driver of sustained, long-term competitiveness and success.

Recall from Chapter 2 that an organization's environment is composed of many different parts—government, suppliers, competitors, and the like. Perhaps no other aspect of the environment has had a more profound impact on organizing in recent years than a focus on customers. Dr. Kenichi Ohmae points out that any business unit must take into account three key players: the *company* itself, the *competition*, and the *customer*. These components form what Ohmae refers to as the *strategic triangle*, as shown in Figure 9.2. Managers need to balance the strategic triangle, and successful

FIGURE 9.2
The Strategic Triangle   SOURCE: From K. Ohmae et al., *The Mind of the Strategist, p. 92.* © 1982 The McGraw-Hill Companies.

organizations use their strengths to create value by meeting customer requirements better than competitors do. In this section, we will discuss in some depth how organizations organize to maintain and extend a competitive advantage with their customers.

Customer Relationship Management

Customer relationship management (CRM) is a multifaceted process, typically mediated by a set of information technologies, that focuses on creating two-way exchanges with customers so that firms have an intimate knowledge of their needs, wants, and buying patterns. In this way, CRM helps companies understand, as well as anticipate, the needs of current and potential customers. And in that way, it is part of a business strategy for managing customers to maximize their long-term value to an enterprise.[32]

customer relationship management (CRM)

A multifaceted process focusing on creating two-way exchanges with customers to foster intimate knowledge of their needs, wants, and buying patterns.

Bankers are using CRM software to collect and sift through data about their customers to learn more about them and the ways to give them everything they want—and still make a profit. Whereas the first generation of such software simply gathered the data, the new generation helps bankers anticipate needs and provide service—sometimes before customers even know what they want. "Delivering something that I expect is one thing, but when you . . . start solving problems that I don't even know I've got yet, that's where you feel well taken care of," says Debbie Wood of industry research firm Jack Henry & Associates. David Sardilli of Oracle Corp. adds, "Meeting the . . . goals of both the members and the customers is paramount." Effective CRM essentially provides a three-dimensional (3-D) view of the customer, the ability to see the customer from different viewpoints and needs.

Many banks find they are falling short of their customers' expectations and genuinely want to correct that. At the consumer level, it could be something as simple as adding more tellers during busy hours like lunchtime and after work. At the commercial level, it could be offering certain financial products or services. "The CRM mindset has to permeate the organization," advises Sardilli. "If there's a customer relationship mindset, when someone makes a call to change their address, the system will know to prompt someone to change the address on their other accounts."[34]

As discussed throughout this book, customers want quality goods and services, low cost, innovative products, and speed. Traditional thinking considered these basic customer wants as a set of potential trade-offs. For instance, customers wanted high quality or low costs passed along in the form of low prices. But world-class companies today know that the "trade-off" mentality no longer applies. Customers want it *all*, and they are learning that an organization exists somewhere that will provide it all.

But if all companies seek to satisfy customers, how can a company realize a competitive advantage? World-class companies have learned that almost any advantage is temporary, because competitors will strive to catch up. Simply stated—although obviously not

The American Customer Satisfaction Index measures consumers' ratings of the price, quality, and customer service associated with buying a variety of goods and services. During this period, the ACSI fell during the months just before a recession and then began to climb. Perhaps this means companies try harder when it's harder to make a sale.[35]

American Customer Satisfaction Index*

* The baseline index of 74.8 was measured in summer 1994.

"Our business is about technology, yes. But it's also about operations and customer relationships."

—Michael Dell

simply done—a company attains and retains competitive advantage by continuing to improve. This concept—*kaizen*, or continuous improvement—is an integral part of Japanese operations strategy.

In the realm of customer relations, continuous improvement includes continually changing in order to connect with customers, even without waiting for customers to make the first move. Comcast Cable, Dell, and other companies have adopted Salesforce.com's Service Cloud application, which lets companies find customers who take their questions and problems to Facebook, Twitter, or other social networking communities. Customer service agents can locate messages about their products and then offer to help, potentially saving a customer relationship. Chase Paymentech Solutions is using collaboration software called Greenhouse to invite customers into conversations about new-product ideas. Customers can critique and vote on ideas; their feedback not only helps Chase figure out which ideas have potential but also strengthens customer commitment.[36]

As organizations focus on responding to customer needs, they soon find that the traditional meaning of a customer expands to include "internal customers." The word *customer* now refers to the *next process*, or *wherever the work goes next.*[37] This highlights the idea of interdependence among related functions and means that all functions of the organization—not just marketing people—have to be concerned with customer satisfaction. Any recipient of a person's work, whether coworker, boss, subordinate, or external party, should be viewed as the customer.

A deeper way to understand how organizations can add customer value to their products has been provided by Michael Porter, who popularized the concept of the value chain. A **value chain** is the sequence of activities that flow from raw materials to the delivery of a good or service, with additional value created at each step. You can see a generic value chain illustrated in Figure 9.3. Each step in the chain adds value to the product or service:

> *Research and development* focus on innovation and new products.
> *Inbound logistics* receive and store raw materials and distribute them to operations.
> *Operations* transform the raw materials into final product.
> *Outbound logistics* warehouse the product and handle its distribution.

value chain

The sequence of activities that flow from raw materials to the delivery of a good or service, with additional value created at each step.

FIGURE 9.3
Generic Value Chain

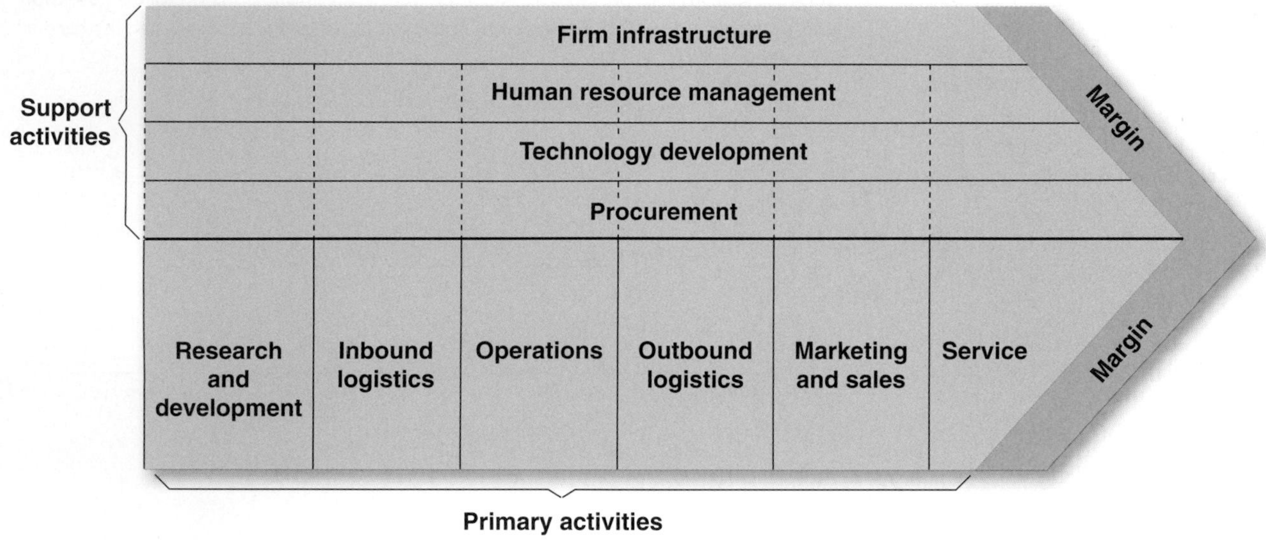

Primary activities

SOURCE: Michael Porter, *Competitive Advantage: Creating and Sustaining Superior Performance* (New York: Free Press, 1985).

Marketing and sales identify customer requirements and get customers to
  purchase the product.
Service offers customer support, such as repair, after the item has been bought.

When the total value created—that is, *what customers are willing to pay*—exceeds the
cost of providing the good or service, the result is the organization's profit *margin*.[38]

Managers can add customer value and build competitive advantage by paying close
attention to their organization's value chain—not only each step in it, but the way
each step interacts with the others. For example, they can achieve economies of scale,
as Walmart has, so that their materials and operations costs are lowered, or they can
develop innovative distribution channels, as Amazon has done, and add customer
value that way. They can also create structures and systems that link the elements of
the value chain in innovative ways.

One of the most effective ways to leverage an organization's value chain is to bring
together elements of the chain to collaborate to add customer value and build competitive advantage. For example, long-term relationships can be established with suppliers to encourage investment in new technologies and practices that speed product
development and turnaround. Nike chooses its suppliers—what it calls its "strategic
partners"—to that end and shares its business plans and strategies with them to reinforce close collaboration. Sales staff can communicate with operations staff, before
the manufacturing process even starts, to develop products jointly that customers will
value highly. Service managers can constantly report back to operations about defects
and work with operations and suppliers to reduce and eliminate them. When managers create that type of collaboration, their organization's agility and responsiveness
increase significantly.

Total Quality Management

Total quality management (TQM) is a way of managing in which everyone is
committed to continuous improvement of his or her part of the operation. In business, success depends on having high-quality products. As described in Chapter 1
and throughout the book, TQM is a comprehensive approach to improving product
quality and thereby customer satisfaction. It is characterized by a strong orientation
toward customers (external and internal) and has become an umbrella theme for organizing work. TQM re-orients managers toward involving people across departments
in improving all aspects of the business. Continuous improvement requires integrative
mechanisms that facilitate group problem solving, information sharing, and cooperation across business functions. As a consequence, the walls that separate stages and
functions of work tend to come down, and the organization operates more in a team-
oriented manner.[39]

One of the founders of the quality management movement was W. Edwards Deming. When he started, his work was largely ignored by American companies, but it
was adopted eagerly by Japanese firms that wanted to shed their products of their
post–World War II reputation for shoddiness. The quality emphasis of Japanese car
manufacturing was one direct result of Deming's work, which has since been adopted
by many American and other companies worldwide. Deming's "14 points" of quality
emphasized a holistic approach to management that demands intimate understanding
of the process—the delicate interaction of materials, machines, and people that determines productivity, quality, and competitive advantage:

1. Create constancy of purpose—strive for long-term improvement rather than
   short-term profit.
2. Adopt the new philosophy—don't tolerate delays and mistakes.
3. Cease dependence on mass inspection—build quality into the process on the
   front end.
4. End the practice of awarding business on price tag alone—build long-term
   relationships.

**total quality
management (TQM)**

An integrative approach to
management that supports
the attainment of customer
satisfaction through a
wide variety of tools and
techniques that result in
high-quality goods and
services.

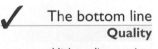

The bottom line
Quality

High quality requires
organizationwide commitment.

5. Improve constantly and forever the system of production and service—at each stage.
6. Institute training and retraining—continually update methods and thinking.
7. Institute leadership—provide the resources needed for effectiveness.
8. Drive out fear—people must believe it is safe to report problems or ask for help.
9. Break down barriers among departments—promote teamwork.
10. Eliminate slogans, exhortations, and arbitrary targets—supply methods, not buzzwords.
11. Eliminate numerical quotas—they are contrary to the idea of continuous improvement.
12. Remove barriers to pride in workmanship—allow autonomy and spontaneity.
13. Institute a vigorous program of education and retraining—people are assets, not commodities.
14. Take action to accomplish the transformation—provide a structure that enables quality.

One of the most important contributors to total quality management has been the introduction of statistical tools to analyze the causes of product defects, in an approach called *Six Sigma Quality*. Sigma is the Greek letter used to designate the estimated standard deviation or variation in a process. (The higher the "sigma level," the lower the amount of variation.) The product defects analyzed may include anything that results in customer dissatisfaction—for example, late delivery, wrong shipment, or poor customer service, as well as problems with the product itself. When the defect has been identified, managers then engage the organization in a determined, comprehensive effort to eliminate its causes and reduce it to the lowest practicable level. At Six Sigma, a product or process is defect-free 99.99966 percent of the time—less than 3.4 defects or mistakes per million. Reaching that goal almost always requires managers to restructure their internal processes and relationships with suppliers and customers in fundamental ways. For example, managers may have to create teams from all parts of the organization to implement the process improvements that will prevent defects from arising. Motorola, where Six Sigma was developed, and General Electric, whose success with Six Sigma helped to make the technique popular, credit the method with helping them improve efficiency and quality. Of course, a technique for measuring and improving processes cannot guarantee business success. A study by QualPro, which markets its own process management method, found that among companies using Six Sigma, the stock prices of some, including Caterpillar, Target, and Whirlpool, beat the overall stock market, while others, including Ford and Xerox, fell short.[40] Thus, any quality improvement method is just one item in the manager's tool kit. We will discuss Six Sigma in more detail in Chapter 16.

The Bama Companies, a family-owned manufacturer of frozen foods, has won the Malcolm Baldrige National Quality Award.

Commitment to total quality requires a thorough, extensive, integrated approach to organizing. To encourage American companies to make that commitment and achieve excellence, the Malcolm Baldrige National Quality Award was established in 1987. Named after a former U.S. Secretary of Commerce, the award is given every year to companies and nonprofit organizations that have met specified criteria in seven areas: (1) leadership; (2) strategic planning; (3) customer and market focus; (4) measurement, analysis, and knowledge management; (5) workforce focus; (6) process management; and (7) business results. Recent winners include MESA Products, a small manufacturer of systems that protect metal from corrosion, which has dramatically cut cycle time and improved productivity while boosting customer service, and the North Mississippi Medical Center, which has reduced errors and streamlined processes by connecting all the caregivers in its system to electronic medical records.[41]

ISO 9001

The influence of TQM on the organizing process has become even more acute with the emergence of ISO 9000 standards. **ISO 9001** is a series of voluntary quality standards developed by a committee working under the International Organization for Standardization (known as ISO), a network of national standards institutions in more than 150 countries. In contrast to most ISO standards, which describe a particular material, product, or process, the ISO 9001 standards apply in a general way to management systems at any organization. These standards aim to improve total quality in all businesses for the benefit of producers and consumers alike. To do this, ISO 9001 sets standards of management that address eight principles:[42]

1. *Customer focus*—learning and addressing customer needs and expectations.
2. *Leadership*—establishing a vision and goals, establishing trust, and providing employees with the resources and inspiration to meet goals.
3. *Involvement of people*—establishing an environment in which employees understand their contribution, engage in problem solving, and acquire and share knowledge.
4. *Process approach*—defining the tasks needed to successfully carry out each process and assigning responsibility for them.
5. *System approach to management*—putting processes together into efficient systems that work together effectively.
6. *Continual improvement*—teaching people how to identify areas for improvement and rewarding them for making improvements.
7. *Factual approach to decision making*—gathering accurate performance data, sharing the data with employees, and using the data to make decisions.
8. *Mutually beneficial supplier relationships*—working in a cooperative way with suppliers.

U.S. companies first became interested in ISO 9001 because overseas customers, particularly those in the European Union, embraced it. Companies that comply with the quality guidelines of ISO 9001 can apply for official certification; some countries and companies demand certification as an acknowledgment of compliance before they will do business. Now some U.S. customers as well are making the same demand. Consequently, the number of companies receiving ISO 9001 certification continues to grow; hundreds of thousands of companies in manufacturing and services industries around the world are ISO-certified. For example, UniFirst Corporation, a Massachusetts-based provider of workplace uniforms and protective work clothing, obtained ISO certification for its two Mexican plants through a process that included documenting all the facilities' processes and training employees in quality control. UniFirst's general manager Jose Del Angel expects that the effort will give the company an advantage, because none of its major competitors are certified so far. And in Cedar Rapids, Iowa, Physicians' Clinic of Iowa (PCI) received certification after two and a half years of preparation that included writing a quality policy, defining objectives, and standardizing medical records. PCI, whose members include 50 physicians and 200 staff employees, found that it had to define quality measures and establish methods for tracking quality.[43]

Certification is not the end of the quality effort but a beginning step. Rather than defining how to operate perfectly, ISO 9001 standards establish practices that enable the organization to keep improving—assuming that it continues to follow those practices.

ISO 9001

A series of quality standards developed by a committee working under the International Organization for Standardization to improve total quality in all businesses for the benefit of producers and consumers.

Reengineering

Extending from TQM and a focus on organizing around customer needs, organizations also have embraced the notion of reengineering (introduced in Chapter 1). The principal idea of reengineering is to revolutionize key organizational systems and processes to answer the question: "If you were the customer, how would you like us to operate?" The answer to this question forms a vision for how the organization should run, and then decisions are made and actions are taken to make the organization operate like the vision. Processes such as product development, order fulfillment, customer service, inventory management, billing, and production are redesigned from scratch as if the organization were brand new and just starting out.

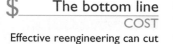

The bottom line
COST
Effective reengineering can cut costs significantly.

For example, Procter & Gamble used reengineering to make its products more competitive. The company learned that the average family buying its products rather than private-label or lower-price brands paid an extra $725 per year. That figure, P&G realized, was far too high and warned that the company's high prices could drive the company to extinction. Other data also signaled the need for P&G to change. Market shares of famous brands such as Comet, Mr. Clean, and Ivory had been dropping for 25 years. P&G was making 55 price changes *daily* on about 80 brands, and inaccurate billings were common. Its plants were inefficient, and the company had the highest overhead in the business. It clearly had to cut prices, and to do that, it had to cut costs.

In response, P&G reengineered. The company tore down and rebuilt nearly every activity that contributed to its high costs. It redesigned the way it develops, manufactures, distributes, prices, markets, and sells products. The reengineering was difficult, time-consuming, and expensive. But after the changes, price changes became rare, factories became far more efficient, inventory levels fell, and sales and profits rose. P&G was able to price its brands nearer to the prices of store brands. P&G might have reinvented itself as a leader in the industry once again and created for itself a long-term competitive advantage that others have scrambled to match.[44]

The kind of reengineering that P&G undertook requires much more than a management directive from the top, a change in the formal organization structure, the introduction of new technology, or even a well-communicated change in strategy. Rather, to be fully effective and successful, reengineering often requires a fundamental change in the way the parts of the organization work together. They need to see each other as partners in a common effort rather than as members of a particular department or unit. Teams made up of all levels of the organization may be involved in the reengineering effort, and information on problems and possible solutions needs to be fully shared between them. Customers and other stakeholders may be interviewed to get their contribution. Often several teams will be working simultaneously. In this way, all the information that is available within and outside the organization can be brought to bear on a problem—and the solution developed will have wider acceptance and can be implemented faster.

As you can see, reengineering is not about making minor organizational changes here and there. It is about completely overhauling the operation, in revolutionary ways, to achieve the greatest possible benefits to the customer and to the organization.

Technology and Organizational Agility

LO 6

technology

The systematic application of scientific knowledge to a new product, process, or service.

We have discussed the strategic, size, and customer influences on organizational design and agility. We now turn to one more critical factor affecting an organization's structure and responsiveness: its *technology*.

Broadly speaking, **technology** can be viewed as the methods, processes, systems, and skills used to transform resources (inputs) into products (outputs). Although we will discuss technology—and innovation—more fully in Chapter 17, in this chapter we want to highlight some of the important influences technology has on organizational design.

> "Information technology and business are becoming inextricably interwoven. I don't think anyone can talk meaningfully about one without talking about the other."
> —Bill Gates

Types of Technology Configurations

Research by Joan Woodward laid the foundation for understanding technology and structure. According to Woodward, three basic technologies characterize how work is done: small batch, large batch, and continuous process technologies. These three classifications are equally useful for describing either service or manufacturing technologies. Each differs in terms of volume produced and variety of goods/services offered. Each also has a different influence on how managers organize and structure the work of their organizations.[45]

Small Batch Technologies   When goods or services are provided in very low volume or **small batches,** a company that does such work is called a *job shop.* A fairly typical example of a job shop is PMF Industries, a small custom metalworking company in Williamsport, Pennsylvania, that produces stainless steel assemblies for medical and other uses. Less formally, in the service industry, restaurants or doctors' offices are examples of job shops, because they provide a high variety of low-volume, customized services.

In a small batch organization, structure tends to be very organic. There tend not to be a lot of rules and formal procedures, and decision making tends to be decentralized. The emphasis is on mutual adjustment among people.

Large Batch Technologies   As volume increases, product variety usually decreases. Companies with higher volumes and lower varieties than a job shop tend to be characterized as **large batch,** or mass production technologies. Examples of large batch technologies include the auto assembly operations of General Motors, Ford, and Chrysler. In the service sector, McDonald's and Burger King are good examples. Their production runs tend to be more standardized, and all customers receive similar (if not identical) products. Machines tend to replace people in the physical execution of work. People run the machines.

With a large batch technology, structure tends to be more mechanistic. There tend to be more rules and formal procedures, and decision making tends to be centralized with higher spans of control. Communication tends to be more formal in companies where hierarchical authority is more prominent.

Continuous Process Technologies   At the very-high-volume end of the scale are companies that use **continuous process** technologies, technologies that do not stop and start. Domino Sugar and Shell Chemical, for example, use continuous process technologies where a very limited number of products are produced. People are completely removed from the work itself. It is done entirely by machines and/or computers. In some cases, people run the computers that run the machines.

Ironically, with continuous process technology, structure can return to a more organic form because less monitoring and supervision are needed. Communication tends to be more informal in companies where fewer rules and regulations are established.

Organizing for Flexible Manufacturing

Although issues of volume and variety often have been seen as trade-offs in a technological sense, today

small batch

Technologies that produce goods and services in low volume.

large batch

Technologies that produce goods and services in high volume.

continuous process

A process that is highly automated and has a continuous production flow.

Dell has revolutionized the concept of mass customization. The production process from order to delivery is managed electronically, which allows Dell to build servers very efficiently and their customers to know where their server is during each step of the process.

mass customization

The production of varied, individually customized products at the low cost of standardized, mass-produced products.

organizations are trying to produce both high-volume and high-variety products at the same time. This is referred to as **mass customization.**[46] Automobiles, clothes, computers, and other products are increasingly being manufactured to match each customer's taste, specifications, and budget. While this seemed only a fantasy a few years ago, mass customization is quickly becoming more prevalent among leading firms. You can now buy clothes cut to your proportions, supplements with the exact blend of the vitamins and minerals you like, CDs with the music tracks you choose, and textbooks whose chapters are picked out by your professor.

How do companies organize to pull off this type of customization at such low cost? As shown in Table 9.2, they organize around a dynamic network of relatively independent operating units.[47] Each unit performs a specific process or task—called a *module*—such as making a component, performing a credit check, or performing a particular welding method. Some modules may be performed by outside suppliers or vendors.

Different modules join forces to make the good or provide a service. How and when the various modules interact with one another are dictated by the unique requests of each customer. The manager's responsibility is to make it easier and less costly for modules to come together, complete their tasks, and then recombine to meet the next

TABLE 9.2

Key Features in Mass Customization

Products	High variety and customization
Product design	Collaborative design; significant input from customers
	Short product development cycles
	Constant innovation
Operations and processes	Flexible processes
	Business process reengineering (BPR)
	Use of modules
	Continuous improvement (CI)
	Reduced setup and changeover times
	Reduced lead times
	JIT delivery and processing of materials and components
	Production to order
	Shorter cycle times
	Use of information technology (IT)
Quality management	Quality measured in customer delight
	Defects treated as capability failures
Organizational structure	Dynamic network of relatively autonomous operating units
	Learning relationships
	Integration of the value chain
	Team-based structure
Workforce management	Empowerment of employees
	High value on knowledge, information, and diversity of employee capabilities
	New product teams
	Broad job descriptions
Emphasis	Low-cost production of high-quality, customized products

SOURCE: Reprinted with permission of APICS—The Educational Society for Resource Management, *Production and Inventory Management* 41, no. 1, 2000, pp. 56–65.

customer demand. The ultimate goal of mass customization is a never-ending campaign to expand the number of ways a company can satisfy customers. The Internet has also made it easy for customers to choose their product preferences online and for companies to take an order straight to the manufacturing floor.

Computer-Integrated Manufacturing   One technological advance that has helped make mass customization possible is **computer-integrated manufacturing (CIM),** which encompasses a host of computerized production efforts linked together. Two examples are computer-aided design and computer-aided manufacturing, which offer the ultimate in computerized process technologies. The magazine-printing industry has adopted CIM, with editorial and advertising content on publishers' computers linked directly with printing and binding networks at printing plants, producing customized versions of the same magazine for different subscribers.

These systems can produce high-variety and high-volume products at the same time.[48] They may also offer greater control and predictability of production processes, reduced waste, faster throughput times, and higher quality. But managers cannot "buy" their way out of competitive trouble simply by investing in superior technology alone. They must also ensure that their organization has the necessary strategic and people strengths and a well-designed plan for integrating the new technology within the organization.

Flexible Factories   As the name implies, **flexible factories** provide more production options and a greater variety of products. They differ from traditional factories in three primary ways: lot size, flow patterns, and scheduling.[49]

First, the traditional factory has long production runs, generating high volumes of a standardized product. Flexible factories have much shorter production runs, with many different products. Second, traditional factories move parts down the line from one location in the production sequence to the next. Flexible factories are organized around products, in work cells or teams, so that people work closely together and parts move shorter distances with shorter or no delays. Third, traditional factories use centralized scheduling, which is time-consuming, inaccurate, and slow to adapt to changes. Flexible factories use local or decentralized scheduling in which decisions are made on the shop floor by the people doing the work.

Lean Manufacturing   Another organizing approach is **lean manufacturing,** based on a commitment to making an operation both efficient and effective; it strives to achieve the highest possible productivity and total quality, cost effectively, by eliminating unnecessary steps in the production process and continually striving for improvement. Rejects are unacceptable, and staff, overhead, and inventory are considered wasteful. In a lean operation, the emphasis is on quality, speed, and flexibility more than on cost, efficiency, and hierarchy. If an employee spots a problem, the employee is authorized to halt the operation and signal for help to correct the problem at its source so that processes can be improved and future problems avoided. With a well-managed lean production process, a company can develop, produce, and distribute products with half or less of the human effort, space, tools, time, and overall cost.[50]

Toyota receives much of the credit for modeling and teaching a commitment to "think lean." Many manufacturing companies have tried to adopt a similar lean approach, but Toyota and others have also applied lean methods to nonmanufacturing processes. Toyota's product development, for example, also uses lean principles. The process begins with identifying what customers define as valuable, so that employees don't waste time and money on things that customers don't care about. Early in the design process, teams bring together experts from various functions to identify potential problems and identify as many solutions as they can, to avoid the need to make design changes later in the process. Managers use their experience with past product development efforts to predict staffing requirements, and employees and technicians working

The bottom line

COST

Today's technologies offer customization at low cost.

computer-integrated manufacturing (CIM)

The use of computer-aided design and computer-aided manufacturing to sequence and optimize a number of production processes.

flexible factories

Manufacturing plants that have short production runs, are organized around products, and use decentralized scheduling.

lean manufacturing

An operation that strives to achieve the highest possible productivity and total quality, cost effectively, by eliminating unnecessary steps in the production process and continually striving for improvement.

Lean manufacturing strives for high quality, speed, and low cost.

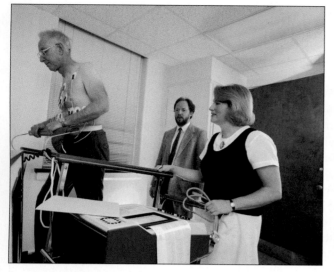

Some hospitals have been using lean principles to reduce costs and patient waiting times while improving safety.

for suppliers are assigned to projects only as they are needed. Further adding to efficiency and quality, the company uses standard parts, procedures, and skill sets wherever possible; detailed checklists help engineers ensure they are using best practices. With methods such as these, Toyota has been able to develop top-quality products faster and more consistently than its competitors. Similar approaches have also been used to improve services, such as operations at hospitals. For instance, St. Agnes Hospital in Baltimore has used lean principles to reduce costs and patient waiting times while improving safety, and the ThedaCare health system in Wisconsin saved more than $3 million in one year of using lean methods.[51]

For the lean approach to result in more effective operations, the following conditions must be met:[52]

People are broadly trained rather than specialized.
Communication is informal and horizontal among line workers.
Equipment is general purpose.
Work is organized in teams, or cells, that produce a group of similar products.
Supplier relationships are long-term and cooperative.
Product development is concurrent, not sequential, and is done by cross-functional teams.

In recent years, many companies have tried to become leaner by cutting overhead costs, laying off operative-level workers, eliminating layers of management, and utilizing capital equipment more efficiently. But if the move to lean manufacturing is simply a harsh, haphazard cost-cutting approach, the result will be chaos, overworked people, and low morale.

Getting lean makes each employee more valuable to the organization, because in lean processes, each employee's activities are essential. With waste already eliminated, companies have little to cut if demand falls. In the latest recession, manufacturers did lay off workers, but not as many as an equally severe downturn would have caused in the past, when companies weren't so streamlined.

An example is Parker Hannifin Corporation's factory in Spartanburg, South Carolina, where workers produce a variety of plastic parts. Lean operations and high-tech manufacturing systems enable the company to operate with a few skilled workers. For example, to make seals for aerosol cans, just five workers operate high-speed machinery, each handling a different step of the process. If demand slows, work can be divided so that two workers start the production on one day and the other three finish on a second day, or everyone can work only part of the week. Laying off any of the five workers would be difficult, because someone would have to be trained to run that person's machine. Similarly, only two workers are needed to run each shift that produces plastic tubes for blasting caps, down from eight a decade ago. If the company doesn't have enough demand to run two shifts, fewer jobs are at risk.

Parker Hannifin's production levels also are more closely tied to order volume, so fewer goods sit around in inventory. That means staffing is more closely matched to demand as well.[53]

Organizing for Speed: Time-Based Competition

Companies worldwide have devoted so much energy to improving product quality that high quality is now the standard attained by all top competitors. Competition has driven quality to such heights that quality products no longer are enough to distinguish one company from another. *Time* has emerged as the key competitive advantage that can separate market leaders from also-rans.[54]

Companies today must learn what the customer needs and meet those needs as quickly as possible. **Time-based competition (TBC)** refers to strategies aimed at reducing the total time needed to deliver the good or service. TBC has several key organizational elements: logistics, just-in-time (JIT), and simultaneous engineering. JIT production systems reduce the time to manufacture products. Logistics speeds the delivery of products to customers. Both are essential steps toward bringing products to customers in the shortest time possible. In today's world, speed is essential.

Logistics   The movement of resources into the organization (inbound) and products from the organization to its customers (outbound) is called **logistics.** Like the supply chain, which we discussed in Chapter 2, an organization's logistics is often a critical element in its responsiveness and competitive advantage.

The world of logistics includes the great mass of parts, materials, and products moving via trucks, trains, planes, and ships from and to every region of the globe. Depending on the product, duplication and inefficiency in distribution can cost far more than making the product itself, and slowdowns can cause products to go out of stock so that consumers choose alternatives. One technological advance that is helping some companies improve logistics efficiency and speed is the use of radio-frequency identification (RFID) tags. When manufacturers label their products with RFID tags, automated readers can easily track where each product is in the distribution system, including which particular items are selling in each store. Best Buy has had great success with RFID tagging; stores using the system are seeing sales increases as employees more efficiently keep track of which products need to be restocked and where they are located in the backroom. Walmart, in contrast, is trying to keep its well-known leadership role in distribution by asking suppliers to use RFID, but many of them are finding they cannot afford to institute the new system at this stage of its development while also meeting Walmart's demands to keep prices at a minimum.[55]

In some industries, speedy logistics are essential because products are perishable. For example, Flora-Holland, a flower auctioneer based in the Netherlands, acquires flowers from 8,000 suppliers and stores them in a massive warehouse for auction and distribution to buyers. Using RFID tagging on each cart of flowers, the company can process more than 60,000 transactions within hours. Whenever a pallet of flowers is sorted or moved, the RFID chip transmits the information about its place in the distribution system, along with data about its freshness.[56]

Just-in-Time Operations   An additional element of TBC involves **just-in-time (JIT)** operations. JIT calls for subassemblies and components to be manufactured in very small lots and delivered to the next stage in the process precisely at the time needed, or "just in time." A customer order triggers a factory order and the production process. The supplying work centers do not produce the next lot of product until the consuming work center requires it. Even external suppliers deliver to the company just in time.

Just-in-time is a companywide philosophy oriented toward eliminating waste throughout all operations and improving materials throughout. In this way, excess inventory is eliminated and costs are reduced. The ultimate goal of JIT is to serve the customer better by providing higher levels of quality and service. An example of an effective just-in-time operation is provided by Dell, which does not begin production of a computer customized to a consumer's specifications until after the customer's order has been received. Contrast this approach with traditional production methods, which require extremely costly warehousing of inventory

time-based competition (TBC)

Strategies aimed at reducing the total time needed to deliver a good or service.

logistics

The movement of the right goods in the right amount to the right place at the right time.

just-in-time (JIT)

A system that calls for subassemblies and components to be manufactured in very small lots and delivered to the next stage of the production process just as they are needed.

"Big will not beat small any more. It will be the fast beating the slow."
—Rupert Murdoch

Saturn has earned a reputation for superior customer satisfaction. Some of that reputation is due to Saturn's world-class distribution system. Why is it important that companies have a seamless logistics system in place?

and parts, uncertain production runs, considerable waste, no customizing capability, and lengthy delivery times.

JIT represents a number of key production and organizational concepts, including the following:

Elimination of waste. Eliminate all waste from the production process, including waste of time, people, machinery, space, and materials.

Perfect quality. Produce perfect parts even when lot sizes are reduced, and produce the product exactly when it is needed in the exact quantities that are needed.

Reduced cycle times. Accomplish the entire manufacturing process more rapidly. Reduce setup times for equipment, move parts only short distances (machinery is placed in closer proximity), and eliminate all delays. The goal is to reduce action to the time spent working on the parts. For most manufacturers today, the percentage of time parts are worked on is about 5 percent of the total production time. JIT seeks to eliminate the other 95 percent, that is, to reduce to zero the time spent not working on the parts.

Employee involvement. In JIT, employee involvement is central to success. The workers are responsible for production decisions. Managers and supervisors are coaches. Top management pledges that there will never be layoffs due to improved productivity.

Value-added manufacturing. Do only those things (actions, work, etc.) that add value to the finished product. If it doesn't add value, don't do it. For example, inspection does not add value to the finished product, so make the product correctly the first time and inspection will not be necessary.

Discovery of problems and prevention of recurrence. Foolproofing, or fail-safing, is a key component of JIT. To prevent problems from arising, their cause(s) must be known and acted on. Thus, in JIT operations, people try to find the "weak link in the chain" by forcing problem areas to the surface so that preventive measures may be determined and implemented.

Many believe that only a fraction of JIT's potential has been realized and that its impact will grow as it is applied to other processes, such as service, distribution, and new-product development.[57] Many stores, for example, are using variations of JIT to minimize the expense of storing products in back rooms. One specialty clothing retailer aims to have shipments move from receiving to the selling floor on the same day. A chain of 30 stores selling furniture and home accessories arranged to have daily deliveries of furniture, so that it could convert storage space to selling space; when a furniture item sells, the store arranges to have the piece replaced the same day.[58] However, it's important to keep in mind that JIT offers efficiency only when the costs of storing items are greater than the costs of frequent delivery.[59]

simultaneous engineering

A design approach in which all relevant functions cooperate jointly and continually in a maximum effort aimed at producing high-quality products that meet customers' needs.

Simultaneous Engineering   JIT is a vital component of TBC, but JIT concentrates on reducing time in only one function: manufacturing. TBC attempts to deliver speed in *all* functions—product development, manufacturing, logistics, and customer service. Customers will not be impressed if you manufacture quickly but it takes weeks for them to receive their products or get a problem solved.

Many companies are turning to simultaneous engineering as the cornerstone of their TBC strategy. **Simultaneous engineering**—also an important component of total quality management—is a major departure from the old development process in which tasks were assigned to various functions in sequence. When R&D completed its part of the project, the work was "passed over the wall" to engineering, which completed its task and passed it over the wall to manufacturing, and so on. This process was highly inefficient, and errors took a long time to correct.

In contrast, simultaneous engineering incorporates the issues and perspectives of all the functions—and customers and suppliers—from the beginning of the process. This team-based approach results in a higher-quality product that is designed for efficient manufacturing *and* customer needs.[60] In the automobile industry, tools such as computer-aided design and computer-aided manufacturing support simultaneous engineering by letting various engineers submit elements and showing how these submissions affect the overall design and the manufacturing process. With a modern CAD system, automobile engineers can enter performance requirements into a spreadsheet, and the system will identify a design that meets cost and manufacturing requirements. This technology has helped automakers reduce product development time dramatically.[61] In the realm of computing, some organizations have taken this idea much further, making the programming code for their products available to the public so that anyone at any time can develop new ideas to use with their product, and the organization can decide to license any ideas that seem to have market potential. For some examples, see the "From the Pages of *BusinessWeek*" feature.

> **The bottom line**
> SPEED
> Time-based competition brings speed to all organization processes.

Opening Up to Collaboration

FROM THE PAGES OF **BusinessWeek**

As president of SAP's Product & Technology Group, Shai Agassi runs product development for the world's largest applications-software company. Ask him to name the most important development in the software industry of the last decade, and he won't say Linux, Web 2.0, or industry consolidation. He will tell you it's the Amazon.com cloud. Officially called Amazon Elastic Cloud Compute (EC2), it's the equivalent of a 21st-century utility. Users pay 10 cents an hour to harness its nearly unlimited computing capacity, allowing anyone to leverage the size and reach of the world's greatest e-commerce engine.

Amazon's EC2 is one of many new low-cost collaborative infrastructures—such as free Internet telephony, open-source software, and global outsourcing—that allow individuals and small producers to harness world-class capabilities, access markets, and serve customers in ways that only large corporations could in the past.

Unlike the previous generations, today's entrepreneurs can buy, off the shelf, practically any function they need to run a company. With storage, computing services, and other digital utilities on tap, business infrastructures that used to be expensive and complicated are increasingly cheap and easy to use. Tantek Celik, chief technologist for Technorati, says such services have "made it much easier and a whole lot cheaper to get up and running."

The potential of these modern-day platforms goes way beyond providing digital utilities. They can be a force for growth and competitiveness. As long as you're smart about how and when to take advantage of them, you can use open platforms as a foundation on which to build a successful business ecosystem.

A growing number of companies are leveraging such platforms to create on-the-fly partnerships with large communities of programmers who use the common infrastructure and toolset to innovate and create value.

Open platforms enable the small to become mighty—something today's generation of Web entrepreneurs learned from the open-source software community. Start-ups like flickr, 43 Things, Del.icio.us, and Technorati, for example, opened up their software services and databases via application programming interfaces (APIs)—bits of code that allow third-party applications to work with a company's core software—as a way to crank out new features, attract users, and scale up their business quickly. Using the popular flickr API, for example, users have added applications for plotting on a map the locations where photos were taken and displaying flickr pictures through your TiVo.

"It comes down to a question of limited time and, frankly, limited creativity," says Technorati's Celik. "No matter how smart you are and no matter how hard you work, three or four people in a start-up—or even small companies with 30 people—can only come up with so many great ideas."

By opening up their APIs, companies create an environment for low-risk experimentation in which anybody who wants to develop on top of their platforms can do so. "No need to send you a formal request," says Celik. "They can just take those APIs and innovate. Then, if someone builds a great new service or capability, we will work out a commercial licensing agreement so that everyone makes money."

Even relatively mature companies are getting involved. For example, Microsoft is turning its Xbox 360 home entertainment console into a platform for amateur game developers. The company recently released a free game development kit, called the XNA Game Studio, to encourage avid game consumers to become game developers and market their own titles through the Xbox Live marketplace.

The strategy addresses a number of challenges facing the company, including a shortage of top programming and design talent, escalating development costs, and a paucity of games for its new console.

The plummeting costs of collaboration and the advantages of harnessing a larger talent pool are causing many to rethink their assumptions about innovation. "Do you take your core assets and processes and keep them to yourself," asks SAP's Agassi, "or do you expose them to every software company on the planet and entice them to come in and help develop those assets?" For Agassi, it comes down to a basic principle of our networked world: There are always more smart people outside your enterprise boundaries than there are inside.

SOURCE: Excerpted from Don Tapscott and Anthony D. Williams, "Opening Up to Collaboration," *Business-Week*, March 9, 2007, downloaded from Business & Company Resource Center, http://galenet.galegroup.com.

Some managers resist the idea of simultaneous engineering. Why should marketing, product planning and design, and R&D "allow" manufacturing to get involved in "their" work? The answer is because the decisions made during the early, product-concept stage determine most of the manufacturing cost and quality. Furthermore, manufacturing can offer ideas about the product because of its experience with the prior generation of the product and with direct customer feedback. Also, the other functions must know early on what manufacturing can and cannot do. Finally, when manufacturing is in from the start, it is a full and true partner and will be more committed to decisions it helped make.

Final Thoughts on Organizational Agility

As we pointed out in the previous chapter, *any* approach to organizing has its strengths and limitations. The advantages of even the innovative, leading-edge structures and systems we have discussed in this chapter are likely to be short-lived if they become fixed rather than remain flexible. Smart managers and smart competitors soon catch up. Today's advantages are tomorrow's "table stakes," the minimum requirements that need to be met if an organization expects to be a major player.

To retain, or gain, a competitive edge, managers may want to keep in mind the principle with which we opened this chapter: Successful organizations—and that includes the successful managers within them—do not sit still. They do not follow rigid models but maintain structures, systems, organizational designs, and relationships that are adaptive—always sensitive to changes in their environment and able to respond quickly, efficiently, and effectively to them. Their managers focus constantly on exceeding customer expectations and on continuous quality improvement, designing their systems and structures to help them do just that.

The emphasis on agility, quality, flexibility, learning, and leanness to which you have been exposed in this chapter is likely to be a constant in your managerial career—ideally in your own organization, but perhaps as well in the competition you confront. When Jack Welch was chairman of GE, he saw his goal as the creation of the *boundaryless organization*, one in which there were no meaningful barriers between the organization and its environment. In such an organization, structures, technologies, and systems are perfectly aligned with the external challenges and opportunities it confronts. Many forward-thinking managers have embraced this goal.[62]

Management Close-Up

ASSESSING OUTCOMES AND SEIZING OPPORTUNITIES

Today, Wendell Weeks and Corning face another crisis. A global economic downturn that began in 2008 caused the market for LCD glass to drop precipitously. Consumers are buying fewer big-ticket items like flat-screen TVs and computers. What's more, industry observers say consumers who are spending money on TVs are buying smaller-screen models, so TV manufacturers don't need as much Corning glass.

Although Corning initially predicted a big year for 2008, with double-digit increases over 2007, the recession blunted sales and production. With production down, revenues are down. Corning was forced to pull back, and industry observers predicted even tougher times ahead. Facing declining demand and uncertainty, Corning was forced to cut 3,500 jobs in 2009.

Meanwhile, Weeks is focusing on Corning's materials engineering expertise to identify new customer needs and satisfy them. Corning devotes 10 percent of its revenues to research and development. Weeks reduces the risk his company faces in such heavy investment of cutting-edge products by spreading sales between consumer and industrial markets and among different regions of the world. Looking at a number of high-potential businesses, such as diesel filters and scientific instruments for pharmaceutical firms, Corning is betting on new projects that currently show promise. The company is also developing a "green" laser that will enable cell-phone users to use their phone like a projector. Another project, the mercury filter, can remove the poisonous metal from the emissions of coal-fired power plants. Made from the same ceramic as a catalytic converter, the filters offer a more cost-effective way to rid the air of toxic mercury. As more companies and nations become concerned about the environment, mercury abatement is expected to become an important business.[63]

- How did Corning's core strengths help Wendell Weeks turn the company around after the telecom industry fell apart and the fiber-optics business stopped?
- What has Weeks done to ensure that Corning stays profitable during an economic downturn? What else could he do?

KEY TERMS

Computer-integrated manufacturing (CIM), p. 327

Continuous process, p. 325

Customer relationship management, (CRM), p. 319

Downsizing, p. 317

Economies of scope, p. 315

Flexible factories, p. 327

High-involvement organization, p. 313

ISO 9001, p. 323

Just-in-time (JIT), p. 329

Large batch, p. 325

Lean manufacturing, p. 327

Learning organization, p. 312

Logistics, p. 329

Mass customization, p. 326

Mechanistic organization, p. 308

Organic structure, p. 308

Rightsizing, p. 317

Simultaneous engineering, p. 330

Small batch, p. 325

Strategic alliance, p. 311

Survivor's syndrome, p. 318

Technology, p. 324

Time-based competition (TBC), p. 329

Total quality management, (TQM), p. 321

Value chain, p. 320

SUMMARY OF LEARNING OBJECTIVES

Now that you have studied Chapter 9, you should be able to:

LO 1 Discuss why it is critical for organizations to be responsive.

Organizations have a formal structure to help control what goes on within them. But to survive today, firms need more than control—they need responsiveness. They must act quickly and adapt to fast-changing demands.

LO 2 Describe the qualities of an organic organization structure.

The organic form emphasizes flexibility. Organic organizations are decentralized, informal, and dependent on the judgment and expertise of people with broad responsibilities. The organic form is not a single formal structure but a concept that underlies all the new forms discussed in this chapter.

LO **3** **Identify strategies and dynamic organizational concepts that can improve an organization's responsiveness.**

New and emerging organizational concepts and forms include core competencies, strategic alliances, learning organizations, and high-involvement organizations.

LO **4** **Explain how a firm can be both big and small.**

Historically, large organizations have had important advantages over small organizations. Today, small size has advantages, including the ability to act quickly, respond to customer demands, and serve small niches. The ideal firm today combines the advantages of both. It creates many small, flexible units, while the corporate levels add value by taking advantage of its size and power.

LO **5** **Summarize how firms organize to meet customer requirements.**

Firms have embraced principles of continuous improvement and total quality management to respond to customer needs.

Baldrige criteria and ISO 9001 standards help firms organize to meet better quality specifications. Extending these, reengineering efforts are directed at completely overhauling processes to provide world-class customer service.

LO **6** **Identify ways that firms organize around different types of technology.**

Organizations tend to move from organic structures to mechanistic structures and back to organic structures as they transition from small batch to large batch and continuous process technologies. To organize for flexible manufacturing, organizations pursue mass customization via computer-integrated manufacturing and lean manufacturing. To organize for time-based competition, firms emphasize their logistics operations, just-in-time operations, and simultaneous engineering.

DISCUSSION QUESTIONS

1. Discuss evidence you have seen of the imperatives for change, flexibility, and responsiveness faced by today's firms.

2. Describe large, bureaucratic organizations with which you have had contact that have not responded flexibly to customer demands. Also describe examples of satisfactory responsiveness. What do you think accounts for the differences between the responsive and nonresponsive organizations?

3. Considering the potential advantages of large and small size, would you describe the "feel" of your college or university as big, small, or small within big? Why? What might make it feel different?

4. What is a core competence? What would you say are the core competencies of Toyota, Walmart, and Apple? Brainstorm some creative new products and markets to which these competencies could be applied.

5. If you were going into business for yourself, what would be your core competencies? What competencies do you have

now, and what competencies are you going to develop? Describe what your role would be in a network organization, and the competencies and roles of other firms you would want in your network.

6. Using an Internet search engine, search for "strategic alliance," and identify three recently formed alliances. For each alliance, identify whether the companies' other products are generally competitors or complementary products. What are the goals of each alliance? What brought them together? Discuss whether you think a strategic alliance is an effective way for these organizations to meet their goals.

7. What skills will you need to work effectively in (a) a learning organization and (b) a high-involvement organization? Be specific, generating long lists. Would you enjoy working in these environments? Why or why not? What can you do to prepare yourself for these eventualities?

CONCLUDING CASE

Rocky Mountain Leaders

Beth Cronin is a licensed mountain guide. She also has a degree in management. About five years ago, she started her own consulting firm called Rocky Mountain Leaders in a suburb near Denver, Colorado. She arranges training sessions for executives and managers at small to medium-sized firms, teaching them interpersonal and leadership skills. Cronin uses the great outdoors as her classroom and arranges hiking, camping, and occasional backpacking or rock climbing trips for her clients, creating scripted challenges for participants designed to help them build their management skills. She also finds that the time preparing dinner over a small camp stove, setting up a tent, and packing gear for a hike can be great team training exercises. Currently, Cronin has two assistants—

part-time employees with backgrounds similar to hers. One is in the process of earning an MBA, while the other majored in psychology. Both employees are skilled outdoorspeople, and both will need full-time jobs in the near future. Cronin wants Rocky Mountain Leaders to grow.

Cronin wants to begin offering workshops and seminars designed to help client organizations become responsive organizations in a fast-paced, competitive business environment. She wants to be able to help them organize around their core competencies, create strategic alliances, develop superior customer relationship management, and evaluate their organizational agility. To accomplish this, she needs to evaluate her own company, making sure it emphasizes its own core competencies as it grows. She knows she will have to turn her two part-time positions into full-time, and potentially hire more employees. She will have to create alliances with other companies—possibly training firms, campgrounds, climbing instructors, transportation companies, GPS satellite device providers, and the like. She will have to focus on her own customer relationship management as she enters new markets. In short, Cronin knows that the next phase for Rocky Mountain Leaders will be challenging—but no more difficult than climbing a mountain.

QUESTIONS

1. Describe Rocky Mountain Leaders' core competencies.

2. What steps can Beth Cronin take to make sure Rocky Mountain Leaders is a responsive organization as it grows? Is Rocky Mountain Leaders better off as a big company or a small one? Why?

3. Create an exercise or challenge that Rocky Mountain Leaders could use to help a client firm become a high-involvement organization.

EXPERIENTIAL EXERCISES

9.1 Mechanistic and Organic Structures

OBJECTIVES

1. To think about your own preferences when it comes to working in a particular organizational structure.

2. To examine aspects of organizations by using as an example this class you are a member of.

INSTRUCTIONS

1. Complete the Mechanistic and Organic Worksheet below.

2. Meet in groups of four to six persons. Share your data from the worksheet. Discuss the reasons for your responses, and analyze the factors that probably encouraged your instructor to choose the type of structure that now exists.

Mechanistic and Organic Worksheet

1. Indicate your general preference for working in one of these two organizational structures by circling the appropriate response:

Mechanistic		1	2	3	4	5	6	7	8	9	10	Organic

2. Indicate your perception of the form of organization that is used in this class by circling the appropriate response for each item:

A. **Task-role definition**

Rigid	1	2	3	4	5	6	7	8	9	10	Flexible

B. **Communication**

Vertical	1	2	3	4	5	6	7	8	9	10	Multidirectional

C. **Decision making**

Centralized	1	2	3	4	5	6	7	8	9	10	Decentralized

D. **Sensitivity to the environment**

Closed	1	2	3	4	5	6	7	8	9	10	Open

SOURCE: Keith Davis and John W. Newstrom, *Human Behavior at Work*, 9th ed., p. 358. © 1993 The McGraw-Hill Companies.

9.2 The Woody Manufacturing Company

OBJECTIVE

To apply the concepts learned about structure and agility at the individual, group, and organizational levels in designing the Woody Manufacturing Company.

TASK 1 (INDIVIDUAL ASSIGNMENT)

a. Read the following case study of the Woody Manufacturing Company.

b. Review the chapter carefully, and choose the organizational design orientation that you feel can best guide you in developing the design for Mr. Woody.

c. Write down your thoughts on alternative management structures, pay systems, and allocation of work to individuals and groups.

TASK 2 (TEAM ASSIGNMENT)

a. Get together with your team and develop a proposal for Mr. Woody that, if followed, would help him fulfill his vision.

b. Prepare a five-minute presentation. Your typewritten team proposal is due prior to your team presentation in Mr. Woody's conference room.

Designing a New Furniture Company

Mr. Woody, the owner/operator of a small furniture company specializing in the manufacture of high-quality bar stools, has experienced a tremendous growth in demand for his products. He has standing orders for $750,000. Consequently, Mr. Woody has decided to expand his organization and attack the market aggressively. His stated mission is "to manufacture world-class products that are competitive in the world market in quality, reliability, performance, and profitability." He would like to create a culture where "pride, ownership, employment security, and trust" are a way of life. He just finished a set of interviews, and he has hired 32 new workers with the following skills:

Four skilled craftspeople.

Ten people with some woodworking experience.

Twelve people with no previous woodworking experience or other skills.

One nurse.

One schoolteacher.

One bookkeeper.

Three people with some managerial experience in nonmanufacturing settings.

Mr. Woody (with your help) must now decide how to design his new organization. This design will include the management structure, pay system, and the allocation of work to individuals and groups. The bar stool–making process has 15 steps:

1. Wood is selected.
2. Wood is cut to size.
3. Defects are removed.
4. Wood is planed to exact specifications.
5. Joints are cut.
6. Tops are glued and assembled.
7. Legs/bases are prepared.
8. Legs/bases are attached to tops.
9. Bar stools are sanded.
10. Stain is applied.
11. Varnish is applied.
12. Bar stools are sanded.
13. Varnish is reapplied.
14. Bar stools are packaged.
15. Bar stools are delivered to the customer.

Mr. Woody currently manufactures three kinds of bar stools (pedestal, four-legged corner, and four-legged recessed). There is no difference in the difficulty of making the three types of bar stools. Major cost variations have been associated with defective wood, imprecise cuts, and late deliveries to customers. Mr. Woody must decide how to organize his company to maintain high quality and profits.

He has thought about several options. He could have some individuals perform the first step for all types of bar stools; he could have an individual perform several steps for one type of bar stool; or he could have a team perform some combination of steps for one or more bar stools. He wonders whether how he organized would affect quality or costs. He's also aware that while the demand for all types of bar stools has been roughly equal over the long run, there were short periods where one type of bar stool was in greater demand than the others. Because Mr. Woody wants to use his people effectively, he has committed an expert in work design to help him set up an optimal organization.

SOURCE: A. B. (Rami) Shani and James B. Lau, *Behavior in Organizations: An Experimental Approach* (New York: McGraw-Hill/Irwin, 2005), p. 370. © 2005 The McGraw-Hill Companies.

10 Human Resources Management

> *You can get capital and erect buildings, but it takes people to build a business.*
>
> — Thomas J. Watson, Founder, IBM

LEARNING OBJECTIVES

After studying Chapter 10, you should be able to:

LO 1 Discuss how companies use human resources management to gain competitive advantage. p. 340

LO 2 Give reasons companies recruit both internally and externally for new hires. p. 346

LO 3 Identify various methods for selecting new employees. p. 348

LO 4 Evaluate the importance of spending on training and development. p. 357

LO 5 Explain alternatives for who appraises an employee's performance. p. 360

LO 6 Describe the fundamental aspects of a reward system. p. 364

LO 7 Summarize how unions and labor laws influence human resources management. p. 371

CHAPTER OUTLINE

Strategic Human Resources Management
The HR Planning Process

Staffing the Organization
Recruitment
Selection
Workforce Reductions

Developing the Workforce
Training and Development

Performance Appraisal
What Do You Appraise?
Who Should Do the Appraisal?
How Do You Give Employees Feedback?

Designing Reward Systems
Pay Decisions
Incentive Systems and Variable Pay
Executive Pay and Stock Options
Employee Benefits
Legal Issues in Compensation and Benefits
Health and Safety

Labor Relations
Labor Laws
Unionization
Collective Bargaining
What Does the Future Hold?

Management Close-Up

In 1981, Pam Nicholson needed a job. Nicholson was a senior at the University of Missouri, and graduation was looming. So, when recruiters from Enterprise Rent-A-Car appeared on campus, she jumped at the chance to interview. For Nicholson, whose long-range goal was to manage a small business, getting an offer to work behind the counter at an Enterprise rental location in St. Louis seemed like a dream come true.

Nicholson worked hard and progressed steadily at Enterprise. After several years of promotions and challenging job responsibilities, in 2008 she was named president and chief operating officer. Industry observers might say Nicholson's career success has something to do with Enterprise founder Jack Taylor and his simple formula for running a business:

{ The career path of Enterprise Rent-A-Car president and COO Pam Nicholson offers a stunning success story. As you read this chapter, consider how Enterprise built its business and how the strategic use of people plays a central role in its success. }

- Hire recent college grads with a thirst for management experience.
- Provide extensive training and mentoring along the way.
- Promote from within.
- Put customers and employees first, and success will follow.

Pam Nicholson's career path illustrates Taylor's philosophy. During her first year at Enterprise, she was named assistant branch manager at her rental location. Shortly thereafter, Enterprise relocated her to southern California, where the company was just breaking into the market. In six years, Nicholson helped Enterprise grow from six offices to more than 300. The company made her a vice president and brought her back to headquarters, where she set up the first national preferred-provider arrangements with top automakers, enabling car owners to drive Enterprise rentals while the dealer services their vehicle.

In 1997, Nicholson's career led her to New York, where, in two years, she reorganized a slumping Enterprise unit, doubling its profits and growing its fleet from 20,000 to 30,000 cars. A 1999 promotion made her senior vice president for North American operations.

As for Nicholson's dream of running a small business? She now oversees a global organization with annual revenues near $10 billion, as well as 75,000 employees in 8,000 locations.[1]

**human resources
management (HRM)**

Formal systems for the
management of people within
an organization.

The opening quote by Thomas Watson, founder of IBM, summarizes our view of the importance of people to any organization. Enterprise Rent-A-Car's decades-old practice of recruiting new college graduates and providing opportunities for advancement has differentiated the company in important ways. **Human resources management (HRM),** historically known as personnel management, deals with formal systems for managing people at work. For that reason, it is one of the fundamental aspects of organizational and managerial life. Your first formal interaction with an organization you wish to join will likely involve some aspect of its human resource function, and throughout your career as a manager you will be a part of, as well as be affected by, your organization's human resource management.

We begin this chapter by describing HRM as it relates to strategic management. We will also discuss more of the "nuts and bolts" of HRM: staffing, training, performance appraisal, rewards, and labor relations. Throughout the chapter, we discuss legal issues that influence each aspect of HRM. In the next chapter, we expand this focus to address related issues of managing a diverse workforce.

Strategic Human Resources Management

LO 1

HRM has assumed a vital strategic role in recent years as organizations attempt to compete through people. Recall from Chapter 4 that firms can create a competitive advantage when they possess or develop resources that are valuable, rare, inimitable, and organized. We can use the same criteria to talk about the strategic impact of human resources:

1. *Creates value.* People can increase value through their efforts to decrease costs or provide something unique to customers or some combination of the two. Empowerment programs, total quality initiatives, and continuous improvement efforts at companies such as Corning and Xerox are intentionally designed to increase the value that employees bring to the bottom line.
2. *Is rare.* People are a source of competitive advantage when their skills, knowledge, and abilities are not equally available to all competitors. Top companies invest a great deal to hire and train the best and the brightest employees to gain advantage over their competitors. Dow Chemical went to court to stop General Electric from hiring away its engineers. This case shows that some companies recognize both the value and the rareness of certain employees.

Southwest Airlines is known for creating a unique culture that gets the most from employees. Southwest rewards its employees for excellent performance and maintains loyalty by offering free airfare, profit sharing, and other incentives. What benefits would you need to stay motivated?

3. *Is difficult to imitate.* People are a source of competitive advantage when their capabilities and contributions cannot be copied by others. Disney, Southwest Airlines, and Whole Foods are known for creating unique cultures that get the most from employees (through teamwork) and are difficult to imitate.
4. *Is organized.* People are a source of competitive advantage when their talents can be combined and deployed rapidly to work on new assignments at a moment's notice. Teamwork and cooperation are two pervasive methods for ensuring an organized workforce. But companies such as Spyglass

(a software company) and AT&T have invested in information technology to help allocate and track employee assignments to temporary projects.

These four criteria highlight the importance of people and show the closeness of HRM to strategic management. In a recent survey by the Society for Human Resource Management, among HR departments with a strategic plan for human resources, 56 percent worked closely with senior management to create strategies for the organization, and 68 percent worked closely to implement organizational strategies.[2] The evidence is growing that this focus brings positive business results. For example, a study by Deloitte & Touche associated the use of effective human resources practices with higher valuation of a company in the stock market.[3] Global trends make this focus even more important. Competition is intensifying. Rising educational standards and access to technology are increasingly available worldwide. *Innovation*—useful new ideas that emerge from the focused creativity of organization members—has become ever more critical to gaining and maintaining competitive advantage. Because employee skills, knowledge, and abilities are among the most distinctive and renewable resources on which a company can draw, their strategic management is more important than ever. Increasingly, organizations are recognizing that their success depends on what people know, that is, their knowledge and skills. The term **human capital** (or, more broadly, *intellectual capital*) often is used today to describe the strategic value of employee knowledge and abilities.

As more executives have come to appreciate that their employees can be their organization's most valuable resources, human resources managers have played a greater role in contributing to the organization's strategic planning. That means human resources (HR) specialists are challenged to know their organization's business, and line managers are challenged to excel at selecting and motivating the best people. As contributors to the organization's strategy, HR managers also face greater ethical challenges. When they were merely a specialized staff function, they could focus on, say, legal requirements for hiring decisions. But strategy decisions require them to be able to link decisions about staffing, training, and other HR matters to the organization's business success. For example, as members of the top management team, HR managers may be faced with the need for drastic downsizing of the workforce while still retaining top executives through generous salaries or bonuses, or they may fail to aggressively investigate and challenge corrupt practices of colleagues. Such dilemmas are complex and challenging. In the long run, however, organizations are best served when HR leaders are a strong advocate for at least four sets of values: strategic, ethical, legal, and financial.[4]

human capital

The knowledge, skills, and abilities of employees that have economic value.

Tough economic times deliver exciting HR opportunities as well as tough HR challenges. Well-managed firms seize the opportunities and meet the challenges.

One company that prepares well for a slowdown is PriceSpective, a consulting firm. The company's four co-owners meet monthly with senior managers to determine whether their current staffing levels are appropriate for their coming needs. Whenever sales are slow, PriceSpective institutes a temporary hiring freeze. Because these actions are part of a regular planning process, employees don't worry; they know managers are simply making course adjustments to keep the company efficient. Also, even when clients are not signing up for services, PriceSpective keeps talking to prospective employees. For the firm's specialized practice serving pharmaceutical firms, it needs many employees with doctoral degrees, who would be difficult to find and hire quickly when business picks up. Of course, when interviewing during a hiring freeze, managers are careful to explain the company' situation and plans for the future.

Other firms are able to hire during a recession, gaining access to a huge pool of talented people. The recent recession drove more shoppers from higher-priced retailers to Family

Dollar Stores, so the company opened more stores, receiving applications from workers with better-than-usual credentials. The company also needed specialists for its information technology department; it found experienced IT workers who left Circuit City when that chain went out of business. Companies that, like Family Dollar, build up their staff when talented people are hungry for work can boost sales, improve efficiency, and gain an advantage over competitors—if they can keep and motivate these employees.[5]

Managing human capital to sustain a competitive advantage is perhaps the most important part of an organization's HR function. But on a day-to-day basis, HR managers also have many other concerns regarding their workers and the entire personnel puzzle. These concerns include attracting talent; maintaining a well-trained, highly motivated, and loyal workforce; managing diversity; devising effective compensation systems; managing layoffs; and containing health care and pension costs. Balancing these issues is difficult, and the best approach varies depending on the circumstances of the organization. A steel producer facing a cutback in business may need human resources activities to assist with layoffs, whereas a semiconductor company may need more staff to produce enough microchips to meet the demands of the consumer electronics market. The emphasis on different HR activities depends on whether the organization is growing, declining, or standing still. This leads to the practical issues involved in HR planning.

"Hire the best. Pay them fairly. Communicate freely. Provide challenges and rewards. Get out of their way. They'll knock your socks off."

—Mary Ann Allison

The HR Planning Process

"Get me the right kind and the right number of people at the right time." It sounds simple enough, but meeting an organization's staffing needs requires strategic human resources planning: an activity with a strategic purpose derived from the organization's plans.

The HR planning process occurs in three stages: planning, programming, and evaluating. First, HR managers need to know the organization's business plans to ensure that the right number and types of people are available—where the company is headed, in what businesses it plans to be, what future growth is expected, and so forth. Few actions are more damaging to morale than having to lay off recently hired college graduates because of inadequate planning for future needs. Second, the organization conducts programming of specific human resources activities, such as recruitment, training, and layoffs. In this stage, the company's plans are implemented. Third, human resources activities are evaluated to determine whether they are producing the results needed to contribute to the organization's business plans. Figure 10.1 illustrates the components of the human resources planning process. In this chapter, we focus on human resources planning and programming. Many of the other factors listed in Figure 10.1 are discussed in later chapters.

Demand Forecasts   Perhaps the most difficult part of human resources planning is conducting *demand* forecasts, that is, determining how many and what type of people are needed. Demand forecasts for people needs are derived from organizational plans. To develop the iPhone, Apple had to determine how many engineers and designers it needed to ensure such a complex product was ready for a mid-2007 U.S. launch, given that the company was collaborating with a phone service provider. Managers also needed to estimate how many iPhones the company would sell. Based on a forecast of selling 10 million units the first full year, they needed to determine how many production employees would be required, along with the staff who would market the phone, handle publicity for the product launch, and answer phone and online inquiries from customers learning how to use the new product. Similarly, companies selling an

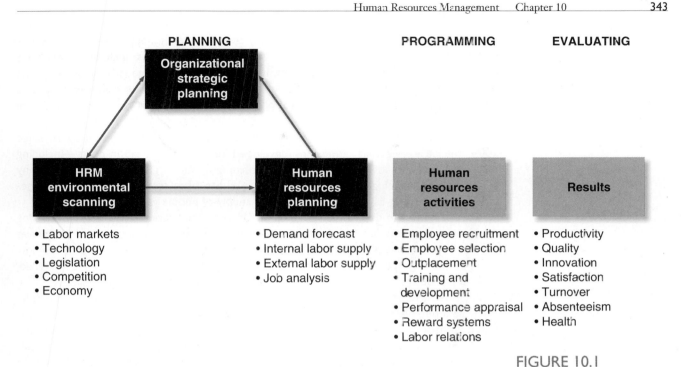

PLANNING   PROGRAMMING   EVALUATING

| Organizational strategic planning | | |

| HRM environmental scanning | Human resources planning | Human resources activities | Results |

- Labor markets
- Technology
- Legislation
- Competition
- Economy

- Demand forecast
- Internal labor supply
- External labor supply
- Job analysis

- Employee recruitment
- Employee selection
- Outplacement
- Training and development
- Performance appraisal
- Reward systems
- Labor relations

- Productivity
- Quality
- Innovation
- Satisfaction
- Turnover
- Absenteeism
- Health

FIGURE 10.1
An Overview of the HR Planning Process

existing product consider current sales and projected future sales growth as they estimate the plant capacity needed to meet future demand, the sales force required, the support staff needed, and so forth. They calculate the number of labor-hours required to operate a plant, sell the product, distribute it, serve customers, and so forth. These estimates are used to determine the demand for different types of workers.

Labor Supply Forecasts   Along with forecasting demand, managers must forecast the *supply of labor*, that is, how many and what types of employees the organization actually will have. In performing a supply analysis, the organization estimates the number and quality of its current employees as well as the available external supply of workers. To estimate internal supply, the company typically relies on its experiences with turnover, terminations, retirements, promotions, and transfers. A computerized human resources information system assists greatly in supply forecasting.

Externally, organizations have to look at workforce trends to make projections. Worldwide, as we discussed in Chapter 6, the highly skilled, higher-paid jobs have been generated mostly in the cities of the industrialized world, where companies have scrambled to find enough qualified workers. At the same time, companies in industrialized nations have used offshoring to move much of their routine and less-skilled work to nations with a large population willing to work for lower pay. However, as described in the "From the Pages of *BusinessWeek*" feature, the resulting demand for overseas talent has made a variety of jobs difficult to fill throughout the world.

Where Are All the Workers?

FROM THE PAGES OF
BusinessWeek

Employers in some unlikely places say they're having trouble filling jobs. Factory managers in Ho Chi Minh City report many of their $62-a-month workers went home for the Tet holiday in February and never came back. In Bulgaria, computer experts are in such demand they can't be bothered to answer the want ads of a Los Angeles movie studio. And in Peoria, Illinois, Caterpillar Inc. is struggling to train enough service technicians. The problem in each case: not enough people who are both able and willing to do the work for the posted pay. "We've got a global problem . . . and it's only going to continue to get worse," says Stephen Hitch, a human resources manager at Caterpillar.

A global labor crunch, already being felt by some employers, appears to have intensified in recent months. That's in spite of widely publicized layoffs, including Citigroup's plans to shed as many as 15,000 staffers. In fact, U.S. unemployment remains low—just 4.5 percent in February 2007—and even companies in countries with higher jobless rates are feeling pinched. "It's not just a U.S. phenomenon," says Jeffrey A. Joerres, CEO of Manpower, the staffing agency.

What's going on here? With global growth running at a strong 5 percent a year since 2004, the strategies that companies developed to hold down labor costs—including offshoring work to low-wage countries—are running out of gas far sooner than many expected. The seemingly inexhaustible pools of cheap labor from China, India, and elsewhere are drying up as demand outstrips the supply of people with the needed skills.

Corporations are determined to keep labor costs under control, so they're reaching deeper into their bag of tricks. Some are doing more in-house training so they don't have to recruit pricey talent on the open market. Some are lowering their standards for new hires or moving operations to virgin territories other outsourcers haven't discovered, such as the Belarusian capital, Minsk, or smaller cities in Bulgaria and Romania.

For now, though, workers with skills that are in short supply are enjoying the ride. If you're a petroleum engineer in Colorado, you can write your own ticket. Pittsburgh-based Consol Energy is so desperate for coal miners that it's staging a media campaign that includes billboards, the Internet, and its first-ever television commercials. In agriculture, the crackdown on illegal immigration has dried up farm labor so much that crops were left rotting in the fields in 2006. Even Michigan, which has the nation's highest unemployment rate, is reaching out to migrant farmworkers from Texas and, soon, Florida.

The job U.S. employers say is hardest to fill is sales representative. The trouble is, companies can't find people with the technical expertise and business savvy to explain complex products to customers, Manpower says. Right behind them on U.S. employers' wish lists are teachers, mechanics, and technicians.

Economists, of course, will tell you there's no such thing as a labor shortage. From a worker's viewpoint, many so-called shortages could quickly be solved if employers were to offer more money. And worldwide, millions of people still can't find jobs. The strongest evidence that there's no general shortage today is that overall worker pay has barely outpaced inflation. In the United States, the share of national income going to corporate profit, rather than, say, labor, is hovering around a 50-year high. With so many people newly available for work in China, India, and the former Soviet Union, the only thing that could cause a real shortage would be "a global pandemic that kills millions of people," Harvard University economist Richard B. Freeman wrote in a research paper in 2006.

But try telling that to employers whose workforce strategies, developed for a period of surplus labor, don't fit the new realities. The challenge is finding people who can do the jobs on offer. Manufacturers in Japan are suffering a lack of skilled workers because of the country's aging population as well as downsizing during the 1990s. China, although far more youthful than Japan, could soon feel the same pinch. Sure, its biggest problem at the moment continues to be creating jobs for the millions of workers pouring into cities, and wages are barely rising overall. But that may be starting to change as the government boosts incentives for people to stay in rural areas and most factories remain concentrated in a few coastal regions. And while India produces 400,000 engineering graduates a year, few have the skills and language abilities to work in an advanced multinational corporation. Some 1.3 million people applied to tech-services giant Infosys Technologies in 2006, but the company says only 2 percent of those were employable.

For business, it seems, there's no shortage of work involved in easing worker shortages.

SOURCE: Excerpted from Peter Coy and Jack Ewing, "Where Are All the Workers?" *BusinessWeek*, April 9, 2007, http://www.businessweek.com.

In the United States, demographic trends have contributed to a shortage of workers with the appropriate skills and education level. Traditional labor-intensive jobs, in agriculture, mining, and assembly-line manufacturing, are making way for jobs in technical, financial, and customized goods and service industries. These jobs often require much more training and schooling than the jobs they are replacing—or that the education system may currently be producing. Demand for highly qualified employees continues to outpace supply—one reason some jobs are being transferred overseas. Some demographic trends we discussed in Chapter 2 may worsen this situation. For example, the upcoming retirement of the baby-boomer generation will remove a large number of educated and trained employees from the workforce. And in math, science, and engineering graduate schools, fewer than half of the students receiving graduate degrees are American born. (To fill U.S. jobs, companies must hire U.S. citizens or immigrants with permission to work in the United States.)

One response managers have made to deal with this skills shortage has been to increase significantly the remedial and training budgets within their own organizations.[6] Another response has been to increase the labor supply by recruiting workers from other countries. The supply of legal immigrant labor is restricted by various laws and regulations. For example, each year the U.S. government awards H-1B visas to 65,000 college-educated workers in high-skilled, highly demanded jobs such as engineers and scientists. Those people are permitted to work temporarily in the United States. Managers at high-tech companies including Microsoft, Oracle, and Intel complain that the number of H-1B visas is too small to enable companies to meet the demand for technical workers, and some companies address that challenge by aggressively hiring early each year, before the quota has been met. Immigrant workers are also attractive to companies with a low-cost strategy, because strong labor demand in the United States enables U.S. workers to insist on higher pay.[7] Retraining downsized workers is yet another approach to increasing the workforce labor pool.

Health care is an industry that is growing—in some areas, faster than organizations can hire and train staff. Manufacturing, on the other hand, is shrinking. As sales decline and companies downsize or close altogether, workers are laid off without other job prospects. Recently, some companies and not-for-profit organizations have begun collaborating to meet the needs of both industries by retraining laid-off manufacturing workers to enter the health-care field.

The Manufacturers Association of Central New York teamed up with the Northern Area Health Education Center and Syracuse University to evaluate and retrain displaced workers in health care fields. Applicants take aptitude tests to determine what skills they already possess—for example, interpersonal skills, including teamwork, or the ability to interpret graphics. Those who already show a level of proficiency in certain areas can obtain a certificate of competency for those skills. A Web site hosted by the Northern Area Health Education Center posts the credential information so that interested employers such as hospitals or nursing homes can find potential job candidates; the site also shows candidates what types of jobs they would qualify for. "We are focusing on jobs that do not have degrees or licenses," says Tom Hadlick, director of the assessment program, which is called WorkKeys. Nursing assistants, pharmacy technicians, and paramedics fall into this category. This collaboration is a way to benefit both the people who need work and the industry that needs them.[8]

On the plus side, earlier forecasts of a diverse workforce have become fact, adding greatly to the pool of available talent. The business world is no longer the exclusive domain of white males. In fact, two-career families have become the norm. Minorities, women, immigrants, older and disabled workers, and other groups have made the management of diversity a fundamental activity of the modern manager. Because of the importance of managing the "new workforce," the next chapter is devoted entirely to this topic.

Reconciling Supply and Demand   Once managers have a good idea of the supply of and the demand for various types of employees, they can start developing approaches for reconciling the two. In some cases, organizations find they need more people than they currently have (i.e., a labor deficit). In such cases, organizations can hire new employees, promote current employees to new positions, or outsource work to contractors. In other cases, organizations may find that they have more people than they need (i.e., a labor surplus). If this is detected far enough in advance, organizations can use attrition—the normal turnover of employees—to reduce the surplus. In other instances, the organization may lay off employees or transfer them to other areas.

When managers do need to hire, one tool they can use is their organization's compensation policy. Large companies in particular spend a lot of time gathering information about pay scales for the various jobs they have available and making sure their compensation system is fair and competitive. We discuss pay issues later in this chapter.

Job Analysis   Although issues of supply and demand are fairly "macro" activities—conducted at an organizational level—HR planning also has a "micro" side called *job analysis*. **Job analysis** does two things.[9] First, it tells the HR manager about the job itself: the essential tasks, duties, and responsibilities involved in performing the job. This information is called a *job description*. The job description for an accounting manager might specify that the position will be responsible for monthly, quarterly, and annual financial reports, getting bills issued and paid, preparing budgets, ensuring the company's compliance with laws and regulations, working closely with line managers on financial issues, and supervising an accounting department of 12 people.

Second, job analysis describes the skills, knowledge, abilities, and other characteristics needed to perform the job. This is called the *job specification*. For our accounting manager example, the job requirements might include a degree in accounting or business, knowledge of computerized accounting systems, prior managerial experience, and excellent communication skills.

Job analysis provides the information required by virtually every human resources activity. It assists with the essential HR programs: recruitment, training, selection, appraisal, and reward systems. It may also help organizations defend themselves in lawsuits involving employment practices—for example, by clearly specifying what a job requires if someone claims unfair dismissal.[10] Ultimately, job analysis helps increase the value added by employees to the organization because it clarifies what is really required to perform effectively.

job analysis

A tool for determining what is done on a given job and what should be done on that job.

Staffing the Organization

LO 2

Once HR planning is completed, managers can focus on staffing the organization. The staffing function consists of three related activities: recruitment, selection, and outplacement.

Recruitment

recruitment

The development of a pool of applicants for jobs in an organization.

Recruitment activities help increase the pool of candidates that might be selected for a job. Recruitment may be internal to the organization (considering current employees for promotions and transfers) or external. Each approach has advantages and disadvantages.[11]

Internal Recruiting The advantages of internal recruiting are that employers know their employees, and employees know their organization. External candidates who are unfamiliar with the organization may find they don't like working there. Also, the opportunity to move up within the organization may encourage employees to remain with the company, work hard, and succeed. Recruiting from outside the company can be demoralizing to employees. Many companies, such as Sears and Eli Lilly, prefer internal to external recruiting for these reasons.

Internal staffing has some drawbacks. If existing employees lack skills or talent, internal recruitment yields a limited applicant pool, leading to poor selection decisions. Also, an internal recruitment policy can inhibit a company that wants to change the nature or goals of the business by bringing in outside candidates. In changing from a rapidly growing, entrepreneurial organization to a mature business with more stable growth, Dell went outside the organization to hire managers who better fit those needs.

Just over this employee's shoulder is an internal job listing board, typical for companies who prefer internal recruiting. Companies are increasingly utilizing their intranet sites to post jobs as well.

Many companies that rely heavily on internal recruiting use a job-posting system. A *job-posting system* is a mechanism for advertising open positions, typically on a bulletin board or the company's intranet. Texas Instruments uses job posting. Employees complete a request form indicating interest in a posted job. The posted job description includes a list of duties and the minimum skills and experience required.

External Recruiting External recruiting brings in "new blood" to a company and can inspire innovation. Among the most frequently used sources of outside applicants are Internet job boards, company Web sites, employee referrals, newspaper advertisements, and college campus recruiting.

Recent surveys suggest that employers place the greatest emphasis on referrals by current employees and online job boards.[12] Some companies actively encourage employees to refer their friends by offering cash rewards. In fact, surveys show word-of-mouth recommendations are the way most job positions get filled. Not only is this recruitment method relatively inexpensive, but employees also tend to know who will be a good fit with the company. Web job boards such as CareerBuilder, Monster, and Yahoo HotJobs have exploded in popularity as a job-recruitment tool because they easily reach a large pool of job seekers. They have largely supplanted newspaper want ads, although print recruiting has grown somewhat, partly as a result of forming alliances with the job boards. Most companies also let people apply for jobs at their corporate Web site, and many even list open positions. Employment agencies are another common recruitment tool, and for important management positions companies often use specialized executive-search firms. Some companies also are buying search engine

 **The bottom line**

Innovation

Outside hires often bring new ideas to the organization.

Some college graduates know exactly what they want to do when they graduate, and others have trouble deciding. Wendy Kopp has an option—put aside your ultimate career goals for two years and teach at a school that really needs you. Kopp founded her not-for-profit organization, Teach for America (TFA), nearly 20 years ago with the idea that some of the nation's best and brightest college graduates could—and would—make a real difference to students attending inner city and rural schools where resources are slim or nonexistent. The idea has resonated so greatly among graduating seniors and young professionals that Teach for America has become the largest hiring employer of college seniors in the nation. During a single year, nearly 20,000 students and graduates apply for roughly 2,400 positions. "We recruit insanely aggressively," admits Kopp. Applicants endure rigorous interviews, testing, and training before they are placed in a school, and they are asked to give a two-year commitment to the project.

All of this activity has not been lost on some of the biggest U.S. companies. In fact, investment bank J.P. Morgan found itself competing with Teach for America for a number of job candidates. So the bank and TFA teamed up to hold joint recruiting events at various colleges. J.P. Morgan has committed to deferring job offers to seniors who are accepted by both its training program and TFA, giving those graduates a chance to fulfill their TFA assignment. Why would the bank make this concession? "We want employees who are committed to serving the community as well as serving shareholders," explains David Puth, Morgan's head of global currency and commodities. Amgen has followed suit, in an effort to grab the best math and science students. Wachovia redesigned its recruiting efforts to mirror those of TFA. Shannon McFayden, head of the bank's human resources department, explains why. "We think Teach for America is the best college recruiting organization in the U.S."[15]

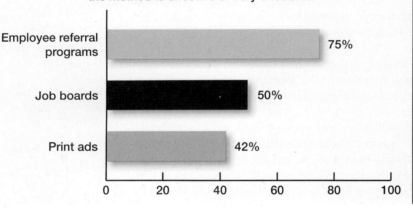

What recruiting methods are most valuable?[14]

Percentage of respondents who say the method is effective or very effective:

ads to display next to the results for relevant terms such as *nurse*. Another online tool is to obtain leads through networking sites such as LinkedIn and Craigslist. Campus recruiting can be helpful for companies looking for applicants who have up-to-date training and innovative ideas. However, companies that rely heavily on campus recruiting and employee referrals have to take extra care to ensure that these methods do not discriminate by generating pools of applicants who are, say, mostly women or primarily white.[13]

Most companies use some combination of the methods we have been discussing, depending on the particular job or situation. For example, they might use internal recruiting for existing jobs that need replacements, and external recruiting when the firm is expanding or needs to acquire some new skill.

LO 3

selection

Choosing from among qualified applicants to hire into an organization.

Selection

Selection builds on recruiting and involves decisions about whom to hire. As important as these decisions are, they are—unfortunately—at times made in very careless or cavalier ways. In this section we describe a number of selection instruments to which you may soon be exposed in your own career.

Applications and Résumés   Application blanks and résumés provide basic information to prospective employers. To make a first cut through candidates, employers review the profiles and backgrounds of various job applicants. Applications and résumés typically include information about the applicant's name, educational background, citizenship, work experiences, certifications, and the like. Their appearance and accuracy also say something about the applicant—spelling mistakes, for example, are almost always immediately disqualifying (something to keep in mind when preparing your own). While providing important information, applications and résumés tend not to be extremely useful for making final selection decisions.

Interviews The most popular selection tool is interviewing, and every company uses some type of interview. However, employment interviewers must be careful about what they ask and how they ask it. As we will explain later in the chapter, federal law requires that employers avoid discriminating against people based on criteria such as sex and race; questions that distinguish candidates according to protected categories may be seen as evidence of discrimination.

In an unstructured (or nondirective) interview, the interviewer asks different interviewees different questions. The interviewer may also use probes, that is, ask follow-up questions to learn more about the candidate.[16]

In a **structured interview,** the interviewer conducts the same interview with each applicant. There are two basic types of structured interview. The first approach—called the *situational interview*—focuses on hypothetical situations. Zale Corporation, a major jewelry chain, uses this type of structured interview to select sales clerks. A sample question is: "A customer comes into the store to pick up a watch he had left for repair. The watch is not back yet from the repair shop, and the customer becomes angry. How would you handle the situation?" An answer that says "I would refer the customer to my supervisor" might suggest that the applicant felt incapable of handling the situation on his or her own. The second approach—called the *behavioral description interview*—explores what candidates have actually done in the past. In selecting accountants, Bill Bufe of Plante & Moran asks candidates how they handled a difficult person they have worked with, and Art King asks how candidates have handled a stressful situation, because he believes this shows how candidates "think on their feet."[17] Because behavioral questions are based on real events, they often provide useful information about how the candidate will actually perform on the job.

Each of these interview techniques offers a manager different advantages and disadvantages, and many interviewers use more than one technique during the same interview. Unstructured interviews can help establish rapport and provide a sense of the applicant's personality, but they may not provide the manager with specific information about the candidate's ability. Structured interviews tend to be more reliable predictors of job performance because they are based on the job analysis that has been done for the position. They are also more likely to be free of bias and stereotypes. And because the same questions are being asked of all candidates for the job, an interview that is at least partially structured allows the manager to compare responses across different candidates.[18]

Reference Checks Résumés, applications, and interviews rely on the honesty of the applicant. To make an accurate selection decision, employers have to be able to trust the words of each candidate. Unfortunately, some candidates may hide criminal backgrounds that could pose a risk to the employer or exaggerate their qualifications. In a highly publicized incident, the dean of admissions at the Massachusetts Institute of Technology resigned after nearly three decades on the job because the school learned that she had provided false information about her educational background.[19] Although she had certainly demonstrated an ability to perform the job functions, she could no longer claim the level of integrity required by that position. Once lost, a reputation is hard to regain.

Because these and more ambiguous ethical gray areas arise, employers supplement candidate-provided information with other screening devices, including *reference checks.* Virtually all organizations contact references or former employers and educational institutions listed by candidates. Although checking references makes sense, reference information is becoming increasingly difficult to obtain as a result of several highly publicized lawsuits. In one case, an applicant sued a former boss on the grounds

During an interview, employers may opt to hold unstructured interviews, where they ask each potential employee different questions, or they may choose to hold structured interviews where the employer asks all potential employees the same questions.

structured interview

Selection technique that involves asking all applicants the same questions and comparing their responses to a standardized set of answers.

that the boss told prospective employers the applicant was a "thief and a crook." The jury awarded the applicant $80,000.[20] Nevertheless, talking to an applicant's previous supervisor is a common practice and often does provide useful information, particularly if specific job-related questions are asked ("Can you give me an example of a project candidate X handled particularly well?").

Background Checks   For a higher level of scrutiny, background investigations also have become standard procedure for many companies. Some state courts have ruled that companies can be held liable for negligent hiring if they fail to do adequate background checks. The different types of checks include Social Security verification, past employment and education verification, and a criminal records check. A number of other checks can be conducted if they pertain to the job being hired for, including a motor vehicle record check (for jobs involving driving) and a credit check (for money-handling jobs).

Internet tools have made basic background checks fast and easy to perform. A recent survey of executive recruiters learned that more than three-quarters use search engines such as Google to find out about candidates.[21] Such searches can turn up a variety of information, including what people have written on blogs or posted under their name on MySpace or Facebook. Internet users are advised to remember that anything that carries their name online may become information for potential employers, even years down the road.

Figure 10.2 shows the various screening tools used by many *Fortune* 1000 companies.

FIGURE 10.2

Use of Preemployment Selection Tools (tools that 212 security representatives at *Fortune* 1000 companies said their companies use consistently)

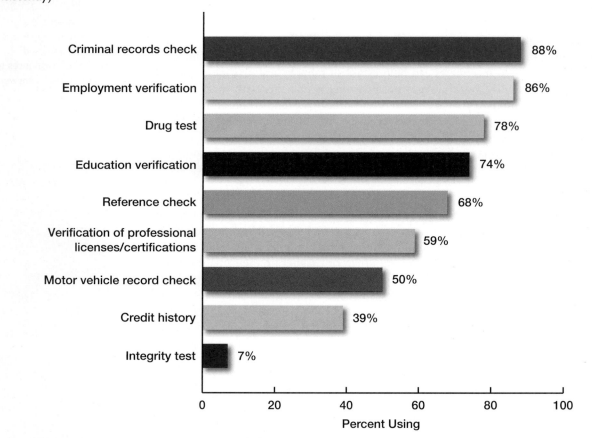

SOURCE: *Top Security Threats and Management Issues Facing Corporate America,* Pinkerton Consulting and Investigations Inc., 2003.

Personality Tests   Employers have been more hesitant to use personality tests for employee selection, largely because they are hard to defend in court.[22] However, some personality types have been associated with greater job satisfaction and performance, especially in situations in which the organization can build groups of people with similar positive traits.[23] As a result, personality tests are regaining popularity, and chances are that at some point in your career you will complete some personality tests. A number of well-known paper-and-pencil inventories measure personality traits such as sociability, adjustment, and energy. Typical questions are "Do you like to socialize with people?" and "Do you enjoy working hard?" Some personality tests try to determine the type of working conditions that the candidate prefers, to see if he or she would be motivated and productive in the particular job. For example, if the candidate prefers making decisions on his or her own but the job requires gaining the cooperation of others, another candidate might be a better fit.

Drug Testing   *Drug testing* is now a frequently used screening instrument. Since the passage of the Drug-Free Workplace Act of 1988, applicants and employees of federal contractors and Department of Defense contractors and those under Department of Transportation regulations have been subject to testing for illegal drugs. Well over half of all U.S. companies conduct preemployment drug tests.

Genetic testing tries to identify the likelihood of contracting a disease (such as emphysema) on the basis of a person's genetic makeup. It is far less common than drug testing and remains controversial.[24]

Cognitive Ability Tests   Among the oldest employment selection devices are cognitive ability tests. These tests measure a range of intellectual abilities, including verbal comprehension (vocabulary, reading) and numerical aptitude (mathematical calculations). About 20 percent of U.S. companies use cognitive ability tests for selection purposes.[25] Figure 10.3 shows some examples of cognitive ability test questions.

Performance Tests   In a performance test, the test taker performs a sample of the job. Most companies use some type of performance test, typically for administrative assistant and clerical positions. The most widely used performance test is the typing test. However, performance tests have been developed for almost every occupation, including managerial positions. Assessment centers are the most notable offshoot of the managerial performance test.[26]

Assessment centers originated during World War II. A typical **assessment center** consists of 10 to 12 candidates who participate in a variety of exercises or situations; some of the exercises involve group interactions, and others are performed individually. Each exercise taps a number of critical managerial dimensions, such as leadership, decision-making skills, and communication ability. Assessors, generally line managers from the organization, observe and record information about the candidates' performance in each exercise. The first organization to use assessment centers was AT&T. Since then, a number of large organizations have used or currently are using the assessment center technique, including the FBI and Sears.

assessment center

A managerial performance test in which candidates participate in a variety of exercises and situations.

Integrity Tests   To assess job candidates' honesty, employers may administer integrity tests. Two forms of integrity tests are polygraphs and paper-and-pencil honesty tests. Polygraphs, or lie detector tests, have been banned for most employment purposes.[27] Paper-and-pencil honesty tests are more recent instruments for measuring integrity. These tests include questions such as whether a person has ever thought about stealing and whether he or she believes other people steal ("What percentage of people take more than $1 from their employer?"). Although companies including Payless ShoeSource reported that losses due to theft declined following the introduction of integrity tests, the accuracy of these tests is still debatable.[28]

Verbal	1. What is the meaning of the word surreptitious?

1. What is the meaning of the word surreptitious?
   - a. covert
   - b. winding
   - c. lively
   - d. sweet

2. How is the noun clause used in the following sentence: "I hope that I can learn this game."
   - a. subject
   - b. predicate nominative
   - c. direct object
   - d. object of the preposition

Quantitative

3. Divide 50 by .5 and add 5. What is the result?
   - a. 25
   - b. 30
   - c. 95
   - d. 105

4. What is the value of 144^2?
   - a. 12
   - b. 72
   - c. 288
   - d. 20736

Reasoning

5. _____ is to boat as snow is to _____
   - a. sail, ski
   - b. water, winter
   - c. water, ski
   - d. engine, water

6. Two women played 5 games of chess. Each woman won the same number of games, yet there were no ties. How can this be so?
   - a. There was a forfeit.
   - b. One player cheated.
   - c. They played different people.
   - d. One game was still in progress.

Mechanical

7. If gear A and gear C are both turning counter-clockwise, what is happening to gear B?
   - a. It is turning counter-clockwise.
   - b. It is turning clockwise.
   - c. It remains stationary.
   - d. The whole system will jam.

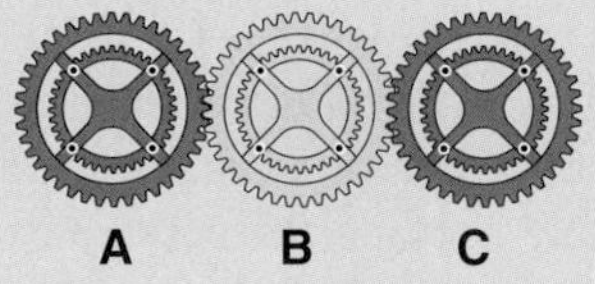

A   B   C

Answers: 1a, 2c, 3d, 4d, 5c, 6c, 7b.

SOURCE: From George Bohlander, Scott Snell, and Arthur Sherman, *Managing Human Resources,* 12th ed. Copyright © 2001. Reprinted by permission of South-Western, a division of Thomson Learning, www.thomsonrights.com. Fax 800 730-2215.

FIGURE 10.3

Sample Measures of Cognitive Ability

reliability

The consistency of test scores over time and across alternative measurements.

validity

The degree to which a selection test predicts or correlates with job performance.

Reliability and Validity   Regardless of the method used to select employees, two crucial issues that need to be addressed are a test's reliability and its validity. **Reliability** refers to the consistency of test scores over time and across alternative measurements. For example, if three different interviewers talked to the same job candidate but drew very different conclusions about the candidate's abilities, we might suspect that there were problems with the reliability of one or more of the selection tests or interview procedures.

Validity moves beyond reliability to assess the accuracy of the selection test. The most common form of validity, *criterion-related validity*, refers to the degree to which a test actually predicts or correlates with job performance. For example, in the academic world, a recent study found that the Graduate Management Admission Test (GMAT) was more valid than undergraduate grade point average in predicting performance in business school—but the two together were highly valid.[29] In the context of staffing, such validity is usually established through studies comparing test performance and job performance for a large enough sample of employees to enable a fair conclusion to be reached. For example, if a high score on a cognitive ability test is strongly predictive of good job performance, then candidates who score well will usually be preferred over those who do not. Still, no test by itself perfectly predicts performance. Managers usually rely on other criteria as well before making a final selection.

Another form of validity, *content validity*, concerns the degree to which selection tests measure a representative sample of the knowledge, skills, and abilities required for the job. The best-known example of a content-valid test is a keyboarding test for administrative assistants, because keyboarding is a task a person in that position almost always performs. However, to be completely content-valid, the selection process also should measure other skills the assistant would be likely to perform, such as answering the telephone, duplicating and faxing documents, and dealing with the public. Content validity is more subjective (less statistical) than evaluations of criterion-related validity but is no less important, particularly when one is defending employment decisions in court.

Due to tough economic times, workforce reductions in companies throughout the U.S. have become commonplace. Job seekers are shown here standing in line to attend a job fair in Chicago.

Workforce Reductions

Unfortunately, staffing decisions do not simply focus on hiring employees. As organizations evolve and markets change, the demand for certain employees rises and falls. Also, some employees simply do not perform at a level required to justify continued employment. For these reasons, managers sometimes must make difficult decisions to terminate their employment.

Layoffs   As a result of the massive restructuring of American industry brought about by mergers and acquisitions, divestiture, and increased competition, many organizations have been downsizing—laying off large numbers of managerial and other employees. As mentioned in Chapter 9, dismissing any employee is tough, but when a company lays off a substantial portion of its workforce, the results can rock the foundations of the organization.[30] The victims of restructuring face all the difficulties of being let go—loss of self-esteem, demoralizing job searches, and the stigma of being out of work. To some extent, employers can help employees with these problems by offering **outplacement,** the process of helping people who have been dismissed from the company regain employment elsewhere. Even then, the impact of layoffs goes further than the employees who leave. For many of the employees who remain with the company, disenchantment, distrust, and lethargy overshadow the comfort of still having a job. In many respects, how management deals with dismissals will affect the productivity and satisfaction of those who remain. A well-thought-out dismissal process eases tensions and helps remaining employees adjust to the new work situation.

Organizations with strong performance evaluation systems benefit because the survivors are less likely to believe the decision was arbitrary. In addition, if care is taken during the actual layoff process—that is, if workers are offered severance pay and help in finding a new job—remaining workers will be comforted. Companies also should avoid stringing out layoffs by dismissing a few workers at a time.

outplacement

The process of helping people who have been dismissed from the company regain employment elsewhere.

Termination   People sometimes "get fired" for poor performance or other reasons. Should an employer have the right to fire a worker? In 1884, a Tennessee court ruled: "All may dismiss their employee(s) at will for good cause, for no cause, or even for cause morally wrong." The concept that an employee may be fired for any reason is known as **employment-at-will** or *termination-at-will* and was upheld in a 1908 Supreme Court ruling.[31] The logic is that if the employee may quit at any time, the employer is free to dismiss at any time.

employment-at-will

The legal concept that an employee may be terminated for any reason.

Since the mid-1970s, courts in most states have made exceptions to this doctrine. Under the public policy exception (i.e., a ruling designed to protect the public from harm), employees cannot be fired for such actions as refusing to break the law, taking time off for jury duty, or "whistle-blowing" to report illegal company behavior. For example, if a worker reports an environmental violation to the regulatory agency and the company fires him or her, the courts may argue that the firing was unfair because the employee acted for the good of the community. Union contracts that limit an employer's ability to fire without cause are another major exception to the employment-at-will doctrine.

Employers can avoid the pitfalls associated with dismissal by developing progressive and positive disciplinary procedures.[32] By *progressive*, we mean that a manager takes graduated steps in attempting to correct a workplace behavior. For example, an employee who has been absent receives a verbal reprimand for the first offense. A second offense invokes a written reprimand. A third offense results in employee counseling and probation, and a fourth results in a paid-leave day to think over the consequences of future rule infractions. The employer is signaling to the employee that this is the "last straw." Arbitrators are more likely to side with an employer that fires someone when they believe the company has made sincere efforts to help the person correct his or her behavior.

termination interview

A discussion between a manager and an employee about the employee's dismissal.

The **termination interview,** in which the manager discusses the company's position with the employee, is a stressful situation for both parties. Most experts believe that the immediate superior should be the one to deliver the bad news to employees. However, it is a wise precaution to have a third party, such as an HR manager, present to provide guidance and take notes on the meeting. Because announcing a termination is likely to upset the employee and occasionally leads to a lawsuit, the manager should prepare carefully. Preparation should include knowing all the facts of the situation and reviewing any documents to make sure they are consistent with the reason for the termination. During the termination interview, ethics and common sense dictate that the manager should be truthful but respectful, stating the facts and avoiding arguments.[33] Table 10.1 provides some other guidelines for conducting a termination interview.

TABLE 10.1
Advice on Termination

Do's	Don'ts
• Give as much warning as possible for mass layoffs.	• Don't leave room for confusion when firing. Tell the individual in the first sentence that he or she is terminated.
• Sit down one on one with the individual, in a private office.	• Don't allow time for debate during a termination session.
• Complete a termination session within 15 minutes.	• Don't make personal comments when firing someone; keep the conversation professional.
• Provide written explanations of severance benefits.	
• Provide outplacement services away from company headquarters.	• Don't rush a fired employee offsite unless security is an issue.
• Be sure the employee hears about his or her termination from a manager, not a colleague.	• Don't fire people on significant dates, like the 25th anniversary of their employment or the day their mother died.
• Express appreciation for what the employee has contributed, if appropriate.	• Don't fire employees when they are on vacation or have just returned.

SOURCE: Wall Street Journal. Eastern Edition by S. Alexander, "Firms Get Plenty of Practice at Lyoffs, but They Often Bungle the Firing Process," Copyright (c)1991 by Dow Jones & Company via Copyright Clearance Center.

Legal Issues and Equal Employment Opportunity   Many laws have been passed governing employment decisions and practices. They will directly affect a good part of your day-to-day work as a manager, as well as the human resource function of your organization. Most of these laws are designed to protect job candidates and employees against discrimination or sexual harassment and to establish standards of pay and hours worked for certain classes of employee. For example, the 1938 *Fair Labor Standards Act* (FLSA), among other provisions, creates two employee categories: exempt and nonexempt. Employees are normally exempt from overtime pay if they have considerable discretion in how they carry out their jobs and if their jobs require them to exercise independent judgment. Managers usually fall in this category. Non-exempt employees are usually paid by the hour and must be paid overtime if they work more than 40 hours in a week. As a manager you will almost certainly need to specify the exempt or nonexempt status of anyone you hire.

The 1964 *Civil Rights Act* prohibits discrimination in employment based on race, sex, color, national origin, and religion. Title VII of the act specifically forbids discrimination in such employment practices as recruitment, hiring, discharge, promotion, compensation, and access to training.[34] The *Americans with Disabilities Act*, passed in 1990, prohibits employment discrimination against people with disabilities. Recovering alcoholics and drug abusers, cancer patients in remission, and AIDS patients are covered by this legislation. The 1991 *Civil Rights Act* strengthened all these protections and permitted punitive damages to be imposed on companies that violate them.

Failure to comply with any of these laws may expose the organization to charges of unfair practices, expensive lawsuits, and civil and even criminal penalties in some cases. For example, Walmart recently paid $17.5 million to settle a lawsuit in which employees said the company had discriminated against African American workers seeking positions as truck drivers. According to these workers, the company had placed stiffer requirements on African American job candidates. In another case, Union Pacific Railroad paid $75,000 to settle a sex discrimination lawsuit in which a woman was not hired as system material foreman, even though she had more experience than men who applied for the position. And Nordstrom paid $292,500 to settle a lawsuit in which Florida workers said their manager had harassed them because of their race.[35]

One common reason employers are sued is **adverse impact**—when a seemingly neutral employment practice has a disproportionately negative effect on a group protected by the Civil Rights Act.[36] For example, if equal numbers of qualified men and women apply for jobs but a particular employment test results in far fewer women being hired, the test may be considered to cause an adverse impact and, therefore, be subject to challenge on that basis.

adverse impact

When a seemingly neutral employment practice has a disproportionately negative effect on a protected group.

Because of the importance of these issues, many companies have established procedures to ensure compliance with labor and equal-opportunity laws. For example, companies frequently monitor and compare salaries by race, gender, length of service, and other categories to make sure employees across all groups are being fairly paid. Written policies can also help ensure fair and legal practices in the workplace, although the company may also have to demonstrate a record of actually following those procedures and making sure they are implemented. In this sense, smart and effective management practices not only help managers motivate employees to do their best work but often help provide legal protection as well. For example, managers who provide their employees with regular, specific evaluations can often prevent misunderstandings that can lead to lawsuits. And a written record of those evaluations is often useful in demonstrating fair and objective treatment.

Many other important staffing laws affect employment practices. For example, the *Age Discrimination in Employment Act* of 1967 and its amendments in 1978 and 1986 prohibit discrimination against people age 40 and over. One reason for this legislation was the common practice of dismissing older workers to replace them with younger workers who were not as highly paid. The *Worker Adjustment and Retraining Notification Act* of 1989, commonly known as the *WARN Act* or *Plant Closing Bill*, requires covered employers to give affected employees 60 days' written notice of plant closings or mass layoffs. Table 10.2 summarizes many of these major employment laws.

TABLE 10.2   U.S. Equal Employment Laws

Act	Major Provisions	Enforcement and Remedies
Fair Labor Standards Act (1938)	Creates exempt (salaried) and nonexempt (hourly) employee categories, governing overtime and other rules; sets minimum wage, child-labor laws.	Enforced by Department of Labor, private action to recover lost wages; civil and criminal penalties also possible.
Equal Pay Act (1963)	Prohibits gender-based pay discrimination between two jobs substantially similar in skill, effort, responsibility, and working conditions.	Fines up to $10,000, imprisonment up to 6 months, or both; enforced by Equal Employment Opportunity Commission (EEOC); private actions for double damages up to 3 years' wages, liquidated damages, reinstatement, or promotion.
Title VII of Civil Rights Act (1964)	Prohibits discrimination based on race, sex, color, religion, or national origin in employment decisions: hiring, pay, working conditions, promotion, discipline, or discharge.	Enforced by EEOC; private actions, back pay, front pay, reinstatement, restoration of seniority and pension benefits, attorneys' fees and costs.
Executive Orders 11246 and 11375 (1965)	Requires equal opportunity clauses in federal contracts; prohibits employment discrimination by federal contractors based on race, color, religion, sex, or national origin.	Established Office of Federal Contract Compliance Programs (OFCCP) to investigate violations; empowered to terminate violator's federal contracts.
Age Discrimination in Employment Act (1967)	Prohibits employment discrimination based on age for persons over 40 years; restricts mandatory retirement.	EEOC enforcement; private actions for reinstatement, back pay, front pay, restoration of seniority and pension benefits; double unpaid wages for willful violations; attorneys' fees and costs.
Vocational Rehabilitation Act (1973)	Requires affirmative action by all federal contractors for persons with disabilities; defines disabilities as physical or mental impairments that substantially limit life activities.	Federal contractors must consider hiring disabled persons capable of performance after reasonable accommodations.
Americans with Disabilities Act (1990)	Extends affirmative action provisions of Vocational Rehabilitation Act to private employers; requires workplace modifications to facilitate disabled employees; prohibits discrimination against disabled.	EEOC enforcement; private actions for Title VII remedies.
Civil Rights Act (1991)	Clarifies Title VII requirements: disparate treatment impact suits, business necessity, job relatedness; shifts burden of proof to employer; permits punitive damages and jury trials.	Punitive damages limited to sliding scale only in intentional discrimination based on sex, religion, and disabilities.
Family and Medical Leave Act (1991)	Requires 12 weeks' unpaid leave for medical or family needs: paternity, family member illness.	Private actions for lost wages and other expenses, reinstatement.

Developing the Workforce

Today's competitive environment requires managers to continually upgrade the skills and performance of employees—and their own. Such constant improvement increases both personal and organizational effectiveness. It makes organization members more useful in their current job and prepares them to take on new responsibilities. And it helps the organization as a whole handle new challenges and take advantage of new methods and technologies that emerge. Developing the workforce in this way involves training and development activities. It also involves appraising employees' performance and giving them effective feedback so they will be motivated to perform at their best. We will discuss each of these activities in turn.

✓ **The bottom line**
Quality
Training improves employee quality.

Training and Development

U.S. businesses spend more than $55 billion to provide their employees with formal training annually. The greatest share of that spending goes to sales training, management and supervisory training, and training in information systems and information technology. Spending on training is growing fastest among companies in the health care, technology, and financial services industries.[37]

Fortune 500 companies such as General Electric and Procter & Gamble have invested heavily in training. IBM's annual training costs have at times exceeded Harvard University's annual operating expenses. But competitive pressures require that companies consider the most efficient training methods. That means traditional classroom settings are often giving way to computerized methods.

The American Society for Training and Development has argued that as a percentage of total payroll, the average organizational investment in training is too small.[38] This lack of commitment is a great concern in light of the fact that today's jobs require more education but that the education level of U.S. workers has not kept pace. What's more, companies need to ensure that employees who have survived layoffs can lead their organizations through tough times.

Cold Stone Creamery spends a portion of their training budget in developing computerized simulations to show how employee actions affect store performance. The company uses computer games because they are familiar and attractive to its young employees.

Overview of the Training Process   Although we use the general term *training* here, training sometimes is distinguished from development. **Training** usually refers to teaching lower-level employees how to perform their present jobs, while **development** involves teaching managers and professional employees broader skills needed for their present and future jobs.

Phase one of training usually starts with a **needs assessment**. Managers conduct an analysis to identify the jobs, people, and departments for which training is necessary. Job analysis and performance measurements are useful for this purpose.

Phase two involves the design of training programs. Based on needs assessment, training objectives and content can be established. For example, Recreational Equipment Inc. (REI) wants its sales associates to learn how to tell whether they are being approached by a transactional customer, who simply wants to find and pay for a specific product, and a consultative customer, who wants to spend some time discussing alternative features and benefits.[39]

Phase three involves decisions about the training methods to be used and whether the training will be provided on-the-job or off-the-job. Common training methods are listed in Figure 10.4. Examples of training methods include lectures, role playing, business simulation, behavior modeling (watching a video and imitating what is observed), conferences, vestibule training (practicing in a simulated job environment),

training

Teaching lower-level employees how to perform their present jobs.

development

Helping managers and professional employees learn the broad skills needed for their present and future jobs.

needs assessment

An analysis identifying the jobs, people, and departments for which training is necessary.

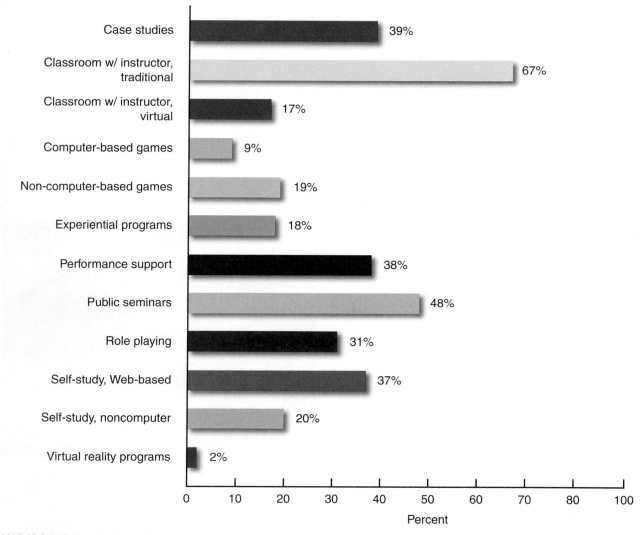

Training Method	Percent
Case studies	39%
Classroom w/ instructor, traditional	67%
Classroom w/ instructor, virtual	17%
Computer-based games	9%
Non-computer-based games	19%
Experiential programs	18%
Performance support	38%
Public seminars	48%
Role playing	31%
Self-study, Web-based	37%
Self-study, noncomputer	20%
Virtual reality programs	2%

SOURCE: From *Training: The Human Side of Business* by Holly Dfalezalek, *"Industry Report 2004."* Copyright © 2004 by *VNU BUS Publications* USA Reproduced with permission of VNU BUS Publications via Copyright Clearance Center.

FIGURE 10.4
Most Frequently Used Training Methods

and apprenticeships. The method should be well suited to the objectives defined in phase two. At REI, where the company wants sales associates to identify and respond to various interpersonal situations, much of the training involves role-playing, supplemented with video presentations. The Home Depot emphasizes mentoring for sales associates who work the aisles but has a more efficient computer-based training program for the cashiers, whose jobs are more routine.[40] Job rotation, where employees are assigned to different jobs in the organization to broaden their experience and improve their skills, is another popular training method. It is frequently applied to managers as well as lower-level employees. In fact, smart managers often request assignment to jobs where they can be challenged and their skills broadened.

Finally, *phase four* of training should evaluate the program's effectiveness. Measures of effectiveness include employee reactions (surveys), learning (tests), improved behavior on the job, and bottom-line results (e.g., an increase in sales or reduction in defect rates following the training program).

Types of Training   Companies invest in training to enhance individual performance and organizational productivity. Programs to improve an employee's computer, technical, or communication skills are quite common, and some types of training have become fairly standard across many organizations. **Orientation training** is typically used to familiarize new employees with their new jobs, work units, and the organization in general. Done well, orientation training has a number of benefits, including lower employee turnover, increased morale, better productivity, and lower recruiting and training costs.

Team training has taken on more importance as organizations reorganize to facilitate individuals working together. Team training teaches employees the skills they need to work together and facilitates their interaction. After General Mills acquired Pillsbury, it used a team training program called Brand Champions to combine the marketing expertise of the two companies and share knowledge among employees handling various functions such as sales and research and development. Most of the time, trainees engaged in team exercises to analyze brands, target customers, and develop marketing messages.[41]

Diversity training focuses on building awareness of diversity issues and providing the skills employees need to work with others who are different from them. This topic is so important that the next chapter is devoted solely to managing diversity.

Today's decentralized and leaner organizations put more demands and responsibility on managers, as has an increasingly competitive environment. And as managers rise in the organization, their technical skills generally become less and less important than their ability to motivate others. For these reasons, *management training programs* have become another widely used development tool. Such programs often seek to improve managers' *people skills*—their ability to delegate effectively, increase the motivation of their subordinates, and communicate and inspire the achievement of organization goals. *Coaching*—being trained by a superior—is usually the most effective and direct management-development tool. Managers may also participate in training programs that are used for all employees, such as job rotation, or attend seminars and courses specifically designed to help them improve their supervisory skills or prepare them for future promotion.

orientation training

Training designed to introduce new employees to the company and familiarize them with policies, procedures, culture, and the like.

team training

Training that provides employees with the skills and perspectives they need to collaborate with others.

diversity training

Programs that focus on identifying and reducing hidden biases against people with differences and developing the skills needed to manage a diversified workforce.

NetApp, a data management company based in Sunnyvale, California, has an engaging approach to management training. The company hired BTS Group to develop a simulation game, modeled on NetApp's real-life business. NetApp first used the BTS simulation at a strategy meeting of its top managers. The executives were so enthusiastic and creative about the ways they solved the simulation problem that the company invited middle managers to play the game as a form of training for top posts, where strategic thinking is essential.

In the simulation, the managers were divided into five teams, bringing together managers from various functions. Each team was told to run an imaginary high-growth company named Pet-a-Toaster for three years, competing against the other teams. In the simulation, a year's worth of events were packed into one day of the training program. Each team received a booklet with details about Pet-a-Toaster, based on the market conditions that were actually facing NetApp. Teams allocated the resources they were given, selected from among possible strategies, and reacted to events posed by the game (for example, a request from a big customer). BTS's simulation software analyzed the actions and provided feedback.

At the end of the simulation, BTS reported each team's total sales and operating profits and described the impact of each team's decisions about where to invest resources. Now NetApp's middle managers have a greater appreciation for what it takes to run a company—and a heightened respect for their leaders.[42]

Performance Appraisal

performance appraisal (PA)

Assessment of an employee's job performance.

One of the most important responsibilities you will have as a manager is **performance appraisal (PA),** the assessment of an employee's job performance. Done well, it can help employees improve their performance, pay, and chances for promotion; foster communication between managers and employees; and increase the employees' and the organization's effectiveness. Done poorly, it actually can have a negative effect—it can cause resentment, reduce motivation, diminish performance, and even expose the organization to legal action.

Performance appraisal has two basic purposes. First, appraisal serves an *administrative* purpose. It provides managers with the information they need to make salary, promotion, and dismissal decisions; helps employees understand and accept the basis of those decisions; and, if necessary, provides documentation that can justify those decisions in court. Second, and at least as important, appraisal serves a *developmental* purpose. The information gathered in the appraisal can be used to identify and plan the additional training, learning, experience, or other improvement employees require. In addition, the manager's feedback and coaching based on the appraisal help employees improve their day-to-day performance and can help prepare them for greater responsibilities in the future.

> "A leader is best when people barely know he exists. Not so good when people obey and acclaim him. Worse when they despise him. But of a good leader who talks little when his work is done, his aim fulfilled, they will say 'We did it ourselves.'"
>
> —Lao-tse

What Do You Appraise?

Performance appraisals can assess three basic categories of employee performance: traits, behaviors, and results. *Trait appraisals* involve subjective judgments about employee characteristics related to performance. They contain dimensions such as initiative, leadership, and attitude, and they ask raters to indicate how much of each trait an employee possesses. Usually the manager will use a numerical *ratings scale* to specify the extent to which an employee possesses the particular traits being measured. For example, if the measured trait is "attitude," the employee might be rated anywhere from 1 (very negative attitude) to 5 (very positive attitude). Trait scales are quite common, because they are simple to use and provide a standard measure for all employees. But they are often not valid as performance measures. Because they tend to be ambiguous as well as highly subjective—does the employee really have a bad attitude, or is he or she just shy?—they often lead to personal bias and may not be suitable for providing useful feedback.

Behavioral appraisals, while still subjective, focus more on observable aspects of performance. They were developed in response to the problems of trait appraisals. These scales focus on specific, prescribed behaviors that can help ensure that all parties understand what the ratings are really measuring. Because they are less ambiguous, they also can help provide useful feedback. Figure 10.5 contains an example of a behaviorally anchored rating scale (BARS) for evaluating quality.

Another common behaviorally focused approach is the *critical incident* technique. In this technique, the manager keeps a regular log and records each significant behavior by the subordinate that reflects the quality of his or her performance. ("Juanita impressed the client with her effective presentation today." "Joe was late with his report.") This approach can be subjective as well as time-consuming, and it may give some employees the feeling that everything they do is being recorded. But it does have the advantage of reminding managers in advance of a performance review what the employee actually did.

Results appraisals tend to be more objective and can focus on production data such as sales volume (for a salesperson), units produced (for a line worker), or profits (for

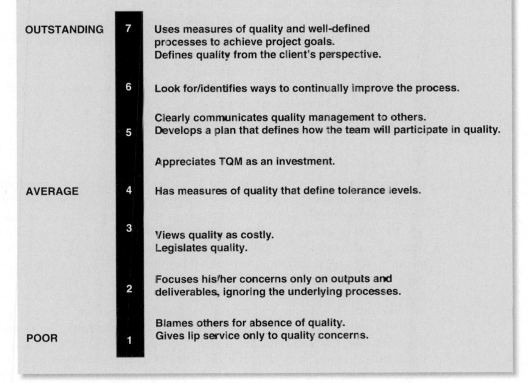

Performance Dimension: Total Quality Management. This area of performance concerns the extent to which a person is aware of, endorses, and develops proactive procedures to enhance product quality, ensure early disclosure of discrepancies, and integrate quality assessments with cost and schedule performance measurement reports to maximize client's satisfaction with overall performance.

OUTSTANDING	7	Uses measures of quality and well-defined processes to achieve project goals. Defines quality from the client's perspective.
	6	Look for/identifies ways to continually improve the process.
	5	Clearly communicates quality management to others. Develops a plan that defines how the team will participate in quality.
		Appreciates TQM as an investment.
AVERAGE	4	Has measures of quality that define tolerance levels.
	3	Views quality as costly. Legislates quality.
	2	Focuses his/her concerns only on outputs and deliverables, ignoring the underlying processes.
POOR	1	Blames others for absence of quality. Gives lip service only to quality concerns.

SOURCE: Landy, Jacobs, and Associates. Used with permission.

FIGURE 10.5
Example of BARS Used for Evaluating Quality

a manager). One approach to results appraisals—called **management by objectives (MBO)**—involves a subordinate and a supervisor agreeing *in advance* on specific performance goals (objectives). They then develop a plan that describes the time frame and criteria for determining whether the objectives have been reached. The aim is to agree on a set of objectives that are clear, specific, and reachable. For example, an objective for a salesperson might be "Increase sales by 25 percent during the following year." An objective for a computer programmer might be "Complete two projects within the next six months."

MBO has several important advantages. First, it avoids the biases and measurement difficulties of trait and behavioral appraisals. At the end of the review period, the employee either has or has not achieved the specified objective. The employee is judged on actual job performance. Second, because the employee and manager have agreed on the objective at the outset, the employee is likely to be more committed to the outcome, and there is less chance for misunderstanding. Third, because the employee is directly responsible for achieving the objective, MBO can be useful when managers want to empower employees to adapt their behavior to achieve the desired results. But the approach has disadvantages as well. It can result in unrealistic objectives being set, frustrating the employee and the manager. The objectives can also be too rigid, leaving the employee with insufficient flexibility should circumstances change. Finally, MBO often focuses too much on short-term achievement at the expense of long-term goals.

management by objectives (MBO)

A process in which objectives set by a subordinate and a supervisor must be reached within a given time period.

None of these performance appraisal systems is easy to conduct properly, and all have drawbacks that must be guarded against. In choosing an appraisal method, the following guidelines may prove helpful:

1. Base performance standards on job analysis.
2. Communicate performance standards to employees.
3. Evaluate employees on specific performance-related behaviors rather than on a single global or overall measure.
4. Document the PA process carefully.
5. If possible, use more than one rater (discussed in the next section).
6. Develop a formal appeal process.
7. Always take legal considerations into account.[43]

Who Should Do the Appraisal?

Just as multiple methods can be used to gather performance appraisal information, several different sources can provide PA information. *Managers* and *supervisors* are the traditional source of appraisal information because they are often in the best position to observe an employee's performance. However, companies are also turning to peers and team members to provide input to the performance appraisal. *Peers* and *team members* often see different dimensions of performance and are often best at identifying leadership potential and interpersonal skills.

One increasingly popular source of appraisal is a person's subordinates. Appraisal by *subordinates* has been used by companies such as Xerox and IBM to give superiors feedback on how their employees view them. Often this information is given in confidence to the manager, and not shared with superiors. Even so, this approach can make managers uncomfortable initially, but the feedback they get is often extremely useful and can help them significantly improve their management style. Because this process gives employees power over their bosses, it is generally used for development purposes only, and not for salary or promotion decisions.

Internal and external customers also are used as sources of performance appraisal information, particularly for companies, such as Ford and Honda, that are focused on total quality management. External customers have been used for some time to appraise restaurant employees, but internal customers can include anyone inside the organization who depends on an employee's work output. Finally, it is usually a good idea for employees to evaluate their own performance. Although *self-appraisals* may be biased upward, the process of self-evaluation helps increase the employee's involvement in the review process and is a starting point for establishing future goals.

Because each source of PA information has some limitations, and because different people may see different aspects of performance, Shell, Eastman Kodak, and many other companies have used approaches that involve more than one source for appraisal information. In a process known as **360-degree appraisal**, feedback is obtained from subordinates, peers, and superiors—every level involved with the employee. Often the person being rated can select the appraisers, subject to a manager's approval, with the understanding that the individual appraisals are kept confidential; returned forms might not include the name of the appraiser, for example, and the results may be consolidated for each level.

The 360-degree appraisal offers many advantages. It provides a much fuller picture of the employee's strengths and weaknesses, and it often captures qualities other appraisal methods miss. For example, an employee may have a difficult relationship with his or her supervisor yet be highly regarded by peers and subordinates. The approach can lead to significant improvement, with employees often very motivated to improve their ratings. Improvements in management performance following 360-degree appraisals have been observed in various countries, but cultural differences can affect the impact of this method. Using the cultural measures defined by

360-degree appraisal

Process of using multiple sources of appraisal to gain a comprehensive perspective on one's performance.

Geert Hofstede (described in Chapter 6), researchers found that 360-degree appraisals were most effective with managers in cultures that were individualistic and had relatively low power distance.[44] On the downside, employees are often unwilling to rate their colleagues harshly, so a certain uniformity of ratings may result. In addition, the 360-degree appraisal is less useful than more objective criteria, like financial targets, in measuring performance. Its objective is usually the employee's development, not to provide a basis for administrative decisions like raises. For those, appraisal methods like MBO are more appropriate.[45]

How Do You Give Employees Feedback?

Appraisals are most effective when they are based on an ongoing relationship with employees, and not just a top-down formal judgment issued once a year. Managers of sports teams do not wait until the season is over to perform an appraisal. Instead, they work with team members throughout the season, and with the team as a whole, to improve the team's performance. Similarly, in high-functioning regular organizations informal appraisal and feedback are constantly taking place. Managers discuss the goals of the organization regularly and often to create a shared understanding of the job performance those goals require. They try to create an atmosphere in which they and their employees are working together on a common agenda. And they communicate with their employees on a day-to-day basis, praising or coaching as appropriate and together assessing progress toward goals. When managers and employees have open communication and employees feel fairly and effectively managed, the kind of appraisal they receive should rarely come as a surprise to them.

Giving PA feedback can be a stressful task for both managers and subordinates. The purposes of PA conflict to some degree. Providing growth and development requires understanding and support; however, the manager must be impersonal and be able to make tough decisions. Employees want to know how they are doing, but typically they are uncomfortable about getting feedback. Finally, the organization's need to make HR decisions conflicts with the individual employee's need to maintain a positive image.[46] These conflicts often make a PA interview difficult; therefore, managers should conduct such interviews thoughtfully.

There is no one "best" way to do a PA interview. In general, appraisal feedback works best when it is *specific* and *constructive*—related to clear goals or behaviors and clearly intended to help the employee rather than simply criticize. Managers have an interest not just in rating performance but in raising it, and effective appraisals take that into account. In addition, the appraisal is likely to be more meaningful and satisfying when the manager gives the employee an opportunity to discuss his or her performance and respond to the appraisal.

One of the most difficult interviews takes place with an employee who is performing poorly. Here is a useful PA interview format to use when an employee is performing below acceptable standards:

1. Summarize the employee's specific performance. Describe the performance in behavioral or outcome terms, such as sales or absenteeism. Don't say the employee has a poor attitude; rather, explain which employee behaviors indicate a poor attitude.
2. Describe the expectations and standards, and be specific.
3. Determine the causes for the low performance; get the employee's input.
4. Discuss solutions to the problem, and have the employee play a major role in the process.
5. Agree to a solution. As a supervisor, you have input into the solution. Raise issues and questions, but also provide support.
6. Agree to a timetable for improvement.
7. Document the meeting.

✔ **The bottom line**
Quality

Effective feedback raises employee performance.

"Outstanding leaders go out of their way to boost the self-esteem of their personnel. If people believe in themselves, it's amazing what they can accomplish."
—Sam Walton

Follow-up meetings may be needed. Here are some guidelines for giving feedback to an average employee:

1. Summarize the employee's performance, and be specific.
2. Explain why the employee's work is important to the organization.
3. Thank the employee for doing the job.
4. Raise any relevant issues, such as areas for improvement.
5. Express confidence in the employee's future good performance.

If all goes well, PA interviews will result in improved outlook and performance. But what if an employee has an addiction to drugs or alcohol, exhibits dangerous behavior, or is volatile? The manager must still give feedback. About 500 million work days are lost each year due to alcoholism, and about 80 percent of alcoholics are employed either full- or part-time. Instead of looking the other way, many firms today try to offer help. Because of privacy and discrimination laws, it is often difficult for a manager to point out the problem directly. "Managers can't identify the problem, even if they are sure, because that would mean they are making a diagnosis, and they aren't qualified to do that," explains Bill Arnold, corporate director of substance abuse counseling services for Quad/Graphics. Human resource experts advise managers to treat the situation as a job-performance issue instead, referring to lost productivity, missed meetings, and the like—and help the employee make plans for improvement.[47]

A potentially violent employee is another situation that needs feedback. Workers who shout threats or have angry outbursts "must be taken seriously," says Carmeline Procaccini, vice president of human resources at Pegasystems, a software company. "We've trained our managers not to take any chances," she continues. She advises supervisors to contact HR staff and executives immediately about any employee who seems overly upset or potentially violent. The appropriate manager can recommend counseling or other assistance, but in the end, the firm must act in the best interests of its other employees.[48]

Designing Reward Systems

LO 6

Another major set of HRM activities involves reward systems. Most of this section will be devoted to monetary rewards such as pay and fringe benefits. (We discuss other motivational tools in Chapter 13.) Although traditionally pay has been the primary monetary reward considered, in recent years benefits have received increased attention. Benefits currently make up a far greater percentage of the total payroll than they did in past decades.[49] The typical employer today pays about 30 percent of payroll costs in benefits. Throughout most of the past two decades, benefits costs have risen faster than wages and salaries, fueled by the rapidly rising cost of medical care. Accordingly, employers are attempting to reduce benefits costs, even as their value to employees is rising. Benefits are also receiving more management attention because of their increased complexity. Many new types of benefits are now available, and tax laws affect myriad fringe benefits, such as health insurance and pension plans.

$ **The bottom line**

COST

Organizations today seek new ways to reduce benefits costs.

Pay Decisions

Reward systems can serve the strategic purposes of attracting, motivating, and retaining people. The wages paid to employees are based on a complex set of forces. Beyond the body of laws governing compensation, a number of basic decisions must be made in choosing the appropriate pay plan. Figure 10.6 illustrates some of the factors that influence the wage mix.

Internal factors

Compensation policy
of organization

Worth of job

Employee's
relative worth

Employer's ability to pay

**Wage
mix**

External factors

Conditions of the
labor market

Area wage rates

Cost of living

Collective bargaining

Legal requirements

FIGURE 10.6
Factors Affecting the Wage
Mix

SOURCE: From George Bohlander, Scott Snell, and Arthur Sherman, *Managing Human Resources*, 12th ed. Copyright © 2001. Reprinted by permission of South-Western, a division of Thomson Learning, www.thomsonrights.com. Fax 800 730-2215.

Three types of decisions are crucial for designing an effective pay plan: pay level, pay structure, and individual pay.

Pay level refers to the choice of whether to be a high-, average-, or low-paying company. Compensation is a major cost for any organization, so low wages can be justified on a short-term financial basis. But being the high-wage employer—the highest-paying company in the region—ensures that the company will attract many applicants. Being a wage leader may be important during times of low unemployment or intense competition.

These chefs from Tersiguel's French Country Restaurant in Maryland have a reason to be smiling: their employer offers reward systems that include employer-matched 401(k), profit sharing, and health benefits.

The *pay structure* decision is the choice of how to price different jobs within the organization. Jobs that are similar in worth usually are grouped together into job families. A pay grade, with a floor and a ceiling, is established for each job family. Figure 10.7 illustrates a hypothetical pay structure.

Finally, *individual pay decisions* concern different pay rates for jobs of similar worth within the same family. Differences in pay within job families are decided in two ways. First, some jobs are occupied by individuals with more seniority than others. Second, some people may be better performers who are therefore deserving of a higher level of pay. Setting an individual's pay lower than that of coworkers—like choosing an overall low pay level—may become more difficult for employers to sustain in the future, as more employees use online resources such as Salary.com and PayScale.com to check whether their pay is above or below the average amount for similar job titles.[50]

Unlike many other types of decisions in organizations, decisions about pay, especially at the individual level, often are kept confidential. Is that practice advantageous for organizations? Surprisingly, there is little evidence about this practice even though it affects almost every private-sector employee.[51] Some possible ways the organization may benefit from keeping pay decisions secret are by avoiding conflicts, protecting individuals' privacy, and reducing the likelihood that employees will leave to seek better pay if they are earning less than the average for their position. However, if decisions about pay are kept secret, employees may worry that decisions are unfair and may be less motivated because the link between performance and pay is unclear. Also,

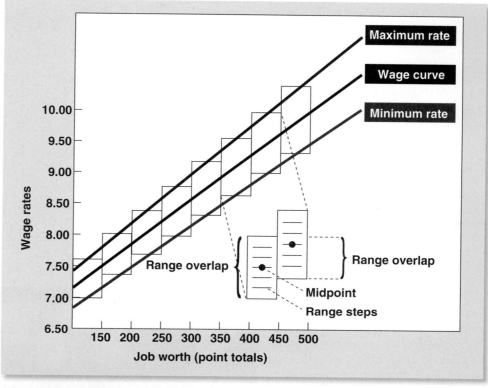

FIGURE 10.7
Pay Structure

SOURCE: From *Managing Human Resources*, 11th ed., by Bohlander, Snell, and Sherman. Copyright © 1998. Reprinted with permission of South-Western, a division of Thomson Learning, www.thomsonrights.com. Fax 800 730-2215.

in an economic sense, labor markets are less efficient when information is unavailable, which can reduce organizations' ability to get the best workers at the optimum rate of pay. Given these possible pros and cons of pay secrecy, do you think this practice is wise? Is it ethical? And what about you—do you want to know how much your coworkers earn?

Incentive Systems and Variable Pay

Incentives can help raise all aspects of organization performance.

Various incentive systems have been devised to encourage and motivate employees to be more productive.[52] (See Chapter 13 for more discussion of rewarding performance.) *Individual incentive plans* are the most common type of incentive plan. An individual incentive system consists of an objective standard against which a worker's performance is compared. Pay is determined by the employee's performance. Individual incentive plans are used frequently in sales jobs—for example, a salesperson will receive extra compensation for exceeding a sales target. Another widely used individual incentive tool is management bonuses. If effectively designed, individual incentive plans can be highly motivating. Some companies, including Walmart, are even beginning to apply them for nonmanagers. Walmart hopes that using bonuses to reward hourly employees for meeting sales, profit, and inventory targets at their stores each quarter will build employees' job satisfaction and reduce turnover.[53]

Several types of group incentive plans, in which pay is based on group performance, are increasingly used today. The idea behind these plans is to give employees a sense of shared participation and even ownership in the performance of the firm. *Gainsharing plans* concentrate on rewarding employees for increasing productivity or saving money in areas under their direct control.[54] For example, if the usual waste allowance in a production line has been 5 percent and the company wants production employees to try to reduce that number, the company may offer to split any savings gained with the employees.

Profit-sharing plans are usually implemented in the division or organization as a whole, although some incentives may still be tailored to unit performance. In most companies, the profit-sharing plan is based on a formula for allocating an annual amount to each employee if the company exceeds a specified profit target. One disadvantage of profit-sharing plans is that they do not reward individual performance. However, they do give all employees a stake in the company's success and motivate efforts to improve the company's profitability. In the "Management Close-Up: Taking Action" feature, consider how profit sharing at Enterprise Rent-A-Car supports the company's strategy and dovetails with its recruiting goals.

Management Close-Up | TAKING ACTION

The rise in air travel in the 1960s and 1970s helped the car-rental industry grow, with competitors like Hertz and Avis locating rental offices within airports to serve travelers. But Enterprise founder Jack Taylor pursued an entirely different business model. Recognizing that travel is not the only reason to rent a car, he established Enterprise branches within local communities, targeting customers who needed transportation while their own vehicle was in the shop. Not only was his a low-cost strategy, but it also proved to be a significant differentiator that created a huge competitive advantage for Enterprise.

Recruiting at Enterprise is a broad-based function. About 225 recruiters visit nearly a thousand universities and colleges looking for new prospects. Since college students appreciate both high-tech and high-touch recruiting methods, recruiters reach out to job candidates through meetings and phone calls, as well as through an award-winning interactive Web site that includes video clips and testimonials from current trainees.

For several years, Enterprise has led the nation's employers in college recruiting, including the recruiting of women and minorities. In recent years it has hired as many as 8,000 college graduates for entry-level positions, and it offers paid internships to an additional 2,000 students.

Enterprise's decentralized management system gives branch managers great latitude to shape their business to fit the wants and needs of their local market. Managers are given the authority and responsibility for their own success. An incentive pay system allows local offices to share in the profits they have generated. Employees receive promotions based on their performance. The arrangement is especially attractive to employees with an entrepreneurial streak; Enterprise branch managers are highly motivated to prove themselves.[55]

- Enterprise president and COO Pam Nicholson began her career path at the company like thousands of other recent college grads do each year: as a management trainee in a local branch. How do Enterprise's recruiting system and decentralized management style contribute to employees' successes? How do they help the company?
- Today, Enterprise's workforce is a blend of baby boomers, Generation Xers, and others. As president and COO how can Nicholson ensure that Enterprise continues to provide its workforce with the right rewards to keep them engaged and productive?

Aon, a large insurance and consulting firm with 47,000 employees in 500 offices around the world, recently instituted a compensation program for its top and middle managers based on three areas of performance: the individual business unit's performance, the geographic region's performance, and the performance of the company as a whole. The breakdown of payments—cash, stock, and the amount—varies depending on the level of the manager. In addition, lower-level employees receive matching contributions to their 401(k) retirement accounts if the company does well.[56]

When objective performance measures are not available but the company still wants to base pay on performance, it uses a *merit pay system*. Individuals' pay raises and bonuses are based on the merit rating they receive from their boss. In Rochester, Minnesota, the school superintendent's bonus is an example of merit pay. The school board rates the superintendent's performance in several predetermined areas, such as promoting teamwork between the board and school district staff and supporting the board in developing a strategic plan. In a recent year, the superintendent received an average score of 3 on a four-point scale, so the board awarded him three-quarters of the maximum bonus.[57]

Executive Pay and Stock Options

In recent years the issues of executive pay and stock options, particularly for CEOs, have become major sources of controversy. One reason is that the gap between the pay of top executives and the average pay of employees has widened considerably. In the 1980s CEOs made less than 40 times the average worker's pay. By the next decade, CEOs were earning 140 times more, and the multiple has now reached 500 times the average worker's pay. This gap is considerably wider in the United States than it is abroad. For example, the average CEO of a large British company earns roughly 130 times that of a U.K. worker, and the average top executive in Australia earns about 50 times more than the average Australian worker. In Japan, where the details of executive pay are less public, executive pay has risen relatively slowly, and companies avoid huge income gaps between the top and bottom of the organization, out of concern for employee morale and teamwork.[58]

Besides the difference between executive and average-worker pay, the sheer size and growth of CEO compensation has also contributed to criticism by shareholders and the general public. Top-earning CEOs today can make tens of millions of dollars a year. Still, it's important to keep in mind that the huge awards that make headlines are not necessarily typical. In a recent year, CEOs of companies in the Standard & Poor's stock index earned on average $4.5 million, but the median was $2.5 million, because a few executives with far higher earnings pushed the average higher. Also, if we consider only the biggest companies, those in the Standard & Poor's 500, CEO pay averaged $9 million because CEOs of the biggest companies tend to earn more than most CEOs.[59]

Even with these considerations, $9 million or even $2.5 million is a lot of money to earn in one year, and the amount of compensation paid to top executives is growing. While salaries and bonuses have risen at a moderate pace, the fastest-growing part of executive compensation comes from stock grants and *stock options*. Such options give the holder the right to purchase shares of stock at a specified price. For example, if the company's stock price is $8 a share, the company may award a manager the right to purchase a specific number of shares of company stock at that price. If the price of the stock rises to, say, $10 a share after a specified holding period—usually three years or more—the manager can *exercise* the option. He or she can purchase the shares from the company at $8 per share, sell the shares on the stock market at $10, and keep the difference. (Of course, if the stock price never rises above $8, the options will be worthless.) For many top managers, large option grants, along with sharply rising share prices on the stock market, became a major source of additional compensation. Nearly one-third of CEOs' compensation (and more than one-fourth of non-CEO executives' compensation) comes in the form of stock options.[60] Adding to the scrutiny over this practice is the striking number of situations in which options were dated just before the company's stock price rose, increasing their value—and the suspicion that at least some of these options were backdated to unethically make them more valuable, rather than give executives the incentive to improve the company's performance in the stock market.[61]

Companies issue options to managers to align their interests with those of the company's owners, the shareholders. The assumption is that managers will become even more focused on making the company successful, leading to a rise in its stock price. Assuming that the executives continue to own their stock year after year, the amount of their wealth that is tied to the company's performance—and their incentive to work hard for the company—should continually increase.[62] However, many critics have suggested that excessive use of options encouraged executives to focus on short-term results to drive up the price of their stock, at the expense of their firm's long-run competitiveness. Others suggested that lucrative options motivated questionable or even unethical behavior, as we mentioned in Chapter 2. More recently, a plunging stock market highlighted another problem with stock options: many options became essentially worthless, so they failed to reward employees.[63] While it makes business sense to give employees an incentive to contribute to their company's value, few if any employees could have prevented a widespread global economic downturn. In the future, employees may be wary about accepting stock options in lieu of less risky forms of pay.

Traditionally, companies incurred no expense when they issued stock options. This was another reason options were considered an attractive incentive tool and were sometimes even issued to nonmanagers. However, because of corporate scandals and to curb excessive use of options, the rules were changed in 2004 so that options have to be treated as an expense by companies that issue them. This means that compensation committees have to focus more on whether options motivate executives to focus on what is important for the company's future.

Employee Benefits

Like pay systems, employee benefit plans are subject to regulation. Employee benefits are divided into those required by law and those optional for an employer.

The three basic required benefits are workers' compensation, Social Security, and unemployment insurance. *Workers' compensation* provides financial support to employees suffering a work-related injury or illness. *Social Security*, as established in the Social Security Act of 1935, provides financial support to retirees; in subsequent amendments, the act was expanded to cover disabled employees. The funds come from payments made by employers, employees, and self-employed workers. *Unemployment insurance* provides financial support to employees who are laid off for reasons they cannot control. Companies that have terminated fewer employees pay less into the unemployment insurance fund; thus, organizations have an incentive to keep terminations at a minimum.

A large number of benefits are not required to be employer-provided. The most common are pension plans and medical and hospital insurance. Both of these are undergoing significant change. One major reason is that in a global economy they have put U.S. firms at a competitive disadvantage. For example, U.S. employers spend an average of $9,000 for each employee with health insurance.[64] Overseas firms generally do not bear these costs, which are usually government funded, and so are able to compete more effectively on price. As a result, with U.S. medical costs rising rapidly, companies have reduced health benefits or asked employees to share more of their cost. A growing share of U.S. companies (more than one-third) offer no medical benefits at all, or they staff more positions with part-time workers and offer coverage only to full-time employees. At the same time, retirement benefits have been shifting away from guaranteed pension payments. While a promised monthly payout used to be the norm, almost no company offers this approach to new employees today.[65] Instead, in many companies, the employer, and perhaps the employee, may contribute to an individual retirement account or 401(k) plan, which is invested. When the employee retires, he or she gets the total amount that has accumulated in the account.

Rapidly rising medical costs have made health care coverage an expensive part of employers' benefits packages.[66] Some employers—especially small ones—have coped by dropping health insurance altogether.

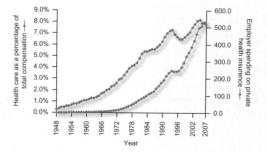

Because of the wide variety of possible benefits and the considerable differences in employee preferences and needs, companies often use **cafeteria** or **flexible benefit programs.** In this type of program, employees are given credits that they "spend" on benefits they desire. Then employees use their credits toward individualized packages of benefits—medical and dental insurance, dependent care, life insurance, and so on.

cafeteria benefit program

An employee benefit program in which employees choose from a menu of options to create a benefit package tailored to their needs.

flexible benefit programs

Benefit programs in which employees are given credits to spend on benefits that fit their unique needs.

comparable worth

Principle of equal pay for different jobs of equal worth.

Legal Issues in Compensation and Benefits

Several laws affect employee compensation and benefits. We have already mentioned the FLSA, which in addition to distinguishing between exempt and nonexempt employees also sets minimum wage, maximum hour, and child labor provisions.[67] The *Equal Pay Act (EPA)* of 1963, now enforced by the EEOC, prohibits unequal pay for men and women who perform equal work. Equal work means jobs that require equal skill, effort, and responsibility and are performed under similar working conditions. The law does permit exceptions in which the difference in pay is due to a seniority system, a merit system, an incentive system based on quantity or quality of production, or any other factor other than sex, such as market demand. Although equal pay for equal work may sound like common sense, many employers have fallen victim to this law by rationalizing that men, traditionally the "breadwinners," deserve more pay than women or by giving equal jobs different titles (senior assistant versus office manager) as the sole basis for pay differences.

One controversy concerns male and female pay differences within the same company. **Comparable-worth** doctrine implies that women who perform *different* jobs of *equal* worth as those performed by men should be paid the same wage.[68] In contrast to the equal-pay-for-equal-work notion, comparable worth suggests that the jobs need *not* be the same to require the same pay. For example, nurses (predominantly female) were found to be paid considerably less than skilled craftworkers (predominantly male), even though the two jobs were found to be of equal value or worth.[69] Under the Equal Pay Act, this would not constitute pay discrimination because the jobs are very different. But under the comparable-worth concept, these findings would indicate discrimination because the jobs are of equal worth.

To date, no federal law requires comparable worth, and the Supreme Court has made no decisive rulings about it. However, some states have considered developing comparable-worth laws, and others already have implemented comparable-worth changes, raising the wages of female-dominated jobs. For example, Minnesota passed a comparable-worth law for public-sector employees after finding that women on average were paid 25 percent less than men. Several other states, including Iowa, Idaho, New Mexico, Washington, and South Dakota, have comparable-worth laws for public-sector employees.[70]

Some laws influence mostly benefit practices. The *Pregnancy Discrimination Act* of 1978 states that pregnancy is a disability and qualifies a woman to receive the same benefits that she would with any other disability. The *Employee Retirement Income Security Act (ERISA)* of 1974 protects private pension programs from mismanagement. ERISA requires that retirement benefits be paid to those who vest or earn a right to draw benefits and ensures retirement benefits for employees whose companies go bankrupt or who otherwise cannot meet their pension obligations.

Health and Safety

The *Occupational Safety and Health Act (OSHA)* of 1970 requires employers to pursue workplace safety. Employers must maintain records of injuries and deaths caused by workplace accidents and submit to onsite inspections. Large-scale industrial accidents and nuclear power plant disasters worldwide have focused attention on the importance of workplace safety.

Coal mining is one of many industries that benefit from safety laws. Mining is one of the five most dangerous jobs to perform, according to the U.S. Bureau of Labor Statistics. Nearly every coal miner can name a friend or family member who has been killed, maimed, or stricken with black lung disease. "You die quick or you die slow," reports one mine worker. Mine safety tragically returned to American consciousness in January 2006, when 12 miners died after being trapped by an explosion in the International Coal Group (ICG) mine in Sago, West Virginia. Critics of ICG's safety practices noted that more than 200 safety citations had been issued against the mine in the previous year, but fines totaled only $24,000.[71] However, according to the Mine Safety and Health Administration, mines have become safer. In the 1960s, hundreds of coal miners died in mine accidents every year; in 1986, 89 miners died (4.8 percent of coal miners), and even with the Sago tragedy in 2006, 47 miners (3.9 percent) died that year.[72]

Another area of concern is the safety of young workers, who may lack the confidence to speak up if they see health or safety problems. A recent study of teenage workers found that many were exposed to hazards and used equipment that should have been off-limits to teens under federal regulations. For example, almost half of teenaged grocery store employees said they had performed prohibited tasks such as using box crushers and dough mixers.[73]

Labor Relations

LO 7

Labor relations is the system of relations between workers and management. Labor unions recruit members, collect dues, and ensure that employees are treated fairly with respect to wages, working conditions, and other issues. When workers organize for the purpose of negotiating with management to improve their wages, hours, or working conditions, two processes are involved: unionization and collective bargaining. These processes have evolved since the 1930s in the United States to provide important employee rights.[74]

labor relations

The system of relations between workers and management.

Labor Laws

Try to imagine what life would be like with unemployment at 25 percent. Pretty grim, you would say. Legislators in 1935 felt that way too. Therefore, organized labor received its Magna Carta with the passage of the National Labor Relations Act.

The *National Labor Relations Act* (also called the *Wagner Act* after its legislative sponsor) ushered in an era of rapid unionization by (1) declaring labor organizations legal, (2) establishing five unfair employer labor practices, and (3) creating the National Labor Relations Board (NLRB). Prior to the act, employers could fire workers who favored unions, and federal troops were often provided to put down strikes. Today, the NLRB conducts unionization elections, hears complaints of unfair labor practices, and issues injunctions against offending employers. The Wagner Act greatly assisted the growth of unions by enabling workers to use the law and the courts to organize and

These protestors in Fontana, California, accuse Walmart of paying low wages, offering no health care or benefits, and trying to prevent employees from forming unions. The protest resulted in seven arrests. How might the retail giant respond to these accusations?

collectively bargain for better wages, hours, and working conditions. Many of the improvements all of us take for granted in the workplace, including minimum wages, health benefits, maternity leave, the 35-hour work-week, and worker protections in general were largely the result of collective bargaining over many years by unions.

Public policy began on the side of organized labor in 1935, but over the next 25 years, the pendulum swung toward the side of management. The *Labor-Management Relations Act*, or *Taft-Hartley Act* (1947), protected employers' free-speech rights, defined unfair labor practices by unions, and permitted workers to decertify (reject) a union as their representative.

Finally, the *Labor-Management Reporting and Disclosure Act*, or *Landrum-Griffin Act* (1959), swung the public policy pendulum midway between organized labor and management. By declaring a bill of rights for union members, establishing control over union dues increases, and imposing reporting requirements for unions, Landrum-Griffin was designed to curb abuses by union leadership and rid unions of corruption.

Unionization

How do workers join unions? Through a union organizer or local union representative, workers learn what benefits they may receive by joining.[75] The union representative distributes authorization cards that permit workers to indicate whether they want an election to be held to certify the union to represent them. The National Labor Relations Board will conduct a certification election if at least 30 percent of the employees sign authorization cards. Management has several choices at this stage: to recognize the union without an election, to consent to an election, or to contest the number of cards signed and resist an election.

If an election is warranted, an NLRB representative will conduct the election by secret ballot. A simple majority of those voting determines the winner. Thus, apathetic workers who do not show up to vote in effect support the union. If the union wins the election, it is certified as the bargaining unit representative.

During the campaign preceding the election, management and the union each try to persuade the workers how to vote. Most workers, though, are somewhat resistant to campaign efforts, having made up their minds well before the NLRB appears on the scene. If the union wins the election, management and the union are legally required to bargain in good faith to obtain a collective bargaining agreement or contract.

Why do workers vote for a union? The four factors that play a significant role are presented in Figure 10.8.[76] First, economic factors are important, especially for workers in low-paying jobs; unions attempt to raise the average wage rate for their members. Second, job dissatisfaction encourages workers to seek out a union. Poor supervisory practices, favoritism, lack of communication, and perceived unfair or arbitrary discipline and discharge are specific triggers of job dissatisfaction. Third, the belief that the union can obtain desired benefits can generate a pro-union vote. Finally, the image of the union can determine whether a dissatisfied worker will seek out the union. Headline stories of union corruption and dishonesty can discourage workers from unionization.

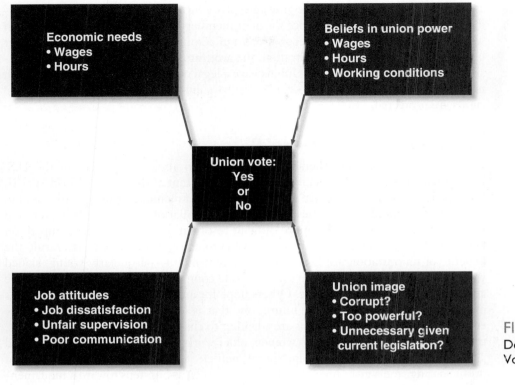

FIGURE 10.8
Determinants of Union
Voting Behavior

Collective Bargaining

In the United States, management and unions engage in a periodic ritual (typically every three years) of negotiating an agreement over wages, benefits, hours, and working conditions. Two types of disputes can arise during this process. First, before an agreement is reached, the workers may go on strike to compel agreement on their terms. Such an action is known as an *economic strike* and is permitted by law. However, today strikes are less likely to be used as a bargaining tool, although they sometimes do still occur as a last resort. Strikers are not paid if they are on strike, and few workers want to undertake this hardship unnecessarily. In addition, managers may legally hire replacement workers during a strike, offsetting some of the strike's effect. Finally, workers are as aware as managers of the tougher competition companies face today, and if treated fairly, they will usually share management's interest in coming to an agreement.

Once an agreement is signed, management and the union sometimes disagree over *interpretation* of the agreement. Usually they settle their disputes through arbitration. **Arbitration** is the use of a neutral third party, typically jointly selected, to resolve the dispute. The United States uses arbitration while an agreement is in effect to avoid *wildcat strikes* (in which workers walk off the job in violation of the contract) or unplanned work stoppages.

What does a collective bargaining agreement contain? In a **union shop,** a union security clause specifies that workers must join the union after a set period of time. **Right-to-work** states, through restrictive legislation, do not permit union shops; that is, workers have the right to work without being forced to join a union. The southern United States has many right-to-work states. The wage component of the contract spells out rates of pay, including premium pay for overtime and paid holidays. Individual rights usually are specified in terms of the use of seniority to determine pay increases, job bidding, and the order of layoffs.

arbitration

The use of a neutral third party to resolve a labor dispute.

union shop

An organization with a union and a union security clause specifying that workers must join the union after a set period of time.

right-to-work

Legislation that allows employees to work without having to join a union.

A feature of any contract is the grievance procedure. Through the grievance procedure, unions perform a vital service for their membership by giving workers a voice in what goes on during contract negotiations and administration.[77] In about 50 percent of discharge cases that go to arbitration, the arbitrator overturns management's decision and reinstates the worker.[78] Unions have a legal duty of fair representation, which means they must represent all workers in the bargaining unit and ensure that workers' rights are protected.

What Does the Future Hold?

In recent years union membership has declined to about 12 percent of the U.S. labor force—down from a peak of more than 33 percent at the end of World War II. Increased automation eliminated many of the types of manufacturing jobs that used to be union strongholds. Employees in today's white-collar office jobs are less interested in joining unions and are also more difficult to organize. Tough global competition has made managers much less willing to give in to union demands, and as a result, the benefits of unionization are less clear to many workers—particularly young, skilled workers who no longer expect to stay with one company all their lives. Some people applaud unions' apparent decline. Others hope for an eventual reemergence. Unions may play a different role in the future, one that is less adversarial and more cooperative with management. Unions are adapting to changing workforce demographics; they are paying more attention to women, older workers, government employees, and people who work at home. Elimination of inefficient work rules, the introduction of profit sharing, and a guarantee of no layoffs were seen as big steps toward a fundamentally different, cooperative long-term relationship.

What seems clear is that when companies recognize that their success depends on the talents and energies of employees, the interests of unions and managers may begin to converge. Rather than one side exploiting the other, unions and managers can find common ground in developing, valuing, and involving employees. Particularly in knowledge-based companies, the balance of power is shifting toward employees. Individuals, not companies, own their own human capital. And these employees are free, within limits, to leave the organization, taking their human capital with them. This leaves organizations in a particularly vulnerable position if they manage poorly. To establish a strong competitive capability, organizations are searching for ways to obtain, retain, and engage their most valuable resources: human resources. The processes and practices outlined in this chapter form the foundation for effective people management. In the next chapter, we discuss one particularly important people-related issue: managing a diverse workforce.

Management Close-Up

ASSESSING OUTCOMES AND SEIZING OPPORTUNITIES

When Pam Nicholson was named president of Enterprise Rent-A-Car in 2008, one of her first responsibilities was to complete the integration of her company's 2007 acquisition of Tulsa-based Vanguard Car Rental, owner of Alamo and National car rentals. Acquiring the Alamo and National brands has helped Enterprise penetrate other market segments. Alamo targets vacationers, and National caters to frequent business travelers. Both firms operate chiefly in airports. Pursuing its strategy of locating in communities, Enterprise did not begin locating rental branches in airports until 1995, opening its first such office in Denver. Since then, the company has also discovered that the revenue stream from local rental branches is smoother than that from airport locations, where business can be cyclical.

Operating a total fleet of 1.1 million rental vehicles—the world's largest—Enterprise takes its environmental responsibility seriously. To reduce its environmental impact, the company aims to buy wisely. Enterprise has the world's largest fleet of fuel-efficient cars: more than 440,000 vehicles that get better than 28 miles to the gallon on the highway. Its fleet includes 5,000 hybrid vehicles and 73,000 "flex-fuel" cars—vehicles that can operate on E85 fuel, a combination of 85 percent ethanol and 15 percent gasoline. Enterprise typically places the flex-fuel vehicles near gas stations that sell E85.

In another nod to the environment, Enterprise offers hourly car rentals and recently launched its nationwide WeCar program for vehicle sharing in corporations and at universities and colleges. These short-term rentals reduce the need for car purchases by companies and college students.

Recently, the Taylor family gave $25 million to create the Enterprise Rent-A-Car Institute for Renewable Fuels, to research alternative fuels that reduce dependency on fossil fuels and cut greenhouse gas emissions. That same year, it pledged to plant 1 million trees in America for the next 50 years to reduce carbon dioxide in the atmosphere. The company already uses recycled paper products in much of its operations. Enterprise also became the first major car-rental company to offer a carbon-offset program. Under the optional program, customers can elect to pay $1.25 to offset the pollution created by their rental vehicle. Enterprise matches customers' payments dollar for dollar to $1 million. About a thousand customers a day buy the carbon offset, and Enterprise plans to extend the program to the United Kingdom. Next on Enterprise's "to do" list is finding a way to mitigate the environmental impact of the waste generation and electricity and water use in its 8,000 offices worldwide.[79]

- Enterprise Rent-A-Car differentiated itself from its largest competitors by locating primarily where people live and work. But now the company has expanded to airport rentals. What can president and COO Pam Nicholson do to ensure that Enterprise branch offices continue to mirror their local communities? How might its environmental programs play a part in those local efforts?
- According to a recent survey of the rental-car industry, customer satisfaction with airport car rentals declined for the second consecutive year. Yet, for the fifth year running, Enterprise ranks first among car-rental companies in customer satisfaction. In your opinion, how does this rating relate to the human resource management policies and practices at Enterprise? How should Nicholson use such survey findings?

KEY TERMS

Adverse impact,   p. 355

Arbitration,   p. 373

Assessment center,   p. 351

Cafeteria benefit programs,   p. 370

Comparable worth,   p. 370

Development,   p. 357

Diversity training,   p. 359

Employment-at-will,   p. 353

Flexible benefit programs,   p. 370

Human capital,   p. 341

Human resources management (HRM),   p. 340

Job analysis,   p. 346

Labor relations,   p. 371

Management by objectives (MBO), p. 361

Needs assessment,   p. 357

Orientation training,   p. 359

Outplacement,   p. 353

Performance appraisal (PA),   p. 360

Recruitment,   p. 346

Reliability,   p. 352

Right-to-work,   p. 373

Selection,   p. 348

Structured interview,   p. 349

360-degree appraisal,   p. 362

Team training,   p. 359

Termination interview,   p. 354

Training,   p. 357

Union shop,   p. 373

Validity,   p. 352

SUMMARY OF LEARNING OBJECTIVES

Now that you have studied Chapter 10, you should be able to:

LO 1   Discuss how companies use human resources management to gain competitive advantage.

To succeed, companies must align their human resources to their strategies. Effective planning is necessary to make certain that the right number and type of employees are available to implement a company's strategic plan. It is clear that hiring the most competent people is a very involved process. Companies that compete on cost, quality, service, and so on also should use their staffing, training, appraisal, and reward systems to elicit and reinforce the kinds of behaviors that underlie their strategies.

LO 2   Give reasons companies recruit both internally and externally for new hires.

Some companies prefer to recruit internally to make certain that employees are familiar with organizational policies and values. In other instances, companies prefer to recruit externally, such as through employee referrals, job boards, newspaper advertising, and campus visits, to find individuals with new ideas and fresh perspectives. External recruiting is also necessary to fill positions when the organization is growing or needs skills that do not exist among its current employees.

LO 3   Identify various methods for selecting new employees.

There are myriad selection techniques from which to choose. Interviews and reference checks are the most common. Personality tests and cognitive ability tests measure an individual's aptitude and potential to do well on the job. Other selection techniques include assessment centers and integrity tests. Background and reference checks verify that the information supplied by employees is accurate. Regardless of the approach used, any test should be able to demonstrate reliability (consistency across time and different interview situations) and validity (accuracy in predicting job performance). In addition, selection methods must comply with equal opportunity laws, which are intended to ensure that companies do not discriminate in any employment practices.

LO 4   Evaluate the importance of spending on training and development.

People cannot depend on a set of skills for all of their working lives. In today's changing, competitive world, old skills quickly become obsolete, and new ones become essential for success. Refreshing or updating an individual's skills requires a great deal of continuous training, designed with measurable goals and methods that will achieve those goals. Companies understand that gaining a competitive edge in quality of service depends on having the most talented, flexible workers in the industry.

LO 5   Explain alternatives for who appraises an employee's performance.

Many companies are using multiple sources of appraisal because different people see different sides of an employee's performance. Typically, a superior is expected to evaluate an employee, but peers and team members are often well positioned to see aspects of performance that a superior misses. Even an employee's subordinates are being asked more often today to give their input to get yet another perspective on the evaluation. Particularly in companies concerned about quality, internal and external customers also are surveyed. Finally, employees should evaluate their own performance, if only to get them thinking about their own performance, as well as to engage them in the appraisal process.

LO 6   Describe the fundamental aspects of a reward system.

Reward systems include pay and benefits. Pay systems have three basic components: pay level, pay structure, and individual pay determination. To achieve an advantage over competitors, executives may want to pay a generally higher wage to their company's employees, but this decision must be weighed against the need to control costs (pay-level decisions often are tied to strategic concerns such as these). To achieve internal equity (paying people what they are worth relative to their peers within the company), managers must look at the pay structure, making certain that pay differentials are based on knowledge, effort, responsibility, working conditions, seniority, and so on. Individual pay determination is often based on merit or the different contributions of individuals. In these cases, it is important to make certain that men and women receive equal pay for equal work, and managers may wish to base pay decisions on the idea of comparable worth (equal pay for an equal contribution). Also, the Occupational Safety and Health Act requires that employees have a safe and healthy work environment.

LO 7   Summarize how unions and labor laws influence human resources management.

Labor relations involve the interactions between workers and management. One mechanism by which this relationship is conducted is unions. Unions seek to present a collective voice for workers, to make their needs and wishes known to management. Unions negotiate agreements with management regarding a range of issues such as wages, hours, working conditions, job security, and health care. One important tool that unions can use is the grievance procedure established through collective bargaining. This mechanism gives employees a way to seek redress for wrongful action on the part of management. In this way, unions make certain that the rights of all employees are protected. Labor laws seek to protect the rights of both employees and managers so that their relationship can be productive and agreeable.

DISCUSSION QUESTIONS

1. How will changes in the labor force affect HRM practices for the next decade?

2. Describe the major regulations governing HRM practices.

3. Define job analysis. Why is job analysis relevant to each of the six key HRM activities discussed in the chapter (i.e., planning, staffing, training, performance appraisal, reward systems, labor relations)?

4. What are the various methods for recruiting employees? Why are some better than others? In what sense are they better?

5. What is a "test"? Give some examples of tests used by employers.

6. What purpose does performance appraisal serve? Why are there so many different methods of appraisal?

7. What are some key ideas to remember when conducting a performance interview?

8. How would you define an effective reward system? What role do benefits serve in a reward system?

9. Why do workers join unions? What implications would this have for an organization that wishes to remain nonunion?

10. Discuss the advantages and disadvantages of collective bargaining for the employer and the employee.

CONCLUDING CASE

The University of Dissension

This is a case about unions.

This case involves one of the divisions of the workforce of a state university near you. The personnel of that university are structured like many others around the country, with four distinct divisions of labor. *Administrators* include the president, a number of vice presidents, and many other executive-level administrative assistants positioned throughout the various departments. *Faculty* make up the second tier, and include assistant, associate, and full professors. *Professional associates* are the "white-collar" support staff; most of these individuals have a college education and work as middle managers, day-to-day operations administrators, technical support staff, and so on. *Operating staffers* are the "blue-collar" workers; they include administrative assistants, clerical workers, physical plant and grounds maintenance people, and custodians.

Operating staffers represent the largest and lowest-paid division of the workforce. Most of those individuals have no education or formal training beyond high school. Their pay scale ranges from minimum wage to $12–$15 per hour. Their benefit package includes some provisions for health and life insurance and retirement. It is far less comprehensive than the other three divisions and is considered to be somewhat comparable to employees in similar positions in the surrounding area.

The operating staffers have always maintained a central committee made up of a cross-representation of the various departments around campus. The committee was originally established to serve as a liaison between labor and management for communication purposes. In reality, it has functioned almost exclusively as a fundraising and community service arm for that group. The operating staffers have always been the most generous division on campus when it comes to community outreach volunteers and for the annual fundraising drives of the traditional nonprofit community service organizations.

For the first time ever, the central committee finds itself talking about unions. Operating staffers have begun to show up for the meetings in growing numbers to voice their displeasure about changes in working conditions and to encourage the committee to go ahead and take a serious look at unionizing.

During the past few years, administrative assistants, groundskeepers, maintenance workers, and custodians have not been replaced as positions become vacant. Supervisors have simply asked existing workers to "pick up the slack" because "the school cannot afford to fill those vacant positions." In addition, operating staffers have been required to contribute more of their paychecks each year to cover an increasing percentage of their health care costs, while the extent of their health care coverage has diminished.

Administrators claim that "times are tough, outside funding is down, and we must all share in the burden of maintaining our school." In the meantime, wages and benefits of administrators and faculty continue to increase, as do student enrollments. The increase in student enrollments also means more work for operating staffers.

The situation is beginning to "heat up" on both sides. Operating staffers have held public rallies on campus that include speeches by disgruntled workers and posters and banners depicting wages, working conditions, and prounion slogans. The central committee was able to organize a "bitch session" with the president as the result of an aggressive and relentless push for that meeting. The president listened quietly to the concerns and demands of the group and finally thanked them for their dedication to the school.

Supervisors and administrators have "informally encouraged" workers to give up the idea of unionizing. Many conversations are taking place off the record. Those conversations warn workers about the very real possibility of losing their jobs to outside vendors who are eager for the opportunity to provide their services to the school.

QUESTIONS

1. What steps would you take as a school administrator to resolve this issue and avoid unionization of the operating staffers?

2. If unionization appears imminent, what position and actions would you take to work through the process in the most collaborative and least disruptive manner?

3. Consider the labor force/supply in your area. Would subcontracting and/or outside recruiting be a means to quell this union movement?

EXPERIENTIAL EXERCISES

10.1 The "Legal" Interview

OBJECTIVES

1. To introduce you to the complexities of employment law.
2. To identify interview practices that might lead to discrimination in employment.

INSTRUCTIONS

1. Working alone, review the text material on interviewing and discrimination in employment.
2. In small groups, complete the "Legal" Interview Worksheet.
3. After the class reconvenes, group spokespersons present group findings.

"Legal" Interview Worksheet

The employment interview is one of the most critical steps in the employment selection process. It also may be an occasion for discriminating against individual employment candidates.

The following represents questions that interviewers often ask job applicants. Identify the legality of each question by circling *L* (legal) or *I* (illegal) and briefly explain your decision.

Interview Question	Legality	Explanation
1. Could you provide us with a photo for our files?	L I	_____
2. Have you ever used another name (previous married name or alias)?	L I	_____
3. What was your maiden name?	L I	_____
4. What was your wife's maiden name?	L I	_____
5. What was your mother's maiden name?	L I	_____
6. What is your current address?	L I	_____
7. What was your previous address?	L I	_____
8. What is your social security number?	L I	_____
9. Where was your place of birth?	L I	_____
10. Where were your parents born?	L I	_____
11. What is your national origin?	L I	_____
12. Are you a naturalized citizen?	L I	_____
13. What languages do you speak?	L I	_____
14. What is your religious/church affiliation?	L I	_____
15. What is your racial classification?	L I	_____
16. How many dependents do you have?	L I	_____
17. What are the ages of your dependent children?	L I	_____
18. What is your marital status?	L I	_____
19. How old are you?	L I	_____
20. Do you have proof of your age (birth certificate or baptismal record)?	L I	_____
21. Whom do we notify in case of an emergency?	L I	_____
22. What is your height and weight?	L I	_____
23. Have you ever been arrested?	L I	_____
24. Do you own your own car?	L I	_____
25. Do you own your own house?	L I	_____
26. Do you have any charge accounts?	L I	_____
27. Have you ever had your salary garnished?	L I	_____
28. To what organizations do you belong?	L I	_____
29. Are you available to work on Saturdays and Sundays?	L I	_____
30. Do you have any form of disability?	L I	_____

10.2 The Pay Raise

OBJECTIVES

1. To further your understanding of salary administration.

2. To examine the many facets of performance criteria, performance criteria weighting, performance evaluation, and rewards.

INSTRUCTIONS

1. Working in small groups, complete the Pay Raise Worksheet.

2. After the class reconvenes, group spokespersons present group findings.

Pay Raise Worksheet

April Knepper is the new supervisor of an assembly team. It is time for her to make pay raise allocations for her subordinates. She has been budgeted $30,000 to allocate among her seven subordinates as pay raises. There have been some ugly grievances in other work teams over past allocations, so Knepper has been advised to base the allocations on objective criteria that can be quantified, weighted, and computed in numerical terms. After she makes her allocations, Knepper must be prepared to justify her decisions. All of the evaluative criteria available to Knepper are summarized as follows:

Employee	Seniority	Output Rating*	Absent Rate	Supervisory Ratings			
				Skills	Initiative	Attitude	Personal
David Bruce	15 yrs.	0.58	0.5%	Good	Poor	Poor	Nearing retirement. Wife just passed away. Having adjustment problems.
Eric Cattalini	12 yrs.	0.86	2.0	Excellent	Good	Excellent	Going to night school to finish his BA degree.
Chua Li	7 yrs.	0.80	3.5	Good	Excellent	Excellent	Legally deaf.
Marilee Miller	1 yr.	0.50	10.0	Poor	Poor	Poor	Single parent with three children.
Victor Munoz	3 yrs.	0.62	2.5	Poor	Average	Good	Has six dependents. Speaks little English.
Derek Thompson	11 yrs.	0.64	8.0	Excellent	Average	Average	Married to rich wife. Personal problems.
Sarah Vickers	8 yrs.	0.76	7.0	Good	Poor	Poor	Women's activist. Wants to create a union.

*Output rating determined by production rate less errors and quality problem.

Managing the Diverse Workforce

"e pluribus unum"

LEARNING OBJECTIVES

After studying Chapter 11, you will be able to:

LO **1** Describe how changes in the U.S. workforce make diversity a critical organizational and managerial issue. p. 384

LO **2** Distinguish between affirmative action and managing diversity. p. 394

LO **3** Explain how diversity, if well managed, can give organizations a competitive edge. p. 395

LO **4** Identify challenges associated with managing a diverse workforce. p. 398

LO **5** Define monolithic, pluralistic, and multicultural organizations. p. 400

LO **6** List steps managers and their organizations can take to cultivate diversity. p. 402

CHAPTER OUTLINE

Diversity: A Brief History

Diversity Today
    The Size of the Workforce
    The Workers of the Future
    The Age of the Workforce

Managing Diversity versus Affirmative Action
    Competitive Advantage through Diversity and Inclusion
    Challenges of Diversity and Inclusion

Multicultural Organizations

How Organizations Can Cultivate a Diverse Workforce
    Top Management's Leadership and Commitment
    Organizational Assessment
    Attracting Employees
    Training Employees
    Retaining Employees

Management Close-Up

Marriott International traces its origins to a root-beer stand opened in 1927 by J. Willard Marriott and his wife Alice in Washington, DC. Even then, the Marriotts were focused on providing hospitality. Today, Marriott International is one of the world's leading lodging companies, with 300,000 associates and nearly 3,000 properties in the United States and 67 other countries and territories. How did the Marriotts achieve such success?

Then as now, the Marriotts believed that taking care of the customer begins with taking care of their associates. As the Marriott empire grew, top managers recognized that embracing the fundamental differences in their workers would be important to building broad-based customer service tailored to all of their customers—what the company calls "culturally competent" customer service. To help associates understand and appreciate cultural differences, Marriott established the company's diversity program in 1989. Today,

{ By making diversity a central feature in the company's operations, Marriott International has set the standard—and created a competitive advantage—in the hospitality industry. As you read this chapter, consider what managers need to know to work with employees of highly diverse backgrounds. What special challenges face global diversity officer Jimmie Walton Paschall as she moves Marriott to the next level? }

three of every five Marriott associates are members of a minority group. Women make up 55 percent of the workforce.

Diversity training is mandated for all new Marriott employees. Aside from race and ethnicity, the program includes training in generational diversity. Offered monthly, the program is widely regarded and duplicated by other employers. To further support diversity in its workforce, Marriott sponsors 11 employee-resource groups. Each special-interest group has been operating for more than a decade and includes senior-executive champions who oversee the groups. The groups help the company recruit and retain associates from traditionally underrepresented population segments.

In an effort to extend Marriott's U.S.-based diversity program throughout the organization, the company created the position of global diversity officer and named Jimmie Walton Paschall to the post.[1]

In Chapter 10, we described the laws that require equal opportunity and fair treatment in the workplace. In this chapter, we discuss why a proactive approach to developing and managing a diverse workforce has become not only a legal or moral obligation, but a fundamental business requirement as well. Executives at Marriott International point to their company's exemplary record on diversity as a key element in its success. Managers who lack the ability to work with and effectively manage men and women of different colors, cultures, ages, abilities, and backgrounds will be at a significant disadvantage in their careers. And organizations that do not take the issue of managing diversity seriously will leave their organizations not only open to legal challenge but also far less able to compete effectively, at home and abroad.

In the United States, as we shall see, the number of racial and ethnic minorities is increasing at a far faster rate than the growth in the white, nonminority population, and women make up a sizable share of the workforce. American workers, customers, and markets are already highly diverse and becoming even more so every day. In addition, as we discussed in Chapter 6, businesses are increasingly global. Managers need to be much more aware of, and sensitive to, cultural differences to succeed in a world economy. We have also discussed throughout this book how vital creativity and innovation have become for organization success. These qualities are fostered in an atmosphere where different perspectives and bright people from all walks of life are celebrated. Few societies have access to the range of talents available in the United States, with its immigrant tradition and racially and ethnically diverse population. Yet getting people from widely divergent backgrounds to work together effectively is not easy. For this reason, managing diversity is one of America's biggest challenges—and opportunities.

managing diversity

Managing a culturally diverse workforce by recognizing the characteristics common to specific groups of employees while dealing with such employees as individuals and supporting, nurturing, and utilizing their differences to the organization's advantage.

Managing diversity involves, first, such basic activities as recruiting, training, promoting, and utilizing to full advantage individuals with different backgrounds, beliefs, capabilities, and cultures. But it means more than just hiring women and minorities and making sure they are treated equally and encouraged to succeed. It also means understanding and deeply valuing employee differences to build a more effective and profitable organization.

This chapter examines the meaning of diversity and the management skills and organizational processes involved in managing the diverse workforce effectively. We also explore the social and demographic changes and economic and employment shifts that are creating this changing U.S. workforce.

Diversity: A Brief History

Managing diversity is not a new management issue. From the late 1800s to the early 1900s, most of the groups that immigrated to the United States were from Italy, Poland, Ireland, and Russia. Members of those groups were considered outsiders because most did not speak English and had different customs and work styles. They struggled, often violently, to gain acceptance in industries such as steel, coal, automobile manufacturing, insurance, and finance. In the 1800s, it was considered poor business practice for white Protestant–dominated insurance companies to hire Irish, Italians, Catholics, or Jews. As late as the 1940s, and in some cases even later than that, colleges routinely discriminated against immigrants, Catholics, and Jews, establishing strict quotas that limited their number, if any were admitted at all. The employment prospects of these groups were severely diminished by this kind of discrimination, and it wasn't until the 1960s that the struggle for acceptance by the various white ethnic and religious groups had on the whole succeeded.

Women's struggle for acceptance in the workplace was in some ways even more difficult. When the Women's Rights Movement was launched in Seneca Falls in 1848, most occupations were off-limits to women, and colleges and professional schools were totally closed to them. Women could not vote and lost all property rights once they were married. In the first part of the 20th century, when women began to be accepted into professional schools, they were subject to severe quotas. There was also a widespread, persistent assumption that certain jobs were done only by men, and other jobs only by women. Even into the 1970s, less than 40 years ago, classified ad sections in newspapers listed different jobs by sex, with sections headed "Help Wanted—Males" and "Help Wanted—Females." Women who wanted a bank loan needed a male cosigner, and married women were not issued credit cards in their own name.[2] Only when the Civil Rights Act of 1964 (see Chapter 10) and other legislation began to be enforced was this kind of sex discrimi-

Many of the rights all of us take for granted today—equal opportunity, fair treatment in housing, the illegality of religious, racial, and sex discrimination—received their greatest impetus from the Civil Rights Movement.

nation gradually eliminated. As we shall see, women are still underrepresented at the most senior levels of corporate life, and major disparities in other areas, like pay, still exist. But most jobs today once considered the exclusive province of men—including front-line military units as well as the executive suite—are now open to and occupied by increasing numbers of women.

The most difficult and wrenching struggle for equality involved America's non-white minorities. Rigid racial segregation remained a fact of American life for 100 years after the end of the Civil War. Black voting rights, particularly in the South, were often viciously suppressed, and racial discrimination in education, employment, and housing throughout the United States was a harsh, daily reality. Years of difficult, courageous protest and struggle gradually began to eat away at both legal and social barriers to equality. Organizations like the NAACP, formed by a group of blacks and whites, began to use America's court system and the Constitution to bring equality to African Americans and other people of color. The unanimous *Brown v. Board of Education* Supreme Court decision in 1954 declared segregation unconstitutional, setting the stage for other legislation we discussed in the last chapter, including the Civil Rights Act of 1964. The consequences of America's bitter racial legacy are still with us; the struggle for equality is far from complete. But many of the rights all of us take for granted today—equal opportunity, fair treatment in housing, the illegality of religious, racial, and sex discrimination—received their greatest impetus from the Civil Rights Movement.

Today, nearly half of the U.S. workforce consists of women, 14 percent of U.S. workers identify themselves as Hispanic or Latino, and 11 percent are black. Two-thirds of all global migration is into the United States. One-third of all businesses in the United States are owned by women, employing about 20 percent of America's workers.[3]

The traditional American image of diversity has been one of assimilation. The United States was considered the "melting pot" of the world, a country in which ethnic and racial differences were blended into an American purée. In real life, many ethnic and most racial groups retained their identities, but they did not express them at work. Employees often abandoned most of their ethnic and cultural distinctions while at work to keep their jobs and get ahead. Many Europeans came to the United States, Americanized their names, perfected their English, and tried to enter the mainstream as quickly as possible.

Today's immigrants are willing to be part of an integrated team, but they no longer are willing to sacrifice their cultural identities to get ahead. Nor will they have to do so. Companies are recognizing that they should be more accommodating of differences, and that doing so pays off in business. Managers are also realizing that their customers have become increasingly diverse and that retaining a diversified workforce can provide a significant competitive advantage in the marketplace.

Diversity Today

LO 1

Today *diversity* refers to far more than skin color and gender. It is a broad term used to refer to all kinds of differences, as summarized in Figure 11.1. These differences include religious affiliation, age, disability status, military experience, sexual orientation, economic class, educational level, and lifestyle in addition to gender, race, ethnicity, and nationality.

Although members of different groups (white males, people born during the Depression, homosexuals, Iraq war veterans, Hispanics, Asians, women, blacks, etc.) share within their groups many common values, attitudes, and perceptions, much diversity also exists within each of these categories. Every group is made up of individuals who are unique in personality, education, and life experiences. There may be more differences among, say, three Asians from Thailand, Hong Kong, and Korea than among a white, an African American, and an Asian all born in Chicago. And not all white males share the same personal or professional goals and values or behave alike.

Thus, managing diversity may seem a contradiction within itself. It means being acutely aware of characteristics *common* to a group of employees, while also managing these employees as *individuals*. Managing diversity means not just tolerating or accommodating all sorts of differences, but supporting, nurturing, and utilizing these differences to the organization's advantage. Borders Books, for example, tries to match up the demographics of its workforce with the demographics of the communities in which its stores operate. Top managers at the company say that sales are better as a result. U.S. businesses will not have a choice of whether to have a diverse workforce; if they want to survive, they must learn to manage a diverse workforce sooner or better than their competitors do.

As Figure 11.2 shows, a sizable number of HR executives say their companies need to or plan to expand their diversity training programs. Although many companies initially instituted diversity programs to prevent discrimination, more are beginning to see such programs as a crucial way to expand their customer bases both domestically and worldwide. In fact, two out of three companies said they had broadened their diversity programs because of increasing globalization, according to a survey of 1,780 HR and training executives by the Boston-based consulting firm Novations/J. Howard and Associates. A separate survey by Korn/Ferry International showed that approximately 85 percent of European recruiters, 88 percent of recruiters in Asia, and 95 percent of recruiters in Latin America either "strongly agreed" or "somewhat agreed" that being at least bilingual is critical to succeed in today's business environment.

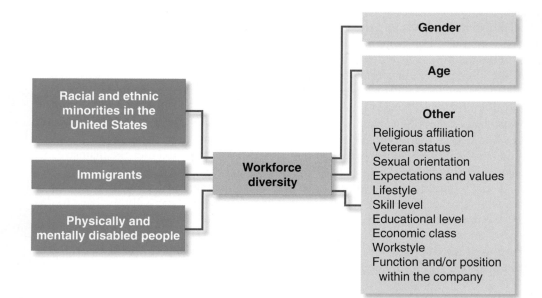

FIGURE 11.1

Components of a
Diversified Workforce

The Size of the Workforce

During most of its history, the United States experienced a surplus of workers. But that is now expected to change. Lower birthrates in the United States and other developed countries are resulting in a smaller labor force. An even more substantial slowdown in the pace of growth of the labor force is projected for the decade ending in 2016, as the baby-boom generation retires.[4]

Employers are likely to outsource some work to factories and firms in developing nations where birthrates are high and the labor supply is more plentiful. But they will have to compete for the best candidates from a relatively smaller and more diverse U.S. labor pool. Employers will need to know who these new workers are—and must be prepared to meet their needs.

> "Human diversity makes tolerance more than a virtue; it makes it a requirement for survival."
>
> —Rene Dubos

The Workers of the Future

Until recently, white American-born males dominated the U.S. workforce. Businesses catered to their needs. However, while this group still constitutes the largest percentage of workers—about 80 percent of U.S. workers are white, and more than half of them are male—its share of the labor force is declining. Although the number of white male workers is expected to continue growing, the number of women and the numbers of Asian American, black, and Hispanic workers are expected to grow faster.[5] This significant change in the workforce parallels trends in the overall U.S. population. Recently, the Census Bureau announced that, for the first time, about one in three residents of the United States is a racial or ethnic minority—a unique milestone in the nation's history. The largest and fastest-growing minority group is Hispanics, closely followed by African Americans. In several states—California, Hawaii, New Mexico, and Texas—and the District of Columbia, these minority groups plus Asians, Native Americans, and Pacific Islanders combine to make a population that is "majority minority."[6] These population trends affect not only the nature of the workforce but also the varied customers and markets managers must attract.

Gender Issues   One of the most important developments in the U.S. labor market has been the growing number of women working outside the home. Social changes during the 1960s and 1970s coupled with financial necessity caused women to enter the workforce and redefine their roles. Consider this:

Women make up about 47 percent of the workforce.

The overall labor force participation rate of women rose throughout the 1970s

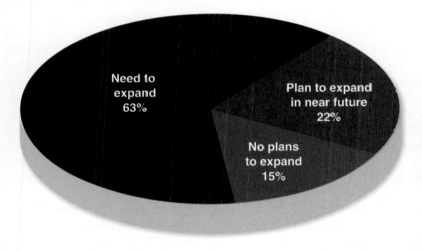

SOURCE: From *Training*, September 2004. "Time To Broaden Diversity," by Gail Johnson. Copyright © 2004 by *VNU BUS Publications* USA Reproduced with permission of VNU BUS Publications via Copyright Clearance Center.

FIGURE 11.2

The Expansion of Diversity Programs in U.S. Companies

Irene Rosenfeld has broken through the glass ceiling as CEO of Kraft Foods, overseeing the company with revenues upwards of $30 billion.

through the 1990s and is now holding steady even as the participation rate of men gradually declines. Almost 60 percent of marriages are dual-earner marriages.

One of every four married women in two-income households earns more than her husband does.[7]

For many women, as well as their spouses, balancing work life with family responsibilities and parenting presents an enormous challenge. Although men's roles in our society have been changing, women still adopt the bulk of family responsibilities, including homemaking, child care, and care of elderly parents. Yet some companies may still expect their employees, particularly at the managerial level, to put in long hours and sacrifice their personal lives for the sake of their jobs, organizations, and careers. Not only may these expectations put many women at a disadvantage in the workplace, but they also may cause companies to lose valuable talent. Companies that offer their employees the opportunity to balance work and family commitments are better able to recruit and retain women. These companies are offering family-friendly benefits such as onsite child care, in-home care for elderly family members, and flexible work schedules, and they are taking advantage of newer technologies to permit more work from home. Still, weighing employees' needs for flexibility against the organization's need for productivity entails complex decisions that take into account different job requirements, as well as each employee's contributions and motivation to meet goals under the flexible arrangement. Michele Coleman Mayes, senior vice president and general counsel of Pitney Bowes, agreed to let one attorney leave promptly at five o'clock each evening; the attorney works on her laptop at night as needed to meet her deadlines. But Mayes refused another employee's request to work part-time because the person in that position needed to be available each day to handle requests for other departments. Mayes tells her employees that scheduling decisions "may not always be equal, but I will try to be fair."[8]

The desire for flexible scheduling is often cited as a reason significant pay disparities still exist between men and women. The average full-time working woman earns about 80 percent as much as men in the same job (recall the discussion in Chapter 10 about equal pay and comparable worth). However, the gap has shrunk most years since the 1970s; women's earnings were just 63 percent of men's in 1979. Still, a recent study found that the gap between the earnings of college-educated men and women actually increased after they spent 10 years in the workforce. Some of the difference is explained by women tending to choose lower-paid occupations, work fewer hours, and devote time to bearing and raising children. But even when the researchers controlled for these and other known variables, one-quarter of the pay gap remained unexplained. One of the researchers, Catherine Hill, speculated, "Part of the wage difference . . . is employers' assumptions of what people's choices will be. . . . Employers assume that young women are going to leave the workforce when they have children, and, therefore, don't promote them."[9]

Another concern involving female workers is the low representation of women in top jobs. As women—along with minorities—move up the corporate ladder, they encounter a "glass ceiling." The *glass ceiling* is an invisible barrier that makes it difficult for women and minorities to move beyond a certain level in the corporate hierarchy.

For example, just 12 women are chief executives of *Fortune* 500 companies—that's 12 out of 500. Looking at all corporate officers of those companies, 16 percent are women, and less than 2 percent are minority women.[10] Still, one positive trend is that women's leadership is beginning to be seen at a broader range of companies. Besides Andrea Jung at the helm of Avon and Irene Rosenfeld at Kraft Foods, the executive ranks now include the likes of Pat Woertz at Archer Daniels Midland and Ursula Burns at Xerox. Table 11.1. lists top women executives and the companies for which they work.

> The percentage of female CEOs is expected to increase, but only slightly, reaching about 6 percent of *Fortune* 1000 CEOs by 2016.[11]

TABLE 11.1   The A-List: Top Women Executives

Rank	Name	Company	Title
1	Indra Nooyi	PepsiCo	Chairman and CEO
2	Irene Rosenfeld	Kraft Foods	CEO
3	Pat Woertz	Archer Daniels Midland	President and CEO
4	Anne Mulcahy	Xerox	Chairman
5	Angela Braly	Wellpoint	President and CEO
6	Andrea Jung	Avon Products	Chairman and CEO
7	Susan Arnold	Procter & Gamble	Vice Chair, Beauty and Health
8	Oprah Winfrey	Harpo	Chairman
9	Brenda Barnes	Sara Lee	Chairman and CEO
10	Ursula Burns	Xerox	CEO
11	Ann Livermore	Hewlett-Packard	Exec. VP, Technology Solutions Group
12	Anne Sweeney	Disney Media Networks	Co-Chair, and President, Disney–ABC Television Group
13	Susan Desmond-Hellmann	Genentech	President, Product Development
14	Ginni Rometty	IBM	Sr. VP, Global Business Services
15	Ellen Kullman	DuPont	Exec. VP, Safety and Protection, Coating and Color
16	Safra Catz	Oracle	President
17	Heidi Miller	J. P. Morgan Chase	CEO, Treasury and Securities Services
18	Judy McGrath	Viacom	Chairman and CEO, MTV Networks
19	Carol Meyrowitz	TJX	President and CEO
20	Ann Moore	Time Inc.	Chairman and CEO
21	Christina Gold	Western Union	President and CEO
22	Amy Brinkley	Bank of America	Chief Risk Officer
23	Susan Ivey	R. J. Reynolds Tobacco	Chairman and CEO
24	Colleen Goggins	Johnson & Johnson	Worldwide Chairman, Consumer and Personal Care Group
25	Susan Chambers	Walmart	Exec. VP

Some companies are helping women break through the glass ceiling. Accenture sponsors monthly networking events for its female employees and offers flexible schedules and part-time arrangements. Such efforts may be behind the results of a survey of managers in which 79 percent of female respondents said they could envision themselves holding a senior management post, compared with only 66 percent feeling that way at the start of their career.[12] Table 11.2 shows the best companies for women executives according to the National Association of Female Executives.

As women have gained more presence and power in the workforce, some have drawn attention to the problem of **sexual harassment,** which is unwelcome sexual conduct that is a term or condition of employment. Sexual harassment falls into two different categories. The first, *quid pro quo harassment*, occurs when "submission to or rejection of sexual conduct is used as a basis for employment decisions." The second type of harassment, *hostile environment*, occurs when unwelcome sexual conduct "has the purpose or effect of unreasonably interfering with job performance or creating an intimidating, hostile, or offensive working environment." Behaviors that can cause a hostile work environment include persistent or pervasive displays of pornography, lewd or suggestive remarks, or demeaning taunts or jokes. Both categories of harassment violate Title VII of the Civil Rights Act of 1964, regardless of the sex of the harasser and the victim; in a recent year, more than 15 percent of complaints filed with the federal government came from males. If an employee files a complaint of sexual harassment with the Equal Employment Opportunity Commission (EEOC), the commission may investigate and, if it finds evidence for the complaint, may request mediation, seek a settlement, or file a lawsuit with the potential for stiff fines—and negative publicity that may damage the company's ability to recruit the best employees in the future.

Harassment by creation of a hostile work environment is now more typical than quid pro quo harassment. But because it may involve more subjective standards of behavior, it puts an extra burden on managers to maintain an appropriate work environment by ensuring that all employees know what conduct is and is not appropriate and that there are serious consequences for this behavior. In fact, even when managers do not themselves engage in harassment, if they fail to prevent it or to take

sexual harassment

Conduct of a sexual nature that has negative consequences for employment.

TABLE 11.2
Top 30 Companies for Executive Women

Aetna, Hartford, CT	Marriott International, Washington, DC
Allstate Insurance, Northbrook, IL	Merck & Co., Whitehouse Station, NJ
American Electric Power (AEP), Columbus, OH	MetLife, New York, NY
American Express, New York, NY	New York Times Co., New York, NY
Bristol-Myers Squibb, New York, NY	Office Depot, Delray Beach, FL
Chubb & Son, Warren, NJ	Patagonia, Ventura, CA
Colgate-Palmolive, New York, NY	Pfizer, New York, NY
Federated Department Stores, Cincinnati, OH	Principal Financial Group, Des Moines, IA
Gannett Co., McLean, VA	Procter & Gamble, Cincinnati, OH
Gap Inc., San Francisco, CA	Prudential Financial, Newark, NJ
General Mills, Minneapolis, MN	Rodale, Emmaus, PA
Hewlett-Packard, Palo Alto, CA	Sallie Mae, Reston, VA
IBM Corporation, Armonk, NY	Texas Instruments, Dallas, TX
Kraft Foods, Northfield, IL	Walmart Stores, Bentonville, AR
Liz Claiborne Inc., North Bergen, NJ	Xerox Corporation, Stamford, CT

SOURCE: Re printed courtesy of NAFE (www.nafe.com) and Inkstoneditorial (www.inkstoneditorial.com).

appropriate action after receiving legitimate complaints about it, they may still be held liable, along with their companies, if a lawsuit is filed. It is also important for managers to know that the "hostile work environment" standard applies to same-sex harassment, as well as to non-gender-related cases, such as a pattern of racial or ethnic slurs. Teenaged workers are a particularly vulnerable population, because they are inexperienced, tend to hold lower-status jobs, and often feel hesitant or embarrassed to speak up. The federal EEOC has made this concern a priority and launched a teen-focused page called "Youth at Work" on its Web site (at http://www.youth.eeoc.gov). The National Restaurant Association and National Retail Federation also have stepped up efforts to protect teens from harassment.[13]

One way managers can help their companies prevent harassment from arising, or avoid punitive damages if a lawsuit is filed, is to make sure their organizations have an effective and comprehensive policy on harassment in place. Table 11.3 shows the basic components of such a policy. Companies such as Avon, Corning, and Metro-Goldwyn-Mayer have found that a strong commitment to diversity leads to fewer problems with sexual harassment.[14]

Before moving on, it is important to note that gender issues and the changing nature of work do not apply just to women. In some ways, the changing status of women has given men the opportunity to redefine their roles, expectations, and lifestyles. Some men are deciding that there is more to life than corporate success and are choosing to scale back work hours and commitments to spend time with their families. Worker values are shifting toward personal time, quality of life, self-fulfillment, and family. Workers today, both men and women, are looking to achieve a balance between career and family.

Minorities and Immigrants   In addition to gender issues, the importance and scope of diversity are evident in the growth of racial minorities and immigrants in the workforce. Consider these facts:

Black, Asian, and Hispanic workers hold more than one of every four jobs in the United States.
Asian and Hispanic workforces are growing the fastest in the United States, followed by the African American workforce.

1. Develop a comprehensive organizationwide policy on sexual harassment and present it to all current and new employees. Stress that sexual harassment will not be tolerated under any circumstances. Emphasis is best achieved when the policy is publicized and supported by top management.
2. Hold training sessions with supervisors to explain Title VII requirements, their role in providing an environment free of sexual harassment, and proper investigative procedures when charges occur.
3. Establish a formal complaint procedure in which employees can discuss problems without fear of retaliation. The complaint procedure should spell out how charges will be investigated and resolved.
4. Act immediately when employees complain of sexual harassment. Communicate widely that investigations will be conducted objectively and with appreciation for the sensitivity of the issue.
5. When an investigation supports employee charges, discipline the offender at once. For extremely serious offenses, discipline should include penalties up to and including discharge. Discipline should be applied consistently across similar cases and among managers and hourly employees alike.
6. Follow up on all cases to ensure a satisfactory resolution of the problem.

TABLE 11.3
Basic Components of an Effective Sexual Harassment Policy

SOURCE: From George Bohlander, Scott Snell, and Arthur Sherman, *Managing Human Resources*, 12th ed. Copyright © 2001. Reprinted by permission of South-Western, a division of Thomson Learning, www.thomsonrights.com. Fax 800 732-2215.

Three in 10 college enrollees are people of color.

By 2020, most of California's entry-level workers will be Hispanic.

English has become the second language for much of the population in California, Texas, and Florida.

Foreign-born workers make up more than 15 percent of the U.S. civilian labor force. About half of these workers are Hispanic, and 22 percent are Asian.

The younger Americans are, the more likely they are to be persons of color.

One in 40 people in the United States identifies himself or herself as multiracial, and the number could soar to 1 in 5 by 2050.[15]

These numbers indicate that the term *minority*, as it is used typically, may soon become outdated. Particularly in urban areas where white males do not predominate, managing diversity means more than eliminating discrimination; it means capitalizing on the wide variety of skills available in the labor market. Organizations that do not take full advantage of the skills and capabilities of minorities and immigrants are severely limiting their potential talent pool and their ability to understand and capture minority markets. Those markets are growing rapidly. As the minority share of the population expands, so does their share of purchasing power. And if you sell to businesses, you are likely to deal with some minority-owned companies, because the number of businesses started by Asian American, African American, and Hispanic entrepreneurs is growing much faster than the overall growth in new companies in the United States. For example, more than half of the companies that started in California's high-tech Silicon Valley were founded by immigrants, and in a recent year, one-fourth of patent applications in the United States identified an immigrant as the inventor or a co-inventor.[16]

In many urban areas with large Asian, Hispanic, or African American populations, banks have deliberately increased the diversity of their managers and tellers to reflect the population mix in the community and attract additional business. If they did not, customers would readily notice and switch to other banks in the area where they would feel more welcome and comfortable. Such diversity—and collaboration among employees—permits increased customer service, helping banks maintain their competitiveness. For example, tellers approached by new immigrants who do not yet speak English immediately call on their bilingual colleagues for help. The bilingual colleagues are also in a better position to assist the bank customers with special problems, such as income transfers from abroad.

Even so, the evidence shows some troubling disparities in employment and earnings. Unemployment rates are higher for black and Hispanic workers than for whites—twice as high in the case of black men. Earnings of black and Hispanic workers have consistently trailed those of white workers; recent figures put the median earnings for African American employees at 77 percent of median earnings for white workers and the median earnings of Hispanics at just 70 percent. African Americans and Hispanic Americans are also underrepresented in management and professional occupations.[17] This underrepresentation may itself help perpetuate the problem, as it can leave many aspiring young minorities with fewer role models or mentors that are so helpful in an executive career.

This disparity may exist even for similar jobs. There is also considerable evidence that discrimination may account for at least some of the disparities in employment and earnings. For example, in one recent study fictitious résumés were used to respond to help-wanted ads in Boston and Chicago newspapers. Each résumé used either African American names like Lakisha and Jamal or white-sounding names like Emily and Greg. The résumés with white-sounding names were 50 percent more likely to get a callback for an interview than the same résumés with African American names. Despite equivalence in credentials, the often unconscious assumptions about different racial groups are very difficult to overcome.[18]

Nevertheless, significant progress has been made. As you can see from the examples in Table 11.4, talented members of minority groups are among the executives running companies and their divisions in a wide variety of industries. And some individuals and groups are highly successful. Average pay and unemployment rates for Asian Americans actually exceed those for white workers.

In addition, virtually every large organization today has policies and programs dedicated to increasing minority representation—including compensation systems that reward managers for increasing the diversity of their operations. Major companies such as FedEx, Xerox, Morgan Stanley Shell, and Sun Microsystems have corporate diversity officers who assist organization managers in their efforts to attract, retain, and promote minority and women executives. Many organizations are also working to ensure a continuing supply of minority candidates by supporting minority internships and MBA programs. Dun and Bradstreet, for example, sponsors summer internship programs for minority MBA students. Lockheed Martin has partnered with the American Management Association's Operation Enterprise to establish two-week paid summer internship programs for high school and college students. These internship programs

TABLE 11.4   Executives of Color: Selected Examples

Name	Company	Title
Alvin Aviles	New York City Health and Hospitals Corp.	President and CEO
Harvey Brownlee	KFC	Chief Operating Officer
Mei-Mei Chan	Seattle Times Co.	Vice President, Advertising
Kenneth I. Chenault	American Express	Chairman and CEO
Karen Clark	Horizon NJ Health	President and Chief Operating Officer
Richard Cordova	Children's Hospital Los Angeles	President and CEO
Lorenzo Creighton	MGM Mirage	President and Chief Operating Officer, New York–New York Hotel & Casino
Digby A. Solomon Diez	Daily Press, Newport News, VA	President, Publisher, and CEO
Ann Fudge	Young & Rubicam Brands	Chairwoman and CEO
Darryl B. Hazel	Ford Motor Co.	Senior Vice President, Ford; President, Customer Service
Douglas V. Holloway	NBC Universal	President, Cable Investments
Margaret Jenkins	Denny's	Chief Marketing Officer
Cleve Killingsworth	Blue Cross and Blue Shield of Massachusetts	President and CEO
William Lamar Jr.	McDonald's USA	Chief Marketing Officer
David Lopez	Harris County Hospital District	President and CEO
Sam Odle	Methodist Hospital and Indiana University Hospital	President and CEO
Clarence Otis Jr.	Darden Restaurants	Chairman and CEO
Carol Terakawa	Yahoo!	Regional Vice President–Southwest
Don Thompson	McDonald's USA	Executive Vice President and Chief Operating Officer
John Thompson	Symantec	Chairman and CEO
Ronald Williams	Aetna	President and CEO

SOURCE: Sonia Alleyne, "The 40 Best Companies for Diversity," *Black Enterprise,* July 2006, downloaded from Business & Company Resource Center, http://galenet. galegroup.com; Nicole Voges, "Diversity in the Executive Suite," *Modern Healthcare,* April 10, 2006, http://galenet.galegroup.com; and National Association of Minority Media Executives. "Board of Directors," NAMME Web site, http://www.namme.org. accessed May 21, 2007.

In a recent magazine ranking based on companies' representation of African Americans in four key areas—procurement, corporate board, senior management, and total workforce—Denny's stood out as making the most improvement following their discrimination lawsuits several years back.

help students and organizations learn about one another and, ideally, turn into full-time employment opportunities. Table 11.5 shows the top 10 companies for diversity according to DiversityInc.com. For all these companies, developing, hiring, and retaining minority executives is critical for their ability to manage an ever-more-diverse workforce and to serve an increasing number of clients and customers with varied backgrounds.

Mentally and Physically Disabled People   The largest unemployed minority population in the United States is people with disabilities. It is composed of people of all ethnic backgrounds, cultures, and ages. The share of the population with a disability is growing as the average worker gets older and heavier.[19] According to the U.S. Census Bureau, 18 percent of the population reports having some degree of disability, and 6 percent of the working-age population say they have a disability that makes it hard for them to get and keep a job.[20] Still, more than half of people with a disability held jobs during the year in which they were surveyed. And among those who are unemployed, many would like to find work.

The Americans with Disabilities Act (ADA), mentioned in Chapter 10, defines a disability as a physical or mental impairment that substantially limits one or more major life activities. Examples of such physical or mental impairments include those resulting from conditions such as orthopedic, visual, speech, and hearing impairments; cerebral palsy; epilepsy; multiple sclerosis; HIV infections; cancer; heart disease; diabetes; mental retardation; psychological illness; specific learning disabilities; drug addiction; and alcoholism.[21]

New assistive technologies are making it easier for companies to comply with the ADA and for those with disabilities to be productive on the job. In many cases, state governments will pay for special equipment or other accommodations that workers need. Companies are discovering that making these accommodations can result in unanticipated fringe benefits, too. The National Industries for the Blind (NIB), a Wisconsin company that markets products under the Skilcraft brand name, is a case in point. Seventy-five percent of NIB employees are visually impaired. Because the company's warehouse pickers have trouble reading instructions on paper, NIB installed a voice technology system that conveys instructions to workers through headsets. An added benefit is that the technology has raised the productivity of the entire operation. Accuracy has improved, and workers—both blind and sighted—are able to pick and ship orders faster using the headsets.

For most businesses, mentally and physically disabled people represent an unexplored but fruitful labor market. Frequently, employers have found that disabled employees are more dependable than other employees, miss fewer days of work, and exhibit lower turnover. Tax credits are also available to companies who hire disabled workers. In addition, managers who hire and support employees with disabilities are signaling to other employees and outside stakeholders their strong interest in creating an inclusive organization culture.

TABLE 11.5
Top 10 Companies for Diversity Recruitment and Retention

1. Bank of America	7. Xerox
2. Pepsi Bottling Group	8. Consolidated Edison Company of New York
3. AT&T	
4. Coca-Cola Company	9. J. P. Morgan Chase
5. Ford Motor Company	10. PepsiCo
6. Verizon Communications	

SOURCE: "The 2007 DiversityInc Top 50 Companies for Diversity," Copyright © 2007, DiversityInc.com. Reproduced with permission.

Education Levels   When the United States was primarily an industrial economy, many jobs required physical strength, stamina, and skill in a trade, rather than college and professional degrees. In today's service and technology economy, more positions require a college education, and even a graduate or professional degree. Today's prospective employees have responded by applying to college in record numbers. The proportion of the workforce with at least some college education has been growing steadily since the 1970s. The share of workers with a bachelor's degree has more than doubled since 1970. At the same time, the share of workers with less than a high school diploma has tumbled from nearly 4 out of 10 in 1970 to below 1 out of 10 today. People with degrees in science and technology are in especially high demand. Employers often expand their search for scientists and computer professionals overseas, but visa requirements limit that supply. At the other end of the spectrum, in the current labor pool, 28 percent of foreign-born workers have not completed high school.[22]

The Age of the Workforce

The baby-boom generation (those born between 1946 and 1964) is aging. Today, almost 4 out of 10 workers are age 45 or older, and the median age of America's workforce is rising as the number of older workers swells, while the number of young workers grows only slightly. Industries such as nursing and manufacturing are already facing a tremendous loss of expertise as a result of downsizing and a rapidly aging workforce. Other industries will soon be in similar straits.[23] As a result of these trends, the Bureau of Labor Statistics projects that entry-level workers will be in short supply.

On the plus side, almost 70 percent of workers between the ages of 45 and 74 told researchers with AARP (formerly the America Association of Retired Persons) that they intend to work in retirement. Retirees often return to the workforce at the behest of their employers, who can't afford to lose the knowledge accumulated by longtime

> For every young worker entering the workforce, two baby boomers are retiring.[24]

employees, their willingness to work nontraditional shifts, and their reliable work habits, which have a positive effect on the entire work group.

To prevent an exodus of talent, employers need strategies to help retain and attract skilled and knowledgeable older workers. Phased retirement plans that allow older employees to work fewer hours per week is one such strategy. Almost one-third of retiring faculty members at 16 University of North Carolina campuses take advantage of phased retirement, and the concept is catching on in many other public and private organizations. Other strategies include making workplace adaptations to help older workers cope with the physical problems they experience as they age, such as poorer vision, hearing, and mobility. This trend is a significant change from the practice in recent decades, when older workers were given incentives to leave to allow companies to reduce overhead and perhaps hire less-expensive replacements. Table 11.6 shows how creative companies are rethinking their retirement policies and solving their skilled-labor shortage by finding ways to attract and retain people over 55. These companies save on turnover and training costs and capitalize on the experience of their older employees.

At the same time, companies need to compete hard for the smaller pool of young talent, being prepared for applicants who know the job market and are ready to demand the working conditions they value and the praise they were raised to expect. Bruce Tulgan, founder of Rainmaker Thinking, which specializes in researching generational differences, says Generation Y—today's young workers—tend to be "high-maintenance" but also "high-performing," having learned to process the flood of information that pours in over the Internet.[25] Many of these workers were raised by highly involved parents who filled their lives with "quality" experiences, so employers are scrambling to design work arrangements that are stimulating, involve teamwork, keep work hours reasonable to allow for outside activities, and provide for plenty of positive feedback. Employers are also updating their recruiting tactics to reach young

TABLE 11.6

Top Five Approaches for More Fully Utilizing Older Employees

Approaches to More Fully Utilizing Older Employees	Approaches Considered Very or Moderately Effective	Businesses That Have Implemented the Approach
Benefit packages targeted toward older employees	68%	18%
Part-time work arrangements with continuation of benefits	64	30
Educating managers about ways to utilize older employees	60	25
Increased availability of part-time work for older employees (regardless of benefits)	55	36
Skill training for older employees	55	44

SOURCE: From "American Business and Older Employees: A Survey of Findings," Copyright © 2002 AARP. (WWW.AARP.ORG). Reprinted with permission via Copyright Clearance Center.

workers where they are—online. Intermedia, which operates computer centers to host large-scale Web and e-mail software for small companies, says the social networking site LinkedIn helps the company reach well-qualified information technology workers. In the government sector, the Central Intelligence Agency and National Security Agency have set up pages on Facebook, where members who register for access can read information about job openings.[26]

Today's companies are learning the value of both young and older workers—and finding new ways to encourage them to collaborate. Pooling the knowledge of experienced workers with the energy and fresh ideas of younger workers can create a powerful workforce. Carolyn Martin of Rainmaker Thinking Inc. encourages her clients to develop mentoring programs so that important company and industry knowledge is passed from older to younger employees. "[Older workers] are walking out the door with a gold mine of experience, product knowledge, and historical perspective, and we're letting them go," she said at a recent economic conference. "Knowledge as power is out. Knowledge shared is in. Everyone, no matter what their age, is a teacher and a learner."

Martin even suggests that employers seek to hire older workers who can teach younger ones. Typically, she says, members of the baby boom generation—who are now beginning to retire—go on to start second careers anyway. "Proactively recruit 50-plus people," she advises. "The older worker is cool. There are not enough Gen-X and -Y to replace them all."[27]

Managing Diversity versus Affirmative Action

LO 2

affirmative action

Special efforts to recruit and hire qualified members of groups that have been discriminated against in the past.

For many organizations, the original impetus to diversify their workforces was social responsibility and legal necessity (recall Chapters 5 and 10). To correct the past exclusion of women and minorities, companies introduced **affirmative action**—special efforts to recruit and hire qualified members of groups that have been discriminated against in the past. The intent is not to prefer these group members to the exclusion of others, but to correct for the long history of discriminatory practices and exclusion. Viewed from this perspective, amending these wrongs is seen as the moral, ethical, and legal approach.

In Portland, Oregon, about one-fifth of the city's population consists of various ethnic minorities, but only 12 percent of new construction employees are minorities. To ensure that opportunities in this industry will be more available to minorities, the city government, Portland Development Commission, Port of Portland, and regional and state transportation departments have in the past few years established affirmative action programs to increase minority group members' participation in public contracts. In the private sector, a recent agreement among the development commission, developers, and unions established a goal that 35 percent of the workforce engaged in projects along the Willamette River in Portland would be minorities and women.[28]

Such efforts, along with legal remedies to end discrimination, have had a powerful impact, transforming our society and organizations in positive ways that would have been unimaginable only a few decades ago. Today the immigrant nature of American society is virtually taken for granted—even seen as a source of pride. And women, African Americans, Hispanics, and other minorities routinely occupy positions that in years past would have been totally closed to them.

Nevertheless, as we have seen, a legislated approach tends to result in fragmented efforts that have not yet fully achieved the integrative goals of diversity. Employment discrimination still persists, and even after decades of government legislation, equal employment opportunity (EEO) and affirmative action laws have not adequately improved the upward mobility of women and minorities. To move beyond correcting past wrongs to truly inclusive organizations requires a change in organization culture—one in which diversity is seen as contributing directly to the attainment of organization goals.

Do you think that the election of our first African-American President will have an impact on affirmative action programs and the management of diversity in companies throughout the country?

Seen in this way, affirmative action and diversity are complementary, not the same. In contrast to EEO and affirmative action programs, managing diversity means moving beyond legislated mandates to embrace a proactive business philosophy that sees differences as a positive value. In the end, *all* employees are different. These differences may include the fundamental attributes of race, ethnicity, age, and gender we have been discussing, but they also may include less obvious attributes such as employees' place of origin, their education, or their life experience. All these elements add to the richness of talents and perspectives managers can draw on. Managing diversity in this broader sense involves organizations making changes in their systems, structures, and practices to eliminate barriers that may keep people from reaching their full potential. It means treating people as individuals—*equally*, but not necessarily the *same*—recognizing that each employee has different needs and will need different things to succeed. But it also asks managers to recognize and value the uniqueness of each employee and to see the different ideas and perspectives each brings to the organization as a source of competitive advantage. In short, managing diversity is not just about getting more minorities and women into the organization. It is about creating an environment in which employees from *every* background listen to each other and work better together so that the organization as a whole will become more effective. This emphasis on coming together to benefit the whole has led many companies to now refer to diversity and *inclusion* as their objective.

Competitive Advantage through Diversity and Inclusion

Today many organizations are approaching diversity and inclusion from a more practical, business-oriented perspective. Increasingly, diversity can be a powerful tool for building competitive advantage. A study by the Department of Labor's Glass Ceiling Institute showed that the stock performance of firms that were high performers on diversity-related goals was over twice as high as that of other firms. Another recent study found that companies with the highest percentage of women among senior

Women are almost as likely as men to take jobs in science, engineering, and technology but are far more likely to quit, primarily because they feel isolated, lack mentors, find the work culture hostile, and are pressured to work long or rigid hours.[30]

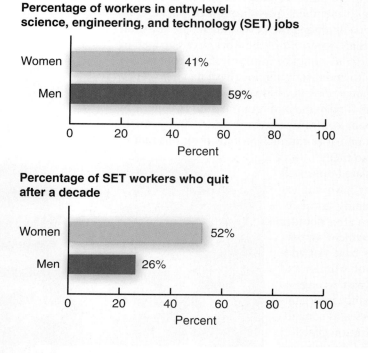

Percentage of workers in entry-level science, engineering, and technology (SET) jobs

Women — 41%
Men — 59%

Percentage of SET workers who quit after a decade

Women — 52%
Men — 26%

managers had a significantly higher return to shareholders than companies with the lowest percentage. Conversely, announcements of damage awards from discrimination lawsuits frequently have had a negative effect on stock returns.[29]

There are many advantages—and some obvious challenges—to managing a diverse workforce. We discuss some of them in this section.

Ability to Attract and Retain Motivated Employees For companies facing changing demographics and business needs, diversity makes good sense. Companies with a reputation for providing opportunities for diverse employees will have a competitive advantage in the labor market and will be sought out by the most qualified employees. In addition, when employees believe their differences are not merely tolerated but valued, they may become more loyal, productive, and committed.

Better Perspective on a Differentiated Market Companies such as Avon, Prudential, Eastman Kodak, and Toys "R" Us are committed to diversity because as the composition of the American workforce changes, so does the customer base of these companies. Just as women and minorities may prefer to work for an employer that values diversity, they may prefer to patronize such organizations.

Many Asian Americans, African Americans, Hispanic Americans, and women have entered the middle class and now control consumer dollars. Similarly, each new generation has its own set of values and experiences, so diversity in ages can help the organization relate to more age groups of customers. As described in the "From the Pages of *BusinessWeek*" feature, a diverse workforce can provide a company with greater knowledge of the preferences and consuming habits of this diversified marketplace. This knowledge can assist companies in designing products and developing marketing campaigns to meet those consumers' needs. In addition, for at least some goods and services, a multicultural sales force may help an organization sell to diverse groups. A diverse workforce also can give a company a competitive edge in a global economy by facilitating understanding of other customs, cultures, and marketplace needs.

☆ **The bottom line**

Service

Diversity can help the organization succeed in new markets.

FROM THE PAGES OF

BusinessWeek

A "McKinsey of Pop Culture"?

Several months into his new job as vice president of U.S. marketing and advertising for General Motors, Mike Jackson came to the conclusion that the automaker was just not cool enough. Young, urban trendsetters on the East and West Coasts were not paying attention to GM's cars. The message being sent to consumers, Jackson says, was all wrong. "We worried far too much about the sheet metal, color, etc.," he explains. "What we really needed to worry about was connecting emotionally with our consumers." So Jackson picked up the phone and called Steve Stoute.

More executives overseeing brands that have gone stale are turning to the 36-year-old consultant and former music executive for help. Stoute's agency, Translation Consultation & Brand Imaging, offers to imbue brands with a combination of hip-hop ethos and practicality to help reposition products, from Chevy Impalas to Crest Whitestrips to Reese's peanut butter cups. The end result is for brands to resonate with a younger, more trendy audience. His message: companies have not embraced the changes in the culture to be able to talk to a new generation of consumers.

As an African American with strong relationships to hip-hop artists (Jay-Z is a good friend and business partner), Stoute knows how easy it is to pigeonhole Translation as a black ad agency. He immodestly characterizes his firm as "a McKinsey of pop culture." By that he means that Translation is called upon by companies facing strategic challenges. "These are companies who know they have to take advantage of global trends, but at the same time are afraid of jeopardizing core businesses," says Stoute. "We show them how to walk that thin line. It often comes down to showing them the language and tonality needed to reach consumers."

But Stoute also says he's helping executives understand a phenomenon that he refers to as the "tanning of America." It's a generation of black, Latino, and white consumers who have the same "mental complexion," he says, based on "shared experiences and values." Rap and hip-hop, starting in the late 1980s when white suburban kids began snapping up music by mostly inner-city artists, provided the first glimpse into this shift.

To connect McDonald's to this world, Stoute helped create its "I'm lovin' it" ad campaign featuring pop star Justin Timberlake. That was relatively easy. To top executives, it was all about coming up with a new ad. Stoute has encouraged them to go much further and told them they could be blowing a big opportunity for reaching young adults. They have a million-plus young people working for them who come to the job every day ashamed of what they are wearing. "The uniforms are ugly," says Stoute. "If the workers were actually proud of what they were wearing, it could be a huge opportunity to promote the brand." Stoute suggested McDonald's hire top designers to redo the uniforms under urban-centric brands such as Sean John, Rocawear, FUBU, American Apparel, and Tommy Hilfiger. The chain is considering the move.

Stoute's most important test will be changing perceptions about GM. The assignment is to help the carmaker increase awareness for its models among a growing and influential buyer group, 18- to 34-year-olds who live in clustered metro areas on the coasts and along the perimeter of the southern United States. The task is to get them to think about GM the way they were already thinking about Toyota and other Japanese models. The mandate, says Stoute, was "to think of ways to spark contagious consumer behavior."

So far, Translation has helped GM redeploy Tiger Woods from the Buick brand to what Stoute believes is a more convincing role, as a spokesman for all of GM. "Tiger and GM share similar values of integrity and, most importantly, diversity," he says. Stoute also connected GM with Jay-Z on Jay-Z Blue, a branded, lavender-tinted, electric blue that will be available on the GMC Yukon. Translation is also creating a campaign for the reissue of the Camaro, the iconic 1970s muscle car. Stoute is talking with the advertising agencies responsible for all GM models about marketing alternatives, such as social media, that go beyond traditional TV and print outlets.

It's still too early to tell if GM is reaching new consumers. Unsurprisingly Stoute believes the results so far are positive. Look no further, he says, than the January 2007 debut of Jay-Z Blue. From Detroit to Beijing, the news was featured on the front pages of 26 national and international Sunday papers.

SOURCE: Excerpted from Tom Lowry, "A McKinsey of Pop Culture?" *BusinessWeek*, March 26, 2007. © 2007 Time Inc. All rights reserved.

The bottom line

Innovation

Diversity can bring new ideas to the organization.

Ability to Leverage Creativity and Innovation in Problem Solving   Work team diversity promotes creativity and innovation, because people from different backgrounds hold different perspectives on issues. Diverse groups have a broader base of experience from which to approach a problem; when effectively managed, they invent more options and create more solutions than homogeneous groups do. In addition, diverse work groups are freer to deviate from traditional approaches and practices. The presence of diversity also can help minimize "groupthink" (recall Chapter 3).[31]

Many law firms now routinely have diverse legal teams working together on a case. Fresh "out of the box" ideas are often required in complex cases, and a group of lawyers from the same background who all think the same way may not be able to be as innovative as a team that is more diverse. In addition, in jury trials, the impression that a legal team makes on a jury can help or badly hurt the client, and diverse jurors are more likely to be receptive to a visibly diverse team, with different kinds of lawyers participating. The increased importance of legal-team diversity has caused some law firms to form alliances with minority firms, so they can collaborate on cases.

The bottom line

SPEED

A diverse workforce can lead to greater responsiveness.

Enhancement of Organizational Flexibility   A diverse workforce can enhance organizational flexibility, because managing diversity successfully requires a corporate culture that tolerates many different styles and approaches. Less restrictive policies and procedures and less standardized operating methods enable organizations to become more flexible and thus better able to respond quickly to environmental changes (recall Chapters 2 and 9). Executives at Aetna, Denny's, and FedEx are so convinced of the competitive potential of a diverse workforce that they tie a portion of management compensation to success in recruiting and promoting minorities and women.[32]

Challenges of Diversity and Inclusion

LO 4

We have discussed the laws guaranteeing equal opportunity and the significant and growing business advantages of diversity and inclusion. Yet every year thousands of lawsuits are filed over issues of discrimination and fair treatment, some involving even the largest and most respected firms.[33] Even when there is no overt discrimination in hiring and pay, managing diversity can be difficult. Often minorities and women who have been hired find themselves in an organization culture or environment that does not give them the opportunity to do their best work. And managers with all the goodwill in the world find it harder than they expected to get people from different backgrounds to work together for a common goal.[34]

To become effective managers of the diverse organization, we first have to identify and overcome a number of challenges. These include unexamined assumptions, lower cohesiveness, communication problems, mistrust and tension, and stereotyping.

Unexamined Assumptions   For most of us, seeing the world from someone else's perspective is difficult, because our own assumptions and viewpoints seem so normal and familiar. For example, heterosexuals may not even think about whether to put a picture of their loved ones on their desks; it is a routine, even automatic decision, repeated in a million workplaces across the country. But for gay employees in many companies, displaying such a picture may cause considerable anxiety—if they feel able to consider it at all. Other unexamined assumptions involve the roles of men and women; for example, many people assume that women will shoulder the burden of caring for children, even if it conflicts with the demands of work. In a recent study, researchers sent employers résumés that were identical except that some bore a male name and others a female name, and half implied that the person submitting the résumé was a parent. Employers were less likely to invite the fictional candidate for an interview when the résumé

> "Among CEOs of *Fortune* 500 companies, 58 percent are six feet or taller . . . Most of us, in ways we are not entirely aware of, automatically associate leadership with imposing physical stature."
>
> —Malcolm Gladwell

implied the candidate was a parent—but only if the name was female.[35] Because the résumés were otherwise identical, the results suggest that people make assumptions about mothers that do not apply to fathers or to childless women.

In an organization that is oblivious to these different perspectives and does not take an active role in making people from diverse backgrounds feel welcome and valued, managers may find it more difficult to develop an enthusiastically shared sense of purpose.

Lower Cohesiveness   Diversity can create a lack of cohesiveness. *Cohesiveness* refers to how tightly knit the group is and the degree to which group members perceive, interpret, and act on their environment in similar or mutually agreed-upon ways. Because of their lack of similarity in language, culture, and/or experience, diverse groups typically are less cohesive than homogeneous groups. Often mistrust, miscommunication, stress, and attitudinal differences reduce cohesiveness, which in turn can diminish productivity. This may be one explanation for the results of a study that showed greater turnover among store employees who feel they are greatly outnumbered by coworkers from other racial or ethnic groups.[36] In a diverse group, managers are challenged to take the lead in building cohesiveness by establishing common goals and values. Group cohesiveness will be discussed in greater detail in Chapter 14.

Communication Problems   Perhaps the most common negative effect of diversity is communication problems. These difficulties include misunderstandings, inaccuracies, inefficiencies, and slowness. Speed is lost when not all group members are fluent in the same language or when additional time is required to explain things. Sometimes diversity may decrease communication, as when white male managers feel less comfortable giving feedback to women or minorities, for fear of how criticism may be received. The result may be employees who do not have a clear idea of what they need to do to improve their performance.

Diversity can also lead to errors and misunderstandings. Group members may assume they interpret things similarly when they in fact do not, or they may disagree because of their different frames of reference.[37] For example, if managers do not actively encourage and accept the expression of different points of view, some employees may be afraid to speak up at meetings, leaving the manager with a false impression that consensus has been reached. We discuss other problems in communication and how to avoid them in Chapter 15.

Mistrust and Tension   People prefer to associate with others who are like themselves. This is a normal, understandable tendency. But it can often lead to misunderstanding, mistrust, and even fear of those who are different, because of a lack of contact and low familiarity. For example, if women and minority-group members are routinely excluded, as they sometimes are, from joining white male colleagues at business lunches or after-hour gatherings, they may come to feel isolated from their colleagues. Similarly, tension often develops between people of different ages—for example, what one generation might see as a tasteless tattoo may be a creative example of body art for a member of a different generation. Such misunderstandings can cause stress, tension, and even resentment, making it more difficult to reach agreement on solutions to problems.

Stereotyping   We learn to see the world in a certain way on the basis of our backgrounds and experiences. Our interests, values, and cultures act as filters and distort, block, and select what we see and hear. We see and hear what we expect to see and hear. Group members often inappropriately stereotype their "different" colleagues rather than accurately perceiving and evaluating those individuals' contributions, capabilities, aspirations, and motivations. Such stereotypes are usually negative or condescending. Women may be stereotyped as not dedicated to their careers, older workers as unwilling to learn new skills, minority-group members as less educated or capable. But even so-called positive stereotypes can be burdensome. For example, the common stereotype that Asians are good at math may well leave unrecognized other attributes that a particular Asian employee might have. Many women and minorities even dislike being stereotyped as members of groups that need special help or support, very much preferring to be treated as individuals.

Stereotypes may cost the organization dearly by stifling employees' ambition so that they don't fully contribute. Research supports the idea that people perform better when they expect that they can. In a study where undergraduate students were purportedly "pretesting" a new graduate admissions test, half the subjects were told that males had greater ability in the test's subject matter. Although all subjects were told they received the same score, the females exposed to the biased message rated their abilities in the subject lower than the males who heard the message, and they set lower goals for their future performance in that area. In another study, playing off the stereotypes that males and Asians excel at math, Asian American women were given a math test after they answered a set of questions either about their Asian identity or about their gender. When asked about their ethnic background, they performed better; when asked about gender, they performed worse.[38] In a corporate setting, managers want their employees to perform to their full ability; stereotypes that dampen individual employees' ambition and performance also detract from the organization's success.

Unless managers are aware of their stereotypes, either their own or those held by others, the stereotypes can directly affect how people in their organizations are treated. Employees stereotyped as unmotivated or emotional will be given less-stress-provoking (and perhaps less important) jobs than their coworkers. Those job assignments will create frustrated employees, perhaps resulting in lower commitment, higher turnover, and underused skills.[39]

The Challenge Ahead   For all these reasons, and more, managing diversity is not easy. U.S. organizations are not isolated from the continuing effects of America's racial legacy or the remaining barriers to equal opportunity. Nor are managers immune to the biases, stereotypes, lack of experience, and tensions that make communication, teamwork, and leadership in a diverse workforce much more challenging. Yet managers very much need to confront these issues. They need to develop the skills and strategies diversity requires if they and their organizations are to succeed in our increasingly multicultural business environment. We address some of the ways they might do that in the remainder of the chapter.

Multicultural Organizations

To capitalize on the benefits and minimize the costs of a diverse workforce, perhaps one of the first things managers need to do is examine their organization's prevailing assumptions about people and cultures. Table 11.7 shows some of the fundamental assumptions that may exist. Based on these assumptions, we can classify organizations as one of three types and describe their implications for managers.

Some organizations are **monolithic.** This type of organization has very little *cultural integration;* in other words, it employs few women, minorities, or any other groups that differ from the majority. For example, in its hiring, an organization might favor alumni of the same college, perhaps even more specifically targeting members of fraternities who are enthusiastic about the school's football team. Such an organization is highly homogeneous in terms of its employee population. In monolithic organizations, if groups other than the norm are employed, they are found primarily in low-status jobs. Minority group members must adopt the norms of the majority to survive. This fact, coupled with small numbers, keeps conflicts among groups low. Discrimination and prejudice typically prevail, informal integration is almost nonexistent, and minority group members do not identify strongly with the company.

monolithic organization

An organization that has a low degree of structural integration—employing few women, minorities, or other groups that differ from the majority—and thus has a highly homogeneous employee population.

TABLE 11.7   Diversity Assumptions and Their Implications for Management

Common and Misleading Assumptions		Less Common and More Appropriate Assumptions	
Homogeneity	*Melting pot myth:* We are all the same.	**Heterogeneity**	*Image of cultural pluralism:* We are not all the same; groups within society differ across cultures.
Similarity	*Similarity myth:* "They" are all just like me.	**Similarity and difference**	*They are not just like me:* Many people differ from me culturally. Most people exhibit both cultural similarities and differences when compared with me.
Parochialism	*Only-one-way myth:* Our way is the only way. We do not recognize any other way of living or working.	**Equifinality**	*Our way is not the only way:* There are many culturally distinct ways of reaching the same goal, of working, and of living one's life.
Ethnocentrism	*One-best-way myth:* Our way is the best way. All other approaches are inferior versions of our way.	**Culture contingency**	*Our way is one possible way:* There are many different and equally good ways to reach the same goal. The best way depends on the culture of the people involved.

SOURCE: From "Diversity Assumptions and Their Implications for Management" by Nancy J. Adler, *Handbook of Organization*, 1996. Reprinted courtesy of Marcel Dekker Inc., New York.

Most large U.S. organizations made the transition from monolithic to *pluralistic* organizations in the 1960s and 1970s because of changing demographics as well as societal forces such as the civil rights and women's movements. **Pluralistic organizations** have a more diverse employee population and take steps to involve persons from different gender, racial, or cultural backgrounds. These organizations use an affirmative action approach to managing diversity: they actively try to hire and train a diverse workforce and to ensure against any discrimination against minority group members. They typically have much more integration than do monolithic organizations, but like monolithic organizations, they often have minority group members clustered at certain levels or in particular functions within the organization.

Because of greater cultural integration, affirmative action programs, and training programs, the pluralistic organization has some acceptance of minority group members into the informal network, much less discrimination, and less prejudice. Improved employment opportunities create greater identification with the organization among minority group members. Often the resentment of majority group members, coupled with the increased number of women and minorities, creates more conflict than exists in the monolithic organization.

The pluralistic organization fails to address the cultural aspects of integration. In contrast, in **multicultural organizations** diversity not only exists but is valued. These organizations fully integrate gender, racial, and minority group members both formally and informally. But managers in such organizations do not focus primarily on the visible differences between employees, like race or sex. Rather, managers value and draw on the different *experience* and *knowledge* employees bring to the organization and help it achieve agreed-upon strategies and goals.[40] The multicultural organization is marked by an absence of prejudice and discrimination and by low levels of intergroup conflict. Such an organization creates a *synergistic* environment in which all members contribute to their maximum potential and the advantages of diversity can be fully realized.[41] As you read the "Management Close-Up: Taking Action" feature, consider whether Marriott International offers the qualities of a multicultural or a pluralistic organization.

pluralistic organization

An organization that has a relatively diverse employee population and makes an effort to involve employees from different gender, racial, or cultural backgrounds.

multicultural organization

An organization that values cultural diversity and seeks to utilize and encourage it.

Management Close-Up | TAKING ACTION

When Jimmie Paschall became senior vice president of external affairs and global diversity officer of Marriott International in 2008, it was actually her second stint at the company. Paschall got her start in a Marriott gift shop, working part-time while attending classes at Howard University in Washington, DC. After graduation, Paschall parlayed her gift-shop job into a full-time position, working her way up the ranks eventually to become director of human resources for Marriott's lodging division. She left the company in 1999 to pursue another career opportunity but was enticed to return to Marriott nine years later.

As global diversity officer, Paschall works to broaden the company's diversity efforts among its 300,000 associates, as well as its property owners, franchisees, suppliers, and customers. Her activities include building a system to capture the best practices in diversity and to identify how to generate and manage diversity in Marriott's global operations. Paschall also has a role in the Marriott Foundation for People with Disabilities and its national program "Bridges . . . from school to work," which provides access to job opportunities for people with disabilities.

As mentioned, diversity at Marriott extends beyond recruiting and retaining a multifaceted workforce. Several years ago, the company established its Diversity Ownership Initiative, which is aimed to help guide minority business owners through the process of hotel ownership. Marriott set itself the goal of having in five years 500 Marriott properties owned or operated by women or minorities. To date, more than 400 of its properties are woman or minority owned or in development.

Marriott also pledged to spend at least $1 billion with diverse suppliers by 2010, and within four years it had exceeded its goal by nearly double. In addition, the company recently expanded its definition of diversity to include businesses in the lesbian, gay, bisexual, and transgender communities.[42]

- Global diversity officer Jimmie Paschall said that as a college student working in a Marriott hotel gift shop she received good advice from a colleague: If you can obtain many different experiences in the hotel business, you'll become skilled at seeing an issue from many sides. How do you think the ability to see an issue from several perspectives would be an asset to Paschall in her current role?
- The text discusses both the challenges and the advantages of managing diversity. What special challenges and advantages might managers at Marriott face in the lodging industry? Do you think Marriott is a true multicultural organization? Why or why not?

How Organizations Can Cultivate a Diverse Workforce

LO 6

An organization's plans for becoming multicultural and making the most of its diverse workforce should include (1) securing top management's leadership and commitment, (2) assessing the organization's progress toward goals, (3) attracting employees, (4) training employees in diversity, and (5) retaining employees. A recent study examining the performance of hundreds of companies over a 30-year period found that organizations that assigned responsibility for achieving diversity targets to certain individuals or groups made the most progress in increasing the share of female and black workers on their payrolls. Moderate change occurred in companies that set up programs for mentoring and networking, but formal diversity training programs had little effect unless the organizations also use the other methods.[43] Thus, cultivating diversity needs to be a well-planned, organizationwide effort in which each element is supported by the personal commitment of individual managers, who address this issue as seriously as they do other management challenges. These managers actively seek to develop the skills, understanding, and practices that enable people of every background to do their best work in the common pursuit of the organization's goals.

The National Basketball Association (NBA) is one organization that has cultivated diversity throughout its history; in fact, it currently has the highest percentage of minority vice presidents and league office managers in the history of men's sports. Fifteen percent of NBA team vice presidents and 34 percent of the professionals who work in the league office are minorities. The NBA also has 12 African American head coaches, the highest number in pro sports. NBA spokesperson Brian McIntyre reports that this is business as usual for the organization. He says that NBA commissioner David Stern "has long felt that a diverse workplace is the only workplace."[44]

Top Management's Leadership and Commitment

Obtaining top management's leadership and commitment is critical for diversity programs to succeed. Otherwise, the rest of the organization will not take the effort seriously. One way to communicate this commitment to all employees—as well as to the external environment—is to incorporate the organization's attitudes toward diversity into the corporate mission statement and into strategic plans and objectives. Managerial compensation can be linked directly to accomplishing diversity goals. Adequate funding must be allocated to the diversity effort to ensure its success. Also, top management can set an example for other organization members by participating in diversity programs and making participation mandatory for all managers.

Joe Dumars is one of the high percentage of minority NBA presidents.

As we mentioned earlier, some organizations have established corporate offices or committees to coordinate the companywide diversity effort and provide feedback to top management. Honeywell hired a "director of workforce diversity," and Avon, a "director of multicultural planning and design." Other companies prefer to incorporate diversity management into the function of director of affirmative action or EEO.

The work of managing diversity cannot be done by top management or diversity directors alone. Many companies rely on minority advisory groups or task forces to monitor organizational policies, practices, and attitudes; assess their impact on the diverse groups within the organization; and provide feedback and suggestions to top management.

For example, at Equitable Life Assurance Society, employee groups meet regularly with the CEO to discuss issues pertaining to women, African Americans, and Hispanics and make recommendations for improvement. At Honeywell, disabled employees formed a council to discuss their needs.

"Diversity: The art of thinking independently together."
—Malcolm Forbes

They proposed and accepted an accessibility program that went beyond federal regulations for accommodations of disabilities.

As you can see, progressive companies are moving from asking managers what they think minority employees need and toward asking the employees themselves what they need.

Organizational Assessment

The next step in managing diversity is to establish an ongoing assessment of the organization's workforce, culture, policies, and practices in areas such as recruitment, promotions, benefits, and compensation. As part of this assessment, managers may evaluate whether they are attracting their share of diverse candidates from the labor pool and whether the needs of their customers are being addressed by the current composition of their workforce. The objective is to identify areas where there are problems or opportunities and to make recommendations where changes are needed. At Aetna, one measure is the percentage of employees who are multilingual; one way the company builds this number is by offering noontime language lessons for interested employees.[45]

Many women and Asians can be at a disadvantage when aggressiveness is a valued part of an organization's culture. Analysis might reveal that this value exists and that it excludes employees who do not share it from full participation. Managers can then decide that the organizational values need to be changed so that other styles of interacting are equally acceptable. Managers can also change their own behaviors to reflect this change—for example, by calling on all individuals in a meeting for their ideas instead of letting more assertive participants dominate. Corporate values and norms should be identified and critically evaluated regarding their necessity and their impact on the diverse workforce.

Attracting Employees

Companies can attract a diverse, qualified workforce by using effective recruiting practices, accommodating employees' work and family needs, and offering alternative work arrangements.

Recruitment   A company's image can be a strong recruiting tool. Companies with reputations for hiring and promoting all types of people have a competitive advantage. Xerox gives prospective minority employees reprints of an article that rates the company as one of the best places for African Americans to work. Hewlett-Packard ensures that its female candidates are familiar with its high rating by *Working Woman* magazine. Many employers are implementing policies to attract more women, ensure that women's talents are used to full advantage, and avoid losing their most capable female employees.

Diversity is built into the origins of the Philadelphia law firm of Caesar Rivise. The firm's founder was Abraham Caesar, an attorney specializing in intellectual property (for example, patents and trademarks). Back in 1926, Caesar could not land a job at one of the local law firms because he was Jewish. Instead, he founded his own firm, joined the next year by partner Charles Rivise. Together, the two attorneys built their practice and wrote important reference books on patents, establishing their reputation as experts in the field.

Given Caesar's early experiences, it's not surprising that his law firm committed itself to diversity in hiring. Stanley Cohen, now a partner, noticed that when he joined the firm in the 1960s. Back then, he recalls, his secretary was an African American man. Another Caesar Rivise employee since the 1960s is Bernice Mims. Although Mims graduated at the top of her South Philadelphia High School class, jobs were offered to other students and not Mims because she was black and the employer stipulated "no Jews or Negroes." However, Caesar hired her as a law clerk, and she remained loyal to the firm, eventually working her way up to manager of human resources.

Today Caesar Rivise builds on its historical commitment to diversity in recruiting by sponsoring diversity fellowships at Drexel University's Earle Mack School of Law. The firm assists qualified minority law students with tuition and offers them work experience. Partnering with Drexel is a good strategic fit for the firm, because the university emphasizes technology and science, backgrounds that are important for working with corporate clients on technical matters. Cohen, for example, has a chemical engineering degree from Drexel.[46]

Many minorities, disabled persons, and economically disadvantaged people are physically isolated from job opportunities. Companies can bring information about job opportunities to the source of labor, or they can transport the labor to the jobs. Polycast Technology in Stamford, Connecticut, contracts with a private van company to transport workers from the Bronx in New York City to jobs in Stamford. Days Inn recruits homeless workers in Atlanta and houses them in a motel within walking distance of their jobs. Burger King has done a lot to recruit and hire immigrants in its fast-food restaurants.

Accommodating Work and Family Needs   More job seekers are putting family needs first. Corporate work and family policies are now one of the most important recruiting tools.

Employers that have adopted onsite child care report decreased turnover and absenteeism and improved morale. In addition to providing child care, many companies now assist with care for elderly dependents, offer time off to care for sick family members, provide parental leaves of absence, and offer a variety of benefits that can be tailored to individual family needs. Some companies are accommodating the needs and concerns of dual-career couples by limiting relocation requirements or providing job search assistance to relocated spouses.

Alternative Work Arrangements   Another way managers accommodate diversity is to offer flexible work schedules and arrangements. Stiff demand for engineering talent is motivating manufacturing companies to accommodate the needs of employees with family responsibilities. Autodesk, which sells design software, sees flexible scheduling as a way to attract and keep female employees. At Freescale Semiconductor, the focus is on meeting performance targets, not on working a set schedule. Section manager Amy Oesch says this approach has enabled her to juggle family responsibilities while moving up to positions of greater authority and earning a graduate degree.[47]

Other creative work arrangements include compressed workweeks (e.g., four 10-hour days) and job sharing, in which two part-time workers share one full-time job. Another option to accommodate working mothers and disabled employees is teleworking (working from home) or telecommuting (working from home via computer hookup to the main work site). This option has been slow to catch on, but the organizations that have tried it report favorable results.

Training Employees

As you learned in Chapter 10, employees can be developed in a variety of ways. Traditionally, most management training was based on the unstated assumption that "managing" means managing a homogeneous, often white-male, full-time workforce. But gender, race, culture, age, educational, and other differences create an additional layer of complexity.[48] Diversity training programs attempt to identify and reduce hidden biases and develop the skills needed to manage a diversified workforce effectively.

The majority of U.S. organizations sponsor some sort of diversity training. Typically, diversity training has two components: awareness building and skill building.

Awareness Building   *Awareness building* is designed to increase awareness of the meaning and importance of valuing diversity.[49] Its aim is not to teach specific skills but to sensitize employees to the assumptions they make about others and the way those assumptions affect their behaviors, decisions, and judgment. For example, male managers who have never reported to a female manager may feel awkward the first time they are required to do so. Awareness building can reveal this concern in advance and help the managers address it.

To build awareness, trainers teach people to become familiar with myths, stereotypes, and cultural differences as well as the organizational barriers that inhibit the full contributions of all employees. They develop a better understanding of corporate culture, requirements for success, and career choices that affect opportunities for advancement.

In most companies, the "rules" for success are ambiguous, unwritten, and perhaps inconsistent with written policy. A common problem for women, minorities, immigrants, and young employees is that they are unaware of many of the unofficial rules that are obvious to people in the mainstream. For example, organizations often have informal networks and power structures that may not be apparent or readily available to women and minority-group members. As a result, these employees are less likely to know where to go when they need to get something approved or when they want to build support and alliances. For managers, valuing diversity means teaching the unwritten "rules" or cultural values to those who need to know them and changing the rules when necessary to benefit employees and hence the organization. It also requires inviting "outsiders" in and giving them access to information and meaningful relationships with people in power.

Skill Building   Diversity training that merely identifies problems without giving participants the tools they need to be able to act on what they have learned may leave participants feeling that the training was not useful or worthwhile. For this reason, many organizations include skill building as part of a diversity program. *Skill building* is designed to allow all employees and managers to develop the skills they need to deal effectively with one another and with customers in a diverse environment. Most of the skills taught are interpersonal, such as active listening, coaching, and giving feedback. Ideally, the skills taught are based on the organizational assessment, so the training can be tailored to the specific business issues managers have identified. For example, if too many women and minorities believe they are not getting enough helpful feedback, the skills-building program can be designed to address that issue. Likewise, training in flexible scheduling can help managers meet the company's needs while accommodating and valuing workers who want to be able to set aside time to advance their education, participate in community projects, or look after elderly parents. Tying the training to specific, measurable business goals increases its usefulness and also allows managers to assess whether it is working.

The Transportation Security Administration (TSA) recently provided a combination of awareness training and skill building to prepare its airport security personnel to screen Muslim travelers without violating their civil rights. The TSA employees were taught that the religious customs of Islam include the hajj, an annual pilgrimage to Saudi Arabia. As a result, once a year air travelers include many groups of these pilgrims. The employees learned to recognize that, especially at the time of the hajj, women in head scarves traveling with men in beards may well be devoutly religious Muslims who were engaging in a deeply personal religious journey. Besides teaching about the customs and practices of Islam, the training prepared TSA employees to perform their jobs without discriminating; for example, they learned how to effectively screen passengers who were wearing head coverings and what to do if passengers were transporting holy water.[50]

Experiential exercises and videotapes, DVDs, and software often are used in the training programs to help expose stereotypes and encourage employees to discuss fears, biases, and problems. Again, the best exercises are related to the actual problems employees are likely to encounter in the workplace. For example, employees in a hospital diversity-training program may practice how to handle a white patient who asks to be treated only by a white doctor or a male patient who only wants to be treated

TABLE 11.8
Guidelines for Diversity
Training

1. **Position training in your broad diversity strategy.** Training is one important element of managing diversity, but or its own it will probably fail. Culture change means altering underlying assumptions and systems that guide organizational behavior. Training programs must be internally consistent with, and complement, other initiatives focused on culture change.

2. **Do a thorough needs analysis.** Do not start training prematurely. As with any training program, eagerness to "do something" may backfire unless you have assessed what specific aspects of diversity need attention first. Focus groups help identify what employees view as priority issues.

3. **Distinguish between education and training.** Education helps build awareness and understanding but does not teach usable skills. Training involves activities that enhance skills in areas such as coaching, conducting performance appraisals, and adapting communications styles. Education and training are both important but they're not the same.

4. **Use a participative design process.** Tap a multitude of parties to ensure that the content and tone of the program are suitable to everyone involved. Outsider consultants often provide fresh perspectives, and have credibility. Insiders have specific company knowledge, sensitivity to local issues, and long-standing relationships with company members. Balance these various sources.

5. **Test the training thoroughly before rollout.** Given the sensitivity, even volatility, of diversity issues, use diversity councils and advocacy groups to pilot the programs. Build in ample feedback time to allow these groups to address sensitive concerns, and refine the training.

6. **Incorporate diversity programs into the core training curriculum.** One-time programs do not have a lasting impact. Blend the program's content into other training programs such as performance appraisal, coaching, and so on.

by a male doctor. Training ABC, Advanced Training Source, and American Training Resources are among the companies that offer such products. Table 11.8 provides a set of guidelines for designing effective diversity training.

Retaining Employees

As replacing qualified and experienced workers becomes more difficult and costly, retaining good workers will become much more important. Nationwide, turnover rates have been rising, with companies needing to replace more than 1 percent of their workers every month—and far more in the retailing and services industries. A number of policies and strategies, like the following, can be used to increase retention of all employees, especially those who are "different" from the norm.[51]

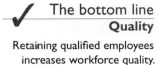
The bottom line
Quality
Retaining qualified employees increases workforce quality.

Support Groups   Companies can help form minority networks and other support groups to promote information exchange and social support. Support groups, sometimes called affinity groups, provide emotional and career support for members who traditionally have not been included in the majority's informal groups. They also can help diverse employees understand work norms and the corporate culture.

At Apple headquarters in Cupertino, California, support groups include a Jewish cultural group, a gay/lesbian group, an African American group, and a technical women's group. Avon encourages employees to organize into African American, Hispanic, and Asian networks by granting them official recognition and assigning a senior manager to provide advice. These groups help new employees adjust and provide direct feedback to management on problems that concern the groups.

Darden Restaurants' president and chief operating officer Drew Madsen (left) and chief executive officer Clarence Otis are shown in Darden's offices in Orlando, Florida. Improvement at Darden's Red Lobster, combined with continuing strong momentum from its Italian chain, Olive Garden, and the steady growth of its Smoky Bones barbecue chain, could lead Darden to its strongest stock performance in years. The company has 1,400 restaurants, making it the world's biggest casual dining operator.

Darden Restaurants started support groups, known as employee networks, at its Orlando, Florida, headquarters. Today there are five such groups: the Family Network, aimed at providing support to employees with families; Women's Network; Asian American Network; African American Network; and Hispanic Network. Each network sponsors social activities for the whole company, provides educational activities, and works with executives to develop mentoring relationships and share insights about groups served by Darden's various restaurant chains, including Red Lobster and Olive Garden.

Darden's employee networks are not meant only to help employees; they also must contribute to business goals. Each network prepared a three-year business plan that details how the network expects to support Darden's growth. For instance, the Family Network sponsored a Take Your Child to Work Day at which children participated in focus groups that generated insights into children's menus. The Hispanic Network hosts events and an intranet where all employees, Hispanic and otherwise, can learn about Hispanic culture and develop ideas for better targeting that part of their clientele.

About 40 percent of Darden's headquarters employees belong to at least one of the networks, which are open to any interested employee. Based on the success of the groups in Orlando, the company is rolling out network membership to its restaurant employees. Darden also trains its managers in diversity issues, such as how to motivate a work group with a wide age range. Given that its restaurants employ both high-schoolers and semi-retired elders, managers need this opportunity to examine their assumptions about age groups and figure out how to cross the generational divide.[52]

Mentoring   Many people have been puzzled at the apparent inability of women and minorities to move up beyond a certain point on the corporate ladder (the glass ceiling). To help these groups enter the informal network that provides exposure to top management and access to information about organizational politics, many companies have implemented formal mentoring programs. **Mentors** are higher-level managers who help ensure that high-potential people are introduced to top management and socialized into the norms and values of the organization.

Aflac's efforts to develop a diverse workforce include programs aimed at retaining employees by offering them opportunities for development and advancement. The insurance company's mentoring program aims to prepare agents from minority groups to move up into management ranks. This program is part of a culture that demonstrates respect for all employees in a variety of ways, including forums where employees can share information about their ethnic customs. Abbott Laboratories

mentors

Higher-level managers who help ensure that high-potential people are introduced to top management and socialized into the norms and values of the organization.

operates a mentoring program where employees can find mentors online. Employees interested in having or being a mentor submit profiles about themselves, and software suggests possible matches based on their experiences, skills, and interests. The advantage of the online relationships is that employees aren't limited by their geographic location or their likelihood of meeting in the course of their daily work.[53]

Career Development and Promotions   Because they are hitting a glass ceiling, many of the most talented women and minority group members are leaving their organizations in search of better opportunities elsewhere. In response, companies such as Deloitte & Touche and Honeywell have established teams to evaluate the career progress of women, minorities, and employees with disabilities and to devise ways to move them up through the ranks. One extremely important step is to make sure deserving employees get a chance at line positions. Women in particular are often relegated to staff positions, like Human Resources, with less opportunity to demonstrate they can earn money for their employers. Career development programs that give a wide range of employees exposure and experience in line jobs can make senior management positions more available to them.

Systems Accommodation   Managers can support diversity by recognizing cultural and religious holidays, differing modes of dress, and dietary restrictions, as well as accommodating the needs of individuals with disabilities. One important disabling condition is AIDS. Under the ADA, organizations must accommodate employees with AIDS as they would persons with any other disability, permitting and even encouraging them to continue working for as long as they are able and, if warranted, allowing flexible scheduling. Also, accommodations for disability may become increasingly important in the future, as the median age of the workforce continues to rise. In addition, the rise in the *weight* of the average U.S. worker may raise disability concerns. Not only are the familiar health consequences such as heart disease, joint problems, and diabetes associated with increased weight, but one study found that obese workers (with a body mass index of 40 or more) had many more workplace injury claims and absences related to injuries.[54] This pattern suggests that managers of the future will be even more concerned than in the past with keeping their workers of all sizes on the job by maintaining safe workplaces and offering benefits that encourage healthy lifestyles (possibly through company-sponsored fitness programs).

Accountability   As we noted at the beginning of this section, one of the most effective ways to ensure that diversity efforts succeed is to hold managers accountable for hiring and developing a diverse workforce. Organizations must ensure that their performance appraisal and reward systems reinforce the importance of effective diversity management. At PepsiCo, each executive reporting to the CEO is assigned responsibility for employee development of a different group—for example, the company's women or Latinos or gay and lesbian employees. The executive responsible for that group must identify leadership talent, learn group members' concerns, identify areas where support is needed, and identify plans for addressing these issues.[55]

For decades, U.S. corporations were striving to integrate their workforces because of regulatory and social responsibility pressures. Today globalization, changing demographics, and the expansion of ethnic markets at home have made managing a diverse workforce a bottom-line issue. Managers at companies like Marriott realize that to remain competitive in the coming years, they will have to make managing diversity a strategic priority to attract, develop, keep, and apply the knowledge of their top talent.

Management Close-Up

ASSESSING OUTCOMES AND SEIZING OPPORTUNITIES

Jimmie Paschall's boss, Marriott CEO J. W. "Bill" Marriott, is a powerful champion for diversity, and he declares that companies must lead by example. In 2003, the company established its Committee for Excellence, a board consisting of external directors and Marriott senior leadership. The body, the first of its kind in the hospitality industry, is responsible for identifying the goals and objectives of Marriott's diversity efforts and regularly measuring the company's progress.

At Marriott, executives' compensation is tied to the success of their diversity efforts. For employees who report directly to Bill Marriott, an individual's performance on this dimension accounts for 13 percent of his or her annual bonus. Bill Marriott also chairs the company's internal diversity council, which meets quarterly.

With Marriott's emphasis on diversity, more than 50 languages are spoken among its workforce. Because English fluency is important to meet U.S. customer needs, in 2007 Marriott introduced "Sed de Saber," an English-language program for Spanish-speaking associates. As the program's popularity grew, Marriott expanded Sed de Saber—in English, the name means

"thirst for knowledge"—to offer Spanish instruction for English-speaking associates.

Marriott offers an additional resource, Global Language Learning, to encourage associates to build their language fluency. Using Rosetta Stone language-learning software, Marriott associates can learn up to 30 languages.

Marriott International has won recognition for its diversity programs from well-known publications and organizations *Black Enterprise* magazine, *DiversityInc., Fortune, Latina Style, Working Mother,* and others. For the ninth consecutive year, *Fortune* named Marriott the Most Admired company in the hospitality industry for its work on behalf of women and minorities.[56]

- Marriott CEO Bill Marriott has said the company's approach to diversity is more than a goal: it's their business. Do you think he is right about Marriott's diversity strategy? If so, how can Jimmie Paschall safeguard her company's leading position?
- Bill Marriott has also said the company's associates are its greatest asset. The company spends a great deal of time training and developing its employees' skills. What else could Jimmie Paschall do to ensure that Marriott's associates understand the important role they play in the company's success?

KEY TERMS

Affirmative action,   p. 394

Managing diversity,   p. 382

Mentors,   p. 408

Monolithic organization,   p. 400

Multicultural organization,   p. 401

Pluralistic organization,   p. 401

Sexual harassment,   p. 388

SUMMARY OF LEARNING OBJECTIVES

Now that you have studied Chapter 11, you should be able to:

LO 1   Describe how changes in the U.S. workforce make diversity a critical organizational and managerial issue.

The labor force is getting older and more racially and ethnically diverse, with a higher proportion of women. And while the absolute number of workers is increasing, the growth in jobs is outpacing the numerical growth of workers. In addition, the jobs that are being created frequently require higher skills than the typical worker can provide; thus, we are seeing a growing skills gap. To be competitive, organizations can no longer take the traditional approach of depending on white males to form the core of the workforce. Today, managers must look broadly to make use of talent wherever it can be found. As the labor market changes, organizations that can recruit, develop, motivate, and retain a diverse workforce will have a competitive advantage.

LO 2   Distinguish between affirmative action and managing diversity.

Affirmative action is designed to correct past exclusion of women and minorities from U.S. organizations. But despite the accomplishments of affirmative action, it has not eliminated barriers that prevent individuals from reaching their full potential. Managing diversity goes beyond hiring people who are different from the norm and seeks to support, nurture, and use employee differences to the organization's advantage.

LO 3   Explain how diversity, if well managed, can give organizations a competitive edge.

Managing diversity is a bottom-line issue. If managers are effective at managing diversity, they will have an easier time attracting, retaining, and motivating the best employees. They will be more effective at marketing to diverse consumer groups in the United States and globally. They will have a workforce that is more creative, more innovative, and better able to solve problems. In addition, they are likely to increase the flexibility and responsiveness of the organization to environmental change.

 Identify challenges associated with managing a diverse workforce.

The challenges for managers created by a diverse workforce include decreased group cohesiveness, communication problems, mistrust and tension, and stereotyping. These challenges can be turned into advantages by means of training and effective management.

LO 5   Define monolithic, pluralistic, and multicultural organizations.

These categories are based on the organization's prevailing assumptions about people and cultures. Monolithic organizations have a low degree of structural integration, so their population is homogeneous. Pluralistic organizations have a relatively diverse employee population and try to involve various types of employees (e.g., engaging in affirmative action and avoiding discrimination). Multicultural organizations not only have diversity but value it, and they fully integrate men and women of various racial and ethnic groups, as well as people with different types of expertise. Conflict is greatest in a pluralistic organization.

LO 6   List steps managers and their organizations can take to cultivate diversity.

To be successful, organizational efforts to manage diversity must have top management support and commitment. Organizations should first undertake a thorough assessment of their cultures, policies, and practices, as well as the demographics of their labor pools and customer bases. Only after this diagnosis has been completed is a company in position to initiate programs designed to attract, develop, motivate, and retain a diverse workforce.

DISCUSSION QUESTIONS

1. What opportunities do you see as a result of changes in our nation's workforce?

2. Is prejudice declining in our society? In our organizations? Why or why not?

3. What distinctions can you make between affirmative action and managing diversity?

4. How can managers overcome obstacles to diversity such as mistrust and tension, stereotyping, and communication problems?

5. How can organizations meet the special needs of different groups (e.g., work and family issues) without appearing to show favoritism to those particular sets of employees?

6. How can diversity give a company a competitive edge? Can diversity really make a difference in the bottom line? How?

CONCLUDING CASE

The New Frontier for Fresh Foods Supermarkets

Fresh Foods Supermarkets is a grocery store chain that was established in the Southeast 20 years ago. The company is now beginning to expand to other regions of the United States. First, the firm opened new stores along the eastern seaboard, gradually working its way up through Maryland and Washington, DC, then through New York and New Jersey, and on into Connecticut and Massachusetts. It has yet to reach the northern New England states, but executives have decided to turn their attention to the Southwest, particularly because of the growth of population there.

Vivian Noble, the manager of one of the chain's most successful stores in the Atlanta area, has been asked to relocate to Phoenix, Arizona, to open and run a new Fresh Foods Supermarket. She has decided to accept the job, but she knows it will be a challenge. As an African American woman, she has faced some prejudice during her career, but she refuses to be stopped by a glass ceiling or any other barrier. She understands that she will be living and working in an area where several cultures combine and collide, and she will be hiring and managing a diverse workforce. Noble has the support of top management at Fresh Foods, which wants the store to reflect the surrounding community—in both staff makeup and product selection. So she will be looking to hire employees with Hispanic and Native American roots, as well as older workers who can relate to the many retired residents in the area. And she will be seeking their input on the selection of certain food products, including popular ethnic brands, so that customers know they can buy what they need and want at Fresh Foods.

In addition, Noble wants to make sure that Fresh Foods provides services above and beyond those of a standard supermarket to attract local consumers. For instance, she wants the store to offer free delivery of groceries to homebound customers who are either senior citizens or physically disabled. She wants to be sure that the store has enough bilingual employees to translate for and otherwise assist customers who speak little or no English. Noble believes that she is a pioneer of sorts, guiding Fresh Food Supermarkets into a new frontier. "The sky is almost always blue here," she says of her new home state. "And there's no glass ceiling between me and the sky."

QUESTIONS

1. What steps can Vivian Noble take to recruit and develop her new workforce?

2. What other ways can Noble help her company reach out to the community?

3. How will Fresh Foods Supermarkets as a whole benefit from successfully moving into this new region of the country?

EXPERIENTIAL EXERCISES

11.1 Being Different

OBJECTIVES

1. To increase your awareness of the feeling of "being different."

2. To better understand the context of "being different."

INSTRUCTIONS

1. Working alone, complete the Being Different Worksheet.

2. In small groups, compare worksheets, and prepare answers to the discussion questions.

3. When the class reconvenes, group spokespersons present group findings.

DISCUSSION QUESTIONS

1. Were there students who experienced being different in situations that surprised you?

2. How would you define "being different"?

3. How can this exercise be used to good advantage?

Being Different Worksheet

Think back to a recent situation in which you experienced "being different," and answer the following questions:

1. Describe the situation in which you experienced "being different."

   _____

   _____

2. Explain how you felt.

   _____

   _____

3. What did you do as a result of "being different"? (That is, in what way was your behavior changed by the feeling of "being different"?)

   _____

   _____

4. What did others in the situation do? How do you think they felt about the situation?

   _____

   _____

5. How did the situation turn out in the end?

   _____

   _____

6. As a result of that event, how will you probably behave differently in the future? In what way has the situation changed you?

   _____

   _____

11.2 Gender Stereotypes

PART I

Your instructor will divide the group into smaller groups based on gender, resulting in male-only and female-only groups. Groups are to brainstorm a list in response to the following statements. It is not necessary for all members to agree with everything the group generates. Add all inputs to the list.

Female groups complete the following:

- All men are _____
- Men think all women are _____

Male groups complete the following:

- All women are _____
- Women think all men are _____

PART II

After generating your lists, your groups will present a role-play to the class based on the following scenarios by switching gender roles (females portray males, and males portray females):

> Two friends (of the same gender) meeting each other back at school for the first time this year.

> A person flirting with a member of the opposite sex at a party. (Females play a male flirting with a female; males play a female flirting with a male.)

Questions

1. What aspects of the role-plays were accurate, distorted, or inaccurate?

2. How did you feel portraying the opposite gender and how did it feel to see your gender portrayed?

3. On what stereotypes or experiences were these role-plays based?

PART III

Your group will now write its brainstorm lists on the board for discussion. Remember that these lists are a product of a group effort and are generally based on stereotypes and not necessarily the view of any one individual.

Analyze the lists for positive and negative results in both personal and professional settings. Generate a list of ways to dispel, reduce, or counter negative stereotypes.

Questions

1. What similarities, patterns, or trends developed from the groups?

2. How do you feel about the thoughts presented about your gender?

3. What implications do these thoughts have on actions and situations in the work environment?

4. What can you do to reduce the negative effects of these stereotypes? What can you do to help dispel these stereotypes? (Brainstorm with your group or class.)

SOURCE: Portions of this exercise were adapted from concepts in Susan F. Fritz, William Brown, Joyce Lunde, and Elizabeth Banset, *Interpersonal Skills for Leadership* (Englewood Cliffs, NJ: Prentice Hall, 1999); and A. B. Shani and James B. Lau, *Behavior in Organizations: An Experiential Approach*, 6th ed. (New York: Irwin, 1996).

11.3 He Works, She Works

INSTRUCTIONS

1. Complete the He Works, She Works Worksheet. In the appropriate spaces, write what you think the stereotyped responses would be. Do not spend too much time considering any one item. Rather, respond quickly and let your first impression or thought guide your answer.

2. Compare your individual responses with those of other class members or participants. It is interesting to identify and discuss the most frequently used stereotypes.

He Works, She Works Worksheet

The family picture is on *his* desk: *He's a solid, responsible family man.*

His desk is cluttered: _____

_____

He's talking with coworkers: _____

_____

He's not at his desk: _____

_____

He's not in the office: _____

_____

The family picture is on *her* desk: *Her family will come before her career.*

Her desk is cluttered: _____

_____

She's talking with coworkers: _____

_____

She's not at her desk: _____

_____

She's not in the office: _____

_____

The family picture is on *his* desk: *He's a solid, responsible family man.*

He's having lunch with the boss: _____

_____

The boss criticized *him:* _____

_____

He got an unfair deal: _____

_____

He's getting married: _____

_____

He's going on a business trip: _____

_____

He's leaving for a better job: _____

_____

The family picture is on *her* desk: *Her family will come before her career.*

She's having lunch with the boss: _____

_____

The boss criticized *her:* _____

_____

She got an unfair deal: _____

_____

She's getting married: _____

_____

She's going on a business trip: _____

_____

She's leaving for a better job: _____

_____

PART 3 SUPPORTING CASE

Pension Benefits Guaranty Corporation to the Rescue: Is It Time for Pension Reform?

On September 2, 1974, President Gerald R. Ford signed the Employee Retirement Income Security Act (ERISA) into law, and created the Pension Benefits Guaranty Corporation (PBGC), a "government-sponsored insurer of private pension plans," to protect the pensions of workers. When participating companies declare bankruptcy or face other pension-related problems, PBGC races to the rescue and guarantees employees will continue to receive a pension. PBGC covers retirees who receive "defined" or "fixed" benefits. Under this pension scheme, retirees are paid a monthly payout based on their salary and years of service to a company.

PBGC offers two types of pension insurance: (1) a single-employer program that includes some 35 million working and retired people enrolled in nearly 30,000 pension plans and (2) a multi-employer program which includes almost 10 million working and retired people enrolled in more than 1,500 pension plans. It pays more than 500,000 retired people in nearly 3,500 terminated pension funds. PBGC generates revenues from several sources: insurance premiums paid by participating employers, its investments, and when it absorbs failing pension plans.

In recent years, the airline industry has caused PBGC to work overtime. Some airline companies have inadequately funded their pension plans and they are unable to continue paying pensions to their retirees. For example, when Pan Am went bankrupt some 15 years ago and many employees who worked at the company for 20 to 30 years lost their pensions, PBGC came to the rescue and bailed out Pan Am's pension program. More recently, two major airlines, US Airways and United Airlines, have fallen into serious financial troubled times. In 2003, PBGC took over US Airways' pilots' pension obligations. In December 2004, PBGC took over United Airlines pilots' pension program to the tune of about $1.4 billion. In 2005, PBGC took over US Airways' flight attendants and mechanics' pension plan. All told, the bailouts of these two airlines cost PBGC approximately $4 billion and have placed a tremendous financial strain on the government-sponsored agency's resources. Recent financial analyses of Delta Airlines suggest that it too may be headed down the same path as US Airways and United Airlines.

According to the Center on Federal Financial Institution (CFFI), a nonprofit Washington, DC, policy institute, all is not well at PBGC. This nonpartisan organization has raised serious concerns about the financial health of PBGC, and its continued ability to bail out failing pension plans. In 2003, PBGC had an $11 billion deficit, which more than doubled in 2004 to $23 billion. The agency's current and future financial obligations to pensioners are projected to include more than 1 million retired people. Moreover, one projection by CFFI suggests that PBGC may not have enough money to support payments to pensioners in 15 years. Such gloomy projections caused Elaine Chao, the U.S. Secretary of Labor, in January 2005, to develop a plan so that the government-sponsored agency can survive. Perhaps it is time for companies to change defined benefits pension plans in favor of other plans, such as a defined contribution plans that provide benefits based on employee and employer contributions rather than a monthly guarantee.

QUESTIONS

1. As a future full-time employee, would you prefer a defined pension benefit or a defined contribution plan? Why?

2. Pension benefits are costly, yet workers need them desperately. Are there any ways managers can ensure employee pension plans are protected?

3. When a company goes bankrupt, should the federal government bail out pension funds? Why? Why not?

Sources: This case was prepared by Joseph C. Santora, who is a professor of business administration at Essex County College, Newark, New Jersey. N. Byrnes, "The Coming Pension Crunch," *BusinessWeek Online,* September 15, 2004, www.businessweek.com; D. Elliot, "PBGC: Effects of US Air and UAL Terminations," Center on Federal Financial Institutions, 2004, http://www.coffi.org; and A. Newman, ed., "Pension Reform: Next?" *BusinessWeek,* January 24, 2005, p. 46, http://www.pbgc.gov/about/default.htm.

chapter

12

Leadership

Every soldier has a right to competent command.

—Julius Caesar

LEARNING OBJECTIVES

After studying Chapter 12, you will be able to:

CHAPTER OUTLINE

Management Close-Up

When it comes to leaders, Amory Lovins isn't a "larger than life" kind of guy. He doesn't have a flamboyant rock star personality. Nor is he likely to be hogging the media spotlight, detailing the shortcomings of business or government. Instead, Lovins works quietly but determinedly to persuade people and organizations to accept his point of view. He believes we can make the world secure, prosperous, and life-sustaining by using energy more efficiently and avoiding fossil fuels—and make money by doing so.

Lovins, a scientist, environmentalist, and entrepreneur, first attracted notice with an essay in which he pointed out that the inefficient use of natural resources is responsible for the world's energy crisis. A physicist by training, Lovins was also one of the first to recognize the dangers of global warming. In 1982, Lovins cofounded the Rocky Mountain Institute (RMI), a not-for-profit "think and do" tank in Colorado that conducts research and advises business, the government, and the military about strategies for using less energy *and* saving money. Tucked into a mountainside with thick insulating walls, RMI's solar-paneled headquarters lacks a furnace and yet uses energy and heat so efficiently that its greenhouse can grow tropical fruit in the dead of a raging Rocky Mountain winter.

Lovins and his RMI staff have advised more than 80 *Fortune* 500 organizations, 19 heads of state, and the U.S. government about energy and environmental matters. Lovins is the author of 29 books, and in his 2004 text *Winning the Oil Endgame,* he outlines how the United States can eliminate its use of imported oil by 2040 and all oil by 2050—and still operate profitably.[1]

> Becoming an effective leader doesn't require adherence to a single path. In fact, leaders exhibit a wide range of personal styles. As you read this chapter, consider how Amory Lovins's leadership style is effective yet different from that of other leaders you know.

People get excited about the topic of leadership. They want to know: what makes a great leader? Managers in all industries are interested in this question. They believe the answer will bring improved organizational performance and personal career success. They hope to acquire the skills that will transform an "average" manager into a true leader.

Amory Lovins would likely agree that leadership can be learned. Based on similar thinking, many large organizations such as Home Depot and Union Pacific actively recruit retired military personnel in the belief that military training and experience prepare those individuals to lead. Of course, you don't have to join the armed services to acquire leadership skills. According to one source, "Leadership seems to be the marshaling of skills possessed by a majority but used by a minority. But it's something that can be learned by anyone, taught to everyone, denied to no one."[2]

LO 1 What is leadership? To start, a leader is one who influences others to attain goals. The greater the number of followers, the greater the influence. And the more successful the attainment of worthy goals, the more evident the leadership. But we must explore beyond this bare definition to capture the excitement and intrigue that devoted followers and students of leadership feel when they see a great leader in action, to understand what organizational leaders really do, and to learn what it really takes to become a truly outstanding leader.

Outstanding leaders combine good strategic substance and effective interpersonal processes to formulate and implement strategies that produce results and sustainable competitive advantage.[3] They may launch enterprises, build organization cultures, win wars, or otherwise change the course of events.[4] They are strategists who seize opportunities others overlook, but "they are also passionately concerned with detail—all the small, fundamental realities that can make or mar the grandest of plans."[5]

What Do We Want from Our Leaders?

LO 2 What do people want from their leaders? Broadly speaking, they want help in achieving their goals.[6] These goals include not just more pay and promotions, but support for their personal development; clearing obstacles so that they can perform at high levels; and treatment that is respectful, fair, and ethical. Leaders serve people best when they help them develop their own initiative and good judgment, enable them to grow, and help them become better contributors. People want competence and proper management—the kinds of things you will read about in this chapter and that are found in other chapters in this book.

Financial executives ought to know what their company's most valuable resources are. In a recent survey, chief financial officers put the emphasis on leadership and people.[8]

- Strong company leadership
- Focus on hiring the best people
- Up-to-date-technology
- Ability to develop and implement new ideas quickly
- Up-to-date intelligence on competitors, markets
- Other/Don't know

What do organizations need? Organizations need people at all levels to be leaders. Leaders throughout the organization are needed to do the things that their people want, but also to help create and implement strategic direction. Thus, organizations place people in formal leadership roles so that these leaders will achieve, not their personal goals, but the organization's goals. Marilyn Nelson, CEO of Carlson Companies, which operates Radisson Hotels, TGI Friday's, and Regent Seven Seas Cruises, recognizes that any chief executive's leadership role is to serve the company:

"You actually have to subordinate your own emotions, your own desires, even make decisions on behalf of the whole that might conflict with what you would do on an individual basis."[7]

These two perspectives—what people want and what organizations need—are neatly combined in a set of five key behaviors identified by James Kouzes and Barry Posner, two well-known authors and consultants.[9] The best leaders

1. *Challenge the process.* They challenge conventional beliefs and practices, and they create change.
2. *Inspire a shared vision.* They appeal to people's values and motivate them to care about an important mission.
3. *Enable others to act.* They give people access to information and give them the power to perform to their full potential.
4. *Model the way.* They don't just tell people what to do, they are living examples of the ideals they believe in.
5. *Encourage the heart.* They show appreciation, provide rewards, and use various approaches to motivate people in positive ways.

You will read about these and other aspects of leadership in this and the following chapters. The topics we discuss will not only help you become a better leader but give you benchmarks that will help you assess the competence and fairness with which your boss manages you.

Vision

LO 3

"The leader's job is to create a vision," stated Robert L. Swiggett, former chair of Kollmorgen Corporation.[10] Until a few years ago, *vision* was not a word one heard managers utter. But today, having a vision for the future and communicating that vision to others are known to be essential components of great leadership. "If there is no vision, there is no business," maintains entrepreneur Mark Leslie.[11] Joe Nevin, an MIS director, described leaders as "painters of the vision and architects of the journey."[12] Practicing businesspeople are not alone in this belief; academic research shows that a clear vision and communication of that vision lead to higher venture growth in entrepreneurial firms.[13]

A **vision** is a mental image of a possible and desirable future state of the organization. It expresses the leader's ambitions for the organization.[14] A leader can create a vision that describes high performance aspirations, the nature of corporate or business strategy, or even the kind of workplace worth building. The best visions are both ideal and unique.[15] If a vision conveys an *ideal*, it communicates a standard of excellence and a clear choice of positive values. If the vision is also *unique*, it communicates and inspires pride in being different from other organizations. The choice of language is important; the words should imply a combination of realism and optimism, an action orientation, and resolution and confidence that the vision will be attained.[16]

Visions can be small or large and can exist at any organizational level as well as at the very top. The important points are that (1) a vision is necessary for effective leadership; (2) a person or team can develop a vision for any job, work unit, or organization; and (3) many people, including managers who do not develop into strong leaders, do not develop a clear vision—instead, they focus on performing or surviving on a day-by-day basis.

Put another way, leaders must know what they want.[17] And other people must understand what that is. The leader must be able to articulate the vision, clearly and often. Other people throughout the organization should understand the

vision

A mental image of a possible and desirable future state of the organization.

Imagine trying to complete a challenging jigsaw puzzle without the "vision" of what you're working toward.

vision and be able to state it clearly themselves. That's a start. But the vision means nothing until the leader and followers take action to turn the vision into reality.[18]

One leader who articulates and models a clear vision is A. G. Lafley, chief executive of Procter & Gamble. Lafley expresses his vision for the company with the slogan "The consumer is boss." According to this vision, every decision should be aimed at getting consumers to try P&G products and ensuring they like the products so much that they remember the experience as—at a minimum—satisfying. The vision guides major decisions such as restructuring research and development to bring in outside ideas and speed them to market, as well as Lafley's practice of visiting consumers in stores and homes, listening to their comments about using detergents and lotions. By following Lafley's vision, P&G has more than doubled the number of its brands with sales of at least $1 billion.[19]

> You can't perform in the long run if you don't have a vision of what you want to accomplish.

A metaphor reinforces the important concept of vision.[20] Putting a jigsaw puzzle together is much easier if you have the picture on the box cover in front of you. Without the picture, or vision, the lack of direction is likely to result in frustration and failure. That is what communicating a vision is all about: making clear where you are heading.

Not just any vision will do. Visions can be inappropriate, and even fail, for a variety of reasons.[21] First, an inappropriate vision may reflect merely the leader's personal needs. Such a vision can be unethical, or it may fail because of lack of acceptance by the market or by those who must implement it. Second (and related to the first), an inappropriate vision may ignore stakeholder needs. Third, the leader must stay abreast of environmental changes. Although effective leaders maintain confidence and persevere despite obstacles, the time may come when the facts dictate that the vision must change. You will learn more about change and how to manage it later in the text.

Where do visions come from?[22] Leaders should be sensitive to emerging opportunities, develop the right capabilities or worldviews, and not be overly invested in the status quo. You also can capitalize on networks of insightful individuals who have ideas about the future. Some visions are accidental; a company may stumble into an opportunity, and the leader may get credit for foresight. Some leaders and companies launch many new initiatives and, through trial and error, occasionally hit home runs. If the company learns from these successes, the "vision" emerges.

City administrator Steve Hewitt desperately needed a vision when a powerful tornado smashed his town of Greensburg, Kansas. Hewitt emerged after the storm to discover that the tornado had destroyed his own house plus the homes of most of the town's 1,400 residents. It also wiped out Greensburg's hospital, fire station, elementary and high schools, water tower, and business district. Hewitt immediately contacted employees and assessed the extent of the damage. He found a safe place for his family to stay and then turned his full attention to rescue and recovery.

First, Hewitt had to deal with the emergency at hand. Supervising crews of city workers and volunteers operating out of tents, Hewitt directed the search and rescue, and later the cleanup. Even as these activities continued, Hewitt had to begin making decisions about the future. Though a small town might understandably give up, Hewitt was determined to rebuild. And out of that tragedy, he seized an opportunity.

Hewitt envisioned a town that would model an energy-efficient and sustainable way of living. He persuaded the city council to pass a resolution that all new municipal buildings meet the stiff LEED (Leadership in Energy and Environmental Design) Platinum certification for "green" buildings, for major energy savings. Hewitt communicated his vision and encouragement in radio broadcasts and flyers handed out at emergency checkpoints. He educated the community about the practical advantages of rebuilding homes to meet LEED standards, persuading many homeowners and store owners to adopt the standards themselves. He developed plans for wind farms to supply electricity to the town. Besides inspiring the locals, these efforts have drawn publicity and donations, including an eco-friendly playground.[23]

Leading and Managing

Effective managers are not necessarily true leaders. Many administrators, supervisors, and even top executives perform their responsibilities successfully without being great leaders. But these positions afford an opportunity for leadership. The ability to lead effectively, then, will set the excellent managers apart from the average ones.

Whereas management must deal with the ongoing, day-to-day complexities of organizations, true leadership includes effectively orchestrating important change.[24] While managing requires planning and budgeting routines, leading includes setting the direction (creating a vision) for the firm. Management requires structuring the organization, staffing it with capable people, and monitoring activities; leadership goes beyond these functions by inspiring people to attain the vision. Great leaders keep people focused on moving the organization toward its ideal future, motivating them to overcome whatever obstacles lie in the way.

Good leadership, unfortunately, is all too rare. Managers may focus on the activities that earn them praise and rewards, such as actions that cause a rise in the company's stock price, rather than making tough ethical choices or investing in long-term results. Some new managers, learning that "quick wins" will help them establish their credibility as leaders, push a pet project while neglecting the impact on the very people they were assigned to lead. This approach tends to backfire, because employees distrust this type of manager and lose any commitment they might have had to the team's long-term success. Successful leaders, in contrast, enlist the team in scoring *collective* quick wins that result from working together toward a shared vision.[25]

It is important to be clear here about several things. First, management and leadership are both vitally important. To highlight the need for more leadership is not to minimize the importance of management or managers. But leadership involves unique processes that are distinguishable from basic management processes.[26] Moreover, just because they involve different processes does not mean that they require different, separate people. The same individual can exemplify effective managerial processes, leadership processes, both, or neither.

Some people dislike the idea of distinguishing between management and leadership, maintaining that it is artificial or derogatory toward the managers and the management processes that make organizations run. Perhaps a better or more useful distinction is between supervisory and strategic leadership.[27] **Supervisory leadership** is behavior that provides guidance, support, and corrective feedback for day-to-day activities. **Strategic leadership** gives purpose and meaning to organizations. Strategic leadership involves anticipating and envisioning a viable future for the organization, and working with others to initiate changes that create such a future.[28]

Leading and Following

Organizations succeed or fail not only because of how well they are led but because of how well followers follow. Just as managers are not necessarily good leaders, people are not always good followers. As one leadership scholar puts it, "Executives are given subordinates; they have to earn followers."[29] But it's also true that good followers help produce good leaders.

As a manager, you will be asked to play the roles of both leader and follower. As you lead the people who report to you, you will report to your boss. You will be a member of some teams and committees, and you may head others. While the leadership roles

**supervisory
leadership**

Behavior that provides guidance, support, and corrective feedback for day-to-day activities.

strategic leadership

Behavior that gives purpose and meaning to organizations, envisioning and creating a positive future.

Georgetown head coach John Thompson III talks to his players during practice for the NCAA East Regional basketball tournament.

What are the failures of followership? Here's one answer: apathy, passivity, cynicism, and noninvolvement that invite leaders' abuse of power.[32]

get the glamour and therefore are the roles that many people covet, followers must perform their responsibilities conscientiously and well. Good followership doesn't mean merely obeying orders, although some bosses may view it that way. The most effective followers are capable of independent thinking and at the same time are actively committed to organizational goals.[30] Robert Townsend, who led a legendary turnaround at Avis, says that the most important characteristic of a follower may be the willingness to tell the truth.[31]

Effective followers also distinguish themselves from ineffective ones by their enthusiasm and commitment to the organization and to a person or purpose—an idea, a product—other than themselves or their own interests. They master skills that are useful to their organizations, and they hold performance standards that are higher than required. Effective followers may not get the glory, but they know their contributions to the organization are valuable. And as they make those contributions, they study leaders in preparation for their own leadership roles.[33]

Power and Leadership

LO 4

Central to effective leadership is **power**—the ability to influence other people. In organizations, this influence often means the ability to get things done or accomplish one's goals despite resistance from others.

power

The ability to influence others.

Sources of Power

One of the earliest and still most useful approaches to understanding power, offered by French and Raven, suggests that leaders have five important potential sources of power in organizations.[34] Figure 12.1 shows those power sources.

Legitimate Power   The leader with *legitimate power* has the right, or the authority, to tell others what to do; employees are obligated to comply with legitimate orders. For example, a supervisor tells an employee to remove a safety hazard, and the employee removes the hazard because he has to obey the authority of his boss. In contrast, when a staff person lacks the authority to give an order to a line manager, the staff person has no legitimate power over the manager. As you might guess, managers have more legitimate power over their direct reports than they do over their peers, bosses, and others inside or outside their organizations.[35]

Reward Power   The leader who has *reward power* influences others because she controls valued rewards; people comply with the leader's wishes to receive those rewards. For example, a manager works hard to achieve her performance goals to get a positive performance review and a big pay raise from her boss. On the other hand, if company policy dictates that everyone receive the same salary increase, a leader's reward power decreases because he or she is unable to give higher raises.

Coercive Power   The leader with *coercive power* has control over punishments; people comply to avoid those punishments. For instance, a manager implements an absenteeism policy that administers disciplinary actions to offending employees. A manager has less coercive power if, say, a union contract limits her ability to punish. In general, lower-level managers have less legitimate, coercive, and reward power than do middle- and higher-level managers.[36]

Referent Power   The leader with *referent power* has personal characteristics that appeal to others; people comply because of admiration, personal liking, a desire for

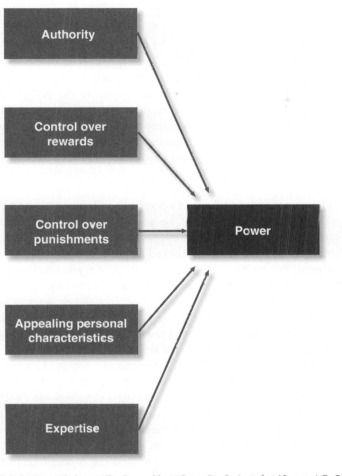

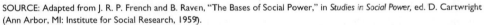

SOURCE: Adapted from J. R. P. French and B. Raven, "The Bases of Social Power," in *Studies in Social Power*, ed. D. Cartwright (Ann Arbor, MI: Institute for Social Research, 1959).

FIGURE 12.1
Sources of Power

approval, or a desire to be like the leader. For example, young, ambitious managers emulate the work habits and personal style of a successful, charismatic executive. An executive who is incompetent, disliked, and commands little respect has little referent power.

Expert Power   The leader who has *expert power* has certain expertise or knowledge; people comply because they believe in, can learn from, or can otherwise gain from that expertise. For example, a sales manager gives her salespeople some tips on how to close a deal. The salespeople then alter their sales techniques because they respect the manager's expertise. However, this manager may lack expert power in other areas, such as finance; thus, her salespeople may ignore her advice concerning financial matters.

People who are in a position that gives them the right to tell others what to do, who can reward and punish, who are well liked and admired, and who have expertise on which other people can draw will be powerful members of the organization. All of these sources of power are potentially important. Although it is easy to assume that the most powerful bosses are those who have high legitimate power and control major rewards and punishments, it is important not to underestimate the more "personal" sources such as expert and referent power.

Management Close-Up   TAKING ACTION

Rocky Mountain Institute chairman and chief scientist Amory Lovins has always been a problem solver and driven to succeed. As a child, he showed great interest in gadgets and experiments, often playing in the basement workshop where his father, the head of research for a scientific instruments company, created unique and unusual devices. As an undergraduate student at Harvard, Lovins continued to explore his broad interests but dropped out after two years when Harvard required him to declare a major. Lovins later explained that he thought drawing the line at one or two main areas of interest was too limiting.

In 1967 he transferred to England's prestigious Oxford University, where he earned a master's degree in physics. However, he left Oxford in 1971 without completing the doctoral degree because Oxford didn't offer a program in energy, his area of interest. Two years later, the Arab oil embargo rocked the U.S. economy with a shortage of oil and gas. For Lovins, that event and the years following it crystallized his belief that a country's dependence on foreign oil represents a national security risk.

Increasingly, Lovins conducted research and focused on ways to make efficient use of the world's resources. In a 1976 essay in *Foreign Affairs*, he introduced the idea of a "soft energy path," advocating the use of renewable energy and creating efficiency through better planning and design. Lovins also coined the term "negawatt" to refer to a watt of electricity that doesn't need to be generated as a result of an energy-saving measure. A former employee describes Lovins as a problem solver and a constant tinkerer. He is known for working odd hours when pondering a problem—to reach the solution for a client or to conduct research.

Lovins continues to take a fresh perspective on the world's energy needs and attempts to persuade others of the need for change. He maintains that earlier discussions of energy conservation focused on sacrifice, which framed the problem from the wrong perspective. He claims instead that energy efficiency generates profits, jobs, and competitive advantage—and that savvy employers are beginning to figure this out.[37]

- What types of power does Amory Lovins possess to make him a good leader of an organization focusing on environmental issues?
- Rather than preach to people about changing how they use energy, Amory Lovins says he attempts to lead by example. How does this behavior influence the behavior of others?

Traditional Approaches to Understanding Leadership

LO 5

Three traditional approaches to studying leadership are the trait approach, the behavioral approach, and the situational approach.

Leader Traits

trait approach

A leadership perspective that attempts to determine the personal characteristics that great leaders share.

The **trait approach** is the oldest leadership perspective; it focuses on individual leaders and attempts to determine the personal characteristics (traits) that great leaders share. What set Winston Churchill, Alexander the Great, Gandhi, and Martin Luther King Jr. apart from the crowd? The trait approach assumes the existence of a leadership personality and assumes that leaders are born, not made.

From 1904 to 1948, researchers conducted more than 100 leadership trait studies.[38] At the end of that period, management scholars concluded that no particular set of traits is necessary for a person to become a successful leader. Enthusiasm for the trait approach diminished, but some research on traits continued. By the mid-1970s, a more balanced view emerged: Although no traits ensure leadership success, certain characteristics are potentially useful. The current perspective is that some personality characteristics—many of which a person need not be born with but can strive to acquire—do distinguish effective leaders from other people:[39]

Sol Trujillo, CEO of Telstra, says, "Listening is a great leadership strength. When you speak, be measured, be knowledgeable, and have conviction in what you say. Be passionate. And always remember, you lead by example."

1. *Drive.* Drive refers to a set of characteristics that reflect a high level of effort. Drive includes high need for achievement, constant striving for improvement, ambition, energy, tenacity (persistence in the face of obstacles), and initiative. In several countries, the achievement needs of top executives have been shown to be related to the growth rates of their organizations.[40] But the need to achieve can be a drawback if leaders focus on personal achievement and get so personally involved with the work that they do not delegate enough authority and responsibility. And whereas need for achievement has been shown to predict organizational effectiveness in entrepreneurial firms, it does not predict success for division heads in larger and more bureaucratic firms.[41]

2. *Leadership motivation.* Great leaders not only have drive; they *want* to lead. In this regard, it helps to be *extraverted*—extraversion is consistently related to both leadership emergence and leadership effectiveness.[42] Also important is a high need for power, a preference to be in leadership rather than follower positions.[43] A high power need induces people to attempt to influence others and sustains interest and satisfaction in the process of leadership. When the power need is exercised in moral and socially constructive ways, rather than to the detriment of others, leaders inspire more trust, respect, and commitment to their vision.

3. *Integrity.* Integrity is the correspondence between actions and words. Honesty and credibility, in addition to being desirable characteristics in their own right, are especially important for leaders because these traits inspire trust in others.

4. *Self-confidence.* Self-confidence is important for a number of reasons. The leadership role is challenging, and setbacks are inevitable. Self-confidence allows a leader to overcome obstacles, make decisions despite uncertainty, and instill confidence in others. Of course, you don't want to overdo this; arrogance and cockiness have triggered more than one leader's downfall.

A senior partner in a law firm told his attorneys about the importance of trust. When a young, ambitious lawyer asked how one can gain trust, the senior partner replied, "Try being trustworthy."[44]

5. *Knowledge of the business.* Effective leaders have a high level of knowledge about their industries, companies, and technical matters. Leaders must have the intelligence to interpret vast quantities of information. Advanced degrees are useful in a career, but ultimately less important than acquired expertise in matters relevant to the organization.[45]

Percy Sutton is one leader who appears to have all of these leadership traits. The founder of Inner City Broadcasting and, more recently, cofounder of information technology company Synematics, Sutton has always exhibited drive, motivation, integrity, self-confidence, and knowledge.

Sutton and a partner bought a radio station and incorporated it into Inner City Broadcasting, which now includes 19 stations, run by Sutton's son Pierre. In 1980, Sutton bought the failing Apollo Theater in New York City's Harlem and brought it out of bankruptcy. He says he lost $31 million on the project but is proud of rescuing this landmark in African American history, which has bolstered the local economy. "When I look out on the street I see all of the activity, and there is a great comfort in knowing that I started it," he says. "This street was dead, and I was very alive. For me it has never been about the money."

What are Sutton's secrets to success? He says he reads seven newspapers a day because "it's good to know what other people are thinking. This is one of my recommendations to people—read, read, read." And he observes, "I'm a happy person. I'm a good lawyer. I challenge things. And in spite of the injuries that have been inflicted on me in my life, I manage to like people."[46]

Finally, there is one personal skill that may be the most important: the ability to perceive the needs and goals of others and to adjust one's personal leadership approach accordingly.[47] Effective leaders do not rely on one leadership style; rather, they are capable of using different styles as the situation warrants.[48] This quality is the cornerstone of the situational approaches to leadership, which we will discuss shortly.

Leader Behaviors

behavioral approach

A leadership perspective that attempts to identify what good leaders do—that is, what behaviors they exhibit.

The **behavioral approach** to leadership attempts to identify what good leaders do. Should leaders focus on getting the job done or on keeping their followers happy? Should they make decisions autocratically or democratically? In the behavioral approach, personal characteristics are considered less important than the actual behaviors that leaders exhibit.

Three general categories of leadership behavior have received particular attention: behaviors related to task performance, group maintenance, and employee participation in decision making.

task performance behaviors

Actions taken to ensure that the work group or organization reaches its goals.

Task Performance   Leadership requires getting the job done. **Task performance behaviors** are the leader's efforts to ensure that the work unit or organization reaches its goals. This dimension is variously referred to as *concern for production, directive leadership, initiating structure,* or *closeness of supervision.* It includes a focus on work speed, quality and accuracy, quantity of output, and following the rules.[49] This type of leader behavior improves leader job performance and group and organizational performance.[50]

Task performance behaviors focus on achieving work goals.

group maintenance behaviors

Actions taken to ensure the satisfaction of group members, develop and maintain harmonious work relationships, and preserve the social stability of the group.

Group Maintenance   In exhibiting **group maintenance behaviors,** leaders take action to ensure the satisfaction of group members, develop and maintain harmonious work relationships, and preserve the social stability of the group. This dimension is sometimes referred to as *concern for people, supportive leadership,* or *consideration.* It includes a focus on people's feelings and comfort, appreciation of them, and stress reduction.[51] This type of leader behavior has a strong positive impact on follower satisfaction, motivation, and leader effectiveness.[52]

What *specific* behaviors do performance- and maintenance-oriented leadership imply? To help answer this question, assume you are asked to rate your boss on these two dimensions. If a leadership study were conducted in your organization, you would be asked to fill out a questionnaire similar to the one in Table 12.1. The behaviors indicated in the first set of questions represent performance-oriented leadership; those indicated in the second set represent maintenance-oriented leadership.

Leader-Member Exchange (LMX) theory

Highlights the importance of leader behaviors not just toward the group as a whole but toward individuals on a personal basis.

Leader-Member Exchange (LMX) theory highlights the importance of leader behaviors not just toward the group as a whole but toward individuals on a personal basis.[53] The focus in the original formulations, which has since been expanded, is primarily on the leader behaviors historically considered group maintenance.[54] According to LMX theory, and as supported by research evidence, maintenance behaviors such as trust, open communication, mutual respect, mutual obligation, and mutual loyalty form the cornerstone of relationships that are satisfying and perhaps more productive.[55]

Task Performance Leadership

1. Is your superior strict about observing regulations?
2. To what extent does your superior give you instructions and orders?
3. Is your superior strict about the amount of work you do?
4. Does your superior urge you to complete your work by a specified time?
5. Does your superior try to make you work to your maximum capacity?
6. When you do an inadequate job, does your superior focus on the inadequate way the job is done?
7. Does your superior ask you for reports about the progress of your work?
8. How precisely does your superior work out plans for goal achievement each month?

Group Maintenance Leadership

1. Can you talk freely with your superior about your work?
2. Does your superior generally support you?
3. Is your superior concerned about your personal problems?
4. Do you think your superior trusts you?
5. Does your superior give you recognition when you do your job well?
6. When a problem arises in your workplace, does your superior ask your opinion about how to solve it?
7. Is your superior concerned about your future benefits, such as promotions and pay raises?
8. Does your superior treat you fairly?

TABLE 12.1

Questions Assessing Task Performance and Group Maintenance Leadership

SOURCE: Reprinted from J. Misumi and M. Peterson, "The Performance-Maintenance (PM) Theory of Leadership: Review of a Japanese Research Program," *Administrative Science Quarterly* 30, no. 2 (June 1985), by permission of *Administrative Science Quarterly*, © 1985 by Johnson Graduate School of Management, Cornell University.

Remember, though, the potential for cross-cultural differences. Maintenance behaviors are important everywhere, but the specific behaviors can differ from one culture to another. For example, in the United States, maintenance behaviors include dealing with people face-to-face; in Japan, written memos are preferred over giving directions face-to-face, thus avoiding confrontation and permitting face-saving in the event of disagreement.[57]

> "A leader's job is to see possibility in people."
> —Carly Fiorina, former CEO, Hewlett-Packard[56]

Participation in Decision Making   How should a leader make decisions? More specifically, to what extent should leaders involve their people in making decisions?[58] As a dimension of leadership behavior, **participation in decision making** can range from autocratic to democratic. **Autocratic leadership** makes decisions and then announces them to the group. **Democratic leadership** solicits input from others. Democratic leadership seeks information, opinions, and preferences, sometimes to the point of meeting with the group, leading discussions, and using consensus or majority vote to make the final choice.

The Effects of Leader Behavior   How the leader behaves influences people's attitudes and performance. Studies of these effects focus on autocratic versus democratic decision styles or on performance- versus maintenance-oriented behaviors.

Decision Styles   The classic study comparing autocratic and democratic styles found that a democratic approach resulted in the most positive attitudes, whereas an

participation in decision making

Leader behaviors that managers perform in involving their employees in making decisions.

autocratic leadership

A form of leadership in which the leader makes decisions on his or her own and then announces those decisions to the group.

democratic leadership

A form of leadership in which the leader solicits input from subordinates.

laissez-faire

leadership philosophy characterized by an absence of managerial decision making.

autocratic approach resulted in somewhat higher performance.[59] A **laissez-faire** style, in which the leader essentially made no decisions, led to more negative attitudes and lower performance. These results seem logical and probably represent the prevalent beliefs among managers about the general effects of these approaches.

Democratic styles, appealing though they may seem, are not always the most appropriate. When speed is of the essence, democratic decision making may be too slow, or people may want decisiveness from the leader.[60] Whether a decision should be made autocratically or democratically depends on the characteristics of the leader, the followers, and the situation.[61] Thus, a situational approach to leader decision styles, discussed later in the chapter, is appropriate.

Performance and Maintenance Behaviors   The performance and maintenance dimensions of leadership are independent of each other. In other words, a leader can behave in ways that emphasize one, both, or neither of these dimensions. Some research indicates that the ideal combination is to engage in both types of leader behaviors.

A team of Ohio State University researchers investigated the effects of leader behaviors in a truck manufacturing plant of International Harvester.[62] Generally, supervisors who were high on *maintenance behaviors* (which the researchers termed *consideration*) had fewer grievances and less turnover in their work units than supervisors who were low on this dimension. The opposite held for *task performance behaviors* (which the research team called *initiating structure*). Supervisors high on this dimension had more grievances and higher turnover rates.

When maintenance and performance leadership behaviors were considered together, the results were more complex. But one conclusion was clear: when a leader is high on performance-oriented behaviors, he or she should *also* be maintenance oriented. Otherwise, the leader will face high rates of employee turnover and grievances.

At about the same time the Ohio State studies were being conducted, a research program at the University of Michigan was studying the impact of the same leader behaviors on groups' job performance.[63] Among other things, the researchers concluded that the most effective managers engaged in what they called *task-oriented behavior:* planning, scheduling, coordinating, providing resources, and setting performance goals. Effective managers also exhibited more *relationship-oriented behavior:* demonstrating trust and confidence, being friendly and considerate, showing appreciation, keeping people informed, and so on. As you can see, these dimensions of leader behavior are essentially the task performance and group maintenance dimensions.

After the Ohio State and Michigan findings were published, it became popular to talk about the ideal leader as one who is always both performance and maintenance oriented. The best-known leadership training model to follow this style is Blake and Mouton's Leadership Grid®.[64] In grid training, managers are rated on their performance-oriented behavior (called *concern for production*) and maintenance-oriented behavior (*concern for people*). Then their scores are plotted on the grid shown in Figure 12.2. The highest score is a 9 on both dimensions.

As the figure shows, joint scores can fall at any point on the grid. Managers who did not score a 9,9—for example, those who were high on concern for people but low on concern for production—would then receive training on how to become a 9,9 leader.

For a long time, grid training was warmly received by U.S. business and industry. Later, however, it was criticized for embracing a simplistic, one-best-way style of leadership and ignoring the possibility that 9,9 is not best under all circumstances. For example, even 1,1 can be appropriate if employees know their jobs (and therefore don't need to receive directions). Also, they may enjoy their jobs and their coworkers enough that whether the boss shows personal concern for them is not very important. Nonetheless, if the manager is uncertain how to behave, it probably is best to exhibit behaviors that are related to both task performance and group maintenance.[65]

In fact, a wide range of effective leadership styles exists. Organizations that understand the need for diverse leadership styles will have a competitive advantage in the modern business environment over those that believe there is only "one best way."

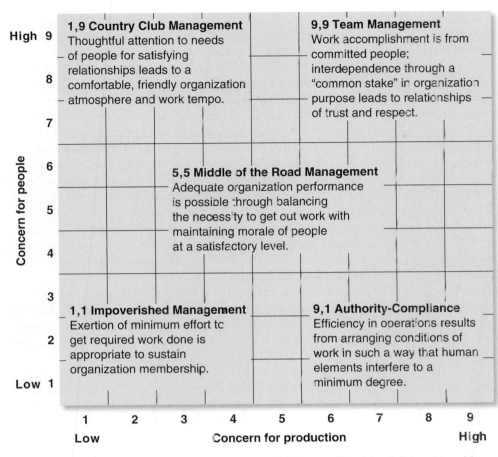

High 9   **1,9 Country Club Management**
Thoughtful attention to needs
of people for satisfying
relationships leads to a
comfortable, friendly organization
atmosphere and work tempo.

9,9 Team Management
Work accomplishment is from
committed people;
interdependence through a
"common stake" in organization
purpose leads to relationships
of trust and respect.

5,5 Middle of the Road Management
Adequate organization performance
is possible through balancing
the necessity to get out work with
maintaining morale of people
at a satisfactory level.

1,1 Impoverished Management
Exertion of minimum effort to
get required work done is
appropriate to sustain
organization membership.

9,1 Authority-Compliance
Efficiency in operations results
from arranging conditions of
work in such a way that human
elements interfere to a
minimum degree.

Concern for people

Low   Concern for production   High

SOURCE: The Leadership Grid® Figure from *Leadership Dilemmas—Grid Solutions*, p. 29, by Robert R. Blake and Anne Adams McCanse. Copyright © 1991, by Robert R. Blake and the Estate of Jane S. Mouton. Used with permission. All rights reserved.

FIGURE 12.2
The Leadership Grid®

situational approach

Leadership perspective proposing that universally important traits and behaviors do not exist, and that effective leadership behavior varies from situation to situation.

Situational Approaches to Leadership

According to proponents of the **situational approach** to leadership, universally important traits and behaviors don't exist. They believe effective leader behaviors vary from situation to situation. *The leader should first analyze the situation and then decide what to do.* In other words, look before you lead.

A head nurse in a hospital described her situational approach to leadership:

My leadership style is a mix of all styles. In this environment I normally let people participate. But in a code blue situation where a patient is dying I automatically become very autocratic: "You do this; you do that; you, out of the room; you all better be quiet; you, get Dr. Mansfield." The staff tell me that's the only time they see me like that. In an emergency like that, you don't have time to vote, talk a lot, or yell at each other. It's time for someone to set up the order.

I remember one time, one person saying, "Wait a minute, I want to do this." He wanted to do the mouth-to-mouth resuscitation. I knew the person behind him did it better, so I said, "No, he does it." This fellow told me later that I hurt him so badly to yell that in front of all the staff and doctors. It was like he wasn't good enough. So I explained it to him: that's the way it is. A life was on the line. I couldn't give you warm fuzzies. I couldn't make you look good because you didn't have the skills to give the very best to that patient who wasn't breathing anymore."[66]

Nurses experience situational leadership on a daily basis. How would you handle a leadership role under pressure?

This nurse has her own intuitive situational approach to leadership. She knows the potential advantages of the participatory approach to decision making, but she also knows that in some circumstances she must make decisions herself.

The first situational model of leadership was proposed in 1958 by Tannenbaum and Schmidt. In their classic *Harvard Business Review* article, these authors described how managers should consider three factors before deciding how to lead: forces in the manager, forces in the subordinate, and forces in the situation.[67] Forces in the manager include the manager's personal values, inclinations, feelings of security, and confidence in subordinates. Forces in the subordinate include his or her knowledge and experience, readiness to assume responsibility for decision making, interest in the task or problem, and understanding and acceptance of the organization's goals. Forces in the situation include the type of leadership style the organization values, the degree to which the group works effectively as a unit, the problem itself and the type of information needed to solve it, and the amount of time the leader has to make the decision.

Consider which of these forces makes an autocratic style most appropriate and which dictates a democratic, participative style. By engaging in this exercise, you are constructing a situational theory of leadership.

Although the Tannenbaum and Schmidt article was published more than a half-century ago, most of its arguments remain valid. Since that time, other situational models have emerged. We will focus here on four: the Vroom model for decision making, Fiedler's contingency model, Hersey and Blanchard's situational theory, and path-goal theory.

The Vroom Model of Leadership   This situational model follows in the tradition of Tannenbaum and Schmidt. The **Vroom model** emphasizes the participative dimension of leadership: how leaders go about making decisions. The model uses the basic situational approach of assessing the situation before determining the best leadership style.[68]

Table 12.2 shows the situational factors used to analyze problems. Each is based on an important attribute of the problem the leader faces and should be assessed as either high or low.

The Vroom model, shown in Figure 12.3, operates like a funnel. You answer the questions one at a time, choosing high or low for each, sometimes skipping questions as you follow the appropriate path. Eventually, you reach one of 14 possible endpoints. For each endpoint, the model states which of five decision styles is most

Vroom model

A situational model that focuses on the participative dimension of leadership.

TABLE 12.2
Situational Factors for Problem Analysis

Decision significance:	The significance of the decision to the success of the project or organization.
Importance of commitment:	The importance of team members' commitment to the decision.
Leader's expertise:	Your knowledge or expertise in relation to this problem.
Likelihood of commitment:	The likelihood that the team would commit itself to a decision that you might make on your own.
Group support for objectives:	The degree to which the team supports the organization's objectives at stake in this problem.
Group expertise:	Team members' knowledge or expertise in relation to this problem.
Team competence:	The ability of team members to work together in solving problems.

SOURCE: V. Vroom, "Leadership and the Decision-Making Process," *Organizational Dynamics*, Spring 2000, pp. 82–94. Copyright © 2000 with permission from Elsevier Science.

Time-Driven Model

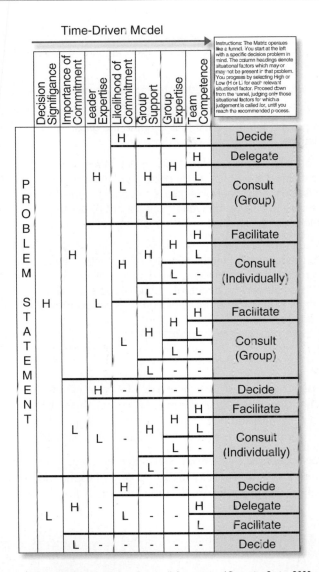

Instructions: The Matrix operates like a funnel. You start at the left with a specific decision problem in mind. The column headings denote situational factors which may or may not be present in that problem. You progress by selecting High or Low (H or L) for each relevant situational factor. Proceed down from the funnel, judging only those situational factors for which a judgement is called for, until you reach the recommended process.

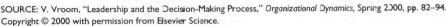

SOURCE: V. Vroom, "Leadership and the Decision-Making Process," *Organizational Dynamics*, Spring 2000, pp. 82–94. Copyright © 2000 with permission from Elsevier Science.

FIGURE 12.3
Vroom's Model of Leadership Style

appropriate. Several different decision styles may work, but the style recommended is the one that takes the least amount of time.

Table 12.3 defines the five leader decision styles. The five styles indicate that there are several shades of participation, not just autocratic or democratic.

Of course, not every managerial decision warrants this complicated analysis. But the model becomes less complex after you work through it a couple of times. Also, using the model for major decisions ensures that you consider the important situational factors and alerts you to the most appropriate style to use.

Fiedler's Contingency Model
According to **Fiedler's contingency model of leadership effectiveness,** effectiveness depends on two factors: the personal style of the leader and the degree to which the situation gives the leader power, control, and influence over the situation.[9] Figure 12.4 illustrates the contingency model. The upper half of the figure shows the situational analysis, and the lower half indicates the appropriate style. In the upper portion, three questions are used to analyze the situation:

1. Are leader-member relations good or poor? (To what extent is the leader accepted and supported by group members?)

Fiedler's contingency model of leadership effectiveness

A situational approach to leadership postulating that effectiveness depends on the personal style of the leader and the degree to which the situation gives the leader power, control, and influence over the situation.

TABLE 12.3
Vroom's Leader Decision Styles

Decide: You make the decision alone and either announce or "sell" it to the group. You may use your expertise in collecting information that you deem relevant to the problem from the group or others.
Consult individually: You present the problem to the group members individually, get their suggestions, and then make the decision.
Consult the group: You present the problem to the group members in a meeting, get their suggestions, and then make the decision.
Facilitate: You present the problem to the group in a meeting. You act as a facilitator, defining the problem to be solved and the boundaries within which the decision must be made. Your objective is to get concurrence on a decision. Above all, you take care to ensure that your ideas are not given any greater weight than those of others simply because of your position.
Delegate: You permit the group to make the decision within prescribed limits. The group undertakes the identification and diagnosis of the problem, developing alternative procedures for solving it, and deciding on one or more alternative solutions. While you play no direct role in the group's deliberations unless explicitly asked, your role is an important one behind the scenes, providing needed resources and encouragement.

SOURCE: V. Vroom, "Leadership and the Decision-Making Process," *Organizational Dynamics,* Spring 2000, pp. 82–94. Copyright © 2000 with permission from Elsevier Science.

2. Is the task structured or unstructured? (To what extent do group members know what their goals are and how to accomplish them?)
3. Is the leader's position power strong or weak (high or low)? (To what extent does the leader have the authority to reward and punish?)

FIGURE 12.4
Fiedler's Analysis of Situations in Which the Task- or Relationship-Motivated Leader Is More Effective

These three sequential questions create a decision tree (from top to bottom, in the figure) in which a situation is classified into one of eight categories. The lower the category number, the more favorable the situation is for the leader; the higher the

Leader–member relations	Good				Poor			
Task structure	Structured		Unstructured		Structured		Unstructured	
Leader position power	High	Low	High	Low	High	Low	High	Low
	1	2	3	4	5	6	7	8

Favorable for leader →→→→→→→→→→→→→→→→→→→→→→→→→ Unfavorable for leader

Type of leader most effective in the situation	Task-motivated	Task-motivated	Task-motivated	Relation-ship-motivated	Relation-ship-motivated	Relation-ship-motivated	Relation-ship-motivated	Task-motivated

SOURCE: D. Organ and T. Bateman, *Organizational Behavior,* 4th ed., McGraw-Hill, 1990. © 1990 by The McGraw-Hill Companies.

number, the less favorable the situation. Fiedler originally called this variable "situational favorableness" but now it is "situational control." Situation 1 is the best: relations are good, task structure is high, and power is high. In the least favorable situation (8), in which the leader has very little situational control, relations are poor, tasks lack structure, and the leader's power is weak.

Different situations dictate different leadership styles. Fiedler measured leadership styles with an instrument assessing the leader's *least preferred coworker* (LPC); that is, the attitude toward the follower the leader liked the least. This was considered an indication more generally of leaders' attitudes toward people. If a leader can single out the person she likes the least, but her attitude is not all that negative, she received a high score on the LPC scale. Leaders with more negative attitudes toward others would receive low LPC scores.

Based on the LPC score, Fiedler considered two leadership styles. **Task-motivated leadership** places primary emphasis on completing the task and is more likely exhibited by leaders with low LPC scores. **Relationship-motivated leadership** emphasizes maintaining good interpersonal relationships and is more likely from high-LPC leaders. These leadership styles correspond to task performance and group maintenance leader behaviors, respectively.

The lower part of Figure 12.4 indicates which style is situationally appropriate. For situations 1, 2, 3, and 8, a task-motivated leadership style is more effective. For situations 4 through 7, relationship-motivated leadership is more appropriate.

Fiedler's theory was not always supported by research. It is better supported if three broad rather than eight specific levels of situational control are assumed: low, medium, and high. The theory was quite controversial in academic circles; among other arguable things, it assumed that leaders cannot change their styles but must be assigned to situations that suit their styles. However, the model has withstood the test of time and still receives attention. Most important, it initiated and continues to emphasize the importance of finding a fit between the situation and the leader's style.

Hersey and Blanchard's Situational Theory   Hersey and Blanchard developed a situational model that added another factor the leader should take into account before deciding whether task performance or maintenance behaviors are more important. Originally called the *life-cycle theory of leadership*, **Hersey and Blanchard's situational theory** highlights the maturity of the followers as the key situational factor.[70] **Job maturity** is the level of the follower's skills and technical knowledge relative to the task being performed; **psychological maturity** is the follower's self-confidence and self-respect. High-maturity followers have both the ability and the confidence to do a good job.

The theory proposes that the more mature the followers, the less the leader needs to engage in task performance behaviors. The required amount of maintenance behaviors is a bit more complex: Maintenance behaviors are not important with followers of low or high levels of maturity but are important for followers of moderate maturity. For low-maturity followers, the emphasis should be on performance-related leadership; for moderate-maturity followers, performance leadership is somewhat less important and maintenance behaviors become more important; and for high-maturity followers, neither dimension of leadership behavior is important.

Little academic research has been done on this situational theory, but the model is popular in management training seminars. Regardless of its scientific validity, Hersey and Blanchard's model provides a reminder that it is important to treat different people differently. Moreover, it suggests the importance of treating the same individual differently from time to time as he or she changes jobs or acquires more maturity in her or his particular job.[71]

Path-Goal Theory   Perhaps the most comprehensive and generally useful situational model of leadership effectiveness is path-goal theory. Developed by Robert

task-motivated leadership

Leadership that places primary emphasis on completing a task.

relationship-motivated leadership

Leadership that places primary emphasis on maintaining good interpersonal relationships.

Hersey and Blanchard's situational theory

A life-cycle theory of leadership postulating that a manager should consider an employee's psychological and job maturity before deciding whether task performance or maintenance behaviors are more important.

job maturity

The level of the employee's skills and technical knowledge relative to the task being performed.

psychological maturity

An employee's self-confidence and self-respect.

path-goal theory

A theory that concerns how leaders influence subordinates' perceptions of their work goals and the paths they follow toward attainment of those goals.

House, **path-goal theory** gets its name from its concern with how leaders influence followers' perceptions of their work goals and the paths they follow toward goal attainment.[72]

The key situational factors in path-goal theory are (1) personal characteristics of followers and (2) environmental pressures and demands with which followers must cope to attain their work goals. These factors determine which leadership behaviors are most appropriate.

The four pertinent leadership behaviors are as follows:

1. *Directive leadership*, a form of task performance-oriented behavior.
2. *Supportive leadership*, a form of group maintenance-oriented behavior.
3. *Participative leadership*, or decision style.
4. *Achievement-oriented leadership*, or behaviors geared toward motivating people, such as setting challenging goals and rewarding good performance.

These situational factors and leader behaviors are merged in Figure 12.5. As you can see, appropriate leader behaviors—as determined by characteristics of followers and the work environment—lead to effective performance.

The theory also specifies *which* follower and environmental characteristics are important. There are three key follower characteristics. *Authoritarianism* is the degree to which individuals respect, admire, and defer to authority. *Locus of control* is the extent to which individuals see the environment as responsive to their own behavior. People with an *internal* locus of control believe that what happens to them is their own doing; people with an *external* locus of control believe that it is just luck or fate. Finally, *ability* is people's beliefs about their own abilities to do their assigned jobs.

Path-goal theory states that these personal characteristics determine the appropriateness of various leadership styles. For example, the theory makes the following propositions:

- A directive leadership style is more appropriate for highly authoritarian people, because such people respect authority.
- A participative leadership style is more appropriate for people who have an internal locus of control, because these individuals prefer to have more influence over their own lives.
- A directive style is more appropriate when subordinates' ability is low. The directive style helps people understand what has to be done.

Appropriate leadership style is also determined by three important environmental factors: people's tasks, the formal authority system of the organization, and the primary work group.

- Directive leadership is inappropriate if tasks already are well structured.
- If the task and the authority or rule system are dissatisfying, directive leadership will create greater dissatisfaction.
- If the task or authority system is dissatisfying, supportive leadership is especially appropriate, because it offers one positive source of gratification in an otherwise negative situation.

FIGURE 12.5
The Path-Goal Framework

- If the primary work group provides social support to its members, supportive leadership is less important.

Path-goal theory offers many more propositions. In general, the theory suggests that the functions of the leader are to (1) make the path to work goals easier to travel by providing coaching and direction, (2) reduce frustrating barriers to goal attainment, and (3) increase opportunities for personal satisfaction by increasing payoffs to people for achieving performance goals. The best way to do these things depends on your people and on the work situation. Again, analyze, and then adapt your style accordingly.

Substitutes for Leadership   Sometimes leaders don't have to lead, or situations constrain their ability to lead effectively. The situation may be one in which leadership is unnecessary or has little impact. **Substitutes for leadership** can provide the same influence on people that leaders otherwise would have.

substitutes for leadership

Factors in the workplace that can exert the same influence on employees as leaders would provide.

Certain follower, task, and organizational factors are substitutes for task performance and group maintenance leader behaviors.[73] For example, group maintenance behaviors are less important and have less impact if people already have a closely knit group, they have a professional orientation, the job is inherently satisfying, or there is great physical distance between leader and followers. Thus, physicians who are strongly concerned with professional conduct, enjoy their work, and work independently do not need social support from hospital administrators.

Task performance leadership is less important and will have less of a positive effect if people have a lot of experience and ability, feedback is supplied to them directly from the task or by computer, or the rules and procedures are rigid. If these factors are operating, the leader does not have to tell people what to do or how well they are performing.

The concept of substitutes for leadership does more than indicate when a leader's attempts at influence will and will not work. It provides useful and practical prescriptions for how to manage more efficiently.[74] If the manager can develop the work situation to the point where a number of these substitutes for leadership are operating, less time will need to be spent in direct attempts to influence people. The leader will be free to spend more time on other important activities.

Research indicates that substitutes for leadership may be better predictors of commitment and satisfaction than of performance.[75] These substitutes are helpful, but you can't put substitutes in place and think you've completed your job as leader. And as a follower, consider this: If you're not getting good leadership, and if these substitutes are not in place, create your own "substitute" for leadership—self-leadership. Take the initiative to motivate yourself, lead yourself, create positive change, and lead others.

Contemporary Perspectives on Leadership

So far, you have learned the major classic approaches to understanding leadership, all of which remain useful today. Now we will discuss a number of new developments that are revolutionizing our understanding of this vital aspect of management.

LO 7

Welches: How Obama Is Doing

FROM THE PAGES OF

Jack and Suzy Welch disagree with the President on points of policy but think he's earned an A thus far. "So . . . how's Obama doing?"

This was the question floated by our host at a recent dinner party. In response, two people said they were disappointed, seven claimed to be on the fence, four asserted it was too early to tell, and three said flat-out great. Where were we in the mix? Allow us to issue a preliminary "report card" on President Obama's leadership since taking office to explain.

But first, note that we just used the word leadership. This column isn't about policy. If it were, we'd probably be on the fence, too. We passionately oppose the President's position on doing away with secret ballots for unionization votes, and we're suspicious of his cap-and-trade proposal, a version of which has done little for Europe. We also find the new budget alarming—with its optimistic forecasts and staggering short-term deficits. On the other hand, we're generally positive about the Administration's reaction to the economic crisis. And we're strongly supportive of his foreign policy, which strikes us as sound and progressive.

But forget all that. Our grade for Obama is based on how he's doing on critical performance criteria as our country's CEO.

VISION AND TEAM-BUILDING

Let's start with vision, the "thing" without which a person simply cannot lead. And look, whether you like his politics or not, Obama's obviously got it. From the economy to the environment, education to health care, the President has articulated his goals to the nation.

http://www.businessweek.com/magazine/content/09_16/b4127000327461.htm

QUESTION

What do you think of President Obama now as a leader? How well can you separate your opinions of his leadership from opinions about policy?

SOURCE: J. Welch and S. Welch, "Obama: A Leadership Report Card," *BusinessWeek*, April 20, 2009, p. 96.

Martin Luther King was a brilliant, charismatic leader who had a compelling vision, a dream for a better world.

charismatic leader

A person who is dominant, self-confident, convinced of the moral righteousness of his or her beliefs, and able to arouse a sense of excitement and adventure in followers.

Charismatic Leadership

Like many great leaders, Ronald Reagan had charisma. So does Barack Obama. Thomas Watson, Alfred Sloan, Steve Jobs, and Richard Branson are good examples of charismatic leaders in industry.

Charisma is a rather elusive concept; it is easy to spot but hard to define. What *is* charisma, and how does one acquire it? According to one definition, "Charisma packs an emotional wallop for followers above and beyond ordinary esteem, affection, admiration, and trust . . . The charismatic is an idolized hero, a messiah and a savior."[76] As you can see from this quotation, many people, particularly North Americans, value charisma in their leaders. But some people don't like the term *charisma*; it can be associated with the negative charisma of evil leaders whom people follow blindly.[77] Nevertheless, charismatic leaders who display appropriate values and use their charisma for appropriate purposes serve as ethical role models for others.[78]

Charismatic leaders are dominant, exceptionally self-confident, and have a strong conviction in the moral righteousness of their beliefs.[79] They strive to create an aura of competence and success and communicate high expectations for and confidence in followers. Ultimately, charismatic leaders satisfy other peoples' needs.[80]

The charismatic leader articulates ideological goals and makes sacrifices in pursuit of those goals.[81] Martin Luther King Jr. had a dream for a better world, and John F. Kennedy spoke of landing a human on the moon. In other words, such leaders have a compelling vision. The charismatic leader also arouses a sense of excitement and adventure. He or she is an eloquent speaker who exhibits superior verbal skills, which helps communicate the vision and motivate followers. Walt Disney mesmerized people with his storytelling; had enormous creative talent; and instilled in his organization strong values of good taste, risk taking, and innovation.[82]

Leaders who possess these characteristics or do these things inspire in their followers trust, confidence, acceptance, obedience, emotional involvement, affection, admiration, and higher performance.[83] For example, having charisma not only helps CEOs inspire other employees in the organization but also may enable them to influence external stakeholders, including customers and investors.[84] Evidence for the positive effects of charismatic leadership has been found in a wide variety of groups, organizations, and management levels, and in countries including India, Singapore, the Netherlands, China, Japan, and Canada.[85]

Charisma has been shown to improve corporate financial performance, particularly under conditions of uncertainty—that is, in risky circumstances or when environments are changing and people have difficulty understanding what they should do.[86] Uncertainty is stressful, and it makes people more receptive to the ideas and actions of charismatic leaders. By the way, too, as an organization's performance improves under a person's leadership, that person becomes seen as more charismatic as a result of the higher performance.[87]

Transformational Leadership

Charisma contributes to transformational leadership. **Transformational leaders** get people to transcend their personal interests for the sake of the larger community.[88] They generate excitement and revitalize organizations. At Hewlett-Packard, the ability to generate excitement is an explicit criterion for selecting managers. In the United Kingdom, Richard Branson of Virgin Group is a transformational leader who built a global business empire.[89]

The transformational process moves beyond the more traditional *transactional* approach to leadership. **Transactional leaders** view management as a series of transactions in which they use their legitimate, reward, and coercive powers to give commands and exchange rewards for services rendered. Unlike transformational leadership, transactional leadership is dispassionate; it does not excite, transform, empower, or inspire people to focus on the interests of the group or organization. However, transactional approaches may be more effective for individualists than for collectivists (recall Chapter 6).[90]

transformational leader

A leader who motivates people to transcend their personal interests for the good of the group.

transactional leaders

Leaders who manage through transactions, using their legitimate, reward, and coercive powers to give commands and exchange rewards for services rendered.

Generating Excitement   Transformational leaders generate excitement in several ways.[91] First, they are *charismatic*, as described earlier. Second, they give their followers *individualized attention*. Transformational leaders delegate challenging work to deserving people, keep lines of communication open, and provide one-on-one mentoring to develop their people. They do not treat everyone alike, because not everyone *is* alike.

Third, transformational leaders are *intellectually stimulating*. They arouse in their followers an awareness of problems and potential solutions. They articulate the organization's opportunities, threats, strengths, and weaknesses. They stir the imagination and generate insights. Therefore, problems are recognized, and high-quality solutions are identified and implemented with the full commitment of followers.

Jim McCluney, CEO of data storage firm Emulex, likes his employees to tease him a little. He believes it's good management to let people relax and poke fun at him. He also believes that doing so helps people think outside the box to come up with new ideas and solutions to problems. "He's really a lot of fun to be around," says one colleague. "He just kind of has a way to get everybody to lower their walls." McCluney is known for hosting pizza days and appearing in employees' offices or at their desks to chat.

McCluney explains the reason for his approach. "If you make your management team really on board, working and adding their unique skills and getting as much diversity of views and opinion on a given problem, the company really thrives." He doesn't abdicate his responsibilities as a leader, but he values the brainpower of his managers and employees. He also knows the pitfalls of trying to do everything himself instead of giving managers some free rein. "At the same time, I have to be able to step in quickly and decisively if there are issues, or we're not making timely decisions," he notes. "So it's a balance between knowing when to be authoritative and when to be collaborative."[92]

Skills and Strategies   At least four skills or strategies contribute to transformational leadership.[93] First, transformational leaders *have a vision*—a goal, an agenda, or a results orientation that grabs people's attention. Second, they *communicate their vision;* through words, manner, or symbolism, they relate a compelling image of the ultimate goal. Third, transformational leaders *build trust* by being consistent, dependable, and persistent. They position themselves clearly by choosing a direction and staying with it, thus projecting integrity. Finally, they have a *positive self-regard.* They do not feel self-important or complacent; rather, they recognize their personal strengths, compensate for their weaknesses, nurture and continually develop their talents, and know how to learn from failure. They strive for success rather than merely try to avoid failure.

Transformational leadership has been identified in industry, the military, and politics.[94] Examples of transformational leaders in business include Henry Ford (founder of Ford Motor Company), Herb Kelleher (former CEO of Southwest Airlines), Jeff Bezos (founder of Amazon.com), David Neeleman (in his former role as leader of JetBlue), and Lee Iacocca (who led Chrysler's turnaround during the 1980s).[95] As with studies of charisma, transformational leadership and its positive impact on follower satisfaction and performance have been demonstrated in countries the world over, including Egypt, Germany, China, England, and Japan.[96] A study in Korean companies found that transformational leadership predicted employee motivation, which in turn predicted creativity.[97] Under transformational leadership, people view their jobs as more intrinsically motivating (see Chapter 13 for more on this) and are more strongly committed to work goals.[98] And top management teams agree more clearly about important organizational goals, which translates into higher organizational performance.[99]

Transforming Leaders   Importantly, transformational leadership is not the exclusive domain of presidents and chief executives. In the military, leaders who received transformational leadership training had a positive impact on followers' personal development. They also were successful as *indirect* leaders: military recruits under the transformational leaders' direct reports were stronger performers.[100] Don't forget, though: the best leaders are those who can display both transformational and transactional behaviors.[101]

Transformational leadership is good for people and good for the bottom line.

Ford Motor Company, in collaboration with the University of Michigan School of Business, put thousands of middle managers through a program designed to stimulate transformational leadership.[102] The training included analysis of the changing business environment, company strategy, and personal reflection and discussion about the need to change. Participants assessed their own leadership styles and developed a specific change initiative to implement after the training—a change that would make a needed and lasting difference for the company.

Over the next six months, the managers implemented change on the job. Almost half of the initiatives resulted in transformational changes in the organization or work unit; the rest of the changes were smaller, more incremental, or more personal. Whether managers made small or transformational changes depended on their attitude going into the training, their level of self-esteem, and the amount of support they received from others on the job for their efforts. Thus, some managers did not respond as hoped. But almost half embraced the training, became more transformational in orientation, and tackled significant transformational changes for the company.

Level 5 leadership, a term well-known among executives, is considered by some to be the ultimate leadership style. Level 5 leadership is a combination of strong professional will (determination) and personal humility that builds enduring greatness.[103] Thus, a Level 5 leader is relentlessly focused on the organization's long-term success while behaving with modesty, directing attention toward the organization rather than him- or herself. Examples include John Chambers, CEO of Cisco Systems, and IBM's former chief executive Louis Gerstner. Gerstner is widely credited for turning around a stodgy IBM by shifting its focus from computer hardware to business solutions. Following his retirement, Gerstner wrote a memoir that details what happened at the company but says little about himself. Although Level 5 leadership is seen as a way to transform organizations to make them great, it requires also that the leader exhibit a combination of transactional and transformational styles.[104]

> ### Level 5 leadership
>
> A combination of strong professional will (determination) and humility that builds enduring greatness.

Before his 30th birthday, Robert Chapman stepped into the job of chief executive of his family's business, Barry-Wehmiller Companies (B-W), following the sudden death of his father. Revenues at B-W, which makes packaging equipment and sells related services, grew rapidly during the early years of Chapman's leadership but then plunged as market demand dried up.

Chapman reacted by assembling his management team to evaluate what had gone wrong. The group determined that the earlier growth had been "undisciplined," not directed toward areas where long-term success would be most likely. The team developed a company vision aimed at balanced and sustainable growth. Since then, says Chapman, the company has "never varied" from "executing our vision with discipline and passion."

The passion comes from a commitment to "people-centric leadership." At B-W under Chapman, managers must care about their employees, give them authority to make important decisions, and clarify how their contributions enhance the company's vision. In terms of corporate structure, this is expressed in an Organizational Empowerment Team, staffed with people who develop leaders and apply methods such as lean manufacturing (see Chapter 9) through which employees contribute to improved operations.

Chapman believes companies can literally change the world through their impact on individual employees. Challenging employees to contribute to the corporate vision gives them a chance to feel that their efforts matter; recognition programs show them that they are appreciated. The result is what Chapman calls an "inspirational environment." Oh, and the company is growing again, too.[105]

Authenticity

In general, consider **authentic leadership** to be rooted in the ancient Greek philosophy "To thine own self be true."[106] In your own leadership, strive for authenticity in the form of honesty, genuineness, reliability, integrity, and trustworthiness. Authentic transformational leaders care about public interests (community, organizational, or group), not just their own.[107] They are willing to sacrifice their own interests for others, and they can be trusted. They are ethically mature; people view leaders who exhibit moral reasoning as more transformational than leaders who do not.[108]

Pseudotransformational leaders are the opposite: they talk a good game, but they ignore followers' real needs as their own self-interests (power, prestige, control, wealth, fame) take precedence.[109]

> ### authentic leadership
>
> A style in which the leader is true to himself or herself while leading.
>
> ### pseudo-transformational leaders
>
> Leaders who talk about positive change but allow their self-interest to take precedence over followers' needs.

Opportunities for Leaders

A common view of leaders is that they are superheroes acting alone, swooping in to save the day. But especially in these complex times, leaders cannot and need not act alone. Business guru John Hersey advises today's leader to be a "SAGE." The letters in *sage* remind leaders to *seek out* other people, *ask* good questions that focus on the other person, *get involved* with other people, and *enrich* people's lives. That outward-looking approach helps leaders identify fresh solutions to vexing problems and invites followers to engage fully with the cause.[110]

GE is famous for developing the leadership skills of employees with potential so that the organization will have strong leaders at many levels. Pictured here are Jack Welch (left) and Jeffrey Immelt (right).

Effective leadership must permeate the organization, not reside in one or two superstars at the top. The leader's job becomes one of spreading leadership abilities throughout the firm.[113] Make people responsible for their own performance. Create an environment in which each person can figure out what needs to be done and then do it well. Point the way and clear the path so that people can succeed. Give them the credit they deserve. Make heroes out of *them*.

Thus, what is now required of leaders is less the efficient management of resources, and more the effective unleashing of people and their intellectual capital.

This perspective uncovers a variety of nontraditional leadership roles that are emerging as vitally important.[112] The term **servant-leader** was coined by Robert Greenleaf, a retired AT&T executive. The term is paradoxical in the sense that "leader" and "servant" are usually opposites; the servant-leader's relationship with employees is more like that of serving customers. For the individual who wants to both lead and serve others, servant-leadership is a way of relating to others to serve their needs and enhance their personal growth while strengthening the organization. For example, when David Wolfskehl, founder of Action Fast Print, stopped telling his employees what to do and instead asked how he could help them solve their problems, productivity jumped 30 percent.[113]

A number of other nontraditional roles provide leadership opportunities. **Bridge leaders** are those who leave their cultures for a significant period of time.[114] They live, go to school, travel, or work in other cultures. Then they return home, become leaders, and through their expanded repertoire they serve as bridges between conflicting value systems within their own cultures or between their culture and other cultures.

With work often being team-based (see Chapter 14), **shared leadership** occurs when leadership rotates to the person with the key knowledge, skills, and abilities for the issue facing the team at a particular time.[115] Shared leadership is most important when tasks are interdependent, are complex, and require creativity. High-performing teams engaged in such work exhibit more shared leadership than poor-performing teams. In consulting teams, the higher the shared leadership, the higher their clients rated the teams' performance.[116] The role of vertical leader remains important—the formal leader still designs the team, manages its external boundaries, provides task direction, emphasizes the importance of the shared leadership approach, and engages in the transactional and transformational activities described in this chapter. But at the same time, the metaphor of geese in V-formation adds strength to the group: the lead goose periodically drops to the back, and another goose "steps up" and takes its place at the forefront.

Lateral leadership does not involve a hierarchical, superior–subordinate relationship but instead invites colleagues at the same level to solve problems together.[117] You alone can't provide a solution to every problem, but you can create processes through which people work collaboratively. If you can get people working to improve methods

servant-leader

A leader who serves others' needs while strengthening the organization.

bridge leaders

A leader who bridges conflicting value systems or different cultures.

shared leadership

Rotating leadership, in which people rotate through the leadership role based on which person has the most relevant skills at a particular time.

lateral leadership

Style in which colleagues at the same hierarchical level are invited to collaborate and facilitate joint problem solving.

collaboratively, you can help create an endless stream of innovations. In other words, it's not about you providing solutions to problems; it's about creating better interpersonal processes for finding solutions. Strategies and tactics can be found throughout this book, including the chapters on decision making, organization structure, teams, communication, and change.

A Note on Courage

To be a good leader, you need the courage to create a vision of greatness for your unit; identify and manage allies, adversaries, and fence sitters; and execute your vision, often against opposition. This does not mean you should commit career suicide by alienating too many powerful people; it does mean taking reasonable risks, with the good of the firm at heart, in order to produce constructive change.

For example, Charles Elachi needed courage when he took a position at NASA's Jet Propulsion Laboratories (JPL) at the beginning of the decade, when a series of budget cuts and efforts to cut corners had resulted in two failed attempts to gather data from Mars exploration projects. In that environment, morale was poor, and public support for JPL was weak. But rather than looking for people to blame, Elachi, a physicist and JPL veteran, got everyone focused on the ambitious next project, the Mars Exploration Rover, which would involve sending two spacecraft to the red planet and landing rovers on the surface to conduct exploration—with the first launch just 27 months away. Undaunted by the two previous failures, Elachi clearly but politely communicated to everyone that another failure was out of the question. At the beginning of the project, he had team leaders list every test that would be necessary before the first spacecraft was sent into orbit. Two years later, he pulled out his "Incompressible Test List" and insisted that team members carry out every procedure—and that the agency fund them. In the end, the mission exceeded expectations.[118]

"When you connect with a purpose greater than yourself, you are fearless; you think big."
—Nancy Barry, on leaving her executive position at the World Bank to become president of Women's World Banking, which makes microloans to impoverished women around the world[119]

Specifically, fulfilling your vision will require some of the following acts of courage:[120] (1) seeing things as they are and facing them head-on, making no excuses and harboring no wishful illusions; (2) saying what needs to be said to those who need to hear it; and (3) persisting despite resistance, criticism, abuse, and setbacks. Courage includes stating the realities, even when they are harsh, and publicly stating what you will do to help and what you want from others. This means laying the cards on the table honestly: Here is what I want from you . . . What do you want from me?[121]

Developing Your Leadership Skills

LO 9

As with other things, you must work at *developing* your leadership abilities. Great musicians and great athletes don't become great on natural gifts alone. They also pay their dues by practicing, learning, and sacrificing. Leaders in a variety of fields, when asked how they became the best leader possible, offered the following comments:[122]

- "I've observed methods and skills of my bosses that I respected."
- "By taking risks, trying, and learning from my mistakes."
- "Reading autobiographies of leaders I admire to try to understand how they think."
- "Lots of practice."
- "By making mistakes myself and trying a different approach."
- "By purposely engaging with others to get things done."
- "By being put in positions of responsibility that other people counted on."

Julie Sajda, Foodservice Director at Hearst Tower in Manhattan, developed herself as a leader by seeking out challenging assignments including catering at the Salt Lake City Winter Olympics and opening the catering program at the Time Warner Center, and by tapping into expertise from mentors.

How Do I Start?

How do you go about developing your leadership abilities? You don't have to wait until you land a management job or even finish your education. You can begin establishing credibility by behaving with integrity, learning from your mistakes, and becoming competent in your chosen field. You should look for—and then seize—opportunities to take actions that will help the groups you already belong to. Even before you are a supervisor, you can practice empowering others by listening carefully when you are in a group and by sharing what you know so that the whole group will be better informed. Finally, begin building a network of personal contacts by reaching out to others to offer help, not just to request it.[123]

When you are searching for your next job, look for a position with an employer that is committed to developing leadership talent. Ideally, leadership development is connected to opportunities to practice the skills you are learning about, so ask about chances to lead a project or a team, even for short periods of time.[124] Companies that excel at leadership development include Johnson & Johnson, Hewlett-Packard, and General Electric.[125]

More specifically, here are some developmental experiences you should seek:[126]

- *Assignments:* Building something from nothing; fixing or turning around a failing operation; taking on project or task force responsibilities; accepting international assignments.
- *Other people:* Having exposure to positive role models; increasing visibility to others; working with people of diverse backgrounds.
- *Hardships:* Overcoming ideas that fail and deals that collapse; confronting others' performance problems; breaking out of a career rut.
- *Other events:* Formal courses; challenging job experiences; supervision of others; experiences outside work.

What Are the Keys?

The most effective developmental experiences have three components: assessment, challenge, and support.[127] *Assessment* includes information that gives you an understanding of where you are now, what your strengths are, your current levels of performance and leadership effectiveness, and your primary development needs. You can think about what your past feedback has been, what previous successes and failures you have had, how people have reacted to your ideas and actions, what your personal goals are, and what strategies you should implement to make progress. You can seek answers from your peers at work, bosses, family, friends, customers, and anyone else who knows you and how you work. The information you collect will help clarify what you need to learn, improve, or change.

The most potent developmental experiences provide *challenge*—they stretch you. We all think and behave in habitual, comfortable ways. This is natural, and perhaps sufficient to survive. But you've probably heard people say how important it can be to get out of your comfort zone—to tackle situations that require new skills and abilities, that are confusing or ambiguous, or that you simply would rather not deal with. Sometimes the challenge comes from lack of experience; other times, it requires changing old habits. It may be uncomfortable, but this is how great managers learn. Remember, some people don't bother to learn or refuse to learn. Make sure you think about your experiences along the way and reflect on them afterward, introspectively and in discussion with others.

You receive *support* when others send the message that your efforts to learn and grow are valued. Without support, challenging developmental experiences can be overwhelming. With support, it is easier to handle the struggle, stay on course, open up to learning, and actually learn from experiences. Support can come informally from other people; more formally through the procedures of the organization; and through learning resources in the forms of training, constructive feedback, talking with others, and so on.

What develops in leadership development? Through such experiences, you can acquire more self-awareness and self-confidence, a broader perspective on the organizational system, creative thinking, the ability to work more effectively in complex social systems, and the ability to learn from experience. As part of your training, take a few notes on the qualities that have made Amory Lovins a success in the "Management Close-Up: Assessing Outcomes and Seizing Opportunities" feature.

Management Close-Up

ASSESSING OUTCOMES AND SEIZING OPPORTUNITIES

Amory Lovins was once considered an eccentric—someone whose ideas were interesting yet radical. But with the recent shocks to the global economy from wild swings in oil prices, the world is beginning to catch up with Lovins and the vision he's been espousing since the 1970s. "I'm getting painfully respectable," he said.

Corporate America and U.S. and foreign government officials have been turning to Lovins and his institute for help, and he and his staff have been working long hours to provide advice and assistance. In fact, in the nearly 30 years since the nonprofit Rocky Mountain Institute was established, the organization has grown to a staff of nearly 100, with offices in Snowmass and Boulder. The organization has also spun off three for-profit businesses. Of the growth Lovins said, "We thought we'd just grow from a handful of people to at most a dozen."

Which companies have RMI staffers been assisting? Faced with the decision to build its next computer-chip fabrication plant in the United States or overseas, Texas Instruments sought RMI's expertise. Together, client and consultant generated ideas for building and operating the plant more efficiently. Texas Instruments used those ideas during construction of its $300 million state-of-the-art U.S. facility, saving nearly $150 million in construction costs alone. Moreover, the facility is designed to use 20 percent less energy and 35 percent less water, with only half the nitrous oxide emissions of conventional facilities.

Walmart also sought RMI's help to improve the energy efficiency of its global truck fleet. RMI's recommendations enabled Walmart to retrofit its fleet. The fleet's fuel efficiency, once a paltry 6 miles per gallon, will get 16 to 18 miles per gallon by 2015. The changes will save Walmart an estimated $500 million a year. In addition, RMI's $13.2 million retrofit of New York's landmark Empire State Building is expected to reduce its energy consumption by 35 to 40 percent, saving more than $4 million a year.

RMI currently works with 10 of the world's top 50 companies, helping them create environmentally sustainable business strategies. Its work in recent years has helped clients redesign more than $30 billion in projects for more energy efficiency. In 2009 Lovins was named to *Rolling Stone*'s list of 100 people who are changing America and *Time* magazine's 100 most influential people. The National Design Awards recently bestowed its Design Mind honor on Lovins. Despite the recognition, Lovins maintains that he is motivated by public service.[128]

- Would you consider Amory Lovins to be a charismatic leader? A transformational leader? Explain.
- RMI staff and clients say Amory Lovins is a consensus builder. How does consensus building make a leader more effective? Does the recent world focus on global warming and the environment enhance Amory Lovins's leadership capabilities? Explain.

KEY TERMS

Authentic leadership,   p. 439

Autocratic leadership,   p. 427

Behavioral approach,   p. 427

Bridge leaders,   p. 440

Charismatic leader,   p. 436

Democratic leadership,   p. 427

Fiedler's contingency model of
    leadership effectiveness,   p. 431

Group maintenance behaviors,   p. 426

Hersey and Blanchard's situational
    theory,   p. 433

Job maturity,   p. 433

Laissez-faire,   p. 428

Lateral leadership,   p. 440

Leader-Member Exchange (LMX)
    theory,   p. 426

Level 5 leadership,   p. 439

Participation in decision making,   p. 427

Path-goal theory,   p. 434

Power,   p. 422

Pseudotransformational leaders,   p. 439

Psychological maturity,   p. 433

Relationship-motivated leadership,
    p. 433

Servant-leader,   p. 440

Shared leadership,   p. 440

Situational approach,   p. 429

Strategic leadership,   p. 421

Substitutes for leadership,   p. 435

Supervisory leadership,   p. 421

Task-motivated leadership,   p. 433

Task performance behaviors,   p. 426

Trait approach,   p. 424

Transactional leaders,   p. 437

Transformational leader,   p. 437

Vision,   p. 419

Vroom model,   p. 430

SUMMARY OF LEARNING OBJECTIVES

Now that you have studied Chapter 12, you should be able to:

LO 1   Discuss what it means to be a leader.

A leader is one who influences others to attain goals. Leaders orchestrate change, set direction, and motivate people to overcome obstacles and move the organization toward its ideal future.

LO 2   Summarize what people want and organizations need from their leaders.

People want help in achieving their goals, and organizations need leaders at all levels. The best leaders challenge the process, inspire a shared vision, enable others to act, model the way, and encourage the heart.

LO 3   Explain how a good vision helps you be a better leader.

Outstanding leaders have vision. A vision is a mental image that goes beyond the ordinary and perhaps beyond what others thought possible. The vision provides the direction in which the leader wants the organization to move and inspiration for people to pursue it.

LO 4   Identify sources of power in organizations.

Having power and using it appropriately are essential to effective leadership. Managers at all levels of the organization have five potential sources of power: Legitimate power is the company-granted authority to direct others. Reward power is control over rewards valued by others in the organization. Coercive power is control over punishments that others in the organization want to avoid. Referent power consists of personal characteristics that appeal to others, so they model their behavior on the leader's and seek the leader's approval. Expert power is expertise or knowledge that can benefit others in the organization.

LO 5   List personal traits and skills of effective leaders.

Important leader characteristics include drive, leadership, motivation, integrity, self-confidence, and knowledge of the business. Perhaps the most important skill is the ability to accurately perceive the situation and then change behavior accordingly.

LO 6   Describe behaviors that will make you a better leader, and identify when the situation calls for them.

Important leader behaviors include task performance behaviors, group maintenance, and participation in decision making. According to the Vroom model, the leadership style should involve individual decisions, consultation with followers, facilitation, or delegation depending on the qualities such as the significance of the decision and the importance of followers' commitment. Fiedler's contingency model says a task-motivated leader is more successful when leader–member relations are good and the task is highly structured, or with an unstructured task but low position power for the leader, or with poor leader–member relations when the task structure and leader's position power are both low. In other situations, a relationship-oriented leader will perform better. Hersey and Blanchard's situational theory says that task performance behaviors become less important as the follower's job maturity and psychological maturity increase. Path-goal theory assesses characteristics of the followers, the leader, and the situation; it then indicates the appropriateness of directive, supportive, participative, or achievement-oriented leadership behaviors.

LO 7   Distinguish between charismatic and transformational leaders.

To have charisma is to be dominant and self-confident, to have a strong conviction of the righteousness of your beliefs, to create an aura of competence and success, and to communicate high expectations for and confidence in your followers. Charisma is one component of transformational leadership. Transformational leaders translate a vision into reality by getting people to transcend their individual interests for the good of the larger community. They do this through charisma, individualized attention to followers, intellectual stimulation, formation and communication of their vision, building of trust, and positive self-regard.

LO 8 Describe types of opportunities to be a leader in an organization.

There's plenty of opportunity to be a leader; being a manager of others who report to you is just the traditional one. You can also take or create opportunities to be a servant-leader or bridge leader and engage in shared leadership and lateral leadership. A servant-leader serves others' needs while strengthening the organization. A bridge leader uses experiences of other cultures to bridge conflicts between value systems. Shared leadership involves taking on a leadership role when your skills are most relevant to a particular situation. Lateral leadership is inspiring people to work collaboratively and solve problems together.

LO 9 Discuss how to further your own leadership development.

You can develop your own leadership skills not only by understanding what effective leadership is all about but also by seeking challenging developmental experiences. Such important life experiences come from taking challenging assignments, through exposure in working with other people, by overcoming hardships and failures, by taking formal courses, and by other actions. The most important elements of a good developmental experience are assessment, challenge, and support.

DISCUSSION QUESTIONS

1. What do you want from your leader?
2. Is there a difference between effective management and effective leadership? Explain your views and learn from others' views.
3. Identify someone you think is an effective leader. What traits and skills does this person possess that make him or her effective?
4. Do you think most managers can be transformational leaders? Why or why not?
5. In your own words, define courage. What is the role of courage in leadership? Give examples of acts of leadership you consider courageous.
6. Do you think men and women differ in their leadership styles? If so, how? Do men and/or women prefer different styles in their bosses? What evidence do you have for your answers?
7. Who are your heroes? What makes them heroes, and what can you learn from them?
8. Assess yourself as a leader based on what you have read in this chapter. What are your strengths and weaknesses?
9. Identify the developmental experiences you have had that may have strengthened your ability to lead. What did those experiences teach you? Also identify some developmental experiences you need to acquire, and how you will seek them. Be specific.
10. Consider a couple of decisions you are facing that could involve other people. Use the Vroom model to decide what approach to use to make the decisions.
11. Consider a job you hold or held in the past. Consider how your boss managed you. How would you describe him or her as a leader? What substitutes for leadership would you have enjoyed seeing put into place?
12. Consider an organization of which you are a leader or a member. What could great transformational leadership accomplish in the organization?
13. Name some prominent leaders whom you would describe as authentic and inauthentic and discuss.
14. Name some leaders you consider servant-leaders, and discuss.
15. Identify some opportunities for you to exhibit shared leadership and lateral leadership.

CONCLUDING CASE

The Law Offices of Jeter, Jackson, Guidry, and Boyer

THE EVOLUTION OF THE FIRM

David Jeter and Nate Jackson started a small general law practice in 1992 near Sacramento, California. Prior to that, the two had spent five years in the district attorney's office after completing their formal schooling. What began as a small partnership—just the two attorneys and a paralegal/assistant—had now grown into a practice that employed more than 27 people in three separated towns. The current staff included 18 attorneys (three of whom have become partners), three paralegals, and six secretaries.

For the first time in the firm's existence, the partners felt that they were losing control of their overall operation. The firm's current caseload, number of employees, number of clients, travel requirements, and facilities management needs had grown far beyond anything that the original partners had ever imagined.

Attorney Jeter called a meeting of the partners to discuss the matter. Before the meeting, opinions about the pressing problems of the day and proposed solutions were sought from the entire staff. The meeting resulted in a formal decision to create a new position, general manager of operations. The partners proceeded to compose a job description and job announcement for recruiting purposes.

Highlights and major responsibilities of the job description include:

- Supervising day-to-day office personnel and operations (phones, meetings, word processing, mail, billings, payroll, general overhead, and maintenance).
- Improving customer relations (more expeditious processing of cases and clients).
- Expanding the customer base.
- Enhancing relations with the local communities.
- Managing the annual budget and related incentive programs.
- Maintaining an annual growth in sales of 10 percent while maintaining or exceeding the current profit margin.

The general manager will provide an annual executive summary to the partners, along with specific action plans for improvement and change. A search committee was formed, and two months later the new position was offered to Brad Howser, a longtime administrator from the insurance industry seeking a final career change and a return to his California roots. Howser made it clear that he was willing to make a five-year commitment to the position and would then likely retire.

Things got off to a quiet and uneventful start as Howser spent the first few months just getting to know the staff; observing day-to-day operations; and reviewing and analyzing assorted client and attorney data and history, financial spreadsheets, and so on.

About six months into the position, Howser became more outspoken and assertive with the staff and established several new operational rules and procedures. He began by changing the regular working hours. The firm previously had a flex schedule in place that allowed employees to begin and end the workday at their choosing within given parameters. Howser did not care for such a "loose schedule" and now required that all office personnel work from 9:00 to 5:00 each day. A few staff members were unhappy about this and complained to Howser, who matter-of-factly informed them that "this is the new rule that everyone is expected to follow, and anyone who could or would not comply should probably look for another job." Sylvia Bronson, an administrative assistant who had been with the firm for several years, was particularly unhappy about this change. She arranged for a private meeting with Howser to discuss her child care circumstances and the difficulty that the new schedule presented. Howser seemed to listen half-heartedly and at one point told Bronson that "assistants are essentially a-dime-a-dozen and are readily available." Bronson was seen leaving the office in tears that day.

Howser was not happy with the average length of time that it took to receive payments for services rendered to the firm's clients (accounts receivable). A closer look showed that 30 percent of the clients paid their bills in 30 days or less, 60 percent paid in 30 to 60 days, and the remaining 10 percent stretched it out to as many as 120 days. Howser composed a letter that was sent to all clients whose outstanding invoices exceeded 30 days. The strongly worded letter demanded immediate payment in full and went on to indicate that legal action might be taken against anyone who did not respond in a timely fashion. While a small number of "late" payments were received soon after the mailing, the firm received an even larger number of letters and phone calls from angry clients, some of whom had been with the firm since its inception.

Howser was given an advertising and promotion budget for purposes of expanding the client base. One of the paralegals suggested that those expenditures should be carefully planned and that the firm had several attorneys who knew the local markets quite well and could probably offer some insight and ideas on the subject. Howser thought about this briefly and then decided to go it alone, reasoning that most attorneys know little or nothing about marketing.

In an attempt to "bring all of the people together to form a team," Howser established weekly staff meetings. These mandatory, hour-long sessions were run by Howser, who presented a series of overhead slides, handouts, and lectures about "some of the proven management techniques that were successful in the insurance industry." The meetings typically ran past the allotted time frame and rarely if ever covered all of the agenda items.

Howser spent some of his time "enhancing community relations." He was very generous with many local groups such as the historical society, the garden clubs, the recreational sports programs, the middle- and high-school band programs, and others. In less than six months he had written checks and authorized donations totaling more than $25,000. He was delighted about all of this and was certain that such gestures of goodwill would pay off handsomely in the future.

As for the budget, Howser carefully reviewed each line item in search of ways to increase revenues and cut expenses. He then proceeded to increase the expected base or quota for attorneys' monthly billable hours, thus directly affecting their profit sharing and bonus program. On the cost side, he significantly reduced the attorneys' annual budget for travel, meals, and entertainment. He considered these to be frivolous and unnecessary. Howser decided that one of the two full-time administrative assistant positions in each office should be reduced to part-time with no benefits. He saw no reason why the current workload could not be completed within this model. Howser wrapped up his initial financial review and action plan by posting notices throughout each office with new rules regarding the use of copy machines, phones, and supplies.

Howser completed the first year of his tenure with the required executive summary report to the partners that included his analysis of the current status of each department and his action plan. The partners were initially impressed both with Howser's approach to the new job and with the changes that he made. They all seemed to make sense and were directly in line with the key components of his job description. At the same time, "the office rumor mill and grapevine" had "heated up" considerably. Company morale, which had always been quite high, was now clearly waning. The water coolers and hallways became the frequent meeting place of disgruntled employees.

As for the marketplace, while the partners did not expect to see an immediate influx of new clients, they certainly did not expect to see shrinkage in their existing client base. A number of individual and corporate clients took their business elsewhere, still fuming over the letter they had received.

The partners met with Howser to discuss the situation. Howser urged them to "sit tight and ride out the storm." He had seen this happen before and had no doubt that in the long run the firm would achieve all of its goals. Howser pointed out that people in general are resistant to change. The partners met for drinks later that day and looked at each other with a great sense of uncertainty. Should they ride out the storm as Howser suggested? Had they done the right thing in creating the position and in hiring Howser? What had started as a seemingly wise, logical, and smooth sequence of events had now become a crisis.

QUESTIONS

1. Do you agree with Howser's suggestion to "sit tight and ride out the storm," or should the partners take some action immediately? If so, what actions specifically?

2. Assume that the creation of the GM–Operations position was a good decision. What leadership style and type of individual would you try to place in this position?

3. Consider your own leadership style. What types of positions and situations should you seek? What types of positions and situations should you seek to avoid? Why?

EXPERIENTIAL EXERCISES

12.1 Power and Influence

OBJECTIVE

To explore the nature of power and influence, and your attitudes toward different kinds of power and influence.

INSTRUCTIONS

Read the introductions and complete sections A, B, and C.

Power and Influence Worksheet

A. Power

Many well-known people have made statements about power and winning (e.g., P. T. Barnum, Mao Tse-tung, Leo Durocher, Lord Acton, Vince Lombardi). Some of these statements are listed in the table that follows. Indicate how you feel about each of the statements by circling number 1 if you strongly disagree, and so on.

	Strongly Disagree	Disagree	Neutral	Agree	Strongly Agree
Winning is everything.	1	2	3	4	5
Nice guys finish last.	1	2	3	4	5
There can only be one winner.	1	2	3	4	5
There's a sucker born every minute.	1	2	3	4	5
You can't completely trust anyone.	1	2	3	4	5
All power rests at the end of the gun.	1	2	3	4	5
Power seekers are greedy and can't be trusted.	1	2	3	4	5
Power corrupts; absolute power corrupts absolutely.	1	2	3	4	5
You get as much power as you pay for.	1	2	3	4	5

B. Influence

During the past week or so you have come in contact with many people. Some have influenced you positively, some negatively. Try to recall recent experiences with employers, peers, teachers, parents, clergy, and the like who may have influenced you in some way. Then try to think about how and why they influenced you as they did.

1. On the following table, list the names of all those who influenced you during the past week or so according to the kind of power that person used. The same person's name may appear under more than one type of power if that person used multiple power bases. Also, indicate whether the influence was positive (+) or negative (−).

Power Base	Names and Whether (+) or (−)
Legitimate authority	_____
Reward	_____
Coercive	_____
Referent	_____
Expert	_____

2. After examining your list, check (√) the following questions.

	Yes	No
a. Was there one person who had + marks appearing under several power bases?	_____	_____
b. Was there one person who had − marks appearing under several power bases?	_____	_____
c. Did you find that most of the people with + marks tended to fall under the same power bases?	_____	_____
d. Did you find that most of the people with − marks tended to fall under the same power bases?	_____	_____

3. From your answers to the last two questions, list which power bases you found to be positive (+) and which you found to be negative (−).

+	−
_____	_____
_____	_____
_____	_____
_____	_____
_____	_____

Do you think you personally prefer to use those power bases you listed under + when you try to influence people? Do you actually use them?

C. Power and Influence

From the table in Part B, find the one person who you think had the strongest positive influence on you (Person 1), and the one who had the strongest negative influence (Person 2). These are most likely the persons whose names appear most frequently.

In the following table, place a 1 on the line for each statement that best indicates how you think Person 1 would respond to that statement. Put a 2 on the line for each statement that reflects how you think Person 2 would respond to that item.

	Strongly Disagree	Disagree	Neutral	Agree	Strongly Agree
Winning is everything.	_____	_____	_____	_____	_____
Nice guys finish last.	_____	_____	_____	_____	_____
There can only be one winner.	_____	_____	_____	_____	_____
There's a sucker born every minute.	_____	_____	_____	_____	_____
You can't completely trust anyone.	_____	_____	_____	_____	_____
All power rests at the end of the gun.	_____	_____	_____	_____	_____
Power seekers are greedy and can't be trusted.	_____	_____	_____	_____	_____
Power corrupts; absolute power corrupts absolutely.	_____	_____	_____	_____	_____
You get as much power as you pay for.	_____	_____	_____	_____	_____

Now compare your responses in Part A to those in Part C. Do you more closely resemble Person 1 or Person 2? Do you prefer to use the kinds of power that person uses? Which kinds of power do you use most frequently? Which do you use least frequently? When do you feel you have the greatest power? When do you have the least power? How do these answers compare to what you found in Part B3?

SOURCE: Excerpted from Lawrence R. Jauch, Arthur G. Bedeian, Sally A. Coltin, and William F. Glueck, *The Managerial Experience: Cases, Exercises, and Readings*, 5th ed. Copyright © 1989. Reprinted with permission of South-Western, a division of Thomson Learning, www.thomsonrights.com. Fax 800 730-2215.

12.2 Evaluating Your Leadership Style

OBJECTIVES

1. To examine your personal style of leadership.
2. To study the nature of the leadership process.
3. To identify ways to improve or modify your leadership style.

INSTRUCTIONS

1. Working alone, complete and score the Leadership Style Survey.
2. In small groups, exchange scores, compute average scores, and develop responses to the discussion questions.
3. After the class reconvenes, group spokespersons present group findings.

DISCUSSION QUESTIONS

1. In what ways did your experience or lack of experience influence your responses to the survey?
2. In what ways did student scores and student responses to survey test items converge? In what ways did they diverge?
3. What do you think accounts for differences in student leadership attitudes?
4. How can students make constructive use of the survey results?

Leadership Style Survey

This survey describes various aspects of leadership behavior. To measure your leadership style, respond to each statement according to the way you would act (or think you would act) if you were a work group leader.

	Always	Frequently	Occasionally	Seldom	Never
1. I would allow team members the freedom to do their jobs in their own way.	5	4	3	2	1
2. I would make important decisions on my own initiative without consulting the workers.	5	4	3	2	1
3. I would allow the team members to make their own decisions.	5	4	3	2	1
4. I would not try to socialize with the workers.	5	4	3	2	1
5. I would allow team members to do their jobs as they see fit.	5	4	3	2	1
6. I would consider myself to be the group's spokesperson.	5	4	3	2	1
7. I would be warm, friendly, and approachable.	5	4	3	2	1
8. I would be sure that the workers understand and follow all the rules and regulations.	5	4	3	2	1
9. I would demonstrate a real concern for the workers' welfare.	5	4	3	2	1
10. I would be the one to decide what is to be done and how it is to be done.	5	4	3	2	1
11. I would delegate authority to the workers.	5	4	3	2	1
12. I would urge the workers to meet production quotas.	5	4	3	2	1
13. I would trust the workers to use good judgment in decision making.	5	4	3	2	1
14. I would assign specific tasks to specific people.	5	4	3	2	1
15. I would let the workers establish their own work pace.	5	4	3	2	1
16. I would not feel that I have to explain my decisions to workers.	5	4	3	2	1
17. I would try to make each worker feel that his or her contribution is important.	5	4	3	2	1
18. I would establish the work schedules.	5	4	3	2	1
19. I would encourage workers to get involved in setting work goals.	5	4	3	2	1
20. I would be action oriented and results oriented.	5	4	3	2	1
21. I would get the workers involved in making decisions.	5	4	3	2	1
22. I would outline needed changes and monitor action closely.	5	4	3	2	1
23. I would help the group achieve consensus on important changes.	5	4	3	2	1
24. I would supervise closely to ensure that standards are met.	5	4	3	2	1
25. I would consistently reinforce good work.	5	4	3	2	1
26. I would nip problems in the bud.	5	4	3	2	1
27. I would consult the group before making decisions.	5	4	3	2	1

chapter 13

Motivating for Performance

LEARNING OBJECTIVES

After studying Chapter 13, you will be able to:

LO 1 Identify the kinds of behaviors managers need to motivate in people. p. 454

LO 2 List principles for setting goals that motivate employees. p. 455

LO 3 Summarize how to reward good performance effectively. p. 457

LO 4 Describe the key beliefs that affect people's motivation. p. 461

LO 5 Discuss ways in which people's individual needs affect their behavior. p. 463

LO 6 Define ways to create jobs that motivate. p. 468

LO 7 Summarize how people assess fairness and how to achieve fairness. p. 473

LO 8 Identify causes and consequences of a satisfied workforce. p. 476

CHAPTER OUTLINE

Motivating for Performance

Setting Goals
Goals That Motivate
Stretch Goals
Limitations of Goal Setting
Set Your Own Goals

Reinforcing Performance
(Mis)Managing Rewards and Punishments
Managing Mistakes
Providing Feedback

Performance-Related Beliefs
The Effort-to-Performance Link
The Performance-to-Outcome Link
Impact on Motivation
Managerial Implications of Expectancy Theory

Understanding People's Needs
Maslow's Need Hierarchy
Alderfer's ERG Theory
McClelland's Needs
Need Theories: International Perspectives

Designing Motivating Jobs
Job Rotation, Enlargement, and Enrichment
Herzberg's Two-Factor Theory
The Hackman and Oldham Model of Job Design
Empowerment

Achieving Fairness
Assessing Equity
Restoring Equity
Procedural Justice

Job Satisfaction
Quality of Work Life
Psychological Contracts

Management Close-Up

Who says that handling customer orders has to be drudgery? If you work at Zappos.com, you are encouraged—even expected—to have fun on the job. Zappos, a Las Vegas–based online shoe seller, calls itself "a service company that just happens to sell shoes." Zappos's employees—who call themselves Zapponians—belong to a dedicated sales staff who aim to delight customers. Order from Zappos, and you'll enjoy free shipping, a 365-day return policy, and top-notch care from service representatives who go the extra mile.

According to Zappos's CEO Tony Hsieh, a company's most important differentiator is excellent customer service, and the key to happy customers is happy employees. When it comes to hiring, Zappos is selective. Although candidates do not need to be crazy about shoes, they do need to be outgoing, open-minded, and passionate about service. All new hires—whether they are working a phone or sitting in a corner office—undergo four weeks of training that includes a stint in the call center. Those who decide the company is not for them can exit with a check for $2,000, no questions asked. Hsieh says about 3 percent leave at that point, and that is fine with him. Hsieh wants to make sure that every new employee fits in with the company culture because the culture *is* the Zappos brand.

Zappos's employees enjoy a wide array of benefits. In addition to free lunch, snacks, and beverages daily, they receive company-paid medical and dental insurance, a 40 percent discount on merchandise, a nap room, regular happy hours, a profit-sharing plan, a library stocked with free business and management books, and access to a full-time on-site life coach. Employees who feel the need to vent—or get some career counseling—sit on a red-velvet throne during their coaching session.[1]

> As CEO of Zappos, Tony Hsieh recognizes that motivated employees are key to the success of his company. As you read this chapter, consider how Hsieh has boosted Zappos's growth and morale.

This chapter tackles an age-old question: How can a manager motivate people to work hard and perform at their best levels? Tony Hsieh of Zappos.com has shown how important a company's culture can be in encouraging people to do their best work.

A sales manager in one company had another unique approach to this question. Each month, the person with the worst sales performance took home a live goat for the weekend. The manager hoped the goat-of-the-month employee would be so embarrassed that he or she would work harder the next month to increase sales.[2] This sales manager may get high marks for creativity. But if he is graded by results, as he grades his salespeople, he will fail. He may succeed in motivating a few of his people to increase sales, but some good people will be motivated to quit the company.

Motivating for Performance

motivation

Forces that energize, direct, and sustain a person's efforts.

Understanding why people do the things they do on the job is not an easy task for a manager. *Predicting* their response to management's latest productivity program is harder yet. Fortunately, enough is known about motivation to give the thoughtful manager practical, effective techniques for increasing people's effort and performance.

Motivation refers to forces that energize, direct, and sustain a person's efforts. All behavior, except involuntary reflexes like eye blinks (which have little to do with management), is motivated. A highly motivated person will work hard toward achieving performance goals. With adequate ability, understanding of the job, and access to the necessary resources, such a person will be highly productive.

To be effective motivators, managers must know what behaviors they want to motivate people to exhibit. Although productive people appear to do a seemingly limitless number of things, most of the important activities can be grouped into five general categories.[3] Managers must motivate people to (1) *join the organization*, (2) *remain in the organization*, and (3) *come to work regularly*. On these points, you should reject the common recent notion that loyalty is dead and accept the challenge of creating an environment that will attract and energize people so that they commit to the organization.[4]

Of course, companies also want people to (4) *perform*—that is, once employees are at work, they should work hard to achieve high *output* (productivity) and high *quality*. Finally, managers want employees to (5) *exhibit good citizenship*. Good citizens of the organization are committed, satisfied employees who perform above and beyond the call of duty by doing extra things that can help the company. The importance of citizenship behaviors may be less obvious than productivity, but these behaviors help the organization function smoothly. They also make managers' lives easier.

"Employee loyalty exists, but it depends upon what the company is willing to do for its employees."
    —Vinnie, an employee at a New York investment bank, on why he turned down a job paying 30 percent more to stay with his current employer, who allows him to telecommute[5]

Many ideas have been proposed to help managers motivate people to engage in these constructive behaviors. The most useful of these ideas are described in the following pages. We start with the most fundamental *processes* that influence the motivation of all people. These processes—described by goal-setting, reinforcement, and expectancy theories—suggest basic and powerful actions for managers to take. Then we discuss the *content* of what people want and need from work, how individuals differ from one another, and how understanding people's needs leads to powerful prescriptions about designing motivating jobs and empowering people to perform at the highest possible levels. Finally, we discuss the most important beliefs and perceptions about fairness that people hold toward their work, and the implications for motivation.

Setting Goals

LO 2

Providing work-related goals for people is an extremely effective way to stimulate motivation. In fact, it is perhaps the most important, valid, and useful single approach to motivating performance. Therefore, we discuss it first.

Goal-setting theory states that people have conscious goals that energize them and direct their thoughts and behaviors toward a particular end.[6] Keeping in mind the principle that goals matter, managers set goals for employees or collaborate with employees on goal setting. For example, a satellite TV company might set goals for increasing the number of new subscribers, the number of current subscribers who pay for premium channels, or the timeliness of responses to customer inquiries.[7] Goal setting works for any job in which people have control over their performance.[8] You can set goals for performance quality and quantity, plus behavioral goals like cooperation or teamwork.[9] In fact, you can set goals for whatever is important.[10]

goal-setting theory

A motivation theory stating that people have conscious goals that energize them and direct their thoughts and behaviors toward a particular end.

Goals That Motivate

The most powerful goals are *meaningful;* noble purposes that appeal to people's "higher" values add extra motivating power.[11] Johnson & Johnson pursues profit, but it's also about improving health care. Ben & Jerry's makes great ice cream but also is socially responsible. ServiceMaster, the cleaning and maintenance company, has a religious commitment that appeals to its employees, and Huntsman Chemical has goals of paying off corporate debt but also relieving human suffering—it sponsors cancer research and a number of charities. Meaningful goals also may be based on data about competitors; exceeding competitors' performance can stoke people's competitive spirit and desire to succeed in the marketplace.[12] This point is not just about

 You can set goals for cost, quality, speed, service, innovation— anything that's important.

the values companies espouse and the lofty goals they pursue; it's also about leadership at a more personal level. Followers of transformational leaders view their work as more important and as highly congruent with their personal goals compared with transactional leaders[13] (recall Chapter 12).

More specifically, much is known about how to manage goals in ways that motivate high job performance. Goals should be *acceptable* to employees. This means, among other things, that they should not conflict with people's personal values and that people have reasons to pursue the goals. Allowing people to participate in setting their work goals—as opposed to having the boss set goals for them—is often a great way to generate goals that people accept and pursue willingly.

Ben & Jerry's is known for making some of the world's finest ice cream. But its social responsibility is also highly important to many employees and customers. Ben & Jerry are shown here with the rock band Daughtry to launch their latest ice cream flavor "ONE Cheesecake Brownie" with proceeds going to help fight global poverty.

Acceptable, maximally motivating goals are *challenging but attainable.* In other words, they should be high enough to inspire better performance but not so high that people can never reach them. One team of consultants to an international corporation created more than 40 programs aimed at increasing quality. The company announced it did not expect significant quality improvement until the *fourth year* of the program. Such a goal is not nearly demanding enough.[14]

Ideal goals do not merely exhort employees in general terms to improve performance, start doing their best, increase productivity, or decrease the length of time customers must wait to receive service. Goals should be more like Esco's target that by 2011 it will generate at least 5 percent of its revenue from selling products it has newly invented, or Guitar Center's objective that whenever a phone rings in one of its stores, a salesperson will pick it up before the fourth ring.[15] Such deadlines and measurable performance goals are specific, quantifiable goals that employees are motivated to achieve. Microsoft uses the acronym SMART to create motivating goals: specific, measurable, achievable, results-based, and time-specific.[16]

Stretch Goals

stretch goals

Targets that are particularly demanding, sometimes even thought to be impossible.

Some firms today set **stretch goals**—targets that are exceptionally demanding, and that some people would never even think of. There are two types of stretch goals: vertical stretch goals, aligned with current activities including productivity and financial results, and horizontal stretch goals, which involve people's professional development like attempting and learning new, difficult things.[17] Impossible though stretch goals may seem to some, they often are in fact attainable.

Stretch goals can generate a major shift away from mediocrity and toward tremendous achievement. But if someone tries in good faith but doesn't meet their stretch goals, don't punish—remember how difficult they are! Base your assessment on how much performance has improved, how the performance compares with others, and how much progress has been made.[18]

Limitations of Goal Setting

Goal setting is an extraordinarily powerful management technique. But even specific, challenging, attainable goals work better under some conditions than others. For example, if people lack relevant ability and knowledge, a better course to follow might be simply urging them to do their best or setting a goal to learn rather than a goal to achieve a specific performance level.[19] Individual performance goals can be dysfunctional if people work in a group and cooperation among team members is essential to team performance.[20] Individualized goals can create competition and reduce cooperation. If cooperation is important, performance goals should be established *for the team.*

Goals can generate manipulative game-playing and unethical behavior. For example, people can sometimes find ingenious ways to set easy goals and convince their bosses that they are difficult.[21] Or they may find ways to meet goals simply to receive a reward, without necessarily performing in desirable ways. For example, when Rockford Acromatic Products Company promoted employee health by offering bonuses to employees who quit smoking for several months, several workers first *started* smoking so they could quit and earn the bonus.[22] In addition, people who don't meet their goals are more likely to engage in unethical behavior than are people who are trying to do their best but have no specific performance goals. This is true regardless of whether they have financial incentives, and it is particularly true when people fall just short of reaching their goals.[23]

Another familiar example comes from the pages of financial reports. Some executives have mastered the art of "earnings management"—precisely meeting Wall Street analysts' earnings estimates or beating them by a single penny.[24] The media trumpet, and investors reward, the company that meets or beats the estimates. People sometimes meet this goal by either manipulating the numbers or initiating whispering campaigns to persuade analysts to lower their estimates, making them more attainable.

Vickie Stringer set a goal to publish her life story and pursued that goal with determination, eventually selling 100,000 copies. Along the way, she developed relationships with book distributors and eventually founded her firm, Triple Crown Publications.

The marketplace wants short-term, quarterly performance, but long-term viability is ultimately more important to a company's success.

It is important *not* to establish a single productivity goal if there are other important dimensions of performance.[25] For instance, if the acquisition of knowledge and skills is important, you can also set a specific and challenging learning goal like "identify 10 ways to develop relationships with end users of our products." Productivity goals will likely enhance productivity, but they may also cause employees to neglect other areas, such as learning, tackling new projects, or developing creative solutions to job-related problems. A manager who wants to motivate creativity can establish creativity goals along with productivity goals for individuals or for brainstorming teams.[26]

Set Your Own Goals

Goal setting works for yourself, as well—it's a powerful tool for self-management. Set goals for yourself; don't just try hard or hope for the best. Create a statement of purpose for yourself comprising three elements: an inspiring distant vision, a mid-distant goal along the way (worthy in its own right), and near-term objectives to start working on immediately.[27] So, if you are going into business, you might articulate your goal for the type of businessperson you want to be in five years, the types of jobs that could create the opportunities and teach you what you need to know to become that businessperson, and the specific schoolwork and job search activities that can get you moving in those directions. And on the job, apply SMART and other goal-setting advice for yourself.

Reinforcing Performance

Goals are universal motivators. So are the processes of reinforcement described in this section. In 1911, psychologist Edward Thorndike formulated the **law of effect:** Behavior that is followed by positive consequences probably will be repeated.[28] This powerful law of behavior laid the foundation for countless investigations into the effects of the positive consequences, called **reinforcers,** that motivate behavior. **Organizational behavior modification (or OB mod)** attempts to influence people's behavior, and improve performance,[29] by systematically managing work conditions and the consequences of people's actions.

Four key consequences of behavior either encourage or discourage people's behavior (see Figure 13.1):

1. **Positive reinforcement**—applying a positive consequence that increases the likelihood that the person will repeat the behavior that led to it. Examples of positive reinforcers include compliments, letters of commendation, favorable performance evaluations, and pay raises.[30] Chris Kinnersley, vice president of safety and organizational development at Staker & Parson Company, has helped the company's managers learn to select rewards that are immediate and personal. For example, at the construction materials and services company, the loader operators who work most efficiently might be rewarded by being assigned to the equipment known to be most comfortable.[31]

2. **Negative reinforcement**—removing or withholding an undesirable consequence. For example, a manager takes an employee (or a school takes a student) off probation because of improved performance. One way to understand the success of Capital One's Future of Work project is that it is a kind of negative reinforcement. This project recognizes that keeping a job can be a strain if you have family or personal obligations that conflict with the structured routine of a 9-to-5 job in an office away from home. The Future of Work project alleviates some of this strain by letting employees use a company-provided laptop, iPod, and BlackBerry so they can avoid some of the schedule conflicts of full-time work by getting work done at home or on the road, as well as in Capital One's flexible facilities.[32]

LO 3

law of effect

A law formulated by Edward Thorndike in 1911 stating that behavior that is followed by positive consequences will likely be repeated.

reinforcers

Positive consequences that motivate behavior.

organizational behavior modification (OB mod)

The application of reinforcement theory in organizational settings.

positive reinforcement

Applying consequences that increase the likelihood that a person will repeat the behavior that led to it.

negative reinforcement

Removing or withholding an undesirable consequence.

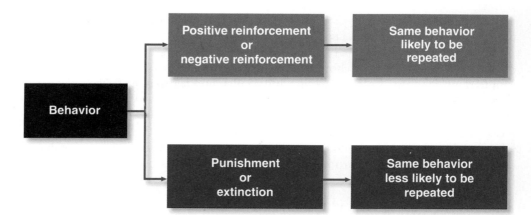

FIGURE 13.1
The Consequences of
Behavior

punishment

Administering an aversive
consequence.

extinction

Withdrawing or failing
to provide a reinforcing
consequence.

3. **Punishment**—administering an aversive consequence. Examples include criticizing or shouting at an employee, assigning an unappealing task, and sending a worker home without pay. Negative reinforcement can involve the *threat* of punishment by not delivering punishment when employees perform satisfactorily. Punishment is the actual delivery of the aversive consequence. Managers use punishment when they think it is warranted or when they believe others expect them to, and they usually concern themselves with following company policy and procedure.[33]

4. **Extinction**—withdrawing or failing to provide a reinforcing consequence. When this occurs, motivation is reduced and the behavior is *extinguished*, or eliminated. Ways that managers may unintentionally extinguish desired behaviors include not giving a compliment for a job well done, forgetting to say thanks for a favor, and setting impossible performance goals so that the person never experiences success. Extinction may be used to end undesirable behaviors, too. The manager might ignore long-winded observations during a meeting or fail to acknowledge unimportant e-mail in the hope that the lack of feedback will discourage the employee from continuing.

The first two consequences, positive and negative reinforcement, are positive for the person receiving them—the person either gains something or avoids something negative. Therefore, the person who experiences these consequences will be motivated to behave in the ways that led to the reinforcement. The last two consequences, punishment and extinction, are negative outcomes for the person receiving them: Motivation to repeat the behavior that led to the undesirable results will be reduced.

Managers should be careful to match consequences to what employees will actually find desirable or undesirable. At Staker & Parson, a supervisor once made the mistake of "punishing" an employee for tardiness by suspending him for three days during fishing season. The employee was delighted.[34]

(Mis)Managing Rewards and Punishments

You've learned about the positive effects of a transformational leadership style, but giving rewards to high-performing people is also essential.[35] Unfortunately, sometimes organizations and managers reinforce the wrong behaviors.[36] For example, compensation plans that include stock options are intended to reinforce behaviors that add to the company's value, but stock options also can reinforce decisions that artificially deliver short-term gains in stock prices, even if they hurt the company in the long run. Likewise, programs that punish employees for absenteeism beyond a certain limit may actually encourage them to be absent. People may use up all their allowable absences and fail to come to work regularly until they reach the point where their next absence will result in punishment. Sometimes, employees are reinforced with admiration and positive performance evaluations for multitasking—say, typing e-mail while on the phone or checking text messages during meetings. This behavior may look efficient and send a signal that the employee is busy and valuable, but multitasking actually slows down the brain's efficiency and can contribute to mistakes.[37] Scans of brain activity show that the brain is not able to concentrate on two tasks at once; it needs time to switch among the multitasker's activities. As a result, managers who praise the hard work of multitaskers may be unintentionally reinforcing inefficiency and failure to think deeply about problems.

To use reinforcement effectively, managers must identify which kinds of behaviors they reinforce and which they discourage (see Table 13.1). The reward system has to support the firm's strategy, defining people's performance in ways that pursue strategic objectives.[38] Reward employees for developing themselves in strategically important ways—for building new skills that are critical to strengthening core competencies and creating value.

Managers should be creative in their use of reinforcers. Sprint, where many workers spend their day sitting in front of a computer, reinforces healthy behavior by providing onsite exercise facilities, where employees can enjoy workouts during their lunch hours.[39] For Steven T. Bigari, owner of 12 McDonald's restaurants, the basic

Methodist Hospital System, located in Houston, recently gave each of its employees a $250 gift card to buy gasoline.[41]

challenge was how to motivate low-wage workers to stay on the job when faced with struggles to find affordable day care and transportation. Facing stiff competition from Taco Bell, Bigari concluded he couldn't afford higher wages, but he helped a local church set up a day care program, and he visited police auctions during his Saturday lunch breaks to purchase low-priced but reliable cars, which he resold at cost.[40]

Innovative managers use nonmonetary rewards, including intellectual challenge, greater responsibility, autonomy, recognition, flexible benefits, and greater influence over decisions. Julian Duncan, an assistant brand manager at Nike, has felt valued and encouraged because top-level managers take time to listen to him and address his concerns. For example, a vice president spent half an hour with Duncan, discussing a question Duncan had e-mailed to him.[42] These and other rewards for high-performing employees, when creatively devised and applied, can continue to motivate when pay and promotions are scarce. Employees at Brown Flynn—a firm that provides services to help companies exercise social responsibility—receive practical benefits such as profit sharing and creative ones like jewelry and shopping sprees, but the intangibles may be what matter most. Employees describe Brown Flynn as offering challenges and rewards, mutual respect, recognition for hard work, and opportunities to exercise leadership.[43] And one of Steven Bigari's McDonald's employees said she preferred

TABLE 13.1
The Greatest Management Principle in the World

"The things that get rewarded get done" is what one author called The Greatest Management Principle in the World. With this in mind, Michael LeBoeuf offered prescriptions for effectively motivating high performance. Companies, and individual managers, should reward the following:

1. *Solid solutions* instead of quick fixes.
2. *Risk taking* instead of risk avoiding.
3. *Applied creativity* instead of mindless conformity.
4. *Decisive action* instead of paralysis by analysis.
5. *Smart work* instead of busywork.
6. *Simplification* instead of needless complication.
7. *Quietly effective behavior* instead of squeaky wheels.
8. *Quality work* instead of fast work.
9. *Loyalty* instead of turnover.
10. *Working together* instead of working against.

SOURCE: From *The Greatest Management Principle in the World* by Michael LeBoeuf. Copyright © 1985 by Michael LeBoeuf. Used by permission of the author.

Managers who inappropriately yell at their staff or overuse punishment often create a climate of fear and anxiety in the workplace. How would you deal with a situation like this?

working for him to earning slightly more at a corporate-owned restaurant, because of the way Bigari treats employees: "He's not in it for himself; he's in it for the people."[44]

Managing Mistakes

How a manager reacts to people's mistakes has a big impact on motivation. Punishment is sometimes appropriate, as when people violate the law, ethical standards, important safety rules, or standards of interpersonal treatment, or when they fail to attend or perform like a slacker. But sometimes managers punish people when they shouldn't—when poor performance isn't the person's fault or when managers take out their frustrations on the wrong people.

Managers who overuse punishment or use it inappropriately create a climate of fear in the workplace.[45] Fear causes people to focus on the short term, sometimes creating problems in the longer run. Fear also creates a focus on oneself, rather than on the group and the organization. B. Joseph White, president of the University of Illinois, recalls consulting for a high-tech entrepreneur who heard a manager present a proposal and responded with brutal criticism: "That's the . . . stupidest idea I ever heard in my life. I'm disappointed in you." According to White, this talented manager was so upset she never again felt fully able to contribute.[46] For managers to avoid such damage, the key is how to think about and handle mistakes.

Recognize that everyone makes mistakes, and that mistakes can be dealt with constructively by discussing and learning from them. Don't punish, but praise, people who deliver bad news to their bosses. Treat failure to act as a failure but don't punish unsuccessful, good-faith efforts. If you're a leader, talk about your failures with your people, and show how you learned from them. Give people second chances, and maybe third chances (Donald Trump claims to give second chances, but never third). Encourage people to try new things, and don't punish them if what they try doesn't work out.

Providing Feedback

Make sure that you reward the right things, not the wrong things. Sound obvious? You'd be surprised how often this principle is violated!

Most managers don't provide enough useful feedback, and most people don't receive or ask for feedback enough.[47] As a manager, you should consider all potential causes of poor performance, pay full attention when employees ask for feedback or want to discuss performance issues, and give feedback according to the guidelines you read about in Chapter 10.

Feedback can be offered in many ways.[48] Customers sometimes give feedback directly: you also can request customer feedback and give it to the employee. You can provide statistics on work that the person has directly influenced. A manufacturing firm—high tech or otherwise—can put the phone number or Web site of the production team on the product so customers can contact the team directly. Performance reviews, described in Chapter 11, should be conducted regularly. And bosses should give more regular, ongoing feedback—it helps correct problems immediately, provides immediate reinforcement for good work, and prevents surprises when the formal review comes.

For yourself, try not to be afraid of receiving feedback; in fact, you should actively seek it. But whether or not you seek the feedback, when you get it, don't ignore it. Try to avoid negative emotions like anger, hurt, defensiveness, or resignation. Think: It's up to me to get the feedback I need; I need to know these things about my performance and my behavior; learning what I need to know about myself will help me identify needs and create new opportunities; it serves my interest best to know rather than not know; taking initiative on this gives me more power and influence over my career.[49]

Performance-Related Beliefs

In contrast to reinforcement theory, which describes the processes by which factors in the work environment affect people's behavior, expectancy theory considers some of the cognitive processes that go on in people's heads. According to **expectancy theory**, the person's work *efforts* lead to some level of *performance*.[50] Then performance results in one or more *outcomes* for the person. This process is shown in Figure 13.2. People develop two important beliefs linking these three events: expectancy, which links effort to performance, and instrumentality, which links performance to outcomes.

The Effort-to-Performance Link

The first belief, **expectancy**, is people's perceived likelihood that their efforts will enable them to attain their performance goals. An expectancy can be high (up to 100 percent), such as when a student is confident that if she studies hard, she can get a good grade on the final. An expectancy can also be low (down to a 0 percent likelihood), such as when a suitor is convinced that his dream date will never go out with him.

All else equal, high expectancies create higher motivation than do low expectancies. In the preceding examples, the student is more likely to study for the exam than the suitor is to pursue the dream date, even though both want their respective outcomes.

Expectancies can vary among individuals, even in the same situation. For example, a sales manager might initiate a competition in which the top salesperson wins a free trip to Hawaii. In such cases, the few top people, who have performed well in the past, will be more motivated by the contest than will the historically average and below-average performers. The top people will have higher expectancies—stronger beliefs that their efforts can help them turn in the top performance.

The Performance-to-Outcome Link

The example about the sales contest illustrates how performance results in some kind of **outcome**, or consequence, for the person. Actually, it often results in several outcomes. For example, turning in the best sales performance could lead to (1) a competitive victory, (2) the free trip to Hawaii, (3) feelings of achievement, (4) recognition from the boss, (5) prestige throughout the company, and (6) resentment from other salespeople.

But how certain is it that performance will result in all of those outcomes? Will winning the contest really lead to resentment? Will it really lead to increased prestige?

These questions address the second key belief described by expectancy theory: instrumentality.[51] **Instrumentality** is the perceived likelihood that performance will be followed by a particular outcome. Like expectancies, instrumentalities can be high (up to 100 percent) or low (approaching 0 percent). For example, you can be fully confident that if you do a good job, you'll get a promotion, or you can feel that no matter how well you do, the promotion will go to someone else.

Also, each outcome has an associated valence. **Valence** is the value the person places on the outcome. Valences can be positive, as a Hawaiian vacation would be for most people, or negative, as in the case of the other salespeople's resentment.

LO **4**

expectancy theory

A theory proposing that people will behave based on their perceived likelihood that their effort will lead to a certain outcome and on how highly they value that outcome.

expectancy

Employees' perception of the likelihood that their efforts will enable them to attain their performance goals.

outcome

A consequence a person receives for his or her performance.

instrumentality

The perceived likelihood that performance will be followed by a particular outcome.

valence

The value an outcome holds for the person contemplating it.

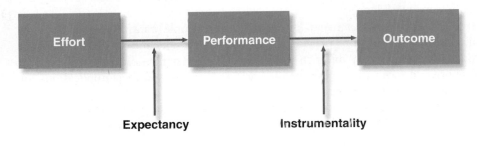

FIGURE 13.2
Basic Concepts of Expectancy Theory

Winning a competition for a free trip to Hawaii would be great, but what about all the losers?

Impact on Motivation

For motivation to be high, expectancy, instrumentalities, and total valence of all outcomes must all be high. A person will not be highly motivated if any of the following conditions exist:

1. He believes he can't perform well enough to achieve the positive outcomes that he knows the company provides to good performers (high valence and high instrumentality but low expectancy).
2. He knows he can do the job and is fairly certain what the ultimate outcomes will be (say, a promotion and a transfer). However, he doesn't want those outcomes or believes other, negative outcomes outweigh the positive (high expectancy and high instrumentality but low valence).
3. He knows he can do the job and wants several important outcomes (a favorable performance review, a raise, and a promotion). But he believes that no matter how well he performs, the outcomes will not be forthcoming (high expectancy and positive valences but low instrumentality).

Managerial Implications of Expectancy Theory

Expectancy theory helps the manager zero in on key leverage points for influencing motivation. Three implications are crucial:

1. *Increase expectancies.* Provide a work environment that facilitates good performance, and set realistically attainable performance goals. Provide training, support, required resources, and encouragement so that people are confident they can perform at the levels expected of them. Recall from Chapter 12 that charismatic leaders excel at boosting their followers' confidence.

2. *Identify positively valent outcomes.* Understand what people want to get out of work. Think about what their jobs provide them and what is not, but could be, provided. Consider how people may differ in the valences they assign to outcomes. Know the need theories of motivation, described in the next section, and their implications for identifying important outcomes.

3. *Make performance instrumental toward positive outcomes.* Make sure that good performance is followed by personal recognition and praise, favorable performance reviews,

pay increases, and other positive results. Also, make sure that working hard and doing things well will have as few negative results as possible. The way you emphasize instrumentality may need to be tailored to employees' locus of control, which we discussed in the context of leadership in Chapter 12. For people who have an external locus of control, tending to attribute results to luck or fate, you may need to make sure that they see a connection between what they do and what you reward. It is useful to realize, too, that bosses usually provide (or withhold) rewards, but others do so as well. Peers, direct reports, customers, and others tend to provide rewards in the form of compliments, help, and praise.

Organizations may set up formal reward systems as well. Umpqua Bank in Roseburg, Oregon, set up a link called "Brag Box" on its intranet. Employees visit the Brag Box to post comments about good things their coworkers have done. Sandy Hunt, Umpqua's vice president for rewards and recognition, regularly checks the Brag Box and notifies managers when their employees have received a compliment so that the managers can further reinforce compliments with praise. In addition, every team at Umpqua has a "recognition fund," which any team member can spend to recognize coworkers for going the extra mile.[52]

Recent experiments on how people make decisions provide additional insights into how managers can motivate employees. For example, in an effort to lower the health care costs of its employees, a billing and records firm called MED3000 invited them to fill out assessments of their health risks; employees with certain risks are steered to programs aimed at managing those risks. But what valued outcomes can the company provide? The general chance to improve one's health is not sufficient. The company divided its employees into three groups: one received $25 for filling out the assessment; a second group received the cash plus a $25 gift card to the supermarket; and a third group was enrolled in a weekly lottery with a chance to win up to $150 for completing the assessment. The lottery generated the best response rate.

Another company concerned about its employees' health is Amica Mutual Insurance. Amica offers a variety of wellness programs, including an on-site fitness center at its headquarters, subsidies for participating in Weight Watchers, free flu shots, and stop-smoking programs. Still, a sizable share of its employees had diabetes, a condition that can become serious—and expensive—if poorly managed. One problem, the company determined, was that there were too many choices, so it was easier to ignore the wellness programs than to set priorities. Amica began offering a program tailored to its employees with diabetes. Those who complete a series of preventive-health exams receive 100 percent coverage of the cost of their diabetes medications. The exams actually cut costs associated with complications, the free medicine is a valued reward, and visiting the doctor five times feels more doable than, say, a weight loss program.[53]

Understanding People's Needs

LO 5

So far we have focused on *processes* underlying motivation. The manager who appropriately applies goal-setting, reinforcement, and expectancy theories is creating essential motivating elements in the work environment. But motivation also is affected by characteristics of the person. The second type of motivation theory, *content theories*, indicates the kinds of needs that people want to satisfy. People have different needs energizing and motivating them toward different goals and reinforcers. The extent to which and the ways in which a person's needs are met or not met at work affect his or her behavior on the job.

The most important theories describing the content of people's needs are Maslow's need hierarchy, Alderfer's ERG theory, and McClelland's needs.

Maslow's Need Hierarchy

Maslow's need hierarchy

A conception of human needs organizing needs into a hierarchy of five major types.

Abraham Maslow organized five major types of human needs into a hierarchy, as shown in Figure 13.3.[54] **Maslow's need hierarchy** illustrates his conception of people satisfying their needs in a specified order, from bottom to top. The needs, in ascending order, are

1. *Physiological* (food, water, sex, and shelter).
2. *Safety or security* (protection against threat and deprivation).
3. *Social* (friendship, affection, belonging, and love).
4. *Ego* (independence, achievement, freedom, status, recognition, and self-esteem).
5. *Self-actualization* (realizing one's full potential, becoming everything one is capable of being).

According to Maslow, people are motivated to satisfy the lower needs before they try to satisfy the higher needs. In today's workplace, physiological and safety needs generally are well satisfied, making social, ego, and self-actualization needs preeminent. But safety issues are still very important in manufacturing, mining, and other work environments. And for months after the terrorist attacks of September 2001, employees still felt fear, denial, and anger—especially among people with children, women, and those close to the events.[55] To deal with such safety issues, managers can show what the firm will do to improve security and manage employee risk, including crisis management plans as discussed in Chapter 3.

Once a need is satisfied, it is no longer a powerful motivator. For example, labor unions negotiate for higher wages, benefits, safety standards, and job security. These bargaining issues relate directly to the satisfaction of Maslow's lower-level needs. Only after these needs are reasonably satisfied do the higher-level needs—social, ego, and self-actualization—become dominant concerns.

Maslow's hierarchy, however, is a simplistic and not altogether accurate theory of human motivation.[56] For example, not everyone progresses through the five needs in hierarchical order. But Maslow made three important contributions. First, he identified important need categories, which can help managers create effective positive reinforcers. Second, it is helpful to think of two general levels of needs, in which lower-level

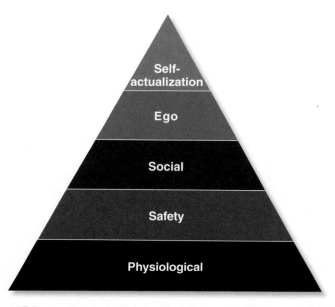

FIGURE 13.3
Maslow's Need Hierarchy

SOURCE: D. Organ and T. Bateman, *Organizational Behavior*, 4th ed., McGraw-Hill, 1990. Copyright © 1990 by The McGraw-Hill Companies.

needs must be satisfied before higher-level needs become important. Third, Maslow alerted managers to the importance of personal growth and self-actualization.

Self-actualization is the best-known concept arising from this theory. According to Maslow, the average person is only 10 percent self-actualized. In other words, most of us are living our lives and working at our jobs with a large untapped reservoir of potential. The implication is clear: managers should help create a work environment that provides training, resources, autonomy, responsibilities, and challenging assignments. This type of environment gives people a chance to use their skills and abilities in creative ways and allows them to achieve more of their full potential.

So treat people not merely as a cost to be controlled but an asset to be developed. Many companies have embarked on programs that provide personal growth experiences for their people. An employee at Federal Express said, "The best I can be is what I can be here. Federal Express . . . gave me the confidence and self-esteem to become the person I had the potential to become."[57] Individual managers also can promote employee growth. Pete Wamsteeker's first supervisor, at a feed company, routinely invited him to discuss his career plans, and Wamsteeker does the same for his employees now that he has become general manager of Cargill Animal Nutrition. When Wamsteeker took that position, he started by learning about his employees so that he could ensure each was in the job where he or she could contribute best. For example, he determined that an employee with a technical background and a quiet, analytical nature would thrive in a job that involves determining how pork producers can be more productive.[58]

Organizations gain by making full use of their human resources. Employees also gain by capitalizing on opportunities to meet their higher-order needs on the job. At Campbell Soup Company, managers are rewarded for developing their employees, and Lisa Walker, business director of Campbell USA's wellness team, rises to that challenge. She worked with one employee to help him collaborate better so that he would be seen as a team player with promotion potential. Walker's employee appreciated that her coaching gave him an opportunity for greater achievement, status, and self-esteem, and he thanked Walker for taking an interest in his success.[59]

Alderfer's ERG Theory

A theory of human needs that is more advanced than Maslow's is Alderfer's ERG theory.[60] Maslow's theory has general applicability, but Alderfer aims his theory expressly at understanding people's needs at work.

Alderfer's ERG theory postulates three sets of needs: existence, relatedness, and growth. *Existence* needs are all material and physiological desires. *Relatedness* needs involve relationships with other people and are satisfied through the process of mutually sharing thoughts and feelings. *Growth* needs motivate people to productively or creatively change themselves or their environment. Satisfaction of the growth needs comes from fully utilizing personal capacities and developing new capacities.

What similarities do you see between Alderfer's and Maslow's needs? Roughly speaking, existence needs subsume physiological and security needs, relatedness needs are similar to social and esteem needs, and growth needs correspond to self-actualization.

ERG theory proposes that several different needs can be operating at once. Thus, whereas Maslow would say that self-actualization is important to people only after other sets of needs are satisfied, Alderfer maintains that people—particularly working people in our postindustrial society—can be motivated to satisfy existence, relatedness, and growth needs at the same time.

Federal Express treats employees not as a cost to be controlled but as an asset to be developed.

Alderfer's ERG theory

A human needs theory postulating that people have three basic sets of needs that can operate simultaneously.

Yarde Metals set up a "nap room" with couches, pillows, soft lighting, and an alarm clock at its headquarters in Southington, Connecticut. Studies suggest that workers who nap may stay healthier—and that means fewer absences and lower costs for health insurance.[61] What do you think, is it worth it to the company?

Consider which theory best explains the motives identified by Diane Schumaker-Krieg to describe her successful career in the financial services industry. Schumaker-Krieg says she was "driven . . . by fear" in October 1987, when she was working for investment firm Dillon Read at the time of the stock market crash. Layoffs were spreading throughout the industry, jobs were scarce, and she was supporting her son following a divorce. Out of determination to take care of her son, Schumaker-Krieg reacted to being laid off by writing a plan for a new business. She persuaded Dillon Read to fund the idea for a year, began building the business, moved it to Credit Suisse, and within years was earning $150 million in profits for her employer. During that time she remarried and earned enough to retire, but she continues working, now as managing director of Credit Suisse's U.S. Equity Research. She sees her current motivation as enjoyment of her accomplishments, her business relationships, and opportunities to continue innovating.[62] Certainly, lower-level needs dominated the early years of Schumaker-Krieg's career, but did the basis for her motivation move one step at a time through all the levels of Maslow's hierarchy?

Maslow's theory is better known to American managers than Alderfer's, but ERG theory has more scientific support.[63] Both have practical value in that they remind managers of the types of reinforcers or rewards that can be used to motivate people. Regardless of whether the manager prefers the Maslow or the Alderfer theory of needs, he or she can motivate people by helping them satisfy their needs, particularly by offering opportunities for self-actualization and growth.

McClelland's Needs

David McClelland also identified a number of basic needs that guide people. The most important needs for managers, according to McClelland, are the needs for achievement, affiliation, and power.[64] Different needs predominate for different people. As you read about these needs, think about yourself—which ones are most and least important to you?

"The degree to which you will find the right recognition [of employees' successes] is equal to the degree to which you know the employee, you know their wants and needs."

—Erika Anderson, organizational development consultant[65]

The need for *achievement* is characterized by a strong orientation toward accomplishment and an obsession with success and goal attainment. Most managers and entrepreneurs in the United States have high levels of this need and like to see it in their employees.

The need for *affiliation* reflects a strong desire to be liked by other people. Individuals who have high levels of this need are oriented toward getting along with others and may be less concerned with performing at high levels.

The need for *power* is a desire to influence or control other people. This need can be a negative force—termed *personalized power*—if it is expressed through the aggressive manipulation and exploitation of others. People high on the personalized-power need want power purely for the pursuit of their own goals. But the need for power also can be a positive motive—called *socialized power*—because it can be channeled toward the constructive improvement of organizations and societies.

Low need for affiliation and moderate to high need for power are associated with managerial success for both higher- and lower-level managers.[66] One reason the need for affiliation is not necessary for leadership success is that people high on this need have difficulty making tough but necessary decisions that will make some people unhappy. To review McClelland's theory, along with the theories of Maslow and Alderfer, read the "Management Close-Up: Taking Action" feature, and consider which needs have motivated Tony Hsieh and his employees.

Management Close-Up | TAKING ACTION

Zappos.com is the inspiration of Tony Hsieh, a 30-something Harvard graduate with a penchant for launching successful businesses. In his first commercial enterprise at age 12, he made and sold buttons. As an undergrad, Hsieh sold pizzas out of his dorm room. After college, he founded LinkExchange, an advertising network that enabled small businesses to barter for banner ads. He sold the business to Microsoft two years later for a cool $265 million.

Not long afterward, Hsieh became involved with a struggling online shoe store that he renamed Zappos—after the Spanish word *zapatos*, "shoes." He quickly identified excellent customer service as a key success factor to differentiate his company and saw that employees who were happy would make sure that customers were, too. He moved the company to Las Vegas because of the city's reputation for service businesses and its 24/7 culture—the same as a customer service representative's time schedule. In nine years, Zappos soared from zero revenue to the $1 billion sales mark.

The pay at Zappos is not the determining factor in motivating employees. In fact, Zappos's salaries are generally at or below the general market level. In addition, the higher the position in the company, the more below-market the salary. Hsieh himself earns only $36,000 but claims pay does not motivate him; it's the challenge of creating something new.

If it's not the money, then what keeps Zappos's customer service reps motivated? Hsieh points to the company's culture. Workers are encouraged to do their best, use their own good judgment, and be themselves. Sales reps do not follow a canned script, and no one pushes them to keep service calls short. Instead, employees are encouraged to chat with customers since, Hsieh says, "For us, every interaction is [an] opportunity." He recites with pride specific instances in which employees listened to customer problems and went beyond a routine response. For instance, one woman who had ordered boots for her husband called for help in returning them because he had died in a car accident. The Zappos rep not only arranged for free return of the boots, but sent her flowers.[67]

- Zappos CEO Tony Hsieh said he decided to sell his business LinkExchange after it no longer felt rewarding. Instead, he wanted a company where he and his employees could be happy. What types of needs does the Zappos culture help fulfill?
- Hsieh sees customer service not as a company expense but as an opportunity to develop a relationship with customers. The company celebrates the on-the-spot decisions that its service reps make to satisfy customers. How does this help motivate employees?

Need Theories: International Perspectives

How do the need theories apply abroad?[68] Whereas managers in the United States care most strongly about achievement, esteem, and self-actualization, managers in Greece and Japan are motivated more by security. Social needs are most important in Sweden, Norway, and Denmark. "Doing your own thing"—the phrase from the 1960s that describes an American culture oriented toward self-actualization—is not even translatable into Chinese. "Achievement," too, is difficult to translate into most other languages. Researchers in France, Japan, and Sweden would have been unlikely to even conceive of McClelland's achievement motive because people of those countries are more group-oriented than individually oriented.

The Japanese are more group-oriented while Americans are more individually oriented when it comes to motivation. How do you think this affects how these two countries do business together?

Clearly, achievement, growth, and self-actualization are profoundly important in the United States, Canada, and Great Britain. But these needs are not universally important. Every manager must remember that need importance varies from country to country and that people may not be motivated by the same needs. One study found that employees in many countries are highly engaged at companies that have strong leadership, work/life balance, a good reputation, and opportunities for employees to contribute, while another found variations from country to country:[69] Employees in Canada were attracted by competitive pay, work/life balance, and opportunities for advancement; workers in Germany by autonomy; in Japan by high-quality coworkers; in the Netherlands by a collaborative work environment; and in the United States by competitive health benefits. Generally, no single way is best, and managers can customize their approaches by considering how individuals differ.[70]

Designing Motivating Jobs

extrinsic rewards

Rewards given to a person by the boss, the company, or some other person.

intrinsic reward

Reward a worker derives directly from performing the job itself.

Here's an example of a company that gave a "reward" that didn't motivate. One of Mary Kay Ash's former employers gave her a sales award: a flounder fishing light. Unfortunately, she doesn't fish. Fortunately, she later was able to design her own organization, Mary Kay Cosmetics, around *intrinsic* as well as *extrinsic* motivators that *mattered* to her people.[71] **Extrinsic rewards** are given to people by the boss, the company, or some other person. An **intrinsic reward** is a reward the person derives directly from performing the job itself. An interesting project, an intriguing subject that is fun to study, a completed sale, and the discovery of the perfect solution to a difficult problem all can give people the feeling that they have done something well. This is the essence of the motivation that comes from intrinsic rewards.

Intrinsic rewards are essential to the motivation underlying creativity.[72] A challenging problem, a chance to create something new, and work that is exciting in and of itself can provide intrinsic motivation that inspires people to devote time and energy to the task. So do managers who allow people some freedom to pursue the tasks that interest them most. The opposite situations result in routine, habitual behaviors that interfere with creativity.[73] A study in manufacturing facilities found that employees initiated more applications for patents, made more novel and useful suggestions, and were rated by their managers as more creative when their jobs were challenging and their managers did not control their activities closely.[74]

Conversely, some managers and organizations create environments that quash creativity and motivation.[75] The classic example of a demotivating job is the highly specialized assembly line job; each worker performs one boring operation before passing the

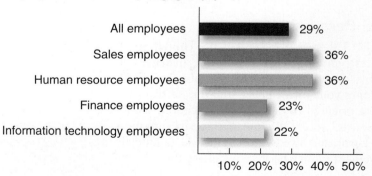

When employees are fully engaged, they are satisfied with their job and employer and they are enthusiastic about and committed to their work. Their personal goals are aligned with their organization's goals. A recent study by the consulting firm BlessingWhite investigated the percentages of employees who are fully engaged.[77]

Employees who are fully engaged (%)

All employees	29%
Sales employees	36%
Human resource employees	36%
Finance employees	23%
Information technology employees	22%

10% 20% 30% 40% 50%

work along to the next worker. Such specialization, or the "mechanistic" approach to job design, was the prevailing practice through most of the 20th century.[76] But jobs that are too simple and routine result in employee dissatisfaction, absenteeism, and turnover.

Especially in industries that depend on highly motivated knowledge workers, keeping talented employees may require letting them design their own jobs so that their work is more interesting than it would be elsewhere.[78] Jobs can be designed in the following ways to increase intrinsic rewards and therefore motivation.

Job Rotation, Enlargement, and Enrichment

With **job rotation,** workers who spend all their time in one routine task can instead move from one task to another. Rather than dishing out the pasta in a cafeteria line all day, a person might work the pasta, then the salads, and then the vegetables or desserts. Job rotation is intended to alleviate boredom by giving people different things to do at different times.

As you may guess, however, the person may just be changing from one boring job to another. But job rotation can benefit everyone when done properly, with people's input and career interests in mind. At Thomson, an international publishing company, new information technology (IT) employees can participate in a job rotation program that helps them learn about the company's diverse business units and identify the area that best fits their talents and interests. Harrah's Entertainment also uses job rotation for its IT workers, which gives them a broad knowledge of the business that enhances their value to the company at the same time it opens up opportunities for career development. About one out of five IT employees at Harrah's choose to participate in the job rotation program.[79]

Job enlargement is similar to job rotation in that people are given different tasks to do. But whereas job rotation involves doing one task at one time and changing to a different task at a different time, job enlargement means that the worker has multiple tasks at the same time. Thus, an assembly worker's job is enlarged if he or she is given two tasks rather than one to perform. In a study of job enlargement in a financial services organization, enlarged jobs led to higher job satisfaction, better error detection by clerks, and improved customer service.[80]

With job enlargement, the person's additional tasks are at the same level of responsibility. More profound changes occur when jobs are enriched. **Job enrichment** means that jobs are restructured or redesigned by adding higher levels of responsibility. This practice includes giving people not only more tasks but higher-level ones, such as when decisions are delegated downward and authority is decentralized. Efforts to redesign jobs by enriching them are now common in American industry. Herzberg's two-factor theory was the first approach to job enrichment, followed by the Hackman and Oldham model.

Herzberg's Two-Factor Theory

Frederick Herzberg's **two-factor theory** distinguished between two broad categories of factors that affect people working on their jobs.[81] The first category, **hygiene factors,** are *characteristics of the workplace:* company policies, working conditions, pay, coworkers, supervision, and so forth. These factors can make people unhappy if they are poorly managed. If they are well managed, and viewed as positive by employees, the employees will no longer be dissatisfied. However, no matter how good these factors are, they will not make people truly satisfied or motivated to do a good job.

According to Herzberg, the key to true job satisfaction and motivation to perform lies in the second category: the motivators. The **motivators** describe the *job itself,* that is, what people *do* at work. Motivators are the nature of the work itself, the actual job responsibilities, opportunity for personal growth and recognition, and the feelings of achievement the job provides. When these factors are present, jobs are presumed to be both satisfying and motivating for most people.

job rotation
Changing from one routine task to another to alleviate boredom.

job enlargement
Giving people additional tasks at the same time to alleviate boredom.

job enrichment
Changing a task to make it inherently more rewarding, motivating, and satisfying.

two-factor theory
Herzberg's theory describing two factors affecting people's work motivation and satisfaction.

hygiene factors
Characteristics of the workplace, such as company policies, working conditions, pay, and supervision, that can make people dissatisfied.

motivators
Factors that make a job more motivating, such as additional job responsibilities, opportunities for personal growth and recognition, and feelings of achievement.

Herzberg's theory has been criticized by many scholars, and for that reason we will not go into more detail about his original theory. But Herzberg was a pioneer in the area of job design and still is a respected name among American managers. Furthermore, even if the specifics of his theory do not hold up to scientific scrutiny, he made several very important contributions. First, Herzberg's theory highlights the important distinction between extrinsic rewards (from hygiene factors) and intrinsic rewards (from motivators). Second, it reminds managers not to count solely on extrinsic rewards to motivate workers but to focus on intrinsic rewards as well. Third, it set the stage for later theories, such as the Hackman and Oldham model, that explain more precisely how managers can enrich people's jobs.

The Hackman and Oldham Model of Job Design

Following Herzberg's work, Hackman and Oldham proposed a more complete model of job design.[82] Figure 13.4 illustrates their model. As you can see, well-designed jobs lead to high motivation, high-quality performance, high satisfaction, and low absenteeism and turnover. These outcomes occur when people experience three critical psychological states (noted in the middle column of the figure):

1. They believe they are doing something meaningful because their work is important to other people.
2. They feel personally responsible for how the work turns out.
3. They learn how well they perform their jobs.

These psychological states occur when people are working on enriched jobs, that is, jobs that offer the following five core job dimensions:

1. *Skill variety*—different job activities involving several skills and talents. For example, management trainees at Enterprise Rent-A-Car try their hands at every area of the business, including hiring employees, washing cars, waiting on customers, working with body shops, and ordering supplies. Assistant manager Sarah Ruddell defines the

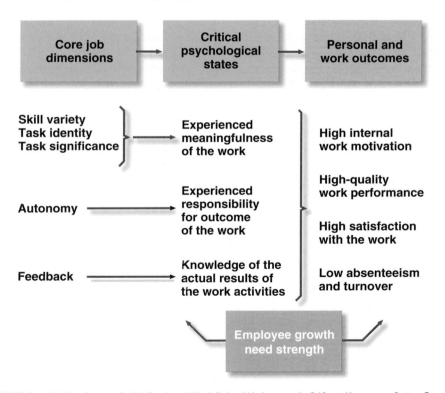

FIGURE 13.4
The Hackman and Oldham
Model of Job Enrichment

SOURCE: From "A New Strategy for Job Enrichment" by J. Richard Hackman et al., *California Management Review.* Copyright © 1975 by the Regents of the University of California. Reprinted from the *California Management Review* 17, no. 4. By permission of The Regents.

broad responsibilities as a plus: "You're not stuck doing the same thing over and over again."[83]

2. *Task identity*—the completion of a whole, identifiable piece of work. At State Farm Insurance, agents are independent contractors who sell and provide service for State Farm products exclusively. They have built and invested in their own businesses. As a result, agent retention and productivity are far better than industry norms.[84]

3. *Task significance*—an important, positive impact on the lives of others. According to Diane Castiglione, the director of recruitment for the U.S. State Department, people are drawn to careers in the Foreign Service because the work matters. Castiglione says Foreign Service employees are aware that they are serving the interests of their country, "whether that means helping an American citizen who has lost his passport or who has been arrested, or whether it means trying to figure out a way to help a U.S. business engage in business in another country, . . . whether it means trying to work on issues involving human rights."[85] Similarly, James Perry, an expert on motivation of government employees, says these workers generally have a strong commitment to serving the public good, including public welfare and stewardship of public resources.[86]

4. *Autonomy*—independence and discretion in making decisions. In a research hospital, a department administrator told her people to do the kinds of research they wanted as long as it was within budget (and legal!). With no other guidelines—that is, complete autonomy—productivity increased sixfold in a year.[87]

5. *Feedback*—information about job performance. Many companies post charts or provide computerized data indicating productivity, number of rejects, and other data. At Whole Foods Market, teams are responsible for hiring and scheduling in their area of the store. Team leaders get information about each month's payroll expense versus the budgeted amount. If the team comes in under budget, everyone knows, because everyone gets a share of the savings. This practical feedback inspires teams to hire carefully and work hard.[88]

The most effective job enrichment increases all five core dimensions.

A person's growth need strength will help determine just how effective a job enrichment program might be. **Growth need strength** is the degree to which individuals want personal and psychological development. Job enrichment would be more successful for people with high growth need strength. But very few people respond negatively to job enrichment.[89]

growth need strength

The degree to which individuals want personal and psychological development.

According to a recent survey of 27,000 people, those most likely to be satisfied with their jobs were clergy members, firefighters, physical therapists, authors, and special-education teachers. Job satisfaction was lowest among laborers (except construction), clothing salespeople, hand packers and packagers, food preparers, and roofers.[90] Can you see how the most satisfying jobs have more of Hackman and Oldham's job characteristics?

Empowerment

Today one frequently hears managers talk about "empowering" their people. Individuals may—or may not—feel empowered, and groups can have a "culture" of empowerment that predicts work-unit performance.[91] **Empowerment** is the process of sharing power with employees, thereby enhancing their confidence in their ability to perform their jobs and their belief that they are influential contributors to the organization. Unfortunately, empowerment doesn't always live up to its hype. One problem is that managers undermine it by sending mixed messages like "Do your own thing—the way we tell you."[92] But empowerment can be profoundly motivating when done properly.[93]

Empowerment results in changes in employees' beliefs—from feeling powerless to believing strongly in their own personal effectiveness.[94] The result is that people take more initiative and persevere in achieving their goals and their leader's vision even in the face of obstacles.[95] Specifically, empowerment encourages the following beliefs among employees.[96] First, they perceive *meaning* in their work: their job fits their values. Second, they feel *competent*, or capable of performing their jobs with skill. Third,

empowerment

The process of sharing power with employees, thereby enhancing their confidence in their ability to perform their jobs and their belief that they are influential contributors to the organization.

they have a sense of *self-determination*, of having some choice in regard to the tasks, methods, and pace of their work. Fourth, they have an *impact*—that is, they have some influence over important strategic, administrative, or operating decisions or outcomes on the job.

Whole Foods Market empowers store managers with decision-making authority on a number of issues. For instance, the chain provides managers with a $150,000 marketing budget that they can spend in ways they think best—without oversight from top corporate executives. As a result, managers can tailor messages to their local communities, rather than run mass-market national or regional ads. In addition, the company's top executives realize that competition in the grocery business is on a local level, so they rely on the knowledge and creativity of their store employees, called *team members,* to devise ways to sell the vast array of products. The chain sells everything from organic foods, to prepared foods at special islands, to gourmet delicacies. And local managers are allowed to stock items produced by small, local vendors. Thus, each store has a customized mix of goods, all of which the store's team leaders have selected. "I liked coming to work because it was never boring," says one employee who worked in the company's first store and came out of retirement to work at the flagship store in Austin, Texas.[97]

When speaking of times when they felt disempowered, people mentioned:[98]

- I had no input into a hiring decision of someone who was to report directly to me. I didn't even get to speak to the candidate.
- They treated us like mushrooms. They fed us and kept us in the dark.
- I worked extremely hard—long hours and late nights—on an urgent project, and then my manager took full credit for it.
- My suggestions, whether good or bad, were either not solicited or, worse, ignored.
- The project was reassigned without my knowledge or input.

In contrast, people felt empowered in the following examples:

- I was able to make a large financial decision on my own. I got to write a large check without being questioned.
- After having received a memo that said, "Cut travel," I made my case about why it was necessary to travel for business reasons, and I was told to go ahead.
- I was five years old, and my dad said, "You'll make a great mechanic one day." He planted the seed. Now I'm an engineer.
- My president supported my idea without question.
- All the financial data were shared with me.

Job enrichment and empowerment don't work magic overnight; people may resist the new approaches and make mistakes along the way. But done right, their potential to achieve real results is undeniable.

To foster empowerment, management must create an environment in which all the employees feel they have real influence over performance standards and business effectiveness within their areas of responsibility.[99] An empowering work environment provides people with *information* necessary for them to perform at their best, *knowledge* about how to use the information and how to do their work, *power* to make decisions that give them control over their work, and the *rewards* they deserve for the contributions they make.[100] Such an environment reduces costs because fewer people are needed to supervise, monitor, and coordinate. It improves quality and service because high performance is inspired at the source, the people who do the work. It also allows quick action because people on the spot see problems, solutions, and opportunities for innovation on which they are empowered to act.

It is essential to give people clear strategic direction but to leave some room for flexibility and calculated risk taking. For example, Southwest Airlines' strategic principle of "meet customers' short-haul travel needs at fares competitive with the cost of automobile travel" helps employees keep strategic objectives in mind and use their discretion in making complicated decisions about service offerings, route selection, cabin design, ticketing procedures, and pricing.[101] More specific actions include increasing signature authority at all levels; reducing the number of rules and approval steps; assigning nonroutine jobs; allowing independent judgment, flexibility, and creativity; defining jobs more broadly as projects rather than tasks; and providing more access to resources and people throughout the organization.[102]

Empowerment does not mean allowing people to decide trivial things like what color to paint the lunchroom. For empowerment to make a difference, people must have an impact on things about which they care, such as quality and productivity.[103] Companies that have successfully used empowerment programs include Lord Corporation in Dayton, Ohio (which produces engine mounts for aircraft), and Herman Miller (the Michigan-based furniture manufacturer).[104]

You should not be surprised when empowerment causes some problems, at least in the short term. This often occurs with virtually any change, including changes for the better. It's important to remember that with empowerment comes responsibility, and employees don't necessarily like the accountability at first.[105] People may make mistakes at first, especially until they have had adequate training. And because more training is needed, costs are higher. Also, because people acquire new skills and make greater contributions, they may demand higher wages. But if they are well-trained and truly empowered, they will deserve them—and both they and the company will benefit.

The Loyalty Fallacy

FROM THE PAGES OF

BusinessWeek

Faithful but marginal employees often think they're safe. Play fair: Enlighten them.

How should leaders manage loyalty? Some bosses hang their hats on it; to them, loyalty differentiates good employees from bad. But I've seen weak employees who are retained because they're loyal drag a company down. When and where is loyalty important?—George DeTellis Jr., Orlando

For starters, we can certainly tell you when loyalty feels like the most important thing in the world: during layoffs. Under such fraught circumstances, longtime employees very naturally tend to think of all the years they've served, all the hours they've toiled, all the times they've "been there" for the team or company. And they wonder: "Didn't my loyalty mean anything?"

Meanwhile, their managers are also feeling shaken, although not from shock and anger but from embarrassment and guilt. Because most managers know full well that employees shouldn't discover which corporate values matter most on their last day of work. Values should be a first-day, every-day topic, especially in recessionary times when people deserve to understand which behaviors constitute job-protecting performance.

And that's rarely loyalty alone.

Now, we're not revving up here to announce, "Loyalty is dead," a line that's been bandied about since the early 1980s, when foreign rivals forced many American corporations to lay off armies of people who presumed they had guaranteed lifetime work.

http://www.businessweek.com/magazine/content/09_03/b4116068842178.htm

SOURCE: J. Welch and S. Welch, "The Loyalty Fallacy," *BusinessWeek,* January 19, 2009, p. 58.

Achieving Fairness

Ultimately, one of the most important issues in motivation surrounds how people view their contributions to the organization and what they receive from the organization. Ideally, they will view their relationship with their employer as a well-balanced, mutually beneficial exchange. As people work and realize the outcomes or consequences of their actions, they assess how fairly the organization treats them.

The starting point for understanding how people interpret their contributions and outcomes is equity theory.[106] **Equity theory** proposes that when people assess how fairly they are treated, they consider two key factors: outcomes and inputs. *Outcomes*, as in expectancy theory, refer to the various things the person receives on the job: recognition, pay, benefits, satisfaction, security, job assignments, punishments, and so forth. *Inputs* refer to the contributions the person makes to the organization: effort, time, talent, performance, extra commitment, good citizenship, and so forth. People have a general expectation that the outcomes they receive will reflect, or be proportionate to, the inputs they provide—a fair day's pay (and other outcomes) for a fair day's work (broadly defined by how people view all their contributions).

But this comparison of outcomes to inputs is not the whole story. People also pay attention to the outcomes and inputs others receive. At salary review time, for example, most people—from executives on down—try to pick up clues that will tell them who got the high raises. As described in the following section, they compare ratios, try to restore equity if necessary, and derive more or less satisfaction based on how fairly they believe they have been treated.

Assessing Equity

Equity theory suggests that people compare the ratio of their own outcomes to inputs against the outcome-to-input ratio of some comparison person. The comparison person can be a fellow student, a coworker, a boss, or an average industry pay scale. Stated more succinctly, people compare:

$$\text{Their own } \frac{\text{Outcomes}}{\text{Inputs}} \text{ versus Others' } \frac{\text{Outcomes}}{\text{Inputs}}$$

If the ratios are equivalent, people believe the relationship is equitable, or fair. Equity causes people to be satisfied with their treatment. But the person who believes his or her ratio is lower than another's will feel inequitably treated. Inequity causes dissatisfaction and leads to an attempt to restore balance to the relationship.

Inequity and the negative feelings it creates may appear anywhere. As a student, perhaps you have been in the following situation. You stay up all night and get a C on the exam. Meanwhile another student studies a couple of hours, goes out for the rest of the evening, gets a good night's sleep, and gets a B on the exam. You perceive your inputs (time spent studying) as much greater than the other student's, but your outcomes are lower. You are displeased at the seeming unfairness. In business, the same thing sometimes happens with pay raises. One manager puts in 60-hour weeks, has a degree from a prestigious university, and believes she is destined for the top. When her archrival—whom she perceives as less deserving ("she never comes into the office on weekends, and all she does when she is here is butter up the boss")—gets the higher raise or the promotion, she experiences severe feelings of inequity. Motivation problems resulting from perceived pay inequities may be the reason major league baseball teams that have great differences in their player salaries tend to win fewer games.[107]

equity theory

A theory stating that people assess how fairly they have been treated according to two key factors: outcomes and inputs.

Equity theory suggests that people compare the ratio of their outcomes-to-inputs against the outcome-to-input ratio of some comparison person. How would you deal with someone you perceive to be a slacker who gets promoted over you?

Many people have felt inequity when they learn about large sums paid to high-profile CEOs. Ironically, one reason for rising CEO pay is an effort to set pay using a method that looks something like the equity comparison: the board of directors compares the CEO's pay with that of chief executives at organizations in a "peer group." Until 2006, companies did not have to disclose which companies were in the peer group, but one example exposed in the courtroom has suggested how inequity can arise. Richard A. Grasso received $140 million in compensation as chairman of the New York Stock Exchange. A compensation expert hired by New York's attorney general learned that the companies of the peer group used as a basis for setting Grasso's pay had median revenues more than 25 times that of the NYSE, media assets 125 times the NYSE's, and a median number of employees that was about 30 times that of the NYSE.[108] And even when a company chooses an appropriate peer group, many boards try to pay their executives in the top one-fourth of the group. The drive to keep everyone's pay above average means the average keeps climbing.

Assessments of equity are not made objectively. They are subjective perceptions or beliefs. In the preceding examples, the person who got the higher raise probably felt she deserved it. Even if she admits she doesn't put in long workweeks, she may convince herself she doesn't need to because she's so talented. The student who got the higher grade may believe it was a fair, equitable result because (1) she kept up all semester, while the other student did not, and (2) she's smart (ability and experience, not just time and effort, can be seen as inputs).

Restoring Equity

People who feel inequitably treated and dissatisfied are motivated to do something to restore equity. They have a number of options that they carry out to change the ratios or to reevaluate the situation and decide it is equitable after all.

The equity equation shown earlier indicates a person's options for restoring equity. People who feel inequitably treated can *reduce their inputs* by giving less effort, performing at lower levels, or quitting. ("Well, if that's the way things work around here, there's no way I'm going to work that hard [or stick around].") Or they can attempt to *increase their outcomes*. ("My boss [or teacher] is going to hear about this. I deserve more; there must be some way I can get more.") On the positive side, employees may also put forth extra effort to keep a situation equitable for the group. In the first few months of each year, many accountants face a flood of work related to annual reports and tax preparation. At Gramkow, Carnevale, Seifert & Company, an accounting firm in Oradell, New Jersey, Kenneth Benkow works six days a week and many evenings during tax time. He explains, "What helps motivate me is that I look around the office and I see people who are working as hard or harder than I am. You feel guilty if you're not pulling your own weight."[109]

Other ways of restoring equity focus on changing the other person's ratio. A person can *decrease others' outcomes*. For example, an employee may sabotage work to create problems for his company or his boss.[110] A person can also change her perceptions of inputs or outcomes. ("That promotion isn't as great a deal as he thinks. The pay is not that much better, and the headaches will be unbelievable.") It is also possible to *increase others' inputs*, particularly by changing perceptions. ("The more I think about it, the more I see he deserved it. He's worked hard all year, he's competent, and it's about time he got a break.")

Thus, a person can restore equity in a number of ways by behaviorally or perceptually changing inputs and outcomes.

Procedural Justice

procedural justice

Using fair process in decision making and making sure others know that the process was as fair as possible.

Inevitably, managers make decisions that have outcomes more favorable for some than for others. Those with favorable outcomes will be pleased; those with worse outcomes, all else equal, will be more displeased. But managers desiring to put salve on

Robert Lane, former CEO of John Deere, stands next to a riding lawn mower produced by his company. Deere & Company is the world's leading manufacturer of agricultural machinery. As mentioned in the text, he believes in treating people with dignity, even when delivering bad news.

the wounds—say, of people they like or respect or want to keep and motivate—still can take actions to reduce the dissatisfaction. The key is for people to believe that managers provide **procedural justice**—using fair process in decision making and helping others know that the process was as fair as possible. When people perceive procedural fairness, they are more likely to support decisions and decision makers.[111] For example, one year after layoffs, managers' use of procedural justice (in the form of employee participation in decisions) still predicted survivors' organizational commitment, job satisfaction, and trust toward management.[112]

Even if people believe that their *outcome* was inequitable and unfair, they are more likely to view justice as having been served if the *process* was fair. You can increase people's beliefs that the process was fair by making the process open and visible; stating decision criteria in advance rather than after the fact; making sure that the most appropriate people—those who have valid information and are viewed as trustworthy—make the decisions; giving people a chance to participate in the process; and providing an appeal process that allows people to question decisions safely and receive complete answers.[113] A good example of this kind of treatment is expressed by Deere and Company's former chief executive, Bob Lane. Lane says that even when "we have to let people go" because the company is struggling, "each and every individual has inherent worth," so management must treat employees with dignity and help them understand the reasons behind the actions.[114]

At an elevator plant in the United States, an army of consultants arrived one day, unexplained and annoying.[115] The rumor mill kicked in; employees thought the plant was to be shut down or that some of them would be laid off. Three months later, management unveiled its new plan, involving a new method of manufacturing based on teams. As the changes were implemented, management did not adequately answer questions about the purpose of the changes, employees resisted, conflicts arose, and the formerly popular plant manager lost the trust of his people. Costs skyrocketed, and quality plummeted.

Concerned, management conducted an employee survey. Employees were skeptical that the survey results would lead to any positive changes and were worried that management would be angry that people had voiced their honest opinions. But management reacted by saying, "We were wrong, we screwed up, we didn't use the right process." They went on to share with employees critical business information, the limited options available, and the dire consequences if the company didn't change. Employees saw the dilemma and came to view the business problem as theirs as well as management's, but they were scared that some of them would lose their jobs. Management retained the right to lay people off if business conditions grew worse but also made several promises: no layoffs as a result of changes made; cross-training programs for employees; no replacements of departing people until conditions improved; a chance for employees to serve in new roles, as consultants on quality issues; and sharing of sales and cost data on a regular basis.

The news was bad, but people understood it and began to share responsibility with management. This was the beginning of the restoration of trust and commitment, and of steady improvements in performance.

Job Satisfaction

LO 8

If people feel fairly treated from the outcomes they receive or the processes used, they will be satisfied. A satisfied worker is not necessarily more productive than a dissatisfied one; sometimes people are happy with their jobs because they don't have to work hard! But job dissatisfaction, aggregated across many individuals, creates a workforce that is more likely to exhibit (1) higher turnover; (2) higher absenteeism; (3) less good citizenship among employees;[116] (4) more grievances and lawsuits; (5) strikes; (6) stealing, sabotage, and vandalism; (7) poorer mental and physical health (which can mean higher job stress, higher insurance costs, and more lawsuits);[117] (8) fewer injuries;[118] (9) poor customer service;[119] and (10) lower productivity and profits.[120] All of these consequences of dissatisfaction, either directly or indirectly, are costly to organizations. Sadly, a survey of U.S. households found that a majority of workers are dissatisfied with their jobs, with the greatest amount of dissatisfaction among workers aged 25 and younger.[121]

Job satisfaction is especially important for relationship-oriented service employees such as realtors, hair stylists, and stockbrokers. Customers develop (or don't develop) a commitment to a specific service provider. Satisfied service providers are less likely to quit the company and more likely to provide an enjoyable customer experience.[122]

A single satisfied person doesn't necessarily produce well on every performance dimension. But an organization full of people with high job satisfaction will likely perform well in countless ways.

Quality of Work Life

Quality of work life (QWL) programs create a workplace that enhances employee well-being and satisfaction. The general goal of QWL programs is to satisfy the full range of employee needs. People's needs apparently are well met at First Horizon National, which offers a flexible benefits package including health and dental insurance, paid vacation, tuition reimbursement, discounts for child care and financial products, and reimbursement for adoption-related expenses. More unusually, First Horizon extends those benefits to workers who telecommute and work part-time. The company repeatedly appears on *Fortune*'s list of the 100 Best Companies to Work For, but more important is the impact on workers like Brenda Fung, a 13-year veteran and recently part-time designer of the company's intranet, who says, "This company has been so generous to me. There's no way I could even think of leaving."[123]

QWL has eight categories:[124]

quality of work life (QWL) programs

Programs designed to create a workplace that enhances employee well-being.

1. Adequate and fair compensation.
2. A safe and healthy environment.
3. Jobs that develop human capacities.
4. A chance for personal growth and security.
5. A social environment that fosters personal identity, freedom from prejudice, a sense of community, and upward mobility.
6. Constitutionalism, or the rights of personal privacy, dissent, and due process.
7. A work role that minimizes infringement on personal leisure and family needs.
8. Socially responsible organizational actions.

Organizations differ drastically in their attention to QWL. Critics claim that QWL programs don't necessarily inspire employees to work harder if the company does not tie rewards directly to individual performance. Advocates of QWL claim that it improves organizational effectiveness and productivity. The term *productivity*, as applied by QWL programs, means much more than each person's quantity of work output.[125] It also includes turnover, absenteeism, accidents, theft, sabotage, creativity, innovation, and especially the quality of work.

Psychological Contracts

The relationship between individuals and employing organizations typically is formalized by a written contract. But in employees' minds there also exists a **psychological contract**—a set of perceptions of what they owe their employers and what their employers owe them.[126] This contract, whether it is seen as being upheld or violated—and whether the parties trust one another or not—has important implications for employee satisfaction and motivation and the effectiveness of the organization.

Historically, in many companies the employment relationship was stable and predictable. Now mergers, layoffs, and other disruptions have thrown asunder the "old

psychological contract

A set of perceptions of what employees owe their employers, and what their employers owe them.

deal."[127] As a McGraw-Hill executive put it, "The 'used-to-be's' must give way to the realities of 'What is and what will be.'"[128] The fundamental "used-to-be" of traditionally managed organizations was that employees were expected to be loyal and employers would provide secure employment. Today the implicit contract goes something like this:[129] If people stay, do their own job plus someone else's (who has been downsized), and do additional things like participating in task forces, the company will try to provide a job (if it can), provide gestures that it cares, and keep providing more or less the same pay (with periodic small increases). The likely result of this not-very-satisfying arrangement: uninspired people and a business trying to survive.

But a better deal is possible, for both employers and employees.[130] Ideally, your employer will provide continuous skill updating and an invigorating work environment in which you can use your skills and are motivated to stay even though you may have other job options.[131] An example of such a modern psychological contract is Allstate's general employment contract, shown in Table 13.2. Thus, you could work for a company that provides the following deal: If you develop the skills we need, apply them in ways that help the company succeed, and behave consistently with our values, we will provide for you a challenging work environment, support for your development, and full, fair rewards for your contributions. The results of such a "contract" are much more likely to be a mutually beneficial and satisfying relationship and a high-performing, successful organization.

Consider how business coach Ram Charan assumed this new psychological contract in advising a frustrated human resource (HR) manager.[132] The manager had asked Charan for guidance in coping with bureaucratic red tape that was frustrating

TABLE 13.2
Allstate Employability Contract

You should expect Allstate to:

1. Offer work that is meaningful and challenging.
2. Promote an environment that encourages open and constructive dialogue.
3. Recognize you for your accomplishments.
4. Provide competitive pay and rewards based on your performance.
5. Advise you on your performance through regular feedback.
6. Create learning opportunities through education and job assignments.
7. Support you in defining career goals.
8. Provide you with information and resources to perform successfully.
9. Promote an environment that is inclusive and free from bias.
10. Foster dignity and respect in all interactions.
11. Establish an environment that promotes a balance of work and personal life.

Allstate expects you to:

1. Perform at levels that significantly increase our ability to outperform the competition.
2. Take on assignments critical to meeting business objectives.
3. Continually develop needed skills.
4. Willingly listen to and act upon feedback.
5. Demonstrate a high level of commitment to achieving company goals.
6. Exhibit no bias in interactions with colleagues and customers.
7. Behave consistently with Allstate's ethical standards.
8. Take personal responsibility for each transaction with our customers and for fostering their trust.
9. Continually improve processes to address customers' needs.

SOURCE: Courtesy of Allstate Insurance Company. Cited in E. E. Lawler III, *Treat People Right!* (San Francisco: Jossey-Bass, 2003).

to him as a leader and to the employees in his group. Charan encouraged the manager to reframe the situation as a need for learning, creativity, and leadership. The manager, said Charan, should investigate what the managers in other departments need from HR so that his people would truly be serving business needs and helping to solve business problems. Charan also encouraged the manager to learn about his employees' career goals and interests so that he can focus on ways to develop his people's strengths through assignments and greater decision-making authority within the department. If the HR manager accepts Charan's guidance, he and his people will face more interesting challenges than they would by simply defining themselves as a static part of a bureaucracy.

Finally, consider how these ideas for motivation apply at Zappos. Read the "Management Close-Up: Assessing Outcomes and Seizing Opportunities" feature and ask yourself whether old-fashioned stable employment relationships can—or should—be the norm at a fast-growing Internet company.

Management Close-Up

ASSESSING OUTCOMES AND SEIZING OPPORTUNITIES

Each year, Zappos's employees are invited to write a short essay describing their company. Their entries are published, unedited, in the annual *Zappos Culture Book* and distributed companywide. Although the essays are as different as the people who write them, each profiles the personal connection that the employee feels to Zappos. The essays also reflect the company's core values. Created by CEO Tony Hsieh early in Zappos's history, the core values guide all of the company's decisions. They include such principles as "Deliver WOW through service," "Create fun and a little weirdness," and "Build a positive team and family spirit."

While many employees yearn for greater balance between their home and work lives and work to keep them separate, Zappos creates employee job satisfaction by blending home and work life. Managers are encouraged to spend 10 to 20 percent of their time with their team away from the job. The objective is to ensure that people get to know each other outside the workplace. The end result is greater trust, better communication, and enhanced productivity for the workforce as a whole.

Hsieh believed that building a community was essential to the growth of his online business. He reasoned that by creating satisfied customers, he would not only create customer loyalty but also generate positive word-of-mouth communication for the business. In this way, Zappos grew by creating a community of satisfied customers and avoided big expenditures on advertising and marketing. Currently Zappos has 7.7 million customers in its database; about three of every four orders come from repeat customers.

Fortune recently named Zappos to its "100 Best Companies to Work For" list. Its dedicated workers would stand behind that award wholeheartedly.[133]

- Zappos's CEO Tony Hsieh says he sees his customers as human beings, not just consumers. How do you suppose that viewpoint affects the way he deals with his workforce?
- Zappos encourages employees to use their best judgment and to be themselves. Having fun at work every day is a priority for the firm. How does this motivate people?

KEY TERMS

SUMMARY OF LEARNING OBJECTIVES

Now that you have studied Chapter 13, you should be able to:

LO 1 Identify the kinds of behaviors managers need to motivate in people.

All important work behaviors are motivated. Managers need to motivate employees to join and remain in the organization and to exhibit high attendance, job performance, and citizenship.

LO 2 List principles for setting goals that motivate employees.

Goal setting is a powerful motivator. Specific, quantifiable, and challenging but attainable goals motivate high effort and performance. Goal setting can be used for teams as well as for individuals. Care should be taken to avoid setting single goals to the exclusion of other important dimensions of performance. Managers also should keep sight of the other potential downsides of goals.

LO 3 Summarize how to reward good performance effectively.

Organizational behavior modification programs influence behavior at work by arranging consequences for people's actions. Most programs use positive reinforcement as a consequence, but other important consequences are negative reinforcement, punishment, and extinction. Care must be taken to reinforce appropriate, not inappropriate, behavior. Innovative managers use a wide variety of rewards for good performance. They also understand how to "manage mistakes" and provide useful feedback.

LO 4 Describe the key beliefs that affect people's motivation.

Expectancy theory describes three important work-related beliefs. That is, motivation is a function of people's (1) expectancies, or effort-performance links; (2) instrumentalities, or performance-outcome links; and (3) the valences people attach to the outcomes of performance. In addition, people care about equity and justice, as described later.

LO 5 Discuss ways in which people's individual needs affect their behavior.

According to Maslow, important needs arise at five levels of a hierarchy: physiological, safety, social, ego, and self-actualization needs. Focusing more on the context of work, Alderfer's ERG theory describes three sets of needs: existence, relatedness, and growth. McClelland says people vary in the extent to which they have needs for achievement, affiliation, and power. Because people are inclined to satisfy their various needs, these theories help to suggest to managers the kinds of rewards that motivate people.

LO 6 Define ways to create jobs that motivate.

One approach to satisfying needs and motivating people is to create intrinsic motivation through the improved design of jobs. Jobs can be enriched by building in more skill variety, task identity, task significance, autonomy, and feedback. Empowerment, the most recent development in the creation of motivating jobs, includes the perceptions of meaning, competence, self-determination, and impact. These qualities come from an environment in which people have necessary information, knowledge, power, and rewards.

LO 7 Summarize how people assess fairness and how to achieve fairness.

Equity theory states that people compare their inputs and outcomes to the inputs and outcomes of others. Perceptions of equity (fairness) are satisfying; feelings of inequity (unfairness) are dissatisfying and motivate people to change their behavior or their perceptions to restore equity. In addition to fairness of outcomes, as described in equity theory, fairness is also appraised and managed through procedural justice.

LO 8 Identify causes and consequences of a satisfied workforce.

A satisfied workforce has many advantages for the firm, including lower absenteeism and turnover; fewer grievances, lawsuits, and strikes; lower health costs; and higher-quality work. One general approach to generating higher satisfaction for people is to implement a quality of work life program. QWL seeks to provide a safe and healthy environment, opportunity for personal growth, a positive social environment, fair treatment, and other improvements in people's work life. These and other benefits from the organization, exchanged for contributions from employees, create a psychological contract. Over time, how the psychological contract is upheld or violated, and changed unfairly or fairly, will influence people's satisfaction and motivation.

DISCUSSION QUESTIONS

1. Think of a significant mistake made by someone on a job. How did the boss handle it, and what was the effect?

2. Why do you think it is so difficult for managers to empower their people?

3. Think of a job you hold currently or held in the past. How would you describe the psychological contract? How does(did) this affect your attitudes and behaviors on the job?

4. If a famous executive or sports figure were to give a passionate motivational speech, trying to persuade people to work harder, what do you think the impact would be? Why?

5. Give some examples of situations in which you wanted to do a great job but were prevented from doing so. What was the impact on you, and what would this suggest to you in your efforts to motivate other people to perform?

6. Discuss the similarities and differences between setting goals for other people and setting goals for yourself. When does goal setting fail, and when does it succeed?

7. Identify four examples of people inadvertently reinforcing the wrong behaviors, or punishing or extinguishing good behaviors.

8. Assess yourself on McClelland's three needs. On which need are you highest, and on which are you lowest? What are the implications for you as a manager?

9. Identify a job you have held, and appraise it on Hackman and Oldham's five core job dimensions. Also describe the degree to which it made you feel empowered. As a class, choose one job and discuss together how it could be changed to be more motivating and empowering.

10. Using expectancy theory, analyze how you have made and will make personal choices, such as a major area of study, a career to pursue, or job interviews to seek.

11. Describe a time when you felt unfairly treated and explain why. How did you respond to the inequity? What other options might you have had?

12. Provide examples of how outcomes perceived as unfair can decrease motivation. Then discuss how procedural justice, or fair process, can help overcome the negative effects.

13. What are the implications for your career of, and how will you prepare for, the psychological contracts described at the end of the chapter?

14. Set some goals for yourself, considering the discussion about goal setting in the chapter.

CONCLUDING CASE

Green Mountain Camp: It's More than a Summer Job

Nick and Carol Randall had a dream for themselves and their two sons: to live at summer camp, re-creating their own memories of swimming in a lake, hiking the mountains, and laughing around the campfire every evening. So, when Green Mountain Camp in Vermont went up for sale, they scraped together their savings and bought the property and the business. Soon they learned why the camp was for sale: the cabins were run down, the kitchen was below health standards, the dock was falling into the lake. But as they assessed the situation, adding up the repairs necessary to open for a summer session of school-age boys, they realized they had an even more serious problem: a lack of employees. When they bought the camp, the previous owners were vague about the commitment of camp staff from year to year; when the Randalls tried to contact both the camp chef and head counselor, neither answered phone calls or e-mails.

Something was clearly wrong. Why weren't Green Mountain staff members motivated to return to work at the camp? After they hired contractors to make the necessary physical repairs to the camp, the Randalls set about recruiting job candidates—talking with them to learn what they needed and wanted in their jobs and how to motivate them not only to serve the camp and its campers but also to stay. One way the Randalls decided to spread the word about the change in ownership was a Web site. The new Web site included an introduction to the Randalls and an invitation to previous staffers to contact them. The site offered job descriptions with meager benefits, but it promised a welcoming, positive atmosphere with opportunities for forming new camp programs, social time, and more comfortable accommodations.

Inquiries from both past staff members and interested newcomers began to trickle in, as did registration applications from campers themselves. Nick and Carol interviewed candidates to learn not only what their skills were but also what would motivate them to commit themselves to the job for more than one summer. Candidates included school teachers, recent college graduates, and even one retired businessman who just wanted to spend his summers outdoors teaching kids how to kayak and sail. The Randalls hired him immediately, hoping to tap his business knowledge in addition to his outdoor skills. All the candidates said they simply wanted to be treated fairly, given some freedom to make decisions on the spot that might benefit or enrich the children, and be paid promptly. They were pleased to hear that the campground itself was under renovation. By late June, the Randalls had filled all the staff positions and had only a few empty spots left for campers. As the first campers began to arrive, the Randalls believed their dream of living at summer camp might really come true.

QUESTIONS

1. What steps might the Randalls take to design motivating jobs for camp staff?

2. What needs might they be able to fill for camp staff?

3. In what ways might the empowerment of camp staff affect the success of the camp?

EXPERIENTIAL EXERCISES

13.1 Assessing Yourself

Circle the response that most closely correlates with each item below.

	Agree		Neither Agree Not Disagree		Disagree
1. I have developed a written list of short-and long-term goals I would like to accomplish.	1	2	3	4	5
2. When setting goals for myself, I give consideration to what my capabilities and limits are.	1	2	3	4	5
3. I set goals that are realistic and attainable.	1	2	3	4	5
4. My goals are based on my hopes and beliefs, not on those of my parents, friends, or significant other.	1	2	3	4	5
5. When I fail to achieve a goal, I get back on track.	1	2	3	4	5
6. My goals are based on my personal values.	1	2	3	4	5
7. I have a current mission statement and have involved those closest to me in formulating it.	1	2	3	4	5
8. I regularly check my progress toward achieving the goals I have set.	1	2	3	4	5
9. When setting goals I strive for performance, not outcomes.	1	2	3	4	5
10. I have a support system in place—friends, family members, and/or colleagues who believe in me and support my goals.	1	2	3	4	5
11. I apply SMART characteristics to my goals.	1	2	3	4	5
12. I prioritize my goals, focusing only on the most important or valuable ones at a particular point in time.	1	2	3	4	5
13. I reward myself when I achieve a goal, or even when I reach a particular milestone.	1	2	3	4	5
14. I revisit my goals periodically, and add and modify goals as appropriate.	1	2	3	4	5

Sum your circled responses. If your total is 42 or higher, you might want to explore ways to improve your skill in the area of goal setting.

SOURCE: Suzanne C. de Janasz, Karen O. Dowd, and Beth Z. Schneider, *Interpersonal Skills in Organizations*, McGraw-Hill/Irwin, 2002, pp. 56–61. © The McGraw-Hill Companies.

13.2 Personal Goal Setting

1. In the spaces provided, brainstorm your goals in the following categories. Write down as many as you wish, including goals that are short, mid, and long term.

Career, job

Academic, intellectual

Financial

Health, fitness

Other

Social: family, friends, significant other, community

2. Of the goals you have listed, select from each of the six categories the two most important goals that you would like to pursue in the short term (next 6–12 months). Write these below.

a. _____

b. _____

c. _____

d. _____

e. _____

f. _____

g. _____

h. _____

i. _____

j. _____

k. _____

l. _____

3. From the 12 goals listed, choose the 3 that are the most important to you at this time: the 3 you commit to work on in the next few months. Write a goal statement for each one, using the following guidelines:

Begin each with the word "To . . ."

Be specific.

Quantify the goal if possible.

Each goal statement should be realistic, attainable, and within your control.

Each goal statement should reflect your aspirations—not those of others such as parents roommates, significant others, and the like.

a. _____
_____

b. _____
_____

c. _____
_____

4. On a separate sheet of paper, develop an action plan for each goal statement. For each action plan:

List the steps you will take to accomplish the goal.

Include dates (by when) and initials (who's responsible) for each step.

Visualize completing the goal and, working backward, specify each step necessary between now and then to reach the goal.

Identify any potential barriers you might experience in attaining the goal. Problem-solve around these obstacles, and convert them into steps in your action plan.

Identify the resources you will need to accomplish these goals, and build in steps to acquire the necessary information into your action plan.

5. Transfer the dates of each step for each goal in your action plan to a daily calendar.

6. Keep an ongoing daily or weekly record of the positive steps you take toward meeting each goal.

SOURCE: Suzanne C. de Janasz, Karen O. Dowd, and Beth Z. Schneider, *Interpersonal Skills in Organizations*, McGraw-Hill/Irwin, 2002, pp. 56–61. © 2002 The McGraw-Hill Companies.

13.3 What Do Students Want from Their Jobs?

OBJECTIVES

1. To demonstrate individual differences in job expectations.

2. To illustrate individual differences in need and motivational structures.

3. To examine and compare extrinsic and intrinsic rewards.

INSTRUCTIONS

1. Working alone, complete the "What I Want from My Job" survey.

2. In small groups, compare and analyze differences in the survey results and prepare group responses to the discussion questions.

3. After the class reconveres, group spokespersons present group findings.

DISCUSSION QUESTIONS

1. Which items received the highest and lowest scores from you? Why?

2. On which items was there most and least agreement among students? What are the implications?

3. Which job rewards are extrinsic, and which are intrinsic?

4. Were more response differences found in intrinsic or in extrinsic rewards?

5. In what ways do you think blue-collar workers' responses would differ from those of college students?

What I Want from My Job

Determine what you want from a job by circling the level of importance of each of the following job rewards.

	Very Important	Important	Indifferent	Unimportant	Very Unimportant
1. Advancement opportunities	5	4	3	2	1
2. Appropriate company policies	5	4	3	2	1
3. Authority	5	4	3	2	1
4. Autonomy and freedom on the job	5	4	3	2	1
5. Challenging work	5	4	3	2	1
6. Company reputation	5	4	3	2	1
7. Fringe benefits	5	4	3	2	1
8. Geographic location	5	4	3	2	1
9. Good coworkers	5	4	3	2	1
10. Good supervision	5	4	3	2	1
11. Job security	5	4	3	2	1
12. Money	5	4	3	2	1
13. Opportunity for self-development	5	4	3	2	1
14. Pleasant office and working conditions	5	4	3	2	1
15. Performance feedback	5	4	3	2	1
16. Prestigious job title	5	4	3	2	1
17. Recognition for doing a good job	5	4	3	2	1
18. Responsibility	5	4	3	2	1
19. Sense of achievement	5	4	3	2	1
20. Training programs	5	4	3	2	1
21. Type of work	5	4	3	2	1
22. Working with people	5	4	3	2	1

Teamwork

" No one can whistle a symphony. It takes an orchestra to play it. "

— Halford E. Luccock

LEARNING OBJECTIVES

After studying Chapter 14, you will be able to:

LO 1 Discuss how teams can contribute to an organization's effectiveness. p. 488

LO 2 Distinguish the new team environment from that of traditional work groups. p. 489

LO 3 Summarize how groups become teams. p. 493

LO 4 Explain why groups sometimes fail. p. 494

LO 5 Describe how to build an effective team. p. 496

LO 6 List methods for managing a team's relationships with other teams. p. 504

LO 7 Identify ways to manage conflict. p. 505

CHAPTER OUTLINE

Management Close-Up

From the moment Cisco Systems began producing Internet routers and switches, the networking giant has been riding the high-tech wave. Given its central role in providing the equipment that forms the backbone of the Internet, it wouldn't be much of an exaggeration to say Cisco also *owns* the wave machine.

A key player in Cisco's remarkable success is John Chambers, Cisco president and CEO since 1995 and one of the longest-tenured CEOs in California's Silicon Valley. Under his leadership, Cisco revenues skyrocketed from $1.2 billion in 1995 to about $40 billion today. While the bulk of these revenues comes from the Cisco routers, switches, and related technologies that direct traffic on the Net, Chambers is constantly innovating and diversifying to keep the company profitable.

In the Internet's first years, the firm's primary goal was simple: installing systems and connecting users. Now, however, the Internet has entered the Web 2.0 phase, with new uses such as social networking and blogging. In other words, networks have changed from being mere conduits of information to an infrastructure that enables problem solving and collaboration.

Chambers says Web 2.0 technologies are revolutionizing the way work is done because they make collaboration possible and require new knowledge and skills for employees to be effective. For a business to operate best in a networked world, he concluded, it would need to facilitate communication and collaboration at every level— a far cry from the "command and control" power most executives used to wield.

Armed with the new technologies, over a six-year period Chambers reconfigured Cisco and pushed much of the creative and decision-making power down to teams at all levels of the organization worldwide. Now Cisco is able to accomplish significantly more than it did when Chambers made all the decisions.[1]

{ In shedding the traditional "command and control" mindset, Cisco CEO John Chambers has brought new meaning to the word *teamwork*. As you read this chapter, consider how teamwork can add value to today's organizations. }

Sometimes teams "work," and sometimes they don't. The goal of this chapter is to help make sure that your management and work teams succeed. The innovative team structure at Cisco illustrates one way a company can apply teamwork, with extraordinary results.

While perhaps few organizations are as innovative as Cisco, teams are transforming the ways organizations do business.[2] Almost all companies now use teams to produce goods and services, to manage projects, and to make decisions and run the company.[3] For you, this has two vital implications. First, you *will* be working in and perhaps managing teams. Second, the *ability* to work in and lead teams is valuable to your employer and important to your career. Fortunately, coursework focusing on team training can enhance students' teamwork knowledge and skills.[4]

The Contributions of Teams

LO I

Well-managed teams are powerful forces that can deliver all desired results.

Team-based approaches to work have generated excitement. Used appropriately, teams can be powerfully effective as a *building block for organization structure*. Organizations such as Semco, Whole Foods, and Kollmorgen, manufacturer of printed circuits and electro-optic devices, are structured entirely around teams. 3M's breakthrough products emerge through the use of teams that are small entrepreneurial businesses within the larger corporation.

Teams also can increase *productivity*, improve *quality*, and reduce *costs*. By adopting a team structure and culture, Battle Creek, Michigan–based Summit Pointe, a mental health organization, has saved millions of dollars while improving patient care.[5] Honeywell's teams saved more than $11 million after reducing production times and shipping more than 99 percent of orders on time.[6] Using engineering teams for its 777 jumbo passenger jet, Boeing received the fastest flight certification ever for a new commercial aircraft. According to Boeing managers, the company could not have developed the 777 without cross-functional teams; it would have been prohibitively expensive.[7] At Nucor's steel plant in Decatur, Alabama, general manager Rex Query credits teamwork for high productivity and improved safety.[8]

Teams also can enhance *speed* and be powerful forces for *innovation* and *change*. 3M and many other companies are using teams to create new products faster. Lenders cut home mortgage approval times from weeks to hours, and life insurance companies cut time to issue new policies from six weeks to one day.[9] At KPMG Netherlands, a strategic integration team of 12 partners, with 100 other professionals divided into 14 task forces, led strategic and cultural changes by studying future trends and scenarios, defining core competencies, and dealing with organizational challenges.[10] General Mills uses a team approach to make decisions about the packaging for its products. For product divisions such as Big G cereals, Yoplait yogurt, or Green Giant vegetables, Packaging Partners teams bring together employees from brand design, engineering, production, research and development, and other relevant functions to figure out how packaging can reduce waste, cut costs, and send a clearer marketing message. In addition, Strategy Map teams convene employees from various product divisions to study packaging using a particular material and determine ways to work more efficiently with suppliers.[11]

Teams also provide many *benefits for their members*.[12] The team is a very useful learning mechanism. Members learn about the company and themselves, and they acquire new skills and performance strategies. The team can satisfy important personal needs, such as affiliation and esteem. Other needs are met as team members receive tangible organizational rewards that they could not have achieved working alone. After General Mills acquired Pillsbury, the managers leading the combined companies' meals division decided they needed to develop a common culture that would promote employee engagement. So they set up a Spirit Team of staff members to select activities that would support that goal. This insightful group of employees realized that just having fun together would not develop a deeper sense of purpose.

Instead, the team identified a more meaningful process: they would partner with a nonprofit organization, Perspectives Family Center, and support this organization with several events each year. Employees who participate not only feel great about what they do but also connect their experience of service with a sense that their company cares about its local community.[13]

Team members can provide one another with feedback; identify opportunities for growth and development; and train, coach, and mentor.[14] A marketing representative can learn about financial modeling from a colleague on a new-product development team, and the financial expert can learn about consumer marketing. Experience working together in a team, and developing strong problem-solving capabilities, is a vital supplement to specific job skills or functional expertise. And the skills are transferable to new positions.

The New Team Environment

The words *group* and *team* often are used interchangeably.[15] Modern managers sometimes use the word *teams* to the point that it has become a cliché; they talk about teams while skeptics perceive no real teamwork. Thus, making a distinction between groups and teams can be useful. A *working group* is a collection of people who work in the same area or have been drawn together to undertake a task but do not necessarily come together as a unit and achieve significant performance improvements. A real **team** is formed of people (usually a small number) with complementary skills who trust one another and are committed to a common purpose, common performance goals, and a common approach for which they hold themselves mutually accountable.[16]

LO 2

Athletic teams are built with people of varying skill levels who work toward a common goal—to win. Teams in a business are often formed with the same mindset.

team

A small number of people with complementary skills who are committed to a common purpose, set of performance goals, and approach for which they hold themselves mutually accountable.

You might not initially think of writing as a team activity, but Evolved Media Network is a small firm whose entire mission is to collaboratively produce documents. One recent project involved writing a 450-page book on the SAP enterprise resource planning software program using two editors and five writers. The team accomplished this feat by using a Web site called a *wiki* (from the Hawaiian phrase *wiki wiki*, which means "faster, faster"). A wiki allows users to compose, delete, and edit content. Everyone can keep track of what everyone else is working on. "The value of wikis comes from a group of people who are now working together in a different way," says company founder Dan Woods. "Content is shared, and everybody's progress is visible to each other. It's no longer my chapter or your chapter. Now it is the book, and we're working on it together."

Although collaboration is the main thrust of wiki participation, Woods does recommend choosing a team leader. The leader oversees the entering of information, motivates team members to contribute, and makes sure the information included is valuable to the project. The leader can train team members new to the technology and ensure that the wiki is functioning properly.[17]

Organizations have been using groups for a long time, but today's workplaces are different.[18] Teams are used in many different ways, and to far greater effect, than in the past. Table 14.1 highlights just a few of the differences between the traditional work environment and the way true teams work today. Ideally, people are far more involved, they are better trained, cooperation is higher, and the culture is one of learning as well as producing.

TABLE 14.1
The New Team
Environment

Traditional Environment	Team Environment
Managers determine and plan the work.	Managers and team members jointly determine and plan the work.
Jobs are narrowly defined.	Jobs require broad skills and knowledge.
Cross-training is viewed as inefficient.	Cross-training is the norm.
Most information is "management property."	Most information is freely shared at all levels.
Training for nonmanagers focuses on technical skills.	Continuous learning requires interpersonal, administrative, and technical training for all.
Risk taking is discouraged and punished.	Measured risk taking is encouraged and supported.
People work alone.	People work together.
Rewards are based on individual performance.	Rewards are based on individual performance and contributions to team performance.
Managers determine "best methods."	Everyone works to continuously improve methods and processes.

SOURCE: From *Leading Teams* by J. Zenger and Associates. Reprinted by permission.

Types of Teams

Your organization may have hundreds of groups and teams, but they can be classified into just a few primary types.[19] **Work teams** make or do things such as manufacture, assemble, sell, or provide service. They typically are well defined; a clear part of the formal organizational structure; and composed of a full-time, stable membership. Work teams are what most people think of when they think of teams in organizations.[20]

Project and development teams work on long-term projects, often over a period of years. They have specific assignments, such as research or new-product development, and members usually must contribute expert knowledge and judgment. These teams work toward a one-time product, disbanding once their work is completed. Then new teams are formed for new projects.

Parallel teams operate separately from the regular work structure of the firm on a temporary basis. Members often come from different units or jobs and are asked to do work that is not normally done by the standard structure. Their charge is to recommend solutions to specific problems. They usually do not have authority to act, however. Examples include task forces and quality or safety teams formed to study a particular problem. Whenever Baltimore's Bradford Bank acquires or starts up another operation, it assembles a team of employees drawn from various divisions to smooth the transition for customers. For example, when Bradford signed a deal to acquire deposits from American Bank, a team of employees from branch management, deposit services, and information technology studied American's products to make sure Bradford was ready to offer similar services to its new customers.[21]

Management teams coordinate and provide direction to the subunits under their jurisdiction and integrate work among subunits.[22] The management team is based on authority stemming from hierarchical rank and is responsible for the overall

work teams

Teams that make or do things like manufacture, assemble, sell, or provide service.

project and development teams

Teams that work on long-term projects but disband once the work is completed.

parallel teams

Teams that operate separately from the regular work structure, and exist temporarily.

management teams

Teams that coordinate and provide direction to the subunits under their jurisdiction and integrate work among subunits.

One example of a project and development team is the Omnica product development team. The 28-person team is responsible for producing medical and high-tech products for their clients faster and more efficiently than they could by any other means.

performance of the business unit. Managers responsible for different subunits form a team together, and at the top of the organization resides the executive management team that establishes strategic direction and manages the firm's overall performance.

Transnational teams are work teams composed of multinational members whose activities span multiple countries.[23] Such teams differ from other work teams not only by being multicultural but also by often being geographically dispersed, being psychologically distant, and working on highly complex projects having considerable impact on company objectives.

Transnational teams tend to be **virtual teams,** communicating electronically more than face-to-face, although other types of teams may operate virtually as well. Virtual teams create difficult challenges: building trust, cohesion, and team identity, and overcoming the isolation of virtual team members.[24] Table 14.2 suggests ways that managers can improve the effectiveness of virtual teams.

transnational teams

Work groups composed of multinational members whose activities span multiple countries.

virtual teams

Teams that are physically dispersed and communicate electronically more than face-to-face.

TABLE 14.2

Practices of Effective Virtual Team Leaders

Leadership Practices of Virtual Team Leader	How Do Virtual Team Leaders Do It?
Establish and maintain trust through the use of communication technology	Focusing the norms on how information is communicated
	Revisiting and adjusting the communication norms as the team evolves ("virtual get-togethers")
	Making progress explicit through use of team virtual workspace
	Equal "suffering" in the geographically distributed world
Ensure diversity in the team is understood, appreciated, and leveraged	Prominent team expertise directory and skills matrix in the virtual workspace
	Virtual subteaming to pair diverse members and rotate subteam members
Manage virtual work cycle and meetings	Use the start of virtual meeting (each time) for social relationship building
	During meeting—ensure through "check-ins" that everyone is engaged and heard from
	End of meeting—ensure that the minutes and future work plan are posted to team repository
Monitor team progress through the use of technology	Make progress explicit through balanced scorecard measurements posted in the team's virtual workspace
Enhance external visibility of the team and its members	Frequent report-outs to a virtual steering committee (comprising local bosses of team members)
Ensure individuals benefit from participating in virtual teams	Virtual reward ceremonies
	Individual recognition at the start of each virtual meeting
	Making each team member's "real location" boss aware of the member's contribution

SOURCE: Excerpted from A. Malhotra, A. Majchrzak, and B. Rosen, "Leading Virtual Teams," *Academy of Management Perspectives,* February 2007, pp. 60–70, table 1.

self-managed teams

Autonomous work groups in which workers are trained to do all or most of the jobs in a unit, have no immediate supervisor, and make decisions previously made by frontline supervisors.

traditional work groups

Groups that have no managerial responsibilities.

quality circles

Voluntary groups of people drawn from various production teams who make suggestions about quality.

semiautonomous work groups

Groups that make decisions about managing and carrying out major production activities but get outside support for quality control and maintenance.

autonomous work groups

Groups that control decisions about and execution of a complete range of tasks.

self-designing teams

Teams with the responsibilities of autonomous work groups, plus control over hiring, firing, and deciding what tasks members perform.

Self-Managed Teams

Today many different types of work teams exist, with many different labels. The terms can be confusing and sometimes are used interchangeably out of a lack of awareness of actual differences. Figure 14.1 shows the different types according to how much autonomy they have.[25] To the left, teams are more traditional with little decision-making authority, being under the control of direct supervision. To the right the teams have more autonomy, decision-making power, and self-direction.

The trend today is toward **self-managed teams,** in which workers are trained to do all or most of the jobs in the unit, they have no immediate supervisor, and they make decisions previously made by frontline supervisors.[26] Self-managed teams are most frequently found in manufacturing. People often resist self-managed work teams, in part because they don't want so much responsibility and the change is difficult.[27] In addition, people often don't like to do performance evaluation of teammates or to fire people, and poorly managed conflict may be a particular problem in self-managed teams.[28] But compared with traditionally managed teams, self-managed teams appear to be more productive, have lower costs, provide better customer service, provide higher quality, have better safety records, and are more satisfying for members.

Referring to Figure 14.1, **traditional work groups** have no managerial responsibilities. The frontline manager plans, organizes, staffs, directs, and controls them, and other groups provide support activities, including quality control and maintenance. **Quality circles** are voluntary groups of people drawn from various production teams who make suggestions about quality but have no authority to make decisions or execute. **Semiautonomous work groups** make decisions about managing and carrying out major production activities but still get outside support for quality control and maintenance. **Autonomous work groups,** or *self-managing teams,* control decisions about and execution of a complete range of tasks—acquiring raw materials and performing operations, quality control, maintenance, and shipping. They are fully responsible for an entire product or an entire part of a production process. **Self-designing teams** do all of that and go one step further—they also have control over the design of the team. They decide themselves whom to hire, whom to fire, and what tasks the team will perform.

Movement from left to right on the continuum corresponds with more and more worker participation. Toward the right, the participation is not trivial and not merely advisory. It has real substance, including not just suggestions but action and impact. When companies have introduced teams that reach the point of being truly self-managed, results have included lower costs and greater levels of team productivity, quality, and customer satisfaction.[29] Overall, semiautonomous and autonomous teams are known to improve the organization's financial and overall performance, at least in North America.[30]

Such results have inspired U.S.-based multinational firms to use self-managed teams in their foreign facilities. For example, Goodyear Tire & Rubber initiated self-managed work teams in Europe, Latin America, and Asia; Sara Lee in Puerto Rico and Mexico; and Texas Instruments in Malaysia. These companies are learning—and other companies

FIGURE 14.1

Team Autonomy Continuum

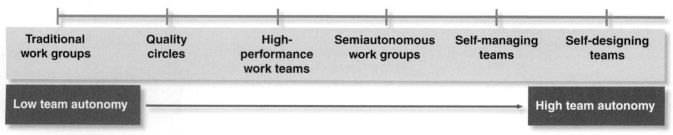

SOURCE: R. Banker, J. Field, R. Schroeder, and K. Sinha, "Impact of Work Teams on Manufacturing Performance: A Longitudinal Field Study," *Academy of Management Journal.* Copyright © 1996 by Academy of Management. Reproduced with permission of Academy of Management via Copyright Clearance Center.

should be forewarned—of the different ways different cultures might respond to self-managed teams, and to customize implementation according to cultural values.[31]

How Groups Become Real Teams

As a manager, you will want your group to become an effective team. To accomplish this, you need to understand how groups can become true teams and why groups sometimes fail to become teams. Groups become true teams via basic group activities, the passage of time, and team development activities.

Group Activities

Assume you are the leader of a newly formed group—actually a bunch of people. What will you face as you attempt to develop your group into a high-performing team? If groups are to develop successfully, they will engage in various activities, including these broad categories:[32]

- *Forming*—group members attempt to lay the ground rules for what types of behavior are acceptable.
- *Storming*—hostilities and conflict arise, and people jockey for positions of power and status.
- *Norming*—group members agree on their shared goals, and norms and closer relationships develop.
- *Performing*—the group channels its energies into performing its tasks.

Groups that deteriorate move to a *declining* stage, and temporary groups add an *adjourning* or terminating stage. Groups terminate when they complete their task or when they disband due to failure or loss of interest and new groups form, as the cycle continues.

Virtual teams also go through these stages of group development.[33] The forming stage is characterized by unbridled optimism: "I believe we have a great team and will work well together. We all understand the importance of the project and intend to take it seriously." Optimism turns into reality shock in the storming stage: "No one has taken a leadership role. We have not made the project the priority that it deserves." The norming stage comes at about the halfway point in the project life cycle, in which people refocus and recommit: "You must make firm commitments to a specific time schedule." The performing stage is the dash to the finish, as teammates show the discipline needed to meet the deadline.

Many teams do training exercises to learn team-building techniques. This is the classic "trust fall." The blindfolded person falls backwards, trusting that his teammates will catch him and not let him fall. Trust must be earned, not demanded.

Passage of Time

A key aspect of group development is the passage of time. Groups pass through critical periods, or times when they are particularly open to formative experiences.[34] The first such critical period is in the forming stage, at the first meeting, when rules and roles are established that set long-lasting precedents. A second critical period is the midway point between the initial meeting and a deadline (e.g., completing a project or making a presentation). At this point, the group has enough experience to understand its work; it comes to realize that time is becoming a scarce resource and it must "get on with it"; and there is enough time left to change its approach if necessary.

In the initial meeting, the group should establish desired norms, roles, and other determinants of effectiveness, which are discussed throughout this chapter. At the second critical period (the midpoint), groups should renew or open lines of communication with outside constituencies. The group can use fresh information from its external environment to revise its approach to performing its task and ensure that it meets the needs of customers and clients. Without these activities, groups may get off on the wrong foot from the beginning, and members may never revise their behavior in the appropriate direction.[35]

Developmental Sequence: From Group to Team

As a manager or group member, you should expect the group to engage in all the activities just discussed at various times. But groups are not always successful. They do not always engage in the developmental activities that turn them into effective, high-performing teams.

A useful developmental sequence is depicted in Figure 14.2. The figure shows the various activities as the leadership of the group moves from traditional supervision, through a more participative approach, to true team leadership.[36]

It is important to understand a couple of points about this model. Groups do not necessarily keep progressing from one "stage" to the next; they may remain permanently in the supervisory level or become more participative but never make it to true team leadership. As a result, progress on these dimensions must be a conscious goal of the leader and the members, and all should strive to meet these goals. Your group can meet these goals—and become a true team—by engaging in the activities in the figure.

Why Groups Sometimes Fail

Team building does not necessarily progress smoothly through such a sequence, culminating in a well-oiled team and superb performance.[37] Some groups never do work out. Such groups can be frustrating for managers and members, who may feel teams are a waste of time and that the difficulties outweigh the benefits.

It is not easy to build high-performance teams. *Teams* is often just a word used by management to describe merely putting people into groups. "Teams" sometimes are launched with little or no training or support systems. For example, both managers and group members need new skills to make a group work. These skills include learning the art of diplomacy, tackling "people issues" head on, and walking the fine line between encouraging autonomy and rewarding team innovations without letting the team get too independent and out of control.[39] Giving up some control is very difficult for managers from traditional systems, but they have to realize they will gain control in the long run by creating stronger, better-performing units.

Building a team can be challenging.[38]

What barriers make it hard for teams to succeed?

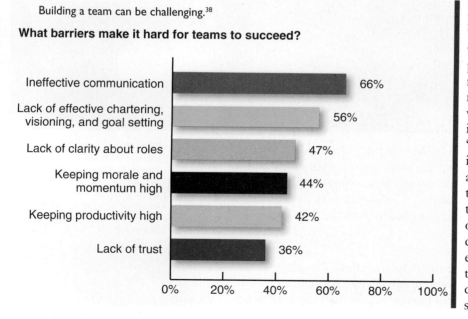

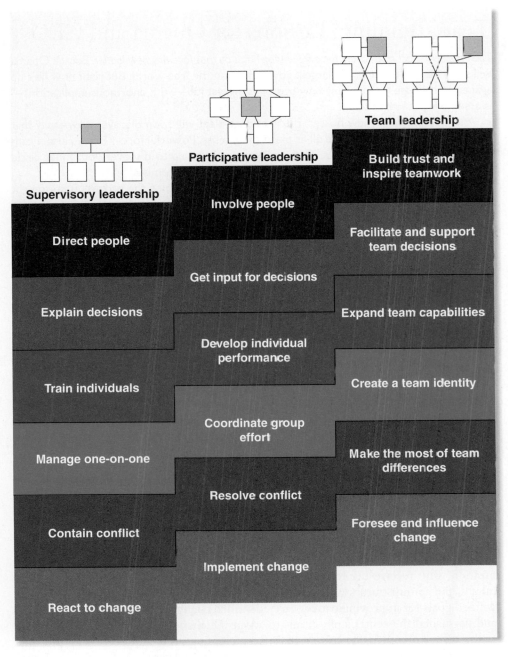

Supervisory leadership

Direct people

Explain decisions

Train individuals

Manage one-on-one

Contain conflict

React to change

Participative leadership

Involve people

Get input for decisions

Develop individual performance

Coordinate group effort

Resolve conflict

Implement change

Team leadership

Build trust and inspire teamwork

Facilitate and support team decisions

Expand team capabilities

Create a team identity

Make the most of team differences

Foresee and influence change

SOURCE: From *Leading Teams* by J. Zenger and Associates. Reprinted by permission.

FIGURE 14.2
Stepping up to Team Leadership

Teams should be truly empowered, as discussed in Chapter 13. The benefits of teams are reduced when they are not allowed to make important decisions—in other words, when management doesn't trust them with important responsibilities. If teams must acquire permission for every innovative idea, they will revert to making safe, traditional decisions.[40]

Empowerment enhances team performance even among virtual teams. Empowerment for virtual teams includes thorough training in using the technologies and strong technical support from management. Some virtual teams have periodic face-to-face interactions, which help performance; empowerment is particularly helpful for virtual teams that don't often meet face-to-face.[41]

Failure lies in not knowing and doing what makes teams successful. To be successful, you must apply clear thinking and appropriate practices.[42] That is what the rest of the chapter is about.

FROM THE PAGES OF

BusinessWeek

Team Building: Lessons for Obama and CEOs

The President-elect must avoid the same hiring hazards that face any new leader. Barack Obama will soon be the leader of the largest government in the free world. But right now he's up against a challenge faced by any new boss. His biggest job—with enormous implications— is assembling the right team.

And just like other new bosses, the President-elect will soon discover how easily that process can go wrong. Trusted allies plead their cases. Powerful forces block certain candidates. Time pressure mounts. Then one day you look up to discover your inner circle is not the A-Team you dreamed of but an all-around compromise.

What then should a leader do to build the best team? Since the process is so fraught with pitfalls, it might help to look at three missteps that commonly undermine a dream team in the making.

Automatically reward loyalists. No matter how long you've worked for the top job, once you get it, the impulse is to "endorse" your own early endorsers. We know of a new CEO, for instance, who appointed his longtime HR chief as president of the company's digital division. His gratitude for her support simply outweighed her limited experience.

What a shortcut to mediocrity, if not disaster.

http://www.businessweek.com/magazine/content/08_47/b4109130824219.htm

SOURCE: Jack Welch and Suzy Welch, "Team Building: Wrong and Right," *Business Week*, November 24, 2008, p. 130.

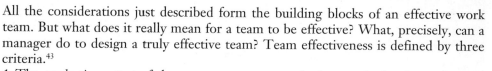

Building Effective Teams

LO 5

All the considerations just described form the building blocks of an effective work team. But what does it really mean for a team to be effective? What, precisely, can a manager do to design a truly effective team? Team effectiveness is defined by three criteria.[43]

1. The *productive output* of the team meets or exceeds the standards of quantity and quality; the team's output is acceptable to the customers, inside or outside the organization, who receive the team's goods or services. As examples, a team of doctors, nurses, and administrators at the University of Texas's M. D. Anderson Cancer Center defined goals for improving patient care, identified changes that would meet the goals, and persuaded the center's physicians to adopt the changes. As a result, performance at the center exceeded the team's goals for increasing visits and decreasing the time that elapses between a patient's first visit and his or her surgery.[44] At Lockheed Martin, Clarence L. "Kelly" Johnson's group designed, built, and flew the first U.S. tactical jet fighter, XP80, in 143 days.[45]

2. Team members realize *satisfaction* of their personal needs. Johnson gave his Lockheed teams the freedom to innovate and stretch their skills. Team members were enthusiastic and realized great pride and satisfaction in their work.

3. Team members remain *committed* to working together again; that is, the group doesn't burn out and disintegrate after a grueling project. Looking back, the members are glad they were involved. In other words, effective teams remain viable and have good prospects for repeated success in the future.[46]

For help in developing these qualities, teams may use team-building activities or work with an outside coach. Team building usually involves activities focused on relationships among team members. Whether these activities are as simple as a group discussion or as elaborate as a weekend retreat with physical challenges, the team-building event should be followed by an opportunity for participants to evaluate what they learned and how they will apply those lessons at work.[47] Coaching a team should be different from coaching individual team members because it focuses on how the group as a whole operates and how it can improve interactions so that it will accomplish its goals.[48] Thus, the process doesn't have the confidentiality of one-on-one coaching, and the coach has to pace the process so that everyone is included. Team coaching addresses issues such as what the team is focused on, how it sets goals, how it can improve communication and decision making. Ideally, the coaching helps a team develop enough that it can begin to coach itself.

Based on years of studying team performance, Richard Hackman has identified common barriers to team effectiveness. One is so simple that it would seem obvious: teams need to properly define their membership. However, many don't establish or communicate clear boundaries, perhaps because of discomfort over excluding people. When a team problem came to light, the chief executive of a financial services company determined that the chief financial officer was unable to collaborate effectively with others on the executive team. So the CEO asked the financial executive to skip the "boring" team meetings, keeping their communications one-on-one. Without the CFO, the executive team began to function at a much higher level.

Another barrier is that people tend to focus too much on harmony, assuming that when team members feel good about their participation, the team is effective. In fact, Hackman says, effectiveness comes first: team members feel satisfied when their team works effectively. In a study of symphony orchestras, dissatisfied musicians tended to perform better, and the relevant measure of satisfaction was how the musicians felt *after* a performance.

A third mistake that Hackman often encounters is the assumption that team members can be together too long. According to this assumption, when the team's membership never changes, the team runs out of ideas. But besides a need for research and development teams to add a new member every few years, Hackman has found that the more common problem is too little continuity: team members haven't been together long enough to learn to work well together. Airplane cockpit crews, for example, perform much better when they have flown together previously.[49]

To ensure the safety of themselves and each other, Boots & Coots firefighters need to maintain trust and communicate under some of the toughest circumstances.

Performance Focus

The key element of effective teamwork is commitment to a common purpose.[50] The best teams are those that have been given an important performance challenge by management and then have reached a common understanding and appreciation of their purpose. Without such understanding and commitment, a group will be just a bunch of individuals.

The best teams also work hard at developing a common understanding of how they will work together to achieve their purpose.[51] They discuss and agree on such details as how tasks and roles will be allocated and how they will make decisions. The team should develop norms for examining its performance strategies and be amenable to changing them when appropriate. For example, work teams usually standardize at least some processes, but they should be willing to try creative new ideas if the situation calls for them.[52] With a clear, strong, motivating purpose and effective performance strategies, people

Teams, with guidance from internal and external customers, should identify the nature of the results they want to achieve.

will pull together into a powerful force that has a chance to achieve extraordinary things.

The team's general purpose should be translated into specific, measurable performance goals.[53] You learned in Chapter 13 about how goals motivate individual performance. Performance can be defined by collective end products, instead of an accumulation of individual products.[54] Team-based performance goals help define and distinguish the team's product, encourage communication within the team, energize and motivate team members, provide feedback on progress, signal team victories (and defeats), and ensure that the team focuses clearly on results. Teams with both difficult goals and specific incentives to attain them achieve the highest performance levels.[55]

The best team-based measurement systems inform top management of the team's level of performance and help the team understand its own processes and gauge its own progress. Ideally, the team plays the lead role in designing its own measurement system. This responsibility is a great indicator of whether the team is truly empowered.[56]

Teams, like individuals, need feedback on their performance. Feedback from customers is especially crucial. Some customers for the team's products are inside the organization. Teams should be responsible for satisfying them and should be given or should seek performance feedback. Better yet, wherever possible, teams should interact directly with external customers who make the ultimate buying decisions about their goods and services. External customers typically provide the most honest, and most crucial and useful, performance feedback of all.[57]

Motivating Teamwork

social loafing

Working less hard and being less productive when in a group.

social facilitation effect

Working harder when in a group than when working alone.

Sometimes individuals work less hard and are less productive when they are members of a group. Such **social loafing** occurs when individuals believe that their contributions are not important, others will do the work for them, their lack of effort will go undetected, or they will be the lone sucker if they work hard but others don't. Perhaps you have seen social loafing in some of your student teams.[58] Conversely, sometimes individuals work harder when they are members of a group than when they are working alone. This **social facilitation effect** occurs because individuals usually are more motivated when others are present, they are concerned with what others think of them, and they want to maintain a positive self-image.

A social facilitation effect is maintained—and a social loafing effect can be avoided—when group members know each other, they can observe and communicate with one another, clear performance goals exist, the task is meaningful to the people working on it, they believe that their efforts matter and others will not take advantage of them, and the culture supports teamwork.[59] Thus, under ideal circumstances, everyone works hard, contributes in concrete ways to the team's work, and is accountable to other team members. Accountability to one another, rather than just to "the boss," is an essential aspect of good teamwork. Accountability inspires mutual commitment and trust.[60] Trust in your teammates—and their trust in you—may be the ultimate key to effectiveness.

Team effort is also generated by designing the team's task to be motivating. Techniques for creating motivating tasks appear in the guidelines for job enrichment discussed in Chapter 13. Tasks are motivating when they use a variety of member skills and provide high task variety, identity, significance, autonomy, and performance feedback.

Ultimately, teamwork is motivated by tying rewards to team performance.[61] If team performance can be measured validly, team-based rewards can be given accordingly. It is not easy to move from a system of rewards based on individual performance to one based on team performance and cooperation. It also may not be appropriate, unless people are truly interdependent and must collaborate to attain true team goals.[62] Team-based rewards are often combined with regular salaries and rewards based on individual performance. At Nucor, where production employees work in teams of 12 to 20, team members earn bonuses based on the tons of steel shipped each week. To ensure high quality, the amount of any bad product is subtracted from total shipments—and if defective products reach the customer, the amount subtracted is multiplied by 3. On average, the amount of the team bonuses equals 170 to 180 percent of the team members' base salary. This type of motivation works because Nucor teams are empowered to make decisions aimed at improving their productivity, and the company actively shares performance data with its employees.[63]

If team performance is difficult to measure validly, then desired behaviors, activities, and processes that indicate good teamwork can be rewarded. Individuals within teams can be given differential rewards based on teamwork indicated by active participation, cooperation, leadership, and other contributions to the team. As you read the "Management Close-Up: Taking Action" feature, consider how these approaches to rewarding team performance would apply to teamwork at Cisco.

If team members are to be rewarded differentially, such decisions are better *not* left only to the boss.[65] They should be made by the team itself, through peer ratings or multi-rater evaluation systems. Why? Team members are in a better position to observe, know, and make valid reward allocations. Finally, the more teams the organization has, and the more a full team orientation exists, the more valid and effective it will be to distribute rewards via gainsharing and other organizationwide incentives.

Management Close-Up | TAKING ACTION

As the Internet radically changed how people live, learn, and work, new opportunities were emerging in many areas. Cisco president and CEO John Chambers knew that the Internet's and Cisco's rapid growth had increased the difficulty for one top person to review new ideas, gather information, and make timely decisions. For Cisco to continue to grow, he reasoned, it needed to be more nimble and bring more products to market faster—in short, to innovate with speed.

Chambers saw collaborative teams as the solution and designed a new, broader, and more inclusive system in which decision-making responsibility is pushed deeper into the organization. The new configuration includes an operating committee of 11 people, Chambers plus other top executives; several councils that manage $10 billion projects; boards that handle $1 billion opportunities; and working groups that support the councils and boards and perform other activities. The teams are cross-functional, interdepartmental, and even transnational. Each is organized around promising initiatives or product lines; other teams can spring up at the drop of a hat when needed. In the new company, to not share what you know is unacceptable, so few turn down an invitation to collaborate.

Chambers says collaborative technologies permit almost instant access to information and to other people, providing new ways to interact. Cisco promotes all types of social networking: blogs, videos, and even an internal "MyCisco" system that employees use like an internal Facebook network. There employees can share what they have learned and provide details about their expertise.

Initially, not everyone embraced the new teamwork structure. The old Cisco sported a "cowboy culture," with leaders competing aggressively for resources. Nearly 20 percent of them left the company, deciding they couldn't work under Chambers' new setup. Leaders now share responsibility for each other's success. They are measured on how well they collaborate and are compensated on how well all businesses perform, not just their own unit.[64]

- As president and CEO of Cisco, John Chambers needs to focus several years into the future to keep the company successful. How do you think this long-term perspective helped shape his view of teamwork?
- How do you suppose Chambers overcame managers' initial resistance in forming collaborative teams?

Member Contributions

Team members should be selected and trained so that they become effective contributors to the team. The teams themselves often hire their new members.[66] MillerCoors Brewing Company and Eastman Chemical teams select members based on the results of tests designed to predict how well they will contribute to team success in an empowered environment. At Texas Instruments, Human Resources screens applicants, and then team members interview them and make selection decisions.

Generally, the skills required by teams include technical or functional expertise, problem-solving and decision-making skills, and interpersonal skills. Some managers and teams mistakenly overemphasize some skills, particularly technical or functional ones, and underemphasize the others. In fact, social skills can be critical to team functioning; one worker with a persistently negative attitude—for example, someone who bullies or constantly complains—can and often does put an entire team into a downward spiral.[67] It is vitally important that all three types of skills be represented, and developed, among team members.

Along with knowledge about their subject area, teams need members to contribute interpersonal skills, especially listening and building trust.[68]

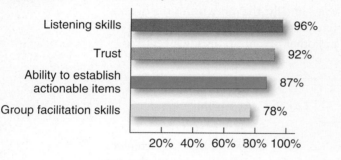

Percentage of survey respondents selecting element as critical for team performance

Element	Percentage
Listening skills	96%
Trust	92%
Ability to establish actionable items	87%
Group facilitation skills	78%

Norms

Norms are shared beliefs about how people should think and behave. For example, some people like to keep information and knowledge to themselves, but teams should try to establish a norm of knowledge sharing because it can improve team performance.[69] From the organization's standpoint, norms can be positive or negative. In some teams, everyone works hard; in other groups, employees are antimanagement and do as little work as possible. Some groups develop norms of taking risks, others of being conservative.[70] A norm could dictate that employees speak either favorably or critically of the company. Team members may show concern about poor safety practices, drug and alcohol abuse, and employee theft, or they may not care about these issues (or may even condone such practices). Health consciousness is the norm among executives at some companies, but smoking is the norm at tobacco companies. Some groups have norms of distrust and of being closed toward one another, but as you might guess, norms of trust and open discussion about conflict can improve group performance.[71]

A professor described his consulting experiences at two companies that exhibited different norms in their management teams.[72] At Federal Express Corporation, a young manager interrupted the professor's talk by proclaiming that a recent decision by top management ran counter to the professor's point about corporate planning. He was challenging top management to defend its decision. A hot debate ensued, and after an hour everyone went to lunch without a trace of hard feelings. But at another corporation, the professor opened a meeting by asking a group of top managers to describe the company's culture. There was silence. He asked again. More silence. Then someone passed him an unsigned note that read, "Dummy, can't you see that we can't speak our minds? Ask for the input anonymously, in writing." As you can see, norms are important, and can vary greatly from one group to another.

Roles

Roles are different sets of expectations for how different individuals should behave. Whereas norms apply generally to all team members, different roles exist for different members within the norm structure.

Two important sets of roles must be performed.[73] **Task specialist** roles are filled by individuals who have particular job-related skills and abilities. These employees keep the team moving toward accomplishment of the objectives. **Team maintenance specialists** develop and maintain harmony within the team. They boost morale, give support, provide humor, soothe hurt feelings, and generally exhibit a concern with members' well-being.

Note the similarity between these roles and the important task performance and group maintenance leadership behaviors you learned about in Chapter 12. As suggested in that chapter, some of these roles will be more important than others at different times and under different circumstances. But these behaviors need not be carried out only by one or two leaders; any member of the team can assume them at any time. Both types of roles can be performed by different individuals to maintain an effectively functioning work team.

What roles should leaders perform? Superior team leaders are better at relating, scouting, persuading, and empowering than are average team leaders.[74] *Relating* includes exhibiting more social and political awareness, caring for team members, and trust-building. *Scouting* means seeking information from managers, peers, and specialists, and investigating problems systematically. *Persuading* means not only influencing the team members but also obtaining external support for teams. *Empowerment* includes delegating authority, being flexible regarding team decisions, and coaching. Leaders also should roll up their sleeves and do real work to accomplish team goals, not just supervise.[75]

Finally, recall from Chapter 12 the importance of team leadership, in which group members rotate or share leadership roles.[76]

Self-managed teams report to a management representative who sometimes is called the *coach*. In true self-managed teams, the coach is not an actual member of the team.[77] The reason this is so is that the group is supposed to make its own decisions and also that the perceived power of the management representative could have a dampening effect on the team's openness and autonomy. The role of the coach, then, is to help the team understand its role in the organization and to serve as a resource for the team. The coach can provide information, resources, and insight that team members do not or cannot acquire on their own. And the coach should be an advocate for the team in the rest of the organization.

Cohesiveness

One of the most important properties of a team is cohesiveness.[78] **Cohesiveness** refers to how attractive the team is to its members, how motivated members are to remain in the team, and the degree to which team members influence one another. In general, it refers to how tightly knit the team is.

The Importance of Cohesiveness   Cohesiveness is important for two primary reasons. First, it contributes to *member satisfaction*. In a cohesive team, members communicate and get along well with one another. They feel good about being a part of the team. Even if their jobs are unfulfilling or the organization is oppressive, people gain some satisfaction from enjoying their coworkers.

Second, cohesiveness has a major impact on *performance*. A recent study of manufacturing teams led to a conclusion that performance improvements in both quality

---

roles

Different sets of expectations for how different individuals should behave.

Pictured is the Cassini Imaging Science Team whose mission is to guide the cameras that take photos of the outer reaches of space. Though the team is widely dispersed (members' locations include New York, California, and Belgium), they are united by a shared sense of purpose and a high value placed on scientific knowledge and technical excellence.

task specialist

An individual who has more advanced job-related skills and abilities than other group members possess.

team maintenance specialist

Individual who develops and maintains team harmony.

cohesiveness

The degree to which a group is attractive to its members, members are motivated to remain in the group, and members influence one another.

Cohesive groups are better than noncohesive groups at attaining the goals they want to attain; as a manager you need to ensure that your team's goals represent good business results.

and productivity occurred in the most cohesive unit, whereas conflict within another team prevented any quality or productivity improvements.[79] Sports fans read about this all the time. When teams are winning, players talk about the team being close, getting along well, and knowing one another's games. In contrast, losing is attributed to infighting and divisiveness. Generally, cohesiveness clearly can and does have a positive effect on performance.[80]

But this interpretation is simplistic; exceptions to this intuitive relationship occur. Tightly knit work groups can also be disruptive to the organization, such as when they sabotage the assembly line, get their boss fired, or enforce low performance norms. When does high cohesiveness lead to good performance, and when does it result in poor performance? The ultimate outcome depends on (1) the task, and (2) whether the group has high or low performance norms.

The Task   If the task is to make a decision or solve a problem, cohesiveness can lead to poor performance. Groupthink (discussed in Chapter 3) occurs when a tightly knit group is so cooperative that agreeing with one another's opinions and refraining from criticizing others' ideas become norms. For a cohesive group to make good decisions, it should establish a norm of constructive disagreement. This type of debating is important for groups up to the level of boards of directors.[81] In top-management teams it has been shown to improve the financial performance of companies.[82]

The effect of cohesiveness on performance, in contrast, can be positive, particularly if the task is to produce some tangible output. In day-to-day work groups for which decision making is not the primary task, cohesiveness can enhance performance. But that depends on the group's performance norms.[83]

Performance Norms   Some groups are better than others at ensuring that their members behave the way the group prefers. Cohesive groups are more effective than noncohesive groups at norm enforcement. But the next question is: Do they have norms of high or low performance?

As Figure 14.3 shows, the highest performance occurs when a cohesive team has high-performance norms. But if a highly cohesive group has low-performance norms, that group will have the worst performance. In the group's eyes, however, it will have succeeded in achieving its goal of poor performance. Noncohesive groups with high-performance norms can be effective from the company's standpoint. However, they won't be as productive as they would be if they were more cohesive. Noncohesive groups with low-performance norms perform poorly, but they will not ruin things for management as effectively as can cohesive groups with low-performance norms.

Self-managed teams can have a positive impact on productivity. But people often resist self-managed teams, in part because they don't want to accept so much responsibility and it is difficult for them to adjust to the change in the decision-making process.

Building Cohesiveness and High-Performance Norms

As Figure 14.3 suggests, managers should build teams that are cohesive and have high performance norms. The following actions can help create such teams:[84]

1. *Recruit members with similar attitudes, values, and backgrounds.* Similar individuals are more likely to get along with one another. Don't do this, though, if the team's task requires heterogeneous skills and inputs. For example, a homogeneous committee or board might make poor decisions, because it will lack different

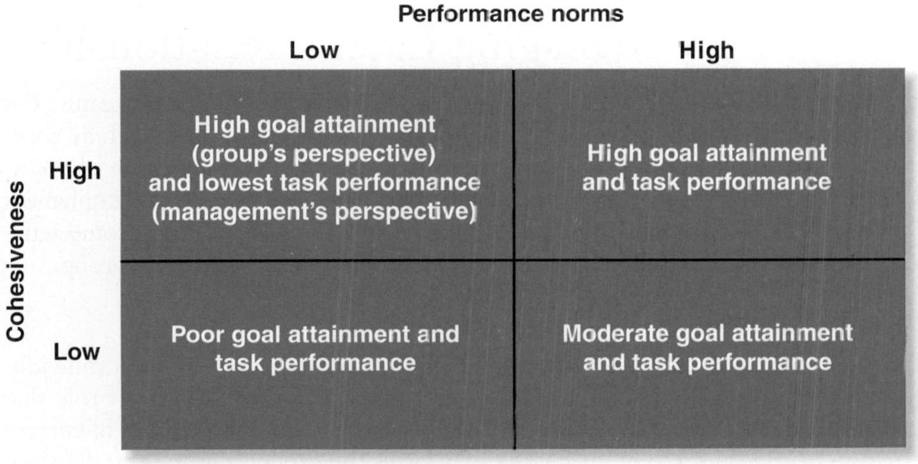

Performance norms

	Low	High
High Cohesiveness	High goal attainment (group's perspective) and lowest task performance (management's perspective)	High goal attainment and task performance
Low	Poor goal attainment and task performance	Moderate goal attainment and task performance

FIGURE 14.3

Cohesiveness, Performance Norms, and Group Performance

information and viewpoints and may succumb to groupthink. Recent research has shown that educational diversity and national diversity provide more benefits than limitations to groups' use and application of information.[85]

2. *Maintain high entrance and socialization standards.* Teams and organizations that are difficult to get into have more prestige. Individuals who survive a difficult interview, selection, or training process will be proud of their accomplishment and feel more attachment to the team.

3. *Keep the team small* (but large enough to get the job done). The larger the group, the less important members may feel. Small teams make individuals feel like large contributors.

4. *Help the team succeed, and publicize its successes.* You read about empowerment in the last chapter; you can empower teams as well as individuals.[86] Be a path-goal leader who facilitates success; the experience of winning brings teams closer together. Then, if you inform superiors of your team's successes, members will believe they are part of an important, prestigious unit. Teams that get into a good performance track continue to perform well as time goes on; groups that don't often enter a downward spiral in which problems compound over time.[87]

5. *Be a participative leader.* Participation in decisions gets team members more involved with one another and striving toward goal accomplishment. Too much autocratic decision making from above can alienate the group from management.

6. *Present a challenge from outside the team.* Competition with other groups makes team members band together to defeat the enemy (witness what happens to school spirit before the big game against an archrival). Some of the greatest teams in business and in science have been completely focused on winning a competition.[88] But don't *you* become the outside threat. If team members dislike you as a boss, they will become more cohesive—but their performance norms will be against you, not with you.

7. *Tie rewards to team performance.* To a large degree, teams are motivated just as individuals are—they do the activities that are rewarded. Make sure that high-performing teams get the rewards they deserve and that poorly performing groups get fewer rewards. You read about this earlier. Bear in mind that not just monetary rewards but also recognition for good work are powerful motivators. Recognize and celebrate team accomplishments. The team will become more cohesive and perform better to reap more rewards. Performance goals will be high, the organization will benefit from higher team motivation and productivity, and the individual needs of team members will be better satisfied. Ideally, being a member of a high-performing team, recognized as such throughout the organization, will become a badge of honor.[89]

But keep in mind that strong cohesiveness encouraging "agreeableness" can be dysfunctional. For problem solving and decision making, the team should establish norms promoting an open, constructive atmosphere including honest disagreement over issues without personal conflict and animosity.[90]

Managing Lateral Relationships

 LO 6

Teams do not function in a vacuum; they are interdependent with other teams. For example, at MillerCoors Brewing Company, major team responsibilities include coordinating with other teams and policy groups. At Texas Instruments, teams are responsible for interfacing with other teams to eliminate production bottlenecks and implement new processes and also for working with suppliers on quality issues.[91] Thus, some activities crucial to the team are those that entail dealing with people *outside* the group.

Managing Outward

gatekeeper

A team member who keeps abreast of current developments and provides the team with relevant information.

Several vital roles link teams to their external environments, that is, to other individuals and groups both inside and outside the organization. A specific type of role that spans team boundaries is the **gatekeeper,** a team member who stays abreast of current information in scientific and other fields and informs the group of important developments. Information useful to the group can also include information about resources, trends, and political support throughout the corporation or the industry.[92]

informing

A team strategy that entails making decisions with the team and then informing outsiders of its intentions.

The team's strategy dictates the team's mix of internally versus externally focused roles and the ways the mix changes over time. General team strategies include informing, parading, and probing.[93] The **informing** strategy entails making decisions with the team and then telling outsiders of the team's intentions. **Parading** means the team's strategy is to simultaneously emphasize internal team building and achieve external visibility. **Probing** involves a focus on external relations. This strategy requires team members to interact frequently with outsiders; diagnose the needs of customers, clients, and higher-ups; and experiment with solutions before taking action.

parading

A team strategy that entails simultaneously emphasizing internal team building and achieving external visibility.

The appropriate balance between an internal and external strategic focus and between internal and external roles depends on how much the team needs information, support, and resources from outside. When teams have a high degree of dependence on outsiders, probing is the best strategy. Parading teams perform at an intermediate level, and informing teams are likely to fail. They are too isolated from the outside groups on which they depend.

probing

A team strategy that requires team members to interact frequently with outsiders, diagnose their needs, and experiment with solutions.

Informing or parading strategies may be more effective for teams that are less dependent on outside groups, for example, established teams working on routine tasks in stable external environments. But for most important work teams of the future—task forces, new-product teams, and strategic decision-making teams tackling unstructured problems in a rapidly changing external environment—effective performance in roles that involve interfacing with the outside will be vital.

Lateral Role Relationships

Managing relationships with other groups and teams means engaging in a dynamic give-and-take that ensures proper coordination throughout the management system. To many managers, this process often seems like a chaotic free-for-all. To help understand the process and make it more productive, we can identify and examine the different types of lateral role relationships and take a strategic approach to building constructive relationships.

Different teams, like different individuals, have roles to perform. As teams carry out their roles, several distinct patterns of working relationships develop:[94]

1. *Work-flow relationships* emerge as materials are passed from one group to another. A group commonly receives work from one unit, processes it, and sends it to the next unit in the process. Your group, then, will come before some groups and after others in the process.

2. *Service relationships* exist when top management centralizes an activity to which a large number of other units must gain access. Common examples are technology services, libraries, and clerical staff. Such units must assist other people to help them accomplish their goals.

3. *Advisory relationships* are created when teams with problems call on centralized sources of expert knowledge. For example, staff members in the human resources or legal department advise work teams.

4. *Audit relationships* develop when people not directly in the chain of command evaluate the methods and performances of other teams. Financial auditors check the books, and technical auditors assess the methods and technical quality of the work.

5. *Stabilization relationships* involve auditing before the fact. In other words, teams sometimes must obtain clearance from others—for example, for large purchases—before they take action.

6. *Liaison relationships* involve intermediaries between teams. Managers often are called on to mediate conflict between two organizational units. Public relations people, sales managers, purchasing agents, and others who work across organizational boundaries serve in liaison roles as they maintain communications between the organization and the outside world.

By assessing each working relationship with another unit (From whom do we receive, and to whom do we send work? What permissions do we control, and to whom must we go for authorizations?), teams can better understand whom to contact and when, where, why, and how to do so. Coordination throughout the working system improves, problems are avoided or short-circuited before they get too serious, and performance improves.[95]

Managing Conflict

The complex maze of interdependencies throughout organizations provides many opportunities for conflict to arise among groups and teams. Some conflict is constructive for the organization, as we discussed in Chapter 3. Typically, conflict can foster creativity when it is about ideas, rather than personalities. In contrast, at a nonprofit organization, team members were committed to maintaining harmony during meetings, but their unresolved differences spilled over into nasty remarks outside of the office.[96]

Many factors cause great potential for destructive conflict: the sheer number and variety of contacts, ambiguities in jurisdiction and responsibility, differences in goals, intergroup competition for scarce resources, different perspectives held by members of different units, varying time horizons in which some units attend to long-term considerations and others focus on short-term needs, and others. Tensions and anxieties are likely to arise in teams that are demographically diverse, include members from different parts of the organization, or are composed of contrasting personalities. Both demographic and cross-functional heterogeneity initially lead to problems such as stress, lower cooperation, and lower cohesiveness.[97]

As chief executive of Global Adjustments, a firm specializing in relocations and cross-cultural issues, Ranjini Manian sees firsthand some of the challenges that arise in multicultural teams. Manian has often observed how people from different cultures face the challenge of coping with uncertainty. She finds that Europeans and North Americans tend to try minimizing uncertainty through rules, plans, and schedules, whereas her Indian colleagues are more likely to focus on adapting to surprises as they occur. The apparently more relaxed approach of the latter group can frustrate Western colleagues, who may interpret that behavior as a lack of commitment to goals. And when an Indian-style belief that uncertainty is inevitable leads to vague or incomplete plans, Western businesspeople tend to view those plans as unprofessional.

The solution for such differences, in Manian's view, is to learn about, respect, and adapt to team members' cultural practices. In the case of coping with uncertainty, Manian appreciates the value of careful planning but sees virtue in balancing this skill with flexibility and calm in the face of unexpected problems or opportunities. When team members can do both, their team will be both forward-thinking and agile.[98]

Over time and with communication, diverse groups actually tend to become more cooperative and perform better than do homogeneous groups. Norms of cooperation can improve performance, as does the fact that cross-functional teams engage in more external communication with more areas of the organization.[99]

Conflict Styles

Teams inevitably face conflicts and must decide how to manage them. The aim should be to make the conflict productive, that is, to make those involved believe they have benefited rather than lost from the conflict.[100] People believe they have benefited from a conflict when (1) a new solution is implemented, the problem is solved, and it is unlikely to emerge again, and (2) work relationships have been strengthened and people believe they can work together productively in the future.

People handle conflict in different ways. You have your own style; others' styles may be similar or may differ. Their styles depend in part on their country's cultural norms. For example, Chinese people are more concerned with collective than with individual interests, and they are more likely than managers in the United States to turn to higher authorities to make decisions rather than resolve conflicts themselves.[101] But culture aside, any team or individual has several options regarding how they deal with conflicts.[102] These personal styles of dealing with conflict, shown in Figure 14.4, are distinguished based on how much people strive to satisfy their own concerns (the assertiveness dimension) and how much they focus on satisfying the other party's concerns (the cooperation dimension).

For example, a common reaction to conflict is **avoidance.** In this situation, people do nothing to satisfy themselves or others. They either ignore the problem by doing nothing at all or address it by merely smoothing over or deemphasizing the disagreement. This, of course, fails to solve the problem or clear the air. When Paul Forti was a middle manager in a management consulting firm, he was passed over for a promotion, and the organization brought in an outsider who was at first too busy to discuss his disappointment and future role in the firm. He handled the situation with avoidance, and as a result, their working relationship suffered for weeks.[103]

Accommodation means cooperating on behalf of the other party but not being assertive about one's own interests. **Compromise** involves moderate attention to both parties' concerns, being neither highly cooperative nor highly assertive. This style results in satisficing but not optimizing solutions. **Competing** is a highly competitive response in which people focus strictly on their own wishes and are unwilling to recognize the other person's concerns. Finally, **collaboration** emphasizes both cooperation and assertiveness. The goal is to maximize satisfaction for both parties. Collaboration changed Paul Forti's relationship with his boss at the consulting firm. The

avoidance
A reaction to conflict that involves ignoring the problem by doing nothing at all, or deemphasizing the disagreement.

accommodation
A style of dealing with conflict involving cooperation on behalf of the other party but not being assertive about one's own interests.

compromise
A style of dealing with conflict involving moderate attention to both parties' concerns.

competing
A style of dealing with conflict involving strong focus on one's own goals and little or no concern for the other person's goals.

collaboration
A style of dealing with conflict emphasizing both cooperation and assertiveness to maximize both parties' satisfaction.

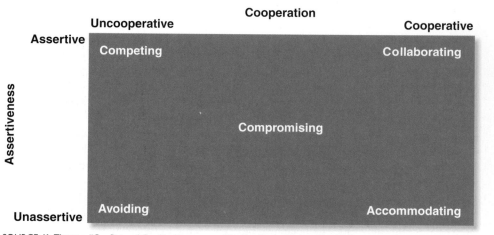

FIGURE 14.4
Conflict Management Strategies

SOURCE: K. Thomas, "Conflict and Conflict Management." In *Handbook of Industrial and Organizational Psychology,* ed. M. D. Dunnette. Copyright © 1976. Reprinted by permission of the editor.

new approach literally started by accident, when the senior manager slipped on some ice, Forti came to her aid, and she commented that she would like to get to know him better. Over lunch, she expressed her respect for Forti, and they developed a better working relationship in which she gave him interesting assignments and made sure clients knew about his expertise. Thus, although Forti hadn't gotten the promotion, he did get many opportunities to develop his career.[104]

So, imagine you and a friend want to go to a movie together, and you have different movies in mind. If he insists that you go to his movie, he is showing the competing style. If you agree, even though you prefer another movie, you are accommodating. If one of you mentions a third movie that neither of you is excited about but both of you are willing to live with, you are compromising. If you realize you don't know all the options, do some research, and find another movie that you're both enthusiastic about, you are collaborating.

Different approaches are necessary at different times.[105] For example, competing can be necessary when cutting costs or dealing with other scarce resources. Compromise may be useful when people are under time pressure, when they need to achieve a temporary solution, or when collaboration fails. People should accommodate when they learn they are wrong or to minimize loss when they are outmatched. Even avoiding may be appropriate if the issue is trivial or resolving the conflict should be someone else's responsibility.

But when the conflict concerns important issues, when both sets of concerns are valid and important, when a creative solution is needed, and when commitment to the solution is vital to implementation, collaboration is the ideal approach. Collaboration can be achieved by airing feelings and opinions, addressing all concerns, and avoiding goal displacement by not letting personal attacks interfere with problem solving. An important technique is to invoke **superordinate goals**—higher-level organizational goals toward which everyone should be striving and that ultimately need to take precedence over personal or unit preferences.[106] Using team-based rewards can give the group a "superordinate identity" that can reduce differences among team members and enhance performance.[107] Collaboration offers the best chance of reaching mutually satisfactory solutions based on the ideas and interests of all parties, and of maintaining and strengthening work relationships.

Being a Mediator

Managers spend a lot of time trying to resolve conflict between *other* people. You already may have served as a **mediator**, a "third party" intervening to help settle a conflict between other people. Third-party intervention, done well, can improve working relationships and help the parties improve their own conflict-management, communication, and problem-solving skills.[108]

Some insight comes from a study of human resource (HR) managers and the conflicts with which they deal.[109] HR managers encounter every type of conflict imaginable: interpersonal difficulties from minor irritations to jealousy to fights; operations issues, including union issues, work assignments, overtime, and sick leave; discipline over infractions ranging from drug use and theft to sleeping on the job; sexual harassment and racial bias; pay and promotion issues; and feuds or strategic conflicts among divisions or individuals at the highest organizational levels.

superordinate goals

Higher-level goals taking priority over specific individual or group goals.

mediator

A third party who intervenes to help others manage their conflict.

Conflicts can arise for any team—the trick is to make them productive. This ad promotes the American Arbitration Association's mission to train professionals on how to effectively minimize and manage conflict—"before the mud starts flying."

In the study, the HR managers successfully settled most of the disputes. These managers typically follow a four-stage strategy. They *investigate* by interviewing the disputants and others and gathering more information. While talking with the dis-

In a recent survey of 1,000 employees, 55 percent said they experience high levels of stress at work. The biggest headache: people issues, such as coworkers who annoy others, compete excessively, or add to workplace pressures.[110]

putants, they seek both parties' perspectives, remaining as neutral as possible. The discussion should stay issue oriented, not personal. They *decide* how to resolve the dispute, often in conjunction with the disputants' bosses. In preparing to decide what to do, blame should not be assigned prematurely; at this point they should be exploring solutions. They *take action* by explaining their decisions and the reasoning, and advise or train the disputants to avoid future incidents. And they *follow up* by making sure everyone understands the solution, documenting the conflict and the resolution, and monitoring the results by checking back with the disputants and their bosses. Throughout, the objectives of the HR people are to be fully informed so that they understand the conflict; to be active and assertive in trying to resolve it; to be as objective, neutral, and impartial as humanly possible; and to be flexible by modifying their approaches according to the situation.

Here are some other recommendations for more effective conflict management.[111] Don't allow dysfunctional conflict to build, or hope or assume that it will go away. Address it before it escalates. Try to resolve it, and if the first efforts don't work, try others. And remember the earlier discussion (Chapter 13) of procedural justice. Even if disputants are not happy with your decisions, there are benefits to providing fair treatment, making a good-faith effort, giving them a voice in the proceedings, and so on. Caring about others' goals as well as your own will help ensure a collaborative process. Remember, too, that you may be able to ask HR specialists to help with difficult conflicts.

Electronic and Virtual Conflict

When teams are geographically dispersed, as is often the case for virtual teams, team members tend to experience more conflict and less trust.[112] Conflict management affects the success of virtual teams.[113] In a recent study, avoidance hurt performance. Accommodation—conceding to others to maintain harmony rather than assertively attempting to negotiate integrative solutions—had no effect on performance. Collaboration had a positive effect on performance. The researchers also uncovered two surprises: compromise hurt performance, and competition helped performance. Compromises hurt because they often are watered-down, middle-of-the-road, suboptimal solutions. Competitive behavior was useful because the virtual teams were temporary and under time pressure, so having some individuals behave dominantly and impose decisions to achieve efficiency was useful rather than detrimental.

When people have problems in business-to-business e-commerce (e.g., costly delays), they tend to behave competitively and defensively rather than collaboratively.[114] Technical problems and recurring problems test people's patience. The conflict will escalate unless people use more cooperative, collaborative styles. Try to prevent conflicts before they arise; for example, make sure your information system is running smoothly before linking with others. Monitor and reduce or eliminate problems as soon as possible. When problems arise, express your willingness to cooperate, and then *actually be* cooperative. Even technical problems require the social skills of good management. Consider, for example, the management skills required to lead virtual teams at Cisco. As described in the "Management Close-Up: Assessing Outcomes and Seizing Opportunities" feature, Cisco's team leaders rely on skills such as communicating, the subject of the next chapter.

Management Close-Up

ASSESSING OUTCOMES AND SEIZING OPPORTUNITIES

Cisco CEO John Chambers admits it took him a few months to trust his new idea about collaboration—an arrangement that he calls "leading from the middle." He began to feel more comfortable however, when he discovered that not only were teams coming to good conclusions on their own but they also were reaching decisions more quickly.

Today, the company is juggling nearly two dozen large business initiatives; in the past it could handle only one or two simultaneously. Projects that once took six months to complete now get done in a week. With the new teamwork structure, Cisco employees kicked off 26 new businesses in a single year; the new businesses are expected to deliver one-fourth of the firm's revenue in the next five years.

A recent team innovation, Stadium Vision, enables stadium owners to broadcast video and digital content—even targeted advertising—to a stadium audience. Already sold to the Arizona Cardinals and Dallas Cowboys football teams and Major League Baseball's New York Yankees, Stadium Vision represents a multimillion-dollar business for Cisco. Its teams developed the product from initial concept through completion in a mere 120 days.

Cisco sees video as the next big thing on the Internet, and it completed a number of acquisitions to boost its video-technology capability. In 2006, it introduced TelePresence, a $300,000 high-definition videoconferencing system that permits corporate clients to hold virtual meetings efficiently. Besides the high-quality resolution, TelePresence offers real-time translation: a speaker's words are translated into English and transmitted via computerized voice and in subtitles on the screen. Currently, translation is available in Spanish, French, Italian, and Chinese, with plans for up to 20 languages eventually.

The company's fastest-growing product, TelePresence is used for Cisco's own meetings, allowing the company to trim 20 percent off its corporate travel budget in its first year alone—a saving of nearly $68 million. Additional savings are projected for future years. As Chambers points out, TelePresence helps companies become more efficient (employees don't lose time in transit) and reduces their consumption of fossil fuels for business travel. And less travel means lower greenhouse gas emissions.[115]

- Why do you think Cisco operates more efficiently in its new collaborative-team structure than it did under the old "command and control" format?
- Consider the role that virtual teams play at Cisco. How has the use of technology fostered teamwork and company success?

KEY TERMS

Accommodation,   p. 506

Autonomous work groups,   p. 492

Avoidance,   p. 506

Cohesiveness,   p. 501

Collaboration,   p. 506

Competing,   p. 506

Compromise,   p. 506

Gatekeeper,   p. 504

Informing,   p. 504

Management teams,   p. 490

Mediator,   p. 507

Norms,   p. 500

Parading,   p. 504

Parallel teams,   p. 490

Probing,   p. 504

Project and development teams, p. 490

Quality circles,   p. 492

Roles,   p. 501

Self-designing teams,   p. 492

Self-managed teams,   p. 492

Semiautonomous work groups,   p. 492

Social facilitation effect,   p. 498

Social loafing,   p. 498

Superordinate goals,   p. 507

Task specialist,   p. 501

Team,   p. 489

Team maintenance specialist,   p. 501

Traditional work groups,   p. 492

Transnational teams,   p. 492

Virtual teams,   p. 491

Work teams,   p. 490

SUMMARY OF LEARNING OBJECTIVES

Now that you have studied Chapter 14, you should be able to:

LO 1 Discuss how teams can contribute to an organization's effectiveness.

Teams are building blocks for organization structure and forces for productivity, quality, cost savings speed, change, and innovation. They have the potential to provide many benefits for both the organization and individual members.

LO 2 Distinguish the new team environment from that of traditional work groups.

Compared with traditional work groups that were closely supervised, today's teams have more authority and often are self-managed. Teams now are used in many more ways, for many more purposes, than in the past. Generally, types of teams include work teams, project and development teams, parallel teams, management teams, transnational teams, and virtual teams. Types of work teams range from traditional groups with low autonomy to self-designing teams with high autonomy.

LO 3 Summarize how groups become teams.

Groups carry on a variety of important developmental activities, including forming, storming, norming, and performing. For a group to become a team, it should move beyond traditional supervisory leadership, become more participative, and ultimately enjoy team leadership. A true team has members who complement one another; who are committed to a common purpose, performance goals, and approach; and who hold themselves accountable to one another.

LO 4 Explain why groups sometimes fail.

Teams do not always work well. Some companies underestimate the difficulties of moving to a team-based approach. Teams require training, empowerment, and a well-managed transition to make them work. Groups may fail to become effective teams unless managers and team members commit to the idea, understand what makes teams work, and implement appropriate practices.

LO 5 Describe how to build an effective team.

Create a team with a high-performance focus by establishing a common purpose, translating the purpose into measurable team goals, designing the team's task so it is intrinsically motivating, designing a team-based performance measurement system, and providing team rewards.

Work to develop a common understanding of how the team will perform its task. Make it clear that everyone has to work hard and contribute in concrete ways. Establish mutual accountability and build trust among members. Examine the team's strategies periodically and be willing to adapt.

Make sure members contribute fully by selecting them appropriately, training them, and checking that all important roles are carried out. Take a variety of steps to establish team cohesiveness and high performance norms.

And don't just manage inwardly. Manage the team's relations with outsiders, too.

LO 6 List methods for managing a team's relationships with other teams.

Perform important roles such as gatekeeping, informing, parading, and probing. Identify the types of lateral role relationships you have with outsiders. This can help coordinate efforts throughout the work system.

LO 7 Identify ways to manage conflict.

Managing lateral relationships well can prevent some conflict. But conflict arises because of the sheer number of contacts, ambiguities, goal differences, competition for scarce resources, and different perspectives and time horizons. Depending on the situation, five basic interpersonal approaches to managing conflict can be used: avoidance, accommodation, compromise, competition, and collaboration. Superordinate goals offer a focus on higher-level organizational goals that can help generate a collaborative relationship. Techniques for managing conflict between other parties include acting as a mediator and managing virtual conflict.

DISCUSSION QUESTIONS

1. Why do you think some people resist the idea of working in teams? How would you deal with their resistance?

2. Consider a job you have held, and review Table 14.1 about the traditional and new team environment. Which environment best describes your job? Assess your job on each of the dimensions described in the table.

3. Assess your job as in question 2, using Figure 14.2. Which leadership "stage" characterized your job environment?

4. Identify some things from a previous job that could have been done differently to move your work group closer toward the "team leadership" depicted in Figure 14.2.

5. Experts say that teams are a means, not an end. What do you think they mean? What do you think happens in a company that creates teams just for the sake of having teams because it's a fad or just because it sounds good? How can this pitfall be avoided?

6. Choose a sports team with which you are familiar. Assess its effectiveness and discuss the factors that contribute to its level of effectiveness.

7. Assess the effectiveness, as in Question 6, of a student group with which you have been affiliated. Could anything have been done to make it more effective?

8. Consider the various roles members have to perform for a team to be effective. Which roles would play to your strengths, and which to your weaknesses? How can you become a better team member?

9. Discuss personal examples of virtual conflict and how they were managed, well or poorly.

10. What do you think are your own most commonly used approaches to handling conflict? Least common? What can you do to expand your repertoire and become more effective at conflict management?

11. Generate real examples of how superordinate goals have helped resolve a conflict. Identify some current conflicts and provide some specific ideas for how superordinate goals could be used to help.

12. Have you ever been part of a group that was "self-managed"? What was good about it, and what not so good? Why do many managers resist this idea? Why do some people love the idea of being a member of such a team, while others don't?

13. How might self-managed teams operate differently in different cultures? What are the advantages, disadvantages, and implications of homogeneous versus highly diverse self-managed teams?

CONCLUDING CASE

Rocky Gagnon, General Contractor

Rocky Gagnon is a 50-year-old journeyman carpenter, laborer, and craftsman. Over the past 30 years, he has worked in almost every job and phase of the house building process. Gagnon is getting older and his back is getting sore. He loves the construction business and feels that now is the time for him to start working more with his mind than his back. Gagnon wants to become a general contractor.

Some general contractors have their own facilities, equipment, and employees. Others simply work out of their homes and subcontract all of the work required to complete a particular project.

Gagnon has an idea and a vision for something a little different. He wants to put together a team of tradespeople who will agree to work together toward the successful completion of about 8 to 15 homes per year. At the same time, each individual will be able to continue to operate as an independent contractor during off hours.

One of the results of working for 30 years in the local building trades is a large and varied network of friends and acquaintances. Gagnon has enjoyed many a drink with the local plumbing and heating contractors, roofers, insulation people, land surveyors, and others. He wants to take advantage of those relationships. The general profile of local contractors, according to Gagnon, is that of a highly skilled, very independent group of people with poor communication skills. The workmanship is generally very good—when it finally gets done.

Many jobs and phases of the house-building process take place in a logical sequence. For example, insulation people cannot do their work until the "rough" electrical, plumbing, and heating work is completed. If any of those contractors falls behind schedule or does not complete his or her task, the process is disrupted. Outside factors such as weather, availability of materials, and overlapping schedules and deadlines with other jobs further complicates the challenge of meeting deadlines. Gagnon wants to coordinate all of this and make house building more efficient.

The spirit of cooperation is also severely lacking, according to Gagnon. It seems that many contractors could not care less about the crew that will follow them in the building process.

For example, a framing crew should know about the exact plans for the fireplace, hearth, and chimney on each job and should leave the site properly set up for that contractor. According to Gagnon, the all-too-typical response of the framer (as well as others) is, "That's not my job, so don't tell me about it." Independent contractors are also notorious for leaving their messes behind for someone else to clean up, such as the general contractor or next crew.

Gagnon wants to change all of this by bringing together a group of tradespeople who will agree to work together as a team for the common good. If done right, Gagnon sees this as a win-win situation for all parties.

Rocky Gagnon knows that the opportunity for success clearly exists. New home construction is very strong in his area and is expected to stay that way for a long time. He also knows that the key to his success will be the presence of strong organizational and communication skills. Gagnon feels that all of the pieces of the puzzle are there for the taking, and that all he needs is some help in setting up the right team and an organizational structure and work process that will achieve the desired results.

During the past few months, Gagnon put together a list and has met separately with the individuals he considers to be the best craftsmen in the area and, most important, who he knows have the potential and willingness to form the team and working relationship that he envisions. The first of several meetings has been set up for the entire group to meet and work through the particulars. Gagnon has hired a well-known and respected business professor from the local community to serve as an adviser and mediator for the group.

QUESTIONS

1. What type of team would work best in this situation? Support your answer with concepts from the text that apply to this proposed venture.

2. What kinds of problems would you expect this group to encounter? What is the best way to work through those?

3. What are the likely keys to success in motivating these individuals to cooperate and communicate as a team?

EXPERIENTIAL EXERCISES

14.1 Prisoners' Dilemma: An Intergroup Competition

INSTRUCTIONS

1. The instructor explains what will take place in this exercise and assigns people to groups. Two types of teams are formed and named Red and Blue (with no more than eight per group) and are not to communicate with the other team in any way, verbally or nonverbally, except when told to do so by the instructor. Groups are given time to study the Prisoners' Dilemma Tally Sheet.

2. (3 min.) Round 1. Each team has three minutes to make a team decision. Write your decisions when the instructor says time is up.

3. (2 min.) The choices of the teams are announced for Round 1. The scores are entered on the Tally Sheet.

4. (4–5 min.) Round 2 is conducted in the same manner as Round 1.

5. (6 min.) Round 3 is announced as a special round, for which the payoff points are doubled. Each team is instructed to

send one representative to chairs in the center of the room. After representatives have conferred for three minutes, they return to their teams. Teams then have three minutes, as before, in which to make their decisions. When recording their scores, they should be reminded that points indicated by the payoff schedule are doubled for this round only.

6. (8–10 min.) Rounds 4, 5, and 6 are conducted in the same manner as the first three rounds.

7. (6 min.) Round 7 is announced as a special round, in which the payoff points are "squared" (multiplied by themselves: e.g., a score of 4 would be $4^2 = 16$). A minus sign would be

retained (e.g., $-(3)^2 = -9$). Team representatives meet for three minutes; then the teams meet for three minutes. At the instructor's signal, the teams write their choices, and then the two choices are announced.

8. (6 min.) Round 8 is handled exactly as Round 7 was. Payoff points are squared.

9. (10–20 min.) The point total for each team is announced, and the sum of the two team totals is calculated and compared with the maximum positive or negative outcomes (+108 or −108 points).

Prisoners' Dilemma Tally Sheet

Instructions:

For 10 successive rounds, the Red team will choose either an A or a B and the Blue team will choose either an X or a Y.

Payoff Schedule:

AX—Both teams win 3 points.
AY—Red team loses 6 points; Blue team wins 6 points.

The score each team receives in a round is determined by the pattern made by the choices of both teams, according to the schedule below.

BX—Red team wins 6 points; Blue team loses 6 points.
BY—Both teams lose 3 points.

Scorecard:

Round	Minutes	Choice		Cumulative Points	
		Red Team	Blue Team	Red Team	Blue Team
1	3				
2	3				
3*	3 (reps.), 3 (teams)				
4	3				
5	3				
6*	3 (reps.), 3 (teams)				
7**	3 (reps.), 3 (teams)				
8**	3 (reps.), 3 (teams)				

*Payoff points are doubled for this round.
**Payoff points are squared for this round. (Retain the minus sign.)
SOURCE: Dorothy Hai, "Prisoner's Dilemma," in *Organizational Behavior: Experiences and Cases.* Copyright © 1986. Reprinted with permission of South-Western College Publishing, a division of Thomson Learning.

14.2 The Traveler's Check Scam Group Exercise

INSTRUCTIONS

1. (3 min.) Group selects an observer. The observer remains silent during the group problem-solving process, recording the activities of the group on the Observer's Report Form.

2. (15 min.) Group members read the following problem and proceed to solve it.

3. (2 min.) When the group has a solution to the problem upon which all members agree, it will be written on a note and handed to the instructor.

4. (5 min.) The observer briefs the group on the problem-solving processes observed during the exercise.

5. (25 min.) The small group discusses the following topics:

a. Did the group decide on a problem solution process before it attempted to solve the problem? If so, what was it?

b. Was the solution of the problem hindered in any way by the lack of an appropriate agreed-upon group problem-solving process? Explain.

c. Who were the leaders of the group during the exercise? What did they do? Critique their leadership activities.

d. What communications patterns were used by the group during the exercise? Who participated the most? Who participated the least? Describe individual behaviors.

e. Did the group solve the problem? How many members of the group discovered the correct answer on their own?

f. Was using the group to solve this problem better than assigning the problem to one person? Explain the rationale for your answer.

THE CASE OF MICKEY THE DIP

Mickey the Dip, an expert pickpocket and forger, liked to work the Los Angeles International Airport on busy days. His technique was to pick the pockets of prosperous-looking victims just before they boarded planes to the East Coast. This gave Mickey five hours to use stolen credit cards before the owners could report their losses.

One morning Mickey snatched a fat wallet from a traveler and left the airport to examine his loot. To his surprise he found no credit cards but instead $500 in traveler's checks. After 20 minutes of practice, Mickey could sign a perfect imitation of the victim's signature. He then proceeded to a large department store where all suits were being sold for 75 percent of the regular price. Mickey purchased a suit for $225 and paid for it with $300 in stolen traveler's checks. After the clerk who served him went to lunch, he bought another suit for $150 and paid for it with the remaining $200 of stolen traveler's checks. Later, Mickey switched the labels on the two suits and, using the receipt from the $225 suit, returned the $150 suit at a centralized return desk for a refund. The refund clerk took the suit and

gave Mickey eleven $20 bills, which he stuffed into his pocket and disappeared.

When the department store deposited the traveler's checks, they were returned as forgeries. Assuming the store normally sold suits at twice their wholesale price and used 10 percent of sales as an overhead cost figure, what was the cash value of the loss suffered by the store as a result of Mickey's caper? Do not consider taxes in your computations.

THE TRAVELER'S CHECK SCAM EXERCISE OBSERVER'S REPORT

1. What happened during the first few minutes the group met after members finished reading the problem? (List behaviors of specific group members.)

2. Identify the group role played by each group member during the exercise. Give examples of the behavior of each.

3. Were there any conflicts within or among group members during the exercise? Explain the nature of the conflicts and the behavior of the individual(s) involved.

4. How were decisions made in the group? Give specific examples.

5. How could the group improve its problem-solving skills?

SOURCE: Peter P. Dawson, *Fundamentals of Organizational Behavior.* Copyright © 1985 Pearson Education, Inc. Reprinted by permission of Pearson Education, Inc., Upper Saddle River, NJ.

Communicating

> *The single biggest problem with communication is the illusion that it has taken place.*
>
> — G. B. Shaw

LEARNING OBJECTIVES

After studying Chapter 15, you will be able to:

LO 1 Discuss important advantages of two-way communication. p. 516

LO 2 Identify communication problems to avoid. p. 517

LO 3 Describe when and how to use the various communication channels. p. 520

LO 4 Summarize ways to become a better "sender" and "receiver" of information. p. 527

LO 5 Explain how to improve downward, upward, and horizontal communication. p. 534

LO 6 Summarize how to work with the company grapevine. p. 539

LO 7 Describe the boundaryless organization and its advantages. p. 540

CHAPTER OUTLINE

Interpersonal Communication
One-Way versus Two-Way Communication
Communication Pitfalls
Mixed Signals and Misperception
Oral and Written Channels
Electronic Media
Media Richness

Improving Communication Skills
Improving Sender Skills
Nonverbal Skills
Improving Receiver Skills

Organizational Communication
Downward Communication
Upward Communication
Horizontal Communication
Informal Communication
Boundarylessness

Management Close-Up

Bill Gates is not the only college dropout to hit the technology jackpot. Like Gates, Digg.com founder Kevin Rose left school before graduation because he saw an opportunity that wouldn't wait. Seeking his fortune in Silicon Valley, Rose has become one of the richest computer geeks in America.

Rose was only in his twenties in 2004 when, with some user-friendly blogging software and $1,200 to his name, he launched Digg. By that time, thanks to newly emerging Web technologies, almost anyone with Internet access could start an interactive Web site. But it was Rose's vision—harnessing the power of social networking to enable Web users to have a say in what news they want to read—that struck a chord with his audience. According to some observers, the social-media bookmarking site has democratized journalism and revolutionized the way millions of people get their news.

{ Kevin Rose has built a new-media empire with Digg as its cornerstone. As you read this chapter, consider how his ability to communicate has enabled him not only to connect with his audience base but also to become an Internet icon with a loyal following. }

About 1.2 million Digg users, or "Diggers," pore over the Internet seeking stories for others to review and vote on. If enough people like it, the story moves to the front page of Digg.com, where it can be seen by as many as 2.5 million daily viewers.

At the beginning, Digg attracted mostly techies who were surfing the Web for computer technology stories. The site grew by word of mouth and eventually broadened its reach beyond tech news to include stories from many general news and Web sources, including *The Wall Street Journal,* Fox News, magazines, other Web sites, podcasts, blogs, and a host of other outlets.[1]

Effective communication is a fundamental component of job performance and managerial effectiveness.[2] It is a primary means by which managers carry out the responsibilities described throughout this book, such as making group decisions, sharing a vision, coordinating individuals and work groups within the organization's structure, hiring and motivating employees, and leading teams. In these and other areas of management, managers such as Kevin Rose of Digg have to be able to share ideas clearly and convincingly, and they have to listen effectively to others. In this chapter, we present important communication concepts and some practical guidelines for improving your effectiveness. We also discuss communication at the interpersonal and organizational levels.

Interpersonal Communication

communication

The transmission of information and meaning from one party to another through the use of shared symbols.

When people in an organization conduct a meeting, share stories in the cafeteria, or deliver presentations, they are making efforts to communicate. To understand why communication efforts sometimes break down and find ways to improve your communication skills, it helps to identify the elements of the communication process. **Communication** is the transmission of information and meaning from one party to another through the use of shared symbols. Figure 15.1 shows a general model of how one person communicates with another.

The *sender* initiates the process by conveying information to the *receiver*—the person for whom the message is intended. The sender has a *meaning* he or she wishes to communicate and *encodes* the meaning into symbols (the words chosen for the message). Then the sender *transmits*, or sends, the message through some *channel*, such as a verbal or written medium.

The receiver *decodes* the message (e.g., reads it) and attempts to *interpret* the sender's meaning. The receiver may provide *feedback* to the sender by encoding a message in response to the sender's message.

The communication process often is hampered by *noise*, or interference in the system, that blocks perfect understanding. Noise could be anything that interferes with accurate communication: ringing telephones, thoughts about other things, or simple fatigue or stress.

The model in Figure 15.1 is more than a theoretical treatment of the communication process: it points out the key ways in which communications can break down. Mistakes can be made at each stage of the model. A manager who is alert to potential problems can perform each step carefully to ensure more effective communication. The model also helps explain the topics discussed next: the differences between one-way and two-way communication, communication pitfalls, misperception, and the various communication channels.

LO 1

One-Way versus Two-Way Communication

one-way communication

A process in which information flows in only one direction—from the sender to the receiver, with no feedback loop.

In **one-way communication,** information flows in only one direction—from the sender to the receiver, with no feedback loop. A manager sends an e-mail to a subordinate without asking for a response. An employee phones the information technology (IT) department and leaves a message requesting repairs for her computer. A supervisor scolds a production worker about defects and then storms away.

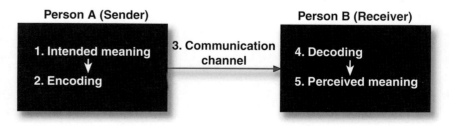

FIGURE 15.1

A Model of One-Way Communication

When receivers respond to senders—Person B becomes the sender and Person A the receiver—**two-way communication** has occurred. One-way communication in situations like those just described can become two-way if the manager's e-mail invites the receiver to reply with any questions, the IT department returns the employee's call and asks for details about the computer problem, and the supervisor calms down and listens to the production worker's explanation of why defects are occurring.

True two-way communication means not only that the receiver provides feedback but also that the sender is receptive to the feedback. In these constructive exchanges, information is shared between both parties rather than merely delivered from one person to the other.

Because it is faster and easier for the sender, one-way communication is much more common than it should be. A busy executive finds it easier to dash off an e-mail message than to discuss a nagging problem with a subordinate. Also, he doesn't have to deal with questions or be challenged by someone who disagrees.

Two-way communication is more difficult and time-consuming than one-way communication. However, it is more accurate; fewer mistakes occur, and fewer problems arise. When receivers have a chance to ask questions, share concerns, and make suggestions or modifications, they understand more precisely what is being communicated and what they should do with the information.[3]

Consider what happened to Dick Nicholson when he was a sales manager attending a company reception for the sales department. Out of Nicholson's earshot, his company's chairman asked the vice president why a particular employee—a chronic underperformer—was "still a salesman." The vice president then told Nicholson what he thought the chairman meant: the chairman wanted to promote the salesperson. If communication were limited to one way, Nicholson could have simply carried out the chairman's apparent order, but instead he visited the chairman later and asked for an explanation. He was relieved when the chairman explained that he was wondering why the ineffective salesperson was still working for the company at all.[4]

Communication Pitfalls

As we know from personal experience, the sender's intended message does not always get across to the receiver. You are operating under an illusion if you think there is a perfect correlation between what you say and what people hear.[5] Errors can occur in all stages of the communication process. In the encoding stage, words can be misused, decimal points entered in the wrong places, facts left out, or ambiguous phrases inserted. In the transmission stage, a memo may get lost on a cluttered desk, the words on the screen could be too small to read from the back of the room, or words might be spoken with ambiguous inflections.

Decoding problems arise when the receiver doesn't listen carefully or reads too quickly and overlooks a key point. And, of course, receivers can misinterpret the message, as a reader draws the wrong conclusion from an unclear text message, a listener takes a general statement by the boss too personally, or a sideways glance is taken the wrong way.

More generally, people's perceptual and filtering processes create misinterpretations. **Perception** is the process of receiving and interpreting information. As you know, such processes are not perfectly objective. They are subjective, as people's self-interested motives and attitudes toward the sender and toward the message create

Two-way communication is more difficult and time-consuming than one-way communication. However, it is more accurate with fewer mistakes occurring and fewer problems arising.

two-way communication

A process in which information flows in two directions—the receiver provides feedback, and the sender is receptive to the feedback.

LO 2

Don't expect to deliver results without communicating effectively in all directions of the compass.

perception

The process of receiving and interpreting information.

When George Franks started a new job, his boss always seemed too busy to talk. A mentor suggested that Franks make a habit of asking his boss how he could help. But his boss interpreted the repeated questions as meaning the boss couldn't keep up with his job; offended, he retaliated by "dumping all the projects no one else wanted" on Franks.[6]

biased interpretations. People often assume that others share their views, and naturally pay more attention to their own views than to those of others.[7] But perceptual differences get in the way of shared consensus. To remedy this situation, it helps to remember that others' viewpoints are legitimate and to incorporate others' perspectives into your interpretation of issues.[8] Generally, adopting another person's viewpoint is fundamental to working collaboratively. And your ability to take others' perspectives—for instance, to really understand the viewpoints of customers or suppliers—can result in higher assessments of your performance.[9]

filtering

The process of withholding, ignoring, or distorting information.

Filtering is the process of withholding, ignoring, or distorting information. Senders do this, for example, when they tell the boss what they think the boss wants to hear or give unwarranted compliments rather than honest criticism. Receivers also filter information; they may fail to recognize an important message or attend to some aspects of the message but not others.

Filtering and subjective perception pervade one interesting aspect of the communications dynamic: how men and women differ in their communicating styles. A manager at a magazine who tended to phrase the assignments she gave her reporters as questions—"How would you like to do the X project with Y?" and "I was thinking of putting you on the X project; is that okay?"—was criticized by her male boss, who told her she did not assume the proper demeanor with her staff.[10] Another, the owner of a retail operation, told one of her store managers to do something by saying, "The bookkeeper needs help with the billing. How would you feel about helping her out?" He said fine but didn't do it. Whereas the boss thought he meant he would do it, he said he meant to indicate how he would feel about helping. He decided he had better things to do.[11]

Because of such filtering and perceptual differences, you cannot assume the other person means what you think he means or understands the meanings you intend. Managers need to excel at reading interactions and adjusting their communication styles and perceptions to the people with whom they interact.[12] The very human tendencies to filter and perceive subjectively underlie much of the ineffective communication and the need for more effective communication practices that you will read about in the rest of this chapter.

Mixed Signals and Misperception

A common thread underlying the discussion so far is that people's perceptions can undermine attempts to communicate. People do not pay attention to everything going on around them. They inadvertently send mixed signals that can undermine the intended messages. Different people attend to different things, and people interpret the same thing in different ways. All of this creates problems in communication.

If the communication is between people from different cultures, these problems are magnified.[13] Communication breakdowns often occur when business transactions take place between people from different countries. Chapter 6 introduced you to the importance of these cultural issues. Table 15.1 offers suggestions for communicating effectively with someone who speaks a different language.

The following example further highlights the operation of mixed signals and misperceptions. A bank CEO knew that to be competitive he had to downsize his organization, and the employees who remained would have to commit to customer service, become more empowered, and really *earn* customer loyalty.[14] Knowing that his employees would have doubts and concerns about the coming reorganization, he decided to make a promise to them that he would do his best to guarantee employment to the survivors.

TABLE 15.1
What Do I Do if They Do
Not Speak My Language?

Verbal Behavior

- *Clear, slow speech.* Enunciate each word. Do not use colloquial expressions.
- *Repetition.* Repeat each important idea using different words to explain the same concept.
- *Simple sentences.* Avoid compound, long sentences.
- *Active verbs.* Avoid passive verbs.

Nonverbal Behavior

- *Visual restatements.* Use as many visual restatements as possible, such as pictures, graphs, tables, and slides.
- *Gestures.* Use more facial and appropriate hand gestures to emphasize the meaning of words.
- *Demonstrations.* Act out as many themes as possible.
- *Pauses.* Pause more frequently.
- *Summaries.* Hand out written summaries of your verbal presentation.

Accurate Interpretation

- *Silence.* When there is a silence, wait. Do not jump in to fill the silence. The other person is probably just thinking more slowly in the nonnative language or translating.
- *Intelligence.* Do not equate poor grammar and mispronunciation with lack of intelligence; it is usually a sign of nonnative language use.
- *Differences.* If unsure, assume difference, not similarity.

Comprehension

- *Understanding.* Do not just assume that they understand; assume that they do not understand.
- *Checking comprehension.* Have colleagues repeat their understanding of the material back to you. Do not simply ask if they understand or not. Let them explain what they understand to you.

Design

- *Breaks.* Take more frequent breaks. Second language comprehension is exhausting.
- *Small modules.* Divide the material to be presented into smaller modules.
- *Longer time frame.* Allocate more time for each module than you usually need for presenting the same material to native speakers of your language.

Motivation

- *Encouragement.* Verbally and nonverbally encourage and reinforce speaking by nonnative language participants.
- *Drawing out.* Explicitly draw out marginal and passive participants.
- *Reinforcement.* Do not embarrass novice speakers.

SOURCE: N. Adler, *International Dimensions of Organizational Behavior,* 1st edition. Copyright © 1986. Reprinted with permission of SouthWestern College Publishing, a division of Thomson Learning. www.thomsonrights.com.

What signals did the CEO communicate to his people by his promises? One positive signal was that he cared about his people. But he also signaled that *he* would take care of *them*, thus undermining his goal of giving them more responsibility and empowering them. The employees wanted management to take responsibility for the market challenge that *they* needed to face—to handle things for them when *they* needed to learn the new ways of doing business. Inadvertently, the CEO spoke to their

Any interpersonal situation holds potential for perceptual errors, filtering, and other communication breakdowns.

backward-looking need for security when he had meant to make them see that the bank's future depended on *their* efforts. However, the CEO did avoid one common pitfall at companies that announce plans for downsizing or outsourcing: ignoring the emotional significance of their message.[15] Sometimes managers are so intent on delivering the business rationale for the changes that they fail to acknowledge the human cost of layoffs. When employees hear a message that neglects to address their feelings, they generally interpret the message to mean that managers don't care.

Consider how many problems can be avoided—and how much more effective communication can be—if people take the time to (1) ensure that the receivers attend to the message they are sending, (2) consider the other party's frame of reference and attempt to convey the message with that viewpoint in mind, (3) take concrete steps to minimize perceptual errors and improper signals in both sending and receiving, and (4) send *consistent* messages. You should make an effort to predict people's interpretations of your messages and think in terms of how they could *misinterpret* your messages. It helps to say not only what you mean but also what you *don't* mean. Every time you say "I am not saying *X*, I am saying *Y*," you eliminate a possible misinterpretation.[16]

Oral and Written Channels

LO 3

Communication can be sent through a variety of channels (step 3 in the Figure 15.1 model), including oral, written, and electronic. Each channel has advantages and disadvantages.

Oral communication includes face-to-face discussion, telephone conversations, and formal presentations and speeches. Advantages are that questions can be asked and answered, feedback is immediate and direct, the receiver(s) can sense the sender's sincerity (or lack thereof), and oral communication is more persuasive and sometimes less expensive than written. However, oral communication also has disadvantages: It can lead to spontaneous, ill-considered statements (and regret), and there is no permanent record of it (unless an effort is made to record it).

Written communication includes e-mail, memos, letters, reports, computer files, and other written documents. Advantages to using written messages are that the message can be revised several times, it is a permanent record that can be saved, the message stays the same even if relayed through many people, and the receiver has more time to analyze the message. Disadvantages are that the sender has no control over where, when, or if the message is read; the sender does not receive immediate feedback; the receiver may not understand parts of the message; and the message must be longer to contain enough information to answer anticipated questions.[17]

You should weigh these considerations when deciding whether to communicate orally or in writing. Also, sometimes use both channels, such as following up a meeting with a confirming memo or writing a letter to prepare someone for your phone call.

Electronic Media

A vital category of communication channels is electronic media. Managers use computers not only to gather and distribute quantitative data but to "talk" with others electronically. In electronic decision rooms, software supports simultaneous access to shared files and allows people to share views and do work collectively.[18] Other means of electronic communication include *teleconferencing*, in which groups of people in different locations interact over telephone lines and perhaps also see one another on television monitors as they participate in group discussions (*videoconferencing*). And you probably are intimately familiar with e-mail, instant messaging, text messaging, and blogging.

E-mail has become a fundamental tool of workplace communication, with the average corporate user handling 171 messages a day.[19] Instant messaging (IMing) is less widespread in business settings, but its use is growing. According to a recent survey, 35 percent of employees engage in IMing at work.[20] New versions of e-mail software may encourage workers to use a wider variety of electronic communication tools. IBM's recent update to Lotus Notes, called Notes 8, lets e-mail users use tabs to launch an IM session or open word-processing or spreadsheet files to create attachments. Users can also organize documents, messages, and calendars by project, letting all project participants review the information and receive notifications when it changes. The latest version of Microsoft's Outlook e-mail program lets users make Internet phone calls as well as write and review documents in a SharePoint collaborative workspace. The advantage of a collaborative workspace is that all participants can go directly to a central location and work directly on a project, without the intervening step of an e-mail.[21] These technology advances encourage collaboration along with communication.

E-mail is one of the most convienent forms of communication, but what are some of the pitfalls? How often have you sent an e-mail, whether personal or professional, and found someone had misinterpreted the message?

Blogging—posting text to a Web site—also has arrived in the business world. Some companies use blogs to communicate with the external environment, for example, by sharing information about product uses or corporate social responsibility. Blogs also may foster communication within the organization.[22]

A project team might have a blog where the team leader posts frequent updates along with relevant presentations and spreadsheets. When team members need information about the project, searching the blog site can be an easy way to find it. They also can post ideas and comments in response to the blogger's entries. Similarly, blogs can be used to encourage collaboration among employees with a shared interest in particular products, functions, or customers.

The most recently developed tools for electronic communication generally fall into a category called **Web 2.0**, a set of Internet-based applications that encourage user-provided content and collaboration. Some of the most widely used Web 2.0 applications are social networking, podcasts, RSS (really simple syndication, where users subscribe to receive news, blogs, or other information they select), and wikis (online publications created with contributions from many authors/users). These communication methods became popular at such sites as Facebook, YouTube, and Wikipedia, but users have brought the experience to work and applied online collaboration to business needs. Unlike the first generation of Internet applications, Web 2.0 tends not to be formally introduced to organizations when IT departments evaluate it and make a purchase. Instead, employees simply begin using the tools to meet a need. Rod Smith, IBM's vice president for emerging Internet technologies, recalls a meeting at which he told Royal Bank of Scotland's IT head about wikis. The IT chief said the bank didn't use them, but when Smith asked the other participants, more than two dozen said *they* did.[23] Web 2.0 technology is at the heart of both Kevin Rose's business strategy for Digg and his communication methods, as described in the "Management Close-Up: Taking Action" feature.

Web 2.0

A set of Internet-based applications that encourage user-provided content and collaboration.

Management Close-Up   TAKING ACTION

Within two years after founder Kevin Rose launched Digg.com, the site had captured 11 million users and become one of the nation's most popular Web sites. Today, its monthly readership numbers 30 million, eclipsing such major online news sites as the *New York Times* and *The Wall Street Journal.*

Clearly, Rose had hit on something that filled Web users' communications needs and provided them a sense of community. Only months after Digg launched, Rose was offered—and declined—$4 million for the site. He was right to refuse the offer: after its first 18 months online, Digg was worth an estimated $60 million.

Use of the Digg Web site seems simple. But Digg uses complex mathematical algorithms to identify those who might be interested in the site. Rose refers to these people as "prescient users"—the Diggers who are the most likely candidates to "digg" stories that eventually become very popular with the vast user audience.

In addition to the Web site, Rose hosts a video podcast called Diggnation. That video feature allows him an opportunity to comment on the week's stories, make jokes and comments, and generally connect with his viewers. The podcasts convey a party-boy image that has made Rose a cult hero with his mostly male audience. The weekly show attracts about 250,000 viewers.[24]

- How does Rose facilitate two-way communication with Digg users?
- Although in real life Kevin Rose is a successful business owner worth millions of dollars, to his Web followers he seems to be simply a computer nerd who's cool. What types of electronic media does Rose use to communicate with his audience?

Advantages   *Advantages* of electronic communication are numerous and dramatic. Within firms, the advantages include the sharing of more information and the speed and efficiency in delivering routine messages to large numbers of people across vast geographic areas. Business-related wikis such as Socialtext let project teams post their ideas in one forum for others to add contributions. Socialtext allows project leaders to grant users access based on their need to know and participate. Web Crossing uses wikis for product development. Michael Krieg, vice president of marketing, says the wikis save the company "untold amounts of paper, postage, meetings, travel budgets, conference calls, and the time required to coordinate it all."[25]

Communicating electronically can reduce time and expenses devoted to traveling, photocopying, and mailing. When a fire caused by a truck accident closed a major freeway route in the San Francisco Bay area, Valerie Williamson skipped the traffic mess by visiting with her colleague Brian Friedlander at her company's virtual office in Second Life, the online virtual world. Williamson and Friedlander used avatars (animated images of themselves) to navigate their meeting in the online conference room of their real-world business, Electric Sheep Company.[26] Participants in Second Life can use their avatars to perform such business communication activities as giving PowerPoint presentations, streaming audio and video, and asking questions.

Some companies, including Boeing, use brainstorming software that allows anonymous contributions, presuming it will add more honesty to internal discussions. Some research indicates more data sharing and critical argumentation, and higher-quality decisions, with a group decision support system than is found in face-to-face meetings.[27] But anonymity also offers great potential for lies, gossip, insults, threats, harassment, and the release of confidential information.[28]

Disadvantages   *Disadvantages* of electronic communication include the difficulty of solving complex problems that require more extended, face-to-face interaction and

$ Imagine how much time you would lose if you couldn't communicate electronically; imagine the savings you could create if your company and its people sought and used the most cost effective ways to communicate.

Cisco employees in New York, left, and San Jose, California, on screen, meeting via monitor. What are the advantages and disadvantages to using this type of technology to communicate?

the inability to pick up subtle, nonverbal, or inflectional clues about what the communicator is thinking or conveying. In online bargaining—even before it begins—negotiators distrust one another more than in face-to-face negotiations. After the negotiation (compared with face-to-face negotiators), people usually are less satisfied with their outcomes, even when the outcomes are economically equivalent.[29]

Although organizations rely heavily on computer-aided communication for group decision making, face-to-face groups generally take less time, make higher-quality decisions, and are more satisfying for members.[30] E-mail is most appropriate for routine messages that do not require the exchange of large quantities of complex information. It is less suitable for confidential information, resolving conflicts, or negotiating.[31] Employees have reported being laid off via e-mail and even text messages.[32] Not only do these more impersonal forms of communication cause hurt feelings, but an upset employee can also easily forward messages, and forwarding often has a snowball effect that can embarrass everyone involved. Like e-mail, IMs can help people work together productively, but they can also leak sensitive information.

Companies are worried about leaks and negative portrayals, and they may require employees to agree to specific guidelines before starting blogs. Some general guidelines are to remember that blogs posted on a company's Web site should avoid anything that could embarrass the company or disclose confidential information. Bloggers should stick to the designated topic of any company-sponsored blog. If members of the media contact you about reporting on a blog you have written, get official approval before proceeding.[33]

Most electronic communications are quick and easy, and some are anonymous. As a result, one inevitable consequence of electronic communication is "flaming": hurling insults, sending "nastygrams," venting frustration, snitching on coworkers to the boss, and otherwise breaching protocol. E-mail, blogs, and IMing liberate people to send messages they would not say to a person's face. The lack of nonverbal cues can result in "kidding" remarks being taken seriously, causing resentment and regret.[34] Some people try to clear up confusion with emoticons such as smiley faces, but those efforts can further muddy the intent. Also, it is not unheard of for confidential messages—including details about people's personal lives and insulting, embarrassing remarks—to become public knowledge through electronic leaks.

Other downsides to electronic communication are important to know.[35] Different people and sometimes different working units latch onto different channels as their medium of choice. For example, an engineering division might use e-mail most, but a design group might rely primarily on instant messaging and neglect e-mail. Another disadvantage is that electronic messages sometimes are monitored or seen inadvertently by those for whom they are not intended. Be careful with your IMs: make sure you don't accidentally send them to the wrong person and that they don't pop up on the screen during a PowerPoint presentation.[36] One way to avoid sending to the wrong person is to close all IM windows except those you're currently using for active conversations. Deleting electronic messages—whether e-mail, IMs, or cell phone text messages—does not destroy them; they are saved elsewhere. Recipients can forward them to others, unbeknownst to the original sender. Many companies use software to monitor e-mail and IMs. And the messages can be used in court cases to indict individuals or companies. Electronic messages sent from work and on company-provided devices are private property—but they are private property of the system's owner, not of the sender.

An e-mail golden rule (like the sunshine rule in the ethics chapter): Don't hit "send" unless you'd be comfortable having the contents on the front page of a newspaper, being read by your mother or a competitor. And it's not a bad idea to have a colleague read nonroutine e-mails before sending.

Managing the Electronic Load   Electronic communication media seem essential these days, and people wonder how they ever worked without them. But the sheer volume of communication can be overwhelming, especially when it doesn't let up during meetings, breaks, or after work.[37]

Fortunately, a few rules of thumb can help you in your electronic communications.[39] For the problem of information overload, the challenge is to separate the truly important from the routine. Effective managers find time to think about bigger business issues and don't get too bogged down in responding to every message that seems urgent but may be trivial. Essential here is to think strategically about your goals, identify the items that are most important, and prioritize your time around those goals. This is easier said than done, of course, but it is essential, and it helps. Most communication software has tools that can help. For example, with instant messaging, set your "away" message when you want to concentrate on something else. And Lotus is developing a feature that lets e-mail users see immediately whether messages in their in-box are addressed only to them or to a group of recipients. Often a group e-mail is a lower priority. Of course, management also has a role to play. Often, employees check messages constantly because they believe (perhaps correctly) that this is what their bosses expect of them. Managers can help employees by limiting and communicating the times during which they expect a prompt response.[40]

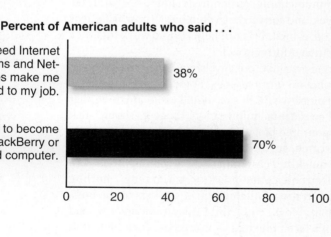

Americans are cautious about electronic overload.[38]

Percent of American adults who said . . .

High-speed Internet connections and Net-enabled devices make me too connected to my job.   38%

It's possible to become addicted to a BlackBerry or other handheld computer.   70%

0   20   40   60   80   100

A few more specific suggestions: with e-mail, don't hit "reply to all" when you should hit just "reply." Get organized by creating folders sorted by subject, priority, or sender, and flag messages that require follow-up. If you receive a copy, you don't need to respond; it's just for your information.

Some companies are recognizing the downsides of electronic media overuse. At U.S. Cellular, executive vice president Jay Ellison took the step of banning e-mail altogether on Fridays. After some resistance, employees found that they were building deeper working relationships through phone calls and face-to-face visits.[41] And at PBD Worldwide Fulfillment Services, Fridays without e-mail have taught new (or old) communication habits that spilled over into the rest of the week. E-mail volume at PBD dropped 75 percent and translated into greater efficiency.[42]

As overwhelming as electronic communications can be, you can take steps to simplify them. For example, a global customer-account-management team established two ground rules: (1) whenever a member communicated with a customer, the member was to send a briefing to all team members, and (2) they designated a primary contact on the team for each customer, with no one else on the team authorized to discuss or decide strategies or policies with the customer. If contacted by a customer, team members would direct the customer to the appropriate contact person. These steps simplified communication channels and greatly reduced contradictory and confusing messages.[43]

The Virtual Office   Many entrepreneurs conduct business via open "offices" on the Internet, working off their computers from wherever they happen to be. Similarly, major companies such as IBM, GE, and Prudential California Realty are slashing office space and giving people laptop or notebook computers, telecommunications software, voice mail, and other communications technologies so that they can work virtually anywhere, anytime.[44] Based on the philosophy that management's focus should be on what people do, not where they are, the **virtual office** is a mobile office in which people can work anywhere—their home, car, airport, customers' offices—as long as they have the tools to communicate with customers and colleagues.

As computer processing power has increased, some companies have begun taking the virtual office to a new, more interactive level. As mentioned earlier, Electric Sheep Company set up a virtual office on the Second Life Web site, where people can use avatars to watch themselves interact in a virtual world. Another organization that has set up a virtual office in Second Life is the American Library Association's Washington office. The ALA's virtual office is in Second Life's Cybrary City, near several libraries. Visitors can seek library services such as help in building a collection or consulting references.[45]

In the short run, at least, the benefits of virtual offices appear substantial. Saving money on rent and utilities is an obvious advantage. In Merced, California, Prudential California Realty's 10 agents stay connected with each other and their clients via the Internet, sharing information on individual Web sites and through e-mail.[46] A virtual office also gives employees access to whatever information they need from the company, whether they are in a meeting, visiting a client, or working from home.[47] Hiring and retaining talented people is easier because virtual offices support scheduling flexibility and even may make it possible to keep an employee who wants to relocate—for example, with a spouse taking a new job in another city.

But what will be the longer-term impact on productivity and morale? We may be in danger of losing too many "human moments," those authentic encounters that happen only when two people are physically together.[48] Some people hate being forced to work at home. Some send faxes, e-mail, and voice mail in the middle of the night—and others receive them. Some work around the clock and still feel they are not doing enough. The long hours of being constantly close to the technical tools of work can cause burnout. And some companies are learning that direct supervision at the office is necessary to maintain the quality of work, especially when employees are inexperienced and need guidance. The virtual office requires changes in human beings and presents technical challenges, so although it is much hyped and useful, it will not completely replace real offices and face-to-face work.

virtual office

A mobile office in which people can work anywhere, as long as they have the tools to communicate with customers and colleagues.

Consulting giant Accenture has offices in 150 cities around the globe, but its employees spend most of their time at clients' workplaces. Under those conditions, cultivating teamwork is difficult for managers, and developing a career is challenging for consultants, who may have a client on one continent, a supervisor on another, and support staff in a third country.

As a result, Accenture has programs in place to foster communication and maintain strong working relationships. The company assigns each new consultant to a career counselor, a senior employee in the same specialty who is available to help the employee develop his or her career. For example, consultant Keyur Patel is a retailing consultant with Accenture. Whether he is at a client's location in San Francisco or at home in Atlanta, Patel checks in with his career counselor about once a month. The counselor advised Patel to spend Fridays at the Atlanta office, making face-to-face connections with his colleagues there.

Of course, Patel also has to keep in touch with his manager, based in Detroit. They check in by phone monthly. Accenture trains its managers on leading virtual teams, including considerations such as scheduling conference calls to account for time differences and to allow plenty of opportunity for casual conversation that maintains a sense of belonging to the team. Accenture also uses a Web conferencing system for online meetings, as well as a company networking site called People Pages, where employees can read each other's profiles and send messages.[49]

Media Richness

media richness

The degree to which a communication channel conveys information.

Some communication channels convey more information than others. The amount of information a medium conveys is called **media richness**.[50] The more information or cues a medium sends to the receiver, the "richer" the medium is.[51] The richest media are more personal than technological, provide quick feedback, allow lots of descriptive language, and send different types of cues. Thus, face-to-face communication is the richest medium because it offers a variety of cues in addition to words: tone of voice, facial expression, body language, and other nonverbal signals. It also allows more descriptive language than, say, a memo does. In addition, it affords more opportunity for the receiver to give feedback to and ask questions of the sender, turning one-way into two-way communication.

The telephone is less rich than face-to-face communication, electronic mail is less rich yet, and memos are the least rich medium. In general, you should send difficult and unusual messages through richer media, transmit simple and routine messages through less rich media like memos, and use multiple media for important messages that you want to ensure people attend to and understand.[52] You should also consider factors such as which medium your receiver prefers, the preferred communication style in your organization, and cost.[53] Table 15.2 gives some sample situations for

TABLE 15.2
What Communication Channel Would You Use?

Situation 1: A midsize construction firm wants to announce a new employee benefit program.
Situation 2: A manager wishes to confirm a meeting time with 10 employees.
Situation 3: Increase enthusiasm in a midsize insurance company for a program that asks employees from different departments to work on the same project team.
Situation 4: A group of engineers who are geographically dispersed want to exchange design ideas with one another.
Situation 5: Describe a straightforward but somewhat detailed and updated version of a voice mail system to 1,000 employees who are geographically dispersed.

SOURCE: From *Communicating for Managerial Effectiveness* by P. G. Clampitt. Copyright © 1991 by Sage Publications Inc. Reprinted by permission of Sage Publications Inc.

choosing channels based on the message and the audience. Select a channel for each situation, and then compare your answers with those in Table 15.3.

Improving Communication Skills

LO 4

In recent years, employers have been dismayed by college graduates' poor communication skills. A demonstrated ability to communicate effectively makes a job candidate more attractive and distinguishes him or her from others. You can do many things to improve your communication skills, both as a sender and as a receiver.

Improving Sender Skills

To start, be aware that honest, direct, straight talk is important but all too rare. CEOs are often coached on how to slant their messages for different audiences—the investment community, employees, or the board. That's not likely to be straight talk. The focus of the messages can differ, but they can't be inconsistent. People should be able to identify your perspective, your reasoning, and your intentions.[54]

Beyond this basic point, senders can improve their skills in making persuasive presentations, writing, language use, and sending nonverbal messages. Table 15.4 offers some useful tips on formal presentations; the following discussion focuses more on other keys to persuasion.

Presentation and Persuasion Skills   Throughout your career, you will be called on to state your case on a variety of issues. You will have information and perhaps an opinion or proposal to present to others. Typically, your goal will be to "sell" your idea. In other words, your challenge will be to persuade others to go along with your personal recommendation. As a leader, you will find that some of your toughest

Situation	Poor Choice	Better Choice
1	Memo	Small group meetings
Rationale: The memo does not offer the feedback potential necessary to explain what may be seen as obscure information. Moreover, with these employees there is a possibility of literacy problems. A group meeting will allow for an oral explanation after which participants can more easily ask questions about any of the complex materials.		
2	Phone	Voice mail or e-mail
Rationale: For a simple message like this, there is no need to use a rich medium when a lean one will do the job.		
3	E-mail, voice mail	Face-to-face, telephone
Rationale: In situations requiring persuasion the sender must be able to quickly adapt the message to the receiver in order to counter objections. This is not a feature of either e-mail or voice mail. Face-to-face communication offers the sender the greatest flexibility. The phone is the next best alternative.		
4	Teleconference	Fax, computer conference
Rationale: A teleconference is apt to overly accentuate the status and personality differences among the engineers. Fax or computer conferencing would allow the quality of the ideas to be the central focus of interaction. Moreover, quick feedback is still possible with these media.		
5	Newsletter	Video
Rationale: If employees are already persuaded of the updated system's merit, you can probably use the newsletter. But a videotape graphically conveys information that requires demonstration, and will educate people about procedures.		

TABLE 15.3
Suggested Media Choices for Scenarios in Table 15.2

TABLE 15.4

Ten Ways to Add Power to Your Presentations

"All the great speakers were bad speakers at first." Ralph Waldo Emerson
1. *Spend adequate time on the* **content** *of your presentation.* It's easy to get so distracted with PowerPoint slides or concern about delivery skills that the actual content of a presentation is neglected. Know your content inside and out; you'll be able to discuss it conversationally and won't be tempted to memorize. If you believe in what you're saying and *own* the material, you will convey enthusiasm and will be more relaxed.
2. *Clearly understand the* **objective** *of your presentation.* Answer this question with one sentence: "What do I want the audience to believe following this presentation?" Writing down your objective will help you focus on your *bottom line.* Everything else in a presentation—the structure, the words, the visuals—should support your objective.
3. **Tell** *the audience the* **purpose** *of the presentation.* As the saying goes, "Tell them what you're going to tell them, then tell them, then tell them what you've told them." Use a clear preview statement early on to help the audience know where you're taking them.
4. *Provide* **meaning,** *not just data.* Today, information is widely available; you won't impress people by overloading them with data. People have limited attention spans and want presenters to help *clarify the meaning* of data.
5. **Practice, practice, practice.** Appearing polished and relaxed during a presentation requires rehearsal time. Practice making your points in a variety of ways. Above all, don't memorize a presentation's content.
6. *Remember that a presentation is more like a* **conversation** *than a speech.* Keep your tone conversational, yet professional. Audience members will be much more engaged if they feel you are talking *with* them rather than *at* them. Rely on PowerPoint slides or a broad outline to jog your memory.
7. *Remember the incredible power of* **eye contact.** Look at individual people in the audience. Try to have a series of one-on-one conversations with people in the room. This will calm you and help you connect with your audience.
8. **Allow imperfection.** If you forget what you were going to say, simply pause, look at your notes, and go on. Don't "break character" and effusively apologize or giggle or look mortified. Remember that an audience doesn't know your material nearly as well as you do and won't notice many mistakes.
9. *Be prepared to* **answer tough questions.** Try to anticipate the toughest questions you might receive. Plan your answers in advance. If you don't have an answer, acknowledge the fact and offer to get the information later.
10. *Provide a* **crisp wrap-up** *to a question-and-answer session.* Whenever possible, follow the Q&A period with a brief summary statement. Set up the Q&A session by saying, "We'll take questions for 10 minutes and then have a few closing remarks." This prevents your presentation from just winding down to a weak ending. Also, if you receive hostile or hard-to-answer questions, you'll have a chance to have the final word.

SOURCE: Lynn Hamilton, class handout (with permission).

challenges arise when people do not want to do what has to be done. Leaders have to be persuasive to get people on board.[55]

Your attitude in presenting ideas and persuading others is very important. Persuasion is not what many people think: merely selling an idea or convincing others to see things your way. Don't assume that it takes a "my way or the highway" approach, with a one-shot effort to make a hard sell and resisting compromise.[56] It usually is more constructive to consider persuasion a process of learning from each other and negotiating a shared solution. Persuasive speakers are seen as authentic, which happens when speakers are open with the audience, make a connection, demonstrate passion, and show they are listening as well as speaking. As a speaker, you can practice this kind of authenticity by noticing and adopting the type of body language you use when you're around people you're comfortable with, planning how to engage directly with your listeners, identifying the reasons why you care about your topic, and watching for nonverbal cues as well as fully engaging yourself when you listen to audience comments and questions.[57]

The most powerful and persuasive messages are simple and informative, are told with stories and anecdotes, and convey excitement.[58] People are more likely to remember and buy into your message if you can express it as a story that is simple, unexpected, concrete, and credible and that includes emotional content. For example, Nordstrom motivates employees by passing along stories of times when its people have provided extraordinary service, such as warming up customers' cars while they shopped or ironing a shirt so that a customer could wear it to a meeting. And Rubal Jain sold a customer on his India-based express-delivery service Safexpress by recounting how the company had delivered 69,000 copies of the latest Harry Potter release to bookstores around the country all at the precise release time—a far more dramatic case than data about on-time deliveries.[59] To be credible, a communicator backs up the message with actions consistent with the words.

Writing Skills   Effective writing is more than correct spelling, punctuation, and grammar (although these help!). Good writing above all requires clear, logical thinking.[60] The act of writing can be a powerful aid to thinking, because you have to think about what you really want to say and what the logic is behind your message.[61]

You want people to find your memos and reports readable and interesting. Strive for clarity, organization, readability, and brevity.[62] Brevity is much appreciated by readers who are overloaded with documents, including wordy memos. Use a dictionary and a thesaurus, and avoid fancy words.

Your first draft rarely is as good as it could be. If you have time, revise it. Take the reader into consideration. Go through your entire letter, memo, or report and delete all unnecessary words, sentences, and paragraphs. Use specific, concrete words rather than abstract phrases. Instead of saying, "A period of unfavorable weather set in," say, "It rained every day for a week."

Be critical of your own writing. If you want to improve, start by reading *The Elements of Style* by William Strunk and E. B. White and the most recent edition of *The Little, Brown Handbook*.[63]

Financial guru Suze Orman has been ranked as one of the best presenters by *BusinessWeek* magazine for her ability to relay information in an easy to understand format. She delivers financial information using clear, concise, and direct language. Great business communicators use simple language to discuss complex issues.

The principles of effective writing apply to online communications, including the creation of Web sites. The key is to focus on the audience's viewpoint. That avoids common pitfalls, such as planning a Web site based on what online marketing expert Seth Rosenblatt calls the "highest-paid person's opinion"—for example, featuring a photo of the chief executive officer on the home page. Simple, positive language also is important, especially online, where visitors are likely to skim the page for answers.

One company that has revamped its Web site to communicate more effectively with customers is A. C. Moore, which sells arts and crafts supplies. The original Web site offered only corporate information and instructional materials for using its products, and the company hoped that some of the millions of visitors would make purchases online, if it were easy enough. In improving the site, A. C. Moore simplified the process of requesting e-mail about products. Originally, to get on a mailing list, Web site visitors had to register as members. Now they can just click a link on the bottom of every page.

Most important, A. C. Moore listens as well as sends messages. Its Web site includes a customer forum, where participants can trade craft ideas and comment about their experiences with the company and its products. At one point, customers began posting complaints about shipping costs; employees took note and developed an alternative. They posted the idea of switching to a low flat rate for all orders, and the forum participants reacted positively, so the company made the change. Such customer-oriented changes have increased A. C. Moore's Web site traffic and sales.[64]

Language   Word choice can enhance or interfere with communication effectiveness. For example, jargon is actually a form of shorthand and can make communication more effective when both the sender and the receiver know the buzzwords. But when the receiver is unfamiliar with the jargon, misunderstandings result. When people from different functional areas or disciplines communicate with one another, misunderstandings often occur because of "language" barriers. As in writing, simplicity usually helps.

> "When [cultivated people] look, they see clearly. When they listen, they think of how to hear keenly . . . In their demeanor, they think of how to be respectful. In their speech, they think of how to be truthful . . . When in doubt, they think of how to pose questions."
>
> —Confucius

Therefore, whether speaking or writing, you should consider the receiver's background—cultural as well as technical—and adjust your language accordingly. When

you are receiving, don't assume that your understanding is the same as the speaker's intentions. Cisco CEO John Chambers, whose background is in business, simply asks the engineering managers in his high-tech company to explain any jargon. He says, "They do it remarkably well."[65] At the same time, Chambers shows respect and enhances his credibility by being truly interested in their work. Whenever Chambers travels with or reviews engineers, he asks them to teach him a topic—and he listens.

The meaning of word choices also can vary by culture. Japanese people use the simple word *hai* (yes) to convey that they understand what is being said; it does not necessarily mean that they agree. Asian businesspeople rarely use the direct "no," using more subtle or

Global teams fail when members have difficulty communicating because of language, cultural, and geographic barriers. What could you do to overcome these barriers?

tangential ways of disagreeing.[66] Global teams fail when members have difficulties communicating because of language, cultural, and geographic barriers. Heterogeneity harms team functioning at first. But when they develop ways to interact and communicate, teams develop a common identity and perform well.[67]

When conducting business overseas, try to learn something about the other country's language and customs. Americans are less likely to do this than people from some other cultures; most Americans do not consider a foreign language necessary for doing business abroad, and a significant majority of U.S. firms do not require employees sent abroad to know the local language.[68] But those who do will have a big edge over their competitors who do not.[69] Making the effort to learn the local language builds rapport, sets a proper tone for doing business, aids in adjustment to culture shock, and especially can help you "get inside" the other culture.[70] You will learn more about how people think, feel, and behave, both in their lives and in their business dealings.

Nonverbal Skills

As you know, people send and interpret signals other than those that are spoken or written. Nonverbal messages can support or undermine the stated message. Often, nonverbal cues make a greater impact than other signals. In employees' eyes, managers' actions often speak louder than the words managers choose. Project manager Steve Bailey had already given many presentations when he attended a presentation skills workshop. There, a facilitator pointed out Bailey's habit of clasping and unclasping his hands as he spoke. The behavior was distracting and made him appear less in authority. When Bailey stopped making that gesture, he discovered that his audiences tended to be more convinced by his presentations.[71]

In conversation, except when you intend to convey a negative message, you should give nonverbal signals that express warmth, respect, concern, a feeling of equality, and a willingness to listen. Negative nonverbal signals show coolness, disrespect, lack of interest, and a feeling of superiority.[72] The following suggestions can help you send positive nonverbal signals.

First, use *time* appropriately. Avoid keeping your employees waiting to see you. Devote sufficient time to your meetings with them, and communicate frequently with them to signal your interest in their concerns. Second, make your *office arrangement* conducive to open communication. A seating arrangement that avoids separation of people helps establish a warm, cooperative atmosphere (in contrast, an arrangement in which you sit behind your desk and your subordinate sits before you creates a more intimidating, authoritative environment).[73] Third, remember your *body language*. Research indicates that facial expression and tone of voice can account for 90 percent of the communication between two people.[74] Several nonverbal body signals convey a positive attitude toward the other person: assuming a position close to the person; gesturing frequently; maintaining eye contact; smiling; having an open body orientation, such as facing the other person directly; uncrossing the arms; and leaning forward to convey interest in what the other person is saying.

Silence is an interesting nonverbal situation. The average American is said to spend about twice as many hours per day in conversation as the average Japanese.[75] North Americans tend to talk to fill silences. Japanese allow long silences to develop, believing they can get to know people better. Japanese believe that two people with good rapport will know each other's thoughts. The need to use words implies a lack of understanding.

Nonverbal Signals in Different Countries   Here are just a few nonverbal mistakes that Americans might make in other countries.[76] Nodding the head up and down in Bulgaria means no. The American thumb-and-first-finger circular A-OK gesture is vulgar in Brazil, Singapore, Russia, and Paraguay. The head is sacred in Buddhist cultures, so you must never touch someone's head. In Muslim cultures, never touch or eat with the left hand, which is thought unclean. Crossing your ankle over your knee is rude in Indonesia, Thailand, and Syria. Don't point your finger toward yourself in Germany or Switzerland—it insults the other person.

You also need to correctly interpret the nonverbal signals of others. Chinese scratch their ears and cheeks to show happiness. Greeks puff air after they receive a compliment. Hondurans touch their fingers below their eyes to show disbelief or caution. Japanese indicate embarrassment or "no" by sucking in air and hissing through their teeth. Vietnamese look to the ground with their heads down to show respect. Compared with Americans, Russians use fewer facial expressions, and Scandinavians fewer hand gestures, whereas people in Mediterranean and Latin cultures may gesture and touch more. Brazilians are more likely than Americans to interrupt, Arabs to speak loudly, and Asians to respect silence.

Use these examples not to stereotype but to remember that people in other cultures have different styles and to aid in communication accuracy.

Improving Receiver Skills

Once you become effective at sending oral, written, and nonverbal messages, you are halfway home toward becoming a complete communicator. However, you must also develop adequate receiving capabilities. Receivers need good listening, reading, and observational skills.

Listening   In today's demanding work environment, managers need excellent listening skills. Although people frequently assume that good listening is easy and natural, in fact it is difficult and not nearly as common as needed. Catherine Coughlin practiced her listening skills as a customer service representative for Union Electric Company during the summers of the years she was earning her college degree. Whether an individual was calling about an unpaid bill, a power outage, or just looking for an excuse to talk to somebody, Coughlin found that "you've got to respect everyone and their story" and then decide how to respond. Over the following decades, Coughlin used that experience to build a successful career with Southwestern Bell Telephone and its successor companies. She is now president and chief executive officer of AT&T Midwest and is still committed to careful listening.[77]

A basic technique called *reflection* will help a manager listen effectively.[79] **Reflection** is a process by which a person states what he or she believes the other person is saying. This technique places a greater emphasis on listening than on talking. When both parties actively engage in reflection, they get into each other's frame of reference rather than listening and responding from their own. The result is more accurate two-way communication.

"You never learn anything while you're talking."
—Catherine Coughlin, CEO, AT&T Midwest[78]

Besides using reflection, you can improve how well you listen by practicing the techniques described in Table 15.5. For managers, the stakes are high; failure to listen not only causes managers to miss good ideas but can even drive employees away. When Ben Berry was a senior systems analyst at a hospital, he was assigned to help lead a team charged with developing computer applications for the hospital. The other team leader, a doctor, had little interest in hearing the ideas that came from Berry and the team members. He was more focused on issuing directions. Team members and Berry himself felt discouraged from participating. Berry tried discussing the issue with his supervisor and with the doctor, but when the doctor never saw the need to listen and involve his team in decisions, Berry left the organization to take another job.[80]

Listening begins with personal contact. Staying in the office, keeping the door closed, and eating lunch at your desk are sometimes necessary to get pressing work done, but that is no way to stay on top of what's going on. Better to walk the halls, initiate conversations and go to lunch even with people outside your area, have coffee in a popular gathering place, and maybe even move your desk onto the factory floor.[81]

When a manager takes time to really listen to and get to know people, those same people think, "She's showing an interest in me" or "He's letting me know that I matter" or "She values my ideas and contributions." Trust develops. Listening and learning from others are even more important for innovation than for routine work. Successful change and innovation come through lots of human contact.

Reading   Illiteracy is a significant problem in the United States. Even if illiteracy is not a problem in your organization, reading mistakes are common and costly. As a receiver, for your own benefit, read memos and e-mail as soon as possible, before it's

TABLE 15.5
Ten Keys to Effective
Listening

1. *Find an area of interest.* Even if you decide the topic is dull, ask yourself, "What is the speaker saying that I can use?"

2. *Judge content, not delivery.* Don't get caught up in the speaker's personality, mannerisms, speaking voice, or clothing. Instead, try to learn what the speaker knows.

3. *Hold your fire.* Rather than getting immediately excited by what the speaker seems to be saying, withhold evaluation until you understand the speaker's message.

4. *Listen for ideas.* Don't get bogged down in all the facts and details; focus on central ideas.

5. *Be flexible.* Have several systems for note taking, and use the system best suited to the speaker's style. Don't take too many notes or try to force everything said by a disorganized speaker into a formal outline.

6. *Resist distraction.* Close the door, shut off the radio, move closer to the person talking, or ask him or her to speak louder. Don't look out the window or at papers on your desk.

7. *Exercise your mind.* Some people tune out when the material gets difficult. Develop an appetite for a good mental challenge.

8. *Keep your mind open.* Many people get overly emotional when they hear words referring to their most deeply held convictions, for example, *union, subsidy, import, Republican* or *Democrat,* and *big business.* Try not to let your emotions interfere with comprehension.

9. *Capitalize on thought speed.* Take advantage of the fact that most people talk at a rate of about 125 words per minute, but most of us think at about four times that rate. Use those extra 400 words per minute to think about what the speaker is saying rather than turning your thoughts to something else.

10. *Work at listening.* Spend some energy. Don't just pretend you're paying attention. Show interest. Good listening is hard work, but the benefits outweigh the costs.

SOURCE: Ralph G. Nichols, "Listening Is a 10-Part Skill," *Nation's Business* 45 (July 1957), pp. 56–60. Cited in R. C. Huseman, C. M. Logue, and D. L. Freshley, eds., *Readings in Interpersonal and Organizational Communication* (Boston: Allyn & Bacon, 1977).

too late to respond. You may skim most of your reading materials, but read important messages, documents, and passages slowly and carefully. Note important points for later referral. Consider taking courses to increase your reading speed and comprehension skills. Finally, don't limit your reading to items about your particular job skill or technical expertise; read materials that fall outside your immediate concerns. You never know when a creative idea that will help you in your work will be inspired by a novel, a biography, a sports story, or an article about a problem in another business or industry.

Observing   Effective communicators are also capable of observing and interpreting nonverbal communications. (As Yogi Berra said, "You can observe a lot by watching.") For example, by reading nonverbal cues, a presenter can determine how her talk is going and adjust her approach if necessary. Some companies train their sales forces to interpret the nonverbal signals of potential customers. People can also decode nonverbal signals to determine whether a sender is being truthful or deceitful. Deceitful communicators tend to maintain less eye contact, make either more or fewer body movements than usual, and smile either too much or too little. Verbally, they offer fewer specifics than do truthful senders.[82]

A vital source of useful observations comes from personally visiting people, plants, and other locations to get a firsthand view.[83] Many corporate executives rely heavily on reports from the field and don't travel to remote locations to observe firsthand what is going on. Reports are no substitute for actually seeing things happen in practice. Frequent visits to the field and careful observation can help a manager develop deep understanding of current operations, future prospects, and ideas for how to fully exploit capabilities.[84]

Of course, you must *accurately interpret* what you observe. A Canadian conducting business with a high-ranking official in Kuwait was surprised that the meeting was held in an open office and was interrupted constantly.[85] He interpreted the lack of a big, private office and secretary to mean that the Kuwaiti was of low rank and uninterested in doing business, and he lost interest in the deal. The Canadian observed the facts accurately, but his perceptual biases and lack of awareness regarding how norms differ across cultures caused him to misinterpret what he saw.

The Japanese are particularly skilled at interpreting every nuance of voice and gesture, putting most Westerners at a disadvantage.[86] When one is conducting business in Asian or other countries, local guides can be invaluable not only to interpret language but to "decode" behavior at meetings, what subtle hints and nonverbal cues mean, who the key people are, and how the decision-making process operates.

FROM THE PAGES OF

BusinessWeek

Frank Luntz: A New Lexicon for the Business Leader

The pollster, political consultant, and author of "Words That Work" offers five words for right now that have the power to persuade. U.S. business leaders are searching for the right lexicon. They need it. Their customers and employees are in a funk, worried that the days of a good job with a steady income are to be replaced forever by living paycheck to paycheck. That lexicon is beginning to take shape. In my travels across the linguistic landscape of contemporary American life to research a book, I have discovered five words that really resonate in the world of business right now. They should become part of every executive's vocabulary.

The most powerful among them is "consequences." Seemingly neutral—there can be good consequences as well as bad—the word instantly personalizes and dramatizes the potential result of a particular action. When someone talks about consequences, the listener immediately thinks: What does this mean for me? When union leaders, shareholders, or community activists talk about the consequences of a particular corporate action, they're putting the company on the defensive and using words that work.

ACCENT ON RELIABILITY

Focusing on "impact" also makes a listener pay attention. This one word causes people to assume they will see a measurable difference. People want results. Talking about "effort," or even "solutions," doesn't work; Americans don't care about good intentions.

http://www.businessweek.com/magazine/content/08_44/b4106106197381.htm

SOURCE: Frank Luntz, "Words that Pack Power, *BusinessWeek,* November 3, 2008, p. 106. © Time Inc. All rights reserved.

Organizational Communication

LO 5

Being a skilled communicator is essential to being a good manager and team leader. But communication must also be managed throughout the organization. Every minute of every day, countless bits of information are transmitted through an organization. The flow of information affects how well people perform. When a group's success depends on discovering new information, individuals who independently tap information from a variety of sources help achieve that success. For evaluating information and arriving at decisions, people in the most effective groups communicate extensively with their team members (a richly connected network). The most productive teams switch back and forth between using centralized networks and using richly connected networks.[87] These patterns of communication may include communications traveling downward, upward, horizontally, and informally within the organization.

Downward Communication

Downward communication refers to the flow of information from higher to lower levels in the organization's hierarchy. Examples include a manager giving an assignment to an assistant, a supervisor making an announcement to his subordinates, and a company president delivering a talk to her management team. Downward communication that provides relevant information enhances employee identification with the company, supportive attitudes, and decisions consistent with the organization's objectives.[88]

downward communication

Information that flows from higher to lower levels in the organization's hierarchy.

People must receive the information they need to perform their jobs and become—and remain—loyal members of the organization. But they often lack adequate information.[89] One problem is *information overload:* they are bombarded with so much information that they fail to absorb everything. Much of the information is not very important, but its volume causes a lot of relevant information to be lost.

A second problem is a *lack of openness* between managers and employees. Managers may believe "No news is good news," "I don't have time to keep them informed of everything they want to know," or "It's none of their business, anyway." Some managers withhold information even if sharing it would be useful.

A third problem is *filtering*, introduced earlier in the chapter. When messages are passed from one person to another, some information is left out. When a message passes through many people, each transmission may cause further information losses. The message can also be distorted as people add their own words or interpretations.

Filtering poses serious problems in organizations. As messages are communicated downward through many organizational levels, much information is lost. The data in Figure 15.2 suggest that by the time messages reach the people for whom they are intended, the receivers may get very little useful information. The smaller the number of authority levels through which communications must pass, the less information will be lost or distorted. Flatter organization offers the advantage of fewer problems caused by filtering of information as it cascades through many layers.

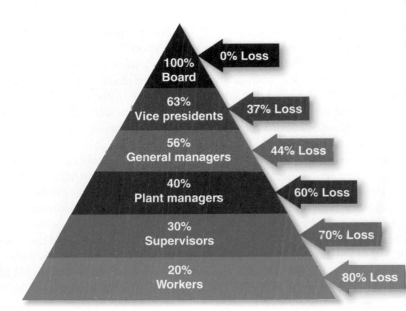

FIGURE 15.2
Information Loss in Downward Communication

coaching

Dialogue with a goal of helping another be more effective and achieve his or her full potential on the job.

Coaching   Some of the most important downward communications occur when managers give performance feedback to their direct reports. We discussed earlier the importance of giving feedback and positive reinforcement when it is deserved. It is also important to explicitly discuss poor performance and areas that can be improved.

Coaching is dialogue with a goal of helping another be more effective and achieve his or her full potential on the job.[90] When done properly, coaching develops executives and enhances performance.[91] When people have performance problems, or exhibit behaviors that need to be changed, coaching is often the best way to help a person change and succeed. And coaching is not just for poor performers; as even the greatest athletes know, it is for anyone who is good and aspires to excellence. Although coaches for executives sometimes are hired from the outside, coaches from outside your organization may not understand fully the context in which you are working.[92] So don't take advice automatically. The best use of coaches is as sounding boards, helping you think through the potential impact of your ideas, generate new options, and learn from experience.

Companies such as Coca-Cola use coaching as an essential part of their executive development process. When done well, coaching is true dialogue between two committed people engaged in joint problem solving. Thus, it is far more than an occasion for highlighting poor performance, delivering reprimands, or giving advice. Good coaching requires achieving real understanding of the problem, the person, and the situation; jointly generating ideas for what to do; and encouraging the person to improve. Good coaches ask a lot of questions, listen well, provide input, and also encourage others to think for themselves. Effective coaching requires honesty, calmness, and supportiveness—all aided by a sincere desire to help. The ultimate and longest lasting form of help is to help people think through and solve their own problems.

Downward Communication in Difficult Times   Adequate downward communication can be particularly valuable during difficult times. During corporate mergers and acquisitions, employees are anxious as they wonder how the changes will affect them. Ideally—and ethically—top management should communicate with employees about the change as early as possible.

But some argue against that approach, maintaining that informing employees about the reorganization might cause them to quit too early. Then too, top management often cloisters itself, prompting rumors and anxiety. CEOs and other senior execs are surrounded by lawyers, investment bankers, and so on—people who are paid merely to make the deal happen, not to make it work. Yet with the people who are affected by the deal, you must increase, not decrease, communication.[93]

In a merger of two *Fortune* 500 companies, two plants received very different information.[94] All employees at both plants received the initial letter from the CEO announcing the merger. But after that, one plant was kept in the dark while the other was continually filled in on what was happening. Top management gave employees information about layoffs; transfers; promotions and demotions; and changes in pay, jobs, and benefits.

Which plant do you think fared better as the difficult transitional months unfolded? In both plants, the merger decreased employees' job satisfaction and commitment to the organization and increased their belief that the company was untrustworthy, dishonest, and uncaring. In the plant whose employees got little information, these problems persisted for a long time. But in the plant where employees received complete information, the situation stabilized and attitudes improved toward their normal levels. Full communication not only helped employees survive an anxious period but also served a symbolic value by signaling care and concern for employees. Without such communications, employee reactions to a merger or acquisition may be so negative as to undermine the corporate strategy.

Open-Book Management   Executives often are proud of their newsletters, staff meetings, videos, and other vehicles of downward communication. More often than not, the information provided concerns company sports teams, birthdays, and new copy machines. But today a more unconventional philosophy is gathering steam. **Open-book management** is the practice of sharing with employees at all levels of the organization vital information previously meant for management's eyes only. This information includes financial goals, income statements, budgets, sales, forecasts, and other relevant data about company performance and prospects. This practice is dramatically different from the traditional closed-book approach in which people may or may not have a clue about how the company is doing, may or may not believe the things that management tells them, and may or may not believe that their personal performance makes a difference. Open-book management is controversial, as many managers prefer to keep such information to themselves. Sharing strategic plans and financial information with employees could lead to leaks to competitors or to employee dissatisfaction with compensation. But the companies that share this information claim a favorable impact on motivation and productivity. Cecil Ursprung, president and CEO of Reflexite Corporation in New Britain, Connecticut, said, "Why would you tell 5 percent of the team what the score was and not the other 95 percent?"[95]

Father of scientific management Frederick Taylor, early in the 20th century, would have considered opening the books to all employees "idiotic."[96] But then Jack Stack tried it at Springfield ReManufacturing Corporation, which was on the brink of collapse.[97] The results? A reporter calls Jack Stack's SRC "the most highly motivated and business-savvy workforce I ever encountered." In addition, "I met fuel-injection-pump rebuilders who knew the gross margins of every nozzle and pump they produced. I met crankshaft grinders and engine assemblers who could discuss the ROI of their machine tools." The rewards they deserve are part of the picture here, too: "I met a guy who worked on turbochargers and ran his area as if it were his own small business. Then again, why shouldn't he? Like the other employees, he was an owner of SRC."[98]

Upward Communication

Upward communication travels from lower to higher ranks in the hierarchy. Adequate upward communication is important for several reasons.[99] First, managers learn what's going on. Management gains a more accurate picture of subordinates' work, accomplishments, problems, plans, attitudes, and ideas. Second, employees gain from the opportunity to communicate upward. People can relieve some of their frustrations, achieve a stronger sense of participation in the enterprise, and improve morale. Third, effective upward communication facilitates downward communication as good listening becomes a two-way street.

> "Many people believe that if you are doing a good job and accomplishing something, your bosses necessarily know this, but they don't."
> —Jeffrey Pfeffer, professor of organizational behavior, Stanford[100]

The problems common in upward communication are similar to those for downward communication. Managers, like their subordinates, are bombarded with information and may neglect or miss information from below. Furthermore, some employees are not always open with their bosses; in other words, filtering occurs upward as well as downward. People tend to share only good news with their bosses and suppress bad news, because they (1) want to appear competent; (2) mistrust their boss and fear that if he or she finds out about something they have done they will be punished; (3) fear the boss will punish the messenger, even if the reported problem is not that person's fault; or (4) believe they are helping their boss if they shield him or her from problems.

For these and other reasons, managers may not learn about important problems. As one leadership expert put it, "If the messages from below say you are doing a flawless job, send back for a more candid assessment."[101]

---

open-book management

Practice of sharing with employees at all levels of the organization vital information previously meant for management's eyes only.

The more management communicates cost, quality, and other data, the more people will care about and pay attention to performance and find new ways to improve.

upward communication

Information that flows from lower to higher levels in the organization's hierarchy.

Managing Upward Communication Generating useful information from below requires managers to both *facilitate* and *motivate* upward communication. For example, they could have an open-door policy and encourage people to use it, have lunch or coffee with employees, use surveys, institute a productivity program for suggestions, or have town-hall meetings. They can ask for employee advice, make informal visits to plants, really think about and respond to employee suggestions, and distribute summaries of new ideas and practices inspired by employee suggestions and actions.[102]

Some executives practice MBWA (management by wandering around). That term, coined by Ed Carlson of United Airlines, refers simply to getting out of the office, walking around, and talking frequently and informally with employees.[103] At the headquarters of Secura Insurance in Appleton, Wisconsin, CEO John Bykowski makes a habit of walking through the building to talk with and listen to employees.[104] And in the offices of the *South Florida Sun-Sentinel*, editor Earl Maucker is known for dropping in to employees' offices and cubicles. Maucker is known among his editorial staff for being accessible and frank, so they trust what he says.[105]

Useful upward communication must be reinforced and not punished. The person who tries to talk to the manager about a problem must not be brushed off consistently. An announced open-door policy must truly be open-door. Also, people must trust their supervisor and know that the manager will not hold a grudge if they deliver negative information. To get honesty, managers must truly listen, not punish the messenger for being honest, and act on valid comments.

Horizontal Communication

Much information needs to be shared among people on the same hierarchical level. Such **horizontal communication** can take place among people in the same work team or in different departments. For example, a purchasing agent discusses a problem with a production engineer and a task force of department heads meets to discuss a particular concern. Communicating with others outside the firm, including potential investors, is another vital type of horizontal communication.[106]

Horizontal communication has several important functions.[107] First, it allows sharing of information, coordination, and problem solving among units. Second, it helps solve conflicts. Third, by allowing interaction among peers, it provides social and emotional support to people. All these factors contribute to morale and effectiveness. For example, David Carere, vice president, finance–credit and account settlement for Rich Products, emphasizes that his staff needs to collaborate with employees in other functions, especially sales and customer service. This horizontal collaboration helps the frozen-dessert company ensure that its sales are profitable and that bad debt is kept to a minimum. To foster communication between his employees and those in other departments, Carere sets up meetings where the credit department

Today's office workers engage in four modes of work: *focus work* (concentrating on a task that may involve thinking, writing, and reflecting), *collaborating* (working with others to generate and evaluate ideas), *learning* (acquiring new knowledge), and *socializing* (developing relationships). Employees of top-performing companies devote more time to the work modes requiring more horizontal communication—including 16 percent more time socializing.[109]

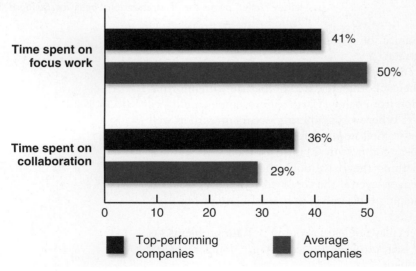

explains its role to employees of other departments and learns more about what they do.[108]

Managing Horizontal Communication

Managing Horizontal Communication   The need for horizontal communication is similar to the need for integration, discussed in Chapter 8. Particularly in complex environments, in which decisions in one unit affect another, information must be shared horizontally. As examples of good horizontal communication, Motorola holds an annual conference for sharing best learnings across functional and business groups throughout the company. NASA co-locates scientists from different disciplines. Hewlett-Packard uses common databases for different product groups to share information and ideas.[110]

General Electric offers a great example of how to use productive horizontal communication as a competitive weapon.[111] GE's businesses could operate independently, but each is supposed to help the others. They transfer technical resources, people, information, ideas, and money among themselves. GE accomplishes this high level of communication and cooperation through easy access between divisions and to the CEO; a culture of openness, honesty, trust, and mutual obligation; and quarterly meetings in which all the top executives get together to share information and ideas. The same kinds of activities are done at lower levels as well.

Informal Communication

Organizational communications differ in formality. *Formal communications* are official, organization-sanctioned episodes of information transmission. They can move upward, downward, or horizontally and often are prearranged and necessary for performing some task.

Informal communication is more unofficial. People gossip; employees complain about their bosses; people talk about their favorite sports teams; work teams tell newcomers how to get by.[112]

The **grapevine** is the social network of informal communications. Informal networks provide people with information, help them solve problems, and teach them how to do their work successfully. You should develop a good network of people willing and able to help.[113] However, the grapevine can be destructive when irrelevant or erroneous gossip and rumors proliferate and harm operations.[114]

grapevine

Informal communication network.

No one knows how rumors get started, but we do know they happen. The so-called grapevine can be managed if you talk to the key people involved, suggest ways to prevent the rumors, and neutralize rumors once they've started.

What does this mean for you personally? Don't engage in e-gossip. Embarrassing episodes become public, and lawsuits based on defamation of character and invasion of privacy have used e-mail evidence. But don't avoid the grapevine, either.[115] Listen, but evaluate before believing what you hear. Who is the source? How credible is he or she? Does the rumor make sense? Is it consistent or inconsistent with other things you know or have heard? Seek more information. Don't stir the pot.

Managing Informal Communication

Managing Informal Communication   Rumors start over any number of topics, including who's leaving, who's getting a promotion, salaries, job security, and costly mistakes. Rumors can destroy people's faith and trust in the company—and in each other. But the grapevine cannot be eliminated. Therefore, managers need to *work with* the grapevine.

The grapevine can be managed in several ways.[116] First, if a manager hears a story that could get out of hand, he or she should *talk to the key people* involved to get the facts and their perspectives. Don't allow malicious gossip.

Second, suggestions for *preventing* rumors from starting include explaining events that are important but have not been explained, dispelling uncertainties by providing facts, and working to establish open communications and trust over time. These efforts are especially important during times of uncertainty, such as after a merger or layoff or when sales slow down, because rumors increase along with anxiety. For example, when advertising revenues fell at R. H. Donnelley, which publishes yellow-pages directories, management stepped up efforts to make sure employees heard any company news straight from management, rather than on the news. Donnelley also encouraged its managers to make regular visits to salespeople to answer their questions.[117]

Third, *neutralize* rumors once they have started: disregard the rumor if it is ridiculous; openly confirm any parts that are true; make public comments (no comment is seen as a confirmation of the rumor); deny the rumor, if the denial is based in truth (don't make false denials); make sure communications about the issue are consistent; select a spokesperson of appropriate rank and knowledge; and hold town meetings if needed.[118]

LO 7 Boundarylessness

boundaryless organization

Organization in which there are no barriers to information flow.

Many executives and management scholars today consider free access to information in all directions to be an organizational imperative. Jack Welch, when he was CEO of General Electric, coined the term *boundarylessness*. A **boundaryless organization** is one in which no barriers to information flow exist. Instead of separating people, jobs, processes, and places with boundaries, ideas, information, decisions, and actions move to where they are most needed.[119] This free flow does not imply a random free-for-all of unlimited communication and information overload. It implies information available *as needed* moving quickly and easily enough so that the organization functions far better as a whole than as separate parts.

GE's chief learning officer uses the metaphor of the organization as a house having three kinds of boundaries: the floors and ceilings, the walls that separate the rooms, and the outside walls. These barriers correspond in organizations to the boundaries between different organizational levels, different units and departments, and the organization and its external stakeholders—for example, suppliers and customers. GE adds a fourth wall: global boundaries separating domestic from global operations.[120]

GE's famous Workout program is a series of meetings for business members across multiple hierarchical levels, characterized by extremely frank, tough discussions that break down vertical boundaries. Workout has involved over hundreds of thousands of GE people; in any given week thousands may be participating in a Workout program.[121] Workout is also done with customers and suppliers, breaking down outside boundaries. GE has also reached out to the community by providing this expertise to nonprofits, such as CommonBond Communities, a provider of affordable housing. A GE employee led a Workout session in which CommonBond employees identified how to improve processes and horizontal communication.[122]

GE uses plenty of other techniques to break down boundaries, as well. It relentlessly benchmarks competitors and companies in other industries to learn best practices all over the world. GE places different functions together physically, such as engineering and manufacturing. It shares services across units. And it sometimes shares physical locations with its customers.

Boundaryless organizations intentionally create dialogue across boundaries, turning barriers into permeable membranes. As the GE people put it, people from different parts of the organization need to learn "how to talk."[123] They must also learn "how to walk." That is, dialogue is essential, but it must be followed by commensurate action.

Management Close-Up

ASSESSING OUTCOMES AND SEIZING OPPORTUNITIES

Digg founder Kevin Rose uses several media to promote and create greater awareness of his site. Besides the weekly Digg-nation video podcasts, Rose partners with Digg chief financial officer Jay Adelson to produce and host programming for an online tech channel called Revision3. Rose and Adelson also hold periodic town hall meetings to chat with their public.

Each month Rose also does an hour-long segment on alternative rock radio station KTIS in San Francisco. During the program, he reads from Digg posts and answers questions from listeners who call in.

In addition, Rose publishes a blog, www.kevinrose.com. The blog includes Rose's thoughts, tips, and random musings, such as his 2009 New Year's resolutions (examples: "Read a book a month," "Drink more water," "Go on a date w/Jennifer Aniston," "Start a small tea Web site" and "Fish w/my Dad"). With all his methods of communication to reach his dedicated audience, Rose has been named one of *BusinessWeek*'s 25 most influential people on the Web.

In 2009 Digg launched WeFollow, a Twitter directory that includes a number of popular categories like Actor, Blogger, Music, Politics, Sports, Tech, and TV. Twitter users can add themselves to the category of their choice, ultimately creating a directory of like-minded followers.

What's on the horizon for Digg? Rose has pledged to expand Digg's features. The company is also taking steps to learn more about its online community, members' interests, and their preferences to keep its readers engaged. Rose and his staff are also focusing on additional ways to link users with similar niche interests and create tools that allow them to share the news of interest to them. In addition, Rose plans to expand Digg internationally. Currently, Digg copycat sites are up and running in Germany, Japan, and Spain.[124]

- Only about one-tenth of Digg's monthly visitors are registered users. What more can Kevin Rose do to encourage two-way communications with his customers and engage them further with Digg?
- What types of communication could Kevin Rose use to make Digg more relevant to the average user? Are there risks in doing so? If so, what?

KEY TERMS

Boundaryless organization,   p. 540

Coaching,   p. 536

Communication,   p. 516

Downward communication,   p. 535

Filtering,   p. 518

Grapevine,   p. 539

Horizontal communication,   p. 538

Media richness,   p. 526

One-way communication,   p. 516

Open-book management,   p. 537

Perception,   p. 517

Reflection,   p. 532

Two-way communication,   p. 517

Upward communication,   p. 537

Virtual office,   p. 525

Web 2.0,   p. 521

SUMMARY OF LEARNING OBJECTIVES

Now that you have studied Chapter 15, you should be able to:

LO 1   Discuss important advantages of two-way communication.

One-way communication flows from the sender to the receiver, with no feedback loop. In two-way communication, each person is both a sender and a receiver as both parties provide and react to information. One-way communication is faster and easier but less accurate than two-way; two-way communication is slower and more difficult but is more accurate and results in better performance.

LO 2   Identify communication problems to avoid.

The communication process involves a sender who conveys information to a receiver. Problems in communication can occur in all stages: encoding, transmission, decoding, and interpreting.

Noise in the system further complicates communication, creating more distortion. Moreover, feedback may be unavailable or misleading. Subjective perceptions and filtering add to the possibility of error.

LO 3   Describe when and how to use the various communications channels.

Communications are sent through oral, written, and electronic channels. All have important advantages and disadvantages that should be considered before choosing a channel. Electronic media have a huge impact on interpersonal and organizational communications and make possible the virtual office. Key advantages of electronic media are speed, cost, and efficiency, but the downsides are also significant, including information overload. Media richness, or how much and what sort of information a channel conveys, is one factor to consider as you decide which channels to use and how to use them both efficiently and effectively.

LO 4   Summarize ways to become a better "sender" and "receiver" of information.

Practice writing, be critical of your work, and revise. Train yourself as a speaker. Use language carefully and well, and work to overcome cross-cultural language differences. Be alert to the nonverbal signals that you send, including your use of time as perceived by other people. Know the common bad listening habits, and work to overcome them. Read widely, and engage in careful, firsthand observation and interpretation.

LO 5   Explain how to improve downward, upward, and horizontal communication.

Actively manage communications in all directions. Engage in two-way communication more than one-way. Make information available to others. Useful approaches to downward communication include coaching, special communications during difficult periods, and open-book management. You should also both facilitate and motivate people to communicate upward. Many mechanisms exist for enhancing horizontal communications.

LO 6   Summarize how to work with the company grapevine.

The informal flow of information can contribute as much as formal communication can to organizational effectiveness and morale. Managers must understand that the grapevine cannot be eliminated and should be managed actively. Many of the suggestions for managing formal communications apply also to managing the grapevine. Moreover, managers can take steps to prevent rumors or neutralize the ones that do arise.

LO 7   Describe the boundaryless organization and its advantages.

Boundaries—psychological if not physical—exist between different organizational levels, units, and organizations and external stakeholders. The ideal boundaryless organization is one in which no barriers to information flow exist. Ideas, information, decisions, and actions move to where they are most needed. Information is available as needed and freely accessible so that the organization as a whole functions far better than as separate parts.

DISCUSSION QUESTIONS

1. Think of an occasion when you faced a miscommunication problem. What do you think caused the problem? How do you think it should have been handled better?

2. Have you ever *not* given someone information or opinions that perhaps you should have? Why? Was it the right thing to do? Why or why not? What would cause you to be glad that you provided (or withheld) negative or difficult information? What would cause you to regret providing/withholding it?

3. Think back to discussions you have heard or participated in. Consider the differences between one-way and two-way communication. How can two "one-ways" be turned into a true "two-way"?

4. Share with the class some of your experiences—both good and bad—with electronic media.

5. Report examples of mixed signals you have received (or sent). How can you reduce the potential for misunderstanding and misperception as you communicate with others?

6. What makes you want to say to someone, "You're not listening!"?

7. What do you think about the practice of open-book management? What would you think about it if you were running your own company?

8. Discuss organizational rumors you have heard: what they were about, how they got started, how accurate they were, and how people reacted to them. What lessons can you learn from these episodes?

9. Refer to the section on "The Virtual Office." What do you think will be the long-term impact of the mobile office on job satisfaction and performance? If you were a manager, how would you maximize the benefits and minimize the drawbacks? If you worked in this environment, how would you manage yourself to maximize your performance and avoid burnout?

10. Have you ever made or seen mistakes due to people not speaking a common language well? How do you or will you deal with others who do not speak the same language as you?

11. Have you ever tried to coach someone? What did you do well, and what mistakes did you make? How can you become a better coach?

12. Have you ever been coached by someone? What did he or she do well, and what mistakes were made? How was it for you to be on the receiving end of the coaching, and how did you respond? What is required to be successful as the "receiver" of someone else's coaching attempts?

13. Think about how companies communicate with Wall Street and the media, and how analysts on TV communicate with viewers. What concepts from the chapter apply, and how can you become a more astute "consumer" of such information?

CONCLUDING CASE

Rock On

A small coastal New England town is home to a group of dedicated musicians who practice hard and play regularly to enthusiastic audiences. The band Rock On has been together for more than 10 years, has completed three successful tours around the United States, and has produced and distributed three CDs.

The group wants to become famous. They want to get on MTV and other shows with high visibility. They want to enter into a lucrative big-name recording contract. They want to be heard regularly on radio shows nationwide. They also want to tour again, but this time before large audiences with big name groups.

The band members are all pushing 30 and feel as though their time is running out. They are discouraged to constantly see bands of obviously lesser talent achieving the goals that they are after.

The group consists of Dave on vocals and rhythm guitar, Big Nate on lead guitar, Nomar on bass, and The Animal on drums. Most of the songs they play are originals. Unlike many other bands, they offer a wide range of music that greatly enhances audience appeal. With the exception of Big Nate, a full-time musician who performs solo and with another smaller group, all other band members hold full-time jobs on the outside.

Historically, the band has reinvested almost all of the money it has earned back into recording fees, CD production, equipment upgrades, radio, and benefit performances and travel.

The group recently used college interns as marketing/consulting agents. Those students made phone connections with radio station people nationwide and followed up on those calls with the mailing of press kits that included sample CDs, posters of the band, biographical information, and a sample stack of press clippings. The student team also researched different aspects of the music business in search of ways to help the band achieve its goals.

The band plays in many venues between Portland, Maine, and New York City, including both the small towns and the larger cities such as Boston, Hartford, and New Haven. They are well known in Boston and well networked throughout the entire region. They are often part of a show that includes two or three other bands. They use a combination of booking agents and direct selling to club owners to get gigs.

Most agree that they are a great band of great people who play great music. All of their press releases and reviews are excellent.

They seem to be doing all of the right things but have yet to achieve their goals.

QUESTIONS

1. What specific communication techniques from the text should this group begin to incorporate into their activities, both on and off stage?

2. Effective communication with the right people could lead this group to the achievement of its goals. Once these meetings and opportunities are established, how would you recommend that the group proceed?

3. What forms of nonverbal communication should this group incorporate into its efforts to achieve success?

EXPERIENTAL EXERCISES

15.1 Nonverbal Communication

OBJECTIVE

To become more conscious of nonverbal messages.

INSTRUCTIONS

Following is a list of nonverbal communication "methods." Pick a day on which you will attempt to keep track of these methods. Think back at the end of the day to three people with whom you communicated in some way. Record how you responded to these people in terms of their nonverbal communication methods. Identify those that had the greatest and least effect on your behavior.

Nonverbal Communication Worksheet

Medium	What Was the Message?	How Did You Respond?	Which Affected Your Behavior Most and Least?
How they shook hands			
Their posture			
Their facial expressions			
Their appearance			
Their voice tones			
Their smiles			
The expressions in their eyes			
Their confidence			
The way they moved			
The way they stood			
How close they stood to you			
How they smelled			
Symbols or gestures they used			
How loudly they spoke			

15.2 Listening Skills Survey

OBJECTIVES

1. To measure your skills as a listener.
2. To gain insight into the factors that determine good listening habits.
3. To demonstrate how you can become a better listener.

INSTRUCTIONS

1. Working alone, complete the Listening Skills Survey.
2. In small groups, compare scores, discuss survey test items, and prepare responses to the discussion questions.
3. After the class reconvenes, group spokespersons present group findings.

DISCUSSION QUESTIONS

1. In what ways did students' responses on the survey agree or disagree?
2. What do you think accounts for the differences?
3. How can the results of this survey be put to practical use?

Listening Skills Survey

To measure your listening skills, complete the following survey by circling the degree to which you agree with each statement.

	Strongly Agree	Agree	Neither Agree nor Disagree	Disagree	Strongly Disagree
1. I tend to be patient with the speaker, making sure she or he is finished speaking before I respond in any fashion.	5	4	3	2	1
2. When listening I don't doodle or fiddle with papers and things that might distract me from the speaker.	5	4	3	2	1
3. I attempt to understand the speaker's point of view.	5	4	3	2	1
4. I try not to put the speaker on the defensive by arguing or criticizing.	5	4	3	2	1
5. When I listen, I focus on the speaker's feelings.	5	4	3	2	1
6. I let a speaker's annoying mannerisms distract me.	5	4	3	2	1
7. While the speaker is talking, I watch carefully for facial expressions and other types of body language.	5	4	3	2	1
8. I never talk when the other person is trying to say something.	5	4	3	2	1
9. During a conversation, a period of silence seems awkward to me.	5	4	3	2	1
10. I want people to just give me the facts and allow me to make up my own mind.	5	4	3	2	1
11. When the speaker is finished, I respond to his or her feelings.	5	4	3	2	1
12. I don't evaluate the speaker's words until she or he is finished talking.	5	4	3	2	1
13. I formulate my response while the speaker is still talking.	5	4	3	2	1
14. I never pretend that I'm listening when I'm not.	5	4	3	2	1
15. I can focus on message content even if the delivery is poor.	5	4	3	2	1
16. I encourage the speaker with frequent nods, smiles, and other forms of body language.	5	4	3	2	1
17. Sometimes I can predict what someone is going to say before she or he says it.	5	4	3	2	1
18. Even if a speaker makes me angry, I hold my temper.	5	4	3	2	1
19. I maintain good eye contact with the speaker.	5	4	3	2	1
20. I try to focus on the speaker's message, not his or her delivery.	5	4	3	2	1
21. If I am confused by a statement someone makes, I never respond until I have asked for and received adequate clarification.	5	4	3	2	1

15.3 Active Listening

This exercise involves triads. Each triad counts off into threes: 1, 2, 3, 1, 2, 3, and so on. In the first round, all the 1s in their respective triads take the pro position (see topics given later in exercise), all the 2s take the con position, and all the 3s act as observers. After a topic is given, two individuals representing opposing viewpoints have one minute to collect their thoughts, and then five to seven minutes to arrive at a *mutually agreeable position* on that topic.

The observer should use the form below to capture *actual examples* of what the individuals said or did that indicated active and less-than-active listening. When time is called, the pro individuals share their opinion of which listening behaviors they performed well and which ones they'd like to improve. Then the con individuals do the same. Finally, the observers share their observations and insights, using examples to reinforce their feedback.

If additional rounds are used, rotate the roles so that each person plays a speaking role, and if possible an observing role.

Round 1:
Topic selected: _____
Notes:

Round 2:
Topic selected: _____
Notes:

Listening Feedback Form

Indicators of Active Listening	Pro	Con
1. Asked questions for clarification		
2. Paraphrased the opposing view		
3. Responded to nonverbal cues (e.g., body posture, tone of voice)		
4. Appeared to move toward a mutually satisfying solution		
Indicators of Less-Than-Active Listening		
5. Interrupted before allowing the other person to finish		
6. Was defensive about their position		
7. Appeared to dominate the conversation		
8. Ignored nonverbal cues		

Potential topics to be used:
 1. Gun control
 2. Capital punishment
 3. Race as a criterion for college admission
 4. Prison reform
 5. U.S. intervention in wars outside of the United States
 6. Legalization of marijuana
 7. Mandatory armed forces draft
 8. Interracial adoption
 9. Premarital and extramarital sex
10. Prayer in schools
11. Diversity in the workplace
12. Pornography on the Internet

QUESTIONS

1. Did you arrive at a mutually agreeable solution? What helped you get there?

2. What were some factors that hindered this process?

3. How comfortable did you feel "arguing" the position you were given? How did this influence your ability to actively listen?

4. If the position you were given was exactly opposite your values or beliefs, did you see this topic differently now than before the exercise?

5. What steps can you take to improve your ability to listen actively to friends or associates, especially when you don't agree with their viewpoint?

PART 4 SUPPORTING CASE

Leadership at AIG: Does Style Matter?

"The King Is Dead, Long Live the King." These indeed may be the very words echoed by employees at American International Group, the world's largest insurance company. Its legendary CEO Maurice "Hank" Greenberg, age 79, was deposed by AIG's board of directors after Elliot Spitzer, New York State's attorney general, leveled charges against the company for possibly manipulating its earnings.

Headquartered in New York, AIG has been in business for nearly 90 years, has some $170 billion in market capitalization, and has approximately 80,000 employees worldwide. Greenberg, an attorney and a much heralded figure in the insurance business, worked at AIG for more than four decades. In 1967, he became president, replacing company founder Cornelius Vander Starr. Greenberg transformed the company from a midlevel insurance company into a major international player. With a reputation as an autocratic leader, Greenberg was known to scream at employees. One source likened Greenberg's tenure to a "reign of terror." Another source offered insights to Greenberg's leadership and managerial style: He "calls employees with detailed questions about contracts and other minutiae." At one meeting in the late 1990s, he told a high-ranking manager: "This is one of the worst presentations I've seen in years . . . Go back, get your stuff and don't come back until you can tell me something I don't already know."

Greenberg also had trouble with his sons, Jeffrey and Evan, when they worked for him at AIG. Jeffrey, the older of the two, worked there for 17 years before quitting in 1995; Evan, who had been designated as his father's successor at AIG, resigned a few years later, in 2000. In some circles people believed their father "pushed" his sons too much by expecting more from them than from other company executives. His sons—Evan, in particular— were concerned about their father's so-called succession plan. Apparently, the senior Greenberg had given only lip service to the idea of succession with no intention of retiring any time soon.

In early March 2005, AIG's board of directors replaced Greenberg with 50-year-old vice chairman and co–chief operating officer (COO) Martin Sullivan, who had worked at the company and for Greenberg in various capacities for more than 30 years. His years in the company made him the consummate insider to lead the company. However, like Greenberg, he was considered a micromanager, known to get involved in some of the nitty-gritty deal-making instead of enabling subordinates to play that role. Had he continued micromanaging instead of delegating, he might have created some serious problems for himself and the company. Yet, despite any managerial similarities to his former boss, staff viewed him as more pleasant and more amicable. One source stated that his "greatest strength is the respect he gets from people who work for him . . . He doesn't scream and shout like Mr. Greenberg."

QUESTIONS

1. AIG chairman and CEO Maurice "Hank" Greenberg was considered an autocratic leader and a micromanager by many employees. yet the company grew dramatically during his reign as CEO. Does leadership style matter as long as the company performs well and shareholders are satisfied with their return on investment?

2. AIG's CEO Sullivan was labeled a micromanager, but with a more pleasant personality. Could he, as a micromanager, have developed a more participative leadership style? How?

3. Greenberg named his son Evan as the heir apparent. Yet Greenberg never set a departure date. Should a good leader set a date for departure? When should he name a successor?

SOURCES: D. Brady, "AIG Needs New Policies," *BusinessWeek Online,* March 1, 2005; E. Kelleher and A. Felsted, "New AIG Chief Has a Softer Touch," *Financial Times,* March 21, 2005, p. 18; I. McDonald, "Insurance Industry's First Family Fades," *The Wall Street Journal,* March 15, 2005, p. C13; N. Scheiber, "Sins of the Son," *New York Magazine,* 2004; J. Weil, M. Langley, and N. Deogun, "AIG's Greenberg Plans to Depart as Woes Mount," *The Wall Street Journal,* March 14, 2005, pp. 1, 14.

This case was prepared by Joseph C. Santora, professor of business administration at Essex County College, Newark, New Jersey.

16

Managerial Control

More than at any time in the past, companies will not be able to hold themselves together with the traditional methods of control: hierarchy, systems, budgets, and the like . . . The bonding glue will increasingly become ideological.

— Collins and Porras[1]

Use your good judgment in all situations. There will be no additional rules.

— Nordstrom's employee manual

LEARNING OBJECTIVES

After studying Chapter 16, you will be able to:

LO 1 Explain why companies develop control systems for employees. p. 550

LO 2 Summarize how to design a basic bureaucratic control system. p. 551

LO 3 Describe the purposes for using budgets as a control device. p. 559

LO 4 Define basic types of financial statements and financial ratios used as controls. p. 564

LO 5 List procedures for implementing effective control systems. p. 569

LO 6 Identify ways in which organizations use market control mechanisms. p. 574

LO 7 Discuss the use of clan control in an empowered organization. p. 577

CHAPTER OUTLINE

Bureaucratic Control Systems
The Control Cycle
Approaches to Bureaucratic Control
Management Audits
Budgetary Controls
Financial Controls
The Downside of Bureaucratic Control
Designing Effective Control Systems

The Other Controls: Markets and Clans
Market Control
Clan Control: The Role of Empowerment and Culture

Management Close-Up

HOW DOES ROGER BERKOWITZ MAINTAIN CONTROL AT LEGAL SEA FOODS?

Go ahead—order whatever your heart desires. Is it the baked Boston scrod, the classic fish and chips, or a lobster roll with fries and slaw? It doesn't matter. At Legal Sea Foods, your favorite dish will be fresh and delicious. It will also taste the same every time, whether you're dining in Philadelphia, Atlanta, or terminal B at Boston's Logan Airport.

Legal Sea Foods traces its origins to the fish market George Berkowitz opened in 1950 next to his father's grocery story in Cambridge, Massachusetts. By 1968, next door to the fish market he also had launched a little seafood restaurant where patrons sitting at picnic tables enjoyed freshly prepared seafood served on paper plates. The Berkowitzes are fanatical about quality. "If it isn't Fresh,

{ Legal Sea Foods has evolved from humble beginnings into a seafood empire. As you read this chapter, consider how the diligent use of managerial control systems has helped this company become a leader in its industry. }

it isn't Legal!" says the Legal Sea Foods slogan, and that sentiment is echoed more than half a century later by president and CEO Roger Berkowitz, George's son.

Owing its success in part to its attention to tightly controlling factors in its operations, the Legal Sea Foods name is synonymous with quality. The company has grown by word of mouth to become an East Coast regional favorite. With more than 30 restaurants from Boston to Boca Raton, Florida, Legal Sea Foods generates more than $200 million in annual revenues. No wonder travel author Patricia Schultz recommended Legal Sea Foods in her best-selling guide *1,000 Things to See Before You Die*.[2]

The controls in place at Legal Sea Foods have helped the Boston-based restaurant group write a business success story. Another control-based success was Dell in its early years, when it gained market share as it perfected an individualized but rapid system for getting desktop and laptop PCs into the hands of consumers and business users. But more recently, Dell has stumbled.[3] Consumers have been more interested in low prices from discounters than in Dell's customization. Efforts to save money by outsourcing customer service led to widespread complaints about poor quality. Then the federal government announced that it was investigating financial irregularities in its reporting systems. When Dell said it would restate its earnings, the NASDAQ stock market nearly removed the company from its listing. How can a company that once was so successful run into so many problems, and how can a restaurant success story like Legal Sea Foods occur in an industry loaded with competitors and subject to numerous variables? These examples are two sides of one coin: control—a means or mechanism for regulating the behavior of organization members. Left on their own, people may act in ways that they perceive to be beneficial to them individually but that may work to the detriment of the organization as a whole. Even well-intentioned people may not know whether they are directing their efforts toward the activities that are most important. Thus, control is one of the fundamental forces that keep the organization together and heading in the right direction.

control

Any process that directs the activities of individuals toward the achievement of organizational goals.

Control is defined as any process that directs the activities of individuals toward the achievement of organizational goals. It is how effective managers make sure that activities are going as planned. Some managers don't want to admit it (see Table 16.1), but control problems—the lack of controls or the wrong kinds of controls—frequently cause irreparable damage to organizations. Ineffective control systems result in problems ranging from employee theft to peeling tire tread problems. Research in Motion was publicly embarrassed when failure to fully test a "noncritical system routine" for updating its computer servers caused the e-mail service on its BlackBerry devices to crash for hours throughout North America.[4] Employees simply wasting time cost U.S. employers billions of dollars each year![5]

Control has been called one of the Siamese twins of management. The other twin is *planning*. Some means of control are necessary because once managers form plans and strategies, they must ensure that the plans are carried out. They must make sure that other people are doing what needs to be done and not doing inappropriate things. If plans are not carried out properly, management must take steps to correct the problem. This process is the primary control function of management. By ensuring creativity, enhancing quality, and reducing cost, managers must figure out ways to control the activities in their organizations.

Control is essential for the attainment of any management objective.

Not surprisingly, effective planning facilitates control, and control facilitates planning. Planning lays out a framework for the future and, in this sense, provides a

TABLE 16.1
Symptoms of an Out-of-Control Company

• **Lax top management**—senior managers do not emphasize or value the need for controls, or they set a bad example.
• **Absence of policies**—the firm's expectations are not established in writing.
• **Lack of agreed-upon standards**—organization members are unclear about what needs to be achieved.
• **"Shoot the messenger" management**—employees feel their careers would be at risk if they reported bad news.
• **Lack of periodic reviews**—managers do not assess performance on a regular, timely basis.
• **Bad information systems**—key data are not measured and reported in a timely and easily accessible way.
• **Lack of ethics in the culture**—organization members have not internalized a commitment to integrity.

blueprint for control. Control systems, in turn, regulate the allocation and use of resources and, in so doing, facilitate the process of the next phases of planning. In today's complex organizational environment, both functions have become more difficult to implement while they have become more important in every department of the organization. Managers today must control their people, inventories, quality, and costs, to mention just a few of their responsibilities.

According to William Ouchi of the University of California at Los Angeles, managers can apply three broad strategies for achieving organizational control: bureaucratic control, market control, and clan control.[6] **Bureaucratic control** is the use of rules, regulations, and formal authority to guide performance. It includes such items as budgets, statistical reports, and performance appraisals to regulate behavior and results. **Market control** involves the use of pricing mechanisms to regulate activities in organizations as though they were economic transactions. Business units may be treated as profit centers and trade resources (services or goods) with one another via such mechanisms. Managers who run these units may be evaluated on the basis of profit and loss. **Clan control**, unlike the first two types, does not assume that the interests of the organization and individuals naturally diverge. Instead, clan control is based on the idea that employees may share the values, expectations, and goals of the organization and act in accordance with them. When members of an organization have common values and goals—and trust one another—formal controls may be less necessary. Clan control is based on many of the interpersonal processes described in the organization culture section of Chapter 2, in Chapter 12 on leadership, and in Chapter 14 on groups and teams (e.g., group norms and cohesiveness).

Table 16.2 summarizes the main features of bureaucratic, market, and clan controls. We use this framework as a foundation for our discussions throughout the chapter.

Government Motors? General Motors former Chairman and CEO Rick Wagoner is shown here talking about the company's restructuring plans during a news conference in February 2009. He later resigned under pressure from the White House, as Fritz Henderson took over as the new CEO. Two months later a historic restructuring plan was implemented that would give the majority ownership of the ailing automaker to the federal government to help them fight off bankruptcy. What type of control is exemplified by this action?

Bureaucratic Control Systems

Bureaucratic (or formal) control systems are designed to measure progress toward set performance goals and, if necessary, to apply corrective measures to ensure that performance achieves managers' objectives. Control systems detect and correct significant variations, or discrepancies, in the results of planned activities.

The Control Cycle

As Figure 16.1 shows, a typical control system has four major steps:

LO 2

bureaucratic control

The use of rules, regulations, and authority to guide performance.

market control

Control based on the use of pricing mechanisms and economic information to regulate activities within organizations.

clan control

Control based on the norms, values, shared goals, and trust among group members.

System Control	Features and Requirements
Bureaucratic control	Uses formal rules, standards, hierarchy, and legitimate authority. Works best where tasks are certain and workers are independent.
Market control	Uses prices, competition, profit centers, and exchange relationships. Works best where tangible output can be identified and market can be established between parties.
Clan control	Involves culture, shared values, beliefs, expectations, and trust. Works best where there is "no one best way" to do a job and employees are empowered to make decisions.

SOURCES: W. G. Ouchi, "A Conceptual Framework for the Design of Organizational Control Mechanisms," *Management Science* 25 (1979), pp. 833–48; W. G. Ouchi, "Markets, Bureaucracies, and Clans." *Administrative Science Quarterly* 25 (1980), pp. 129–41; and Richard D. Robey and C. A. Sales, *Designing Organizations* (Burr Ridge, IL: Richard D. Irwin, 1994).

TABLE 16.2
Characteristics of Controls

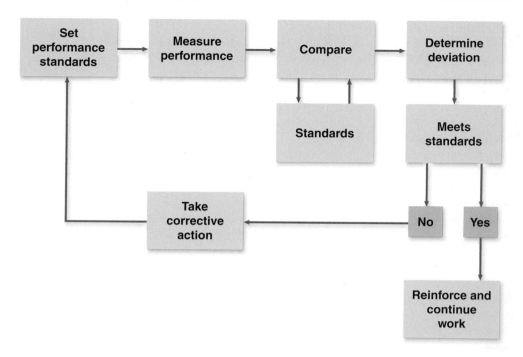

FIGURE 16.1
The Control Process

1. Setting performance standards.
2. Measuring performance.
3. Comparing performance against the standards and determining deviations.
4. Taking action to correct problems and reinforce successes.

Step 1: Setting Performance Standards   Every organization has goals: profitability, innovation, satisfaction of customers and employees, and so on. A **standard** is the level of expected performance for a given goal. Standards are targets that establish desired performance levels, motivate performance, and serve as benchmarks against which to assess actual performance. Standards can be set for any activity—financial activities, operating activities, legal compliance, charitable contributions, and so on.[7]

We have discussed setting performance standards in other parts of the text. For example, employee goal setting for motivation is built around the concept of specific, measurable performance standards. Such standards should be challenging and should aim for improvement over past performance. Typically, performance standards are derived from job requirements, such as increasing market share by 10 percent, reducing costs 20 percent, and answering customer complaints within 24 hours. But performance standards don't apply just to people in isolation—they frequently reflect the integration of both human and system performance. HealthPartners, a Bloomington, Minnesota, nonprofit organization that operates clinics and a hospital and offers health insurance plans, sets ambitious standards for patient care. To achieve a goal of reducing diabetes complications by 30 percent, HealthPartners measured existing practices and results, and then set up a standard protocol for exams and treatments, including the requirement that any abnormal results receive an immediate response. To encourage its physicians to follow the protocol, HealthPartners offers financial incentives for compliance. In little more than a decade, HealthPartners exceeded its goal for improved diabetes care. A local eye doctor commented that it was easy to tell which diabetic patients have coverage through HealthPartners because so few of them suffer diabetes-related damage to their retinas. HealthPartners has similar programs for treatment of cardiovascular disease and depression and for improving the health status of patients who are obese or smoke.[8]

Performance standards can be set with respect to (1) quantity, (2) quality, (3) time used, and (4) cost. For example, production activities include volume of output

standard

Expected performance for a given goal: a target that establishes a desired performance level, motivates performance, and serves as a benchmark against which actual performance is assessed.

Standards must be set for all bottom-line practices.

(quantity), defects (quality), on-time availability of finished goods (time use), and dollar expenditures for raw materials and direct labor (cost). Many important aspects of performance, such as customer service, can be measured by the same standards— adequate supply and availability of products, quality of service, speed of delivery, and so forth.

One word of caution: The downside of establishing performance targets and standards is that they may not be supported by other elements of the control system. Each piece of the system is important and depends on the others. Otherwise, the system can get terribly out of balance.

> Sometimes quality standards involve meeting or exceeding standards set by government agencies. Recently, the U.S. Food and Drug Administration proposed loosening its standards for the ingredients in products labeled "chocolate" to allow the use of vegetable fats other than cocoa butter. If the rule change takes effect, candies like Whoppers malted milk balls and PayDay Chocolatey Avalanche could put "chocolate" in their names. Some true chocolate lovers are horrified, but Nick Malgieri, director of the baking program at the Institute of Culinary Education in New York, says, "No one is going to force a high-class chocolate maker to add vegetable fat to chocolate."[9] At companies that seek a reputation for premium quality, the recipe standards can remain as strict as ever, and chocolate afficionados will be on the alert.

Step 2: Measuring Performance   The second step in the control process is to measure performance levels. For example, managers can count units produced, days absent, papers filed, samples distributed, and dollars earned. Performance data commonly are obtained from three sources: written reports, oral reports, and personal observations.

Written reports include computer printouts and on-screen reports. Thanks to computers' data-gathering and analysis capabilities and decreasing costs, both large and small companies can gather huge amounts of performance data.

One common example of *oral reports* occurs when a salesperson contacts his or her immediate manager at the close of each business day to report the accomplishments, problems, or customers' reactions during the day. The manager can ask questions to gain additional information or clear up any misunderstandings. When necessary, tentative corrective actions can be worked out during the discussion.

Personal observation involves going to the area where activities take place and watching what is occurring. The manager can directly observe work methods, employees' nonverbal signals, and the general operation. Personal observation gives a detailed picture of what is going on, but it also has some disadvantages. It does not provide accurate quantitative data; the information usually is general and subjective. Also, employees can misunderstand the purpose of personal observation as mistrust or lack of confidence. Still, many managers believe in the value of firsthand observation. As you learned in earlier chapters, personal contact can increase leadership visibility and upward communication. It also provides valuable information about performance to supplement written and oral reports.

Regardless of the performance measure used, the information must be provided to managers on a timely basis. For example, consumer-goods companies such as General Foods carefully track new-product sales in selected local markets first, so they can make any necessary adjustments well before a national rollout. Information that is not available is of little or no use to managers.

At the Baccarat factory in France, the workers in the quality control area are responsible for the quality and selection of these fine cut crystal glasses.

Step 3: Comparing Performance with the Standard   The third step in the control process is comparing performance with the standard. In this process, the manager evaluates the performance. For some activities, relatively small deviations from the standard are acceptable, while in others a slight deviation may be serious. In many manufacturing processes, a significant deviation in either direction (e.g., drilling a hole that is too small or too large) is unacceptable. In other cases, a deviation in one direction, such as sales or customer satisfaction that fall below the target level, is a problem, but a deviation in the other, exceeding the sales target or customer expectations, is a sign employees are getting better-than-expected results. As a result, managers who perform the oversight must analyze and evaluate the results carefully.

principle of exception

A managerial principle stating that control is enhanced by concentrating on the exceptions to or significant deviations from the expected result or standard.

The managerial **principle of exception** states that control is enhanced by concentrating on the exceptions to, or significant deviations from, the expected result or standard. In other words, in comparing performance with the standard, managers need to direct their attention to the exception—for example, a handful of defective components produced on an assembly line or the feedback from customers who are upset or delighted with a service. Atlanta-based US Security Associates uses information technology to gather performance data on its uniformed security guards and dispatches supervisors to investigate any variances from performance norms, such as a failure of a guard to sign in at a client's location on time.[10]

With the principle of exception, only exceptional cases require corrective action. This principle is important in controlling. The manager is not concerned with performance that equals or closely approximates the expected results. Managers can save much time and effort if they apply the principle of exception.

The accounting and consulting firm of Moody, Famiglietti & Andronico (MFA) uses a formal control process to ensure that it provides exceptional service that is tailored to each client's needs and preferences. The Tewksbury, Massachusetts, firm adopted the U.S. Army's practice of conducting before-action reviews and after-action reviews to learn from its experiences and apply those lessons to future challenges.

At MFA, when employees are preparing to handle an assignment, they begin by calling a short meeting with everyone who has worked with that client during the previous year, as well as employees who have handled similar assignments for other clients. During this before-action review, the participants trade experiences and tidbits of knowledge about the client—say, questions that are likely to arise, efforts that have pleased this client in the past, or existing tools for handling common problems. The input from this meeting helps the team establish goals for the assignment.

During the assignment, team members meet periodically to assess progress and identify any adjustments needed based on what they learn about the client. Within a couple of days of the project's completion, the team reassembles to evaluate its results, comparing outcomes with goals. Participants identify successful actions to recommend in the future, as well as mistakes to avoid next time. Besides noting whether they helped the client meet goals, they also record what they learned about serving the client—data that will be valuable input at the next before-action review for that client. Because the lessons they learn will be the topic of discussion at future before-action reviews, MFA employees are highly motivated to fix mistakes and improve methods.[11]

Step 4: Taking Action to Correct Problems and Reinforce Successes

The last step in the control process is to take appropriate action when there are significant deviations. This step ensures that operations are adjusted to achieve the planned results—or to continue exceeding the plan if the manager determines that is possible. In cases in which significant variances are discovered, the manager usually takes immediate and vigorous action.

"Mistakes and problems are inevitable in complex enterprises. . . . We shouldn't expect heads of established organizations to be perfect, but we should expect them to catch and correct their mistakes quickly."

— Rosabeth Moss Kanter, professor, Harvard Business School[12]

An alternative approach is for the corrective action to be taken, not by higher-ups, but by the operator at the point of the problem. In computer-controlled production technology, two basic types of control are feasible: specialist control and operator control. With *specialist control*, operators of computer-numerical-control (CNC) machines must notify engineering specialists of malfunctions. With this traditional division of labor, the specialist takes corrective action. With *operator control*, multi-skilled operators can rectify their own problems as they occur. Not only is this second strategy more efficient because deviations are controlled closer to their source, but it is also more satisfying because operators benefit by having a more enriched job. At Microscan System, which makes bar-code scanners, every employee is responsible for ensuring the quality of his or her work, resulting in efficient operations. Engineers are responsible for preventing and correcting problems in product and process design, and production workers are responsible for preventing and correcting defects in the processes they carry out.[13]

When corrective action is needed to solve a systemic problem, such as major delays in work flow, often a team approach is most effective. A corrective action is more likely to have greater acceptance in the organization if it is based on a common effort and takes into account multiple points of view. As we discussed in Chapter 14, teams often bring a greater diversity of resources, ideas, and perspectives to problem solving. Knowledgeable team members can often prevent managers from implementing simplistic solutions that don't address the underlying causes of a problem. They are more likely to take into account the effects of any solution on other parts of the organization, preventing new problems from arising later. And they may well develop solutions that managers might not have considered on their own. As a result, any corrective action that is finally adopted will probably be more effective. An important added benefit of bringing employees together to develop corrective actions is that it helps managers build and reinforce an organizationwide culture of high standards.

The selection of the corrective action depends on the nature of the problem. The corrective action may involve a shift in marketing strategy (if, say, the problem is lower-than-expected sales), a disciplinary action, a new way to check the accuracy of manufactured parts, or a major modification to a process or system. Sometimes managers learn they can get better results if they adjust their own practices. Yum Brands, whose franchise restaurants include KFC, Taco Bell, Pizza Hut, and Long John Silver's, conducts regular surveys to learn whether employees feel strong commitment to their jobs. These data are shared with managers to help them measure their performance as leaders and motivators. Jonathan McDaniel, a Houston KFC manager, once learned that his employees were unhappy with their work hours. He began asking them ahead of time whether they wanted particular days off each month—information that helped him create better schedules and end a cause of employee dissatisfaction.[14]

Approaches to Bureaucratic Control

The three approaches to bureaucratic control are feedforward, concurrent, and feedback. **Feedforward control** takes place before operations begin and includes policies, procedures, and rules designed to ensure that planned activities are carried out properly. Examples include inspection of raw materials and proper selection and training of employees. **Concurrent control** takes place while plans are being carried out. It includes directing, monitoring, and fine-tuning activities as they occur. **Feedback control** focuses on the use of information about results to correct deviations from the acceptable standard after they arise.

Feedforward Control   Feedforward control (sometimes called *preliminary control*) is future oriented; its aim is to prevent problems before they arise. Instead of waiting for results and comparing them with goals, a manager can exert control by limiting activities in advance. For example, companies have policies defining the scope within which decisions are made. A company may dictate that managers must adhere to clear ethical and legal guidelines when making decisions. Formal rules and procedures also prescribe people's actions before they occur. For example, legal experts advise

feedforward control

The control process used before operations begin, including policies, procedures, and rules designed to ensure that planned activities are carried out properly.

concurrent control

The control process used while plans are being carried out, including directing, monitoring, and fine-tuning activities as they are performed.

feedback control

Control that focuses on the use of information about previous results to correct deviations from the acceptable standard.

companies to establish policies forbidding disclosure of proprietary information or making clear that employees are not speaking for the company when they post messages on blogs, microblogging sites such as Twitter, or social-networking sites such as Facebook. Human resource policies defining what forms of body art are acceptable to display at work can avoid awkward case-by-case conversations about a tattoo that offends coworkers or piercings that are incompatible with the company's image.[15]

Recently, more managers have grown concerned about the organizational pitfalls of workplace romances, and some have sought a solution in feedforward controls. As wonderful as it is to find love, problems can arise if romantic activities between a supervisor and subordinate create a conflict of interest or charges of sexual harassment. Other employees might interpret the relationship wrongly—that the company sanctions personal relationships as a path to advancement. In addition, romantic ups-and-downs can spill over into the workplace and affect everyone's mood and motivation. Controls aimed at preventing such problems in an organization include training in appropriate behavior (including how to avoid sexual harassment) and even requiring executives and their romantic interests to sign "love contracts" in which they indicate that the relationship is voluntary and welcome. A copy of the contract goes into the company's personnel files in case the attachment disintegrates and an unhappy employee wants to blame the company for having allowed it in the first place.[16]

Concurrent Control   Concurrent control, which takes place while plans are carried out, is the heart of any control system. On a manufacturing floor, all efforts are directed toward producing the correct quantity and quality of the right products in the specified amount of time. In an airline terminal, the baggage must get to the right airplanes before flights depart. In factories, materials must be available when and where needed, and breakdowns in the production process must be repaired immediately. Concurrent control also is in effect when supervisors watch employees to ensure they work efficiently and avoid mistakes.

Advances in information technology have created powerful concurrent controls. Computerized systems give managers immediate access to data from the most remote corners of their companies. For example, managers can update budgets instantly based on a continuous flow of performance data. In production facilities, monitoring systems that track errors per hour, machine speeds, and other measures allow managers to correct small production problems before they become disasters. Point-of-sale terminals in store checkout lines send sales data back to a retailer's headquarters to show which products are selling in which locations.

For James Skinner, CEO of McDonald's, paying attention to what is happening in the restaurants is critical. Launches of new menu items such as McCafé premium coffee drinks, breakfast burritos, and McGriddle sandwiches have been hits with McDonald's customers looking for value in their food purchases. Skinner and his staff check sales monthly in all stores to assess what is selling well throughout the global chain and to make adjustments. Monitoring these details as they occur has allowed McDonald's to grow even during the recent recession.[17]

Feedback Control   Feedback control is involved when performance data have been gathered and analyzed and the results have been returned to someone (or something) in the process to make corrections. When supervisors monitor behavior, they are exercising concurrent control. When they point out and correct improper performance, they are using feedback as a means of control.

Timing is an important aspect of feedback control. Long time lags often occur between performance and feedback, such as when actual spending is compared with the quarterly budget, instead of weekly or monthly, or when some aspect of performance is compared with the projection made a year earlier. Yet, if feedback on performance is not timely, managers cannot quickly identify and eliminate the problem and prevent more serious harm.[18]

Some feedback processes are under real-time (concurrent) control, such as a computer-controlled robot on an assembly line. Such units have sensors that continually determine whether they are in the correct position to perform their functions. If they are not, a built-in control device makes immediate corrections.

In other situations, feedback processes require more time. Some companies that value innovation are applying social network analysis, which uses data from surveys to create diagrams showing which employees collaborate with which colleagues. Employees who are at a hub of information sharing are the organization's "innovation catalysts"—people who actively participate in information sharing. Managers can use the social network analysis to reward innovation catalysts, give them important assignments, and, in areas where not enough collaboration is occurring, train and motivate employees to share knowledge.[19]

The Role of Six Sigma   One of the most important quality-control tools to emerge is Six Sigma, which we first discussed in Chapter 9. It is a particularly robust and powerful application of feedback control. Six Sigma is designed to reduce defects in all organization processes—not just product defects but anything that may result in customer dissatisfaction, such as inadequate service, delayed delivery, and excessively high prices due to high costs or inefficiency. The system was developed at Motorola in the late 1980s, when the company found it was being beaten consistently in the competitive marketplace by foreign firms that were able to produce higher-quality products at a lower cost. Since then, the technique has been widely adopted and even improved on by many companies, such as GE, Allied Signal, Ford, and Xerox.

Sigma is the Greek letter used in statistics to designate the estimated standard deviation, or variation in a process. It indicates how often defects in a process are likely to occur. The lower the sigma number, the higher the level of variation or defects; the higher the sigma number, the lower the level of variation or defects. For example, as you can see in Table 16.3, a two-sigma-level process has more than 300,000 defects per million opportunities (DPMO)—not a very well-controlled process. A three-sigma-level process has 66,807 DPMO, which is roughly a 93 percent level of accuracy. Many organizations operate at this level, which on its face does not sound too bad, until we consider its implications—for example, 7 items of airline baggage lost for every 100 processed. The additional costs to organizations of such inaccuracy are enormous. As you can see in the table, even at just above a 99 percent defect-free rate, or 6,210 DPMO, the accuracy level is often unacceptable—the statistical equivalent of about 50 dropped newborn babies a day.[20]

At a six-sigma level, a process is producing fewer than 3.4 defects per million, which means it is operating at a 99.99966 percent level of accuracy. Six Sigma companies have not only close to zero product or service defects but also substantially lower production costs and cycle times and much higher levels of customer satisfaction. The methodology isn't just for the factory floor, either. Accountants have used Six Sigma to improve the quality of their audits investigating risks faced by their clients.[21]

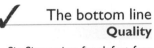

The bottom line
Quality

Six Sigma aims for defect-free performance

Sigma Level	DPMO	Is Four Sigma Good Enough?
2σ	308,537	Consider these everyday examples of four sigma quality . . .
3σ	66,807	• 20,000 lost articles of mail per hour
4σ	6,210	• Unsafe drinking water 15 minutes per day
5σ	233	• 5,000 incorrect surgical operations per week
6σ	3.4	• 200,000 wrong prescriptions each year
		• No electricity for 7 hours each month

TABLE 16.3
Relationship between Sigma Level and Defects per Million Opportunities

SOURCE: Tom Rancour and Mike McCracken, "Applying 6 Sigma Methods for Breakthrough Safety Performance," *Professional Safety* 45, no. 10 (October 2000), pp. 29–32. Reprinted with permission.

The Six Sigma approach is based on an intense statistical analysis of business processes that contribute to customer satisfaction. For example, a business process could be assembling a product or delivering products to customers. For the given process, the effort begins by defining the outputs and information that flow through each stage of the process and then measuring performance at each stage. A variety of tools are available for analyzing the results. These might include looking for all the root causes of any problem. Suppose some customers are dissatisfied with a company's customer service. Asking "why?" over and over could reveal that customers are dissatisfied because phone calls go unanswered, which happens because support staff cannot keep up with the call volume, which happens because the department is understaffed, which is the result of frozen hiring levels, the result of budget cuts. Any solution will have to address the budget restrictions, either by increasing the budget or by finding a way that a small department can satisfy customers. After the problems are analyzed, process improvements are identified and implemented, and the new process is evaluated again. This cycle continues until the desired quality level is achieved. In this way, the Six Sigma process leads to continuous improvement in an organization's operations.

Six Sigma has come under some criticism for not always delivering business results.[22] One likely reason Six Sigma doesn't always improve the bottom line is that it focuses only on how to eliminate defects in a process, not whether the process is the best one for the organization. So, for example, at 3M, a drive to improve efficiency through Six Sigma has been blamed for slowing the flow of innovative ideas. At Home Depot, Six Sigma has been credited with improving such processes as customer checkout and deciding where to place products in stores, but some say the effort took store workers away from customers. One way managers can apply the strengths of Six Sigma and minimize the drawbacks is by setting different goals and control processes for the company's mature products than for its areas of innovation.

The Columbus Metropolitan Library used Six Sigma to the benefit of its workers, customers, and its overall processes. Because the library is a not-for-profit organization, its profits were not the issue. Instead, working within a limited—in fact, frozen—budget was the challenge. As the budget began to squeeze staff and services more tightly, the library's top managers had to figure out how to do more, perform better, and achieve results with fewer resources. To accomplish this, they turned to the Lean Six Sigma (LSS) approach, which combines Six Sigma quality improvement methods with efforts to eliminate waste—in time, complex processes, and materials. They settled on areas needing improvement, formed teams, and began to identify and define the specific problems the library was facing.

Some of the improvement projects were broad in scope, and others were quite narrow. For example, one of the narrower projects involved reviewing how long a customer had to wait to speak to a staff member after dialing the library's information line. The line is a crucial link to the public, handling nearly 400,000 calls a year. Despite its importance, customers sometimes had to wait as much as five minutes to speak with someone—creating general dissatisfaction with the library. At first glance, it seemed that more staff would be needed to alleviate the problem. But when the project team dug deeper and applied statistical analysis through the Six Sigma approach, they discovered that the wait time was really caused by the length of the recorded menu and the way staff was trained to handle it. With reprogramming of the menu and retraining of the current staff, more than 80 percent of calls to the information line are now answered in less than 15 seconds.

The library has also undertaken projects involving community relations and development, requests for printed documents, human resources, and finance. "Of course, true system-wide quality improvement will require more than a handful of successful projects," writes library executive Shaunessy Everett. "Change is risky, it's scary, and it takes time." But the Columbus Metropolitan Library is now a true devotee of the Six Sigma approach.[23]

Management Audits

Over the years, **management audits** have developed as a means of evaluating the effectiveness and efficiency of various systems within an organization, from social responsibility programs to accounting control. Management audits may be external or internal. Managers conduct external audits of other companies and internal audits of their own companies. Some of the same tools and approaches are used for both types of audit.[24]

External Audits An **external audit** occurs when one organization evaluates another organization. Typically an external body such as a CPA firm conducts financial audits of an organization (accounting audits are discussed later). But any company can conduct external audits of competitors or other companies for its own strategic decision-making purposes. This type of analysis (1) investigates other organizations for possible merger or acquisition, (2) determines the soundness of a company that will be used as a major supplier, or (3) discovers the strengths and weaknesses of a competitor to maintain or better exploit the competitive advantage of the investigating organization. Publicly available data usually are used for these evaluations.[25]

External audits provide essential feedback control when they identify legal and ethical lapses that could harm the organization and its reputation. They also are useful for preliminary control because they can prevent problems from occurring. If a company seeking to acquire other businesses gathers adequate, accurate information about possible candidates, it is more likely to acquire the most appropriate companies and avoid unsound acquisitions.

Internal Audits An organization may assign a group to conduct an **internal audit** to assess (1) what the company has done for itself and (2) what it has done for its customers or other recipients of its goods or services. The company can be evaluated on a number of factors, including financial stability, production efficiency, sales effectiveness, human resources development, earnings growth, energy use, public relations, civic responsibility, and other criteria of organizational effectiveness. The audit reviews the company's past, present, and future, including any risks the organization should be prepared to face.[26] A recent study found that the stock prices of companies with highly rated audit committees tended to rise faster than shares of companies with lower-rated internal auditors. It is likely that the higher-rated audit committees do a better job of finding and eliminating undesirable practices.[27]

To perform a management audit, auditors compile a list of desired qualifications and weight each qualification. Among the most common undesirable practices uncovered by a management audit are the performance of unnecessary work, duplication of work, poor inventory control, uneconomical use of equipment and machines, procedures that are more costly than necessary, and wasted resources. At Capital One Financial Corporation, the human resource (HR) department performed an audit of facilities usage. Over several months, staff members walked through headquarters, noting which desks were occupied. The audit determined that more than 4 out of 10 desks were unused each day, and another 3 out of 10 were unused at least part of the day. Employees were away at meetings, visiting clients, or working flexible schedules. The HR staff developed a plan for Capital One to operate more efficiently in one-third of its space. Now most employees keep their work items in a cart, which they take to a desk when they need one. The change saves the company $3 million a year.[28]

Budgetary Controls

Budgetary control is one of the most widely recognized and commonly used methods of managerial control. It ties together feedforward control, concurrent control, and feedback control, depending on the point at which it is applied. *Budgetary control* is the process of finding out what's being done and comparing the results with the corresponding budget data to verify accomplishments or remedy differences. Budgetary control commonly is called **budgeting.**

management audit

An evaluation of the effectiveness and efficiency of various systems within an organization.

external audit

An evaluation conducted by one organization, such as a CPA firm, on another.

internal audit

A periodic assessment of a company's own planning, organizing, leading, and controlling processes.

budgeting

The process of investigating what is being done and comparing the results with the corresponding budget data to verify accomplishments or remedy differences; also called *budgetary controlling.*

LO 3

Fundamental Budgetary Considerations   In private industry, budgetary control begins with an estimate of sales and expected income. Table 16.4 shows a budget with a forecast of expected sales (the *sales budget*) on the top row, followed by several categories of estimated expenses for the first three months of the year. In the bottom row, the profit estimate is determined by subtracting each month's budgeted expenses from the sales in that month's sales budget. Columns next to each month's budget provide space to enter the actual accomplishments so that managers can readily compare expected amounts and actual results.

Although this discussion of budgeting focuses on the flow of money into and out of the organization, budgeting information is not confined to finances. The entire enterprise and any of its units can create budgets for their activities, using units other than dollars, if appropriate. For example, many organizations use production budgets forecasting physical units produced and shipped, and labor can be budgeted in skill levels or hours of work required.

A primary consideration of budgeting is the length of the budget period. All budgets are prepared for a specific time period. Many budgets cover one, three, or six months or one year. The length of time selected depends on the primary purpose of the budgeting. The period chosen should include the enterprise's complete normal cycle of activity. For example, seasonal variations should be included for production and for sales. The budget period commonly coincides with other control devices, such as managerial reports, balance sheets, and statements of profit and loss. In addition, the extent to which reasonable forecasts can be made should be considered in selecting the length of the budget period.

Budgetary control proceeds through several stages. *Establishing expectancies* starts with the broad plan for the company and the estimate of sales, and it ends with budget approval and publication. Next, the *budgetary operations* stage deals with finding out what is being accomplished and comparing the results with expectancies. The last stage, as in any control process, involves responding appropriately with some combination of reinforcing successes and correcting problems.

Although practices differ widely, a member of top management often serves as the chief coordinator for formulating and using the budget. Usually the chief financial officer (CFO) has these duties. He or she needs to be less concerned with the details than with resolving conflicting interests, recommending adjustments when needed, and giving official sanction to the budgetary procedures. In a small company, budgeting responsibility generally rests with the owner. To understand why budgeting is a critical responsibility even in small start-ups, and to receive some practical advice on using budgets, read the "From the Pages of *BusinessWeek*" feature.

TABLE 16.4   A Sales-Expense Budget

	January Estimate	January Actual	February Estimate	February Actual	March Estimate	March Actual
Sales	$1,200,000		$1,350,000		$1,400,000	
Expenses						
General overhead	310,000		310,000		310,000	
Selling	242,000		275,000		288,000	
Producing	327,000		430,500		456,800	
Research	118,400		118,400		115,000	
Office	90,000		91,200		91,500	
Advertising	32,500		27,000		25,800	
Estimated gross profit	80,100		97,900		112,900	

Better Business through Budgeting

Creating a budget can help a start-up entrepreneur set goals and evaluate the viability of a business idea. It can also help established small-business owners gauge the financial health of their companies and measure progress. No business should be without a working budget, yet many small companies do operate without formal budgets, or they seldom consult the budgets they draw up, says Wendy Alexander, director of small business for Capital One Financial. Here are edited excerpts of Alexander's interview with columnist Karen E. Klein.

Q: Why does a would-be entrepreneur or a small-business owner need to devote the time to creating a working budget?

A: For a start-up CEO, a well-planned budget is crucial to assess whether an idea is realistic, from a business and financial perspective. Once a company is in motion, it's a tool that tells you whether or not your financials are on track. If you experience unexpected windfalls or expenses, your budget acts as an early-warning system to alert you to those things. And, of course, a budget is key to getting loans, bringing on new partners, and attracting investors. With a budget, you'll have a history of performance that allows you to show what you planned to do with your company and what you have achieved.

Q: Don't most companies have budgets?

A: Most, but not all. A substantial number of the micro-businesses we counsel do not have working budgets. The reality is, most small-business owners found their companies because they love whatever it is they are producing or providing as a service. Managing the finances is secondary to most of them. So, if they feel like the financial matters are more or less under control, they don't bother to create a formal budget. Also, small-business owners are always strapped for time, and the last thing they want to spend a lot of time on are financial details. What's key is to make the commitment to do a budget, and then make it as simple—but also as effective—as possible.

Q: How do you define a budget, and what elements should it include?

A: Very simply, it involves identifying the income that the company is bringing in and the expenses that are going out. Every company should track its income, expenses, and profits and project those numbers about a year out, or even a couple of years out. Doing that shows how the company is expected to do in the future, and as time passes, those expectations can be compared to how the company actually does. That comparison shows the entrepreneur how the company is performing and whether or not goals are being met.

Q: How do small-business owners make realistic projections about what their financial performance will be over time?

A: If they are already in business, they should have a lot of historical data they can look at and go from there. A new business owner will need to do some research. Start by pulling together all your anticipated sources of income. Then think about whether the business is seasonal, what additional income sources might come along in the near future, and what your marketing plan is likely to generate in terms of increased income. Next, you do the same thing for your fixed costs and variable expenses, thinking about each major line item and what it is expected to cost. Once you've pulled the pieces of the puzzle together, you need to plug in the numbers.

Q: How do you come up with those?

A: You research prices and what things are likely to cost. If you can, you research the sales of other people in the same market you're in. Something to remember is that it always pays to be a little conservative with your numbers. It's always great to have some contingency funds. So don't constrict your business from taking advantage of good opportunities, but do build a financial cushion into your budget.

Q: What are the dangers of not having a budget?

A: The biggest danger is running blindly into a nasty surprise. Some of those surprises could even put your company out of business. For a start-up company that doesn't establish a budget, it may find that even if it is selling as much product as expected, the numbers just don't add up. It may simply be impossible to make a profit at the business. A lot of times with start-ups, entrepreneurs are focused so completely on recruiting customers that they don't realize how much their expenses are going to eat into their income.

Q: What are some of the common mistakes you see in budgeting, and how can entrepreneurs avoid them?

A: The biggest mistake is for a business owner to treat a budget as a one-time exercise, or a once-a-year exercise, rather than as a living document that they're using to run the business day to day. Often we see entrepreneurs who have prepared budgets, but only because they are trying to get a loan or they're doing their taxes. They put all this time and effort into drawing up the budget, then they set it aside and never consult it again.

SOURCE: Excerpted from Karen E. Klein, "Better Business through Budgeting," *BusinessWeek,* January 19, 2006, http://www.businessweek.com (interview with Wendy Alexander).

Types of Budgets   There are many types of budgets. Some of the more common types are as follows:

- *Sales budget.* Usually data for the sales budget include forecasts of sales by month, sales area, and product.
- *Production budget.* The production budget commonly is expressed in physical units. Required information for preparing this budget includes types and capacities of machines, economic quantities to produce, and availability of materials.
- *Cost budget.* The cost budget is used for areas of the organization that incur expenses but no revenue, such as human resources and other support departments. Cost budgets may also be included in the production budget. Costs may be fixed, or independent of the immediate level of activity (such as rent) or variable, rising or falling with the level of activity (such as raw materials).

As indicated in the text, there are many types of budgets, but the master budget is the one that brings together and coordinates the activities of the other budgets. It can be referred to as the "budget of budgets."

- *Cash budget.* The cash budget is essential to every business. It should be prepared after all other budget estimates are completed. The cash budget shows the anticipated receipts and expenditures, the amount of working capital available, the extent to which outside financing may be required, and the periods and amounts of cash available.
- *Capital budget.* The capital budget is used for the cost of fixed assets like plant and equipment. Such costs are usually treated, not as regular expenses, but as investments because of their long-term nature and importance to the organization's productivity.
- *Master budget.* The master budget includes all the major activities of the business. It brings together and coordinates all the activities of the other budgets and can be thought of as a "budget of budgets."

Traditionally, budgets were often imposed *top-down,* with senior management setting specific targets for the entire organization at the beginning of the budget process. In today's more complex organizations, the budget process is much more likely to be *bottom-up*, with top management setting the general direction, but with lower-level and middle-level managers actually developing the budgets and submitting them for approval. When the budgets are consolidated, senior managers can then determine whether the budget objectives of the organization are being met. The budget will then be either approved or sent back down the organization for additional refinement.

Accounting records must be inspected periodically to ensure they were properly prepared and are correct. **Accounting audits,** which are designed to verify accounting reports and statements, are essential to the control process. This audit is performed by members of an outside firm of public accountants. Knowing that accounting records are accurate, true, and in keeping with generally accepted accounting practices (GAAP) creates confidence that a reliable base exists for sound overall controlling purposes.

accounting audits

Procedures used to verify accounting reports and statements.

Activity-Based Costing   Traditional methods of cost accounting may be inappropriate in today's business environment because they are based on outdated methods of rigid hierarchical organization. Instead of assuming that organizations are bureaucratic "machines" that can be separated into component functions such as human resources, purchasing, and maintenance, companies such as Hewlett-Packard and GE have used **activity-based costing (ABC)** to allocate costs across business processes.

ABC starts with the assumption that organizations are collections of people performing many different but related activities to satisfy customer needs. The ABC system is designed to identify those streams of activity and then to allocate costs across particular business processes. The basic procedure is outlined in Figure 16.2 and works as follows: First, employees are asked to break down what they do each day in order to define their *basic activities*. For example, employees in Dana Corporation's material control department engage in a number of activities that range from processing sales orders and sourcing parts to requesting engineering changes and solving problems. These activities form the basis for ABC. Second, managers look at total expenses computed by traditional accounting—fixed costs, supplies, salaries, fringe benefits, and so on—and spread total amounts over the activities according to the amount of time spent on each activity. At Dana, customer service employees spend nearly 25 percent of their time processing sales orders and only about 3 percent scheduling parts. Thus, 25 percent of the total cost ($144,846) goes to order processing, and 3 percent

activity-based costing (ABC)

A method of cost accounting designed to identify streams of activity and then to allocate costs across particular business processes according to the amount of time employees devote to particular activities.

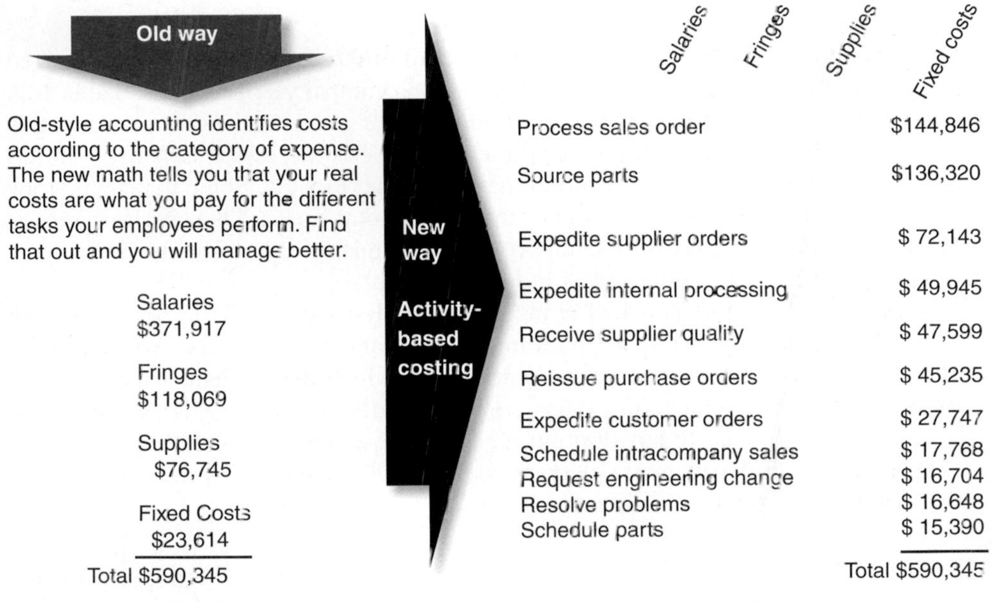

Old way

Old-style accounting identifies costs according to the category of expense. The new math tells you that your real costs are what you pay for the different tasks your employees perform. Find that out and you will manage better.

Salaries $371,917

Fringes $118,069

Supplies $76,745

Fixed Costs $23,614

Total $590,345

SOURCE: Courtesy Dana Corporation.

New way

Activity-based costing

	Salaries	Fringes	Supplies	Fixed costs
Process sales order				$144,846
Source parts				$136,320
Expedite supplier orders				$ 72,143
Expedite internal processing				$ 49,945
Receive supplier quality				$ 47,599
Reissue purchase orders				$ 45,235
Expedite customer orders				$ 27,747
Schedule intracompany sales				$ 17,768
Request engineering change				$ 16,704
Resolve problems				$ 16,648
Schedule parts				$ 15,390
Total				$590,345

FIGURE 16.2
How Dana Discovers What Its True Costs Are

($15,390) goes to scheduling parts. As can be seen in Figure 16.2, both the traditional and ABC systems reach the same bottom line. However, because the ABC method allocates costs across business processes, it provides a more accurate picture of how costs should be charged to products and services.[29]

This heightened accuracy can give managers a more realistic picture of how the organization is actually allocating its resources. It can highlight where wasted activities are occurring or whether activities cost too much relative to the benefits provided. Managers can then take action to correct the problem. For example, Dana's most expensive activity is sales-order processing. Its managers might try to find ways to lower that cost, freeing up resources for other tasks. By providing this type of information, ABC has become a valuable method for streamlining business processes.

Financial Controls

In addition to budgets, businesses commonly use other statements for financial control. Two financial statements that help control overall organizational performance are the balance sheet and the profit and loss statement.

The Balance Sheet   The **balance sheet** shows the financial picture of a company at a given time. This statement itemizes three elements: (1) assets, (2) liabilities, and (3) stockholders' equity. **Assets** are the values of the various items the corporation owns. **Liabilities** are the amounts the corporation owes to various creditors. **Stockholders' equity** is the amount accruing to the corporation's owners. The relationship among these three elements is as follows:

$$\text{Assets} = \text{Liabilities} + \text{Stockholders' equity}$$

Table 16.5 shows an example of a balance sheet. During the year, the company grew because it enlarged its building and acquired more machinery and equipment by means of long-term debt in the form of a first mortgage. Additional stock was sold to help finance the expansion. At the same time, accounts receivable were increased, and work in process was reduced. Observe that Total assets ($3,053,367) = Total liabilities ($677,204 + $618,600) + Stockholders' equity ($700,000 + $981,943 + $75,620).

Summarizing balance sheet items over a long period of time uncovers important trends and gives a manager further insight into overall performance and areas in which adjustments need to be made. For example, at some point, the company might decide that it would be prudent to slow down its expansion plans.

The Profit and Loss Statement   The **profit and loss statement** is an itemized financial statement of the income and expenses of a company's operations. Table 16.6 shows a comparative statement of profit and loss for two consecutive years. In this illustration, the operating revenue of the enterprise has increased. Expense also has increased, but at a lower rate, resulting in a higher net income. Some managers draw up tentative profit and loss statements and use them as goals. Then performance is measured against these goals or standards. From comparative statements of this type, a manager can identify trouble areas and correct them.

Controlling by profit and loss is most commonly used for the entire enterprise and, in the case of a diversified corporation, its divisions. However, if controlling is by departments, as in a decentralized organization in which department managers have control over both revenue and expense, a profit and loss statement is used for each department. Each department's output is measured, and a cost, including overhead, is charged to each department's operation. Expected net income is the standard for measuring a department's performance.

Financial Ratios   An effective approach for checking on the overall performance of an enterprise is to use key financial ratios. Ratios help indicate possible strengths

---

$ The bottom line
COST
Activity-based costing can highlight overspending.

balance sheet

A report that shows the financial picture of a company at a given time and itemizes assets, liabilities, and stockholders' equity.

assets

The values of the various items the corporation owns.

liabilities

The amounts a corporation owes to various creditors.

stockholders' equity

The amount accruing to the corporation's owners.

profit and loss statement

An itemized financial statement of the income and expenses of a company's operations.

Comparative Balance Sheet for the Years Ending December 31		
	This Year	**Last Year**
Assets		
Current assets:		
Cash	$161,870	$119,200
U.S. Treasury bills	250,400	30,760
Accounts receivable	825,595	458,762
Inventories:		
Work in process and finished products	429,250	770,800
Raw materials and supplies	251,340	231,010
Total current assets	1,918,455	1,610,532
Other assets:		
Land	157,570	155,250
Building	740,135	91,784
Machinery and equipment	172,688	63,673
Furniture and fixtures	132,494	57,110
Total other assets before depreciation	1,202,887	367,817
Less: Accumulated depreciation and amortization	67,975	63,786
Total other assets	1,134,912	304,031
Total assets	$3,053,367	$1,914,563
Liabilities and stockholders' equity		
Current liabilities:		
Accounts payable	$287,564	$441,685
Payrolls and withholdings from employees	44,055	49,580
Commissions and sundry accruals	83,260	41,362
Federal taxes on income	176,340	50,770
Current installment on long-term debt	85,985	38,624
Total current liabilities	667,204	622,021
Long-term liabilities:		
15-year, 9 percent loan, payable in each of the years 2002–2015	210,000	225,000
5 percent first mortgage	408,600	
Registered 9 percent notes payable		275,000
Total long-term liabilities	618,600	500,000
Stockholders' equity:		
Common stock: authorized 1,000,000 shares, outstanding last year 492,000 shares, outstanding this year 700,000 shares at $1 par value	700,000	492,000
Capital surplus	981,943	248,836
Earned surplus	75,620	51,706
Total stockholders' equity	1,757,563	792,542
Total liabilities and stockholders' equity	$3,053,367	$1,914,563

TABLE 16.5

A Comparative Balance Sheet

TABLE 16.6
A Comparative Statement
of Profit and Loss

Comparative Statement of Profit and Loss for the Years Ending June 30			
	This Year	Last Year	Increase or Decrease
Income:			
Net sales	$253,218	$257,636	$4,418*
Dividends from investments	480	430	50
Other	1,741	1,773	32
Total	255,439	259,839	4,400*
Deductions:			
Cost of goods sold	180,481	178,866	1,615
Selling and administrative expenses	39,218	34,019	5,199
Interest expense	2,483	2,604	121*
Other	1,941	1,139	802
Total	224,123	216,628	7,495
Income before taxes	31,316	43,211	11,895*
Provision for taxes	3,300	9,500	6,200*
Net income	$ 28,016	$ 33,711	$5,695*

*Decrease.

and weaknesses in a company's operations. Key ratios are calculated from selected items on the profit and loss statement and the balance sheet. We will briefly discuss three categories of financial ratios: liquidity, leverage, and profitability:

current ratio

A liquidity ratio that indicates the extent to which short-term assets can decline and still be adequate to pay short-term liabilities.

debt-equity ratio

A leverage ratio that indicates the company's ability to meet its long-term financial obligations.

return on investment (ROI)

A ratio of profit to capital used, or a rate of return from capital.

- *Liquidity ratios.* Liquidity ratios indicate a company's ability to pay short-term debts. The most common liquidity ratio is *current assets to current liabilities*, called the **current ratio** or *net working capital ratio*. This ratio indicates the extent to which current assets can decline and still be adequate to pay current liabilities. Some analysts set a ratio of 2 to 1, or 2.00, as the desirable minimum. For example, referring back to Table 16.5, the liquidity ratio there is about 2.86 ($1,918,455/$667,204). The company's current assets are more than capable of supporting its current liabilities.
- *Leverage ratios.* Leverage ratios show the relative amount of funds in the business supplied by creditors and shareholders. An important example is the **debt-equity ratio,** which indicates the company's ability to meet its long-term financial obligations. If this ratio is less than 1.5, the amount of debt is not considered excessive. In Table 16.5, the debt-equity ratio is only 0.35 ($618,600/$1,757,563). The company has financed its expansion almost entirely by issuing stock rather than by incurring significant long-term debt.
- *Profitability ratios.* Profitability ratios indicate management's ability to generate a financial return on sales or investment. For example, **return on investment (ROI)** is a ratio of profit to capital used, or a rate of return from capital (equity plus long-term debt). This ratio allows managers and shareholders to assess how well the firm is doing compared with other investments. For example, if the net income of the company in Table 16.5 were $300,000 this year, its return on capital would be 12.6 percent [$300,000/($1,757,563/$618,600)], normally a very reasonable rate of return.

Using Financial Ratios   Although ratios provide both performance standards and indicators of what has occurred, exclusive reliance on financial ratios can have negative consequences. Because ratios usually are expressed in compressed time horizons (monthly, quarterly, or yearly), they often cause **management myopia**—managers focus on short-term earnings and profits at the expense of their longer-term strategic obligations.[30] Control systems using long-term (e.g., three- to six-year) performance targets can reduce management myopia and focus attention further into the future.

A second negative outcome of ratios is that they relegate other important considerations to a secondary position. Research and development, management development, progressive human resource practices, and other considerations may receive insufficient attention. Therefore, the use of ratios should be supplemented with other control measures. Organizations can hold managers accountable for market share, number of patents granted, sales of new products, human resource development, and other performance indicators.

management myopia

Focusing on short-term earnings and profits at the expense of longer-term strategic obligations.

The Downside of Bureaucratic Control

So far you have learned about control from a mechanical viewpoint. But organizations are not strictly mechanical; they are composed of people. While control systems are used to constrain people's behavior and make their future behavior predictable, people are not machines that automatically fall into line as the designers of control systems intend. In fact, control systems can lead to dysfunctional behavior. A control system cannot be effective without consideration of how people will react to it. For effective control of employee behavior, managers should consider three types of potential responses to control: rigid bureaucratic behavior, tactical behavior, and resistance.[31]

Rigid Bureaucratic Behavior   Often people act in ways that will help them look good on the control system's measures. This tendency can be useful, because it focuses people on the behaviors management requires. But it can result in rigid, inflexible behavior geared toward doing *only* what the system requires. For example, in the earlier discussion of Six Sigma, we noted that that control process emphasizes efficiency over innovation. After 3M began using Six Sigma extensively, it slipped from its goal of having at least one-third of sales come from newly released products. When George Buckley took the CEO post, only one-fourth of sales were coming from new products, and Buckley began relying less extensively on efficiency controls. Buckley explained to a reporter, "Invention is by its very nature a disorderly process."[32] The control challenge, of course, is for 3M to be both efficient and creative.

Rigid bureaucratic behavior occurs when control systems prompt employees to stay out of trouble by following the rules. Unfortunately, such systems often lead to poor customer service and make the entire organization slow to act (recall the discussion of bureaucracy in Chapter 10). Some companies, including General Motors and UPS, enforce rules that employees must keep their desks neat. Of course, a chaotic workplace has its problems, but one survey found that people who said their desks were "very neat" spent more of their day looking for items than people who said their desks were "fairly messy."[33] By that measure, controlling neatness actually makes employees less efficient. Likewise, trying to control your own productivity by limiting phone calls and e-mail to certain times of day is beneficial only if you don't have the kind of job where ignoring the phone or e-mail causes you to annoy customers or miss important problems.

We have all been victimized at some time by rigid bureaucratic behavior. Reflect for a moment on this now classic story of a "nightmare" at a hospital:

At midnight, a patient with eye pains enters an emergency room at a hospital. At the reception area, he is classified as a nonemergency case and referred to the hospital's eye clinic. Trouble is, the eye clinic doesn't open until the next morning. When he arrives at the clinic, the nurse asks for his referral slip, but the emergency room doctor had forgotten to give it to him. The patient has to return to the emergency room and wait for another physician to screen him. The physician refers him back to the eye clinic and to a social worker to arrange payment. Finally, a third doctor looks into his eye, sees a small piece of metal, and removes it—a 30-second procedure.[34]

Stories such as these have, of course, given bureaucracy a bad name. Some managers will not even use the term *bureaucratic control* because of its potentially negative connotation. That is unfortunate because the control system itself is not the problem. The problems occur when the systems are no longer viewed as tools for running the business but instead as rules for dictating rigid behavior.

Tactical Behavior   Control systems will be ineffective if employees engage in tactics aimed at "beating the system." The most common type of tactical behavior is to manipulate information or report false performance data. People may produce two kinds of invalid data: about what *has* been done and about what *can* be done. False reporting about the past is less common, because it is easier to identify someone who misreports what happened than someone who gives an erroneous prediction or estimate of what might happen. Still, managers sometimes change their accounting systems to "smooth out" the numbers. Also, people may intentionally feed false information into a management information system to cover up errors or poor performance. Recently, several customs inspectors at Orlando Sanford International Airport said their supervisors had pressured them to speed up the processing of passengers by entering "generic" data instead of actually questioning the passengers. According to the inspectors, when the system flagged passengers for additional screening during busy periods, they were told to guess at the information, such as race and length of stay, rather than asking the passengers to provide the information. The justification for this behavior was that time pressure gave them no more than a minute to screen each passenger and keep the line moving, so that the public would be satisfied with their agency's work.[35]

More commonly, people falsify their predictions or requests for the future. When asked to give budgetary estimates, employees usually ask for larger amounts than they need. On the other hand, they sometimes submit unrealistically *low* estimates when they believe a low estimate will help them get a budget or a project approved. Budget-setting sessions can become tugs-of-war between subordinates trying to get slack in the budget and superiors attempting to minimize slack. Similar tactics are exhibited when managers negotiate unrealistically low performance standards so that subordinates will have little trouble meeting them; when salespeople project low forecasts so that they will look good by exceeding them; and when workers slow down the work pace while time-study analysts are setting work pace standards. In these and other cases, people are concerned only with their own performance figures rather than with the overall performance of their departments or companies.

Resistance to Control   Often people strongly resist control systems. They do so for several reasons. First, comprehensive control systems increase the accuracy of performance data and make employees more accountable for their actions. Control systems uncover mistakes, threaten people's job security and status, and decrease people's autonomy.

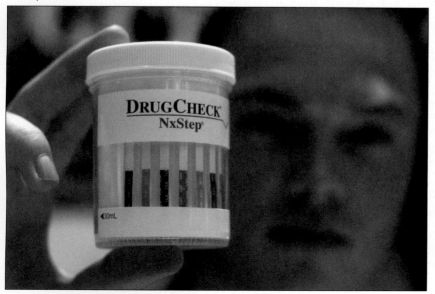

Drug testing is one of the ways organizations monitor employees. Some people favor the control measure but change their minds when personally asked to submit a urine specimen.

When Ford CEO Alan Mulally toured the automobile testing facility at product-rating organization Consumer Reports, he and two senior engineers received a lot of criticism from the Consumer Reports team about the inefficient design of the new Ford Edge crossover SUV. The Ford Edge doesn't have an electronic door opener like many of its rivals do. Although that doesn't sound like a major shortcoming, consider the shopper who arrives at the vehicle with arms full of groceries on a rainy day and has to drop all packages just to open the door or rear hatch. To that customer, it's a big deal. But as the engineers received this criticism, they began to become more and more defensive about their design. Mulally identified this behavior as one of his company's biggest problems—the tendency of employees to explain away mistakes instead of tackling them. "We seek to be understood more than we seek to understand," he commented.

Back at headquarters, Mulally examined the history of Ford compacts, where he learned that every time a Ford dealer sells a compact instead of a truck or SUV, the company loses $3,000. He was told that this is because Ford needed to sell a high number of these cars to reach the firm's corporate average fuel economy number. But Mulally wasn't satisfied with the answer. "Why haven't you figured out a way to make a profit [on these cars]?" he asked. The answer is that for years, Ford has accepted the inevitability of losing money. When executive chairman Bill Ford Jr. learned that the company still used letter grades to assess its performance—and that executives were content with Cs—he pantomimed aiming a gun at his head and replied, "We still do that?"[36]

Second, control systems can change expertise and power structures. For example, management information systems can make the costing, purchasing, and production decisions previously made by managers much quicker. Those individuals may fear a loss of expertise, power, and decision-making authority as a result.

Third, control systems can change the social structure of an organization. They can create competition and disrupt social groups and friendships. People may end up competing against those with whom they formerly had comfortable, cooperative relationships. Because people's social needs are so important, they will resist control systems that reduce social need satisfaction.

Fourth, control systems may be seen as an invasion of privacy, lead to lawsuits, and cause low morale.

Designing Effective Control Systems

LO 5

Effective control systems maximize potential benefits and minimize dysfunctional behaviors. To achieve this, management needs to design control systems that

1. Establish valid performance standards.
2. Provide adequate information to employees.
3. Ensure acceptablity to employees.
4. Maintain open communication.
5. Use multiple approaches.

Establish Valid Performance Standards   An effective control system must be based on valid and accurate performance standards. The most effective standards, as discussed earlier, tend to be expressed in quantitative terms; they are objective rather than subjective. Also, the measures should not be capable of being easily sabotaged or faked. Moreover, the system must incorporate all important aspects of performance. For example, a company that just focused on sales volume without also looking at profitability might soon go out of business. As you learned earlier, unmeasured behaviors are neglected. Often, performance standards for delivering training and other HR programs emphasize trainee satisfaction as reported on surveys. But the Philadelphia Department of Licenses and Inspections instead verified that its training actually

North American companies aren't just interested in the price and quality of their information technology; most companies also are creating "green" IT strategies that minimize energy consumption, an important financial consideration today. In a recent survey, 91 percent of companies rated energy efficiency in IT products as an important or very important standard—a value that shows up in IT budgets.[38]

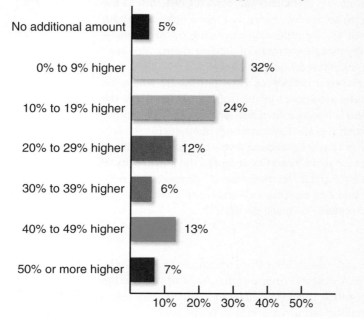

Higher price companies would be willing to pay for an equivalent IT product with greater energy efficiency

No additional amount	5%
0% to 9% higher	32%
10% to 19% higher	24%
20% to 29% higher	12%
30% to 39% higher	6%
40% to 49% higher	13%
50% or more higher	7%

10% 20% 30% 40% 50%

improved employee performance. The department was notorious for its long lines and rude workers, so it turned for help to the Philadelphia Ritz-Carlton Hotel—part of a chain known for its superb customer service. The hotel's area general manager provided training initially to 40 department workers in how to improve their service skills. As part of its posttraining measurement process, the department checked the wait times for license applicants, which dropped from 82 minutes to 14 minutes. The department is continuing its partnership program with Ritz-Carlton through additional employee training and attendance at each other's management meetings.[37]

But management also must defend against another problem: too many measures that create overcontrol and employee resistance. To make many controls tolerable, managers can devote attention to a few key areas while setting "satisfactory" performance standards in others. Or they can establish simple priorities. The purchasing agent may have to meet targets in the following sequence: quality, availability, cost, inventory level. Finally, managers can set tolerance ranges. For example, in financial budgeting optimistic, expected, and minimum levels sometimes are specified.`

Many companies' budgets set cost targets only. This causes managers to control spending but also to neglect earnings. At Emerson Electric, profit and growth are key measures. If an unanticipated opportunity to increase market share arises, managers can spend what they need to go after it. The phrase "it's not in the budget" is less likely to stifle people at Emerson than it is at most other companies.

This principle applies to nonfinancial aspects of performance as well. At many customer service call centers, control aims to maximize efficiency by focusing on the average amount of time each agent spends handling each phone call. But the business objectives of call centers should also include other measures such as cross-selling products or improving customer satisfaction and repeat business. Carlson Leisure Travel Services is one of a growing number of companies using new technology to analyze the content—not just the duration—of each call and capture information about the amount sold by call-center agents.[39]

Business consultant Michael Hammer summarizes these points in terms of what he calls seven "deadly sins" of performance measurement to avoid:[40]

1. *Vanity*—using measures that are sure to make managers and the organization look good. For example, a company might measure order fulfillment in terms of whether products are delivered by the latest date promised by the organization, rather than by the tougher and more meaningful measure of when the customers request to receive the products.

2. *Provincialism*—limiting measures to functional or departmental responsibilities, rather than the organization's overall objectives. If a company's transportation

department measures only shipping costs, it won't have an incentive to consider that shipping reliability (delivery on a given date) will affect performance at the company's stores or distribution centers.

3. *Narcissism*—measuring from the employee's, manager's, or company's point of view, rather than the customer's. For example, a maker of computer systems measured on-time shipping of each component; if 90 percent of the system's components arrived at the customer on time, it was 90 percent on time. But from the customer's point of view, the system wasn't on time at all, because the customer needed *all* the components to use the system.

4. *Laziness*—not expending the effort to analyze what is important to measure. An electric power company simply assumed customers cared about installation speed, but in fact, customers really cared more about receiving an accurate installation schedule.

5. *Pettiness*—measuring just one component of what affects business performance. An example would be clothing manufacturers that assume they should just consider manufacturing cost, rather than the overall costs of making exactly the right products available in stores when customers demand them.

6. *Inanity*—failing to consider the way standards will affect real-world human behavior and company performance. A fast-food restaurant targeted waste reduction and was surprised when restaurant managers began slowing down operations by directing their employees to hold off on cooking anything until orders were placed.

7. *Frivolity*—making excuses for poor performance rather than taking performance standards seriously. In some organizations, more effort goes to blaming others than to correcting problems.

According to Hammer, the basic correction to these "sins" is to carefully select standards that look at entire business processes, such as product development or order fulfillment, and identify which actions make those processes succeed. Then managers should measure performance against these standards precisely, accurately, and practically, making individuals responsible for their achievement and rewarding success.

Provide Adequate Information   Management must communicate to employees the importance and nature of the control system. Then people must receive feedback about their performance. Feedback motivates people and provides information that enables them to correct their own deviations from performance standards. Allowing people to initiate their own corrective action encourages self-control and reduces the need for outside supervision. *Open-book management*, described in Chapter 15, is a powerful use of this control principle.

Information should be as accessible as possible, particularly when people must make decisions quickly and frequently. For example, a national food company with its own truck fleet had a difficult problem. The company wanted drivers to go through customer sales records every night, insert new prices from headquarters every morning, and still make their rounds—an impossible set of demands. To solve this control problem, the company installed personal computers in more than 1,000 delivery trucks. Now drivers use their PCs for constant communication with headquarters. Each night drivers send information about the stores, and each morning headquarters sends prices and recommended stock mixes.

In general, a manager designing a control system should evaluate the information system in terms of the following questions:

1. Does it provide people with data relevant to the decisions they need to make?
2. Does it provide the right amount of information to decision makers throughout the organization?
3. Does it provide enough information to each part of the organization about how other, related parts of the organization are functioning?[41]

Ritz-Carlton sets performance measures for maintaining its impressive reputation and ensures that employees see how they contribute. The measures are based on the key factors behind the company's success: its mystique, employee engagement, customer engagement, product service excellence, community involvement, and financial performance. Financial performance is viewed as the result of achieving the other goals. For each success factor, cross-functional teams identify targets as detailed as the number of scuff marks on elevator doors or the percentage of satisfied employees at a location. The teams include frontline employees, so that early in the control process, employees already feel their input matters.

At each location, at the beginning of every shift, all employees gather for a meeting to discuss activities, issues, and Ritz-Carlton's business philosophy. They compare recent performance against the company's targets in each area. These conversations reinforce the key performance factors and help employees appreciate the importance of what they do.

Each business unit has up to three priorities to focus on, with each employee working to improve customer, employee, or financial results. Employees appreciate their role in giving each guest a special experience. When Joanne Hanna checked into a Ritz-Carlton after a grueling series of airport delays that caused her to miss several meetings, a hotel employee carried her bags and listened to her frustration. He suggested a spa visit or a masseuse, and when he learned she didn't have time, he brought her a scented candle—and had the information entered into Ritz-Carlton's database. Now, on every visit, Hanna finds a candle in her room, reminding her of one employee's empathy.[42]

Ensure Acceptability to Employees   Employees are less likely to resist a control system and exhibit dysfunctional behaviors if they accept the system. They are more likely to accept systems that have useful performance standards but are not overcontrolling. Employees also will find systems more acceptable if they believe the standards are possible to achieve.

The control system should emphasize positive behavior rather than focusing on controlling negative behavior alone. McBride Electric, an electrical contracting company, uses an electronic monitoring system called DriveCam to encourage its drivers to behave responsibly in terms of safety and fuel consumption. A DriveCam video monitor in each truck records activity inside and outside the cab; it saves that recording only if the truck is involved in a specified "trigger event" such as braking hard or swerving. Management explained the system to the drivers, emphasizing that it would help the company improve profits (a relevant message in a company that practices open-book management) and would protect the workers if they were ever accused falsely of unsafe practices. Not only did McBride immediately begin seeing improvements in safety and vehicle wear and tear, but it was also able to make good on its promise to defend employees. An anonymous phone caller complained that poor driving by a McBride driver had caused him to wreck his car. The McBride manager who took the call explained that he would be able to review a video taken from the truck that day—and the caller quickly hung up.[43] This approach exhibits the motivational quality of "procedural justice," described in Chapter 13. It gave employees the feeling that they were being evaluated by a fair process and was therefore more likely to be accepted by them.

One of the best ways to establish reasonable standards and thus gain employee acceptance of the control system is to set standards participatively. As we discussed in Chapter 4, participation in decision making secures people's understanding and cooperation and results in better decisions. Allowing employees to collaborate in control-system decisions that affect their jobs directly will help overcome resistance and foster acceptance of the system. In addition, employees on the "front line" are more likely to know which standards are most important and practical, and they can inform a manager's judgment on these issues. Finally, if standards are established in collaboration with employees, managers will more easily obtain cooperation on solving the problem when deviations from standards occur.

Maintain Open Communication   When deviations from standards occur, it is important that employees feel able to report the deviations so that the problem can be addressed. If employees come to feel that their managers want to hear only good news or, worse, if they fear reprisal for reporting bad news, even if it is not their fault, then any controls that are in place will be much less likely to be effective. Problems may go unreported or, even worse, may reach the point where they become much more expensive or difficult to solve. But if managers create an environment of openness and honesty, one in which employees feel comfortable sharing even negative information and are appreciated for doing so in a timely fashion, then the control system is much more likely to work effectively. In the "Management Close-Up: Taking Action" feature, for example, consider how communication comes into play in ensuring excellent service from the types of employees hired by Legal Sea Foods.

Nevertheless, managers may sometimes need to discipline employees who are failing to meet important standards. In such cases, an approach called *progressive discipline* is usually most effective. In this approach, clear standards are established, but failure to meet them is dealt with in a progressive or step-by-step process. For

> "I've learned that mistakes can often be as good a teacher as success."
> — Jack Welch, former CEO, General Electric

Management Close-Up   TAKING ACTION

Legal Sea Foods wins rave reviews from patrons, partly because of its dedication to high standards. The company views the use of control systems across all of its functions—supply chain, finance, information technology, and human resources—as the key to success.

In 2003 the company opened its $18 million Quality Control Center (QCC) in Boston, a 35,000-square-foot refrigerated space for testing and processing the 120 tons of fish and seafood that travel weekly through its doors. Legal Sea Foods buys seafood daily; every catch is tested for bacteria, and swordfish and tuna are tested for mercury as well. Not a government regulation, this testing is part of Legal Sea Foods' own quality protocols.

With fresh fish, turnaround time is critical. Once a catch is deemed forkworthy, it is packaged into vacuum-sealed portions. Product tested today at the QCC will ship the following day by truck or air to restaurants up and down the Eastern Seaboard.

The quality story extends to hiring the right people and helping them grow. Believing the best dining experience comes when waitstaff connect with customers on an "emotional" level, Legal Sea Foods uses an assessment tool to gauge how well a candidate can create such moments with guests. A weeklong orientation for new hires begins with presentations on the company's history, culture, and values and continues with interactive training. Hourly workers have a "learning coach" who mentors them and helps them develop new skills. Computer classes, instruction on seafood, and other learning opportunities are available on an ongoing basis to ensure that the staff understand Legal Sea Foods standards and can carry them out.[44]

- Legal Sea Foods CEO Roger Berkowitz regularly meets with waitstaff in his restaurants. How can the input of employees on the front line change operational protocols?
- Berkowitz says a good leader must think four to five years in the future. How could such thinking impact an organization's operational controls?

example, the first time an employee's sales performance has been worse than it should have been, the supervising manager may offer verbal counseling or coaching. If problems persist, the next step might be a written reprimand. This type of reasonable and considered approach signals to all employees that the manager is interested in improving their performance, not in punishing them.

Use Multiple Approaches   Multiple controls are necessary. For example, banks need controls on risk so that they don't lose a lot of money from defaulting borrowers, as well as profit controls including sales budgets that aim for growth in accounts and customers.

As you learned earlier in this chapter, control systems generally should include both financial and nonfinancial performance targets and incorporate aspects of preliminary, concurrent, and feedback control. In recent years, a growing number of companies have combined targets for managers into a **balanced scorecard,** a combination of four sets of performance measures: (1) financial, (2) customer satisfaction, (3) business processes (quality and efficiency), and (4) learning and growth.[45] The goal is generally to broaden management's horizon beyond short-term financial results so that the company's long-term success is more likely. For example, Hyde Park Electronics had been using a variety of financial controls when it adopted a business scorecard that added metrics such as on-time delivery, employee satisfaction, and sales impact of marketing activities. Profits under the balanced scorecard reached record levels.[46] The balanced scorecard also is adaptable to nonprofit settings. Ocean-Monmouth Legal Services, which provides legal services to poor people in New Jersey, uses a balanced scorecard to track progress in meeting strategic, operational, financial, and client satisfaction goals. The organization's executive director, Harold E. Creacy, credits the approach with helping to cope with the rising costs and tight resources that so often plague nonprofits.[47]

Effective control will also require managers and organizations to use many of the other techniques and practices of good management. For example, compensation systems will grant rewards for meeting standards and impose consequences if they are not met. And to gain employee acceptance, managers may also rely on many of the other communication and motivational tools that we discussed in earlier chapters, such as persuasion and positive reinforcement.

balanced scorecard

Control system combining four sets of performance measures: financial, customer, business process, and learning and growth.

The Other Controls: Markets and Clans

Although the concept of control has always been a central feature of organizations, the principles and philosophies underlying its use are changing. In the past, control was focused almost exclusively on bureaucratic (and market) mechanisms. Generations of managers were taught that they could maximize productivity by regulating what employees did on the job—through standard operating procedures, rules, regulations, and close supervision. To increase output on an assembly line, for example, managers in the past tried to identify the "one best way" to approach the work and then to monitor employees' activities to make certain that they followed standard operating procedures. In short, they controlled work by dividing and simplifying tasks, a process we referred to in Chapter 1 as *scientific management.*

Although formal bureaucratic control systems are perhaps the most pervasive in organizations (and the most talked about in management textbooks), they are not always the most effective. *Market controls* and *clan controls* may both represent more flexible, though no less potent, approaches to regulating performance.

LO 6   Market Control

In contrast to bureaucratic controls, market controls involve the use of economic forces—and the pricing mechanisms that accompany them—to regulate performance.

The system works like this: in cases where output from an individual, department, or business unit has value to other people, a price can be negotiated for its exchange. As a market for these transactions becomes established, two effects occur:

- Price becomes an indicator of the value of the good or service.
- Price competition has the effect of controlling productivity and performance.

The basic principles that underlie market controls can operate at the corporate level, the business unit (or department) level, and the individual level. Figure 16.3 shows a few different ways in which market controls are used in an organization.

Market Controls at the Corporate Level   In large, diversified companies, market controls often are used to regulate independent business units. Particularly in large conglomerate firms that act as holding companies, business units typically are treated as profit centers that compete with one another. Top executives may place very few bureaucratic controls on business unit managers but use profit and loss data for evaluating performance. While decision making and power are decentralized to the business units, market controls ensure that business unit performance is in line with corporate objectives.

Use of market control mechanisms in this way has been criticized by those who insist that economic measures do not reflect the complete value of an organization adequately. Employees often suffer as diversified companies are repeatedly bought and sold based on market controls.

Market Controls at the Business Unit Level   Market control also can be used within business units to regulate exchanges among departments and functions. Transfer pricing is one method that organizations use to try to reflect market forces for internal transactions. A **transfer price** is the charge by one unit in the organization for a good or service that it supplies to another unit of the same organization. For example, in automobile manufacturing, a transfer price may be affixed to components

The bottom line

$ COST

Market controls help maintain low prices.

transfer price

Price charged by one unit for a good or service provided to another unit within the organization.

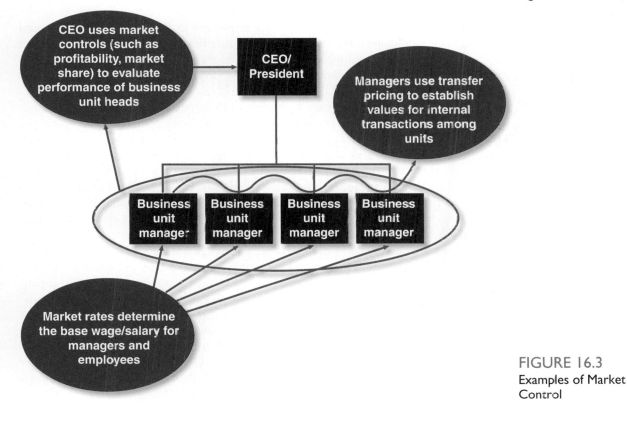

FIGURE 16.3
Examples of Market Control

As much as it would seem that market controls play a significant role in the salary of a professional baseball player or any other professional athlete, are the sometimes ridiculously high salaries that are paid for players today truly indicative of a player's skill—or something else? If the player doesn't live up to the expectation of the previously perceived skill level or, put another way, has a "bad year," should the organization be allowed to cut his pay?

and subassemblies before they are shipped to subsequent business units for final assembly. Ideally, the transfer price reflects the price that the receiving business unit would have to pay for that product or service in the marketplace.

As organizations have more options to outsource goods and services to external partners, market controls such as transfer prices provide natural incentives to keep costs down and quality up. Managers stay in close touch with prices in the marketplace to make sure their own costs are in line, and they try to improve the service they provide to increase their department's value to the organization. Consider the situation in which training and development activities can be done internally by the human resources department or outsourced to a consulting firm. If the human resources department cannot supply quality training at a reasonable price, there may be no reason for that department to exist inside the firm. Similarly, Penske Truck Leasing Company began outsourcing many of its finance processes to a company called Genpact, not only for lower prices but also for the expertise developed by that specialized firm to compete in the marketplace. Penske's senior vice president of finance, Frank Cocuzza, says the department spends $20 million less per year than it did to perform the same functions in-house while it has improved its rate of collections and learned thousands of ways to make his own operation more efficient, modeled after Genpact's lean practices.[48]

Market Controls at the Individual Level   Market controls also are used at the individual level. For example, in situations where organizations are trying to hire employees, the supply and demand for particular skills influence the wages employees can expect to receive and the rate organizations are likely to pay. Employees or job candidates who have more valuable skills tend to be paid a higher wage. Of course, wages don't always reflect market rates—sometimes they are based (perhaps arbitrarily) on internal resource considerations—but the market rate is often the best indicator of an employee's potential worth to a firm.

Market-based controls such as these are important in that they provide a natural incentive for employees to enhance their skills and offer them to potential firms. Even after individuals gain employment, market-based wages are important as controls in that persons with higher economic value may be promoted faster to higher positions in the organization.

Market controls often are used by boards of directors to manage CEOs of major corporations. Ironically, CEOs usually are seen as the ones controlling everyone else in the company, but the fact is that the CEO is accountable to the board of directors, and the board must devise ways to ensure that the CEO acts in its interest. Absent board control, CEOs may act in ways that make them look good personally (such as making the company bigger or more diversified) but that do not lead to higher profits for the firm. And as recent corporate scandals have shown, without board control CEOs may also artificially inflate the firm's earnings, or not fully declare expenses, making the firm look much more successful than it really is.

Traditionally, boards have tried to control CEO performance mainly through the use of incentive plans, in addition to base salary. These typically include some type of bonus tied to short-term profit targets. In large U.S. companies, most CEO compensation is now at risk, meaning it depends mainly on the performance of the company. In addition to short-term incentives, boards use some type of long-term incentives linked to the firm's share price, usually through stock options, which we discussed in Chapter 10. Also, balanced scorecards are intended to keep CEOs focused on the company's longer-term health. And under the Sarbanes-Oxley Act, described in Chapter 5, board members are expected to exercise careful control over the company's financial performance, including oversight of the CEO's compensation package.

Clan Control: The Role of Empowerment and Culture

Increasingly, managers are discovering that control systems based solely on bureaucratic and market mechanisms are insufficient for directing today's workforce. There are several reasons for this:

- *Employees' jobs have changed.* The nature of work is evolving. Employees working with computers, for example, have more variability in their jobs, and much of their work is intellectual and therefore invisible. Because of this, there is no one best way to perform a task, and programming or standardizing jobs becomes extremely difficult. Close supervision is also unrealistic, because it is nearly impossible to supervise activities such as reasoning and problem solving.
- *The nature of management has changed.* The role of managers is evolving, too. Managers used to know more about the job than employees did. Today, it is typical for employees to know more about their jobs than anyone else does. We refer to this as the shift from touch labor to knowledge work. When real expertise in organizations exists at the very lowest levels, hierarchical control becomes impractical.[49]
- *The employment relationship has changed.* The social contract at work is being renegotiated. It used to be that employees were most concerned about issues such as pay, job security, and the hours of work. Today, however, more and more employees want to be more fully engaged in their work, taking part in decision making, devising solutions to unique problems, and receiving assignments that are challenging and involving. They want to use their brains.

For these three reasons, the concept of *empowerment* not only has become more popular in organizations but has become a necessary aspect of a manager's repertoire of control. With no "one best way" to approach a job and no way to scrutinize what employees do every day, managers must empower employees to make

> "As a manager the important thing is not what happens when you are there, but what happens when you are not there."
>
> —Ken Blanchard

decisions and trust that they will act in the best interests of the firm. But this does not mean giving up control. It means creating a strong culture of high standards and integrity so that employees will exercise effective control on their own.

Recall our extensive discussion of organization culture in Chapter 2. If the organization's culture encourages the wrong behaviors, then an effort to impose effective controls will be severely hindered. But if managers create and reinforce a strong culture that encourages correct behavior, one in which everyone understands management's values and expectations and is motivated to act in accordance with them, then clan control can be a very effective control tool.[50] As we noted at the beginning of this chapter, *clan control* involves creating relationships built on mutual respect and encouraging each individual to take responsibility for his or her actions. Employees work within a guiding framework of values, and they are expected to use good judgment. For example, at NetApp, an IT company specializing in data storage and protection, a commitment to employee empowerment prompted the switch from a 12-page travel policy to some simple guidelines for employees who need to go on a business trip: "We are a frugal company. But don't show up dog-tired to save a few bucks. Use your common sense."[51] The emphasis in an empowered organization is on satisfying customers, not on pleasing the boss. Mistakes are tolerated as the unavoidable by-product of dealing with change and uncertainty and are viewed as opportunities to learn. And team members learn together. Table 16.7 provides a set of guidelines for managing in an empowered world.

The resiliency and time investment of clan control are a double-edged sword. Clan control takes a long time to develop and an even longer time to change. This gives an organization stability and direction during periods of upheaval in the environment or

Clan control empowers employees to meet performance standards.

TABLE 16.7

Management Control in an Empowered Setting

1. **Put control where the operation is.** Layers of hierarchy, close supervision, and checks and balances are quickly disappearing and being replaced with self-guided teams. For centuries even the British Empire—as large as it was—never had more than six levels of management including the Queen.
2. **Use "real time" rather than after-the-fact controls.** Issues and problems must be solved at the source by the people doing the actual work. Managers become a resource to help out the team.
3. **Rebuild the assumptions underlying management control to build on trust rather than distrust.** Today's "high-flex" organizations are based on empowerment, not obedience. Information must facilitate decision making, not police it.
4. **Move to control based on peer norms.** Clan control is a powerful thing. Workers in Japan, for example, have been known to commit suicide rather than disappoint or lose face within their team. Although this is extreme, it underlines the power of peer influence. The Japanese have a far more homogeneous culture and set of values than we do. In North America, we must build peer norms systematically and put much less emphasis on managing by the numbers.
5. **Rebuild the incentive systems to reinforce responsiveness and teamwork.** The twin goals of adding value to the customer and team performance must become the dominant raison d'être of the measurement systems.

SOURCE: Gerald H. B. Ross, "Revolution in Management Control," *Management Accounting*, November 1990, pp. 23–27. Reprinted by permission.

the organization (e.g., during changes in the top management). Yet if managers want to establish a new culture—a new form of clan control—they must help employees unlearn the old values and embrace the new. We will talk about this transition process more in the final chapter of this book.

Management Close-Up

ASSESSING OUTCOMES AND SEIZING OPPORTUNITIES

By establishing and following precise managerial controls, Legal Sea Foods has achieved consistency in its operations. Many of its operational controls have become industry standards. For example, the company worked with the Department of Commerce to develop criteria to protect against foodborne illness. That program—the Hazard Analysis Critical Control Point program—has served as the industry standard since 1997 and is still used by the U.S. Food and Drug Administration today. Legal Sea Foods' practice of sending its seafood vendors quality reports and copying the Massachusetts Department of Public Health motivates vendors to perform at the highest standards while keeping the government in the loop.

Years before the anti–trans fat campaign was fashionable, Legal Sea Foods president and CEO Roger Berkowitz launched a crusade of his own, to remove trans fats from the restaurant's menu. The company has also partnered with the Harvard School of Public Health to monitor research findings on seafood nutrition.

Legal Sea Foods was among the first in its industry to identify the need to preserve the environment and focus on sustainable seafood sources. Years ago it began recycling its vegetable oil into biodiesel fuels to conserve energy. Berkowitz regularly visits the Gloucester fish auctions, maintaining contact with fishermen who bring in the catch. He recognizes the importance of protecting fishing stocks but also sees firsthand where federal regulations threaten to become onerous for the fishing industry. He serves as a vocal industry advocate with members of Congress.[52]

- Legal Sea Foods' CEO Roger Berkowitz has this comment about quality: "Anybody can be good once in a while, but very few people can be good all the time." How do you think this perspective affects the control processes in place at Legal Sea Foods?

- Legal Sea Foods' management thinks of it as a seafood company in the restaurant business—not a restaurant group that sells seafood. How does this distinction drive the type of managerial controls the company imposes?

KEY TERMS

Accounting audits,   p. 563

Activity-based costing (ABC),   p. 563

Assets,   p. 564

Balanced scorecard,   p. 574

Balance sheet,   p. 564

Budgeting,   p. 559

Bureaucratic control,   p. 551

Clan control,   p. 551

Concurrent control,   p. 555

Control,   p. 550

Current ratio,   p. 566

Debt-equity ratio,   p. 566

External audit,   p. 559

Feedback control,   p. 555

Feedforward control,   p. 555

Internal audit,   p. 559

Liabilities,   p. 564

Management audit,   p. 559

Management myopia,   p. 567

Market control,   p. 551

Principle of exception,   p. 554

Profit and loss statement,   p. 564

Return on investment (ROI),   p. 566

Standard,   p. 552

Stockholders' equity,   p. 564

Transfer price,   p. 575

SUMMARY OF LEARNING OBJECTIVES

Now that you have studied Chapter 16, you should be able to:

LO 1 Explain why companies develop control systems for employees.

Left to their own devices, employees may act in ways that do not benefit the organization. Control systems are designed to eliminate idiosyncratic behavior and keep employees directed toward achieving the goals of the firm. Control systems are a steering mechanism for guiding resources, for helping each individual act on behalf of the organization.

LO 2 Summarize how to design a basic bureaucratic control system.

The design of a basic control system involves four steps: (1) setting performance standards, (2) measuring performance, (3) comparing performance with the standards, and (4) eliminating unfavorable deviations by taking corrective action. Performance standards should be valid and should cover issues such as quantity, quality, time, and cost. Once performance is compared with the standards, the principle of exception suggests that the manager needs to direct attention to the exceptional cases that have significant deviations. Then the manager takes the action most likely to solve the problem.

LO 3 Describe the purposes for using budgets as a control device.

Budgets combine the benefits of feedforward, concurrent, and feedback controls. They are used as an initial guide for allocating resources, a reference point for using funds, and a feedback mechanism for comparing actual levels of sales and expenses with their expected levels. Recently, companies have modified their budgeting processes to allocate costs over basic processes (such as customer service) rather than to functions or departments. By changing the way they prepare budgets, many companies have discovered ways to eliminate waste and improve business processes.

LO 4 Define basic types of financial statements and financial ratios used as controls.

The basic financial statements are the balance sheet and the profit and loss statement. The balance sheet compares the value of company assets to the obligations the company owes to owners and creditors. The profit and loss statement shows company income relative to costs incurred. In addition to these statements, companies look at liquidity ratios (whether the company can pay its short-term debts), leverage ratios (the extent to which the company is funding operations by going into debt), and profitability ratios (profit relative to investment). These ratios provide a goal for managers as well as a standard against which to evaluate performance.

LO 5 List procedures for implementing effective control systems.

To maximize the effectiveness of controls, managers should (1) establish valid performance standards, (2) provide adequate information to employees, (3) ensure acceptability, (4) maintain open communication, and (5) see that multiple approaches are used (such as bureaucratic, market, and clan control).

LO 6 Identify ways in which organizations use market control mechanisms.

Market controls can be used at the level of the corporation, the business unit or department, or the individual. At the corporate level, business units are evaluated against one another based on profitability. At times, less profitable businesses are sold while more profitable businesses receive more resources. Within business units, transfer pricing may be used to approximate market mechanisms to control transactions among departments. At the individual level, market mechanisms control the wage rate of employees and can be used to evaluate the performance of individual managers.

LO 7 Discuss the use of clan control in an empowered organization.

Approaching control from a centralized, mechanistic viewpoint is increasingly impractical. In today's organizations, it is difficult to program "one best way" to approach work, and it is often difficult to monitor performance. To be responsive to customers, companies must harness the expertise of employees and give them the freedom to act on their own initiative. To maintain control while empowering employees, companies should (1) use self-guided teams, (2) allow decision making at the source of the problems, (3) build trust and mutual respect, (4) base control on a guiding framework of norms, and (5) use incentive systems that encourage teamwork.

DISCUSSION QUESTIONS

1. What controls can you identify in the management of your school or at a company where you now work (or recently worked)? If you can, interview a manager or employee of the organization to learn more about the controls in use there. How might the organization's performance change if those controls were not in place?

2. How are leadership and control different? How are planning and control different? How are structure and control different?

3. Imagine you are the sales manager of a company that sells medical supplies to hospitals nationwide. You have 10 salespeople reporting to you. You are responsible for your department achieving a certain level of sales each year. In general terms, how might you go about taking each step in the control cycle?

4. In the situation described in Question 3, what actions would you need to take if sales fell far below the budgeted level? What, if any, actions would you need to take if sales far exceeded the sales budget? If sales are right on target, does effective controlling require any response from you? (Would your answer differ if the department were on target overall, but some salespeople fell short and others exceeded their targets?)

5. Besides sales and expenses, identify five other important control measures for a business. Include at least one nonfinancial measure.

6. What are the pros and cons of bureaucratic controls such as rules, procedures, and supervision?

7. Suppose a company at which executives were rewarded for meeting targets based only on profits and stock price switches to a balanced scorecard that adds measures for customer satisfaction, employee engagement, employee diversity, and ethical conduct. How, if at all, would you expect executives' performance to change in response to the new control system? How, if at all, would you expect the company's performance to change?

8. Google has recently begun offering Google Apps, such as Gmail, Google Calendar, and Docs & Spreadsheets, as collaboration tools for employees. Describe how the company could use market controls to determine whether Google employees will use these software programs or competing software (e.g., Word and Excel).

9. How effective is clan control as a control mechanism? What are its strengths? Its limitations? When would a manager rely on clan control the most?

10. Does empowerment imply the loss of control? Why or why not?

11. Some people use the concept of "personal control" to describe the application of business control principles to individual careers. Thinking about your school performance and career plans, which steps of the control process (Figure 16.1) have you been applying effectively? How do you keep track of your performance in meeting your career and life goals? How do you measure your success? Does clan control help you meet your personal objectives?

CONCLUDING CASE

The Grizzly Bear Lodge

Diane and Rudy Conrad own a small lodge outside Yellowstone National Park. Their lodge has 15 rooms that can accommodate up to 40 guests, with some rooms set up for families. Diane and Rudy serve a continental breakfast on weekdays and a full breakfast on weekends, included in the room rates they charge. Their busy season runs from May through September, but they remain open until Thanksgiving and reopen in April for a short spring season. They currently employ one cook and two waitpersons for the breakfasts on weekends, handling the other breakfasts themselves. They also have several housekeeping staff members, a groundskeeper, and a front-desk employee. The Conrads take pride in the efficiency of their operation, including the loyalty of their employees, which they attribute to their own form of clan control. If a guest needs something—whether it's a breakfast catered to a special diet or an extra set of towels—Grizzly Bear workers are empowered to supply it.

The Conrads are considering expanding their business. They have been offered the opportunity to buy the property next door, which would give them the space to build an annex containing an additional 20 rooms. Currently, their annual sales total $300,000. With expenses running at $230,000—including mortgage, payroll, maintenance, and so forth—the Conrads' annual income is $70,000. They want to expand and make improvements without cutting back on the personal service they offer to their guests. In fact, in addition to hiring more staff to handle the larger facility, they are considering collaborating with more local businesses to offer guided rafting, fishing, hiking, and horseback riding trips. They also want to expand their food service to include dinner during the high season, which means renovating the restaurant area of the lodge and hiring more kitchen and wait staff. Ultimately, the Conrads would like the lodge to be open year-round, offering guests opportunities to cross-country ski, ride snowmobiles, or hike in the winter. They hope to offer holiday packages for Thanksgiving, Christmas, and New Year's celebrations in the great outdoors. The Conrads report that their employees are enthusiastic about their plans and want to stay with them through the expansion process. "This is our dream business," says Rudy. "We're only at the beginning."

QUESTIONS

1. Discuss how Rudy and Diane can use feedforward, concurrent, and feedback controls both now and in the future at the Grizzly Bear Lodge to ensure their guests' satisfaction.

2. What might be some of the fundamental budgetary considerations the Conrads would have as they plan the expansion of their lodge?

3. Describe how the Conrads could use market controls to plan and implement their expansion.

EXPERIENTIAL EXERCISES

16.1 Safety Program

OBJECTIVE

To understand some of the specific activities that fall under the management functions *planning, organizing, controlling and staffing,* and *directing.*

INSTRUCTIONS

After reading the following case, briefly describe the kinds of steps you would take as production manager in trying to solve your safety problem. Be sure to relate your answer specifically to the activities of *planning, organizing, controlling and staffing,* and *directing.*

MANAGING THE VAMP CO. SAFETY PROGRAM

If there are specific things that a manager does, how are they done? What does it "look like" when one manages? The following describes a typical situation in which a manager performs managerial functions:

As production manager of the Vamp Stamping Company, you've become quite concerned over the metal stamping shop's safety record. Accidents that resulted in operators' missing time on the job have increased quite rapidly in the past year. These more serious accidents have jumped from 3 percent of all accidents reported to a current level of 10 percent.

Because you're concerned about your workers' safety as well as the company's ability to meet its customers' orders, you want to reduce this downtime accident rate to its previous level or lower within the next six months.

You call the accident trend to the attention of your production supervisors, pointing out the seriousness of the situation and their continuing responsibility to enforce the gloves and safety goggles rules. Effective immediately, every supervisor will review his or her accident reports for the past year, file a report summarizing these accidents with you, and state their intended actions to correct recurring causes of the accidents. They will make out weekly safety reports as well as meet with you every Friday to discuss what is being done and any problems they are running into.

You request the union steward's cooperation in helping the safety supervisor set up a short program on shop safety practices.

Because the machine operators are having the accidents, you encourage your supervisors to talk to their workers and find out what they think can be done to reduce the downtime accident rate to its previous level.

While the program is going on, you review the weekly reports, looking for patterns that will tell you how effective the program is and where the trouble spots are. If a supervisor's operators are not decreasing their accident rate, you discuss the matter in considerable detail with the supervisor and his or her key workers.

SOURCE: From Theodore T. Herbert, *The New Management: Study Guide,* 4th ed., p. 41. Copyright © 1983 Pearson Education. Reprinted by permission of Pearson Education, Inc., Upper Saddle River, NJ.

16.2 Preliminary, Concurrent, and Feedback Control

OBJECTIVES

1. To demonstrate the need for control procedures.

2. To gain experience in determining when to use preliminary, concurrent, and feedback controls.

INSTRUCTIONS

1. Read the text materials on preliminary, concurrent, and feedback control.

2. Read the Control Problem Situation and be prepared to resolve those control problems in a group setting.

3. Your instructor will divide the class into small groups. Each group completes the Preliminary, Concurrent, and Feedback

Control Worksheet by achieving consensus on the types of control that should be applied in each situation. The group also develops responses to the discussion questions.

4. After the class reconvenes, group spokespersons present group findings.

DISCUSSION QUESTIONS

1. For which control(s) was it easier to determine application? For which was it harder?

2. Would this exercise be better assigned to groups or to individuals?

CONTROL PROBLEM SITUATION

Your management consulting team has just been hired by Technocron International, a rapidly growing producer of electronic surveillance devices that are sold to commercial and government end users. Some sales are made through direct selling, and some through industrial resellers. Direct-sale profits are being hurt by what seem to be exorbitant expenses paid to a few of the salespeople, especially those who fly all over the world in patterns that suggest little planning and control. There is trouble among the resellers because standard contracts have not been established and each reseller has an entirely different contractual relationship. Repayment schedules vary widely from customer to customer. Also, profits are reduced by the need to customize most orders, making mass production almost impossible. However, no effort has been made to create interchangeable components. There are also tremendous inventory problems. Some raw materials and parts are bought in such small quantities that new orders are being placed almost daily. Other orders are so large that there is hardly room to store everything. Many of these purchased components are later found to be defective and unusable, causing production delays. Engineering changes

are made that make large numbers of old components still in storage obsolete. Some delays result from designs that are very difficult to assemble, and assemblers complain that their corrective suggestions are ignored by engineering. To save money, untrained workers are hired and assigned to experienced "worker-buddies" who are expected to train them on the job. However, many of the new people are too poorly educated to understand their assignments, and their worker-buddies wind up doing a great deal of their work. This, along with the low pay and lack of consideration from engineering, is causing a great deal of worker unrest and talk of forming a union. Last week alone nine new worker grievances were filed, and the U.S. Equal Employment Opportunity Commission has just announced intentions to investigate two charges of discrimination on the part of the company. There is also a serious cash-flow problem, as a number of long-term debts are coming due at the same time. The cash-flow problem could be relieved somewhat if some of the accounts payable could be collected.

The CEO manages corporate matters through five functional divisions: operations, engineering, marketing, finance, and human resources management and general administration.

Preliminary, Concurrent, and Feedback Control Worksheet

Technocron International is in need of a variety of controls. Complete the following matrix by noting the preliminary, concurrent, and feedback controls that are needed in each of the five functional divisions.

Divisions	Preliminary Controls	Concurrent Controls	Feedback Controls
HRM and general administration			
Operations	_____	_____	_____
Engineering	_____	_____	_____
Marketing	_____	_____	_____
Finance	_____	_____	_____

Managing Technology and Innovation

> *The imperatives of technology and organization, not the images of ideology, are what determine the shape of economic society.*
>
> —John Kenneth Galbraith

LEARNING OBJECTIVES

After studying Chapter 17, you will be able to:

LO 1 List the types of processes that spur development of new technologies. p. 586

LO 2 Describe how technologies proceed through a life cycle. p. 587

LO 3 Discuss ways to manage technology for competitive advantage. p. 589

LO 4 Summarize how to assess technology needs. p. 594

LO 5 Identify alternative methods of pursuing technological innovation. p. 596

LO 6 Define key roles in managing technology. p. 604

LO 7 Describe the elements of an innovative organization. p. 605

LO 8 List characteristics of successful development projects. p. 608

CHAPTER OUTLINE

Management Close-Up

CAN TAKANOBU ITO EXTEND HONDA'S INNOVATION WINNING STREAK?

Although the name "Honda" may have originated in Japan, after a half-century in North America, it has become a household word for American consumers. When you think "Honda," think "engine." Producing high-quality motorized products is Honda's special expertise. Not only does the company market scooters, motorcycles, and automobiles, but it also produces everything from lawn mowers, snow blowers, and tillers to all-terrain vehicles, outboard motors, and even light jets.

Honda first established a presence in the United States in 1959 and during the 1970s began to invest heavily to construct U.S. manufacturing sites. At the time, among foreign automakers, only Volkswagen made cars in U.S. factories. With the opening of its first assembly plant in 1979, Honda became the first Japanese automaker to build motor vehicles in the United States. Today, Honda facilities are nationwide, with a U.S. workforce numbering nearly 27,000.

{ Through its commitment to research and development, management at Honda says it sees the world "not as it is, but as it could be." As you read this chapter, consider how this commitment to innovation has helped Honda capture market share and build a loyal following. }

During the 1990s, Honda poured $400 million into its three Ohio-based assembly plants to create a streamlined, flexible production process. The flexible system enables Honda to switch from making one model to another in a matter of minutes—a procedure that takes its competitors weeks, even months, and millions of dollars.

At the center of Honda's redesigned manufacturing system is ASIMO, a two-legged robot the company developed to work alongside—and sometimes with—its human counterparts. The only humanoid robot that can walk and climb stairs, ASIMO even recharges itself.

Amid a global economic downturn that brought the auto industry to its knees, Honda's $400 million "gamble" is paying off. With its two strongest competitors, Toyota and Nissan, projecting a year in the red and other carmakers filing for bankruptcy, Honda's focus on innovation through technology has not only given it a significant competitive edge but helped the company remain profitable.[1]

Technological innovation is daunting in its complexity and pace of change. And as Honda's leadership has figured out, it is vital for a firm's competitive advantage. Not long ago, new products took years to plan and develop, were standardized and mass produced, and were pushed onto the market through extensive selling and promotional campaigns. With sales lives for these products measured in decades, production processes used equipment dedicated to making only those standardized products and achieved savings through economies of scale. But today's customers often demand products that have yet to be designed. Product development is now a race to become the first to introduce innovative products—products whose lives often are measured in months as they are quickly replaced by other, even more technologically sophisticated products.

Today's managers and organizations depend on effective management of technology not only to carry out their basic tasks but, even more important, to ensure the continuing competitiveness of their goods or services. In a marketplace where technology and rapid innovation are critical for success, managers must understand how technologies emerge, develop, and change the ways organizations compete and the ways people work. This chapter discusses how technology can affect an organization's competitiveness and how to integrate technology into the organization's competitive strategy. Then we assess the technological needs of the organization and the means by which these needs can be met.

🔆 **The bottom line**

Innovation

Innovation is a key to competitiveness.

Technology and Innovation

LO 1

technology

The systematic application of scientific knowledge to a new product, process, or service.

innovation

A change in method or technology; a positive, useful departure from previous ways of doing things.

In Chapter 9, we defined **technology** as the methods, processes, systems, and skills used to transform resources into products. More broadly speaking, we can think of technology as the commercialization of science: the systematic application of scientific knowledge to a new product, process, or service. In this sense, technology is embedded in every product, service, and procedure used or produced.[2]

If we find a better product, process, or procedure to accomplish our task, we have an innovation. **Innovation** is a change in method or technology—a positive, useful departure from previous ways of doing things. Two fundamental types of innovation are process and product innovation. *Process innovations* are changes that affect the way outputs are produced. In Chapter 9 we discussed flexible manufacturing practices such as just-in-time, mass customization, and simultaneous engineering. Each of these innovations has changed the way products are manufactured and distributed. In contrast, *product innovations* are changes in the actual outputs (goods and services) themselves.[3] These two categories cover a multitude of creative new ideas, which in businesses can involve changes in product offerings, the basic "platforms" or common features and processes that underlie product creation, the customer problems the organization can solve, the types of customers the organization serves, the nature of the experience provided by the organization, the way the organization earns money from what it does, the efficiency and effectiveness of its processes, the structure of the organization, the supply chain through which it delivers goods and services, the physical or virtual points at which it interacts with customers, the ways the organization communicates, and the brand associated with the organization and its products.[4]

There are definable and predictable patterns in the way technologies emerge, develop, and are replaced. Critical forces converge to create new technologies, which then follow well-defined life cycle patterns. Understanding the forces driving technological development and the patterns they follow can help a manager anticipate, monitor, and manage technologies more effectively.

"I think there is a world market for maybe five computers."
—Thomas Watson, IBM chairman, in 1943

- First, there must be a *need*, or *demand*, for the technology. Without this need driving the process, there is no reason for technological innovation to occur.

- Second, meeting the need must be theoretically possible, and the *knowledge* to do so must be available from basic science.
- Third, we must be able to *convert* the scientific knowledge into practice in both engineering and economic terms. If we can theoretically do something but doing it is economically impractical, the technology cannot be expected to emerge.
- Fourth, the *funding, skilled labor, time, space,* and *other resources* needed to develop the technology must be available.
- Finally, *entrepreneurial initiative* is needed to identify and pull all the necessary elements together.

Technology Life Cycle

Technological innovations typically follow a relatively predictable pattern called the **technology life cycle.** Figure 17.1 depicts the pattern. The cycle begins with the recognition of a need and a perception of a means by which the need can be satisfied through applied science or knowledge. The knowledge and ideas are brought together and developed, culminating in a new technological innovation. Early progress can be slow in these formative years as competitors continually experiment with product design and operational characteristics to meet consumer needs. This stage is where the rate of product innovation tends to be highest. For example, during the early years of the auto industry, companies tried a wide range of machines, including electric and steam-driven cars, to determine which product would be most effective. Eventually the internal combustion engine emerged as the dominant design, and the number of product innovations leveled off.

Once early problems are resolved and a dominant design emerges, improvements come more from process innovations to refine the technology. At this point managers can gain an advantage by pursuing process efficiencies and cost competitiveness. In the auto example, as companies settled on a product standard, they began leveraging the benefits of mass production and vertical integration to improve productivity. These process innovations were instrumental in lowering production costs and bringing the price of automobiles in line with consumer budgets.[5]

Consider United Parcel Service (UPS), whose drivers have been delivering packages to businesses and consumers for decades. A little more than a decade ago, drivers used paper maps, 3- by 5-inch cards, and their own memories to determine the most efficient way to drive their routes. Then, in 2005, UPS rolled out its $600 million route optimization system, software that designs each route so precisely that it limits the number of inefficient left turns, stop lights, and other obstacles that might slow a driver down. Not only does this technology reduce the amount of time a driver spends making each delivery, but t also cuts down on gasoline used idling at stop signs, lights, and waiting for that left-hand turn.

UPS is continually updating the system, which in one month alone reduced the number of miles logged by drivers by as much as 3 million. One new feature is a global positioning system (GPS) technology that actually beeps if a driver pulls into the wrong driveway. The technology also sends a driver to a pickup destination more quickly because it knows which driver is closest. UPS is also planning to update the system further so that a customer can reroute a package during delivery, if necessary. "We're trying to become a paradox: to be the biggest [delivery] company, but also the most flexible," says Kurt Kuehn, senior vice president of worldwide sales and marketing. "We have not reached the endgame."[6]

Eventually the new technology begins to reach the upper limits of both its performance capabilities and the spread of its usage. Development slows and becomes increasingly costly, and the market becomes saturated (i.e., there are few new

LO 2

technology life cycle

A predictable pattern followed by a technological innovation, from its inception and development to market saturation and replacement.

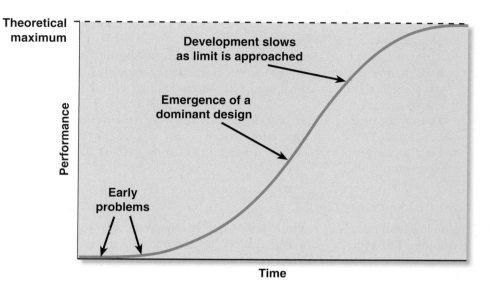

FIGURE 17.1
The Technology Life Cycle

customers). The technology can remain in this mature stage for some time—as in the case of autos—or can be replaced quickly by another technology offering superior performance or economic advantage. The life cycles can take decades or even centuries, as in the case of iron- and steel-making technologies. A dramatic example of technology evolution can be found in the recorded-music industry, which moved from the relatively primitive device Thomas Edison invented through the vinyl record to the cassette tape to the digitally recorded CD and then to highly miniaturized but memory-intensive MP3 players like the iPod, which are now being challenged by cell phones that will download a large number of songs through wireless connections.

As this example shows, a technology life cycle can be made up of many individual *product* life cycles. Each of these products performs a similar task—delivering recorded music to a listener—yet each product is an improvement over its predecessors. In this way, technological development involves significant innovations, often representing entirely new technologies, followed by a large number of small, incremental innovations. Ongoing development of a technology increases the benefits gained through its use, makes the technology easier to use, and allows more applications. In the process, the use of the technology expands to new adopters.

Diffusion of Technological Innovations

Like the technology life cycle, the adoption of new technology over time follows an S-shaped pattern (see the top line in Figure 17.2). The percentage of people using the technology is small in the beginning but increases dramatically as the technology succeeds and spreads through the population. Eventually the number of users peaks and levels off when the market for the technology is saturated. This pattern, first observed in 1903, has been verified with many new technologies and ideas in a wide variety of industries and settings.[7]

The adopters of a new technology fall into five groups (see the bottom line in Figure 17.2). Each group presents different challenges and opportunities to managers who want to market a new technology or product innovation.

The first group, representing approximately 2.5 percent of adopters, consists of the *innovators*. Typically, innovators are adventurous and willing to take risks. They are willing to pay a premium for the latest and newest technology or product to come along and to champion it if it meets with their approval. The enthusiasm of innovator-adopters is no guarantee of success—for example, the product may still be too expensive for the general market. But a lack of enthusiasm among this group is often a sign that the new technology has serious problems and more development is needed.

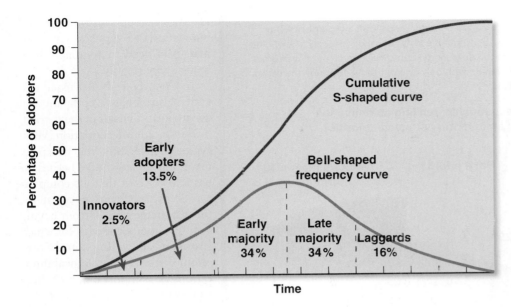

FIGURE 17.2
Technology Dissemination
Pattern and Adopter
Categories

The next 13.5 percent of adopters are *early adopters*. This group is critical to the success of a new technology, because its members include well-respected opinion leaders. Early adopters often are the people or organizations to which others look for leadership, ideas, and up-to-date technological information. Innovators and early adopters are extremely important in new-product launches, and marketing managers often spend heavily in promotion among these groups to generate a groundswell of enthusiasm.

The next group, representing 34 percent of adopters, is the *early majority*. These adopters are more deliberate and take longer to decide to use something new. Often they are important members of a community or industry, but typically not the leaders. It may take a while for the technology or new product to spread to this group, but once it does, use will begin to proliferate into the mainstream.

Representing the next 34 percent are the *late majority*. Members of this group are more skeptical of technological change and approach innovation with great caution, often adopting only out of economic necessity or increasing social pressure.

The final 16 percent are *laggards*. Often isolated and highly conservative in their views, laggards are extremely suspicious of innovation and change.

The speed with which an innovation spreads depends largely on five attributes. An innovation will spread quickly if it:

1. Has a great advantage over its predecessor.
2. Is compatible with existing systems, procedures, infrastructures, and ways of thinking.
3. Has less rather than greater complexity.
4. Can be tried or tested easily without significant cost or commitment.
5. Can be observed and copied easily.

Designing products with these technological considerations in mind can make a critical difference in their success.

Technological Innovation in a Competitive Environment

LO 3

Discussions about technology life cycles and diffusion patterns may imply that technological change occurs naturally or automatically. Just the opposite; change is neither easy nor natural in organizations (we discuss change more fully in the next chapter).

Executives at a majority of companies consider innovation a top priority, but only about half are satisfied with their company's return on innovation spending. Companies are most likely to measure innovation success in terms of customer satisfaction and growth in revenue, with only one out of five tracking the return on their investment in innovation.[8]

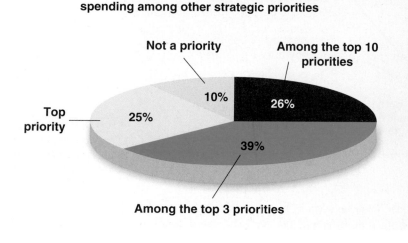

Survey respondents' ranking of innovation spending among other strategic priorities

Not a priority

Among the top 10 priorities

10%

26%

Top priority

25%

39%

Among the top 3 priorities

Decisions about technology and innovation are very strategic, and managers need to approach them in a systematic way.

In Chapter 4, we discussed two generic strategies a company can use to position itself in the market: low cost and differentiation. With *low-cost* leadership, the company maintains an advantage because it has a lower cost than its competitors. With a *differentiation* strategy, the advantage comes from having a unique good or service for which customers are willing to pay a premium price.[9] Technological innovations can support either of these strategies: they can be used to gain cost advantage through pioneering lower-cost product designs and creating low-cost ways to perform needed operations, or they can support differentiation by pioneering unique goods or services that increase buyer value and thus command premium prices.

In some cases, a new technology can completely change the rules of competition within an industry.[10] Leading companies that respond ineffectively to technological opportunities can falter while new companies emerge as the dominant competitors. For example, Bill Gates's shrewd decision to make the details of Microsoft's operating system widely available let software writers easily develop products for it, helping Microsoft achieve its dominant position today.

But industries seldom are transformed overnight. Typically, signals of a new technology's impact are visible well in advance, leaving time for companies and people to respond. For example, almost any competitor in the telecommunications industry fully understood the value of cellular technology. Often the key issue is not *whether* to adopt a new technology but *when* to adopt it and how to integrate the change with the organization's operating practices and strategies.

Innovation can improve any bottom-line practice.

Technology Leadership

The adage "timing is everything" is applied to many things, ranging from financial investments to telling jokes. It also applies to the development and exploitation of new technologies. Industry leaders such as Xerox, 3M, Hewlett-Packard, and Merck built and now maintain their competitive positions through early development and application of new technologies. However, technology leadership imposes costs and risks, and it is not the best approach for every organization (see Table 17.1).[11] Apple is well known for its technology leadership, beginning with its Macintosh computer, which pioneered the use of a mouse and graphical desktop icons instead of strings of typed computer commands, and advancing through the wildly popular iPod and iPhone. And as described in "Management Close-Up: Taking Action," Honda was a technology leader in its development of flexible factories.

Management Close-Up | TAKING ACTION

At Honda's helm these days is Takanobu Ito, named president and CEO in 2009. Ito, who joined Honda in 1978 in research and development, served as chief of automobile operations before becoming CEO. Ito assumed the reins at Honda during historically unprecedented times for automakers. A global recession and widespread unemployment, coupled with volatile gas prices, diminished consumers' appetite for big-ticket items like cars, particularly big gas-guzzlers. In addition, recently the yen has been strong against the dollar, making it costly to import from Japan.

But Ito, described by former Honda CEO Takeo Fukui as "tough," has never shied away from a challenge. Earlier, he led the team that developed the first-ever all-aluminum uniframe body, used in the Honda NSX sports car. He later directed the design of Acura's first SUV, the MDX.

Besides being president and CEO, Ito heads Honda Research & Development—the first individual since 1992 to simultaneously lead both businesses. Wearing two hats, Ito says, streamlines decision making at a time when speed is essential to survival.

Ito's plans call for intensifying Honda's already strong emphasis on R&D. As he does so, the company will benefit further from what industry observers call its key strategic advantage: the flexible assembly lines it built more than 10 years ago. Widely regarded as the nimblest player in the industry, when gas prices soared, Honda was able to slow production of its pickup truck and step up the assembly of smaller, more fuel-efficient models. It also relocated the assembly of some models to other plants, gaining even greater efficiencies.[12]

- While they may have different parts, all Honda vehicle models are assembled using the same process. How can Honda president and CEO Takanobu Ito use this fact to the company's advantage as he strives to keep it profitable?
- Industry observers say Honda has never "followed the crowd" or patterned itself after its competitors. Instead, it has pursued its own path. What changes do you think Ito will make during his tenure? Why?

Advantages of Technology Leadership

What makes innovators and technology leadership attractive is the potential for high profits and first-mover advantages. Being the first to market with new technologies can provide significant competitive advantage. If technology leadership increases an

Advantages	Disadvantages
First-mover advantage	Greater risks
Little or no competition	Cost of technology development
Greater efficiency	Costs of market development and customer education
Higher profit margins	Infrastructure costs
Sustainable advantage	Costs of learning and eliminating defects
Reputation for innovation	
Establishment of entry barriers	Possible cannibalization of existing products
Occupation of best market niches	
Opportunities to learn	

TABLE 17.1
Advantages and Disadvantages of Technology Leadership

organization's efficiency relative to competitors, it achieves a cost advantage. The organization can use the advantage to reap greater profits than competitors or attract more customers by charging lower prices. Similarly, if a company is first to market with a new technology, it may be able to charge a premium price because it faces no competition. Higher prices and greater profits can defray the costs of developing new technologies.

This one-time advantage of being the technology leader can be turned into a sustainable advantage. Sustainability of a lead depends on competitors' ability to duplicate the technology and the organization's ability to keep building on the lead quickly enough to outpace competitors. It can do this in several ways. The reputation for being an innovator can create an ongoing advantage and even spill over to the company's other products. For example, 3M's reputation for innovation and quality differentiates some of its standard products, such as adhesive tape, and allows a product to command a premium price. A competitor may be able to copy the product but not the reputation. Patents and other institutional barriers also can be used to block competitors and maintain leadership. The big players in the pharmaceutical industry invest heavily in research and development; they depend on patents to give them several years of selling new drugs without competition before generic versions of their drugs are permitted. For example, the blood thinner Plavix, which has the second-largest level of sales in the world, is protected by patent until 2011. In that year and the next, the patents for one-fifth of current drugs will expire, so pharmaceutical companies face a tremendous challenge to develop new drugs in the meantime.[13]

An older Apple iPhone is shown next to an advertisement for the new iPhone 3G at an AT&T store in Palo Alto, California. To sustain the momentum of the original iPhone's success, Apple's competitive strategy was to release the next generation of iPhones with faster Internet access and lower retail prices.

The first mover also can preempt competitors by occupying the best market niches. If it can establish high switching costs (recall Chapter 2) for repeat customers, these positions can be difficult for competitors to capture. Microsoft dominates the software market with its Windows and Vista operating systems because of the large library of software that is packaged with each. Although other companies can offer more advanced software, their products are not as attractive because they are not bundled as the Windows- and Vista-based systems are.

Technology leadership can provide a significant learning advantage. While competitors may be able to copy or adopt a new technology, ongoing learning by the technology leader can keep a company ahead by generating minor improvements that are difficult to imitate. Many Japanese manufacturers use several small, incremental improvements generated with their *kaizen* programs (recall Chapter 9) to upgrade the quality of their products and processes continuously. All these minor improvements cannot be copied easily by competitors, and collectively they can provide a significant advantage.[14]

Disadvantages of Technology Leadership   Being the first to develop or adopt a new technology does not always lead to immediate advantage and high profits, however. While such potential may exist, technology leadership does impose high costs and risks that followers do not have to bear. Being the leader thus can be more costly than being the follower. These costs include educating buyers unfamiliar with the new technology, building an infrastructure to support the technology, and developing complementary products to achieve the technology's full potential. For example, when the personal computer was first developed in the 1970s, dozens of computer companies entered the market. Almost all of them failed, usually because they lacked the financial, marketing, and sales ability required to attract and service customers. Also, many new products require regulatory approval. For example, the cost of developing a new drug, including testing and the expense of obtaining FDA approval, can run from hundreds of millions of dollars to almost $2 billion. While followers do not get the benefits of being first to market, they can copy the drug for a fraction of the cost once the original patents expire. This strategy can be highly profitable if the drug is widely used or has few close substitutes, enabling producers to charge a high price.[15]

Being a pioneer carries other risks. If raw materials and equipment are new or have unique specifications, a ready supply at a reasonable cost may not be available. Or the technology may not be fully developed and may have problems yet to be resolved. In addition, the unproved market for the technology creates uncertainty in demand. Finally, the new technology may have an adverse impact on existing structures or business. It may cannibalize current products or make existing investments obsolete.

Technology Followership

Not all organizations are equally prepared to be technology leaders, nor would leadership benefit each organization equally. In deciding whether to be a technology leader or follower, managers will consider their company's competitive strategy, the benefits gained through use of the technology, and the characteristics of their organization.

Interestingly, technology followership also can be used to support both low-cost and differentiation strategies. If the follower learns from the leader's experience, it can avoid the costs and risks of technology leadership, thereby establishing a low-cost position. The makers of generic drugs use this type of strategy. Followership also can support differentiation. By learning from the leader, the follower can adapt the products or delivery systems to fit buyers' needs more closely. Microsoft is famous for having built a successful company on this type of followership. The company's original operating system, MS-DOS, was purchased from Seattle Computer Works to compete with the industry's first desktop operating system, CP/M, sold by Digital Research. Marketing strength, combined with incremental product innovations, enabled Microsoft to steal the lead in software categories (e.g., Excel's spreadsheet program beat Lotus 1-2-3, which had taken share from the first mover, VisiCalc).[16] Microsoft products, including music players, videogame consoles, and Web browsers, have been launched after technology leaders have paved the way.

A manager's decision on when to adopt new technology also depends on the potential benefits of the new technology, as well as the organization's technology skills. As discussed earlier, technologies do not emerge in their final state; rather, they exhibit *ongoing development* (see Figure 17.3). Such development eventually makes the technology easier to use and more adaptable to various strategies. For example, the development of high-bandwidth communication networks has enabled many more companies

$ **The bottom line**
COST
Following the technology leader can save development expense.

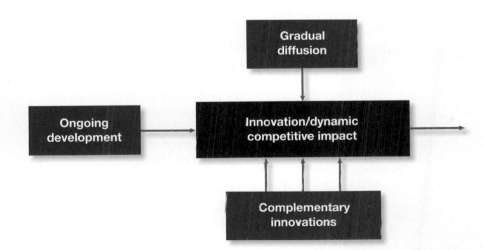

SOURCE: D. M. Schroeder, "A Dynamic Perspective on the Impact of Process Innovation upon Competitive Strategies," *Strategic Management Journal* 11 (January 1990), pp. 25–42.

FIGURE 17.3
Dynamic Forces of a Technology's Competitive Impact

to work with suppliers located abroad. At the same time, *complementary products and technologies* may be developed and introduced that make the main technology more useful. For example, the combination of the personal computer with disk drives, printers, e-mail, and other software turned it into an essential business tool.

These complementary products and technologies combine with the *gradual diffusion* of the technology to form a shifting competitive impact from the technology. The appropriate time for an organization to adopt technological innovations is when the costs and risks of switching to the technology are outweighed by the benefits. This point will be different for each organization, with some organizations benefiting from a leadership, early adopter role, and others from a followership role, depending on each organization's characteristics and strategies.[17]

Assessing Technology Needs

LO 4

The biggest industry sector in the U.S. economy is health care services, where spending is soaring, much to the dismay of the insurers and patients paying the medical bills. One reason U.S. health care costs so much is that the industry has been slower than others to adopt types of technology that can make day-to-day operations more efficient. According to a RAND Corporation study, Americans could save $162 billion a year if health care providers made better investments in information technology. For example, fewer than one out of five hospitals are using a complete bar code system for dispensing medicine, which could save money and reduce medication errors.[18] In today's increasingly competitive environment, failure to correctly assess the technology needs of the organization can fundamentally impair the organization's effectiveness.

Assessing the technology needs of the organization involves measuring current technologies as well as external trends affecting the industry.

Measuring Current Technologies

technology audit

Process of clarifying the key technologies on which an organization depends.

Airborne Networks—technology that NASA and the U.S. Air Force are developing—will create an "Internet in the sky" that could let planes fly safely without ground controllers. The U.S. Air Force plans to actively develop and test the network from 2008 to 2012.

Before organizations can devise strategies for developing and exploiting technological innovation, they must gain a clear understanding of their current technology base. A **technology audit** helps clarify the key technologies on which an organization depends. The most important dimension of a new technology is its competitive value. One technique for measuring competitive value categorizes technologies as emerging, pacing, key, and base.[19]

- *Emerging technologies* are still under development and thus are unproved. They may, however, significantly alter the rules of competition in the future. Managers will want to monitor the development of emerging technologies but may not yet need to invest in them until they have been more fully developed.

- *Pacing technologies* have yet to prove their full value but have the potential to alter the rules of competition by providing significant advantage. For example, when first installed, computer-aided manufacturing (see Chapter 9) was a pacing technology. Its full potential was not yet widely realized, but companies that used it effectively developed significant speed and cost advantages. Managers will want to focus on developing or investing in pacing technologies because of the competitive advantages they can provide.
- *Key technologies* have proved effective, but they also provide a strategic advantage because not everyone uses them. Knowledge and dissemination of these technologies are limited, and they continue

to provide some first-mover advantages. For example, a more powerful, proprietary processing chip by Intel is a key technology for that organization. Eventually, alternatives to key technologies can emerge. But until then key technologies can give organization managers a significant competitive edge and make it much more difficult for new entrants to threaten the organization.

- *Base technologies* are those that are commonplace in the industry; everyone must have them to be able to operate. Thus, they provide little competitive advantage. Managers have to invest only to ensure their organization's continued competence in the technology.

Technologies can evolve rapidly through these categories. For example, electronic word processing was considered an emerging technology in the late 1970s. By the early 1980s, it could have been considered pacing. While promising advantages, the technology's cost and capabilities restricted its usefulness to a limited number of applications. With continued improvements and more powerful computer chips, electronic word processing quickly became a key technology. Its costs dropped, its usage spread, and it demonstrated the capacity to enhance productivity. By the late 1980s, it was considered a base technology in most applications. Word-processing technology is now used so widely that it is viewed as a routine activity in almost every office.

Assessing External Technological Trends

Just as with any planning, decisions about technology must balance internal capabilities (strengths and weaknesses) with external opportunities and threats. There are several techniques that managers use to better understand how technology is changing within an industry.

Benchmarking   As mentioned in Chapter 4, benchmarking is the process of comparing the organization's practices and technologies with those of other companies. The ability to benchmark technologies against those of competitors varies among industries. While competitors understandably are reluctant to share their secrets, information trading for benchmarking is not uncommon and can prove highly valuable. For example, Harley-Davidson's recovery of its reputation for manufacturing quality motorcycles began only after company executives toured Honda's plant and witnessed firsthand the weaknesses of Harley's manufacturing technologies and the vast potential for improvement.

Benchmarking against potential competitors in other nations is also important. Companies may find key or pacing technologies in use that can be imported easily and offer significant advantage. Also, overseas firms may be more willing to share their knowledge if they are not direct competitors and if they are eager to exchange information to benefit both companies.

Scanning   Whereas benchmarking focuses on what is being done currently, scanning focuses on what can be done and what is being developed. In other words, benchmarking examines key and perhaps some pacing technologies, while scanning seeks out pacing and emerging technologies—those just being introduced and still in development.

Scanning typically involves a number of tactics, many of them the same as those used in benchmarking. However, scanning places greater emphasis on identifying and monitoring the sources of new technologies for an industry. It also may dictate that executives read more cutting-edge research journals and attend research conferences and seminars. The extent to which scanning is done depends largely on how close to the cutting edge of technology an organization needs to operate.

Benchmarking can lower cost and raise speed, quality, and customer service.

Japanese companies, such as Nissan, are often willing to show U.S. competitors their operations because they believe the U.S. companies are unwilling or unable to use what they have learned.

Key Factors to Consider in Technology Decisions

LO 5   Once managers have thoroughly analyzed their organization's current technological position, they can plan how to either develop or exploit emerging technological innovations for the future. Managers must balance many interrelated factors in their decisions, such as the technology's potential to support the organization's strategic needs and the organization's skills and capabilities to exploit the technology successfully. The organization's competitive strategy, the technical abilities of its employees to deal with the new technology, the fit of the technology with the company's operations, and the company's ability to deal with the risks and ambiguities of adopting a new technology all must be considered in conjunction with the dynamic forces of a developing technology. This process does not always mean waiting for the technology to develop. Often it requires changing the capabilities and strategies of the organization to match the needs of the technology, including hiring new people, training existing employees, changing internal policies and procedures, and changing strategies. These considerations are discussed next.

Anticipated Market Receptiveness

The first consideration that needs to be addressed in developing a strategy around technological innovation is market potential. In many cases, innovations are stimulated by external demand for new goods and services. For example, the share of Internet users who use a language other than English has been growing rapidly. This trend, along with the globalization of business, has fueled demand for the ability to search the Web in different languages. Companies are creating a variety of software innovations to meet this demand. Google will translate a searcher's query into a dozen languages and also translate Web pages to present results in the searcher's language. Yahoo Answers will send queries to a native speaker of the user's language. It indexes those responses so that they can be searched by future users in that language.[20]

English is still the Internet's top language, but most users speak other languages.[21]

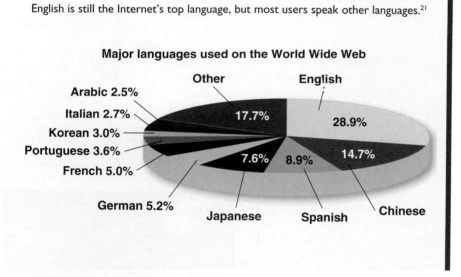

Major languages used on the World Wide Web

Other 17.7%
English 28.9%
Chinese 14.7%
Spanish 8.9%
Japanese 7.6%
German 5.2%
French 5.0%
Portuguese 3.6%
Korean 3.0%
Italian 2.7%
Arabic 2.5%

In assessing market receptiveness, executives need to make two determinations:

1. In the short run, the new technology should have an immediate, valuable application.
2. In the long run, the technology must be able to satisfy a market need or needs.

For example, when prescribing medicine, physicians view the traditional method of scribbling on a pad and handing the prescription to a patient or nurse as very simple to use. Learning to use new technology for that purpose must be worthwhile. Hospitals that move to electronic management of drug distribution need to roll out entire systems, but those systems let doctors tap into information networks where they can look up drug interactions, side effects, and so on. When doctors see how the system helps them deliver better care and reduce errors, most are quick to embrace the new technology.[22]

Drawing on a decade of experience in designing computer games, Damion Schubert has identified several important pitfalls to avoid if a game is to be well received by its market. Schubert, the lead combat designer for BioWare (where his credits include *Star Wars: The Old Republic*), says the first mistake is to innovate too much. He points out that trying to execute every new idea for a game inevitably confuses the message about what is exciting in that game, and it is probably impossible to do well. Instead, designers have to think about what they can accomplish well within the constraints of a schedule and then select innovations that users are most likely to enjoy.

Schubert learned of a team that was designing a multiplayer game and thought it would be interesting to allow players to set each others' houses on fire. Really, though, that innovation was something that fed the designers' wish to try something new, not an idea that players would really appreciate. Instead, Schubert says, designers need to ask gamers what *they* think would make the game better.

Similarly, Schubert says, game designers often confuse features with benefits. They might count up the number of races in a game, or the number of creatures or quests. Then they think of ways to add more races, creatures, or quests. But in most genres, the number of such features is limited in the best games, because what provides genuine quality in a game is for each choice to be interesting, detailed, and well crafted. Thus, it is more important to thoroughly test every innovation so that it works well than to heap on new features. Gamers, Schubert insists, are not just looking for designers "to show them something new" but rather "to show them something better."[23]

Technological Feasibility

In addition to market receptiveness, managers must consider the feasibility of technological innovations. Visions can stay unrealized for a long time. Technical obstacles may represent barriers to progress. For example, limitations on battery miniaturization and storage have hindered the development of battery-powered vehicles. And the makers of computer chips face continual hurdles in developing newer and faster models. Since Intel brought the first microprocessor to market in 1971, chip makers have made dramatic advances in computing. The number of transistors on a chip, and its resulting performance, has doubled nearly every 18 to 24 months, upholding what has become known as Moore's Law (Gordon Moore is the cofounder of Intel). But the frontier of microprocessor technology is restricted by the combined forces of physics and economics. The wires that run between transistors are 400 times thinner than a human hair, and the task of continually doubling the speed of electrons passing wires of near-zero width is tricky—and may become impossible at some point. To continue boosting processor speed economically, developers have had to be creative, using techniques such as shrinking components and embedding two or more processor cores on one microchip to shorten the distance data must travel between processors.[24]

> "I have not failed. I've just found 10,000 ways that don't work."
> —Thomas Edison

Other industries face similar technological hurdles. In the oil industry, for example, technological barriers prevent exploration and drilling in the deepest parts of the ocean. In medicine, scientists and doctors work continuously to identify the causes of and cures for diseases such as cancer and AIDS. Automakers' efforts to develop electric cars have been constrained by the difficulty of designing a battery that can power the long trips Americans love to take. General Motors' widely touted Volt has a range of 40 miles between charges, the same range as an experimental car being tested by Toyota for city driving.[25] Each of these potentially valuable innovations is slowed by the technical limits of currently available technologies.

Economic Viability

Closely related to technological feasibility is economic viability. Apart from whether a firm can "pull off" a technological innovation, executives must consider whether there is a good financial incentive for doing so. The use of hydrogen-powered fuel-cell technology for automobiles is almost feasible technically, but its costs are still too high. In addition, even if those costs were brought down to more acceptable levels, the absence of a supporting infrastructure in the society as a whole—such as the lack of hydrogen refueling stations—would represent another barrier to economic viability. However, if organizations can find niche markets for a high-priced new technology, they often can advance the technology to the point that applications become more affordable. For example, three-dimensional (3D) printers can read plans and translate them into physical objects by applying light or chemicals to plastic to harden it into a desired shape. Originally costing $100,000, today's versions of the machine sell for $15,000 and are used by industrial designers to test part designs before they go into full-scale production. Investing in this technology makes sense because it saves manufacturers the major expense of setting up production processes to make models of parts still in development. The price of a 3D printer is expected to drop as low as $2,000 within a few years, and assuming companies could eventually develop simple versions for under $1,000, 3D printers could start showing up in people's homes. Then if a plastic part of a toy or appliance breaks, you could go online for the plans and "print" out a replacement instantly.[26]

Less futuristic innovations also require a careful assessment of economic viability and costs. New technologies often represent an expensive and long-term commitment of resources. And integrating them effectively within an organization can require a great deal of management time. Once an organization commits to a technological innovation, a change in direction becomes extremely difficult and costly. For these reasons, a careful, objective analysis of technology costs versus benefits is essential. Of course, benefits can be substantial as well. Fast-food restaurants can adopt a system called Hyperactive Bob. The system scans the parking lot to count vehicles that are arriving; compiles that data with information about time of day, cooking times, ordering patterns, and so on; and then issues orders to employees, directing them which items and how many to begin cooking. Employees touch a screen to indicate when they accept a task and when they are finished. The system, made by Hyperactive Technologies, costs $5,000 to install and $3,000 a year for software licensing, but it saves thousands a year in reduced food waste plus much more in reduced employee turnover—because Bob is an alternative to being shouted at by an anxious supervisor.[27]

The issue of economic viability takes us back to our earlier discussion of adoption timing. Earlier adopters may have first-mover advantages, but costs are associated with this strategic approach. The development costs of a particular technological innovation may be quite high, as in pharmaceuticals, chemicals, and software. Patents and copyrights often help organizations recoup the costs of their investments in technological innovations. Without such protection, the investments in research and development might not be justifiable.

Hyperactive Bob applies robotics technology (computer vision and artificial intelligence) to fast-food operations to make them more efficient. Using this technology is economically feasible because it reduces waste, improves customer satisfaction, and reduces employee turnover.

Conversion of paper medical records into electronic systems has been widely touted as an important money-saving technological advance. Savings can come from recommending generic versions of medicines when available, keeping records in one centralized database rather than duplicating them in various locations, and avoiding errors from misreading handwritten orders or prescribing medicines that interact with other drugs the patient is already taking. The hurdle is how to pay for the conversion.

Managers of Midland Memorial Hospital wanted electronic medical records. Nurses were wasting too much time hunting for charts, squinting at messy handwriting, and filling out repetitive forms, but creating a computer system would be expensive. A system with all the features could cost $20 million or more. Midland found the answer at the Veterans Health Administration. When VA facilities went electronic, they put the source code for their software in the public domain, so other programmers could use it, adding unique features for their clients. Using the new system, Midland has lower rates of infection and death and incurred fewer medication errors. The hospital also caught up on its billing backlog.

Doctors face a similar challenge. So far, fewer than two out of ten have computerized medical records. Many are intimidated by the expense and have few if any computer experts on staff. The federal government has addressed the economic hurdle with incentives of about $40,000 for installing and using electronic-records systems. Also, in New York City, the Primary Care Information Project developed software and helped more than 1,000 physicians implement it. The project's head concludes that doctors will change but only if they have enough help—financial and technical.[28]

Unfortunately, the exploding growth in piracy or even fakery of patented pharmaceuticals, software, and other products has added new barriers to economic viability. Globalization has created a worldwide market for goods produced by low-cost counterfeiters and pirates overseas, who have the added advantage that they do not have to incur research and development expense. In addition, technology has made it easy to copy software without paying for it. Pfizer's anti-impotence drug Viagra, Hewlett-Packard inkjet cartridges, Intel computer chips, GM car designs, Coach handbags, Nike Air Jordan shoes, and countless music and movie recordings—all these and much more have been counterfeited or illegally copied and sold. Worldwide lost sales as a result of this illegal activity—the theft of *intellectual property*—have been estimated at more than $500 billion a year. A major contributor to the problem is China, which accounted for about 80 percent of the fake or pirated goods seized by the U.S. government in a recent year. Some companies have also taken action on their own. Auto parts maker Bendix set up a team charged with enforcing intellectual property rights, has adapted packaging so that it is harder to counterfeit, and educates customers by setting up trade show displays with side-by-side comparisons of its product and knock-offs. Other companies, including Pfizer, are using radio-frequency tags on their packages so that they can more accurately track products throughout the distribution process. All these measures are designed to help organizations—and countries—maintain the economic viability of their innovations.[29]

> $ **The bottom line**
> COST
> Innovation requires financial feasibility.

Anticipated Competency Development

We have stated repeatedly in this text that organizations should (and do) build their strategies based on core competencies. This advice applies to technology and innovation strategies as well. Frequently, we can view technological innovations that are the tangible product of intangible—or tacit—knowledge and capabilities that make up a firm's core competence. Merck and Intel are examples of companies in which core competencies in research and development lead to new technological innovations.

By contrast, firms that are not technology oriented must develop new competencies to survive. For example, when Amazon.com changed the face of e-retailing in the 1990s, traditional brick-and-mortar bookstores had to adapt quickly. To regain competitiveness, they had to bolster their information technology competencies, which wasn't always an easy thing to do.

The upshot of this is that while certain technologies may have tremendous market applicability, managers must have (or develop) the internal competencies needed to execute their technology strategies. Without the skills needed to implement an innovation, even promising technological advances may prove disastrous.

Organizational Suitability

The final issues that tend to be addressed in deciding on technological innovations have to do with the culture of the organization, the interests of managers, and the expectations of stakeholders. Companies such as 3M and Google, which are seen as proactive "technology-push" innovators, tend to have cultures that are more outward-looking and opportunistic. Executives in these *prospector* firms give considerable priority to developing and exploiting technological expertise, and decision makers tend to have bold intuitive visions of the future. Typically they have technology champions who articulate competitively aggressive, first-mover technological strategies. In many cases, executives are more concerned about the opportunity costs of not taking action than they are about the potential to fail.

By contrast, *defender* firms, such as Kroger and Safeway, tend to adopt a more circumspect posture toward innovation. These firms tend to operate in stable environments. As a result, their strategies are focused more on deepening their capability base through complementary technologies that extend rather than replace their current ones. Strategic decisions are likely to be based on careful analysis and experience in the industry setting. In the United States, supermarkets have competed for decades by emphasizing low-cost distribution over large distances. That strategy has helped the companies survive low-cost pressure from Walmart but has not always translated well when U.S.-based supermarket chains have tried to expand into other parts of the world.[30]

A hybrid *analyzer* firm, such as Microsoft, needs to stay technologically competitive but tends to allow others to demonstrate solid demand in new arenas before it responds. Microsoft's Xbox game console, Office software, and Zune music player all contain innovations, but other companies pioneered the original path-breaking product concepts. As we noted earlier, these types of firms tend to adopt an early-follower strategy to grab a dominant position more from their strengths in marketing and manufacturing than through technological innovation.

Every company has different capabilities to deal with new technology. As discussed previously, early adopters have characteristics different from those of late adopters. Early adopters of new technologies tend to be larger, more profitable, and more specialized. Therefore, they are in an economic position to absorb the risks associated with early adoption while profiting more from its advantages. In addition, the people involved in early adoption are more highly educated, have a greater ability to deal with abstraction, can cope with uncertainty more effectively, and have strong problem-solving capabilities. Thus, early adopters can more effectively manage the difficulties and uncertainty of a less fully developed technology.[31]

One additional consideration managers need to take into account when introducing new technology is the impact the new technology will have on employees. Often, new technology brings with it work-flow and other changes that directly affect the organization's work environment. If the organization does not endorse and implement innovation, these changes may create anxiety and even resistance among employees, making integration of the technology more difficult. When managers communicate well in advance about the new technology, explain its purpose, and provide the necessary training, the process of integrating the new technology into the organization's

Considerations	Examples
Market receptiveness—assess external demand for the technology (short/long run).	Cell phones, MP3, personal digital assistants (PDAs), HDTV
Technological feasibility—evaluate technical barriers to progress.	Deep-sea oil exploration, physical size of PC microprocessors
Economic viability—examine any cost considerations, and forecast profitability.	Solar fusion, fuel cells for automobiles, missile defense system
Competency development—determine whether current competencies are sufficient.	Information technology in hospitals, digital technology in cameras
Organizational suitability—assess the fit with culture and managerial systems.	Steel companies focusing on creativity and innovation

TABLE 17.2
Framing Decisions about Technological Innovation

existing processes becomes easier. The cooperation of employees is often a major factor in determining how difficult and costly the introduction of new technology will be. We discuss the issue of managing change in more detail in the next chapter.

Table 17.2 briefly summarizes the five major factors we have been discussing: market receptiveness, technological feasibility, economic viability, anticipated competency development, and organizational suitability. All of these considerations jointly influence the decisions managers will make about technology innovations. A lack in even one of them can derail an otherwise promising project.

Sourcing and Acquiring New Technologies

Developing new technology may conjure up visions of scientists and product developers working in research and development (R&D) laboratories like that of Bell Labs. However, new technology also can come from many other sources, including suppliers, manufacturers, users, other industries, universities, the government, and overseas companies. While every source of innovation should be explored, each industry usually has specific sources for most of its new technologies. For example, because of the limited resources of most farming operations, innovations in farming most often come from manufacturers, suppliers, and government extension services. Seed manufacturers develop and market new, superior hybrids; chemical producers improve pesticides and herbicides; and equipment manufacturers design improved farm equipment. Land-grant universities develop new farming techniques, and extension agents spread their usage.

In many industries, however, the primary sources of new technology are the organizations that use it. For instance, more than three-fourths of scientific innovations are developed by the users of the scientific instruments being improved and subsequently may be licensed or sold to manufacturers or suppliers.[32]

The airline industry is constantly striving to cut costs to keep flight travel affordable. A decade ago, the German airline Deutsche Lufthansa developed route-mapping software for its own use to calculate the most efficient routes for its flights. But the airline now sells versions of its Lido system to about 30 other carriers, including British Airways, Air Canada, Singapore Airlines, and Emirates Airlines.

The software tracks such data as weather, airport locations, and runways; the weight and performance of aircraft; fixed air routes; temporarily blocked airspace and the like; and then searches through multiple scenarios to find the best for each flight. British Airways estimates that the software saves the firm $15 million to $20 million a year. Air Canada reports similar results. "In the operating world of an airline, the flight-planning system is absolutely critical to cost control," says Captain Richard Sowden of Air Canada's flight technical department. So technology that was originally developed by one firm for its own internal use has become an option for purchase by many of its competitors.[33]

make-or-buy decision

The question an organization asks itself about whether to acquire new technology from an outside source or develop it itself.

Essentially, the question of how to acquire new technology is a **make-or-buy decision.** In other words, should the organization develop the technology itself or acquire it from an outside source? However, the decision is not that simple. There are many alternatives, and each has advantages and disadvantages. Some of the most common options are discussed in the following sections.

Internal Development

Developing a new technology within the company has the potential advantage of keeping the technology proprietary—exclusive to the organization. This provides an important advantage over competitors. The disadvantage of internal development is that it usually requires additional staff and funding for an extended period. Even if the development succeeds, considerable time may elapse before practical benefits are realized. Managers must carefully weigh the potential benefits of proprietary technology against the cost of developing it. Intel balances these risks and benefits by operating research and development laboratories in several locations, including Oregon, Israel, India, and China. Engineers in the various labs have come up with breakthrough ideas in the projects they have tackled, and labs in offshore locations can get around legal restrictions on technology imports, as well as save money relative to the cost of hiring talent in the United States.[34]

$ Purchasing may be faster and cheaper than internal development.

Purchase

Most technology already is available in products or processes that can be purchased openly. For example, a bank that needs sophisticated information-processing equipment need not develop the technology itself. It can simply purchase the technology from manufacturers or suppliers. In most situations, this is the simplest, easiest, and most cost-effective way to acquire new technology. However, in this case, the technology itself will not offer a competitive advantage.

Contracted Development

If the technology is not available and a company lacks the resources or time to develop it internally, it may choose to contract the development from outside sources. Possible contractors include other companies, independent research laboratories, and university and government institutions. Usually outside contracting involves an agreed-upon series of objectives and timetables for the project, with payments made as each part of the project is tested and achieved.

Licensing

Certain technologies that are not easily purchased as part of a product can be licensed for a fee. Television producers license the right to install V-chips (paying a royalty of about $1 per TV set) because the U.S. government requires them so that parents can limit the content to which their children are exposed. Companies that develop videogames often license technology, including the software that models the physics behind the activities depicted in the game. The artwork, characters, and music for a particular game may be unique, but the basic laws of real-world physics apply to the action shown in most of today's sophisticated games, so there is no advantage to programming that aspect of each game. Licensing is more economical.[35]

Technology Trading

Another way to gain access to new technologies is with technology trading. Representatives from Scotsman Ice Systems have studied other manufacturers' information technology applications. Whether or not those companies were in the same industry, their experiences have provided Scotsman with lessons that would have been expensive to learn from trial and error. Similarly, Mary Jo Cartwright, a director of manufacturing operations for Batesville Casket Company, toured a John Deere farm equipment plant and took note of a technology called visual management screens, which display how-to information for production workers. Although the technology wasn't worthwhile for Batesville at the time, when it later became involved in more customization, the company introduced visual management screens to give workers detailed and understandable assembly instructions.[36]

Sometimes even rival companies use technology trading. Not all industries are amenable to this kind of sharing, but technology trading is becoming increasingly common because of the high cost of developing advanced technologies independently.[37]

Research Partnerships and Joint Ventures

Research partnerships are arrangements designed to jointly pursue specific new-technology development. Typically, each member enters the partnership with different skills or resources needed for development to succeed. An effective combination is an established company and a start-up. Joint ventures are similar in most respects to research partnerships, but they tend to have greater permanence, and their outcomes result in entirely new companies.[38] But as we described in our discussion on strategic alliances in Chapter 9, sometimes even powerful competitors collaborate on projects. An example is the strategic alliance formed by Tyson Foods, the giant meat producer, and ConocoPhillips, one of the big U.S. oil companies, to develop a renewable diesel fuel that includes beef, pork, and poultry fat discarded during meat processing. This alliance brings together Tyson's knowledge in applying protein chemistry and Conoco's knowledge of refinery technology.[39]

Acquisition of an Owner of the Technology

If a company lacks the needed technology but wishes to acquire proprietary ownership of it, one option is to purchase the company that owns the technology. This transaction can take a number of forms, ranging from an outright purchase of the entire company to a minority interest sufficient to gain access to the technology. For example, Motorola purchased shares of Global Locate, which developed the technology for fast-working global positioning systems. Customers are increasingly interested in GPS applications in cell phones and other mobile devices. More recently, a semiconductor supplier called Broadcom acquired Global Locate outright. That move positions Broadcom to supply semiconductors featuring GPS navigation without having to license that technology or depend on an outside supplier.[40]

Choosing among these alternatives is simpler if managers ask the following basic questions:

1. Is it important (and possible) in terms of competitive advantage that the technology remain proprietary?
2. Are the time, skills, and resources for internal development available?
3. Is the technology readily available outside the company?

As Figure 17.4 illustrates, the answers to these questions guide the manager to the most appropriate technology acquisition option.

If the preferred decision is to acquire a company, managers take additional steps to ensure the acquisition will make sense for the long term. For example, they try to make sure that key employees will remain with the firm, instead of leaving and perhaps taking essential technical expertise with them. Similarly, as with any large investment, managers carefully assess whether the financial benefits of the acquisition will justify the purchase price.

Technology and Managerial Roles

chief information officer (CIO)

Executive in charge of information technology strategy and development.

In organizations, technology traditionally has been the responsibility of vice presidents for research and development. These executives are directly responsible for corporate and divisional R&D laboratories. Typically, their jobs have a functional orientation. But increasingly companies have the position of **chief information officer (CIO)**, often also called the *chief technology officer (CTO)*. The CIO is a senior position at the corporate level with broad, integrative responsibilities. CIOs coordinate the technological efforts of the various business units; act as a voice for technology in the top management team; identify ways that technology can support the company's strategy; supervise new-technology development; and assess the technological implications of major strategic initiatives such as acquisitions, new ventures, and strategic alliances. They also manage their organization's *information technology (IT)* group.[41]

Without the CIO's integrative role, different departments in an organization could easily adopt different technology tools and standards, leading to much higher equipment and maintenance expense and difficulties in connecting the different parts of the organization. Also, because organization technologists often have a very specialized expertise, managers without such expertise may have difficulty supervising them effectively. A CIO can help managers ensure that the work technologists do is aligned with the strategic goals of the organization.

Chief technology officers also perform an important boundary role: they work directly with outside organizations. For example, they work with universities for funding research to stay abreast of technical developments and with regulatory agencies to ensure compliance with regulations, identify trends, and influence the regulatory process.

Sophie Vandebroek, Chief Technology Officer of Xerox, has the goal of making Xerox's systems simpler, speedier, smaller, smarter, more secure, and socially responsible, what she calls the "six S's." Her own innovations include launching a research center on an island in the virtual world of Second Life, so that geographically separated employees can collaborate online.

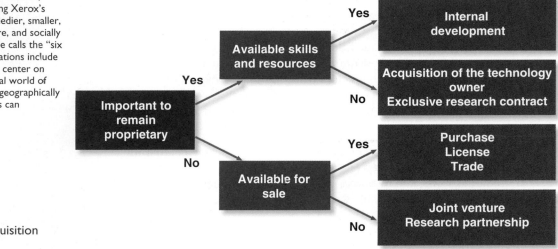

FIGURE 17.4
Technology Acquisition Options

Other people play a variety of critical roles in developing new technology. Recall from Chapter 7 that it is the *entrepreneur* who, in an effort to exploit untried technologies, invents new products or finds new ways to produce old products. The entrepreneur opens up new possibilities that change the competitive structure of entire industries. For example, Steve Jobs started Apple Computer in his garage, helping to popularize the personal computer and years later the MP3 music player.

Key roles in acquiring and developing new technologies are the technical innovator, product champion, and executive champion.[43] The **technical innovator** develops the new technology or has the key skills needed to install and operate the technology. This person possesses the requisite technical skills, but he or she may not have the managerial skills needed to push the idea forward and secure acceptance within the organization. This is where the product champion gets involved. Introducing new technology into an organization requires that someone promote the idea. The **product champion**—often at the risk of his or her position and prestige—promotes the idea throughout the organization, searching for support and acceptance. The champion can be a high-level manager but often is not. If the champion lacks the power and financial resources to make the required changes independently, she or he must convince people who have such authority to support the innovation. In other words, product champions must get sponsorship.

Sponsorship comes from the **executive champion,** who has the status, authority, and financial resources to support the project and protect the product champion. Without this support and protection, the product champion, and thus the new technology, could not succeed. Resources needed to develop the innovation would be unavailable, and without protection, the champion would not be allowed to continue promoting the change.

> "Cost management will never, ever go away. If you can't manage your costs, you can't qualify for the other stuff. Just being strategic isn't sufficient [for a CIO]."
> —Karl Wachs, CIO, Celanese Corporation[42]

technical innovator

A person who develops a new technology or has the key skills to install and operate the technology.

product champion

A person who promotes a new technology throughout the organization in an effort to obtain acceptance of and support for it.

executive champion

An executive who supports a new technology and protects the product champion of the innovation.

Organizing for Innovation

Successful innovation is a lot more than a great idea. A study by the Boston Consulting Group found that lack of good ideas is hardly ever the obstacle to profitable innovation. More often, ideas fail to generate financial returns because the organization isn't set up to innovate. The culture is risk averse, projects get bogged down, efforts aren't coordinated, and management can't figure out where to direct the company's money.[44]

In Chapter 6 we introduced the concept of "learning organizations"—companies that excel at solving problems, seeking and finding new approaches, and sharing new knowledge with all members of an organization. Such learning organizations are particularly well positioned to develop useful innovations. The innovations may involve *exploiting* existing capabilities—to improve production speed or product quality, for example. Or the innovation may involve *exploring* new knowledge—seeking to develop new products or services.[45] Both innovation processes are necessary. Innovative learning organizations use their existing strengths to improve their operations and thus improve their bottom lines. But they also learn to unleash people's creative energies and capabilities to develop new products and processes that will ensure their long-term competitiveness. In this section we discuss some of the approaches managers use to organize for innovation.

Unleashing Creativity

As discussed in Chapter 7, 3M has a strong orientation toward *intrapreneurship* and derives about one-third of its revenues from new products. 3M, Merck, Hewlett-Packard, and

A culture that permits failure is crucial for fostering the creative thinking and risk taking required for innovation. If 3M hadn't kept Francis G. Okie on board after a few failed inventions, Okie would never have come up with 3M's first success—waterproof sandpaper.

Rubbermaid have well-established histories of producing many successful new technologies and products. What sets these and other continuous innovators apart? The one thing these companies have in common is an organizational culture that encourages innovation.[46]

Consider the 3M legend from the early 1920s of inventor Francis G. Okie. Okie dreamed up the idea of using sandpaper instead of razor blades for shaving. The aim was to reduce the risk of nicks and avoid sharp instruments. The idea failed, but rather than being punished for the failure, Okie was encouraged to champion other ideas, which included 3M's first blockbuster success: waterproof sandpaper. A culture that permits failure is crucial for fostering the creative thinking and risk taking required for innovation.

As strange as it may seem, *celebrating* failure can be vital to the innovation process.[47] Failure is the essence of learning, growing, and succeeding. Innovative companies have many balls in the air at all times, with many people trying many new ideas. A majority of the ideas will fail, but it is only through this process that the few big "hits" will emerge that make a company an innovative star. Madison Mount, who leads the design work for food and beverage clients of IDEO, says, "If I'm not taking risks, I feel uncomfortable, because I'm not learning."[48] This type of attitude from a manager can foster creative thinking throughout the ranks.

3M uses the simple set of rules listed in Table 17.3 to help foster innovation. These rules can be—and are—copied by other companies. But 3M has an advantage in that it has followed these rules since its inception and ingrained them in its culture. This culture is shared and passed on in part through stories. One such legend is about the 3M engineer who was fired because he refused to stop working on a project that his boss thought was wasting resources. Despite being fired, the engineer came to work as usual, finished the project, and demonstrated the value of his innovation. The engineer eventually was promoted to head a new division created to manufacture and market the innovation.

> "Failure is the best way to clear the fog to see a path to success."
> —Diego Rodriguez and Ryan Jacoby, IDEO, an innovative design firm[49]

TABLE 17.3
3M's Rules for an Innovative Culture

• **Set goals for innovation.** By corporate decree, 25 to 30 percent of annual sales must come from new products that are five years old or less.
• **Commit to research and development.** 3M invests in R&D at almost double the rate of the average U.S. company. One R&D goal is to cut in half the time it takes to introduce new products.
• **Inspire intrapreneurship.** Champions are encouraged to run with new ideas, and they get a chance to manage their products as if they were running their own businesses. 3Mers are allowed to spend 15 percent of their time pursuing personal research interests unrelated to current company projects.
• **Facilitate, don't obstruct.** Divisions are kept small and are allowed to operate with a great deal of independence but have constant access to information and technical resources. Researchers with good ideas are awarded $50,000 Genesis grants to develop their brainstorms into new products.
• **Focus on the customer.** 3M's definition of quality is to demonstrate that the product can do what the customer—not some arbitrary standard—dictates.
• **Tolerate failure.** 3Mers know that if their ideas fail, they still will be encouraged to pursue other innovative ideas. Management knows that mistakes will be made and that destructive criticism kills initiative.

SOURCES: Company reports; R. Mitchell, "Masters of Innovation: How 3M Keeps Its New Products Coming," *BusinessWeek*, April 10, 1989, pp. 58–63; T. Katauskas, "Follow-Through: 3M's Formula for Success," *R&D*, November 1990; and Thomas J. Martin, "Ten Commandments for Managing Creative People," *Fortune*, January 16, 1995, pp. 135–36.

IBM has been helping other firms unleash creativity with its collaborative Lotus software. Whereas in the past new ideas might only be shared in a conference room or around the water cooler, new technologies allow a flow from one employee to another anytime, anywhere.

One of IBM's newest products, Lotus Connections, is a package of five software applications that allow coworkers to share a variety of information rapidly. The package contains profiles, where employees can post information about their expertise and interests; communities, which are formed and managed by colleagues who share common interests; activities, which can be used for managing group projects; bookmarks, which contain shared documents and Web sites; and blogs, where employees can post their own views and commentary. "The business market is showing a lot of interest in using social networking tools to improve productivity. It's about helping people find experts and the information they need to get their jobs done," explains Steve Mills, general manager of the software group at IBM.

Some observers refer to Lotus Connections as the business world's answer to MySpace. But managers realize that shared knowledge is one of the most important resources a firm has. "While social computing software is perceived as being at the fringe of most large businesses, it's actually moving to the center fast—because it's about how the next generation of employees communicate, and create and share ideas," explains Frank Gens, senior vice president for research at IDC.[50]

Bureaucracy Busting

Bureaucracy is an enemy of innovation. While bureaucracy is useful to maintain orderliness and gain efficiencies, it also can work directly against innovativeness. Developing radically different technologies requires a more fluid and flexible (organic) structure that does not restrict thought and action. However, such a structure can be chaotic and disruptive to normal operations. Thus, although 3M has been admired for its culture of innovation, during the previous decade, it became inefficient, with unpredictable profits and an unimpressive stock price. An efficiency drive beginning in 2001 impressed investors and drove up profits, but breakthrough innovations dried up.[51]

To balance innovation with other business goals, companies often establish special temporary project structures that are isolated from the rest of the organization and allowed to operate under different rules. These units go by many names, including "skunkworks" (recall Chapter 7), "greenhouses," and "reserves."

To foster a culture that values innovation, software maker Intuit set up a program called Innovation Lab. Adapting a policy that Google made famous, the company allows employees to spend 10 percent of their time on unstructured activities aimed at generating and developing new ideas. They can choose an idea they personally feel passionate about or can devote the time to learning about new technologies. Intuit also sponsors "idea jams"—days set aside for employees with an idea to assemble a team to develop the idea. Idea jams are one-day events that take place every three months. Employees also have access to workgroup software called Brainstorm, which helps them share ideas and recruit team members to work on the ideas during the idea jams and their unstructured time. Review groups and mentors ensure that ideas are practical and successful. Intuit provides cash awards for winning ideas, but the excitement of Innovation Lab and idea jams is what really motivates Intuit employees to contribute to innovations such as the mobile version of QuickBooks Online.[52]

Bureaucracy-busting managerial systems that encourage collaboration can facilitate innovation. At steel companies such as Chaparral and Nucor, for example, employees work in cross-functional teams to solve problems and create innovative solutions. These flat structures help create an environment that encourages creativity and cooperation. Teams focus on current issues and problems as well as future concerns and

The bottom line

Innovation

Bureaucracy busting encourages innovation.

opportunities. In addition, teams collaborate with outside partners to bring knowledge into the organization so that it can be integrated with existing ideas and information to create innovations. All the while, teams are supported by values of egalitarianism, information sharing, openness to outside ideas, and positive risk. The aim is to destroy the traditional boundaries between functions and departments to create collaborative, less bureaucratic "learning laboratories."[53]

LO 8

development project

A focused organizational effort to create a new product or process via technological advances.

Implementing Development Projects

A powerful tool for managing technology and innovations is the **development project**.[54] A development project is a focused organizational effort to create a new product or process via technological advances. For example, when MTV launched channels aimed at various Asian American markets, the company used development projects embedded in a culture that values innovation. To learn about the effort, see the "From the Pages of *BusinessWeek*" feature.

FROM THE PAGES OF
BusinessWeek

How MTV Channels Innovation

With all the talk about innovation, the creation of corporate innovation departments, and the hiring of chief innovation officers, it's worth noting that some companies with long track records of innovative product and service development have little to no formal innovation structure. Take MTV. In its 25 years, the company has established the music video as one of the most bankable currencies in pop culture, put reality programming on the map, presided over the Heavy Metallization and Hip-Hoppification of pop music, and spawned numerous international editions. Yet look at MTV's organization chart, and you won't see any mention of the I-word. "We don't have a chief innovation officer," says Nusrat Durani, MTV World General Manager. "We don't even think about innovation formally as other companies do." Instead, the company has fostered a culture of innovation, an open and active environment in which new ideas are encouraged from a variety of personalities and perspectives. If a concept holds up to quantitative and qualitative business analysis, it can spawn a new venture no matter whose idea it was.

MTV's culture of innovation stems, in part, from the network's eclectic hiring tendencies. One of the company's founders had been an importer of textiles. The head of MTV International is an Army man. And the chairperson of the company used to be a copywriter. As Durani puts it, "We have a diversity of talent, backgrounds, and experiences. We bring these diverse experiences with us."

As for Durani, he was raised in the Middle East by Indian parents and educated in India. His career spans businesses in India and the United States, where he now lives. So it was no accident that when he learned of MTV's exploratory efforts to serve the growing Asian American community, he had a strong opinion.

MTV World began within the business development team, which had noted the growth in numbers and cultural significance of the Asian American market. To serve these audiences, the initial plan was to leverage MTV International's assets by bringing content directly from MTV India, China, and Korea to U.S. viewers. Durani was working for MTV Interactive and had been brought into the MTV World planning process along with a group of staffers from around the company to vet the idea. And he disagreed with the initial concept. The 20-something Indian American kid is different from his 20-something counterpart in Bombay, he argued, and that called for a unique hybrid. "You have to make a channel that's bicultural. As soon as the people involved in the decision making heard that, they said, 'Of course.'"

For the next 18 months or so, Durani had two roles: finessing the plan with the business development team and reaching out at night for input from his MTV International counterparts in Asia—and also his day job at MTV Interactive. By the time the team was ready to present the plan for MTV World, MTV's annual budget had already been set. But because the organization eschews hard-and-fast rules about how and when innovation happens, MTV World got the green light anyway.

MTV Desi, the first of the MTV World channels, went live in 2006. Its aim is to "super-serve" Indian Americans born in the United States or raised here. The first-generation Indian American, according to Durani, wants "old-school Bollywood and cricket culture." MTV Desi targets the bicultural kids who want the same experiences as other native-born Americans. They love Bangra but also Shakira; they've grown up with MTV but also Bollywood.

To get going, a "pre-launch advisory council" included MTV staffers from News, Music, and MTV World; musical artists; and members of the greater Indian community. The team evaluated the market with demographic and behavioral research on Asian American youth, using methods such as focus groups, house parties, and online surveys, and opened the floor to debate how best to serve them. And though Durani and MTV president Christina Norman finalized most decisions, just about every aspect of the new channel was open to suggestion and discussion. Younger members of the production staff, for example, came up with the idea of featuring young spoken-word artists, and this team continues to be involved in programming this content.

Collaboration extended across MTV divisions as well, and such cross-pollination was key to the development of MTV Desi, which draws roughly 15 percent of its programming from MTV India. The first video shown on MTV Desi, for example, was from an Indian Sikh artist. And this year, MTV India and MTV Desi collaborated on the simultaneous promotion of the Bollywood hit *Kabhi Alvida Na Kahena* (Never Say Good-Bye). In addition, a behind-the-scenes documentary on Shakira's Bollywood-inspired performance at the 2006 Video Music Awards was produced to air on both MTV India and MTV Desi. There are similar links between the various channels of MTV World (MTV Chi for Chinese Americans and MTV K for Korean Americans) and the core MTV News operation. This interaction is usually not formalized; direct ad hoc collaboration is the principal conduit between MTV teams.

SOURCE: Brad Nemer, "How MTV Channels Innovation," *BusinessWeek*, November 6, 2006. © 2006 Time Inc.

Development projects typically feature a special cross-functional team that works together on an overall concept or idea. Like most cross-functional teams, its success depends on how well individuals work together to pursue a common vision. And in the case of development projects, teams must interact with suppliers and customers frequently, making the complexity of their task that much greater. Because of their urgency and strategic importance, most development projects are conducted under intense time and budget pressures, thus presenting a real-time test of the company's ability to innovate.

Managers should recognize that development projects have multiple benefits. Not only are they useful for creating new products and processes, but they frequently cultivate skills and knowledge that can be used for future endeavors. In other words, the capabilities that companies derive from a development project frequently can be turned into a source of competitive advantage. For example, when Ford created a development project to design an air-conditioning compressor to outperform its Japanese rival, executives also discovered that they had laid the foundation for new processes that Ford could use in future projects. Their new

The success of a project is determined by how well a cross-functional team can work together. What traits do good team players have?

capability in integrated design and manufacturing helped Ford reduce the costs and lead times for other product developments. Thus, *organizational learning* had become an equally important criterion for evaluating the success of the project.

For development projects to achieve their fullest benefit, they should build on core competencies (recall Chapters 4 and 9); have a guiding vision about what must be accomplished and why (Chapter 12); have a committed team (Chapters 12 and 14); instill a philosophy of continuous improvement (Chapter 9); and generate integrated, coordinated efforts across all units (Chapters 8 and 9).

Technology, Job Design, and Human Resources

Adopting a new technology typically requires changes in the way jobs are designed. Often the way the task is redefined fits people to the demands of the technology to maximize the technology's operation. But this often fails to maximize total productivity, because it ignores the human part of the equation. The social relationships and human aspects of the task may suffer, lowering overall productivity.

sociotechnical systems

An approach to job design that attempts to redesign tasks to optimize operation of a new technology while preserving employees' interpersonal relationships and other human aspects of the work.

The **sociotechnical systems** approach to work redesign specifically addresses this problem. This approach redesigns tasks in a manner that jointly optimizes the social and technical efficiency of work. Beginning with studies on the introduction of new coal-mining technologies in 1949, the sociotechnical systems approach to work design focused on small, self-regulating work groups.[55] Later it was found that such work arrangements could operate effectively only in an environment in which bureaucracy was limited. Today's trends in bureaucracy "bashing," lean and flat organizations, work teams, and an empowered workforce are logical extensions of the sociotechnical philosophy of work design. At the same time, the technologies of the information age—in which people at all organizational levels have access to vast amounts of information—make these leaner and less bureaucratic organizations possible.

Managers face several choices regarding how to apply a new technology. Technology can be used to limit the tasks and responsibilities of workers and "de-skill" the workforce, thus turning workers into servants of the technology. Alternatively, managers can select and train workers to master the technology, using it to achieve great accomplishments and improve the quality of their lives. Technology, when managed effectively, can empower workers as it improves the competitiveness of organizations.

TABLE 17.4 Compensation Practices in Traditional and Advanced Manufacturing Firms

Type of Compensation Practice	Traditional Factory	Integrated Manufacturing
Performance-contingent	Focus on *individual incentives* reflects division of labor and separation of stages and functions.	Extensive use of *group incentives* to encourage teamwork, cooperation, and joint problem solving.
Job-contingent	Use of *hourly wage* assumes that differences in employee contribution are captured in job classifications and that performance is determined largely by the production system.	Use of *salary* assumes that the employees' contributions transcend the job per se to substantially affect output. The distinctions between classes of employment are diminished.
Person-contingent	*Seniority pay* rewards experience as a surrogate for knowledge and skill in a stable environment and rewards loyalty to reduce uncertainty within the system.	*Skill-based* pay rewards continuous learning and the value added from increased flexibility in a dynamic environment.

SOURCE: Scott A. Snell and James W. Dean Jr., "Strategic Compensation for Integrated Manufacturing: The Moderating Effects of Jobs and Organizational Inertia," *Academy of Management Journal* 37 (1994), pp. 1109–40.

However, as managers make decisions about how to design jobs and manage employees, they also need to consider other human resource systems that complement the introduction of new technology. Table 17.4, for example, shows how compensation systems can be changed to facilitate the implementation of advanced manufacturing technology. In the contemporary setting, the use of group incentives, salary, and skill-based pay systems helps reinforce the collective effort (recall the use of cross-functional teams), professionalism, empowerment, and flexibility required for knowledge work. If a company's pay system is not aligned with the new technologies, it may not reward behavior that is needed to make the changes work. Worse, existing reward systems actually may reinforce old behaviors that run counter to what is needed for the new technology.

Taken as a whole, these ideas provide a set of guidelines for managing the strategic and organizational issues associated with technology and innovation. In Chapter 18, we expand this discussion to focus on how organizations can reshape themselves to adapt to a dynamic marketplace. Managing change and organizational learning are central elements of what it takes to become a world-class organization. Honda is a case in point.

Management Close-Up

ASSESSING OUTCOMES AND SEIZING OPPORTUNITIES

Honda introduced the world's first gasoline–electric hybrid car, the Insight, in 1999. It discontinued the three-door hatchback in 2006, only to reintroduce it in 2009 as a second-generation, five-door hatchback. Priced at $19,800, the 2010 Insight was the least-expensive hybrid available. Honda also markets hybrid versions of its Civic and Accord, but to date, its hybrid sales have not been as strong as those of the Toyota Prius, which outsells Honda hybrids 4 to 1. Nevertheless, Honda doesn't seem overly concerned.

That may be because Honda doesn't regard the lithium-ion battery technology—which powers the Prius—as the wave of the future. Honda cites significant weaknesses in that technology, such as a tendency to overheat and take too long to charge. What is superior to the lithium-ion battery, the company believes, is hydrogen fuel-cell technology. In 2009 the company introduced the FCX Clarity, a four-passenger sedan whose motor runs on electricity generated by a hydrogen fuel cell. Although the Clarity is currently available for lease only in areas where hydrogen fuel-pump stations exist, Honda expresses confidence that the infrastructure will catch up.

Twice as efficient as a hybrid and three times more efficient than a gas-powered vehicle, the Clarity's only emission is water,

a by-product of the hydrogen fuel cell. While hybrid models powered by lithium-ion batteries take hours to charge, Honda's Clarity charges in a minute. What's more, the company claims, within 10 years Clarity owners will be able to charge their cars at home. Environmental experts named the Clarity the 2009 World Green Car.

On the horizon for Honda is an array of affordable electric hybrids, including a hybrid version of its subcompact Honda Fit as well as the redesigned Insight. Company management expects hybrids to account for 10 percent of its sales by 2012.

Honda acknowledges that gasoline will likely continue to be the most frequently used fuel for the near term, but its engineers are working to identify additional alternatives. Current projects include the development of a next-generation clean diesel engine and the production of ethanol from cellulosic biomaterials, not corn.[56]

- What can Honda president and CEO Takanobu Ito do to make Honda hybrid models more appealing during an economic downturn?
- In 2008, Honda discontinued its sponsorship of Formula One racing. The move is expected to save the company about $500 million a year. In your opinion, should Ito reevaluate this decision made by his predecessor? Why?

KEY TERMS

SUMMARY OF LEARNING OBJECTIVES

Now that you have studied Chapter 17, you should be able to:

LO 1 List the types of processes that spur development of new technologies.

Forces that compel the emergence of a new technology include (1) a need for the technology, (2) the requisite scientific knowledge, (3) the technical convertibility of this knowledge, (4) the capital resources to fund development, and (5) the entrepreneurial insight and initiative to pull the components together.

LO 2 Describe how technologies proceed through a life cycle.

New technologies follow a predictable life cycle. First, a workable idea about how to meet a market need is developed into a product innovation. Early progress can be slow as competitors experiment with product designs. Eventually, a dominant design emerges as the market accepts the technology, and further refinements to the technology result from process innovations. As the technology begins to approach both the theoretical limits to its performance potential and market saturation, growth slows and the technology matures. At this point the technology can remain stable or be replaced by a new technology.

LO 3 Discuss ways to manage technology for competitive advantage.

Adopters of new technologies are categorized according to the timing of their adoption: innovators, early adopters, the early majority, the late majority, and laggards. Technology leadership has many first-mover advantages but also poses significant disadvantages. The same may be said for followership. After that, technology that helps improve efficiency will support a low-cost strategy, while technologies that help make products more distinctive or unique will support a differentiation strategy. Determining an appropriate technology strategy depends on the degree to which the technology supports the organization's competitive requirements and, if a technology leadership strategy is chosen, the company's ability, in terms of skills, resources, and commitment, to deal with the risks and uncertainties of leadership.

LO 4 Summarize how to assess technology needs.

Assessing the technology needs of a company begins by benchmarking, or comparing, the technologies it employs with those of both competitors and noncompetitors. Benchmarking should be done on a global basis to understand practices used worldwide. Technology scanning helps identify emerging technologies and those still under development in an effort to project their eventual competitive impact.

LO 5 Identify alternative methods of pursuing technological innovation.

New technologies can be acquired or developed. Options include internal development, purchase, contracted development, licensing, trading, research partnerships and joint ventures, and acquisition. The approach used depends on the existing availability of the technology; the skills, resources, and time available; and the importance of keeping the technology proprietary.

LO 6 Define key roles in managing technology.

People play many different roles in managing technology. For example, the chief information officer is the person with broad, integrative responsibility for technological innovation. In addition, the entrepreneur is the person who recognizes the competitive potential of the technology and finds new ways to exploit opportunities. The technical innovator has the key skills needed to develop or install and operate the technology. The product champion is the person who promotes the new idea(s) to gain support throughout the organization. The executive champion is the person with the status and resources to support the project.

LO 7 Describe the elements of an innovative organization.

Organizing for innovation involves unleashing the creative energies of employees while directing their efforts toward meeting market needs in a timely manner. Companies can unleash creativity by establishing a culture that values intrapreneurship; accepts and even celebrates failure as a sign of innovation; and reinforces innovation through goal setting, rewards, and stories of creative employees. The organization's structure should balance bureaucracy for controlling existing processes with a flexibility that allows innovation to take place. Development projects provide an opportunity for cross-functional teamwork aimed at innovation. Job design should take into account both social relationships and the technical efficiency of work so that jobs are within employees' ability but also empower them to work cooperatively and creatively.

LO 8 List characteristics of successful development projects.

For development projects to achieve the fullest benefit, they should (1) build on core competencies; (2) have a guiding vision about what must be accomplished and why; (3) have a committed team; (4) instill a philosophy of continuous improvement; and (5) generate integrated, coordinated efforts across all teams and units.

DISCUSSION QUESTIONS

1. According to Francis Bacon, "A wise man will make more opportunities than he finds." What does this have to do with technology and innovation? What does it have to do with competitive advantage?

2. What examples of technological innovation can you identify? What forces led to the commercialization of the science behind those technologies? Did the capability exist before the market demand, or was the demand there before the technology was available?

3. Thomas Edison once said that most innovations are 10 percent inspiration and 90 percent perspiration. How does this match what you know about technology life cycles?

4. Why would a company choose to follow rather than lead technological innovations? Is the potential advantage of technological leadership greater when innovations are occurring rapidly, or is it better in this case to follow?

5. If you were in the grocery business, whom would you benchmark for technological innovations? Would the companies be inside or outside your industry? Why?

6. How would you see the executive champion, the chief information officer, and the product champion working together? Could the roles all be played by the same individual? Why or why not?

CONCLUDING CASE

S & Z East Coast Importers

OVERVIEW

Herbie Shapiro has worked as a retail footwear salesman in the New York City area for nearly 20 years. The New York City native has always worked for someone else, but he knows the business and its people very well. Shapiro has always felt that the supply side of the retail footwear business is poorly organized and that few if any distributors provide good service to the hundreds of retail outlets in the metropolitan area.

Mei Zhao, a native of China, is a longtime acquaintance of Shapiro, and a manufacturer's rep for several of the Pacific Rim footwear manufacturers. Zhao functions primarily as a foreign agent and freight forwarder for the Asian manufacturers, overseeing the unloading and trucking of container ship cargo.

Zhao shares many of the same views as Shapiro when it comes to the distribution and supply side of the retail footwear business. Both men are at the midpoint of their careers: have built a solid business and personal relationship with one another; and, following several meetings, have decided to form a partnership. S & Z East Coast Importers has the opportunity to lease a 60,000-square-foot warehouse with a buy option in northern New Jersey for purposes of establishing a distribution center for the metropolitan area retail footwear business.

Zhao already has many good links and relationships with the major suppliers and shippers of retail footwear. The partners plan to import a wide range of products, including casual shoes, athletic footwear, fashion and outdoor boots, slippers, socks, laces, pads, and inserts. Zhao has access to all of the major national brands as well as the bargain-priced no-name lines.

In addition to his long association and membership in local and national footwear organizations, Shapiro knows many store owners and employees within the New York–New Jersey metro area. Shapiro is well liked and well respected. The partners believe that their strong combination of supply-side and retail experience will provide them with access to many good markets.

As is the case in many industries, retail footwear has a very small number of large suppliers of manufactured products coupled with a very large number of small retail stores. One of the major keys to success therefore is the existence of an efficient, well-organized system of distribution. Shapiro and Zhao are focusing their efforts on doing a better job than the competition and on filling that niche in the footwear market.

LOGISTICAL ISSUES AND CHALLENGES

Most of the aforementioned footwear products arrive at the West Coast on giant container ships. After clearing customs, the containers are offloaded onto tractors for local (western) delivery and onto railcars for Midwestern and East Coast distribution. Shapiro and Zhao plan to set up their building as a warehouse and distribution center.

Warehouse and distribution centers must purchase virtually all of their products in large quantities. Shapiro and Zhao will typically be faced with buying shipments of 500,000 pairs of shoes, 1,000,000 pairs of socks, 600,000 pairs of running shoes, and so on. Retailers, on the other hand, typically must purchase very small quantities of mixed loads of products, primarily because of a lack of retail and storage space. Shapiro and Zhao will typically be faced with orders that call for 50 to 150 pairs of shoes, 50 to 100 pairs of socks, 100 to 300 pairs of running shoes, and so on.

Warehouse and distribution centers must therefore be set up to receive, unload, and store large shipments of product (railroad cars/tractor trailers); to "break bulk" (unpack, count, inventory, and repack); and to load and deliver small mixed loads to retail establishments. Many metro-area retailers are located on cramped and busy streets with limited access.

The financial side of Shapiro and Zhao's business looks very promising. Thanks to Zhao's connections with suppliers and Shapiro's connections with the New York–New Jersey metro market, the partners anticipate an average markup of 30 percent for their products. That is nearly twice as much as Zhao earns as a manufacturer's rep.

For their business to succeed, several variables and logistics must fall into place and be properly managed. The warehouse and distribution process, quality of service, and financial management must operate at maximum efficiency. In addition to in-house efficiency and cost control, the company must also buy and sell enough volume of product to cover all costs and generate profits.

Retail customers are looking for timely and frequent deliveries of small quantities of specific products. Some of those customers may need merchandising help as well. If products are not selling, the distribution centers and manufacturers will soon be backed up with product as well. Retail sales are the key to avoiding a bottleneck in the process and flow of manufacturing and distribution.

The financial side of this business requires close and careful management of receivables and payables. Manufacturers typically expect and receive payment for their products in about 10 days. This is essential to the sustained cash flow of those operations (primarily for payroll and raw materials purposes). Retailers, on the other hand, expect and receive accounts payable terms ranging from 30 to 60 days. This is essential to the sustained cash flow of those operations, as customer sales are the primary source of funds. So while the prospect of a 30 percent markup is clearly attractive, the cash flow situation and challenge must be met.

Shapiro and Zhao are unsure about the best way to facilitate and manage trucking and insurance. They have the option of buying or leasing their own trucks on both the supply and delivery side and also have the option of using independent trucking companies. They could select some combination of those two options. In addition, merchandise must be insured, but who exactly is responsible for that coverage, and when does that "ownership" change hands?

The partners project monthly warehouse operating expenses of $55,000 (building, payroll, administration, and salaries). This does not include merchandise, trucking, or insurance. Given their 30 percent average markup on products, monthly sales of about $180,000 will be needed to break even. The partners have conservatively projected first-year sales to be $3 million.

Their warehouse inventory capabilities are in excess of $30 million. Shapiro and Zhao realize that it will take some time to approach that level from both a sales and cash flow perspective.

Their facility and market base clearly present the potential to achieve sales of $40 million or more. Cash flow is the current obstacle. They have just over $1 million in working capital for their start-up and believe that that will accommodate first-year sales of $3 million given their logistics of inventory purchase, sales, and cash flow.

From a distance, the prospect of success is promising. The partners have the opportunity to buy low and sell high in large volume. A market niche is waiting to be filled. The partners have the experience and the connections on both the supply and sales sides of the business.

QUESTIONS

1. How can Herbie Shapiro and Mei Zhao use technology to achieve success in their new venture? Be sure to address each of the major categories presented—purchasing, transportation, operations, distribution, and financial management.

2. Select a specific business or industry that you may become a part of. How would you incorporate the technological aspects of the text into your day-to-day operations?

EXPERIENTIAL EXERCISES

17.1 Planning for Innovation

OBJECTIVES

1. To brainstorm innovative ideas for a company that has become stagnant.
2. To explore the elements of a good innovation plan.

INSTRUCTIONS

1. Read the Mason Inc. scenario.
2. Individually or in small groups, offer a plan for encouraging innovation at Mason Inc. Discuss staffing, rewards, organizational structure, work design, and any other facets of organizational behavior that apply.
3. In small groups, or with the entire class, share the plans you developed.

MASON INC. SCENARIO

Mason Inc. designs, develops, and manufactures personal grooming products. From 1950 to 1980 it was a leader in introducing new, profitable products into the marketplace. Its Research and Development Division grew from 20 to 150 professionals during that time. Since 1980, however, the company has relied on its past successes and has failed to introduce any significant innovative product into the marketplace. Top management wants to reestablish Mason's reputation as the number-one innovator in the industry.

DISCUSSION QUESTIONS

1. What elements do these plans have in common?
2. How well do the plans follow the innovation process?
3. Do the plans incorporate provisions for fulfilling the various roles required for innovation?
4. What are the strengths and weaknesses of each plan?
5. What should be the components of an effective plan?

SOURCE: J. Gordon, *A Diagnostic Approach to Organizational Behavior* (Englewood Cliffs, NJ: Prentice-Hall, 1983), p. 654. Reprinted by permission of Prentice-Hall, Inc., Englewood Cliffs, N.J.

17.2 Innovation for the Future

OBJECTIVE

To look ahead into the future.

INSTRUCTIONS

Choose a partner. Together, develop an innovative product or service that will be popular in the year 2025. As you develop your product or service, ask yourselves the following questions:

1. What trends lead you to believe that this product or service will be successful?
2. What current technologies, services, or products will be replaced by your idea?

Present your idea to the class for discussion.

Operations Management in the New Economy

The business of a company—any company—is to take certain inputs and, by means of a process, transform them into outputs. Bringing these outputs (the product) to market cost-effectively will ensure the company's continued existence and well-being. The methods, systems, and mental framework by which a company transforms its inputs into outputs characterize its *operations*. A company maintains the health of its transformation process through *management* of these operations. *Operations management* is the analysis and implementation of this process.

Many varied factors impinge on a company's operations and managers. As company size increases, so do the number of variables. Effective management of the operation and its variables contributes in no small measure to the company's success, whether the company is small or large, diversified or devoted to core businesses, a network organization or a highly structured, centralized body. It holds true whether the company sells a tangible product (goods) or an intangible one (services), for in both cases, the customer is buying the object of a desire, or the satisfaction of a need.

EFFECTS OF CHANGE

We often read that operations management is in transition today. In actuality, it has always been in transition, because the world is always changing. Changes may take the form of new products (imagine the first traders bringing spices to Europe in the early Middle Ages), new distribution channels (Federal Express completely revamped our expectations about package delivery), alterations in the labor pool (women assumed many factory jobs during World War II, when men were at war), or new technologies (gunpowder altered all the rules of war in 14th-century Europe).

Characteristic of the current age is the quickening *rate* at which change occurs, placing pressure on individuals to adapt quickly and rewarding those able to shift mental gears, personal habits, and priorities easily. Indeed, survival of the fittest applies not only to physical attributes but also to mental agility. Operations managers must be among the most "fit" to function effectively in today's world.

THE CONTEXT OF OPERATIONS MANAGEMENT

What does it mean to be an effective manager of an operation? It means responding to the needs of diverse parties *within* the company, ensuring smooth movement through all stages of the transformation process. We can even take the viewpoint that, within the process, the "customer" is the department receiving the result of the preceding stage. For example, in a printing company, the operator of the press is the customer of the prepress area. An effective manager works with this awareness, ensuring that each area supplies what the next one expects.

Operations management also means satisfying parties in the *larger* arena. For example, investors may want to know how well a new product line is faring in the market or whether a new manufacturing process is delivering as promised. The community may want assurances that wastes from the production process will not cause quality of life to suffer. The government may demand an accounting of any number of activities covered by regulations. Thus, the manager of an operation does not exist in isolation but is part of an ongoing interaction among any number of parties.

In ages past, the world was home to many different societies or cultures, which were mostly different one from another, but each was more homogeneous than is the case today. Buyers in a given community needed the same products. Everyone knew what those products were, and common agreement on quality prevailed. Also prevalent was a common understanding of the entitlements of various social levels (what goods of what quality were the prerogative of the wealthy, for example). Because items were individually made, customization was the norm, for there was no other way to do business.

As the industrial age dawned in the 19th century, this situation changed. Suddenly the "customer" was no longer a few identifiable individuals, but a growing mass of less well-defined persons, any of whom, with money, could have what was formerly the prerogative of the few. With industrialization came mass production, and one product for all buyers became the norm, because there was no other cost-effective way to do business.

The modern-day corporation took shape against this background, and marketing was born. Now in the digital age, we are witnessing a phenomenon that once would have sounded like an oxymoron: mass customization. What are the implications for today's managers?

When the product is static or has few variations, operations management quite justifiably focuses on the product (and its cost). This perspective has produced the orientation of traditional operations management. With the ability to manufacture many variations of the same product, with access to increasing amounts of information, the focus today has shifted to the customer's *experience* of the product: how he or she perceives to have been served by the vendor. The customer assesses whether the product contains the desired characteristics and quality, at the best price. Management of an operation with this awareness probably will spell the success or failure of the company in today's environment.

But is today's customer truly different? Yes and no, for despite the fact that things change, things also stay the same. Human beings still engage in the same activities: they create community; they raise the next generation; they trade; they provide for themselves; and in the process, they learn, fight, and play. And today's managers still shuttle inputs through the transformation process into successful outputs. Most of the traditional notions about human activity still apply.

To explain any activity, however, one may use a variety of lenses (Galileo's lens was different from Ptolemy's, and so he derived a different explanation of the universe). A manager may view the process from the standpoint of product specifications, cost limitations, customer satisfaction, or any number of viewpoints. The lens chosen will reflect a particular view of the world and its priorities, as well as the company's priorities.

Sometimes there are no right or wrong choices, only consequences. The lens that adequately explained a given phenomenon at one time may not serve today. What is reflected through the lens will form the guidelines for decisions, however, and so the choice has far-reaching repercussions.

NEW PERSPECTIVES

From time to time, particular orientations or viewpoints burst onto the stage, altering perceptions and leaving changed priorities in their wake. Such is the case with W. Edwards Deming's *total quality management,* now an article of faith for many of today's managers. The Japanese readily embraced Deming's principles, taking an enviable and now imitated approach to

FROM THE PAGES OF
BusinessWeek

Streamlined Plane Making

Bitter rivals Airbus and Boeing Co. don't agree on much, but these days their production gurus chant a common mantra: Let's copy Toyota, the company that reinvented car making. The giant jet makers and their suppliers are going back to school to learn about efficient production from companies that churn out vehicles that are just a fraction of a plane's size and complexity.

Cutting production costs and speeding assembly is a vital step in the Airbus–Boeing duel to stay competitive. So airplane people are now designing parts with an eye to how fast they can be assembled. Both Boeing and Airbus have slashed their parts inventories, copied the way carmakers organize factories, and trimmed production times. Boeing has also managed to apply to gargantuan planes a technique long ago adopted by Henry Ford: assembly lines.

Not long ago, the idea of aping a mass-market car manufacturer seemed preposterous. Carmakers churned out millions of light vehicles last year, each priced in the tens of thousands of dollars. Annual output at Boeing and Airbus together was just 605 planes, some priced at almost $200 million. Car models change every few years, while jetliner models change over decades. "We always thought airplanes were different because they had four million parts," says Alan Mulally, head of Boeing's commercial aircraft division. "Well, airplanes aren't different. This is manufacturing."

Airbus aims to build a single-aisle plane from scratch in just six months, half the time taken in 2003. Working faster means Airbus can produce more planes at its existing factories, and it expects to free up more than $1.3 billion in cash by shortening the time it keeps its parts in stock—another economy pioneered by carmakers.

As Boeing prepares to build its proposed fuel-efficient 787 Dreamliner jet, project manager Mike Bair wants to make the plane so modular that the last stage of assembly takes just three days. Its predecessor model, the 767, took up to a month to assemble. Because individuality sends costs soaring, he is also emulating car companies by offering a standard set of features on the 787. Customers can no longer dictate cockpit layouts and have limited choice on items such as electronics and interiors. Airbus and Boeing have also started outsourcing entire components, just as carmakers outsource systems like transmissions.

On shop floors, the plane makers have also learned from carmakers. At an Airbus factory in Wales, production teams used to walk far to the stockroom for bags of bolts and rivets, and frequently left them scattered about because they lacked nearby storage. Using work-analysis methods developed by the auto industry, project teams studied which fasteners were needed where, and when, and then organized racks on the shop floor. Now, carefully labeled bins contain tidy sets of supplies needed for specific tasks. The change has sped up work and saved over $100,000 in rivets and bolts at the Welsh factory alone, Airbus says.

But swapping one production method for another can require huge investments in new equipment and staff training. That's a big reason why aviation manufacturers have moved slowly. Airbus, for example, moves planes through successive stations during assembly but still maintains much of the old piecework approach. Production managers say this gives flexibility because a glitch that slows one plane won't stall a whole assembly line. Boeing, though, made one of the most dramatic production changes yet when it began putting together planes on a huge moving line. Top Boeing executives made multiple visits to Toyota when they were first beginning to study how to convert the production process to a moving line. When many workers initially balked at the production line and unions filed complaints, Boeing took extra pains to win them over. The change paid off: Boeing halved the time it takes to assemble a single-aisle 737, and has started putting its other planes— including its oldest and largest product, the 747—on moving lines.

SOURCE: Daniel Michaels and J. Lynn Lunsford, "Streamlined Plane Making," *The Wall Street Journal,* April 1, 2005, p. B1. © 2005 Time Inc. All rights reserved.

Streamlined Plane Making

Boeing, Airbus Look to Car Companies' Methods to Speed Up Jetliner Production

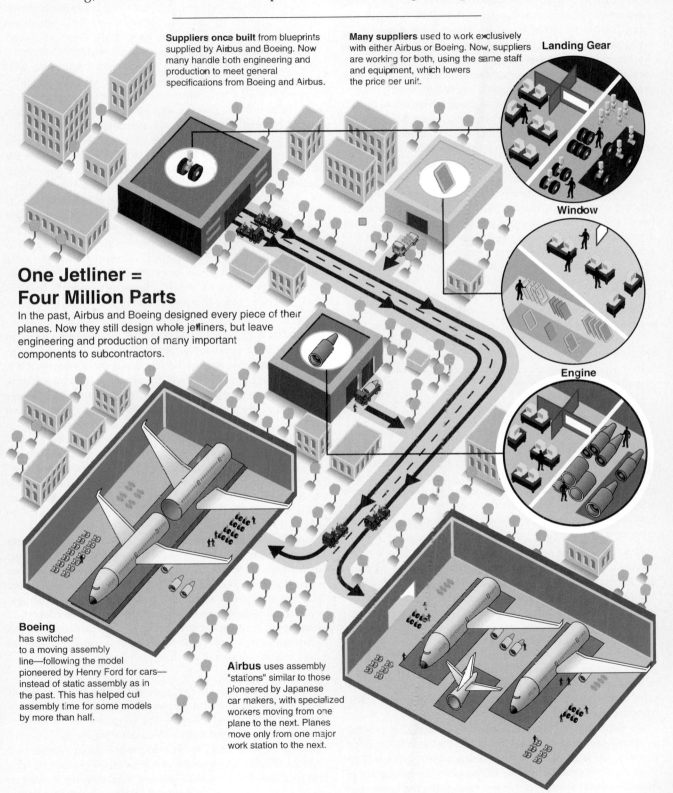

Suppliers once built from blueprints supplied by Airbus and Boeing. Now many handle both engineering and production to meet general specifications from Boeing and Airbus.

Many suppliers used to work exclusively with either Airbus or Boeing. Now, suppliers are working for both, using the same staff and equipment, which lowers the price per unit.

Landing Gear

Window

Engine

One Jetliner = Four Million Parts

In the past, Airbus and Boeing designed every piece of their planes. Now they still design whole jetliners, but leave engineering and production of many important components to subcontractors.

Boeing has switched to a moving assembly line—following the model pioneered by Henry Ford for cars—instead of static assembly as in the past. This has helped cut assembly time for some models by more than half.

Airbus uses assembly "stations" similar to those pioneered by Japanese car makers, with specialized workers moving from one plane to the next. Planes move only from one major work station to the next.

SOURCE: *The Wall Street Journal*, April 1, 2005, p. B1.

customer satisfaction (see Chapter 9 of the text for Deming's 14 points). Western nations paid scant attention until they saw the results of offering quality in a customer-oriented operation.

For most of us, quality is what we see in the end result (does the product meet manufacturing specifications?). In his lengthy essay *Zen and the Art of Motorcycle Maintenance*, Robert Pirsig associated achievement of quality with a state of mind: "Skilled mechanics and machinists of a certain sort . . . have patience, care and attentiveness to what they're doing, a kind of inner peace of mind that isn't contrived but results from a kind of harmony with the work . . . "[1] More characteristic of the Eastern mindset, this statement means that quality (good or bad) is not an attribute of the end product, but rather is inherent in the way an individual interacts with the subject of his or her attention.

To achieve good quality requires knowing what is good, and then having the mindset suitable for achieving it. This attentiveness is related to the Japanese *kaizen,* a willingness and desire to improve constantly. Since the 1980s, Japanese business practices have been the object of study and implementation by Westerners, from specific procedures (such as *kanban,* the basis of just-in-time inventory management) to general philosophies (the *kaizen* that is part of Japanese general operations strategy). A manager anywhere today would be ill served by neglect of these concepts. As you can see from the "From the Pages of *Business-Week*" features, even airplane manufacturers are finding new relevance in Japan's manufacturing philosophy and techniques.

Likewise, companies that involve employees in the process are on the way to understanding that the people who interface with the product are crucial to its success. We will see how important this view is in a few pages.

CORPORATE ORGANIZATION

There are many ways to structure a company, and some of today's companies have taken their present form as a result of trends in the economy: mergers or acquisitions, diversification, alliances. With all, there are still certain functions identifiable in most corporate organizations. The operation of that function is what commands the attention of its managers. Let us consider how some of these common functions support the operations management system.

Strategic Planning On the highest level, guiding the corporation from the broadest perspective is strategic, or long-range, planning. The firm's upper-level managers provide the corporation's direction, defining and refining its mission in the process. Management of this function entails answering questions such as: What business are we in? What business should or will we be in? Who are our customers? How can or should we serve them? Do we want to focus on core businesses or diversify? Answers to these questions will help develop corporate goals, which, filtered through the company's management levels, give direction to its operation.

As stated earlier, the world is always changing. Good strategic planning seeks to *anticipate* change and then plan for it. Good planners also foster a feeling of confidence about what is likely to produce success. During the 1990s, when the rallying cry of much of corporate management was to stick to core businesses, GE chief Jack Welch built a successful conglomerate of widely diverse businesses, finding people with the mindset to operate

well within that structure, and achieving effective coordination of all functions through its many divisions.

Marketing Of all the company's functions, marketing is closest to the customer. Its job is to identify customer needs (latent or manifest) and translate them back to the firm for its reaction. Its role in supporting the operations management system is therefore critical. Operations managers must then restate what marketing has communicated in terms that will bring about the needed response from the production mechanism. To support its efforts, marketing works with advertising to state the company's offerings in terms that are attractive to the buyer. Sales is a part of the marketing function also, salespeople being those who take action to sell within an identified market. This is the front line, the place where information about customer needs and desires penetrates and gains the attention of the company.

A story told in sales circles is about the ABC Company (a shoe manufacturer), whose marketing head visited a remote area of the world to assess the market. He returned to report to his boss, "There's no market; they don't wear shoes." The marketing head of competitor XYZ Company made the same trip for the same purpose, reporting to *his* boss: "It's a terrific market! They've got no shoes!" Marketing's response to a circumstance can take a firm into new areas.

Research and Engineering Suppose the marketing function has identified a new need or potential market. Enter the design and engineering people, whose function is the development and refinement of the product and the processes that manufacture it. They design, develop, and test the product through all stages until it is ready for market launch. They interact with customers who participate in the testing of a new product prior to launching. They also interact with operations—the product attributes and the processes required to make them will become the responsibility of the operations management system. Even as a product is still on the drawing board, its design may change based on customer response, manufacturing procedures (i.e., what is feasible in the current setup), or prices of material or labor.

As researchers and developers, this part of the company is most in touch with what will be available in the future, and one of its functions is identification and implementation of solutions not currently in use. The end result of the designers' work will affect purchasing (of parts, equipment, materials), inventory management (quantities of items to keep on hand), shop floor operation (equipment may need rearrangement), capacity requirements (maximum rate of production), and human resources (human skills needed and cost of acquisition).

Human Resources This brings us to the next function: human resources. A company *is* its people. They form the culture, produce the product, and deliver it. The human resources function must seek, attract, and keep individuals having the skills, human qualities, and experience required by the operations management system. Effective management of human resources thus directly affects the entire production process. Any company wishing to build a plant in a geographically desirable area would be foolish not to take into account the human component: educational level, work ethic, habits, and expectations of the labor pool.

Some believe that there are no bad employees, only employees placed in wrong positions. Effective use of employees will provide operations managers with a valuable source of innovation and productivity gains, for the employees are actually in contact with the product (and with the customer, in the case of a service business). They are the interface where quality is born. It cannot be stressed too heavily that one of the most valuable attributes of any employee is the ability to communicate: to articulate what's right about the work experience, what's wrong, and how to improve it. Dissatisfaction unexpressed is potential trouble; ideas not presented represent lost potential.

Purchasing Just as human inputs matter, so do materials. Selecting inputs that will support the company's orientation and vision is the crucial role played by the purchasing function. Optimally, it is a source of expertise for the operations management system, providing information about the variety of materials and systems available for use by the production process. The performance of any operating division is ultimately dependent on goods and services supplied to it by purchasing. Will the materials produce the result intended by the design of the product? Will they allow themselves to be molded as intended by the production process? Will they support the level of quality promised?

Cost-effective supply of the right materials potentially represents enormous savings for the company. A purchasing manager was once heard to say: "The sales division would have to close $500,000 in new business to produce the money I just saved by changing suppliers."

Logistics The logistics of moving inputs through transformation may or may not benefit from an overview of the entire process, for the flow may take different names, depending on its location in the process. It may be called *inventory management* as inputs arrive, *scheduling* while in the transformation process, and *distribution* when outputs are en route to the customer. Smooth or poor coordination of the flow from supplier of materials to delivery to the customer has repercussions throughout the channel. If materials are not ready for a specific section of the production apparatus at the right time, equipment and machinery sit idle (a drain on profitability). Delays in delivery to customers mean delays in payment received, and that has an impact on the company's cash flow.

Finance This brings us to the finance area. This function serves as an interface between the firm's managers and the financial community: banks, investment firms, and stockholders. These entities have a stake in the company's success or failure, and at all times are poised to assist, advise, provide support, or withdraw it. Finance must explain the company's performance adequately to elicit the maximum amount of support from financial institutions. In so doing, it makes use of the accounting department. Not merely a mechanism for tracking costs, the accounting department provides information useful to managers in understanding the cost implications of their decisions. Such cost-monitoring information can help managers understand how their own costs compare with standard costs, for example. Accounting also can help derive the cost implications of introducing new equipment or technologies.

In another of its roles, the finance function must be knowledgeable about the firm's creditworthiness. Any decline in the company's ability to pay its bills will weaken its position vis-à-vis competitors. Finance also must monitor the creditworthiness of suppliers. If suppliers are not financially able to deliver what they promise, the operations management system will feel the impact immediately. The financial community watches the impact of all these decisions, basing its ratings (and therefore support) on the wisdom of the decision makers.

A Team Operation The fineness with which one breaks down the preceding functions can vary, but it should be clear at this point that the operations management system is only one of those operating within the corporate context. In the best of all possible worlds, operations management works hand in glove with the other functions, alert to any harmful fragmentation or lack of communication. Communication is, of course, a two-way street, and just as operations people must be aware of the workings of the other functions, the latter must know what the operations management system perceives, needs, and expects.

Satisfying customer expectations is a corporate activity, the work of one body (from *corpus*, Latin for "body"), with the whole dependent on how well its parts work individually and how well they work together. Neglect of any one organ affects the body's ability to perform at optimum level.

PREPARING FOR THE FUTURE IN THE NEW ECONOMY

In addition to awareness of how the company is operating at present, every good manager will give thought to what *could* happen, what is *likely* to happen, and what is possible, both for the company as a whole and for his or her own sphere of influence. Stated another way, an effective manager has a sense of vision. This means being aware of changes or potential changes in customer demands and changes in the company's resources (technology, labor pool, financial support). A good manager must listen, being attentive to all facts, and then select the useful facts from among the many supplied. A manager must constantly ask, "What if . . . ?"

With good vision and a healthy curiosity, a manager will more adequately handle factors impinging on the operations management system. The objective is to develop a sense of vision adequate to anticipate conceivable consequences. Let us consider some of today's challenges in what is often referred to as the **new economy.**

Globalization A company's sphere of activity has always been what could be reached easily by current means of communication and transportation. What is reachable has constantly expanded. The entire world is today's operating arena, both for buying inputs and for selling outputs. This circumstance presents the operations management system with a new range of possibilities.

The possibility of *outsourcing* has always been present. That is, do we make a particular component of the product, or do we send it out for manufacture pursuant to our specifications? Today, a manager may outsource locally or to any facility in the world offering the capability of supplying the need. It takes a lot of information, as well as sound judgment, to know which part of the process would benefit from being handled out of house.

The success of producing elsewhere depends in part on the characteristics of the "elsewhere." In the 20th century, U.S.

companies based in northern states sometimes would move certain manufacturing operations to the southern part of the country, taking advantage of lower labor costs. While this required some adjustment in expectations, the adjustment is slight compared to manufacturing in Pacific Rim countries or Latin America, for example. The reason is simple: Each culture handles things in a particular way. A wise manager will not assume that a different culture will respond to expectations in the same manner as an American labor force would, and this circumstance may work to one's advantage or to one's detriment. Those who can anticipate potential problem areas are ahead of the game in the decision to manufacture offshore.

Then there is the globe as *marketplace*. To sell globally requires product design that accounts for differing tastes throughout the world's cultures. A small manufacturer of skin-care products based on formulas from India began marketing her line in America some years ago. She reports that she had to make alterations to account for the fact that Americans would not use a product with an unusual smell, no matter how beneficial for the skin.[2] Nescafe markets its products all over the globe, but the instant coffee sold in Brazil does not taste like that sold in the United States—in each instance, the product must satisfy the taste of a different culture.[3]

The ease with which the operations management system can make these alterations has increased dramatically in the last few decades. Digital technology has made flexibility in manufacturing a much more attainable situation than was previously the case, offering enormous potential to vary the product.

Environment   Another challenge facing today's manager is the environment, meaning both the world and the milieu in which the company operates. In an earlier time, negative effects from a manufacturing process were absorbed unobtrusively by the surroundings. As population density increased and consumption skyrocketed, particularly in the Western nations, this ceased to be true. What occurs in one place on the planet has an impact on the rest of it. The manager's challenge is to care enough about the future without imperiling today's operations, and the decisions are not simple.

It is unfortunate that the issue of environmental responsibility traditionally has been cast in ethical terms. While this stance is valid, and ultimately *the* reason for being good stewards of the planet, it does not help managers handle all the information required to make good decisions or quantify what is needed for decision making. In addition, consumers are often inconsistent, demanding recycled paper, for instance, and then choosing to buy whiter paper that is not recycled.

Certainly the last few decades have witnessed significant progress in the handling of the most blatantly offensive effects of manufacturing processes (waste streaming, emissions control). But making the right decision is not a clear-cut path. Consider the simple example of the supermarket checkout stand. "Would you like paper or plastic for your groceries?" The environmentally responsible buyer must choose between less than desirable alternatives. Paper (even if recycled) uses trees; plastic uses hydrocarbons and is not as easy to recycle. Decisions faced by operations managers are infinitely more complex.

Furthermore, if managers do not see to their societal responsibility, others will demand compliance. A corporation is not its own island in community waters, for others are affected by its decisions: property owners, investors, the larger public, and tomorrow's adults. Surely we have learned by now that groups that do not police their own ranks effectively are sure targets for policing by others, be they governmental agencies or community organizations.

The alternatives for an operations manager are therefore to react or to take a leadership role, becoming knowledgeable about potential negative effects of the process managed by him or her and proposing ways to handle them. In the long term, if we are to manage our economy's activities for tomorrow rather than today, responsibility for the environment is not a choice.

Knowledge and Information   One of the features of the new economy is that in the transformation process, the major input is intellectual property: knowledge, research, information, and design. These inputs have supplanted (in value) the material inputs required to build physical units. When knowledge is the major raw material, launching the first unit of a product represents millions of dollars; the cost of the second and thereafter is minuscule.

The products themselves are of a different nature, and it often takes greater sophistication to use a new-economy product—thus, for example, people's reluctance to switch from a PC to a Mac, or vice versa. As a result, customers are not as likely to be swayed by advertising, but rather by their increasing knowledge of the product and its technology. Successful companies will be those that increase a customer's knowledge base in general, and skill with their own products in particular.

As the information explosion continues to feed today's consumers and today's workforce, the knowledge acquired gives rise to expectations. As we will discuss later, today's consumers are far from being locked into only a few sources for their information. Rather, they swim in an ocean of facts, figures, perspectives, and opportunities.

Nor are today's employees like those of yesteryear. It is instead the case that, depending on his or her own personal needs or aspirations, an employee is drawn to (and will stay with) a specific job in a given company for two reasons: (1) the possibility of experiencing personal satisfaction or growth and (2) satisfaction in the human interaction prevalent at that company. The balance of these factors varies with the individual, but everyone draws from these two wells. Today's managers therefore must provide more than the means for an employee to put bread on the table. The company must offer ongoing professional development, opportunity for increased responsibility in the firm, and a satisfying place to work. Today's employees do not expect to be *supervised,* but rather *coached* along the path of success. Clearly, the manager also must be knowledgeable and continue to grow, increasing in value as a mentor.

Technology   The challenge of technology will occupy us for the rest of these pages. Technology has always existed and has always been neutral. That is, just as a knife serves to feed the family or to kill an adversary, new technologies can be used to help or harm. As with any challenge, managers can view technological innovation as something to react to, something to anticipate, something to plan for, or something from which to derive potential improvements and growth.

Technologies exist in various stages of development; that is, some are ready and available for use by the operations management system, some will be cost-effective in 5 or 10 years, and some are in embryo. Any forward-looking manager will be aware of all three. Technology companies (those which market the latest of a given technology, e.g., cellular phones) must monitor technology on two fronts. They must be aware of similar products on the market, constantly assessing the limits of their own products. They also must be aware of technologies potentially usable by their own operations, just as any nontechnology company would.

In its development, a technology tends to move to the hands of the user. Take the clock as an example. At one time in history, the only clock in the community was the one in the town square. Then wealthier people could purchase large timepieces known as "grandfather clocks." By the middle of the 20th century most adults owned a wristwatch, often a special gift received at graduation. Today children and adults have access to many timepieces, from those on their wrists to the many in the home, office, or car. We could trace a similar progression for other technologies, such as engines and, of course, computers (where the transition from mainframes to portable PCs occurred within a few decades of the last century).

The shift of a technology to the user is not always smooth. One of the potential stumbling blocks when a company embraces a technology is to discount the human factor involved in its use. We see this in small businesses constantly. The local copy shop brings in the latest copying and finishing equipment, offering everything from double-sided, spiral-bound reports graced with photos to personalized, artistic party invitations. The resulting product, however, is in part dependent on the skill and experience of the operator and the availability of sufficient personnel to work with customers.

Larger industrial equipment offers a similar scenario. At an earlier time in history, the operator of, for example, a multi-story printing press would have 30 years to become familiar with the operation of that equipment before a new generation came on stream. In today's offices, employees barely become proficient at using the current popular software before a new or different version of it comes out. These "improvements" provide fertile ground for inefficiencies, for in the final analysis, technology can advance only at the rate at which human beings can use it effectively.

With this knowledge, any effective operations manager will have some type of formal technology management in place—some means of looking ahead, preparing for the effects of new technologies. When envisioning the potential of new technology (or technology in embryo), the best human characteristics to bring to the table are:

1. Awareness (information plus perspective) and
2. Imagination (the ability to create new scenarios from existing ones).

Awareness is the easiest to acquire. In fact, it can be bought from the many consultants standing ready to assist corporations in preparing for the future. One must cultivate powers of imagination within oneself.

THE INTERNET

That brings us to the current challenge for one's imaginative powers: the Internet. Opportunities and pitfalls abound on the Web. What follows are some noteworthy experiences gained from successful and unsuccessful uses of the Internet. By the time this material sees print, much will have changed.

Several methods have emerged as options for exploiting an Internet operation. A regular **bricks and mortar** business can create its own in-house Web group, or it can partner with a dot-com company that will operate the Web end of its business for it. For example, when the three largest retailers in the country decided to jump on the **e-tailing** bandwagon in the late 1990s, their strategies differed: JC Penney and Sears formed their own in-house Web site divisions; Kmart, in contrast, contracted with a subsidiary, bluelight.com, to get its site up and running. Last, a business can elect to sell its products only on the Internet. Internet-only companies are referred to as **pure-play** operations. Amazon.com is an example.

Managers also have to figure out how to integrate Web activities seamlessly into their operations. Poorly integrated systems can wreak havoc within an organization. For instance, the first Christmas Toys 'R' Us did business on the Web, the company had to turn away customers because it couldn't fill the number of orders the site generated. To solve the problem, Toys 'R' Us formed an alliance with Amazon.com. Amazon handled the Web site and the online ordering process, and Toys 'R' Us managed inventory and shipping. Each company had expertise the other needed to sell toys online.

Alongside Web sales, retailers are in various stages of deploying new technologies to offer the benefits of online shopping at the retail site. For example, a kiosk on the shopping floor can make information available electronically, providing shoppers the information they need to make a buying decision. Lamps Plus gives its customers access to high-resolution images they can zoom in on and manipulate to review fabric textures and sample different colors and products in a 360-degree view. Pacific Sunwear lets its customers search for and display clothing for boys or girls by item, color, and price. Other sites, like eBags and Amazon, offer online guides or customer reviews to help buyers make decisions.

These retailers, along with others such as Nordstrom, Eddie Bauer, and Radio Shack, are building on brand-name presence and a familiarity already created at the mall, in the dealership, and through catalog sales—an advantage not enjoyed by companies operating exclusively on the Web.

Not long ago, the online auctioneer eBay and a few companies that built e-stores for other firms were the only ones operating in the black. However, pure-play companies can be successful. Approximately one-quarter of the 200 public Internet companies that survived the dot-bomb shakeout are profitable

Amazon.com was slow to make a profit because of its initial start-up costs—for product and warehouses, for example. However, e-tailers offering travel products, software, and financial services have low overhead and can see a profit much faster.

now under standard accounting rules. The biggest moneymakers are online travel, software, and financial services. Why? Because they sell pure information products—there are no products to store or ship. But even Amazon.com, which has long operated in the red, is finally showing a profit despite the fact that every time someone buys a book on Amazon, the company must turn around and purchase a copy from the publisher. Also, once pure-play companies recoup their initial start-up costs, they don't need to spend much more money as sales rise. No additional stores need to be built to reach consumers, for example.[4]

Nonetheless, technology tricks and novel business ideas are not enough. Customers still want speed, convenience, quality, and good service. In this regard, the Web is no different from conventional stores and catalogs. Customers ultimately will cast their votes for the companies that provide the best product experience whether they see the product on the Web or can touch it in stores.

COMPANYWIDE RESONANCE

Sales and marketing data collection is turned on its head by the Internet, as companies record information about a user's habits during a Web site visit. For instance, if you buy a product on Amazon.com, during future visits, the site will make suggestions about similar products in which you might be interested. Many retailers are of the opinion that this type of **data mining** will make or break the operation in the future. That is, the ability to collect and use information from online customers will be crucial to successful marketing decisions.

Moreover, a company's Web page can make it easy or hard for the customer to get the information leading to a purchase. As some have learned the hard way, it is not enough to simply take images that are successful in print and place them on the Web, for each medium has its own characteristics.

The design of the company's Web site has a companywide impact. For example, if a customer on the Web can verify that an item is available, the chances of closing the sale are increased. If a customer can find out the expected delivery date of the product and the means, the chances of a sale are increased even more. In this scenario, front- and back-end operations touch, and delivering the goods is still key to success.

Mountains of Data The purchasing function benefits from the Web through sheer availability of information, as well as ease of response to questions. Today, a purchasing manager need not wait for a visit from a sales representative. In fact, under the impact of the Web, businesses are seeing a realignment of the traditional relationships among producers, wholesalers, distributors, and retailers. In the business-to-business world, buyers previously faced a number of obstacles to getting the best deal: Suppliers were distant, research time was scarce, and intermediaries controlled most of the information. Enter Ariba, a Web-based marketplace for industrial goods. Purchasing need only put out a contract on the Web, and a flood of bids from suppliers may be the response. In a sense, Web-based companies are becoming the new intermediaries, the conduit between producers and buyers.

Purchasing managers can go online to Ariba for industrial goods, National Transportation Exchange for trucking, Chemdex for biochemical supplies, and IMX Exchange for mortgage brokers to find loans, and this is only the start.

The Internet has also become the intermediary between employers and employees. Human resources departments can avail themselves of numerous Web-based tools to find candidates. Not only are there gigantic job exchanges such as Monster.com, but intranets exist to keep job searches within companies. Job seekers and potential employers can access one another's information based on geographic preference, salary range, or skill sets.

Logistics, scheduling, and distribution tasks increasingly are plugged into Web-based networks, benefiting from the ease of gathering weather data, traffic patterns, and late-breaking news. Tracking information about shipments can be downloaded from Federal Express. Zip codes are available online from the U.S. Postal Service. These factors affect the company's ability to deliver the product on time and the availability of materials from suppliers, effects ultimately felt by the operations management system.

Changing Information Patterns To reduce printing costs and make documents widely available, companies are digitizing information. In some instances, they are posting it on the Web. Different people residing in distant places can view the same information this way. Still, digitizing information is not without its obstacles. Not all people have the same hardware and software used for viewing and printing out information. Additionally, miscommunications can occur that otherwise might not if all employees were working under one roof.

Corporations must take these circumstances into account when deciding how to make use of the Web, for the decisions affect each of the company's functioning units. Posting certain kinds of information does not usually cause problems. For example, providing company address(es), phone numbers, hours of operation, and the like, is more economically done on the Web than by a live employee answering the telephone. Many inquiries that in the print age were handled by mailing out an annual report, for example, may be handled more cost-effectively on the Web.

Supplying other types of information, however, might not be as free of repercussions as in the preceding examples. Depending on whether the company is a business-to-business or a business-to-consumer operation, buyers will want product information,

Companies can easily track their shipments by downloading the information directly from FedEx.

forms and terms of payment, special sales, return policies, status of an order, shipping rates and turnaround, possibility of changing a current order, tracking information, or status of an order.

Providing and maintaining only one piece of this information—for example, change in an order—affects at least three departments: accounting, distribution, and marketing. Each department supplying the information must be aware of the consequences of making the information available and have a mechanism for handling changes. Coordination becomes an issue as well. For example, charges to a credit-card account must not occur before the merchandise is shipped. Whether selling to another business or to consumers, online operation requires new networks. Companies forge ahead nonetheless in this burgeoning technology, realizing that the potential advantages are well worth the temporary discomforts.

INTELLECTUAL PROPERTY

We have mentioned that a characteristic of the new economy is the nature of the product: knowledge, design, and engineering, rather than hard manufacturing. Let us look at an environmental engineering firm and how the Web affects its operation. The business of such a firm might include devising solutions to improve power-plant operation. The activities of firms involved in the planning of any such industrial facility are subject to compliance with government regulations. Handling engineering projects, for example, a new power plant, requires submission of an enormous amount of data to demonstrate that the firm has complied with and planned for all impacts on the community. A requirement might be, for example, that notification be given to every property owner within a certain radius of the plant. Downloading that information from title companies and then monitoring the notification process is only one of a multitude of tasks potentially manageable on the Web.

The firm must provide the information to the various parties in certain forms, which gives rise to new information needs. For example, one way to verify that it has indeed shipped the requisite print or CD-ROM copies is by downloading tracking information from Federal Express. It also can make its compliance documentation available in a read-only format on the Web, allowing printing of sections by those who wish to do so.

In preparing to build a plant, all federal, state, and local regulations must be accounted for. The firm must provide information on how its power plant will affect traffic patterns, cultural resources, schools, water supply, flora and fauna, and air quality. It also must state its plans for handling hazardous materials generated during the construction and operation of the plant.

Managing the enormous body of information to respond in the ways illustrated would have been a near impossibility before computer management of data.

PITFALLS

What have been the experiences of those who have succeeded in e-commerce and those who have failed, and what can we learn from them? We already mentioned Toys 'R' Us and its inability to fill its orders on the Web. In addition to losing business, it, along with other retailers such as Macys.com and CDNow, was subject to Federal Trade Commission investigation and fines regarding rules for order fulfillment. The FTC regulation states that if retailers cannot meet promised deadlines, they must notify customers, giving them the option of canceling the order. Could the management of these companies have foreseen the inability to fill orders, and if so, how?

Confidentiality of information is an issue. A recent Gallup poll revealed that 66 percent of Americans favor new laws to protect their privacy amid the high-tech revolution.[5] Amazon.com found itself under fire after it began charging different consumers different prices on the basis of information it had collected on them. Toys 'R' Us was hit with a class-action lawsuit claiming that it allowed market researchers to access consumer data from its Web site. The retailer responded that it had hired the firm to analyze customers' data in order to improve their shopping experience. Although breach of confidentiality predates the Web, the enormity of any breach is compounded by the staggering amounts of digital data available for tapping. The Federal Trade Commission and Congress are attempting to pass laws and institute regulations to protect consumers.

Customer familiarity with the Web is another issue. Despite what seems to be a flurry of online buying, media reports suggest that many customers are not buying online at all, or only infrequently, or only certain products. As with catalog shopping, the online industry will mature as consumers become more familiar with offerings and as Web retailers improve in presentation and fulfillment.

Some customers are concerned about credit-card data transmitted online and are therefore hesitant to shop. The misuse of credit-card data is present, however, every time a clerk in a store records the data during a purchase. Although this is more a perception than a real problem, perception motivates people's actions, preventing some from making the leap into cybershopping.

Circumstances such as these are forcing the formation of new business models as companies grapple with all the variables, spurred on by the potential benefits.

NEW NEEDS AND DESIRES

Customers themselves are changing as it becomes possible to satisfy latent needs or desires. We have alluded to mass customization. Here are some specific examples of varying product features.

Setting up an assembly line or installing production equipment is part of the cost of manufacturing. Speaking of color choice in automobiles, Henry Ford once said: "They can have any color they want, as long as it's black." Alteration of a manufacturing process to vary a product feature was very costly. With the flexible manufacturing available in the digital age, manufacturers have the option of producing multiple flavors of bottled water, blue jeans tailored for different bodies, and a veritable artist's palette for automobile colors. Levi Strauss and Brooks now offer machine-customized garments, accommodating a vast array of body measurements. Barbie's friends can have hair and skin color, clothing, and even personalities picked by their young owners. Digital technology fuels the manufacturing capability; the Web spurs demand.

The result is that customers' desire for customization and personalization has been moved to a new level. Shoppers previously settled for a product that was mostly, or approximately, what they wanted. They are now beginning to see that sometimes they can have a product endowed with *precisely* the features they want. The experience of product acquisition is therefore changing.

THE VALUE OF HUMAN ATTRIBUTES

What are the implications of all this change for traditional operations management? Changes are remembered as negative or positive, depending on how well one has survived them. There is no reason to believe that technological change is any more threatening than other kinds of change. Traditional human qualities still serve: vision, awareness, alertness, imagination, courage, steadfastness, persistence, flexibility, attentiveness, and goodwill.

Today's managers must be aware, noticing shifts in trends, habits and customs, possibilities, and ground rules. They must have or develop the vision to foresee the range of possibilities, and then the imagination to create solutions. They must have the courage to strike out in new directions and be alert to adjustments required by the new direction. An effective manager will be flexible enough to make an adjustment and steadfast in the face of misunderstandings and mistakes. A manager will need to be persistent in following the chosen path, with attentiveness to all facets of the surroundings. Chances of success in any challenge are enhanced by goodwill.

Finally, he or she will need luck. Some say "it comes to you," and some say "you make your own." Most think that both are true.

KEY TERMS

bricks and mortar, p. 621

data mining, p. 622

e-tailing, p. 621

new economy, p. 619

pure-play, p. 621

DISCUSSION QUESTIONS

1. What is "mass customization"? How can products be mass-produced yet still be differentiated to appeal to individual market sectors? How has mass customization affected management's focus on the product?

2. Why was Deming's "total quality management" embraced by the Japanese long before Deming's philosophy became key to U.S. operations management? How does it relate to operations management?

3. How has the new economy changed operations management? What is the major input in the operations process as a result?

4. What must businesses consider in deciding to take advantage of new technology? How does new technology affect operations management decisions?

5. Why were many dot-com companies so short-lived at the end of the 20th century? Why would Amazon and Toys 'R' Us form an alliance? Which firm is likely to benefit more? Explain.

6. How can the Internet improve a firm's operations management?

7. What are the implications for operations management of customers being able to satisfy purchasing needs immediately by using the Internet? Have e-business functions fundamentally changed the way firms do business? Explain.

Creating and Managing Change

> *The world hates change, yet that is the only thing that has brought progress.*
>
> — Charles Kettering
>
> *My interest is in the future because I am going to spend the rest of my life there.*
>
> — Charles Kettering

LEARNING OBJECTIVES

After studying Chapter 18, you will be able to:

LO 1 Discuss what it takes to be world class. p. 628

LO 2 Describe how to manage and lead change effectively. p. 632

LO 3 List tactics for creating a successful future. p. 646

CHAPTER OUTLINE

Management Close-Up

Have you ever cleaned your car's windshield? Sprayed yourself with insect repellant before hiking in the forest? Treated a stain on your favorite T-shirt? Packed your lunch? If you answered "yes" to any of these questions, chances are you've used products from Racine, Wisconsin–based SC Johnson. This family business got its start in 1886 installing wood parquet floors. After owner Samuel Curtis Johnson created a special wax to care for his customers' floors, the company changed its direction—from installing parquet to manufacturing home cleaning products. Now, SC Johnson sells a broad array of products for air care, cleaning, personal care, pest control, and food storage. Its industry-leading brands include Fantastik, Glade, Off!, Pledge, Shout, Windex, and Ziploc.

An $8 billion business with 12,000 employees, SC Johnson operates in more than 70 countries. For seven years running, it has been named one of *Fortune*'s "100 Best Companies to Work For," ranking in the top 10 three times. It recently made its 20th appearance on *Working Mother*'s annual list of "100 Best Companies for Working Mothers" as well as its third consecutive appearance as one of AARP's top companies for workers over age 50.

While SC Johnson wins praise for its comprehensive programs benefiting employees, what earns even greater respect is how the company leads the way on the critical issues facing our planet. SC Johnson worked to protect the environment even before environmentalism became popular. For example, as early as 1935, the company explored Brazil in search of a sustainable source of wax for use in making its popular Johnson's Wax. When the hazards of chlorofluorocarbons (CFCs)—which were used as propellants in aerosol cans—to Earth's ozone layer were revealed during the 1970s, SC Johnson became the first manufacturer to eliminate CFCs from its cans. It did so three years ahead of a U.S. government deadline. Since 2000, the company has aggressively expanded its quest for sustainable practices under the leadership of CEO H. Fisk Johnson, great-great-grandson of the founder.[1]

{ The very existence of SC Johnson as a company depends on the profitable sale of household products that contain chemicals. Yet the company has taken the lead in the fight to save the environment from hazardous chemicals. As you read this chapter, consider how being at the forefront on important issues helps an organization achieve world-class distinction. }

These experts are all talking about the same things: the importance and challenges of creating change and the need to improve constantly to achieve world-class excellence and competitive advantage for the future.

"Managing change is a way of thinking, and there are some people it just comes naturally to. When you find those people, you grab them and use them."

—Donna Curry, recruitment program manager, Tennessee Valley Authority[2]

"Ever-increasing change is inevitable and will be the hallmark of our lives."

—Daryl R. Conner, *Managing at the Speed of Change*[3]

"Almost everyone is more enthusiastic about change when the change is their own idea, and less enthusiastic if they feel the change is being imposed on them."

—Maggie Bayless, managing partner, ZingTrain[4]

"Even when you can get people all pumped up about the 'new' and they understand what's needed and why, all people need to do is hit the same old barriers about four times and their enthusiasm drops like a rock."

—John Kotter, professor, Harvard Business School[5]

"During the last two to three years, we have experienced more change than this company has ever experienced."

—Sharon Rues Pettid, human resource manager, Mutual of Omaha[9]

Change happens—constantly and unpredictably. Whatever competitive advantage you may have depends on particular circumstances at a particular time, but circumstances change.[6] The economic environment shifts; competitors pop up everywhere; markets emerge and disappear. The challenge for organizations is not just to produce innovative new products but to balance a culture that is innovative and that builds a sustainable business.[7] And for individuals, the ability to cope with change is related to their job performance, the rewards they receive,[8] and their career success.

Becoming World Class

LO **1**

It's a worthy aspiration: becoming world class at every one of your competitive goals.

Managers today want, or *should* want, their organizations to become world class.[10] Being world class requires applying the best and latest knowledge and ideas and having the ability to operate at the highest standards of any place anywhere.[11] Thus, becoming world class does not mean merely improving. It means becoming one of the very best in the world at what you do. To some people, striving for world-class excellence seems a lofty, impossible, unnecessary goal. But it is a goal that is essential to survival and success in today's intensely competitive business world.

World-class companies create high-value products and earn superior profits over the long run. They demolish the obsolete methods, systems, and cultures of the past that impeded their competitive progress and apply more effective and competitive organizational strategies, structures, processes, and management of human resources. The result is an organization capable of competing successfully on a global basis.[12]

Sustainable, Great Futures

Two Stanford professors, James Collins and Jerry Porras, studied 18 corporations that had achieved and maintained greatness for half a century or more.[13] The companies included Sony, American Express, Motorola, Marriott, Johnson & Johnson, Disney, 3M, Hewlett-Packard, Citicorp, and Walmart. Over the years, these companies have been widely admired, been considered the premier institutions in their industries, and made a real impact on the world. Although every company goes through periodic downturns—and these firms are no exceptions over their long histories—these companies have consistently prevailed across the decades. They turn in extraordinary performance *over the long run*, rather than fleeting greatness.

The researchers sought to identify the essential characteristics of enduringly great companies. These great companies have strong core values in which they believe deeply, and they express and live the values consistently. They are driven by goals—not just incremental improvements or business-as-usual goals, but stretch goals (recall Chapter 13). They change continuously, driving for progress via adaptability, experimentation, trial and error, entrepreneurial thinking, and fast action. And they do not focus on beating the competition; they focus primarily on beating themselves. They continually ask, "How can we improve ourselves to do better tomorrow than we did today?"

But underneath the action and the changes, the core values and vision remain steadfast and uncompromised. Table 18.1 displays the core values of several of the companies that were "built to last." Note that the values are not all the same. In fact, no set of common values consistently predicted success. Instead, the critical factor is that the great companies *have* core values, *know* what they are and what they mean, and *live* by them—year after year after year.

Boeing has advanced the technology of airplane design with this carbon-fiber plane, the 787 Dreamliner. In this design, carbon-fiber composites are "baked" in huge sections, reducing manufacturing and maintenance time. The plane is also lighter than its aluminum counterparts, allowing the airlines to buy less fuel. Shown here is its world premiere in front of 15,000 cheering employees, customers, and suppliers outside of the Boeing assembly plant in Everett, Washington.

Organizations operating on a small scale can achieve greatness within their niche. A case in point is Neil Kelly Company (NKC), a home construction, remodeling, and repair firm that operates in Oregon. Under the leadership of Tom Kelly, son of the company's founder, Neil, the company meets difficult sales goals through creative marketing and maintains a strong culture based on a commitment to craftsmanship and environmentally friendly building practices.

Tom Kelly's passion for green construction led him to set up a "home performance" division that conducts energy-efficiency audits, assesses indoor air quality, and fixes any problems that turn up in either assessment. The company also recently acquired a maker of "green" cabinets. NKC's concern for the environment is attractive to potential employees and prospective customers—especially in the Pacific Northwest, where environmental values are important to a sizable share of the population.

Of course, the company isn't great simply because of its high ideals. Tom Kelly is an aggressive and creative marketer. Even when the economy took a sharp downturn, Kelly increased his marketing budget, helping him build sales even as other companies were cutting back. For example, he set up a deal with a local television station to do a series of five stories about a green home-rebuilding project featuring NKC's new line of cabinetry. This creative arrangement not only gave the company media exposure, it also continues to serve as a teaching tool about green construction. For Tom Kelly, this kind of "enlightened self-interest" is "very much a legacy of my father's. He was somebody who really gave back to the community and built that into our corporate soul."[14]

The Tyranny of the *Or*

Many companies, and individuals, are plagued by the **tyranny of the *or***. This refers to the belief that things must be either A or B and cannot be both. The authors provide many common examples: beliefs that you must choose either change or stability; be conservative or bold; have control and consistency or creative freedom; do well in the short term or invest for the future; plan methodically or be opportunistic; create shareholder wealth or do good for the world; be pragmatic or idealistic.[15] Such beliefs, that only one goal but not another can be attained, often are invalid and certainly are constraining—unnecessarily so.

tyranny of the *or*

The belief that things must be either A or B and cannot be both; that only one goal and not another can be attained.

The Genius of the *And*

In contrast to the tyranny of the *or*, the **genius of the *and***—more academically, **organizational ambidexterity**—refers to being able to achieve multiple objectives at the same time.[16] It develops via the actions of many individuals throughout the organization. We discussed earlier in the book the importance of delivering multiple

genius of the *and*; organizational ambidexterity

Ability to achieve multiple objectives simultaneously.

TABLE 18.1
Core Ideologies in Built-to-Last Companies

3M	Innovation—"Thou shalt not kill a new product idea"
	Absolute integrity
	Respect for individual initiative and personal growth
	Tolerance for honest mistakes
	Product quality and reliability
	"Our real business is solving problems"
American Express	Heroic customer service
	Worldwide reliability of services
	Encouragement of individual initiative
Boeing	Being on the leading edge of aeronautics; being pioneers
	Tackling huge challenges and risks
	Product safety and quality
	Integrity and ethical business
	To "eat, breathe, and sleep the world of aeronautics"
Sony	To experience the sheer joy that comes from the advancement, application, and innovation of technology that benefits the general public
	To elevate the Japanese culture and national status
	Being pioneers—not following others, but doing the impossible
	Respecting and encouraging each individual's ability and creativity
Walmart	"We exist to provide value to our customers"—to make their lives better via lower prices and greater selection; all else is secondary
	Swim upstream, buck conventional wisdom
	Be in partnership with employees
	Work with passion, commitment, and enthusiasm
	Run lean
	Pursue ever-higher goals
Walt Disney	No cynicism allowed
	Fanatical attention to consistency and detail
	Continuous progress via creativity, dreams, and imagination
	Fanatical control and preservation of Disney's "magic" image
	"To bring happiness to millions" and to celebrate, nurture, and promulgate "wholesome American values"

SOURCE: From *Built to Last* by James C. Collins and Jerry I. Porras, Copyright © 1997 by James C. Collins and Jerry I. Porras. Reprinted by permission of the authors, HarperCollins Publishers, Inc. and Random House Group Limited.

competitive values to customers, performing all the management functions, reconciling hard-nosed business logic with ethics, leading and empowering, and others. Authors Collins and Porras have their own list:[17]

- Purpose beyond profit *and* pragmatic pursuit of profit.
- Relatively fixed core values *and* vigorous change and movement.
- Conservatism with the core values *and* bold business moves.

- Clear vision and direction *and* experimentation.
- Stretch goals *and* incremental progress.
- Control based on values *and* operational freedom.
- Long-term thinking and investment *and* demand for short-term results.
- Visionary, futuristic thinking *and* daily, nuts-and-bolts execution.

You have learned about all of these concepts throughout this course and should not lose sight of any of them—either in your mind or in your actions. To achieve them requires the continuous and effective management of change.

Organization Development

How do organizations become more ambidextrous and move in the other positive directions described throughout this book? This chapter discusses several general approaches that will create positive change. We begin here with an umbrella concept called organization development.

Organization development (OD) is a systemwide application of behavioral science knowledge to develop, improve, and reinforce the strategies, structures, and processes that lead to organization effectiveness.[18] Throughout this course, you have acquired knowledge about behavioral science and the strategies, structures, and processes that help organizations become more effective. The "systemwide" component of the definition means that OD is not a narrow improvement in technology or operations but a broader approach to changing organizations, units, or people. The "behavioral science" component means that OD is not *directly* concerned with economic, financial, or technical aspects of the organization—although they may benefit, through changes in the behavior of the people in the organization. The other key part of the definition—to develop, improve, and reinforce—refers to the actual process of changing, for the better and for the long term.

Two features of organization development are important to note.[19] First, it aims to increase organizational effectiveness—improving the organization's ability to deal with customers, stockholders, governments, employees, and other stakeholders, which results in better-quality products, higher financial returns, and high quality of work life. Second, OD has an important underlying value orientation: it supports human potential, development, and participation in addition to performance and competitive advantage.

Many specific OD techniques fit under this philosophical umbrella.[20] The basic types are *strategic interventions*, including helping organizations conduct mergers and acquisitions, change their strategies, and develop alliances; *technostructural interventions* relating to organization structure and design, employee involvement, and work design; *human resources management interventions*, including attracting good people, setting goals, and appraising and rewarding performance; and *human process interventions*, including conflict resolution, team building, communication, and leadership. As you can see, you learned about these topics throughout your management course. You also will learn more about the process of creating change in the rest of this chapter.

organization development (OD)

The systemwide application of behavioral science knowledge to develop, improve, and reinforce the strategies, structures, and processes that lead to organizational effectiveness.

The strategy of Cirque du Soleil is one of constant innovation: combining circus and theater, and studying other industries like car design, fashion, and restaurants to get ideas for new shows.

Achieving Greatness

A recent study of 200 management techniques employed by 160 companies over 10 years identified the specific management practices that lead to sustained, superior performance.[21] The authors boiled their findings down to four key factors:

1. *Strategy*—focused on customers, continually fine-tuned based on marketplace changes, and clearly communicated to employees.
2. *Execution*—good people, with decision-making authority on the front lines, doing quality work and cutting costs.
3. *Culture*—one that motivates, empowers people to innovate, rewards people appropriately (psychologically as well as economically), entails strong values, challenges people, and provides a satisfying work environment.
4. *Structure*—making the organization easy to work in and easy to work with, characterized by cooperation and the exchange of information and knowledge throughout the organization.

You have been learning about these concepts throughout this course.

Becoming world class doesn't apply only to the private sector. People worry about globalization's negative effects on local communities as plants shut down and people lose their jobs to overseas workers. But local communities do have options—not easy ones, but doable. A locality can strive to become a world-class center of *thinkers, makers,* or *traders.*[22] Thus, Boston creates new ideas and technologies that often dominate world markets; Spartanville–Greenville, South Carolina, is a world-class manufacturing region that has attracted direct foreign investment from more than 200 companies in 18 countries; and Miami, Florida, connects Latino and Anglo cultures the way Hong Kong and Singapore have historically bridged Chinese and British cultures. The keys to creating world-class local communities include visionary leadership, a climate friendly to business, a commitment to training workers, and collaboration among businesses and between business and local government.[23]

People are the key to successful change.[24] For an organization to be great, or even just to survive, people have to care about its fate and know how they can contribute. But typically, leadership lies with only a few people at the top. Too few take on the burden of change; the number of people who care deeply, and who make innovative contributions, is too small. People throughout the organization need to take a greater interest and a more active role in helping the business as a whole. They have to identify with the entire organization, not just with their unit and close colleagues.

Managing Change

LO 2

Shared leadership is crucial to the success of most change efforts—people must be not just *supporters* of change but also *implementers.*[25]

This shared responsibility for change is not unusual in start-ups and very small organizations. But too often it is lost with growth and over time. In large, traditional corporations, it is all too rare. Organizations need to permanently rekindle individual creativity and responsibility, instituting a true change in the behavior of people throughout the ranks. The essential task is to motivate people fully to keep changing in response to new business challenges.

Change Agents

Change agents are, as the name implies, people who create change. Throughout this chapter, you will read about change agents—in some cases what they have created, in other cases what they have learned. These change agents are examples of people who recognized opportunities to get better results by making a change. As you read these stories, keep in mind that what these change agents do, you can, too, wherever you find yourself working.

What Change Agents Are made Of?

They've got power, vision, bravery, and support—which may be why they're rare. **What kind of person is a change agent? Anil Kale, PUNE, INDIA**

Apparently, any person running for President! Change-Agent-In-Chief is a title claimed by both Barack Obama and John McCain, setting off a veritable firestorm of debate about what kind of person is truly best equipped to shake things up.

Count us in. Not on picking whether Obama or McCain is more likely to transform America: both will, just in very different ways. But count us in on the debate about what kind of person in general—and especially, what kind of person in business—has the qualities to really make change happen. Because, as your question implies, change agents are distinctly different from the pack. In fact, we'd estimate that in most organizations, they comprise no more than 10% of all employees.

http://www.businessweek.com/magazine/content/08_42/b4104096917161.htm

Motivating People to Change

People must be *motivated* to change. But often they resist changing. Some people resist change more than others, but managers tend to underestimate the amount of resistance they will encounter.[27]

People at all levels of their organizations, from entry-level workers to top executives, resist change. When Foremost Farms USA asked workers to switch goals—instead of making American cheese as fast as they could, they had to aim for getting each block to weigh precisely 640 pounds—the workers complied only as long as managers kept checking. When management's attention turned elsewhere, they reverted to the more familiar emphasis on speed.[28] At IBM, many changes have been necessary to keep bureaucracy from stifling innovation, and all of them have been challenging. At one point, executives learned that lower-level managers were getting bogged down because they had to invest so much time and effort in obtaining approval from higher-ups. CEO Sam Palmisano announced that he would give first-level managers authority to spend $5,000 without prior approval—a daring move, considering that the authority applied to 30,000 managers. However, the managers felt uncomfortable with their new authority, and in the first year of the new program, they spent only $100,000 of the $150 million Palmisano had entrusted to them.[29] In other words, they were reluctant to change the way they worked, even though it stood to make their job easier.

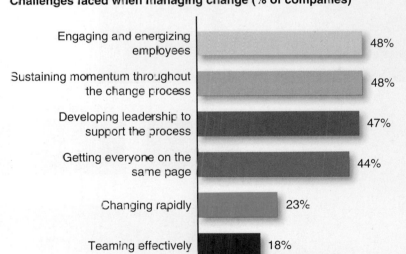

According to human resources leaders surveyed by the Ken Blanchard Companies, some of the toughest challenges in managing change entail getting everyone on board so employees care about and work hard for success.[26]

Challenges faced when managing change (% of companies)

Challenge	%
Engaging and energizing employees	48%
Sustaining momentum throughout the change process	48%
Developing leadership to support the process	47%
Getting everyone on the same page	44%
Changing rapidly	23%
Teaming effectively	18%

Many people settle for mediocrity rather than aspire to world-class status. They resist the idea of striving mightily for excellence. When told by their managers, "We have to become world class," their reactions resemble the following statements:

- "Those world-class performance numbers are ridiculous! I don't believe them, they are impossible! Maybe in some industries, some companies . . . but ours is unique . . ."
- "Sure, maybe some companies achieve those numbers, but there's no hurry . . . We're doing all right. Sales were up 5 percent this year, costs were down 2 percent. And we've got to keep cutting corners . . ."
- "We can't afford to be world class like those big global companies; we don't have the money or staff . . ."
- "We don't believe this stuff about global markets and competitors. We don't need to expand internationally. One of our local competitors tried that a few years ago and lost its shirt."
- "It's not a level playing field . . . the others have unfair advantages . . ."

To deal with such reactions and successfully implement positive change, managers must understand why people often resist change. Figure 18.1 shows the common reasons for resistance. Some reasons are general and arise in most change efforts. Other reasons for resistance relate to the specific nature of a particular change.

General Reasons for Resistance   Several reasons for resistance arise regardless of the actual content of the change:[30]

Fear of the unknown and mistrust can prompt resistance to change. This scene shows thousands of protestors rallying against the federal government's Wall Street bailout policy in front of the New York Stock Exchange in September of 2008.

- *Inertia.* Usually people don't want to disturb the status quo. The old ways of doing things are comfortable and easy, so people don't want to shake things up and try something new. For example, it is easier to keep living in the same apartment or house than to move to another.
- *Timing.* People often resist change because of poor timing. Maybe you would like to move to a different place to live, but do you want to move this week? Even if a place were available, you probably couldn't take the time. If managers or employees are unusually busy or under stress, or if relations between management and workers are strained,

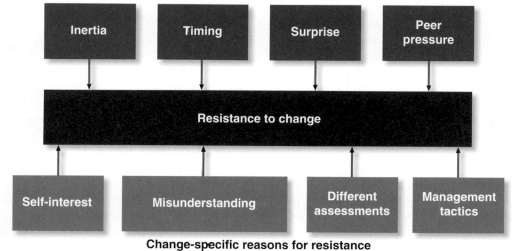

FIGURE 18.1
Reasons for Resistance to Change

the timing is wrong for introducing new proposals. Where possible, managers should introduce change when people are receptive.

- *Surprise.* One key aspect of timing and receptivity is surprise. If the change is sudden, unexpected, or extreme, resistance may be the initial—almost reflexive—reaction. Suppose your university announced an increase in tuition, effective at the beginning of next term. Wouldn't you at least want more warning, so you might be prepared? Managers or others initiating a change often forget that others haven't given the matter much thought; the change leaders need to allow time for others to think about the change and prepare for it.
- *Peer pressure.* Sometimes work teams resist new ideas. Even if individual members do not strongly oppose a change suggested by management, the team may band together in opposition. If a group is highly cohesive and has anti-management norms (recall Chapter 14), peer pressure will cause individuals to resist even reasonable changes. Of course, peer pressure can be a positive force, too. Change leaders who invite—and listen to—ideas from team members may find that peer pressure becomes a driving force behind the change's success.

Change-Specific Reasons for Resistance   Other causes of resistance arise from the specific nature of a proposed change. Change-specific reasons for resistance include:[32]

- *Self-interest.* Most people care less about the organization's best interest than they do about their own best interests. They will resist a change if they think it will cause them to lose something of value. What could people fear to lose? At worst, their jobs, if management is considering closing down a plant. A merger, reorganization, or technological change could create the same fear. Other possible fears include loss of the feeling of being competent in a familiar job, expectations that the job will become more difficult or time-consuming, uncertainty about whether enough training or other resources will be provided for succeeding at the change, and concerns about the organization's future, given that management wasn't satisfied with the status quo.

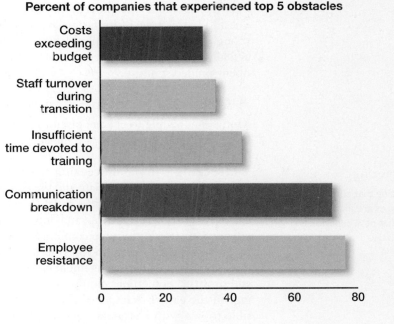

Employee resistance is the most common obstacle to major organizational change.[31]

Percent of companies that experienced top 5 obstacles

- *Misunderstanding.* Even when management proposes a change that will benefit everyone, people may resist because they don't fully understand it. People may not see how the change fits with the firm's strategy, or they simply may not see the change's advantage over current practices.[33] One company met resistance to the idea of introducing flexible working hours, a system in which workers have some say regarding the hours they work. This system can benefit employees, but a false rumor circulated among plant employees that people would have to work evenings, weekends, or whenever their supervisors wanted. The employees' union demanded that management drop the flexible-hours idea. The president was caught completely off guard by this unexpected resistance, and complied with the union's demand.

- *Different assessments.* Employees receive different—and usually less— information than management receives. Even within top management ranks, some executives know more than others do. Such discrepancies cause people to develop different assessments of proposed changes. Some may be aware that the benefits outweigh the costs, while others may see only the costs and not perceive the advantages. This is a common problem when management announces a change, say, in work procedures, and doesn't explain to employees why the change is needed. Management expects advantages in terms of increased efficiency, but workers may see the change as another arbitrary, ill-informed management rule that causes headaches for those who must carry it out.
- *Management tactics.* Sometimes a change that is successful elsewhere is undertaken in a new location, and problems may arise during the transfer.[34] Management may attempt to force the change and may fail to address concerns in order to develop employee commitment. Or it may fail to provide the necessary resources, knowledge, or leadership to help the change succeed. Sometimes a change receives so much exposure and glorification that employees resent it and resist. Managers who overpromise what they—or the change—can deliver may discover that the next time they want to introduce a change, they have lost credibility, so employees resist.

It is important to recognize that employees' assessments can be more accurate than management's; employees may know a change won't work even if management doesn't. In this case, resistance to change is beneficial for the organization. Thus, even though management typically considers resistance a challenge to be overcome, it may actually represent an important signal that a proposed change requires further, more open-minded scrutiny.[35]

A General Model for Managing Resistance

Motivating people to change often requires three basic stages, shown in Figure 18.2: unfreezing, moving to institute the change, and refreezing.[36]

unfreezing

Realizing that current practices are inappropriate and that new behavior is necessary.

Unfreezing   In the **unfreezing** stage, management realizes that its current practices are no longer appropriate and the company must break out of (unfreeze) its present mold by doing things differently. People must come to recognize that some of the past ways of thinking, feeling, and doing things are obsolete.[37] A direct and sometimes effective way to do this is to communicate the negative consequences of the old ways by comparing the organization's performance with that of its competitors'. As discussed in Chapter 15, management can share with employees data about costs, quality, and profits.[38] Sometimes employees just need to understand the rationale for changing. In the earlier example of Foremost Farms, big competitors had made it impossible to win with a strategy of working efficiently and selling cheese at a low price. Management had decided to sell more profitable customized products, such as the

FIGURE 18.2
Motivating People to Change

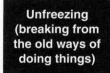

640-pound blocks of cheese that one customer planned to repackage in smaller sizes. After Foremost managers took the time to explain the situation to employees, the workers understood the new requirements and began performing as requested.[39]

When managers communicate a problem, they need to take care not to arouse people's defensiveness. Instead of unfreezing resistance, managers are likely to place employees on the defensive when they pin the blame for shortcomings directly and entirely on the workers.[40] Similarly, bombarding employees with facts aimed at inducing fear may only add to their resistance. When a problem seems huge, people often decide it is hopeless and don't face it. In *Change or Die*, journalist Alan Deutschman uses that pattern of behavior to explain why heart attack victims often fail to follow diet and exercise plans, even though doctors tell them they will literally die if they don't take care of themselves.[41] Deutschman sees a similar pattern playing out in companies where executives rely on threats of layoffs and corporate bankruptcy to motivate employees to adopt new work practices. In these difficult situations, leaders more effectively unfreeze negative behavior with a message of hope and a commitment to collaborate with others so that they can accomplish successful change together.

Sometimes, it's the manager—not the employee—who resists change. But managers and employees can work together to bring about change. Here are a few tips you might use as an employee to get your manager's attention and perhaps convince your boss that it's time to make a change for the good of your work group, division, or company. However you approach it, always be tactful and respectful.

- Educate your boss. Talk with him or her about the situation and your ideas. Offer reading material if it is available.
- Provide feedback when it's appropriate—when asked, in private, in an e-mail or (better) face-to-face.
- Offer to schedule a guest speaker who is an expert in the type of change you propose. Do all the homework and legwork to carry out your idea.
- Find a mentor in the company, even if the person works outside your division. The relationship can help you gain influence with your own manager.
- Perform your very best on the job. Doing so will attract the attention of your boss and establish your credibility. If you are the best at what you do, your opinion will carry more weight.[42]

An important contributor to unfreezing is the recognition of a performance gap, which can be a precipitator of major change. A **performance gap** is the difference between actual performance and the performance that should or could exist.[43] A gap typically implies poor performance; for example, sales, profits, stock price, or other financial indicators are down. This situation attracts management's attention, and management introduces changes to try to correct things.

Another, very important form of performance gap can exist. This type of gap can occur when performance is good but someone realizes that it could be better. Thus, the gap is between what is and what *could be*. This realization is where entrepreneurs seize opportunities and where companies that engage in strategic maneuvering gain a competitive edge.

In the realm of change management, employees are best motivated by situations that combine the sense of urgency that comes from identifying a problem with the sense of excitement that comes from identifying an opportunity. Furthermore, managers communicating a performance gap should keep in mind that employees care about more than market share and revenues. Employees want to know how making a change can help them have a positive impact on their work group, their customers, their company, their community, and themselves. For example, a financial services company

performance gap

The difference between actual performance and desired performance.

met resistance when it tried to persuade employees that a change would enhance the company's competitive position. Employees got on board only after the change leaders also started talking about how the change would help employees reduce errors, enable teams to avoid duplication of effort, make jobs more interesting, and help the organization fulfill its mission to deliver affordable housing.[44]

As an impetus for change, a performance gap can apply to the organization as a whole; it also can apply to departments, groups, and individuals. If a department or work group is not performing as well as others in the company, or if it sees an opportunity that it can exploit, that unit will be motivated to change. Similarly, an individual may receive negative performance feedback or see a personal opportunity on which to capitalize. Under these circumstances, unfreezing begins, and people can be more motivated to change than if they identify no such gap.

Lawrence Ellison, CEO of Oracle, is well-versed in what it takes to convey a vision of change within his organization. Oracle has often acquired other companies, bringing tumultuous change for individual employees and managers within both organizations.

moving

Instituting the change.

Moving   The next step, **moving** to institute the change, begins with establishing a vision of where the company is heading. You learned about vision in the leadership chapter. The vision can be realized through strategic, structural, cultural, and individual change. Strategic ideas are discussed throughout the book. Changes in structure may involve moving to the divisional, matrix, or some other appropriate form (discussed in Chapters 8 and 9). Cultural changes (Chapter 2) are institutionalized through effective leadership (Chapters 12 through 15). Individuals will change as new people join the company (Chapters 10 and 11) and as people throughout the organization adopt the leader's new vision for the future.

The bottom line
Innovation

A useful tactic for innovating toward a positive future is to imagine the difference between what *is* and what *could be*.

force-field analysis

An approach to implementing the unfreezing/ moving/refreezing model by identifying the forces that prevent people from changing and those that will drive people toward change.

> ## Change agent: Jerry L. Rhoads
>
> The Fox Valley Nursing Center, located northwest of Chicago in Elgin, Illinois, was struggling to maintain its certification several years ago when an early winter storm dropped 16 inches of snow in 24 hours. Roads were nearly impassable, and staff members were calling in to report they couldn't make it to work. CEO Jerry Rhoads learned of the staff shortage in a phone call from the assistant director of nursing, and he told her she should simply list all the critical tasks that needed to be done for each resident, and the staff members should work in teams to get those tasks done. Rhoads was surprised by the result: staff members worked cheerfully and diligently for 72 hours, rotating through work and rest breaks so that no one became exhausted. Rhoads saw an opportunity for meaningful change. He began reorganizing the nursing center's staff into teams handling specific processes. Under the new system, absenteeism and turnover fell, while morale and occupancy rates improved. Some people predicted that the snowstorm's effects had simply been an exception, but staff members told Rhoads that "they knew how to provide this level of care all along, but no one would let them do it." He adds, "I believed them, and they were the ones who made it work."
>
> SOURCE: Jerry L. Rhoads, "A Storm-Inspired Makeover," *Contemporary Long Term Care*, April–May 2007, downloaded from General Reference Center Gold, http://find.galegroup.com.

One technique that helps to manage the change process, **force-field analysis,** involves identifying the specific forces that prevent people from changing and the specific forces that will drive people toward change.[45] Managers operating under this concept investigate forces acting in opposite directions at a particular time. Change leaders assess organizational strengths and select forces to add or remove in order to create change. Eliminating the restraining forces helps people unfreeze, and increasing the driving forces helps and motivates them to move forward.

Use of force-field analysis demonstrates that often a range of forces are pressing on an organization at a particular time. This analysis can increase people's optimism that it is possible to strategize and plan for change. The great social psychologist Kurt Lewin developed force-field analysis (and the unfreezing/moving/refreezing model). Lewin theorized that although driving forces may be more easily affected, shifting them may increase opposition (tension and/or conflict) within the organization and add restraining forces. Therefore, to create change, it may be more effective to remove restraining forces. An exercise at the end of the chapter provides an example and takes you through this process.

Refreezing   Finally, **refreezing** means strengthening the new behaviors that support the change. The changes must be diffused and stabilized throughout the company. Refreezing involves implementing control systems that support the change (Chapter 16), applying corrective action when necessary, and reinforcing behaviors and performance (Chapter 13) that support the agenda. Management should consistently support and reward all evidence of movement in the right direction.[46]

> **refreezing**
> Strengthening the new behaviors that support the change.

In today's organizations, refreezing is not always the best third step if it creates new behaviors that are as rigid as the old ones. The ideal new culture is one of continuous change. Refreezing is appropriate when it permanently installs behaviors that maintain essential core values, such as a focus on important business results and those values maintained by the companies that are "built to last." But refreezing should not create new rigidities that might become dysfunctional as the business environment continues to change.[47] The behaviors that should be refrozen are those that promote continued adaptability, flexibility, experimentation, assessment of results, and continuous improvement—in other words, lock in key values, capabilities, and strategic mission, but not necessarily specific management practices and procedures.

Specific Approaches to Enlist Cooperation

You can try to command people to change, but the key to long-term success is to use other approaches.[48] Developing true support is better than "driving" a program forward.[49] How, specifically, can managers motivate people to change?

Most managers underestimate the variety of ways they can influence people during a period of change.[50] Several effective approaches to managing resistance and enlisting cooperation are available, as described in Table 18.2 and expanded here.

Education and Communication   Management should educate people about upcoming changes before they occur. It should communicate not only the *nature* of the change but its *logic*. This process can include one-on-one discussions, presentations to groups, or reports and memos. As we discussed in Chapter 15, effective communication includes feedback and listening. Whenever Round Table Pizza introduces a new project or process, managers set up meetings with their employees to discuss the change and bring up any concerns they have.[51] That provides an environment in which management can explain the rationale for the change—and perhaps improve it.

Participation and Involvement   As discussed in Chapter 15, change requires reflection and dialogue.[52] It is important to listen to the people who are affected by the change. They should be involved in the change's design and implementation. For major, organizationwide change, participation in the process can extend from the top to the very bottom of the organization.[53] When feasible, management should use the advice of people throughout the organization.

TABLE 18.2
Methods for Managing
Resistance to Change

Approach	Commonly Used in Situations	Advantage	Drawbacks
Education and communication	Where there is a lack of information or inaccurate information and analysis.	Once persuaded, people will often help with the implementation of the change.	Can be very time-consuming if lots of people are involved.
Participation and involvement	Where the initiators do not have all the information they need to design the change, and where others have considerable power to resist.	People who participate will be committed to implementing change, and any relevant information they have will be integrated into the change plan.	Can be very time-consuming if participators design an inappropriate change.
Facilitation and support	Where people are resisting because of adjustment problems.	No other approach works as well with adjustment problems.	Can be time-consuming and expensive, and still fail.
Negotiation and rewards	Where someone or some group will clearly lose out in a change, and where that group has considerable power to resist.	Sometimes it is a relatively easy way to avoid major resistance.	Can be too expensive in many cases if it alerts others to negotiate for compliance.
Manipulation and cooptation	Where other tactics will not work, or are too expensive.	It can be a relatively quick and inexpensive solution to resistance problems.	Can lead to future problems if people feel manipulated.
Explicit and implicit coercion	Where speed is essential, and the change initiators possess considerable power.	It is speedy and can overcome any kind of resistance.	Can be risky if it leaves people angry at the initiators.

SOURCE: Reprinted by permission of the *Harvard Business Review*. An exhibit from "Choosing Strategies for Change" by John P. Kotter and Leonard A. Schlesinger (March–April 1979). Copyright © 1979 by the Harvard Business School Publishing Corporation; all rights reserved.

As you learned in Chapter 3, people who are involved in decisions understand them more fully and are more committed to them. People's understanding and commitment are important ingredients in the successful implementation of a change. Participation also provides an excellent opportunity for education and communication.

Facilitation and Support   Management should make the change as easy as possible for employees and support their efforts. Facilitation involves providing the training and other resources people need to carry out the change and perform their jobs under the new circumstances. This step often includes decentralizing authority and empowering people, that is, giving them the power to make the decisions and changes needed to improve their performance.

Offering support involves listening patiently to problems, being understanding if performance drops temporarily or the change is not perfected immediately, and generally being on the employees' side and showing consideration during a difficult period.

Negotiation and Rewards   When necessary and appropriate, management can offer concrete incentives for cooperation with the change. Perhaps job enrichment is acceptable only with a higher wage rate, or a work rule change is resisted until management agrees to a concession on some other rule (say, regarding taking breaks). Even among higher-level managers, one executive might agree to another's idea for a policy change only in return for support on some other issue of more personal importance. Rewards such as bonuses, wages and salaries, recognition, job assignments, and perks can be examined and perhaps restructured to reinforce the direction of the change.[54]

When people trust one another, change is easier. But change is further facilitated by demonstrating its benefits to people.[55] When a pharmaceutical company was trying to make improvements in the way it managed its supply chain, the vice president in charge set a positive tone by calling a meeting at which participants would start by sharing stories of their successes in carrying out their roles within the supply chain. Although suspicious at first, the participants gained enthusiasm and commitment before turning their energy toward making changes. The company was able to measure the improvement: 20 days shaved off the product lead time, saving the company more than $250,000.[56] The participants not only saw themselves as effective problem solvers but also had a dramatic measure of the improvement they could initiate in one meeting.

Change agent: Wenda Harris Millard

In the 1990s, when advertisers were wary of using the Internet, Yahoo! management hired someone it could trust as head of its sales force: Wenda Harris Millard. Millard was a 50-year-old veteran of the magazine industry. She taught her young and brash salespeople to work respectfully with their older ad agency clients, and she showed those clients that online ads could benefit them. Agency creative types loved TV ads but thought of Internet advertising as mainly boring pop-ups with a box saying "Click here." Yahoo! under Millard brought them together at educational summits and established the Yahoo Big Idea Chair award for the most creative online advertising. Seeing what innovative companies were doing, ad agency people became able to envision online advertising as a medium that allowed plenty of room for creativity—and Yahoo! began selling ads to big companies, reaching millions of Web visitors every day.

SOURCE: Alan Deutschman, *Change or Die* (Los Angeles: Regan, 2007), pp. 187–93.

Manipulation and Cooptation   Sometimes managers use more subtle, covert tactics to implement change. One form of manipulation is cooptation, which involves giving a resisting individual a desirable role in the change process. The leader of a resisting group often is coopted. For example, management might invite a union leader to be a member of an executive committee or ask a key member of an outside organization to join the company's board of directors. As a person becomes involved in the change, he or she may become less resistant to the actions of the coopting group or organization.

Explicit and Implicit Coercion   Some managers apply punishment or the threat of punishment to those who resist change. With this approach, managers use force to make people comply with their wishes. For example, a manager might insist that subordinates cooperate with the change and threaten them with job loss, denial of a promotion, or an unattractive work assignment. Sometimes you just have to lay down the law.

Each approach to managing resistance has advantages and drawbacks and, like many of the other situational management approaches described in this book, each is useful in different situations. Look back at Table 18.2, which summarizes the advantages, drawbacks, and appropriate circumstances for these approaches to managing resistance to change. As the table implies, managers should not use just one or two general approaches, regardless of the circumstances. Effective change managers are familiar with the various approaches and know how to apply them according to the situation.

Throughout the process, change leaders need to build in stability. Recall from the companies that were "built to last" that they all have essential core characteristics of which they don't lose sight. In the midst of change, turmoil, and uncertainty, people need anchors onto which they can latch.[57] Making an organization's values and mission constant and visible can often serve this stabilizing function. In addition, strategic principles can be important anchors during change.[58] Maintaining the visibility of key people, continuing key assignments and projects, and making announcements about which organizational components will *not* change can also promote stability. Such anchors will reduce anxiety and help overcome resistance.

Harmonizing Multiple Changes

total organization change

Introducing and sustaining multiple policies, practices, and procedures across multiple units and levels.

There are no "silver bullets" or single-shot methods of changing organizations successfully. Single shots rarely hit a challenging target. Usually, many issues need simultaneous attention, and any single, small change will be absorbed by the prevailing culture and disappear. **Total organization change** involves introducing and sustaining multiple policies, practices, and procedures across multiple units and levels.[59] Such change affects the thinking and behavior of everyone in the organization, can enhance the organization's culture and success, and can be sustained over time.

A survey at a Harvard Business School conference found that the average attendee's company had five major change efforts going on at once.[60] The most common change programs were practices you have studied in this course: continuous improvement; quality programs; time-based competition; and creation of a learning organization, a team-based organization, a network organization, core competencies, and strategic alliances. The problem is, these efforts usually are simultaneous but not coordinated. As a result, changes get muddled; people lose focus.[61] The people involved suffer from confusion, frustration, low morale, and low motivation.

Because companies introduce new changes constantly, many people complain about their companies' "flavor of the month" approach to change. That is, employees often see many change efforts as just the company's jumping on the latest bandwagon or fad. The more these change fads come and go, the more cynical people become, and the more difficult it is to get them committed to making the change a success.[62]

So an important question is, Which change efforts are really worth undertaking? Here are some specific questions to ask before embarking on a change project:[63]

- What is the evidence that the approach really can produce positive results?
- Is the approach relevant to your company's strategies and priorities?
- Can you assess the costs and potential benefits?
- Does it really help people add value through their work?
- Does it help the company focus better on customers and the things they value?
- Can you go through the decision-making process described in Chapter 3, understand what you're facing, and feel that you are taking the right approach?

The need for change was obvious when Janet Frank took the top job at California's State Compensation Insurance Fund, an agency with a state-appointed governing board and civil-service workers but no taxpayer funding. The State Fund, which provides workers' compensation insurance for many California companies, was in deep trouble after several of its leaders were accused of conflict of interest in awarding contracts. Two directors and two executives resigned; the government launched investigations and evaluated whether to press criminal charges.

Under fire, the board of directors brought in Frank, then an executive with CNA Financial Corporation, to clean up the agency. The mandate for change was a given. The dilemma was where to begin, considering that Frank had to placate angry citizens, legislators looking for evidence of better oversight, and business customers concerned about insurance costs. The state's insurance commissioner, Steve Poizner, delivered 150 recommended changes during Frank's first two months on the job.

Frank started with governance and communication. She brought in a finance executive and a chief risk officer to lead audits, looking for opportunities and weaknesses. She began requiring the internal-audit department to report its results directly to the board of directors, independent of management. She reorganized the communications department so it can deliver clearer messages to the agency's constituencies. She set up a public-records department to meet a newly passed disclosure requirement. Communication efforts also target employees worried about the future. In frequent appearances at meetings, Frank not only shares goals but also gathers ideas.[64]

Management also needs to connect the dots—that is, integrate the various efforts into a coherent picture that people can see, understand, and get behind.[65] You connect the dots by understanding each change program and its goals, by identifying similarities among the programs and also their differences, and by dropping programs that don't meet priority goals or demonstrate clear results. Most important, you do it by communicating to everyone concerned the common themes among the various programs: their common rationales, objectives, and methods. You show them how the various parts fit the strategic big picture and how the changes will make things better for the company and its people. You must communicate these benefits thoroughly, honestly, and frequently.[66]

Symantec's John Thompson, recently named as Chairman of the Board of Directors of the company, has been called "a relentless upbeat" leader who uses "big, bold, and optimistic language" to convey a positive vision, even through difficult changes.

Leading Change

Successful change requires managers to actively lead it. The essential activities of leading change are summarized in Figure 18.3.

The companies that lead change most effectively *establish a sense of urgency.*[67] To do so, managers must examine current realities and pressures in the marketplace and the competitive arena, identify both crises and opportunities, and be frank and honest about them. In this sense, urgency is a reality-based sense of determination, not just fear-based busyness. The immediacy of the need for change is an important component, in part because so many large companies grow complacent.

Figure 18.4 shows some of the common reasons for complacency. To stop complacency and create urgency, a manager can talk candidly about the organization's weaknesses compared with competitors, making a point to back up statements with data. Other tactics include setting stretch goals, putting employees in direct contact with unhappy customers and shareholders, distributing worrisome information to all employees instead of merely engaging in management "happy talk," eliminating excessive perks, and highlighting to everyone the future opportunities that exist but that the organization so far has failed to pursue.

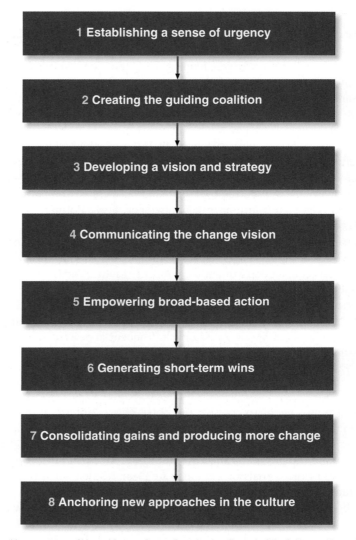

FIGURE 18.3
Leading Change

Ultimately, urgency is driven by compelling business reasons for change. Survival, competition, and winning in the marketplace are compelling; they provide a sense of direction and energy around change. Change becomes not a hobby, a luxury, or something nice to do, but a business necessity.[68]

To *create a guiding coalition* means putting together a group with enough power to lead the change. Change efforts fail when a sufficiently powerful coalition is not formed.[69] Major organization change requires leadership from top management, working as a team. But over time, the support must gradually expand outward and downward throughout the organization. Middle managers and supervisors are essential. Groups at all levels are the glue that can hold change efforts together, the medium for communicating about the changes, and the means for enacting new behaviors.[70]

Developing a vision and strategy, as discussed in earlier chapters, directs the change effort. This process involves determining the idealized, expected state of affairs after the change is implemented. Because confusion is common during major organizational change, the clearest possible image of the future state must be developed and conveyed to everyone.[71] This image, or vision, is a target or guideline that can clarify expectations, dispel rumors, and mobilize people's energies. The portrait of the future also should communicate how the transition will occur, why the change is

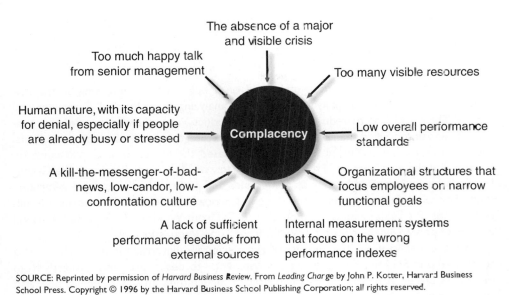

FIGURE 18.4
Sources of Complacency

being implemented, and how people will be affected by the change. The power of a compelling vision is one of the most important aspects of change and should not be underestimated or underutilized.

Communicating the change vision requires using every possible channel and opportunity to talk up and reinforce the vision and required new behaviors. It is said that aspiring change leaders undercommunicate the vision by a factor of 10, or even 100 or 1,000, seriously undermining the chances of success.[72] In contrast, when Virginia Blood Services (VBS) launched an effort to improve its organizational culture to lower employee turnover and accident rates, management made communication a central part of the change effort. The communication program at VBS includes employee meetings every three months, an employee newsletter distributed every two weeks, and messages from the president addressing key topics. In each site's break room, the organization replaced its bulletin boards—where no one bothered to read the memos and government posters—with wall-mounted display cases featuring colorful posters and motivational, sometimes humorous messages about safety, quality, and teamwork. The items in the displays are changed every week to maintain interest. The communication program, which supports practical measures like safety training and new scheduling procedures, has helped build support for the new organizational culture, motivating employees to stay safe and on the job.[73]

Empowering broad-based action means getting rid of obstacles to success, including systems and structures that constrain rather than facilitate. Encourage risk taking and experimentation, and empower people by providing information, knowledge, authority, and rewards, as described in Chapter 13.

Generate short-term wins. Don't wait for the ultimate grand realization of the vision. You need results. As small victories accumulate, you make the transition from an isolated initiative to an integral part of the business.[74] Plan for and create small victories that indicate to everyone that progress is being made. Recognize and reward the people who made the wins possible, doing it visibly so that people notice and the positive message permeates the organization.

Make sure you *consolidate gains and produce more change*. With the well-earned credibility of previous successes, keep changing things in ways that support the vision. Hire, promote, and develop people who will further the vision. Reinvigorate the organization and your change efforts with new projects and change agents. For example, as discussed in "Management Close-Up: Taking Action," SC Johnson built on its original successes with environmentally friendly initiatives by launching further efforts that express and reinforce the company's commitment to the environment.

Management Close-Up   TAKING ACTION

In 2001, scientists at SC Johnson embarked on a huge task: inventorying all the raw materials used in their company's products and analyzing them for their environmental impact. Their goal was to reduce SC Johnson products' negative effects wherever possible. The team classified the raw materials into five categories—insecticides, propellants, resins, solvents, and surfactants—and then evaluated the impact of each substance on humans and the environment. Through this project, which became known as the Greenlist, SC Johnson identified hazardous compounds and potential pollutants and eliminated them. For example, as a result of the Greenlist process, the company removed 1.8 million pounds of volatile organic compounds (VOCs) from Windex's formula and 4 million pounds of polyvinylidene chloride (PVDC) from Saran Wrap's formula.

As the Greenlist grew, the process of examining raw materials for toxicity became a routine step in SC Johnson's product development—to design products correctly from the outset rather than reformulate them later to reduce their impact. Greenlist now also is used when the company designs packaging materials. It was through Greenlist, in fact, that SC Johnson decided to eliminate chlorine-based plastic packaging from its products. The company also licenses the use of its patented Greenlist software at no charge to interested organizations.

In 2003, SC Johnson broke ground on a cogeneration energy plant, a $5 million system in which a turbine burns methane gas from landfill waste and produces electricity and steam for one of its largest manufacturing facilities. The plant is one of only a few in the United States that recover energy from waste methane. The plant's savings in greenhouse gas emissions are roughly equivalent to keeping 3,200 cars off the road each year—or driving around the Earth 7,630 times. Also, the energy produced by the cogeneration plant saves SC Johnson about $2.4 million in energy costs per year and has greatly reduced its use of polluting coal-generated electricity.[75]

- Since he became company CEO in 2000, Fisk Johnson needed to take on the role of change agent at SC Johnson. Why would top management's commitment be important in creating the change for greater environmental responsibility? List as many reasons as you can for this commitment.
- Under Fisk Johnson's leadership, SC Johnson's Greenlist was developed by a team of scientists who believed the initiative was important for the environment. Why might a consumer products company want to lead such a change in its industry?

"Change is a verb."

—Mimi Silbert, founder, Delancey Street Foundation[76]

reactive change

A response that occurs under pressure; problem-driven change.

Finally, *anchor new approaches in the culture.*[77] Highlight positive results, communicate the connections between the new behaviors and the improved results, and keep developing new change agents and leaders. Continually increase the number of people joining you in taking responsibility for change.[78]

Shaping the Future

LO 3

proactive change

A response that is initiated before a performance gap has occurred.

Most change is reactive. A better way to change is to be proactive. **Reactive change** means responding to pressure, after the problem has arisen. It also implies being a follower. **Proactive change** means anticipating and preparing for an uncertain future. It implies being a leader and *creating* the future you want.

The road to the future includes drivers, passengers, and road kill. Put another way: on the road to the future, who will be the windshield, and who will be the bug?[79]

Needless to say, it's best to be a driver.[80] How do you become a driver? By being proactive more than merely reactive, by really thinking about the future, and by *creating* futures.

Thinking about the Future

If you think only about the present or wallow in the uncertainties of the future, your future is just a roll of the dice. It is far better to exercise foresight, set an agenda for the future, and pursue it with everything you've got. So contemplate and envision the future.

As of 75 years ago, we had no safe and effective antibiotics, no TV, no computers, and no commercial air travel. In recent years we have gone to the moon, created the Internet, and read the human genome. *BusinessWeek* asks, Will the next 75 years bring the same mega-transformations? Or will progress be more incremental, elaborating on current knowledge more than creating new technologies and industries?[81]

BusinessWeek answers its own question: "The global economy could be on the cusp of an age of innovation equal to that of the past 75 years. All the right factors are in place: science is advancing rapidly, more countries are willing to devote resources to research and development and education, and corporate managers, too, are convinced of the importance of embracing change."[82] *BusinessWeek* cites nanotechnology, energy technologies, and the biological sciences as examples. Innovation will be the key to the world's future.

Shoshana Zuboff and Jim Maxim, authors of *The Support Economy*, claim that the era of industrial capitalism is over, traditional business enterprises are disappearing, vast new markets exist, new kinds of companies are ready to be created, and the new business model hasn't yet emerged.[83]

BE FEARLESS.

Don't think taking risks and being fearless is only for companies; think of your own quest for personal competitive advantage in the same way. Ultimately, where you go, what you do, who you become, all are up to you. So, be fearless.

Creating the Future

Companies can try different strategic postures to prepare to compete in an uncertain future. **Adapters** take the current industry structure and its future evolution as givens. They choose where to compete. This posture is taken by most companies by conducting standard strategic analysis and choosing how to compete within given environments. In contrast, **shapers** try to change the structure of their industries, creating a future competitive landscape of their own design.[84]

Researchers studying corporate performance over a 10-year period found that 17 companies in the *Fortune* 1000 grew total shareholder return by 35 percent or more per year.[85] How did they do it? They completely reinvented industries. Harley-Davidson turned around by selling not just motorcycles, but nostalgia. Amgen broke the rules of the biotech industry by focusing not on what customers wanted, but on great science. Starbucks took a commodity and began selling it in trendy stores. CarMax and other companies reinvented the auto industry.

You need to create advantages. The challenge is, not to maintain your position in the current competitive arena, but to create new competitive arenas, transform your industry, and imagine a future that others don't see. Creating advantage is better than playing catch-up. At best, doing things to catch up buys time; it cannot get you out ahead of the pack or buy world-class excellence.[86] To create new markets or transform industries—these are perhaps the ultimate forms of proactive change.[87]

Figure 18.5 illustrates the vast opportunity to create new markets. Articulated needs are those that customers acknowledge and try to satisfy. Unarticulated needs are those that customers have not yet experienced. Served customers are those to whom your company is now selling, and unserved customers are untapped markets.

Business-as-usual concentrates on the lower-left quadrant. The leaders who re-create the game are constantly trying to create new opportunities in the other three quadrants.[88] For example, you can pursue the upper-left quadrant by imagining how you can satisfy a larger proportion of your customers' total needs. Caterpillar appreciates

adapters

Companies that take the current industry structure and its evolution as givens, and choose where to compete.

shapers

Companies that try to change the structure of their industries, creating a future competitive landscape of their own design.

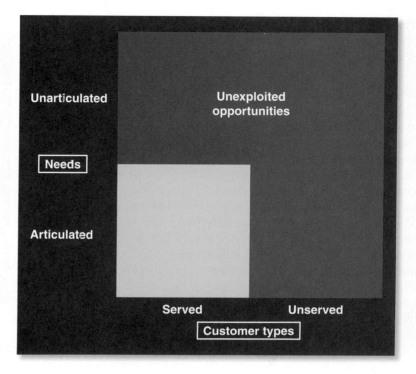

FIGURE 18.5
Vast Opportunity

that its customers want more than its heavy equipment; they also need excellent service so that they can use that equipment to meet their own customers' needs. As a result, if a customer anywhere in the world needs a Caterpillar part, the company will ship it there within 24 hours. And Lands' End expanded both its product offerings and number of served customers by offering customization—the ability to specify exact measurements when ordering jeans and other selected items of clothing.[89]

Other companies hope to meet unarticulated needs by developing and exploiting cutting-edge technology. The nanometer—one-billionth of a meter, 1/100,000 the width of a human hair, or about the size of 10 hydrogen atoms in a row—is the building block of a new industry, nanotechnology. Why is the nanometer so important?[90] Because matter of this size often behaves differently—transmitting light or electricity, or becoming harder than diamonds, or becoming powerful chemical catalysts. Large and small companies are beginning to rush nano-based products into the marketplace. Early applications include coatings and light-emitting dots for more efficient semiconductors and nanoparticles that clean up polluted water by forming chemical bonds with contaminants.[91] Applications under development include 50-nanometer capsules containing vitamins and other nutrients that can be added to beverages without changing their taste or that can be activated by microwaves.[92]

Is nanotech—for that matter, are most "industries of the future"—being overhyped? By one account, companies had sold $50 billion in nano-related products in 2006, and the National Science Foundation has forecast the market to reach $1 trillion by 2015.[93] However, there are concerns that the technology is untested and perhaps risky.[94] The particles are so small that they can pass through most filters, and their ability to react at the atomic level could cause unforeseen chemical and biological consequences. Can the industry convince consumers of its safety, or will there be a global backlash, as with genetically modified foods in Europe? What regulations will appear? Which nanotechnologies will create what new industries? Which companies will emerge as winners? And what will it take to do so? As you've read, technological change is a central part of the changing landscape, and competition often arises between newcomers and established companies.

All things considered, which should you and your firm do?

- Preserve old advantages or create new advantages?
- Lock in old markets or create new markets?
- Take the path of greatest familiarity or the path of greatest opportunity?
- Be only a benchmarker or a pathbreaker?
- Place priority on short-term financial returns or on making a real, long-term impact?
- Do only what seems doable or what is difficult and worthwhile?
- Change what is or create what isn't?
- Look to the past or live for the future?[95]

Shaping Your Own Future

If you are an organizational leader and your organization operates in traditional ways, your key goal should be to create a revolution, genetically reengineering your company before it becomes a dinosaur of the modern era.[96] What should be the goals of the revolution? You've been learning about them throughout this course.

But maybe you are not going to lead a revolution. Maybe you just want a successful career and a good life. You still must be able to deal with an economic environment that is increasingly competitive and fast-moving.[97] Creating the future you want for yourself requires setting high personal standards. Don't settle for mediocrity; don't assume that "good" is necessarily good enough—for yourself or for your employer. Think about how not just to meet expectations but to exceed them; to not merely "live with" apparent constraints but break free of the unimportant, arbitrary, or imagined ones; and to seize opportunities instead of letting them pass by.[98]

| Change agent: Matthew Kirchner

Matthew Kirchner is chief executive of American Finishing Resources, a company that serves manufacturers by removing coatings (for example, from improperly painted parts) and by making customized fixtures used for applying coatings. While his industry may not seem glamorous, Kirchner is as buffeted as any manager by demands from his customers, regulators, bankers, and suppliers. In that situation, change could become something that just happens to his career and his company. Instead, Kirchner takes the reins of his career and his future by starting each day with a meeting scheduled for himself alone to plan for the changes he wants to see. During that hour, Kirchner reviews his personal mission statement (his expression of why he comes to work each day), the major efforts under way to land new business, basic measures of revenue and expenses, and schedules of work in process. By refreshing his view of the big picture, Kirchner starts his day focused on what he has determined is most important.

SOURCE: Matthew Kirchner, "One Hour a Day," *Products Finishing*, September 2008, downloaded from Business & Company Resource Center, http://galenet.galegroup.com.

Table 18.3 helps you think about how you can continually add value to your employer—and also to yourself—as you upgrade your skills, your ability to contribute, your security with your current employer, and your ability to find alternative employment if necessary. The most successful individuals take charge of their own development the way an entrepreneur takes charge of a business.[99]

More advice from the leading authors on career management:[100] consciously and actively manage your own career. Develop marketable skills, and keep developing more. Make career choices based on personal growth, development, and learning opportunities. Look for positions that stretch you, and for bosses who develop their

TABLE 18.3
Adding Value, Personally

Go beyond your job description:	Learn something new every week.
• Volunteer for projects.	Discover new ways to make a contribution.
• Identify problems.	Engage in active thought and deliberate action.
• Initiate solutions.	
Seek out others and share ideas and advice.	Take risks based on what you know and believe.
Offer your opinions and respect those of others.	Recognize, research, and pursue opportunity.
Take an inventory of your skills every few months.	Differentiate yourself.

SOURCE: Compiled from C. Hakim, *We Are All Self-Employed* (San Francisco: Barrett-Koehler, 1994).

protégés. Seek environments that provide training and the opportunity to experiment and innovate. And know yourself: assess your strengths and weaknesses, your true interests, and ethical standards. If you are not already thinking in these terms and taking commensurate action, you should start now.

Additionally, become indispensable to your organization. Be happy and enthusiastic in your job and committed to doing great work, but don't be blindly loyal to one company. Be prepared to leave, if necessary. View your job as an opportunity to prove what you can do and increase what you can do, not as a comfortable niche for the long term.[101] Go out on your own if it meets your skills and temperament.

This points out the need to maintain your options. More and more, contemporary careers can involve leaving behind a large organization and going entrepreneurial, becoming self-employed in the "postcorporate world."[102] In such a career, independent individuals are free to make their own choices. They can flexibly and quickly respond to demands and opportunities. Developing start-up ventures, consulting, accepting temporary employment, doing project work for one organization and then another, working in professional partnerships, being a constant deal maker—these can be the elements of a successful career. Ideally, this self-employed model can help provide a balanced approach to working and to living life at home and with family, because people have more control over their work activities and schedules.

This go-it-alone approach can sound ideal, but it also has downsides. Independence can be frightening, the future unpredictable. It can isolate "road warriors" who are always on the go, working from their cars and airports, and interfere with social and family life.[103] Effective self-management is needed to keep career and family obligations in perspective and in control. Coping with uncertainty and change is also easier if you develop resilience. To become more resilient, practice thinking of the world as complex but full of opportunities; expect change, but see it as interesting and potentially rewarding, even if changing is difficult. Also, keep a sense of purpose, set priorities for your time, be flexible when facing uncertainty or a need to change, and take an active role in the face of change rather than waiting for change to happen to you.[104]

Continuous learning provides a fundamental competitive advantage by helping you and your organization achieve difficult goals.

Learning and Leading

Continuous learning is a vital route to renewable competitive advantage.[105] People in your organization—and you, personally—should constantly explore, discover, and take action, as illustrated in Figure 18.6. With this approach, you can learn what is effective and what is not and adjust and improve accordingly. The philosophy of continuous learning helps your company achieve lower cost, higher quality, better service, superior innovation, and greater speed—and helps you grow and develop on a personal level.

Explore

The first step is to explore current reality.
The aim is to be as honest and open as possible
about what is happening at present.

- Identify the problem/opportunity area
- Check with the customers, suppliers, or
  other key stakeholders
- Reveal hidden issues
- Gather data
- Look for root causes
- Rethink the issue

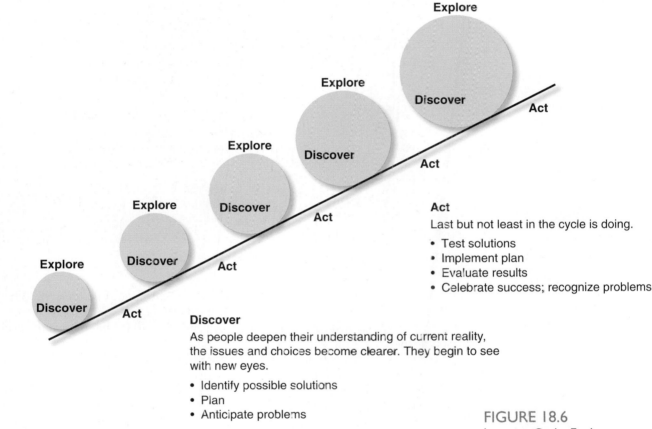

Act

Last but not least in the cycle is doing.

- Test solutions
- Implement plan
- Evaluate results
- Celebrate success; recognize problems

Discover

As people deepen their understanding of current reality,
the issues and choices become clearer. They begin to see
with new eyes.

- Identify possible solutions
- Plan
- Anticipate problems

FIGURE 18.6

Learning Cycle: Explore,
Discover, Act

SOURCE: From *Leaning into the Future Charging the Way People Change Organizctions* by George Binney and Colin Williams;
published by Nicholas Brealey Publishing Ltd., 1997. Tel: (0171) 430-0224, Fax: (0171) 404-8311. Reprinted by permission.

Commit to lifelong learning. Lifelong learning includes being willing to seek new challenges and to reflect honestly on successes and failures.[106] Lifelong learning requires occasionally taking risks, moving outside your "comfort zone," honestly assessing the reasons behind your successes and failures, asking for and listening to other people's information and opinions, and being open to new ideas.

Through a career, a person can "inhabit" and grow through the hierarchy of stages illustrated in Figure 18.7. The descriptions in the hierarchy suggest not only that you do these things, but that you should do them *well*. Your first job may not include managerial responsibilities, but it will require you to be an individual contributor and probably to be part of a team. Level 3 is where managerial competencies are required, while Level 4 distinguishes true leadership from competent management. Level 5 represents a leadership style that you read about briefly in Chapter 12, which combines strong will and determination with personal humility. The figure shows that Level 5 leadership represents a peak achievement: it is the ultimate contribution of a leader

FIGURE 18.7
Level 5 Hierarchy

LEVEL 5 — **LEVEL 5 EXECUTIVE**
Builds enduring greatness through a paradoxical blend of personal humility and professional will.

LEVEL 4 — **EFFECTIVE LEADER**
Catalyzes commitment to and vigorous pursuit of a clear and compelling vision, stimulating higher performance standards.

LEVEL 3 — **COMPETENT MANAGER**
Organizes people and resources toward the effective and efficient pursuit of predetermined objectives.

LEVEL 2 — **CONTRIBUTING TEAM MEMBER**
Contributes individual capabilities to the achievement of group objectives and works effectively with others in a group setting.

LEVEL 1 — **HIGHLY CAPABLE INDIVIDUAL**
Makes productive contributions through talent, knowledge, skills, and good work habits.

SOURCE: J. Collins, *Good to Great* (New York: Harper Business 2001).

who can turn a good company into a great one.[107] You might ask yourself, What is my level now (or where will I be after graduation)? What do I aspire to? What have I learned at this point that can help me progress, and what do I need to learn to develop myself further?

A leader—and this could include you—should be able to create an environment in which "others are willing to learn and change so their organizations can adapt and innovate [and] inspire diverse others to embark on a collective journey of continual learning and leading."[108] *Learning leaders* exchange knowledge freely; commit to their own continuous learning as well as to others'; are committed to examining their own behaviors and defensiveness that may inhibit their learning; devote time to their colleagues, suspending their own beliefs while they listen thoughtfully; and develop a broad perspective, recognizing that organizations are an integrated system of relationships.[109]

Honored as one of the best management books of the year in Europe, *Leaning into the Future* gets its title from a combination of the words *leading* and *learning*.[110] The two perspectives, on the surface, appear very different. But they are powerful and synergistic when pursued in complementary ways. A successful future derives from adapting to the world *and* shaping the future; being responsive to others' perspectives *and* being clear about what you want to change; encouraging others to change *while* recognizing what you need to change about yourself; understanding current realities *and* passionately pursuing your vision; learning *and* leading.

This is another example of an important concept from the beginning of the chapter. For yourself, as well as for your organization, be ambidextrous. At SC Johnson, as described in "Management Close-Up: Assessing Outcomes and Seizing Opportunities," success comes not only from learning what consumers and regulators demand but also from "doing what's right."

Management Close-Up

ASSESSING OUTCOMES AND SEIZING OPPORTUNITIES

Under Fisk Johnson's leadership, SC Johnson continues to reduce its impact on the environment. More than revamping the formulation of its products and packaging, the efforts involve examining manufacturing, distribution, and other processes in the firm's supply chain. In 2005, the company set a five-year plan for reducing waste and greenhouse gas emissions and using clean energy for its manufacturing plants worldwide. The firm has made great progress so far: in the United States alone, SC Johnson has already exceeded, by double, its goal for reducing greenhouse gas emissions.

Another energy initiative of which Fisk Johnson is proud is the company's step into wind power. In 2008, SC Johnson launched a windmill project to provide green energy for one of its largest plants in Bay City, Michigan. The project provides nearly half of the plant's energy needs, an amount comparable to supplying electricity to 1,800 homes for a year. What's more, the clean energy keeps nearly 30,000 tons of carbon dioxide out of the atmosphere each year—the equivalent of taking nearly 3,000 cars off the road in a year.

The company has also discovered a way to save on its fossil fuel use during distribution. By the end of Year One of its five-year plan, its revised system for loading trucks to ensure that they carried full loads to their destinations had improved the fleet's efficiency, cut fuel use by 168,000 gallons, and saved the company $1.6 million.

SC Johnson has also made the move to hybrid cars for its sales force. First offered as an option in 2007, a hybrid vehicle such as a Toyota Camry or Prius has become the choice of nearly two-thirds of SC Johnson's salespeople. The ultimate goal set for the company's sales force is to achieve, on average, 40 miles to the gallon.

For a family-owned company that stretches back five generations, SC Johnson seems squarely focused on the future.[111]

- Recently, SC Johnson voluntarily provided more information on its product labels than the U.S. government requires and discontinued the use of compounds known as phthalates, which were used to make the fragrances of some of its products last longer, because of questions about their safety. How do such behaviors differentiate SC Johnson from other companies—and CEO Fisk Johnson from other leaders?
- Fisk Johnson has said that while winning is about performance, it's also about "doing what's right—right for the planet, right for people, right for the next generation." How do these words relate to the definition of "world class"?

KEY TERMS

Adapters, p. 647

Force-field analysis, p. 638

Genius of the *and*, p. 629

Moving, p. 638

Organization development (OD), p. 631

Organizational ambidexterity, p. 629

Performance gap, p. 637

Proactive change, p. 646

Reactive change, p. 646

Refreezing, p. 639

Shapers, p. 647

Total organization change, p. 642

Tyranny of the *or*, p. 629

Unfreezing, p. 636

SUMMARY OF LEARNING OBJECTIVES

Now that you have studied Chapter 18, you should be able to:

LO 1 Discuss what it takes to be world class.

You should strive for world-class excellence, which means using the very best and latest knowledge and ideas to operate at the highest standards of any place anywhere. Sustainable greatness comes from, among other things, having strong core values, living those values constantly, striving for continuous improvement, experimenting, and always trying to do better tomorrow than today. It is essential to not fall prey to the tyranny of the *or;* that is, the belief that one important goal can be attained only at the expense of another. The genius of the *and* is that multiple important goals can be achieved simultaneously and synergistically.

LO 2 Describe how to manage and lead change effectively.

Effective change management occurs when the organization moves from its current state to a desired future state without excessive cost to the organization or its people. People resist change for a variety of reasons, including inertia, poor timing, surprise, peer pressure, self-interest, misunderstanding, different information about (and assessments of) the change, and management's tactics.

Motivating people to change requires a general process of unfreezing, moving, and refreezing, with the caveat that appropriate and not inappropriate behaviors be "refrozen." More specific techniques to motivate people to change include education and communication, participation and involvement, facilitation and support, negotiation and rewards, manipulation and cooptation, and coercion. Each approach has strengths, weaknesses, and appropriate uses, and multiple approaches can be used. It is important to harmonize the multiple changes that are occurring throughout the organization.

Effective change requires active leadership, including creating a sense of urgency, forming a guiding coalition, developing a vision and strategy, communicating the change vision, empowering broad-based action, generating short-term wins, consolidating gains and producing more change, and anchoring the new approaches in the culture.

LO 3   **List tactics for creating a successful future.**

Preparing for an uncertain future requires a proactive approach. You can proactively forge the future by being a shaper more than an adapter, creating new competitive advantages, actively managing your career and your personal development, and becoming an active leader and a lifelong learner.

DISCUSSION QUESTIONS

1. Review the quotes on page 634, describing "resistance to becoming world class." Why do some people resist the goal of becoming world class? What lies behind the quotes? How can this resistance be overcome?

2. Generate specific examples of world-class business that you have seen as a consumer. Also, generate examples of poor business practice. Why and how do some companies inspire world-class practices, while others do not?

3. How might blogging affect the process of managing change? What are the professional and career implications of blogging for you?

4. Generate and discuss examples of problems and opportunities that have inspired change, both in businesses and in you, personally.

5. Review the methods for dealing with resistance to change. Generate specific examples of each that you have seen, and analyze the reasons why they worked or failed to work.

6. Choose some specific types of changes you would like to see happen in groups or organizations with which you are familiar. Imagine that you were to try to bring about these changes. What sources of resistance should you anticipate? How would you manage the resistance?

7. Develop a specific plan for becoming a "continuous learner."

8. In your own words, what does the idea of "creating the future" mean to you? How can you put this concept to good use? Again, generate some specific ideas that you can really use.

9. In what ways do you think the manager's job will be different in 20 years than it is today? How can you prepare for that future?

CONCLUDING CASE

Barbara's World of Windows, Fabrics, and Accessories—Home Consultant Division

BUSINESS OVERVIEW AND PERSPECTIVE

Shortly after World War II, Barbara and Jerry Klein opened a small retail store in the northern New Jersey metropolitan area. Their major product lines included cotton, wool, and other fabrics that Jerry was able to buy from a few of his old war buddies who worked in mills located throughout the southeastern United States. The fabrics were purchased by an almost exclusively female clientele from the local area for use in making curtains, clothing, slipcovers, pillows, and other related home furnishings. The store also sold curtain rods, hardware, zippers, sewing supplies, and related accessories.

The store was a great success throughout the 1950s, 1960s, and 1970s. During that time, sales grew from $150,000 to more than $2,500,000 annually. The store employed 30 people, mostly homemakers from the local area who were sewers and clothing makers themselves. The warm, cozy, and friendly atmosphere made the store a favorite of the local and surrounding townspeople. Several competitors came and went over the years—those that survived were very small, posing little threat to Barbara and Jerry, who essentially enjoyed the fruits of a monopoly.

Barbara's (comfortable) world came crashing down during the 1980s, as sales steadily declined to less than $1,800,000 by the decade's end. Their original clientele had gradually retired, moved away, or passed on by that time. The modern-day women from the area were now going to college and establishing professional careers rather than staying at home sewing curtains or making clothes. At the same time, a number of new and more diversified competitors had come onto the scene, capturing more and more market share.

Those new stores carried a much wider range of products, including bridal wear; tablecloths and napkins; miniblinds and assorted shades; quilts; blankets; and limited lines of furniture, lamps, candles, and complementary products.

Barbara and Jerry's daughter Sandy, a recent business school graduate who grew up working part-time in the business, came on board as assistant manager of operations. Sandy was being trained and groomed to eventually take over the business. Given her many years of direct work experience and her newly acquired business management skills, Sandy was given some freedom and encouragement to effect change and turn things around.

A NEW ERA

The store's entire merchandise inventory was counted, assessed, and reorganized. Sandy got rid of slow-moving and stagnant inventory. High-turnover, high-profit merchandise was given more and better shelf space. A number of new products were added to challenge the competition and better reflect the buying trends and needs of the modern-day consumer.

The most significant change was the addition of a new Home Consultant Division. Recognizing the needs and characteristics of today's professional woman shopper, Sandy proceeded to bring the business to the customer in the comfort of her own home. During evening and weekend hours, sales associates visited the homes of working women. Offered a variety of full-color catalogs and fabric samples, customers could simply select the blinds, shades, draperies, wall coverings, slipcovers, and so on of their choosing and write a check for one-half of the total invoice as a deposit. The sales associate took the necessary measurements while on site. The finished products were delivered and installed in approximately two to four weeks. The remaining balance was paid at the time of delivery and installation.

The Home Consultant Division was a huge start-up success. Sales reached $1,000,000 during the first year of operation and $1,500,000 during year 2. As the division grew, so too did a number of problems and inefficiencies. A shortage of qualified installers caused the lag time between orders and installations to grow to as much as 6 to 12 weeks. On the home appointment side, where a customer could once expect to have a sales associate visit within a week or two of inquiring, the wait for an appointment had grown to average about one month. On top of all of this, Sandy knew that there was a lot more business out there to capture.

Customers became impatient and unhappy, as Sandy now faced her first serious problem that needed to be fixed fast. The complacency and lack of marketing savvy of her parents had allowed a number of able competitors to come onto the scene, two of which were gearing up to offer their own home shopping divisions.

Sandy asked Barbara Johnson, one of the sales associates, to document the complete and exact process that takes place from the time an inquiry is received to the time that an installation is completed, in the hope of identifying specific inefficiencies and production bottlenecks. Johnson's report can be summarized as follows:

- The process begins with a phone call from people responding to newspaper ads or from in-store shoppers. No programs are currently in place to actively solicit prospective customers.
- The secretary or whoever happens to answer the phone records the information (name, address, phone number, nature of inquiry) and places a note in the sales associate's mailbox.
- A sales associate (currently two full-time, one part-time) places a phone call to set up an appointment in the order in which the inquiry was received. Most clients are within a 25-mile radius of the store.
- A typical day for a sales associate might include a 4:00 p.m. appointment in one town followed by a 7:30 p.m. appointment in another town. On Saturdays, the sales associate typically has a 9:00 a.m. appointment in one town followed by a 12:00 p.m. appointment in another town.
- The associate then meets with the client, equipped with catalogs and samples, order forms, and measuring equipment. Most appointments result in a sale. The sales associate takes the necessary measurements (window sizes, sofa dimensions, and so on), and leaves with a check for an estimated 50 percent deposit.

- The sales associates spend about one day per week processing orders (calculating the yardage and best source of material, locating the appropriate curtain rod, tabulating the exact invoice total, and so on).
- When all of the materials arrive at the store for a particular order, the sales associate is notified and then proceeds to contact and schedule an installer; this also includes a scheduling call to the client.
- The installer completes the delivery and installation and collects the final payment for the store.

Johnson also provided the following breakdown of each sales associate's average distribution of time spent on the job:

- 40 percent of the time is spent selling at the client's home.
- 30 percent of the time is spent processing orders.
- 30 percent of the time is spent traveling between appointments.

Barbara's report concluded with a summary from the installation side of the division: "Most deliveries and installations are made by two independent subcontractors that have been with the company since the start-up of the division. They have a reputation for doing good work. Several others have come and gone—this due to either poor workmanship or lack of availability or reliability.

"Several customers have complained about the appearance and presentation of the installers and their equipment. Many of the clients are women who live in suburban neighborhoods. These women are often home alone when the deliveries and installations are made. They are apprehensive and fearful when they see unshaven young men with old clothes pull up to their home in a battered old van. A few customers have actually refused to let the installer into their home without first speaking with someone at the store.

"The two primary installers are working hard and are steadily falling further and further behind the order file."

As for the many untapped markets and additional new business that is out there, Sandy wants her staff to become more proactive—to go after orders rather than just waiting for the phone to ring or for a shopper to inquire while in the store.

Sandy feels that the company is making a big mistake by completely ignoring the local industrial and governmental markets. For example, on the industrial side, hotels, restaurants, banks, offices, and many other establishments regularly purchase and update their furniture, window coverings, and other interior decor. The same is true for prospective governmental customers such as schools, city and town offices, and federal buildings. Sandy also notes that all of the customers, both in the store and in the home, continue to be almost exclusively women.

QUESTIONS

1. You have inherited a company that must make several internal changes to survive and thrive. How would you plan for and manage each of the changes that must occur? Be sure to address both strategic and tactical aspects of your plan.

2. The text lists and describes a number of operational aspects and components; select each of those that are relevant to this case, and provide a specific example of a technique that you would incorporate into the new operation.

3. In general, what interpersonal skills and management techniques will you use to successfully effect change?

EXPERIENTIAL EXERCISES

18.1 A Force-Field Analysis

OBJECTIVE

To introduce you to force-field analysis for managing organizational change.

INSTRUCTIONS

Read the following force-field analysis, and come up with an organizational problem of your own to analyze.

FORCE-FIELD ANALYSIS

As described in the chapter, a force-field analysis is one way to assess change in an organization. The change leader identifies the driving and restraining forces at work at a particular time, assesses organizational strengths, and selects forces to add or remove in order to create change. Using force-field analysis demonstrates the range of forces pressing on an organization at a particular time and can increase optimism that change is possible.

Example—Trying to increase student participation in student government.

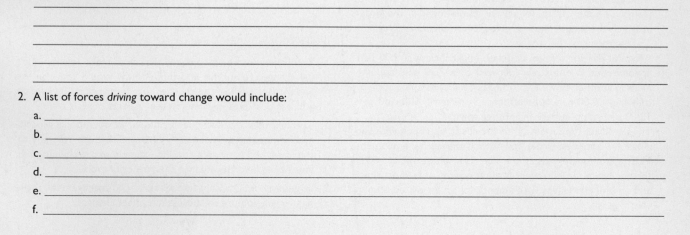

Driving Forces	Restraining Forces
More money allocated for student government activities. ⟶	⟵ High emphasis on grades—a need to study more.
Better publicity and public relations programs for student government. ⟶	⟵ Other activities—cultural, social, sports— divert interest.
Student government representatives go to classes and explain positive effects of student decisions. ⟶	⟵ Not much public relations work in the past.
Special career programs offered for student government participants. ⟶	⟵ Students do not see student government as effective or helping them get a job.

Present balance point

Force-Field Analysis Worksheet

1. Choose an organizational change in process, complete the Problem Analysis section, and fill in the model. (10–15 min.)

2. In groups of three or four, discuss the driving and restraining forces in each person's problem. (20 min.)

3. Class discussion (10 min.)

   a. Why is it useful to break a problem situation up into driving and restraining forces?

   b. Would the model be used any differently whether applied to an individual or organizational problem?

PROBLEM ANALYSIS

1. Describe the problem in a few words.

   _____

   _____

   _____

   _____

   _____

2. A list of forces *driving* toward change would include:

   a. _____

   b. _____

   c. _____

   d. _____

   e. _____

   f. _____

3. A list of forces *restraining* change would include:

a. _____

b. _____

c. _____

d. _____

e. _____

f. _____

4. Put the driving and restraining forces of the problem on this force-field analysis, according to their degree of impact on change.

Driving Forces	Restraining Forces
→	←

Present balance point

SOURCE: Dorothy Hai, "Force-Field Analysis" in *Organizational Behavior: Experiences and Cases* (St. Paul, MN: West, 1986), pp. 259–61. Copyright © 1986. Reprinted by permission by South-Western College Publishing, a division of Thomson Learning.

18.2 Networking Scenarios

1. Working on your own, develop a networking strategy for the following three scenarios. (10 min.)

2. Working with your partner or small group, collaborate on identifying the best strategy for dealing with each of the three scenarios. Each group should develop one best strategy for each scenario. (20 min.)

3. Each group reports, sharing its best strategies for each of the three scenarios (or at least one if not enough time is available). (2–3 min. per group per strategy).

4. The large group or class engages in discussion, using the questions at the end. (10 min.)

SCENARIOS

I. You are running for Student Government President. What steps would you take to make your candidacy a success?

1. _____

2. _____

3. _____

4. _____

5. _____

6. _____

II. You are in an internship and are interested in becoming a permanent full-time employee at the organization. What people would you approach and what steps could you take to obtain an offer?

1. _____

2. _____

3. _____

4. _____

5. _____

6. _____

III. You just moved to a new community and your company's business growth relies heavily on referrals. How do you make contacts in a place where you don't know anyone? How can you build a client base?

1. _____

2. _____

3. _____

4. _____

5. _____

6. _____

QUESTIONS

1. What was difficult about this exercise?

2. What creative means were devised to build networks of contacts in these scenarios?

3. Which of these ideas would be easy to implement? Which would be difficult? What makes some strategies easier to do than others?

4. What personal qualities are needed to actually use these strategies?

5. How can someone who is shy about approaching new people use (some or all of) these strategies successfully?

6. What did you learn about yourself and others from this exercise?

SOURCE: Suzanne C. de Janasz, Karen O. Dowd, and Beth Z. Schneider, *Interpersonal Skills in Organizations,* McGraw-Hill/Irwin, 2002, p. 212. © 2002 The McGraw-Hill Companies.

PART 5 SUPPORTING CASE

The Transformation at General Electric

Jack Welch Jr. was appointed chairman and chief executive officer of General Electric in April 1981. Welch retired in 2001. His tenure in the job was characterized by constant strategic and organizational change at GE. Among the initiatives with which Welch is associated are:

1. *Changing the shape of the business portfolio.* Welch established two sets of criteria for redefining the business portfolio of GE. The first was to declare, "We will only run businesses that are number one or number two in their global markets—or, in the case of services, that have a substantial position—and are of a scale and potential appropriate to a $50 billion enterprise." Second, Welch defined three broad areas of business for GE: core, high-technology, and service businesses. As a result of these criteria, during the 1980s GE sold or closed businesses accounting for $10 billion in assets and acquired businesses amounting to $18 billion in assets. Divestment included Utah International, housewares and small appliances, consumer electronics, and semiconductors. Additions included RCA; Employers Reinsurance Corp.; Kidder Peabody Group; Navistar Financial; several new plastics ventures; Thomson's medical electronics business;

and joint ventures with Fanuc (factory automation), Robert Bosch (electric motors), GEC (major appliances and electrical equipment), and Ericsson (mobile communications).

2. *Changing strategic planning.* Welch largely dismantled the highly elaborate strategic planning system that had been built up at GE over the previous decade. Documentation was drastically reduced, and the planning review process was made more informal—the central element was a meeting between Welch, his two vice chairmen, and top management of each SBU (strategic business unit), which focused on identifying and discussing a few key themes. By 1984 the 200-strong corporate planning staff had been halved. The broad objective was "to get general managers talking to general managers about strategy rather than planners talking to planners."

3. *Delayering.* The changes in planning were one aspect of a more general change in the role of headquarters staff from being "checker, inquisitor, and authority figure to facilitator, helper, and supporter." This change involved a substantial reduction in reporting and paper generation and an increase in individual decision-making authority. These changes permitted a substantial widening of spans of control and the removal of

several layers of hierarchy. In most of GE, levels of management were reduced from nine to four.

4. *Destaffing.* Divesting pressures, removing management layers, reducing corporate staffs, and increasing productivity resulted in enormous improvements. Between 1980 and 1990, GE's sales more than doubled while its numbers of employees fell from 402,000 to 298,000.

5. *Values.* A persistent theme in Welch's leadership was a commitment to values. Welch continually emphasized the importance of the company's "software" (values, motivation, and commitment) over its "hardware" (businesses and management structure). Welch's philosophy was articulated in 10 key principles and values:

Being number one or two in each business.

Becoming and staying lean and agile.

"Ownership"—individuals taking responsibility for decisions and actions.

"Stewardship"—individuals ensuring that GE's resources were leveraged to the full.

"Entrepreneurship."

"Excellence"—the highest personal standards.

"Reality."

"Candor."

"Open communications"—both internally and externally.

Financial support—earning a return needed to support success.

This emphasis on values was supported by a type of leadership that put a huge emphasis on communicating and disseminating these values throughout the company. Welch devoted a large portion of his time to addressing meetings of employees and management seminars at GE's Crotonville Management Development Institute.

NEW CULTURE, NEW SYSTEMS

During his first five years in office, Welch's priorities were strategy and structure. GE's business portfolio was radically transformed, and within its main businesses GE's strategies gave a much greater emphasis to local presence and global success and to the development and application of new technology. In terms of organizational structure, Welch's crusade against excess costs, complacency, and administrative inefficiencies resulted in a drastic pruning of the corporate hierarchy and a much flatter organization.

At the root of the "new culture' that Welch sought to build at GE was a redefinition of the relational contract between GE and its employees:

Like many other large companies in the United States, Europe and Japan, GE has had an implicit psychological contract based upon perceived lifetime employment . . . This produced a paternal, feudal, fuzzy kind of loyalty. You put in your time, worked hard, and the company took care of you for life. That kind of loyalty tends to focus people inward . . . The psychological contract has to change. People at all levels have to feel the risk-reward tension.

My concept of loyalty is not "giving time" to some corporate entity and, in turn, being shielded and protected from the outside world. Loyalty is an affinity among people who want to grapple with the outside world and win . . . The new psychological contract, if

there is such a thing, is that jobs at GE are the best in the world for people who are willing to compete. We have the best training and development resources and an environment committed to providing opportunities for personal and professional growth.

Creating a new attitude requires a shift from an internal focus to an external focus:

What determines your destiny is not the hand you're dealt, it's how you play your hand. The best way to play your hand is to face reality—see the world as it is and act accordingly . . . For me, the idea is: to shun the incremental and go for the leap. Most bureaucracies—and ours is no exception—unfortunately still think in incremental terms rather than in terms of fundamental change. They think incrementally because they think internally. Changing the culture—opening it up to quantum change—means constantly asking, not how fast am I going, how well am I doing versus how well I did a year or two before, but rather, how fast and how well am I doing versus the world outside.

Critical to building a new culture and changing the "old ways" of GE was not just the bureaucracy itself, but the habits and attitudes that had been engendered by bureaucracy:

The walls within a big, century-old company don't come down like Jericho's when management makes some organizational changes or gives a speech. There are too many persistent habits propping them up. Parochialism, turf battles, status, "functionalities" and, most important, the biggest sin of a bureaucracy, the focus on itself and its inner workings, are always in the background.

THE WORK-OUT PROGRAM—A GENERIC VIEW

GE's Work-Out Program was a response to the desire to speed the process of organizational change in GE. Welch conceived the idea of Work-Out in September 1988. Welch conducted a session at every class of GE managers attending Management Development Institute at Crotonville, New York. He was impressed by the energy, enthusiasm, and flow of ideas that his open discussion sessions with managers were capable of generating. At the same time, he was frustrated by the resilience of many of GE's bureaucratic practices and the difficulty of transferring the ideas that individual managers possessed into action. After a particularly lively session at Crotonville, Welch and GE's education director, James Braughman, got together to discuss how the interaction in these seminars could be replicated throughout the company in a process that would involve all employees and would generate far-reaching changes within GE. In the course of a helicopter ride from Crotonville to GE's Fairfield headquarters, Welch and Braughman sketched the concept and the framework for the Work-Out process.

A model for GE's Work-Out was a traditional New England town hall meeting where citizens gather to vent their problems, frustrations, and ideas, and people eventually agree on certain civic actions. Welch outlined the goals of Work-Out as follows:

Work-Out has a practical and an intellectual goal. The practical objective is to get rid of thousands of bad habits accumulated since the creation of General Electric . . . The second thing we want to achieve, the intellectual part, begins by putting the leaders of each business in front of 100 or so of their people, eight to ten times a year, to let them hear what their people think. Work-Out will expose the leaders to the vibrations of their business opinions, feelings, emotions, resentments, not abstract theories of organization and management.

A generic summary of the Work-Out Program reveals three interrelated purposes: to fuel a process of continuous improvement and change; to foster cultural transformation characterized by trust, empowerment, elimination of unnecessary work, and a boundaryless organization; and to improve business performance.

THE STRUCTURE OF THE WORK-OUT PROCESS

The central idea of the Work-Out process was to create a forum where a cross section of employees in each business could speak their minds about how their business was managed without fear of retribution. Because those doing the work were often the best people to recommend improvements in how their work should be managed, such interaction was seen as a first step in taking actions to remove unnecessary work and improve business processes. In January 1989, Welch announced Work-Out at an annual meeting of GE's 500 top executives. A broad framework was set out, but considerable flexibility was given to each of GE's 14 core businesses in how they went about the program. The key elements of Work-Out were:

- *Off-site meetings*. Work-Out was held as a forum and to get away from the company environment. Two-to-three-day Work-Out events were held off site.
- *Focus on issues and key processes*. There was a strong bias toward action-oriented sessions. The initial Work-Out events tended to focus on removing unnecessary work. This is what Braughman referred to as the "low-hanging fruit." As the programs developed, Work-Out focused more on more complex business processes. For example, in GE Lighting, groupwide sessions were held to accelerate new product development, improve fill rates, and increase integration between component production and assembly. In plastics the priorities were quality improvement, lower cycle times, and increased cross-functional coordination.
- *Cross-sectional participation*. Work-Out sessions normally involved between 50 and 100 employees drawn from all levels and all functions of a business. Critical to the process was the presence of the top management of the particular business.
- *Small groups and town meetings*. Work-Out events normally involved a series of small group meetings that began with a brainstorming session followed by a plenary session (or "town meeting") in which the suggestions developed by the small groups were put to senior managers and then openly debated. At the end of each discussion, the leader was required to make an immediate decision: to adopt, reject, or defer for further study.
- *Follow-up*. A critical element of Work-Out was a follow-up process to ensure that what had been decided was implemented.

THE RESULTS OF WORK-OUT

The results from Work-Out were remarkable. During its first four years, more than 3,000 Work-Out sessions had been conducted in GE, resulting in thousands of small changes eliminating "junk work" as well as much more complex and further-reaching changes in organizational structure and management processes. The terms *rattlers* and *pythons* were introduced to describe the two types of problems. Rattlers were simple problems that could be "shot" on sight. Pythons were more complex issues that needed unraveling.

As well as tangible structural changes and performance gains, some of the most important effects were changes in organizational culture. In GE Capital, one of the most centralized and bureaucratized of GE's businesses, one employee described the changes as follows: "We've been suppressed around here for a long time. Now that management is finally listening to us, it feels like the Berlin Wall is coming down."

In five years, more than 300,000 employees, customers, and suppliers went through Work-Out sessions. A large variety of impressive and significant performance and efficiency improvements are reported in GE's internal documents, following introduction of the Work-Out processes. For example, the Gas Engine Turbines business unit at Albany, New York, reported an 80 percent decrease in production time to build gas engine turbines; Aircraft Engines at Lynn, Massachusetts, reduced jet engine production time from 30 weeks to 4 weeks. GE's Financial Services Operation reported a reduction in operating costs from $5.10 to $4.55 per invoice, invoices paid per employee were up 34 percent, costs per employee paid fell 19 percent, and employees paid per payroll worker rose 32 percent. The Aerospace plant at Syracuse, New York, reported that as a result of the Work-Out Program, beyond achieving 100 percent compliance with pollution regulations, the production of hazardous waste materials was reduced from 759 tons in 1990 to 275 tons in 1992.

MANAGING WORK-OUT

Work-Out was intended as a bottom-up process in which (1) employees throughout each business would be free to challenge their leaders and (2) management's role was primarily to perpetuate the program and to ensure that decisions, once made, were implemented. But Work-Out could not be just a populist movement within the corporation. It needed to be directed toward creating the kind of corporation that GE needed to be to survive and prosper. To this extent Jack Welch saw his role as communicating and disseminating the principles, values, and themes that would permit GE's continued success.

In 1989 Welch crystallized his ideas about GE's management around three themes: speed, simplicity, and self-confidence:

We found in the 1980s that becoming faster is tied to becoming simpler. Our businesses, with tens of thousands of employees, will not respond to visions that have sub-paragraphs and foot-notes. If we're not simple we can't be fast . . . and if we're not fast, we can't win.

Simplicity, to an engineer, means clean, functional, winning designs, no bells and whistles. In marketing it might manifest itself as clear, unencumbered proposals. For manufacturing people it would produce a logical process that makes sense to every individual on the line. And on an individual, interpersonal level it would take the form of plain speaking, directness, honesty.

But as surely as speed flows from simplicity, simplicity is grounded in self-confidence. Self-confidence does not grow in someone who is just another appendage on the bureaucracy; whose authority rests on little more than a title. People who are freed from the confines of their box on the organization chart, whose status rests on real world achievement—those are the people who develop the self-confidence to be simple, to share every bit of information available to them, to listen to those above, below and around them and then move boldly.

But a company cannot distribute self-confidence. What it can do—what we must do—is to give our people an opportunity to win, to contribute, and hence earn self-confidence themselves. They don't get that opportunity, they can't taste winning if they spend their days wandering in the muck of a self-absorbed bureaucracy.

Speed . . . simplicity . . . self-confidence. We have it in increasing measure. We know where it comes from . . . and we have plans to increase it in the 1990s.

BEST PRACTICES

One of the Work-Out Program's many impressive outcomes is that it's a catalyst for new improvement programs. One such program, Best Practices, is aimed at increasing productivity. The GE business-development staff focused on 24 credible companies from an initial pool of 200 that had achieved faster productivity growth than GE and sustained it for at least 10 years. From this list, one dozen companies agreed to take part in GE's proposal to send its employees to their companies to learn their secrets to success. In exchange, GE offered to share the results of the study as well as success stories with the participating companies. This learning for the Best Practices program involved companies such as Ford, Hewlett-Packard, Xerox, and Chaparral Steel plus three Japanese firms.

GE was less concerned with the actual work done at the companies than with management practices and attitudes of the employees. The difference between Best Practices and traditional benchmarking is that the former does not require keeping score. The focus on learning alternative successful management practices and managing processes was identified as the most critical component for long-term productivity improvements. The basic

assumption that through multiple exposure to alternative management practices, managers and employees will be stimulated to continuously improve their own practices, continues to guide the program. Best Practices has evolved into a formal course taught to at least one dozen employees and managers per month in each business unit.

QUESTIONS

1. Based on the information presented, describe the overall planned change approach and phases led by Jack Welch.

2. Identify and briefly describe the major characteristics of the Work-Out Program.

3. Discuss how the organizational culture changed. What caused the change? What effects did the culture change have on human behavior and organizational performance and effectiveness?

4. Assess the case using the models and concepts presented in the last chapter and other parts of the book.

SOURCES: This case was written by R. Grant and A. B. (Rami) Shani for classroom use. The case draws heavily on the following sources: N. M. Tichy and S. Sherman, *Control Your Destiny or Someone Else Will* (New York: Doubleday, 1992); R. Slater, *The New GE: How Jack Welch Revived an American Institution* (Burr Ridge, IL: Irwin, 1993); R. N. Ashkenas and T. D. Jick, "From Dialogue to Action in GE Work-Out," in W. A. Pasmore and R. Woodman (eds.), *Research in Organization Change and Development,* vol. 6 (Greenwich, CT: JAI Press, 1993), pp. 267–87; and "Jack Welch's Lessons for Success," *Fortune,* February 25, 1993, pp. 86–90.

CASE INCIDENTS

Robot Repercussion

Victor Principal, vice president of industrial relations for General Manufacturing, Inc., sat in his office reviewing the list of benefits the company expected to realize from increasing its use of industrial robots. In a few minutes, he would walk down to the labor-management conference room for a meeting with Ralph McIntosh, president of the labor union local representing most of the company's industrial employees. The purpose of this meeting would be to informally exchange views and positions preliminary to the opening for formal contract negotiations later in the month, which would focus on the use of computer-integrated robotics systems and the resulting impact on employment, workers, and jobs.

Both Principal and McIntosh had access to similar information flows relevant to industrial robots, including the following. Unlike single-task machines, installed in earlier stages of automation, robots can be programmed to do one job and then reprogrammed to do another one. The pioneering generation of robots was mainly programmed to load machines, weld, forge, spray paint, handle materials, and inspect auto bodies. The latest generation of robots includes vision-controlled robots, which enable the machines to approximate the human ability to recognize and size up objects by using laser-beam patterns recorded by television cameras and transmitted to "smart" computers. The computer software interprets and manipulates the images relayed by the camera in a "smart" or artificially intelligent way.

Experts concluded that the impact of robot installation on employment would be profound, although the extent of the worker replacement was not clear. The inescapable conclusion was that robot usage had the capacity to increase manufacturing performance and to decrease manufacturing employment.

Principal walked down to the conference room. Finding McIntosh already there, Principal stated the company's position regarding installation of industrial robots: "The company needs the cooperation of the union and our workers. We don't wish to be perceived as callously exchanging human workers for robots." Then Principal listed the major advantages associated with robots: (1) improved quality of product as a result of the accuracy of robots; (2) reduced operating costs, as the per-hour operational cost of robots was about one-third of the per-hour cost of wages and benefits paid to an average employee; (3) reliability improvements, as robots work tirelessly and don't require behavioral support; and (4) greater manufacturing flexibility, because robots are readily reprogrammable for different jobs. Principal concluded that these advantages would make the company more competitive, which would allow it to grow and increase its workforce.

McIntosh's response was direct and strong: "We aren't Luddites racing around ruining machines. We know it's necessary to increase productivity and that robotic technology is here. But we can't give the company a blank check. We need safeguards and protection." McIntosh continued, "We intend to bargain for the following contract provisions:

1. Establishment of labor–management committees to negotiate *in advance* about the labor impact of robotics technology and, of equal importance, to have a voice in deciding how and whether it should be used.

2. Rights to advance notice about installation of new technology.

3. Retraining rights for workers displaced, to include retraining for new positions in the plant, the community, or other company plants.

4. Spreading the work among workers by use of a four-day workweek or other acceptable plan as an alternative to reducing the workforce."

McIntosh's final sentence summed up the union's position: "We in the union believe the company is giving our jobs to robots to reduce the labor force."

Their meeting ended amiably, but Principal and McIntosh each knew that much hard bargaining lay ahead. As Principal returned to his office, the two opposing positions were obvious. On his yellow tablet, Principal listed the requirements as he saw them: (1) a clearly stated overall policy was needed to guide negotiation decisions and actions; (2) it was critical to decide on a company position regarding each of the union's announced demands and concerns; and (3) a plan had to be developed.

As Principal considered these challenges, he idly contemplated a robot possessing artificial intelligence and vision capability that could help him in his work. Immediately a danger alarm sounded in his mind. A robot so constructed might be more than helpful and might take over this and other important aspects of his job. Slightly chagrined, Principal returned to his task. He needed help—but not from any "smart" robot.

SOURCE: J. Champion and J. James, *Critical Incidents in Management: Decision and Policy Issues,* 6th ed. (Burr Ridge, IL: McGraw-Hill/Irwin, 1989). © 1989 The McGraw-Hill Companies.

Implementing Strategic Change

James Fulmer, chief executive officer of Allied Industries, reviewed three notes he had exchanged with Frank Curtis, director of fiscal affairs, now president of a company owned by Allied. The two executives were going to meet in a few minutes to discuss problems that had recently surfaced. During the past decade, Allied had aggressively pursued a growth objective based on a conglomerate strategy of acquiring companies in distress. CEO Fulmer's policy was to appoint a new chief operating officer for each acquisition with instructions to facilitate a turnaround. Fulmer reviewed two of the notes he had written to Curtis.

Date: January 15, 2007

Memorandum

To: Frank Curtis, Director of Fiscal Affairs, Allied Industries

From: James Fulmer, Chairman, Allied Industries

Subject: Your Appointment as President, Lee Medical Supplies

You are aware that Allied Industries recently acquired Lee Medical Supplies. Mr. John Lee, founder and president of the company, has agreed to retire, and I am appointing you to replace him. Our acquisitions group will brief you on the company, but I want to warn you that Lee Medical Supplies has a history of mismanagement. As a distributor of medical items, the company's sales last year totaled approximately $300 million, with net earnings of only $12 million. Your job is to make company sales and profits compatible with Allied standards. You are reminded that it is my policy to call for an independent evaluation of company progress and your performance as president after 18 months.

Date: September 10, 2007

Memorandum

To: Frank Curtis, President, Lee Medical Supplies

From: James Fulmer, Chairman, Allied Industries

Subject: Serious Problems at Lee Medical Supplies

In accord with corporate policy, consultants recently conducted an evaluation of Lee Medical Supplies. In a relatively short period of time, you have increased sales and profits to meet Allied's standards, but I am alarmed at other aspects of your performance. I am told that during the past 18 months, three of your nine vice presidents have resigned and that you have terminated four others. An opinion survey conducted by the consultants indicates that a low state of morale exists and that your managerial appointees are regarded by their subordinates as hard-nosed perfectionists obsessed with quotas and profits. Employees report that ruthless competition now exists between divisions, regions, and districts. They also note that the collegial, family-oriented atmosphere fostered by Mr. Lee has been replaced by a dog-eat-dog situation characterized by negative management attitudes toward employee feelings and needs. After you have studied the enclosed report from the consultants, we will meet to discuss their findings. I am particularly concerned with their final conclusion that "a form of corporate cancer seems to be spreading throughout Lee Medical Supplies."

As Fulmer prepared to read the third note, written by Frank Curtis, he reflected on his interview with the consultants. While Fulmer considered Curtis a financial expert and a turnaround specialist, his subordinates characterized Curtis as an autocrat and better suited to be a Marine boot camp commander.

Date: September 28, 2007

Memorandum

To: James Fulmer

From: Frank Curtis

Subject: The So-Called Serious Problems at Lee Medical Supplies

I have received your memorandum dated September 10, and reviewed the consultants' report. When you appointed me to my present position I was instructed to take over an unprofitable company and make it profitable. I have done so in 18 months, although I inherited a family-owned business that by your own admission had been mismanaged for years. I found a group of managers and salespeople with an average company tenure of 22 years. Mr. Lee had centralized all personnel decisions so that only he could terminate an employee. He tolerated mediocre performance. All employees were paid on a straight salary basis, with seniority the sole criterion for advancement. Some emphasis was given to increasing sales each year, but none was given to reducing costs and increasing profits. Employees did indeed find the company a fun place to work, and the feeling of being a part of a family did permeate the company. Such attitudes were, however, accompanied by mediocrity, incompetence, and poor performance.

I found it necessary to implement immediate strategic changes in five areas: the organization's structure, employee rewards and incentives, management information systems, allocation of resources, and managerial leadership style. As a result, sales areas were reorganized into divisions, regions, and districts. Managers who I felt were incompetent and/or lacking in commitment to my objectives and methods were replaced. Unproductive and mediocre employees were encouraged to find jobs elsewhere. Authority for staffing and compensation decisions was decentralized to units at the division, region, and district levels. Managers of those units were informed that along with their authority went responsibility for reducing costs and for increasing sales and profits. Each unit was established as a profit center. A new department was established and charged with reviewing performance of those units. Improved accounting and control systems were implemented. A management-by-objectives program was developed to establish standards and monitor performance. Performance appraisals are now required for all employees. To encourage more aggressive

action, bonuses and incentives are offered to managers of units showing increased profits. A commission plan based on measurable sales and profit performances has replaced straight salaries. Resources are allocated to units based on their performance.

My own leadership style has probably represented the most traumatic change for employees. Internal competition is a formally mandated policy throughout the company. It has been responsible for much of the progress achieved to date. Progress, however, is never made without costs, and I recognize that employees are not having as much fun as in the past. I was employed to achieve results and not to ensure that employees remain secure and happy in their work. Don't let a few crybabies unable to adjust to changes lead you to believe that problems take precedence over profits. Does it mean that I am not people oriented if I believe it is unlikely that a spirit of aggressiveness and competitiveness can coexist with an atmosphere of cooperativeness and family orientation? Do you feel that we are obligated to employees because of past practices? Frankly, I thought I had your support to do whatever was necessary to get this company turned around. In our meeting, tell me if you think my approaches have been wrong and, if so, tell me what I should have done differently.

Just as Fulmer finished reviewing the third memorandum, his secretary informed him that Curtis had arrived for their scheduled meeting. He realized he was undecided about how to communicate to Curtis his ideas and beliefs regarding how changes in an organization can best be implemented. One thing he did know: He didn't appreciate how Curtis had expressed his views in his memorandum, but he recognized that he probably should set aside emotions and respond to the questions Curtis posed.

SOURCE: J. Champion and J. James, *Critical Incidents in Management: Decision and Policy Issues*, 6th ed. (Burr Ridge, IL: McGraw-Hill/Irwin, 1989). © 1989 The McGraw-Hill Companies.

Glossary

accommodation   A style of dealing with conflict involving cooperation on behalf of the other party but not being assertive about one's own interests.

accountability   The expectation that employees will perform a job, take corrective action when necessary, and report upward on the status and quality of their performance.

accounting audits   Procedures used to verify accounting reports and statements.

acquisition   One firm buying another.

activity-based costing (ABC)   A method of cost accounting designed to identify streams of activity and then to allocate costs across particular business processes according to the amount of time employees devote to particular activities.

adapters   Companies that take the current industry structure and its evolution as givens, and choose where to compete.

adverse impact   When a seemingly neutral employment practice has a disproportionately negative effect on a protected group.

advertising support model   Charging fees to advertise on a site.

affective conflict   Emotional disagreement directed toward other people.

affiliate model   Charging fees to direct site visitors to other companies' sites.

affirmative action   Special efforts to recruit and hire qualified members of groups that have been discriminated against in the past.

Alderfer's ERG theory   A human needs theory postulating that people have three basic sets of needs that can operate simultaneously.

arbitration   The use of a neutral third party to resolve a labor dispute.

assessment center   A managerial performance test in which candidates participate in a variety of exercises and situations.

assets   The values of the various items the corporation owns.

authentic leadership   A style in which the leader is true to himself or herself while leading.

authority   The legitimate right to make decisions and to tell other people what to do.

autocratic leadership   A form of leadership in which the leader makes decisions on his or her own and then announces those decisions to the group.

autonomous work groups   Groups that control decisions about and execution of a complete range of tasks.

avoidance   A reaction to conflict that involves ignoring the problem by doing nothing at all, or deemphasizing the disagreement.

B

balance sheet   A report that shows the financial picture of a company at a given time and itemizes assets, liabilities, and stockholders' equity.

balanced scorecard   Control system combining four sets of performance measures: financial, customer, business process, and learning and growth.

barriers to entry   Conditions that prevent new companies from entering an industry.

behavioral approach   A leadership perspective that attempts to identify what good leaders do—that is, what behaviors they exhibit.

benchmarking   The process of comparing an organization's practices and technologies with those of other companies.

bootlegging   Informal work on projects, other than those officially assigned, of employees' own choosing and initiative.

boundaryless organization   Organization in which there are no barriers to information flow.

bounded rationality   A less-than-perfect form of rationality in which decision makers cannot be perfectly rational because decisions are complex and complete information is unavailable or cannot be fully processed.

brainstorming   A process in which group members generate as many ideas about a problem as they can; criticism is withheld until all ideas have been proposed.

bridge leaders   A leader who bridges conflicting value systems or different cultures.

broker   A person who assembles and coordinates participants in a network.

budgeting   The process of investigating what is being done and comparing the results with the corresponding budget data to verify accomplishments or remedy differences; also called budgetary controlling.

buffering   Creating supplies of excess resources in case of unpredictable needs.

bureaucratic control   The use of rules, regulations, and authority to guide performance.

business ethics   The moral principles and standards that guide behavior in the world of business.

business incubators   Protected environments for new, small businesses.

business plan   A formal planning step that focuses on the entire venture and describes all the elements involved in starting it.

business strategy   The major actions by which a business competes in a particular industry or market.

C

cafeteria benefit program   An employee benefit program in which employees choose from a menu of options to create a benefit package tailored to their needs.

Caux Principles   Ethical principles established by international executives based in Caux, Switzerland, in collaboration with business leaders from Japan, Europe, and the United States.

centralized organization   An organization in which high-level executives make most decisions and pass them down to lower levels for implementation.

certainty   The state that exists when decision makers have accurate and comprehensive information.

charismatic leader   A person who is dominant, self-confident, convinced of the moral righteousness of his or her beliefs, and able to arouse a sense of excitement and adventure in followers.

chief information officer (CIO)   Executive in charge of information technology strategy and development.

clan control   Control based on the norms, values, shared goals, and trust among group members.

coaching   Dialogue with a goal of helping another be more effective and achieve his or her full potential on the job.

coalitional model   Model of organizational decision making in which groups with differing preferences use power and negotiation to influence decisions.

cognitive conflict   Issue-based differences in perspectives or judgments.

cohesiveness   The degree to which a group is attractive to its members, members are motivated to remain in the group, and members influence one another.

collaboration   A style of dealing with conflict emphasizing both cooperation and assertiveness to maximize both parties' satisfaction.

communication   The transmission of information and meaning from one party to another through the use of shared symbols.

comparable worth   Principle of equal pay for different jobs of equal worth.

competing   A style of dealing with conflict involving strong focus on one's own goals and little or no concern for the other person's goals.

competitive environment The immediate environment surrounding a firm; includes suppliers, customers, rivals, and the like.

competitive intelligence Information that helps managers determine how to compete better.

compliance-based ethics programs Company mechanisms typically designed by corporate counsel to prevent, detect, and punish legal violations.

compromise A style of dealing with conflict involving moderate attention to both parties' concerns.

computer-integrated manufacturing (CIM) The use of computer-aided design and computer-aided manufacturing to sequence and optimize a number of production processes.

concentration A strategy employed for an organization that operates a single business and competes in a single industry.

concentric diversification A strategy used to add new businesses that produce related products or are involved in related markets and activities.

conceptual and decision skills Skills pertaining to the ability to identify and resolve problems for the benefit of the organization and its members.

concurrent control The control process used while plans are being carried out, including directing, monitoring, and fine-tuning activities as they are performed.

conflict Opposing pressures from different sources, occurring on the level of psychological conflict or of conflict between individuals or groups.

conglomerate diversification A strategy used to add new businesses that produce unrelated products or are involved in unrelated markets and activities.

contingency plans Alternative courses of action that can be implemented based on how the future unfolds.

continuous process A process that is highly automated and has a continuous production flow.

control Any process that directs the activities of individuals toward the achievement of organizational goals.

controlling The management function of monitoring performance and making needed changes.

cooperative strategies Strategies used by two or more organizations working together to manage the external environment.

coordination The procedures that link the various parts of an organization for the purpose of achieving the organization's overall mission.

coordination by mutual adjustment Units interact with one another to make accommodations to achieve flexible coordination.

coordination by plan Interdependent units are required to meet deadlines and objectives that contribute to a common goal.

core competence A unique skill and/or knowledge an organization possesses that give it an edge over competitors.

corporate governance The role of a corporation's executive staff and board of directors in ensuring that the firm's activities meet the goals of the firm's stakeholders.

corporate social responsibility (CSR) Obligation toward society assumed by business.

corporate strategy The set of businesses, markets, or industries in which an organization competes and the distribution of resources among those entities.

cost competitiveness Keeping costs low to achieve profits and be able to offer prices that are attractive to consumers.

culture shock The disorientation and stress associated with being in a foreign environment.

current ratio A liquidity ratio that indicates the extent to which short-term assets can decline and still be adequate to pay short-term liabilities.

customer relationship management (CRM) A multifaceted process focusing on creating two-way exchanges with customers to foster intimate knowledge of their needs, wants, and buying patterns.

custom-made solutions New, creative solutions designed specifically for the problem.

D

debt-equity ratio A leverage ratio that indicates the company's ability to meet its long-term financial obligations.

decentralized organization An organization in which lower-level managers make important decisions.

defenders Companies that stay within a stable product domain as a strategic maneuver.

delegation The assignment of new or additional responsibilities to a subordinate.

democratic leadership A form of leadership in which the leader solicits input from subordinates.

demographics Measures of various characteristics of the people who make up groups or other social units.

departmentalization Subdividing an organization into smaller subunits.

development Helping managers and professional employees learn the broad skills needed for their present and future jobs.

development project A focused organizational effort to create a new product or process via technological advances.

devil's advocate A person who has the job of criticizing ideas to ensure that their downsides are fully explored.

dialectic A structured debate comparing two conflicting courses of action.

differentiation An aspect of the organization's internal environment created by job specialization and the division of labor.

differentiation strategy A strategy an organization uses to build competitive advantage by being unique in its industry or market segment along one or more dimensions.

discounting the future A bias weighting short-term costs and benefits more heavily than longer-term costs and benefits.

diversification A firm's investment in a different product, business, or geographic area.

diversity training Programs that focus on identifying and reducing hidden biases against people with differences and developing the skills needed to manage a diversified workforce.

divestiture A firm selling one or more businesses.

divisional organization Departmentalization that groups units around products, customers, or geographic regions.

division of labor The assignment of different tasks to different people or groups.

domain selection Entering a new market or industry with an existing expertise.

downsizing The planned elimination of positions or jobs.

downward communication Information that flows from higher to lower levels in the organization's hierarchy.

dynamic network Temporary arrangements among partners that can be assembled and reassembled to adapt to the environment.

E

ecocentric management Its goal is the creation of sustainable economic development and improvement of quality of life worldwide for all organizational stakeholders.

economic responsibilities To produce goods and services that society wants at a price that perpetuates the business and satisfies its obligations to investors.

economies of scope Economies in which materials and processes employed in one product can be used to make other, related products.

egoism An ethical system defining acceptable behavior as that which maximizes consequences for the individual.

emotional intelligence The skills of understanding yourself, managing yourself, and dealing effectively with others.

employment-at-will The legal concept that an employee may be terminated for any reason.

empowerment The process of sharing power with employees, thereby enhancing their confidence in their ability to perform their jobs and their belief that they are influential contributors to the organization.

entrepreneur Individual who establishes a new organization without the benefit of corporate sponsorship.

entrepreneurial orientation The tendency of an organization to identify and capitalize successfully on opportunities to launch new ventures by entering new or established markets with new or existing goods or services.

entrepreneurial venture A new business having growth and high profitability as primary objectives.

entrepreneurship The pursuit of lucrative opportunities by enterprising individuals.

environmental scanning Searching for and sorting through information about the environment.

environmental uncertainty Lack of information needed to understand or predict the future.

equity theory A theory stating that people assess how fairly they have been treated according to two key factors: outcomes and inputs.

ethical climate In an organization, the processes by which decisions are evaluated and made on the basis of right and wrong.

ethical issue Situation, problem, or opportunity in which an individual must choose among several actions that must be evaluated as morally right or wrong.

ethical leader One who is both a moral person and a moral manager influencing others to behave ethically.

ethical responsibilities Meeting other social expectations, not written as law.

ethics The system of rules that governs the ordering of values.

ethnocentrism The tendency to judge others by the standards of one's group or culture, which are seen as superior.

executive champion An executive who supports a new technology and protects the product champion of the innovation.

expatriates Parent-company nationals who are sent to work at a foreign subsidiary.

expectancy Employees' perception of the likelihood that their efforts will enable them to attain their performance goals.

expectancy theory A theory proposing that people will behave based on their perceived likelihood that their effort will lead to a certain outcome and on how highly they value that outcome.

external audit An evaluation conducted by one organization, such as a CPA firm, on another.

external environment All relevant forces outside a firm's boundaries, such as competitors, customers, the government, and the economy.

extinction Withdrawing or failing to provide a reinforcing consequence.

extrinsic rewards Rewards given to a person by the boss, the company, or some other person.

F

failure rate The number of expatriate managers of an overseas operation who come home early.

feedback control Control that focuses on the use of information about previous results to correct deviations from the acceptable standard.

feedforward control The control process used before operations begin, including policies, procedures, and rules designed to ensure that planned activities are carried out properly.

Fiedler's contingency model of leadership effectiveness A situational approach to leadership postulating that effectiveness depends on the personal style of the leader and the degree to which the situation gives the leader power, control, and influence over the situation.

filtering The process of withholding, ignoring, or distorting information.

final consumer Those who purchase products in their finished form.

flexible benefit programs Benefit programs in which employees are given credits to spend on benefits that fit their unique needs.

flexible factories Manufacturing plants that have short production runs, are organized around products, and use decentralized scheduling.

flexible processes Methods for adapting the technical core to changes in the environment.

force-field analysis An approach to implementing the unfreezing/moving/refreezing model by identifying the forces that prevent people from changing and those that will drive people toward change.

forecasting Method for predicting how variables will change the future.

formalization The presence of rules and regulations governing how people in the organization interact.

framing effects A decision bias influenced by the way in which a problem or decision alternative is phrased or presented.

franchising An entrepreneurial alliance between a franchisor (an innovator who has created at least one successful store and wants to grow) and a franchisee (a partner who manages a new store of the same type in a new location).

frontline managers Lower-level managers who supervise the operational activities of the organization.

functional organization Departmentalization around specialized activities such as production, marketing, and human resources.

functional strategies Strategies implemented by each functional area of the organization to support the organization's business strategy.

G

garbage can model Model of organizational decision making depicting a chaotic process and seemingly random decisions.

gatekeeper A team member who keeps abreast of current developments and provides the team with relevant information.

genius of the *and*; organizational ambidexterity Ability to achieve multiple objectives simultaneously.

global model An organizational model consisting of a company's overseas subsidiaries and characterized by centralized decision making and tight control by the parent company over most aspects of worldwide operations; typically adopted by organizations that base their global competitive strategy on cost considerations.

goal A target or end that management desires to reach.

goal displacement A condition that occurs when a decision-making group loses sight of its original goal and a new, less important goal emerges.

goal-setting theory A motivation theory stating that people have conscious goals that energize them and direct their thoughts and behaviors toward a particular end.

grapevine Informal communication network.

group maintenance behaviors Actions taken to ensure the satisfaction of group members, develop and maintain harmonious work relationships, and preserve the social stability of the group.

groupthink A phenomenon that occurs in decision making when group members avoid disagreement as they strive for consensus.

growth need strength The degree to which individuals want personal and psychological development.

H

Hersey and Blanchard's situational theory A life-cycle theory of leadership postulating that a manager should consider an employee's psychological and job maturity before deciding whether task performance or maintenance behaviors are more important.

hierarchy The authority levels of the organizational pyramid.

high-involvement organization A type of organization in which top management ensures that there is consensus about the direction in which the business is heading.

horizontal communication Information shared among people on the same hierarchical level.

host-country nationals Natives of the country where an overseas subsidiary is located.

human capital The knowledge, skills, and abilities of employees that have economic value.

human resources management (HRM) Formal systems for the

management of people within an organization.

hygiene factors   Characteristics of the workplace, such as company policies, working conditions, pay, and supervision, that can make people dissatisfied.

I

illusion of control   People's belief that they can influence events, even when they have no control over what will happen.

incremental model   Model of organizational decision making in which major solutions arise through a series of smaller decisions.

independent strategies   Strategies that an organization acting on its own uses to change some aspect of its current environment.

informing   A team strategy that entails making decisions with the team and then informing outsiders of its intentions.

initial public offering (IPO)   Sale to the public, for the first time, of federally registered and underwritten shares of stock in the company.

innovation   The introduction of new goods and services.

innovation   A change in method or technology; a positive, useful departure from previous ways of doing things.

inpatriate   A foreign national brought in to work at the parent company.

inputs   Goods and services organizations take in and use to create products or services.

instrumentality   The perceived likelihood that performance will be followed by a particular outcome.

integration   The degree to which differentiated work units work together and coordinate their efforts.

integrity-based ethics programs   Company mechanisms designed to instill in people a personal responsibility for ethical behavior.

intermediary model   Charging fees to bring buyers and sellers together.

intermediate consumer   A customer who purchases raw materials or wholesale products before selling them to final customers.

internal audit   A periodic assessment of a company's own planning, organizing, leading, and controlling processes.

international model   An organizational model that is composed of a company's overseas subsidiaries and characterized by greater control by the parent company over the research function and local product and marketing strategies than is the case in the multinational model.

interpersonal and communication skills   People skills; the ability to lead, motivate, and communicate effectively with others.

intrapreneurs   New-venture creators working inside big companies.

intrinsic reward   Reward a worker derives directly from performing the job itself.

ISO 9001   A series of quality standards developed by a committee working under the International Organization for Standardization to improve total quality in all businesses for the benefit of producers and consumers.

J

job analysis   A tool for determining what is done on a given job and what should be done on that job.

job enlargement   Giving people additional tasks at the same time to alleviate boredom.

job enrichment   Changing a task to make it inherently more rewarding, motivating, and satisfying.

job maturity   The level of the employee's skills and technical knowledge relative to the task being performed.

job rotation   Changing from one routine task to another to alleviate boredom.

just-in-time (JIT)   A system that calls for subassemblies and components to be manufactured in very small lots and delivered to the next stage of the production process just as they are needed.

K

knowledge management   Practices aimed at discovering and harnessing an organization's intellectual resources.

Kohlberg's model of cognitive moral development   Classification of people based on their level of moral judgment.

L

labor relations   The system of relations between workers and management.

laissez-faire   A leadership philosophy characterized by an absence of managerial decision making.

large batch   Technologies that produce goods and services in high volume.

lateral leadership   Style in which colleagues at the same hierarchical level are invited to collaborate and facilitate joint problem solving.

law of effect   A law formulated by Edward Thorndike in 1911 stating that behavior that is followed by positive consequences will likely be repeated.

Leader-Member Exchange (LMX) theory   Highlights the importance of leader behaviors not just toward the group as a whole but toward individuals on a personal basis.

leading   The management function that involves the manager's efforts to stimulate high performance by employees.

lean manufacturing   An operation that strives to achieve the highest possible productivity and total quality, cost effectively, by eliminating unnecessary steps in the production process and continually striving for improvement.

learning organization   An organization skilled at creating, acquiring, and transferring knowledge, and at modifying its behavior to reflect new knowledge and insights.

legal responsibilities   To obey local, state, federal, and relevant international laws.

legitimacy   People's judgment of a company's acceptance, appropriateness, and desirability, generally stemming from company goals and methods that are consistent with societal values.

Level 5 leadership   A combination of strong professional will (determination) and humility that builds enduring greatness.

liabilities   The amounts a corporation owes to various creditors.

life-cycle analysis (LCA)   A process of analyzing all inputs and outputs, through the entire "cradle-to-grave" life of a product, to determine total environmental impact.

line departments   Units that deal directly with the organization's primary goods and services.

logistics   The movement of the right goods in the right amount to the right place at the right time.

low-cost strategy   A strategy an organization uses to build competitive advantage by being efficient and offering a standard, no-frills product.

M

macroenvironment   The general environment; includes governments, economic conditions, and other fundamental factors that generally affect all organizations.

make-or-buy decision   The question an organization asks itself about whether to acquire new technology from an outside source or develop it itself.

management   The process of working with people and resources to accomplish organizational goals.

management audit   An evaluation of the effectiveness and efficiency of various systems within an organization.

management by objectives (MBO)   A process in which objectives set by a subordinate and a supervisor must be reached within a given time period.

management myopia   Focusing on short-term earnings and profits at the expense of longer-term strategic obligations.

management teams   Teams that coordinate and provide direction to the subunits under their jurisdiction and integrate work among subunits.

managing diversity   Managing a culturally diverse workforce by recognizing the characteristics common to specific groups of employees while dealing with such employees as individuals and supporting, nurturing, and utilizing their differences to the organization's advantage.

market control   Control based on the use of pricing mechanisms and economic information to regulate activities within organizations.

Maslow's need hierarchy A conception of human needs organizing needs into a hierarchy of five major types.

mass customization The production of varied, individually customized products at the low cost of standardized, mass-produced products.

matrix organization An organization composed of dual reporting relationships in which some managers report to two superiors—a functional manager and a divisional manager.

maximizing A decision realizing the best possible outcome.

mechanistic organization A form of organization that seeks to maximize internal efficiency.

media richness The degree to which a communication channel conveys information.

mediator A third party who intervenes to help others manage their conflict.

mentors Higher-level managers who help ensure that high-potential people are introduced to top management and socialized into the norms and values of the organization.

merger One or more companies combining with another.

middle-level managers Managers located in the middle layers of the organizational hierarchy, reporting to top-level executives.

mission An organization's basic purpose and scope of operations.

monolithic organization An organization that has a low degree of structural integration—employing few women, minorities, or other groups that differ from the majority—and thus has a highly homogeneous employee population.

moral philosophy Principles, rules, and values people use in deciding what is right or wrong.

motivation Forces that energize, direct, and sustain a person's efforts.

motivators Factors that make a job more motivating, such as additional job responsibilities, opportunities for personal growth and recognition, and feelings of achievement.

moving Instituting the change.

multicultural organization An organization that values cultural diversity and seeks to utilize and encourage it.

multinational model An organizational model that consists of the subsidiaries in each country in which a company does business, with ultimate control exercised by the parent company.

N

needs assessment An analysis identifying the jobs, people, and departments for which training is necessary.

negative reinforcement Removing or withholding an undesirable consequence.

network organization A collection of independent, mostly single-function firms that collaborate on a good or service.

nonprogrammed decisions New, novel, complex decisions having no proven answers.

norms Shared beliefs about how people should think and behave.

North American Free Trade Agreement (NAFTA) An economic pact that combined the economies of the United States, Canada, and Mexico into one of the world's largest trading blocs.

O

offshoring Moving work to other countries.

one-way communication A process in which information flows in only one direction—from the sender to the receiver, with no feedback loop.

open-book management Practice of sharing with employees at all levels of the organization vital information previously meant for management's eyes only.

open systems Organizations that are affected by, and that affect, their environment.

operational planning The process of identifying the specific procedures and processes required at lower levels of the organization.

opportunity analysis A description of the good or service, an assessment of the opportunity, an assessment of the entrepreneur, specification of activities and resources needed to translate your idea into a viable business, and your source(s) of capital.

optimizing Achieving the best possible balance among several goals.

organic structure An organizational form that emphasizes flexibility.

organizational behavior modification (OB mod) The application of reinforcement theory in organizational settings.

organization chart The reporting structure and division of labor in an organization.

organization culture The set of important assumptions about the organization and its goals and practices that members of the company share.

organization development (OD) The systemwide application of behavioral science knowledge to develop, improve, and reinforce the strategies, structures, and processes that lead to organizational effectiveness.

organizing The management function of assembling and coordinating human, financial, physical, informational, and other resources needed to achieve goals.

orientation training Training designed to introduce new employees to the company and familiarize them with policies, procedures, culture, and the like.

outcome A consequence a person receives for his or her performance.

outplacement The process of helping people who have been dismissed from the company regain employment elsewhere.

outputs The products and services organizations create.

outsourcing Contracting with an outside provider to produce one or more of an organization's goods or services.

P

parading A team strategy that entails simultaneously emphasizing internal team building and achieving external visibility.

parallel teams Teams that operate separately from the regular work structure, and exist temporarily.

participation in decision making Leader behaviors that managers perform in involving their employees in making decisions.

path-goal theory A theory that concerns how leaders influence subordinates' perceptions of their work goals and the paths they follow toward attainment of those goals.

perception The process of receiving and interpreting information.

performance appraisal (PA) Assessment of an employee's job performance.

performance gap The difference between actual performance and desired performance.

philanthropic responsibilities Additional behaviors and activities that society finds desirable and that the values of the business support.

planning The management function of systematically making decisions about the goals and activities that an individual, a group, a work unit, or the overall organization will pursue.

plans The actions or means managers intend to use to achieve organizational goals.

pluralistic organization An organization that has a relatively diverse employee population and makes an effort to involve employees from different gender, racial, or cultural backgrounds.

positive reinforcement Applying consequences that increase the likelihood that a person will repeat the behavior that led to it.

power The ability to influence others.

principle of exception A managerial principle stating that control is enhanced by concentrating on the exceptions to or significant deviations from the expected result or standard.

proactive change A response that is initiated before a performance gap has occurred.

probing A team strategy that requires team members to interact frequently with outsiders, diagnose their needs, and experiment with solutions.

procedural justice Using fair process in decision making and making sure others know that the process was as fair as possible.

product champion A person who promotes a new technology throughout the organization in an effort to obtain acceptance of and support for it.

profit and loss statement An itemized financial statement of the income and expenses of a company's operations.

programmed decisions Decisions encountered and made before, having objectively correct answers, and solvable by using simple rules, policies, or numerical computations.

project and development teams Teams that work on long-term projects but disband once the work is completed.

prospectors Companies that continuously change the boundaries for their task environments by seeking new products and markets, diversifying and merging, or acquiring new enterprises.

pseudotransformational leaders Leaders who talk about positive change but allow their self-interest to take precedence over followers' needs.

psychological contract A set of perceptions of what employees owe their employers, and what their employers owe them.

psychological maturity An employee's self-confidence and self-respect.

punishment Administering an aversive consequence.

Q

quality The excellence of your product (goods or services).

quality circles Voluntary groups of people drawn from various production teams who make suggestions about quality.

quality of work life (QWL) programs Programs designed to create a workplace that enhances employee well-being.

R

reactive change A response that occurs under pressure; problem-driven change.

ready-made solutions Ideas that have been seen or tried before.

recruitment The development of a pool of applicants for jobs in an organization.

reflection Process by which a person states what he or she believes the other person is saying.

refreezing Strengthening the new behaviors that support the change.

reinforcers Positive consequences that motivate behavior.

relationship-motivated leadership Leadership that places primary emphasis on maintaining good interpersonal relationships.

relativism Philosophy that bases ethical behavior on the opinions and behaviors of relevant other people.

reliability The consistency of test scores over time and across alternative measurements.

resources Inputs to a system that can enhance performance.

responsibility The assignment of a task that an employee is supposed to carry out.

return on investment (ROI) A ratio of profit to capital used, or a rate of return from capital.

rightsizing A successful effort to achieve an appropriate size at which the company performs most effectively.

right-to-work Legislation that allows employees to work without having to join a union.

risk The state that exists when the probability of success is less than 100 percent and losses may occur.

roles Different sets of expectations for how different individuals should behave.

S

Sarbanes-Oxley Act An act passed into law by Congress in 2002 to establish strict accounting and reporting rules in order to make senior managers more accountable and to improve and maintain investor confidence.

satisficing Choosing an option that is acceptable, although not necessarily the best or perfect.

scenario A narrative that describes a particular set of future conditions.

selection Choosing from among qualified applicants to hire into an organization.

self-designing teams Teams with the responsibilities of autonomous work groups, plus control over hiring, firing, and deciding what tasks members perform.

self-managed teams Autonomous work groups in which workers are trained to do all or most of the jobs in a unit, have no immediate supervisor, and make decisions previously made by frontline supervisors.

semiautonomous work groups Groups that make decisions about managing and carrying out major production activities but get outside support for quality control and maintenance.

servant-leader A leader who serves others' needs while strengthening the organization.

service The speed and dependability with which an organization delivers what customers want.

sexual harassment Conduct of a sexual nature that has negative consequences for employment.

shapers Companies that try to change the structure of their industries, creating a future competitive landscape of their own design.

shared leadership Rotating leadership, in which people rotate through the leadership role based on which person has the most relevant skills at a particular time.

simultaneous engineering A design approach in which all relevant functions cooperate jointly and continually in a maximum effort aimed at producing high-quality products that meet customers' needs.

situational analysis A process planners use, within time and resource constraints, to gather, interpret, and summarize all information relevant to the planning issue under consideration.

situational approach Leadership perspective proposing that universally important traits and behaviors do not exist, and that effective leadership behavior varies from situation to situation.

skunkworks A project team designated to produce a new, innovative product.

small batch Technologies that produce goods and services in low volume.

small business A business having fewer than 100 employees, independently owned and operated, not dominant in its field, and not characterized by many innovative practices.

smoothing Leveling normal fluctuations at the boundaries of the environment.

social capital Goodwill stemming from your social relationships; a competitive advantage in the form of relationships with other people and the image other people have of you.

social facilitation effect Working harder when in a group than when working alone.

social loafing Working less hard and being less productive when in a group.

sociotechnical systems An approach to job design that attempts to redesign tasks to optimize operation of a new technology while preserving employees' interpersonal relationships and other human aspects of the work.

span of control The number of subordinates who report directly to an executive or supervisor.

specialization A process in which different individuals and units perform different tasks.

speed Fast and timely execution, response, and delivery of results.

staff departments Units that support line departments.

stakeholders Groups and individuals who affect and are affected by the achievement of the organization's mission, goals, and strategies.

standard Expected performance for a given goal: a target that establishes a desired performance level, motivates performance, and serves as a benchmark against which actual performance is assessed.

standardization Establishing common routines and procedures that apply uniformly to everyone.

stockholders' equity The amount accruing to the corporation's owners.

strategic alliance A formal relationship created among independent organizations with the purpose of joint pursuit of mutual goals.

strategic control system A system designed to support managers in evaluating the organization's progress regarding its strategy and, when discrepancies exist, taking corrective action.

strategic goals Major targets or end results relating to the organization's long-term survival, value, and growth.

strategic leadership Behavior that gives purpose and meaning to organizations, envisioning and creating a positive future.

strategic management A process that involves managers from all parts of the organization in the formulation and implementation of strategic goals and strategies.

strategic maneuvering An organization's conscious efforts to change the boundaries of its task environment.

strategic planning A set of procedures for making decisions about the organization's long-term goals and strategies.

strategic vision The long-term direction and strategic intent of a company.

strategy A pattern of actions and resource allocations designed to achieve the organization's goals.

stretch goals Targets that are particularly demanding, sometimes even thought to be impossible.

structured interview Selection technique that involves asking all applicants the same questions and comparing their responses to a standardized set of answers.

subscription model Charging fees for site visits.

substitutes for leadership Factors in the workplace that can exert the same influence on employees as leaders would provide.

subunits Subdivisions of an organization.

superordinate goals Higher-level goals taking priority over specific individual or group goals.

supervisory leadership Behavior that provides guidance, support, and corrective feedback for day-to-day activities.

supply chain management The managing of the network of facilities and people that obtain materials from outside the organization, transform them into products, and distribute them to customers.

survivor's syndrome Loss of productivity and morale in employees who remain after a downsizing.

sustainable growth Economic growth and development that meets present needs without harming the needs of future generations.

switching costs Fixed costs buyers face when they change suppliers.

SWOT analysis A comparison of strengths, weaknesses, opportunities, and threats that helps executives formulate strategy.

T

360-degree appraisal Process of using multiple sources of appraisal to gain a comprehensive perspective on one's performance.

tactical planning A set of procedures for translating broad strategic goals and plans into specific goals and plans that are relevant to a distinct portion of the organization, such as a functional area like marketing.

task-motivated leadership Leadership that places primary emphasis on completing a task.

task performance behaviors Actions taken to ensure that the work group or organization reaches its goals.

task specialist An individual who has more advanced job-related skills and abilities than other group members possess.

team A small number of people with complementary skills who are committed to a common purpose, set of performance goals, and approach for which they hold themselves mutually accountable.

team maintenance specialist Individual who develops and maintains team harmony.

team training Training that provides employees with the skills and perspectives they need to collaborate with others.

technical innovator A person who develops a new technology or has the key skills to install and operate the technology.

technical skill The ability to perform a specialized task involving a particular method or process.

technology The systematic application of scientific knowledge to a new product, process, or service.

technology audit Process of clarifying the key technologies on which an organization depends.

technology life cycle A predictable pattern followed by a technological innovation, from its inception and development to market saturation and replacement.

termination interview A discussion between a manager and an employee about the employee's dismissal.

third-country nationals Natives of a country other than the home country or the host country of an overseas subsidiary.

time-based competition (TBC) Strategies aimed at reducing the total time needed to deliver a good or service.

top-level managers Senior executives responsible for the overall management and effectiveness of the organization.

total organization change Introducing and sustaining multiple policies, practices, and procedures across multiple units and levels.

total quality management (TQM) An integrative approach to management that supports the attainment of customer satisfaction through a wide variety of tools and techniques that result in high-quality goods and services.

traditional work groups Groups that have no managerial responsibilities.

training Teaching lower-level employees how to perform their present jobs.

trait approach A leadership perspective that attempts to determine the personal characteristics that great leaders share.

transactional leaders Leaders who manage through transactions, using their legitimate, reward, and coercive powers to give commands and exchange rewards for services rendered.

transaction fee model Charging fees for goods and services.

transcendent education An education with five higher goals that balance self-interest with responsibility to others.

transfer price Price charged by one unit for a good or service provided to another unit within the organization.

transformational leader A leader who motivates people to transcend their personal interests for the good of the group.

transnational model An organizational model characterized by centralizing certain functions in locations that best achieve cost economies; basing other functions in the company's national subsidiaries to facilitate greater local responsiveness; and fostering communication among subsidiaries to permit transfer of technological expertise and skills.

transnational teams Work groups composed of multinational members whose activities span multiple countries.

two-factor theory Herzberg's theory describing two factors affecting people's work motivation and satisfaction.

two-way communication A process in which information flows in two directions—the receiver provides feedback, and the sender is receptive to the feedback.

tyranny of the or The belief that things must be either A or B and cannot be both; that only one goal and not another can be attained.

U

uncertainty The state that exists when decision makers have insufficient information.

unfreezing Realizing that current practices are inappropriate and that new behavior is necessary.

union shop An organization with a union and a union security clause specifying that workers must join the union after a set period of time.

unity-of-command principle A structure in which each worker reports to one boss, who in turn reports to one boss.

universalism The ethical system stating that all people should uphold certain values that society needs to function.

upward communication Information that flows from lower to higher levels in the organization's hierarchy.

utilitarianism An ethical system stating that the greatest good for the greatest number should be the overriding concern of decision makers.

V

valence The value an outcome holds for the person contemplating it.

validity The degree to which a selection test predicts or correlates with job performance.

value The monetary amount associated with how well a job, task, good, or service meets users' needs.

value chain The sequence of activities that flow from raw materials to the delivery of a good or service, with additional value created at each step.

vertical integration The acquisition or development of new businesses that produce parts or components of the organization's product.

vigilance A process in which a decision maker carefully executes all stages of decision making.

virtual office A mobile office in which people can work anywhere, as long as they have the tools to communicate with customers and colleagues.

virtual teams Teams that are physically dispersed and communicate electronically more than face-to-face.

virtue ethics Perspective that what is moral comes from what a mature person with "good" moral character would deem right.

vision A mental image of a possible and desirable future state of the organization.

Vroom model A situational model that focuses on the participative dimension of leadership.

W

Web 2.0 A set of Internet-based applications that encourage user-provided content and collaboration.

work teams Teams that make or do things like manufacture, assemble, sell, or provide service.

Notes

Chapter 1

1. Arnie Cooper, "Charging Ahead," *Popular Science*, December 15, 2008, http://www.popsci.com; Rebecca Buckman, "Tesla Cuts 20% of Workforce," *Forbes*, October 28, 2008, http://www.forbes.com; Fareed Zakaria, "A Tesla in Your Future?" *Newsweek*, July 21, 2008, http://www.newsweek.com.
2. Michael Abramowitz and Steve Vogel, "Apologies, Anger at Walter Reed Hearing," *Washington Post*, March 6, 2007, http://www.washingtonpost.com. See also Dana Priest and Anne Hull, "Soldiers Face Neglect, Frustration at Army's Top Medical Facility," *Washington Post*, February 18, 2007, http://www.wasingtonpost.com.
3. "Former Hospital Commanders Apologize," *UPI NewsTrack*, March 5, 2007, downloaded from Business & Company Resource Center, http://galenet.galegroup.com.
4. John Christoffersen, "Global Ambition: GE Looks Outside U.S. for Growth," *Cincinnati Post*, January 18, 2007, downloaded from Business & Company Resource Center, http://galenet.galegroup.com.
5. Ibid.
6. Nandini Lakshman, "Cisco's Grand India Ambitions," *BusinessWeek Online*, January 3, 2007, downloaded from Business & Company Resource Center, http://galenet.galegroup.com.
7. Gregory T. Huang, "Over the Border," *New Scientist*, January 20, 2007, downloaded from Business & Company Resource Center, http://galenet.galegroup.com (interview of Ethan Zuckerman).
8. Stephanie Clifford, "How to Get Ahead in China," *Inc.*, May 2008, pp. 96–104.
9. Sue Shellenbarger, "Time-Zoned: Working Around the Round-the-Clock Workday," *The Wall Street Journal*, February 15, 2007, http://online.wsj.com.
10. S. Green, F. Hassan, J. Immelt, M. Marks, and D. Meiland, "In Search of Global Leaders," *Harvard Business Review*, August 2003, pp. 38–45.
11. Betsy Morris, "The Pepsi Challenge," *Fortune*, February 19, 2008, http://money.cnn.com.
12. T. Bisoux, "Corporate CounterCulture," *BizEd*, November/December 2004, pp. 16–20, quoted on p. 19.
13. G. Huber, *The Necessary Nature of Future Firms* (Thousand Oaks, CA: Sage, 2004).
14. Jay Greene and Cliff Edwards, "Desktops Are So Twentieth Century," *BusinessWeek*, December 8, 2006, http://www.businessweek.com.
15. F. Cairncross, *The Company of the Future* (Cambridge, MA: Harvard Business School Press, 2002).
16. Jean Chatzky, "Confessions of an E-Mail Addict," *Money*, March 2007, downloaded from Business & Company Resource Center, http://galenet.galegroup.com.
17. George Avalos, "Shackled to Technology," *Contra Costa Times (Walnut Creek, CA)*, January 14, 2007, downloaded from Business & Company Resource Center, http://galenet.galegroup.com.
18. Chatzky, "Confessions of an E-Mail Addict."
19. Robert Austin, "Managing Knowledge Workers," *Science*, July 21, 2006, accessed at ScienceCareers.org, http://sciencecareers.sciencemag.org.
20. David Raths, "Hospital IT Departments Prescribe Portals for Physicians," *KMWorld*, February 2007, downloaded from Business & Company Resource Center, http://galenet.galegroup.com.
21. M. Hansen and B. von Oetinger, "Introducing T-Shaped Managers: Knowledge Management's Next Generation," *Harvard Business Review*, March 2001, pp. 106–16.
22. John Teresko, "Toyota's Real Secret," *Industry Week*, February 2007, downloaded from Business & Company Resource Center, http://galenet.galegroup.com.
23. Ibid.
24. Bruce Horovitz, "Cranium Guys Have Their Inner Child on Speed Dial," *USA Today*, May 9, 2006, http://www.usatoday.com.
25. L. Willcocks and R. Plant, "Pathways to E-Business Leadership: Getting from Bricks to Clicks," *Sloan Management Review*, Spring 2001, pp. 50–59.
26. Suzanne Vranica, "P&G Boosts Social-Networking Efforts," *The Wall Street Journal*, January 8, 2007, http://online.wsj.com.
27. John D. Stoll, Monica Langley, and Sharon Terlep, "New GM CEO Says More Cuts Coming," *The Wall Street Journal*, March 31, 2009, http://online.wsj.com; Jeffrey McCracken, John D. Stoll, and Neil King Jr., "U.S. Threatens Bankruptcy for GM, Chrysler," *The Wall Street Journal*, March 31, 2009, http://online.wsj.com; and Mike Barris, "Auto Makers [sic] Sales Drop," *The Wall Street Journal*, April 1, 2009, http://online.wsj.com.
28. Adam Lashinsky, "Chaos by Design," *Fortune*, October 2, 2006, http://money.cnn.com.
29. Alexandria Sage, "Love Is Blind in Pitch Black Restaurant," Reuters, December 8, 2006, http://news.yahoo.com; Opaque–Dining in the Dark, "What Is Opaque?" http://www.opaque-events.com, accessed March 8, 2007; and Opaque–Dining in the Dark, "First Ever 'Dining in the Dark' Experience Coming to Los Angeles July 23," news release, n.d., accessed at http://www.opaque-events.com, March 8, 2007.
30. "Home and Abroad," *The Economist*, February 10, 2007, Business & Company Resource Center, http://galenet.galegroup.com.
31. R. I. Sutton, "The Weird Rules of Creativity," *Harvard Business Review*, September, 2001, pp. 94–103.
32. Laura Landro, "Hospitals Take Consumers' Advice," *The Wall Street Journal*, February 7, 2007, http://online.wsj.com.
33. Ibid.
34. O. Port, "The Kings of Quality," *BusinessWeek*, August 30, 2004, p. 20.
35. Karla Ward, "Attracting Opposites," *Lexington Herald-Leader*, December 12, 2006; and Lisa McTigue Pierce, "How to Do It 'My Way,' " *Food & Drug Packaging*, January 2007, both downloaded from Business & Company Resource Center, http://galenet.galegroup.com.
36. Pierce, "How to Do It 'My Way' "; and MyJones Web site, http://www.myjones.com, accessed March 9, 2007.
37. D. A. Garvin, "Manufacturing Strategic Planning," *California Management Review*, Summer 1993, pp. 85–106.
38. Reported in "Hospital Ratings May Not Be True Quality Measure," *Washington Post*, December 13, 2006, http://www.washingtonpost.com.
39. U.S. Census Bureau, *Statistical Abstract of the United States*, 2007, Table 650, p. 431, http://www.census.gov/prod/www/statistical-abstract.html.
40. Ibid., Tables 607 and 608, pp. 394–95.
41. Mindy Fetterman, "Best Buy Gets in Touch with Its Feminine Side," *USA Today*, December 20, 2006, http://www.usatoday.com.
42. Sherri Begin, "The Art of Service," *Crain's Detroit Business*, February 12,

2007, downloaded from Business & Company Resource Center, http://galenet.galegroup.com.

43. Lashinsky, "Chaos by Design."

44. Teresko, "Toyota's Real Secret."

45. Ibid.

46. Gary McWilliams, "Wal-Mart's Radio-Tracked Inventory Hits Static," *The Wall Street Journal*, February 15, 2007, http://online.wsj.com.

47. Kris Maher, "Wal-Mart Seeks New Flexibility in Worker Shifts," *The Wall Street Journal*, January 3, 2007, http://online.wsj.com.

48. Adam Bluestein, Leigh Buchanan, Max Chafkin, Jason Del Rey, April Joyner, and Ryan McCarthy, "The Ultimate Business Tune-Up for Times Like These," *Inc.*, January 2009, http://www.inc.com.

49. Julie Johnsson, "Jets Reach New Heights," *Chicago Tribune*, February 25, 2007, sec. 5, pp. 1, 4.

50. Adam Lashinsky, "Mark Hurd's Moment," *Fortune*, March 2, 2009, http://money.cnn.com, updated March 3, 2009.

51. Vanessa Fuhrmans, "A Novel Plan Helps Hospital Wean Itself off Pricey Tests," *The Wall Street Journal*, January 12, 2007, http://online.wsj.com.

52. "Avon Regains Some Allure," *BusinessWeek*, February 7, 2007, http://www.businessweek.com.

53. Claudia H. Deutsch, "A Chance to Save Their Skin," *New York Times*, January 19, 2007, downloaded from Business & Company Resource Center, http://galenet.galegroup.com.

54. J. W. Cortada, *21st Century Business* (London: Financial Times/Prentice Hall, 2001).

55. D. Lepak, K. Smith, and M. S. Taylor, "Value Creation and Value Capture: A Multilevel Perspective," *Academy of Management Review* 23 (2007): 180–94.

56. Randstad USA, "Focusing on Employees Can Pay Future Dividends," news release, October 20, 2008, www.us.ranstad.com/about/mediaRoom.html.

57. Julia Werdigier, "Chief's Bonus Is Cut at BP," *New York Times*, March 7, 2007, downloaded from Business & Company Resource Center, http://galenet.galegroup.com.

58. Rob Johnson, "Local Restaurants Check Their Peanut Butter," *Roanoke (Va.) Times*, February 24, 2007, downloaded from Business & Company Resource Center, http://galenet.galegroup.com; Joe Ruff, "FDA Finds Salmonella Strain at ConAgra Plant," *Omaha World-Herald*, March 2, 2007, http://galenet.galegroup.com; Centers for Disease Control and Prevention, "Salmonellosis—Outbreak Investigation, February 2007," news release, March 7, 2007, http://www.cdc.gov; Food and Drug Administration, "FDA Update on Peanut Butter Recall," news release, March 9, 2007, http://www.fda.gov; and ConAgra Foods, "ConAgra Foods

Presents Business Update at Consumer Conference," news release, February 20, 2007, http://investor.conagrafoods.com.

59. David R. Baker, "Electric Car Startup Downshifts for Rough Road," *San Francisco Chronicle*, December 28, 2008, http://www.sfgate.com; Buckman, "Tesla Cuts 20% of Workforce"; Claire Cain Miller, "Musk Unplugged: Tesla C.E.O. Discusses Car Troubles," *New York Times*, October 24, 2008, http://bits.blogs.nytimes.com; Martin LaMonica, "Tesla Motors Replaces CEO, Plans Layoff," *CNET News*, October 15, 2008, http://news.cnet.com; Michael V. Copeland, "Tesla's Wild Ride," *Fortune*, July 11, 2008, http://cnnmoney.printthis.clickability.com.

60. R. Webber, "General Management Past and Future," *Financial Times Mastering Management*, 1997.

61. Pui-Wing Tam, "CIO Jobs Morph from Tech Support into Strategy," *The Wall Street Journal*, February 20, 2007, http://online.wsj.com.

62. Ibid.

63. Q. N. Huy, "In Praise of Middle Managers," *Harvard Business Review*, September 2001, pp. 72–79.

64. L. A. Hill, "New Manager Development for the 21st Century," *Academy of Management Executive*, August 2004, pp. 121–26.

65. C. Bartlett and S. Goshal, "The Myth of the Generic Manager: New Personal Competencies for New Management Roles," *California Management Review* 40, no. 1 (1997), pp. 92–116.

66. L. R. Sayles, "Doing Things Right: A New Imperative for Middle Managers," *Organizational Dynamics*, Spring 1993, pp. 5–14.

67. H. Mintzberg, *The Nature of Managerial Work* (New York: Harper & Row, 1973).

68. R. Katz, "Skills of an Effective Administrator," *Harvard Business Review* 52 (September–October), pp. 90–102.

69. Hill, "New Manager Development for the 21st Century."

70. H. Mintzberg, "The Manager's Job: Folklore and Fact," *Harvard Business Review* 53 (July–August 1975), pp. 49–61.

71. Francesca Di Meglio, "Columbia Gets Personal," *BusinessWeek Online*, October 18, 2006 (interview with Michael Morris), downloaded from Business & Company Resource Center, http://galenet.galegroup.com.

72. "To Get That Job, Bring on the Charm," *Internet Week*, August 23, 2006, downloaded from Business & Company Resource Center, http://galenet.galegroup.com.

73. Di Meglio, "Columbia Gets Personal."

74. Colin Stewart, "Program Teaches Corporate Skills to Cure What Ails Them," *Orange County Register*, December 28, 2006, downloaded from Business & Company Resource Center, http://galenet.galegroup.com.

75. Hill, "New Manager Development for the 21st Century."

76. D. Goleman, R. Boyatzis, and A. McKee, *Primal Leadership: Realizing the Power of Emotional Intelligence* (Boston: Harvard Business School Press, 2002).

77. Debbie Kelley, "Rita Burns: Memorial Hospital's Public Voice," *(Colorado Springs) Gazette*, October 9, 2006, downloaded from Business & Company Resource Center, http://galenet.galegroup.com.

78. R. Boyatzis, "Get Motivated," *Harvard Business Review*, January 2004, p. 30.

79. W. George, "Find Your Voice," *Harvard Business Review*, January 2004, p. 35.

80. Stephen Xavier, "Control Yourself: What Role Does Emotional Intelligence Play in Executive Leadership?" *US Business Review*, March 2006, downloaded from Business & Company Resource Center, http://galenet.galegroup.com.

81. Ibid.

82. W. Kiechel III, "A Manager's Career in the New Economy," *Fortune*, April 4, 1994, pp. 68–72.

83. Elizabeth Garone, "Leading the Environmental Charge at Xerox," *The Wall Street Journal*, March 25, 2009, http://online.wsj.com.

84. Lisa Takeuchi Cullen, "The Zeal for the Job," *Time*, March 19, 2007, http://www.time.com.

85. Diane Hess, "How I Got Where I Am Today: A Videogame Marketing Director," *CareerJournal.com*, May 11, 2006, http://www.careerjournal.com.

86. K. Inkson and M. B. Arther, "How to Be a Successful Career Capitalist," *Organizational Dynamics*, Summer 2001, pp. 48–60.

87. Geoffrey Colvin, "What It Takes to Be Great," *Fortune*, October 19, 2006, http://money.cnn.com.

88. L. M Roberts, J. Dutton, G. Spreitzer, E. Heaphy, and R. Quinn, "Composing the Reflected Best-Self Portrait: Building Pathways for Becoming Extraordinary in Work Organizations," *Academy of Management Review* 30 (2005), pp. 712–36.

89. L. M. Roberts, "Changing Faces: Professional Image Construction in Diverse Organizational Settings," *Academy of Management Review* 30 (2005), pp. 685–711.

90. M. E. P. Seligman, *Authentic Happiness: Using the New Positive Psychology to Realize Your Potential for Lasting Fulfillment* (New York: Free Press, 2002).

91. E. W. Morrison, "Newcomers' Relationships: The Role of Social Network Ties During Socialization," *Academy of Management Journal* 45 (2002), pp. 1149–60.

92. P. Adler and S. Kwon, "Social Capital: Prospects for a New Concept," *Academy of Management Review* 27 (2002), pp. 17–40.

93. Esther Shein, "Six Degrees of Irritation," *CFO*, March 2007, downloaded from Business & Company Resource Center, http://galenet.galegroup.com.

94. T. Peters, *Liberation Management* (New York: Alfred A. Knopf, 1992).
95. P. Drucker, "What Makes an Effective Executive?" *Harvard Business Review*, June 2004, pp. 58–63.
96. Marshall Goldsmith, "Three Obstacles to a Career Move," *BusinessWeek*, March 7, 2007, downloaded from Business & Company Resource Center, http://galenet.galegroup.com.
97. "Tesla Model S Revealed: Sedan to Hit 60 in under Six Seconds, Seat 7, Go 300 Miles," *Wide Open Throttle: Motor Trend*, March 26, 2009, http://wot.motortrend.com; Jerry Garrett, "Tesla Model S Electric Sedan Breaks Cover," *New York Times*, March 26, 2009, http://wheels.blogs.nytimes.com; Andrew Ross Sorkin, "The Roadster Points the Way for Tesla," *New York Times*, March 23, 2009, http://dealbook.blogs.nytimes.com; Hannah Elliott, "Hottest Electric Cars to Hit the Roads," *Forbes*, March 18, 2009, http://www.forbes.com; David R. Baker, "Electric Car Startup Downshifts for Rough Road," *San Francisco Chronicle*, December 28, 2008, http://www.sfgate.com; "Extended Interview: Tesla Motors Chairman Elon Musk," *Online Newshour*, June 25, 2008, http://www.pbs.org; Michael S. Malone, "From Rockets to Electric Cars: Marveling at Musk," *ABC News*, May 23, 2008, http://abcnews.go.com.

Appendix A

1. C. George, *The History of Management Thought* (Englewood Cliffs, NJ: Prentice-Hall, 1972).
2. Ibid.
3. A. D. Chandler, *Scale and Scope: The Dynamic of Industrial Capitalism* (Cambridge, MA: Belknap Press of Harvard University Press, 1990).
4. Ibid.
5. J. Schlosser and E. Florian, "Fortune 500 Amazing Facts!" *Fortune*, April 5, 2004, pp. 152–59.
6. J. Baughman, *The History of American Management* (Englewood Cliffs, NJ: Prentice-Hall, 1969), chap. 1.
7. George, *The History of Management Thought*, chaps. 5–7; F. Taylor, *The Principles of Scientific Management* (New York: Harper & Row, 1911).
8. J. Case, "A Company of Businesspeople," *Inc.*, April 1993, pp. 70–93.
9. Schlosser and Florian, "Fortune 500 Amazing Facts!"
10. H. Kroos and C. Gilbert, *The Principles of Scientific Management* (New York: Harper & Row, 1911).
11. H. Fayol, *General and Industrial Management*, trans. C. Storrs (Marshfield, MA: Pitman Publishing, 1949).
12. George, *The History of Management Thought*, chap. 9; J. Massie, "Management Theory," in *Handbook of Organizations*, ed. J. March (Chicago: Rand McNally, 1965), pp. 387–422.

13. C. Barnard, *The Functions of the Executive* (Cambridge, MA: Harvard University Press, 1938).
14. George, *The History of Management Thought*; Massie, "Management Theory."
15. Schlosser and Florian, "Fortune 500 Amazing Facts!"
16. E. Mayo, *The Human Problems of Industrial Civilization* (New York: Macmillan, 1933); F. Roethlisberger and W. Dickson, *Management and the Worker* (Cambridge, MA: Harvard University Press, 1939).
17. A. Maslow, "A Theory of Human Motivation," *Psychological Review* 50 (July 1943), pp. 370–96.
18. A. Carey, "The Hawthorne Studies: A Radical Criticism," *American Sociological Review* 32, no.3 (1967), pp. 403–16.
19. M. Weber, *The Theory of Social and Economic Organizations*, trans. T. Parsons and A. Henderson (New York: Free Press, 1947).
20. George, *The History of Management Thought*, chap. 11.
21. D. McGregor, *The Human Side of Enterprise* (New York: McGraw-Hill, 1960).
22. C. Argyris, *Personality and Organization* (New York: Harper & Row, 1957).
23. R. Likert, *The Human Organization* (New York: McGraw-Hill, 1967).
24. L. von Bertalanffy, "The History and Status of General Systems Theory," *Academy of Management Journal* 15 (1972), pp. 407–26; D. Katz and R. Kahn, *The Social Psychology of Organizations*, 2nd ed. (New York: John Wiley & Sons, 1978).
25. J. Thompson, *Organizations in Action* (New York: McGraw-Hill, 1967); J. Galbraith, *Organization Design* (Reading, MA: Addison-Wesley, 1977); D. Miller and P. Friesen, *Organizations: A Quantum View* (Englewood Cliffs, NJ: Prentice-Hall, 1984).
26. Schlosser and Florian, "Fortune 500 Amazing Facts!"

Chapter 2

1. Company Web site and "Brewing a Better World," Corporate Social Responsibility Report, Fiscal Year 2007, http://www.greenmountaincoffee.com, accessed March 25, 2009; Rick Aristotle Munarriz, "Warm Up to Green Mountain Coffee Roasters," *The Motley Fool*, January 29, 2009, http://www.fool.com; "Green Mountain Coffee Roasters, Inc., Releases 'Brewing a Better World' Corporate Social Responsibility Report," *CSR Wire*, January 12, 2009, http://www.csrwire.com; Paul Rolfes, "Green Mountain Coffee Roasters: Grounds for Growth," *Smallcapinvestor.com*, July 23, 2008, http://www.smallcapinvestor.com; Alliston Ackerman, "Retail Coffee Favored in Volatile Economy," *Consumer Goods Technology*, July 22,

2008, http://www.consumergoods.com; "Green Mountain Coffee Roasters Founder Bob Stiller Will Step Down," *Automatic Merchandiser*, July 8, 2008, http://www.amonline.com.
2. Mike Hughlett, "Web Radio Fears Going Bust," *Chicago Tribune*, March 8, 2007; and "Recording Labels Should Negotiate Royalty System," *San Jose Mercury News*, March 14, 2007, both downloaded from Business & Company Resource Center, http://galenet.galegroup.com.
3. "CEO Dough," *USA Today*, January 20, 2006, http://www.usatoday.com.
4. Kate Galbraith, "Economy Shifts, and the Ethanol Industry Reels," *New York Times*, November 4, 2008, http://www.nytimes.com.
5. Kelly Evans, "Economy Dives as Goods Pile Up," *The Wall Street Journal*, January 31, 2009, http://online.wsj.com.
6. Joseph Fuller and Michael C. Jensen, "Just Say No to Wall Street," *Journal of Applied Corporate Finance* 14, no. 4 (Winter 2002), pp. 41–46.
7. Jad Mouawad, "Oil Innovations Pump New Life into Old Wells," *New York Times*, March 5, 2007, http://www.nytimes.com.
8. Bureau of Labor Statistics, "BLS Releases 2004–14 Employment Projections," news release, December 7, 2005, http://www.bls.gov.
9. Martha M. Hamilton, "Age 65 and Not Ready or Able to Go," *Washington Post*, January 14, 2007, http://www.washingtonpost.com.
10. Lori Aratani, "Teens Can Multitask, But What Are Costs?" *Washington Post*, February 26, 2007, http://www.washingtonpost.com.
11. Bureau of Labor Statistics, "Charting the U.S. Labor Market in 2005," June 2006, http://www.bls.gov/cps/labor2005/home.htm.
12. See, for example, Ben Arnoldy, "Too Prosperous, Massachusetts Is Losing Its Labor Force," *Christian Science Monitor*, January 9, 2007, http://www.csmonitor.com.
13. Mitra Toossi, "A New Look at Long-Term Labor Force Projections to 2050," *Monthly Labor Review*, November 2006, pp. 19–39.
14. Ibid.; and Bureau of Labor Statistics, "Charting the U.S. Labor Market."
15. "Gaming Goes for the Burn," *PR Week*, February 19, 2007, downloaded from Business & Company Resource Center, http://galenet.galegroup.com.
16. Michael Zitz, "Nintendo Winning Game System Red Hot," *Free Lance–Star* (Fredericksburg, VA), February 23, 2007, downloaded from Business & Company Resource Center, http://galenet.galegroup.com.
17. Dean Takahashi, "Nintendo Responds to Multiple Gamer Complaints on Game Controller Safety," *Design News*, February 5, 2007, downloaded from Business & Company Resource Center, http://galenet.galegroup.com.

18. Charles J. Murray, "Fast and Cool," *Design News*, February 5, 2007, downloaded from Business & Company Resource Center, http://galenet.galegroup.com.

19. Matt Richtel, "Nintendo's Wii, Radiating Fun, Is Eclipsing Sony," *New York Times*, January 31, 2007, Business & Company Resource Center, http://galenet.galegroup.com; "EA: Sony's Video Game Dominance Is Over," *ExtremeTech.com*, March 6, 2007, Business & Company Resource Center, http://galenet.galegroup.com; and Kerry E. Grace, "Sony Cuts Price on PlayStation 2 to $99," *The Wall Street Journal*, March 31, 2009, http://online.wsj.com.

20. David J. Collis and Cynthia A. Montgomery, *Corporate Strategy: Resources and Scope of the Firm* (New York: McGraw-Hill/Irwin, 1997).

21. Adam Plowright, "New Wireless Internet Service Set to Leave Its Asian Niche," *Agence France Presse*, February 24, 2007, http://news.yahoo.com; and John Blau, "WiMax Likely Choice for 'Net Access in Emerging Markets," *InfoWorld*, February 14, 2007, http://www.infoworld.com.

22. John DeGaspari, "Pfizer Retrenches," *MMR*, February 12, 2007, downloaded from Business & Company Resource Center, http://galenet.galegroup.com.

23. Aaron Ricadela, "Console Wars: Sony Fights Back," *BusinessWeek*, March 8, 2007, downloaded from Business & Company Resource Center, http://galenet.galegroup.com; and Grace, "Sony Cuts Price on PlayStation 2."

24. Eric Gwinn, "Shootout at the Top," *Chicago Tribune*, February 27, 2007, downloaded from Business & Company Resource Center, http://galenet.galegroup.com.

25. Ricadela, "Console Wars."

26. "Looking Forward to the Next Level: Electronic Arts," *The Economist*, February 10, 2007, downloaded from Business & Company Resource Center, http://galenet.galegroup.com.

27. Yukari Iwatani Kane, "Look It's Mii—on Wii!" *The Wall Street Journal*, March 16, 2007, http://online.wsj.com.

28. Arthur Sherman, George Bohlander, and Scott Snell, *Managing Human Resources*, 11th ed. (Cincinnati, OH: South-Western Publishing, 1998).

29. Brian Bremner, "Nintendo Storms the Gaming World," *BusinessWeek*, January 29, 2007, downloaded from Business & Company Resource Center, http://galenet.galegroup.com.

30. Adapted from Hau L. Lee and Corey Billington, "The Evolution of Supply-Chain-Management Models and Practice at Hewlett-Packard," *Interfaces* 25, no. 5 (September–October 1995), pp. 42–63.

31. Tracy Maylett and Kate Vitasek, "For Closer Collaboration, Try Education," *Supply Chain Management Review*, January–February 2007, downloaded from Business & Company Resource Center, http://galenet.galegroup.com.

32. Company Web site and "Brewing a Better World," http://www.greenmountaincoffee.com; "Changing Climate Change: Green Mountain Coffee Roasters, Inc., to Award $800,000 in Grants to Find Solutions," *Business Wire*, February 16, 2009, http://markets.on.nytimes.com; "Green Mountain Coffee Roasters, Inc., Releases 'Brewing a Better World,'" *CSR Wire*; Katy Marquardt, "Brewing Profits, a Cup at a Time," *U.S. News & World Report*, November 17/24, 2008, pp. 55–58; and "From Hotel Rooms and Offices to Homes and Supermarkets—Keurig Brewer Success Allows Green Mountain to Expand," *Flexnews*, June 16, 2008, http://www.flex-news-food.com.

33. Don Tapscott and Anthony D. Williams, "Hack This Product, Please!" *BusinessWeek*, February 23, 2007, downloaded from Business & Company Resource Center, http://galenet.galegroup.com.

34. See, for example, "PS3 on Store Shelves at Wal-Mart," http://youtube.com/watch?v=thV53ZJlbng, added December 31, 2006; and "Wii60: Why Can't We Be Friends," http://youtube.com/watch?v=-mdAnzsnTy4, added May 18, 2006.

35. P. Kotler, *Marketing Management: Analysis, Planning, Implementation and Control*, 9th ed. (Englewood Cliffs, NJ: Prentice Hall, 1990).

36. Aaron A. Buchko, "Conceptualization and Measurement of Environmental Uncertainty: An Assessment of the Miles and Snow Perceived Environmental Uncertainty Scale," *Academy of Management Journal* 37, no. 2 (April 1994), pp. 410–25.

37. Abdalla F. Hagen, "Corporate Executives and Environmental Scanning Activities: An Empirical Investigation," *SAM Advanced Management Journal* 60, no. 2 (Spring 1995), pp. 41–47; Richard L. Daft, "Chief Executive Scanning, Environmental Characteristics, and Company Performance: An Empirical Study," *Strategic Management Journal* 9, no. 2 (March/April 1988), pp. 123–39; and Masoud Yasai-Ardekani, "Designs for Environmental Scanning Systems: Tests of a Contingency Theory," *Management Science* 42, no. 2 (February 1996), pp. 187–204.

38. Sumantra Ghoshal, "Building Effective Intelligence Systems for Competitive Advantage," *Sloan Management Review* 28, no. 1 (Fall 1986), pp. 49–58; and Kenneth D. Cory, "Can Competitive Intelligence Lead to a Sustainable Competitive Advantage?" *Competitive Intelligence Review* 7, no. 3 (Fall 1996), pp. 45–55.

39. Paul J. H. Schoemaker, "Multiple Scenario Development: Its Conceptual and Behavioral Foundation," *Strategic Management Journal* 14, no. 3 (March 1993), pp. 193–213.

40. Robin R. Peterson, "An Analysis of Contemporary Forecasting in Small Business," *Journal of Business Forecasting Methods & Systems* 15, no. 2 (Summer 1996), pp. 10–12; and Spyros Makridakis. "Business Forecasting for Management: Strategic Business Forecasting," *International Journal of Forecasting* 12, no. 3 (September 1996), pp. 435–37.

41. Dale Russakoff, "Building a Career Path Where There Was Just a Dead End," *Washington Post*, February 26, 2007, http://www.washingtonpost.com.

42. Bureau of Labor Statistics, "Contingent and Alternative Employment Arrangements, February 2005," news release, July 27, 2005, http://www.bls.gov/cps/.

43. Martin B. Meznar, "Buffer or Bridge? Environmental and Organizational Determinants of Public Affairs Activities in American Firms," *Academy of Management Journal* 38, no. 4 (August 1995), pp. 975–96.

44. David Lei, "Advanced Manufacturing Technology: Organizational Design and Strategic Flexibility," *Organization Studies* 17, no. 3 (1996), pp. 501–23; and James W. Dean Jr. and Scott A. Snell, "The Strategic Use of Integrated Manufacturing: An Empirical Examination," *Strategic Management Journal* 17, no. 6 (June 1996), pp. 459–80.

45. C. Zeithaml and V. Zeithaml, "Environmental Management: Revising the Marketing Perspective," *Journal of Marketing* 48 (Spring 1984), pp. 46–53.

46. "Washington Wire," *The Wall Street Journal*, March 16, 2007, http://blogs.wsj.com/washwire/.

47. Willem P. Burgers, "Cooperative Strategy in High Technology Industries," *International Journal of Management* 13, no. 2 (June 1996), pp. 127–34; and Jeffrey E. McGee, "Cooperative Strategy and New Venture Performance: The Role of Business Strategy and Management Experience," *Strategic Management Journal* 16, no. 7 (October 1995), pp. 565–80.

48. Adam Bluestein, Leigh Buchanan, Max Chafkin, Jason Del Rey, April Joyner, and Ryan McCarthy, "The Ultimate Business Tune-Up for Times Like These," *Inc.*, January 2009, http://www.inc.com.

49. Center for Responsive Politics, "PACs by Industry," *OpenSecrets*, http://www.opensecrets.org, accessed April 6, 2009 (based on data from the Federal Election Commission, released March 2, 2009).

50. Richard A. D'Aveni, *Hypercompetition—Managing the Dynamics of Strategic Maneuvering* (New York: Free Press, 1994); and Michael A. Cusumano, "Strategic Maneuvering and Mass-Market

Dynamics: The Triumph of VHS over Beta," *Business History Review* 66, no. 1 (Spring 1992), pp. 51–94.

51. Model adapted from C. Zeithaml and V. Zeithaml, "Environmental Management: Revising the Marketing Perspective," *Journal of Marketing,* Spring 1984. Published by the American Marketing Association.

52. Bremner, "Nintendo Storms the Gaming World."

53. See, for example, Hiawatha Bray, "Analysis: IPod Likely to Be Apple's Strongest Player," *Boston Globe*, January 16, 2007, http://www.boston.com; and Brian Garrity, "IWin," *Billboard,* December 23, 2006, http://www.billboard.com.

54. "Bayer to Axe 6,100 Jobs Worldwide after Schering Takeover," news release, March 2, 2007, *Agence France Presse,* http://www.afp.com.

55. Ricadela, "Console Wars."

56. Steve McGrath and John D. Stoll, "Ford to Sell Aston Martin Unit in Deal Valued at $848 Million," *The Wall Street Journal,* March 12, 2007, http://online.wsj.com.

57. R. Miles and C. Snow, *Organizational Strategy, Structure, and Process* (New York: McGraw-Hill, 1978).

58. Sarah E. Needleman, "Restaurateur Fights Online Mudslinging," *Startup Journal,* http://www.startupjournal.com, accessed October 24, 2006.

59. Sarah E. Needleman, "Tips on Safeguarding Your Online Reputation," *Startup Journal,* http://www.startupjournal.com, accessed October 24, 2006.

60. Ralph H. Kilmann, Mary J. Saxton, and Roy Serpa, *Gaining Control of the Corporate Culture* (San Francisco: Jossey-Bass, 1985); and Kim S. Cameron and Robert E. Quinn, *Diagnosing and Changing Organizational Culture: Based on the Competing Values Framework* (Englewood Cliffs, NJ: Addison-Wesley, 1998).

61. Jessica E. Vascellaro and Scott Morrison, "Google Gears Down for Tougher Times," *The Wall Street Journal,* December 3, 2008, http://online.wsj.com.

62. Carol Hymowitz, "In Deal-Making, Keep People in Mind," *The Wall Street Journal,* May 12, 2008, http://online.wsj.com.

63. Cameron and Quinn, *Diagnosing and Changing Organizational Culture.*

64. Sebastian Desmidt and Aime Heene, "Mission Statement Perception: Are We All on the Same Wavelength? A Case Study in a Flemish Hospital," *Health Care Management Review,* January–March 2007, downloaded from Business & Company Resource Center, http://galenet.galegroup.com.

65. Carmine Gallo, "How Ritz-Carlton Maintains Its Mystique," *BusinessWeek,* February 13, 2007, http://www.businessweek.com.

66. R. Leifer and P. K. Mills, "An Information Processing Approach for Deciding upon Control Strategies and Reducing Control Loss in Emerging Organizations," *Journal of Management* 22, no. 1 (1996), pp. 113–37; Scott A. Dellana and Richard D. Hauser, "Toward Defining the Quality Culture," *Engineering Management Journal* 11, no. 2 (June 1999), pp. 11–15; and Don Cohen and Lawrence Prusak, *In Good Company: How Social Capital Makes Organizations Work* (Cambridge, MA: Harvard Business School Press, 2001).

67. John Koob, "Early Warnings on Culture Clash," *Mergers & Acquisitions,* July 1, 2006, downloaded from Business & Company Resource Center, http://galenet.galegroup.com.

68. Company Web site and "Brewing a Better World," http://www.greenmountaincoffee.com; Ed Marcum, "Green Mountain Coffee Plant to Expand," *Knoxville News Sentinel,* January 29, 2009, http://www.knoxnews.com; Melissa Allison, "Tully's Sells Bulk of Business to Green Mountain Coffee," *Seattle Times,* September 15, 2008, http://www.seattletimes.com; "Green Mountain Coffee Roasters Founder Bob Stiller Will Step Down," *Automatic Merchandiser,* July 8, 2008, http://www.amonline.com; "From Hotel Rooms and Offices to Homes and Supermarkets," *Flexnews,* June 16, 2008, http://www.flex-news-food.com.

Chapter 3

1. Bill George, "The Courage to Say 'No' to Wall Street," *U.S. News & World Report,* December 1/December 8, 2008, pp. 50–51; Michael Fitzgerald, "X Woman," *Portfolio,* October 2008, http://www.portfolio.com; Don Tennant, "Anne Mulcahy on Getting the Color Back into Xerox," *Computerworld,* June 17, 2008, http://www.computerworld.com; "Anne Mulcahy Becomes the First Woman CEO to Receive Chief Executive Magazine's 'CEO of the Year' Award," *Reuters,* June 3, 2008, http://www.reuters.com; and Andrew Davidson, "Anne Mulcahy: Xerox Saviour in the Spotlight," *TimesOnline,* June 1, 2008, http://business.timesonline.co.uk.

2. Nancy Doucette, "Stuff Happens," *Rough Notes,* December 2006, downloaded from OCLC FirstSearch, http://firstsearch.oclc.org.

3. M. Magasin and F. L. Gehlen, "Unwise Decisions and Unanticipated Consequences," *Sloan Management Review* 41 (1999), pp. 47–60.

4. M. McCall and R. Kaplan, *Whatever It Takes: Decision Makers at Work* (Englewood Cliffs, NJ: Prentice-Hall, 1985); and Luda Kopeikina, "The Elements of a Clear Decision," *MIT Sloan Management Review* 47 (Winter 2006), pp. 19–20.

5. B. Bass, *Organizational Decision Making* (Homewood, IL: Richard D. Irwin, 1983).

6. J. March, "Bounded Rationality, Ambiguity, and the Engineering of Choice," *Bell Journal of Economics* 9 (1978), pp. 587–608.

7. D. Messick and M. Bazerman, "Ethical Leadership and the Psychology of Decision Making," *Sloan Management Review* (Winter 1996), pp. 9–22.

8. Karen Robinson-Jacobs, "Friday's Cutting Portions and Prices," *Dallas Morning News,* March 2, 2007, downloaded from Business & Company Resource Center, http://galenet.galegroup.com; and T.G.I. Friday's, "T.G.I. Friday's Restaurants Take Leadership Role with Portion Control," news release, March 2, 2007, http://fridays.mediaroom.com.

9. Susumu Ogawa and Frank T. Piller, "Reducing the Risks of New Product Development," *MIT Sloan Management Review* 47 (Winter 2006), pp. 65–71.

10. McCall and Kaplan, *Whatever It Takes.*

11. Max Chafkin, "Case Study: When the Bank Called in a Loan, Larry Cohen Had to Act Fast to Save the Family Business," *Inc.,* June 2006, pp. 58–60.

12. Del Jones, "Cisco CEO Sees Tech as Integral to Success," *USA Today,* March 19, 2007, p. 4B (interview of John Chambers).

13. Chafkin, "Case Study," p. 58.

14. Q. Spitzer and R. Evans, *Heads, You Win! How the Best Companies Think* (New York: Simon & Schuster, 1997).

15. Jeffrey A. Trachtenberg, "Borders Business Plan Gets a Rewrite," *The Wall Street Journal,* March 22, 2007, http://online.wsj.com.

16. C. Gettys and S. Fisher, "Hypothesis Plausibility and Hypotheses Generation," *Organizational Behavior and Human Performance* 24 (1979), pp. 93–110.

17. E. R. Alexander, "The Design of Alternatives in Organizational Contexts: A Pilot Study," *Administrative Science Quarterly* 24 (1979), pp. 382–404.

18. Ogawa and Piller, "Reducing the Risks," p. 68.

19. A. R. Rao, M. E. Bergen, and S. Davis, "How to Fight a Price War," *Harvard Business Review,* March–April 2000, pp. 107–16.

20. Chafkin, "Case Study."

21. Ibid.

22. Dana Mattioli and Sara Murray, "Employers Hit Salaried Staff with Furloughs," *The Wall Street Journal,* February 24, 2009, http://online.wsj.com.

23. OfficeTeam, "On Your Best Behaviour: Survey Shows the Boss' Assistant Can Influence the Hiring Decision," news release, *CNW Group,* March 19, 2009, downloaded from Business & Company Resource Center, http://galenet.galegroup.com.

24. Spitzer and Evans, *Heads, You Win!*

25. K. Labich, "Four Possible Futures," *Fortune*, January 25, 1993, pp. 40–48.

26. "Is Executive Hubris Ruining Companies?" *Industry Week*, January 31, 2007, http://www.industryweek.com (interview of Matthew Hayward).

27. McCall and Kaplan, *Whatever It Takes.*

28. George, "The Courage to Say 'No'"; Tennant, "Anne Mulcahy on Getting the Color Back"; and Davidson, "Anne Mulcahy."

29. J. Pfeffer and R. Sutton, *The Knowing–Doing Gap* (Boston: Harvard Business School Press, 2000).

30. D. Siebold, "Making Meetings More Successful," *Journal of Business Communication* 16 (Summer 1979), pp. 3–20.

31. Chafkin, "Case Study."

32. I. Janis and L. Mann, *Decision Making* (New York: Free Press, 1977); and Bass, *Organizational Decision Making.*

33. Kopeikina, "The Elements of a Clear Decision."

34. Brittany Hite, "Deciding to Ditch a Successful Ad Campaign," *The Wall Street Journal*, February 23, 2009, http://online.wsj.com.

35. J. W. Dean Jr. and M. Sharfman, "Does Decision Process Matter? A Study of Strategic Decision-Making Effectiveness," *Academy of Management Journal* 39 (1996), pp. 368–96.

36. R. Nisbett and L. Ross, *Human Inference: Strategies and Shortcomings* (Englewood Cliffs, NJ: Prentice-Hall, 1980).

37. Messick and Bazerman, "Ethical Leadership."

38. Phred Dvorak, "Dangers of Clinging to Solutions of the Past," *The Wall Street Journal*, March 2, 2009, http://online.wsj.com.

39. T. Bateman and C. Zeithaml, "The Psychological Context of Strategic Decisions: A Model and Convergent Experimental Findings," *Strategic Management Journal* 10 (1989), pp. 59–74.

40. Erin White, "Why Good Managers Make Bad Decisions," *The Wall Street Journal*, February 12, 2009, http://online.wsj.com.

41. Messick and Bazerman, "Ethical Leadership."

42. N. Adler, *International Dimensions of Organizational Behavior* (Boston: Kent, 1990).

43. Joann S. Lublin, "Recall the Mistakes of Your Past Bosses, So You Can Do Better," *The Wall Street Journal*, January 2, 2007, http://online.wsj.com.

44. L. Perlow, G. Okhuysen, and N. Repenning, "The Speed Trap: Exploring the Relationship between Decision Making and Temporal Context," *Academy of Management Journal* 45 (2002), pp. 931–55.

45. K. M. Esenhardt, "Speed and Strategic Choice: How Managers Accelerate Decision Making," *California Management Review* 32 (Spring 1990), pp. 39–54.

46. Q. Spitzer and R. Evans, "New Problems in Problem Solving," *Across the Board*, April 1997, pp. 36–40.

47. G. W. Hill, "Group versus Individual Performance: Are *n* + 1 Heads Better than 1?" *Psychological Bulletin* 91 (1982), pp. 517–39.

48. N. R. F. Maier, "Assets and Liabilities in Group Problem Solving: The Need for an Integrative Function," *Psychological Review* 74 (1967), pp. 239–49.

49. Ibid.

50. D. A. Garvin and M. A. Roberto, "What You Don't Know about Making Decisions," *Harvard Business Review*, September 2001, pp. 108–16.

51. R. Cosier and C. Schwenk, "Agreement and Thinking Alike: Ingredients for Poor Decisions," *The Executive*, February 1990, pp. 69–74.

52. A. Amason, "Distinguishing the Effects of Functional and Dysfunctional Conflict on Strategic Decision Making: Resolving a Paradox for Top Management Teams," *Academy of Management Journal* 39 (1996), pp. 123–48; and R. Dooley and G. Fyxell, "Attaining Decision Quality and Commitment from Dissent: The Moderating Effects of Loyalty and Competence in Strategic Decision-Making Teams," *Academy of Management Journal* (August 1999), pp. 389–402.

53. C. De Dreu and L. Weingart, "Task versus Relationship Conflict, Team Performance, and Team Member Satisfaction: A Meta-Analysis," *Journal of Applied Psychology* 88 (2003), pp. 741–49.

54. Cosier and Schwenk, "Agreement and Thinking Alike."

55. Ibid.

56. P. LaBerre, "The Creative Revolution," *Industry Week*, May 16, 1994, pp. 12–19.

57. J. V. Anderson, "Weirder Than Fiction: The Reality and Myths of Creativity," *Academy of Management Executive* (November 1992), pp. 40–47; J. Krohe Jr., "Managing Creativity," *Across the Board* (September 1996), pp. 17–21; and R. I. Sutton, "The Weird Rules of Creativity," *Harvard Business Review* (September 2001), pp. 94–103.

58. J. Perry-Smith and C. Shalley, "The Social Side of Creativity: A Static and Dynamic Social Network Perspective," *Academy of Management Review* 28 (2003), pp. 89–106; and J. Perry-Smith, "Social yet Creative: The Role of Social Relationships in Facilitating Individual Creativity," *Academy of Management Journal* 49 (2006), pp. 85–101.

59. "Innovation from the Ground Up," *Industry Week*, March 7, 2007, http://www.industryweek.com (interview of Erika Andersen); A. Farnham, "How to Nurture Creative Sparks," *Fortune*, January 10, 1994, pp. 94–100; and T. M. Amabile, "A Model of Creativity and Innovation in Organizations," in *Research in Organizational Behavior*, ed. B. Straw and L. Cummings, vol. 10 (Greenwich, CT: JAI Press, 1988), pp. 123–68.

60. T. Amabile, C. Hadley, and S. Kramer, "Creativity under the Gun," *Harvard Business Review* (August 2002), pp. 52–61.

61. S. Farmer, P. Tierney, and K. Kung-McIntyre, "Employee Creativity in Taiwan: An Application of Role Identity Theory," *Academy of Management Journal* 46 (2003), pp. 618–30.

62. "Innovation from the Ground Up."

63. Mike Larson, "LEEDing by Example," *Western Builder*, April 6, 2009, downloaded from Business & Company Resource Center, http://galenet.galegroup.com.

64. L. Thompson, "Improving the Creativity of Organizational Work Groups," *Academy of Management Executive* 17 (2003), pp. 96–109.

65. T. Levitt, "Creativity Is Not Enough," *Harvard Business Review* (August 2002), pp. 137–44.

66. Dean and Sharfman, "Does Decision Process Matter?"

67. K. Eisenhardt, J. Kahwajy, and L. J. Bourgeois III, "How Management Teams Can Have a Good Fight," *Harvard Management Review*, July–August 1997, pp. 77–85.

68. C. M. Pearson and I. I. Mitroff, "From Crisis Prone to Crisis Prepared: A Framework for Crisis Management," *Academy of Management Executive* (February 1993), pp. 48–59.

69. Jordan Robertson and Eileen Sullivan, "U.S. Power Grid Hacked, Officials Say," *Chicago Tribune*, April 9, 2009, http://www.chicagotribune.com.

70. S. Moore, "Disaster's Future: The Prospects for Corporate Crisis Management and Communication," *Business Horizons*, January–February 2004, pp. 29–36.

71. G. Meyers with J. Holusha, *When It Hits the Fan: Managing the Nine Crises of Business* (Boston: Houghton Mifflin, 1986); and S. Bacharach and P. Bamberger, "9/11 and New York City Firefighters' post hoc Unit Support and Control Climates: A Context Theory of the Consequences of Involvement in Traumatic Work-Related Events," *Academy of Management Journal* 50 (2007), pp. 849–68.

72. McCall and Kaplan, *Whatever It Takes.*

73. Allison Sebolt, "Becoming Stronger in the Midst of a Disaster," *Electrical Wholesaling*, July 1, 2006, downloaded from Business & Company Resource Center, http://galenet.galegroup.com.

74. J. Dutton, P. Frost, M. Worline, J. Lilius, and J. Kanov, "Leading in Times of Trauma," *Harvard Business Review* (January 2002), pp. 54–61.

75. George, "The Courage to Say 'No' to Wall Street"; Fitzgerald, "X Woman"; Don Tennant, "The Grill: Xerox CEO Anne Mulcahy on Making Hard

Choices to Bring the Company Back to Life," *Computerworld*, September 1, 2008, http://www.computerworld.com; "The 100 Most Powerful Women: #10, Anne Mulcahy," *Forbes*, August 27, 2008, http://www.forbes.com; Jacquie McNish, "Xerox's Success Is a Reflection of Her Dedication," *Toronto Globe and Mail*, September 11, 2008, http://0-www.lexisnexis.com; "Anne Mulcahy Becomes the First Woman CEO," *Reuters;* and Davidson, "Anne Mulcahy."

Chapter 4

1. "10 Most 'Accountable' Big Companies," *Fortune*, November 14, 2008, http://money.cnn.com; Elise Ackerman, "Mercury News Interview: Nokia CEO Maps Out U.S. Strategy," *San Jose Mercury News*, October 20, 2008, http://www.mercurynews.com; Dianne See Morrison, "Nokia Chief Olli-Pekka Kallasvuo: Hats Off to Apple, Jury Still Out on Google," *Yahoo! Finance*, October 2, 2008, http://biz.yahoo.com; Peter Clarke, "Nokia Tops Greenpeace Green Guide," *EETimes*, September 17, 2008, http://www.eetimes.com.

2. J. Bracker and J. Pearson, "Planning and Financial Performance of Small Mature Firms," *Strategic Management Journal* 7 (1986), pp. 503–22; and P. Waalewijn and P. Segaar, "Strategic Management: The Key to Profitability in Small Companies," *Long Range Planning* 26, no. 2 (April 1993), pp. 24–30.

3. W. M. Bulkeley, "How an IBM Lifer Built Software Unit into a Rising Star," *The Wall Street Journal*, April 2, 2007, http://online.wsj.com.

4. J. Robison, "Are You Ready for Disaster?" *Las Vegas Review-Journal*, September 11, 2006, downloaded from Business & Company Resource Center, http://galenet.galegroup.com. Data for companies with 500 or fewer workers.

5. A. Murray, "JetBlue: Now Just Another Airline in a Lousy Business," *The Wall Street Journal*, February 21, 2007, http://online.wsj.com.

6. Brent Bowers, "In Tough Times, Tackle Anxiety First," *New York Times*, November 13, 2008, downloaded from Business & Company Resource Center, http://galenet.galegroup.com.

7. G. Farrell, "CEO Profile: Wells Fargo's Kovacevich Banks on Success as a One-Stop Shop," *USA Today*, March 26, 2007, http://www.usatoday.com.

8. D. C. Hambrick and J. W. Fredrickson, "Are You Sure You Have a Strategy?" *Academy of Management Executive* 19, no. 4 (2005), pp. 51–62.

9. J. L. Bower and C. G. Gilbert, "How Managers' Everyday Decisions Create or Destroy Your Company's Strategy," *Harvard Business Review*, February 2007, pp. 72–79.

10. J. L. Lunsford, "Gradual Ascent: Burned by Last Boom, Boeing Curbs Its Pace," *The Wall Street Journal*, March 26, 2007, http://online.wsj.com; Boeing, "Boeing in Brief," About Us, http://www.boeing.com, February 2007; and Boeing, "About Us: Culture," http://www.boeing.com/aboutus/culture/index.html, accessed April 15, 2009.

11. R. Kaplan and D. Norton, "Plotting Success with 'Strategy Maps,'" *Optimize*, February 2004, http://www.optimizemag.com; and R. S. Kaplan and D. P. Norton, "Having Trouble with Your Strategy? Then Map It," *Harvard Business Review*, September–October 2000.

12. Bower and Gilbert, "Managers' Everyday Decisions"; and "Business: Fading Fads," *The Economist*, April 22, 2000, pp. 60–61.

13. S. W. Floyd and P. J. Lane, "Strategizing throughout the Organization: Management Role Conflict in Strategic Renewal," *Academy of Management Review* 25, no. 1 (January 2000), pp. 154–77.

14. Mission statements quoted from the corporate Web sites: McDonald's, "Student Research," http://www.mcdonalds.com; Microsoft, "Mission and Values," http://www.microsoft.com; and Allstate, Corporate Press Kit, http://www.allstate.com, all accessed April 3, 2007.

15. Vision statements quoted from the organizations' Web sites: DuPont, "Our Company: DuPont Vision," http://www2.dupont.com; City of Redmond, "City of Redmond Vision Statement," http://www.ci.redmond.wa.us; and Great Lakes Naval Museum Association, "Vision Statement," http://www.greatlakesnavalmuseum.org, all accessed April 3, 2007.

16. Andrew Martin, "The Happiest Meal: Hot Profits," *New York Times*, January 11, 2009, http://www.nytimes.com.

17. A. A. Thompson and A. J. Strickland III, *Strategic Management Concepts and Cases*, 8th ed. (New York: Richard D. Irwin, 1995), p. 23; R. Edward Freeman, J. S. Harrison, and A. C. Wicks, *Managing for Stakeholders* (New Haven, CT: Yale University Press, 2007).

18. Reyna Gobel, "Inspiring Innovation," *Success*, April 2009, pp. 24–26.

19. M. Kanelios, "Full Steam Ahead for Nevada Solar Project," *CNet News.com*, March 20, 2007, http://news.com.com.

20. David Porter, "One Man's Garbage Becomes Another's Power Plant," *Yahoo News*, October 28, 2008, http://news.yahoo.com.

21. D. Michaels, "Pact Ushers in Competitive Skies," *The Wall Street Journal*, March 23, 2007, http://online.wsj.com.

22. D. J. Collis and C. A. Montgomery, *Corporate Strategy: A Resource-Based Approach*, 2nd ed. (New York, McGraw-Hill/Irwin, 2005).

23. R. L. Priem, "A Consumer Perspective on Value Creation," *Academy of Management Review* 32, no. 1 (2007), pp. 219–35.

24. Farrell, "CEO Profile."

25. A. Wilcox King, "Disentangling Interfirm and Intrafirm Causal Ambiguity: A Conceptual Model of Causal Ambiguity and Sustainable Competitive Advantage," *Academy of Management Review* 32, no. 1 (2007), pp. 156–78.

26. S. Hamm and W. C. Symonds, "Mistakes Made on the Road to Innovation," *BusinessWeek*, November 27, 2006, http://www.businessweek.com.

27. G. Naik, "A Hospital Races to Learn Lessons of Ferrari Pit Stop," *The Wall Street Journal*, November 14, 2006, http://online.wsj.com.

28. R. A. Guth, "Microsoft May Shift Strategy to Keep Up," *The Wall Street Journal*, March 29, 2007, http://online.wsj.com.

29. R. A. Guth, D. K. Berman, and K. J. Delaney, "Google Joins Race to Buy DoubleClick," *The Wall Street Journal*, April 2, 2007, http://online.wsj.com.

30. Scott Moritz, "Nokia's Back on Its Feet," *TheStreet.com*, March 26, 2009, http://www.thestreet.com; Andrew Nusca, "How Nokia Ovi Store Will Trump Apple on Global Stage," *The ToyBox*, March 25, 2009, http://blogs.zdnet.com; "Moments of Truth: Global Executives Talk about the Challenges That Shaped Them as Leaders," *Harvard Business Review*, December 1, 2008, http://www.hbrideacast.org; Lionel Laurent, "Nokia's Trickle-Up Success," *Forbes*, June 16, 2008, http://www.forbes.com; Marguerite Reardon, "Nokia's Success Tied to Emerging Markets," *CNET News*, January 24, 2008, http://news.cnet.com.

31. D. G. Sirmon, M. A. Hitt, and R. D. Ireland, "Managing Firm Resources in Dynamic Environments to Create Value: Looking inside the Black Box," *Academy of Management Review* 32, no. 1 (2007), pp. 273–92.

32. Adam Bluestein, "The Success Gene," *Inc.*, April 2008, pp. 83–94.

33. D. Barboza, "Google Acquires Stake in Chinese Web Site," *The New York Times*, January 5, 2007, http://www.nytimes.com.

34. P. Haspeslagh, "Portfolio Planning: Uses and Limits," *Harvard Business Review* 60, no.1 (1982), pp. 58–67; R. Hamermesh, *Making Strategy Work* (New York: John Wiley & Sons, 1986); and R. A. Proctor, "Toward a New Model for Product Portfolio Analysis," *Management Decision* 28, no. 3 (1990), pp. 14–17.

35. A. Johnson, "Abbott's Makeover Attracts Investors," *The Wall Street Journal*, January 19, 2007, http://online.wsj.com.

36. "M&A Activity: U.S. and U.S. Cross-Border Transactions," FactSet Mergerstat Free Reports, updated April 14, 2009, http://www.mergerstat.com.

37. Bulkeley, "How an IBM Lifer Built Software Unit into a Rising Star."

38. M. Porter, *Competitive Advantage* (New York: Free Press, 1985), pp. 11–14.

39. J. Ewers, "Making It Stick," *U.S. News & World Report*, February 5, 2007, pp. EE3–EE8.

40. R. Varadarajan, "Think Small," *The Wall Street Journal*, February 14, 2007, http://online.wsj.com.

41. F. F. Suarez and G. Lanzolla, "The Role of Environmental Dynamics in Building a First Mover Advantage Theory," *Academy of Management Review* 32, no. 2 (2007), pp. 377–92.

42. Bulkeley, "How an IBM Lifer Built Software Unit into a Rising Star"; Farrell, "CEO Profile"; and Lunsford, "Gradual Ascent."

43. Justin Scheck and Paul Glader, "R&D Spending Holds Steady in Slump," *The Wall Street Journal*, April 6, 2009, http://online.wsj.com.

44. R. A. Eisenstat, "Implementing Strategy: Developing a Partnership for Change," *Planning Review*, September–October 1993, pp. 33–36.

45. Daniel Michaels and J. Lynn Lunsford, "Lack of Seats, Galleys Delays Boeing, Airbus," *The Wall Street Journal*, August 8, 2008, http://online.wsj.com; and John Flowers, "Boeing Announces Further Delays to 787 Dreamliner Program," *The Wall Street Journal*, April 9, 2008, http://online.wsj.com.

46. Sara Silver and Dana Cimilluca, "Nokia Siemens Makes Offer for Parts of Nortel," *The Wall Street Journal*, April 8, 2009, http://online.wsj.com; Moritz, "Nokia's Back on Its Feet"; Claire Cain Miller, "Nokia Sends $35 Million to Obopay to Develop Mobile Payments," *New York Times*, March 25, 2009, http://bits.blogs.nytimes.com; "Nokia Device to Challenge RIM and Apple Next Year," *Yahoo! Finance*, December 2, 2008, http://tech.yahoo.com; Ackerman, "Mercury News Interview"; Amarenda Bhushan, "Nokia CEO Olli-Pekka Kallasvuo Likes iPhone!" *CEOWORLD Magazine*, October 2, 2008, http://ceoworld.biz; Richard Wray, "Nokia's Future Is Green," *The Guardian*, February 13, 2008, http://www.guardian.co.uk; Marguerite Reardon, "Nokia Unveils 'Green' Handset Design," *CNET News*, February 13, 2008, http://news.cnet.com

Chapter 5

1. Suzanne Kapner, "Changing of the Guard at Wal-Mart," *Fortune*, February 18, 2009, http://money.cnn.com; Cathryn Creno, "Wal-Mart's Sustainability Efforts Draw Praise," *Arizona Republic*, May 26, 2008, http://www.azcentral.com; and Erica L. Plambeck, "The Greening of Wal-Mart's Supply Chain," *Supply Chain Management Review*, July 1, 2007, http://www.scmr.com.

2. V. Anand, B. Ashforth, and M. Joshi, "Business as Usual: The Acceptance and Perpetuation of Corruption in Organizations," *Academy of Management Executive* (May 2004), pp. 39–53; and B. Ashforth, D. Gioia, S. Robinson, and L. Trevino, "Re-viewing Organizational Corruption," *Academy of Management Review* 33 (July 2008), 670–684.

3. Edelman, "Business More Trusted than Media and Government in Every Region of the Globe," news release, January 22, 2007, *Trust Barometer 2007* pages of Edelman Web site, http://www.edelman.com/trust/2007/.

4. M. Banaji, M. Bazerman, and D. Chugh, "How (Un)Ethical Are You?" *Harvard Business Review*, December 2003, pp. 56–64.

5. S. L. Grover, "The Truth, the Whole Truth, and Nothing but the Truth: The Causes and Management of Workplace Lying," *Academy of Management Executive* 19 (May 2005), pp. 148–57.

6. David Gelles, "Blogs That Spin a Web of Deception," *Financial Times*, February 12, 2009, downloaded from Business & Company Resource Center, http://galenet.galegroup.com.

7. B. L. Toffler, "Five Ways to Jump-Start Your Company's Ethics," *Fast Company*, October 2003, p. 36.

8. M. E. Guy, *Ethical Decision Making in Everyday Work Situations* (New York: Quorum Books, 1990).

9. B. Sleeper, K. Schneider, and P. Weber, "Scale and Study of Student Attitudes toward Business Education's Role in Addressing Social Issues," *Journal of Business Ethics* 68 (2006), pp. 381–91; Y. J. Chen and T. L. P. Tang, "Attitude toward and Propensity to Engage in Unethical Behavior: Measurement Invariance across Major among University Students," *Journal of Business Ethics* 69 (2006), pp. 77–93; and B. A. Ritter, "Can Business Ethics Be Trained? A Study of the Ethical Decision-Making Process in Business Students," *Journal of Business Ethics* 68 (2006), pp. 153–64.

10. O. C. Ferrell and J. Fraedrich, *Business Ethics: Ethical Decision Making and Cases*, 3rd ed. (Boston: Houghton Mifflin, 1997).

11. Ibid.

12. Guy, *Ethical Decision Making*.

13. Ferrell and Fraedrich, *Business Ethics*.

14. J. Hechinger and D. Armstrong, "Universities Resolve Kickback Allegations," *The Wall Street Journal*, April 3, 2007, http://online.wsj.com; J. Hechinger, "Probe into College-Lender Ties Widens," *The Wall Street Journal*, April 5, 2007, http://online.wsj.com; and Associated Press, "CIT Executives Placed on Leave Amid Student Loan Investigation," *The Wall Street Journal*, April 9, 2007, http://online.wsj.com.

15. Hechinger and Armstrong, "Universities Resolve Kickback Allegations"; and AP, "CIT Executives."

16. Transparency International, "Persistently High Corruption in Low-Income Countries Amounts to an 'Ongoing Humanitarian Disaster,'" news release, September 23, 2008, http://www.transparency.org.

17. A. Spicer, T. Dunfee, and W. Biley, "Does National Context Matter in Ethical Decision Making? An Empirical Test of Integrative Social Contracts Theory," *Academy of Management Journal* 47 (2004), pp. 610–20. W. Bailey & A. Spicer, "When does National Identity Matter? Convergence and Divergence in International Business Ethics," *Academy of Management Journal*, 2007, 1462–1480. And K. Martin, J. Cullen, J. Johnson, & K. Parboteeah, "Deciding to Bribe: A Cross-level Analysis of Firm and Home Country Influences on Bribery Activity," *Academy of Management Journal*, 2007, 1401–1422.

18. L. Kohlberg and D. Candee, "The Relationship of Moral Judgment to Moral Action" in *Morality, Moral Behavior, and Moral Development*, ed. W. M. Kurtines and J. L. Gerwitz (New York: John Wiley & Sons, 1984).

19. L. K. Trevino, "Ethical Decision Making in Organizations: A Person-Situation Interactionist Model," *Academy of Management Review*, 1992, pp. 601–17.

20. Ferrel and Fraedrich, *Business Ethics*.

21. J. Badarocco Jr. and A. Webb, "Business Ethics: A View from the Trenches," *California Management Review*, Winter 1995, pp. 8–28; and G. Laczniak, M. Berkowitz, R. Brookes, and J. Hale, "The Business of Ethics: Improving or Deteriorating?" *Business Horizons*, January–February 1995, pp. 39–47.

22. M. Gunther, "God and Business," *Fortune*, July 9, 2001, pp. 58–80.

23. Anand, Ashforth, and Joshi, "Business as Usual."

24. Thompson Hine LLP, "U.S. Sentencing Commission Announces Stiffened Organization Sentencing Guidelines in Response to the Sarbanes-Oxley Act," advisory bulletin, June 1, 2004, last modified August 31, 2006, http://www.thompsonhine.com; and R. J. Zablow, "Creating and Sustaining an Ethical Workplace," *Risk Management* 53, no. 9 (September 2006), downloaded from OCLC FirstSearch, http://firstsearch.oclc.org.

25. R. E. Allinson, "A Call for Ethically Centered Management," *Academy of Management Executive*, February 1995, pp. 73–76.

26. R. T. De George, *Business Ethics*, 3rd ed. (New York: Macmillan, 1990).

27. B. W. Heineman Jr., "Avoiding Integrity Land Mines," *Harvard Business Review*, April 2007, pp. 100–108.

28. R. A. Cooke, "Danger Signs of Unethical Behavior: How to Determine if Your Firm Is at Ethical Risk," *Journal of Business Ethics*, April 1991, pp. 249–53.

29. E. Nakashima, "Harsh Words Die Hard on the Web," *Washington Post*, March 7, 2007, http://www.washingtonpost.com.

30. L. K. Trevino and M. Brown, "Managing to Be Ethical: Debunking Five Business Ethics Myths," *Academy of Management Executive*, May 2004, pp. 69–81.

31. Ibid.

32. Heineman, "Avoiding Integrity Land Mines."

33. S. Brenner and E. Molander, "Is the Ethics of Business Changing?" in *Ethics in Practice: Managing the Moral Corporation*, ed. K. Andrews (Cambridge, MA: Harvard Business School Press, 1989).

34. D. Messick and M. Bazerman, "Ethical Leadership and the Psychology of Decision Making," *Sloan Management Review*, Winter 1996, pp. 9–22.

35. C. Handy, *Beyond Uncertainty: The Changing Worlds of Organizations* (Boston: Harvard Business School Press, 1996).

36. J. Stevens, H. Steensma, D. Harrison, and P. Cochran, "Symbolic or Substantive Document? The Influence of Ethics Codes on Financial Executives' Decisions," *Strategic Management Journal* 26 (2005), pp. 181–95; and J. Weber, "Does It Take an Economic Village to Raise an Ethical Company?" *Academy of Management Executive* 19 (May 2005), pp. 158–59.

37. J. B. Ciulla, "Why Is Business Talking about Ethics? Reflections on Foreign Conversations," *California Management Review*, Fall 1991, pp. 67–80.

38. R. J. Zablow, "Creating and Sustaining an Ethical Workplace: Ethics Resource Center (ERC), "Code Construction and Content," *The Ethics Resource Center Toolkit*, http://www.ethics.org, accessed April 10, 2007; and J. Brown, "Ten Writing Tips for Creating an Effective Code of Conduct," Ethics Resource Center, http://www.ethics.org, accessed April 10, 2007.

39. G. R. Weaver, L. K. Trevino, and P. L. Cochran, "Corporate Ethics Programs as Control Systems: Influences of Executive Commitment and Environmental Factors," *Academy of Management Journal* 42 (1999), pp. 41–57.

40. Ethics Resource Center, "Performance Reviews Often Skip Ethics, HR Professionals Say," news release, June 12, 2008, http://www.ethics.org.

41. L. S. Paine, "Managing for Organizational Integrity," *Harvard Business Review*, March–April 1994, pp. 106–17.

42. F. Hall and E. Hall, "The ADA: Going beyond the Law," *Academy of Management Executive*, February 1994, pp. 7–13; and A. Farnham, "Brushing Up Your Vision Thing," *Fortune*, May 1, 1995, p. 129.

43. L. O'Brien, "Yahoo Betrayed My Husband," *Wired News*, March 15, 2007, http://www.wired.com.

44. G. R. Weaver, L. K. Trevino, and P. L. Cochran, "Integrated and Decoupled Corporate Social Performance: Management Commitments, External Pressures, and Corporate Ethics Practices" *Academy of Management Journal* 42 (1999), pp. 539–52.

45. Trevino and Brown, "Managing to Be Ethical," p. 70.

46. Ibid.

47. Banaji, Bazerman, and Chugh, "How (Un)Ethical Are You?"

48. Andrew Taylor, "Execs' Posh Retreat after Bailout Angers Lawmakers," *Yahoo News*. October 7, 2008, http://news.yahoo.com.

49. Anand, Ashforth, and Joshi, "Business as Usual." Remi Trudel and June Cotte, "Does Being Ethical Pay?" *The Wall Street Journal*, May 12, 2008, http://online.wsj.com.

50. T. Thomas, J. Schermerhorn Jr., and J. Dienhart, "Strategic Leadership of Ethical Behavior in Business," *Academy of Management Executive*, May 2004, pp. 56–66.

51. Trevino and Brown, "Managing to Be Ethical."

52. "Ex-Aide at Coke Is Guilty in Plot to Steal Secrets," *The Wall Street Journal*, February 5, 2007, http://online.wsj.com.

53. Allard, "Ethics at Work."

54. D. Dahl, "Learning to Love Whistleblowers," *Inc.*, March 2005, downloaded from OCLC FirstSearch, http://firstsearch.oclc.org.

55. M. E. Schreiber and D. R. Marshall, "Reducing the Risk of Whistleblower Complaints," *Risk Management* 53, no. 11 (November 2006), downloaded from OCLC FirstSearch, http://firstsearch.oclc.org.

56. R. Bies, J. Bartunek, T. Fort, and M. Zald, "Corporations as Social Change Agents: Individual, Interpersonal, Institutional. and Environmental Dynamics," *Academy of Management Review*, 2007, pp. 788–793.

57. L. Preston and J. Post, eds., *Private Management and Public Policy* (Englewood Cliffs, NJ: Prentice-Hall, 1975).

58. Ferrel and Fraedrich, *Business Ethics*.

59. D. Matten and J. Moon, "'Implicit' and 'Explicit' CSR: A Conceptual Framework for a Comparative Understanding of Corporate Social Responsibility," *Academy of Management Review*, 2008, pp. 404–424.

60. A. Carroll, "Managing Ethically with Global Stakeholders: A Present and Future Challenge," *Academy of Management Executive*, May 2004, pp. 114–20.

61. L. Etter, "Smithfield to Phase Out Crates," *The Wall Street Journal*, January 25, 2007, http://online.wsj.com.

62. P. C. Godfrey, "The Relationship between Corporate Philanthropy and Shareholder Wealth: A Risk Management Perspective," *Academy of Management Review* 30 (2005), pp. 777–98.

63. E. Giacalone, "A Transcendent Business Education for the 21st Century," *Academy of Management Learning & Education*, 2004, pp. 415–20.

64. M. Witzel, "Not for Wealth Alone: The Rise of Business Ethics," *Financial Times Mastering Management Review*, November 1999, pp. 14–19.

65. D. C. Korten, *When Corporations Ruled the World* (San Francisco: Berrett-Koehler, 1995).

66. Handy, *Beyond Uncertainty*.

67. D. Quinn and T. Jones, "An Agent Morality View of Business Policy," *Academy of Management Review* 20 (1995), pp. 22–42.

68. B. McKay, "Why Coke Aims to Slake Global Thirst for Safe Water," *The Wall Street Journal*, March 15, 2007, http://online.wsj.com.

69. N. Varchaver, "Chemical Reaction," *Fortune*, April 2, 2007, downloaded from Business & Company Resource Center, http://galenet.galegroup.com.

70. D. Schuler and M. Cording, "A Corporate Social Performance–Corporate Financial Performance Behavioral Model for Consumers," *Academy of Management Review* 31 (2006), pp. 540–58.

71. M. Orlitzky, F. Schmidt, and S. Rynes, "Corporate Social and Financial Performance: A Meta-Analysis," *Organization Studies*, 24 (2003), pp. 403–441.

72. D. Turban and D. Greening, "Corporate Social Performance and Organizational Attractiveness to Prospective Employees," *Academy of Management Journal* 40 (1997), pp. 658–72.

73. A. McWilliams and D. Siegel, "Corporate Social Responsibility: A Theory of the Firm Perspective," *Academy of Management Review* 26 (2001), pp. 117–27.

74. M. E. Porter and M. R. Kramer, "Strategy and Society: The Link between Competitive Advantage and Corporate Social Responsibility," *Harvard Business Review*, December 2006, pp. 78–92.

75. Ibid., p. 89.

76. S. L. Hart and M. B. Milstein, "Global Sustainability and the Creative Destructions of Industries," *Sloan Management Review*, Fall 1999, pp. 23–33.

77. P. M. Senge and G. Carstedt, "Innovating Our Way to the Next Industrial Revolution," *Sloan Management Review*, Winter 2001, pp. 24–38.

78. C. Holliday, "Sustainable Growth, the DuPont Way," *Harvard Business Review*, September 2001, pp. 129–34.

79. Dexter Roberts, "Wal-Mart Plans a Crackdown on Chinese Suppliers," *BusinessWeek*, October 24, 2008, http://www.businessweek.com; "Wal-Mart Launches Web-Based Innovation Tool to Drive Sustainability Progress," *SpaceDaily*, February 27, 2008, http://www.spacedaily.com; and "Report from Wal-Mart Sustainability Summit: 'In It for the Long Haul,'" *GreenBiz*, October 12, 2007, http://www.greenbiz.com.

80. M. Gunther, "Green Is Good," *Fortune*, March 22, 2007, http://money.cnn.com; and M. LaMonica, "GE Chief: All Engines Go for Alternative Energy," *C/Net News.com*, March 12, 2007, http://news.com.com.

81. P. Shrivastava, "Ecocentric Management for a Risk Society," *Academy of Management Review* 20 (1995), pp. 118–37.

82. Ibid.

83. Ibid.

84. D. Wright, "Lockheed Gets More Time," *Bradenton (Fla.) Herald*, March 7, 2006, downloaded from Business & Company Resource Center, http://galenet.galegroup.com.

85. M. Herbst, "Gore Rings a Green Alarm," *BusinessWeek*, March 22, 2007; E. Osnos, "In China's Toxic Air, Winds of Change," *Chicago Tribune*, March 13, 2007; and Xinhua News Agency, "Unclean Drinking Water Threatens Health of 320M Chinese: Report," *BBC Monitoring International Reports*, March 13, 2007, all downloaded from Business & Company Resource Center, http://galenet.galegroup.com.

86. Shrivastava, "Ecocentric Management."

87. Gunther, "Green Is Good."

88. S. Waddock, "Leadership Integrity in a Fractured Knowledge World," *Academy of Management Learning & Education*, 2007, pp. 543–557.

89. J. O'Toole, "Do Good, Do Well: The Business Enterprise Trust Awards," *California Management Review*, Spring 1991, pp. 9–24.

90. Alexandra Alter, "Yet Another 'Footprint' to Worry About: Water," *The Wall Street Journal*, February 17, 2009, http://online.wsj.com.

91. O'Toole, "Do Good, Do Well"; and Shrivastava, "Ecocentric Management."

92. M. Russo and P. Fouts, "A Resource-Based Perspective on Corporate Environmental Performance and Profitability," *Academy of Management Journal* 40 (1997), pp. 534–59; and R. D. Klassen and D. Clay Whybark, "The Impact of Environmental Technologies on Manufacturing Performance," *Academy of Management Journal* 42 (1999), pp. 599–615.

93. M. LaMonica, "IBM Sees Green in Environmental Tech," *C/Net News.com*, March 6, 2007, http://news.com.com.

94. Jeffrey Ball, "Green Goal of 'Carbon Neutrality' Hits Limit," *The Wall Street Journal*, December 30, 2008, http://online.wsj.com; and Google Inc., "Going Green at Google," Corporate Overview: Green Initiatives, Google Corporate home page, http://www.google.com/corporate/green/, accessed April 21, 2009.

95. G. Pinchot and E. Pinchot, *The Intelligent Organization* (San Francisco: Berrett-Koehler, 1996).

96. S. L. Hart, "Beyond Greening: Strategies for a Sustainable World," *Harvard Business Review*, January–February 1997, pp. 66–76.

97. Kapner, "Changing of the Guard at Wal-Mart"; Nicole Maestri, "Duke to Lead Wal-Mart as It Gains Clout," *Reuters*, November 21, 2008, http://www.reuters.com; Andrew C. Revkin, "Wal-Mart's New Sustainability Push," *New York Times*, October 23, 2008, http://dotearth.blogs.nytimes.com; Stephanie Rosenbloom, "Wal-Mart to Toughen Standards," *New York Times*, October 22, 2008, http://www.nytimes.com; Julie Sturgeon, "Wal-Mart Seeks to Tie Low Prices, Sustainability," *Supermarket News*, October 10, 2008, http://supermarketnews.com; Kate Bertrand Connolly, "Wal-Mart's Scorecard Drives Sustainable Packaging," *FoodProcessing.com*, [no month] 2008, http://www.foodprocessing.com; Creno, "Wal-Mart's Sustainability Efforts Draw Praise"; "Wal-Mart Sustainability Campaign Makes Bad Business Sense," *Reuters*, March 31, 2008, http://www.reuters.com; "Wal-Mart Launches Web-Based Innovation Tool" *SpaceDaily*; Dominique Patton, "Wal-Mart Chief Pledges Higher Prices for Sustainable Suppliers," *AP-foodtechnology.com*, January 24, 2008, http://www.ap-foodtechnology.com; Sami Grover, "Wal-Mart's Sustainability Summit: Greenwash It Was Not," *TreeHugger*, October 11, 2007, http://www.treehugger.com.

Appendix B

1. P. Hawken, A. Lovins, and L. Hunter Lovins, *Natural Capitalism* (Boston: Little Brown, 1999).

2. F. Rice, "Who Scores Best on the Environment?" *Fortune*, July 26, 1993, p. 114–22.

3. J. K. Hammitt, "Climate Change Won't Wait for Kyoto," *The Washington Post*, November 29, 2000, p. A39.

4. A. Brown, "Business Leaders Respond to Rio with Self-Regulation," *International Herald Tribune*, June 23, 1997, p. 17.

5. Ibid.

6. K. W. Chilton, "Reengineering U.S. Environmental Protection," *Business Horizons*, March–April 2000, pp. 7–16.

7. K. Dechant and B. Altman, "Environmental Leadership: From Compliance to Competitive Advantage," *Academy of Management Executive*, August 1994, pp. 7–20.

8. R. Stavins, letter in "The Challenge of Going Green," *Harvard Business Review*, July–August 1994, pp. 37–50.

9. N. Walley and B. Whitehead, "It's Not Easy Being Green," *Harvard Business Review*, May–June 1994, pp. 46–51; and C. J. Corbett and L. N. Van Wassenhove, "The Green Fee: Internationalizing and Operationalizing Environmental Issues," *California Management Review*, Fall 1993, pp. 116–33.

10. Walley and Whitehead, "It's Not Easy Being Green."

11. Stavins, "The Challenge of Going Green."

12. Ibid.

13. F. B. Cross, "The Weaning of the Green: Environmentalism Comes of Age in the 1990s," *Business Horizons*, September–October 1990, pp. 40–46.

14. Stavins, "The Challenge of Going Green."

15. J. Singh, "Making Business Sense of Environmental Compliance," *Sloan Management Review*, Spring 2000, pp. 91–100.

16. H. Ellison, "Saving Nature While Earning Money," *International Herald Tribune*, June 23, 1997, p. 18.

17. E. Smith and V. Cahan, "The Greening of Corporate America," *BusinessWeek*, April 23, 1990, pp. 96–103.

18. M. E. Porter, "America's Green Strategy," *Science*, April 1991, p. 168.

19. A. Kleiner, "What Does It Mean to Be Green?" *Harvard Business Review*, July–August 1991, pp. 38–47.

20. D. C. Kinlaw, *Competitive and Green: Sustainable Performance in the Environmental Age* (Amsterdam: Pfeiffer & Co., 1993).

21. Rice, "Who Scores Best on the Environment?"

22. Rice, "Who Scores Best on the Environment?"; J. O'Toole, "Do Good, Do Well: The Business Enterprise Trust Awards," *California Management Review*, Spring 1991, pp. 9–24.

23. O'Toole, "Do Good, Do Well."

24. G. Hardin, "The Tragedy of the Commons," *Science* 162 (1968), pp. 1243–48.

25. D. Kirkpatrick, "Environmentalism: The New Crusade," *Fortune*, February 12, 1990, pp. 44–55.

26. Ibid.

27. R. Carson, *The Silent Spring* (Boston: Houghton Mifflin, 1962); R. Paehlke, *Environmentalism and the Future of Progressive Politics* (New Haven, CT: Yale University Press, 1989), pp. 13–41, 76–143; R. Nash, ed., *The American Environment* (Reading, MA: Addison-Wesley, 1968); R. Revelle and

H. Landsberg, eds., *America's Changing Environment* (Boston: Beacon Press, 1970); L. Caldwell, *Environment: A Challenge to Modern Society* (Garden City, NY: Anchor Books, 1971); and J. M. Petulla, *Environmental Protection in the United States* (San Francisco: San Francisco Study Center, 1987).

28. B. Commoner, *Science and Survival* (New York: Viking Press, 1963); and B. Commoner, *The Closing Circle: Nature, Man and Technology* (New York: Bantam Books; 1971).

29. R. Paehlke, *Environmentalism and the Future of Progressive Politics* (New Haven: Yale University Press, 1989).

30. P. Shrivastava, "Ecocentric Management for a Risk Society," *Academy of Management Review* 20 (1995), pp. 118–37.

31. Commoner, *The Closing Circle.*

32. Paehlke, *Environmentalism.*

33. Ibid.

34. Ibid.

35. P. Hawken, J. Ogilvy, and P. Schwartz, *Seven Tomorrows: Toward a Voluntary History* (New York: Bantam Books, 1982); and Paehlke, *Environmentalism.*

36. Porter, "America's Green Strategy."

37. R. Y. K. Chan, "An Emerging Green Market in China: Myth or Reality?" *Business Horizons*, March–April 2000, pp. 55–60.

38. S. Waddock and N. Smith, "Corporate Responsibility Audits: Doing Well by Doing Good," *Sloan Management Review*, Winter 2000, pp. 75–83.

39. C. Morrison, *Managing Environmental Affairs: Corporate Practices in the U.S., Canada, and Europe* (New York: Conference Board, 1991).

40. Ibid.

41. Kleiner, "What Does It Mean to Be Green?"

42. K. Fischer and J. Schot, *Environmental Strategies for Industry* (Washington, DC: Island Press, 1993).

43. J. Howard, J. Nash, and J. Ehrenfeld, "Standard or Smokescreen? Implementation of a Voluntary Environmental Code," *California Management Review*, Winter 2000, pp. 63–82.

44. Rice, "Who Scores Best on the Environment?"

45. M. P. Polonsky and P. J. Rosenberger III, "Reevaluating Green Marketing: A Strategic Approach," *Business Horizons*, September–October 2001, pp. 21–30.

46. Rice, "Who Scores Best on the Environment?"

47. Ibid.

48. Polansky and Rosenberger, "Reevaluating Green Marketing."

49. S. Hart and M. Milstein, "Global Sustainability and the Creative Destruction of Industries," *Sloan Management Review*, Fall 1999, pp. 23–32; Ellison, "Saving Nature While Earning Money."

50. Dechant and Altman, "Environment Leadership."

51. Smith and Cahan, "The Greening of Corporate America."

52. J. Elkington and T. Burke, *The Green Capitalists* (London: Victor Gullanez, 1989); and M. Zetlin, "The Greening of Corporate America," *Management Review*, June 1990, pp. 10–17.

53. Smith and Cahan, "The Greening of Corporate America."

54. J. Carey, "Global Warming," *BusinessWeek*, August 16, 2004, pp. 60–69.

55. J. Stevens, "Assessing the Health Risks of Incinerating Garbage," *EURA Reporter*, October 1989, pp. 6–10.

56. Carey, "Global Warming."

57. A. Lovins, L. Hunter Lovins, and P. Hawken, "A Road Map for Natural Capitalism," *Harvard Business Review*, May–June 1999, pp. 145–58.

58. A. Kolk, "Green Reporting," *Harvard Business Review*, January–February 2000, pp. 15–16.

59. L. Blumberg and R. Gottlieb, "The Resurrection of Incineration" and "The Economic Factors," in *War on Waste*, ed. L. Blumberg and R. Gottlieb (Washington, DC: Island Press, 1989).

60. Carey, "Global Warming."

61. L. Blumberg and R. Gottlieb, "Recycling's Unrealized Promise," in Blumberg and Gottlieb; *War on Waste*, pp. 191–226.

62. Carey, "Global Warming."

63. Lovins, Lovins, and Hawken, "A Road Map for Natural Capitalism."

64. J. Elkington, "Towards the Sustainable Corporation: Win-Win-Win Business Strategies for Sustainable Development," *California Management Review*, Winter 1994, pp. 90–100.

65. Lovins, Lovins, and Hawken, "A Road Map for Natural Capitalism."

66. Carey, "Global Warming."

67. Dechant and Altman, "Environmental Leadership."

68. Brown, "Business Leaders Respond to Rio with Self-Regulation."

69. H. Ellison, "Joint Implementation Promotes Cooperation on World Climate," *International Herald Tribune*, June 23, 1997, p. 21.

70. Corbett and Van Wassenhove, "The Green Fee."

71. Polansky and Rosenberger, "Reevaluating Green Marketing."

72. Carey, "Global Warming."

73. Corbett and Van Wassenhove, "The Green Fee."

74. R. D. Klassen and D. Clay Whybark, "The Impact of Environmental Technologies on Manufacturing Performance," *Academy of Management Journal* 42 (1999), pp. 599–615.

75. D. Machalaba, "New Recyclables Market Emerges: Plastic Railroad Ties," *The Wall Street Journal*, October 19, 2004, p. B1.

76. Hart and Milstein, "Global Sustainability."

77. Ibid.

78. Polansky and Rosenberger, "Reevaluating Green Marketing."

79. N. Stein, "Yes, We Have No Profits," *Fortune*, November 26, 2001, pp. 183–96.

80. Hart and Milstein, "Global Sustainability."

81. Ibid.

82. M. Fong, "Soy Underwear? China Targets Eco-Friendly Clothes Market," *The Wall Street Journal*, December 17, 2004, pp. B1, B4.

83. Ibid.

84. Polansky and Rosenberger, "Reevaluating Green Marketing."

85. Ibid.

86. Elkington, "Towards the Sustainable Corporation."

87. F. S. Rowland, "Chlorofluorocarbons and the Depletion of Stratospheric Ozone," *American Scientist*, January–February 1989, pp. 36–45.

88. Elkington, "Towards the Sustainable Corporation."

89. Corbet and Van Wasserhove, "The Green Fee."

90. Ellison, "Joint Implementation Promotes Cooperation on World Climate."

91. Elkington, "Towards the Sustainable Corporation."

92. H. Ellison, "The Balance Sheet," *International Herald Tribune*, June 23, 1997, p. 21.

93. Ibid.

94. P. B. Gray and D. Devlin, "Heroes of Small Business," *Fortune Small Business*, November 2000, pp. 50–64.

95. S. Tully, "Water, Water Everywhere," *Fortune*, May 15, 2000, pp. 343–54.

Chapter 6

1. Kraft Foods Web site, http://www.kraftfoodscompany.com, accessed April 16, 2009; Ishmiel Kaput, "Independence from Altria Group Positive for Kraft Foods," *Seeking Alpha*, June 20, 2007, http://seekingalpha.com; Andrew Martin, "Irene Rosenfeld Tries to Spark Renewal at Kraft," *International Herald Tribune*, February 21, 2007, http://www.iht.com; "Kraft Foods Unveils Plan to Lift Sales; Shares Fall 3%," *Los Angeles Times*, February 21, 2007, http://www.latimes.com; Ashley M. Heher, "Kraft Foods Outlines New Plan to Turn Company around by 2009," *USA Today*, February 20, 2007, http://www.usatoday.com.

2. European Union, "The EU at a Glance," http://www.europa.eu, accessed April 16, 2007; Central Intelligence Agency, "European Union," *The World Factbook*, http://www.cia.gov, last updated March 15, 2007; and Bureau of Economic Analysis, "Gross Domestic Product: Fourth Quarter 2006 (Final), Corporate Profits: Fourth Quarter 2006," news release, March 29, 2007, http://www.bea.gov.

3. "Not What It Was," *The Economist*, February 10, 2007, downloaded from

Business & Company Resource Center, http://galenet.galegroup.com.

4. "Nokia to Build Mobile Phone Factory in Romania," *Agence France Presse*, March 26, 2007, http://news.yahoo.com; and D. Rocks, K. Zachovalova, and N. Saminathaer, "Made in China—er, Veliko Turnovo," *BusinessWeek*, January 8, 2007, downloaded from Business & Company Resource Center, http://galenet.galegroup.com.

5. R. Casert, "EU Waves New Fines in Face of Microsoft," *Seattle Times*, March 2, 2007; and D. Litterick, "Regulation EU Losing Patience with Reluctant Microsoft," *Daily Telegraph (London)*, March 2, 2007, both downloaded from Business & Company Resource Center, http://galenet.galegroup.com.

6. "EC Investigates Sony-BMG Merger," *Billboard*, March 10, 2007; J. Wardell, "Warner Renews Interest in EMI Group," *Star-Ledger (Newark, NJ)*, February 21, 2007; and D. Gow, "Sell Note: Britney on the Block," *Guardian (London)*, March 16, 2007, all downloaded from Business & Company Resource Center, http://galenet.galegroup.com.

7. "China Surpasses U.S. in Exports," *The Wall Street Journal*, April 12, 2007, http://online.wsj.com.

8. World Trade Organization, *Trade Profiles 2008* (Geneva: WTO, 2009), p. 38, available at http://www.wto.org; World Trade Organization, *International Trade Statistics 2008* (Geneva: WTO, 2008), p. 5, available at http://www.wto.org; and World Trade Organization, "WTO Sees 9% Global Trade Decline in 2009 as Recession Strikes," new release, March 24, 2009, http://www.wto.org.

9. J. McDonald, "Intel Plant to Boost Beijing Tech Plans," *Associated Press*, March 26, 2007, http://news.yahoo.com; and M. Kanellos, "Intel to Produce Chips in China," *C/Net News*, March 26, 2007, http://news.com.com.

10. James T. Areddy and Peter Sanders, "Chinese Learn English the Disney Way," *The Wall Street Journal*, April 20, 2009, http://online.wsj.com.

11. Bureau of Labor Statistics, "International Comparisons of Hourly Compensation Costs in Manufacturing, 2007," news release, March 26, 2009, http://www.bls.gov/ilc.

12. A. van Agtmael, "Industrial Revolution 2.0," *Foreign Policy*, January–February 2007, downloaded from Business & Company Resource Center, http://galenet.galegroup.com.

13. Asia-Pacific Economic Cooperation, "Scope of Work" and "Frequently Asked Questions," APEC Web site, http://www.apec.org, accessed April 17, 2007.

14. Agtmael, "Industrial Revolution 2.0"; CEMEX Web site, http://www.cemex.com, accessed April 17, 2007.

15. P. Engardio, "Emerging Giants," *BusinessWeek*, July 31, 2006, http://www.businessweek.com.

16. Agtmael, "Industrial Revolution 2.0."

17. Department of Commerce, International Trade Administration, "U.S.–CAFTA–DR Free Trade Agreement: How Can U.S. Companies Benefit," http://www.export.gov, accessed April 17, 2007; and P. S. Goodman, "Labor Rights in Guatemala Aided Little by Trade Deal," *Washington Post*, March 16, 2007, http://www.washingtonpost.com.

18. See, for example, D. Chapman, "Atlanta's Trade Dream Fizzles Out," *Atlanta Journal-Constitution*, January 30, 2007; and "Bye Bye Free Trade Area of the Americas?" *Managing Exports and Imports*, November 2006, both downloaded from Business & Company Resource Center, http://galenet.galegroup.com.

19. "Citigroup Plans More Branches in India," *Associated Press*, March 26, 2007, http://my.earthlink.net.

20. S. Faris, "Starbucks vs. Ethiopia," *Fortune International*, March 5, 2007, http://galenet.galegroup.com; and J. Adamy and R. Thurow, "Ethiopia Battles Starbucks Over Rights to Coffee Names," *The Wall Street Journal*, March 5, 2007, http://online.wsj.com.

21. World Trade Organization (WTO), *International Trade Statistics 2008*; and WTO, "WTO Sees 9% Global Trade Decline."

22. See, for example, M. Mandel, "What Spending Slowdown?" *BusinessWeek*, April 23, 2007, http://www.businessweek.com.

23. Census Bureau, *Statistical Abstract of the United States: 2007*, http://www.census.gov, table 1273, p. 797; and Council on Competitiveness, "Trade Deficit Doesn't Capture U.S. Competitive Edge," news release, November 13, 2006, http://www.compete.org.

24. Engardio, "Emerging Giants."

25. C. Zappone, "China Poised for Global Shopping Spree," *CNNMoney*, March 30, 2007, http://money.cnn.com.

26. Engardio, "Emerging Giants"; and P. Engardio, "Haier: Taking a Brand Name Higher," *BusinessWeek*, July 31, 2006, http://www.businessweek.com.

27. Joseph B. White, "What Is an American Car?" *The Wall Street Journal*, January 26, 2009, http://online.wsj.com.

28. T. Heston, "Fitting into the Global Puzzle," *Fabricating and Metalworking*, February 2007, downloaded from Business & Company Resource Center, http://galenet.galegroup.com.

29. N. Sandler, "Software That Will This Sentence Fix," *BusinessWeek*, February 22, 2007, downloaded from Business & Company Resource Center, http://galenet.galegroup.com.

30. D. W. Drezner, "The Outsourcing Bogeyman," *Foreign Affairs*, May/June 2004, online.

31. D. Wessel and B. Davis, "Pain from Free Trade Spurs Second Thoughts," *The Wall Street Journal*, March 28, 2007, http://online.wsj.com.

32. Wessel and Davis, "Pain from Free Trade"; P. Levy, "Trade Truths for Turbulent Times: A Reply to Vladimir Masch," *BusinessWeek*, February 14, 2007, downloaded from Business & Company Resource Center, http://galenet.galegroup.com; P. Restuccia, "Profs Claim the Threat of Outsourcing Is Overblown," *Boston Herald*, February 12, 2007, http://galenet.galegroup.com; and D. Blanchard, "Compete or Retreat," *Industry Week*, January 2007, http://galenet.galegroup.com.

33. "Report: Offshoring's Cost Advantage Slips," *CIOInsight*, March 21, 2007, downloaded from Business & Company Resource Center, http://galenet.galegroup.com.

34. Council on Competitiveness, "Trade Deficit Doesn't Capture U.S. Competitive Edge."

35. C. Lombardi, "Survey: Software Companies Increasing Offshoring Work," *C/Net News*, January 12, 2007, http://news.com.com.

36. "When Staying Put Trumps Offshoring," *McKinsey Quarterly*, December 7, 2004, online.

37. David Blanchard, "The Latest Global Hotspot: The USA," *Industry Week*, October 1, 2008, http://www.industryweek.com; Barbara Kiviat, "Sewn in the U.S.A.," *Time*, April 28, 2008, pp. Global 1–2; and Timothy Aeppel, "Stung by Soaring Transport Costs, Factories Bring Jobs Home Again," *The Wall Street Journal*, June 13, 2008, http://online.wsj.com.

38. Brad Dorfman, "Corporate News," *LiveMint.com*, September 3, 2008, http://www.livemint.com; Devon Pendleton, "The 100 Most Powerful Women," *Forbes*, August 27, 2008, http:www.forbes.com; Jay Palmer, "Kraft: Tastier Than You Think," *SmartMoney*, May 19, 2008, http://www.smartmoney.com; "Kraft Reports Strong Revenue Growth in 2007," *Asia Food Journal*, February 8, 2008, http://www.asiafoodjournal.com; "Report: Kraft Nearing Deal to Sell Post Cereal," *USA Today*, November 5, 2007, http://www.usatoday.com; "Kraft Foods Appoints Mary Beth West as CMO," *Business Wire*, October 29, 2007, http://www.businesswire.com; "Markets: Kraft Makes Offer for Danone Unit—The Company Whose Brands Include Oreo Bids $7.2 Billion for the Group's Cookie Division," *Los Angeles Times*, July 4, 2007, http://articles.latimes.com; Ashley M. Heher, "Kraft Bids $7.2B for Danone Cookie Unit," *USA Today*, July 3, 2007, http://www.usatoday.com; Kaput, "Independence from Altria Group"; "Kraft Foods Unveils Plan to Lift

Sales," *Los Angeles Times;* Martin, "Irene Rosenfeld Tries to Spark Renewal."

39. See, for example, "India's Bharti Says to Sign Wal-Mart Deal in April," *Reuters,* April 11, 2007, http://news.yahoo.com.

40. G. A. Fowler, B. Steinberg, and A. O. Patrick, "Mac and PC's Overseas Adventures," *The Wall Street Journal,* March 1, 2007, http://online.wsj.com.

41. P. B. Kavilanz, "U.S. Slaps Tariffs on Chinese Imports," *CNNMoney.com,* March 30, 2007, http://money.cnn.com.

42. Heineken International Web site, http://www.henekeninternational.com, accessed May 30, 2007; and Heineken N.V. profile, *Vintners.com,* http://www.vintners.com, accessed May 30, 2007.

43. A.-W. Harzing, "An Empirical Analysis and Extension of the Bartlett and Ghoshal Typology of Multinational Companies," *Journal of International Business Studies* 31, no. 1 (2000), pp. 101–20.

44. J. Sandberg, "How Long Can India Keep Office Politics out of Outsourcing?" *The Wall Street Journal,* February 27, 2007, http://online.wsj.com.

45. S. E. Prokesch, "Making Global Connections at Caterpillar," *Harvard Business Review* 74, no. 2 (March–April 1996), pp. 88–89; "Caterpillar Gets a Lift," *BusinessWeek,* February 16, 2007, http://www.businessweek.com; *Off-Highway Engineering: Technical Innovations,* http://www.sae.org/ohmag/techinnovations/02-2001/; L. Freeman, "Caterpillar on a Roll," *B to B* 85, no. 14 (September 11, 2000), pp. 3, 44; I. Buchanan, "The US Experience," *Asian Business* 34, no. 5 (May 1998), pp. 14–16; and Caterpillar Web site, http://www.cat.com, accessed April 18, 2007.

46. C. H. Moon, "The Choice of Entry Modes and Theories of Foreign Direct Investment," *Journal of Global Marketing* 11, no. 2 (1997), pp. 43–64; I. Maignan and B. A. Lukas, "Entry Mode Decisions: The Role of Managers' Mental Models," *Journal of Global Marketing* 10, no. 4 (1997), pp. 7–22.

47. A. O. Patrick, "The Race to Get TV Shows Overseas," *The Wall Street Journal,* March 28, 2007, http://online.wsj.com; and B. Barnes, "NBC Faces Trials Bringing 'Law & Order' to France," *The Wall Street Journal,* March 1, 2007, http://online.wsj.com.

48. Suzanne Barlyn, "Call My Lawyer . . . in India," *Time,* April 14, 2008, pp. Global 1–2; and World Trade Organization, *International Trade Statistics 2008,* p. 6.

49. C. Simons and D. Zehr, "Dell Tries to Win Over Chinese with Scaled-Down PCs," *Atlanta Journal-Constitution,* March 22, 2007, downloaded from Business & Company Resource Center, http://galenet.galegroup.com.

50. P. Jitpleecheep, "Auntie Anne's Aims to Double Asia Outlets," *Bangkok Post,* April 10, 2007, downloaded from Business & Company Resource Center, http://galenet.galegroup.com.

51. M. Prewitt, "Breaking Down the Great Wall to Franchising in China," *Nation's Restaurant News,* March 12, 2007, downloaded from Business & Company Resource Center, http://galenet.galegroup.com.

52. "Hershey's Global Gambit," *BusinessWeek,* April 4, 2007, http://www.businessweek.com.

53. R. C. Beasley, "Reducing the Risk of Failure in the Formation of Commercial Partnerships," *Licensing Journal* 24, no. 4 (April 2004), p. 71.

54. M. Nevin Duffy, "3M Lauds China Government Help," *Chemical Market Reporter* 251, no. 1 (January 6, 1997), p. 19.

55. M. Kripalani, "Open Season on Outsourcers," *BusinessWeek,* April 17, 2006, http://www.businessweek.com.

56. "IBM's India Hiring Binge Continues," *Associated Press,* February 28, 2007, http://news.yahoo.com.

57. N. J. Adler and S. Bartholomew, "Managing Globally Competent People," *Academy of Management Executive* 6, no. 3 (1992), pp. 52–65; and C. G. Howard, "Profile of the 21st-Century Expatriate Manager," *HRMagazine,* June 1992, pp. 93–100.

58. T. Purdum, "Chasing the Sun," *IndustryWeek.com,* April 1, 2007, http://www.industryweek.com.

59. A. W. Andreason, "Expatriate Adjustment to Foreign Assignments," *International Journal of Commerce and Management* 13 no. 1 (Spring 2003), pp. 42–61.

60. P. Capell, "Know before You Go: Expats' Advice to Couples," *Career Journal Europe,* May 2, 2006, http://www.careerjournaleurope.com.

61. R. A. Swaak, "Expatriate Failures: Too Many, Too Much Cost, Too Little Planning," *Compensation & Benefits Review,* November/December 1995, pp. 50–52.

62. Capell, "Know before You Go."

63. G. M. Spreitzer, M. W. McCall, and J. D. Mahoney, "Early Identification of International Executive Potential," *Journal of Applied Psychology* 82, no. 1 (1997), pp. 6–29; R. Mortensen, "Beyond the Fence Line," *HRMagazine,* November 1997, pp. 100–9; "Expatriate Games," *Journal of Business Strategy,* July/August 1997, pp. 4–5; and "Building a Global Workforce Starts with Recruitment," *Personnel Journal* (special supplement), March 1996, pp. 9–11.

64. A. Paul, "How the Internet Shrinks the Distance between Us," *The Wall Street Journal,* March 16, 2007, http://online.wsj.com.

65. G. A. Fowler, "In China's Offices, Foreign Colleagues Might Get an Earful," *The Wall Street Journal,* February 13, 2007, http://online.wsj.com.

66. John Slocum, "Coming to America," *Human Resource Executive,* October 2, 2008, http://www.hrexecutive.com.

67. Emily Flitter, "Time Runs Differently in the Emirates," *The Wall Street Journal,* April 16, 2008, http://online.wsj.com.

68. J. Brett, K. Behfar, and M. C. Kern, "Managing Multicultural Teams," *Harvard Business Review,* November 2006, pp. 84–91.

69. D. Stamps, "Welcome to America," *Training,* November 1996, pp. 23–30.

70. L. K. Trevino and K. A. Nelson, *Managing Business Ethics: Straight Talk about How to Do It Right* (New York: John Wiley & Sons, 1995).

71. Transparency International, "Leading Exporters Undermine Development with Dirty Business Overseas," news release, October 4, 2006, http://www.transparency.org.

72. J. G. Longnecker, J. A. McKinney, and C. W. Moore, "The Ethical Issues of International Bribery: A Study of Attitudes among U.S. Business Professionals," *Journal of Business Ethics* 7 (1988), pp. 341–46.

73. K. Q. Seelye, "J&J Reveals Improper Payments," *New York Times,* February 13, 2007, downloaded from Business & Company Resource Center, http://galenet.galegroup.com.

74. A. B. Desai and T. Rittenburg, "Global Ethics: An Integrative Framework for MNEs," *Journal of Business Ethics* 16 (1997), pp. 791–800; and P. Buller, J. Kohls, and K. Anderson, "A Model for Addressing Cross-Cultural Ethical Conflicts," *Business & Society* 36, no. 2 (June 1997), pp. 169–93.

75. Kraft Foods Web site, http://www.kraftfoodscompany.com, accessed April 1, 2009; Dorfman, "Corporate News"; Brad Dorfman, "Price Increases Help Kraft Foods Lift Profits," *Financial Post,* July 28, 2008, http://www.financialpost.com; Palmer, "Kraft: Tastier Than You Think"; Julie Jargon, "Kraft Reformulates Oreo, Scores in China," *The Wall Street Journal,* May 1, 2008, http://online.wsj.com.

Chapter 7

1. Virgin Web site, http://www.virgin.com, accessed April 1, 2009; Sara Wilson, "Branson," *Entrepreneur,* November 2008, pp. 58–62; Emily Benammar, "Richard Branson Forced to Abandon Transatlantic Record Attempt," *Telegraph,* October 24, 2008, http://www.telegraph.co.uk; Jyoti Thottam, "Richard Branson's Flight Plan," *Time,* April 17, 2008, http://www.time.com; Alan Deutschman, "The Enlightenment of Richard Branson," *Fast Company,* December 19, 2007, http://www.fastcompany.com; Kane Farabaugh, "Virgin Group Founder Commits Billions of Dollars to Help

Environment," *Voice of America*, March 19, 2007, http://www.voanews.com; Michael Specter, "Branson's Luck," *New Yorker*, May 14, 2007, http://www.newyorker.com.

2. S. Shane and S. Venkataraman, "The Promise of Entrepreneurship as a Field of Research, *Academy of Management Review* 25 (2000), pp. 217–26.

3. J. A. Timmons, *New Venture Creation* (Burr Ridge, IL: Richard D. Irwin, 1994).

4. G. T. Lumpkin and G. G. Dess, "Clarifying the Entrepreneurial Orientation Construct and Linking It to Performance," *Academy of Management Review* 21 (1996), pp. 135–72.

5. R. W. Smilor, "Entrepreneurship: Reflections on a Subversive Activity," *Journal of Business Venturing* 12 (1997), pp. 341–46.

6. W. Megginson, M. J. Byrd, S. R. Scott Jr., and L. Megginson, *Small Business Management: An Entrepreneur's Guide to Success*, 2nd ed. (Boston: Irwin McGraw-Hill, 1997).

7. J. Timmons and S. Spinelli, *New Venture Creation: Entrepreneurship for the 21st Century*, 6th ed. (New York: McGraw-Hill/Irwin, 2004), p. 3.

8. J. A. Timmons, *The Entrepreneurial Mind* (Andover, MA: Brick House, 1989).

9. Timmons and Spinelli, *New Venture Creation.*

10. A. Loten, "Start-Ups Key to States' Economic Success," *Inc.*, February 7, 2007, http://www.inc.com.

11. Timmons and Spinelli, *New Venture Creation.*

12. Ibid.

13. Ibid.

14. D. Bricklin, "Natural-Born Entrepreneur," *Harvard Business Review* (September 2001), pp. 53–59, quoting p. 58.

15. Alexandra Levit, "'Insider' Entrepreneurs," *The Wall Street Journal*, April 6, 2009, http://online.wsj.com.

16. "For Zappos, the Next Trend Is More Customized Pages for Customers," *InternetRetailer*, February 12, 2009, http://www.internetretailer.com; M. Chafkin, "How I Did It: Tony Hsieh, CEO, Zappos.com," *Inc.*, September 2006, http://www.inc.com.

17. A. Marsh, "Promiscuous Breeding," *Forbes*, April 7, 1997, pp. 74–77; and J. Nocera, "Fewer Eggs, More Baskets in the Incubator," *New York Times*, October 28, 2006, downloaded from Business & Company Resource Center, http://galenet.galegroup.com.

18. L. Kanter, "The Eco-Advantage," *Inc.*, November 2006, pp. 78–103 (NaturaLawn example on page 84).

19. H. Aldrich, *Ethnic Entrepreneurs: Immigrant Business in Industrial Societies* (Newbury Park, CA: Sage, 1990).

20. R. Flandez, "Immigrants Gain Edge Doing Business Back Home," *The Wall Street Journal*, March 20, 2007, http://online.wsj.com.

21. Timmons and Spinelli, *New Venture Creation.*

22. Michael V. Copeland, "Products for the Other 3 Billion," *Fortune*, April 1, 2009, http://money.cnn.com.

23. J. Collins and J. Porras, *Built to Last* (London: Century, 1996).

24. M. V. Copeland, "Start Last, Finish First," *Business 2.0*, January–February 2006, downloaded from Business & Company Resource Center, http://galenet.galegroup.com.

25. Collins and Porras, *Built to Last.*

26. K. H. Vesper, *New Venture Mechanics* (Englewood Cliffs, NJ: Prentice Hall, 1993).

27. Kanter, "The Eco-Advantage," p. 87.

28. Vesper, *New Venture Mechanics.*

29. Kanter, "The Eco-Advantage," p. 84.

30. J. Berg, "Entrepreneurs Develop Errand Service," *Patriot-News (Harrisburg, PA)*, January 23, 2007, http://galenet.galegroup.com.

31. Kanter, "The Eco-Advantage," p. 84.

32. Timmons and Spinelli, *New Venture Creation.*

33. P. J. Sauer, "Serving Up Success," *Inc.*, January 2007, http://www.inc.com.

34. International Franchise Association, "Study Reveals Significant Growth of Franchising Sector," news release, February 23, 2007, http://www.franchise.org; and International Franchise Association, "The Profile of Franchising: 2006," August 3, 2006, http://www.franchise.org/IndustrySecondary.aspx?id = 31604.

35. K. Spors, "Franchised versus Nonfranchised Businesses," *The Wall Street Journal*, February 27, 2007, http://online.wsj.com.

36. Timmons and Spinelli, *New Venture Creation.*

37. R. Gibson, "Learning from Others' Mistakes," *The Wall Street Journal*, March 19, 2007, http://online.wsj.com.

38. M. V. Copeland and S. Hamner, "The 20 Smartest Companies to Start Now," *Business 2.0*, September 2006, downloaded from General Reference Center Gold, http://find.galegroup.com.

39. A. Pasztor, "Sharper Image Sells New Toy: Zero Gravity's Spacey Flights," *The Wall Street Journal*, March 28, 2007, http://online.wsj.com; and B. Spillman, "Nothing to These Flights," *Las Vegas Review–Journal*, March 5, 2007, downloaded from Business & Company Resource Center, http://galenet.galegroup.com.

40. A. M. Kukec, "Two Start-Ups Get State Boost to Fight Terrorism," *Daily Herald (Arlington, IL)*, January 10, 2006; and T. Walsh, "State Venture Capital to Be Put to Work," *Detroit Free Press*, August 28, 2006, both downloaded from Business & Company Resource Center, http://galenet.galegroup.com.

41. J. E. Lange, "Entrepreneurs and the Continuing Internet: The Expanding Frontier," in Timmons and Spinelli, *New Venture Creation*, pp. 183–220.

42. Ibid.

43. Nielsen//NetRatings, "Resources: Free Data and Rankings," February 2007, http://www.nielsen-netratings.com, accessed April 24, 2007.

44. J. E. Vascellaro, "Selling Your Designs Online," *The Wall Street Journal*, April 5, 2007, http://online.wsj.com.

45. A. Sipress, "The New Dot-Economy," *Washington Post*, December 5, 2006, http://www.washingtonpost.com.

46. Timmons, *New Venture Creation.*

47. J. R. Baum and E. A. Locke, "The Relationship of Entrepreneurial Traits, Skill, and Motivation to Subsequent Venture Growth," *Journal of Applied Psychology* 89 (2004), pp. 587–98.

48. E. Pak, "Twenty-Something Entrepreneurs Are Helping Transform the Surf and Skate Industry," *Orange County Register (Santa Ana, CA)*, February 23, 2007, downloaded from Business & Company Resource Center, http://galenet.galegroup.com.

49. Nocera, "Fewer Eggs, More Baskets."

50. Wilson, "Branson"; Richard Branson, "In Defense of Capitalism," *Mail Online*, September 25, 2008, http://www.dailymail.co.uk; Peter Pae, "Richard Branson Unveils His Space Plane," *Newsday*, July 29, 2008, http://www.newsday.com; Deutschman, "The Enlightenment of Richard Branson"; Farabaugh, "Virgin Group Founder Commits Billions of Dollars."

51. M. Sonfield and R. Lussier, "The Entrepreneurial Strategy Matrix: A Model for New and Ongoing Ventures," *Business Horizons*, May–June 1997, pp. 73–77.

52. D. J. Lynch, "Executive Suite—Today's Entrepreneur: Miami Magnate Gives City a Makeover," *USA Today*, March 11, 2007, http://www.usatoday.com.

53. Lange, "Entrepreneurs and the Continuing Internet."

54. S. Venkataraman and M. Low, "On the Nature of Critical Relationships: A Test of the Liabilities and Size Hypothesis," in *Frontiers of Entrepreneurship Research* (Babson Park, MA: Babson College, 1991), p. 97.

55. Timmons and Spinelli, *New Venture Creation.*

56. P. Hoy, "Most Small Businesses Start without Outside Capital," *Inc.*, October 3, 2006, http://www.inc.com.

57. R. Grant, "The Trade-Offs of Venture Capital," *Mortgage Banking*, February 2007, downloaded from Business & Company Resource Center, http://galenet.galegroup.com.

58. "Just the Facts," *Inc.*, September 2008, http://www.inc.com; and "Start-Up Capital," *Inc.*, September 2008, http://www.inc.com.

59. Cari Tuna, "Tough Call: Deciding to Start a Business," *The Wall Street*

Journal, January 8, 2009, http://online.wsj.com.

60. H. Dietrich, "Worried about Future Viaduct Construction Woes, Sound Sports Is Planning Ahead," *Minneapolis–St. Paul Business Journal*, http://twincities.bizjournals.com, accessed June 14, 2006.

61. L. Buchanan, "Create Jobs, Eliminate Waste, Preserve Value," *Inc.*, December 2006, pp. 94–106.

62. M. V. Copeland, "A Studio System for Startups," *Business 2.0*, May 2007, downloaded from Business & Company Resource Center, http://galenet.galegroup.com.

63. Norm Brodsky, "Street Smarts: Our Irrational Fear of Numbers," *Inc.*, January 2009, http://www.inc.com.

64. Chafkin, "How I Did It."

65. Anjali Cordeiro, "Sweet Returns," *The Wall Street Journal*, April 23, 2009, http://online.wsj.com.

66. Gibson, "Learning from Others' Mistakes."

67. Jacob Stokes, "University of Missouri: A New Life for Old Phones," *Inc.*, March 2009, http://www.inc.com.

68. D. McGinn, "Why Size Matters," *Inc.*, Fall 2004, pp. 32–36.

69. L. Buchanan, "Six Ways to Open an Office Overseas," *Inc.*, April 2007, pp. 120–21.

70. H. Sapienza, E. Autio, G. George, and S. Zahra, "A Capabilities Perspective on the Effects of Early Internationalization on Firm Survival and Growth," *Academy of Management Review* 31, no. 4 (2006), pp. 914–33.

71. B. Burlingham, "How Big Is Big Enough?" *Inc.*, Fall 2004, pp. 40–43.

72. Ibid.

73. Kanter, The Eco-Advantage.

74. W. Harris, "Team Players," *Black Enterprise*, January 2007, downloaded from Business & Company Resource Center, http://galenet.galegroup.com.

75. S. Finkelstein, "The Myth of Managerial Superiority in Internet Startups: An Autopsy," *Organizational Dynamics*, Fall 2001, pp. 172–85.

76. Gangemi, "Young, Fearless, and Smart."

77. J. Melloan. "The Big Picture," *Inc.*, September 2006, http://www.inc.com.

78. R. Weisman, "Bootstrappers Avoid Outside Money Ties," *Boston Globe*, February 5, 2007, downloaded from Business & Company Resource Center, http://galenet.galegroup.com

79. Cordeiro, "Sweet Returns."

80. P. F. Drucker, "How to Save the Family Business," *The Wall Street Journal*, August 19, 1994, p. A10.

81. D. Gamer, R. Owen, and R. Conway, *The Ernst & Young Guide to Raising Capital* (New York: John Wiley & Sons, 1991).

82. Ibid.

83. A. Lustgarten, "Warm, Fuzzy, and Highly Profitable," *Fortune*, November 15, 2004, p. 194.

84. R. D. Hisrich and M. P. Peters, *Entrepreneurship: Starting, Developing, and Managing a New Enterprise* (Burr Ridge, IL: Irwin, 1994).

85. Ibid.

86. W. A. Sahlman, "How to Write a Great Business Plan," *Harvard Business Review*, July–August 1997, pp. 98–108.

87. Ibid.

88. Copeland, "Start Last, Finish First."

89. R. D. Atkinson and D. K. Correa, *The 2007 State New Economy Index* (Ewing Marion Kauffman Foundation and Information Technology and Innovation Foundation, 2007), http://www.kauffman.org; and J. Gangemi, "Ranking the States for the New Economy," *BusinessWeek*, February 27, 2007, http://www.businessweek.com.

90. Sahlman, "How to Write a Great Business Plan."

91. Ibid.

92. M. Zimmerman and G. Zeitz, "Beyond Survival: Achieving New Venture Growth by Building Legitimacy," *Academy of Management Review*, 27 (2002), pp. 414–21.

93. A. L. Stinchcombe, "Social Structure and Organizations," in J. G. March, ed., *Handbook of Organizations* (Chicago: Rand McNally. 1965), pp. 142–93.

94. L. Taylor, "Want Your Start-Up to Be Successful? Appearance Is Everything," *Inc.*, February 23, 2007, http://www.inc.com.

95. Ibid.

96. R. A. Baron and G. D. Markman, "Beyond Social Capital: How Social Skills Can Enhance Entrepreneurs' Success," *Academy of Management Executive*, February 2000, pp. 106–16.

97. J. Florin, M. Lubatkin, and W. Schulze, "A Social Capital Model of High-Growth Ventures," *Academy of Management Journal* 46 (2003), pp. 374–84.

98. E. Ramstad, "In the Land of Conglomerates, Brian Ko Goes His Own Way," *CareerJournal.com*, January 4. 2007, http://www.careerjournal.com.

99. L. Buchanan, "How I Did It: Tim Litle, Chairman, Litle & Co.," *Inc.*, September 2006, http://www.inc.com.

100. Gangemi, "Young, Fearless, and Smart."

101. Ibid.

102. Harris, "Team Players."

103. Ibid.

104. J. Markoff, "Searching for Michael Jordan? Microsoft Wants a Better Way," *New York Times*, March 7, 2007, downloaded from Business & Company Resource Center, http://galenet.galegroup.com; and "Microsoft Researchers Collaborate to Change the World," *Agence France Presse*, March 6, 2007, http://www.afp.com.

105. R. M. Kanter, *The Change Masters* (New York: Simon & Schuster, 1983).

106. D. Kuratko, R. D. Ireland, and J. Hornsby, "Improving Firm Performance through Entrepreneurial Actions: Acordia's Corporate Entrepreneurship Strategy," *Academy of Management Executive* 15 (2001), pp. 60–71.

107. Collins and Porras, *Built to Last*.

108. R. M. Kanter, C. Ingols, E. Morgan, and T. K. Seggerman, "Driving Corporate Entrepreneurship," *Management Review* 76 (April 1987), pp. 14–16.

109. J. Argenti, *Corporate Collapse: The Causes and Symptoms* (New York: John Wiley & Sons, 1979).

110. Kanter et al., "Driving Corporate Entrepreneurship."

111. Yan Ling, Zeki Simsek, Michael Lubatkin, and John Veiga, "Transformational Leadership's Role in Promoting Corporate Entrepreneurship: Examining the CEO–TMT Interface," *Academy of Management Journal*, 2008, pp. 557–76.

112. G. T. Lumpkin and G. G. Dess, "Clarifying the Entrepreneurial Orientation Construct and Linking It to Performance," *Academy of Management Review* 21 (1996), pp. 135–72.

113. Sapienza et al., "A Capabilities Perspective."

114. T. Bateman and J. M. Crant, "The Proactive Dimension of Organizational Behavior," *Journal of Organizational Behavior* (1993), pp. 103–18.

115. Lumpkin and Dess, "Clarifying the Entrepreneurial Orientation Construct."

116. C. Pinchot and E. Pinchot, *The Intelligent Organization* (San Francisco: Barrett-Koehler, 1996).

117. "Virgin Rebirth," *Economist*, September 25, 2008, http://www.economist.com; Pae, "Richard Branson Unveils His Space Plane"; "Virgin Launches New Green Fund," *Environmental Leader*, January 21, 2008. http://www.environmentalleader.com; "Virgin to Test 747 on Biofuel," *Environmental Leader*, October 16, 2007, http://www.environmentalleader.com; "Richard Branson's Latest Venture," *BusinessWeek*, July 25, 2007, http://www.businessweek.com; Specter, "Branson's Luck"; "Virgin Trains Launches Green Marketing Blitz," *Environmental Leader*, March 28, 2007, http://www.environmentalleader.com; Farabaugh. "Virgin Group Founder Commits Billions of Dollars"; "Virgin Group, NTR Form Virgin Bioverda," *Environmental Leader*, January 17, 2007, http://www.environmentalleader.com.

Chapter 8

1. Company Web site, http://www.whirlpoolcorp.com, accessed April 8, 2009; Terry Waghorn, "Making Your Company an Innovation Machine," *Forbes*, January 8, 2009, http://www.forbes.com; Fara Warner,

"Recipe for Growth," *Fast Company*, December 19, 2007, http://www.fastcompany.com.

2. R. N. Ashkenas and S. C. Francis, "Integration Managers: Special Leaders for Special Times," *Harvard Business Review* 78, no. 6 (November–December 2000), pp. 108–16.

3. A. West, "The Flute Factory: An Empirical Measurement of the Effect of the Division of Labor on Productivity and Production Cost," *American Economist* 43, no. 1 (Spring 1999), pp. 82–87.

4. P. Lawrence and J. Lorsch, *Organization and Environment* (Homewood, IL: Richard D. Irwin, 1969).

5. Ibid.; and B. L. Thompson, *The New Manager's Handbook* (New York: McGraw-Hill, 1994). See also S. Sharifi and K. S. Pawar, "Product Design as a Means of Integrating Differentiation," *Technovation* 16, no. 5 (May 1996), pp. 255–64; and W. B. Stevenson and J. M. Bartunek, "Power, Interaction, Position, and the Generation of Cultural Agreement in Organizations," *Human Relations* 49, no. 1 (January 1996), pp. 75–104.

6. P. Puranam, H. Singh, and M. Zollo, "Organizing for Innovation: Managing the Coordination-Autonomy Dilemma in Technology Acquisitions," *Academy of Management Journal* 49, no. 2 (2006), pp. 263–80.

7. A. J. Ali, R. C. Camp, and M. Gibbs, "The Ten Commandments Perspective on Power and Authority in Organizations," *Journal of Business Ethics* 26, no. 4 (August 2000), pp. 351–61; and R. F. Pearse, "Understanding Organizational Power and Influence Systems," *Compensation & Benefits Management* 16, no. 4 (Autumn 2000), pp. 28–38.

8. S. F. Shultz, *Board Book: Making Your Corporate Board a Strategic Force in Your Company's Success* (New York: AMACOM, 2000); and R. D. Ward, *Improving Corporate Boards: The Boardroom Insider Guidebook* (New York: John Wiley & Sons, 2000).

9. D. Jones, "Aflac Will Let Shareholders Vote on Pay for Top Executives," *USA Today*, February 14, 2007, http://www.usatoday.com.

10. T. Perkins, "The 'Compliance Board,'" *The Wall Street Journal*, March 2, 2007, http://online.wsj.com.

11. "Board Membership Profiles Have Changed Sharply over the Past Decade," *Corporate Board*, January–February 2009, downloaded from Business & Company Resource Center, http://galenet.galegroup.com; and Spencer Stuart, *2008 Spencer Stuart Board Index*, November 2008, http://www.spencerstuart.com.

12. Jack Tester, "Who's Your 'Lawnmower'?" *Plumbing and Mechanical*, November 2008, downloaded from Business & Company Resource Center, http://galenet.galegroup.com.

13. C. M. Daily and D. R. Dalton, "CEO and Board Chair Roles Held Jointly or Separately: Much Ado about Nothing?" *Academy of Management Executive* 11, no. 3 (August 1997), pp. 11–20.

14. T. Simons, L. H. Pelled, and K. A. Smith, "Making Use of Difference: Diversity, Debate, and Decision Comprehensiveness in Top Management Teams," *Academy of Management Journal* 42, no. 6 (December 1999), pp. 662–73; and C. Carl Pegels, Y. I Song, and B. Yang, "Management Heterogeneity, Competitive Interaction Groups, and Firm Performance," *Strategic Management Journal* 21, no. 3 (September 2000), pp. 911–21.

15. S. Vickery, C. Droge, and R. Germain, "The Relationship between Product Customization and Organizational Structure," *Journal of Operations Management* 17, no. 4 (June 1999), pp. 377–91.

16. Joel Spolsky, "How Hard Could It Be? How I Learned to Love Middle Managers," *Inc.*, September 2008, http://www.inc.com.

17. D. Van Fleet and A. Bedeian, "A History of the Span of Management," *Academy of Management Review* 2 (1977), pp. 356–72.

18. P. Jehiel, "Information Aggregation and Communication in Organizations," *Management Science* 45, no. 5 (May 1999), pp. 659–69; and A. Altaffer, "First-Line Managers: Measuring Their Span of Control," *Nursing Management* 29, no. 7 (July 1998), pp. 36–40.

19. "Span of Control vs. Span of Support," *Journal for Quality and Participation* 23, no. 4 (Fall 2000), p. 15; J. Gallo and P. R. Thompson, "Goals, Measures, and Beyond: In Search of Accountability in Federal HRM," *Public Personnel Management* 29, no. 2 (Summer 2000), pp. 237–48; C. O. Longenecker and T. C. Stansfield, "Why Plant Managers Fail: Causes and Consequences," *Industrial Management* 42, no. 1 (January/February 2000), pp. 24–32.

20. Z. X. Chen and S. Aryee, "Delegation and Employee Work Outcomes: An Examination of the Cultural Context of Mediating Processes in China," *Academy of Management Journal* 50, no. 1 (2007), pp. 226–38.

21. I. Brat, "Turning Managers into Takeover Artists," *The Wall Street Journal*, April 6, 2007, http://online.wsj.com.

22. "How to Delegate More Effectively," *Community Banker*, February 2009, p. 14; B. Nefer, "Don't Be Delegatin-Phobic," *Supervision*, December 2008, downloaded from Business & Company Resource Center, http://galenet.galegroup.com; J. Mahoney, "Delegating Effectively," *Nursing Management* 28, no. 6 (June 1997), p. 62; and J. Lagges, "The Role of Delegation in Improving Productivity," *Personnel Journal*, November 1979, pp. 776–79.

23. G. Matthews, "Run Your Business or Build an Organization?" *Harvard Management Review*, March–April 1984, pp. 34–44.

24. N. Siggelkow and J. W. Rivkin, "When Exploration Backfires: Unintended Consequences of Multi-level Organizational Search," *Academy of Management Proceedings*, 2006, pp. BB1–BB6.

25. "More Than a Bicycle: The Leadership Journey at Harley-Davidson," *Harvard Business School Working Knowledge*, September 5, 2000, online; C. Fessler, "Rotating Leadership and Harley-Davidson: From Hierarchy to Interdependence," *Strategy & Leadership* 25, no. 4 (July/August 1997), pp. 42–43; and J. Young and K. L. Murrell, "Harley-Davidson Motor Company Organizational Design: The Road to High Performance," *Organizational Development Journal* 16, no. 1 (Spring 1998), p. 65.

26. R. Forrester, "Empowerment: Rejuvenating a Potent Idea," *Academy of Management Executive* 14, no. 3 (August 2000), pp. 67–80; and M. L. Perry, C. L. Pearce, and H. P. Sims Jr., "Empowered Selling Teams: How Shared Leadership Can Contribute to Selling Team Outcomes," *Journal of Personal Selling & Sales Management* 19, no. 3 (Summer 1999), pp. 35–51.

27. Geoff Colvin and Jessica Shambora, "J&J: Secrets of Success," *Fortune*, April 22, 2009, http://money.cnn.com.

28. Larry Gard, "Growth Trifecta," *Construction Today*, January 2009, downloaded from Business & Company Resource Center, http://galenet.galegroup.com; and Environmental Systems Design, "About ESD," corporate Web site, http://www.esdesign.com, accessed May 1, 2009.

29. E. E. Lawler III, "New Roles for the Staff Function: Strategic Support and Services," in *Organizing for the Future*, J. Galbraith, E. E. Lawler III, & Associates (San Francisco: Jossey-Bass, 1993).

30. R. Cross and L. Baird, "Technology Is Not Enough: Improving Performance by Building Organizational Memory," *Sloan Management Review* 41, no. 3 (Spring 2000), pp. 69–78; and R. Duncan, "What Is the Right Organizational Structure?" *Organizational Dynamics* 7 (Winter 1979), pp. 59–80.

31. Company Web site, http://www.astrazeneca-us.com, accessed June 11, 2007; B. Heffernan, "Avoiding Disconnected DTC," *DTC Perspectives*, http://www.dtcperspectives, accessed June 11, 2007; and "Cross-Functional Teams: Collaboration

Best Practices for Pharmaceutical Commercialization Success," *PR Newswire*, May 2, 2007, http://www.prnewswire.com.

32. G. S. Day, "Creating a Market-Driven Organization," *Sloan Management Review* 41, no. 1 (Fall 1999), pp. 11–22.

33. R. Boehm and C. Phipps, "Flatness Forays," *McKinsey Quarterly* 3 (1996), pp. 128–43.

34. B. T. Lamont, V. Sambamurthy, K. M. Ellis, and P. G. Simmonds, "The Influence of Organizational Structure on the Information Received by Corporate Strategists of Multinational Enterprises," *Management International Review* 40, no. 3 (2000), pp. 231–52.

35. Linda A. Johnson, "Pfizer Planning to Redraw Its Battle Lines," *America's Intelligence Wire*, October 8, 2008, downloaded from Business & Company Resource Center, http://galenet.galegroup.com.

36. Morten T. Hansen, "When Internal Collaboration Is Bad for Your Company," *Harvard Business Review*, April 2009, pp. 83–88.

37. W. Bernasco, P. C. de WeerdNederhof, H. Tillema, and H. Boer, "Balanced Matrix Structure and New Product Development Process at Texas Instruments Materials and Controls Division," *R&D Management* 29, no. 2 (April 1999), pp. 121–31; J. K. McCollum, "The Matrix Structure: Bane or Benefit to High Tech Organizations?" *Project Management Journal* 24, no. 2 (June 1993), pp. 23–26; R. C. Ford, "Cross-Functional Structures: A Review and Integration of Matrix," *Journal of Management* 18, no. 2 (June 1992), pp. 267–94; and H. Kolodny, "Managing in a Matrix," *Business Horizons*, March–April 1981, pp. 17–24.

38. D. Cackowski, M. K. Najdawi, and Q. B. Chung, "Object Analysis in Organizational Design: A Solution for Matrix Organizations," *Project Management Journal* 31, no. 3 (September 2000), pp. 44–51; J. Barker, "Conflict Approaches of Effective and Ineffective Project Managers: A Field Study in a Matrix Organization," *Journal of Management Studies* 25, no. 2 (March 1988), pp. 167–78; G. J. Chambers, "The Individual in a Matrix Organization," *Project Management Journal* 20, no. 4 (December 1989), pp. 37–42, 50; and S. Davis and P. Lawrence, "Problems of Matrix Organizations," *Harvard Business Review*, May–June 1978, pp. 131–42.

39. A. Ferner, "Being Local Worldwide: ABB and the Challenge of Global Management Relations," *Industrielles* 55, no. 3 (Summer 2000), pp. 527–29; and C. Bartlett and S. Ghoshal, "Matrix Management: Not a Structure, a Frame of Mind," *Harvard Business Review* 68 (July–August 1990), pp. 138–45.

40. J. Tata, S. Prasad, and R. Thorn, "The Influence of Organizational Structure on the Effectiveness of TQM Programs," *Journal of Managerial Issues* 11, no. 4 (Winter 1999), pp. 440–53; and Davis and Lawrence, "Problems of Matrix Organizations."

41. R. E. Miles and C. C. Snow, *Fit, Failure, and the Hall of Fame* (New York: Free Press, 1994); and G. Symon, "Information and Communication Technologies and Network Organization: A Critical Analysis," *Journal of Occupational and Organizational Psychology* 73, no. 4 (December 2000), pp. 389–95.

42. S. Clifford, "How I Did It: Morgan Lynch, CEO, Logoworks," *Inc.*, September 2006, http://www.inc.com.

43. Miles and Snow, *Fit, Failure, and the Hall of Fame*.

44. S. C. Kang, S. S. Morris, and S. A. Snell, "Relational Archetypes, Organizational Learning, and Value Creation: Extending the Human Resource Architecture," *Academy of Management Review* 32, no. 1 (2007), pp. 236–56.

45. J. G. March and H. A. Simon, *Organizations* (New York: John Wiley & Sons, 1958); and J. D. Thompson, *Organizations in Action* (New York: McGraw-Hill, 1967).

46. P. S. Adler, "Building Better Bureaucracies," *Academy of Management Executive* 13, no. 4 (November 1999), pp. 36–49.

47. Kristen B. Frasch, "Best HR Ideas for 2009," *Human Resource Executive Online*, March 2, 2009, http://www.hreonline.com; Waghorn, "Making Your Company an Innovation Machine"; Jill Rose, "Whirlpool: Nurturing Ideas," *American Executive*, September 30, 2008, http://www.americanexecutive.com; Warner, "Recipe for Growth."

48. D. Tapscott, "The Global Plant Floor," *BusinessWeek*, March 20, 2007, http://galenet.galegroup.com.

49. J. Galbraith, "Organization Design: An Information Processing View," *Interfaces* 4 (Fall 1974), pp. 28–36. See also S. A. Mohrman, "Integrating Roles and Structure in the Lateral Organization," in *Organizing for the Future*, ed. J. Galbraith, E. E. Lawler III, and Associates (San Francisco: Jossey-Bass, 1993); and B. B. Flynn and F. J. Flynn, "Information-Processing Alternatives for Coping with Manufacturing Environment Complexity," *Decision Sciences* 30, no. 4 (Fall 1999), pp. 1021–52.

50. Galbraith, "Organization Design," and Mohrman, "Integrating Roles and Structure."

51. Company Web site, http://www.whirlpoolcorp.com, accessed April 8, 2009; Frasch, "Best HR Ideas for 2009"; "The Issue: Whirlpool Cleans Up Its Supply Chain," *Business Week*, October 24, 2008, http://www.businessweek.com; Rose, "Whirlpool: Nurturing Ideas."

Chapter 9

1. Corning Web site, www.corning.com, accessed April 21, 2009; "A Jolt Brings Corning Back to Its Research Roots," *Associated Press*, January 11, 2009, http://www.tech.yahoo.com; "Fast 50: The World's Most Innovative Companies," *Fast Company*, March 2008; "CEO Brought Corning Back from Death's Door." *USA Today*, February 19, 2007, http://www.usatoday.com.

2. P. M. Wright, L. Dyer, and M. G. Takla, "What's Next? Key Findings from the 1999 State-of-the-Art and Practice Study," *Human Resource Planning* 22, no. 4 (1999), pp. 12–20; and Donald Sull, "How to Thrive in Turbulent Markets," *Harvard Business Review*, February 2009, pp. 78–88.

3. T. Burns and G. Stalker, *The Management of Innovation* (London: Tavistock, 1961).

4. D. Krackhardt and J. R. Hanson, "Information Networks: The Company behind the Chart," *Harvard Business Review*, July–August 1993, pp. 104–11.

5. G. Hamel and C. K. Prahalad, "Competing for the Future," *Harvard Business Review*, July–August 1994, pp. 122–28.

6. G. Hamel and C. K. Prahalad, *Competing for the Future* (Boston: Harvard Business School Press, 1994).

7. "A Jolt Brings Corning Back," *Associated Press*, January 11, 2009; Peter Marsh, "Glassmaker That Expanded with Care," *Financial Times*, November 16, 2008, http://www.ft.com; Rich Smith, "Cross-Examining Corning's Flaws," *Motley Fool*, May 1, 2008, http://www.fool.com; Ann Steffora Mutschler, "Corning Opens China LCD Glass Plant," *Electronic News*, March 28, 2008, http://www.edn.com; "CEO Brought Corning Back," *USA Today*, February 19, 2007; Richard M. Smith, "Q&A: Corning's Comeback CEO," *Newsweek*, January 29, 2007, http://www.newsweek.com.

8. D. G. Sirmon, M. A. Hitt, and R. D. Ireland, "Managing Firm Resources in Dynamic Environments to Create Value: Looking inside the Black Box," *Academy of Management Review* 32, no. 1 (2007), pp. 273–92.

9. "Monster, NYT Form Online Jobs Alliance," *Reuters*, February 14, 2007, http://news.yahoo.com.

10. D. Grossman, "Airline Alliances Aim for Integration," *USA Today*, March 25, 2007, http://www.usatoday.com.

11. Gene Slowinski, Edward Hummel, Amitabh Gupta, and Ernest R. Gilmont, "Effective Practices for Sourcing Innovation," *Research-Technology Management*, January–February 2009, pp. 27–34.

12. R. C. Sampson, "R&D Alliances and Firm Performance: The Impact of Technological Diversity and Alliance Organization on Innovation," *Academy of Management Journal* 50, no. 2 (2007), pp. 364–86.

13. R. M. Kanter, "Collaborative Advantage: The Art of Alliances," *Harvard Business Review,* July–August 1999, pp. 96–108; J. B. Cullen, J. L. Johnson, and T. Sakano, "Success through Commitment and Trust: The Soft Side of Strategic Alliance Management," *Journal of World Business* 35, no. 3 (Fall 2000), pp. 223–40; and P. Kale, H. Singh, and H. Perlmutter, "Learning and Protection of Proprietary Assets in Strategic Alliances: Building Relational Capital," *Strategic Management Journal* 21, no. 3 (March 2000), pp. 217–37.

14. P. Senge, *The Fifth Discipline* (New York: Doubleday Currency, 1990).

15. D. A. Garvin, "Building a Learning Organization," *Harvard Business Review,* July–August 1993, pp. 78–91; D. A. Garvin, *Learning in Action: A Guide to Putting the Learning Organization to Work* (Boston: Harvard Business School Press, 2000); and V. J. Marsick and K. E. Watkins, *Facilitating Learning Organizations: Making Learning Count* (Aldershot, Hampshire: Gower, 1999).

16. Ibid.; and N. Anand, H. K. Gardner, and T. Morris, "Knowledge-Based Innovation: Emergence and Embedding of New Practice Areas in Management Consulting Firms," *Academy of Management Journal* 50, no. 2 (2007), pp. 406–28.

17. R. J. Vandenberg, H. A. Richardson, and L. J. Eastman, "The Impact of High Involvement Work Process on Organizational Effectiveness: A Second-Order Latent Variable Approach," *Group & Organization Management* 24, no. 3 (September 1999), pp. 300–39; G. M. Spreitzer and A. K. Mishra, "Giving Up Control without Losing Control: Trust and Its Substitutes' Effects on Managers' Involving Employees in Decision Making," *Group & Organization Management* 24, no. 2 (June 1999), pp. 155–87; and S. Albers Mohrman, G. E. Ledford, and E. E. Lawler III, *Strategies for High Performance Organizations—The CEO Report: Employee Involvement, TQM, and Reengineering Programs in Fortune 1000 Corporations* (San Francisco: Jossey-Bass, 1998).

18. R. Pagnamenta, "Transformation That Could Rescue Unilever from the Slippery Slope," *The Times (London),* January 3, 2007; and "Unilever on Revival Track after Top Managers Culled," *Evening Standard (London),* May 3, 2007, both downloaded from Business & Company Resource Center, http://galenet.galegroup.com.

19. "Why Big Might Remain Beautiful," *The Economist,* March 24, 1990, p. 79; and W. Zellner, "Go-Go Goliaths," *BusinessWeek,* February 13, 1995, pp. 64–70.

20. A. Bianco, "Wal-Mart's Midlife Crisis," *BusinessWeek,* April 30, 2007, http://www.businessweek.com.

21. Pagnamenta, "Transformation That Could Rescue Unilever."

22. L. L. Hellofs and R. Jacobson, "Market Share and Customers' Perceptions of Quality: When Can Firms Grow Their Way to Higher versus Lower Quality?" *Journal of Marketing* 63, no. 1 (January 1999), pp. 16–25.

23. J. Dean, "The Greatly Improbable, Highly Enjoyable, Increasingly Profitable Life of Michael Kobold," *Inc.,* May 2007, pp. 126–34.

24. Bonnie Del Conte, "Manufacturing Plant as Classroom: Reinventing Continuous Learning," *Plant Engineering,* March 1, 2009, downloaded from Business & Company Resource Center, http://galenet.galegroup.com.

25. V. Vara, "After GE," *The Wall Street Journal,* April 12, 2007, http://online.wsj.com.

26. Ibid.

27. R. Flandez, "The Benefits of Plugging a Big Company's Products," *The Wall Street Journal,* May 8, 2007, http://online.wsj.com.

28. W. F. Cascio, "Downsizing: What Do We Know? What Have We Learned?" *Academy of Management Executive* 7 (February 1993), pp. 95–104; and S. J. Freeman, "The Gestalt of Organizational Downsizing: Downsizing Strategies as Package of Change," *Human Relations* 52, no. 12 (December 1999), pp. 1505–41.

29. Ashlee Vance, "Microsoft Slashes Jobs as Sales Fall," *New York Times,* January 23, 2009, http://www.nytimes.com; Ashlee Vance, "Microsoft Profit Falls for First Time in 23 Years," *New York Times,* April 24, 2009, http://www.nytimes.com; and Peter Kafka, "Microsoft Starts the Layoff Machine Again with Thousands of Cuts," *All Things Digital,* http://mediamemo.allthingsd.com.

30. W. F. Cascio, "Strategies for Responsible Restructuring," *Academy of Management Executive* 19, no. 4 (2005), pp. 39–50; Cascio, "Downsizing: What Do We Know?"; Freeman, "The Gestalt of Organizational Downsizing"; and M. Hitt, B. Keats, H. Harback, and R. Nixon, "Rightsizing: Building and Maintaining Strategic Leadership and Long-Term Competitiveness," *Organizational Dynamics,* Fall 1994, pp. 18–31.

31. C. D. Zatzick and R. D. Iverson, "High-Involvement Management and Workforce Reduction: Competitive Advantage or Disadvantage?" *Academy of Management Journal* 49, no. 5 (2006), pp. 999–1015.

32. Cascio, "Strategies for Responsible Restructuring"; Cascio, "Downsizing"; and J. Ciancio, "Survivor's Syndrome," *Nursing Management* 31, no. 5 (May 2000), pp. 43–45.

33. K. Ohmae, *The Mind of the Strategist: Business Planning for Competitive Advantage* (New York: Penguin Books, 1982), Chap. 8; H. Stern, "Succeeding in a 'Customer-Centric' Economy," *Foodservice Equipment & Supplies* 53, no. 10 (September 2000), pp. 27–28.

34. "CRM's Net Generation: Service, Analytics," *American Banker,* February 20, 2007, http://galenet.galegroup.com.

35. Claes Fornell, "ACSI Rises as the Economy Weakens: What Does It Mean?" *ACSI Quarterly Commentaries,* Q4 2008, American Customer Satisfaction Index Web site, http://www.theacsi.org, February 17, 2009; and American Customer Satisfaction Index, "National Quarterly Scores," ACSI Web site, http://wwwtheacsi.org, accessed May 6, 2009.

36. "Salesforce.com Offers Twitter Customer-Service App," *Information Week,* March 23, 2009, downloaded from Business & Company Resource Center, http://galenet.galegroup.com; and Ernest Beck, "Daptiv's Greenhouse: Collaboration Grows," *BusinessWeek Online,* June 12, 2008, Business & Company Resource Center, http://galenet.galegroup.com.

37. K. Ishikawa, *What Is Total Quality Control? The Japanese Way,* trans. David J. Lu (Englewood Cliffs, NJ: Prentice-Hall, 1985); and J. Seibert and J. Lingle, "Internal Customer Service: Has It Improved?" *Quality Progress* 40, no. 3 (March 2007), downloaded from OCLC FirstSearch, http://firstsearch.oclc.org.

38. M. Porter, *Competitive Advantage: Creating and Sustaining Superior Performance* (New York: Free Press, 1985); and Internet Center for Management and Business Administration, "The Value Chain," Strategy pages, *NetMBA,* http://www.netmba.com, accessed May 7, 2007.

39. B. Creech, *The Five Pillars of TQM: How to Make Total Quality Management Work for You* (New York: Plume Publishing, 1995); and J. R. Evans and W. M. Lindsay, *Management and Control of Quality* (Mason, OH: South-Western College Publishing, 1998).

40. K. Richardson, "The 'Six Sigma' Factor for Home Depot," *The Wall Street Journal,* January 4, 2007, http://online.wsj.com.

41. Baldrige National Quality Program, *Criteria for Performance Excellence,* 2007, National Institute of Standards and Technology (NIST), http://www.quality.nist.gov, accessed May 4, 2007; and National Institute of Standards and Technology, "Three to Receive Presidential Award for Excellence," news release, November 21, 2006, http://www.nist.gov.

42. International Organization for Standardization, "ISO 9000/ISO 14000: Understand the Basics," http://www.iso.org, accessed May 7, 2007.

43. "UniFirst Manufacturing Facilities Awarded ISO 9001:2000 Certification," *Modern Uniforms,* February–March 2006; and J. M. Levett, "Implementing

an ISO 9001 Quality Management System in a Multispecialty Clinic," *Physician Executive*, November–December 2005, both downloaded from Business & Company Resource Center, http://galenet.galegroup.com.

44. J. Champy, *Reengineering Management* (New York: HarperBusiness, 1995). See also M. Hammer and J. Champy, *Reengineering the Corporation* (New York: HarperCollins, 1992).

45. J. Woodward, *Industrial Organization: Theory and Practice* (London: Oxford University Press, 1965).

46. J. H. Gilmore and B. J. Pine, eds., *Markets of One: Creating Customer-Unique Value through Mass Customization* (Cambridge, MA: Harvard Business Review Press, 2000); and B. J. Pine, *Mass Customization: The New Frontier in Business Competition* (Cambridge, MA: Harvard Business School Press, 1992).

47. F. Sahin, "Manufacturing Competitiveness: Different Systems to Achieve the Same Results," *Production and Inventory Management Journal* 41, no. 1 (First Quarter 2000), pp. 56–65.

48. S. Wadhwa and K. S. Rao, "Flexibility: An Emerging Meta-Competence for Managing High Technology," *International Journal of Technology Management* 19, no. 7–8 (2000), pp. 820–45.

49. B. A. Peters and L. F. McGinnis, "Strategic Configuration of Flexible Assembly Systems: A Single Period Approximation," *IIE Transaction* 31, no. 4 (April 1999), pp. 379–90.

50. J. K. Liker and J. M. Morgan, "The Toyota Way in Services: The Case of Lean Product Development," *Academy of Management Perspectives* 20, no. 2 (May 2006), pp. 5–20; "Strategic Reconfiguration: Manufacturing's Key Role in Innovation," *Production and Inventory Management Journal* (Summer–Fall 2001), pp. 9–17; S. R. Morrey, "Learning to Think Lean: A Roadmap and Toolbox for the Lean Journey," *Automotive Manufacturing & Production* 112, no. 8 (August 2000), p. 147; and Sahin, "Manufacturing Competitiveness."

51. Liker and Morgan, "The Toyota Way in Services"; and H. Cho, "Squeezing the Fat from Health Care," *Baltimore Sun*, September 17, 2006, downloaded from Business & Company Resource Center, http://galenet.galegroup.com.

52. Sahin, "Manufacturing Competitiveness"; and G. S. Vasilash, "Flexible Thinking: How Need, Innovation, Teamwork & a Whole Bunch of Machining Centers Have Transformed TRW Tillsonburg into a Model of Lean Manufacturing," *Automotive Manufacturing & Production* 111, no. 10 (October 1999), pp. 64–65.

53. Timothy Aeppel and Justin Lahart, "Lean Factories Find It Hard to Cut Jobs Even in a Slump," *The Wall Street Journal*, March 9, 2009, http://online.wsj.com.

54. C. H. Chung, "Balancing the Two Dimensions of Time for Time-Based Competition," *Journal of Managerial Issues* 11, no. 3 (Fall 1999), pp. 299–314; and D. R. Towill and P. McCullen, "The Impact of Agile Manufacturing on Supply Chain Dynamics," *International Journal of Logistics Management* 10, no. 1 (1999), pp. 83–96. See also G. Stalk and T. M. Hout, *Competing against Time: How Time-Based Competition Is Reshaping Global Markets* (New York: Free Press, 1990).

55. M. Hayes Weier, "Best Buy Sees a Growth Future in RFID," *EE Times*, March 27, 2007, http://www.eetimes.com.

56. A. M. Field, "Where Have All the Flowers Gone?" *Journal of Commerce*, April 16, 2007, downloaded from Business & Company Resource Center, http://galenet.galegroup.com.

57. M. Tucker and D. Davis, "Key Ingredients for Successful Implementation of Just-in-Time: A System for All Business Sizes," *Business Horizons*, May–June 1993, pp. 59–65; H. L. Richardson, "Tame Supply Chain Bottlenecks," *Transportation & Distribution* 41, no. 3 (March 2000), pp. 23–28.

58. C. Robbins Gentry, "Back-Room Secrets: Just-in-Time Deliveries Optimize Space," *Chain Store Age*, March 2007, downloaded from Business & Company Resource Center, http://galenet.galegroup.com.

59. See, for example, "Just-in-Time: Has Its Time Passed?" *Baseline*, September 11, 2006, downloaded from Business & Company Resource Center, http://galenet.galegroup.com.

60. J. E. Ettlie, "Product Development—Beyond Simultaneous Engineering," *Automotive Manufacturing & Production* 112, no. 7 (July 2000), p. 18; U. Roy, J. M. Usher, and H. R. Parsaei, eds. *Simultaneous Engineering: Methodologies and Applications* (Newark, NJ: Gordon and Breach, 1999); and M. M. Helms and L. P. Ettkin, "Time-Based Competitiveness: A Strategic Perspective," *Competitiveness Review* 10, no. 2 (2000), pp. 1–14.

61. J. Zygmont, "Detroit Faster on Its Feet," *Ward's Auto World*, July 1, 2006, downloaded from Business & Company Resource Center, http://galenet.galegroup.com.

62. R. Ashkenas, D. Ulrich, T. Jick, and S. Kerr, *The Boundaryless Organization: Breaking the Chains of Organizational Structure* (San Francisco: Jossey-Bass, 1995); R. W. Keidel, "Rethinking Organizational Design," *Academy of Management Executive*, November 1994, pp. 12–27; and R. Ashkenas, T. Jick, D. Ulrich, and C. Paul-Chowdhury, *The Boundaryless Organization Field Guide: Practical Tools for Building the New Organization* (San Francisco: Jossey-Bass, 1999).

63. "With 3,500 Layoffs, Corning Is Latest to Cut Jobs," *Reuters*, January 27, 2009, http://www.nytimes.com; "Corning Seeks New Venture in Mercury Filters," *RedOrbit*, January 12, 2009, http://www.redorbit.com; "A Jolt Brings Corning Back," *Associated Press*, January 11, 2009; Ben Dobbin, "Corning Lowers 4Q Profit Outlook," *USA Today*, November 18, 2008, http://www.usatoday.com; Marsh, "Glassmaker That Expanded with Care"; Rich Smith, "Corning Creamed," *Motley Fool*, September 4, 2008, http://www.fool.com; Rich Smith, "A Steady Picture at Corning," *Motley Fool*, August 1, 2008, http://www.fool.com; Scott Montz, "Corning Sees No Slowdown in the Big Picture," *CNNMoney*, July 30, 2008, http://money.cnn.com; Smith, "Cross-Examining Corning's Flaws"; "CEO Brought Corning Back," *USA Today*, February 19, 2007; Smith, "Q&A: Corning's Comeback CEO."

Chapter 10

1. Company Web site, http://www.erac.com, accessed November 7, 2008; Enterprise Rent-A-Car, "Enterprise Rent-A-Car's Pam Nicholson Named to *Fortune*'s 50 Most Powerful Women in Business 2008," news release, September 29, 2008; "Breaking Barriers: Enterprise Rent-A-Car's Pam Nicholson," *The Wall Street Journal*, August 4, 2008, http://www.wsj.com; Alison Stein Wellner, "Nothing but Green Skies," *Inc.*, November 2007, http://www.inc.com; "Mentoring Is a Mission at Enterprise Rent-A-Car," *Diversity in Action*, April/May 2007, http://www.diversitycareers.com.

2. "How Strategic Is HR Now?" *HR Focus*, December 2006, downloaded from Business & Company Resource Center, http://galenet.galegroup.com.

3. "HR's Impact on Shareholder Value," *Workforce Management*, December 11, 2006, downloaded from Business & Company Resource Center, http://galenet.galegroup.com.

4. P. M. Wright and S. A. Snell, "Partner or Guardian? HR's Challenge in Balancing Value and Values," *Human Resource Management* 44, no. 2 (2005), pp. 177–82.

5. Elaine Pofeldt, "Empty Desk Syndrome: How to Handle a Hiring Freeze," *Inc.*, May 2008, pp. 39–40; and Cari Tuna, "Some Employers See Hiring Opportunity," *The Wall Street Journal*, April 3, 2009, http://online.wsj.com.

6. J. Hopkins, "Small Employers Struggle to Fill Jobs," *USA Today*, January 4, 2007, http://www.usatoday.com; "Most Employers Unprepared for Baby Boomer Retirements"; *CCH Pension*, November 9, 2006, http://hr.cch.com, reporting on a survey of about 100 organizations by ClearRock; and

D. Ellwood, *Grow Faster Together, or Grow Slowly Apart* (Washington, DC: Aspen Institute, 2003), http://www.aspeninstitute.org.

7. S. Lohr, "Parsing the Truths about Visas for Tech Workers," *New York Times*, April 15, 2007, http://www.nytimes.com; "Does Silicon Valley Need More Visas for Foreigners?" *The Wall Street Journal*, March 19, 2007 (interview with Robert Hoffman and Ron Hira), http://online.wsj.com; P. Elstrom, "Work Visas May Work against the U.S.," *BusinessWeek*, February 8, 2007, http://www.businessweek.com; and A. Broache, "Does H-1B Surge Mean Cap Should Be Raised?" *CNet News*, April 5, 2007, http://news.com.com.

8. J. Marquez, "Retrained and Ready," *Workforce Management*, May 7, 2007, http://galenet.galegroup.com.

9. D. E. Hartley, *Job Analysis at the Speed of Reality* (Amherst, MA: HRD Press, 1999); F. P. Morgeson and M. A. Campion, "Accuracy in Job Analysis: Toward an Inference-Based Model," *Journal of Organizational Behavior* 21, no. 7 (November 2000), pp. 819–27; and J. S. Shippmann, R. A. Ash, L. Carr, and B. Hesketh, "The Practice of Competency Modeling," *Personnel Psychology* 53, no. 3 (Autumn 2000), pp. 703–40.

10. J. S. Schippmann, *Strategic Job Modeling: Working at the Core of Integrated Human Resources* (Mahwah, NJ: Lawrence Erlbaum Associates, 1999).

11. D. E. Terpstra, "The Search for Effective Methods," *HR Focus*, May 1996, pp. 16–17; H. G. Heneman III and R. A. Berkley, "Applicant Attraction Practices and Outcomes among Small Businesses," *Journal of Small Business Management* 37, no. 1 (January 1999), pp. 53–74; and J.-M. Hiltrop, "The Quest for the Best: Human Resource Practices to Attract and Retain Talent," *European Management Journal* 17, no. 4 (August 1999), pp. 422–30.

12. G. Ruiz, "Print Ads See Resurgence as Hiring Source," *Workforce Management*, March 26, 2007; and G. Ruiz, "Recruiters Cite Referrals as Top Hiring Tool," *Workforce Management*, October 23, 2006, both downloaded from General Reference Center Gold, http://find.galegroup.com.

13. F. Hansen, "Employee Referral Programs, Selective Campus Recruitment Could Touch Off Bias Charges," *Workforce Management*, June 26, 2006, downloaded from General Reference Center Gold, http://find.galegroup.com.

14. Ruiz, "Recruiters Cite Referrals," reporting data from a survey by ERE Media and Classified Intelligence.

15. P. Sellers, "Schooling Corporate Giants in Recruiting," *Fortune*, December 6, 2006, http://money.cnn.com.

16. R. Myers, "Interviewing Techniques: Tips from the Pros," *Journal of Accountancy* (August 2006), downloaded from Business & Company Resource Center, http://galenet.galegroup.com; M. McDaniel, D. L. Whetzel, F. L. Schmidt, and S. D. Maurer, "The Validity of Employment Interviews: A Comprehensive Review and Meta-Analysis," *Journal of Applied Psychology* 79, no. 4 (August 1994), pp. 599–616; M. A. Campion, J. E. Campion, and P. J. Hudson Jr., "Structured Interviewing: A Note on Incremental Validity and Alternative Question Types," *Journal of Applied Psychology* 79, no. 6 (December 1994), pp. 998–1002; and R. A. Fear, *The Evaluation Interview* (New York: McGraw-Hill, 1984).

17. Myers, "Interviewing Techniques."

18. U.S. Merit Systems Protection Board, "The Federal Selection Interview: Unrealized Potential," February 2003, mspb.gov/studies/interview.htm.

19. T. Lewin, "Dean at M.I.T. Resigns, Ending a 28-Year Lie," *New York Times*, April 27, 2007, http://www.nytimes.com.

20. C. E. Stenberg, "The Role of Pre-Employment Background Investigations in Hiring," *Human Resource Professional* 9, no. 1 (January/February 1996), pp. 19–21; P. Taylor, "Providing Structure to Interviews and Reference Checks," *Workforce*, May 1999, Supplement, pp. 7–10; "Fear of Lawsuits Complicates Reference Checks," *InfoWorld* 21, no. 5 (February 1, 1999), p. 73; D. E. Terpstra, R. B. Kethley, R. T. Foley, and W. Limpaphayom, "The Nature of Litigation Surrounding Five Screening Devices," *Public Personnel Management* 29, no. 1 (Spring 2000), pp. 43–54.

21. C. Bigda, "Web Widens Job-Search Connections," *Chicago Tribune*, March 4, 2007, http://www.chicagotribune.com.

22. See also M. R. Barrick and M. K. Mount, "The Big Five Personality Dimensions and Job Performance: A Meta-Analysis," *Personnel Psychology* 44 (1991), pp. 1–26; D. P. O'Meara, "Personality Tests Raise Questions of Legality and Effectiveness," *HRMagazine*, January 1994, pp. 97–100; and L. A. McFarland and A. M. Ryan, "Variance in Faking across Noncognitive Measures," *Journal of Applied Psychology* 85, no. 5 (October 2000), pp. 812–21.

23. R. E. Ployhart, J. A. Weekley, and K. Baughman, "The Structure and Function of Human Capital Emergence: A Multilevel Examination of the Attraction-Selection-Attrition Model," *Academy of Management Journal* 49, no. 4 (2006), pp. 661–77.

24. "Fewer Employers Are Currently Conducting Psych & Drug Tests," *HR Focus* 77, no. 10 (October 2000), p. 8; D. R. Comer, "Employees' Attitudes toward Fitness-for-Duty Testing," *Journal of Managerial Issues* 12, no. 1 (Spring 2000), pp. 61–75; and "ACLU Report Debunks Workplace Drug Testing," *HR Focus* 76, no. 4 (November 1999), p. 4.

25. P. M. Wright, M. K. Kacmar, G. C. McMahan, and K. Deleeuw, "$P = f(M \times A)$: Cognitive Ability as a Moderator of the Relationship between Personality and Job Performance," *Journal of Management* 21, no. 6 (1995), pp. 1129–2063; P. R. Sackett and D. J. Ostgaard, "Job-Specific Applicant Pools and National Norms for Cognitive Ability Tests: Implications for Range Restriction Corrections in Validation Research," *Journal of Applied Psychology* 79, no. 5 (October 1994), pp. 680–84; F. L. Schmidt and J. E. Hunter, "Tacit Knowledge, Practical Intelligence, General Mental Ability, and Job Knowledge," *Current Directions in Psychological Science* 2, no. 1 (1993), pp. 3–13; M. Roznowski, D. N. Dickter, L. L. Sawin, V. J. Shute, and S. Hong, "The Validity of Measures of Cognitive Processes and Generability for Learning and Performance on Highly Complex Computerized Tutors: Is the G Factor of Intelligence Even More General?" *Journal of Applied Psychology* 85, no. 6 (December 2000), pp. 940–55; and J. M. Cortina, N. B. Goldstein, S. C. Payne, H. K. Davison, and S. W. Gilliland, "The Incremental Validity of Interview Scores over and above Cognitive Ability and Conscientiousness Scores," *Personnel Psychology* 53, no. 2 (Summer 2000), pp. 325–51.

26. W. Arthur Jr., D. J. Woehr, and R. Maldegen, "Convergent and Discriminant Validity of Assessment Center Dimensions: A Conceptual and Empirical Reexamination of the Assessment Center Construct-Related Validity Paradox," *Journal of Management* 26, no. 4 (2000), pp. 813–35; and R. Randall, E. Ferguson, and F. Patterson, "Self-Assessment Accuracy and Assessment Center Decisions," *Journal of Occupational and Organizational Psychology* 73, no. 4 (December 2000), p. 443.

27. McFarland and Ryan, "Variance in Faking across Noncognitive Measures"; and Terpstra et al., "The Nature of Litigation Surrounding Five Screening Devices."

28. D. S. Ones, C. Viswesvaran, and F. L. Schmidt, "Comprehensive Meta-Analysis of Integrity Test Validities: Findings and Implications for Personnel Selection and Theories of Job Performance," *Journal of Applied Psychology* 78 (August 1993), pp. 679–703.

29. N. R. Kuncel, M. Credé, and L. L. Thomas, "A Meta-analysis of the

Predictive Validity of the Graduate Management Admission Test (GMAT) and Undergraduate Grade Point Average (UGPA) for Graduate Student Academic Performance," *Academy of Management Learning and Education* 6, no. 1 (2007), pp. 51–68.

30. R.-L. DeWitt, "The Structural Consequences of Downsizing," *Organization Science* 4, no. 1 (February 1993), pp. 30–40; and P. P. Shah, "Network Destruction: The Structural Implications of Downsizing," *Academy of Management Journal* 43, no. 1 (February 2000), pp. 101–12.

31. See *Adair v. United States*, 2078 U.S. 161 (1908); and D. A. Ballam, "Employment-at-Will: The Impending Death of a Doctrine," *American Business Law Journal* 37, no. 4 (Summer 2000), pp. 653–87.

32. Jonathan A. Segal, "A Warning about Warnings," *HR Magazine*, February 2009, pp. 67–70; International Public Management Association for Human Resources (IPMA-HR), "Progressive Discipline," IPMA-HR Web site, http://www.ipma-hr.org, accessed May 8, 2009; U.S. Chamber of Commerce, "Progressive Discipline," http://business.uschamber.com, accessed May 8, 2009; and Dick Grote, "Positive Approach to Employee Discipline," *ManagerNewz*, March 12, 2007, http://archive.managernewz.com.

33. James W. Bucking, "Employee Terminations: Ten Must-Do Steps When Letting Someone Go," *Supervision*, May 2008, downloaded from Business & Company Resource Center, http://galenet.galegroup.com; and Marie Price, "Employee Termination Process Is Tough for Those on Both Sides," *Journal Record (Oklahoma City, OK)*, October 23, 2008, Business & Company Resource Center, http://galenet.galegroup.com.

34. *Employer EEO Responsibilities* (Washington, DC: Equal Employment Opportunity Commission, U.S. Government Printing Office, 1996); N. J. Edman and M. D. Levin-Epstein, *Primer of Equal Employment Opportunity*, 6th ed. (Washington, DC: Bureau of National Affairs, 1994).

35. Reuters, "Wal-Mart Settles Lawsuit on Hiring," *New York Times*, February 21, 2009, http://www.nytimes.com; Thomas L. Gallagher, "UP Settles Discrimination Suit," *Traffic World*, February 4, 2009, downloaded from Business & Company Resource Center, http://galenet.galegroup.com; and Amy Martinez, "Nordstrom Agrees to Pay to Settle Harassment Suit," *Seattle Times*, April 18, 2009, downloaded from Business & Company Resource Center, http://galenet.galegroup.com.

36. R. Gatewood and H. Field, *Human Resource Selection*, 3rd ed. (Chicago: Dryden Press, 1994), pp. 36–49; and R. A. Baysinger, "Disparate Treatment and Disparate Impact Theories of

Discrimination: The Continuing Evolution of Title VII of the 1964 Civil Rights Act," in *Readings in Personnel and Human Resource Management*, ed. R. S. Schuler, S. A. Youngblood, and V. L. Huber (St. Paul, MN: West Publishing, 1987).

37. "$56 Billion Budgeted for Formal Training," *Training*, December 2006, downloaded from General Reference Center Gold, http://find.galegroup.com.

38. A. P. Carnevale, *America and the New Economy: How New Competitive Standards Are Radically Changing American Workplaces* (San Francisco: Jossey-Bass, 1991); M. Hequet, "Doing More with Less," *Training* 31 (October 1995), pp. 77–82; and R. M. Fulmer, P. A. Gibbs, and M. Goldsmith, "Developing Leaders: How Winning Companies Keep on Winning," *Sloan Management Review* 42, no. 1 (Fall 2000), pp. 49–59.

39. G. Anders, "Companies Find Online Training Has Its Limits," *The Wall Street Journal*, March 26, 2007, http://online.wsj.com.

40. Ibid.

41. J. Gordon, "Building Brand Champions: How Training Helps Drive a Core Business Process at General Mills," *Training*, January–February 2007, downloaded from General Reference Center Gold, http://find.galegroup.com.

42. Phred Dvorak, "Simulation Shows What It's Like to Be Boss," *The Wall Street Journal*, March 31, 2008, http://online.wsj.com.

43. For more information, see K. Wexley and G. Latham, *Increasing Productivity through Performance Appraisal* (Reading, MA: Addison-Wesley, 1994).

44. F. Shipper, R. C. Hoffman, and D. M. Rotondo, "Does the 360 Feedback Process Create Actionable Knowledge Equally across Cultures?" *Academy of Management Learning & Education* 6, no. 1 (2007), pp. 33–50.

45. G. Toegel and J. Conger, "360 Degree Assessment: Time for Reinvention," *Academy of Management Learning and Education* 2, no. 3 (September 2003), p. 297; L. K. Johnson, "Retooling 360s for Better Performance," *Harvard Business School Working Knowledge*, February 23, 2004, online.

46. M. Edwards and A. J. Ewen, "How to Manage Performance and Pay with 360-Degree Feedback," *Compensation and Benefits Review* 28, no. 3 (May/June 1996), pp. 41–46. See also M. N. Vinson, "The Pros and Cons of 360-Degree Feedback: Making It Work," *Training and Development* 50, no. 4 (April 1996), pp. 11–12; and R. S. Schuler, *Personnel and Human Resource Management* (St. Paul, MN: West Publishing, 1984).

47. P. Capell, "When an Employee Is a Problem Drinker," *Career Journal*, December 5, 2006, http://www.careerjournal.com.

48. C. Hymowitz, "Bosses Have to Learn How to Confront Troubled Employees," *The Wall Street Journal*, April 23, 2007, http://online.wsj.com.

49. U.S. Census Bureau, *Statistical Abstract of the United States*, 2007, p. 418; and Bureau of Labor Statistics, *Charting the U.S. Labor Market in 2005*, June 2006, http://www.bls.gov.

50. D. Darlin, "Using the Web to Get the Boss to Pay More," *New York Times*, March 3, 2007, http://www.nytimes.com.

51. A. Colella, R. L. Paetzold, A. Zardkoohi, and M. J. Wesson, "Exposing Pay Secrecy," *Academy of Management Review* 32, no. 1 (2007), pp. 55–71.

52. E. M. Ritzky, "Incentive Pay Programs That Help the Bottom Line," *HRMagazine* 40, no. 4 (April 1995), pp. 68–74; S. Gross and J. Bacher, "The New Variable Pay Programs: How Some Succeed, Why Some Don't," *Compensation and Benefits Review* 25, no. 1 (January–February 1993), p. 51; and G. T. Milkovich and J. M. Newman, *Compensation* (New York: McGraw-Hill/Irwin, 1999).

53. K. Maher and K. Hudson, "Wal-Mart to Sweeten Bonus Plans for Staff," *The Wall Street Journal*, March 22, 2007, http://online.wsj.com.

54. T. Welbourne and L. Gomez-Mejia, "Gainsharing: A Critical Review and a Future Research Agenda," *Journal of Management* 21, no. 3 (1995), pp. 559–609; L. P. Gomez-Mejia, T. M. Welbourne, and R. M. Wiseman, "The Role of Risk Sharing and Risk Taking under Gainsharing," *Academy of Management Review* 25, no. 3 (July 2000), pp. 492–507; D. Collins, *Gainsharing and Power: Lessons from Six Scanlon Plans* (Ithaca, NY: ILR Press, 1998); and P. K. Zingheim and J. R. Schuster, *Pay People Right!* (San Francisco: Jossey-Bass, 2000).

55. "Top Entry Level Employers," *CollegeGrad.com*, accessed November 7, 2008, http://www.collegegrad.com; David LaGesse, "A 'Stealth Company' No Longer," *U.S. News & World Report*, October 27, 2008, http://www.usnews.com; Patricia Sellers, "A Powerful Woman Revs Ahead at Enterprise," *Fortune*, August 4, 2008, http://www.fortune.com; Lindsey Edmonds Wickman, "Enterprise Rent-A-Car: Ahead of the Curve with Personalized Recruitment," *Talent Management* [no date], http://www.talentmgt.com; "Mentoring Is a Mission," *Diversity in Action*.

56. J. Marquez, "Many Businesses, but One Mission," *Workforce Management*, June 12, 2006, http://galenet.galegroup.com.

57. E. Grossfield, "Superintendent Gets a Good Review and Partial Bonus," *Post-Bulletin (Rochester, MN)*, July 13, 2006, downloaded from Business & Company Resource Center, http://galenet.galegroup.com. See also

D. W. Meyers. *Human Management: Principles and Practice* (Chicago: Commerce Clearing House, 1986); and J. P. Guthrie, "Alternative Pay Practices and Employee Turnover: An Organization Economics Perspective," *Group & Organization Management 25*, no. 4 (December 2000), pp. 419–39.

58. R. Kirkland, "The Real CEO Pay Problem," *Fortune*, July 10, 2006, downloaded from Business & Company Resource Center, http://galenet. galegroup.com; K. Drawbaugh, "Soaring Executive Pay Meets Reforms," *Reuters*, March 9, 2007, http://news.yahoo.com; R. Watts and D. Roberts, "FTSE Pay Spirals out of Control," *Sunday Telegraph (London)*, September 24, 2006, http://galenet. galegroup.com; "Study: Australian Execs Outstrip Workers," *UPI NewsTrack*, January 28, 2006, http:// galenet.galegroup.com; and M. Fackler and D. Barboza, "In Asia, Executives Earn Much Less," *New York Times*, June 16, 2006, http://galenet.galegroup. com.

59. M. J. Conyon, "Executive Compensation and Incentives," *Academy of Management Perspectives 20*, no. 1 (February 2006), pp. 25–44.

60. Ibid.

61. C. Forelle and J. Bandler, "The Perfect Payday," *The Wall Street Journal*, March 18, 2006, http://online.wsj.com.

62. Conyon, "Executive Compensation and Incentives."

63. Jonathan D. Glater, "Stock Options Are Adjusted after Many Share Prices Fall," *New York Times*, March 27, 2009, http://www.nytimes.com; and David Nicklaus, "Worthless Options Worry Companies," *St. Louis Post-Dispatch*, April 3, 2009, downloaded from Business & Company Resource Center, http://galenet.galegroup.com.

64. A. Murray, "Why Taxpayers Should Take Note of Chrysler Deal," *The Wall Street Journal*, May 16, 2007, http:// online.wsj.com; and K. Kingsbury, "Pressure on Your Health Benefits," *Time*, November 6, 2006, downloaded from Business & Company Resource Center, http://galenet.galegroup.com.

65. D. Cauchon, "Pension Gap Divides Public and Private Workers," *USA Today*, February 21, 2007, http://www. usatoday.com.

66. Employee Benefit Research Institute, "Employer Spending on Health Insurance," in *EBRI Databook on Employee Benefits*, updated March 2009, http://www.ebri.org.

67. E. C. Kearns and M. Gallagher, eds., *The Fair Labor Standards Act* (Washington, DC: BNA, 1999).

68. C. Fay and H. W. Risher, "Contractors, Comparable Worth and the New OFCCP: Deja Vu and More," *Compensation and Benefits Review 32*, no. 5 (September/October 2000), pp. 23–33; and G. Flynn, "Protect Yourself from an Equal-Pay Audit,"

Workforce 78, no. 6 (June 1999), pp. 144–46.

69. G. W. Bohlander, S. A. Snell, and A. W. Sherman Jr., *Managing Human Resources*, 12th ed. (Mason, OH: South-Western Publishing, 2001).

70. E. Henry, "Wage-Bias Bill: Study Panel Proposed," *Arizona Business Gazette*, February 28, 2002, pp. 2–4; S. E. Gardner and C. Daniel, "Implementing Comparable Worth/Pay Equity: Experiences of Cutting-Edge States," *Public Personnel Management 27*, no. 4 (Winter 1998), pp. 475–89.

71. P. Wingert and A. Campo-Flores, "A Dark Place," *Newsweek*, January 16, 2006; and A. Young, "Mining Regulators to Increase Fines for Safety Violations," *Knight Ridder Washington Bureau*, February 16, 2006, both downloaded from General Reference Center Gold, http://find.galegroup. com.

72. Mine Safety and Health Administration, "MSHA Fatality Statistics," http:// www.msha.gov, accessed May 15, 2007.

73. "U.S. Teens Work Late, Long and in Danger, Study," *Reuters*, March 5, 2007, http://news.yahoo.com; and C. K. Johnson, "Teens Tell about On-the-Job Dangers," *Chicago Tribune*, March 5, 2007, http://www.chicagotribune.com.

74. L. Kahn, *Primer of Labor Relations*, 25th ed. (Washington, DC: Bureau of National Affairs Books, 1994); and A. Sloane and F. Witney, *Labor Relations* (Englewood Cliffs, NJ: Prentice-Hall, 1985).

75. S. Premack and J. E. Hunter; "Individual Unionization Decisions," *Psychological Bulletin 103* (1988), pp. 223–34; L. Troy, *Beyond Unions and Collective Bargaining* (Armonk, NY: M. E. Sharpe, 1999); and J. A. McClendon, "Members and Nonmembers: Determinants of Dues-Paying Membership in a Bargaining Unit," *Relations Industrielles 55*, no. 2 (Spring 2000), pp. 332–47.

76. R. Sinclair and L. Tetrick, "Social Exchange and Union Commitment: A Comparison of Union Instrumentality and Union Support Perceptions," *Journal of Organizational Behavior 16*, no. 6 (November 1995), pp. 669–79. See also Premack and Hunter, "Individual Unionization Decisions."

77. D. Lewin and Richard B. Peterson, *The Modern Grievance Procedure in the United States* (Westport, CT: Quorum Books, 1998).

78. G. Bohlander and D. Blancero, "A Study of Reversal Determinants in Discipline and Discharge Arbitration Awards: The Impact of Just Cause Standards," *Labor Studies Journal 21*, no. 3 (Fall 1996), pp. 3–18.

79. Company Web site, http://www.erac. com, accessed April 29, 2009; "J.D. Power Survey: Enterprise No. 1 in Rental Cars," *Yahoo*, November 17, 2008, http://www.yahoo. com; LaGesse, "A 'Stealth Company'

No Longer"; "Enterprise Rent-A-Car Institute for Renewable Fuels Taps Dr. Richard Sayre, Leading Biofuels Researcher, as Director," *Business Wire*, August 27, 2008, http://www. businesswire.com; Kelsey Volkmann, "Nicholson: Enterprise Rent-A-Car, Vanguard Integration to Be Completed in a Year," *St. Louis Business Journal*, August 4, 2008, http://www.bizjournals. com; Shera Dalin, "Enterprise Drives toward a Cleaner Environment," *St. Louis Commerce Magazine*, April 2008, http://www.stlcommercemagazine.com; Marc Gunther, "Renting 'Green'? Not So Easy," *Fortune*, January 17, 2008, http://www.money.cnn.com; Wellner, "Nothing but Green Skies."

Chapter 11

1. "No. 4: Marriott International," *DiversityInc.*, April 8, 2009, http:// www.diversityinc.com; "DiversityInc Ranks Marriott Fourth among 'Top 50 Companies for Diversity," *PRNewswire*, March 25, 2009, http:// www.prnewswire.com; Company Web site, http://www.marriott.com, accessed January 7, 2009; "2008 50 Companies for Diversity," *DiversityInc.*, no date, http://www.diversityinc.com; Peter Haapaniemi, "Diversity Goes Global," *Capital Thinking*, Fall 2008, http://www. capitalthinkingmagazine.com; Gillian Gaynair, "Marriott International Forms Diversity Position," *Washington Business Journal*, January 15, 2008, http://www. washington.bizjournals.com.

2. B. Eisenberg and M. Ruthsdotter, "Living the Legacy: The Women's Rights Movement 1848–1998," National Women's History Project, http://www.legacy98.org/move-hist. html.

3. Ibid.; and Bureau of Labor Statistics, "Labor Force Statistics from the Current Population Survey," http:// www.bls.gov/cps, accessed May 18, 2007.

4. Bureau of Labor Statistics, "Employment Projections: 2006–16," news release, December 4, 2007, http:// www.bls.gov.

5. Ibid.

6. Census Bureau, "Minority Population Tops 100 Million," news release, May 17, 2007, http://www.census.gov.

7. Bureau of Labor Statistics, "Household Data: Annual Averages," *Labor Force Statistics from the Current Population Survey*, last modified April 3, 2009, http://www.bls.gov/cps/demographis. htm; and Bureau of Labor Statistics, *Women in the Labor Force: A Databook*, Report 1011, December 2008, http:// www.bls.gov/cps/wlf-databook-2008.pdf.

8. C. Hymowitz, "Bend without Breaking: Women Executives Discuss the Art of Flex Schedules," *The Wall Street Journal*, March 6, 2007, http://online. wsj.com.

9. Bureau of Labor Statistics, *Charting the U.S. Labor Market in 2005* (Washington, DC: U.S. Department of Labor, June 2006), http://www.bls.gov; and E. Simon, "Women Make Less One Year after College," *Associated Press*, April 23, 2007, http://news.yahoo.com.

10. C. Hymowitz, "The 50 Women to Watch," *The Wall Street Journal*, November 20, 2006, http://online.wsj.com; and J. Mero, "Fortune 500 Women CEOs," *Fortune*, April 30, 2007, http://money.cnn.com.

11. C. Helfat, D. Harris, and P. Wolfson, "The Pipeline to the Top: Women and Men in the Top Executive Ranks of U.S. Corporations," *Academy of Management Perspectives* (November 2006), pp. 42–64.

12. A. Selko, "Gender Still a Large Hurdle to Career Advancement Say Women Execs," *Industry Week*, March 8, 2007, http://www.industryweek.com.

13. S. Armour, "Companies Try to Educate Teen Workers about Harassment," *USA Today*, October 19, 2006, http://www.usatoday.com.

14. G. Bohlander, S. Snell, and A. Sherman, *Managing Human Resources*, 12th ed. (Mason, OH: South-Western Publishing, 2001); and W. Petrocelli and B. K. Repa, *Sexual Harassment on the Job: What It Is and How to Stop It* (Berkeley, CA: Nolo Press, 1998).

15. Bureau of Labor Statistics, "Labor Force Characteristics of Foreign-Born Workers Summary," news release. April 25, 2007, http://www.bls.gov; and J. Lee and F. D. Bean, "America's Changing Color Lines," *Annual Review of Sociology*, 2004, pp. 221–43.

16. "The United States of Entrepreneurs," *The Economist*, March 14, 2009, accessed at http://www.kauffman.org.

17. Bureau of Labor Statistics, "Labor Force Statistics from the Current Population Survey," http://ftp.bls.gov, accessed May 21, 2007; and BLS, *Charting the U.S. Labor Market*, chart 4-7.

18. M. Bertrand and S. Mullainathan, "Are Emily and Greg More Employable than Lakisha and Jamal?" NBER Working Paper No. 9873, July 2003, http://www.nber.org.

19. M. P. McQueen, "Workplace Disabilities Are on the Rise," *The Wall Street Journal*, May 1, 2007, http://online.wsj.com.

20. Census Bureau, "Facts for Features: Americans with Disabilities Act, July 26," news release, July 19, 2006, http://www.census.gov.

21. Equal Employment Opportunity Commission (EEOC), "Disability Discrimination," http://www.eeoc.gov, accessed May 12, 2009; EEOC, "Notice Concerning the Americans with Disabilities Act (ADA) Amendments Act of 2008," last modified March 10, 2009, http://www.eeoc.gov; and EEOC, "ADA Charge Data by Impairments/Bases: Resolutions, FY1997–FY2008,"

last modified March 11, 2009, http://www.eeoc.gov.

22. Bureau of Labor Statistics, *Charting the U.S. Labor Market in 2006*, last modified September 28, 2007, http://www.bls.gov/cps/labor2006/; and Bureau of Labor Statistics, "Labor Force Characteristics of Foreign-Born Workers Summary," news release, April 25, 2007, http://www.bls.gov.

23. Census Bureau, *Statistical Abstract of the United States: 2007*, table 574, p. 373; and AARP, "Workforce Trends," Money and Work pages of AARP Web site, http://www.aarp.org, accessed May 21, 2007.

24. B. O. Driscoll, "Local Businesses Urged to Build Loyalty, Mentors," *Reno (NV) Gazette-Journal*, February 7, 2007, http://www.rgj.com.

25. N. A. Hira, "Attracting the Twentysomething Worker." *Fortune*, May 15, 2007, http://money.cnn.com.

26. Thomas Hoffman, "Eight New Ways to Target Top Talent in '08," *Computerworld*, January 28, 2008, pp. 34, 36; and Alex Kingsbury, "The CIA and NSA Want You to Be Their Friend on Facebook," *U.S. News & World Report Online*, February 5, 2009, downloaded from Business & Company Resource Center, http://galegroup.com.

27. Driscoll, "Local Businesses Urged to Build Loyalty, Mentors."

28. L. Tucker, "Portland Local and Oregon State Organizations Have Instituted Affirmative Action Programs," *Daily Journal of Commerce, Portland*, January 23, 2006, downloaded from Business & Company Resource Center, http://galenet.galegroup.com.

29. K. Labich, "No More Crude at Texaco," *Fortune*, September 6, 1999, pp. 205–12; *Good for Business: Making Full Use of the Nation's Human Capital* (Washington, DC: Federal Glass Ceiling Commission, 1995); and K. Weisul, "The Bottom Line on Women at the Top," *BusinessWeek*, January 26, 2004, http://www.businessweek.com.

30. Lisa Belkin, "Diversity Isn't Rocket Science, Is It?" *New York Times*, May 15, 2008, http://www.nytimes.com; Tara Weiss, "Science and the Glass Ceiling," *Forbes*, May 12, 2008, http://www.forbes.com; and Center for Work-Life Policy, "The Athena Factor: Reversing the Brain Drain in Science, Engineering, and Technology," news release, May 21, 2008, http://www.worklifepolicy.org.

31. N. Adler, *International Dimensions of Organizational Behavior*, 3rd ed. (Boston: PWS-Kent, 1997); and T. Cox and S. Blake, "Managing Cultural Diversity: Implications for Organizational Competitiveness," *Academy of Management Executives* 5 (August 1991), pp. 45–56.

32. C. Larsen, "Top Companies 2007: Meet the Top Companies," National

Association of Female Executives, http://www.nafe.com, accessed May 17, 2007; and S. Alleyne, "The 40 Best Companies for Diversity," *Black Enterprise*, July 2006, downloaded from Business & Company Resource Center, http://galenet.galegroup.com.

33. See, for example, S. J. Tribble, "Cisco Accused of Bias in Hiring," *San Jose Mercury News*, May 10, 2007, http://www.mercurynews.com; G. Appleson, "Baby Boomers, Often Targeted in Layoffs, Fight Age Discrimination," *St. Louis Post-Dispatch*, April 29, 2007, downloaded from Business & Company Resource Center, http://galenet.galegroup.com; "Class Action Suits in the Workplace Are on the Rise," *HR Focus*, April 2007, http://galenet.galegroup.com; and M. Schoeff Jr., "Walgreen Suit Reflects EEOC's Latest Strategies," *Workforce Management*, March 26, 2007, http://galenet.galegroup.com.

34. R. R. Thomas Jr., "From Affirmative Action to Affirming Diversity," *Harvard Business Review*, March–April 1990.

35. K. Jesella, "Mom's Mad, and She's Organized," *New York Times*, February 22, 2007, http://www.nytimes.com.

36. G. Avalos, "Study Looks at Diversity, Turnover," *Contra Costa Times (Walnut Creek, CA)*, October 13, 2006, downloaded from Business & Company Resource Center, http://galenet.galegroup.com.

37. Adler, *International Dimensions of Organizational Behavior*; and Cox and Blake, "Managing Cultural Diversity."

38. J. D. Nordell, "Positions of Power: How Female Ambition Is Shaped," *Slate*, November 21, 2006, http://www.slate.com.

39. Adler, *International Dimensions of Organizational Behavior*.

40. K. A. Jehn, "Workplace Diversity, Conflict, and Productivity: Managing in the 21st Century," SEI Center for Advanced Studies in Management, Wharton School, University of Pennsylvania, Diversity, http://mktg-sun.wharton.upenn.edu/SEI/diversity.html.

41. A. J. Murrell, F. J. Crosby, and R. J. Ely, *Mentoring Dilemmas: Developmental Relationships within Multicultural Organizations* (Mahwah, NJ: Lawrence Erlbaum Associates, 1999). See a review of this book by M. L. Lengnick-Hall, "Mentoring Dilemmas: Developmental Relationships within Multicultural Organizations," *Personnel Psychology* 53, no. 1 (Spring 2000), pp. 224–27.

42. "Marriott Nearly Doubles Billion Dollar Spending Goal with Diverse Suppliers," *Hospitality Industry*, February 25, 2009, http://www.hospitality-industry.com; Haapaniemi, "Diversity Goes Global"; Deann D. Holcomb, "Marriott Adds Global Hospitality to Diversity and Inclusion," *Minority Business News*, August 12, 2008, http://www.mbnusa.com; "Marriott Expands

Diverse Hotel Ownership Portfolio," *National Harbor*, July 31, 2008, http:// www.nationalharbor.com; "100 Best Companies to Work For," *Fortune*, February 4, 2008, http://money. cnn.com; Anita Huslin, "Marriott's New Diversity Executive Comes Full Circle," *Washington Post*, January 21, 2008, http://www.washingtonpost.com; Gaynair, "Marriott International Forms Diversity Position"; "Marriott Sets New Supplier Diversity Goal," *Smart Brief*, August 16, 2007.

43. A. Kalev, F. Dobbin, and E. Kelly, "Best Practices or Best Guesses? Assessing the Efficacy of Corporate Affirmative Action and Diversity Policies," *American Sociological Review* 71 (2006), pp. 589–617.

44. T. Reed, "NBA Has the Most Diverse Workforce," *Associated Press*, May 9, 2007, http://news.yahoo.com.

45. R. Rodriguez, "Diversity Finds Its Place," *HRMagazine*, August 2006, downloaded from Business & Company Resource Center, http://galenet. galegroup.com.

46. Monica Yant Kinney, "Firm Makes a Case for Loyalty," *Philadelphia Inquirer*, April 5, 2009, downloaded from Business & Company Resource Center, http://galenet.galegroup.com; Robert Hightower, "Law Firm to Celebrate Employee's 50-Year Mark," *Philadelphia Tribune*, April 9, 2009, http://www. phillytrib.com; Caesar, Rivise, Bernstein, Cohen & Pokotilow, "About Us," http://www.crbcp.com, accessed May 12, 2009; Drexel University, "Drexel at a Glance," http://www. drexel.edu, accessed May 12, 2009; and Drexel University Earle Mack School of Law, "Diversity Initiatives," http:// www.drexel.edu/law/diversity.asp, accessed May 12, 2009.

47. A. Selko, "The Changing Faces of the Workplace," *Industry Week*, April 1, 2007, http://www.industryweek.com; and M. D. Lee, S. M. MacDermid, and M. L. Buck, "Organizational Paradigms of Reduced-Load Work: Accommodation, Elaboration, and Transformation," *Academy of Management Journal* 43, no. 6 (December 2000), pp. 1211–34.

48. L. E. Overmyer Day, "The Pitfalls of Diversity Training," *Training and Development* 49, no. 12 (December 1995), pp. 24–29; S. Rynes and B. Rosen, "A Field Survey of Factors Affecting the Adoption and Perceived Success of Diversity Training," *Personnel Psychology* 48, no. 2 (Summer 1995), pp. 247–70; L. Ford, "Diversity: From Cartoons to Confrontations," *Training & Development* 54, no. 8 (August 2000), pp. 70–71; and J. M. Ivancevich and J. A. Gilbert, "Diversity Management: Time for a New Approach," *Public Personnel Management* 29, no. 1 (Spring 2000), pp. 75–92.

49. M. Burkart, "The Role of Training in Advancing a Diversity Initiative,"

Diversity Factor 8, no. 1 (Fall 1999), pp. 2–5.

50. A. Marks, "For Airport Screeners, More Training about Muslims," *Christian Science Monitor*, January 9, 2007, http:// www.csmonitor.com.

51. "How Bad Is the Turnover Problem?" *HR Focus*, March 2007, downloaded from Business & Company Resource Center, http://galenet.galegroup.com; B. Thomas, "Black Entrepreneurs Win, Corporations Lose," *BusinessWeek*, September 20, 2006, General Reference Center Gold, http://find.galegroup. com; and P. Shurn-Hannah, "Solving the Minority Retention Mystery," *The Human Resource Professional* 13, no. 3 (May/June 2000), pp. 22–27.

52. Lisa Bertagnoli, "Group Dynamics: Darden's Employee Networks," *Chain Leader*, September 1, 2008, http://www. chainleader.com; and David Farkas, "Talkin' 'bout Your Generations," *Chain Leader*, April 2009, pp. 38–41.

53. Alleyne, "The 40 Best Companies"; and M. E. Podmolik, "Mentor Match Found Online," *Chicago Tribune*, May 14, 2007, http://www.chicagotribune. com.

54. C. K. Johnson, "Study: Fat Workers Cost Employers More," *Associated Press*, April 23, 2007, http://news.yahoo.com.

55. R. Rodriguez, "Diversity Finds Its Place,"

56. "No. 4: Marriott International," *DiversityInc.*; "DiversityInc Ranks Marriott Fourth," *PRNewswire*; Company Web site, http://www. marriott.com, accessed January 7, 2009; "Marriott International Named by Latina Style As One of the Best Companies for Latinas in the U.S.," *CSR Wire*, September 8, 2008, http:// www.csrwire.com; Holcomb, "Marriott Adds Global Hospitality"; "Marriott Named One of '40 Best Companies for Diversity' by Black Enterprise Magazine," *Reuters*, July 29, 2008, http://www.reuters.com; "100 Best Companies to Work For," *Fortune*.

Chapter 12

1. Company Web site, http://www.rmi. org, accessed April 10, 2009; Kent Garber, "A Bright Light in the Field of New Energy," *U.S. News & World Report*, December 1–8, 2008, pp. 44–45; "Amory Lovins on Energy," *CNN. com*, October 16, 2008, http://www. edition.cnn.com; Lucy Siegle, "This Much I Know: Amory Lovins," *The Observer*, March 23, 2008, http://www. guardian.co.uk; Logan Ward, "Amory Lovins: Solving the Energy Crisis (and Bringing Wal-Mart)," *Popular Mechanics*, November 2007, http:// www.popularmechanics.com; Rob Walton, "Heroes of the Environment: Amory B. Lovins," *Time*, October 25, 2007, http://www.time.com; Warren Karlenzig, "Rocky Mountain Institute

Turns 25: The Distributed Generation of Amory Lovins' Brainpower," *WorldChanging Team*, August 15, 2007, http://www.worldchanging.com; and David Roberts, "All You Need Is Lovins," *Grist*, July 26, 2007, http:// www.grist.org.

2. W. Bennis and B. Nanus, *Leaders* (New York: Harper & Row, 1985), p. 27.

3. J. Petrick, R. Schere, J. Brodzinski, J. Quinn, and M. Fall Ainina, "Global Leadership Skills and Reputational Capital: Intangible Resources for Sustainable Competitive Advantage," *Academy of Management Executive*, February 1999, pp. 58–69.

4. Bennis and Nanus, *Leaders*.

5. Ibid., p. 144.

6. E. E. Lawler III, *Treat People Right! How Organizations and Individuals Can Propel Each Other into a Virtual Spiral of Success* (San Francisco: Jossey-Bass, 2003).

7. B. Kopf and B. Birleffi, "Not Her Father's Chief Executive," *U.S. News and World Report*, October 22, 2006, http://www.usnews.com (interview with Marilyn Nelson).

8. Robert Half Finance and Accounting, "Survey: CFOs Cite Strong Leadership, Talent as Keys to Staying Ahead of the Competition," news release, April 8, 2009, http://www.roberthalffinance. com.

9. J. Kouzes and B. Posner, *The Leadership Challenge*, 2nd ed. (San Francisco: Jossey-Bass, 1995).

10. J. Kouzes and B. Posner, *The Leadership Challenge*, 1st ed. (San Francisco: Jossey-Bass, 1987).

11. Ibid.

12. Ibid.

13. J. Baum, E. A. Locke, and S. Kirkpatrick, "A Longitudinal Study of the Relation of Vision and Vision Communication to Venture Growth in Entrepreneurial Firms," *Journal of Applied Psychology* 83 (1998), pp. 43–54.

14. E. C. Shapiro, *Fad Surfing in the Boardroom* (Reading, MA: Addison-Wesley, 1995).

15. Kouzes and Posner, The Leadership Challenge (1995).

16. Ibid.

17. W. Bennis and R. Townsend, *Reinventing Leadership* (New York: William Morrow, 1995).

18. Ibid.

19. A. Markels, "Turning the Tide at P&G," *U.S. News and World Report*, October 22, 2006, http://www.usnews .com.

20. Kouzes and Posner, *The Leadership Challenge* (1987).

21. J. A. Conger, "The Dark Side of Leadership," *Organizational Dynamics* 19 (Autumn 1990), pp. 44–55.

22. J. Conger, "The Vision Thing: Explorations into Visionary Leadership," in *Cutting Edge Leadership 2000*, ed. B. Kellerman and L. Matusak (College Park, MD: James MacGregor Burns Academy of Leadership, 2000).

23. Bill Wolpin, "The Tough Get Going," *American City & County*, November 1, 2008, downloaded from Business & Company Resource Center, http://galenet.galegroup.com; Mann Jackson, "Come-Back Kid," *American City & County*, November 1, 2008, downloaded from http://galenet.galegroup.com; and Brett Zongker, "Museum Features Kansas Town That Went Green," Associated Press, *Yahoo News*, October 26, 2008, http://news.yahoo.com.

24. J. P. Kotter, "What Leaders Really Do," *Harvard Business Review* 68 (May–June 1990) pp. 103–11.

25. Mark E. Van Buren and Todd Safferstone, "Collective Quick Wins," *Computerworld*, January 26, 2009, pp. 24–25.

26. G. Yukl, *Leadership in Organizations*, 3rd ed. (Englewood Cliffs, NJ: Prentice Hall, 1994).

27. R. House and R. Aditya, "The Social Scientific Study of Leadership: Quo Vadis?" *Journal of Management* 23 (1997), pp. 409–73.

28. R. D. Ireland and M. A. Hitt. "Achieving and Maintaining Strategic Competitiveness in the 21st Century. The Role of Strategic Leadership," *Academy of Management Executive*, February 1999, pp. 43–57.

29. J. Gardner, "The Heart of the Matter: Leader–Constituent Interaction," pp. 239–244, quote at p. 240. *Leading & Leadership*, ed. T. Fuller (Notre Dame, IN: University of Notre Dame Press. 2000), pp. 38–45.

30. R. E. Kelly, "In Praise of Followers," *Harvard Business Review* 66 (November–December 1988), pp. 142–48.

31. Bennis and Townsend, *Reinventing Leadership*.

32. Gardner, "The Heart of the Matter."

33. Kelly, "In Praise of Followers."

34. J. R. P. French and B. Raven, "The Bases of Social Power," in *Studies in Social Power*, ed. D. Cartwright (Ann Arbor, MI: Institute for Social Research, 1959).

35. G. Yukl and C. Falbe, "Importance of Different Power Sources in Downward and Lateral Relations," *Journal of Applied Psychology* 76 (1991), pp. 416–23.

36. Ibid.

37. "Amory Lovins on Energy," *CNN.com*; Siegle, "This Much I Know"; Roger Fillion, "Energy-Efficient Visionary," *Rocky Mountain News*, February 9, 2008, http://www.rockymountainnews.com; Ward, "Amory Lovins"; Karlenzig, "Rocky Mountain Institute Turns 25."

38. R. M. Stogdill, "Personal Factors Associated with Leadership: A Survey of the Literature," *Journal of Psychology* 25 (1948), pp. 35–71.

39. S. Kirkpatrick and E. Locke, "Leadership: Do Traits Matter?" *The Executive* 5 (May 1991), pp. 48–60.

40. G. A. Yukl, *Leadership in Organizations*, 2nd ed. (Englewood Cliffs, NJ: Prentice-Hall, 1989).

41. R. Heifetz and D. Laurie, "The Work of Leadership," *Harvard Business Review*, January–February 1997, pp. 124–34.

42. T. Judge, J. Bono, R. Ilies, and M. Gerhardt, "Personality and Leadership: A Qualitative and Quantitative Review." *Journal of Applied Psychology* 87 (2002), pp. 765–80.

43. R. Foti and N. M. A. Hauenstein, "Pattern and Variable Approaches in Leadership Emergence and Effectiveness," *Journal of Applied Psychology* 92 (2007), pp. 347–55.

44. T. Fuller, *Leading & Leadership, 2000* (Notre Dame, IN: University of Notre Dame Press, 2000), p. 243.

45. J. P. Kotter, *The General Managers* (New York: Free Press, 1982).

46. G. Imperato, "The Adventurer: How I Did It," *Inc.*, May 2007, pp. 115–16.

47. S. Zaccaro, R. Foti, and D. Kenny, "Self-Monitoring and Trait-Based Variance in Leadership: An Investigation of Leader Flexibility across Multiple Group Situations," *Journal of Applied Psychology* 76 (1991), pp. 308–15.

48. D. Goleman, "Leadership that Gets Results," *Harvard Business Review*, March–April 2000, pp. 78–90.

49. J. Misumi and M. Peterson, "The Performance-Maintenance (PM) Theory of Leadership: Review of a Japanese Research Program," *Administrative Science Quarterly* 30 (June 1985), pp. 198–223.

50. T. Judge, R. Piccolo, and R. Ilies, "The Forgotten Ones? The Validity of Consideration and Initiating Structure in Leadership Research," *Journal of Applied Psychology* 89 (2004), pp. 36–51.

51. Misumi and Peterson. "The Performance-Maintenance (PM) Theory."

52. Judge, Piccolo, and Ilies, "The Forgotten Ones?"

53. G. Graen and M. Uhl-Bien, "Relationship-Based Approach to Leadership: Development of Leader-Member Exchange (LMX) Theory of Leadership over 25 Years: Applying a Multi-Level Multidomain Perspective," *Leadership Quarterly* 6, no. 2 (1995), pp. 219–47.

54. House and Aditya, "The Social Scientific Study of Leadership."

55. C. R. Gerstner and D. V. Day, "Meta-Analytic Review of Leader-Member Exchange-Theory: Correlates and Construct Issues," *Journal of Applied Psychology* 82 (1997), pp. 827–44.

56. C. Nobel, "The Smart Business of Diversity," *InfoWorld*, January 22, 2007, http://www.infoworld.com (interview with Carly Fiorina).

57. House and Aditya, "The Social Scientific Study of Leadership."

58. J. Wagner III, "Participation's Effect on Performance and Satisfaction: A Reconsideration of Research," *Academy of Management Review*, April 1994, pp. 312–30.

59. R. White and R. Lippitt, *Autocracy and Democracy: An Experimental Inquiry* (New York: Harper & Brothers, 1960).

60. J. Muczyk and R. Steel, "Leadership Style and the Turnaround Executive," *Business Horizons*, March–April 1999, pp. 39–46.

61. A. Tannenbaum and W. Schmidt, "How to Choose a Leadership Pattern," *Harvard Business Review* 36 (March–April 1958), pp. 95–101.

62. E. Fleishman and E. Harris, "Patterns of Leadership Behavior Related to Employee Grievances and Turnover," *Personnel Psychology* 15 (1962), pp. 43–56.

63. R. Likert. *The Human Organization: Its Management and Value* (New York: McGraw-Hill, 1967).

64. R. Blake and J. Mouton, *The Managerial Grid* (Houston: Gulf, 1964).

65. Misumi and Peterson, "The Performance-Maintenance (PM) Theory."

66. J. Wall, *Bosses* (Lexington, MA: Lexington Books, 1986), p. 103.

67. Tannenbaum and Schmidt, "How to Choose a Leadership Pattern."

68. V. H. Vroom, "Leadership and the Decision-Making Process," *Organizational Dynamics*, Spring 2000, pp. 82–93.

69. F. E. Fiedler, *A Theory of Leadership Effectiveness* (New York: McGraw-Hill, 1967).

70. P. Hersey and K. Blanchard, *The Management of Organizational Behavior* (Englewood Cliffs, NJ: Prentice Hall, 1984).

71. Yukl, *Leadership in Organizations*.

72. R. J. House, "A Path Goal Theory of Leader Effectiveness," *Administrative Science Quarterly* 16 (1971), pp. 321–39.

73. J. Howell, D. Bowen, P. Dorfman, S. Kerr, and P. Podsakoff, "Substitutes for Leadership: Effective Alternatives to Ineffective Leadership," *Organizational Dynamics* 19 (Summer 1990), pp. 21–38.

74. R. G. Lord and W. Gradwohl Smith, "Leadership and the Changing Nature of Performance," in *The Changing Nature of Performance*, ed. D. R. Ilgen and E. D. Pulakos (San Francisco: Jossey-Bass, 1999).

75. S. Dionne, F. Yammarino, L. Atwater, and L. James, "Neutralizing Substitutes for Leadership Theory: Leadership Effects and Common-Source Bias," *Journal of Applied Psychology* 87 (2002), pp. 454–64.

76. B. M. Bass, *Leadership and Performance Beyond Expectations* (New York: Free Press, 1985).

77. Y. A. Nur, "Charisma and Managerial Leadership: The Gift That Never Was," *Business Horizons*, July–August 1998, pp. 19–26; and R. J. House, "A 1976 Theory of Charismatic Leadership," in *Leadership: The Cutting Edge*, ed. J. G. Hunt and L. L. Larson (Carbondale, IL: Southern Illinois University Press, 1977).

78. M. Brown and L. Trevino, "Socialized Charismatic Leadership, Values Congruence, and Deviance in Work Groups," *Journal of Applied Psychology* 91 (2006), pp. 954–62.

79. M. Potts and P. Behr, *The Leading Edge* (New York: McGraw-Hill, 1987).

80. J. Howell and B. Shamir, "The Role of Followers in the Charismatic Leadership Process: Relationships and Their Consequences," *Academy of Management Review* 30 (2005), pp. 96–112.

81. S. Yorges, H. Weiss, and O. Strickland, "The Effect of Leader Outcomes on Influence, Attributions, and Perceptions of Charisma," *Journal of Applied Psychology* 84 (1999), pp. 428–36.

82. Potts and Behr, "Leading Edge."

83. D. A. Waldman and F. J. Yammarino, "CEO Charismatic Leadership: Levels-of-Management and Levels-of-Analysis Effects," *Academy of Management Review* 24 (1999), pp. 266–85.

84. A. Fanelli and V. Misangyi, "Bringing Out Charisma: CEO Charisma and External Stakeholders," *Academy of Management Review* 31 (2006), pp. 1049–61.

85. House and Aditya, "The Social Scientific Study of Leadership."

86. D. A. Waldman, G. G. Ramirez, R. J. House, and P. Puranam, "Does Leadership Matter? CEO Leadership Attributes and Profitability under Conditions of Perceived Environmental Uncertainty," *Academy of Management Journal* 44 (2001), pp. 134–43.

87. B. Agle, N. Nagarajan, J. Sonnenfeld, and D. Srinivasan, "Does CEO Charisma Matter? An Empirical Analysis of the Relationships among Organizational Performance, Environmental Uncertainty, and Top Management Team Perceptions of CEO Charisma," *Academy of Management Journal* 49 (2006), pp. 161–74.

88. J. M. Howell and K. E. Hall-Merenda, "The Ties That Bind: The Impact of Leader-Member Exchange, Transformational and Transactional Leadership, and Distance on Predicting Follower Performance," *Journal of Applied Psychology* 84 (1999), pp. 680–94; and B. M. Bass, "Leadership: Good, Better, Best," *Organizational Dynamics*, Winter 1985, pp. 26–40.

89. F. J. Yammarino, F. Dansereau, and C. J. Kennedy, "A Multiple-Level Multidimensional Approach to Leadership: Viewing Leadership through an Elephant's Eye," *Organizational Dynamics*, Winter 2001, pp. 149–63.

90. D. I. Jung and B. J. Avolio, "Effects of Leadership Style and Followers' Cultural Orientation on Performance in Group and Individual Task Conditions," *Academy of Management Journal* 42 (1999), pp. 208–18.

91. Bass, *Leadership.*

92. G. Hall, "Unconventional Wisdom," *Orange County Register*, January 23, 2007, http://galennet.galegroup.com.

93. Bennis and Nanus, *Leaders.*

94. B. Bass, B. Avolio, and L. Goodheim, "Biography and the Assessment of Transformational Leadership at the World-Class Level," *Journal of Management* 13 (1987), pp. 7–20.

95. K. Albrecht and R. Zemke, *Service America* (Homewood, IL: Dow Jones Irwin, 1985).

96. T. A. Judge and J. E. Bono, "Five-Factor Model of Personality and Transformational Leadership," *Journal of Applied Psychology* 85 (2000), pp. 751–65; and B. Bass, "Does the Transactional-Transformational Paradigm Transcend Organizational and National Boundaries?" *American Psychologist* 22 (1997), pp. 130–42.

97. S. J. Shin and J. Zhou, "Transformational Leadership, Conservation, and Creativity: Evidence from Korea," *Academy of Management Journal* 46 (2003), pp. 703–14.

98. R. Piccolo and J. Colquitt, "Transformational Leadership and Job Behaviors: The Mediating Role of Core Job Characteristics," *Academy of Management Journal* 49 (2006), pp. 327–40.

99. A. Colbert, A. Kristof-Brown, B. Bradley, and M. Barrick, "CEO Transformational Leadership: The Role of Goal Importance Congruence in Top Management Teams," *Academy of Management Journal* 51 (2008), pp. 81–96.

100. T. Dvir, D. Eden, B. Avolio, and B. Shamir, "Impact of Transformational Leadership on Follower Development and Performance: A Field Experiment," *Academy of Management Journal* 45 (2002), pp. 735–44.

101. B. M. Bass, *Transformational Leadership: Industry, Military, and Educational Impact* (Mahwah, NJ: Lawrence Erlbaum Associates. 1998).

102. G. Spreitzer and R. Quinn, "Empowering Middle Managers to Be Transformational Leaders," *Journal of Applied Behavioral Science* 32 (1996), pp. 237–61.

103. J. Collins, "Level 5 Leadership," *Harvard Business Review* 1 (2001), pp. 66–76; and J. Kline Harrison and M. William Clough, "Characteristics of 'State of the Art' Leaders: Productive Narcissism versus Emotional Intelligence and Level 5 Capabilities," *Social Science Journal* 43 (2006), pp. 287–92.

104. D. Vera and M. Crossan, "Strategic Leadership and Organizational Learning," *Academy of Management Review* 29 (2004), pp. 222–40.

105. Esther Herlzfeld, "Leadership Leads to Growth," *Official Board Markets*, April 11, 2009, downloaded from Business & Company Resource Center, http://galenet.galegroup.com; and Barry-

Wehmiller Web site, http://www.barry-wehmiller.com, accessed May 15, 2009.

106. F. Luthans, *Organizational Behavior*, 10th ed. (New York: McGraw-Hill/Irwin, 2005).

107. B. M. Bass, "Thoughts and Plans," in *Cutting Edge Leadership 2000*, ed. B. Kellerman and L. R. Matusak (College Park, MD: James MacGregor Burns Academy of Leadership, 2000), pp. 5–9.

108. N. Turner, J. Barling, O. Epitropaki, V. Butcher, and C. Milner, "Transformational Leadership and Moral Reasoning," *Journal of Applied Psychology* 87 (2002), pp. 304–11.

109. Bass, "Thoughts and Plans."

110. John Hersey, "Some SAGE Advice," *Hardware Retailing*, May 2009, downloaded from Business & Company Resource Center, http://galenet.galegroup.com.

111. W. Bennis, "The End of Leadership: Exemplary Leadership Is Impossible without Full Inclusion, Initiatives, and Cooperation of Followers," *Organizational Dynamics*, Summer 1999, pp. 71–79.

112. L. Spears, "Emerging Characteristics of Servant Leadership," in *Cutting Edge Leadership 2000*, ed. B. Kellerman and L. Matusak (College Park, MD: James MacGregor Burns Academy of Leadership, 2000); and L. Buchanan, "In Praise of Selflessness: Why the Best Leaders Are Servants," *Inc.*, May 2007, pp. 33–35.

113. Buchanan, "In Praise of Selflessness," p. 34.

114. J. Ciulla, "Bridge Leaders," in *Cutting Edge Leadership 2000*, ed. B. Kellerman and L. Matusak (College Park, MD: James MacGregor Burns Academy of Leadership, 2000), pp. 25–28.

115. C. L. Pearce, "The Future of Leadership: Combining Vertical and Shared Leadership to Transform Knowledge Work," *Academy of Management Executive*, February 2004, pp. 47–57.

116. J. Carson, P. Tesluk, and J. Marrone, "Shared Leadership in Teams: An Investigation of Antecedent Conditions and Performance," *Academy of Management Journal* (2007), 50 pp. 1217–34.

117. R. Fisher and A. Sharp, *Getting It Done* (New York: HarperCollins, 1998).

118. A. Markels, "Guiding the Path to Mars," *U.S. News and World Report*, October 22, 2006, http://www.usnews.com.

119. M. Useem, "Thinking Big, Lending Small," *U.S. News and World Report*, October 22, 2006, http://www.usnews.com.

120. P. Block, *The Empowered Manager* (San Francisco: Jossey-Bass, 1991).

121. Ibid.

122. Kouzes and Posner, *The Leadership Challenge* (1995).

123. Larry W. Boone and Monica S. Peborde, "Developing Leadership Skills in College and Early Career Positions," *Review of Business*, Spring 2008, downloaded from Business &

Company Resource Center, http://galenet.galegroup.com.

124. Amanda Gaines, "Straight to the Top," *American Executive,* August 2008, downloaded from Business & Company Resource Center, http://galenet.galegroup.com; and Scott J. Allen and Nathan S. Hartman, "Leadership Development: An Exploration of Sources of Learning," *SAM Advanced Management Journal,* Winter 2008, pp. 10–19, 62–63.

125. R. Fulmer, P. Gibbs, and M. Goldsmith, "Developing Leaders: How Winning Companies Keep on Winning," *Sloan Management Review* (Fall 2000), pp. 49–59.

126. M. McCall, *High Flyers* (Boston: Harvard Business School Press, 1998).

127. E. Van Velsor, C. D. McCauley, and R. Moxley, "Our View of Leadership Development," in *Center for Creative Leadership Handbook of Leadership Development,* ed. C. D. McCauley, R. Moxley, and E. Van Velsor (San Francisco: Jossey-Bass, 1998), pp. 1–25.

128. Company Web site, http://www.rmi.org, accessed April 10, 2009; Julia Levitt, "Worldchanging Interview: Amory Lovins," *Worldchanging,* March 23, 2009, http://www.worldchanging.com; "The 100 People Who Are Changing America," *Rolling Stone,* March 18, 2009, http://www.rollingstone.com; Garber, "A Bright Light in the Field of New Energy"; Fillion, "Energy-Efficiency Visionary"; Ward, "Amory Lovins"; Karlenzig, "Rocky Mountain Institute Turns 25."

Chapter 13

1. Max Chafkin, "Everybody Loves Zappos," *Inc.,* May 2009, pp. 66–73; Jeffrey M. O'Brien, "Zappos Knows How to Kick It," *Fortune,* January 22, 2009, http://money.cnn.com; Brian Morrissey, "Q&A: Zappos CEO Tony Hsieh," *Adweek,* December 22, 2008, http://www.adweek.com; Kim Eugenic, "Live from WOMMA in Las Vegas," *Nielsen Online,* November 13, 2008, http://nielsen-online.com; Claire Cain Miller, "Making Sure the Shoe Fits at Zappos.com," *New York Times,* November 6, 2008, http://bits.blogs.nytimes.com; Brenna Fisher, "How I Do It: Tony Hsieh (Zappos.com)," *Success,* November 2008, pp. 22–23; Helen Coster, "A Step Ahead," *Forbes,* June 2, 2008, http://www.forbes.com; Direct Marketing Association, "NCDM 2007 Keynote Speaker Tony Hsieh Runs a Service Company That Just Happens to Sell Shoes," news release, December 12, 2007, http://www.the-dma.org; and Ken Magill, "Worker's Paradise," *Direct Magazine,* October 1, 2007, http://www.directmag.com.

2. R. Kreitner and F. Luthans, "A Social Learning Approach to Behavioral Management: Radical Behaviorists 'Mellowing Out,'" *Organizational Dynamics,* Autumn 1984, pp. 47–65.

3 D. Katz and R. L. Kahn, *The Social Psychology of Organizations* (New York: John Wiley & Sons, 1966).

4. C. A. Bartlett and S. Ghoshal, "Building Competitive Advantage through People," *Sloan Management Review,* Winter 2002, pp. 34–41.

5. A. Fisher, "Loyalty Isn't Dead, Employers Have to Earn It," *Fortune,* January 16, 2007, http://money.cnn.com.

6. E. Locke, "Toward a Theory of Task Motivation and Incentives," *Organizational Behavior and Human Performance* 3 (1968), pp. 157–89.

7. W. F. Cascio, "Managing a Virtual Workplace," *Academy of Management Executive,* August 2000, pp. 81–90.

8. E. A. Locke, "Guest Editor's Introduction: Goal-Setting Theory and Its Applications to the World of Business," *Academy of Management Executive* 4 (November 2004), pp. 124–25.

9. G. P. Latham, "The Motivational Benefits of Goal-Setting," *Academy of Management Executive* 4 (November 2004), pp. 126–29.

10. E. A. Locke, "Linking Goals to Monetary Incentives," *Academy of Management Executive* 4 (November 2004), pp. 130–33.

11. E. E. Lawler III, *Treat People Right!* (San Francisco: Jossey-Bass, 2003).

12. Ibid.

13. J. Bono and T. Judge, "Self-Concordance at Work: Toward Understanding the Motivational Effects of Transformational Leaders," *Academy of Management Journal* 46 (2003), pp. 554–71.

14. R. H. Schaffer, "Demand Better Results—and Get Them," *Harvard Business Review* 69 (March–April 1991), pp. 142–49.

15. B. Hunsberger, "Entrepreneurial Spirit Keeps Company Fired Up," *Seattle Times,* March 29, 2007, downloaded from Business & Company Resource Center, http://galenet.galegroup.com; and P. Kaihla, "Best-Kept Secrets of the World's Best Companies," *Business 2.0,* April 2006, http://galenet.galegroup.com.

16. K. N. Shaw, "Changing the Goal-Setting Process at Microsoft," *Academy of Management Executive* 4 (November 2004), pp. 139–43.

17. S. Kerr and S. Landauer, "Using Stretch Goals to Promote Organizational Effectiveness and Personal Growth: General Electric and Goldman Sachs," *Academy of Management Executive* 4 (November 2004), pp. 134–38.

18. Ibid.

19. Latham, "Motivational Benefits of Goal-Setting."

20. T. Mitchell and W. Silver, "Individual and Group Goals When Workers Are Interdependent: Effects on Task Strategies and Performance," *Journal of Applied Psychology* 75 (1990), pp. 185–93.

21. Latham, "Motivational Benefits of Goal-Setting."

22. S. Boehle, "The Games Trainers Play," *Training,* August 1, 2006, http://www.trainingmag.com; and M. P. McQueen, "Wellness Plans Reach Out to the Healthy," *The Wall Street Journal,* March 28, 2007, http://online.wsj.com.

23. M. Schweitzer, L. Ordonez, and B. Douma, "Goal Setting as a Motivator of Unethical Behavior," *Academy of Management Journal* 47 (2004), pp. 422–32.

24. M. A. Duran, "Norm-Based Behavior and Corporate Malpractice," *Journal of Economic Issues* 41, no. 1 (March 2007), downloaded from Business & Company Resource Center, http://galenet.galegroup.com; and D. Durfee, "Management or Manipulation?" *CFO,* December 2006, http://galenet.galegroup.com.

25. G. Seijts and G. Latham, "Learning versus Performance Goals: When Should Each Be Used?" *Academy of Management Executive* 19 (February 2005), pp. 124–31; P. C. Early, T. Connolly, and G. Ekegren, "Goals, Strategy Development, and Task Performance: Some Limits on the Efficacy of Goal Setting," *Journal of Applied Psychology* 74 (1989), pp. 24–33; and C. E. Shalley, "Effects of Productivity Goals, Creativity Goals, and Personal Discretion on Individual Creativity," *Journal of Applied Psychology* 76 (1991), pp. 179–85.

26. R. C. Litchfield, "Brainstorming Reconsidered: A Goal-Based View," *Academy of Management Review* 33 (2008), pp. 649–668.

27. R. Fisher and A. Sharp, *Getting It Done* (New York: HarperCollins, 1998).

28. E. Thorndike, *Animal Intelligence* (New York: Macmillan, 1911).

29. A. D. Stajkovic and F. Luthans, "Differential Effects of Incentive Motivators on Work Performance," *Academy of Management Journal* 44 (2001), pp. 580–90.

30. J. Zaslow, "The Most-Praised Generation Goes to Work," *The Wall Street Journal,* April 20, 2007, http://online.wsj.com.

31. Adam Madison, "Positive Results," *Rock Products,* September 1, 2008, downloaded from Business & Company Resource Center, http://galenet.galegroup.com.

32. A. Fisher, "Happy Employees, Loyal Employees," *Fortune,* "100 Best Companies to Work For," January 16, 2007.

33. K. Butterfield, L. K. Trevino, and G. Ball, "Punishment from the Manager's Perspective: A Grounded Investigation and Inductive Model," *Academy of Management Review* 39 (1996), pp. 1479–512.

34. Madison, "Positive Results."

35. T. Judge and R. Piccolo, "Transformational and Transactional Leadership: A Meta-Analytic Test of Their Relative Ability," *Journal of Applied Psychology* 89 (2004), pp. 755–68.

36. S. Kerr, "On the Folly of Rewarding A While Hoping for B," *Academy of Management Journal* 18 (1975), pp. 769–83.

37. See S. Lohr, "Science Finds Advantage in Focusing, Not Multitasking," *Chicago Tribune*, March 25, 2007, sec. 1, p. 10.

38. E. E. Lawler III, *Rewarding Excellence* (San Francisco: Jossey-Bass, 2000).

39. J. Stenson, "Is Your Job Making You Fat?" *MSNBC*, February 6, 2007, http://www.msnbc.msn.com.

40. M. Fitzgerald, "Thinks Big about the Little Guy," *New York Times*, February 4, 2007, downloaded from Business & Company Resource Center, http://galenet.galegroup.com.

41. "100 Best Companies to Work For 2007: Unusual Perks," *Fortune*, January 22, 2007, http://money.cnn.com.

42. Fisher, "Happy Employees, Loyal Employees."

43. J. H. Cho, "Lessons in Employee Appreciation," *Star-Ledger (Newark, NJ)*, February 8, 2007, downloaded from Business & Company Resource Center, http://galenet.galegroup.com.

44. Fitzgerald, "Thinks Big."

45. J. Pfeffer and R. Sutton, *The Knowing–Doing Gap* (Boston: Harvard Business School Press, 2000).

46. J. S. Lublin, "Recall the Mistakes of Your Past Bosses, So You Can Do Better," *The Wall Street Journal*, January 2, 2007, http://online.wsj.com.

47. S. Moss and J. Sanchez, "Are Your Employees Avoiding You? Managerial Strategies for Closing the Feedback Gap," *Academy of Management Executive* 18, no. 1 (February 2004), pp. 32–44.

48. Lawler, *Treat People Right!*

49. S. B. Silverman, C. E. Pogson, and A. B. Cober, "When Employees at Work Don't Get It: A Model for Enhancing Individual Employee Change in Response to Performance Feedback," *Academy of Management Executive* 19, no. 2 (May 2005), pp. 135–47; and J. Jackman and M. Strober, "Fear of Feedback," *Harvard Business Review*, April 2003, pp. 101–7.

50. V. H. Vroom, *Work and Motivation* (New York: John Wiley & Sons, 1964).

51. R. E. Wood, P. W. B. Atkins, and J. E. H. Bright, "Bonuses, Goals, and Instrumentality Effects," *Journal of Applied Psychology* 84 (1999), pp. 703–20.

52. Melanie Scarborough, "The Rewards of Recognition: Six Strategies for Successful Employee Programs," *Community Banker*, January 2009, pp. 24–27.

53. Vanessa Fuhrmans, "Training the Brain to Choose Wisely," *The Wall Street Journal*, April 28, 2009, http://online.wsj.com; and Laura Blue, "Making Good Health Easy," *Time*, February 23, 2009, Wellness 1–2.

54. A. H. Maslow, "A Theory of Human Motivation," *Psychological Review*, July 1943, pp. 370–96.

55. L. Mainicro and D. Gibson, "Managing Employee Trauma: Dealing with the Emotional Fallout from 9-11," *Academy of Management Executive*, August 2003, pp. 130–43.

56. M. Wahba and L. Birdwell, "Maslow Reconsidered: A Review of Research on the Need Hierarchy Theory," *Organizational Behavior and Human Performance* 15 (1976), pp. 212–40.

57. G. Dessler, "How to Earn Your Employees' Commitment," *Academy of Management Executive*, May 1999, pp. 58–67, quoted on p. 63.

58. C. Hymowitz, "Managers Lose Talent When They Neglect to Coach Their Staffs," *The Wall Street Journal*, March 19, 2007, http://online.wsj.com.

59. Ibid.

60. C. Alderfer, *Existence, Relatedness, and Growth. Human Needs in Organizational Settings* (Glencoe, IL: Free Press, 1972).

61. L. Tanner, "Study: Napping Might Help Heart," *Yahoo News*, February 12, 2007, http://news.yahoo.com.

62. C. Hymowitz, "When the Paycheck Isn't Optional, Ambition Is Less Complicated," *The Wall Street Journal*, April 26, 2007, http://online.wsj.com.

63. C. Pinder, *Work Motivation* (Glenview, IL: Scott, Foresman, 1984).

64. D. McClelland, *The Achieving Society* (New York: Van Nostrand Reinhold, 1961).

65. Quoted in Cho, "Lessons in Employee Appreciation."

66. D. McClelland and R. Boyatzis, "Leadership Motive Pattern and Long-Term Success in Management," *Journal of Applied Psychology* 67 (1982), pp. 737–43.

67. Fisher, "How I Do It"; Chafkin, "Everybody Loves Zappos"; Miller, "Making Sure the Shoe Fits"; Magill, "Worker's Paradise."

68. N. Adler, *International Dimensions of Organizational Behavior*, 2nd ed. (Boston: Kent, 1991); and G. Hofstede, *Cultures and Organizations* (London: McGraw-Hill, 1991).

69. N. R. Lockwood, "Leveraging Employee Engagement for Competitive Advantage: HR's Strategic Role," *HRMagazine*, March 2007, downloaded from Business & Company Resource Center, http://galenet.galegroup.com.

70. E. E. Lawler III and D. Finegold, "Individualizing the Organization: Past, Present, and Future," *Organizational Dynamics*, Summer 2000, pp. 1–15.

71. Ibid.

72. T. M. Amabile, "A Model of Creativity and Innovation in Organizations," in *Research in Organizational Behavior*, ed. B. M. Staw and L. L. Cummings (Greenwich, CT: JAI Press, 1988), pp. 10, 123–67.

73. C. M. Ford, "A Theory of Individual Creative Action in Multiple Social Domains," *Academy of Management Review* 21 (1996), pp. 1112–42.

74. G. Oldham and A. Cummings, "Employee Creativity: Personal and Contextual Factors at Work," *Academy of Management Journal* 39 (1996), pp. 607–34.

75. T. Amabile, R. Conti, H. Coon, J. Lazenby, and M. Herron, "Assessing the Work Environment for Creativity," *Academy of Management Journal* 39 (1996), pp. 1154–84.

76. M. Campion and G. Sanborn, "Job Design," in *Handbook of Industrial Engineering*, ed. G. Salvendy (New York: John Wiley & Sons, 1991).

77. BlessingWhite, *The State of Employee Engagement, 2008: North American Overview*, 2008, http://www.blessingwhite.com/research.

78. Lawler and Finegold, "Individualizing the Organization."

79. R. Garretson, "Job Rotation Pays Dividends," *Network World*, February 26, 2007, downloaded from OCLC FirstSearch, http://firstsearch.oclc.org.

80. M. Campion and D. McClelland, "Interdisciplinary Examination of the Costs and Benefits of Enlarged Jobs: A Job Design Quasi-Experiment," *Journal of Applied Psychology* 76 (1991), pp. 186–98.

81. F. Herzberg, *Work and the Nature of Men* (Cleveland: World, 1966).

82. J. R. Hackman, G. Oldham, R. Janson, and K. Purdy, "A New Strategy for Job Enrichment," *California Management Review* 16 (Fall 1975), pp. 57–71.

83. P. Lehman, "No. 5 Enterprise: A Clear Road to the Top," *BusinessWeek*, September 18, 2006, downloaded from General Reference Center Gold, http://find.galegroup.com.

84. R. Rechheld, "Loyalty-Based Management" *Harvard Business Review*, March–April 1993, pp. 64–73.

85. K. Miller, "Buying into the State Department Lifestyle," *BusinessWeek*, November 14, 2006, downloaded from General Reference Center Gold, http://find.galegroup.com.

86. Bill Trahant, "Recruiting and Engaging the Federal Workforce," *Public Manager*, Spring 2008, downloaded from Business & Company Resource Center, http://galenet.galegroup.com.

87. T. Peters and N. Austin, *A Passion for Excellence* (New York: Random House, 1985).

88. Kaihla, "Best-Kept Secrets."

89. Campion and Sanborn, "Job Design."

90. J. Bryner, "Survey Reveals Most Satisfying Jobs," *Yahoo News*, April 18, 2007, http://news.yahoo.com.

91. S. Seibert, S. Silver, and W. A. Randolph, "Taking Empowerment to the Next Level: A Multiple-Level Model of Empowerment, Performance, and Satisfaction," *Academy of Management Journal* 47 (2004), pp. 332–49.

92. C. Argyris, "Empowerment: The Emperor's New Clothes," *Harvard Business Review*, May–June 1998, pp. 98–105.

93. R. Forrester, "Empowerment: Rejuvenating a Potent Idea," *Academy of Management Executive*, August 2000, pp. 67–80.

94. R. C. Liden, S. J. Wayne, and R. T. Sparrowe, "An Examination of the Mediating Role of Psychological Empowerment on the Relations between the Job, Interpersonal Relationships, and Work Outcomes," *Journal of Applied Psychology* 85 (2000), pp. 407–16.

95. Peters and Austin, *A Passion for Excellence.*

96. K. Thomas and B. Velthouse, "Cognitive Elements of Empowerment: An 'Interpretive' Model of Intrinsic Task Motivation," *Academy of Management Review* 15 (1990), pp. 666–81.

97. S. Gray, "Whole Foods' CEO Intends to Stop Growth Slippage," *Pittsburgh Post-Gazette*, December 4, 2006, http://www.post-gazette.com; and "Whole Foods Impressing Customers, Investors," *MSNBC*, April 18, 2006, http://www.msnbc.com.

98. J. Kouzes and B. Posner, *The Leadership Challenge*, 2nd ed. (San Francisco: Jossey-Bass, 1995).

99. Price Waterhouse Change Integration Team, *Better Change* (Burr Ridge, IL: Richard D. Irwin, 1995).

100. E. E. Lawler III, *The Ultimate Advantage: Creating the High Involvement Organization* (San Francisco: Jossey-Bass, 1992).

101. O. Gadiesh and J. L. Gilbert, "Transforming Corner-Office Strategy into Frontline Action," *Harvard Business Review*, May 2001, pp. 72–79.

102. Kouzes and Posner, *The Leadership Challenge.*

103. Price Waterhouse, *Better Change.*

104. J. Jasinowski and R. Hamrin, *Making It in America* (New York: Simon & Schuster, 1995).

105. W. A. Randolph and M. Sashkin, "Can Organizational Empowerment Work in Multinational Settings?" *Academy of Management Executive* 16 (2002), pp. 102–15.

106. J. Adams, "Inequality in Social Exchange," in *Advances in Experimental Social Psychology*, ed. L. Berkowitz (New York: Academic Press, 1965).

107. M. Bloom, "The Performance Effects of Pay Dispersion of Individuals and Organizations," *Academy of Management Journal* 42 (1999), pp. 25–40.

108. G. Morgenson, "Peer Pressure: Inflating Executive Pay," *New York Times*, November 26, 2006, http://www.nytimes.com.

109. D. Prial, "Crunch Time for CPAs," *The Record (Bergen County, NJ)*, April 17, 2007, downloaded from Business & Company Resource Center, http://galenet.galegroup.com.

110. D. Skarlicki, R. Folger, and P. Tesluk, "Personality as a Moderator in the Relationships between Fairness and Retaliation," *Academy of Management Journal* 42 (1999), pp. 100–108.

111. J. Brockner, "Making Sense of Procedural Fairness: How High Procedural Fairness Can Reduce or Heighten the Influence of Outcome Favorability," *Academy of Management Review* 27 (2002), pp. 58–76; and D. De Cremer and D. van Knippenberg, "How Do Leaders Promote Cooperation? The Effects of Charisma and Procedural Fairness," *Journal of Applied Psychology* 87 (2002), pp. 858–66.

112. M. Kernan and P. Hanges, "Survivor Reactions to Reorganization: Antecedents and Consequences of Procedural, Interpersonal, and Informational Justice," *Journal of Applied Psychology* 87 (2002), pp. 916–28.

113. Lawler, *Treat People Right!*

114. A. Pomeroy, "Company Is a Team, Not a Family," *HRMagazine*, April 2007, downloaded from Business & Company Resource Center, http://galenet.galegroup.com.

115. W. C. Kim and R. Mauborgne, "Fair Process: Managing in the Knowledge Economy," *Harvard Business Review*, July–August 1997, pp. 65–75.

116. T. Bateman and D. Organ, "Job Satisfaction and the Good Soldier: The Relationship between Affect and Employee 'Citizenship,' " *Academy of Management Journal* (1983), pp. 587–95.

117. D. Henne and E. Locke, "Job Dissatisfaction: What Are the Consequences?" *International Journal of Psychology* 20 (1985), pp. 221–40.

118. J. Barling, E. K. Kelloway, and R. Iverson, "High-Quality Work, Job Satisfaction, and Occupational Injuries," *Journal of Applied Psychology* 88 (2003), pp. 276–83.

119. D. Bowen, S. Gilliland, and R. Folger, "HRM and Service Fairness: How Being Fair with Employees Spills Over to Customers," *Organizational Dynamics* (Winter 1999), pp. 7–23.

120. J. Harter, F. Schmidt, and T. Hayes, "Business-Unit-Level Relationship between Employee Satisfaction, Employee Engagement, and Business Outcomes: A Meta-Analysis," *Journal of Applied Psychology* 87 (2002), pp. 268–79.

121. T. Schweitzer, "U.S. Workers Hate Their Jobs More than Ever," *Inc.*, March 6, 2007, http://www.inc.com.

122. T. Bisoux, "Corporate CounterCulture," *BizEd*, November/December 2004, pp. 16–20.

123. Fisher, "Happy Employees, Loyal Employees"; "100 Best Companies to Work for 2007," *Fortune* Rankings, January 22, 2007, http://money.cnn.com; and First Horizon National Corp., "Careers" and "Our Benefits," http://www.firsthorizon.com, accessed June 5, 2007.

124. R. E. Walton, "Improving the Quality of Work Life," *Harvard Business Review* (May–June 1974), pp. 12, 16, 155.

125. E. E. Lawler III, "Strategies for Improving the Quality of Work Life," *American Psychologist* 37 (1982), pp. 486–93; and J. L. Suttle, "Improving Life at Work: Problems and Prospects," in *Improving Life at Work*, ed. J. R. Hackman and J. L. Suttle (Santa Monica, CA: Goodyear, 1977).

126. S. L. Robinson, "Trust and Breach of the Psychological Contract," *Administrative Science Quarterly* 41 (1996), pp. 574–99.

127. D. Rousseau, "Changing the Deal While Keeping the People," *Academy of Management Executive* 10 (1996), pp. 50–58.

128. E. Ridolfi, "Executive Commentary," *Academy of Management Executive* 10 (1996), pp. 59–60.

129. E. E. Lawler III, *From the Ground Up* (San Francisco: Jossey-Bass, 1996).

130. Ibid.

131. S. Ghoshal, C. Bartlett, and P. Moran, "Value Creation: The New Management Manifesto," *Financial Times Mastering Management Review*, November 1999, pp. 34–37.

132. Ram Charan, "Stop Whining, Start Thinking," *BusinessWeek*, August 14, 2008, http://www.businessweek.com.

133. Lilly Rockwell, "Zappos Chief Speaks," *Austin American-Statesman*, March 13, 2009, http://www.austin360.com; O'Brien, "Zappos Knows How to Kick It"; Fisher, "How I Do It"; Brian Morrissey, "These Brands Build Community," *Adweek*, May 12, 2008, http://www.adweek.com; Margaret Kane, "New Zappos: Shoes—and Gadget to Boot," *CNET News*, April 18, 2008, http://www.cnet.com; Direct Marketing Association, "NCDM 2007 Keynote Speaker"; Magill, "Worker's Paradise."

Chapter 14

1. St. Lawson, "Cisco to Shift Resources to Consumer Push," *PC World*, December 9, 2008, http://www.pcworld.com; E. McGirt, "How Cisco's CEO John Chambers Is Turning the Tech Giant Socialist," *Fast Company*, November 25, 2008, http://www.fastcompany.com; R. Ando, "Chambers Sees Cisco CEO Role Changing," *Reuters*, July 8, 2008, http://www.reuters.com; J. Doerr, "Builders and Titans: John Chambers," *Time*, May 1, 2008, http://www.time.com; "A Conversation with John Chambers," *Domain News 360 Blog*, April 11, 2008, http://www.domainnews360.com; "Reinventing Cisco Systems," *redOrbit*, January 27, 2008, http://www.redorbit.com; and W. J. Holstein, "Cisco: Is John Chambers Overstaying?" *BNET*, December 21, 2007, http://blogs.bnet.com.

2. E. C. Wenger and W. M. Snyder, "Communities of Practice: The Organizational Frontier," *Harvard Business Review*, January–February 2000, pp. 139–45.

3. S. Cohen and D. Bailey, "What Makes Teams Work: Group Effectiveness Research from the Shop Floor to the Executive Suite," *Journal of Management* 23 (1997), pp. 239–90.

4. G. Chen, L. Donahue, and R. Klimoski, "Training Undergraduates to Work in Organizational Teams," *Academy of Management Learning and Education* 3 (2004), pp. 27–40.

5. Ken Blanchard Companies, "Client Spotlight: Summit Pointe," *Ignite!*, March 2007, http://www.kenblanchard.com/ignite.

6. K. Wexley and S. Silverman, *Working Scared* (San Francisco: Jossey-Bass, 1993).

7. E. E. Lawler III, *From the Ground Up* (San Francisco: Jossey-Bass, 1996).

8. E. Fleischauer, "Nucor Manager Says Teamwork Key to Success; Q1 Earnings Up," *Decatur (AL) Daily*, April 20, 2007, http://www.decaturdaily.com.

9. Lawler, *From the Ground Up*.

10. R. Heifetz and D. Laurie, "The Work of Leadership," *Harvard Business Review*, January–February 1996, pp. 124–34.

11. P. Demetrakakes, "Packaging a Big Part of General Success," *Food and Beverage Packaging*, October 2008, downloaded from Business & Company Resource Center, http://galenet.galegroup.com.

12. D. Nadler, J. R. Hackman, and E. E. Lawler III, *Managing Organizational Behavior* (Boston: Little, Brown, 1979).

13. K. Holland, "How to Build Teamwork after an Awful Season," *New York Times*, December 28, 2008, downloaded from Business & Company Resource Center, http://galenet.galegroup.com.

14. M. Cianni and D. Wnuck, "Individual Growth and Team Enhancement: Moving toward a New Model of Career Development," *Academy of Management Executive* 11 (1997), pp. 105–15.

15. Cohen and Bailey, "What Makes Teams Work."

16. J. Katzenbach and D. Smith, "The Discipline of Teams," *Harvard Business Review*, March–April 1993, pp. 111–20.

17. M. D. Sarrel, "SMB Boot Camp: Wicked Productive Wikis," *PC Magazine*, February 20, 2007, http://galenet.galegroup.com.

18. J. Zenger et al., *Leading Teams* (Burr Ridge, IL: Business One Irwin, 1994).

19. S. Cohen, "New Approaches to Teams and Teamwork," in J. Galbraith, E. E. Lawler III, and Associates, *Organizing for the Future* (San Francisco: Jossey-Bass, 1993).

20. Cohen and Bailey, "What Makes Teams Work."

21. L. Mullins, "Integration Crew for Maryland Bank," *American Banker*, February 13, 2007, downloaded from General Reference Center Gold, http://find.galegroup.com.

22. Ibid.

23. C. Snow, S. Snell, S. Davison, and D. Hambrick, "Use Transnational Teams to Globalize Your Company," *Organizational Dynamics*, Spring 1996, pp. 50–67.

24. B. Kirkman, B. Rosen, C. Gibson, P. Tesluk, and S. McPherson, "Five Challenges to Virtual Team Success: Lessons from Sabre, Inc.," *Academy of Management Executive* 16 (2002), pp. 67–80.

25. R. Banker, J. Field, R. Schroeder, and K. Sinha, "Impact of Work Teams on Manufacturing Performance: A Longitudinal Field Study," *Academy of Management Journal* 39 (1996), pp. 867–90.

26. D. Yeatts, M. Hipskind, and D. Barnes, "Lessons Learned from Self-Managed Work Teams," *Business Horizons*, July–August 1994, pp. 11–18.

27. B. Kirkman and D. Shapiro, "The Impact of Cultural Values on Job Satisfaction and Organizational Commitment in Self-Managing Work Teams: The Mediating Role of Employee Resistance," *Academy of Management Journal* 44 (2001), pp. 557–69.

28. C. Langfred, "The Downside of Self-Management: A Longitudinal Study of the Effects of Conflict on Trust, Autonomy, and Task Interdependence in Self-Managing Teams," *Academy of Management Journal*, 2007, pp. 885–900.

29. B. Kirkman and D. Shapiro, "The Impact of Cultural Values on Employee Resistance to Teams: Toward a Model of Globalized Self-Managing Work Team Effectiveness," *Academy of Management Review* 22 (1997), pp. 730–57.

30. B. Macy and H. Isumi, "Organizational Change, Design, and Work Innovation: A Meta-Analysis of 131 North American Field Studies—1961–1991," *Research in Organizational Change and Development* 7 (1993), pp. 235–313.

31. Ibid.

32. B. W. Tuckman, "Developmental Sequence in Small Groups," *Psychological Bulletin* 63 (1965), pp. 384–99.

33. S. Furst, M. Reeves, B. Rosen, and R. Blackburn, "Managing the Life Cycle of Virtual Teams," *Academy of Management Executive*, May 2004, pp. 6–20. Quotes in this paragraph are from pp. 11 and 12.

34. C. J. G. Gersick, "Time and Transition in Work Teams: Toward a New Model of Group Development," *Academy of Management Journal* 31 (1988), pp. 9–41.

35. J. R. Hackman, *Groups That Work (and Those That Don't)* (San Francisco: Jossey-Bass, 1990).

36. Zenger et al., *Leading Teams*.

37. R. Cross, "Looking before You Leap: Assessing the Jump to Teams in Knowledge-Based Work," *Business Horizons*, September–October 2000, pp. 29–36.

38. Ken Blanchard Companies, "The Critical Role of Teams," *Research Findings*, April 11, 2006, http://www.kenblanchard.com/thoughtleadership (reporting on a March 2006 survey of 962 HR, training, and operations leaders).

39. J. Case, "What the Experts Forgot to Mention," *Inc.*, September 1993, pp. 66–78.

40. A. Nahavandi and E. Aranda, "Restructuring Teams for the Reengineered Organization," *Academy of Management Executive*, November 1994, pp. 58–68.

41. B. Kirkman, B. Rosen, P. Tesluk, and C. Gibson, "The Impact of Team Empowerment on Virtual Team Performance: The Moderating Role of Face-to-Face Interaction," *Academy of Management Journal* 47 (2004), pp. 175–92.

42. J. R. Katzenbach and D. K. Smith, *The Wisdom of Teams* (Boston: Harvard Business School Press, 1993).

43. Nadler et al., *Managing Organizational Behavior*.

44. D. Wood, "Multidisciplinary Team Eliminates Inefficiencies in a Busy GYN Oncology Clinic," *Oncology Nursing News*, April 2009, downloaded from Business & Company Resource Center, http://galenet.galegroup.com.

45. T. Peters and N. Austin, *A Passion for Excellence* (New York: Random House, 1985).

46. Nadler et al., *Managing Organizational Behavior*.

47. S. Adams, "Making All Your Teams into A-Teams," *Training Journal*, August 2008, downloaded from Business & Company Resource Center, http://galenet.galegroup.com.

48. D. Clutterbuck, "How to Coach a Team in the Field: What Is Involved in Team Coaching and What Skills Are Required?" *Training Journal*, February 2007, downloaded from Business & Company Resource Center, http://galenet.galegroup.com.

49. D. Coutu, "Why Teams Don't Work," *Harvard Business Review*, May 2009, pp. 99–105 (interview of J. Richard Hackman).

50. Katzenbach and Smith, "The Discipline of Teams."

51. Ibid.

52. L. Gibson, J. Mathieu, C. Shalley, and T. Ruddy, "Creativity and Standardization: Complementary or Conflicting Drivers of Team Effectiveness?" *Academy of Management Journal* 48 (2005), pp. 521–31.

53. C. Meyer, "How the Right Measures Help Teams Excel," *Harvard Business Review*, May–June 1994, pp. 95–103.

54. J. R. Katzenbach and J. A. Santamaria, "Firing Up the Front Line," *Harvard Business Review*, May–June 1999, pp. 107–17.

55. D. Knight, C. Durham, and E. Locke, "The Relationship of Team Goals, Incentives, and Efficacy to Strategic Risk, Tactical Implementation, and Performance," *Academy of Management Journal* 44 (2001), pp. 326–38.

56. B. L. Kirkman and B. Rosen, "Powering Up Teams," *Organizational Dynamics* (Winter 2000), pp. 48–66.

57. Lawler, *From the Ground Up*.

58. A. Jassawalla, H. Sashittal, and A. Maishe, "Students' Perceptions of Social Loafing: Its Antecedents and

Consequences in Undergraduate Business Classroom Teams," *Academy of Management Learning and Education,* 2009, pp. 42–54.

59. M. Erez, "Is Group Productivity Loss the Rule or the Exception? Effects of Culture and Group-Based Motivation," *Academy of Management Journal* 39 (1996), pp. 1513–37.

60. Katzenbach and Smith, "The Discipline of Teams."

61. M. Bolch, "Rewarding the Team," *HRMagazine,* February 2007, downloaded from General Reference Center Gold, http://find.galegroup.com; P. Pascarelloa, "Compensating Teams," *Across the Board,* February 1997, pp. 16–22; and M. Johnson, J. Hollenbeck, S. Humphrey, D. Ilgen, D. Jundt, and C. Meyer, "Cutthroat Cooperation: Asymmetrical Adaptation to Changes in Team Reward Structures," *Academy of Management Journal,* 2006, 103–19.

62. R. Wageman, "Interdependence and Group Effectiveness," *Administrative Science Quarterly* 40 (1995), pp. 145–80.

63. Bolch, "Rewarding the Team."

64. O. Marks, "From Command and Control to Collaboration and Teamwork," *ZDNet.com,* February 9, 2009, http://blogs.zdnet.com; Lawson, "Cisco to Shift Resources to Consumer Push"; McGirt, "How Cisco's CEO John Chambers Is Turning the Tech Giant Socialist"; B. Fryer, "Cisco CEO John Chambers on Teamwork and Collaboration," *Harvard Business Review,* October 24, 2008, http://www.discussionleader.hbsp.com; Ando, "Chambers Sees Cisco CEO Role Changing"; "Reinventing Cisco Systems"; John Chambers, "Commentary," *Forbes,* January 23, 2008, http://www.forbes.com; and S. Gharib, "One on One with John Chambers, Cisco Chairman and CEO, Shares Success Secrets," *Nightly Business Report,* November 7, 2007, http://www.pbc.org.

65. Lawler, *From the Ground Up.*

66. R. Wellins, R. Byham, and G. Dixon, *Inside Teams* (San Francisco: Jossey-Bass, 1994).

67. J. Allen, "One 'Bad Apple' Does Spoil the Whole Office," *Reuters,* February 12, 2007, http://news.yahoo.com, and J. Wardy, "Don't Let One with Bad Attitude Infect Others," *Daily Record (Morris County, NJ),* April 23, 2007, http://www.dailyrecord.com.

68. Institute for Corporate Productivity, "Virtual Teams Now a Reality," news release, September 4, 2008, http://www.i4cp.com.

69. A. Srivastava, K. Bartol, and E. Locke, "Empowering Leadership in Management Teams: Effects on Knowledge Sharing, Efficacy, and Performance," *Academy of Management Journal,* 2006, pp. 1239–51.

70. J. M. Levine, E. T. Higgins, and H. Choi, "Development of Strategic Norms in Groups," *Organizational Behavior and Human Decision Processes* 82 (2000), pp. 88–101.

71. K. Jehn and E. Mannix, "The Dynamic Nature of Conflict: A Longitudinal Study of Intragroup Conflict and Group Performance," *Academy of Management Journal* 44 (2001), pp. 238–51.

72. J. O'Toole, *Vanguard Management: Redesigning the Corporate Future* (New York: Doubleday, 1985).

73. R. F. Bales, *Interaction Process Analysis: A Method for the Study of Small Groups* (Reading, MA: Addison-Wesley, 1950).

74. V. U. Druskat and J. Wheeler, "Managing from the Boundary: The Effective Leadership of Self-Managing Work Teams," *Academy of Management Journal* 46 (2003), pp. 435–57.

75. Katzenbach and Smith, *The Wisdom of Teams.*

76. J. Carson, P. Tesluk, and J. Marrone. "Shared Leadership in Teams: An Investigation of Antecedent Conditions and Performance," *Academy of Management Journal,* 2007, pp. 1217–34.

77. C. Stoner and R. Hartman. "Team Building: Answering the Tough Questions," *Business Horizons,* September–October 1993, pp. 70–78.

78. S. E. Seashore, *Group Cohesiveness in the Industrial Work Group* (Ann Arbor, MI: University of Michigan Press, 1954).

79. Banker et al., "Impact of Work Teams on Manufacturing Performance."

80. B. Mullen and C. Cooper, "The Relation between Group Cohesiveness and Performance: An Integration," *Psychological Bulletin* 115 (1994), pp. 210–27.

81. D. P. Forbes and F. J. Milliken, "Cognition and Corporate Governance: Understanding Boards of Directors as Strategic Decision-Making Groups," *Academy of Management Review* 24 (1999), pp. 489–505.

82. T. Simons, L. H. Pelled, and K. A. Smith, "Making Use of Difference: Diversity, Debate, and Decision Comprehensiveness in Top Management Teams," *Academy of Management Journal* 42 (1999), pp. 662–73.

83. Seashore, *Group Cohesiveness in the Industrial Work Group.*

84. B. Lott and A. Lott, "Group Cohesiveness as Interpersonal Attraction: A Review of Relationships with Antecedent and Consequent Variables," *Psychological Bulletin,* October 1965, pp. 259–309.

85. K. Dahlin, L. Weingart, and P. Hinds, "Team Diversity and Information Use," *Academy of Management Journal* 48 (2005), pp. 1107–23.

86. B. L. Kirkman and B. Rosen, "Beyond Self-Management: Antecedents and Consequences of Team Empowerment," *Academy of Management Journal* 42 (1999), pp. 58–74.

87. Hackman, *Groups That Work.*

88. W. Bennis, *Organizing Genius* (Reading, MA: Addison-Wesley, 1997).

89. Cianni and Wnuck, "Individual Growth and Team Enhancement."

90. K. Jehn. "A Multimethod Examination of the Benefits and Detriments of Intragroup Conflict," *Administrative Science Quarterly* 40 (1995), pp. 245–82.

91. Wellins et al., *Inside Teams.*

92. D. G. Ancona, "Outward Bound: Strategies for Team Survival in an Organization," *Academy of Management Journal* 33 (1990), pp. 334–65.

93. Ibid.

94. L. Sayles, *Leadership: What Effective Managers Really Do, and How They Do It* (New York: McGraw-Hill, 1979).

95. Ibid.

96. P. Lencioni, "How to Foster Good Conflict," *The Wall Street Journal,* November 13, 2008, http://online.wsj.com; and D. Schachter, "Learn to Embrace Opposition for Improved Decision Making," *Information Outlook,* October 2008, downloaded from Business & Company Resource Center, http://galenet.galegroup.com.

97. J. Chatman and F. Flynn, "The Influence of Demographic Heterogeneity on the Emergence and Consequences of Cooperative Norms in Work Teams," *Academy of Management Journal* 44 (2001), pp. 956–74; and R. T. Keller, "Cross-Functional Project Groups in Research and New Product Development: Diversity, Communications, Job Stress, and Outcomes," *Academy of Management Journal* 44 (2001), pp. 547–55.

93. R. Manian, "Teamwork, Sweat and Tears," *Business Line,* March 23, 2009, downloaded from Business & Company Resource Center, http://galenet.galegroup.com; and A. Homan, J. Hollenbeck, S. Humphrey, D. Van Knippenberg, D. Ilgen, and G. Van Kleef, "Facing Differences with an Open Mind: Openness to Experience, Salience of Intragroup Differences, and Performance of Diverse Work Groups," *Academy of Management Journal,* 2008, pp. 1204–22.

99. "Managing Multicultural Teams: Winning Strategies from Teams around the World," *Computerworld,* November 20, 2006, http://find.galegroup.com.

100. D. Tjosvold, *Working Together to Get Things Done* (Lexington, MA: Lexington Books, 1986).

101. C. Tinsley and J. Brett, "Managing Workplace Conflict in the United States and Hong Kong," *Organizational Behavior and Human Decision Processes* 85 (2001), pp. 360–81.

102. K. W. Thomas, "Conflict and Conflict Management," in *Handbook of Industrial and Organizational Psychology,* ed. M. D. Dunnette (Chicago: Rand McNally, 1976).

103. J. S. Lublin, "How Best to Supervise Internal Runner-Up for the Job You Got," *The Wall Street Journal,* January 30, 2007, http://online.wsj.com.

104. Ibid.

105. K. W. Thomas, "Toward Multidimensional Values in Teaching: The Example of Conflict Behaviors," *Academy of Management Review*, 1977, pp. 484–89.

106. C. O. Longenecker and M. Neubert, "Barriers and Gateways to Management Cooperation and Teamwork," *Business Horizons*, September–October 2000, pp. 37–44.

107. M. Johnson, J. Hollenbeck, S. Humphrey, D. Algen, D. Jundt, and C. Meyer, "Cutthroat Cooperation: Asymmetrical Adaptation to Changes in Team Reward Structures." *Academy of Management Journal* 49 (2006), pp. 103–119.

108. P. S. Nugent, "Managing Conflict: Third-Party Interventions for Managers," *Academy of Management Executive* 16 (2002), pp. 139–54.

109. M. Blum and J. A. Wall Jr., "HRM: Managing Conflicts in the Firm," *Business Horizons*, May–June 1997, pp. 84–87.

110. V. Elmer, "Stressed Out," *The Washington Post*, October 19, 2006, http://www.washingtonpost.com.

111. J. A. Wall Jr. and R. R. Callister, "Conflict and Its Management," *Journal of Management* 21 (1995), pp. 515–58.

112. J. Polzer, C. B. Crisp, S. Jarvenpaa, and J. Kim, "Extending the Faultline Model to Geographically Dispersed Teams: How Collocated Subgroups Can Impair Group Functioning," *Academy of Management Journal* 49 (2006), pp. 679–92.

113. M. Montoya-Weiss, A. Massey, and M. Song, "Getting It Together: Temporal Coordination and Conflict Management in Global Virtual Teams," *Academy of Management Journal* 44 (2001), pp. 1251–62.

114. R. Standifer and J. A. Wall Jr., "Managing Conflict in B2B Commerce," *Business Horizons*, March–April 2003, pp. 65–70.

115. Company Web site, http://newsroom.cisco.com, accessed April 15, 2009; Marks, "From Command and Control to Collaboration and Teamwork"; Lawson, "Cisco to Shift Resources to Consumer Push"; B. Silverstein, "Cisco: Networked," *BrandChannel.com*, December 8, 2008, http://brandchannel.com; and M. Reardon, "Cisco Launches New Video Initiative," *Business Tech*, December 7, 2008, http://news.cnet.com; Doerr, "Builders and Titans."

Chapter 15

1. D. M. Ewalt, "The Web Celeb 25," *Forbes*, January 1, 2009, http://www.forbes.com; M. Chafkin, "The Hottest Company in America," *Inc.*, November 2008, pp. 88–96; C. McCarthy, "Digg's Kevin Rose: We've Got to Be More Than a Fanboy Hub," *CNET News*, October 9, 2008, http://news.cnet.com; "The 25 Most Influential People on the Web," *BusinessWeek*, October 1, 2008, http://images.businessweek.com; and C. Jeffery, "In Digg Nation," *Mother Jones*, June 27, 2007, http://www.motherjones.com.

2. L. Penley, E. Alexander, I. E. Jernigan, and C. Henwood, "Communication Abilities of Managers: The Relationship to Performance," *Journal of Management* 17 (1991), pp. 57–76.

3. W. V. Haney, "A Comparative Study of Unilateral and Bilateral Communication," *Academy of Management Journal* 7 (1964), pp. 128–36.

4. J. Sandberg, "What Exactly Was It That the Boss Said? You Can Only Imagine," *The Wall Street Journal*, September 19, 2006, http://online.wsj.com.

5. M. McCormack, "The Illusion of Communication," *Financial Times Mastering Management Review*, July 1999, pp. 8–9.

6. J. Sandberg, "Not Communicating with Your Boss? Count Your Blessings," *The Wall Street Journal*, May 22, 2007, http://online.wsj.com.

7. R. Cross and S. Brodt, "How Assumptions of Consensus Undermine Decision Making," *Sloan Management Review* 42 (2001), pp. 86–94.

8. S. Mohammed and E. Ringseis, "Cognitive Diversity and Consensus in Group Decision Making: The Role of Inputs, Processes, and Outcomes," *Organizational Behavior and Human Decision Processes* 85 (2001), pp. 310–35.

9. S. Parker and C. Axtell, "Seeing Another Viewpoint: Antecedents and Outcomes of Employee Perspective Taking," *Academy of Management Journal* 44 (2001), pp. 1085–100.

10. D. Tannen, "The Power of Talk: Who Gets Heard and Why," *Harvard Business Review*, September–October 1995, pp. 138–48.

11. Ibid.

12. Ibid.

13. L. K. Larkey, "Toward a Theory of Communicative Interactions in Culturally Diverse Workgroups," *Academy of Management Review*, April 1996, pp. 463–91.

14. C. Argyris, "Good Communication That Blocks Learning," *Harvard Business Review*, July–August 1994, pp. 77–85.

15. E. Krell, "The Unintended Word," *HRMagazine*, August 2006, downloaded from General Reference Center Gold, http://find.galegroup.com.

16. C. Deutsch, "The Multimedia Benefits Kit," *New York Times*, October 14, 1990, sec. 3, p. 25.

17. T. W. Comstock, *Communicating in Business and Industry* (Albany, NY: Delmar, 1985).

18. J. Taylor and W. Wacker, *The 500 Year Delta: What Happens after What Comes Next* (New York: HarperCollins, 1997).

19. M. Totty, "Rethinking the Inbox," *The Wall Street Journal*, March 26, 2007, http://online.wsj.com.

20. K. Lorenz, "WAN2CHAT? 10 Tips for IM-ing at Work," *AOL Jobs*, December 15, 2006, http://jobs.aol.com.

21. Totty, "Rethinking the Inbox."

22. S. J. Leandri, "Five Ways to Improve Your Corporate Blogs," *Information Outlook*, January 2007, downloaded from Business & Company Resource Center, http://galenet.galegroup.com.

23. R. D. Hof, "Web 2.0: The New Guy at Work," *BusinessWeek*, June 19, 2006, downloaded from Business & Company Resource Center, http://galenet.galegroup.com.

24. Chafkin, "The Hottest Company in America"; McCarthy, "Digg's Kevin Rose"; C. McCarthy, "Getting Global with Digg's Kevin Rose," *CNET News*, October 9, 2008, http://www.cnet.com; and Jeffery, "In Digg Nation."

25. J. Dye, "Collaboration 2.0: Make the Web Your Workspace," *EContent*, January–February 2007, downloaded from General Reference Center Gold, http://find.galegroup.com.

26. E. Lee, "The Maze Meltdown: Crash May Virtually Change Commuting," *San Francisco Chronicle*, May 6, 2007, http://www.sfgate.com.

27. S. S. K. Lam and J. Schaubroeck, "Improving Group Decisions by Better Pooling Information: A Comparative Advantage of Group Decision Support Systems," *Journal of Applied Psychology* 85 (2000), pp. 565–73.

28. M. Schrage, "If You Can't Say Anything Nice, Say It Anonymously," *Fortune*, December 6, 1999, p. 352; and B. Stone, "A Call for Manners in the World of Nasty Blogs," *New York Times*, April 9, 2007, http://www.nytimes.com.

29. C. Naquin and G. Paulson, "Online Bargaining and Interpersonal Trust," *Journal of Applied Psychology* 88 (2003), pp. 113–20.

30. B. Baltes, M. Dickson, M. Sherman, C. Bauer, and J. LaGanke, "Computer-Mediated Communication and Group Decision Making: A Meta-Analysis," *Organizational Behavior and Human Decision Processes* 87 (2002), pp. 156–79.

31. R. Rice and D. Case, "Electronic Message Systems in the University: A Description of Use and Utility," *Journal of Communication* 33 (1983), pp. 131–52; and C. Steinfield, "Dimensions of Electronic Mail Use in an Organizational Setting," *Proceedings of the Academy of Management*, San Diego, 1985.

32. M. Gardner, "You've Got Mail: 'We're Letting You Go,' " *Christian Science Monitor*, September 18, 2006, http://www.csmonitor.com; and Linton Weeks, "Read the Blog: You're Fired," *National Public Radio*, December 8, 2008, http://www.npr.org.

33. Leandri, "Five Ways to Improve Your Corporate Blogs."

34. Reuters, "Is That Really What Your E-mail Meant to Say?" *Yahoo News*, February 14, 2007, http://news.yahoo.com.

35. B. Glassberg, W. Kettinger, and J. Logan, "Electronic Communication: An Ounce of Policy Is Worth a Pound of Cure," *Business Horizons*, July–August 1996, pp. 74–80.

36. A. Joyce, "Never Out of IM Reach," *The Washington Post*, December 26, 2004, p. F5; and G. Hughes, "Quick Guide to IM-ing at Work," *Yahoo Tech*, January 24, 2007, http://tech.yahoo.com.

37. Totty, "Rethinking the Inbox"; Reuters, "BlackBerrys, Laptops Blur Work/Home Balance: Poll," *Yahoo News*, April 5, 2007, http://news.yahoo.com; and M. Locher, "BlackBerry Addiction Starts at the Top," *PC World*, March 6, 2007, http://www.pcworld.com.

38. C. McCarthy, "Americans Mixed about Constant Net Access, Poll Finds," *CNet News*, April 16, 2007, http://news.com.com.

39. Taylor and Wacker, *The 500 Year Delta*; Locher, "BlackBerry Addiction"; and Hughes, "Quick Guide to IM-ing."

40. Locher, "BlackBerry Addiction."

41. E. Horng, "No E-mail Fridays Transform Office," *ABC News*, March 10, 2007, http://abcnews.go.com.

42. Ibid.

43. V. Govindarajan and A. Gupta, "Building an Effective Global Team," *Organizational Dynamics* 42 (2001), pp. 63–71.

44. N. B. Kurland and D. E. Bailey, "Telework: The Advantages and Challenges of Working Here, There, Anywhere, Anytime," *Organizational Dynamics*, Autumn 1999, pp. 53–68; and B. Van Der Meer, "Realty Companies Making Internet Home," *Modesto (CA) Bee*, December 15, 2006, downloaded from General Reference Center Gold, http://find.galegroup.com.

45. "ALA Washington Opens Virtual Office," *American Libraries*, March 2007, downloaded from General Reference Center Gold, http://find.galegroup.com.

46. Van Der Meer, "Realty Companies Making Internet Home."

47. T. Mackintosh, "Is This the Year You Move to a Virtual Office?" *Accounting Technology*, May 2007, downloaded from General Reference Center Gold, http://find.galegroup.com.

48. E. M. Hallowell, "The Human Moment at Work," *Harvard Business Review*, January–February 1999, pp. 58–66.

49. J. Marquez, "Connecting a Virtual Workforce," *Workforce Management*, September 22, 2008, downloaded from Business & Company Resource Center, http://galenet.galegroup.com.

50. R. Lengel and R. Daft, "The Selection of Communication Media as an Executive Skill," *Academy of Management Executive* 2 (1988), pp. 225–32.

51. J. R. Carlson and R. W. Zmud, "Channel Expansion Theory and the Experiential Nature of Media Richness Perceptions," *Academy of Management Journal* 42 (1999), pp. 153–70.

52. L. Trevino, R. Daft, and R. Lengel, "Understanding Managers' Media Choices: A Symbolic Interactionist Perspective," in *Organizations and Communication Technology*, ed. J. Fulk and C. Steinfield (London: Sage, 1990).

53. J. Fulk and B. Boyd, "Emerging Theories of Communication in Organizations," *Journal of Management* 17 (1991), pp. 407–46.

54. L. Bossidy and R. Charan, *Confronting Reality: Doing What Matters to Get Things Right* (New York: Crown Business, 2004).

55. M. McCall, M. Lombardo, and A. Morrison, *The Lessons of Experience: How Successful Executives Develop on the Job* (Lexington, MA: Lexington, 1988).

56. J. A. Conger, "The Necessary Art of Persuasion," *Harvard Business Review*, May–June 1998, pp. 84–95.

57. N. Morgan, "How to Become an Authentic Speaker," *Harvard Business Review*, November 2008, pp. 115–19.

58. N. Nohria and B. Harrington, *Six Principles of Successful Persuasion* (Boston: Harvard Business School Publishing Division, 1993).

59. J. Ewers, "Making It Stick," *U.S. News & World Report*, January 29–February 5, 2007, pp. EE2–EE8 (review of *Made to Stick* by Chip Heath and Dan Heath).

60. H. K. Mintz, "Business Writing Styles for the 70's," *Business Horizons*, August 1972. Cited in *Readings in Interpersonal and Organizational Communication*, ed. R. C. Huseman, C. M. Logue, and D. L. Freshley (Boston: Allyn & Bacon, 1977).

61. C. D. Decker, "Writing to Teach Thinking," *Across the Board*, March 1996, pp. 19–20.

62. M. Forbes, "Exorcising Demons from Important Business Letters," *Marketing Times*, March–April 1981, pp. 36–38.

63. W. Strunk Jr. and E. B. White, *The Elements of Style*, 3rd ed. (New York: Macmillan, 1979); and H. R. Fowler and J. E Aaron, *The Little, Brown Handbook*, 10th ed. (New York: Longman, 2006).

64. J. Tsai, "Spiff Up Your Site!" *CRM Magazine*, December 2008, downloaded from Business & Company Resource Center, http://galenet.galegroup.com.

65. D. Jones, "Cisco CEO Sees Tech as Integral to Success," *USA Today*, March 19, 2007, p. 4B (interview with John Chambers).

66. G. Ferraro, "The Need for Linguistic Proficiency in Global Business," *Business Horizons*, May–June 1996, pp. 39–46.

67. P. C. Early and E. Mosakowski, "Creating Hybrid Team Cultures: An Empirical Test of Transnational Team Functioning," *Academy of Management Journal* 43 (2000), pp. 26–49.

68. Ferraro, "The Need for Linguistic Proficiency."

69. C. Chu, *The Asian Mind Game* (New York: Rawson Associates, 1991).

70. Ferraro, "The Need for Linguistic Proficiency."

71. J. S. Lublin, "Improv Troupe Teaches Managers How to Give Better Presentations," *Career Journal*, February 7, 2007, http://www.careerjournal.com.

72. Comstock, *Communicating in Business and Industry*.

73. M. Korda, *Power: How to Get It, How to Use It* (New York: Random House, 1975).

74. A. Mehrabian, "Communication without Words," *Psychology Today*, September 1968, p. 52. Cited in M. B. McCaskey, "The Hidden Message Managers Send," *Harvard Business Review*, November–December 1979, pp. 135–48.

75. Ferraro, "The Need for Linguistic Proficiency."

76. *Business Horizons*, May–June 1993. Copyright 1993 by the Foundation for the School of Business at Indiana University. Used with permission.

77. A. T. Palmer, "Art of Listening Picked Up Young," *Chicago Tribune*, April 29, 2007, sec. 5, p. 3.

78. Ibid.

79. A. Athos and J. Gabarro, *Interpersonal Behavior* (Englewood Cliffs, NJ: Prentice-Hall, 1978).

80. M. K. Pratt, "Five Ways to Drive Your Best Workers out the Door," *Computerworld*, August 25, 2008, pp. 26–27, 30.

81. J. Kouzes and B. Posner, *The Leadership Challenge* (San Francisco: Jossey-Bass, 1995).

82. G. Graham, J. Unruh, and P. Jennings, "The Impact of Nonverbal Communication in Organizations: A Survey of Perceptions," *Journal of Business Communications* 28 (1991), pp. 45–62.

83. Ibid.

84. D. Upton and S. Macadam, "Why (and How) to Take a Plant Tour," *Harvard Business Review*, May–June 1997, pp. 97–106.

85. N. Adler, *International Dimensions of Organizational Behavior*, 2nd ed. (Boston: Kent, 1991).

86. Chu, *The Asian Mind Game*.

87. Alex Pentland, "How Social Networks Network Best," *Harvard Business Review*, February 2009, p. 37.

88. A. Smidts, A. T. H. Pruyn, and C. B. M. van Riel, "The Impact of Employee Communication and Perceived External Prestige on Organizational Identification," *Academy of Management Journal* 49 (2001), pp. 1051–62.

89. J. W. Koehler, K. W. E. Anatol, and R. L. Applebaum, *Organizational Communication: Behavioral Perspectives* (Orlando, FL: Holt, Rinehart & Winston, 1981).

90. J. Waldroop and T. Butler, "The Executive as Coach," *Harvard Business Review*, November–December 1996, pp. 111–17.

91. D. T. Hall, K. L. Otazo, and G. P. Hollenbeck, "Behind Closed Doors: What Really Happens in Executive Coaching," *Organizational Dynamics,* Winter 1999, pp. 39–53.

92. T. Judge and J. Cowell, "The Brave New World of Coaching," *Business Horizons,* July–August 1997, pp. 71–77; E. E. Lawler III, *Treat People Right!* (San Francisco: Jossey-Bass, 2003); and L. A. Hill, "New Manager Development for the 21st Century," *Academy of Management Executive,* August 2004, pp. 121–26.

93. J. Gutknecht and J. B. Keys, "Mergers, Acquisitions, and Takeovers: Maintaining Morale of Survivors and Protecting Employees," *Academy of Management Executive,* August 1993, pp. 26–36.

94. D. Schweiger and A. DeNisi, "Communication with Employees Following a Merger: A Longitudinal Field Experiment," *Academy of Management Journal* 34 (1991), pp. 110–35.

95. J. Case, "The Open-Book Managers," *Inc.,* September 1990, pp. 104–13.

96. J. Case, "Opening the Books," *Harvard Business Review,* March–April 1997, pp. 118–27.

97. T. R. V. Davis, "Open-Book Management: Its Promise and Pitfalls," *Organization Dynamics,* Winter 1997, pp. 7–20.

98. B. Burlingham, "Jack Stack, SRC Holdings," *Inc.,* April 2004, pp. 134–35.

99. W. V. Ruch, *Corporate Communications* (Westport, CT: Quorum, 1984).

100. J. Sandberg, "Working for a Boss Who Only Manages Up Can Be a Real Downer," *The Wall Street Journal,* May 16, 2006, http://online.wsj.com.

101. J. Gardner, "The Heart of the Matter: Leader-Constituent Interaction," in *Leading & Leadership,* ed. T. Fuller (Notre Dame, IN: Notre Dame University Press, 2000), pp. 239–44.

102. R. Ashkenas, D. Ulrich, T. Jick, and S. Kerr, *The Boundaryless Organization* (San Francisco: Jossey-Bass, 1995).

103. Ruch, *Corporate Communications.*

104. P. Bach, "Staying in Touch a Changing Picture," *Post-Crescent* (Appleton, WI), April 18, 2006, downloaded from General Reference Center Gold, http://find.galegroup.com.

105. M. Fitzgerald, "The Earl of Florida," *Editor & Publisher,* February 1, 2007, downloaded from General Reference Center Gold, http://find.galegroup.com.

106. A. Hutton, "Four Rules for Taking Your Message to Wall Street," *Harvard Business Review,* May 2001, pp. 125–32.

107. Koehler et al., *Organizational Communication.*

108. W. Atkinson, "Let's Work Together Right Now," *Collections & Credit Risk,* May 2006, downloaded from Business & Company Resource Center, http://galenet.galegroup.com.

109. Janet Pogue, "Working around the Water Cooler," *Employee Benefit News,* February 1, 2009, downloaded from Business & Company Resource Center, http://galenet.galegroup.com; Gensler, "Gensler Survey Measures Connection between Workplace Design and Business Performance," news release, October 23, 2008, http://www.gensler.com; and Gensler, *2008 Workplace Survey: United States,* 2008, http://www.gensler.com.

110. Ashkenas et al., *The Boundaryless Organization.*

111. D. K. Denton, "Open Communication," *Business Horizons,* September–October 1993, pp. 64–69.

112. N. B. Kurland and L. H. Pelled, "Passing the Word: Toward a Model of Gossip and Power in the Workplace," *Academy of Management Review* 25 (2000), pp. 428–38.

113. L. Abrams, R. Cross, E. Lesser, and D. Levin, "Nurturing Interpersonal Trust in Knowledge-Sharing Networks," *Academy of Management Executive* 17 (November 2003), pp. 64–77.

114. R. L. Rosnow, "Rumor as Communication: A Contextual Approach," *Journal of Communication* 38 (1988), pp. 12–28.

115. L. Burke and J. M. Wise, "The Effective Care, Handling, and Pruning of the Office Grapevine," *Business Horizons,* May–June 2003, pp. 71–76.

116. K. Davis, "The Care and Cultivation of the Corporate Grapevine," *Dun's Review,* July 1973, pp. 44–47.

117. "Office Politics Is on the Rise According to a Survey by Accountemps," *Bradenton (FL) Herald,* October 25, 2008, downloaded from Business & Company Resource Center, http://galenet.galegroup.com; and Alan M. Wolf, "A Morale Boost," *Raleigh (NC) News & Observer,* March 15, 2009, http://galenet.galegroup.com.

118. N. Difonzo, P. Bordia, and R. Rosnow, "Reining in Rumors," *Organizational Dynamics,* Summer 1994, pp. 47–62.

119. Ashkenas et al., *The Boundaryless Organization.*

120. R. M. Hodgetts, "A Conversation with Steve Kerr," *Organizational Dynamics,* Spring 1996, pp. 68–79.

121. R. M. Fulmer, "The Evolving Paradigm of Leadership Development," *Organizational Dynamics,* Spring 1997, pp. 59–72.

122. General Electric, "GE Shares Skills, Intellectual Capital with CommonBond Communities," news release, December 4, 2006, http://www.genewscenter.com.

123. Ashkenas et al., *The Boundaryless Organization.*

124. Kevin Rose blog, http://kevinrose.com, accessed May 15, 2009; Techcrunch, "Interview with Digg's Kevin Rose: The State of the Union," *AjaxWorld Magazine,* April 21, 2009, http://ajax.sys-con.com; A. Zafra, "Kevin Rose Launches WeFollow Twitter Directory," *Search Engine Journal,* March 15, 2009, http://www.searchenginejournal.com; Ewalt, "The Web Celeb 25"; Chafkin, "The Hottest Company in America"; J. Kirk, "Digg's Kevin Rose: 'We Have to Do Better,'" *Network World,* October 9, 2008, http://www.networkworld.com; McCarthy, "Digg's Kevin Rose"; "The 25 Most Influential People on the Web," *BusinessWeek.*

Chapter 16

1. J. C. Collins, and J. I. Porras, *Built to Last: Successful Habits of Visionary Companies* (New York: HarperBusiness, 1994).

2. Company Web site, http://www.legalseafoods.com, accessed April 22, 2009; and E. Elan, "Roger Berkowitz: Legal Sea Foods Leader Fosters Collaboration in Menu Development," *Nation's Restaurant News,* May 5, 2008, http://findarticles.com.

3. B. Kenney, "Dell Inc.: Coach Michael Dell's New Game Plan," *Industry Week,* June 7, 2007, http://www.industryweek.com.

4. "BlackBerry Outage Explained," *Chicago Tribune,* April 21, 2007, sec. 3, p. 2; and N. Weil, "BlackBerry Service Restored, Slow Response Irks Users," *InfoWorld,* April 18, 2007, http://www.infoworld.com.

5. W. G. Ouchi, "Markets, Bureaucracies, and Clans," *Administrative Science Quarterly* 25 (1980), pp. 129–41.

6. R. Simons, A. Davila, and R. S. Kaplan, *Performance Measurement & Control Systems for Implementing Strategy* (Englewood Cliffs, NJ: Prentice Hall, 2000).

7. E. D. Pulakos, S. Arad, M. A. Donovan, and K. E. Plamondon, "Adaptability in the Workplace: Development of a Taxonomy of Adaptive Performance," *Journal of Applied Psychology* 85, no. 4 (August 2000), pp. 12–24; and J. H. Sheridan, "Lean Sigma Synergy," *Industry Week* 249, no. 17 (October 16, 2000), pp. 81–82.

8. E. Gardner, "High-Quality Information," *Modern Healthcare,* March 5, 2007, downloaded from General Reference Center Gold, http://find.galegroup.com.

9. M. S. Rosenwald, "Chocolate Purists Alarmed by Proposal to Fudge Standards," *Washington Post,* April 27, 2007, http://www.washingtonpost.com.

10. J. T. Burr, "Keys to a Successful Internal Audit," *Quality Progress* 30, no. 4 (April 1997), pp. 75–77; and J. Zorabedian, "Uniform Security," *American Executive,* June 2008, downloaded from Business & Company Resource Center, http://galenet.galegroup.com.

11. L. Buchanan, "Leadership: Armed with Data," *Inc.,* March 2009, http://www.inc.com.

12. R. M. Kanter, "The Matter with the Mainstream," *U.S. News & World*

Report, October 30, 2006, downloaded from General Reference Center Gold, http://find.galegroup.com.

13. "Quality Leadership 100," *Quality,* September 2006, downloaded from Business & Company Resource Center, http://galenet.galegroup.com.

14. E. White, "How Surveying Workers Can Pay Off," *The Wall Street Journal,* June 18, 2007, http://online.wsj.com.

15. B. Roberts, "Stay Ahead of the Technology Use Curve," *HRMagazine,* October 2008, downloaded from Business & Company Resource Center, http://galenet.galegroup.com; and K. A. Carr, "Broaching Body Art," *Crain's Cleveland Business,* September 29, 2008, http://galenet.galegroup.com.

16. T. Hals, "Beware the Pitfalls of Office Romance," *Yahoo News,* February 13, 2007, http://news.yahoo.com; and M. Selvin, "'Love Contract'? It's Office Policy," *Los Angeles Times,* February 13, 2007, http://www.latimes.com.

17. "McDonald's Sales Rise 7.1%," *CNNMoney,* February 9, 2009, http://money.cnn.com; and "CEOs Who Don't Get Out Often Enough, and Some Who Do," *24/7 Wall Street,* May 7, 2008, http://247wallst.com.

18. V. U. Druskat, "Effects and Timing of Developmental Peer Appraisals in Self-Managing Work Groups," *Journal of Applied Psychology* 84, no. 1 (February 1999), p. 58.

19. T. Cox, "Finding the Real MVPs in the Business," *Industry Week,* January 17, 2007, http://www.industryweek.com.

20. S. Waddock and N. Smith, "Corporate Responsibility Audits: Doing Well by Doing Good," *Sloan Management Review* 41, no. 2 (Winter 2000), pp. 75–83; L. L. Bergeson, "OSHA Gives Incentives for Voluntary Self-Audits," *Pollution Engineering* 32, no. 10 (October 2000), pp. 33–34.

21. S. Aghili, "A Six Sigma Approach to Internal Audits," *Strategic Finance,* February 2009, downloaded from Business & Company Resource Center, http://galenet.galegroup.com.

22. See, for example, B. Hindo, "At 3M, a Struggle between Efficiency and Creativity," *BusinessWeek,* June 11, 2007, downloaded from General Reference Center Gold, http://find.galegroup.com; B. Hindo and B. Grow, "Six Sigma; So Yesterday?" *BusinessWeek,* June 11, 2007, http://find.galegroup.com; and J. Rae, "Viewpoint: Have It Both Ways," *BusinessWeek,* June 11, 2007, http://find.galegroup.com.

23. S. Everett, "Do More, Better, For Less," *Library Journal,* September 15, 2006, http://galenet.galegroup.com.

24. T. Rancour and M. McCracken, "Applying 6 Sigma Methods for Breakthrough Safety Performance," *Professional Safety* 45, no. 10 (October 2000), pp. 29–32; and G. Eckes. "Making Six Sigma Last," *Ivey Business Journal,* January–February 2002, p. 77.

25. J. L. Colbert, "The Impact of the New External Auditing Standards," *Internal Auditor* 5, no. 6 (December 2000), pp. 46–50.

26. Aghili, "A Six Sigma Approach"; Y. Giard and Y. Nadeau, "Improving the Processes," *CA Magazine,* December 2008, downloaded from Business & Company Resource Center, http://galenet.galegroup.com; and G. Cheney, "Connecting the Dots to the Next Crisis," *Financial Executive,* April 2009, pp. 30–33.

27. J. D. Glater, "The Better the Audit Panel, the Higher the Stock Price," *New York Times,* April 8, 2005, p. C4.

28. B. Roberts, "Data-Driven Human Capital Decisions," *HRMagazine,* March 2007, downloaded from General Reference Center Gold, http://find.galegroup.com.

29. P. C. Brewer and L. A. Vulinec, "Harris Corporation's Experiences with Using Activity-Based Costing," *Information Strategy: The Executive's Journal* 13, no. 2 (Winter 1997), pp. 6–16; and T. P. Pare, "A New Tool for Managing Costs," *Fortune,* June 14, 1993, pp. 124–29.

30. K. Merchant, *Control in Business Organizations* (Boston: Pitman, 1985); and C. W. Chow, Y. Kato, and K. A. Merchant, "The Use of Organizational Controls and Their Effects on Data Manipulation and Management Myopia," *Accounting, Organizations, and Society* 21, nos. 2/3 (February/April 1996), pp. 175–92.

31. E. E. Lawler III and J. Rhode, *Information and Control in Organizations* (Pacific Palisades, CA: Goodyear, 1976); A. Ferner, "The Underpinnings of 'Bureaucratic' Control Systems: HRM in European Multinationals," *Journal of Management Studies* 37, no. 4 (June 2000), pp. 521–39; and M. S. Fenwick, "Cultural and Bureaucratic Control in MNEs: The Role of Expatriate Performance Management," *Management International Review* 39 (1999), pp. 107–25.

32. Hindo, "At 3M, a Struggle between Efficiency and Creativity."

33. D. H. Freedman, "Go Ahead, Make a Mess," *Inc.,* December 2006, pp. 120–25.

34. J. Veiga and J. Yanouzas, *The Dynamics of Organization Theory,* 2nd ed. (St. Paul, MN: West, 1984).

35. P. R. Gutierrez, "Airport Workers Report Breach," *Orlando Sentinel,* May 26, 2007, downloaded from General Reference Center Gold, http://find.galegroup.com.

36. D. Kiley, "The New Heat on Ford," *BusinessWeek,* June 4, 2007, http://www.businessweek.com.

37. M. Gelbart, "L&I Gets Ritz-Carlton Image Tips," *Philadelphia Inquirer,* March 10, 2009, http://www.philly.com.

38. Symantec Corporation, "Symantec Study Reveals Green IT Now Essential

IT Practice," news release, May 27, 2009, http://www.symantec.com; and Symantec Corporation, *Green IT Report: Regional Data—United States and Canada,* May 2009, http://www.symantec.com.

39. J. Fleischer, "New Methods to Measure Performance," *Call Center,* February 1, 2007, downloaded from General Reference Center Gold, http://find.galegroup.com.

40. M. Hammer, "The Seven Deadly Sins of Performance Measurement and How to Avoid Them," *MIT Sloan Management Review* 48, no. 3 (Spring 2007), pp. 19–28.

41. Lawler and Rhode, *Information and Control in Organizations*; and J. A. Gowan Jr. and R. G. Mathieu, "Critical Factors in Information System Development for a Flexible Manufacturing System," *Computers in Industry* 28, no. 3 (June 1996), pp. 173–83.

42. J. Robison, "How the Ritz-Carlton Manages the Mystique," *Gallup Management Journal,* December 11, 2008, downloaded from Business & Company Resource Center, http://galenet.galegroup.com.

43. W. Leavitt, "Twenty-First Century Driver Training," *Fleet Owner,* January 1, 2006, downloaded from Business & Company Resource Center, http://galenet.galegroup.com.

44. Company Web site, http://www.legalseafoods.com, accessed April 22, 2009; L. Buchanan, "The Way I Work: Roger Berkowitz," *Inc.,* July 2008, pp. 84–87; Elan, "Roger Berkowitz"; W. Forrest, "Restaurant Chain Provides Best Practice Supply Chain Example," *Purchasing,* July 14, 2007, http://www.purchasing.com; D. Farkas, "Legal Sea Foods Sharpens Its Hospitality Skills with Ongoing Training for Hourly Employees," *Chain Leader,* May 1, 2007, http://www.chainleader.com.

45. R. S. Kaplan and D. P. Norton, *The Balanced Scorecard: Translating Strategy into Action* (Boston: Harvard Business School Press, 1996); and A. Gumbus and R. N. Lussier, "Entrepreneurs Use a Balanced Scorecard to Translate Strategy into Performance Measures," *Journal of Small Business Management* 44, no. 3 (July 2006), downloaded from General Reference Center Gold, http://find.galegroup.com.

46. Gumbus and Lussier, "Entrepreneurs Use a Balanced Scorecard."

47. M. A. Reed-Woodard, "The Business of Nonprofit," *Black Enterprise,* June 2007, downloaded from General Reference Center Gold, http://find.galegroup.com.

48. R. Myers, "Going Away," *CFO,* May 2007, downloaded from General Reference Center Gold, http://find.galegroup.com.

49. K. Moores and J. Mula, "The Salience of Market, Bureaucratic, and Clan Controls in the Management of Family

Firm Transitions: Some Tentative Australian Evidence," *Family Business Review* 13, no. 2 (June 2000), pp. 91–106; and A. Walker and R. Newcombe, "The Positive Use of Power on a Major-Construction Project," *Construction Management and Economics* 18, no. 1 (January/February 2000), pp. 37–44.

50. P. H. Fuchs, K. E. Mifflin, D. Miller, and J. O. Whitney, "Strategic Integration: Competing in the Age of Capabilities," *California Management Review* 42, no. 3 (Spring 2000), pp. 118–47; M. A. Lando, "Making Compliance Part of Your Organization's Culture," *Healthcare Executive* 15, no. 5 (September/October 1999), pp. 18–22; and K. A. Frank and K. Fahrbach, "Organization Culture as a Complex System: Balance and Information in Models of Influence and Selection," *Organization Science* 10, no. 3 (May/June 1999), pp. 253–77.

51. "100 Best Companies to Work For, 2009," *Fortune*, February 2, 2009, http://money.cnn.com.

52. Company Web site, http://www.legalseafoods.com, accessed April 22, 2009; C. O'Neil, "Chain Fishes for Quality," *Atlanta Journal-Constitution*, October 29, 2008, http://www.ajc.com; Elan, "Roger Berkowitz"; C. LaBan, "Legal Sea Foods," *Philadelphia Inquirer*, July 22, 2007, http://www.philly.com; Buchanan, "The Way I Work."

Chapter 17

1. Company Web site, http://www.honda.com, accessed May 1, 2009; J. Murphy and Y. Takahashi, "Honda Picks New Chief Executive," *The Wall Street Journal*, February 24, 2009, http://online.wsj.com; J. Lorio, "2009 Man of the Year: Takeo Fukui," *Automobile*, November 13, 2008, http://www.automobilmag.com; and K. Linebaugh, "Honda's Flexible Plants Provide Edge," *The Wall Street Journal*, September 23, 2008, http://online.wsj.com.

2. R. A. Burgelman, M. A. Maidique, and S. C. Wheelwright, *Strategic Management of Technology and Innovation* (New York: McGraw-Hill, 2000).

3. D. C. L. Prestwood and P. A. Schumann Jr., "Revitalize Your Organization," *Executive Excellence* 15, no. 2 (February 1998), p. 16; C. Y. Baldwin and K. B. Clark, "Managing in an Age of Modularity," *Harvard Business Review* 75, no. 5 (September–October 1997), pp. 84–93; S. Gopalakrishnan, P. Bierly, and E. H. Kessler, "A Reexamination of Product and Process Innovations Using a Knowledge-Based View," *Journal of High Technology Management Research* 10, no. 1 (Spring 1999), pp. 147–66; and J. Pullin, "Bombardier Commands Top Marks," *Professional Engineering* 13, no. 3 (July 5, 2000), pp. 40–46.

4. M. Sawhney, R. C. Wolcott, and I. Arroniz, "The 12 Different Ways for Companies to Innovate," *MIT Sloan Management Review* 47, no. 3 (Spring 2006), pp. 75–81.

5. G. P. Pisano, *The Development Factory: Unlocking the Potential of Process Innovation* (Boston: Harvard Business School Press, 1996); and R. Leifer, C. M. McDermott, G. C. O'Connor, L. S. Peters, M. Rice, and R. W. Veryzer, *Radical Innovation: How Mature Companies Can Outsmart Upstarts* (Cambridge MA: Harvard Business School Press, 2000).

6. "How Technology Delivers for UPS," *BusinessWeek*, March 5, 2007, http://www.businessweek.com.

7. H. M. O'Neill, R. W. Pounder, and A. K. Buchholtz, "Patterns in the Diffusion of Strategies across Organizations: Insights from the Innovation, Diffusion Literature," *Academy of Management Review* 23, no. 1 (January 1998), pp. 98–114; E. M. Rogers, *Diffusion of Innovations* (New York: Free Press, 1995); and B. Guilhon, ed., *Technology and Markets for Knowledge: Knowledge Creation, Diffusion and Exchange within a Growing Economy*, Economics of Science, Technology and Innovation 22 (Dordrecht, Netherlands: Kluwer Academic Publishing, 2000).

8. J. P. Andrew, K. Haanæs, D. C. Michael, H. L. Sirkin, and A. Taylor, *Innovation 2009: Making Hard Decisions in the Downturn*, Boston Consulting Group Senior Management Survey, http://www.bcg.com.

9. M. E. Porter, *Competitive Strategy* (New York: Free Press, 1980).

10. J. A. Schumpeter, *The Theory of Economic Development* (Boston: Harvard University Press, 1934); and K. DesMarteau, "Information Technology Trends Drive Dramatic Industry Change," *Bobbin* 41, no. 12 (August 2000), pp. 48–58.

11. S. A. Zahra, S. Nash, and D. J. Bickford, "Transforming Technological Pioneering in Competitive Advantage," *Academy of Management Executive* 9, no. 1 (1995), pp. 17–31; and M. Sadowski and A. Roth, "Technology Leadership Can Pay Off," *Research Technology Management* 42, no. 6 (November/December 1999), pp. 32–33.

12. H. Greimel, "New Honda CEO to Focus on R&D," *AutoWeek*, February 25, 2009, http://www.autoweek.com; A. Weber, "How Flexible Is Your Factory?" *Assembly Magazine*, February 25, 2009, http://www.assemblymag.com; I. Rowley, "Honda CEO Fukui Steps Aside," *BusinessWeek*, February 23, 2009, http://www.businessweek.com; Lorio, "2009 Man of the Year"; and Linebaugh, "Honda's Flexible Plants Provide Edge."

13. A. Weintraub, "Who Might Be Eyeing Bristol?" *BusinessWeek*, June 20, 2007, downloaded from General Reference Center Gold, http://find.galegroup.com; and D. Cust, "Pharma Sector Faces 'Perfect Storm,'" *Acquisitions Monthly*, June 2007, http://find.galegroup.com.

14. M. Imai and G. Kaizen, *A Commonsense, Low-Cost Approach to Management* (New York: McGraw-Hill, 1997); and M. Imai and G. Kaizen, *The Key to Japan's Competitive Success* (New York: McGraw-Hill, 1986).

15. N. Masia, "The Cost of Developing a New Drug," *Focus on Intellectual Property Rights*, U.S. Department of State International Information Programs, January 2006, http://usinfo.state.gov/products/pubs; and A. Berenson, "A Cancer Drug's Big Price Rise Is Cause for Concern," *New York Times*, March 12, 2006, http://www.nytimes.com.

16. A. G. Shilling, "First-Mover Disadvantage," *Forbes*, June 18, 2007, downloaded from General Reference Center Gold, http://find.galegroup.com.

17. P. A. Geroski, "Models of Technology Diffusion," *Research Policy* 29, no. 4/5 (April 2000), pp. 603–25; and L. A. Thomas, "Adoption Order of New Technologies in Evolving Markets," *Journal of Economic Behavior & Organization* 38, no. 4 (April 1999), pp. 453–82.

18. G. Colvin, "McKesson: Wiring the Medical World," *Fortune*, February 5, 2007, http://money.cnn.com.

19. R. E. Oligney and M. I. Economides, "Technology as an Asset," *Hart's Petroleum Engineer International* 71, no. 9 (September 1998), p. 27.

20. J. E. Vascellaro, "Found in Translation," *The Wall Street Journal*, May 24, 2007, http://online.wsj.com.

21. Miniwatts Marketing Group, "Internet World Users by Language," *Internet World Stats*, last updated June 2, 2007, http://www.internetworldstats.com.

22. Colvin, "McKesson."

23. D. Schubert, "Focusing Your Innovation," *Game Developer*, February 1, 2009, downloaded from Business & Company Resource Center, http://galenet.galegroup.com.

24. See, for example, B. Ames, "IBM Speeds Chips with DRAM Memory," *PC World*, February 14, 2007, http://www.pcworld.com; S. Ferguson, "Intel Plans Push into Mobility, Emerging Markets," *eWeek*, May 3, 2007, http://www.eweek.com; and S. Ferguson, "AMD's Next-Gen Mobile Chip, Platform to Conserve Power," *eWeek*, May 18, 2007, http://www.eweek.com.

25. A. Taylor III, "The Great Electric Car Race," *Fortune*, April 14, 2009, http://money.cnn.com.

26. S. Hansell, "Beam It Down from the Web, Scotty," *New York Times*, May 7, 2007, http://www.nytimes.com.

27. M. Kanellos, "For Fast-Food Help, Call in the Robots," *CNet News*, March 26, 2007, http://news.com.com.

28. L. Landro, "An Affordable Fix for Modernizing Medical Records," *The Wall Street Journal*, April 30, 2009, http://online.wsj.com; and St. Lohr, "How to Make Electronic Medical

Records a Reality," *New York Times*, March 1, 2009, http://www.nytimes.com.

29. J. Jusko, "Foiling Fakes," *Industry Week*, May 2007, downloaded from General Reference Center Gold, http://find.galegroup.com.

30. "Fresh, but Far from Easy," *The Economist*, June 23, 2007, downloaded from General Reference Center Gold, http://find.galegroup.com.

31. R. Dewan, B. Jing, and A. Seidmann, "Adoption of Internet-Based Product Customization and Pricing Strategies," *Journal of Management Information Systems* 17, no. 2 (Fall 2000), pp. 9–28; P. A. Geroski, "Models of Technology Diffusion," *Research Policy* 29, no. 4/5 (April 2000), pp. 603–25; Rogers, *Diffusion of Innovations*.

32. E. Von Hippel, *The Sources of Innovation* (Oxford, UK: Oxford University Press, 1994); and D. Leonard, *Wellsprings of Knowledge: Building and Sustaining the Sources of Innovation* (Cambridge, MA: Harvard Business School Press, 1998).

33. S. Carey, "Calculating Costs in the Clouds," *The Wall Street Journal*, March 6, 2007, http://online.wsj.com.

34. T. Krazit, "Intel R&D on Slow Boat to China," *CNet News*, April 16, 2007, http://news.com.com.

35. K. MacQueen, "Cashing in His V-Chips," *Maclean's*, June 11, 2007, downloaded from General Reference Center Gold, http://find.galegroup.com; and "Online Gaming's Netscape Moment?" *The Economist*, June 9, 2007, http://find.galegroup.com.

36. T. Purdum, "Benchmarking Outside the Box: Best Practices Can Rise from Where You Least Expect Them," *Industry Week*, March 2007, downloaded from General Reference Center Gold, http://find.galegroup.com.

37. Von Hippel, *The Sources of Innovation*; and Leonard, *Wellsprings of Knowledge*.

38. J. Hagedoorn, A. N. Link, and N. S. Vonortas, "Research Partnerships," *Research Policy* 29, no. 4/5 (April 2000), pp. 567–86; and S.-S. Yi, "Entry, Licensing and Research Joint Ventures," *International Journal of Industrial Organization* 17, no. 1 (January 1999), pp. 1–24.

39. R. Dorn, "Chicken, Pork or Beef?" *Fleet Equipment*, May 2007, downloaded from General Reference Center Gold, http://find.galegroup.com; and "One of the Nation's Largest Producers of Animal Fat and a Major Oil Company Have Decided to Make Diesel Fuel Together," *Diesel Progress*, North American ed., May 2007, http://find.galegroup.com.

40. "Broadcom Acquires GPS Specialist Global Locate for $146 Million," *Information Week*, June 12, 2007, downloaded from General Reference Center Gold, http://find.galegroup.com.

41. T. Hoffman, "Change Agents," *ComputerWorld*, April 23, 2007,

downloaded from General Reference Center Gold, http://find.galegroup.com; Center for CIO Leadership, "Center for CIO Leadership Unveils 2008 Survey Results," news release, November 18, 2008, http://www.marketwire.com; and Center for CIO Leadership, "CIO Leadership Survey Executive Summary," abstract, 2008, http://www.cioleadershipcenter.com, accessed June 3, 2009; and G. H. Anthes, "The CIO/CTO Balancing Act," *ComputerWorld* 34, no. 25 (June 19, 2000), pp. 50–51.

42. Hoffman, "Change Agents."

43. D. L. Day, "Raising Radicals: Different Processes for Championing Innovative Corporate Ventures," *Organization Science* 5, no. 2 (May 1994), pp. 148–72; C. Siporin, "Want Speedy FDA Approval? Hire a 'Product Champion,'" *Medical Marketing & Media*, October 1993, pp. 22–28; C. Siporin, "How You Can Capitalize on Phase 3B," *Medical Marketing & Media*, October 1994, pp. 72–72; and E. H. Kessler, "Tightening the Belt: Methods for Reducing Development Costs Associated with New Product Innovation," *Journal of Engineering and Technology Management* 17, no. 1 (March 2000), pp. 59–92.

44. Andrew et al., *Innovation 2009*, p. 11.

45. J. G. March, "Exploration and Exploitation in Organizational Learning," *Organization Science* 2, no. 1 (1991), pp. 71–87.

46. B. Hindo, "At 3M, a Struggle between Efficiency and Creativity," *BusinessWeek*, June 11, 2007, http://www.businessweek.com; K. Palmer, "Creativity on Demand," *U.S. News & World Report*, April 30, 2007, pp. EE2–EE4; E. Figueroa and P. Conceicao, "Rethinking the Innovation Process in Large Organizations: A Case Study of 3M," *Journal of Engineering and Technology Management* 17, no. 1 (March 2000), pp. 93–109; and D. Howell, "No Such Thing as a Daft Idea," *Professional Engineering* 13, no. 4 (February 23, 2000), pp. 28–29.

47. D. A. Fields, "How to Stop the Dumbing Down of Your Company," *Industry Week*, March 7, 2007, http://www.industryweek.com; L. K. Gundry, J. R. Kickul, and C. W. Prather, "Building the Creative Organization," *Organizational Dynamics* 22, no. 2 (Spring 1994), pp. 22–36; and T. Kuczmarski, "Inspiring and Implementing the Innovation Mind-Set," *Planning Review*, September–October 1994, pp. 37–48.

48. D. Rodriguez and R. Jacoby, "Embracing Risk to Grow and Innovate," *BusinessWeek*, May 16, 2007, http://www.businessweek.com.

49. Ibid.

50. S. Hamm, "IBM's Social Networking Push," *BusinessWeek*, January 23, 2007, http://www.businessweek.com

51. Hindo, "At 3M, a Struggle."

52. D. Tsuruoka, "Intuit Innovation Lab, 'Idea Jams' Aim to Spur Creativity," *Investor's Business Daily*, April 14, 2009, downloaded from Business & Company Resource Center, http://galenet.galegroup.com.

53. D. Leonard, *Wellsprings of Knowledge: Building and Sustaining the Sources of Innovation* (Cambridge MA: Harvard Business School Press, 1998); D. Leonard-Barton, "The Factory as a Learning Laboratory," *Sloan Management Review*, Fall 1992, pp. 23–38; and A. K. Gupta and V. Govindarajan, "Knowledge Management's Social Dimension: Lessons from Nucor Steel," *Sloan Management Review* 42, no. 1 (Fall 2000), pp. 71–80.

54. H. K. Bowen, K. B. Clark, C. A. Holloway, and S. C. Wheelwright, "Development Projects: The Engine of Renewal," *Harvard Business Review*, September–October 1994, pp. 110–20; C. Eden, T. Williams, and F. Ackermann, "Dismantling the Learning Curve: The Role of Disruptions on the Planning of Development Projects," *International Journal of Project Management* 16, no. 3 (June 1998), pp. 131–38; and M. V. Tatikonda and S. R. Rosenthal, "Technology Novelty, Project Complexity, and Product Development Project Execution Success: A Deeper Look at Task Uncertainty in Product Innovation," *IEEE Transactions on Engineering Management* 47, no. 1 (February 2000), pp. 74–87.

55. E. Trist, "The Evolution of Sociotechnical Systems as a Conceptual Framework and as an Action Research Program," in *Perspectives on Organizational Design and Behavior*, ed. A. Van de Ven and W. F. Joyce, pp. 19–75 (New York: John Wiley & Sons, 1981); and A. Molina, "Insights into the Nature of Technology Diffusion and Implementation: The Perspective of Sociotechnical Alignment," *Technovation* 17, nos. 11/12 (November/December 1997), pp. 601–26.

56. Company Web site, http://www.honda.com, accessed May 1, 2009; J. Murphy, "Honda CEO Vies for Green Mantle," *The Wall Street Journal*, June 16, 2009, http://online.wsj.com; I. Rowley, "Honda's High Hopes for Hybrids," *BusinessWeek*, May 21, 2008, http://www.businessweek.com; H. Greimel, "Honda President Takeo Fukui Says Lithium Ion Technology Is Still Too Unreliable for Mass Production," *AutoWeek*, March 24, 2008, http://www.autoweek.com; J. O'Dell, "Honda's Fuel-Cell Electric Car Is No Trailer Queen," *Edmunds*, November 26, 2007, http://www.edmunds.com; and "Honda's Boss Speaks Out: The Thoughts of President Fukui," *Motor Trend*, October 2007, http://www.motortrend.com.

Appendix D

1. Robert M. Pirsig, *Zen and the Art of Motorcycle Maintenance* (New York: William Morrow and Company, 1974).
2. Pratima Raichur, *Absolute Beauty* (New York: HarperPerennial, 1986).
3. Nescafe: Nestle (verified by Terril Haywood via 1/16/01 e-mail that Nescafe and Nesquik flavors are modified for the market in which they are sold).
4. Timothy J. Mullaney and Robert D. Hof, "Information Technology Annual Report," *BusinessWeek Online*, June 24, 2002.
5. Jane Black, "The Fight for Privacy Has Just Begun," *BusinessWeek Online*, January 10, 2002.

Chapter 18

1. Company Web site, http://www.scjohnson.com, accessed May 1, 2009; "SC Johnson Again a Best Place to Work in America," *RedOrbit*, January 22, 2009, urlhttp://www.redorbit.com; and "Ten Green Giants," *Fortune*, July 3, 2007, http://money.cnn.com.
2. N. H. Woodward, "To Make Changes, Manage Them," *HRMagazine*, May 2007, downloaded from General Reference Center Gold, http://find.galegroup.com.
3. D. R. Conner, *Managing at the Speed of Change* (New York: Random House, 2006), p. 45.
4. M. Bayless, "A Recipe for Effective Change," *Gourmet Retailer*, January 2007, downloaded from General Reference Center Gold, http://find.galegroup.com.
5. J. J. Brazil, "Mission: Impossible?" *Fast Company*, April 2007, downloaded from FirstSearch, http://firstsearch.oclc.org.
6. C. M. Christensen, "The Past and Future of Competitive Advantage," *Sloan Management Review*, Winter 2001, pp. 105–9.
7. M. Schrage, "Getting Beyond the Innovation Fetish," *Fortune*, November 13, 2000, pp. 225–32.
8. T. A. Judge, C. J. Thoresen, V. Pucik, and T. M. Welbourne, "Managerial Coping with Organizational Change: A Dispositional Perspective," *Journal of Applied Psychology* 84 (1999), pp. 107–22.
9. Woodward, "To Make Changes, Manage Them."
10. C. Giffi, A. Roth, and G. Seal, *Competing in World-Class Manufacturing: America's 21st Century Challenge* (Homewood, IL: Business One Irwin, 1990).
11. R. M. Kanter, *World Class: Thriving Locally in the Global Economy* (New York: Touchstone, 1995).
12. Giffi, Roth, and Seal, *Competing in World-Class Manufacturing*.
13. J. Collins and J. Porras, *Built to Last* (London: Century, 1996).
14. M. R. Morris, "The Dean of Green," *Professional Remodeler*, November 1, 2008, downloaded from Business &

Company Resource Center, http://galenet.galegroup.com.
15. Collins and Porras, *Built to Last*.
16. C. Gibson and J. Birkinshaw, "The Antecedents, Consequences, and Mediating Role of Organizational Ambidexterity," *Academy of Management Journal* 47 (2004), pp. 209–26.
17. Collins and Porras, *Built to Last*.
18. T. Cummings and C. Worley, *Organization Development and Change*, 8th ed. (Mason, OH: Thomson/South-Western, 2005).
19. Ibid.
20. Ibid.
21. N. Nohria, W. Joyce, and B. Roberson, "What Really Works," *Harvard Business Review*, July 2003, pp. 42–52.
22. R. M. Kanter, "Thriving Locally in the Global Economy," *Harvard Business Review*, August 2003, pp. 119–27.
23. Ibid.
24. Conner, *Managing at the Speed of Change*; and R. Teerlink, "Harley's Leadership U-Turn," *Harvard Business Review*, July–August 2000, pp. 43–48.
25. E. E. Lawler III, *Treat People Right!* (San Francisco: Jossey-Bass, 2003).
26. P. Zigarmi and J. Hoekstra, "Leadership Strategies for Making Change Stick," *Perspectives* (Ken Blanchard Companies, 2008), http://www.kenblanchard.com, accessed May 22, 2009.
27. Conner, *Managing at the Speed of Change*; and S. Oreg, "Resistance to Change: Developing an Individual Differences Measure," *Journal of Applied Psychology*, 2003, pp. 680–93.
28. P. Dvorak, "How Understanding the 'Why' of Decisions Matters," *The Wall Street Journal*, March 19, 2007, http://online.wsj.com.
29. A. Deutschman, *Change or Die* (Los Angeles: Regan, 2007), pp. 164–78.
30. J. Stanislao and B. C. Stanislao, "Dealing with Resistance to Change," *Business Horizons*, July–August 1983, pp. 74–78; and J. D. Ford and L. W. Ford, "Decoding Resistance to Change," *Harvard Business Review*, April 2009, pp. 99–103.
31. A. Benedict, *2007 Change Management Survey Report* (Alexandria, VA: Society for Human Resource Management, 2007), accessed at http://www.shrm.org.
32. J. P. Kotter and L. A. Schlesinger, "Choosing Strategies for Change," *Harvard Business Review*, March–April 1979, pp. 106–114; Ford and Ford, "Decoding Resistance to Change"; and Zigami and Hoekstra, "Leadership Strategies."
33. D. Zell, "Overcoming Barriers to Work Innovations: Lessons Learned at Hewlett-Packard," *Organizational Dynamics*, Summer 2001, pp. 77–85.
34. Ibid.
35. E. B. Dent and S. Galloway Goldberg, "Challenging Resistance to Change," *Journal of Applied Behavioral Science*, March 1999, pp. 25–41. Ford and Ford,

"Decoding Resistance to Change"; Zigarmi and Hoekstra, "Leadership Strategies"; and J. Ford, L. Ford, and A. D'Amelio, "Resistance to Change: The Rest of the Story", *Academy of Management Review* 33, (2008), pp. 362–77.
36. G. Johnson, *Strategic Change and the Management Process* (New York: Basil Blackwell, 1987); and K. Lewin, "Frontiers in Group Dynamics," *Human Relations* 1 (1947), pp. 5–41.
37. E. H. Schein, "Organizational Culture: What It Is and How to Change It," in *Human Resource Management in International Firms*, ed. P. Evans, Y. Doz, and A. Laurent (New York: St. Martin's Press, 1990).
38. M. Beer, R. Eisenstat, and B. Spector, *The Critical Path to Corporate Renewal* (Cambridge, MA: Harvard Business School Press, 1990).
39. Dvorak, "How Understanding the 'Why' of Decisions Matters."
40. E. E. Lawler III, "Transformation from Control to Involvement," in *Corporate Transformation*, ed. R. Kilmann and T. Covin (San Francisco: Jossey-Bass, 1988).
41. Deutschman, *Change or Die*, pp. 1–15.
42. P. Willax, "Getting the Boss to Embrace Change Requires Tact, Ingenuity," *New Hampshire Business Review*, May 11, 2007, http://find.galegroup.com.
43. D. Hellriegel and J. W. Slocum Jr., *Management*, 4th ed. (Reading, MA: Addison-Wesley, 1986).
44. C. Aiken and S. Keller, "The Irrational Side of Change Management," *McKinsey Quarterly*, April 2009, http://www.mckinseyquarterly.com.
45. Lewin, "Frontiers in Group Dynamics."
46. Schein, "Organizational Culture."
47. E. E. Lawler III, *From the Ground Up* (San Francisco: Jossey-Bass, 1995).
48. Q. Nguyen Huy, "Time, Temporal Capability, and Planned Change," *Academy of Management Review* 26 (2001), pp. 601–23.
49. B. Sugarman, "A Learning-Based Approach to Organizational Change: Some Results and Guidelines," *Organizational Dynamics*, Summer 2001, pp. 62–75.
50. Kotter and Schlesinger, "Choosing Strategies for Change."
51. Woodward, "To Make Changes, Manage Them."
52. Sugarman, "A Learning-Based Approach to Organizational Change."
53. R. H. Miles, "Beyond the Age of Dilbert: Accelerating Corporate Transformations by Rapidly Engaging all Employees," *Organizational Dynamics*, Spring 2001, pp. 313–21.
54. D. A. Nadler, "Managing Organizational Change: An Integrative Approach," *Journal of Applied Behavioral Science* 17 (1981), pp. 191–211.
55. D. Rousseau and S. A. Tijoriwala, "What's a Good Reason to Change?

Motivated Reasoning and Social Accounts in Promoting Organizational Change," *Journal of Applied Psychology* 84 (1999), pp. 514–28.

56. E. Oakley, "Leading Change without Authority," *Material Handling Management*, May 2007, downloaded from General Reference Center Gold, http://find.galegroup.com.

57. C. F. Leana and B. Barry, "Stability and Change as Simultaneous Experiences in Organizational Life," *Academy of Management Review* 25 (2000), pp. 753–59.

58. O. Gadiesh and J. Gilbert, "Transforming Corner-Office Strategy into Frontline Action," *Harvard Business Review*, May 2001, pp. 72–79.

59. B. Schneider, A. Brief, and R. Guzzo, "Creating a Climate and Culture for Sustainable Organizational Change," *Organizational Dynamics*, Spring 1996, pp. 7–19.

60. The Price Waterhouse Change Integration Team, *Better Change: Best Practices for Transforming Your Organization* (Burr Ridge, IL: Irwin, 1995).

61. M. Beer and N. Nohria, "Cracking the Code of Change," *Harvard Business Review*, May–June 2000, pp. 133–41.

62. N. Nohria and J. Berkley, "Whatever Happened to the Take-Charge Manager?" *Harvard Business Review*, January–February 1994, pp. 128–37.

63. D. Miller, J. Hartwick, and I. Le Breton-Miller, "How to Detect a Management Fad—and Distinguish It from a Classic," *Business Horizons*, July–August 2004, pp. 7–16.

64. Cari Tuna, "Repairing an Agency's Credibility," *The Wall Street Journal*, March 22, 2009, http://online.wsj.com; and State Compensation Insurance Fund, "Testimony of Janet Frank, President, State Compensation Insurance Fund, to the Senate Banking, Finance and Insurance Committee," February 6, 2008, http://www.scif.com.

65. Price Waterhouse Change Integration Team, *Better Change*.

66. Ibid.

67. E. M. Heffes, "You Need Urgency Now!" *Financial Executive*, January–February 2009, downloaded from Business & Company Resource Center, http://galenet.galegroup.com (interview with John P. Kotter).

68. Lawler, *From the Ground Up*.

69. J. Kotter, *Leading Change* (Boston: Harvard Business School Press, 1996).

70. Schneider, Brief, and Guzzo, "Creating a Climate and Culture."

71. R. Beckhard and R. Harris, *Organizational Transitions* (Reading, MA: Addison-Wesley, 1977).

72. Kotter, *Leading Change*.

73. E. Boens, "Positive Communication," *Industrial Safety and Hygiene News*, June 2006, downloaded from General Reference Center Gold, http://find.galegroup.com.

74. G. Hamel, "Waking Up IBM," *Harvard Business Review*, July–August 2000, pp. 137–46; and Deutschman, *Change or Die*.

75. "Cogeneration at SC Johnson Prevents Greenhouse Gas Emissions Equivalent to Driving around the Earth 7,630 Times," *CSRwire*, August 27, 2007, http://www.csrwire.com; "Ten Green Giants"; and "SC Johnson Shares Environmental Leadership Legacy with Consumers," *CSRwire*, April 6, 2007, http://www.csrwire.com.

76. Deutschman, *Change or Die*, p. 202.

77. Kotter, *Leading Change*.

78. D. Smith, *Taking Charge of Change* (Reading, MA: Addison-Wesley, 1996).

79. G. Hamel, "Killer Strategies That Make Shareholders Rich," *Fortune*, June 23, 1997, pp. 22–34.

80. G. Hamel and C. K. Prahalad, *Competing for the Future* (Boston: Harvard Business School Press, 1994).

81. M. J. Mandel, "This Way to the Future," *BusinessWeek*, October 11, 2004, pp. 92–98.

82. Ibid., p. 93.

83. S. Zuboff and J. Maxim, *The Support Economy* (New York: Penguin, 2004).

84. H. Courtney, J. Kirkland, and P. Viguerie, "Strategy under Uncertainty," *Harvard Business Review*, November–December 1997, pp. 66–79.

85. J. O'Shea and C. Madigan, *Dangerous Company: The Consulting Powerhouses and the Business They Save and Ruin* (New York: Times Books, 1997).

86. Hamel and Prahalad, *Competing for the Future*.

87. Ibid.

88. Ibid.

89. R. D. Hof, "How to Hit a Moving Target," *BusinessWeek*, August 21, 2006, downloaded from General Reference Center Gold, http://find.galegroup.com.

90. S. E. Rickert, "Taking the NanoPulse: Sizing Up Nanotechnology," *Industry Week*, May 9, 2007, http://www.industryweek.com; M. David, "Into the Nano Frontier—Closer Than You Might Think," *Electronic Design*, May 10, 2007, downloaded from General Reference Center Gold, http://find.galegroup.com; and S. Baker and A. Aston, "The Business of Nanotech," *BusinessWeek*, February 14, 2005, pp 569–70.

91. David, "Into the Nano Frontier"; and M. Haiken, "Eight Nanotech Takes on Water Pollution," *Business 2.0*, July 2007, downloaded from General Reference Center Gold, http://find.galegroup.com.

92. M. C. Bellas, "Very Small and Unfathomably Huge," *Beverage World*, June 15, 2007, downloaded from General Reference Center Gold, http://find.galegroup.com.

93. David, "Into the Nano Frontier."

94. See, for example, J. Truini, "EPA Needs to Address Tiny Concerns, Report Says," *Waste News*, May 28, 2007, downloaded from General Reference Center Gold, http://find.galegroup.com.

95. Hamel and Prahalad, *Competing for the Future*.

96. J. Kotter, *The New Rules: How to Succeed in Today's Post-Corporate World* (New York: Free Press, 1995).

97. Ibid.

98. T. Bateman and C. Porath, "Transcendent Behavior," in *Positive Organizational Scholarship*, ed. K. Cameron, J. Dutton, and R. Quinn (San Francisco: Barrett-Koehler, 2003).

99. L. A. Hill, "New Manager Development for the 21st Century," *Academy of Management Executive*, August 2004, pp. 121–26.

100. Lawler, *From the Ground Up*; and Kotter, *The New Rules*.

101. Lawler, *Treat People Right!*

102. M. Peiperl and Y. Baruck, "Back to Square Zero: The Post-Corporate Career," *Organizational Dynamics*, Spring 1997, pp. 7–22.

103. Ibid.

104. Conner, *Managing at the Speed of Change*, pp. 235–45.

105. J. W. Slocum Jr., M. McGill, and D. Lei, "The New Learning Strategy Anytime, Anything, Anywhere," *Organizational Dynamics*, Autumn 1994, pp. 33–37.

106. Kotter, *The New Rules*.

107. J. Collins, *From Good to Great* (New York: HarperBusiness, 2001).

108. Hill, "New Manager Development for the 21st Century," p. 125.

109. J. A. Raelin, "Don't Bother Putting Leadership into People," *Academy of Management Executive*, August 2004, pp. 131–35.

110. G. Binney, and C. Williams, *Leaning into the Future* (London: Nicholas Brealey, 1997).

111. U.S. Environmental Protection Agency, "Partner Profile," April 27, 2009, http://www.epa.gov; "SC Johnson Starts Listing Product Ingredients Publicly," *GreenBiz*, March 13, 2009, http://greenbiz.com; "SC Johnson to Phase Out Phthalates," *Daily Green*, March 12, 2009, http://www.thedailygreen.com; S. Bennett, "SC Johnson Shifts to Hybrid Fleet for Sales Force," *Automotive Fleet*, December 2008, http://www.automotive-fleet.com; "SC Johnson Commits to Additional Renewable Energy Source," *CSRwire*, March 13, 2008, http://www.csrwire.com; D. Blanchard, "SC Johnson Finds a 'Greener' Way to Load Trucks," *Industry Week*, February 1, 2008, http://www.industryweek.com; and "Cogeneration at SC Johnson."

Photo Credits

Chapter 1
Page 5: © Royalty-Free/Corbis/DAL.
Page 7: © AP Photo/Marcio Jose Sanchez.
Page 8: © AP Photo/Elaine Thompson.
Page 9: © AP Photo/Laurent Rebours.
Page 11: © The McGraw-Hill Companies, Inc./Ken Cavanagh, photographer/DAL.
Page 16: Courtesy of Google.com
Page 23: Courtesy of Xerox Corporation.
Page 25: © The McGraw-Hill Companies, Inc./John Flournoy, photographer/DAL.

Appendix A
Page 37: Public domain image from the Library of Congress Prints and Photographs Division/DAL.
Page 38 (left): © Stock Montage, Inc.
Page 38 (right): © Stock Montage, Inc.

Chapter 2
Page 51: © AP Photo/David Zalubowski.
Page 53: © Photodisc/Getty Images/DAL.
Page 56: © AP Photo/Eckehard Schulz.
Page 61: © AP Photo/Toby Talbot.
Page 69: © AP Photo/M. Spencer Grant.
Page 72 (left): Courtesy of Nordstrom, Inc.
Page 72 (right): Courtesy of Nordstrom, Inc.

Chapter 3
Page 88: © Threadless.com/Jérémie Royer
Page 92: © AP Photo/Fiona Hanson.
Page 96: © AP Photo/Peter Cosgrove.
Page 100: © Ryan McVay/Getty Images/DAL.
Page 103: © Photodisc/PunchStock/DAL
Page 107: © AP Photo/Ben Margot.

Chapter 4
Page 129: © Richard Cummins/Corbis.
Page 131: © AP Photo/Charles Rex Arbogast.
Page 136: © AP Photo/The Idaho State Journal, Joshua Duplechian.
Page 141: © Erica Simone Leeds 2007/DAL.
Page 145: © Robert Maass/Corbis.
Page 149: Courtesy of Nordstrom, Inc.

Chapter 5
Page 162: © AP Photo/Louis Lanzano.
Page 165: © Michael Newman/PhotoEdit.
Page 169: © AP Photo/Pat Sullivan.
Page 171: © Royalty-Free/Corbis/DAL.
Page 173: Courtesy of NovaCare.
Page 178: © AP Photo/Dawn Villella.
Page 179: © The McGraw-Hill Companies, Inc./John Flournoy, photographer/DAL.
Page 183: Courtesy of Timberland Company.

Appendix B
Page 193: © Royalty Free/Corbis.
Page 196: Courtesy of Toyota Motor North America, Inc.

Chapter 6
Page 204: © AP Photo/Ling long - Imaginechina.
Page 205: © John Neubauer/PhotoEdit.
Page 211: © AP Photo/Mustafa Quaishi.
Page 215: Image courtesy of The Advertising Archives.
Page 216: Courtesy of Toyota Motor North America, Inc.
Page 220: Courtesy of Cold Stone Creamery.
Page 226: © Digital Vision/Getty Images/DAL.

Chapter 7
Page 238: © AP Photo/The News-Gazette, Heather Coit.
Page 240: Courtesy of Zappos.com. © Zappos.com, Inc.
Page 244: © Dominic Lipinski/PA Wire/AP Images.
Page 245: Courtesy of Scaled Composites.
Page 246: © AP Photo/Pat Sullivan.
Page 249: © AP Photo/Jeff Chiu.
Page 251: © AP Photo/Reed Saxon.
Page 258: Courtesy of Amie Street.

Chapter 8
Page 276: © AP dycj - Imaginechina/AP Images.
Page 279: © Eric Audras/Photoalto/PictureQuest/DAL.
Page 280: © Chris Goodenow/Reuters/Corbis.
Page 286: © AP Photo/Nati Harnik.
Page 293: Courtesy of NASA.
Page 297: ©1997 IMS Communications LTD/Capstone Design. All rights reserved./DAL.
Page 299: © Paul J. Richards/AFP/Getty Images.

Chapter 9
Page 312: © Joe Raedle/Getty Images.
Page 313: © Ryan McVay/Getty Images/DAL.
Page 314: © Davis Barber/PhotoEdit.
Page 322: Courtesy of Bama Companies, Inc.
Page 325: © AP Photo/Paul Sakuma.
Page 328: © Royalty Free/Corbis.
Page 330: © David Graham/Time Life Pictures/Getty Images.

Chapter 10
Page 340: © NBAE/Getty Images.
Page 347: © Tim Boyle/Getty Images.
Page 349: © Ryan McVay/Getty Images/DAL.
Page 353: © AP Photo/M. Spencer Green.
Page 357: Courtesy of Persuasive Games.
Page 365: Courtesy of Tersiguel's; photo by Vickie Goeller.
Page 372: © Robyn Beck/AFP/Getty Images.

Chapter 11
Page 383: © Library of Congress, Prints and Photographs Division, LC-U9-10364-37.
Page 386: © AP Photo/Thibault Camus.
Page 392: © AP Photo/Advantica.
Page 395: © The McGraw-Hill Companies, Inc./David Planchet/DAL.
Page 403: © Alan Einstein/NBAE/Getty Images.
Page 408: © AP Photo/Williams Perry.

Chapter 12
Page 419: © Mel Curtis/Getty Images/DAL.
Page 421: © AP Photo/Chuck Burton.
Page 425: © AP Photo/Mark Baker.
Page 429: © Jupiterimages/Imagesource/DAL.
Page 436: © Associated Press.
Page 440: © AP Photo/Kathy Willens.
Page 442: © davepix.com.

Chapter 13
Page 445: © AP Photo/Tammie Arroyo.
Page 456: © Alyson Aliano.
Page 460: © Imagesource/PictureQuest/DAL.
Page 462: © Robert Glusic/Getty Images/DAL.
Page 465: © AP Photo/Paul Sakuma.
Page 468: © Kaz Chiba/The Image Bank/Getty Images.
Page 474: © Tom & Dee Ann McCarthy/Corbis.
Page 476: © John Zich/zr/Corbis.

Chapter 14
Page 489: © Eyewire/Getty Images/DAL.
Page 490: Courtesy of Omnica Corporation.
Page 493: © Marc Pokempner/Getty Images.
Page 497: Courtesy of Boots & Coots.
Page 501: Courtesy of CICLOPS and the Cassini Imaging Team.
Page 502: © Robert Glusic/Getty Images/DAL.
Page 507: © American Arbitration Association. *Note: This ad is not part of the current advertising campaign.*

Chapter 15
Page 517: © Jack Hollingsworth/Corbis/DAL.
Page 520: © BananaStock Ltd./DAL.
Page 521: © Comstock/PunchStock/DAL.
Page 523: © Hiroko Masuike/The New York Times/Redux.
Page 529: © Frazier Harrison/Getty Images.
Page 530: © Chuan Khoo/Getty Images/DAL.
Page 539: © Bill Varie/Corbis.

Chapter 16

Page 551: © AP Photo/Carlos Osorio.
Page 553: © Chamussy/Sipa/AP Images.
Page 562: © Keith Brofsky/Getty Images/DAL.
Page 568: © Ron Wurzer/Getty Images.
Page 576: © AP Photo/Kevin P. Casey.

Chapter 17

Page 592: © AP Photo/Paul Sakuma.
Page 594: © J. Luke/PhotoLink/Getty Images/DAL.

Page 595: © Tony - Imaginechina/AP Images.
Page 598: Courtesy of HyperActive Technologies.
Page 604: © Alyson Aliano.
Page 606: Courtesy of 3M Company.
Page 609: © Ned Frisk/Corbis/DAL.

Appendix D

Page 621: © Macduff Everton/Corbis.
Page 622: © AP Photo/Mark Humphrey.

Chapter 18

Page 629: © Frank Brandmaier/Corbis.
Page 631: © Simon Fergusson/Getty Images.
Page 634: © AP Photo/Mary Altaffer.
Page 638: © David Paul Morris/Getty Images.
Page 643: © Kim Kulish/Corbis.
Page 647: Copyright © 2008 Symantec Corporation. Reprinted with permission.

Name Index

Woodward, Bob, 14
Woodward, Joan, 325, N-19
Woodward, N. H., N-38
Worley, C., N-38
Worline, M., N-6
Wray, Richard, N-8
Wright, D., N-10
Wright, Patrick M., N-17, N-19, N-20
Wright, Will, 7
Wynn, Gregory, 260

X

Xavier, Stephen, N-2

Y

Yammarino, F. J., N-25, N-26
Yang, Baik, N-16
Yanouzas, J., N-35
Yasai-Ardekani, Masoud, N-4

Yeatts, D., N-30
Yi, Sang-Seung, N-37
Yorges, S., N-26
Young, A., N-22
Young, J., N-16
Youngblood, S. A., N-21
Yukl, G. A., N-25

Z

Zablow, R. J., N-8, N-9
Zaccaro, S., N-25
Zachovalova, K., N-12
Zafra, A., N-34
Zahra, S. A., N-15, N-36
Zakaria, Fareed, N-1
Zald, M., N-9
Zappone, C., N-12
Zardkoohi, A., N-21
Zaslow, J., N-27
Zatzick, C. D., N-18

Zehr, D., N-13
Zeithaml, C., 68, 69, N-4, N-5, N-6
Zeithaml, V., 68, 69, N-4, N-5
Zeitz, G., N-15
Zell, D., N-38
Zeltzer, Alysa, 71
Zemke, R., N-26
Zenger, J., 490, 495, N-30
Zetlin, M., N-11
Zhou, J., N-26
Zigarmi, P., N-38
Zimmerman, M., N-15
Zingheim, P. K., N-21
Zitz, Michael, N-3
Zmud, R. W., N-33
Zollo, M., N-16
Zongker, Brett, N-25
Zorabedian, J., N-34
Zuboff, Shoshana, 647, N-39
Zygmont, J., N-19

Subject Index